THE MATRIX READER

W9-CCD-198

Examining the Dynamics of Oppression and Privilege

Abby Ferber

Christina M. Jiménez

Andrea O'Reilly Herrera

Dena R. Samuels

University of Colorado–Colorado Springs

McGraw-Hill Higher Education

Boston   Burr Ridge, IL   Dubuque, IA   New York   San Francisco   St. Louis
Bangkok   Bogotá   Caracas   Kuala Lumpur   Lisbon   London   Madrid   Mexico City
Milan   Montreal   New Delhi   Santiago   Seoul   Singapore   Sydney   Taipei   Toronto

The McGraw·Hill Companies

McGraw-Hill
Higher Education

Published by McGraw-Hill, an imprint of The McGraw-Hill Companies, Inc., 1221 Avenue of the Americas, New York, NY 10020. Copyright © 2009. All rights reserved. No part of this publication may be reproduced or distributed in any form or by any means, or stored in a database or retrieval system, without the prior written consent of The McGraw-Hill Companies, Inc., including, but not limited to, in any network or other electronic storage or transmission, or broadcast for distance learning.

This book is printed on acid-free paper.

1 2 3 4 5 6 7 8 9 0 DOC/DOC 0 9 8

ISBN: 978-0-07-340411-0
MHID: 0-07-340411-X

Editor in Chief: *Michael J. Ryan*
Sponsoring Editor: *Gina Boedecker*
Marketing Manager: *Leslie Oberhuber*
Developmental Editor: *Kate Scheinman*
Production Editor: *Chanda Feldman*
Manuscript Editor: *Jennifer Gordon*
Design Managers: *Cassandra Chu and Laurie Entringer*
Text Designer: *Glenda King*
Cover Designer: *Pam Verrow*
Art Editor: *Sonia Brown*
Photo Research: *Judy Mason*
Production Supervisor: *Richard DeVitto*
Composition: *10/12 Plantin Light by Aptara, Inc.*
Printing: *45# New Era Matte Plus by R. R. Donnelley & Sons*

Cover: © iStockPhoto

Credits: The credits section for this book begins on page 645 and is considered an extension of the copyright page.

Library of Congress Cataloging-in-Publication Data
Ferber, Abby L.
    The matrix reader / Abby L. Ferber, Andrea O'Reilly Herrera, Christina M. Jimenez, Dena R. Samuels.—1st ed.
        p. cm.
    Includes bibliographical references.
    ISBN: 978-0-07-340411-0; ISBN: 0-07-340411-X (alk. paper)
        1. Feminist Theory. II. O'Reilly Herrera, Andrea. III. Jimenez, Christina M. IV. Samuels, Dena R. V. Title.
HQ1180.B34 2008
305.4201—dc22   200804073

The Internet addresses listed in the text were accurate at the time of publication. The inclusion of a Web site does not indicate an endorsement by the authors or McGraw-Hill, and McGraw-Hill does not guarantee the accuracy of the information presented at these sites.

www.mhhe.com

We dedicate this book

      . . . to those who make our families complete.

      . . . to the allies who have been, and continue to be, involved in the struggle for justice and equality.

      . . . and to you, the reader, for your willingness to take the first step.

I CAN SAY THIS WITH CERTAINTY: If your life is being ground up in economic machinery and the burden of oppression is heavy on your back, you hunger for liberation, and so do those around you. Look for our brightly colored banners coming up over the hill of the past and into your present. Listen for our voices—our protest chants drawing nearer. Join us in the front ranks. We are marching toward liberation.

That's what the characters in *Stone Butch Blues* fought for. The last chapter of this saga of struggle has not yet been written.

—*Leslie Feinberg*

Table of Contents

v

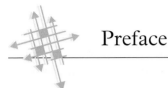

Preface

The Matrix Reader has grown out of two interrelated commitments that each of us has in our own teaching and research: our commitment to a fully interdisciplinary and intersectional approach to teaching about race, class, gender, and sexuality and our dedication to social justice through education and social action. These dual goals have been nurtured by our experiences working together— across disciplines—in the Ethnic Studies and Women's Studies programs at the University of Colorado, Colorado Springs. We have always shared ideas, approaches, and materials for these classes, particularly for the introductory courses to Ethnic and Women's Studies. Each of us brings a different perspective to the table—Andrea's primary disciplinary training is in literature and theory; Christina's is history; and Abby and Dena's is sociology. Over the years we have discovered that our interdisciplinary collaborations greatly enrich not only our course material but also our classroom experiences. In gathering materials for this collection, for example, Andrea suggested the inclusion of poems and reflective literary prose; Christina circulated articles on specific historical events and documents and images drawn from the media; Abby contributed handouts with contemporary statistics of inequalities and suggested that we include visual images; and Dena shared works that focused on empowering students to become agents for social change. Despite our distinct approaches in our classes, we all utilize the concepts of oppression, privilege, and social change as the framework for our courses.

Reflective of our collective teaching experiences, *The Matrix Reader* adopts an intersectional approach based on the work of Patricia Hill Collins and others. Collins examines the ways in which race, gender, and other systems of inequality interact and intersect as part of a matrix of oppression and privilege (Samuels, Ferber, & O'Reilly Herrera 2003). Unlike the majority of texts, which focus almost exclusively on the dynamics of discrimination, our reader highlights the duality of oppression and privilege and the ways in which race, gender, and sexuality shape everyone's lives. In our view, analyzing this duality enables students to better understand the fundamental concept that oppression and privilege function simultaneously at the institutional and individual levels; as a result, students learn how each person plays (perhaps unconsciously) some role in creating, maintaining, and perpetuating inequality in our society. This realization is particularly powerful for students with privileged social identities because it clearly explains how they are also affected by, and benefit from, existing social systems.

In addition to enfranchising students, implementing Collins's concept of the *matrix of domination* as the controlling metaphor in our reader helps students understand in a nonthreatening way that oppression occurs on multiple levels (personal, cultural, and institutional). In this manner each student can envision herself or himself as an agent for social change despite the daunting idea of altering an institutionalized social system. Conversely, students learn they should not feel guilty about participating in social systems that they may directly or indirectly benefit from, but which they did not create. Rather, by contextualizing discrimination and inequality using a sociohistorical backdrop, *The Matrix Reader* culminates in a section that equips students with the tools to become an "ally" and encourages them to become active agents for social change.

Our unique history of collaboration at the University of Colorado at Colorado Springs has mirrored the theoretical convergence of Ethnic and Women's Studies at universities across the country. In fact, these disciplines have long grappled with the intersectional nature of their inquiries. For example, Women's Studies programs have explored the complexities of women's experiences across the lines of race, class, sexual orientation, and nation. Originally growing out of the work of scholars trained in traditional disciplines, many of the methodologies, theories, and debates in Ethnic and Women's Studies borrow from, and simultaneously engage with, cross-disciplinary scholarship. Over the past few decades, explicitly intersectional analysis has accelerated within Ethnic and Women's Studies as well as in Sexuality and Queer Studies. Across the country, a number of departments, programs, and centers of Multicultural and Gender Studies have been created, including our own recently established Women's and Ethnic Studies major and our Matrix Center for the Advancement of Social Equity and Inclusion, which is committed to diversity and social justice work. We believe this intersectional, interdisciplinary, and conceptually driven approach is the wave of the future in Ethnic and Women's Studies not only because it allows us to discuss the complexity of identity as we experience it, but also because this approach empowers students with the knowledge, motivation, and ability to affect social change. As we gradually begin to acknowledge the fact that we as a nation are fundamentally multiethnic and multiracial, our students are increasingly interested in understanding issues surrounding multiracial and multiethnic identity, as well as subjects such as physical ability and religious and sexual orientation. This complex approach to identity is emphasized in *The Matrix Reader.*

ORGANIZATION

The Matrix Reader opens with a general introduction that presents the reader with the overarching concepts of oppression and privilege and discusses our pedagogical approach to introducing students to the subjects of race, gender, and sexuality. *The Matrix* is divided into five sections organized according to specific, interrelated themes. Each section is introduced by a brief essay, that discusses unifying concepts and issues and provides insight into our rationale for selecting and grouping the various readings and literary works.

The essays in Section I, "Constructing Identities and Examining Intersections," are divided into two parts and introduce the fundamental concepts related to the study of race, ethnicity, gender, sexuality, and class. In addition, they examine the complexity of these categories and how they came to be defined. Part A, "Constructing Identity," defines the key identity concepts that recur throughout the volume. The works featured here demonstrate the manner in which each concept is a social construct, subject to political, historical, and cultural variation. The essays in Part B, "Examining the Intersections," emphasize the inherent problems and limitations of the classifications themselves; several highlight multiracial and multiethnic identity formation. In addition, they examine the intersections among these classifications, suggesting some of the ways that race, ethnicity, gender, sexuality, and class—as well as other factors like physical ability—are intertwined in shaping our experiences and opportunities.

In Section II, "Understanding Oppression and Privilege," we introduce and explore the foundational concepts of oppression and privilege and the dynamics that maintain inequality. The readings introduce key theoretical concepts for understanding these issues today. More specifically, they distinguish racism from discrimination; introduce the concept of institutional racism, patriarchy, and homophobia; and explore the manner in which each individual is located within a complex and shifting matrix of oppression and privilege. Employing an intersectional approach, certain essays set their discussion of discrimination/privilege within a comparative, global context, thus creating a framework to discuss issues of U.S. privilege, immigration or migration, and globalization.

Section III, "How We Got Here: The Historical Context," explores the historical roots of institutionalized systems of oppression and privilege as well as movements for social change within the context of U.S. history. In exploring these histories, students will learn how hierarchies of difference based on the primary statuses were intertwined with issues of citizenship, legal protections, social practices, and national identity, and how they inform contemporary systems of inequality. Readings in Part A, "The Big Picture: Understanding the Historical Context," present essays with more expansive perspectives regarding the history of institutional- and societal-based discrimination. Among the subjects treated in this section are the experiences of ethnic Americans during the nineteenth century; the challenges faced by disabled Americans; and the objectification of women's bodies. These essays demonstrate that systems of oppression and privilege have deep roots not only in our history, but also in U.S. law and dominant ideologies of the past. Part B, "Dynamics of Oppression, Dynamics of Change: The Challenges of U.S. History," presents more topic-centered essays focusing on individual and group experiences in diverse historical contexts. Some essays recount what are often *invisible* or marginalized perspectives in U.S. history. Others highlight the social activism of historically oppressed social groups and their continuous struggle for "equal protection under the law," their basic rights as U.S. citizens, and inclusion in the concept of the nation. The civil rights movement, the women's movement, ethnic identity movements (such as the Chicano movement and Black Power), and the gay and lesbian rights movements are presented as twentieth-century examples of community activism that produced profound political and social change. We hope to emphasize the important history of activism and cultural resistance, rather than focusing solely on the history of discrimination and the progress that has been made toward social and institutional change.

Section IV, "Contemporary Institutionalized Oppression and Privilege," examines the manner in which discrimination and inequality manifest themselves at the institutional level in a contemporary context. This section provides a snapshot of oppression and privilege in a wide range of social institutions including the media, health, language, education, and the criminal justice system. The works in this section introduce contemporary examples of ongoing inequality produced in, maintained by, and reinforced across every institution in society. They emphasize, moreover, the construction of categories of difference within specific institutions, where they are assigned differential value and carry differential access to resources and rewards.

In Section V, "Be the Change," we focus the process of social change. In teaching this subject matter over many years, we have found that students sometimes leave race and gender courses with a lingering sense of powerlessness and frustration. They are often unclear regarding how to proceed and are desperate for answers to some of these overwhelming social problems. Part A, "Recognizing Resistance to Change," explores resistance and examines contemporary forms of individual as well as organized backlash to movements for social justice. In order to enact social change, it is critical that we first understand how resistance to change prevents our society from becoming more equitable. Once we become cognizant of what we are up against in terms of working to make a difference, we can begin in earnest to move forward. Part B, "Institutionalizing Social Change," provides specific examples, models, and recommendations for social and institutional change and examines forms of cultural resistance that have proven successful in advancing social justice movements. Part C, "Where Do I Begin?" features a wide range of works that suggest concrete ways to enact social change in our individual lives and circles of influence. Although significant and long-term social change ultimately requires institutional change, even this can begin with individuals. Our goal in this final section is to provide concrete strategies and suggestions for students interested in what they can begin to do right now, in their own lives, to make a difference.

SUPPLEMENTS

Dena Samuels has written a comprehensive Teaching Guide. Visit our book Web site at www.mhhe.com/ferber1 to access this password-protected instructor resource.

ACKNOWLEDGMENTS

We would like to thank the many reviewers who provided encouragement and feedback on *The Matrix Reader* at various stages of development:

Clare Battista, *California Polytechnic State University*
Jan Buhrmann, *Illinois College*
E. Megan Glancy, *Valdosta State University*
Jessica Greenebaum, *Central Connecticut State University*
Melinda D. Kane, *University of Texas at Dallas*
Lora Bex Lempert, *University of Michigan—Dearborn*
Lavonna L. Lovern, *Valdosta State University*
Sheena Malhotra, *California State University, Northridge*
Peter Meiksins, *Cleveland State University*
Jessica Nathanson, *Augustana College*
Joan Toms Olson, *University of Mary Washington*
Chris T. Papaleonardos, *The Ohio State University*
Jo-Ann Pilardi, *Towson University*
Alberto Pulido, *University of San Diego*
S. Rowan Wolf, *Portland Community College*

We would also like to thank Jane Muller for her assistance in preparing our manuscript for publication.

Reference

Samuels, D., Ferber, A., & O'Reilly Herrera, A. 2003. Introducing the concepts of oppression and privilege into the classroom. *Race, Gender, and Class: Special Edition on Privilege, 10* (4), 5–21.

Introduction

Equality and justice for all is one of the basic ideals of American society. It is a tenet that most Americans are socialized to believe is true and for which many would stand up and fight. Throughout history some have argued that the United States is the *land of equal opportunity*—a meritocracy in which everyone can reach their goals and realize their aspirations if they simply work hard and take advantage of the opportunities that surround them. According to this approach, success depends solely upon personal ambition coupled with talent or intellectual ability; conversely, failure is the result of the natural or innate differences among us. The American dream is the desire to live in a society in which *everyone* has the opportunity to be successful and reach their life potential. In reality, however, the American dream has and continues to be unattainable for many of our nation's citizens.

Today, we live in a highly stratified society—a society in which people are divided and ranked hierarchically according to various categories or primary statuses such as race, ethnicity, gender, class, and sexuality. As you will gather from a number of essays included in this volume, ample proof demonstrates that these rankings lead to inequality. Why is this? Have you ever wondered, for example, why there is such a tremendous gap between the very wealthy and the very poor in our society, or why women still earn less money than men working at the same jobs? Why, moreover, are people of color disproportionately less educated and underpaid compared to white people? Some might argue that the answers to these questions lie in the differences among us, that one's chances at success are determined by inherited facets of identity such as race and gender. For many, this answer provides a simple or convenient explanation for the inequality that exists today between men and women and between people of color and whites, and, moreover, it rationalizes and justifies the status quo.

The actual causes of inequality, as you will soon discover, are much more complex. We must, therefore, refuse to accept easy answers and instead be willing to ask more profound and nuanced questions. Modern-day inequality is the result of hundreds of years of history. *The Matrix Reader* thus emphasizes the concrete historical context from which the contemporary legacy of inequality and discrimination springs. In order to fully undertstand this legacy, however, we must first acknowledge the complex nature of identity formation itself. Consider, for example, the idea that our identities are composed of the primary statuses of race, ethnicity, gender, class, and sexuality and informed by factors such as age, religious orientation, and ableism. These primary statuses and factors determine what sociologists term one's *social location,* and, as Michael Omi and Howard Winant suggest in their essay in this volume, their individual or collective significance or meanings are subject to social, political, and historical change. In addition to being mutually dependent, these statuses and factors interact, intersect, and shift according to the various contexts in which we find ourselves. Consider, for example, a Muslim woman who chooses to wear an *abaya.* On September 10, 2001, she might have been significantly less concerned about her safety walking down the street than on September 12. Our personal experiences are considerably impacted by the sociohistorical factors of the society in which we find ourselves. Primary statuses determine not only how we see ourselves, but also the manner in which we are viewed by others and the treatment we subsequently receive at both the individual and institutional levels.

Based on the hierarchical structure of American society, some of our primary statuses, or social locations, benefit us while others put us at a disadvantage. In her article "Toward a New Vision" in Section I, Patricia Hill Collins presents the *matrix of domination,* which examines the ways our social locations intersect and interact in shaping our lives and society. As Collins explains, the interconnected axes of oppression and privilege form a hierarchical matrix of domination that affects our lived experience. Understanding where we each fit in the system is helpful in connecting us to the problem of inequality and provides us with possibilities for growth and change.

Systems of oppression and privilege are not about an individual's personal qualities, but rather address the social systems that shape all of our lives, regardless of individual qualities or personal intentions. The manner in which we are oppressed and privileged affects our life chances, the impressions we make on others, and our own sense of identity. Notably, however, the dynamics of privilege are often invisible to those who benefit most from them (Johnson 2006). For example, a white, heterosexual Protestant male who lacks a college education, earns an income below the poverty line, and does not have access to health insurance may have a hard time believing that he is privileged by nature of his race, gender, sexual and religious orientation. While this person may experience oppression based on class, at the same time he is privileged because of these other aspects of his identity. The matrix of domination illustrates that regardless of where we are situated at any given time, we *all* fit somewhere in the matrix. As a result, we are all, always, implicated in the matrix of domination in some way, for everyone is shaped by some combination of these interacting statuses or social categories, and everyone experiences varying degrees of oppression and privilege depending upon her or his location in society.

In the past, race/ethnicity and gender/sexuality were treated as mutually exclusive categories. Rarely did college courses integrate the study of different systems of inequality. As a result, courses on race tended to focus strictly on the experiences of men of color, whose lives were assumed to be shaped solely by race; likewise, courses on gender focused almost exclusively on white, middle-class heterosexual women as the assumed norm. A groundbreaking co-edited volume published in 1982, *All the Women Are White, All the Blacks Are Men, And Some of Us Are Brave,* challenged this monolithic approach. Women of color, who were systematically excluded from traditional courses and texts, were among the first to effectively question this outdated approach to the study of race and gender. They championed instead the importance of *intersectionality* (the interaction and intersection of categories or primary statuses).

Despite these advances, many academic readers continue to treat the primary statuses as distinct and polarized categories. Textbooks and readers also tend to minimize or overlook entirely subjects such as transsexual, bisexual or transgender, and multiracial identity and thereby ignore the complex realities of a vast portion of the populace. Consider, for example, that a term such as *race* has become part of our commonsense vocabulary, and we are all asked at one time or another to place ourselves within a range of categories listed under this rubric. Then ask yourself the following question: What box would you check if your mother identified as Latina, and your father identified as an African American? In reality, neither of these two categories is clear-cut. By having to choose a single category in which to identify yourself, you are being asked to reduce the vast complexity of your individual identity to a single attribute—a monolithic category.

Researchers and theorists have gradually begun to examine the relationship among the primary statuses that constitute our identities and inform the broader societal dynamics of oppression and privilege (Johnson 2006; Kimmel & Ferber 2003). Failing to acknowledge the intersectional relationships among these basic categories ultimately prevents us from fully understanding the lived experience of most of the people with whom we come in contact on a daily basis. By viewing our identities from an intersectional perspective, we can begin to explore in depth the manner in which systems of oppression and privilege operate. While "as Marilyn Frye describes it, the concept of oppression points to social forces that tend to 'press' on people and hold them down, to hem them in and block their pursuit of a good life" (Johnson 2006, 38), Peggy McIntosh explains in her article in Section II that "privilege exists when one group has something of value that is denied to others simply because of the groups they belong to." Because they exist in relation to each other, oppression and privilege operate hand in hand; in fact, one cannot exist without the other.

Modeled on Collins's groundbreaking concept, our anthology implements the matrix as a framework for understanding how oppression and privilege work, the role these concepts play in identity formation, and how they play out in daily life. Our ultimate goal is to empower students to become agents of change. Once you examine your own social location and place yourself within the matrix of domination, you will begin to understand how your individual actions and behavior can affect society in both positive and negative ways. The matrix of domination thus provides a point of connection among everyone in the class, including the instructor. Focusing solely on oppression only addresses half of the problem. It can also create antagonism between people who are discriminated against on a daily basis and those who are not. Bringing privilege into the discussion enables us to see that we all experience varying degrees of oppression and privilege. Exploring the ways in which each one of us is oppressed and privileged potentially unites us in our effort to enact positive social change.

The Matrix Reader presents an approach that simultaneously highlights the interdisciplinary nature of various fields of study, emphasizes the interdependent and shifting relationship between oppression and privilege, and treats the primary statuses as being inextricably interlinked. In an effort to reflect the manner in which the fields of race, cultures, gender, and sexuality studies interface, *The Matrix Reader* features both essays and cultural expressions drawn from several disciplines including sociology, history, literature, psychology, and education. Selected readings also introduce pertinent issues stemming from historical and contemporary patterns of immigration, civil rights, and language politics. We wish to acknowledge, however, our consciousness of the fact that this collection is neither comprehensive nor all-inclusive. Space limitations have prevented us from treating the experiences of a wider range of groups, as well as from presenting a more expansive, global perspective. Nevertheless, *The Matrix Reader* provides a framework for comprehending oppression and privilege that can be applied to all social locations and institutions.

We also wish to draw attention to the constraints inherent in the very language that we use to speak of people who have been, and continue to be, marginalized and oppressed in U.S. society. At the same time, we recognize that in order to create change, it is important to speak about these various groups and articulate their experiences. We are compelled, therefore, to use language that is currently common in the field with the caveat that the obvious lack of appropriate or more inclusive language is of considerable concern. In our introductions to each section, for example, we employ the phrase "person/people of color" when referring to non-whites with full knowledge of the fact that it puts these groups in opposition to one another. The transgender movement has made great strides in regard to this issue by proposing terms such as *ze* to refer to "s/he," and *hir* to refer to "him/her." Innovation in language and the absorption of such language into disciplines and our culture is something to which we look forward.

Finally, whenever possible we have used forms of self-expression and voice to engage the reader to better understand the central issues treated in our text. Among the overarching themes addressed in *The Matrix Reader* are the concepts of social justice and respect for others. Once we understand that we may be discriminated against or oppressed by one category or social location, yet privileged in another, we can begin to see that oppression and discrimination against any group is unacceptable and that there are no exceptions. For instance, someone may recognize the misogyny involved in telling a sexist joke, and the resulting devaluation and degradation of women, but may still think that it is acceptable to tell a heterosexist or homophobic joke.

Understanding the dynamics of oppression and privilege and the intersectional nature of inequality makes clear that we all must work as allies across social locations to be agents of change. We cannot successfully fight against racism, for example, if we continue simultaneously to perpetuate sexism and homophobia, and visa versa. We hope you find this text inspiring as you begin to "connect to the problem," as Allan Johnson puts it, and, consequently, "become part of the solution" (2006).

REFERENCES

1. Johnson, A. G. 2006. *Privilege, power, and difference,* 2nd ed. New York: McGraw-Hill.
2. Kimmel, M. S., & Ferber, A. L. 2003. *Privilege: A reader.* Boulder, CO: Westview.

I. Constructing Identities and Examining Intersections

Abby L. Ferber

Our bodies are too complex to provide clear-cut answers.
—ANNE FAUSTO-STERLING

While our sense of identity feels very personal and private, identities are simultaneously individual and collective. *Social identity* refers to those aspects of our identity that are shaped by our group memberships. From the very outset of our lives, we begin thinking about individuals as members of social groups. We are often anxious to know the sex of a baby even before it is born. And once the infant enters the world, she or he will be dressed and adorned and offered toys to play with based on the sex. Research shows that even the most egalitarian parents treat infants differently based on their sex. So from the moment of birth on, we are socialized by our families, friends, day care, television, commercials, schools, toys, greeting cards, and bedroom decorations into specific social categories. *Socialization* constitutes

> The total set of experiences in which children become clear about norms and expectations and learn how to function as respected and accepted members of a culture. . . . children are socialized at both conscious and unconscious levels to internalize the dominant values and norms of their culture, and in so doing, develop a sense of self. (Holtzman, cited in Allen 2003)

So our very sense of who we are, our identity, develops in interaction with society and with the social classifications and meanings of our society.

We may identify with the social groups we are a part of, or we may be classified by others as belonging to specific social groups with which we do not identify. Indeed, the ways others classify us is just as important as how we classify ourselves. For example, a child born to an American Indian mother and an African American father may define herself as multiracial and value both sides of her family cultures, but society, and the individuals she encounters on a daily basis, may simply see her and treat her as black. The categories others place us in have a tremendous impact on our lives. For example, many cases of homophobic hate crimes have been perpetrated against heterosexual individuals.

However, because the victims were perceived by others as gay, they were made to suffer the consequences of hate.

Social identities have become so central to our culture that we often feel troubled when we cannot locate someone within our culture's social classifications, especially the categories of race or gender. Michael Omi and Howard Winant point out in the article included in this section,

> One of the first things we notice about people when we meet them . . . is their race. We utilize race to provide clues about *who* a person is. This fact is made painfully obvious when we encounter someone whom we cannot conveniently racially categorize—someone who is, for example, racially "mixed" or of an ethnic/racial group with which we are not familiar. Such an encounter becomes a source of discomfort and momentarily a crisis of racial meaning. Without a racial identity, one is in danger of having no identity.

A growing body of work by multiracial writers details their daily encounters with people asking "What are you?" We may be uneasy when we cannot classify someone into our accepted categories. Have you ever seen someone who you were not quite sure was male or female? You may have asked friends what they thought. You may have examined the individual's clothing or body for clues. The problem may be that we are asking the wrong questions. Instead, we might consider why it is that these social identity categories are so important to us in the first place. Why do we assume they tell us something important about ourselves? And do they really?

Many of our commonsense assumptions about race, gender, and sexuality are embedded in what we call an *essentialist* approach. *Essentialism* is the assumption that "social differences such as those between men and women, people of different races, or social classes are due to intrinsic biological or psychic differences between the members of the different groups" (Clatterbaugh 1995, 49). These differences are believed to be innate and unchanging and are seen as more significant than environmental factors in explaining differences among people. Essentialism, however, is not supported by the research. While our commonsense assumptions may tell us that categories such as race are rooted in biology, biologists today reject such notions.

Most contemporary theories of difference and inequality fall under the broad umbrella of *social constructionism*. A wide range of social constructionist approaches can be found within a diverse array of disciplines, including philosophy, sociology, literature, biology, psychology, and anthropology. While constructionist arguments are not new, they have been most fully embraced and expanded upon over the past two decades. Unlike essentialist approaches, social constructionist approaches emphasize the role of human interaction and culture in shaping classifications of difference and producing inequality. Social constructionist approaches have shaped our understanding of race/ethnicity, sex/gender, sexual orientation, class, and ability, as each of the articles included in this section demonstrates.

Social constructionist approaches emphasize that:

- There is no strictly biological basis for these categories of identity.
- Each of these categories varies tremendously across cultures.
- Each of these categories similarly varies historically.

Because essentialist approaches have become so commonsensical in our culture, it can be difficult to grasp the social constructionist approach at first. After all, identities like race and sex seem purely biological and visible, don't they? We can clearly see that there are differences among us in terms of skin color, and the first thing the doctor pronounces upon the birth of a baby is either "It's a boy!" or "It's a girl!" Yet things are often not as simple as they seem.

Let's consider race as an example and examine these propositions a bit further. We know today that race has no biological basis. Of course, we look different from one another, but there is no such thing as "white blood," "black blood," or "Latino/a blood" and no gene for determining racial identity. In fact, there is greater genetic variety *within* racial groups than *between* them. That means that you are actually more likely to genetically resemble someone from a different racial group than another person who happens to be classified in the same racial group as you. Further, there is no such thing as a "pure" race. We are all the product of tremendous intermixing over centuries.

Sociologists and anthropologists have added to the evidence supporting a constructionist perspective, demonstrating that racial classifications vary from one culture to another. Other cultures have racial classifications that look very different from our own. Many cultures recognize mixed-race individuals as a separate category. Even within the United States, Hawaii has always embraced a very different set of racial classifications, reflecting its history and culture. Just as these categories are different from one culture to the next, we find that people supported different categories in the past. Historians have revealed the ways in which racial classifications change over time. While our commonsense essentialist framework may lead us to assume that racial identity is universal and unchanging, in fact the idea of race was not invented to describe humans until the seventeenth century. Prior to that time, no concept of race existed.

The term *race* is believed to have originated in the Middle Ages in the romance languages and was first used to refer to the breeding of animals. *Race* did not appear in the English language until the sixteenth century and was used as a technical term to describe human groups in the seventeenth century. By the end of the eighteenth century, as emphasis upon the observation and classification of human differences grew, race became the most commonly employed concept for differentiating human groups according to northern European standards. Audrey Smedley argues that because *race* has its roots in the breeding of animal stock, unlike other terms used to categorize humans, it came to imply an innate or inbred quality, believed to be permanent and unchanging (2007). Winthrop

Jordan has suggested that ideas of racial difference and hierarchy, specifically the construction of blacks as savage and primitive, played an essential role in rationalizing slavery (1969). Concepts of race were developed in tandem with racism—they did not exist prior to the rise of racism.

Early religious theories defined non-whites as people to be tamed and civilized, or as savage brutes. These beliefs were used to rationalize taking Native American lands and enslaving Africans. Religious justifications gave way to the rise of scientific racism in the middle of the eighteenth century (Banton & Harwood 1975). Carolus Linnaeus (Carl von Linné), a prominent naturalist in the eighteenth century, developed the first authoritative racial division of humans in his *Natural System,* published in 1735 (West 1982). Considered the founder of scientific taxonomy, he attempted to classify all living things, both plant and animal. Linnaeus defined Europeans as "gentle, acute, inventive . . . governed by customs," while describing Africans as "crafty, indolent, negligent . . . governed by caprice" (in West 1982, 56).

From early on, racial classification has involved hierarchy and the linkage of physical features with character and cultural traits. In 1755 Johann Friedrich Blumenbach, an early founder of modern anthropology, advanced his own systematic racial classification in his study *On the Natural Varieties of Mankind.* He designated five human races—Caucasian, Mongolian, Ethiopian, American, and Malayan—and ranked them on a scale according to their distance from the "civilized" Europeans. Race as a concept was scientifically defined as heritable and unalterable. The authority of science contributed to the quick and widespread acceptance of these ideas and prevented their interrogation.

This evolving system of racial classification is a racial ideology. An *ideology* is a belief system that shapes the way we interpret and make sense of the world and consequently guides our action and behavior. Ideologies are relied upon to provide a justification for inequality and oppression. For example, an ideology that defines certain groups of people as less than human, or as evil and a threat to our own well-being, may justify acts of murder by those who otherwise would not consider themselves as capable of such violence.

Not only are racial classifications relatively new in the history of the world, but they have been in constant flux. For example, if we examine the U.S. census classifications for race, we find that the racial categories one is asked to select from have changed almost every ten years with each new census. In the table that follows, we see that in 1790, the year of the first census, the classifications were Free Whites, All other free persons except Indians, and Slaves. By 1870 the racial categories were expanded to include White, Black, Mulatto, Octoroon, Chinese, Indian, Quadroon, and Japanese. After years of struggle and lobbying by multiracial organizations, the 2000 census was the first that allowed individuals to check more than one racial category. Once we recognize race as a social construct, it is easy to understand why there has been so much confusion, argument, and change over time in our classification systems. After all, there is no *essential*

Categories Used by the U.S. Bureau of the Census to Designate Race, 1790–2000

1790, 1800, 1810

Free Whites	Slaves
All other Free Persons, except Indians not taxed	

1820, 1830, 1840

Free Whites	Free Colored
Foreigners, not naturalized	Slaves

1850, 1860

White	Mulatto
Black	Black slaves
Mulatto slaves	

1870, 1880, 1890, 1900, 1910, 1920

White	Chinese
Black	Indian
Mulatto	Quadroon★
Octoroon★	Japanese

1930

White	All other
Negro	Indian
Chinese	Japanese
Filipino	Hindu
Korean	

1940

White	Japanese
Negro	Filipino
Indian	Hindu
Chinese	Korean

1950

White	Japanese
Negro	Chinese
American Indian	Filipino

1960

White	Hawaiian
Negro	Part Hawaiian
American Indian	Aleut
Japanese	Eskimo
Chinese	

(*continued*)

Categories Used by the U.S. Bureau of the Census to Designate Race, 1790–2000 (*continued*)

1970

White	Chinese
Negro/Black	Filipino
Indian	Hawaiian
Japanese	Korean

1980

White	Indian (American)
Black or Negro	Asian Indian
Japanese	Hawaiian
Chinese	Guamanian
Filipino	Samoan
Korean	Eskimo
Vietnamese	Aleut

1990

White	Samoan
Black or Negro	Guamanian
Indian (American)	Other API
Eskimo	Asian or Pacific Islander
Aleut	Chinese
Vietnamese	Hawaiian
Japanese	Korean
Asian Indian	

2000

White	Native Hawaiian
Black or African American	Guamanian or Chamorro
American Indian or Alaska Native	Samoan
Asian Indian	Other Pacific Islander
Chinese	Vietnamese
Filipino	
Japanese	
Korean	
Other Asian	

*Category applied to 1890 census only.
Source: U.S. Bureau of the Census 1999.

marker of race—no gene or blood type we can look at—to determine how many races exist and who falls into which categories.

Once we see that race is a social rather than a biological concept, many new questions arise. We might ask, if race was not invented until the seventeenth century, why was it invented at that time? What was going on in the world? If classifications of race, class, gender, and sexuality are not rooted simply in nature, then we must ask why they have been constructed and in what ways they have been constructed. Why, for example, do we divide people up into categories based on skin color, or sex, or whom they are sexually attracted to rather than other kinds of differences, such as eye color, or hair color, or height? The construction of social identities is inherently political and tied to relations of power. The readings in this section will reveal that certain institutions—such as science, religion, medicine, law, and government—played a central role in creating these classification systems and enforcing them. While many people today argue that inequality is the result of differences among groups that are rooted in nature, what history reveals is the opposite. Instead, it is the dynamics of oppression and privilege that have produced the idea of essential racial differences.

From a social constructionist approach, our goal is to critically examine how, when, and why these classification systems have been constructed. What purposes did they serve in the past? What purposes do they serve today? Who do they benefit? How do they serve as a source of identity and pride as well as a basis for discrimination, segregation, and inequality?

We often tend to reduce problems to a nature versus nurture perspective; however, the world is not that clear-cut. The social constructionist perspective we embrace does not focus solely on the social and ignore the biological. Instead, these factors are seen as interconnected and inseparable. Like Linnaeus and Blumenbach, scientists who study the body and who have been raised in a given culture cannot step outside of that culture. Our society shapes our understanding of what we consider to be important biological issues to study, what kinds of questions to ask, and how we ask them. We also come to understand the world through the language of our culture, which shapes the way in which we make sense of the biological material we are given. As we shall see, for example, in the English language there are only two gendered pronouns, making it difficult to describe someone who does not fit into our male or female boxes. Other cultures, such as some Native American tribes, have more than two sex and gender categories. Further, biology and the environment are continuously interacting as we develop over the life course. Our bodies change in interaction with our environment. Our intellectual and physical capabilities are shaped by factors such as prenatal care, nutrition, restrictive clothing, exercise, exposure to mental stimulation, and so on. According to biologist Anne Fausto-Sterling, "the more we look for a simple physical basis for 'sex,' the more it becomes clear that 'sex' is not a purely physical category. What bodily signals and functions we define as male or female come already entangled in our ideas about gender" (2000, 4).

For example, think about your male faculty members. If we were to gather together all of the male faculty on your campus and compare them with the male construction workers in your community, which group do you think would be more muscular on average? I am guessing your answer is the construction workers (unless your campus has an exceptional physical fitness program!). Why is that? Is it the case that strong young men decide to go into construction work, while their less endowed brethren pursue careers in higher education? Of course not. The distinctions we would find would be a result of their very different jobs and the ways in which they spend their days and use their bodies. Not surprisingly, the same is true for differences in gender and class. Sociologists have found that women's nurturing skills as mothers are the product of gendered training for motherhood and that men and women in similar occupations often end up displaying the same kinds of learned skills. Male professors are also more likely to come from middle- or upper-class families that encourage them to pursue, and can finance, a higher education. Construction workers are more likely to come from a working-class background and are less likely to be encouraged to pursue higher education. What we see in this example is that difference is a result of circumstance and social context; it is not biologically determined.

Consider another example: the stereotype that the poor are poor because they do not work hard enough and do not possess strong values and work ethics. According to this logic, there is something about these individuals that has led them to poverty. The research does not support this, however. Rather, research illustrates that people who are raised in poverty are likely to have had inadequate schooling, suffer from poor nutrition, lack access to good health care, and in turn have fewer career opportunities, decreased earning potential, greater health risks, shortened life expectancy, and so on. Thus, for children born into poverty, a wide range of factors combine to make it unlikely that they will escape.

At the same time that the poor are scrutinized for their individual failures, many social trends point to other explanations for the rise in poverty. For example, cuts have been made in social services like health care, public schools, drug and alcohol counseling, and mental health care. Patterns of work have shifted as factories have moved overseas resulting in the loss of manufacturing jobs in the United States, and new job growth has been concentrated in the low-paying, part-time service sector. Whether we consider issues of class, race, gender, or other social identities, it is the *social* context that is key to understanding inequality.

As if things were not complicated enough, we must complicate them further. The articles in this section examine the ways in which key social categories are constructed and tied to inequality. We focus here primarily upon the categories of race/ethnicity, sex/gender, sexual orientation, and social class and include one article on the social construction of disability. So far we have talked about these social identities as separate, distinct classifications, but clearly they are not. None of us are *only* Asian American or *only* lesbian. We all have multiple social identities. These identities interact in how they shape our lives. What it means to be white may be very different in our society for white women than it is for white men. What it means to be a man may be very different in our society for heterosexuals and homosexuals. In the past, when researchers or activists have tried to separate these categories, they have ended up focusing on only the dominant group. Many African American women have written and spoken out about their marginalization within the civil rights movement. And, historically, discussion of "women's rights" often focused narrowly on the needs of white, middle- and upper-class, heterosexual women. Women of color were often excluded from the discussion. Women of color have leveled critiques against the first and second waves of the women's movement for ignoring the ways in which women's lives, needs, experiences, and priorities are shaped by other social identities like race, class, and sexual identity. These identities interact in shaping many aspects of our lives, and they are inseparable. We cannot understand one without understanding the others and, moreover, the ways they are constructed together. The chapters in the second half of this section will examine some of these intersections and interactions.

REFERENCES

1. Allen, B. 2003. *Difference matters: Communicating social identity.* Long Grove, IL: Waveland Press.
2. Banton, M., & Harwood, J. 1975. *The race concept.* New York: Praeger.
3. Clatterbaugh, K. 1995. Mythopoetic foundations and new age patriarchy. In *The politics of manhood: Profeminist men respond to the mythopoetic men's movement (and the mythopoetic leaders answer),* ed. M. S. Kimmel. Philadelphia: Temple University Press.
4. Fausto-Sterling, A. 2000. *Sexing the body: Gender politics and the construction of sexuality.* New York: Basic Books.
5. Jordan, W. 1969. *White over black.* Chapel Hill: University of North Carolina Press.
6. Smedley, A. 2007. *Race in North America,* 3rd ed. Boulder, CO: Westview.
7. West, C. 1982. *Prophesy deliverance! An Afro-American revolutionary Christianity.* Philadelphia: Westminster Press.

I Am Not Your Princess

especially for Dee Johnson

BY CHRYSTOS

Sandpaper between two cultures which tear
one another apart I'm not
a means by which you can reach spiritual
   understanding or even

learn to do beadwork
I'm only willing to tell you how to make fry bread
1 cup flour, spoon of salt, spoon of baking powder
Stir   Add milk or water or beer until it holds
    together
Slap each piece into rounds   Let rest
Fry in hot grease until golden
This is Indian food
only if you know that Indian is a government word

which has nothing to do with our names for
   ourselves
I won't chant for you
I admit no spirituality to you
I will not sweat with you or ease your guilt with
   fine turtle tales
I will not wear dancing clothes to read poetry or
explain hardly anything at all
I don't think your attempts to understand us are
   going to work so
I'd rather you left us in whatever peace we can still
scramble up   after all you continue to do
If you send me one more damn flyer about how to
   heal myself
for $300 with special feminist counseling
I'll probably set fire to something
If you tell me one more time that I'm wise I'll
   throw up on you
Look at me
See my confusion   loneliness   fear
   worrying about all our
struggles to keep   what little is left for us
Look at my heart   not your fantasies   Please
   don't ever
again tell me about your Cherokee great-great
   grandmother
Don't assume I know every other Native Activist
in the world personally   That I even know the
   names of all the tribes
or can pronounce names I've never heard
or that I'm expert at the peyote stitch
If you ever
again tell me
how strong I am
I'll lay down on the ground & moan so you'll see
at last   my human weakness   like your own
I'm not strong   I'm scraped
I'm blessed with life while so many I've known
   are dead
I have work to do   dishes to wash a house to clean
   There is no magic
See my simple cracked hands which have washed
   the same things you wash
See my eyes dark with fear in a house by myself
   late at night

See that to pity me or to adore me are the same
1 cup flour, spoon of salt, spoon of baking powder
   & liquid to hold
remember this is only my recipe   There are
   many others
Let me rest
here
at least

A. CONSTRUCTING IDENTITY

 1

Becoming a Visible Man

JAMISON GREEN

HOW DO YOU KNOW?

"You all know what sex you are, right?" That's how I like to start. To most students I look like a professor, a psychologist, or a businessman. I am short, athletically built, with a full, trimmed beard, a balding head, and a deep voice. I seek out the students' eyes, as many as will meet my gaze. They are a mélange of ethnic backgrounds, ages, and life experiences, a generation or two different from the much more homogeneous group with whom I attended college in the late 1960s, and I think how much richer education can be today with so many diverse viewpoints close at hand. That is, provided we are not afraid to listen and give credence to different voices.

Most of the students look blankly at their papers or at the empty chalkboard behind me, but a few stare quizzically at me. Some look at me and look away. Are they afraid? Am I fearful of their judgment, or of their misunderstanding? Can I get through their preconceptions, their resistance, and their various cultural positions that I have no time to explore? I am not their instructor; I'm merely a guest lecturer the instructor wants them to meet. I only have an hour or so with them, and—like everything else—mine is a topic that can be explored in so many ways. I can only skim the surface with them. I can only hope to awaken them, to alert them to the possibilities.

"Come on," I encourage them. "You all know what sex you are, right?"

A few students nod in affirmation.

"So, how do you know? Without looking down . . . no cheating, now. . . . How do you know what sex you are?"

Now some of them start to laugh. "Your mother tells you," someone suggests.

"And you believed her?" I ask, smiling. "Seriously, how do you know?"

"By your chromosomes?" someone asks.

"Okay, I don't mean to embarrass anyone, so don't volunteer information you are not comfortable sharing, but how many people in this room have had their chromosomes checked?" I inquire. In over ten years of lectures like this, speaking to several thousand people, I've encountered only three individuals who confessed to having had their chromosomes checked, all for development-related anomalies. This time not one hand is raised. "Right," I explain, "It's rare that any of us knows what our sex chromosomes actually are. Did you know that 1 in 20,000 men have two X-chromosomes, rather than one X- and one Y-chromosome? They don't find this out until their female partner can't get pregnant and doctors eliminate her infertility as the reason. Sure, there are plenty of reasons for a man to be sterile, but one possibility is that he has two X-chromosomes. One in 20,000 men is a 46-chromosome, XX male; ten percent of those have no Y-chromosome material. That's a pretty high number for something we are led to believe is impossible. That statistic is from Chapter 41 in the 13th edition of *Smith's General Urology,* a standard urology textbook. And what does that tell us about the Y-chromosome? Not that you need a Y to be male, but that you may need a Y to make viable sperm. Maybe! Because there are two species of small rodent-type mammals, called mole voles, in which there is no Y chromosome, yet they are still

reproducing both males and females, still procreating just as other mammals [Graves, 2001]. So if you can be a man with two X-chromosomes, and at least 1 in 20,000 men is, what makes you a man?" Some students, particularly males, are scowling now, confused, possibly getting angry. "That's right: it's all more complicated than we've been led to believe."

"We can identify the sex chromosomes in a developing fetus, but geneticists will tell you we have no idea what genes are firing. We especially don't know what genes are firing during embryogenesis, when the embryo is formed. Our science so far understands certain clusters of gene firing, like those that control the development of limbs or cause the webbing between the fingers to go away, but we do not understand the sequence of gene firings necessary to create an unambiguous male or female result, regardless of what the sex chromosomes are. The fact is, both the XX and XY karyotypes have bi-potential; that is, either karyotype can produce a male or a female result depending on which genes fire. There are gene expressions in each pair that can go down what we might call a male pathway or a female pathway. Those gene expressions, which trigger myriad events in the future, and which combine with myriad other expression events to form combinations we cannot anticipate, are the root of what we don't yet understand about the generalizations we've labeled 'female' and 'male.'

"According to the Intersex Society of North America, 1 in 100 people have bodies that differ from standard male or female. That means that one out of one hundred bodies has some quality that doctors would specify as an abnormality of sexual differentiation. Roughly 1 in 1,000 births involves what's called 'ambiguous genitalia,' in which the doctor can't tell by looking whether the infant is a boy or a girl. One in 1,000 births! That's a pretty high number. And what do you suppose they do in such a situation? Until recently, the standard has been that the doctors will decide what sex to assign the child, based on what kind of genital reconstruction surgery would be easiest or most effective from the doctor's point of view. But now this policy is hotly debated. Do you think they get it right every time? Do you think just because your genitals are a certain shape that this tells you what sex you are?" Horrified looks cross some students' faces. "So how do you know what sex you are?"

"By how you feel?" someone usually suggests. It seems to be the only avenue I've left open to them.

"Certainly that's a big part of it. Most people have feelings that correspond to the type of body they have. We sometimes think of feelings as something having to do with feeling attracted to another person, but certainly we all have feelings about ourselves, too. We have feelings about how we look, and how our personalities and interests correspond with those of other people with whom we identify. Now, what we're talking about today is not sexual orientation. I'm not talking about to whom you are attracted or what kind of sexual role you like to play. I'm talking about your relationship to your own body.

"Most people do feel connected to the type of body they have; that is, generally, the female type or the male type. And people may be attracted to people who have opposite-type bodies, or people who have similar-type bodies, or maybe they're not attracted to body types at all, but to individual people regardless of their bodies, but when we start connecting only feelings about bodies to sexual response and bringing in very complicated social ideas about sexual behavior it's easy to become confused about which idea or feeling or belief leads to what other specific idea, feeling or behavior. So let's not complicate matters just yet with too much talk about sexual attraction and relationship entanglements, though we certainly need to acknowledge that these are important aspects of our social lives that are strongly influenced by our relationship to our own body. What I want to focus on right now is the relationship one has with one's own sense of self, in their body, and the individual's sense of how that body fits or relates in the world. It can help us to understand this if we talk not just about sex, but about gender, too. Sex and gender are not the same things. Who can tell me the difference between sex and gender?"

The students are all watching me closely now, and several volunteer guesses; sometimes someone comes very close to the response I'm seeking. Still, it's likely that I'll need to explain: "Sex is a system of classification that divides body types based on presumed reproductive capacity as determined typically by visual examination of the external genitalia. There's a second meaning of the word 'sex,' which is that sex is also an activity we can engage in, and that activity has complex social meanings itself. We sometimes use the word 'love' as a euphemism for this second meaning of the word sex—having sex and making love. That second meaning leads us right back into sexual orientation, so for now we're going to discuss sex as just that system of classification of body types.

"The language we use to discuss sex as biology is derived from the study of plants. Our science about human sexuality is still very young. Plant biology? People have been studying plants for thousands of years, and we think we have them down pretty well. But we don't understand much about human sexuality. We've only been studying it seriously for a little over a century. It's not as simple as Xs and Ys or in-ies and out-ies. Science cannot tell us exactly what events must occur in the development of a human embryo that will give a completely male or completely female result. Remember, we don't know, in full scientific detail, what constitutes human maleness or femaleness. We're not plants that can be classified by the color of our petals or the shape of our leaves. We're much more complex than the color of our skin and hair or the shape of our genitals. We have social characteristics, too, like gender and sexual orientation, and maybe more characteristics that we don't yet know about. If we look closely enough at people we can see that none of these things—sex, gender, or sexual orientation—is the same, nor are they necessarily causal factors in relationship to each other, though they are certainly intertwined. But for now, to recap, sex is a system of classification of bodies that we call 'male' and 'female.'

"So, what's gender? Gender is another system of classification that describes characteristics and behaviors that we ascribe to bodies, and we call those characteristics and behaviors 'masculine' or 'feminine.' For example, we perceive a high-pitched voice as feminine, and a low-pitched voice as masculine; or we think of fine-motor skills—the ability to do small, dexterous work with the fingers—as feminine, and brute strength as masculine. And, as individuals, we can both express and perceive these qualities, these characteristics or behaviors, so it's an interactive system, this thing called gender. You may see a very beautiful woman, with long hair and a gorgeous body, and think of her as very feminine, but when all of a sudden she lifts up a park bench and says, 'not another step closer, or I'll shove this down your throat' in a deep, menacing growl, you may realize there's more to her than meets the eye. So if you had that experience, what would you think?"

"She's really a man," someone will suggest. After all, they may know I'm there to discuss transsexualism. They want me to get to the juicy part. But I haven't finished laying the foundation yet.

"What makes you think that?"

"Women don't do those things."

"Well, yes, generally, most women can't lift park benches, and most women don't have really low voices. But that doesn't mean this particular woman is not a woman. It could simply mean she's a woman who has a low voice and great strength. I notice you said, 'She's *really* a man.' I think it is interesting to consider why it's so tempting to conclude there is a deception going on. What makes us so confident that we know what's real? I see this as a cognitive process: we make assumptions based on what we observe, and when we find our observations were incorrect according to some arbitrary system of categorization, instead of recalibrating our categories we react with shock, horror, shame, anger, embarrassment, whatever, toward the person or object about which we were incorrect. It can't be our fault we were wrong in our categorization; it had to be that we were deceived, or we wouldn't have been wrong at all. I think it's fascinating that we perceive it this way, instead of saying to ourselves, 'Wow, she's strong, and beautiful, and what a sexy voice, and I guess I'd better back off because it seems she means business!'

"So we make assumptions about what is real or possible based on the gendered characteristics and behaviors that we learn in our culture. Another interesting thing about these gendered qualities is that the category they're assigned to can change between cultures, or change within a culture over time. What were decidedly masculine once, like the occupations of secretary, telephone operator, bank clerk, and tailor, went through a feminine phase and are now more gender-neutral. Another example of this kind of shift occurred in the 1960s and 1970s when some American men began to wear their hair long (again, after a few generations where short hair was the fashion), and people thought a man with long hair was trying to be a woman, or at least was expressing himself as a feminine man, whereas now men can have long or short hair and it's far less likely to be interpreted as a gender statement.

"Changing hairstyles often challenge gender norms. More than a few long-haired men in the 1960s were beaten up because they challenged gender norms. We experienced a culturally similar, though not as physically painful, shift when women began to wear jeans everywhere, not just in the barn. And a man with fine-motor dexterity will be praised for it if he applies his abilities to tying fishing flies, or building model railroads or ships in bottles, or playing a musical instrument, but he'll be ridiculed if he likes to crochet doilies. We tend to prefer our male-bodied people to have masculine gender characteristics and our female-bodied people to have feminine gender characteristics, and when they don't, particularly if the dichotomy is highly visible, it can make some people uncomfortable, even angry, when they feel they don't know how to classify the person they are observing, or when the other person's gender qualities threaten the observer's sense of confidence in her or his own gender. I find this level of response to gender variance fascinating. How is it that someone else's gender can throw a person's sense of confidence or solidarity out of balance? What cognitive mechanism is at work here, and what purpose does it serve? We learn as young children that behaving according to our assigned gender role means doing expected things based upon conformance to the sex we appear to be. If our sex and gender correspond, that's not too difficult for most of us, and we assume everyone feels about themselves the same way we do, and experiences similar difficulty or ease in adjusting behavior and appearance to conform to the gender norms of our culture. And if we travel to a new cultural environment, we quickly learn any new gender norms because we want people to perceive us as 'who we are.' If those new gender norms went against our ability to internalize or express them, we would experience tremendous discomfort.

"Like sex, gender is also more than one thing. It's more than the external presentation of gendered qualities. It's also one's deeply felt sense of self. That's what we call gender identity. Gender *could* be what we call male and female from a social standpoint, without regard to the need for reproduction, and it could be that there are more than two genders. Similarly, intersexed people potentially demonstrate that there are more than two discrete sexes, even though we tend to classify everything in these dichotomies of female and male, feminine and masculine.

"Perhaps this computer analogy will be helpful: think of sex as the hardware; gender as the software. In between there is an operating system that allows the software and hardware to give meaningful instructions to each other so they work together to accomplish tasks. It's easy to see how that works if a person's sex and gender are aligned, but what happens if your body doesn't match your sense of self? Think about that for a moment. Imagine you are exactly who you know yourself to be, you feel great about yourself, you have plans for your future, but when you look down your body is the opposite sex from who you know yourself to be. You know you're a woman, but you have to dress like a man, you have to behave like a man, because you have a male body. And you guys who know you're guys, you have all the feelings you know so well, but imagine your body is female. What's more valid: your feelings and your certain knowledge of yourself, or your body, the thing that other people see which signals to them what they can expect from you? Imagine what it would feel like to live with that

discrepancy. That's something like what many transgendered people feel, what they have to deal with every day.

"For transgendered and transsexual people, their sense of self doesn't line up with their body in various ways, or they may be perceived as belonging to one sex or gender when they actually belong to the other, or they don't feel they belong at all. But people seem to be more closely connected to their gender than to their sex. That's hard to grasp if your sex and gender are aligned, but not so difficult if you are one of the millions of people who are to some extent in-between. All the evidence of the physical body doesn't mean much when a person has a gender identity that doesn't match that body. Gender identity—the sense of self—is stronger than the body, and will find a way to manifest itself.

"To return to the computer analogy, one of the things we really don't know about in people is the interface between the software and the hardware. Take that male person with masculine characteristics: he may actually feel feminine, no matter what he looks or acts like. Or you might see a male person with feminine characteristics and assume that he is gay, but he may very well be straight or bisexual. And he might think of himself as masculine, no matter what you might conclude from observing him. Or he could think of himself as androgynous, and still have a prideful sense of himself as male and as a man. You simply can't tell by looking at someone what his or her sexual orientation is, or what the person's gender identity is. You may see aspects of the person's gender, just as you may see aspects of the person's sex, as in secondary sex characteristics, but those may or may not be the aspects with which the person identifies or experiences affinity, and those may not be the aspects that define that individual as to their gender or their sex by any particular standard. For example, we think of thick body hair as a masculine trait because it is more common for males, but many women have significantly visible hair on their arms or faces. Hair on her arms won't make a woman feel she's a man, nor does it necessarily detract from her femininity. If a woman wears jeans it doesn't mean she has a masculine gender identity. And if a woman is attractive and seems feminine to you, sir, it doesn't mean she is attracted to men, or even that she thinks of herself as a woman.

"This is very complicated human behavior. We can reduce it to this: if you're a girl and you want to wear lipstick because you like the way it makes you look and feel about yourself, and you're not allowed to wear lipstick, you may be able to divert your desire to wear lipstick, but that desire to express that gender-related characteristic will surface somehow, whether by finding times and places where you can wear lipstick with impunity or by finding some other way to express the same motivation. If you're a girl in a male body, those feelings don't change just because you're in a male body. It's your gender identity that's in the driver's seat."

REFERENCE

1. Graves, J. A. (2001). "From brain determinism to testis determination: Evolution of the mammalian sex-determining gene." *Reproduction, Fertility and Development,* 13(7-8): 665–72.

2

Gender Relations

R. W. CONNELL

PATTERNS IN GENDER

[Earlier on] included two studies of organizations, Barrie Thorne's study of American elementary schools and Dunbar Moodie's study of South African mines. Each of these organizations had a regular set of arrangements about gender: who was recruited to do what work (most of the teachers were women, all of the mineworkers were men); what social divisions were recognized (e.g. creating 'opposite sides' in the playground); how emotional relations were conducted (e.g. the 'mine wives'); and how these institutions were related to others (e.g. the families of the workers).

Such a pattern in gender arrangements may be called the *gender regime* of an institution. Research on

a very wide range of organizations has mapped their gender regimes—schools, offices, factories, armies, police forces, sporting clubs. It is clear that gender regimes are a usual feature of organizational life.

These studies make clear that the gender regime of an institution can change—though change is often resisted. An example is the merger of two gender-segregated English secondary schools described in a very interesting ethnography by Joan Draper (1993). After the merger some boys tried to establish dominance in the new social space, some girls accepted subordination, other girls fought it. Meanwhile other boys began experimenting with gender and turned up in dyed hair, eyeshadow and nail polish. The teachers found the turmoil hard to handle and some became distressed at the loss of their previously established place in the educational world. Over time, however, a new gender regime crystallized.

When Thorne went into Oceanside Elementary School and found that most of the teachers were women, she was not exactly surprised. That is the usual arrangement in elementary schools in the United States. Similarly, Moodie was not astonished to find an all-male workforce at the Witwatersrand gold mines he investigated. That is the usual arrangement in South African mines, and in mining all over the world.

The gender regimes of these particular organizations, then, are part of wider patterns, which also endure over time. I call these wider patterns the *gender order* of a society. The gender regimes of institutions usually correspond to the overall gender order, but may depart from it. This is important for change. Some institutions change quickly, others lag; or to put it another way, change often starts in one sector of society and takes time to seep through into other sectors.

When we look at a set of gender arrangements, whether the gender regime of an institution or the gender order of a whole society, we are basically looking at a set of *relationships*—ways that people, groups, and organizations are connected and divided. 'Gender-relations' are the relationships arising in and around the reproductive arena. Not all gender relations are direct interactions between women on one side and men on the other. The relations may be indirect—mediated, for instance, by a market, or by technologies such as TV or the Internet. Relationships may be among men, or among women, but still are gender relations—such as hierarchies of masculinity among men.

Gender relations are always being constituted in everyday life. If we don't bring it into being, gender does not exist. The point is forcibly made by ethnomethodology, a school of sociological research concerned with what we presuppose in everyday conduct. Candace West and Don Zimmerman, in a celebrated article called 'Doing Gender' (1987), show an impressive range of ways in which everyday speech constitutes gender relations. Not only are speakers identified in terms of their gender. Relationships between them, such as dominance, deference, antagonism, solidarity, are constantly being enacted in the course of conversations which are nominally about quite different subjects.

Yet we are not free to enact gender however we like. In reality, gender practice is powerfully constrained. When I, as an Australian academic in the 2000s, relate to people in gendered ways, I am not free to use the practices of a slave-owning Athenian aristocrat of the fifth century BC. Wrong meanings would be attached to my actions, and I would doubtless find time to work out my errors in gender theory from a cell in Long Bay Gaol.

Social theory has attempted to capture the fact of constraint and the patterns in relationships with the concept of *structure*. Relations among people (or among groups or institutions) would have little significance if they were randomly arranged. Patterns in these relations would matter little if they were ephemeral. It is the enduring or extensive patterns among social relations that social theory calls 'structures'.

The gender arrangements of a society involve social structure in this sense. For instance, if religious, political and conversational practices all place men in authority over women, we speak of a patriarchal structure of gender relations. Or if clans of men regularly marry each others' sisters, we speak of a kinship structure of exchange.

A structure of relations does not mechanically determine how people or groups act. That was the error of deterministic marxism. But a structure of relations certainly defines possibilities and consequences. For instance, the structure of gender relations in Australian society did not fix what sexual practices Huey Brown would engage in. But they gave him a definite set of possibilities. When he took up certain of them—continuing sex with men, drag, and domestic partnership—the structure of gender relations defined powerful consequences for his life, which are traced in Gary Dowsett's case study.

In this sense, social structure conditions practice. This does not imply that structures cause, or exist separately from practices. The structure of gender relations has no existence outside the practices through which people and groups conduct those relations. Structures do not continue, cannot be 'enduring', unless they are reconstituted from moment to moment in social action. In this sense gender, even in its most elaborate, abstract or fantastic forms, is always an 'accomplishment', as West and Zimmerman have put it. Gender is something usually done; and done in social life, not something that exists prior to social life.

FOUR DIMENSIONS OF GENDER

When the pioneering British feminist Juliet Mitchell published *Woman's Estate* in 1971, she argued that women's oppression involves not one, but four structures: production, reproduction, socialization and sexuality.

Why make such distinctions? Many discussions of gender do not. For instance, the feminist lawyer Catharine MacKinnon (1989), developing a theory of the state and the gender dimension of law, treats 'gender hierarchy' as a homogeneous whole. The anthropologist Gayle Rubin (1975), in a very influential model of the 'sex/gender system', treated the whole field as a single system. But when we look closely into these theories it becomes clear that each prioritizes a particular kind of relationship (MacKinnon: domination; Rubin: kinship). If we were to put power relations and kinship together in a more comprehensive picture of gender, we would need at least a two-dimensional model.

There are also practical reasons for acknowledging multiple dimensions in gender relations. We often experience disparities in gender relations, as if part of our lives were working on one gender logic, and another part on a different logic. When this happens in public life, not just in personal affairs, the complexity within the gender system becomes highly visible.

For instance, the modern liberal state defines men and women as citizens, that is, as alike. But the dominant sexual code defines men and women as opposites. Meanwhile customary ideas about the division of labour in family life define women as housewives and caretakers of children. Accordingly women entering the public domain—trying to exercise their rights as citizens—have an uphill battle to have their authority recognized. They may try to solve this problem by becoming 'honorary men', tougher than the toughest, like Margaret Thatcher in Britain and Madeleine Albright in the United States. But most women in politics, like Hillary Clinton in the United States and Cheryl Kernot in Australia, have to struggle for credibility.

The political scientist Carole Pateman (1988) dramatized this disparity in her argument that the 'social contract' of liberal society was underpinned by a 'sexual contract', the private subordination of women to men. This gave the whole of liberal democracy the character of a 'fraternal social contract', an agreement among men. The statistics of political participation suggest this is still broadly true around the world.

At times such disparities become so striking that they stimulate a strong cultural response. The sixteenth-century cult of 'Gloriana' is a fascinating example. Elizabeth Tudor became queen of England under rules of inheritance that preferred men but admitted women as residual heirs. She became a skilful politician, riding out rebellion and financial crisis, successfully managing deep religious tensions and the changing social forces represented in parliament—which broke out into revolution a few decades after her death. She was, in the language of the day, a strong monarch. But her authority was in flagrant contradiction with the ideas of a patriarchal society. To maintain legitimacy she and her supporters had to construct a new sexual identity (stalling endlessly on marriage negotiations, and celebrating the 'Virgin Queen') and a mixed-gender position as leader of a new cult of nationality. In a famous speech she gave at the time of the invasion threat from the Spanish Armada, Elizabeth put it this way:

> I know I have the body of a weak and feeble woman, but I have the heart and stomach of a king, and of a king of England too, and think foul scorn that [the duke of] Parma or [the king of] Spain, or any prince of Europe should dare to invade the borders of my realm; to which, rather than any dishonour shall grow by me, I myself will take up arms, I myself will be your general, judge, and rewarder of every one of your virtues in the field.
>
> *(Neale 1960: 302)*

An extraordinary literary cult was fostered, which by late in her reign was almost defining her as a supernatural being. This genre includes Spenser's *The Faerie Queene*, one of the great English epic poems.

There is, then, a strong case for seeing gender relations as internally complex, as involving multiple structures. If that general case is accepted, how are we to identify and map the structures involved?

Mitchell's original model mainly distinguished types of practice—work, child-rearing and sexuality—but also mixed these with social functions, such as 'reproduction' and 'socialization'. Apart from some logical inconsistency, this approach has limitations. It is clear, for instance, that rather different gender relations can exist in the same kind of practice. Consider, for instance, the range of social relations involved in 'sexuality', as shown in Dowsett's study of Harriet Brown.

An alternative approach is to identify different social dynamics, or processes of change, and try to work back to their internal logic. This was the approach taken by classical socialism, which identified the dynamic of class struggle and worked back to a structural analysis of capitalism. It is the approach of single-structure theories of patriarchy, which starts with the political dynamic of feminism and describes the system of power and oppression that feminism confronts.

A sophisticated development of this idea was offered by Sylvia Walby in *Theorizing Patriarchy*

(1990), which distinguishes six structures in contemporary patriarchy: paid employment, household production, culture, sexuality, violence, and the state. This greatly improves the kind of model seen in MacKinnon's work. Walby's model is still a model of patriarchy, that is to say, institutionalized inequality in gender relations. If we want to include in the picture of gender patterns that are not inherently unequal, we need a different formulation.

The model I suggest is a development from the one that I proposed in *Gender and Power* (Connell 1987). It distinguishes four dimensions of gender, describing four main structures in the modern system of gender relations. Later in the chapter I will discuss how these structures change. Here I will outline them and comment on their significance.

POWER RELATIONS

Power, as a dimension of gender, was central to the Women's Liberation concept of 'patriarchy', and to the social analyses that flowed from it: the idea of men as a dominant 'sex class', the analysis of rape as an assertion of men's power over women, and the critique of media images of women as passive, trivial and dumb.

Women's Liberation recognized that patriarchal power was not just a matter of direct control of women by individual men, but was also realized impersonally through the state. A classic example, analysed in a famous article by Catharine MacKinnon (1983), is court procedure in rape cases. Independent of any personal bias of the judge, the procedures by which rape charges are tried effectively place the complainant rather than the defendant 'on trial'. The woman's sexual history, marital situation and motives in laying a charge are all under scrutiny.

Many attempts at legal reform have been made since, and have proved that the inbuilt biases in social assumptions and court procedure about sexual assault are very difficult to eliminate. It can still be a damaging experience for a woman to bring charges. A very public example of the difficulty occurred in Sydney in late 2000. A young woman made a complaint to police about an event during a party in the Parliament buildings involving a sexual approach by a Member of Parliament in his office (he said the approach was consensual, she said it was not). The Speaker of the House (a man who belonged to the same party as the MP in question) responded by collecting derogatory evidence from an aide about the *woman's* behaviour on the night in question. The woman dropped the complaint to avoid the impact of publicity on her private life. Nevertheless an official inquiry was held in a blaze of publicity into the possibility of corrupt conduct by the Speaker, his aide and the MP. All were cleared.

Another important case of the institutionalization of power relations is bureaucracies. Clare Burton, an Australian social scientist who also served in public life as an equal opportunity commissioner, spoke of the 'mobilization of masculine bias' in selection and promotion of staff. By this she meant the impersonal but pervasive tendency, in organizations dominated by men, to favour criteria and procedures that favour men (Burton 1987).

Power also emerged as a major theme in Gay Liberation writing such as Dennis Altman's *Homosexual: Oppression and Liberation* (1972). In this case the focus was on power applied to a specific group of men: criminalization, police harassment, economic discrimination, and violence. Gay Liberation theorists linked the oppression of gay men with the oppression of lesbians and the oppression of women generally. This argument laid the foundation for the analysis of gendered power relations among men, and the distinction of hegemonic from subordinated masculinities (Carrigan, Connell and Lee 1985), which is important in current research on men and masculinities.

Power operating through institutions, power in the form of oppression of one group by another, is an important part of the structure of gender. But there is another approach to power, popularized by the French historian and philosopher Michel Foucault (1977). Foucault was sceptical of the idea that there was a unified, central agency of power in society. Rather, he argued, power is widely dispersed, and operates intimately and diffusely. Especially it operates discursively, through the ways we talk, write and conceptualize. This diffuse but tenacious power operates close up, not at a distance. It impacts directly on people's bodies as 'discipline' as well as on their identities and sense of their place in the world.

This post-structuralist approach appealed to many feminist as well as gay theorists, who saw here a way of understanding the fine texture, as well as the strength, of gendered power. Power is present intimately. The discourse of fashion and beauty, for instance, positions women as consumers, subjects them to humiliating tests of acceptability, enforces arbitrary rules and is responsible for much unhappiness, ill health, and even some deaths (among young women whose dieting goes out of control). Yet there is no Patriarchy Central compelling women to do all this. As the 'lip gloss' in Barrie Thorne's ethnography illustrates, girls and young women enter the world of fashion and beauty because they want to, because it delivers pleasures, and because the regulation and discipline are bound up with the identity they are seeking.

Both these approaches to power contribute to our understanding of gender relations: they are not exclusive. There is both organized, institutional power and diffuse, discursive power. And both approaches raise the crucial question of resistance.

To give a full account of power relations requires an account of the way power is contested, and countervailing power is mobilized. Total domination is extremely rare; even fascist dictatorships could not accomplish that. Gendered power is no more total than other kinds. Oppressive laws are met by campaigns for reform—such as the most famous of all feminist campaigns, the 'suffragette' struggle for the vote. Domestic patriarchy may be weakened, or manoeuvred around, by the inhabitants of the 'red chamber' (as the classic Chinese novel put it), the women of the household.

Discursive power can also be contested or transformed. The remarkable work of the Australian educator Bronwyn Davies shows that challenges to patriarchy need not involve head-on confrontation. In *Shards of Glass* (1993) Davies shows how educators in the classroom can help children and youth gain control of gender discourses. Young people can learn how they are discursively positioned and regulated, and can learn to shift between, or manoeuvre among, identities.

The conditions for resistance change in history. The modern liberal state, which emerged in Europe and North America in the eighteenth and nineteenth centuries, creates possibilities for mass politics which did not exist before. Monarchical states and household patriarchies did not depend on notions of citizenship; the liberal state does. In that sense, the development of patriarchal institutions themselves created the conditions for the emergence of modern feminism.

PRODUCTION RELATIONS

The 'sexual division of labour' was the first structure of gender to be recognized in social science, and remains the centre of most discussions of gender in anthropology and economics. In many societies, and in many situations, certain tasks are performed by men and others are performed by women. So, in the Aboriginal communities of the Australian central desert, hunting wallabies and kangaroos was undertaken by men, collecting root vegetables and seeds was mainly undertaken by women. In contemporary North America teaching young children is mainly done by women; in South Africa underground mining is entirely done by men.

Such divisions of labour are common throughout history and across cultures. But while gender divisions of labour are extremely common, there is not exactly the same division in different cultures or at different points of history. The same task may be 'women's work' in one context, and 'men's work' in another. Agricultural labour—digging and planting—is an important example.

A striking modern case is secretarial work. Being a clerk was originally a man's job—as described in Herman Melville's dark short story "Bartleby the Scrivener" (1853). With the advent of the typewriter and the growing scale of office work, clerical work increasingly involved women; in fact it became archetypical 'women's work', as Rosemary Pringle shows in *Secretaries Talk* (1989). But with the advent of the computer and word processing, 'the secretary' is disappearing as an occupational category. Clerical work is again, increasingly, being done by men.

In modern Western society, gender divisions between jobs are not the whole of the gender division of labour. There is a larger division between 'work'—the realm of paid labour and production for markets—and 'home'. The whole economic sphere is culturally defined as men's world (regardless of the presence of women in it), while domestic life is defined as women's world (regardless of the presence of men in it).

The Norwegian sociologist Øystein Holter (1995, 1997) argues that this division is the structural basis of the modern Western gender order. It is what makes this system different from the gender orders of non-Western, non-capitalist societies. His point is not only that our notions of 'masculinity' and 'femininity' are closely connected with this division. Just as important, the social relations that govern work in these two spheres are different. In the economy, work is done for pay, labour is bought and sold, and the products of labour are placed on a market where profit prevails. In the home, work is done for love (or from mutual obligation), the products of labour are a gift, the logic of gift-exchange prevails. From these structural differences, Holder argues, flow characteristically different experiences for men and women—and our ideas about the different natures of men and women.

This is not exactly a distinction between 'production' and 'consumption', though that has been suggested by others as the economic core of the gender system. Domestic 'consumption' requires work, just as much as factory-based 'production'. Housewives do not spend their time lolling on couches, and scoffing chocolates. Housework and childcare are hard work and the hours have remained long, despite the advent of 'labour-saving' machines like vacuum cleaners and microwave ovens. But housework and job-work are done in different social relations, as Holter correctly observes, and they consequently have very different cultural meanings.

The division of labour itself is only part of a larger process. In a modern economy the shared work of women and men is embodied in every major product, and every major service—therefore, in the process of economic growth. Yet women and men are differently located in that process, and . . . women and men get different benefits from it.

What can be seen here is gendered accumulation process. Maria Mies (1986), the German socialist feminist who has formulated this issue most clearly, suggests that the global economy has developed through a dual process of colonization and 'house-wifization'. Women in the colonized world, formerly full participants in local non-capitalist economies, have been increasingly pressed into the 'housewife' pattern of social isolation and dependence on a male breadwinner.

Accumulation in modern economies is organized through large corporations and global markets. The gender regimes of these institutions make it possible for them to apply the products of men's and women's joint work in gendered ways. The way firms distribute corporate income—through wage structures, benefits packages, etc.—tends to favour men, especially middle-class men. The products that corporations place on the market have gender effects and gendered uses, from cosmetics to armaments.

The gendered accumulation process has many effects beyond the 'economy' narrowly defined. For instance, where there is a gender division of labour in occupations—such as men being the majority in engineering and mechanical trades, women in arts-based and human service jobs—there will be a division in the education systems which prepare people for this work. It is not surprising to find that enrollments in school courses in 'engineering studies' and 'computer sciences' are overwhelmingly boys, while enrolments in 'fine arts' and 'hospitality' are mainly girls.

EMOTIONAL RELATIONS

The importance of emotional attachment in human life was made clear a hundred years ago by Sigmund Freud (1900). Borrowing ideas from neurology but mainly learning from his own case studies, Freud showed how charges of emotion—both positive and negative—were attached, in the unconscious mind, to images of other people. His famous analysis of the 'oedipus complex', the centrepiece of his theory of personality development, showed how important the patterning of these attachments, or cathexes, might be. (For clear and careful definitions of these terms see *The Language of Psycho-Analysis:* Laplanche and Pontalis 1973.)

In fact Freud was speaking not only about the individual mind, but also about the pattern of relationships inside an important social institution, the bourgeois family. He thus opened up for investigation the structure of emotional relations, attachments or commitments. This is an important dimension of gender, often interwoven with power and the division of labour (e.g., in the figures of the father and the mother), but also following its own logic.

Emotional commitments may be positive or negative, favourable or hostile towards the object. For instance, prejudice against women (misogyny), or against homosexuals (homophobia), is a definite emotional relationship. Emotional commitments may also be, as Freud emphasized, both loving and hostile at once. Ambivalence, as this state is called, is common in reality though it tends to be forgotten in gender myths and stereotypes.

A major arena of emotional attachment is sexuality. Anthropological and historical studies have made it clear that sexual relations involve culturally formed bodily relationships, not a simple biological reflex (Caplan 1987). They have a definable social structure. The main axis on which contemporary Western sexuality is organized is gender: the division between cross-gender (heterosexual) and same-gender (homosexual) relations. This distinction is so important that we treat it as defining different kinds of people ('homosexuals', 'heterosexuals'), and certain biologists go looking for a 'homosexual gene' to explain the difference. (However, no one has gone looking for the 'heterosexual gene'.)

But cross-cultural research shows that many societies do not make this distinction. They have both same-gender and cross-gender sexual encounters, but they do not arrange them the way we do, nor think they define different types of people. For instance, the 'Sambia', a community in Papua New Guinea described in a well-known ethnography by Gilbert Herdt, *Guardians of the Flutes* (1981), treat same-gender sexuality as a ritual practice that all men are involved in at a particular stage of life. From a Western point of view, all Sambia men are homosexuals at one age, and all switch over to become heterosexuals at another. That is absurd, of course. From a Sambian point of view, they are simply following the normal development of masculinity.

In contemporary Western society, households are expected to be formed on the basis of romantic love, that is, a strong individual attachment between two partners. This ideal is promoted in mass media and popular fiction, and its importance is confirmed by research with groups who might be thought sceptical of it. They include the men in Gary Dowsett's study (Harriet Brown was not alone wanting to live in a loving couple); and the American college students in an ethnography by Dorothy Holland and Margaret Eisenhart, *Educated in Romance* (1990).

Where this pattern holds, sexual attachment is now the main basis of household formation. The cultural dominance of the West has meant a shift, in many post-colonial situations, from the choice of a marriage partner by one's parents to the choice of a partner by personal attraction—romantic love. The resulting tensions are explored in the recent comedy *East is East*, a film about an Anglo-Pakistani family struggling about arranged marriages, Muslim tradition, and British working-class realities. Curmudgeonly conservatives warned that the shift from marriages arranged by wise parents to marriages contracted by impetuous youth risked the collapse of a household when the sexual interest died. The historically startling level of divorce in the United States—where according to very recent sample survey data, 43 percent of first marriages end in separation or divorce within fifteen years— shows they were right.

Emotional relations are also found in the workplace (and not just in the form of office sex). Rosemary Pringle's study, already mentioned, shows how emotional relations with bosses help to construct the very job of 'secretary'. Arlie Hochschild's classic *The Managed Heart* (1983) analyses emotional labour in the modern economy. There are many jobs where producing a particular emotional relationship with a customer is central to the work being done. These are, typically, gender-typed jobs. Hochschild's main examples are airline hostesses, a job where workers are trained to produce sympathy and induce relaxation; and telephone debt collectors, a job where workers must display aggression and induce fear. Hochschild argues that this kind of labour is becoming more common with the expansion of service industries. If so, alienated relations based on commercialized feelings and gender stereotypes may be increasingly important in modern life.

Hostile emotional relationships are not only symbolic, like the ones enacted by Hochschild's debt collectors. They may involve all too real practices of oppression. Stephen Tomsen's (1998) study of homophobic killings, for instance, shows two major patterns of conduct. One is gang attacks in public places by young men who go looking for gender deviants to punish, a process that depends on mutual encouragement in the group. The other is killings by individuals in private. Some of these involve a violent response to a sexual approach (and perhaps to the killers' own desires) which they think calls their masculinity into question. Both patterns may result in killings of extreme brutality.

Emotional relations go beyond the face-to-face. Nationalism, as Joane Nagel (1998) points out, constantly uses gender imagery in constructing national solidarities. We are all familiar with the 'family of the nation', the 'father of his country', the heroic soldier dying to protect his womenfolk, 'Mother Russia', the nation as goddess. It is no accident that, as Irina Novikova and Svetlana Slapšak (2000) show, new nationalisms in the former communist countries of eastern Europe are reasserting highly traditional gender images.

SYMBOLIC RELATIONS

All social practice involves interpreting the world. As post-structuralists observe, nothing human is 'outside' discourse. Society is unavoidably a world of meanings. At the same time, meanings bear the traces of the social processes by which they were made. This is the fundamental point made by the sociology of knowledge. Cultural systems bear particular social interests, and grow out of historically specific ways of life.

This point applies to gender meanings. Whenever we speak of 'a woman' or 'a man', we call into play a tremendous system of understandings, implications, overtones and allusions that have accumulated through our cultural history. The 'meanings' of these words are enormously greater than the biological categories of male and female. When the Papua New Guinea highland community studied by Marilyn Strathern (1978) say 'our clan is a clan of men', they do not mean that the clan entirely consists of males. When an American football coach yells at his losing team that they are 'a bunch of women', he does not mean they can now get pregnant. But both are saying something meaningful, and in their contexts, important.

The best-known model of the structure of symbolism in gender derives from the French psychoanalyst Jacques Lacan. Lacan's analysis of the phallus as master-symbol gave rise to an interpretation of language as 'phallocentric', a system in which the place of authority, the privileged subjectivity, is always that of the masculine. The potentially infinite play of meaning in language is fixed by the phallic point of reference; culture itself embodies the 'law of the father'. If that is so, the only way to contest patriarchal meanings is to escape known forms of language. Hence feminist thinkers in the 1970s, such as Xavière Gauthier, developed an interest in women's writing as an oppositional practice that had to subvert the laws of culture. (For translations of Gauthier, and other French feminists on this question, see Marks and de Courtivron 1981.)

Chris Weedon (1987) wonders how feminist theory could have adopted so deterministic a psychology, which gives no room for opposition, only for escape. There are certainly other schools of psychoanalysis which offer more open-ended accounts of gender and suggest more possibilities for action.

Nevertheless the dichotomous gender structuring of culture is important, and the Lacanian approach gives us some inkling of why patriarchal gender arrangements are so difficult to abolish. To do so involves uprooting, not just a few intolerant attitudes, but a whole system of communication and meaning. Queen Elizabeth, addressing her men at Tilbury, acknowledged 'the body of a weak and feeble woman', but claimed 'the heart and stomach of a king'. She could not have reversed her symbolism, and claimed 'the heart and stomach of a woman', if she were to motivate her troops to fight.

Though language—speech and writing—is the most analysed site of symbolic gender relations, it is not the only one. Gender symbolism also operates in dress, makeup, gesture, in photography and film, and in more impersonal forms of culture such as the built environment.

Elizabeth Wilson's (1987) elegant study of fashion, *Adorned in Dreams,* shows that women's and men's styles of dress not only symbolize gender difference, but are also a site of struggle over what women and men are allowed to do. The famous 'bloomers' of nineteenth-century dress reform were connected with the struggle to expand the rights of women. For a short while bloomers were adopted by suffrage activists. They were jeered at by conservatives because they symbolized emancipated women (not that they changed women's activities in practice). Similarly in the 1960s the new fashion styles were connected with young women's demand for sexual freedom, and were duly denounced as licentious. Jean Shrimpton, a visiting British fashion model, created a media scandal in Australia by going to the Melbourne Cup races in a mini-dress and—an unforgivable offence—without gloves!

Rosa Linda Fregoso's *The Bronze Screen* (1993) illustrates the play of gender relations in film—in this case, films produced by Chicana/Chicano filmmakers, about the community of Mexican affiliation in the south-western USA. Chicano (men) film-makers, Fregoso observes, have not demeaned their women characters, but they have not given them an active role in discourse. Only with the advent of woman film-makers did films start to explore generational difference, language, religion and relationships from women's standpoints, and show some of the tensions and ambiguities in women's position and responses. Architectural design also reflects assumptions about gender dichotomy and gendered spaces, and grows out of the designers' gendered experience. Annmarie Adams and Peta Tancred in *Designing Women* (2000), a study of gender and architecture in Canada, found that the imagery in professional journals persistently associated women with interiors, especially domestic interiors, but presented architects as 'powerful, virile, and masculine'. However, this pattern of marginalization changed as women arrived in the profession, and became influential in establishing the modernist style.

Symbolic relations in gender include the rules for 'gender attribution' studied by ethnomethodologists. Here we move below the level at which gender categories ordinarily appear, to consider how a person (or action) gets assigned to a gender category. These rules are normally taken for granted in everyday life. But they are painstakingly studied by cross-dressers and transsexuals hoping to 'pass', which requires one to produce an effect of naturalness by deliberate action. Accordingly, transsexuals have appeared to psychiatrists and ethnomethodologists as a kind of natural experiment exposing the cultural underpinnings of the gender system (Kessler and McKenna 1978).

But things get complicated when the transsexuals read the psychiatrists' and ethnomethodologists' books—as some now do. As a warning against over-simplified views of gender, transsexualism itself has now become a gender category, and to a certain extent—a sexual subculture. You can buy the international Tranny Guide (Vicky Lee 1999) to learn how to do it (with serious advice on body care, how to present at the job, etc.) and how to get in touch with the cross-dressing scene around the world. You can even check this scene out on the Internet (try www.wayout-publishing.com). In a recent book Viviane Namaste (2000) urges attention to the real-life situations and experiences of transsexual and transgendered people—which tend to be 'erased' by queer theory, social science and medicine alike.

The tyranny scene is determinedly upbeat, but there is a dark side to violating the cultural categories. Transgender people often face ostracism, loss of jobs, and family hostility, as well as major difficulties in sexual relations. Some have to support themselves by sex work such as stripping and prostitution. As Harriet found, there is a certain clientele of 'straight' men who are excited by transsexuals. But this does not mean they respect them. Roberta Perkins's pioneering book presenting the voices of transsexuals in Sydney includes Naomi, a stripper who remarked:

> I think men have a definite dislike for women in general, that's why women are raped and bashed, and strippers are up there to provide an outlet for this dislike by the yelling of profanities at them. Transsexuals are lower down than women according to men, and look how many men sexually abuse transsexuals.
>
> *(1983: 73)*

Naomi's point about abusive men relates not only to the cultural relations of gender but also to power relations, in the form of sexual violence. She also implies something about production relations—straight men have the economic resources to be the clients of these services. And of course her remarks relate to emotional relations, in terms of sexual desire and hatred. So all four structures of gender are present in this one situation.

This is usual. In distinguishing four structures of gender relations, I do not mean to suggest they operate in separate compartments of life. They are constantly intermingled and interacting in practice. I distinguish structures *analytically* because tracing out their logic helps in understanding an extremely complex reality. This does not imply that reality itself comes in boxes. Naomi, for one, knows that.

GENDER AS HISTORY

Ideologies of 'natural difference' have drawn much of their force from the traditional belief that gender never changes. Adam delved and Eve span, Men must work and Women must weep, Boys will be Boys. Serious analysis begins with the recognition that exactly the opposite is true: *everything about gender is historical.*

What does 'historical' mean? In the whole story of life on earth, human history represents a new process of change. Some time in the last half-million years, social dynamics replaced organic evolution as the central mechanism of change in our biosphere. Sociobiologists and evolutionary psychologists are not absurd in asking how human society is related to the evolution of the natural world. The same question was the centre of nineteenth-century sociology, when books with titles like *Social Evolution* (Kidd 1898) were best-sellers. But these authors, over-anxious to prove the continuity of evolution, miss the deep change in the process of change. A radically new dynamic was introduced when the collective capacities of humans could be mobilized by social relations. This is why human society, and not organic evolution, can produce cloth, pottery, ziggurats, irrigated rice-fields, rock music and gravity-wave detectors.

Some biological features of human ancestors were certainly preconditions of this change. The open architecture (to borrow a computer term) of the human hand, brain, and speech apparatus makes an immense range of applications possible. The human body, equipped with arm and hand, cannot scratch as sharply as a cat, dig as well as a wombat, swim as fast as a seal, manipulate as delicately as a monkey, or crush as powerfully as a bear. But it can do all those things moderately well; and it can make tools to do them all very well. This multiplies the capacities of any one person. Yet the greatest human invention of all is other human beings. We not only create social relations, we teach new generations to operate in, and build on, the social relations already existing. With cumulating effects over time, social relations multiply the capacities of any individual body on the astonishing scale we see all around us. So great a multiplication, ironically, that it now threatens human life by nuclear war or environmental disaster.

The horizon in time where history appears is also the horizon of gender. In the broadest perspective, gender represents the transformation of the system of sexual reproduction by social action. Human collective capacities, organized through social relations, lead to entirely new possibilities. Some are for creativity and pleasure. For instance, sexuality is constructed in culture, and the world of love and eroticism becomes possible. Some are for subjection and exploitation. Patriarchy becomes possible, along with family property, bride-price, convents and prostitution.

Above this horizon is the history of gender: the course of events that has produced the actual gender orders we live in. The history of gender includes the history of practices, and transformations of the body in practice. It includes the production and transformation of the categories of gender. We know these are not fixed; new categories ('the homosexual', 'the housewife') appear and others decline. The history of gender includes the gender regimes of institutions and the gender orders of societies.

This is, in principle, a world history. That idea was first formulated in the nineteenth century, in debates about 'origins' which invented the idea of a primitive matriarchy. The search for origins was resumed in the 1970s in the debate about patriarchy unleashed by Women's Liberation. The search is futile. As the French feminist Christine Delphy (1984) showed in a brilliant critique, origins stories are not history but are a form of myth-making. They create myths in which later social arrangements are explained (and often justified) by a mechanism 'discovered' at the point of origin.

A real history of gender begins with the recognition that the later course of events is *not* contained in any founding moment.

Rather, an open-ended social process is involved, which must be studied in all its complexity by patient examination of the historical records: the archaeological deposits, the written sources, the oral traditions. Local history of this kind has flourished for several decades, being one of the main branches of Women's Studies. It has produced superb work, such as *Family Fortunes* by Leonore Davidoff and Catherine Hall (1987), a social history of gender in the English middle class of the

industrial revolution. A world history of gender has taken longer to develop, but now seems to be emerging from two starting points. One is the archaeological reconstruction of gender relations in prehistory and ancient urban cultures (Gero and Conkey 1991). The other is the study of gender relations in modern imperialism, the global process which has at last reversed the proliferation of cultures and begun to create a single world society.

Recognizing the deeply historical character of gender has an important and intellectual and political consequence. If a structure can come into existence, it can also go out of existence. The history of gender may have an end.

There are several ways in which gender relations might cease to be important conditions of social life. They might be weakened by an internal uncoupling, so that gender patterns in one domain of practice cease to reinforce those in another. Alternatively, gender relations might be overwhelmed by some other historical dynamic. This was expected by marxists like Alexandra Kollontai, who thought that proletarianization and socialist revolution would end the oppression of women. In our day, the total triumph of the market might do the job.

Finally, gender relations might be extinguished by a deliberate de-gendering, in which the reach of gender structure is reduced to zero. A de-gendering logic is found in some current feminist strategies, such as equal opportunity and anti-discrimination policies. Not all feminists agree with the de-gendering approach, and not all theorists assume a complete de-gendering of society is possible. Even if it is impractical, however, a gender-free society remains an important conceptual benchmark for thinking about change.

THE PROCESS OF CHANGE

Most discussions of why gender arrangements change have focused on external pressures on the gender order: changing technology, urban life, the demands of capitalism, mass communications, secularism, modernization or Westernization.

It is true that these social forces can produce change in gender relations. But gender relations also have internal tendencies towards change. Further, some of the 'external' forces are gendered from the start (for instance, the capitalist economic system). In this discussion I will focus on the dynamics of change that arise within gender relations.

Post-structuralist theory has recognized internal tendencies towards change by arguing that gender categories are inherently unstable. For instance, the uncertain and contested character of the category 'women' is a theme of Judith Butler's well-known book *Gender Trouble* (1990). Gender identities are produced discursively. But meanings in discourse are not fixed. Indeed they are inherently unstable, incapable of being fixed.

Further, there is no fixed connection between discursive identities and the bodies to which those identities refer. The signifier is able to float free, in a play of meanings and pleasures. That is sometimes thought to be a general feature of 'postmodern' life, and it certainly suggests that gender identities can be played with, taken up and abandoned, unpacked and recombined. This has been a theme in the 'queer theory' of the 1990s and in other applications of post-structuralist and postmodern ideas.

There are several difficulties with a concept of generalized instability. It can be made true by definition, but in that case is not interesting. If it is open to empirical checking, then it is difficult to avoid the fact that in some historical situations gender identities and relations change slowly, in other situations they change explosively. A good example is Irina Novikova's account of the Soviet and post-Soviet gender orders. Nor does a concept of generalized instability give any grip on why some people would want to change gender arrangements, while others would resist changes. This is a question of central importance for the politics of gender. It raises the issue of the differing material interests that different groups have in an unequal society—a question hard to formulate in a purely discursive theory.

The post-structuralist approach is helpful in emphasizing that identities are always historically constructed and in principle open to change; but we need a more specific theory to understand how change occurs. The key is to recognize that structures develop *crisis tendencies,* that is, internal contradictions or tendencies that undermine current patterns and force change in the structure itself.

This approach to change—which draws from German critical theory, especially Jürgen Habermas (1976)—allows us to distinguish periods when pressures for change are well controlled, or are gradually building, from periods when crisis tendencies erupt into actual crisis and force rapid change. It also allows us to identify interests that can be mobilized for and against change, by examining where different groups are located in the structure under pressure, and how they have come into being within that structure. Crisis tendencies can be identified in each of the four structures of gender relations identified earlier in this chapter.

Power relations show the most spectacular recent change. A global movement for the emancipation of women has appeared, challenging men's control of institutions as well as men's power in the intimate spheres of sexuality and the family.

The main crisis tendency here has often been noticed. There is an underlying contradiction between the subordination of women to men in patriarchal homes and workplaces, and the abstract equality between women and men which is presupposed by citizenship and markets. Over the last two centuries this contradiction has sharpened, as the liberal state has developed, and market relations have come to dominate the economy.

Women are the main group subordinated in patriarchal power structures and so have a structural interest in change. Feminist movements, mobilizing women, have been energized by this contradiction and have used it to break down inequality. They have persistently claimed 'rights' in the public sphere and used those rights to challenge oppression in private spheres. The campaign against domestic violence is a notable example (see Rebecca Dobash and Russell Dobash 1992). This campaign, claiming human rights to safety and freedom from fear, has used the patriarchal state itself to enforce these rights when violated by husbands and de factos.

Production relations have also been the site of massive change. Through the second half of the twentieth century there was a worldwide incorporation of women's labour into the market economy. In the industrialized countries this took the form of a huge growth in married women's 'workforce participation' rates, especially in the service sector. In the developing world it took the form of an even more massive move into cities and into market-based agriculture. By the end of the century adult women's workforce participation was over 90 percent of the men's rate in Cambodia, Ghana, Tanzania, Vietnam, Malawi, Rwanda, Mozambique, Burundi, Guinea, Benin and Sweden—and not far behind that in other parts of Scandinavia, eastern Europe, the former Soviet Union, China, central and west Africa.

There is an underlying contradiction between the equal contribution to social labour by women and men (bearing in mind unpaid as well as paid work) and the gendered appropriation of the products of social labour. The gendered appropriation is seen in the unequal incomes of women and men as groups, the better conditions and career prospects men generally have, and the patriarchal inheritance of wealth. (It is still the general rule in big business that sons may take over the company but daughters hardly ever do.)

Women have a general interest in changing this. One consequence is that women workers make up a growing proportion of union members, and union militants. The story of women's struggle to establish their presence in the union movement is told in Suzanne Franzway's *Sexual Politics and Greedy Institutions* (forthcoming). It is significant that the latest two presidents of the Australian Council of Trade Unions (the unions' peak organization in that country) have been women. But the turbulence of the gendered accumulation process, and its interplay with class and colonial relations, create complex economic situations. An important consequence is that some women—and often the most influential—have an interest in resisting economic reform, because this would disturb the corporate system from which they benefit.

Emotional relations have also seen important recent changes in the industrialized countries. Though lesbians and gay men are still subject to homophobic abuse and violence, homosexual sexuality has to a certain extent achieved legitimacy as an alternative within the heterosexual order. Visible gay and lesbian communities now exist in many cities, anti-discrimination and anti-defamation laws exist in a number of countries, and there is a limited representation of gay and lesbian communities in some political systems and in some areas of policy-making (e.g. in relation to the HIV/AIDS epidemic). As Dennis Altman (1982) pointed out, gay and lesbian communities have achieved a position in some ways resembling that of ethnic minorities.

This is a partial resolution of a long-standing contradiction. The patriarchal gender order prohibits some forms of emotional attachment and pleasure which its own gender arrangements (e.g. homo-social institutions, the oedipal family) produce. A related logic operates within heterosexual relations. The constantly growing incitement to sexual activity (what conservatives call 'permissiveness') contradicts the continuing definition of women as sexually passive, as the objects of men's desire and seduction. The result has been an uneven pattern of change, seen in surveys of sexual behaviour, where women's sexual repertoire has been growing but the 'double standard' for women and men remains.

Symbolic relations are the home ground of generalized-instability arguments, which centre on the discursive construction of identities. It might therefore seem difficult to define crisis tendencies here. But what has made it possible to recognize unstable identities is a tendency towards crisis in the legitimation of patriarchy.

Patriarchy has long been legitimated by belief systems which picture gender as a timeless, unchanging division—whether laid down by God or fixed by the genes—which makes 'woman's place' the right place for ever and ever. Over the last century and a half, social and intellectual movements have chipped away at these assumptions: from the woman suffrage movement and psychoanalysis to

Gay Liberation and post-structuralism. Natural-difference ideas remain very influential in popular culture. But over time their capacity to form the unquestioned common sense of society has been undermined. In an era when 'sex changes' are reported in the media, governments have Equal Opportunity targets, and global conferences on gender reform occur, it is difficult to take for granted a timeless male/female opposition.

A vast change in presuppositions has thus occurred in the cultural-life of the industrial (and many industrializing) countries. A hundred years ago those who claimed equality for women, or rights for homosexuals, had to justify the claim against presuppositions to the contrary. Now those who deny equality or rights have to justify their denial against a presumption for equality and a presumption that change can occur. The boot is on the other foot.

This discussion has focused on crisis tendencies on the large scale. It is also possible for crisis tendencies to emerge on the small scale—in personal life and in intimate relationships. Crisis tendencies arise when personal practice is structured around commitments which are both urgent and contradictory. The classic case is the incompatible desires and fears of the young child in the 'oedipal' crisis, which Freud thought the basis of all later neuroses. We do not have to accept Freud's theory to agree that contradictions often arise in personal life, and drive change in a person's trajectory through life.

These changes may be individual and produce nothing but eccentricity. But they may also move in parallel with other lives, and this can result in sustainable change. The Women's Liberation movement of the 1960s and 1970s was not just a public event; it was fuelled by contradictions in the personal lives of women, especially in their relations with men. Narratives by women from this movement (e.g. those collected by Barbara Laslett and Barrie Thorne, 1997) show how the similarity of these experiences was recognized and became a basis of solidarity. Their actions, in turn, stimulated changes in the trajectories of certain men. One consequence was the 'fair families'

of the 1980s and 1990s, whose story has recently been explored by Barbara Risman (1998).

Since the involvement of the body in gender relations is a social process, crisis tendencies may also arise at the level of the body. Freud's classic analysis of 'hysteria' recognized precisely that: a bodily effect (e.g. a cough, or a paralysed arm) whose cause was a psychological conflict. The bodily effects may be much rougher than Dr. Freud's genteel patients were used to. Asserting masculinity, in a poor neighbourhood or a factory or on the road, may result in violence, industrial injury, or road death. I noted . . . how factory work consumes the workers' bodies, and how exemplary masculinity in professional sport produces over-use, injury, and long-term bodily damage.

Crisis tendencies may even affect bodily sensations. As Lynne Segal observes in *Straight Sex* (1994), there have been many difficulties in heterosexual relations connected with the new feminism. They are not necessarily produced by feminism—arguably, by the same crisis tendencies that gave rise to feminism. Similarly, the violations of gender boundaries in transsexuality do not just occur in people's heads. They often involve bodily sensations such as hallucinations of a body of the other sex, or a sensation of being trapped within the wrong body—see, for instance, Katherine Cummings' account of her transsexual experience in *Katherine's Diary* (1992).

Thus crisis tendencies in gender emerge on the large scale and on the small. All four structures contain crisis tendencies; but they are not the same tendencies, and they do not necessarily develop at the same pace or mature at the same time. There is, thus, complexity and unevenness in the process of historical change. It is not surprising that gender orders are far from homogeneous, and that gender politics are complicated and turbulent.

REFERENCES

1. Adams, Annmarie, and Peta Tancred. 2000. *Designing Women: Gender and the Architectural Profession,* Toronto: University of Toronto Press.
2. Altman, Dennis, 1972. *Homosexual: Oppression and Liberation.* Sydney: Angus & Robertson.

3. _____ 1982. *The Homosexualization of America, the Americanization of the Homosexual.* New York: St Martin's Press.

4. Burton, Clare. 1987. 'Merit and gender: organizations and the mobilisation of masculine bias', *Australian Journal of Social Issues* 22: 424–35.

5. Butler, Judith. 1990. *Gender Trouble: Feminism and the Subversion of Identity.* New York: Routledge.

6. Caplan, Pat, ed. 1987. *The Cultural Construction of Sexuality.* London: Tavistock.

7. Carrigan, Tim, Robert Connell, and John Lee. 1985. 'Toward a new sociology of masculinity', *Theory and Society* 14: 551–604.

8. Connell, R. W. 1987. *Gender and Power: Society, the Person and Sexual Politics.* Cambridge: Polity.

9. Cummings, Katherine. 1992. *Katherine's Diary: The Story of a Transsexual.* Melbourne: Heinemann.

10. Davidoff, Leonore, and Catherine Hall. 1987. *Family Fortunes: Men & Women of the English Middle Class 1780–1850.* London: Hutchinson.

11. Davies, Bronwyn. 1993. *Shards of Glass: Children Reading and Writing beyond Gendered Identities.* Sydney: Allen & Unwin.

12. Delphy, Christine. 1984. *Close to Home: A Materialist Analysis of Women's Oppression.* London: Hutchinson.

13. Dobash, R. Emerson, and Russell P. Dobash. 1992. *Women, Violence and Social Change.* London: Routledge.

14. Dowsett, Gary W. 1996. *Practicing Desire: Homosexual Sex in the Era of AIDS.* Stanford, Calif.: Stanford University Press.

15. Draper, Joan. 1993. 'We're back with Gobbo: the reestablishment of gender relations following a school merger', pp. 49–74 in *Gender and Ethnicity in Schools: Ethnographic Accounts,* edited by P. Woods and M. Hammersley. London: Routledge/Open University.

16. Foucault, Michel. 1977. *Discipline and Punish: The Birth of the Prison,* translated by A. Sheridan. New York: Pantheon.

17. Franzway, Suzanne. forthcoming. *Sexual Politics and Greedy Institutions.* Sydney: Pluto Press.

18. Fregoso, Rosa Linda. 1993. *The Bronze Screen: Chicana and Chicano Film Culture.* Minneapolis: University of Minnesota Press.

19. Freud, Sigmund. 1953 [1900]. *The Interpretation of Dreams,* in *Complete Psychological Works,* vols 4–5. London: Hogarth.

20. Gero, Joan M., and Margaret W. Conkey, eds. 1991. *Engendering Archaeology: Women and Prehistory.* Oxford: Blackwell.

21. Habermas, Jürgen. 1976. *Legitimation Crisis.* London: Heinemann.

22. Herdt, Gilbert H. 1981. *Guardians of the Flutes: Idioms of Masculinity.* New York: McGraw-Hill.

23. Hochschild, Arlie Russell. 1983. *The Managed Heart: Commercialization of Human Feeling.* Berkeley: University of California Press.

24. Holland, Dorothy C., and Margaret A. Eisenhart. 1990. *Educated in Romance: Woman, Achievement, and College Culture.* Chicago: University of Chicago Press.

25. Holter, Øystein Gullvåg. 1995. 'Family theory reconsidered', pp. 99–129 in *Labour of Love: Beyond the Self-Evidence of Everyday Life,* edited by T. Borchgrevink and Ø. G. Holter. Aldershot: Avebury.

26. _____ 1997. *Gender, Patriarchy and Capitalism: A Social Forms Analysis.* Oslo: University of Oslo.

27. Kessler, Suzanne J., and Wendy McKenna. 1978. *Gender: An Ethnomethodological Approach.* New York: Wiley.

28. Kidd, Benjamin. 1898. *Social Evolution,* 3rd edition. London: Macmillan.

29. Laplanche, J., and J.-B. Pontalis. 1973. *The Language of Psycho-Analysis.* New York: Norton.

30. Laslett, Barbara, and Barrie Thorne, eds. 1997. *Feminist Sociology: Life Histories of a Movement.* New Brunswick: Rutgers University Press.

31. Lee, Vicky, ed. 1999. *The Tranny Guide,* 7th edition. London: Way Out Publishing.

32. MacKinnon, Catharine A. 1983. 'Feminism, marxism, method and the state: toward feminist jurisprudence', *Signs* 8: 635–58.

33. _____ 1989. *Toward a Feminist Theory of the State.* Cambridge, Mass.: Harvard University Press.

34. Marks, Elaine, and Isabelle de Courtivron, eds. 1981. *New French Feminisms: An Anthology.* Brighton: Harvester.

35. Melville, Herman. 1969 [1853]. 'Bartleby the Scrivener', pp. 159–90 in *Alienation: A Casebook,* edited by D. J. Burrows and F. R. Lapides. New York: Crowell.

36. Mies, Maria, 1986. *Patriarchy and Accumulation on a World Scale: Women in the International Division of Labour.* London: Zed Books.

37. Mitchell, Juliet. 1971. *Woman's Estate.* Harmondsworth: Penguin.

38. Nagel, Joane. 1998. 'Masculinity and nationalism: gender and sexuality in the making of nations', *Ethnic and Racial Studies* 21: 242–69.

39. Namaste, Viviane K. 2000. *Invisible Lives: The Erasure of Transsexual and Transgendered People.* Chicago: University of Chicago Press.

40. Neale, J. E. 1960. *Queen Elizabeth I.* Harmondsworth: Penguin.

41. Novikova, Irina. 2000. 'Soviet and post-Soviet masculinities: after men's wars in women's memories', pp. 117–29 in *Male Roles, Masculinities and Violence: A Culture of Peace Perspective,* edited by I. Breines, R. Connell and I. Eide. Paris: UNESCO Publishing.

42. Pateman, Carole. 1988. *The Sexual Contract.* Stanford, Calif.: Stanford University Press.

43. Perkins, Roberta. 1983. *The 'Drag Queen' Scene: Transsexuals in Kings Cross.* Sydney: Allen & Unwin.

44. Pringle, Rosemary. 1989. *Secretaries Talk: Sexuality, Power and Work.* Sydney: Allen & Unwin.

45. Risman, Barbara J. 1998. *Gender Vertigo: American Families in Transition.* New Haven: Yale University Press.

46. Rubin, Gayle. 1975. 'The traffic in women: notes on the "political economy" of sex', pp. 157–210 in *Toward an Anthropology of Woman,* edited by R. R. Reiter. New York: Monthly Review.

47. Segal, Lynne. 1994. *Straight Sex: Rethinking the Politics of Pleasure.* Berkeley: University of California Press.

48. Slapšak, Svetlana. 2000. 'Hunting, ruling, sacrificing: tradional male practices in contemporary Balkan culture', pp. 131–42 in *Male Roles, Masculinities and Violence: A*

Culture of Peace Perspective, edited by I. Breines, R. W. Connell and I. Eide. Paris: UNESCO Publishing.

49. Strathern, Marilyn. 1978. 'The achievement of sex: paradoxes in Hagen gender-thinking', pp. 171–202 in *The Yearbook of Symbolic Anthropology,* edited by E. Schwimmer, London: Hurst.

50. Thorne, Barrie. 1993. *Gender Play: Girls and Boys in School.* New Brunswick: Rutgers University Press.

51. Tomsen, Stephen. 1998. '"He had to be a poofter or something": violence, male honour and heterosexual panic', *Journal of Interdisciplinary Gender Studies* 3(2): 44–57.

52. Walby, Sylvia. 1990. *Theorizing Patriarchy.* Oxford: Basil Blackwell.

53. Weedon, Chris. 1987. *Feminist Practice and Poststructuralist Theory.* Oxford: Basil Blackwell.

54. West, Candace, and Don H. Zimmerman. 1987. 'Doing gender', *Gender and Society* 1: 125–51.

55. Wilson, Elizabeth. 1987. *Adorned in Dreams: Fashion and Modernity.* Berkeley: University of California Press.

✳ 3

The Invention of Heterosexuality

JONATHAN NED KATZ

Heterosexuality is old as procreation, ancient as the lust of Eve and Adam. That first lady and gentleman, we assume, perceived themselves, behaved, and felt just like today's heterosexuals. We suppose that heterosexuality is unchanging, universal, essential: ahistorical.

Contrary to that common sense conjecture, the concept of heterosexuality is only one particular historical way of perceiving, categorizing, and imagining the social relations of the sexes. Not ancient at all, the idea of heterosexuality is a modern invention, dating to the late nineteenth century. The heterosexual belief, with its metaphysical claim to eternity, has a particular, pivotal place in the social universe of the late nineteenth and twentieth centuries that it did not inhabit earlier. This essay traces the historical process by which the heterosexual idea was created as ahistorical and taken-for-granted. . . .

By not studying the heterosexual idea in history, analysts of sex, gay and straight have continued to

privilege the "normal" and "natural" at the expense of the "abnormal" and "unnatural." Such privileging of the norm accedes to its domination, protecting it from questions. By making the normal the object of a thoroughgoing historical study we simultaneously pursue a pure truth and a sex-radical and subversive goal: we upset basic preconceptions. We discover that the heterosexual, the normal, and the natural have a history of changing definitions. Studying the history of the term challenges its power.

Contrary to our usual assumption, past Americans and other peoples named, perceived, and socially organized the bodies, lusts, and intercourse of the sexes in ways radically different from the way we do. If we care to understand this vast past sexual diversity, we need to stop promiscuously projecting our own hetero and homo arrangement. Though lip-service is often paid to the distorting, ethnocentric effect of such conceptual imperialism, the category heterosexuality continues to be applied uncritically as a universal analytical tool. Recognizing the time-bound and culturally-specific character of the heterosexual category can help us begin to work toward a thoroughly historical view of sex. . . .

BEFORE HETEROSEXUALITY: EARLY VICTORIAN TRUE LOVE, 1820–1860

In the early nineteenth-century United States, from about 1820 to 1860, the heterosexual did not exist. Middle-class white Americans idealized a True Womanhood, True Manhood, and True Love, all characterized by "purity"—the freedom from sensuality.[1] Presented mainly in literary and religious texts, this True Love was a fine romance with no lascivious kisses. This ideal contrasts strikingly with late nineteenth- and twentieth-century American incitements to a hetero sex.*

---

*Some historians have recently told us to revise our idea of sexless Victorians: their experience and even their ideology, it is said, were more erotic than we previously thought. Despite the revisionists, I argue that "purity" was indeed the dominant, early Victorian, white middle-class standard. For the debate on Victorian sexuality see John D'Emilio and Estelle Freedman, *Intimate Matters: A History of Sexuality in America* (New York: Harper & Row, 1988), p. xii.

Early Victorian True Love was only realized within the mode of proper procreation, marriage, the legal organization for producing a new set of correctly gendered women and men. Proper womanhood, manhood, and progeny—not a normal male-female eros—was the main product of this mode of engendering and of human reproduction.

The actors in this sexual economy were identified as manly men and womanly women and as procreators, not specifically as erotic beings or heterosexuals. Eros did not constitute the core of a heterosexual identity that inhered, democratically, in both men and women. True Women were defined by their distance from lust. True Men, though thought to live closer to carnality, and in less control of it, aspired to the same freedom from concupiscence.

Legitimate natural desire was for procreation and a proper manhood or womanhood; no heteroerotic desire was thought to be directed exclusively and naturally toward the other sex; lust in men was roving. The human body was thought of as a means towards procreation and production; penis and vagina were instruments of reproduction, not of pleasure. Human energy, thought of as a closed and severely limited system, was to be used in producing children and in work, not wasted in libidinous pleasures.

The location of all this engendering and procreative labor was the sacred sanctum of early Victorian True Love, the home of the True Woman and True Man—a temple of purity threatened from within by the monster masturbator, an archetypal early Victorian cult figure of illicit lust. The home of True Love was a castle far removed from the erotic exotic ghetto inhabited most notoriously then by the prostitute, another archetypal Victorian erotic monster. . . .

LATE VICTORIAN SEX-LOVE: 1860–1892

"Heterosexuality" and "homosexuality" did not appear out of the blue in the 1890s. These two eroticisms were in the making from the 1860s on. In late Victorian America and in Germany, from about 1860 to 1892, our modern idea of an eroticized

universe began to develop, and the experience of a heterolust began to be widely documented and named. . . .

In the late nineteenth-century United States, several social factors converged to cause the eroticizing of consciousness, behavior, emotion, and identity that became typical of the twentieth-century Western middle class. The transformation of the family from producer to consumer unit resulted in a change in family members' relation to their own bodies; from being an instrument primarily of work, the human body was integrated into a new economy, and began more commonly to be perceived as a means of consumption and pleasure. Historical work has recently begun on how the biological human body is differently integrated into changing modes of production, procreation, engendering, and pleasure so as to alter radically the identity, activity, and experience of that body.[2]

The growth of a consumer economy also fostered a new pleasure ethic. This imperative challenged the early Victorian work ethic, finally helping to usher in a major transformation of values. While the early Victorian work ethic had touted the value of economic production, that era's procreation ethic had extolled the virtues of human reproduction. In contrast, the late Victorian economic ethic hawked the pleasures of consuming, while its sex ethic praised an erotic pleasure principle for men and even for women.

In the late nineteenth century, the erotic became the raw material for a new consumer culture. Newspapers, books, plays, and films touching on sex, "normal" and "abnormal," became available for a price. Restaurants, bars, and baths opened, catering to sexual consumers with cash. Late Victorian entrepreneurs of desire incited the proliferation of a new eroticism, a commoditized culture of pleasure.

In these same years, the rise in power and prestige of medical doctors allowed these upwardly mobile professionals to prescribe a healthy new sexuality. Medical men, in the name of science, defined a new ideal of male-female relationships that included, in women as well as men, an essential, necessary, normal eroticism. Doctors, who had earlier named and judged the sex-enjoying woman a "nymphomaniac," now began to label women's *lack* of sexual pleasure a mental disturbance, speaking critically, for example, of female "frigidity" and "anesthesia."*

By the 1880s, the rise of doctors as a professional group fostered the rise of a new medical model of Normal Love, replete with sexuality. The new Normal Woman and Man were endowed with a healthy libido. The new theory of Normal Love was the modern medical alternative to the old Cult of True Love. The doctors prescribed a new sexual ethic as if it were a morally neutral, medical description of health. The creation of the new Normal Sexual had its counterpart in the invention of the late Victorian Sexual Pervert. The attention paid the sexual abnormal created a need to name the sexual normal, the better to distinguish the average him and her from the deviant it.

HETEROSEXUALITY: THE FIRST YEARS, 1892–1900

In the periodization of heterosexual American history suggested here, the years 1892 to 1900 represent "The First Years" of the heterosexual epoch, eight key years in which the idea of the heterosexual and homosexual were initially and tentatively formulated by U.S. doctors. The earliest-known American use of the word "heterosexual" occurs in a medical journal article by Dr. James G. Kiernan of Chicago, read before the city's medical society on March 7, 1892, and published that May—portentous dates in sexual history.[3] But Dr. Kiernan's heterosexuals were definitely not exemplars of normality. Heterosexuals, said Kiernan, were defined by a mental condition, "psychical hermaphroditism." Its symptoms were "inclinations to both sexes." These heterodox sexuals also betrayed inclinations "to abnormal methods of gratification," that

is, techniques to insure pleasure without procreation. Dr. Kiernan's heterogeneous sexuals did demonstrate "traces of the normal sexual appetite" (a touch of procreative desire). Kiernan's normal sexuals were implicitly defined by a monolithic other-sex inclination and procreative aim. Significantly, they still lacked a name.

Dr. Kiernan's article of 1892 also included one of the earliest-known uses of the word "homosexual" in American English. Kiernan defined "Pure homosexuals" as persons whose "general mental state is that of the opposite sex." Kiernan thus defined homosexuals by their deviance from a gender norm. His heterosexuals displayed a double deviance from both gender and procreative norms.

Though Kiernan used the new words heterosexual and homosexual, an old procreative standard and a new gender norm coexisted uneasily in his thought. His word heterosexual defined a mixed person and compound urge, abnormal because they wantonly included procreative and nonprocreative objectives, as well as same-sex and different-sex attractions.

That same year, 1892, Dr. Krafft-Ebing's influential *Psychopathia Sexualis* was first translated and published in the United States.[4] But Kiernan and Krafft-Ebing by no means agreed on the definition of the heterosexual. In Krafft-Ebing's book, "heterosexual" was used unambiguously in the modern sense to refer to an erotic feeling for a different sex. "Homo-sexual" referred unambiguously to an erotic feeling for a "same sex." In Krafft-Ebing's volume, unlike Kiernan's article, heterosexual and homosexual were clearly distinguished from a third category, a "psycho-sexual hermaphroditism," defined by impulses toward both sexes.

Krafft-Ebing hypothesized an inborn "sexual instinct" for relations with the "opposite sex," the inherent "purpose" of which was to foster procreation. Krafft-Ebing's erotic drive was still a reproductive instinct. But the doctor's clear focus on a different-sex versus same-sex sexuality constituted a historic, epochal move from an absolute procreative standard of normality toward a new norm. His definition of heterosexuality as other-sex attraction provided

---

*This reference to females reminds us that the invention of heterosexuality had vastly different impacts on the histories of women and men. It also differed in its impact on lesbians and heterosexual women, homosexual and heterosexual men, the middle class and working class, and on different religious, racial, national, and geographic groups.

the basis for a revolutionary, modern break with a centuries-old procreative standard.

It is difficult to overstress the importance of that new way of categorizing. The German's mode of labeling was radical in referring to the biological sex, masculinity or femininity, and the pleasure of actors (along with the procreant purpose of acts). Krafft-Ebing's heterosexual offered the modern world a new norm that came to dominate our idea of the sexual universe, helping to change it from a mode of human reproduction and engendering to a mode of pleasure. The heterosexual category provided the basis for a move from a production-oriented, procreative imperative to a consumerist pleasure principle—an institutionalized pursuit of happiness. . . .

Only gradually did doctors agree that heterosexual referred to a normal, "other-sex" eros. This new standard-model heterosex provided the pivotal term for the modern regularization of eros that paralleled similar attempts to standardize masculinity and femininity, intelligence, and manufacturing.[5] The idea of heterosexuality as the master sex from which all others deviated was (like the idea of the master race) deeply authoritarian. The doctors' normalization of a sex that was hetero proclaimed a new heterosexual separatism—an erotic apartheid that forcefully segregated the sex normals from the sex perverts. The new, strict boundaries made the emerging erotic world less polymorphous—safer for sex normals. However, the idea of such creatures as heterosexuals and homosexuals emerged from the narrow world of medicine to become a commonly accepted notion only in the early twentieth century. In 1901, in the comprehensive *Oxford English Dictionary*, "heterosexual" and "homosexual" had not yet made it.

THE DISTRIBUTION OF THE HETEROSEXUAL MYSTIQUE: 1900–1930

In the early years of this heterosexual century the tentative hetero hypothesis was stabilized, fixed, and widely distributed as the ruling sexual orthodoxy: The Heterosexual Mystique. Starting among pleasure-affirming urban working-class youths,

southern blacks, and Greenwich-Village bohemians as defensive subculture, heterosex soon triumphed as dominant culture.[6]

In its earliest version, the twentieth-century heterosexual imperative usually continued to associate heterosexuality with a supposed human "need," "drive," or "instinct" for propagation, a procreant urge linked inexorably with carnal lust as it had not been earlier. In the early twentieth century, the falling birth rate, rising divorce rate, and "war of the sexes" of the middle class were matters of increasing public concern. Giving vent to heteroerotic emotions was thus praised as enhancing baby-making capacity, marital intimacy, and family stability. (Only many years later, in the mid-1960s, would heteroeroticism be distinguished completely, in practice and theory, from procreativity and male-female pleasure sex justified in its own name.)

The first part of the new sex norm—hetero—referred to a basic gender divergence. The "oppositeness" of the sexes was alleged to be the basis for a universal, normal, erotic attraction between males and females. The stress on the sexes' "oppositeness," which harked back to the early nineteenth century, by no means simply registered biological differences of females and males. The early twentieth-century focus on physiological and gender dimorphism reflected the deep anxieties of men about the shifting work, social roles, and power of men over women, and about the ideals of womanhood and manhood. That gender anxiety is documented, for example, in 1897, in *The New York Times'* publication of the Reverend Charles Parkhurst's diatribe against female "andromaniacs," the preacher's derogatory, scientific-sounding name for women who tried to "minimize distinctions by which manhood and womanhood are differentiated."[7] The stress on gender difference was a conservative response to the changing social-sexual division of activity and feeling which gave rise to the independent "New Woman" of the 1880s and eroticized "Flapper" of the 1920s.

The second part of the new hetero norm referred positively to sexuality. That novel upbeat focus on the hedonistic possibilities of male-female conjunctions also reflected a social transformation—a revaluing of pleasure and procreation, consumption and work in commercial, capitalist society. The democratic attribution of a normal lust to human females (as well as males) served to authorize women's enjoyment of their own bodies and began to undermine the early Victorian idea of the pure True Woman—a sex-affirmative action still part of women's struggle. The twentieth-century Erotic Woman also undercut nineteenth-century feminist assertion of women's moral superiority, cast suspicions of lust on women's passionate romantic friendship with women, and asserted the presence of a menacing female monster, "the lesbian."[8] . . .

In the perspective of heterosexual history, this early twentieth-century struggle for the more explicit depiction of an "opposite-sex" eros appears in a curious new light. Ironically, we find sex-conservatives, the social purity advocates of censorship and repression, fighting against the depiction not just of sexual perversity but also of the new normal heterosexuality. That a more open depiction of normal sex had to be defended against forces of propriety confirms the claim that heterosexuality's predecessor, Victorian True Love, had included no legitimate eros. . . .

THE HETEROSEXUAL STEPS OUT:
1930–1945

In 1930, in *The New York Times,* heterosexuality first became a love that dared to speak its name. On April 30th of that year, the word "heterosexual" is first known to have appeared in *The New York Times Book Review.* There, a critic described the subject of André Gide's *The Immoralist* proceeding "from a heterosexual liaison to a homosexual one." The ability to slip between sexual categories was referred to casually as a rather unremarkable aspect of human possibility. This is also the first known reference by *The Times* to the new hetero/homo duo.[9]

The following month the second reference to the hetero/homo dyad appeared in *The New York Times Book Review,* in a comment on Floyd Dell's *Love in the Machine Age.* This work revealed a prominent antipuritan of the 1930s using the dire threat of homosexuality as his rationale for greater heterosexual freedom. *The Times* quoted Dell's warning that current abnormal social conditions kept the young dependent on their parents, causing "infantilism, prostitution and homosexuality." Also quoted was Dell's attack on the "inculcation of purity" that "breeds distrust of the opposite sex." Young people, Dell said, should be "permitted to develop normally to heterosexual adulthood." "But," *The Times* reviewer emphasized, "such a state already exists, here and now." And so it did. Heterosexuality, a new gender-sex category, had been distributed from the narrow, rarified realm of a few doctors to become a nationally, even internationally, cited aspect of middle-class life.[10] . . .

HETEROSEXUAL HEGEMONY:
1945–1965

The "cult of domesticity" following World War II—the reassociation of women with the home, motherhood, and child-care; men with fatherhood and wage work outside the home—was a period in which the predominance of the hetero norm went almost unchallenged, an era of heterosexual hegemony. This was an age in which conservative mental-health professionals reasserted the old link between heterosexuality and procreation. In contrast, sex-liberals of the day strove, ultimately with success, to expand the heterosexual ideal to include within the boundaries of normality a wider-than-ever range of nonprocreative, premarital, and extramarital behaviors. But sex-liberal reform actually helped to extend and secure the dominance of the heterosexual idea, as we shall see when we get to Kinsey.

The postwar sex-conservative tendency was illustrated in 1947, in Ferdinand Lundberg and Dr. Marnia Farnham's book, *Modern Woman: The Lost Sex.* Improper masculinity and femininity was exemplified, the authors decreed, by "engagement in heterosexual relations . . . with the complete intent to see to it that they do not eventuate in reproduction."[11] Their procreatively defined heterosex was one expression of a postwar ideology of fecundity that,

The study of heterosexuality in time will also help us to recognize the *vast historical diversity of sexual emotions and behaviors*—a variety that challenges the monolithic heterosexual hypothesis. John D'Emilio and Estelle Freedman's *Intimate Matters: A History of Sexuality in America* refers in passing to numerous substantial changes in sexual activity and feeling: for example, the widespread use of contraceptives in the nineteenth century, the twentieth-century incitement of the female orgasm, and the recent sexual conduct changes by gay men in response to the AIDS epidemic. It's now a commonplace of family history that people in particular classes feel and behave in substantially different ways under different historical conditions.[18] Only when we stop assuming an invariable essence of heterosexuality will we begin the research to reveal the full variety of sexual emotions and behaviors.

The historical study of the heterosexual experience can help us *understand the erotic relationships of women and men in terms of their changing modes of social organization.* Such modal analysis actually characterizes a sex history well underway.[19] This suggests that the eros-gender-procreation system (the social ordering of lust, femininity and masculinity, and baby-making) has been linked closely to a society's particular organization of power and production. To understand the subtle history of heterosexuality we need to look carefully at correlations between (1) society's organization of eros and pleasure; (2) its mode of engendering persons as feminine or masculine (its making of women and men); (3) its ordering of human reproduction; and (4) its dominant political economy. This General Theory of Sexual Relativity proposes that substantial historical changes in the social organization of eros, gender, and procreation have basically altered the activity and experience of human beings within those modes.[20]

A historical view locates heterosexuality and homosexuality in time, helping us distance ourselves from them. This distancing can help us formulate new questions that clarify our long-range sexual-political goals: What has been and is the social function of sexual categorizing? Whose interests have been served by the division of the world into heterosexual and homosexual? Do we dare not draw a line between those two erotic species? Is some sexual naming socially necessary? Would human freedom be enhanced if the sex-biology of our partners in lust was of no particular concern, and had no name? In what kind of society could we all more freely explore our desire and our flesh?

As we move [into the year 2000], a new sense of the historical making of the heterosexual and homosexual suggests that these are ways of feeling, acting, and being with each other that we can together unmake and radically remake according to our present desire, power, and our vision of a future political-economy of pleasure.

REFERENCES

1. Barbara Welter, "The Cult of True Womanhood: 1820–1860," *American Quarterly*, vol. 18 (Summer 1966); Welter's analysis is extended here to include True Men and True Love.
2. See, for example, Catherine Gallagher and Thomas Laqueur, eds., "The Making of the Modern Body: Sexuality and Society in the Nineteenth Century," *Representations*, no. 14 (Spring 1986) (republished, Berkeley: University of California Press, 1987).
3. Dr. James G. Kiernan, "Responsibility in Sexual Perversion," *Chicago Medical Recorder*, vol. 3 (May 1892), pp. 185–210.
4. R. von Krafft-Ebing, *Psychopathia Sexualis, with Especial Reference to Contrary Sexual Instinct: A Medico-Legal Study*, trans. Charles Gilbert Chaddock (Philadelphia: F. A. Davis, 1892), from the 7th and revised German ed. Preface, November 1892.
5. For the standardization of gender see Lewis Terman and C. C. Miles, *Sex and Personality, Studies in Femininity and Masculinity* (New York: McGraw Hill, 1936). For the standardization of intelligence see Lewis Terman, *Stanford-Binet Intelligence Scale* (Boston: Houghton Mifflin, 1916). For the standardization of work, see "scientific management" and "Taylorism" in Harry Braverman, *Labor and Monopoly Capital: The Degradation of Work in the Twentieth Century* (New York: Monthly Review Press, 1974).
6. See D'Emilio and Freedman, *Intimate Matters*, pp. 194–201, 231, 241, 295–96; Ellen Kay Trimberger, "Feminism, Men, and Modern Love: Greenwich Village, 1900–1925," in *Powers of Desire: The Politics of Sexuality*, ed. Ann Snitow, Christine Stansell, Sharon Thompson

(New York: Monthly Review Press, 1983), pp. 131–52; Kathy Peiss, "'Charity Girls' and City Pleasures: Historical Notes on Working Class Sexuality, 1880–1920," in *Powers of Desire*, pp. 74–87; and Mary P. Ryan, "The Sexy Saleslady: Psychology, Heterosexuality, and Consumption in the Twentieth Century," in her *Womanhood in America*, 2nd ed. (New York: Franklin Watts, 1979), pp. 151–82.

7. [Rev. Charles Parkhurst], "Woman. Calls Them Andromaniacs. Dr. Parkhurst So Characterizes Certain Women Who Passionately Ape Everything That Is Mannish. Woman Divinely Preferred. Her Supremacy Lies in Her Womanliness, and She Should Make the Most of It—Her Sphere of Best Usefulness the Home," *The New York Times*, May 23, 1897, p. 16:1.

8. See Lisa Duggan, "The Social Enforcement of Heterosexuality and Lesbian Resistance in the 1920s," in *Class, Race, and Sex: The Dynamics of Control*, ed. Amy Swerdlow and Hanah Lessinger (Boston: G. K. Hall, 1983), pp. 75–92; Rayna Rapp and Ellen Ross, "The Twenties Backlash: Compulsory Heterosexuality, the Consumer Family, and the Waning of Feminism," in *Class, Race, and Sex;* Christina Simmons, "Companionate Marriage and the Lesbian Threat," *Frontiers*, vol. 4, no. 3 (Fall 1979), pp. 54–59; and Lillian Faderman, *Surpassing the Love of Men* (New York: William Morrow, 1981).

9. Louis Kronenberger, review of André Gide, *The Immoralist*, New York Times Book Review, April 20, 1930, p. 9.

10. Henry James Forman, review of Floyd Dell, *Love in the Machine Age* (New York: Farrar & Rinehart), *New York Times Book Review*, September 14, 1930, p. 9.

11. Ferdinand Lundberg and Dr. Marnia F. Farnham, *Modern Woman: The Lost Sex* (New York: Harper, 1947).

12. Dr. Howard A. Rusk, *New York Times Book Review*, January 4, 1948, p. 3.

13. Alfred Kinsey, Wardell B. Pomeroy, Clyde E. Martin, *Sexual Behavior in the Human Male* (Philadelphia: W. B. Saunders, 1948), pp. 199–200.

14. Kinsey, *Sexual Behavior*, pp. 637, 639.

15. See Steven Epstein, "Gay Politics, Ethnic Identity: The Limits of Social Constructionism," *Socialist Review* 93/93 (1987), pp. 9–54.

16. Gore Vidal, "Someone to Laugh at the Squares With" [Tennessee Williams], *New York Review of Books*, June 13, 1985; reprinted in his *At Home: Essays, 1982–1988* (New York: Random House, 1988), p. 48.

17. Rosalyn Regelson, "Up the Camp Staircase," *The New York Times*, March 3, 1968, Section II, p. 1:5.

18. D'Emilio and Freedman, *Intimate Matters*, pp. 57–63, 268, 356.

19. Ryan, *Womanhood;* John D'Emilio, "Capitalism and Gay Identity," in *Powers of Desire*, pp. 100–13; Jeffrey Weeks, *Coming Out: Homosexual Politics in Britain from the Nineteenth Century to the Present* (London: Quartet Books, 1977); D'Emilio and Freedman, *Intimate Matters;* Katz, "Early Colonial Exploration, Agriculture, and Commerce: The Age of Sodomitical Sin, 1607–1740," *Gay/Lesbian Almanac*, pp. 23–65.

20. This tripartite system is intended as a revision of Gayle Rubin's pioneering work on the social-historical organization of eros and gender. See "The Traffic in Women: Notes on the Political-Economy of Sex," in *Toward an Anthropology of Women*, ed. Rayna R. Reiter (New York: Monthly Review Press, 1975), pp. 157–210, and "Thinking Sex: Notes for a Radical Theory of the Politics of Sexuality," in *Pleasure and Danger: Exploring Female Sexuality*, ed. Carole S. Vance (Boston: Routledge & Kegan Paul, 1984), pp. 267–329.

4

Masculinity as Homophobia

Fear, Shame, and Silence in the Construction of Gender Identity

MICHAEL S. KIMMEL

We think of manhood as eternal, a timeless essence that resides deep in the heart of every man. We think of manhood as a thing, a quality that one either has or doesn't have. We think of manhood as innate, residing in the particular biological composition of the human male, the result of androgens or the possession of a penis. We think of manhood as a transcendent tangible property that each man must manifest in the world, the reward presented with great ceremony to a young novice by his elders for having successfully competed an arduous initiation ritual. . . .

In this chapter, I view masculinity as a constantly changing collection of meanings that we construct through our relationships with ourselves, with each other, and with our world. Manhood is neither static nor timeless; it is historical. Manhood is not the manifestation of an inner essence; it is socially constructed. Manhood does not bubble up to consciousness from our biological makeup; it is created in culture. Manhood means different things at different times to different people. We come to know what it means to be a man in our culture by setting our definitions in opposition to a set of "others"—racial minorities, sexual minorities, and, above all, women. . . .

★ ★ ★

MASCULINITY AS HISTORY AND THE HISTORY OF MASCULINITY

★ ★ ★

In the late 18th and early 19th centuries, two models of manhood prevailed. The *Genteel Patriarch* derived his identity from landownership. Supervising his estate, he was refined, elegant, and given to casual sensuousness. He was a doting and devoted father, who spent much of his time supervising the estate and with his family. Think of George Washington or Thomas Jefferson as examples. By contrast, the *Heroic Artisan* embodied the physical strength and republican virtue that Jefferson observed in the yeoman farmer, independent urban craftsman, or shopkeeper. Also a devoted father, the Heroic Artisan taught his son his craft, bringing him through ritual apprenticeship to status as master craftsman. Economically autonomous, the Heroic Artisan also cherished his democratic community, delighting in the participatory democracy of the town meeting. Think of Paul Revere at his pewter shop, shirtsleeves rolled up, a leather apron—a man who took pride in his work.

Heroic Artisans and Genteel Patriarchs lived in casual accord, in part because their gender ideals were complementary (both supported participatory democracy and individual autonomy, although patriarchs tended to support more powerful state machineries and also supported slavery) and because they rarely saw one another: Artisans were decidedly urban and the Genteel Patriarchs ruled their rural estates. By the 1830s, though, this casual symbiosis was shattered by the emergence of a new vision of masculinity, *Marketplace Manhood*.

Marketplace Man derived his identity entirely from his success in the capitalist marketplace, as he accumulated wealth, power, status. He was the urban entrepreneur, the businessman. Restless, agitated, and anxious, Marketplace Man was an absentee landlord at home and an absent father with his children, devoting himself to his work in an increasingly homosocial environment—a male-only world in which he pits himself against other men. His efforts at self-making transform the political and economic spheres, casting aside the Genteel Patriarch as an anachronistic feminized dandy—sweet, but ineffective and outmoded, and transforming the Heroic Artisan into a dispossessed proletarian, a wage slave.

★ ★ ★

Marketplace Manhood was a manhood that required proof, and that required the acquisition of tangible goods as evidence of success. It reconstituted itself by the exclusion of "others"—women, nonwhite men, nonnative-born men, homosexual men—and by terrified flight into a pristine mythic homosocial Eden where men could, at last, be real men among other men. The story of the ways in which Marketplace Man becomes American Everyman is a tragic tale, a tale of striving to live up to impossible ideals of success leading to chronic terrors of emasculation, emotional emptiness, and a gendered rage that leave a wide swath of destruction in its wake.

MASCULINITIES AS POWER RELATIONS

Marketplace Masculinity describes the normative definition of American masculinity. It describes his characteristics—aggression, competition, anxiety—and the arena in which those characteristics are deployed—the public sphere, the marketplace. If the marketplace is the arena in which manhood is tested and proved, it is a gendered arena, in which tensions between women and men and tensions among different groups of men are weighted with meaning. These tensions suggest that cultural definitions of gender are played out in a contested terrain and are themselves power relations.

All masculinities are not created equal; or rather, we are all *created* equal, but any hypothetical equality evaporates quickly because our definitions of masculinity are not equally valued in our society.

One definition of manhood continues to remain the standard against which other forms of manhood are measured and evaluated. Within the dominant culture, the masculinity that defines white, middle-class, early middle-aged, heterosexual men is the masculinity that sets the standards for other men, against which other men are measured and, more often than not, found wanting. Sociologist Erving Goffman (1963) wrote that in America, there is only "one complete, unblushing male":

> a young, married, white, urban, northern heterosexual, Protestant father of college education, fully employed, of good complexion, weight and height, and a recent record in sports. Every American male tends to look out upon the world from this perspective. . . . Any male who fails to qualify in any one of these ways is likely to view himself . . . as unworthy, incomplete, and inferior. (p. 128)

This is the definition that we will call "hegemonic" masculinity, the image of masculinity of those men who hold power, which has become the standard in psychological evaluations, sociological research, and self-help and advice literature for teaching young men to become "real men" (Connell, 1987). The hegemonic definition of manhood is a man *in* power, a man *with* power, and a man *of* power. We equate manhood with being strong, successful, capable, reliable, in control. The very definitions of manhood we have developed in our culture maintain the power that some men have over other men and that men have over women.

Our culture's definition of masculinity is thus several stories at once. It is about the individual man's quest to accumulate those cultural symbols that denote manhood, signs that he has in fact achieved it. It is about those standards being used against women to prevent their inclusion in public life and their consignment to a devalued private sphere. It is about the differential access that different types of men have to those cultural resources that confer manhood and about how each of these groups then develop their own modifications to preserve and claim their manhood. It is about the power of these definitions themselves to serve to maintain the real-life power that men have over women and that some men have over other men.

This definition of manhood has been summarized cleverly by psychologist Robert Brannon (1976) into four succinct phrases:

1. "No Sissy Stuff!" One may never do anything that even remotely suggests femininity. Masculinity is the relentless repudiation of the feminine.
2. "Be a Big Wheel." Masculinity is measured by power, success, wealth, and status. As the current saying goes, "He who has the most toys when he dies wins."
3. "Be a Sturdy Oak." Masculinity depends on remaining calm and reliable in a crisis, holding emotions in check. In fact, proving you're a man depends on never showing your emotions at all. Boys don't cry.
4. "Give 'em Hell." Exude an aura of manly daring and aggression. Go for it. Take risks.

These rules contain the elements of the definition against which virtually all American men are measured. Failure to embody these rules, to affirm the power of the rules and one's achievement of them is a source of men's confusion and pain. Such a model is, of course, unrealizable for any man. But we keep trying, valiantly and vainly, to measure up. American masculinity is a relentless test.[2] The chief test is contained in the first rule. Whatever the variations by race, class, age, ethnicity, or sexual orientation, being a man means "not being like women." This notion of antifemininity lies at the heart of contemporary and historical conceptions of manhood, so that masculinity is defined more by what one is not rather than who one is.

* * *

MASCULINITY AS A HOMOSOCIAL ENACTMENT

Other men: We are under the constant careful scrutiny of other men. Other men watch us, rank us, grant our acceptance into the realm of manhood. Manhood is demonstrated for other men's approval. It is other men who evaluate the performance. Literary critic David Leverenz (1991) argues that "ideologies of manhood have functioned primarily in relation to the gaze of male peers and male authority" (p. 769). Think of how men boast to one another of their accomplishments—from their latest sexual conquest to the size of the fish they caught—and how we constantly parade the markers of manhood—wealth, power, status, sexy women— in front of other men, desperate for their approval.

That men prove their manhood in the eyes of other men is both a consequence of sexism and one of its chief props. "Women have, in men's minds, such a low place on the social ladder of this country that it's useless to define yourself in terms of a woman," noted playwright David Mamet. "What men need is men's approval." Women become a kind of currency that men use to improve their ranking on the masculine social scale. (Even those moments of heroic conquest of women carry, I believe, a current of homosocial evaluation.) Masculinity is a *homosocial* enactment. We test ourselves, perform heroic feats, take enormous risks, all because we want other men to grant us our manhood. . . .

MASCULINITY AS HOMOPHOBIA

. . . That nightmare from which we never seem to awaken is that those other men will see that sense of inadequacy, they will see that in our own eyes we are not who we are pretending to be. What we call masculinity is often a hedge against being revealed as a fraud, an exaggerated set of activities that keep others from seeing through us, and a frenzied effort to keep at bay those fears within ourselves. Our real fear "is not fear of women but of being ashamed or humiliated in front of other men, or being dominated by stronger men" (Leverenz, 1986, p. 451).

This, then, is the great secret of American manhood: *We are afraid of other men.* Homophobia is a central organizing principle of our cultural definition of manhood. Homophobia is more than the irrational fear of gay men, more than the fear that we might be perceived as gay. "The word 'faggot' has nothing to do with homosexual experience or even with fears of homosexuals," writes David Leverenz

(1986). "It comes out of the depths of manhood: a label of ultimate contempt for anyone who seems sissy, untough, uncool" (p. 455). Homophobia is the fear that other men will unmask us, emasculate us, reveal to us and the world that we do not measure up, that we are not real men. We are afraid to let other men see that fear. Fear makes us ashamed, because the recognition of fear in ourselves is proof to ourselves that we are not as manly as we pretend, that we are, like the young man in a poem by Yeats, "one that ruffles in a manly pose for all his timid heart." Our fear is the fear of humiliation. We are ashamed to be afraid.

Shame leads to silence—the silences that keep other people believing that we actually approve of the things that are done to women, to minorities, to gays and lesbians in our culture. The frightened silence as we scurry past a woman being hassled by men on the street. That furtive silence when men make sexist or racist jokes in a bar. That clammy-handed silence when guys in the office make gay-bashing jokes. Our fears are the sources of our silences, and men's silence is what keeps the system running. This might help to explain why women often complain that their male friends or partners are often so understanding when they are alone and yet laugh at sexist jokes or even make those jokes themselves when they are out with a group.

The fear of being seen as a sissy dominates the cultural definitions of manhood. It starts so early. "Boys among boys are ashamed to be unmanly," wrote one educator in 1871 (cited in Rotundo, 1993, p. 264). I have a standing bet with a friend that I can walk onto any playground in America where 6-year-old boys are happily playing and by asking one question, I can provoke a fight. That question is simple: "Who's a sissy around here?" Once posed, the challenge is made. One of two things is likely to happen. One boy will accuse another of being a sissy, to which that boy will respond that he is not a sissy, that the first boy is. They may have to fight it out to see who's lying. Or a whole group of boys will surround one boy and all shout "He is! He is!" That boy will either burst into tears and run home crying, disgraced, or he will have to take on several boys at once, to prove that he's not a sissy. (And what will his father or older brothers tell him if he chooses to run home crying?) It will be some time before he regains any sense of self-respect.

Violence is often the single most evident marker of manhood. Rather it is the willingness to fight, the desire to fight. The origin of our expression that one has a chip on one's shoulder lies in the practice of an adolescent boy in the country or small town at the turn of the century, who would literally walk around with a chip of wood balanced on his shoulder—a signal of his readiness to fight with anyone who would take the initiative of knocking the chip off (see Gorer, 1964, p. 38; Mead, 1965).

As adolescents, we learn that our peers are a kind of gender police, constantly threatening to unmask us as feminine, as sissies. One of the favorite tricks when I was an adolescent was to ask a boy to look at his fingernails. If he held his palm toward his face and curled his fingers back to see them, he passed the test. He'd look at his nails "like a man." But if he held the back of his hand away from his face, and looked at his fingernails with arm outstretched, he was immediately ridiculed as sissy.

As young men we are constantly riding those gender boundaries, checking the fences we have constructed on the perimeter, making sure that nothing even remotely feminine might show through. The possibilities of being unmasked are everywhere. Even the most seemingly insignificant thing can pose a threat or activate that haunting terror. On the day the students in my course "Sociology of Men and Masculinities" were scheduled to discuss homophobia and male-male friendships, one student provided a touching illustration. Noting that it was a beautiful day, the first day of spring after a brutal northeast winter, he decided to wear shorts to class. "I had this really nice pair of new Madras shorts," he commented. "But then I thought to myself, these shorts have lavender and pink in them. Today's class topic is homophobia. Maybe today is not the best day to wear these shorts."

Our efforts to maintain a manly front cover everything we do. What we wear. How we talk. How we walk. What we eat. Every mannerism, every movement contains a coded gender language. Think, for example, of how you would answer the question: How do you "know" if a man is homosexual? When I ask this question in classes or workshops, respondents invariably provide a pretty standard list of stereotypically effeminate behaviors. He walks a certain way, talks a certain way, acts a certain way. He's very emotional; he shows his feelings. One woman commented that she "knows" a man is gay if he really cares about her; another said she knows he's gay if he shows no interest in her, if he leaves her alone.

Now alter the question and imagine what heterosexual men do to make sure no one could possibly get the "wrong idea" about them. Responses typically refer to the original stereotypes, this time as a set of negative rules about behavior. Never dress that way. Never talk or walk that way. Never show your feelings or get emotional. Always be prepared to demonstrate sexual interest in women that you meet, so it is impossible for any woman to get the wrong idea about you. In this sense, homophobia, the fear of being perceived as gay, as not a real man, keeps men exaggerating all the traditional rules of masculinity, including sexual predation with women. Homophobia and sexism go hand in hand. . . .

HOMOPHOBIA AS A CAUSE OF SEXISM, HETEROSEXISM, AND RACISM

Homophobia is intimately interwoven with both sexism and racism. The fear—sometimes conscious, sometimes not—that others might perceive us as homosexual propels men to enact all manner of exaggerated masculine behaviors and attitudes to make sure that no one could possibly get the wrong idea about us. One of the centerpieces of that exaggerated masculinity is putting women down, both by excluding them from the public sphere and by the quotidian put-downs in speech and behaviors that organize the daily life of the American man. Women and gay men become the "other" against which heterosexual men project their identities, against whom they stack the decks so as to compete in a situation in which they will always win, so that by suppressing them, men can stake a claim for their own manhood. Women threaten emasculation by representing the home, workplace, and familial responsibility, the negation of fun. Gay men have historically played the role of the consummate sissy in the American popular mind because homosexuality is seen as an inversion of normal gender development. There have been other "others." Through American history, various groups have represented the sissy, the non-men against whom American men played out their definitions of manhood, often with vicious results. In fact, these changing groups provide an interesting lesson in American historical development.

At the turn of the 19th century, it was Europeans and children who provided the contrast for American men. The "true American was vigorous, manly, and direct, not effete and corrupt like the supposed Europeans," writes Rupert Wilkinson (1986). "He was plain rather than ornamented, rugged rather than luxury seeking, a liberty loving common man or natural gentleman rather than an aristocratic oppressor or servile minion" (p. 96). The "real man" of the early 19th century was neither noble nor serf. By the middle of the century, black slaves had replaced the effete nobleman. Slaves were seen as dependent, helpless men, incapable of defending their women and children, and therefore less than manly. Native Americans were cast as foolish and naive children, so they could be infantilized as the "Red Children of the Great White Father" and therefore excluded from full manhood.

By the end of the century, new European immigrants were also added to the list of the unreal men, especially the Irish and Italians, who were seen as too passionate and emotionally volatile to remain controlled sturdy oaks, and Jews, who were seen as too bookishly effete and too physically puny to truly measure up. In the mid-20th century, it was also Asians—first the Japanese during the Second World War, and more recently, the Vietnamese during the Vietnam War—who have served as unmanly templates against which American men have hurled their gendered rage. Asian men were seen as small, soft, and effeminate—hardly men at all.

Such a list of "hyphenated" Americans—Italian-, Jewish-, Irish-, African- Native-, Asian-, gay—composes the majority of American men. So manhood only possible for a distinct minority, and the definition has been constructed to prevent the others from achieving it. Interestingly, this emasculation of one's enemies has a flip side—and one that is equally gendered. These very groups that have historically been cast as less than manly were also, often simultaneously, cast as hypermasculine, as sexually aggressive, violent rapacious beasts, against whom "civilized" men must take a decisive stand and thereby rescue civilization. Thus black men were depicted as rampaging sexual beasts, women as carnivorously carnal, gay men as sexually insatiable, southern European men as sexually predatory and voracious, and Asian men as vicious and cruel torturers who were immorally disinterested in life itself, willing to sacrifice their entire people for their whims. But whether one saw these groups as effeminate sissies or as brutal savages, the terms with which they were perceived were gendered. These groups become the "others," the screens against which traditional conceptions of manhood were developed. . . .

POWER AND POWERLESSNESS IN THE LIVES OF MEN

I have argued that homophobia, men's fear of other men, is the animating condition of the dominant definition of masculinity in America, that the reigning definition of masculinity is a defensive effort to prevent being emasculated. In our efforts to suppress or overcome those fears, the dominant culture exacts a tremendous price from those deemed less than fully manly: women, gay men, nonnative-born men, men of color. This perspective may help clarify a paradox in men's lives, a paradox in which men have virtually all the power and yet do not feel powerful (see Kaufman, 1993).

Manhood is equated with power—over women, over other men. Everywhere we look, we see the institutional expression of that power—in state and national legislatures, on the boards of directors of every major U.S. corporation or law firm, and in every school and hospital administration. . . .

When confronted with the analysis that men have all the power, many men react incredulously. "What do you mean, men have all the power?" they ask. "What are you talking about? My wife bosses me around. My kids boss me around. My boss bosses me around. I have no power at all! I'm completely powerless!"

Men's feelings are not the feelings of the powerful, but of those who see themselves as powerless. These are the feelings that come inevitably from the discontinuity between the social and the psychological, between the aggregate analysis that reveals how men are in power as a group and the psychological fact that they do not feel powerful as individuals. They are the feelings of men who were raised to believe themselves entitled to feel that power, but do not feel it. No wonder many men are frustrated and angry. . . .

Why, then, do American men feel so powerless? Part of the answer is because we've constructed the rules of manhood so that only the tiniest fraction of men come to believe that they are the biggest of wheels, the sturdiest of oaks, the most virulent repudiators of femininity, the most daring and aggressive. We've managed to disempower the overwhelming majority of American men by other means—such as discriminating on the basis of race, class, ethnicity, age, or sexual preference. . . .

Others still rehearse the politics of exclusion, as if by clearing away the playing field of secure gender identity of any that we deem less than manly—women, gay men, nonnative-born men, men of color—middle-class, straight, white men can reground their sense of themselves without those haunting fears and that deep shame that they are unmanly and will be exposed by other men. This is the manhood of racism, of sexism, of homophobia. It is the manhood that is so chronically insecure that it trembles at the idea of lifting the ban on gays in the military, that is so threatened by women in the workplace that women become the targets of sexual harassment, that is so deeply frightened of equality that it must ensure that the playing field of male competition remains stacked against all newcomers to the game.

Exclusion and escape have been the dominant methods American men have used to keep their fears of humiliation at bay. The fear of emasculation by other men, of being humiliated, of being seen as a sissy, is the leitmotif in my reading of the history of American manhood. Masculinity has become a relentless test by which we prove to other men, to women, and ultimately to ourselves, that we have successfully mastered the part. The restlessness that men feel today is nothing new in American history; we have been anxious and restless for almost two centuries. Neither exclusion nor escape has ever brought us the relief we've sought, and there is no reason to think that either will solve our problems now. Peace of mind, relief from gender struggle, will come only from a politics of inclusion, not exclusion, from standing up for equality and justice, and not by running away.

NOTES

1. Much of this work is elaborated in *Manhood: The American Quest* (in press).
2. Although I am here discussing only American masculinity, I am aware that other have located this chronic instability and efforts to prove manhood in the particular cultural and economic arrangements of Western society. Calvin, after all, inveighed against the disgrace "for men to become effeminate," and countless other theorists have described the mechanics of manly proof. (see, for example, Seidler, 1994.)

REFERENCES

1. Connell, R. W. (1987). *Gender and power.* Stanford, CA: Stanford University Press.
2. Goffman, E. (1963). *Stigna.* Englewood Cliffs, NJ: Prentice Hall.
3. Gorer, G. (1964). *The American people: A study in national character.* New York: Norton.
4. Kaufman, M. (1993). *Cracking the armour: Power and pain in the lives of men.* Toronto: Viking Canada.
5. Leverenz, D. (1986). Manhood, humiliation and public life: Some stories. *Southwest Review, 71,* Fall.
6. Leverenz, D. (1991). "The last real man in America: From Natty Bumppo to Batman." *American Literary Review, 3.*
7. Mead, M. (1965). *And keep your powder dry.* New York: William Morrow.
8. Rotundo, E. A. (1993). *American manhood: Transformations in masculinity from the revolution to the modern era.* New York: Basic Books.
9. Seidler, V. J. (1994). *Unreasonable men: Masculinity and social theory.* New York: Routledge.
10. Wilkinson, R. (1986). *American tough: The tough-guy tradition and American character.* New York: Harper & Row.

***The physiognomy of race in the medical
anthropology of the late nineteenth century.***
The Eastern Jew as the exemplary member of the
"dark-skinned" races.

Part of the frontispiece of Carl Ernst Bock, *Das Buch vom
gesunden und kranken Menschen* (Leipzig: Ernst Keil, 1893).

 5

Racial Formations

MICHAEL OMI AND HOWARD WINANT

In 1982–83, Susie Guillory Phipps unsuccessfully
sued the Louisiana Bureau of Vital Records to
change her racial classification from black to white.
The descendant of an eighteenth-century white
planter and a black slave, Phipps was designated

"black" in her birth certificate in accordance with a
1970 state law which declared anyone with at least
one-thirty-second "Negro blood" to be black. The
legal battle raised intriguing questions about the
concept of race, its meaning in contemporary society,
and its use (and abuse) in public policy. Assistant
Attorney General Ron Davis defended the law by
pointing out that some type of racial classification
was necessary to comply with federal record-keeping
requirements and to facilitate programs for the prevention of genetic diseases. Phipps's attorney, Brian
Begue, argued that the assignment of racial categories on birth certificates was unconstitutional and
that the one-thirty-second designation was inaccurate. He called on a retired Tulane University professor who cited research indicating that most
whites have one-twentieth "Negro" ancestry. In the
end, Phipps lost. The court upheld a state law
which quantified racial identity, and in so doing
affirmed the legality of assigning individuals to specific racial groupings.[1]

The Phipps case illustrates the continuing
dilemma of defining race and establishing its
meaning in institutional life. Today, to assert that
variations in human physiognomy are racially
based is to enter a constant and intense debate. *Scientific* interpretations of race have not been alone in
sparking heated controversy; *religious* perspectives
have done so as well.[2] Most centrally, of course,
race has been a matter of *political* contention. This
has been particularly true in the United States, where
the concept of race has varied enormously over time
without ever leaving the center stage of US history.

WHAT IS RACE?

Race consciousness, and its articulation in theories of
race, is largely a modern phenomenon. When European explorers in the New World "discovered" people who looked different than themselves, these "natives" challenged then existing conceptions of the
origins of the human species, and raised disturbing
questions as to whether *all* could be considered in the
same "family of man."[3] Religious debates flared over
the attempt to reconcile the Bible with the existence
of "racially distinct" people. Arguments took place

over creation itself, as theories of polygenesis questioned whether God had made only one species of humanity ("monogenesis"). Europeans wondered if the natives of the New World were indeed human beings with redeemable souls. At stake were not only the prospects for conversion, but the types of treatment to be accorded them. The expropriation of property, the denial of political rights, the introduction of slavery and other forms of coercive labor, as well as outright extermination, all presupposed a worldview which distinguished Europeans—children of God, human beings, etc.—from "others." Such a worldview was needed to explain why some should be "free" and others enslaved, why some had rights to land and property while others did not. Race, and the interpretation of racial differences, was a central factor in that worldview.

In the colonial epoch science was no less a field of controversy than religion in attempts to comprehend the concept of race and its meaning. Spurred on by the classificatory scheme of living organisms devised by Linnaeus in *Systema Naturae,* many scholars in the eighteenth and nineteenth centuries dedicated themselves to the identification and ranking of variations in humankind. Race was thought of as a *biological* concept, yet its precise definition was the subject of debates which, as we have noted, continue to rage today. Despite efforts ranging from Dr. Samuel Morton's studies of cranial capacity[4] to contemporary attempts to base racial classification on shared gene pools,[5] the concept of race has defied biological definition. . . .

Attempts to discern the *scientific meaning* of race continue to the present day. Although most physical anthropologists and biologists have abandoned the quest for a scientific basis to determine racial categories, controversies have recently flared in the area of genetics and educational psychology. For instance, an essay by Arthur Jensen which argued that hereditary factors shape intelligence not only revived the "nature or nurture" controversy, but raised highly volatile questions about racial equality itself.[6] Clearly the attempt to establish a *biological* basis of race has not been swept into the dustbin of history, but is being resurrected in various scientific arenas. All such attempts seek to remove the concept of race from fundamental social, political, or economic determination. They suggest instead that the truth of race lies in the terrain of innate characteristics, of which skin color and other physical attributes provide only the most obvious, and in some respects most superficial, indicators.

RACE AS A SOCIAL CONCEPT

The social sciences have come to reject biologistic notions of race in favor of an approach which regards race as a *social* concept. Beginning in the eighteenth century, this trend has been slow and uneven, but its direction clear. In the nineteenth century Max Weber discounted biological explanations for racial conflict and instead highlighted the social and political factors which engendered such conflict.[7] The work of pioneering cultural anthropologist Franz Boas was crucial in refuting the scientific racism of the early twentieth century by rejecting the connection between race and culture, and the assumption of a continuum of "higher" and "lower" cultural groups. Within the contemporary social science literature, race is assumed to be a variable which is shaped by broader societal forces.

Race is indeed a pre-eminently *sociohistorical* concept. Racial categories and the meaning of race are given concrete expression by the specific social relations and historical context in which they are embedded. Racial meanings have varied tremendously over time and between different societies.

In the United States, the black/white color line has historically been rigidly defined and enforced. White is seen as a "pure" category. Any racial intermixture makes one "nonwhite." In the movie *Raintree County,* Elizabeth Taylor describes the worst of fates to befall whites as "havin' a little Negra blood in ya'—just one little teeny drop and a person's all Negra."[8] This thinking flows from what Marvin Harris has characterized as the principle of *hypo-descent:*

> By what ingenious computation is the genetic tracery of a million years of evolution unraveled and

each man [sic] assigned his proper social box? In the United States, the mechanism employed is the rule of hypo-descent. This descent rule requires Americans to believe that anyone who is known to have had a Negro ancestor is a Negro. We admit nothing in between. . . . "Hypo-descent" means affiliation with the subordinate rather than the superordinate group in order to avoid the ambiguity of intermediate identity. . . . The rule of hypo-descent is, therefore, an invention, which we in the United States have made in order to keep biological facts from intruding into our collective racist fantasies.[9]

The Susie Guillory Phipps case merely represents the contemporary expression of this racial logic.

By contrast, a striking feature of race relations in the lowland areas of Latin America since the abolition of slavery has been the relative absence of sharply defined racial groupings. No such rigid descent rule characterizes racial identity in many Latin American societies. Brazil, for example, has historically had less rigid conceptions of race, and thus a variety of "intermediate" racial categories exist. Indeed, as Harris notes, "One of the most striking consequences of the Brazilian system of racial identification is that parents and children and even brothers and sisters are frequently accepted as representatives of quite opposite racial types."[10] Such a possibility is incomprehensible within the logic of racial categories in the US.

To suggest another example: the notion of "passing" takes on new meaning if we compare various American cultures' means of assigning racial identity. In the United States, individuals who are actually "black" by the logic of hypo-descent have attempted to skirt the discriminatory barriers imposed by law and custom by attempting to "pass" for white.[11] Ironically, these same individuals would not be able to pass for "black" in many Latin American societies.

Consideration of the term "black" illustrates the diversity of racial meanings which can be found among different societies and historically within a given society. In contemporary British politics the term "black" is used to refer to all nonwhites. Interestingly this designation has not arisen through the racist discourse of groups such as the National Front. Rather, in political and cultural movements, Asian as well as Afro-Caribbean youth are adopting the term as an expression of self-identity.[12] The wide-ranging meanings of "black" illustrate the manner in which racial categories are shaped politically.[13]

The meaning of race is defined and contested throughout society, in both collective action and personal practice. In the process, racial categories themselves are formed, transformed, destroyed, and re-formed. We use the term *racial formation* to refer to the process by which social, economic, and political forces determine the content and importance of racial categories, and by which they are in turn shaped by racial meanings. Crucial to this formulation is the treatment of race as a *central axis* of social relations which cannot be subsumed under or reduced to some broader category or conception.

RACIAL IDEOLOGY AND RACIAL IDENTITY

The seemingly obvious "natural" and "common sense" qualities which the existing racial order exhibits themselves testify to the effectiveness of the racial formation process in constructing racial meanings and racial identities.

One of the first things we notice about people when we meet them (along with their sex) is their race. We utilize race to provide clues about *who* a person is. This fact is made painfully obvious when we encounter someone whom we cannot conveniently racially categorize—someone who is, for example, racially "mixed" or of an ethnic/racial group with which we are not familiar. Such an encounter becomes a source of discomfort and momentarily a crisis of racial meaning. Without a racial identity, one is in danger of having no identity.

Our compass for navigating race relations depends on preconceived notions of what each specific racial group looks like. Comments such as, "Funny, you don't look black," betray an underlying image of what black should be. We also become disoriented when people do not act "black," "Latino," or indeed "white." The content of such stereotypes reveals a series of unsubstantiated beliefs about who these groups are and what "they" are like.[14]

In US society, then, a kind of "racial etiquette" exists, a set of interpretative codes and racial meanings which operate in the interactions of daily life. Rules shaped by our perception of race in a comprehensively racial society determine the "presentation of self,"[15] distinctions of status, and appropriate modes of conduct. "Etiquette" is not mere universal adherence to the dominant group's rules, but a more dynamic combination of rules with the values and beliefs of subordinated groupings. This racial "subjection" is quintessentially ideological. Everybody learns some combination, some version, of the rules of racial classification, and of their own racial identity, often without obvious teaching or conscious inculcation. Race becomes "common sense"—a way of comprehending, explaining, and acting in the world.

Racial beliefs operate as an "amateur biology," a way of explaining the variations in "human nature."[16] Differences in skin color and other obvious physical characteristics supposedly provide visible clues to differences lurking underneath. Temperament, sexuality, intelligence, athletic ability, aesthetic preferences and so on are presumed to be fixed and discernible from the palpable mark of race. Such diverse questions as our confidence and trust in others (for example, clerks or salespeople, media figures, neighbors), our sexual preferences and romantic images, our tastes in music, films, dance, or sports, and our very ways of talking, walking, eating, and dreaming are ineluctably shaped by notions of race. Skin color "differences" are thought to explain perceived differences in intellectual, physical, and artistic temperaments, and to justify distinct treatment of racially identified individuals and groups.

The continuing persistence of racial ideology suggests that these racial myths and stereotypes cannot be exposed as such in the popular imagination. They are, we think, too essential, too integral,

to the maintenance of the US social order. Of course, particular meanings, stereotypes, and myths can change, but the presence of a *system* of racial meanings and stereotypes, of racial ideology, seems to be a permanent feature of US culture.

Film and television, for example, have been notorious in disseminating images of racial minorities which establish for audiences what people from these groups look like, how they behave, and "who they are."[17] The power of the media lies not only in their ability to reflect the dominant racial ideology, but in their capacity to shape that ideology in the first place. D.W. Griffith's epic *Birth of a Nation*, a sympathetic treatment of the rise of the Ku Klux Klan during Reconstruction, helped to generate, consolidate, and "nationalize" images of blacks which had been more disparate (more regionally specific, for example) prior to the film's appearance.[18] In US television, the necessity to define characters in the briefest and most condensed manner has led to the perpetuation of racial caricatures, as racial stereotypes serve as shorthand for scriptwriters, directors and actors, in commercials, etc. Television's tendency to address the "lowest common denominator" in order to render programs "familiar" to an enormous and diverse audience leads it regularly to assign and reassign racial characteristics to particular groups, both minority and majority.

These and innumerable other examples show that we tend to view race as something fixed and immutable—something rooted in "nature." Thus we mask the historical construction of racial categories, the shifting meaning of race, and the crucial role of politics and ideology in shaping race relations. Races do not emerge full-blown. They are the results of diverse historical practices and are continually subject to challenge over their definition and meaning.

RACIALIZATION: THE HISTORICAL DEVELOPMENT OF RACE

In the United States, the racial category of "black" evolved with the consolidation of racial slavery. By the end of the seventeenth century, Africans whose specific identity was Ibo, Yoruba, Fulani, etc., were rendered "black" by an ideology of exploitation based on racial logic—the establishment and maintenance of a "color line." This of course did not occur overnight. A period of indentured servitude which was not rooted in racial logic preceded the consolidation of racial slavery. With slavery, however, a racially based understanding of society was set in motion which resulted in the shaping of a specific *racial* identity not only for the slaves but for the European settlers as well. Winthrop Jordan has observed: "From the initially common term *Christian*, at mid-century there was a marked shift toward the terms *English* and *free*. After about 1680, taking the colonies as a whole, a new term of self-identification appeared—*white*."[19]

We employ the term *racialization* to signify the extension of racial meaning to a previously racially unclassified relationship, social practice, or group. Racialization is an ideological process, a historically specific one. Racial ideology is constructed from pre-existing conceptual (or, if one prefers, "discursive") elements and emerges from the struggles of competing political projects and ideas seeking to articulate similar elements differently. An account of racialization processes that avoids the pitfalls of US ethnic history[20] remains to be written.

Particularly during the nineteenth century, the category of "white" was subject to challenges brought about by the influx of diverse groups who were not of the same Anglo-Saxon stock as the founding immigrants. In the nineteenth century, political and ideological struggles emerged over the classification of Southern Europeans, the Irish, and Jews, among other "non-white" categories.[21] Nativism was only effectively curbed by the institutionalization of a racial order that drew the color line *around*, rather than *within*, Europe.

By stopping short of racializing immigrants from Europe after the Civil War, and by subsequently allowing their assimilation, the American racial order was reconsolidated in the wake of the tremendous challenge placed before it by the abolition of racial slavery.[22] With the end of Reconstruction in 1877, an effective program for limiting the emergent class struggles of the later nineteenth century was forged:

the definition of the working class *in racial terms*—as "white." This was not accomplished by any legislative decree or capitalist maneuvering to divide the working class, but rather by white workers themselves. Many of them were recent immigrants, who organized on racial lines as much as on traditionally defined class lines.[23] The Irish on the West Coast, for example, engaged in vicious anti-Chinese race-baiting and committed many pogrom-type assaults on Chinese in the course of consolidating the trade union movement in California.

Thus the very political organization of the working class was in important ways a racial project. The legacy of racial conflicts and arrangements shaped the definition of interests and in turn led to the consolidation of institutional patterns (e.g., segregated unions, dual labor markets, exclusionary legislation) which perpetuated the color line *within* the working class. Selig Perlman, whose study of the development of the labor movement is fairly sympathetic to this process, notes that:

> The political issue after 1877 was racial, not financial, and the weapon was not merely the ballot, but also "direct action"—violence. The anti-Chinese agitation in California, culminating as it did in the Exclusion Law passed by Congress in 1882, was doubtless the most important single factor in the history of American labor, for without it the entire country might have been overrun by Mongolian [sic] labor and *the labor movement might have become a conflict of race instead of one of classes.*[24]

More recent economic transformations in the US have also altered interpretations of racial identities and meanings. The automation of southern agriculture and the augmented labor demand of the postwar boom transformed blacks from a largely rural, impoverished labor force to a largely urban, working-class group by 1970.[25] When boom became bust and liberal welfare statism moved rightwards, the majority of blacks came to be seen, increasingly, as part of the "underclass," as state "dependents." Thus the particularly deleterious effects on blacks of global and national economic shifts (generally rising unemployment rates, changes in the employment structure away from reliance on labor intensive work, etc.) were explained once again in the late 1970s and 1980s (as they had been in the 1940s and mid-1960s) as the result of defective black cultural norms, of familial disorganization, etc.[26] In this way new racial attributions, new racial myths, are affixed to "blacks."[27] Similar changes in racial identity are presently affecting Asians and Latinos, as such economic forces as increasing Third World impoverishment and indebtedness fuel immigration and high interest rates, Japanese competition spurs resentments, and US jobs seem to fly away to Korea and Singapore.[28]. . .

Once we understand that race overflows the boundaries of skin color, superexploitation, social stratification, discrimination and prejudice, cultural domination and cultural resistance, state policy (or of any other particular social relationship we list), once we recognize the racial dimension present to some degree in every identity, institution, and social practice in the United States—once we have done this, it becomes possible to speak of *racial formation*. This recognition is hard-won; there is a continuous temptation to think of race as an *essence*, as something fixed, concrete and objective, as (for example) one of the categories just enumerated. And there is also an opposite temptation: to see it as a mere illusion, which an ideal social order would eliminate.

In our view it is crucial to break with these habits of thought. The effort must be made to understand race as *an unstable and "decentered" complex of social meanings constantly being transformed by political struggle*. . . .

NOTES

1. *San Francisco Chronicle*, 14 September 1982, 19 May 1983. Ironically, the 1970 Louisiana law was enacted to supersede an old Jim Crow statute which relied on the idea of "common report" in determining an infant's race. Following Phipps's unsuccessful attempt to change her classification and have the law declared unconstitutional, a legislative effort arose which culminated in the repeal of the law. See *San Francisco Chronicle*, 23 June 1983.
2. The Mormon church, for example, has been heavily criticized for its doctrine of black inferiority.
3. Thomas F. Gossett notes:
   Race theory . . . had up until fairly modern times no firm hold on European thought. On the other hand, race theory and race prejudice were by no means unknown at the time when the English colonists came to North America.

Undoubtedly, the age of exploration led many to speculate on race differences at a period when neither Europeans nor Englishmen were prepared to make allowances for vast cultural diversities. Even though race theories had not then secured wide acceptance or even sophisticated formulation, the first contacts of the Spanish with the Indians in the Americas can now be recognized as the beginning of a struggle between conceptions of the nature of primitive peoples which has not yet been wholly settled. (Thomas F. Gossett, *Race: The History of an Idea in America* [New York: Schocken Books, 1965], p. 16.)

Winthrop Jordan provides a detailed account of early European colonialists' attitudes about color and race in *White Over Black: American Attitudes Toward the Negro, 1550–1812* (New York: Norton, 1977 [1968]), pp. 3–43.

4. Pro-slavery physician Samuel George Morton (1799–1851) compiled a collection of 800 crania from all parts of the world which formed the sample for his studies of race. Assuming that the larger the size of the cranium translated into greater intelligence, Morton established a relationship between race and skull capacity. Gossett reports that: "In 1849, one of his studies included the following results: The English skulls in his collection proved to be the largest, with an average cranial capacity of 96 cubic inches. The Americans and Germans were rather poor seconds, both with capacities of 90 cubic inches. At the bottom of the list were the Negroes with 83 cubic inches, the Chinese with 82, and the Indians with 79." (Ibid., p. 74.)

   On Morton's methods, see Stephen J. Gould, "The Finagle Factor," *Human Nature* (July 1978).
5. Definitions of race founded upon a common pool of genes have not held up when confronted by scientific research which suggests that the differences *within* a given human population are greater than those *between* populations. See L. L. Cavalli-Sforza, "The Genetics of Human Populations," *Scientific American* (September 1974), pp. 81–89.
6. Arthur Jensen, "How Much Can We Boost IQ and Scholastic Achievement?" *Harvard Educational Review*, vol. 39 (1969), pp. 1–123.
7. Ernst Moritz Manasse, "Max Weber on Race," *Social Research*, vol. 14 (1947), pp. 191–221.
8. Quoted in Edward D.C. Campbell, Jr., *The Celluloid South: Hollywood and the Southern Myth* (Knoxville: University of Tennessee Press, 1981), pp. 168–70.
9. Marvin Harris, *Patterns of Race in the Americas* (New York: Norton, 1964), p. 56.
10. Ibid., p. 57.
11. After James Meredith had been admitted as the first black student at the University of Mississippi, Harry S. Murphy announced that he, and not Meredith, was the first black student to attend "Ole Miss." Murphy described himself as black but was able to pass for white and spent nine months at the institution without attracting any notice. (Ibid., p. 56.)
12. A. Sivanandan, "From Resistance to Rebellion: Asian and Afro-Caribbean Struggles in Britain," *Race and Class*, vol. 23, nos. 2–3 (Autumn–Winter 1981).

13. Consider the contradictions in racial status which abound in the country with the most rigidly defined racial categories—South Africa. There a race classification agency is employed to adjudicate claims for upgrading of official racial identity. This is particularly necessary for the "coloured" category. The apartheid system considers Chinese as "Asians" while the Japanese are accorded the status of "honorary whites." This logic nearly detaches race from any grounding in skin color and other physical attributes and nakedly exposes race as a juridical category subject to economic, social, and political influences. (We are indebted to Steve Talbot for clarification of some of these points.)

14. Gordon W. Allport, *The Nature of Prejudice* (Garden City, New York: Doubleday, 1958), pp. 184–200.

15. We wish to use this phrase loosely, without committing ourselves to a particular position on such social psychological approaches as symbolic interactionism, which are outside the scope of this study. An interesting study on this subject is S. M. Lyman and W. A. Douglass, "Ethnicity: Strategies of Individual and Collective Impression Management," *Social Research,* vol. 40, no. 2 (1973).

16. Michael Billig, "Patterns of Racism: Interviews with National Front Members," *Race and Class,* vol. 20, no. 2 (Autumn 1978), pp. 161–79.

17. "Miss San Antonio USA Lisa Fernandez and other Hispanics auditioning for a role in a television soap opera did not fit the Hollywood image of real Mexicans and had to darken their faces before filming." Model Aurora Garza said that their faces were bronzed with powder because they looked too white. "I'm real Mexican [Garza said] and very dark anyway. I'm even darker right now because I have a tan. But they kept wanting me to make my face darker and darker" (*San Francisco Chronicle,* 21 September 1984). A similar dilemma faces Asian American actors who feel that Asian character lead roles inevitably go to white actors who make themselves up to be Asian. Scores of Charlie Chan films, for example, have been made with white leads (the last one was the 1981 *Charlie Chan and the Curse of the Dragon Queen*). Roland Winters, who played in six Chan features, was asked by playwright Frank Chin to explain the logic of casting a white man in the role of Charlie Chan: "The only thing I can think of is, if you want to cast a homosexual in a show, and you get a homosexual, it'll be awful. It won't be funny . . . and may be there's something there . . . "(Frank Chin, "Confessions of the Chinatown Cowboy," *Bulletin of Concerned Asian Scholars,* vol. 4, no. 3 (Fall 1972)).

18. Melanie Martindale-Sikes, "Nationalizing 'Nigger' Imagery Through 'Birth of a Nation'," paper prepared for the 73rd Annual Meeting of the American Sociological Association, 4–8 September 1978 in San Francisco.

19. Winthrop D. Jordan, op. cit., p. 95; emphasis added.

20. Historical focus has been placed either on particular racially defined groups or on immigration and the "incorporation" of ethnic groups. In the former case the characteristic ethnicity theory pitfalls and apologetics such as functionalism and cultural pluralism may be avoided, but only by sacrificing much of the focus on race. In the latter case, race is considered a manifestation of ethnicity.

21. The degree of antipathy for these groups should not be minimized. A northern commentator observed in the 1850s: "An Irish Catholic seldom attempts to rise to a higher condition than that in which he is placed, while the Negro often makes the attempt with success." Quoted in Gossett, op. cit., p. 288.

22. This analysis, as will perhaps be obvious, is essentially DuBoisian. Its main source will be found in the monumental (and still largely unappreciated) *Black Reconstruction in the United States 1860–1880* (New York: Atheneum, 1977 [1035]).

23. Alexander Saxton argues that:
North Americans of European background have experienced three great racial confrontations: with the Indian, with the African, and with the Oriental. Central to each transaction has been a totally one-sided preponderance of power, exerted for the exploitation of nonwhites by the dominant white society. In each case (but especially in the two that began with systems of enforced labor), white workingmen have played a crucial, yet ambivalent role. They have been both exploited and exploiters. On the one hand, thrown into competition with nonwhites as enslaved or "cheap" labor, they suffered economically; on the other hand, being white, they benefited by that very exploitation which was compelling the nonwhites to work for low wages or for nothing. Ideologically they were drawn in opposite directions. *Racial identification cut at right angles to class consciousness.* (Alexander Saxton, *The Indispensable Enemy: Labor and the Anti-Chinese Movement in California* (Berkeley and Los Angeles: University of California Press, 1971), p. 1, emphasis added.)

24. Selig Perlman, *The History of Trade Unionism in the United States* (New York: Augustus Kelley, 1950), p. 52; emphasis added.

25. Whether Southern blacks were "peasants" or rural workers is unimportant in this context. Some time during the 1960s blacks attained a higher degree of urbanization than whites. Before World War II most blacks had been rural dwellers and nearly 80 percent lived in the South.

26. See George Gilder, *Wealth and Poverty* (New York: Basic Books, 1981); Charles Murray, *Losing Ground* (New York: Basic Books, 1984).

27. A brilliant study of the racialization process in Britain, focused on the rise of "mugging" as a popular fear in the 1970s, is Stuart Hall et al., *Policing the Crisis* (London: Macmillan, 1978).

28. The case of Vincent Chin, a Chinese American man beaten to death in 1982 by a laid-off Detroit auto worker and his stepson who mistook him for Japanese and blamed him for the loss of their jobs, has been widely publicized in Asian American communities. On immigration conflicts and pressures, see Michael Omi, "New Wave Dread: Immigration and Intra-Third World Conflict," *Socialist Review,* no. 60 (November–December 1981).

Crane and Co. advertisement addressed to African Americans.
In The Colored American Magazine, 1903.

6

Failing to See

HARLON DALTON

Most White people, in my experience, tend not to think of themselves in racial terms. They know that they are White, of course, but mostly that translates into being not Black, not Asian-American, and not Native American. Whiteness, in and of itself, has little meaning.[1]

For a significant chunk, the inability to "get" race, and to understand why it figures so prominently in the lives of most people of color, stems from a deep affliction—the curse of rugged individualism. All of us, to some degree, suffer from this peculiarly American delusion that we are individuals first and foremost, captains of our own ships, solely responsible for our own fates: When taken to extremes, this ideal is antagonistic to the very idea of community. Even families cease to be vibrant social organisms; instead they are viewed as mere incubators and support systems for the individuals who happen to be born into them.

For those who embrace the rugged individualist ideal with a vengeance and who have no countervailing experience of community, the idea that a person's sense of self could be tied to that of a group is well-nigh incomprehensible. Collective concerns can only be interpreted as "groupthink"; collective responsibility as some strange foreign ideology. I frankly despair of being able to reach such people. Fortunately, most Americans, whatever their professed ideals, know from personal experience what community feels like. They are meaningfully connected to something smaller than the nation and larger than themselves.

For some, the tie is to a particular region of the country. I have a former colleague, for example, whose West Texas accent seemed to get stronger the longer he remained away from home. For others, the connection is to a religious community, or to a profession, or to a community defined by shared ideals or aspirations, such as Alcoholics Anonymous and the Benevolent and Protective Order of Elks. Perhaps most significantly, marly Americans eagerly lay claim to their ethnic heritage. It is, for them a rich source of comfort, pride, and self-understanding. It provides shape and texture to their lives.

So-called white ethnics are not alone in this respect. Hyphenated Americans of all colors draw great strength from their ethnic roots, and take pride in those characteristics that make their ethnic group distinctive. Ethnicity is as significant a social force for Vietnamese-Americans living in Virginia and Chinese-Americans living in the borough of Queens as it is for Irish-Americans in South Boston and Polish-Americans in Chicago. Chicanos, Salvadorans, Puerto Ricaris, and Cuban-Americans readily distinguish among one another even though their Anglo neighbors can't (or don't bother trying to) tell them apart. West Indians and U.S.-born African-Americans are as distinct from one another as steel drums are from taxophones. Lakota Sioux are not Navajo are not Pequot are hot Crow.

On the other hand, from what I have observed, people who trace their ethnic roots to Europe tend to think quite differently about race than do people who hail from the rest of the world. Most non-White ethnics recognize that, at least in the American context, they have a race as well as anethnicity. They understand full well that the quality of their lives is affected by these two social categories in distinct ways. White ethnics, on the other hand, are much less likely to think of themselves in racial terms. Like Whites who don't identify strongly with any ethnic group, they tend to take race for granted or to view it as somehow irrelevant.

At the same time, many White ethnics rely on their experience of thnicity to draw conclusions about the operation of race in America. Drawing parallels makes sense to them because they regard white ethnicity and non-White race as being more or less equivalent. However, as the average Korean-American or Haitian immigrant can atlest, despite their surface similarities, race and ethnicity are very different creatures.

Ethnicity is the beater of culture. It describes that aspect of our heritage that provides us with a mother tongue and that shapes our values, our worldview, our family structure, our rituals, the foods we eat, our mating behavior, our music—in short, much of our daily lives. We embody our ethnicity without regard for the presence or absence of other ethnic groups. Of course, ethnic groups influence one another in myriad ways and more than occasionally come into conflict. But they do not need each other to exist.

In contrast, races exist only in relation to one another. Whiteness is meaningless in the absence of

Blackness, the same holds in reverse. Moreover, race itself would be meaningless if it were not a fault line along which power, prestige, and respect are distributed. Thus, during the war in Vietnam the North Vietnamese did not distinguish between Black Americans and White ones, since both seemed equally powerful with an M-15 in their hands. White ethnicity determines culture, race determines social position. Although the members of a given ethnic group may, for a time, find themselves on the bottom by virtue of their recent arrival, their lack of language or job skills, or even because of rank discrimination, that position usually is not long-term. *Race* and hierarchy, however, are indelibly wed.

Despite this distinction, much confusion is generated by the fact that for most American Blacks (excluding, for example, recent immigrants from the Caribbean), race and ethnicity are inextricably intertwined. The particulars of our African cultural heritage were largely, though not completely, destroyed by slavery. Part of what made the television miniseries. *Roots* such a powerful experience for so many of us was that the protagonist was able to trace his heritage not only to a genetic African continent but to a particular country particular village, and particular tribe.We long for that kind of deep rootedness, but mostly we have to make do. From the remnants of our various African cultures, the rhythms of our daily existence, and the customs of our new home, especially the rural South and the urban inner city, we developed a nuiquely African-American culture, with its own music, speech patterns, religious practices, and all the rest.

The emergence in the 1980s of the term "African-American" was meant to supply a label for our ethnicity that is distinct from the one used for race. Most people, however, continue to use the term "Black" to refer to both. "White," on the other hand, refers only to race. It has no particular cultural content. In ethnic terms, a random White person wandering through New York's Metropolitan Museum of Art could as easily be Irish-American, an immigrant from Greece, a Lithuanian transplant, or a Texan on vacation.

Why do most White people not see themselves as having a race? In part, race oblivibusness is the natural consequence of being in the driver's seat. We are all much more likely to disregard attributes that seldom produce a ripple than we are those that subject us to discomfort. For example, a Reform Jewish family living in, say, Nacogdoches, Texas, will be more acutely aware of its religious/ethnic heritage than will the Baptist family next door. On the other hand, if that same family moved to the Upper West Side of Manhattan, its Jewishness would probably be worn more comfortably. For most Whites, race—or more precisely, their own race—is simply part of the unseen, unproblematic background.

Whatever the reason, the inability or unwillingness of many White people to think of themselves in racial terms has decidedly negative consequences. For one thing, it produces huge blind spots. It leaves them baffled by the amount of energy many Blacks pour into questions of racial identity. It makes it difficult for them in understand why many (but by no means all) Blacks have a sense of group consciousness that influences the choices they make as individuals. It blinds Whites to the fact that their lives are shaped by race just as much as are the lives of people of color. How they view life's possibilities; whom they regard as heroes; the extent to which they feel the country is theirs; the extent to which that belief is echoed back to them; all this and more is in part a function of their race.

This obliviousness also makes it difficult for many Whites to comprehend why Blacks interact with them on the basis of past dealings with other Whites, and why Blacks sometimes expect them to make up for the sins of their fathers, and of their neighbors as well. Curiously enough, many of the same folk wouldn't think twice about responding to young Black males as a type rather than as individuals.

Far and away the most troublesome consequence of race obliviousness is the failure of many to recognize the privileges our society confers on them because they have white skin.[2] White skin privilege is a birthright, a set of advantages one receives simply by being born with features that society values especially highly.

REFERENCES

1. Wellman, David T. (1993). *Portraits of White Racism*, 2d ed. Cambridge: Cambridge University Press, 194–95.
2. Ibid., 136–37, 163, 186–87.

 7

Los Intersticios:
Recasting Moving Selves

EVELYN ALSULTANY

Ethnicity in such a world needs to be recast so that our moving selves can be acknowledged. . . . Who am I? When am I? The questions that are asked in the street, of my identity, mold me. Appearing in the flesh, I am cast afresh, a female of color—skin color, hair texture, clothing, speech, all marking me in ways that I could scarcely have conceived of.

—MEENA ALEXANDER

I'm in a graduate class at the New School in New York City. A white female sits next to me and we begin "friendly" conversation. She asks me where I'm from. I reply that I was born and raised in New York City and return the question. She tells me she is from Ohio and has lived in New York for several years. She continues her inquiry: "Oh . . . well, how about your parents?" (I feel her trying to map me onto her narrow cartography; New York is not a sufficient answer. She analyzes me according to binary axes of sameness and difference. She detects only difference at first glance, and seeks to pigeonhole me. In her framework, my body is marked, excluded, not from this country. A seemingly "friendly" question turns into a claim to land and belonging.) "My father is Iraqi and my mother Cuban," I answer. "How interesting. Are you a U.S. citizen?"

I am waiting for the NYC subway. A man also waiting asks me if I too am Pakistani. I reply that I'm part Iraqi and part Cuban. He asks if I am Muslim, and I reply that I am Muslim. He asks me if I am married, and I tell him I'm not. In cultural camaraderie he leans over and says that he has cousins in Pakistan available for an arranged marriage if my family so desires. (My Cubanness, as well as my own relationship to my cultural identity, evaporates as he assumes that Arab plus Muslim equals arranged marriage. I can identify: he reminds me of my Iraqi relatives and I know he means well.) I tell him that I'm not interested in marriage but thank him for his kindness. (I accept his framework and respond accordingly, avoiding an awkward situation in which he realizes that I am not who he assumes I am, offering him recognition and validation for his [mis]identification.)

I am in a New York City deli waiting for my bagel to toast. The man behind the counter asks if I'm an Arab Muslim (he too is Arab and Muslim). I reply that yes, I am by part of my father. He asks my name, and I say, "Evelyn." In utter disdain, he tells me that I could not possibly be Muslim; if I were truly Muslim I would have a Muslim name. What was I doing with such a name? I reply (after taking a deep breath and telling myself that it's not worth getting upset over) that my Cuban mother named me and that I honor my mother. He points to the fact that I'm wearing lipstick and have not changed my name, which he finds to be completely inappropriate and despicable, and says that I am a reflection of the decay of the Arab Muslim in America.

I'm on an airplane flying from Miami to New York. I'm sitting next to an Ecuadorian man. He asks me where I'm from. I tell him. He asks me if I'm more Arab, Latina, or American, and I state that I'm all of the above. He says that's impossible. I must be more of one ethnicity than another. He determines that I am not really Arab, that I'm more Latina because of the camaraderie he feels in our speaking Spanish.

I am in Costa Rica. I walk the streets and my brown skin and dark hair blend in with the multiple shades of brown around me. I love this first-time experience of blending in! I walk into a coffee shop for some café con leche, and my fantasy of belonging is shattered when the woman preparing the coffee asks me where I'm from. I tell her that I was born and

raised in New York City by a Cuban mother and an Arab father. She replies, "Que eres una gringa."

I am shocked by the contextuality of identity: that my body is marked as gringa in Costa Rica, as Latina in some U.S. contexts, Arab in others, in some times and spaces not adequately Arab, or Latina, or "American," and in other contexts simply as *other.*

My body becomes marked with meaning as I enter public space. My identity fractures as I experience differing dislocations in multiple contexts. Sometimes people otherize me, sometimes they identify with me. Both situations can be equally problematic. Those who otherize me fail to see a shared humanity and those who identify with me fail to see difference; my Arab or Muslim identity negates my Cuban heritage. Identification signifies belonging or home, and I pretend to be that home for the mistaken person. It's my good deed for the day (I know how precious it can be to find a moment of familiarity with a stranger). The bridge becomes my back as I feign belonging, and I become that vehicle for others, which I desire for myself. Although it is illusory, I do identify with the humanity of the situation—the desire to belong in this world, to be understood. But the frameworks used to (mis)read my body, to disconnect me, wear on me. I try to develop a new identity. What should I try to pass for next time? Perhaps I'll just say I'm Cuban to those who appear to be Arab or South Asian. A friend suggests I say I'm an Italian from Brooklyn. I wonder if I could successfully pass for that. Ethnicity needs to be recast so that our moving selves can be acknowledged.

 8

Social Class Matters

BRENDA J. ALLEN

I would get excited when my grandma brought home hand-me-down clothing from the white families she worked for as a maid. I would eagerly sift through the pile to find something I liked. Although I proudly wore secondhand outfits, my friends and I would taunt members of a family in the projects who often rummaged through the dumpster for castoffs. Even though I knew that the government housing project where I lived was restricted to low income families, I do not remember feeling stigmatized. Every year my elementary school would send "care" packages to needy families overseas. Pleased to help poor children, I would happily donate small items like a bar of soap, a handkerchief, or a box of crayons.

I used to wish my family could get surplus government food like some of my friends' families. But Ma's income was slightly higher than the maximum allowed. Fortunately, her income was low enough to qualify me for the Comprehensive Employment Training Act (CETA) program. In junior high, CETA employed me as an assistant to the home economics teacher; in high school, I worked in the guidance counselors' office. I used my income to start a bank account and help Ma pay for my school clothes.

Kids in the projects enjoyed lots of recreational activities, thanks to government social programs that provided facilities, staff, and other resources. We flocked year round to the settlement house (a recreation and social services center) to do arts and crafts, play sports, put on variety shows, and watch movies. I was a member of the girls' basketball team and an award winning drill team. During the summer, we played in fully equipped and staffed playgrounds. Thanks to the Associated Neighborhood Centers (a city-sponsored program), I worked one summer as a day camp counselor, where the kids nicknamed me "Big Bird."

Employees who managed the projects scheduled tenants, on a rotating basis, to pick up trash, mow the lawn, or clean the laundry room in their section of the huge complex. If members of a household neglected their duties, or if their work did not pass inspection, they had to pay a fine.

My experiences encompass some of the issues that I cover in this chapter. My musings show how class-power dynamics unfold in macrosocietal structures as individuals engage in everyday micropractices. The

fact that my friends and I made fun of the family who could barely afford clothes demonstrates the enduring nature of class consciousness. Combined with my home training, the annual charitable drive at my school socialized me to care about those less fortunate than I. Yet, attitudes toward class vary according to sociohistorical context. When I was younger, the media did not bombard me with advertisements tailored for my age group, although they had begun to target teenagers. I distinctly remember the jingle for Wrangler stretch jeans. I begged Ma to get me a pair, and she did. However, my friends and I were not as concerned about style and brand names as most young people nowadays seem to be. Few children who now live where I was raised would welcome castoffs from strangers. Due to peer pressure, the hype of brand names, and fashion trends, most of them are probably more picky than I was about clothing.

Styles of consumption both define and display class positions. For example, use of space can indicate class. Geographic location can denote class position, as trailer parks often signify "white trash," and "housing projects" are class infused as symbols of the poor.[1] The familiar saying that the most important aspect of real estate is "location, location, location" implies a class bias. Prices of comparable homes can vary sharply based on the neighborhoods where they are located. Most major U.S. cities have identifiable enclaves of wealthy people, as well as "the other side of the tracks" (or the "wrong side") where poor people reside.

Throughout history, the federal government and state and local agencies, to varying degrees and with varying criteria for qualifying for assistance, have intervened to assist members of lower class groups. When I was growing up in the 1960s, the United States was in the midst of social reform. Due in large part to efforts of social activists, the government initiated programs designated for socioeconomically disadvantaged families. As a result, many lower income families had jobs, affordable housing, and food. The programs that employed me as a teenager helped to reinforce the strong work ethic my mother instilled in me and to give me a sense of self-empowerment. My peers and I enjoyed recreational activities that gave us a rich childhood and a strong sense of community. We were among innumerable beneficiaries across the country of the settlement house movement that offered services to poor citizens and poor immigrants. Many of us are proud to be former residents of the neighborhood we affectionately call "Brick City." We were fortunate to grow up during a time when public attitudes toward the needy were benevolent.

My memories imply relationships between hegemony and social class. For example, income often dictates where people live.[2] The United States comprises a class segregated society with poor and rich people residing in different types of "gated" communities, with different ramifications. To live in the projects, we had to follow rigid rules and policies or risk eviction. As I recall, families in the projects never questioned being required to maintain the property.

I delve into these and related issues in this chapter to show how power relationships and ideology affect constructions of social class in the United States. First, I discuss conceptions of class, after which I explain why class matters. Next, I trace the social construction of class in the United States. Then, I explore relationships between class and communication.

WHAT IS SOCIAL CLASS?

What is your social class? If you are like most people in the United States, you consider yourself to be middle class. But how did you draw that conclusion? Many people equate class with economic status.[3] However, economics is not the only defining factor of class distinctions. The word "class" comes from the Roman *classis,* a system used to divide the population into groups for taxation purposes.[4] Since Roman days, class consistently has been based on social stratification, the ranking of groups according to various criteria, with ascending positions afforded more value, respect, status, and privilege than lower positions. Placement in a class system can occur through **ascription,** based on conditions at birth such as family background, race,

sex, or place of birth, or **achievement,** as a result of individual effort or merit such as earning a college degree.[5]

Most social science ideas about class stem from those of Karl Marx and Max Weber. Although their perspectives differ, both men based their work on economics. Marx conceived of two classes related to the means of production: the bourgeoisie, which includes those who own the means of production, and the proletariat or working class (everyone else).[6] Class attribution initially was based on objective terms, such as the amount of **capital** (accumulated goods and their value) one amassed.

Believing there is more to class than just economics, Weber maintained that stratification is based on property, power, and prestige (the three Ps).[7] Property refers not only to ownership, but also to the *control* of property. Weber conceived of power from a "power over" standpoint. He viewed power as the ability to control resources and behaviors of others, contending that this form of control and its results are key factors in social stratification:[8] "Class is about the power some people have over the lives of others, and the powerlessness most people experience as a result."[9] Prestige means esteem or social status. One type of prestige in contemporary society is occupational prestige. Because amount of income and advanced education and training can affect the prestige level of occupations, white-collar occupations generally elicit higher prestige than blue-collar or pink-collar occupations, which include service and clerical jobs.

Weber's conception of class corresponds with contemporary views that economic factors are not the only determinants of class; more subtle factors are involved as well. French sociologist Pierre Bourdieu elaborated the concept of capital to emphasize ideological conditions of existence as well as how people use capital to compete for position and resources. He specified three types of capital: **economic capital,** which includes financial assets; **cultural capital,** which encompasses specialized skills and knowledge such as linguistic and cultural competencies, passed down through one's family or from experiences in social institutions, such as an

Ivy League education,[10] and **social capital,** which consists of networks of connections.[11]

Here's a brief example of Bourdieu's conception of capital. When I won an all-expenses-paid scholarship for college, I could have gone to any college in the world that admitted me because I had earned access to economic capital to pay tuition, room, board, and travel costs. Because I was clueless about how to select a school, I picked the one that another black female student (who had won the same scholarship two years earlier) had chosen. I was not savvy about the college selection process, and the guidance counselors at my school did not offer any assistance. (Research persistently reveals a pattern of differential counseling according to a student's social class.[12]) In essence, because I was a member of a working-class family whose members had never attended college, I had not accrued the appropriate cultural or social capital to navigate the college admission process. Fortunately, I did acquire an important bit of cultural capital by virtue of being tracked according to my IQ and placed in classes with middle- to upper-class white students who understood the ropes of getting into college. I took my cues from them as they discussed the SAT and the ACT (college entrance exams I did not know about), and I persuaded Ma to pay for me to take those tests.

Bourdieu's perspective on class acknowledges "linguistic, social and communication processes that foster class membership and consciousness."[13] For example, an increasing emphasis on educational credentials reflects the primacy of cultural capital in U.S. society. Members of the middle and upper class increasingly seek access to elite institutions that signal an educational experience different from and more valuable than that which has become increasingly available to the masses.[14] Persons in higher socioeconomic brackets often rely on "connections" to gain admission to preferred institutions, which illustrates an underlying premise of social capital: "It's not what you know, it's who you know." Another example of social capital permeates the standard practice within elite institutions of higher education of "legacy admissions,"

or giving preferential treatment to children of alumni. Few people challenge this form of "affirmative action."

When I asked you about your social class, what categories of class did you consider? Although dozens of classification schemes exist, most charts refer to variations of "upper," "middle," and "lower" classes. Some designations subdivide these, for instance: "upper-upper," "lower-upper," "upper-middle," "lower-middle," "working class," and "poor." Synonyms for the upper class include "owning," "capitalist," or "overclass." The lowest of the lower class has been labeled the "underclass."[15]

These classifications explicitly acknowledge power relationships. Members of the working class tend to have relatively little control over their jobs, and they usually do not supervise anyone. Comprising the top stratum, the capitalist class includes those who have control over the means of production; only 2 percent of the population falls in this category.

The preceding ideas correspond with the following definition of **social class:** "an open (to some degree) stratification system that is associated with a systematically unequal allocation of resources and constraints."[16] "Resources and constraints" can refer to various types of capital, including money, savoir-faire or "know-how," social skills, authority, experience, and clout.

WHY SOCIAL CLASS MATTERS

Although class difference and class struggle represent significant themes in U.S. history, rarely does anyone discuss social class. Yet, social class embodies a powerful, persistent predictor of accessibility to resources, potential for longevity and success, and self-esteem. Most people remain in or close to the class position of their family, which may affect their personal identity: "estimation of self-worth, degrees of confidence and feelings of entitlement or lack of entitlement permeate the experience of belonging to one class or another."[17] Social class also can be "a major determinant of individual decisions and social actions."[18]

From womb to tomb, social class can make a major difference in one's life. Most working-class mothers see a doctor for the first time in the last month of pregnancy, whereas most wealthy women get top quality prenatal care throughout their entire pregnancy.[19] As a result, rates of infant mortality, birth defects, and illness are higher among poor families. Poor children lack basic resources and suffer debilitating material conditions, such as constant moving, poor nutrition, lack of warm clothing, and inferior living conditions, which can constrain their potential to learn. Lower-class communities more often are built in old industrial areas, and residents are exposed to environmental hazards such as air pollution, lead paint, and asbestos.[20]

Class is the strongest predictor of achievement in schools.[21] The higher the social class, the more likely the student is to succeed academically. Social class is the strongest predictor of whether or not an individual will go to college, as well as the type of college a student will attend. Suburban schools in wealthy neighborhoods work with budgets two to three times higher per student than poor urban and rural schools. Poor students are disproportionately labeled as low-status and segregated from mainstream students and education. In one poor, Hispanic district, more than one-quarter of the students were classified as "special education," and teachers believed that students' poverty caused their failure rates.[22]

Compared to patients in higher-level social classes, those from lower classes tend to receive more inferior medical care and have limited access to care.[23] Injury at work and work-related fatalities are higher for lower-class workers.[24] Older poor people suffer more from chronic illness, and wealthy people in general live longer than poor and working-class individuals. These distinctions across classes are not limited to stark differences between the poor and the affluent. Throughout the life span, health declines with each successive class group.[25]

Although social discourse implies that the United States is classless, class-based stratification persists.[26] As the preceding paragraph intimates, quality of life varies according to **socioeconomic status** (SES), which is determined by the combination of income, education, and occupation. Even though the United States is an affluent society in general (median in-

come for a family of four in 2001 was $56,061),[27] wealth (defined as total value of money and other assets, minus outstanding debts) is distributed much more unequally than income.

In fact, the United States has the most unequally distributed wealth and income in the world. About 40 percent of families have little or no wealth.[28] In 1999, the annual income of the average poor family was $9,211.[29] In 1996, the richest 20 percent of the population owned approximately 80 percent of the country's entire wealth.[30] Economic statistics indicate that the rich are getting richer, and the gap is widening between the haves and the have-nots. In 1980, CEOs of large corporations earned 42 times the salary of the average factory worker; in 2001, their salary was 411 times greater. Between 1992 and 2002, workers' wages grew 36 percent, while CEO compensation jumped 340 percent.[31]

Social class matters because it affects the political system. Political candidacy and being elected are tied to class issues. To run for office requires a substantial bankroll and extensive social networks. Most candidates for national office garner funding from elite corporations, and most congressional representatives are lawyers or established business persons. Between 1979 and 1993, 90 percent of cabinet members were either members of the upper class or associated with major corporations.[32] In addition, political candidates recognize that class matters. Most of them either tout the fact that they grew up poor, or in working-class families, implying that they understand the plight of the poor, or they admit that they are rich, invoking proof of the American dream.[33]

Finally, a number of startling statistics confirm why we should concern ourselves with social class. Approximately one out of four children is born into poverty in the United States. This rate is 1.5 times greater than that of comparable democracies in the world. The United States provides fewer tax-supported services for infants and youths than other developed countries.[34] Furthermore, 40 percent of people living in poverty are under 18 years of age. Approximately 17 percent of children or 12.1 million under 18 are poor by federal standards. Nine million U.S. children suffer from malnutrition.[35]

Almost two-thirds of poor persons are white. However, relative to their numbers in the population, a disproportionate percentage of blacks and Hispanics are poor. Among blacks who live a normal life span, nine out of every ten will have experienced poverty at some point, as contrasted with five out of every ten whites.[36] The highest rate of poverty in 1999 was among American Indians and Alaskan natives (25.9 percent). Each night, 700,000 homeless people reside in temporary public shelters; among these, 40 percent are families with children.[37] Comprising two-thirds of poor persons over 18, women represent an increasing proportion of the poor. These facts reveal that nondominant members of social identity categories, such as women, children, and people of color, are more likely to be poor than are dominant members. These numbers illustrate once again that intersections of identity matter. Similar to other aspects of social identity we are studying, current conceptions and conditions of social class arise from a variety of sociohistorical developments.

CONSTRUCTING SOCIAL CLASS IN THE UNITED STATES

Power dynamics related to the social construction of social class are evident in the history of how the United States was established and built. In early stages of the country, many white male newcomers arrived with high social and economic status. Others experienced "shipboard mobility," simply by leaving poor circumstances in England to take advantage of opportunities across the ocean. In the seventeenth century, over half of English immigrants were indentured servants who worked five to ten years to pay for their passage to the New World. Almost one-third of them died before paying off their contracts. Those who survived were able to improve their status, though not to a substantial extent.[38]

Meanwhile, few economic opportunities existed for Native Americans, white women, and blacks. Chances for upward mobility were available primarily to certain white men who capitalized on slavery, immigrant labor, tenant farming, sharecropping, farm mortgages, and land grabs from Native Americans, French immigrants, and Mexicans. Consequently, only a few persons accumulated wealth.

The so called "New World" was unlike Europe, which operated under feudalism and a formal class hierarchy. In contrast, the land that would become the United States seemed egalitarian, and numerous authors wrote about abundant opportunities for mobility. Yet, the offspring of wealthy colonialists were the main persons who ascended the economic ladder. During the financial panics in the 1800s, descendants of the colonial elite survived because they were in a sound financial position to take advantage of economic prospects, such as buying up land offered for sale below market value. In the mid-1800s, 95 percent of New York City's wealthiest one hundred persons were born into their wealth.[39] Thus, class was primarily ascriptive.

Across history, the government and politicians played major roles in creating, reinforcing, and changing conceptions of social class, as well as attitudes toward social class. During World War I, President Woodrow Wilson invoked values of thrift and savings to persuade citizens to make personal sacrifices. When times became more prosperous after the war, political figures invoked and inculcated ideals such as individualism, materialism, and hedonism. A consumer ethic arose, encouraging people to acquire material possessions. Mass advertising campaigns sought to convince middle- and working-class people to use credit or installment plans to buy products.

After World War I, the government mainly served the interests of the wealthy. For example, the tax on earnings of one million dollars decreased from $600,000 to $200,000.[40] By reducing the percentage of income taxed, inequalities in the incomes of the rich and the poor became even more pronounced. During the Great Depression (1929–1933), the gross national product dropped by 29 percent and consumer spending fell 18 percent. Unemployment rose from 3.2 percent in 1929 to 24.9 percent in 1933. In essence, "the American dream had turned into the American nightmare."[41]

The economic cycle turned again after the bombing of Pearl Harbor, with the beginning of World War II. Spending and investment increased in the defense industry. Once again, politicians implored citizens to make sacrifices for patriotism.

During the twentieth century, the government established numerous programs to improve economic and material conditions of citizens, including the Social Security Act implemented in 1935 to provide retirement income for workers, and the GI Bill of 1944 to benefit veterans of World War II by opening up educational opportunities for young men of all races from poor backgrounds. By the 1950s, the country was poised to return to prosperity and materialism. Although boundaries of race and gender blocked mobility, class lines became more permeable in the 1950s and 1960s. Working-class families were able to purchase a modest home and a car and to plan for extended summer vacations. Many could afford to send their children to college.[42] In addition, the government created opportunities such as CETA to remove obstacles to class mobility.

Since the 1960s, numerous developments have affected class location. In the 1980s, under Ronald Reagan's administration, the tax structure shifted to benefit the wealthy and to decrease domestic programs for low-income families and children. In 1996, Congress passed the Personal Responsibility and Work Opportunity Reconciliation Act (PRWORA) and the Temporary Assistance for Needy Families (TANF) program to initiate welfare reform that requires recipients to work in exchange for time-limited assistance.[43]

Across history, whenever the federal government created and administered social policies and programs, they often were responding to concerns and demands of citizen groups and individuals, whose attitudes toward poor people and poverty fluctuated. Early perceptions of social inequality were imbued with a Christian attitude of benevolence and compassion toward the less fortunate. This mind-set changed drastically in the late nineteenth century, when most people viewed poverty as a blight on society. Social programs during those times distinguished deserving poor, such as the elderly, orphans,

and widows with young children, from the undeserving poor, such as vagrants. Crimes of vagrancy were punishable by flogging and even death.[44]

During the late nineteenth century, a discourse arose about survival of the fittest and eradication of the unfit. This social Darwinist approach to poverty endorsed the idea of helping nature run its course by weeding out "undesirables," for instance, through sterilization. Included in the list of undesirables were persons with disabilities, people of color, and poor white people. Stereotypes portrayed poor whites as incestuous, alcoholic, stupid, and "genetic defectives." White Anglo-Saxon Protestant families who moved West from the Oklahoma dust bowl during the 1930s were held with contempt and antagonism. Known as "Okies," they were called "dirty, shiftless, ignorant, breeders." This "white trash" stereotype blames the poor for being poor, and it helps to solidify for middle- and upper-class whites a sense of cultural and intellectual superiority.[45]

Across the twentieth century, societal discourse fluctuated between portraying poor people as genetically defective and depicting them as helpless victims of macrosocietal economic conditions.[46] By the beginning of the twenty-first century, attitudes had shifted yet again, as some analysts contend that "poverty" has lost its meaning and that most citizens are apathetic toward poor people.

However, grassroots groups are springing up to narrow the widening gap between the rich and the poor. The living wage movement, established in the 1990s, seeks to raise wage standards at local levels. Advocates of this movement encourage cities and counties to develop ordinances for organizations that contract city and county services. These ordinances require employers to pay workers enough to "survive on what they earn and support their families without relying on welfare for emergency health care and food stamps and other public assistance."[47] Baltimore (Maryland), Los Angeles, San Jose, and Oakland (California) have approved living wage ordinances.

Another example of efforts to improve class positions of citizens is the "I Have a Dream" Foundation.[48] Philanthropist Eugene Lang created this remarkable intervention program in 1981 after returning to the elementary school he had attended 50 years earlier in New York's Harlem. When the school's principal told Lang that three-quarters of the students would probably never complete high school, Lang was so moved that he vowed to pay the college tuition of every sixth grader who would graduate from high school.

Lang's program has blossomed. Across the country, local groups adopt an entire grade from an elementary school or an entire age group from a housing development and offer a variety of services and support systems to children and their families from elementary school through college. Most "Dreamers" who go to college are the first in their families to do so. The U.S. Department of Education has developed a replication of the model called GEAR UP (Gaining Early Awareness and Readiness for Undergraduate Programs),[49] which employs partnerships committed to serving and accelerating the academic achievement of cohorts of students. GEAR UP promotes academic preparation.[50]

This overview samples a multitude of historical developments related to social class in the United States. Inherent in this history are dominant ideologies related to class in the United States.

THE MYTH OF A CLASSLESS SOCIETY

Social discourse often portrays the United States as a classless society.[51] Compared to the class system in England and the caste system in India, systems that are ascriptive, the "classless" United States certainly would seem preferable to most people. However, an irony infuses this myth of classlessness. As feminist scholar bell hooks observes, "for so long everyone has wanted to hold on to the belief that the United States is a class-free society—that anyone who works hard enough can make it to the top. Few people stop to think that in a class-free society there would be no top."[52] Furthermore, the language we use to denote class differences implies hierarchy as well as power differentials, as seen in the terms "upper class" and "lower class."[53]

From its colonialist inception, the United States was vaunted as the land of opportunity. This image, etched into the psyche of many people, helped to generate the fundamental class-based ideology of the American dream: "an American social ideal that stresses egalitarianism and especially material prosperity."[54] This premise arises from a culture of individualism and autonomy that affirms that anyone can get rich in a society that is open and competitive. This ideology rests on an achievement orientation to success rather than ascription. The concept of equal opportunity implies that individuals are responsible for success or failure: "wealth is seen as the result of superior individual effort and talent and poverty as the product of deficiencies in these areas."[55]

The rags-to-riches myth valorizes the few people who manage to beat the odds. Popular since the seventeenth century, this recurring narrative promotes a picture of the United States as a utopia. It focuses on individuals and their potential, claiming that everyone can participate and advance equally, if only they work hard enough. This narrative associates success with virtue and merit. Thus, this perspective ignores the fact that a person's starting point can affect success and overlooks the point that success often depends on access to books, health care, education, professional jobs, travel, and other forms of economic, social, and cultural capital. The rags-to-riches perspective fails to acknowledge structural barriers and systemic obstacles to employment, housing, education, and health care.

Related to this, the "culture of poverty" ideology contends that poor people collectively exhibit traits that keep them down. This perspective on class blames the poor for their plight and ignores the fact that many wealthy people have inherited their wealth and resources or that they were better positioned to attain the American dream. This ideology does not acknowledge that economic, cultural, and social capital can tilt the playing field in favor of those who have accumulated wealth, knowledge, and/or connections. Instead, victim-blaming narratives and cultural deprivation stories ascribe persistent intergenerational poverty to immorality and family dysfunctions.[56]

Belief in the dream seems to be alive and well: 94 percent of Americans think that "people who work full time should be able to earn enough to keep their families out of poverty."[57] Many people in the United States also seem reticent to even entertain the topic of social class: "if we identify and recognize a class system in the United States, we are challenging and questioning the very fiber of democracy. To some of us it may even seem unpatriotic to consider an American class system."[58]

SOCIAL CLASS AND LABOR

Enmeshed in the preceding overview of the social construction of social class are several issues related to labor. By the late nineteenth century, due to the development of large corporations and railroads, the United States had established itself as a capitalist society. Capitalist expansion was a major force in class formations as the industrial revolution provided opportunities for thousands of workers to produce a multitude of goods. Due to industrialization and urbanization, more people became dependent on wage-paying jobs for food, clothing, and shelter. Rapid industrialization fostered the rise of a large class of white-collar workers.[59] By the end of the 1920s, corporations controlled almost half of industry, and two-thirds of industrial wealth was owned by publicly financed corporations.[60]

During the depression, job discrimination escalated for women and blacks, 50 percent of whom became unemployed. Desperate for any type of work, whites took over so called "Negro" occupations such as bellhop, street cleaner, and elevator operator. This type of response recurred across the history of labor in the United States: "the roots of ethnic and racial antagonism usually lie in economic inequality and conflict . . . because subordinate racial and ethnic minorities represent an economic threat to many members of the dominant majority."[61]

As the number of factories rose due to industrialization, workers' safety and health were often threatened. Also, factory owners did not have to pay workers the wages they deserved because a large labor pool provided a steady supply of employees. Consequently, workers began to organize to acquire safe working conditions as well as reasonable compensation. They formed labor unions and took actions such as strikes and organized protests to secure their demands. To retaliate, some capitalist owners took coercive measures.

They enlisted the assistance of local or federal law enforcement groups who used physical force against the workers. Many persons were killed or injured during these interventions. For instance, in 1937, National Guardsmen killed eighteen strikers and arrested two hundred in my hometown (Youngstown, Ohio).[62]

Resistance in the form of organized protests and strikes is an extremely important part of the labor history of the United States, as these activities, usually initiated by unions, resulted in changes in opportunities for economic mobility. Efforts of labor union movements helped to garner such important aspects of employment as an eight-hour workday, a forty-hour workweek, occupational safety laws, wage minimums, unemployment benefits, and so forth. However, many union groups engaged in racist and sexist practices by barring racial minorities and women from their membership.[63] In addition, corporate bosses sometimes used class and race antagonisms to secure consent to domination. Henry Ford mounted a conscious campaign of racial division between black and white workers. To dissuade blacks from joining unions, he reminded them of the United Auto Workers' opposition to black membership.[64]

On the other hand, groups also formed interracial coalitions. These groups realized that economic opportunity and political and civil rights were interrelated.[65] Predominantly white members of the unions representing automobile workers, electrical workers, and garment workers joined with the Brotherhood of Sleeping Car Porters to donate money and organize members to travel to Washington, D.C., in 1963 to march for jobs and freedom.

A pivotal figure in the labor movement was former migrant worker Cesar E. Chavez. In the 1960s, he and Dolores Huerta founded the United Farm Workers union and worked tirelessly for almost three decades to gain better pay and working conditions for laborers. Basing his efforts on Gandhi's nonviolence approach, Chavez went on extended hunger strikes and coordinated numerous boycotts. In 2000, California made his birthday, March 31, a paid holiday for state employees. A campaign is under way to create a paid federal holiday to honor Chavez.[66]

Spotlight on Media

PRINT MEDIA, SOCIAL CLASS, AND RACE

Numerous studies report that the media often portray a disproportionate number of poor people as black.[67] The media often invoke a narrative script of "the welfare queen." This script has two key components—welfare recipients are disproportionately women, and women on welfare are disproportionately African-American.[68] Political scientist Martin Gilens conducted content analysis of print media from the 1960s through 1992. His research found that 62 percent of poverty stories that appeared in *Time, Newsweek,* and *U.S. News and World Report* featured African-Americans.[69] In addition, fewer African-Americans were portrayed in "sympathetic" stories about poverty and welfare. Newsmagazines depicted almost 100 percent of the "underclass" as African-Americans. A similar project yielded similar results of articles about poverty and poor people in newsmagazines published between 1993 and 1998.[70]

This portrayal has imprinted stereotypic race-gender-class images on the minds of many people in the United States. Perhaps this helps to explain why the public significantly overestimates the percentage of blacks among the poor. In a survey published in 1999, 55 percent of the participants thought most of the poor were black, 31 percent thought white and black were "about equal," and 24 percent thought most were white.[71] These portrayals are important because they help to perpetuate stereotypes about blacks as well as misconceptions about poverty. Moreover, because public opinion can affect public policy, "if attitudes on poverty-related issues are driven by inaccurate and stereotypical portrayals of the poor, then the policies favored by the public (and political elites) may not adequately address the true problems of poverty."[72]

COMMUNICATING SOCIAL CLASS IN ORGANIZATIONS

Members of society use communication to disseminate and internalize ideologies and myths about social class. Power dynamics operate as "those in control of linguistic and communicative resources use these to manage the impressions of others."[73] In essence, communication is a fundamental aspect of class formations, and the experience of class occurs primarily through communication. Individuals consciously or subconsciously "read" one another's appearance and behaviors to discern class position. We look for cues such as clothing, accessories, speech style, mode of transportation, and so forth to make decisions about other people's class location. And, we perform class by our (conscious and

unconscious) choices of clothing, accessories, speech style, manners, food preferences, home décor, mode of transportation, and so forth. Persons in similar class positions usually share similar symbols and language systems.

Most organizations reflect the class system of society.[74] Class dynamics are evident in organizational structures, practices, policies, and norms. For example, "in institutional settings, stratification is built into organizational structures, including lines of authority, job descriptions, rules, and spatial and temporal segregation"[75] to identify and delineate organization members who have/don't have power and prestige. The workplace is a crucial site of class production and reproduction: "Of all places where practices, languages, and relations are lived and shared by individual class members, of all places where consent is important to dominant-subordinate relations, of all places where hegemony is constructed, the most important place must be at work."[76] Within organizations, classism occurs in numerous ways.

Organizations tend to exercise varying degrees and types of control of employees depending on their location in the hierarchy. Lower-level workers usually have to account for when and how they expend their time. In contrast, higher-level employees may be less accountable. Because I am a professor, I can come and go freely on campus. I do not have to fill out a time sheet or punch a time card, and I do not have to take timed breaks. If I do not feel well, I can cancel class without consulting anyone, and my pay for that period will not be affected. Yet, most nonfaculty staff members at the university have to call their supervisor by a specific time in order to be paid for sick leave; they also might be required to provide proof of illness.

Organizational hierarchies are necessarily class based, and some are more explicit about distinctions between levels than others. The federal government designates occupations according to a grade system that divides civil servant employees into eighteen ascending categories. Usually, the higher one's position in a hierarchy, the greater that person's status and access to resources, including compensation, benefits, leave policies, parking privileges, bathrooms, dining facilities, and even office furniture. According to author Paul Fussell, furniture salespeople know the hierarchy of office desks: oak is at the bottom, then walnut; mahogany represents the upper middle, and teak is the ultimate wood.[77]

Physical aspects of the workplace also signify class distinctions and forms of control. For example, "space is deliberately ordered to give signals about hierarchy and status."[78] The higher one is in the hierarchy, the more space one is usually allocated, and vice versa. Within office buildings, space is usually allocated according to class location. Executives tend to occupy larger, private offices furnished with more expensive or status-loaded artifacts. Consider,

for instance, the symbolism of the corner office or the key to the executive washroom.

Lower-level personnel not only tend to have less privacy but also less control over their work space. Higher-level employees are more likely to have window(s) and door(s), individual light switches and even a thermostat, whereas lower-level employees tend to have limited (if any) control of ambient conditions. Yet, employees sometimes challenge or subvert control mechanisms by altering their spaces or creating new ones. For example, two women in adjacent cubicles cut a hole in the partition that separated them in order to talk with each other.[79]

Class biases suffuse many routine practices in organizations. Employee recruitment processes often occur through social networks based on class similarities. In some organizations, hiring criteria favor recruiting Ivy League or private college graduates, an example of more obvious class discrimination.[80] As mentioned previously in the discussion on race, interview expectations for certain jobs value dominant language codes, which usually correspond with speech styles used by dominant group members, who tend to belong to middle or upper classes. Requiring employees to pay for items needed for doing the job, such as uniforms, may prohibit some individuals from taking a job. Other examples of practices that reflect class bias include requiring employees to pay their business travel expenses in advance and be reimbursed later or issuing company credit cards, possibly excluding persons with bad credit histories.

When organizations schedule mandatory events such as training or retreats during off-hours, employees responsible for children or other family members may incur family care expenses (e.g., for their children or elderly parents). Organizations may presuppose possession of cultural capital as members expect employees to attend and participate in social events such as black-tie affairs in country club settings. Even though these events may not be mandatory, they can be important sites for networking. Employees who do not attend because of general apprehension or because they do not have funds to purchase the proper clothing and/or to pay child care costs, or those who do attend but are unsure about etiquette, may not accrue networking advantages.

Lower-status organization members, such as custodial staff, often perform their work backstage and/or after-hours, which renders them invisible. Even when they are visible, others in the workplace may tend not to acknowledge them.[81] However, some of these employees note that being backstage allows them some autonomy and independence and limits the potential for demeaning interactions with other employees.[82]

Formal and informal dress codes also signify class. The common distinctions of "blue collar" (less formal: clothes might become soiled on the job) and "white collar" (more formal: clothes are likely to retain a clean, pressed appearance) illustrate a class distinction connected to appearance. Newer labels combine status and other aspects of social identity. For instance, "pink collar" designates clerical workers and implies a female focus. "Brown collar" refers to low-level, physically demanding occupations, such as domestic workers, farm workers, and low-level machine operators in which Latino/a workers are severely overrepresented.[83] Thus, "brown" refers to the ethnicity of the disproportionate number of Latino/a workers who are employed in those types of jobs.

Mode of dress often signals the wearer's status in the organization. In most corporations, executives are expected to wear business suits or business attire. Many organizations require employees to wear uniforms, which can reveal and conceal statuses, certify legitimacy, establish conformity, or suppress individuality.[84] Uniforms "vary in legitimacy and prestige, conferring different degrees of honor upon members."[85] Military uniforms may evoke different responses than working-class uniforms. In addition, "the very existence of a uniform implies a group structure."[86] For example, uniforms clearly signify the hierarchy of armed services personnel.

Among working-class employees such as hotel maids or bellmen, a uniform signals a person's role to customers, clients, and patrons. For members of the working class, a uniform forces conformity and constrains individuality of dress among an

occupational group. It also highlights the wearer's status and differentiates the wearer from other people in an organizational setting. Author Katherine Boo contends that working-class uniforms are not made for the workers, but rather for "the rest of us." Boo reports that a backlash about dress is building among the working class, following members of occupations who have substituted uniforms for street clothes. Nurses report an increase in respect from both patients and doctors when they wear clothing other than their white uniforms, and anthropologists repeatedly find that persons wearing business suits evoke more respect and better responses than those who wear other clothing.[87] However, working-class individuals may resent people whom they call "suits" because "the business suit represents the ability of members of the middle class to command respect for their kind of work. The business suit in our society loudly proclaims that the wearer is involved in dignified work."[88]

In contrast, a working-class uniform may invoke a different response. Parking attendant Jimmy Killens asserts that he would not accept an invitation to go after work to dinner at a fancy restaurant in Washington, D.C., because he fears that patrons would disdain him: "I wear a uniform," he declares, "so it does not matter that I make an honest wage. I'm looked down on in this town. A uniform—it says you're nothing."[89]

Health Care Settings

Social class dynamics affect power relations between and among communicators in a variety of organizational contexts. Examples of these dynamics are evident in research on health care environments. In those settings, patient-provider interactions constitute important communication scenarios. Providers must acquire information to facilitate diagnosis and treatment, and they must persuade patients to comply with treatment plans. Patients need to feel comfortable and respected enough to share personal information and to accept recommendations from providers.

A small, growing body of literature on patient-provider interactions suggests a relationship between patient characteristics, such as social class and race, and provider attitudes and interaction behaviors.[90] Patients of higher socioeconomic status (SES) tend to receive better medical care and to have more access to medical care than those with lower SES.[91] Some providers subscribe to negative stereotypes about poor patients that mirror those of society at large; for instance, they believe that poor patients are lazy, ignorant, and noncompliant.[92] In one study, "upper-middle-class patients received more physician time, more information, more positive talk, and more talk overall than did patients from lower social classes."[93] Another project reported that physicians were less likely to discuss diet and exercise with lower-income patients, but they were more likely to discuss smoking with this group than with middle-class patients.[94]

Because psychotherapy entails speech systems based on dominant language competencies, psychiatrists may differentially treat persons who do not have those communication skills. Psychiatrists may assign more optimistic prognoses to middle-class patients than lower-class patients. In addition, hospital workers tend to treat middle-class psychiatric patients better than lower-class ones.[95]

These biases and their related communication behaviors may stem from disparities between health care providers and their patients. Physicians from lower SES backgrounds may be more effective communicators with lower SES patients. Recent recruiting practices for medical schools tend to focus on applicants from the middle and upper classes. The students with lower SES who graduate from medical school and become physicians provide a disproportionately higher share of care to minority, poor, and Medicaid patients.[96]

Educational Settings

In addition to health care contexts, educational systems are primary sites of social class dynamics, as a 1999 research study reports:

> The educational system replicates the class structure and corporate system of capitalist societies. That is, schools prepare a labor force to assume the

tasks demanded by the corporations. Some schools, dominated by low income and minority youth, teach the skills of punctuality needed to maintain the assembly line. Other schools, populated by majority and high-income youth, teach the skills of independent thought and personnel management necessary for higher levels of the corporation.[97]

Basically, educational experiences "from preschool to high school differentially prepare students for their ultimate positions in the workforce, and a student's placement in various school programs is based primarily on her or his race and class origin."[98] For instance, school personnel counseled students to enroll in either college preparatory or trade-technical courses on the basis of students' social class and assumptions of their parents' ability to pay for their education.[99]

Because members of the middle and upper classes have always controlled educational systems and content, their values suffuse curriculum structures and materials and placement procedures. Consequently, the process of education differs for children according to their social class, and these differences help to reproduce inequalities.

Most children attend schools segregated by race, ethnicity, and class, and poor children still attend inferior schools.[100] Even when schools are integrated, students often are resegregated by tracking or ability grouping.[101] Lower-track classes tend to consist mainly of working-class and minority students. As the quote at the beginning of this section implies, separating and segregating students by social class can perpetuate class distinctions and socialize students regarding "their place" in society. For instance, while working with lower-class students, teachers often apply an approach known as a "pedagogy of poverty," which stresses teacher control and student compliance.[102] In this approach, teachers offer direct instruction to an entire class; they expect all students to comply and respond in similar ways. Under this model, teachers do not employ alternative methods such as cooperative learning, student-devised learning contracts, individualized instruction, or peer tutoring. Instead, they assign students repetitive, nonintellectual tasks as opposed to giving them problem-solving and/or other group/team-oriented or creative classroom activities.[103]

Children from upper-class families tend to enjoy an educational advantage over other classes, because children with higher SES can afford opportunities for enrichment outside of the classroom. They usually come to school better prepared, and better socialized to be educated. Their access to cultural and social capital places them in positions of privilege. Working-class or poor students do not always fare well on standardized tests that are written in language more commonly geared toward and used by higher SES members. Therefore, how well someone speaks and understands white, middle-class English erroneously becomes a common measurement of intelligence, and students not proficient in standard English may have limited opportunity for advancement.

Class differences may also affect parent involvement, a pivotal factor for student success. A review of literature concludes that "low-income parents and working-class parents, as compared with middle-class parents, receive less warm welcomes in their children's schools; their interventions and suggestions are less respected and attended to and they are less able to influence the education of their children."[104] The study cites repeated reports of teachers and administrators who discount and devalue any information that working-class parents might try to share.

However, many teacher in low-income schools strive to develop relationships with low-income parents. Educator Bernice Lott offers recommendations to improve parent-teacher relationships that have obvious communication implications. They also imply effects of power and ideology. Lott believes that schools should take the initiative in building relationships because they have the advantage of resources and power. She advises teachers to encourage informal communication rather than focus only on scheduled meetings that frequently do not correspond to the lifestyle of working parents who may not be able to take time off work, or who may work during nontraditional hours. She also recommends that teacher training programs help prospective teachers to communicate effectively with parents from varying class backgrounds.

A variety of educational reform initiatives seek to change conditions related to class differences. Many school systems are involved in restructuring, which entails strategies such as untracking courses, forming heterogeneous classrooms, redesigning and streamlining curriculum, revising assessment methods, and decentralizing administration.[105] In an in-depth, three-year study of school restructuring in one city, educator Pauline Lipman concludes

Although restructuring schools and teachers' work may be necessary for fundamental change, it will take a profound and protracted engagement of ideas and values, and ultimately a significant challenge to the power of dominant ideologies, to transform education in the interest of all students.[106]

CONCLUSION

Social class encompasses a socially constructed category of identity that involves more than just economic factors; it includes an entire socialization process. Across history, attitudes toward social class have varied, as have the communication processes that create, reinforce, and challenge class distinctions. Although the United States purports to be a classless society, social class distinctions have become solidified, due in part to dominant ideologies such as the culture of poverty and the American dream. To achieve the American dream, many groups have organized and fought to improve important aspects of employment, including equitable pay and safe working conditions. Their efforts have had significant, positive impacts on the quality of work life for many people. However, organizations of all types, from schools, to factories, to health care facilities, to corporations, continue to be sites where members reproduce dominant perspectives on social class. Consequently, a strong need exists to identify and develop strategies for reducing blatant and subtle forms of classism and its effects.

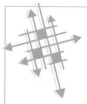

ID Check

1. What is your social class?
2. How important is your social class to you? Explain.
3. What and who have been the primary sources of socialization for you about your social class? As you reflect on who has influenced you, name specific persons. Where appropriate, identify the organization or type of organization with which they were affiliated.
4. How if at all do you express your social class (e.g., through langusocial class, communication style, dress, accessories, music, and so forth)?
5. Does your awareness of your social class ever facilitate how you communicate with others? Explain.
6. Does your awareness of your social class ever hinder how you communicate with others? Explain.
7. What situations, if any, do you avoid because of apprehensions related to your social class?
8. What situations, if any, do you seek because of your social class?
9. What advantages, if any, do you enjoy based upon your social class?
10. Do you know of any stereotypes about your social class? If so, list them.
11. Are you ever aware of stereotypes about your social class as you interact with others? Explain.
12. How do the media tend to depict your social class? Do media depictions correspond with your sense of your social class? Explain.

NOTES

1. Moon, D. G., & Rolison, G. L. (1998). Communication of classism. In M. L. Hecht (Ed.), *Communicating prejudice* (pp. 122–135). Thousand Oaks, CA: Sage.
2. Holtzman, L. (2000). *Media messages: What film, television, and popular music teach us about race, class, gender, and sexual orientation.* Armonk, NY: M. E. Sharpe.
3. Holtzman, p. 99.
4. Stark, R. (2001). *Sociology,* Belmont, CA: Wadsworth.
5. Ellis, D. G. (1999). *Crafting society: Ethnicity, class, and communication theory.* Mahwah, NJ: Lawrence Erlbaum, p. 176.
6. Artz, L., & Murphy, B. O. (2000). *Cultural hegemony in the United States.* Thousand Oaks, CA: Sage.
7. Weber's original categories are class, status, and party. However, according to Stark, most social scientists use the synonymous three Ps to avoid confusion regarding distinctions between Weber's terms.
8. Weber, M. (1947). *The theory of social and economic organization.* T. Parsons (Ed.), A. M. Henderson & T. Parsons (Trans.). New York: The Free Press.
9. Artz & Murphy.
10. Bourdieu, P. (1987). What makes a social class? On the theoretical and practical existence of groups. *Berkeley Journal of Sociology, 22,* 1–18. Bourdieu also cited *symbolic capital,* "the form the different types of capital take once they are perceived and recognized as legitimate," p. 4.
11. Eakin, E. (2001, January 6). The intellectual class struggle. *New York Times,* p. A15.
12. Dworkin, A. G., & Dworkin, R. J. (Eds.). (1999). *The minority report: An introduction to racial, ethnic, and gender relations* (3rd ed.). Fort Worth: Harcourt Brace.
13. Ellis, p. 195.
14. Holtzman.
15. Holtzman.
16. Henry, P. (2001). An examination of the pathways through which social class impacts health outcomes, p. 1. [On-line] http://www.amsreview.org/articles/henry03-2001.pdf
17. Reay, D. (1996). Dealing with difficult differences: Reflexivity and social class in feminist research. *Feminism & Psychology, 6*(3), 443–456, p. 450.
18. Levine, R. F. (Ed.). (1998): *Social class and stratification: Classic statements and theoretical debates.* Lanham, MD: Rowman & Littlefield, p. 63.

19. Holtzman.
20. Henry.
21. Spade, J. Z. (2001). Gender and education in the United States. In D. Vannoy (Ed.), *Gender mosaics: Social perspectives* (pp. 85–93). Los Angeles: Roxbury, p. 89.
22. Brantlinger, E. (2001). Poverty, class, and disability: A historical, social and political perspective. *Focus on exceptional children, 33*(7), 1–19.
23. Magnus, S. A., & Mick, S. S. (2000). Medical schools, affirmative action, and the neglected role of social class. *American Journal of Public Health, 90*(8), 1197–1202.
24. Henry.
25. Markson, E. W., & Hollis-Sawyer, L. A. (Eds.). (2000). *Intersections of aging.* Los Angeles: Roxbury.
26. Lott, B., & Bullock, H. E. (2001). Who are the poor? *Journal of Social Issues, 57*(2), 189–206.
27. U.S. Census Bureau. *Median income for 4-person families, by state.* [On-line] Retrieved April 22, 2003 http://www.census.gov/hhes/income/4person.html
28. Lott & Bullock.
29. U.S. Census Bureau. [On-line] www.census.gov
30. Macionis, J. J. (1999). *Sociology* (7th ed.). Upper Saddle River, NJ: Prentice-Hall.
31. BusinessWeek On-line (2002, May 6). Special report—the crisis in corporate governance. *Executive pay.* [On-line] http://www.businessweek.com/magazine/content/02_18/b3781703.htm
32. Artz & Murphy.
33. Ellis.
34. Artz & Murphy.
35. Lott & Bullock.
36. Rank, M. R., & Hirschl, T. A. (1999). The likelihood of poverty across the American adult life span. *Social Work, 44*(3), 201–216.
37. Lott & Bullock.
38. Holtzman.
39. Holtzman.
40. Artz & Murphy.
41. Holtzman, p. 112.
42. Artz & Murphy.
43. U.S. Department of Health and Human Services. Administration for Children and Families. *Fact Sheet* [On-line] http://www.acf.dhhs.gov/programs/opa/facts/tanf.htm
44. Artz & Murphy.
45. Artz & Murphy.
46. Artz & Murphy.
47. Sammon, P. J. (2000). The living wage movement. *America, 183*(5), 16.
48. Sammon.
49. The "I Have a Dream" Foundation Web site. [On-line] http://www.ihad.org
50. GEAR UP Home Page. [On-line: Accessed 07/03/03] http://www.ed.gov/gearup/
51. Holtzman, p. 98. Some of these perspectives have been critiqued as racist (e.g., the Moynihan report claimed that the matriarchal structure of the black family contributed to black poverty).
52. hooks, b. (2000). *Where we stand: Class matters.* New York: Routledge, p. 5.
53. Lahiri, I., & Jensen, K. (2002, August). *Business Case for Diversity.* Uncovering classism: A checklist for organizations. [On-line] http://www.diversitycentral.com/business/business_case_diversity.html
54. *Merriam-Webster's Collegiate Dictionary.* [On-line] m-w.com/home.htm
55. Allen, R. L., & Kuo, C. (1991). Communication and beliefs about racial equality. *Discourse & Society, 2*(3), 259–279, p. 263.
56. Brantlinger, E. Poverty, class, and disability: A historical, social and political perspective. *Focus on Exceptional Children, 33*(7), 1–19.
57. Ehrenreich, B. (2001). Nickel and dimed: On (not) getting by in America. New York: Metropolitan Books, p. 220.
58. Holtzman, p. 107.
59. Artz & Murphy.
60. Holtzman.
61. Stark, p. 301.
62. Artz & Murphy.
63. Clawson, D., & Clawson, M. (1999). What has happened to the U.S. labor movement? Union decline and renewal. *Annual Review of Sociology, Annual 25,* 95–119.
64. Artz & Murphy.
65. Zweig.
66. Sorokin, E., & Wetstein: C. (2002, May 6). Activists lobby for Chavez holiday (California Journal: News from the golden state). *Insight on the News, 18*(16), p. 31.
67. Clawson, R. A., & Trice, R. (2000). Poverty as we know it (media portrayals of the poor). *Public Opinion Quarterly, 64*(1), 53–64, p. 53.
68. Clawson, R. A., & Kegler, R. A. (2000). The "race coding" of poverty in American government college textbooks. *The Howard Journal of Communications, 11,* 179–188.
69. Lott & Bullock.
70. Clawson & Trice.
71. Clawson & Trice.
72. Clawson & Trice, p. 61
73. Ellis, p. 185.
74. Ellis, p. 190.
75. Nakano-Glenn, E. (1992). From servitude to service work: Historical continuities in the racial division of paid reproductive labor. *Signs 18,* 1–43, p. 32.
76. Acker, J. (1990). Hierarchies, jobs, bodies: A theory of gendered organizations. *Gender & Society 5,* 139–158, p. 145; Artz & Murphy, p. 255.
77. Fussell, P. (1992). *Class: A guide through the American status system.* New York: Simon & Schuster.
78. Baldry, C. (1999). Space—The final frontier. (Critical Essay). *Sociology, 33*(3), 535–553, p. 539.
79. Baldry.
80. Lahiri & Jensen.
81. Nakano-Glenn.
82. Baldry.
83. Catanzarite, L. (2000). Brown-collar jobs: Occupational segregation and earnings of recent-immigrant Latinos. *Sociological Perspectives, 43*(1), 45–76.
84. Joseph, N., & Alex, N. (1972). The uniform: A sociological perspective. *American Journal of Sociology, 77*(4), 719–730.

85. Joseph & Alex, p. 720.
86. Joseph & Alex, p. 722.
87. Boo, K. Excerpt from Pride, prejudice and the not-so-subtle politics of the working class, originally published in *The Washington Post,* March 14, 1993. [On-line] www.pbs.org/peoplelikeus/resources/index.html
88. Gorman, T. J. (2000). Cross-class perceptions of social class. *Sociological Spectrum, 20,* 93–120, p. 107.
89. Boo.
90. Strickland, W. J., & Strickland, D. L. (1996). Partnership building with special populations. *Family Community Health, 19*(3), 21–34.
91. Magnus & Mick.
92. Strickland & Strickland.
93. Strickland & Strickland, p. 23.
94. Strickland & Strickland.
95. Magnus & Mick.
96. Magnus & Mick.
97. Dworkin & Dworkin, p. 63.
98. Magnus & Mick.
99. Dworkin & Dworkin.
100. Dworkin & Dworkin, p. 292.
101. Cooper, R. (2000). Urban school reform from a student-of-color perspective. *Urban Education, 34*(5), 597–622.
102. Haberman, M. (1991). The pedagogy of poverty versus good teaching. *Phi Delta Kappan, 73*(4), 290–294.
103. Dworkin & Dworkin.
104. Lott, B. (2001). Low income parents and the public schools. *Journal of Social Issues, 57*(2), 247–259, p. 249.
105. Ladson-Billings, G. (1998). Foreword. In P. Lipman, *Race, class, and power in school restructuring* (pp. ix–xv). New York: State University of New York Press, p. ix.
106. Lipman, P. (1998). *Race, class, and power in school restructuring.* New York: State University of New York Press, p. 293.

 9

Bringing Classism into the Race and Gender Picture

CHUCK BARONE

Oppression, whether based on gender, race, or class, takes place on multiple levels including the institutional (macro), intergroup (meso), and personal (micro) levels of social interaction. At all three levels structures and human agency are interactive, that is structures constrain the choices and actions of individuals while individual choice and action are at the same time determinant of structures. Yet rarely do we provide a multi-leveled or integrative analysis of any of these oppressions. Much of feminist analysis has tended to emphasize the personal dynamics of sexism, while many racial studies have tended to focus on the nature of intergroup prejudice and discrimination. Studies of class have for the most part emphasized the institutional basis of class oppression. Ferree & Hall (1996) in their survey of introductory sociology texts reach similar conclusions. More recently the class-based experiences of women and people of color have been brought into women's studies and racial/ethnic studies. These efforts have spawned the rapidly growing new field of race, class, and gender, a field that combines all three with emphasis on the intersections.

Despite the tremendous insights of these intellectual traditions into the nature of class oppression, we lack an understanding of class oppression as "classism," as a system of social oppression that operates on multiple levels and that embraces both social structures and human agency. When viewed as a whole there are three shortcomings within the current work on class oppression. The macro structural insights into class oppression of Marxist sociologists, political economists, and historians are largely ignored in the newer race and gender studies. Ignoring the roots of class oppression in capitalist economic structures is like ignoring the structural basis of gender oppression in patriarchy or ignoring racial formations by focusing only on individual prejudice.

On the other, hand, the insights of the newer race and gender studies into the personal and social dynamics of oppression and the role of culture have been largely ignored by those working within some Marxist traditions, particularly political economists. Kandal (1996) provides a cogent summary of the history of race and gender within the Marxist traditions, as well as the current retreat from class on the left. Leaving the personal and social experiences of people aside is like trying to change institutions while ignoring human agency and the personal dynamics of oppression. Finally, and with rare exceptions, most within all of these intellectual traditions, including Marxists, fail to identify class oppression as "classism," as a social system of oppression. This failure has meant an inadequate understanding of class oppression.

Unfortunately in the interdisciplinary work on race, gender, and class, class oppression has analytically often been the poor cousin in this trilogy in spite of the efforts of some (like the recently formed *Race, Gender, & Class* Section of the American Sociological Association) to make class more central. Even when class is explicitly addressed, the concept of classism rarely appears in the literature and when it does appear it is usually conceptually ill-defined. Although there seems to be a general commitment to the importance of class issues and experiences, the focus is often exclusively on the poor and often focused on people of color. Part of the invisibility of class in America can be attributed to a racial formation which has collapsed class-based discourses into race-based ones (Quadagno 1994).

One section of a widely used and otherwise good reader (Rothenberg 1995: Part II) addresses racism, sexism, and "class difference" instead of classism. This is not just a matter of labeling preference; it reflects a lack of conceptual clarity which is then further compounded by the absence of a reading in this section dealing centrally with class oppression. In the section of this same reader dealing with the social construction of race, class, and gender the discussion of class is limited to the so-called "underclass." Such omissions are perhaps understandable when there is such a paucity of literature on classism and on the social construction of class identities.

Another study by a social psychologist that actually develops and utilizes the concept of classism, a rare instance in the literature which must be applauded, fails to structurally locate class oppression and focuses exclusively on the beliefs and behavior of the "middle class" towards the poor (Bullock 1995). This study is illuminating, but its focus on the middle-class poor reinforces the invisibility of the working class majority and the broader structures of class and class oppression. The absence of structurally based definitions of class characterizes much of the work on race, class, and gender which often tends to focus more on the subjective experience of class through personal narratives, oral histories, and ethnographies.

One of the best attempts to integrate race, class, and gender has been by historian Ronald Takaki, whose masterful weaving of the experiences of race, ethnicity, gender, and class in *A Different Mirror* has given us perhaps the best multicultural history of the U.S to date. Yet despite the economic-based struggles of working people that play such a powerful role in binding together the multicultural histories of Americans, the structures of class oppression are all but invisible in Takaki's work.

Classism, rooted in the capitalist macrolevel class structures of exploitation, pits humans against humans. In the dialectics of structure vs. agency, the macrolevel institutions of class exploitation and conflict clearly have a logic and dynamic of their own, independent of the wills of individuals who occupy positions within those structures, constraining what people can and cannot do. Understanding the class structure of capitalism and its class-based dynamics is critical to an understanding of the class oppression of working men and women of all racial/ethnic groups.

Human agency is constrained by the macrolevel class structures of capitalism while at the same time determining (reproducing as well as transforming) those same structures. Understanding both the personal and social dynamics of class as a system of oppression and questions of human agency, voice, and identity are critical to fully grasping the phenomena of class oppression and class struggle. Only through such complex understandings will we be able to meet the challenge of race, gender, and class liberation and to create a society free of classism and based on racial and gender equality.

The purpose of this paper is to sketch out a multilevel analysis of class oppression as part of a social system of oppression (classism) that begins with a macro-level class analysis of capitalism and extends to the personal and social dynamics of class oppression. The analysis draws on studies (particularly ethnographies and personal narratives) from within the social sciences and humanities.

Although many different aspects of class oppression have been studied throughout the social sciences and humanities, they are scattered and there has been no attempt to bring them together in any systematic fashion or view them within a larger class framework of social oppression. Next, although the use of the term "classism" is starting to appear in oppression studies, it is rarely defined and is conceptually underdeveloped compared with the concepts of racism and sexism. Classism is uniquely defined and developed here.

Section I first presents a general definition of oppression as a multi-level social system, drawn from the most recent developments in oppression theory. Then the concept of classism is defined and developed providing the conceptual framework for the rest of the paper. Section II briefly summarizes the political economic (structural) basis of class oppression drawing on the work of political economists. Section III examines the inter-group dynamics of class oppression with an emphasis on class bigotry and prejudice. In Section IV the personal dynamics of classism are examined with an emphasis on the process whereby classist beliefs, attitudes, and behavior are internalized in ways that insure that class members play out their socially expected class roles (social reproduction). Section V provides a multidimensional analysis of schooling and the key role it plays in reproducing classism. Finally, the implications of this multilevel analysis of class oppression are examined.

CLASS OPPRESSION AS A SOCIAL SYSTEM

Oppression can be defined as the "systematic, institutionalized mistreatment of one group of people by another for whatever reason" (Yamato 1995:66). Oppression takes place through a complex of "everyday practices, attitudes, assumptions, behaviors, and institutional rules" (Lott 1995:13). Interactions on the basis of such oppression are relational between oppressor and oppressed, mistreater and victim, dominant and subordinate.

Oppression operates on macro, meso, and micro levels, each interactive with the other. On the macro level oppression is a matter of collectivity—of economic, social, political, and cultural/ideological institutions. At the meso level, oppression operates at the level of group interaction. The micro level is a matter of individuality and identity, our attitudes and interactions with others (Omi & Winant 1994: Ch 4; Ferree & Hall 1996). In other words, oppression operates on personal, inter-group, and cultural/institutional levels.

Both structure, the persistent patterns of social relations, and agency, the self-motivated actions of individuals, are operative on macro, meso, and micro social levels (Ferree & Hall 1996:930). Depending upon the level, oppression manifests itself differently as aware and unaware prejudice (attitudes, stereotypes, and behavior), discrimination (power), and institutionalized oppression (control and social reproduction).

Classism can be defined as the systematic oppression of one group by another based on economic distinctions or, more accurately, one's position within the system of production and distribution. According to Bowles and Gintis (1986), at the institutional level, "Structure allows socially consequential power to be employed against the wills and efforts of those affected thereby."

The primary relation of classism is economic exploitation and consists of squeezing as much labor out of workers as possible and appropriating a disproportionate share of the community's production (surplus product). Class economic exploitation includes the mistreatment of people on the job, forcing people to work long and hard under difficult and often dangerous conditions, and the denial of the democratic rights of people to control their own production/distribution process. In his working class memoir *Rivethead*, Ben Hamper captures the nature of class exploitation:

> I was seven years old the first time I ever set foot inside an automobile factory. The occasion was Family Night at the old Fisher Body plant in Flint . . . If nothing else, this annual peepshow lent a whole world of credence to our father's daily grumble. The assembly line did indeed stink. The noise was very close to intolerable. The heat was one complete bastard . . . we found my old man down the

trim line . . . We stood there for forty minutes or so, a miniature lifetime, and the pattern never changed. Car, windshield. Car, windshield. Drudgery piled atop drudgery. Cigarette to cigarette. Decades of rolling through the rafters, bones turning to dust, stubborn clocks gagging down flesh, another windshield, another cigarette, wars blinking on and off, thunderstorms muttering the alphabet, crows on power lines, asleep or dead, that mechanical octopus squirming against nothing, nothing, *nothingness* (Hamper 1991: 1–2).

Although rooted in the economy, classism also extends to the social, political, and cultural spheres. Anthropologist Karen Sacks defines class as "membership in a community that is dependent upon waged-labor, but that is unable to subsist or reproduce by such labor alone" (Sacks 1989:543). One of the virtues of this community-based definition is that it allows us to view class oppression as part of a larger social system of oppression. Sacks's (1988) study of a union organizing drive at Duke Medical Center is an excellent integrated multilevel analysis of race, gender, and class.

Like other forms of oppression, classism at the intergroup (meso) level consists of prejudice based on negative attitudes toward and classist stereotypes of working class people, and discrimination based on overt behaviors that distance, avoid, and/or exclude on the basis of class distinction (Bullock 1995:119).

As Donna Langston states, class is also clearly a personal experience:

> . . . as a result of the class you are born into and raised in, class is your understanding of the world and where you fit in; it's composed of ideas, behavior, attitudes, values, and language; class is how you think, feel, act, look, talk, move, walk; class is what stores you shop at, restaurants you eat in; class is the schools you attend, the education you attain; class is the very jobs you will work at throughout your adult life. . . . We experience class at every level of our lives . . . In other words, class is socially constructed and all-encompassing. When we experience classism, it will be because of our lack of money . . . and because of the way we talk, think, act, move— because of our culture (Langston 1995:112).

Class experience is an important part of our identity, who we are, how we are, and how we relate to others and how we see the world. (See the special issue "Race, Gender, & Class: Working Class Intellectual Voices" of *Race, Gender, & Class* 4(1) 1996.)

Class oppression ultimately rests upon a structure of rules and social conventions embodied in institutions, linguistic convention, unwritten custom, and legal practice (Bowles & Gintis 1996:94). Like any other oppression, classism exists because people "agree to" play by the rules. When people decide not to play by the rules or try to change the rules, they are confronted by a range of social responses from normative peer pressure to intervention by legal authorities to threats and use of physical violence by the dominant classes or those who act on their behalf, such as the police or military. The so-called "power" of the dominant classes rests upon this structure of rules, the ideology of classism, and the threat or use of violence. Class exploitation, then, is part of a larger social system of class oppression called classism. Like other forms of oppression, classism operates on macro (institutional), meso (inter-group), and micro (individual) social levels.

THE ECONOMIC FACE OF CLASS OPPRESSION

The primary institutional basis of classism is the economic system. Capitalism is structured on the basis of classes. The three key economic institutions that generate classes are private ownership, the hierarchical organization of capitalist factories and offices, and the capitalist division of labor. These three institutions produce a class-based system of domination and subordination between owners and those who do not own, between managers and those who are managed, and between professionals and those without professional credentials. These can be subsumed into two primary structural bases of class oppression:

1. **Capital Ownership:** ownership of the means of production including the land, natural resources, equipment, machinery, factories,

offices, farms, and other business. When it is in the hands of only a few people, such ownership yields structural or institutional power and control over those who do not own capital. Without access to the means of production, people are unable to survive economically and are placed at a structural disadvantage relative to owners.

2. **Command Positions** within organizational hierarchies (managers, administrators) and in terms of educationally credentialed employees (professionals). Although they often serve at the discretion of owners and do not have ultimate power, managers and professionals often have legally enforceable and thus institutionalized command and authority over others.

Those who do not own and do not have command positions make up the working class majority who account for 73% of U.S. families. The capitalist owning class who owns and controls the corporate sector represent 2% of families while the middle class consists of those who own small businesses (13%) or occupy command positions based on hierarchical positions and/or professional credentials within the private or public sectors (12%)(Bowles & Edwards 1993:119). Capitalism is thus structured in a way that generates three primary classes: a capitalist class, a middle class, and working class. These classes are structurally opposed to each other creating a class system of power and authority, social domination and subordination, and economic exploitation. (Other relational class models can be substituted here if the reader prefers. (For a discussion of these class structures see Vanneman & Cannon [1987: Ch 4], Wright [1986], and Belkhir [1996].)

Within these class structures, domination has been extended historically by the use of segmented labor markets and internal labor markets that have separated workers on the basis of artificially created occupational structures and job ladders. Racial and gender differences have also been used to further divide and separate workers. In the face of class struggle, these divide and conquer strategies have been effective methods to split workers into competing groups that have maintained capitalist

exploitation and rates of profit (Albelda, Drago, Shulman 1997: Ch 7–8).

The macrolevel institutional basis of class oppression goes beyond these economic structures. The capitalist mode of production also requires a system of noneconomic institutions and culture. The family, legal/judicial system, government, schools, church, mental health system, culture, and community organizations are all structured in ways that maintain and reproduce the capitalist mode of production and distribution. Although space does not permit a discussion here of these other institutional bases of class oppression (schooling will be discussed in Section V below), understanding the class-based (as well as other oppression-based) nature of these institutions, and the ways in which these reinforce, extend, and challenge class oppression, is important to a complete understanding of how classism works. (See for example Edwards, Reich, & Weisskopf 1986 and McNall, Levine, & Fantasia 1991.)

INTER-GROUP DYNAMICS

Because capitalism lacks an overall coordinating mechanism, people are left on their own to compete for jobs, resources, and income. However, the interests of different economic classes are structured in such a way that their interests are often opposed and power is unequally distributed. Due to limited capital ownership and the limited availability of command positions, some people are able to claim a disproportionate share of the better jobs, resources, and incomes for themselves while denying them to others. The folk wisdom "them that has gits" captures these relationships poignantly.

This is, of course, the basis for economic exploitation and is at the root of all class oppression: the benefits to one class are often at the expense of other classes. It forms the basis for class conflict—for inter-group relations among the three economic classes as they are pitted against each other and struggle for economic advantage, privilege, status and, as is often the case, economic survival. The extreme maldistribution of income and wealth distribution, . . ., reveals the profound degree of economic exploitation that takes place in capitalism.

The worsening of this distribution in recent years reflects a shift in the balance of power away from workers to the owning and middle classes, and away from the United States to the other national centers of capitalist accumulation. Explaining these shifting fortunes requires an understanding of the political economic dynamics of capitalism (see for example Bowles & Edwards 1993), particularly the most recent trends in globalization, deindustrialization, and the forces of economic destablization (see for example Greider 1997). . . .

These distributional struggles form the underlying basis of classism. The actual content of class relations (class culture) is elitist, i.e., class oppression and privileges are defended on the basis of one person/group claiming to be more important, smarter, better, more deserving, more qualified, more productive, etc. than another person/group. These attitudes frame class behavior and thus inter-class social relations. The oppressed person/group (the working class) is viewed as less intelligent, less talented, inferior, and thus not worth very much. Such views can be patronizing ("they are doing the best they can") or they can be vicious ("working class people are stupid, dirty, lazy, and uncivilized").

Carol Tarlen (1994:21), university clerical worker and writer, writes about what it was like growing up working class and being viewed through such a lens:

> I am motivated by the pain and anger that comes from being rejected because of my class background. I want to prove to all those girls whose parents had 'professional jobs'. . . the ones whose hair neatly curled into pageboys; who wore plaid knee-length pleated skirts and lambswool sweaters; the ones who quit associating with me when I said I lived in . . . the housing tract notorious for its Latino and Okie inhabitants; and especially the ones who assumed that having an old mattress on your front lawn was a sign of intellectual inferiority and moral degeneration—I want to prove . . . that tough girls from the other side of the highway can't be shoved to the back of the classroom anymore, that we have lives filled with love, honor, imagination,

risk. See me, I want to say, acknowledge my talent and intelligence.

Classist patterns and attitudes such as these are the source of much prejudice and have been used to denigrate and discriminate against working class people, and to rationalize current and past oppression of millions of people the world over. Widespread anti-union sentiments, attacks on welfare and the poor, and negative media stereotypes of working class people, especially TV sitcoms, are examples of classism in action. The work by Puette (1992) and Bullock (1995:127–130) discusses class bias and the media. Such individual classist beliefs and attitudes frame inter-class relations (behavior) and facilitate the systematic economic exploitation and oppression of working people. The objective structures of class oppression and exploitation require, on a subjective level, socially held classist beliefs and attitudes. On a social level, individually held beliefs are rooted in a cultural belief system, a classist ideology which rationalizes class oppression as just and equitable.

In the U.S. the ideology takes the form of a belief in individual achievement—the myth that individuals rise on the basis of their own effort and ability. Success honors those who make it and failure stigmatizes those who fail. Conservatives tend to emphasize moral failure, criticizing and scorning those who fail, while liberals tend to focus on deficiency, expressing pity and concern for those unfortunate enough to fail (Lewis 1978:10). Although cast in terms of individuals and equal opportunities, this ideology is classist. It casts working class people as inferior and incompetent, middle and owning class people as superior, perhaps blessed by God. It allows people to rationalize and ignore class oppression, to see and understand the social universe as merely the result of individual interaction, and to view class oppression as "normal" and a "natural" part of a secular or divine order. *The Bell Curve*, the recent best-selling book by Herrnstein and Murray, is an attempt to renew and legitimate this view in the face of currently growing class and racial inequality and bigotry.

There are many powerful studies of gender and race supporting the position that while biology (nature) does play some role in explaining gender and racial differences, environment (culture) plays a far more powerful role in explaining social differences (Ortner and Whitehead 1981; Jaggar 1988: Part Two). Although studies on the causes of class differences are not as extensive, there is some evidence, and every reason to assume, that class inequality and class differences are not reflective of natural or innate differences, but are acquired and socially constructed (Argyle 1994). Rather than being part of our innate nature, class differences are culturally constructed and socially enforced by classism.

PERSONAL DYNAMICS OF CLASSISM

At the personal or individual level, the internalization of classist beliefs, attitudes, and behavior is the result of a socializing and conditioning process which instills in individuals patterns of behavior, mannerisms, and beliefs that insure conformity to class roles (Jackins 1972; Barone 1995). Acting out or occupying these roles requires that we give up part of our uniquely human qualities, of choosing our own identities. It is here assumed that these inherent human qualities are our capacity to love, our power to take charge of our universe and effect change, our capacity for rational and intelligent thought, our ability to feel and be completely sensitive to our own and each others humanity, and our capacity for joy and excitement. Occupying oppressive roles requires that we give up some of these human qualities.

We are given the choice as young children to play out our socially expected role(s), a painful process at best, or be punished. If you are female and act like a boy, or white and act black, or owning class and act working class, if you resist role conditioning, you risk humiliation and isolation, being ostracized and subjected to emotional and physical abuse. Material success and economic security are also held out as rewards in return for occupying oppressor roles, replacing genuine human needs with an artificially created materialism which serves both to keep people in their socially constructed roles and fuel capitalist profits. Role conditioning begins at birth, extends through young adulthood and is then reinforced throughout adulthood. When we are young we have little choice but to submit to conditioning and carry out our prescribed social roles.

> We working-class people have been conditioned as children to be submissive, to devalue ourselves, to think we are ignorant compared to other people, to feel powerless, to settle for very little, to accept insecurity as an unavoidable fact of life, to feel 'lucky to have a job', and to despise ourselves and each other for not standing up for ourselves and each other and for giving in to violence at each other and to alcoholism (Jackins 1988:3).

Once conditioned into our respective socially constructed roles (most of us occupy multiple roles, e.g., white gay male working class or black heterosexual female middle class), much of our identity, behavior, actions, and interactions relate back to our socializing experiences as young children (See Barone [1995] for a more complete analysis of the ways these early experiences play themselves out later on in dominant/subordinate social relationships). This process is not without its own structural contradictions. Waites (1993) argues that the socialization and conditioning of females into socially constructed gender roles creates dilemmas and double binds.

For example,

> From birth, little girls are subjected to incessant but contradictory messages about their sexuality. . . . Be attractive, but not seductive; be noticeably feminine, but not provocative; be helpful, but not controlling (45-46).

Taylor, Gilligan, & Sullivan (1995) found similar kinds of dilemmas and double binds based on class, race, and gender in their study of a diverse group of adolescent females from working class families.

Role reproduction is further complicated by the "complex ways in which people mediate and respond to the interface between their own lived experiences and structures of domination and constraint" (MacLeod 1995:19). As a result cultures of resistance may develop alongside cultures of accommodation.

Ethnographic studies show that while working class cultures of resistance have transformative potential they wind up reproducing class roles and structures (MacLeod 1995; Willis 1977).

Even though the structures of class oppression often overwhelm human agency, class struggle and resistance at the micro as well as other social levels is not entirely without effect. Nonetheless, given the generally reproductive outcomes, the contradictory structures of class conditioning and interplay of human agency will be ignored here. Additionally, in spite of the variability of individual working class patterns across race and gender, the focus here is on the more general working class patterns of identity, attitudes, behavior, and interaction.

As a result of social conditioning many of the working class internalize negative beliefs and stereotypes about themselves. We are bombarded daily with thousands of subtle and not so subtle messages about ourselves and others.

> I remember the pain of being humiliated because I was a skinny child who was teased at school for wearing too small dresses and living in a trailer; or a recent humiliation when one of the faculty I work for gave me [a] dirty look because I forgot to give her a message. . . . I remember sitting at my receptionist's desk as two female faculty carried on a conversation literally over my head, discussing the private schools their children were attending, oblivious to my presence (Tarlen 1994:21).

These classist messages have a powerful effect on people, making the social construction of reality appear as the natural state of human beings. Classism experienced on a daily basis by working class people reinforces class conditioning. Working class people tend to view themselves and be seen by others as not very smart, uneducated, inarticulate, poor leaders, lacking in ability, lazy, crude and uncivilized. But they view those in the middle and owning class as superior—more intelligent and ambitious, with greater poise, self-confidence and leadership ability (Argyle 1994:Ch 9). Judy Kujundzic (1988) speaks out about what it's like being working class:

> What's hard about being working-class is never feeling like you're working class enough. Like you don't work hard enough or you're not funny enough. . . . It's hard to speak up. It's hard to notice that you think real well and to go ahead and do it, not just freezing up even after you decide you're going to think and act . . . It's hard to notice how smart you are, that you think all the time . . . It's sometimes hard to remember how clever other working-class people are because they work real hard at covering it up and acting dumb whenever the situation seems like that's what's required . . . It's hard getting people to take action, to move against how they feel, to move as a group, although it can be done . . . The other thing about being working-class is the hopelessness, the sense that you know there are so many things wrong, and you can't figure out where to start to take them on and pull them down (67–68).

This is called internalized oppression and as a result many become resigned to their class fate and show deference to one's "betters." Members of oppressed groups are emotionally, physically, and spiritually abused until they begin to believe that oppression is their lot in life, that it is somehow deserved, natural, right, or conversely, that it does not exist (Yamato 1995:66). Clarissa Sligh, artist and photographer, shares her experience growing up working class:

> . . . I began to notice that people who had more than us felt that because we had to scrape to get by, that they were better than us. I began to believe it too. Momma said they worked harder, had more than one job, and handled their money better than us (Sligh 1994: 254).

Internalized oppression insures the perpetuation (reproduction) of the class system from one generation to the next. Suzanne Lipsky (1987) explains the power and role of internalized oppression:

> Internalized racism has been the primary means by which we have been forced to perpetuate and 'agree' to our own oppression. It has been a major factor preventing us, as black people, from realizing and putting into action the tremendous intelligence and power which in reality we possess.

Class oppression, like racism, requires that individuals internalize class domination and subordination and to the extent that we do we become resigned to our fates. Although there is mobility (up and down), class stability is the norm (MacLeod 1995; Mishel, Bernstein, & Schmitt 1996:97ff). Even those who fight back and rebel often wind up reproducing the very class system they are rebelling against (Willis 1977).

Owning class and middle class children are also conditioned in similar ways and generally internalize the belief that they are superior—smarter, and better leaders—and that working class people are inferior. These beliefs, and the attitudes and behaviors that accompany them, make up the classist oppressor pattern and insure that most middle and owning class young people will occupy middle and owning class positions. Middle class people have been placed in a precarious position between the owning class and the working class; they are both oppressed and oppressor, often plagued by feelings of inadequacy over work and productivity, guilt for complicity in oppression, and fear of failing and moral slippage. Underneath their pretenses, they have been hurt and held prisoner inside their humanly constricted and conditioned roles. Putting a happy face on it all often takes an extraordinary amount of energy, and it takes its toll, in spite of the generally held belief that they are living the "American Dream." (Ehrenreich [1990] provides a very insightful analysis of middle class angst).

Classism distorts the basic humanity and compromises the values of members of the owning class as well. Although Marx recognized the alienation of the bourgeoisie, there are few contemporary studies of the harmful effects of class oppression on the dominant classes (Cookson & Persell 1986; Maccoby 1976; *Coming Home* 1996). However, there is a growing literature on the negative effects of racism on whites (Feagin & Vera 1995:Ch 5; Bowser & Hunt 1996) and sexism on men (Blood, Tuttle, & Lakey 1995; Irwin, Jackins & Kreiner 1992). Like racism and sexism, classism forces members of dominant classes into socially constructed roles that might benefit them . . . in material and other ways, separate them from many of their distinctively human qualities. In their study of elite private schools

Cookson and Persell (1986) describe what they call the "prepping" process of upper class children:

> . . . the systematic wearing down of individual identities into a single collective identity . . . What we found was a conspiracy of forces—powerful institutional controls, peer pressures and personal resignation . . . In order to forge the prep personality, the schools rely on . . . strict discipline, shared rituals, and what we call 'deep structural regulation'.

Quite the opposite of places of privileges, these schools are oppressive, examples of what sociologists call "total institutions" where individual needs are completely subordinated to the goals of the institution. The human cost of owning class conditioning is high:

> The psychological price of prepping includes a relinquishing of personal identity, a loss of innocence and a growth of cynicism. Having paid their dues, students who survive the rite of passage obtain membership in an elite group, which they embrace with a strong sense of psychological and social entitlement.

Cookson and Persell go on to conclude that the "structure of boarding school life prepares many students for a life as prisoners of their class" creating "generations of individuals, some of whom are crippled, rather than empowered, by privilege."

It is important to note that while class conditioning has negative effects on all classes, it is still a way of constructing owning and middle class dominance, creating people who will oppress others. Working class people have borne the brunt of class oppression both through the denial of the fruits of their labor (low and inadequate incomes, poverty, economic hardship) and through mistreatment both on and off the job (overwork, injuries, illness, death, oppressive work conditions, layoffs). Working class people experience on a daily basis subtle and overt class bigotry as they are confronted with middle and owning classist attitudes and behavior. Indeed, the repeated acting out of classism reinforces, across lifetimes, class oppression and the exploitation of working people, in the same way that sexism and racism enforce the oppression of women and people of color.

Other forms of oppression have been submerged in the preceding analysis of class. Within classes there are many important differences such as race, ethnicity, religion, gender, sexuality, nationality, occupation, and geographic location that make our subjective and objective experiences within classes sometimes very different from each other. This often makes class a very confusing experience and creates "fractured identities." It means that there is no single class perspective or standpoint, but rather multiple class perspectives. However, it is important not to lose sight of the overall class structure of exploitation and oppression within which these class differences play themselves out and which shape the choices of individuals. Equally important, the very structures of class oppression are also themselves shaped by race and gender oppression as independent forms of social domination.

CLASSISM, SCHOOLING, AND CLASS REPRODUCTION

A key distinguishing quality of the owning class is that capital ownership can be inherited, whereas the command positions of the middle class cannot. Middle class youth often must become credentialed before they can obtain command positions. Of course, they have all the advantages that their class positions confer upon them—money, confidence, good schools, social connections, and even nepotism. One of my middle-class college students wrote of her class background:

> When I was six years old, my girl friends and I used to sit around and talk about where we would go to college. It wasn't a choice, we just knew that we would go to college and become professionals. . . . When I graduate from college I will work for a large luxury hotel and will manage my own hotel someday (Student Paper).

This student's sense of middle class confidence and entitlement stands out; college and a successful professional career appear as a birthright, not something one must be diligent and lucky to achieve. Contrast this with a working class voice:

> In 1980 I got a clerical job at a university . . . After twelve years, I was laid off [discarded as so much human excrement]. This job meant a lot to me, since I had no hope of ever getting 'professional' employment. Although I attended college, I never finished. I felt alienated from my middle-class peers. Writing papers was agony, because the linear, rational thinking required of them was impossible for someone with my background. Therefore, the working class for me is something there is no escape from. It's an eternal present as well as memory (Joseph 1995:137).

At the institutional level, the school system plays a predominant role in both the social conditioning process and the reproduction and legitimation of class inequality (MacLeod 1995; Willis 1977). Well documented are the "savage inequalities" of property-based school taxes which result in inferior schools in less wealthy working class communities (Kozol 1991). Additionally, next to the family, schools are perhaps the most important conditioning agent, holding out the promise of individual mobility while reinforcing expected social roles and insuring the success of the already successful. Within dominant cultural discourse, education is erroneously viewed as a sorting process where individuals with superior abilities do well academically and are rewarded with command positions and economic privileges. Individuals with inferior abilities or who are not motivated and do not work hard, do not do well in school and wind up in working class positions with low pay and poor working conditions or without a job at all. Class inequality is thus rationalized as a meritocracy.

Jay MacLeod's now classic 1987 working class ethnography, *Ain't No Makin' It*, shows the fallacy of the belief that hard work and motivation always pay off. This study focuses on two groups of working class teens who live in the same housing project. The white Hallway Hangers, who see the system as rigged against them, refuse to go along; they aren't motivated, don't study, and rebel at every chance. The black Brothers, on the other hand, do all the right things; they are motivated, behave themselves, and have the right values for success. Yet both sets of teens wind up not making it. MacLeod explains:

> Conservative and liberal commentators alike often contend that if the poor would only apply themselves, behave responsibly, and adopt bourgeois values, then they will propel themselves into the middle class. The Brothers follow the recipe quite closely but the outcomes are disappointing. They illustrate how rigid and durable the class structure is. Aspiration, application, and intelligence often fail to cut through the firm figurations of structural inequality . . . [The Brothers'] dreams of comfortable suburban bliss currently are dreams deferred, and likely to end up as dreams denied (1995:241).

Perhaps the biggest fraud of all perpetuated by the school system is the underlying belief that individuals differ significantly in terms of innate intelligence (Blum 1978; Ryan 1981; Argyle 1994: Ch 4; Fischer *et al* 1996). School performance data show that on average working class children don't do as well in school as children of the middle or owning classes (Walsh & Witte 1985). Therefore, it is incorrectly assumed that they must not be as bright, smart, or intelligent. This emphasis on intellectual inequality lies at the heart of "higher" education which is structured and based on a whole set of classist, as well as racist and sexist, beliefs. The reality is that schools are systematically biased against working class students. Working class ways of knowing, seeing, and being (often referred to as cultural capital) are systematically depreciated and invalidated in schools (MacLeod 1995:Ch 6). Education and much of what is taught is based on middle and owning class ways of knowing, seeing, and being.

Anthropologist and linguist Shirley Brice Heath (1983) has done an ethnographic study of two Southern working class communities and she documents these class (and race) based educational biases:

> The school is not a neutral objective arena; it is an institution which has the goal of changing people's values, skills, and knowledge bases. Yet some portions of the population, such as [the middle and owning classes], bring with them to school linguistic

and cultural capital accumulated through hundreds of thousands of occasions for practicing the skills and espousing the values the schools transmit. Long before reaching school, [such] children . . have made the transition from home to the larger societal institutions which share the values, skills, and knowledge bases of the school. Their eventual positions of power in the school and the workplace are guaranteed by the conceptual structures which they have learned at home and which are reinforced in school and numerous other institutions (367–368).

According to language and literature professor Janet Zandy(1994)

> Oral language (vocabulary, syntax, inflection, pronunciation, diction, exclamations, blessings, curses) is a giveaway class identity marker . . . Class marks not only our tongues, but also our bodies. Working-class people practice a language of the body that eludes theoretical textual studies. Working-class people do not have the quiet hands or the neutral faces of the privileged classes.

These class markers identify one's social and economic class background, making it difficult to hide one's class background or assimilate into another class or avoid class bigotry and prejudice let alone negotiate the educational terrain that relies on middle and owning class cultural capital.

Linguistic studies (MacLeod 1995:Ch 2; Argyle 1994:Ch 6) show that middle and owning class students, because they often come from a more isolated and individualistic environment, have to explain themselves, their positions, and ideas at length because they cannot assume shared meaning. Everything has to be carefully explained and fully articulated to insure meaning for the listener. Working class students, on the other hand, often come from a more communal environment where they are more connected to others and where meaning is often shared through common experiences. They don't have to explain themselves at length and in such detail because they can assume the listener has a shared context and will understand. Working class use of language and ways of knowing are thus contextual and organic whereas middle and owning class are elaborated and linear. Schooling emphasizes the linguistic patterns and the kinds of thinking that white, male, middle and owning class patterns generate. Anyone whose linguistic patterns or thinking do not fit this norm or who have difficulty adapting to such norms are systematically depreciated and labeled inferior, slow, stupid, or learning disabled and are (de)graded and tracked accordingly.

Because of the inherent classist basis of schooling, working class students often perform poorly, while middle and upper class students do well. Ethnographic studies confirm these results and reveal the ways that middle and owning class behavioral norms are validated while working class norms are punished and invalidated in school (MacLeod 1995; Heath 1983). Many do not attempt to cross these class divides, choosing not to risk failure in what is sometimes perceived as a rigged game as the following statement from one of MacLeod's (1995) working class student interviews illustrates:

> Shorty: Hey, you can't get no education around here unless you're fucking rich, y'know? You can't get no education . . . And you can't get a job once they find out where you come from. 'You from Clarendon Heights? Oh shit. It's them kids again.'

Group loyalty is often valued more highly than upward mobility so there is resistance to being separated from one's class peers. Often individual survival is viewed as dependent upon membership in a group and group membership is valued more highly than individual mobility. The following exchange between MacLeod and another working class student illustrates this point:

> Jinks: I'd say everyone more or less has the same attitudes toward school: fuck it. Except the bookworms-people who just don't hang around outside and drink, get high, who sit at home-they're the ones who get the education.
> JM: And they just decided for themselves?
> Jinks: Yup.
> JM: So why don't more [low income] people decide that way?
> Jinks: Y'know what it is Jay? We all don't break away because we're too tight. Our friends are

important to us. Fuck it. If we can't make it together, fuck it. Fuck it all (119).

Of course there are young people who in spite of these risks do cross school class boundaries. Many are not successful and blame themselves for failure (internalized oppression). For working class students, doing well in school means being bi-cultural and bi-lingual, and it often means a denial of one's self, culture, and people. Carol Faulkner (1994), a teacher at Lane Community College in Oregon, writes about college and the costs of becoming an academic:

> A college education was never my birthright, but something I always knew I had to struggle to get. I was sixteen when my mother came to my school, pulled me out of history class, and told me the shop was closing. My father was already disabled by then, and I went back to class dazed with a picture in my head of having to forget college and go to work to support my parents as my father had done before me. It's hard to explain what getting an education has meant to me, but more and more I ask myself what good is it to have arrived if I have to pretend to be someone else when I get there. What I really want is to be accepted and respected for who I am within the academic community.

Many of the upwardly mobile working class find themselves with a foot in both worlds but do not feel at home in either world. Sennett's and Cobb's classic work, *The Hidden Injuries of Class*, vividly portrays the personal costs experienced by upwardly mobile white working class people, the costs of class assimilation. Jake Ryan's and Charles Sackrey's (1984) collection of stories by academics from the working class, who like Carol Faulkner above have difficulty fitting in, reveals both the difficulty of assimilation as well as the classism on college and university campuses. One faculty member sums his experience up this way:

> Being a working class academic is sometimes very lonely. It's difficult to relate to most colleagues, but it is also difficult to relate to working-class folks, who tend not to trust you since got to be a "Doctor" (Ryan and Sackrey 1984:257).

Although more difficult to identify than sexism or racism, given the existing low level of class awareness, classist patterns of behavior and attitudes among the faculty of college and universities, particularly more elite institutions, make it difficult for those with working class backgrounds to fit in. The same is true for students and more generally for others from the working class in other middle class settings (Tokarozyk and Fay 1993; Penelope 1994; Dews and Law 1995; Zandy 1994; and Barker and Belkhir 1996).

The middle classes in many ways are the standard bearers of U.S. culture and society. Most Americans dream of and aspire to middle class status and it is the middle class, at least the white heterosexual gentile middle class, that set the standards of "normality" by which most people are judged both in and out of school. Middle class standards of cleanliness, demeanor, quietness, pleasantness, hard work, and denial are examples of such behavioral norms or yardsticks. These norms are reinforced by the family, schools, and the mental health system of counselors, psychologists, and psychiatrists (Foner & Alexander 1991). However, these standards or norms were not generated in a social vacuum; they are the characteristics and patterns of behavior required for middle class command positions (managers and professionals). Middle class standards are enforced by the owning class whom the middle classes serve. According to sociologist Edna Bonacich

> In my view, middle class people (including myself) are essentially the sergeants of the system. We professionals and managers are paid by the wealthy and powerful, by corporations and the state, to keep things in order. Our role is one of maintaining the [class] system. . . . We are a semi-elite. We are given higher salaries, social status, better jobs, and better life chances as payment for our service to the system. If we were not useful to the power elite, they would not reward us (Bonacich 1989).

The interplay of class structure and human agency, and the interplay between macro, meso, and micro social levels, are quite complex. Classism, schooling, and the shunting of individuals into capitalist class structures preserves the illusion of just desserts while reproducing class structures and class oppression.

SUMMARY AND IMPLICATIONS

Classism, rooted in the capitalist macrolevel class structures of economic exploitation, pits humans against humans. In the dialectics of structure versus agency, the macrolevel institutions of class exploitation and conflict clearly have a logic and dynamic of their own, independent of the wills of individuals who occupy positions within those institutions, constraining what people can and cannot do. Capitalist class macro-structures reach down into meso and micro social levels, constraining human agency at these levels as well.

The whole purpose of classism as an ideology is to justify past and continuing economic exploitation and alienation of the working class. It is not so much that people are in fundamental conflict with each other as it is that capitalism structures our personal and social relationships with each other in ways that are fundamentally in opposition. Without an essential understanding of these political economic structures of class exploitation and conflict, and the dynamics of class-based economic systems, our understanding of the nature of class oppression will be very limited, as will our understanding of the class-based nature of women's oppression and the oppression of people of color.

However, while human agency is constrained by these class structures on macro, meso, and micro social levels, agency is at the same time determining (reproducing as well as transforming) those same structures. Historically the interplay of structure and agency is clear. People both create institutions and are created by them. The subjective basis of capitalist institutions is the patterned attitudes and behaviors of individuals. Like other forms of oppression, class oppression requires that people be socialized and conditioned to occupy and play out their respective class roles and participate in class oppression. These microlevel forces help to explain how individuals learn their particular class outlook, mannerisms, demeanor, and culture, indeed how individuals within classes think, choose, and act in the world.

At the macro social level, oppression appears to operate independent of human will or volition. In the dialectic of structure and agency, structure appears to win out over human agency. However, the subjective basis of these institutions and culture is the patterned behavior and attitudes of individuals. The same conditioned patterns that form much of the basis for our identity, attitudes, behavior, and interaction at the micro level also provide the underlying basis for macro level economic, social, and political institutions. The patterns or records materialize at this structural level and exist in a frozen, ordered state, as "products" of human creation.

Class patterns of thinking and behavior at the personal level hold classism in place at the intergroup mesolevel and account for the ongoing class bigotry and prejudice experienced by the working class. Pumping surplus labor out of workers (exploitation), the *raison d'etre* of classism, could not happen without classism anymore than the oppression of people of color or women could exist without racism and sexism. The ongoing aware and unaware rehearsal of the patterns of class bigotry and prejudice serves to keep people locked into the system of class oppression, as "prisoners" of their class. Classism prevents people from creating a society characterized by economic structures of cooperation and sharing.

Although all the implications of the analysis of classism sketched out here have yet to be worked out, a couple of preliminary observations can be made. At the most general level, this analysis provides a more inclusive, multilevel framework within which to view and understand class oppression as a social system of oppression. Defining and bringing classism into the picture allows us to see better some of the micro, meso, and macro level dimensions of class-based oppression, social domination, and reproduction/resistance by understanding these as part of a larger system of class oppression that is rooted in and based on economic exploitation. Bringing in a political economic analysis of class-based exploitation and the dynamics of the capitalist econ-

omy allows us to see beyond the individual stories of economic hardship (or success) experienced by working women and men. Class is about more than "difference"; it is about the systematic economic exploitation and the appropriation of economic resources, about the structures of class oppression.

On the other hand, class is more than just economics. The personal and social dynamics of classism are equally important dimensions and are often missed by those who focus more narrowly on the macrostructures of class oppression. The lived experience of workers and their families, the subjective voices and experiences of working people, bring life and a new vibrancy to the more structural-based class research.

From a race, gender, and class perspective the analysis of classism provided here is incomplete because neither race or gender have been explicitly taken into account, even though many of the working class voices contained within these pages have been the voices of women and people of color. However, the task has been to explicitly extend our understanding of class and classism so that we might better understand that particular dimension of race, gender, and class oppression. Clearly all three are at play simultaneously on all three social levels, and as MacLeod (1995:248) has shown in his ethnography, each can magnify or mitigate the effects of the other. Class, as an independent mechanism, can have multiplicative effects on race and gender, as well as having interactive effects where class is intertwined with race and gender.

Of course, what is true here from a class perspective also holds true from a race or gender perspective. While both race and gender are classed experiences, class is both a raced and gendered experience. Indeed, the structures of class oppression are affected by race and gender. For example, capitalism as a class-based mode of production can also be viewed as the latest stage of patriarchy where men have always dominated women no matter whether slavery, feudalism, or capitalism. Each of these class-based modes of production has provided the material basis for the domination of women (Al-Hibri 1981).

While it certainly does not make sense to rank these oppressions, depending upon the location, one or the other may be the more primary shaper of our experiences within particular social sites. Class may be a more primary shaper of our economic experiences even though those experiences are very much influenced by race and gender, while the family or community may be more influenced by race or gender even though class is not an irrelevant determinant of behavior within those sites (Wright 1997:Ch 6).

By viewing class oppression as a multilevel process where social structure and human agency interact, and where race, gender, and class interact, we can begin to see more clearly some of the complexities of the process of social reproduction/ resistance and the ways that people are conditioned and socialized to participate as oppressor and oppressed within the institutions of capitalist class exploitation. Social contradictions abound on all social levels within the mode of production, within the capitalist system as a whole at other institutional sites such as the state, family, schools, or within capitalist culture, and in the social and personal dynamics of class oppression. Much more attention needs to be given to the exact nature of these social contradictions if we are to develop more effective political strategies and policies for class liberation. Ending class oppression will require more than just improving the standard of living of society's poorest citizens or a redistribution of income. It will also take more than just changing people's attitudes. Bringing class oppression to an end requires the elimination of classism on all social levels including the macrolevel structures of capitalism. While class is primarily linked to exploitation and control over economic resources, and has a powerful influence on individual attitudes and actions on all social levels, people are not passive or indifferent in the face of such pressures.

The intellectual and political challenge is to understand and exploit both the oppositional and collaborative forces of human agency for radical reform and revolutionary social structural change. Structure and agency are clearly interactive across multiple levels, sites and locations as shown above in the analysis of schooling. Our failure to understand the personal and social dynamics of classism along with the dynamics of racism and sexism is perhaps one of the principle reasons for the failure of the left to organize and mobilize effective working class reform or revolutionary movements. This is one of the lessons of the feminist and anti-racism movements. Institutional changes are limited by change in the attitudes and behavior of individuals. The slogan "the personal is political" applies with equal force to classism.

On a personal level freeing ourselves (all classes) from classism requires reversing the conditioning process through healing the wounds of class oppression, reclaiming our past and present class experiences, and sorting out how classism presently and in the past prevents us from being ourselves, from shaping our own identities, and from having the kinds of relationships we want with all people. I can personally attest to the liberation value of the healing work that I have done within the International Reevaluation Co-Counseling Community, which provides a model of personal recovery and liberation from the effects of social conditioning and oppression (Jackins 1972).

Reversing class conditioning, particularly working class internalized oppression, is key to successful working class liberation. As scholar activists we are not immune to the larger social and cultural forces of classism, and are thus not free of classism, no matter how much we might champion working class liberation. We need to address the ways that we have personally internalized classism (and racism and sexism) and the way that classism (and racism and sexism) has shaped our own identities. This means eliminating the elitism and arrogance that many of us have internalized. Of course, eliminating classism also requires that we take leadership to organize other members of our class and form alliances that cross class, gender, and racial boundaries in order to get rid of capitalism and create a classless system of production and distribution that is free of classism, free of racism, and free of sexism, and that is democratic, equitable, and humane.

BIBLIOGRAPHY

1. Albelda, R, Drago, R. & Shulman, S. (1997). *Unlevel Playing Fields:Understanding Wage Inequality and Discrimination.* NY: McGraw-Hill.
2. Al-Hibri, A. (1982). Capitalism Is An Advanced Stage of Patriarchy: But Marxism Is Not Feminism. *Women and Revolution.* Lydia Sargent (ed). Boston: South End Press.
3. Apple, M. (1982). *Education and Power.* NY: Routledge & Kegan.
4. Argyle, M. (1994). *The Psychology of Social Class.* NY: Routledge.
5. Barker, J. & Belkhir JA. (eds). (1996). "Working Class Intellectual Voices." Special Issue *Race, Gender, Class (4)1.*
6. Baron, C. (1995). *The Personal and Social Dynamics of Oppression.* Working Paper Dickinson College.
7. Belkhir, JA. (1996). Social Inequality and Race, Gender, Class: A Working Class Intellectual Perspective. *Race, Gender, & Class.,* 4(1):143–194.
8. Blood, P., Tuttle, A. & Lakey, G. (1995). Understanding and Fighting Sexism: A Call to Men. *Race, Class, and Gender.* Margaret Andersen and Partricia Hill Collins (eds). Belmont, CA: Wadsworth Publishing.
9. Blum, JM. (1978). *Pseudoscience and Mental Ability.* NY: Monthly Review Press.
10. Bonacich, E. (1989). Inequality in America: The Failure of the American System for People of Color. *Sociological Spectrum* 9(1).
11. Bowles, S. & Edwards, R. (1993). *Understanding Capitalism.* Second Edition. New York: Harper-Collins.
12. Bowles, S. & Gintis, H. (1986). *Democracy and Capitalism.* New York: Basic Books.
13. Bowser, B. & Hunt, R. (eds). (1996). *Impacts of Racism on White Americans.* Second Edition. Thousand Oaks, CA: Sage Publications.
14. Bullock, H. (1995). Class Acts: Middle-Class Responses to the Poor. Pp 118–159 in *The Social Psychology of Interpersonal Discrimination,* edited by Bernice Lott and Diane Maluso. NY: Guilford Press.
15. Burawoy, M. (1979). *Manufacturing Consent.* Chicago: Chicago University Press.
16. Collins, PH. (1991). *Black Feminist Thought.* New York: Routledge.
17. Cookson, P. & Persell, C. March (1986). The Price of Privilege. *Psychology Today.* (March):30–35.
18. _____ (1986). *Preparing For Power: America's Elite Boarding Schools.* NY: Basic Books.
19. Daniels, J. (1990). *Punching Out.* Detroit, MI: Wayne State University Press.
20. Dews, CLB & Law, CL. (eds). (1995). *This Fine Place So Far From Home: Voices of Academics From the Working Class.* Philadelphia: Temple University Press.
21. Edwards, R., Michael Reich, M., & Weisskopf, T. (eds). (1986). *The Capitalist System: A Radical Analysis of American Society.* New York: Prentice Hall.
22. Ehrenreich, B. (1990). *Fear of Falling: The Inner Life of the Middle Class.* New York: Harper Collins.
23. Fantasia, R. (1988). *Cultures of Solidarity.* Berkeley, CA: University of California Press.
24. Faulkner, C. (1994). My Beautiful Mother. *Liberating Memory.* Janet Zandy (ed). Pp 198–205. New Brunswick, NJ: Rutgers University Press.
25. Feagin, J & Vera, H. (1995). *White Racism,* NY: Routledge.
26. Ferree, MM & Hall. EJ. (1996). Rethinking Stratification From a Feminist Perspective: Gender, Race, and Class In Mainstream Textbooks. *American Sociological Review,* 61(December):929–950.
27. Fischer, C. et al. (1996). *Inequality by Design: Cracking the Bell Curve Myth.* Princeton, NJ: Princeton University Press.
28. Foner, J. & Alexander, J. (1991). *What's Wrong With The "Mental Health" System: And What Can Be Done About It.* Seattle, WA: Rational Island Publishers.
29. Giroux, HA. (1993). *Theory and Resistance in Education.* NY: Heinemann Educational Books.
30. Glen, EN. (1985). Racial Ethnic Women's Labor: The Intersections of Race, Gender and Class Oppression. *Review of Radical Political Economics.* 17(3) 86–108.
31. Greider, W. (1997). *One World, Ready or Not: The Manic Logic of Capitalism.* NY: Simon & Schuster.
32. Hamper, B. (1991). *Rivethead: Tales From The Assembly Line.* NY: Warner Books.
33. Heath, SB. (1983). *Ways With Words.* New York: Cambridge University Press.
34. Irwin, J., Jackins, H. & Charlie Kreiner, C. (1992). *The Liberation of Men.* Seattle, WA: Rational Island Publishers.
35. Jackins, H. (1972). *The Human Side of Human Beings.* Seattle: Rational Island Publishers.
36. _____ (1988). The Facts of Life For Working Class Racers. *Working For A Living* (6) Seattle: Rational Island Publishers.
37. Jaggar, AM. (1988). *Feminist Politics and Human Nature.* Totowa, NJ: Rowman & Littlefield Pub.
38. Joseph, D. (1995). Breaking Through the Sounds of Silence. Pp. 131–142. in *Liberating Memory,* edited by J. Zandy. New Brunswick, NY: Rutgers University Press.
39. Kandal, TR. (1996). Gender, Race, & Ethnicity: Let's Not Forget Class. *Race, Gender, & Class* 4(1):143–165.
40. Kozol, J. (1991). *Savage Inequalities.* NY: Crown.
41. Kujundzio, J. (1988). *Working For A Living* (6) Pp. 67–68. Seattle, WA: Rational Island Publishers.
42. Langston, D. (1995). Tired of Playing Monopoly? *Race, Class, and Gender: An Anthology,* edited by M. Andersen and PH Collins. Belmont, CA: Wadsworth Publishing Co.
43. Lewis, M. (1978). *The Cultural of Inequality.* Amherst, MA: University of Massachusetts Press.
44. Lipsky, S. (1987). *Internalized Racism.* Seattle, WA: Rational Island Publishers.
45. Lott, B. (1995). Distancing From Women: Interpersonal Sexist Discrimination. Pp. 12–49 in *The Social Psychology of Interpersonal Discrimination,* edited by B. Lott and D Maluso. NY: Guilford Press.
46. Lott, B. & Maluso, D. (eds). (1995). *The Social Psychology of Interpersonal Discrimination.* NY: Guilford Press.
47. Maccoby, M. (1976). *The Gamesman.* New York: Simon and Schuster.

48. MacLeod, J. (1995). *Ain't No Makin' It: Aspirations and Attainment in a Low-Income Neighborhood.* Expanded Edition. Boulder, CO: Westview Press.

49. McNall, SG., Levine, R. & Fantasia, R. (eds). (1991). *Bringing Class Back In: Contemporary and Historical Perspectives.* Boulder, CO: Westview Press.

50. Mishel, L. & Bernstein, J. & Schmitt, J. (1996). *The State of Working America 1996–97.* Armonk, NY: M.E. Sharpe.

51. Omi, M. & Winant, H. (1994). *Racial Formations in the United States.* Second Edition. New York: Routledge.

52. Ortner, SB. & Whitehead, H. (eds). (1981). *Sexual Meanings: The Cultural Construction of Gender and Sexuality.* NY: Cambridge University Press.

53. Penelope, J. (ed) (1994). *Out of the Class Closet: Lesbians Speak.* Freedom, CA: Crossings Press.

54. Puette, WJ. (1992). *Through Jaundiced Eyes: How the Media View Organized Labor.* Ithaca, NY: ILR Press.

55. Quadagno, JS. (1994). *The Color of Welfare.* New York: Oxford University Press.

56. Rothenberg, P (ed). (1995). *Race, Class, and Gender in the United States: An Integrated Study.* Third Edition. NY: St. Martin's Press.

57. Ryan, J. & Sackrey, C. (1984). *Strangers In Paradise: Academics from the Working Class.* Boston: South End Press.

58. Ryan, W. (1981). *Equality,* New York: Pantheon.

59. Sacks, K. (1989). "Toward a Unified Theory of Class, Race, and Gender." *American Ethnologist* 16(3).

60. Sacks K. (1984). *Caring By the Hour.* Chicago: University of Illinois Press.

61. Sennett, R. & Cobb, J. (1972). *The Hidden Injuries of Class.* NY: Vintage Books.

62. Sligh, C. (1994). "Reliving My Mother's Struggle." Pp. 250–264 in *Liberating Memory,* edited by J. Zandy. New Brunswick, NJ: Rutgers University Press.

63. Steinberg, S. (1993). *The Ethnic Myth: Race, Ethnicity, and Class in America.* Boston: Beacon Press.

64. Tarlen, C. (1994). The Memory of Class and Intellectual Privilege. Pp. 19–25 in *Liberating Memory,* edited by J. Zandy. New Brunswick, NJ: Rutgers University Press.

65. Taylor, JM & Gilligan, C. & Sullivan. AM. (1995). *Between Voice and Silence.* Cambridge, MA: Harvard University Press.

66. Tokarczyk, MM. & Fay, EA. (eds). (1993). *Working-Class Women in the Academy: Laborers in the Knowledge Factory.* Amherst, MA: University of Massachusets Press.

67. Vanneman, R. & Weber Cannon, L. (1987). *The American Perception of Class.* Philadelphia: Temple University Press.

68. Wachtel, P. (1983). *The Poverty of Affluence.* New York: Free Press.

69. Waites, EA. (1993). *Trauma and Survival.* New York: Norton.

70. Walsh, DJ. & Witte, JF. (1985). *Correlates of Educational Performance.* (Report No. 6). Madison/Milwaukee, WI: Study Commission on the Quality of Education in the Metropolitan Milwaukee Public Schools.

71. Willis, P. (1977). *Learning To Labour: How Working Class Kids Get Working Class Jobs.* NY: Columbia Univ Press.

72. Wright, EO. (1997). *Class Counts: Comparative Studies in Class Analysis.* NY: Cambridge Univ Press.

73. Wright, EO. (1991). The Conceptual Status of Class Structure in Class Analysis. Pp. 17–38 in *Bringing Class Back In: Contemporary and Historical Perspectives,* edited by SG. McNall, R Levine, and R. Fantasia. Boulder, CO: Westview Press.

74. Wright, EO. (1986). What is Middle about the Middle Class? In *Analytical Marxism,* edited by J. Roemer. NY: Cambridge Univ Press.

75. Yamato, G. (1995). Something About the Subject Makes it Hard to Name. In *Race, Class, and Gender: Anthology,* edited by M. Andersen and Patricia Hill Collins. Belmont, CA: Wadsworth Publishing Co.

76. Zandy, J, (ed). (1994). *Liberating Memory.* New Brunswick, NJ: Rutgers University Press.

10

The Social Construction of Disability

SUSAN WENDELL

I maintain that the distinction between the biological reality of a disability and the social construction of a disability cannot be made sharply, because the biological and the social are interactive in creating disability. They are interactive not only in that complex interactions of social factors and our bodies affect health and functioning, but also in that social arrangements can make a biological condition more or less relevant to almost any situation. I call the interaction of the biological and the social to create (or prevent) disability "the social construction of disability.". . .

SOCIAL FACTORS THAT CONSTRUCT DISABILITY

First, it is easy to recognize that social conditions affect people's bodies by creating or failing to prevent sickness and injury. Although, since disability is relative to a person's physical, social, and cultural environment, none of the resulting physical conditions is necessarily disabling, many do in fact cause disability given the demands and lack of support in the environments of the people affected. In this direct sense of damaging people's bodies in ways that are disabling in their environments, much disability is created by the violence of invasions, wars, civil wars, and terrorism, which cause disabilities not only through direct injuries to combatants and non-combatants, but also through the spread of disease and the deprivations of basic needs that result from the chaos they create. In addition, although we more often hear about them when they cause death, violent crimes such as shootings, knifings, beatings, and rape all cause disabilities, so that a society's success or failure in protecting its citizens from injurious crimes has a significant effect on its rates of disability.

The availability and distribution of basic resources such as water, food, clothing, and shelter have major effects on disability, since much disabling physical damage results directly from malnutrition and indirectly from diseases that attack and do more lasting harm to the malnourished and those weakened by exposure. Disabling diseases are also contracted from contaminated water when clean water is not available. Here too, we usually learn more about the deaths caused by lack of basic resources than the (often life-long) disabilities of survivors.

Many other social factors can damage people's bodies in ways that are disabling in their environments, including (to mention just a few) tolerance of high-risk working conditions, abuse and neglect of children, low public safety standards, the degradation of the environment by contamination of air, water, and food, and the overwork, stress, and daily grinding deprivations of poverty. The social factors that can damage people's bodies almost always affect some groups in a society more than others because of racism, sexism, heterosexism, ageism, and advantages of class background, wealth, and education.

Medical care and practices, traditional and Western-scientific, play an important role in both preventing and creating disabling physical damage. (They also play a role in defining disability. . . .) Lack of good prenatal care and dangerous or inadequate obstetrical practices cause disabilities in babies and in the women giving birth to them. Inoculations against diseases such as polio and measles prevent quite a lot of disability. Inadequate medical care of those who are already ill or injured results in unnecessary disablement. On the other hand, the rate of disability in a society increases with improved medical capacity to save the lives of people who are dangerously ill or injured in the absence of the capacity to prevent or cure all the physical damage they have incurred. Moreover, public health and sanitation measures that increase the average life-span also increase the number of old people with disabilities in a society, since more people live long enough to become disabled.

The *pace of life* is a factor in the social construction of disability that particularly interests me, because it is usually taken for granted by non-disabled people, while many people with disabilities are acutely aware of how it marginalizes or threatens to marginalize us. I suspect that increases in the pace of life are important social causes of damage to people's bodies through rates of accident, drug and alcohol abuse, and illnesses that result from people's neglecting their needs for rest and good nutrition. But the pace of life also affects disability as a second form of social construction, the social construction of disability through expectations of performance.

When the pace of life in a society increases, there is a tendency for more people to become disabled, not only because of physically damaging consequences of efforts to go faster, but also because fewer people can meet expectations of 'normal' performance; the physical (and mental) limitations of those who cannot meet the new pace become conspicuous and disabling, even though the same limitations were inconspicuous and irrelevant to full participation in the slower-paced society. . . .

Feminists talk about how the world has been designed for the bodies and activities of men. In many industrialized countries, including Canada and the United States, life and work have been structured as though no one of any importance in the public world, and certainly no one who works outside the home for wages, has to breast-feed a baby or look after a sick child. Common colds can be acknowledged publicly, and allowances are made for them, but menstruation cannot be acknowledged and allowances are not made for it. Much of the public world is also structured as though everyone were physically strong, as though all bodies were shaped the same, as though everyone could walk, hear, and see well, as though everyone could work and play at a pace that is not compatible with any kind of illness or pain, as though no one were ever dizzy or incontinent or simply needed to sit or lie down. (For instance, where could you rest for a few minutes in a supermarket if you needed to?) Not only the architecture, but the entire physical and social organization of life tends to assume that we are either strong and healthy and able to do what the average young, non-disabled man can do or that we are completely unable to participate in public life.

A great deal of disability is caused by this physical structure and social organization of society. For instance, poor architectural planning creates physical obstacles for people who use wheelchairs, but also for people who can walk but cannot walk far or cannot climb stairs, for people who cannot open doors, and for people who can do all of these things but only at the cost of pain or an expenditure of energy they can ill afford. Some of the same architectural flaws cause problems for pregnant women, parents with strollers, and young children. This is no coincidence. Much architecture has been planned with a young adult, non-disabled male paradigm of humanity in mind. In addition, aspects of social organization that take for granted the social expectations of performance and productivity, such as inadequate pubic transportation (which I believe assumes that no one who is needed in the public world needs public transportation), communications systems that are inaccessible to people with visual or hearing impairments, and inflexible work arrangements that exclude part-time work or rest periods, create much disability.

When public and private worlds are split, women (and children) have often been relegated to the private, and so have the disabled, the sick, and the old. The public world is the world of strength, the positive (valued) body, performance and production, the non-disabled, and young adults. Weakness, illness, rest and recovery, pain, death, and the negative (devalued) body are private, generally hidden,

and often neglected. Coming into the public world with illness, pain, or a devalued body, people encounter resistance to mixing the two worlds; the split is vividly revealed. Much of the experience of disability and illness goes underground, because there is no socially acceptable way of expressing it and having the physical and psychological experience acknowledged. Yet acknowledgement of this experience is exactly what is required for creating accessibility in the public world. The more a society regards disability as a private matter, and people with disabilities as belonging in the private sphere, the more disability it creates by failing to make the public sphere accessible to a wide range of people.

. . . Two things are important to remember about the help that people with disabilities may need. One is that most industrialized societies give non-disabled people (in different degrees and kinds, depending on class, race, gender, and other factors) a lot of help in the form of education, training, social support, public communication and transportation facilities, public recreation, and other services. The help that non-disabled people receive tends to be taken for granted and not considered help but entitlement, because it is offered to citizens who fit the social paradigms, who by definition are not considered dependent on social help. It is only when people need a different kind or amount of help than that given to 'paradigm' citizens that it is considered help at all, and they are considered socially dependent. Second, much, though not all, of the help that people with disabilities need is required because their bodies were damaged by social conditions, or because they cannot meet social expectations of performance, or because the narrowly-conceived physical structure and social organization of society have placed them at a disadvantage; in other words, it is needed to overcome problems that were created socially.

Thus disability is socially constructed through the failure or unwillingness to create ability among people who do not fit the physical and mental profile of 'paradigm' citizens. Failures of social support for people with disabilities result in inadequate rehabilitation, unemployment, poverty, inadequate personal and medical care, poor communication services, inadequate training and education, poor protection from physical, sexual, and emotional abuse, minimal opportunities for social learning and interaction, and many other disabling situations that hurt people with disabilities and exclude them from participation in major aspects of life in their societies.

CULTURAL CONSTRUCTION OF DISABILITY

Culture makes major contributions to disability. These contributions include not only the omission of experiences of disability from cultural representations of life in a society, but also the cultural stereotyping of people with disabilities, the selective stigmatization of physical and mental limitations and other differences (selective because not all limitations and differences are stigmatized, and different limitations and differences are stigmatized in different societies), the numerous cultural meanings attached to various kinds of disability and illness, and the exclusion of people with disabilities from the cultural meanings of activities they cannot perform or are expected not to perform.

The lack of realistic cultural representations of experiences of disability not only contributes to the 'Otherness' of people with disabilities by encouraging the assumption that their lives are inconceivable to non-disabled people but also increases non-disabled people's fear of disability by suppressing knowledge of how people live with disabilities. Stereotypes of disabled people as dependent, morally depraved, super-humanly heroic, asexual, and/or pitiful are still the most common cultural portrayals of people with disabilities. Stereotypes repeatedly get in the way of full participation in work and social life. For example, Francine Arsenault, whose leg was damaged by childhood polio and later by gangrene, describes the following incident at her wedding:

> When I got married, one of my best friends came to the wedding with her parents. I had known her parents all the time I was growing up; we visited in each other's homes and I thought that they knew my situation quite well.
>
> But as the father went down the reception line and shook hands with my husband, he said, "You know, I used to think that Francine was intelligent, but to put herself on you as a burden like this shows that I was wrong all along."

Here the stereotype of a woman with a disability as a helpless, dependent burden blots out, in the friend's father's consciousness, both the reality that Francine simply has one damaged leg and the probability that her new husband wants her for her other qualities. Moreover, the man seems to take for granted that the new husband sees Francine in the same stereotyped way (or else he risks incomprehension or rejection), perhaps because he counts on the cultural assumptions about people with disabilities. I think both the stigma of physical 'imperfection' (and possibly the additional stigma of having been damaged by disease) and the cultural meanings attached to the disability contribute to the power of the stereotype in situations like this. Physical 'imperfection' is more likely to be thought to 'spoil' a woman than a man by rendering her unattractive in a culture where her physical appearance is a large component of a woman's value; having a damaged leg probably evokes the metaphorical meanings of being 'crippled,' which include helplessness, dependency, and pitifulness. Stigma, stereotypes, and cultural meanings are all related and interactive in the cultural construction of disability. . . .

It seems that the cultural constructions of disability, including the ignorance, stereotyping, and stigmatization that feed fears of disability, have to be at least partly deconstructed before disability can be seen by more people as a set of social problems and social responsibilities. Until that change in perspective happens, people with disabilities and their families will continue to be given too much individual responsibility for 'overcoming' disabilities, expectations for the participation of people with disabilities in public life will be far too low, and social injustices that are recognized now (at least in the abstract), such as discrimination against people with disabilities, will be misunderstood. . . .

B. EXAMINING THE INTERSECTIONS

One . . .

SHARON HWANG COLLIGAN

1. ONE
Well
the straights talk of
heterosexual thrusting as if it were the only real
    form of
sexual fulfillment and
the straights tense if I touch them and
the gays make jokes about "breeders" and
fall silent if I mention my (male) lover
I look for books on bisexuality but
they are all about married men or
have titles like "two lives to lead"—
Well I am NOT a man and will never
lead two lives   I am one woman

ONE ONE ONE

I thought Gay Rights meant being able
to love who I love

2. YOU SEE
I am white Chinese
I am bisexual Lesbian

3. MY FATHER
is Polish and Irish and German
long blended in America
My mother is the child of
two brave Chinese   who survived
in an alien and hating land
to raise bright and beautiful
middle-class
daughters
who no longer speak Chinese
who work to succeed
to pass
White racism against my yellow

family and self is a crime   The criminals
are of my own white
family, my own pale skin color

4. WE LOVED
Though she and I separated   I
vowed never to forget nor
deny the fires she ignited in my body & soul
I chose at 17 to
claim
the word Dyke   to commit my fate
to that of the lesbians
when the witch hunters came they would have to
    come for me too

even if by that time I had married him

None of the coming-out stories
or other writings I devoured
Seventeen alone and bisexual   never once
validated my reality   never once offered a story
of a relationship
neither abusive nor boring
with a male lover
My new & fragile lesbian world was
as important to me as my own bones   But
in the women's journals were
quiet signs of
You Are Not Welcome   everywhere

I looked at myself and realized

11

Toward a New Vision

Race, Class, and Gender as Categories of Analysis and Connection

PATRICIA HILL COLLINS

The true focus of revolutionary change is never merely the oppressive situations which we seek to escape, but that piece of the oppressor which is planted deep within each of us.

—AUDRE LORDE, *Sister Outsider*, 123

Audre Lorde's statement raises a troublesome issue for scholars and activists working for social change. While many of us have little difficulty assessing our own victimization within some major system of oppression, whether it be by race, social class, religion, sexual orientation, ethnicity, age or gender, we typically fail to see how our thoughts and actions uphold someone else's subordination. Thus, white feminists routinely point with confidence to their oppression as women but resist seeing how much their white skin privileges them. African-Americans who possess eloquent analyses of racism often persist in viewing poor White women as symbols of white power. The radical left fares little better. "If only people of color and women could see their true class interests," they argue, "class solidarity would eliminate racism and sexism." In essence, each group identifies the type of oppression with which it feels most comfortable as being fundamental and classifies all other types as being of lesser importance.

Oppression is full of such contradictions. Errors in political judgment that we make concerning how we teach our courses, what we tell our children, and which organizations are worthy of our time, talents and financial support flow smoothly from errors in theoretical analysis about the nature of oppression and activism. Once we realize that there are few pure victims or oppressors, and that each one of us derives varying amounts of penalty and privilege from the multiple systems of oppression that frame our lives, then we will be in a position to see the need for new ways of thought and action.

To get at that "piece of the oppressor which is planted deep within each of us," we need at least two things. First, we need new visions of what oppression is, new categories of analysis that are inclusive of race, class, and gender as distinctive yet interlocking structures of oppression. Adhering to a stance of comparing and ranking oppressions—

the proverbial, "I'm more oppressed than you"— locks us all into a dangerous dance of competing for attention, resources, and theoretical supremacy. Instead, I suggest that we examine our different experiences within the more fundamental relationship of domination and subordination. To focus on the particular arrangements that race or class or gender takes in our time and place without seeing these structures as sometimes parallel and sometimes interlocking dimensions of the more fundamental relationship of domination and subordination may temporarily ease our consciences. But while such thinking may lead to short-term social reforms, it is simply inadequate for the task of bringing about long-term social transformation.

While race, class and gender as categories of analysis are essential in helping us understand the structural bases of domination and subordination, new ways of thinking that are not accompanied by new ways of acting offer incomplete prospects for change. To get at that "piece of the oppressor which is planted deep within each of us," we also need to change our daily behavior. Currently, we are all enmeshed in a complex web of problematic relationships that grant our mirror images full human subjectivity while stereotyping and objectifying those most different than ourselves. We often assume that the people we work with, teach, send our children to school with, and sit next to . . . will act and feel in prescribed ways because they belong to given race, social class or gender categories. [These judgments by category relationships that transcend the legitimate differences created by race, class and gender as categories of analysis.] We require new categories of connection, new visions of what our relationships with one another can be. . . .

[This discussion] addresses this need for new patterns of thought and action. I focus on two basic questions. First, how can we reconceptualize race, class and gender as categories of analysis? Second, how can we transcend the barriers created by our experiences with race, class and gender oppression in order to build the types of coalitions essential for social exchange? To address these questions I contend that we must acquire both new theories of how race, class and gender have shaped the experiences not just of women of color, but of all groups. Moreover, we must see the connections between the categories of analysis and the personal issues in our everyday lives, particularly our scholarship, our teaching and our relationships with our colleagues and students. As Audre Lorde points out, change starts with self, and relationships that we have with those around us must always be the primary site for social change.

HOW CAN WE RECONCEPTUALIZE RACE, CLASS AND GENDER AS CATEGORIES OF ANALYSIS?

To me, we must shift our discourse away from additive analyses of oppression (Spelman, 1982; Collins, 1989). Such approaches are typically based on two key premises. First, they depend on either/or, dichotomous thinking. Persons, things and ideas are conceptualized in terms of their opposites. For example, Black/White, man/woman, thought/feeling, and fact/opinion are defined in oppositional terms. Thought and feeling are not seen as two different and interconnected ways of approaching truth that can coexist in scholarship and teaching. Instead, feeling is defined as antithetical to reason, as its opposite. In spite of the fact that we all have "both/and" identities (I am both a college professor and a mother—I don't stop being a mother when I drop my child off at school, or forget everything I learned while scrubbing the toilet), we persist in trying to classify each other in either/or categories. I live each day as an African-American woman—a race/gender specific experience. And I am not alone. Everyone has a race/gender/class specific identity. Either/or, dichotomous thinking is especially troublesome when applied to theories of oppression because every individual must be classified as being either oppressed or not oppressed. The both/and position of simultaneously being oppressed and oppressor becomes conceptually impossible.

A second premise of additive analyses of oppression is that these dichotomous differences must be ranked. One side of the dichotomy is typically labeled dominant and the other subordinate. Thus, Whites rule Blacks, men are deemed superior to women, and reason is seen as being preferable to emotion. Applying this premise to discussions of oppression leads to the assumption that oppression can be quantified, and that some groups are oppressed more than others. I am frequently asked, "Which has been most oppressive to you, your status as a Black person or your status as a woman?" What I am really being asked to do is divide myself into little boxes and rank my various statuses. If I experience oppression as a both/and phenomenon, why should I analyze it any differently?

Additive analyses of oppression rest squarely on the twin pillars of either/or thinking and the necessity to quantify and rank all relationships in order to know where one stands. Such approaches typically see African-American women as being more oppressed than everyone else because the majority of Black women experience the negative effects of race, class and gender oppression simultaneously. In essence, if you add together separate oppressions, you are left with a grand oppression greater than the sum of its parts.

I am not denying that specific groups experience oppression more harshly than others—lynching is certainly objectively worse than being held up as a sex object. But we must be careful not to confuse this issue of the saliency of one type of oppression in people's lives with a theoretical stance positing the interlocking nature of oppression. Race, class and gender may all structure a situation but may not be equally visible and/or important in people's self-definitions. In certain contexts, such as the antebellum American South and contemporary South America, racial oppression is more visibly salient, while in other contexts, such as Haiti, El Salvador and Nicaragua, social class oppression may be more apparent. For middle-class White women, gender may assume experiential primacy unavailable to poor Hispanic women struggling with the ongoing issues of low-paid jobs and the frustrations of the welfare bureaucracy. This recognition that one category may have salience over another for a given time and place does not minimize the theoretical importance of assuming that race, class and gender as categories of analysis structure all relationships.

In order to move toward new visions of what oppression is, I think that we need to ask new questions. How are relationships of domination and subordination structured and maintained in the American political economy? How do race, class and gender function as parallel and interlocking systems that shape this basic relationship of domination and subordination? Questions such as these promise to move us away from futile theoretical struggles concerned with ranking oppressions and towards analyses that assume race, class and gender are all present in any given setting, even if one appears more visible and salient than the others. Our task becomes redefined as one of reconceptualizing oppression by uncovering the connections among race, class and gender as categories of analysis.

1. The Institutional Dimension of Oppression

Sandra Harding's contention that gender oppression is structured along three main dimensions—the institutional, the symbolic and the individual—offers a useful model for a more comprehensive analysis encompassing race, class and gender oppression (Harding 1986). Systemic relationships of domination and subordination structured through social institutions such as schools, businesses, hospitals, the workplace and government agencies represent the institutional dimension of oppression. Racism, sexism, and elitism all have concrete institutional locations. Even though the workings of the institutional dimension of oppression are often obscured with ideologies claiming equality of opportunity, in actuality, race, class and gender place Asian-American women, Native American men, White men, African-American women and other groups in distinct institutional niches with varying degrees of penalty and privilege.

Even though I realize that many . . . would not share this assumption, let us assume that the institutions of American society discriminate, whether by design or by accident. While many of us are familiar with how race, gender and class operate separately to structure inequality, I want to focus on how these three systems interlock in structuring the institutional dimension of oppression. To get at the interlocking nature of race, class and gender, I want you to think about the antebellum plantation as a guiding metaphor for a variety of American social institutions. Even though slavery is typically analyzed as a racist institution, and occasionally as a class institution, I suggest that slavery was a race, class, gender specific institution. Removing any one piece from our analysis diminishes our understanding of the true nature of relations of domination and subordination under slavery.

Slavery was a profoundly patriarchal institution. It rested on the dual tenets of White male authority and White male property, a joining of the political and the economic within the institution of the family. Heterosexism was assumed and all Whites were expected to marry. Control over affluent White women's sexuality remained key to slavery's survival because property was to be passed on to the legitimate heirs of the slave owner. Ensuring affluent White women's virginity and chastity was deeply intertwined with maintenance of property relations.

Under slavery, we see varying levels of institutional protection given to affluent White women, working class and poor White women and enslaved African women. Poor White women enjoyed few of the protections held out to their upper class sisters. Moreover, the devalued status of Black women was key in keeping all White women in their assigned places. Controlling Black women's fertility was also key to the continuation of slavery, for children born to slave mothers themselves were slaves.

African-American women shared the devalued status of chattel with their husbands, fathers and sons. Racism stripped Blacks as a group of legal rights, education and control over their own persons. African-Americans could be whipped, branded, sold, or killed, not because they were poor, or because they were women, but because they were Black. Racism ensured that Blacks would continue to serve Whites and suffer economic exploitation at the hands of all Whites.

So we have a very interesting chain of command on the plantation—the affluent White master as the reigning patriarch, his White wife helpmate to serve him, help him manage his property and bring up his heirs, his faithful servants whose production and reproduction were tied to the requirements of the capitalist political economy and largely propertyless, working class White men and women watching from afar. In essence, the foundations for the contemporary roles of elite White women, poor Black women, working class White men and a series of other groups can be seen in stark relief in this fundamental American social institution. While Blacks experienced the most harsh treatment under slavery, and thus made slavery clearly visible as a racist institution, race, class and gender interlocked in structuring slavery's systemic organization of domination and subordination.

Even today, the plantation remains a compelling metaphor for institutional oppression. Certainly the actual conditions of oppression are not as severe now as they were then. To argue, as some do, that things have not changed all that much denigrates the achievements of those who struggled for social change before us. But the basic relationships among Black men, Black women, elite White women, elite White men, working class White men and working class White women as groups remain essentially intact.

A brief analysis of key American social institutions most controlled by elite White men should convince us of the interlocking nature of race, class and gender in structuring the institutional dimension of oppression. For example, if you are from an American college or university, is your campus a modern plantation? Who controls your university's political economy? Are elite White men overrepresented among the upper administrators and trustees controlling your university's finances and policies? Are elite White men being joined by growing numbers of elite White women helpmates? What kinds of people are in your classrooms grooming the next generation who will occupy these and other decision-making positions? Who are the support staff that produce the mass mailings, order the supplies, fix the leaky pipes? Do African-Americans, Hispanics or other people of color form the majority of the invisible workers who feed you, wash your dishes, and clean up your offices and libraries after everyone else has gone home?

If your college is anything like mine, you know the answers to these questions. You may be affiliated with an institution that has Hispanic women as vice-presidents for finance, or substantial numbers of Black men among the faculty. If so, you are fortunate. Much more typical are colleges where a modified version of the plantation as a metaphor for the institutional dimension of oppression survives.

2. The Symbolic Dimension of Oppression

Widespread, societally sanctioned ideologies used to justify relations of domination and subordination comprise the symbolic dimension of oppression. Central to this process is the use of stereotypical or controlling images of diverse race, class and gender groups. In order to assess the power of this dimension of oppression, I want you to make a list, either on paper or in your head, of "masculine" and "feminine" characteristics. If your list is anything like that compiled by most people, it reflects some variation of the following:

Masculine	Feminine
aggressive	passive
leader	follower
rational	emotional
strong	weak
intellectual	physical

Not only does this list reflect either/or dichotomous thinking and the need to rank both sides of the dichotomy, but ask yourself exactly which men and women you had in mind when compiling these characteristics. This list applies almost exclusively to middle class White men and women. The allegedly "masculine" qualities that you probably listed are only acceptable when exhibited by elite White men, or when used by Black and Hispanic men against each other or against women of color. Aggressive Black and Hispanic men are seen as dangerous, not powerful, and are often penalized when they exhibit any of the allegedly "masculine" characteristics. Working class and poor White men fare slightly better and are also denied the allegedly "masculine" symbols of leadership, intellectual competence, and human rationality. Women of color and working class and poor White women are also not represented on this list, for they have never had the luxury of being "ladies." What appear to be universal categories representing all men and women instead are unmasked as being applicable to only a small group.

It is important to see how the symbolic images applied to different race, class and gender groups interact in maintaining systems of domination and subordination. If I were to ask you to repeat the same assignment, only this time, by making separate lists for Black men, Black women, Hispanic women and Hispanic men, I suspect that your gender symbolism would be quite different. In comparing all of the lists, you might begin to see the interdependence of symbols applied to all groups. For example, the elevated images of White womanhood need devalued images of Black womanhood in order to maintain credibility.

While the above exercise reveals the interlocking nature of race, class and gender in structuring the symbolic dimension of oppression, part of its importance lies in demonstrating how race, class and gender pervade a wide range of what appears to be universal language. Attending to diversity in our scholarship, in our teaching, and in our daily lives provides a new angle of vision on interpretations of reality thought to be natural, normal and "true." Moreover, viewing images of masculinity and femininity as universal gender symbolism, rather than as symbolic images that are race, class and gender specific, renders the experiences of people of color and of nonprivileged White women and men invisible. One way to dehumanize an individual or group is to deny the reality of their experiences. So when we refuse to deal with race or class because they do not appear to be directly relevant to gender, we are actually becoming part of someone else's problem.

Assuming that everyone is affected differently by the same interlocking set of symbolic images allows us to move forward toward new analyses. Women of color and White women have different relations to White male authority and this difference explains the distinct gender symbolism applied to both groups. Black women encounter controlling images such as the mammy, the matriarch, the mule and the whore, that encourage others to reject us as fully human people. Ironically, the negative nature of these images simultaneously encourages us to reject them. In contrast, White women are offered seductive images, those that promise to reward them for supporting the status quo. And yet seductive images can be equally controlling. Consider, for example, the views of Nancy White, a 73-year-old Black woman, concerning images of rejection and seduction:

> My mother used to say that the black woman is the white man's mule and the white woman is his dog. Now, she said that to say this: we do the heavy work and get beat whether we do it well or not. But the white woman is closer to the master and he pats them on the head and lets them sleep in the house, but he ain't gon' treat neither one like he was dealing with a person. (Gwaltney, 148)

Both sets of images stimulate particular political stances. By broadening the analysis beyond the confines of race, we can see the varying levels of rejection and seduction available to each of us due to our race, class and gender identity. Each of us lives with an allotted portion of institutional privilege and penalty, and with varying levels of rejection and seduction inherent in the symbolic images applied to us. This is the context in which we make our choices. Taken together, the institutional and symbolic dimensions of oppression create a structural backdrop against which all of us live our lives.

3. *The Individual Dimension of Oppression*

Whether we benefit or not, we all live within institutions that reproduce race, class and gender oppression. Even if we never have any contact with members of other race, class and gender groups, we all encounter images of these groups and are exposed to the symbolic meanings attached to those images. On this dimension of oppression, our individual biographies vary tremendously. As a result of our institutional and symbolic statuses, all of our choices become political acts.

Each of us must come to terms with the multiple ways in which race, class and gender as categories of analysis frame our individual biographies. I have lived my entire life as an African-American woman from a working class family and this basic fact has had a profound impact on my personal biography. Imagine how different your life might be if you had been born Black, or White, or poor, or of a different race/class/gender group than the one with which you are most familiar. The institutional treatment you would have received and the symbolic meanings attached to your very existence might differ dramatically from that you now consider to be natural, normal and part of everyday life. You might be the same, but your personal biography might have been quite different.

I believe that each of us carries around the cumulative effect of our lives within multiple structures of oppression. If you want to see how much you have been affected by this whole thing, I ask you one simple question—who are your close friends? Who are the people with whom you can share your hopes, dreams, vulnerabilities, fears and victories? Do they look like you? If they are all the same, circumstance may be the cause. For the first seven years of my life I saw only low income Black people. My friends from those years reflected the composition of my community. But now that I am an adult, can the defense of circumstance explain the patterns of people that I trust as my friends and colleagues? When given other alternatives, if my friends and colleagues reflect the homogeneity of one race, class and gender group, then these categories of analysis have indeed become barriers to connection.

I am not suggesting that people are doomed to follow the paths laid out for them by race, class and gender as categories of analysis. While these three structures certainly frame my opportunity struc-

ture, I as an individual always have the choice of accepting things as they are, or trying to change them. As Nikki Giovanni points out, "we've got to live in the real world. If we don't like the world we're living in, change it. And if we can't change it, we change ourselves. We can do something" (Tate 1983, 68). While a piece of the oppressor may be planted deep within each of us, we each have the choice of accepting that piece or challenging it as part of the "true focus of revolutionary change."

HOW CAN WE TRANSCEND THE BARRIERS CREATED BY OUR EXPERIENCES WITH RACE, CLASS AND GENDER OPPRESSION IN ORDER TO BUILD THE TYPES OF COALITIONS ESSENTIAL FOR SOCIAL CHANGE?

Reconceptualizing oppression and seeing the barriers created by race, class and gender as interlocking categories of analysis is a vital first step. But we must transcend these barriers by moving toward race, class and gender as categories of connection, by building relationships and coalitions that will bring about social change. What are some of the issues involved in doing this?

1. Differences in Power and Privilege

First, we must recognize that our differing experiences with oppression create problems in the relationships among us. Each of us lives within a system that vests us with varying levels of power and privilege. These differences in power, whether structured along axes of race, class, gender, age or sexual orientation, frame our relationships. African-American writer June Jordan describes her discomfort on a Caribbean vacation with Olive, the Black woman who cleaned her room:

> . . . even though both "Olive" and "I" live inside a conflict neither one of us created, and even though both of us therefore hurt inside that conflict, I may be one of the monsters she needs to eliminate from her universe and, in a sense, she may be one of the monsters in mine (1985, 47).

Differences in power constrain our ability to connect with one another even when we think we are engaged in dialogue across differences. Let me give you an example. One year, the students in my course "Sociology of the Black Community" got into a heated discussion about the reasons for the upsurge of racial incidents on college campuses. Black students complained vehemently about the apathy and resistance they felt most White students expressed about examining their own racism. Mark, a White male student, found their comments particularly unsettling. After claiming that all the Black people he had ever known had expressed no such beliefs to him, he questioned how representative the viewpoints of his fellow students actually were. When pushed further, Mark revealed that he had participated in conversations over the years with the Black domestic worker employed by his family. Since she had never expressed such strong feelings about White racism, Mark was genuinely shocked by class discussions. Ask yourselves whether that domestic worker was in a position to speak freely. Would it have been wise for her to do so in a situation where the power between the two parties was so unequal?

In extreme cases, members of privileged groups can erase the very presence of the less privileged. When I first moved to Cincinnati, my family and I went on a picnic at a local park. Picnicking next to us was a family of White Appalachians. When I went to push my daughter on the swings, several of the children came over. They had missing, yellowed and broken teeth, they wore old clothing and their poverty was evident. I was shocked. Growing up in a large eastern city, I had never seen such awful poverty among Whites. The segregated neighborhoods in which I grew up made White poverty all but invisible. More importantly, the privileges attached to my newly acquired social class position allowed me to ignore and minimize the poverty among Whites that I did encounter. My reactions to those children made me realize how confining phrases such as "well, at least they're not Black," had become for me. In learning to grant human subjectivity to the Black victims of poverty, I had simultaneously learned to demand White victims of poverty. By applying categories of race to the objective conditions confronting me, I was quantifying and ranking oppressions and missing the very real suffering which, in fact, is the real issue.

One common pattern of relationships across differences in power is one that I label "voyeurism." From the perspective of the privileged, the lives of people of color, of the poor, and of women are interesting for their entertainment value. The privileged become voyeurs, passive onlookers who do not relate to the less powerful, but who are interested in seeing how the "different" live. Over the years, I have heard numerous African-American students complain about professors who never call on them except when a so-called Black issue is being discussed. The students' interest in discussing race or qualifications for doing so appear unimportant to the professor's efforts to use Black students' experiences as stories to make the material come alive for the White student audience. Asking Black students to perform on cue and provide a Black experience for their White classmates can be seen as voyeurism at its worst.

Members of subordinate groups do not willingly participate in such exchanges but often do so because members of dominant groups control the institutional and symbolic apparatuses of oppression. Racial/ethnic groups, women, and the poor have never had the luxury of being voyeurs of the lives of the privileged. Our ability to survive in hostile settings has hinged on our ability to learn intricate details about the behavior and world view of the powerful and adjust our behavior accordingly. I need only point to the difference in perception of those men and women in abusive relationships. Where men can view their girlfriends and wives as sex objects, helpmates and a collection of stereotypes categories of voyeurism—women must be attuned to every nuance of their partners' behavior. Are women "naturally" better in relating to people with more power than themselves, or have circumstances mandated that men and women develop different skills?. . .

Coming from a tradition where most relationships across difference are squarely rooted in relations of domination and subordination, we have much less experience relating to people as different but equal. The classroom is potentially one powerful and safe space where dialogues among individuals of unequal power relationships can occur. The relationship between Mark, the student in my class, and the domestic worker is typical of a whole series of relationships that people have when they relate across differences in power and privilege. The relationship among Mark and his classmates represents the power of the classroom to minimize those differences so that people of different levels of power can use race, class and gender as categories of analysis in order to generate meaningful dialogues. In this case, the classroom equalized racial differences so that Black students who normally felt silenced spoke out. White students like Mark, generally unaware of how they had been privileged by their whiteness, lost that privilege in the classroom and thus became open to genuine dialogue. . . .

2. Coalitions around Common Causes

A second issue in building relationships and coalitions essential for social change concerns knowing the real reasons for coalition. Just what brings people together? One powerful catalyst fostering group solidarity is the presence of a common enemy. African-American, Hispanic, Asian-American, and women's studies all share the common intellectual heritage of challenging what passes for certified knowledge in the academy. But politically expedient relationships and coalitions like these are fragile because, as June Jordan points out:

> It occurs to me that much organizational grief could be avoided if people understood that partnership in misery does not necessarily provide for partnership for change. When we get the monsters off our backs all of us may want to run in very different directions (1985, 47).

Sharing a common cause assists individuals and groups in maintaining relationships that transcend their differences. Building effective coalitions involves struggling to hear one another and developing empathy for each other's points of view. The coalitions that I have been involved in that lasted and that worked have been those where commitment to a specific issue mandated collaboration as the best strategy for addressing the issue at hand.

Several years ago, masters degree in hand, I chose to teach in an innercity parochial school in danger of closing. The money was awful, the conditions were poor, but the need was great. In my job, I had to work with a range of individuals who, on the surface, had very little in common. We had White nuns, Black middle class graduate students, Blacks from the "community," some of whom had been incarcerated and/or were affiliated with a range of federal anti-poverty programs. Parents formed another part of this community, Harvard faculty another, and a few well-meaning White liberals from Colorado were sprinkled in for good measure.

As you might imagine, tension was high. Initially, our differences seemed insurmountable. But as time passed, we found a common bond that we each brought to the school. In spite of profound differences in our personal biographies, differences that in other settings would have hampered our ability to relate to one another, we found that we were all deeply committed to the education of Black children. By learning to value each other's commitment and by recognizing that we each had different skills that were essential to actualizing that commitment, we built an effective coalition around a common cause. Our school was successful, and the children we taught benefited from the diversity we offered them.

. . . None of us alone has a comprehensive vision of how race, class and gender operate as categories of analysis or how they might be used as categories of connection. Our personal biographies offer us partial views. Few of us can manage to study race, class and gender simultaneously. Instead, we each know more about some dimensions of this larger story and less about others. . . . Just as the members of the school had special skills to offer to the task of building the school, we have areas of specialization and expertise, whether scholarly, theoretical, pedagogical or within areas of race, class or gender. We do not all have to do the same thing in the same way. Instead, we must support each other's efforts, realizing that they are all part of the larger enterprise of bringing about social change.

3. Building Empathy

A third issue involved in building the types of relationships and coalitions essential for social change concerns the issue of individual accountability. Race, class and gender oppression form the structural backdrop against which we frame our relationship—these are the forces that encourage us to substitute voyeurism . . . for fully human relationships. But while we may not have created this situation, we are each responsible for making individual, personal choices concerning which elements of race, class and gender oppression we will accept and which we will work to change.

One essential component of this accountability involves developing empathy for the experiences of individuals and groups different than ourselves. Empathy begins with taking an interest in the facts of other people's lives, both as individuals and as groups. If you care about me, you should want to know not only the details of my personal biography but a sense of how race, class and gender as categories of analysis created the institutional and symbolic backdrop for my personal biography. How can you hope to assess my character without knowing the details of the circumstances I face?

Moreover, by taking a theoretical stance that we have all been affected by race, class and gender as categories of analysis that have structured our treatment, we open up possibilities for using those same constructs as categories of connection in building empathy. For example, I have a good White woman friend with whom I share common interests and beliefs. But we know that our racial differences have provided us with different experiences. So we talk about them. We do not assume that because I am Black, race has only affected me and not her or that because I am a Black woman, race neutralizes the effect of gender in my life while accenting it in hers. We take those same categories of analysis that have created cleavages in our lives, in this case, categories of race and gender, and use them as categories of connection in building empathy for each other's experiences.

Finding common causes and building empathy is difficult, no matter which side of privilege we inhabit. Building empathy from the dominant side of privilege is difficult, simply because individuals from privileged backgrounds are not encouraged to do so. For example, in order for those of you who are White to develop empathy for the experiences of people of color, you must grapple with how your white skin has privileged you. This is difficult to do, because it not only entails the intellectual process of seeing how whiteness is elevated in institutions and symbols, but it also involves the often painful process of seeing how your whiteness has shaped your personal biography. Intellectual stances against the institutional and symbolic dimensions of racism are generally easier to maintain than sustained self-reflection about how racism has shaped all of our individual biographies. Were and are your fathers, uncles, and grandfathers really more capable than mine, or can their accomplishments be explained in part by the racism members of my family experienced? Did your mothers stand silently by and watch all this happen? More importantly, how have they passed on the benefits of their whiteness to you?

These are difficult questions, and I have tremendous respect for my colleagues and students who are trying to answer them. Since there is no compelling reason to examine the source and meaning of one's own privilege, I know that those who do so have freely chosen this stance. They are making conscious efforts to root out the piece of the oppressor planted within them. To me, they are entitled to the support of people of color in their efforts. Men who declare themselves feminists, members of the middle class who ally themselves with anti-poverty struggles, heterosexuals who support gays and lesbians, are all trying to grow, and their efforts place them far ahead of the majority who never think of engaging in such important struggles.

Building empathy from the subordinate side of privilege is also difficult, but for different reasons. Members of subordinate groups are understandably reluctant to abandon a basic mistrust of members of powerful groups because this basic mistrust has traditionall been central to their survival. As a Black woman, it would be foolish for me to assume that White women, or Black men, or White men or any other group with a history of exploiting African-American women have my best interests at heart. These groups enjoy varying amounts of privilege over me and therefore I must carefully watch them and be prepared for a relation of domination and subordination.

Like the privileged, members of subordinate groups must also work toward replacing judgments by category with new ways of thinking and acting. Refusing to do so stifles prospects for effective coalition and social change. Let me use another example from my own experiences. When I was an undergraduate, I had little time or patience for the theorizing of the privileged. My initial years at a private, elite institution were difficult, not because the coursework was challenging (it was, but that wasn't what distracted me) or because I had to work while my classmates lived of family allowances (I was used to work). The adjustment was difficult because I was surrounded by so many people who took their privilege for granted. Most of them felt entitled to their wealth. That astounded me.

I remember one incident watching a White woman down the hall in my dormitory try to pick out which sweater to wear. The sweaters were piled up on her bed in all the colors of the rainbow, sweater after sweater. She asked my advice in a way that let me know that choosing a sweater was on of the most important decisions she had to make on a daily basis. Standing kneedeep in her sweaters, I realized how different our lives were. She did not have to worry about maintaining a solid academic average so that she could receive financial aid. Because she was in the majority, she was not treated as a representative of her race. She did not have to consider how her classroom comments or basic existence on campus contributed to the treatment her group would receive. Her allowance protected her from having to work, so she ws free to spend her time studying, partying, or in her case, worrying about which sweater to wear. The degree of inequality in our lives and her unquestioned sense of entitlement concerning that

inequality offended me. For a while, I categorized all affluent White women as being superficial, arrogant, overly concerned with material possessions, and part of my problem. But had I continued to classify people in this way, I would have missed out on making some very good friends whose discomfort with their inherited or acquired social class privileges pushed them to examine their position.

Since I opened with the words of Audre Lorde, it seems appropiate to close with another of her ideas. . . .

> Each of us called upon to take a stand. So in these days ahead, as we examie ourselves and each other, our works, our fears, our differences, our sisterhood and survivals, I urge you to tackle what is most difficult for us all, self-scrutiny of our complacencies, the idea that since each of us believes she is one the side of right, she need not examine her position (1985).

I urge you to examine your position.

REFERENCES

1. Acker, Joan. 1994a. The Gender Regime of Swedish Banks. *Scandinavian Journal of Management* 10, no. 2: 117–30.
2. Acker, Joan, and Donald Van Houston. 1974. Differential Recruitment and Control: The Sex Structuring of Organizations. *Administrative Science Quarterly* 19 (June, 1974): 152–63.
3. Amott, Teresa, and Julie Matthaei. 1996. *Race, Gender, and Work: A Multi-cultural Economic History of Women in the United States.* Revised edition. Boston: South End Press.
4. Benería, Lourdes. 1999. Globalization, Gender and the Davos Man. *Feminist Economics* 5, no. 3: 61–83.
5. Bremner, Robert H. 1956. *From the Depths: The Discovery of Poverty in the United States.* New York: New York University Press.
6. Brodkin, Karen. 1998. Race, Class, and Gender: The Metaorganization of American Capitalism. *Transformine Anthropology* 7, no. 2: 46–57.
7. Brown, Michael K., Martin Carnoy, Elliott Currie, Troy Duster, David B. Oppenheimer, Marjorie M. Shultz, and David Wellman. 2003. *White-Washing Race: The Myth of a Color-Blind Society.* Berkeley: University of California Press.
8. Burris, Beverly H. 1996. Technocracy, Patriarchy and Management. In *Men as Managers, Managers as Men,* ed. David L. Collinson and Jeff Hcarn. London: Sage.
9. Cockburn, Cynthia. 1983. *Brothers* London: Pluto Press.
10. ———. 1991. *In the Way of Women: Men's Resistance to Sex Equality in Organization.* Ithaca, N.Y.: ILR Press.
11. Cohn, Samuel. 1985. *The Process of Occupational Sex-Typing: The Femininization of Clerical Labor in Great Britain,* Philadelphia: Temple University Press.

12. Collins, Patricia Hill. 2000. *Black Feminist Thought,* second edition, New York and London: Routledge.
13. Collinson, David L., and Jeff Hearn. 1996. Breaking the Silence: On Men, Masculinities and Managements. In *Men as Managers, Managers as Men,* ed. David L. Collinson and Jeff Hearns. London: Sage.
14. Connell, R. W. 2000. *The Men and the Boys.* Berkeley: University of California Press.
15. ———. 1995. *Masculinities,* Berkeley: University of California Press.
16. ———. 1987. *Gender & Power,* Stanford, Calif.: Stanford University Press.
17. Figart, Deborah M., Ellen Mutarl, and Marilyn Power. 2002. *Living Wages, Equal Wages.* London and New York: Routledge.
18. Foner, Philip S. 1947. *History of the Labor Movement in the United States.* New York: International Publishers.
19. Frankel, Linda. 1984. Southern Textile Women: Generations of Survival and Struggle. In *My Troubles Are Going to Have Trouble with Me,* ed. Karen Brodkin Sacks and Dorothy Remy. New Brunswick, N.J.: Rulgers University Press.
20. Glenn, Evelyn Nakano. 2002. *Unequal Freedom: How Race and Gender Shaped American Citizenship and Labor.* Cambridge: Harvard University Press.
21. Goldin, Claudia. 1990. *Understanding the Gender Gap: An Economic History of American Women.* New York and Oxford: Oxford University Press.
22. Gutman, Herbert G. 1976. *Work, Culture Society in Industrializing America.* New York: Alfred A. Knopf.
23. Hartmann, Heidi. 1976. Capitalism, Patriarchy, and Job Segregation by Sex. *Sigus* 1, no. 3, part 2: 137–69.
24. Hearn, Jeff. 1996. Is Masculinity Dead? A Critique of the Concept of Masculinity/Masculinities. In *Understanding Masculinities: Social Relations and Cultural Arenas,* ed. M. Mac an Ghaill. Buckingham: Oxford University Press.
25. ———. 2004. From Hegomonic Masculinity to the Hegemony of Men. *Feminist Theory* 5, no. 1: 49–72.
26. Hearn, Jeff, and Wendy Parkin. 2001. *Gender, Sexuality and Violence in Organizations.* London: Sage.
27. Janiewski, Dolores. 1996. Southern Honour, Southern Dishonour: Managerial Ideology and the Construction of Gender, Race, and Class Relations in Southern Industry. In *Feminism & History,* ed. Joan Wallach Scott. Oxford: Oxford University Press.
28. Kanter, Rosabeth Moss. 1977. *Men and Women of the Corporation.* New York: Basic Books.
29. Keister, Lisa, 2000. *Wealth in America: Trends in Wealth Inequality.* Cambridge: Cambridge University Press.
30. Kessler-Harris, Alice. 1982. *Out to Work: A History of Wage-Earning Women in the United States,* New York: Oxford University Press.
31. Kilbourne, Barbara, Paula England, and Kurt Beron. 1994. Effects of Individual, Occupational, and Industrial Characteristics on Earnings: Intersections of Race and Gender. *Social Forces* 72: 1149–76.
32. McDowell, Linda. 1997. A Tale of Two Cities? Embedded Organizations and Embodied Workers in the City of London. In *Geographies of Economies,* ed. Roger Lee and Jane Willis, 118–29. London: Arnold.
33. Middleton, Chris. 1983. Patriarchal Exploitation and the Rise of English Capitalism. In *Gender, Class and Work,* ed. Eva Gamarnikow, David H. J. Morgan, June Purvis, and Daphne E. Taylorson. London: Heinemann.
34. Milton, David. 1982. *The Politics of U.S. Labor: From the Great Depression to the New Deal.* New York: Monthly Review Press.
35. Omi, Michael, and Howard Winant. 1994. *Racial Formation in the United States.* New York: Routledge.
36. Padavic, Irene, and Barbara Reskin. 2002. *Women and Men at Work,* second edition. Thousand Oaks, Calif.: Pine Forge Press.
37. Perrow, Charles. 2002. *Organizing America.* Princeton and Oxford: Princeton University Press.
38. Read, Rosslyn. 1996. Entrepreneurialism and Paternalism in Australian Management: A Gender Critique of the "Self-Made" Man. In *Men as Managers, Managers as Men,* ed. David L. Collinson and Jeff Hearn. London: Sage.
39. Reskin, Barbara F., Debra B. McBrier, and Julie A. Kmec. 1999. The Determinants and Consequences of Workplace Sex and Race Composition. *Annual Review of Sociology* vol. 25: 335–61.
40. Royster, Deirdre A. 2003. *Race and the Invisible Hand: How White Networks Exclude Black Men from Blue-Collar Jobs.* Berkeley: University of California Press.
41. Seidler, Victor J. 1989. *Rediscovering Masculinity: Renson, Language, and Sexuality.* London and New York: Routledge.
42. Taylor, Paul F. 1992. *Bloody Harlan: The United Mine Workers in Harlan County, Kentucky, 1931–1941.* Lanham, Md.: University Press of America.
43. Wacjman, Judy. 1998. *Managing Like a Man.* Cambridge: Polity Press.
44. Williams, Eric. 1944. *Capitalism and Slavery.* Chapel Hill: University of North Carolina Press.

12

What White Supremacists Taught a Jewish Scholar About Identity

ABBY L. FERBER

A few years ago, my work on white supremacy led me to the neo-Nazi tract *The New Order,* which proclaims: "The single serious enemy facing the white man is the Jew." I must have read that statement a dozen times. Until then, I hadn't thought of myself as the enemy.

When I began my research for a book on race, gender, and white supremacy, I could not understand why white supremacists so feared and hated Jews. But after being immersed in newsletters and periodicals for months, I learned that white supremacists imagine Jews as the masterminds behind a great plot to mix races and, thereby, to wipe the white race out of existence.

The identity of white supremacists, and the white racial purity they espouse, requires the maintenance of secure boundaries. For that reason, the literature I read described interracial sex as "the ultimate abomination." White supremacists see Jews as threats to racial purity, the villains responsible for desegregation, integration, the civil-rights movement, the women's movement, and affirmative action—each depicted as eventually leading white women into the beds of black men. Jews are believed to be in control everywhere, staging a multipronged attack against the white race. For *WAR*, the newsletter of White Aryan Resistance, the Jew "promotes a thousand social ills . . . [f]or which you'll have to foot the bills."

Reading white-supremacist literature is a profoundly disturbing experience, and even more difficult if you are one of those targeted for elimination. Yet, as a Jewish woman, I found my research to be unsettling in unexpected ways. I had not imagined that it would involve so much self-reflection. I knew white supremacists were vehemently anti-Semitic, but I was ambivalent about my Jewish identity and did not see it as essential to who I was. Having grown up in a large Jewish community, and then having attended a college with a large Jewish enrollment, my Jewishness was invisible to me—something I mostly ignored. As I soon learned, to white supremacists, that is irrelevant.

Contemporary white supremacists define Jews as non-white: "not a religion, they are an Asiatic *race,* locked in a mortal conflict with Aryan man," according to *The New Order.* In fact, throughout white-supremacist tracts, Jews are described not merely as a separate race, but as an impure race, the product of mongrelization. Jews, who pose the ultimate threat to racial boundaries, are themselves imagined as the product of mixed-race unions.

Although self-examination was not my goal when I began, my research pushed me to explore the contradictions in my own racial identity. Intellectually, I knew that the meaning of race was not rooted in biology or genetics, but it was only through researching the white-supremacist movement that I gained a more-personal understanding of the social construction of race. Reading white-supremacist literature, I moved between two worlds: one where I was white, another where I was the non-white seed of Satan; one where I was privileged, another where I was despised; one where I was safe and secure, the other where I was feared and thus marked for death.

According to white-supremacist ideology, I am so dangerous that I must be eliminated. Yet, when I put down the racist, anti-Semitic newsletters, leave my office, and walk outdoors, I am white.

Growing up white has meant growing up privileged. Sure, I learned about the historical persecution of Jews, overheard the hushed references to distant relatives lost in the Holocaust. I knew of my grandmother's experiences with anti-Semitism as a child of the only Jewish family in a Catholic neighborhood. But those were just stories to me. Reading white supremacists finally made the history real.

While conducting my research, I was reminded of the first time I felt like an "other." Arriving in the late 1980s for the first day of graduate school in the Pacific Northwest, I was greeted by a senior graduate student with the welcome: "Oh, you're the Jewish one." It was a jarring remark, for it immediately set me apart. This must have been how my mother felt, I thought, when, a generation earlier, a college classmate had asked to see her horns. Having lived in predominantly Jewish communities, I had never experienced my Jewishness as "otherness." In fact, I did not even *feel* Jewish. Since moving out of my parents' home, I had not celebrated a Jewish holiday or set foot in a synagogue. So it felt particularly odd to be identified by this stranger as a Jew. At the time, I did not feel that the designation described who I was in any meaningful sense.

But whether or not I define myself as Jewish, I am constantly defined by others that way. Jewishness is not simply a religious designation that one may choose, as I once naïvely assumed. Whether or not I see myself as Jewish does not matter to white supremacists.

I've come to realize that my own experience with race reflects the larger historical picture for Jews. As whites, Jews today are certainly a privileged group in the United States. Yet the history of the Jewish experience demonstrates precisely what scholars mean when they say that race is a social construction.

At certain points in time, Jews have been defined as a non-white minority. Around the turn of the last century, they were considered a separate, inferior race, with a distinguishable biological identity justifying discrimination and even genocide. Today, Jews are generally considered white, and Jewishness is largely considered merely a religious or ethnic designation. Jews, along with other European ethnic groups, were welcomed into the category of "white" as beneficiaries of one of the largest affirmative-action programs in history—the 1944 GI Bill of Rights. Yet, when I read white-supremacist discourse, I am reminded that my ancestors were excluded from the dominant race, persecuted, and even killed.

Since conducting my research, having read dozens of descriptions of the murders and mutilations of "race traitors" by white supremacists, I now carry with me the knowledge that there are many people out there who would still wish to see me dead. For a brief moment, I think that I can imagine what it must feel like to be a person of color in our society . . . but then I realize that, as a white person, I cannot begin to imagine that.

Jewishness has become both clearer and more ambiguous for me. And the questions I have encountered in thinking about Jewish identity highlight the central issues involved in studying race today. I teach a class on race and ethnicity, and usually, about midway through the course, students complain of confusion. They enter my course seeking answers to the most troubling and divisive questions of our time, and are disappointed when they discover only more questions. If race is not biological or genetic, what is it? Why, in some states, does it take just one black ancestor out of 32 to make a person legally black, yet those 31 white ancestors are not enough to make that person white? And, always, are Jews a race?

I have no simple answers. As Jewish history demonstrates, what is and is not a racial designation, and who is included within it, is unstable and changes over time—and that designation is always tied to power. We do not have to look far to find other examples: The Irish were also once considered non-white in the United States, and U.S. racial categories change with almost every census.

My prolonged encounter with the white-supremacist movement forced me to question not only my own assumptions about Jewish identity, but also my assumptions about whiteness. Growing up "white," I felt raceless. As it is for most white people, my race was invisible to me. Reflecting the assumption of most research on race at the time, I saw race as something that shaped the lives of people of color—the victims of racism. We are not used to thinking about whiteness when we think about race. Consequently, white people like myself have failed to recognize the ways in which our own lives are shaped by race. It was not until others began identifying me as the Jew, the "other," that I began to explore race in my own life.

Ironically, that is the same phenomenon shaping the consciousness of white supremacists: They embrace their racial identity at the precise moment when they feel their privilege and power under attack. Whiteness historically has equaled power, and when that equation is threatened, their own whiteness becomes visible to many white people for the first time. Hence, white supremacists seek to make racial identity, racial hierarchies, and white power part of the natural order again. The notion that race is a social construct threatens that order. While it has become an academic commonplace to assert that race is socially constructed, the revelation is profoundly unsettling to many, especially those who benefit most from the constructs.

My research on hate groups not only opened the way for me to explore my own racial identity, but also provided insight into the question with which I began this essay: Why do white supremacists express such hatred and fear of Jews? The ambiguity in Jewish racial identity is precisely what white supremacists find so threatening. Jewish history reveals race as a social designation, rather than a God-given or genetic endowment. Jews blur the boundaries between whites and people of color, failing to fall securely on either side of the divide. And it is ambiguity that white supremacists fear most of all.

I find it especially ironic that, today, some strict Orthodox Jewish leaders also find that ambiguity threatening. Speaking out against the high rates of intermarriage among Jews and non-Jews, they issue dire warnings. Like white supremacists, they fear assaults on the integrity of the community and fight to secure its racial boundaries, defining Jewishness as biological and restricting it only to those with Jewish mothers. For both white supremacists and such Orthodox Jews, intermarriage is tantamount to genocide.

For me, the task is no longer to resolve the ambiguity, but to embrace it. My exploration of white-supremacist ideology has revealed just how subversive doing so can be: Reading white-supremacist discourse through the lens of Jewish experience has helped me toward new interpretations. White supremacy is not a movement just about hatred, but even more about fear: fear of the vulnerability and instability of white identity and privilege. For white supremacists, the central goal is to naturalize racial identity and hierarchy, to establish boundaries.

Both my own experience and Jewish history reveal that to be an impossible task. Embracing Jewish identity and history, with all their contradictions, has given me an empowering alternative to white-supremacist conceptions of race. I have found that eliminating ambivalence does not require eliminating ambiguity.

13

Is Capitalism Gendered and Racialized?

JOAN ACKER

The class practices, or practices of provisioning, . . . are, of course, aspects of the ongoing functioning of capitalism. . . . I make the claim that capitalism as an organization of production and distribution is gen-

dered and racialized. I argue, along with R. W. Connell (1987) that "gender divisions . . . are a deepseated feature of production itself. . . . They are not a hangover from pre-capitalist modes of production" (103–104). The same is true for race divisions. I explore the ways in which capitalism can be seen as gendered and racialized and what this analysis means for understanding the ongoing production of gendered and racialized class practices and outcomes such as continuing gender and race segregation and divisions of labor. This exploration builds upon the valuable insights in socialist feminist work of the 1970s and early 1980s.

Although talk about globalizing capitalism is common today, class relations are usually seen as situated within particular nation-states and are usually analyzed within national boundaries. Good reasons exist for doing this: Nation-states and their gendered and racialized class structures have differing national characteristics produced by different political, social, and economic histories. However, to see the historical relations through which capitalism emerged in different countries as gendered and racially structured, a broader view is helpful. Therefore, in the following discussion, which deals primarily with the United States, I give some attention to processes that span state boundaries, or are transnational from the beginning. Organizations are critical locations for many of the activities and practices that comprise capitalism and class. The development of large organizations shaped and still shapes changing class processes (Perrow 2002) that are at the same time gender and race processes. Therefore, looking at these processes requires paying attention to organizations and what people do within them to create, implement, or oppose the practices that constitute relations of power and exploitation. I discuss some actions taken in the name of organizations in this chapter, . . .

Capitalism is racialized and gendered in two intersecting historical processes. First, industrial capitalism emerged in the United States dominated by white males, with a gender- and race-segregated labor force, laced with wage inequalities, and a society-wide gender division of caring labor. The processes of reproducing segregation and wage inequality changed over time, but segregation and inequality were not eliminated. A small group of white males still dominate the capitalist economy and its politics. The society-wide gendered division of caring labor still exists. Ideologies of white masculinity and related forms of consciousness help to justify capitalist practices. In short, conceptual and material practices that construct capitalist production and markets, as well as beliefs supporting those practices, are deeply shaped through gender and race divisions of labor and power and through constructions of white masculinity.

Second, these gendered and racialized practices are embedded in and replicated through the gendered substructures of capitalism. These gendered substructures exist in ongoing incompatible organizing of paid production activities and unpaid domestic and caring activities. Domestic and caring activities are devalued and seen as outside the "main business" (Smith 1999) of capitalism. The commodification of labor, the capitalist wage form, is an integral part of this process, as family provisioning and caring become dependent upon wage labor. The abstract language of bureaucratic organizing obscures the ongoing impact on families and daily life. At the same time, paid work is organized on the assumption that reproduction is of no concern. The separations between paid production and unpaid life-sustaining activities are maintained by corporate claims that they have no responsibility for anything but returns to shareholders. Such claims are more successful in the United States, in particular, than in countries with stronger labor movements and welfare states. These often successful claims contribute to the corporate processes of establishing their interests as more important than those of ordinary people.

THE GENDERED AND RACIALIZED DEVELOPMENT OF U.S. CAPITALISM

Segregations and Wage Inequalities

Industrial capitalism is historically, and in the main continues to be, a white male project, in the sense that white men were and are the innovators, owners, and holders of power.[1] Capitalism developed in Britain and then in Europe and the United States in societies that were already dominated by white men and already contained a gender-based division of labor. The emerging waged labor force was sharply divided by gender, as well as by race and ethnicity with many variations by nation and regions within nations. At the same time, the gendered division of labor in domestic tasks was reconfigured and incorporated in a gendered division between paid market labor and unpaid domestic labor. In the United States, certain white men, unburdened by caring for children and households and already the major wielders of gendered power, buttressed at least indirectly by the profits from slavery and the exploitation of other minorities, were, in the nineteenth century, those who built the U.S. factories and railroads, and owned and managed the developing capitalist enterprises.[2] As far as we know, they were also heterosexual and mostly of Northern European heritage. Their wives and daughters benefited from the wealth they amassed and contributed in symbolic and social ways to the perpetuation of their class, but they were not the architects of the new economy.[3]

Recruitment of the labor force for the colonies and then the United States had always been transnational and often coercive.[4] Slavery existed prior to the development of industrialism in the United States: Capitalism was built partly on profits from that source.[5] Michael Omi and Howard Winant (1994, 265) contend that the United States was a racial dictatorship for 258 years, from 1607 to 1865. After the abolition of slavery in 1865, severe exploitation, exclusion, and domination of blacks by whites perpetuated racial divisions cutting across gender and some class divisions, consigning blacks to the most menial, low-paying work in agriculture, mining, and domestic service. Early industrial workers were immigrants. For example, except for the brief tenure (twenty-five years) of young, native-born white women workers in the Lowell, Massachusetts mills, immigrant women and children were the workers in the first mass production industry in the United States, the textile mills of Massachusetts and Philadelphia, Pennsylvania (Perrow 2002). This was a gender and racial/ethnic division of labor that still exists, but now on a global basis. Waves of European immigrants continued to come to the United States to work in factories and on farms. Many of these European immigrants, such as impoverished Irish, Poles, and eastern European Jews were seen as non-white or not-quite-white by white Americans and were used in capitalist production as low-wage workers, although some of them were actually skilled workers (Brodkin 1998). The experiences of racial oppression built into industrial capitalism varied by gender within these racial/ethnic groups.

Capitalist expansion across the American continent created additional groups of Americans who were segregated by race and gender into racial and ethnic enclaves and into low-paid and highly exploited work. This expansion included the extermination and expropriation of native peoples, the subordination of Mexicans in areas taken in the war with Mexico in 1845, and the recruitment of Chinese and other Asians as low-wage workers, mostly on the west coast (Amott and Matthaei 1996; Glenn 2002).[6]

Women from different racial and ethnic groups were incorporated differently than men and differently than each other into developing capitalism in the late nineteenth and early twentieth centuries. White Euro-American men moved from farms into factories or commercial, business, and administrative jobs. Women aspired to be housewives as the male breadwinner family became the ideal. Married white women, working class and middle class, were housewives unless unemployment, low wages, or death of their husbands made their paid work necessary (Goldin 1990, 133). Young white women with some secondary education moved into the expanding clerical jobs and into elementary school teaching when white men with sufficient education were unavailable (Cohn 1985). African Americans, both women and men, continued to be confined to menial work, although some were becoming factory workers, and even teachers and professionals as black schools and colleges were formed (Collins 2000). Young women from first- and second-generation European immigrant families worked in factories and offices. This is a very sketchy outline of a complex process (Kessler-Harris 1982), but the overall point is that the capitalist labor force in the United States emerged as

deeply segregated horizontally by occupation and stratified vertically by positions of power and control on the basis of both gender and race.

Unequal pay patterns went along with sex and race segregation, stratification, and exclusion. Differences in the earnings and wealth (Keister 2000) of women and men existed before the development of the capitalist wage (Padavic and Reskin 2002). Slaves, of course, had no wages and earned little after abolition. These patterns continued as capitalist wage labor became the dominant form and wages became the primary avenue of distribution to ordinary people. Unequal wages were justified by beliefs about virtue and entitlement. A living wage or a just wage for white men was higher than a living wage or a just wage for white women or for women and men from minority racial and ethnic groups (Figart, Mutari, and Power 2002). African-American women were at the bottom of the wage hierarchy.

The earnings advantage that white men have had throughout the history of modern capitalism was created partly by their organization to increase their wages and improve their working conditions. They also sought to protect their wages against the competition of others, women and men from subordinate groups (for example, Cockburn 1983, 1991). This advantage also suggests a white male coalition across class lines, (Connell 2000; Hartmann 1976), based at least partly in beliefs about gender and race differences and beliefs about the superior skills of white men. White masculine identity and self-respect were complexly involved in these divisions of labor and wages.[7] This is another way in which capitalism is a gendered and racialized accumulation process (Connell 2000). Wage differences between white men and all other groups, as well as divisions of labor between these groups, contributed to profit and flexibility, by helping to maintain growing occupational areas, such as clerical work, as segregated and low paid. Where women worked in manufacturing or food processing, gender divisions of labor kept the often larger female work force in low-wage routine jobs, while males worked in other more highly paid, less routine, positions (Acker and Van Houten 1974). While white men might be paid more, capitalist organizations could benefit from this "gender/racial dividend." Thus, by maintaining divisions, employers could pay less for certain levels of skill, responsibility, and experience when the worker was not a white male.

This is not to say that getting a living wage was easy for white men, or that most white men achieved it. Labor-management battles, employers' violent tactics to prevent unionization, massive unemployment during frequent economic depressions characterized the situation of white industrial workers as wage labor spread in the nineteenth and early twentieth centuries.[8] During the same period, new white-collar jobs were created to manage, plan, and control the expanding industrial economy. This rapidly increasing middle class was also stratified by gender and race. The better-paid, more respected jobs went to white men; white women were secretaries and clerical workers; people of color were absent. Conditions and issues varied across industries and regions of the country. But, wherever you look, those variations contained underlying gendered and racialized divisions. Patterns of stratification and segregation were written into employment contracts in work content, positions in work hierarchies, and wage differences, as well as other forms of distribution.

These patterns persisted, although with many alterations, through extraordinary changes in production and social life. After World War II, white women, except for a brief period immediately after the war, went to work for pay in the expanding service sector, professional, and managerial fields. African Americans moved to the North in large numbers, entering industrial and service sector jobs. These processes accelerated after the 1960s, with the civil rights and women's movements, new civil rights laws, and affirmative action. Hispanics and Asian Americans, as well as other racial/ethnic groups, became larger proportions of the population, on the whole finding work in low-paid, segregated jobs. Employers continued, and still continue, to select and promote workers based on gender and racial identifications, although the processes are more subtle, and possibly less visible, than in the past. (for example, Brown et al. 2003; Royster 2003).[9] These processes continually recreate gender and racial

inequities, not as cultural or ideological survivals from earlier times, but as essential elements in present capitalisms (Connell 1987, 103–106).

Segregating practices are a part of the history of white, masculine-dominated capitalism that establishes class as gendered and racialized. Images of masculinity support these practices, as they produce a taken-for-granted world in which certain men legitimately make employment and other economic decisions that affect the lives of most other people. Even though some white women and people from other-than-white groups now hold leadership positions, their actions are shaped within networks of practices sustained by images of masculinity (Wacjman 1998).

Masculinities and Capitalism

Masculinities are essential components of the ongoing male project, capitalism. While white men were and are the main publicly recognized actors in the history of capitalism, these are not just any white men. They have been, for example, aggressive entrepreneurs or strong leaders of industry and finance (Collinson and Hearn 1996). Some have been oppositional actors, such as self-respecting and tough workers earning a family wage, and militant labor leaders. They have been particular men whose locations within gendered and racialized social relations and practices can be partially captured by the concept of masculinity. "Masculinity" is a contested term. As Connell (1995, 2000), Hearn (1996), and others have pointed out, it should be pluralized as "masculinities," because in any society at any one time there are several ways of being a man. "Being a man" involves cultural images and practices. It always implies a contrast to an unidentified femininity.[10]

Hegemonic masculinity can be defined as the taken-for-granted, generally accepted form, attributed to leaders and other influential figures at particular historical times. Hegemonic masculinity legitimates the power of those who embody it. More than one type of hegemonic masculinity may exist simultaneously, although they may share characteristics, as do the business leader and the sports star at the present time. Adjectives describing hegemonic masculinities closely follow those describing characteristics of successful business organizations, as Rosabeth Moss Kanter (1977) pointed out in the 1970s. The successful CEO and the successful organization are aggressive, decisive, competitive, focused on winning and defeating the enemy, taking territory from others.[11] The ideology of capitalist markets is imbued with a masculine ethos. As R. W. Connell (2000, 35) observes, "The market is often seen as the antithesis of gender (marked by achieved versus ascribed status, etc.). But the market operates through forms of rationality that are historically masculine and involve a sharp split between instrumental reason on the one hand, emotion and human responsibility on the other" (Seidler 1989). Masculinities embedded in collective practices, are part of the context within which certain men made and still make the decisions that drive and shape the ongoing development of capitalism. We can speculate that how these men see themselves, what actions and choices they feel compelled to make and they think are legitimate, how they and the world around them define desirable masculinity, enter into that decision making (Reed 1996). Decisions made at the very top reaches of (masculine) corporate power have consequences that are experienced as inevitable economic forces or disembodied social trends. At the same time, these decisions symbolize and enact varying hegemonic masculinities (Connell 1995). However, the embeddedness of masculinity within the ideologies of business and the market may become invisible, seen as just part of the way business is done. The relatively few women who reach the highest positions probably think and act within these strictures.

Hegemonic masculinities and violence[12] are deeply connected within capitalist history: The violent acts of those who carried out the slave trade or organized colonial conquests are obvious examples. Of course, violence has been an essential component of power in many other socioeconomic systems, but it continues into the rational organization of capitalist economic activities. Violence is frequently a legitimate, if implicit, component of power exercised by bureaucrats as well as "robber barons." Metaphors of violence, frequently military violence, are often linked to notions of the masculinity of corporate leaders, as "defeating the enemy" suggests. In contemporary capitalism, violence and its links to masculinity are often masked by the seeming impersonality of objective conditions. For example, the masculinity of top managers, the ability to be tough, is involved in the implicit violence of many corporate decisions, such as those cutting jobs in order to raise profits and, as a result, producing unemployment. Armies and other organizations, such as the police, are specifically organized around violence. Some observers of recent history suggest that organized violence, such as the use of the military, is still mobilized at least partly to reach capitalist goals, such as controlling access to oil supplies. The masculinities of those making decisions to deploy violence in such a way are hegemonic, in the sense of powerful and exemplary. Nevertheless, the connections between masculinity, capitalism, and violence are complex and contradictory, as Jeff Hearn and Wendy Parkin (2001) make clear. Violence is always a possibility in mechanisms of control and domination, but it is not always evident, nor is it always used.

As corporate capitalism developed, Connell (1995) and others (for example, Burris 1996) argue that a hegemonic masculinity based on claims to expertise developed alongside masculinities organized around domination and control. Hegemonic masculinity relying on claims to expertise does not necessarily lead to economic organizations free of domination and violence, however (Hearn and Parkin 2001). Hearn and Parkin (2001) argue that controls relying on both explicit and implicit violence exist in a wide variety of organizations, including those devoted to developing new technology.

Different hegemonic masculinities in different countries may reflect different national histories, cultures, and change processes.[13] For example, in Sweden in the mid-1980s, corporations were changing the ways in which they did business toward a greater participation in the international economy, fewer controls on currency and trade, and greater emphasis on competition. Existing images of dominant masculinity were changing, reflecting new business practices. This seemed to be happening in the banking sector, where I was doing research on women and their jobs

(Acker 1994a). The old paternalistic leadership, in which primarily men entered as young clerks expecting to rise to managerial levels, was being replaced by young, aggressive men hired as experts and managers from outside the banks. These young, often technically trained, ambitious men pushed the idea that the staff was there to sell bank products to customers, not, in the first instance, to take care of the needs of clients. Productivity goals were put in place; nonprofitable customers, such as elderly pensioners, were to be encouraged not to come into the bank and occupy the staff's attention. The female clerks we interviewed were disturbed by these changes, seeing them as evidence that the men at the top were changing from paternal guardians of the people's interests to manipulators who only wanted riches for themselves. The confirmation of this came in a scandal in which the CEO of the largest bank had to step down because he had illegally taken money from the bank to pay for his housing. The amount of money was small; the disillusion among employees was huge. He had been seen as a benign father; now he was no better than the callous young men on the way up who were dominating the daily work in the banks. The hegemonic masculinity in Swedish banks was changing as the economy and society were changing.

Hegemonic masculinities are defined in contrast to subordinate masculinities. White working class masculinity, although clearly subordinate, mirrors in some of its more heroic forms the images of strength and responsibility of certain successful business leaders. The construction of working class masculinity around the obligations to work hard, earn a family wage, and be a good provider can be seen as providing an identity that both served as a social control and secured male advantage in the home. That is, the good provider had to have a wife and probably children for whom to provide. Glenn (2002) describes in some detail how this image of the white male worker also defined him as superior to and different from black workers.

Masculinities are not stable images and ideals, but shifting with other societal changes. With the turn to neoliberal business thinking and globalization, there seem to be new forms. Connell (2000)

identifies "global business masculinity," while Lourdes Benería (1999) discusses the "Davos man," the global leader from business, politics, or academia who meets his peers once a year in the Swiss town of Davos to assess and plan the direction of globalization. Seeing masculinities as implicated in the ongoing production of global capitalism opens the possibility of seeing sexualities, bodies, pleasures, and identities as also implicated in economic relations.

In sum, gender and race are built into capitalism and its class processes through the long history of racial and gender segregation of paid labor and through the images and actions of white men who dominate and lead central capitalist endeavors. Underlying these processes is the subordination to production and the market of nurturing and caring for human beings, and the assignment of these responsibilities to women as unpaid work. Gender segregation that differentially affects women in all racial groups rests at least partially on the ideology and actuality of women as carers. Images of dominant masculinity enshrine particular male bodies and ways of being as different from the female and distanced from caring. . . . , I argue that industrial capitalism, including its present neoliberal form, is organized in ways that are, at the same time, antithetical and necessary to the organization of caring or reproduction and that the resulting tensions contribute to the perpetuation of gendered and racialized class inequalities. Large corporations are particularly important in this process as they increasingly control the resources for provisioning but deny responsibility for such social goals.

NOTES

1. Omi and Winant (1994) develop the notion of *project* to discuss racial formation. This is a helpful notion that I borrow to assist in thinking about capitalism and class, but use in a somewhat different way. To think about the development of capitalism as a project or as many projects brings actors' bodies and activities, as well as the cultural representation of those bodies and activities of actors, into a central place in "processes."
2. The male identity of the leaders of industrialization is obvious in every history of the process. See, for example, Gutman (1976) or Perrow (2002).

3. Chris Middleton (1983) argued that, in Britain, male heads of households in the emerging capitalist class appropriated the labor of members of the household, including wives and daughters. In the process, patriarchal power was reorganized and women in this class actually saw the range of their contributions to production shrink as they were excluded from various occupations and economic sectors.
4. There is a huge literature on the working lives of women, their history, and present configurations. See, for example, Kessler-Harris (1982), Amott and Matthaei (1996), Glenn (2002) for histories and Padavic and Reskin (2002) for a contemporary overview.
5. See Eric Williams (1944).
6. While race/ethnicity-based dominations of colonial peoples were built into capitalist development in Britain and European countries, these patterns of racial exploitation and oppression did not become integrated into gender and class processes within national boundaries until after World War II. Each country had a different history of colonialism, different labor force recruitment policies in the postwar period, and different policies in regard to immigration. All of these patterns result in different racial patterns, different problems today.
7. For example, Dolores Janiewski (1996) shows how preexisting race and gender ideologies, along with employers' commitments to maintaining the existing sexual and racial order, shaped Southern managerial strategies in the textile and tobacco industries.
8. Many histories of labor struggles exist. See, for example, Foner (1947), Taylor (1992), Milton (1982). For examples of women's participation in labor struggles, see Frankel (1984) and Kessler-Harris (1982).
9. For interpretations of the processes and policies resulting in hierarchical segregation, horizontal segregation between occupations, and manual and non-manual work and the pay gap, see Reskin, McBrier, and Kmec (1999) and Kilbourne, England, and Beron (1994).
10. Connell (2000) defines masculinities as "configurations of practice within gender relations, a structure that includes large-scale institutions and economic relations as well as face-to-face relationships and sexuality" (29). The referent of "masculinities" is often ambiguous (Connell 1995). "Configurations of practice within gender relations" could refer to ideologies, images, ideals, myths, or behaviors and emotions of actual men. Moreover, masculinities are often changing, reproduced through organizational and institutional practices, social interaction, and through images, ideals, myths, or representations of behaviors and emotions. Jeff Hearn (2004) reviews the problems with the concept "hegemonic masculinity" and proposes that talking about "the hegemony of men" and dropping the notion of masculinity may solve some of these problems.
11. Although prescriptions for successful management have included in the last few years human relations skills and softer, more emotional and supportive approaches to supervision usually identified with femininity, these have not, it seems to me, disturbed the images of hegemonic masculinities. See Wacjman (1998).

12. Violence is another ambiguous term. Jeff Hearn and Wendy Parkin (2001) in *Gender, Sexuality and Violence in Organizations,* include sexual harassment and bullying along with physical violence and expand the concept to include "violation," which denotes a wide variety of actions that demean, coerce, and intimidate within work organizations.
13. Linda McDowell's (1997) study of merchant bankers in London describes another embodied hegemonic masculinity, a manly, heterosexual, class-based masculinity that dominates and disempowers many "others."

REFERENCES

1. Acker, Joan. 1994a. The Gender Regime of Swedish Banks. *Scandinavian Journal of Management* 10, no. 2: 117–30.
2. Acker, Joan, and Donald Van Houten. 1974. Differential Recruitment and Control: The Sex Structuring of Organizations. *Administrative Science Quarterly* 19 (June, 1974): 152–63.
3. Amott, Teresa, and Julie Matthaei. 1996. *Race, Gender, and Work: A Multi-cultural Economic History of Women in the United States.* Revised edition. Boston: South End Press.
4. Benería, Lourdes. 1999. Globalization, Gender and the Davos Man. *Feminist Economics* 5, no. 3: 61–83.
5. Bremner, Robert H. 1956. *From the Depths: The Discovery of Poverty in the United States.* New York: New York University Press.
6. Brodkin, Karen. 1998. Race, Class, and Gender: The Metaorganization of American Capitalism. *Transforming Anthropology* 7, no. 2: 46–57.
7. Brown, Michael K., Martin Carnoy, Elliott Currie, Troy Duster, David B. Oppenhcimer, Marjorie M. Shultz, and David Wellman. 2003. *White-Washing Race: The Myth of a Color-Blind Society.* Berkeley: University of California Press.
8. Burris, Beverly H. 1996. Technocracy, Patriarchy and Management. In *Men as Managers, Managers as Men,* ed. David L. Collinson and Jeff Hearn. London: Sage.
9. Cockburn, Cynthia. 1983. *Brothers* London: Pluto Press.
10. ———. 1991. *In the Way of Women: Men's Resistance to Sex Equality in Organization.* Ithaca, N.Y: ILR Press.
11. Cohn, Samuel. 1985. *The Process of Occupational Sex-Typing: The Femininization of Clerical Labor in Great Britain.* Philadelphia: Temple University Press.
12. Collins, Patricia Hill. 2000. *Black Feminist Thought,* second edition. New York and London: Routledge.
13. Collinson, David L., and Jeff Hearn. 1996. Breaking the Silence: On Men, Masculinities and Managements. In *Men as Managers, Managers as Men,* ed. David L. Collinson and Jeff Hearns. London: Sage.
14. Connell, R. W. 2000. *The Men and the Boys.* Berkeley: University of California Press.
15. ———. 1995. *Masculinities.* Berkeley: University of California Press.
16. ———. 1987, *Gender & Power.* Stanford, Calif: Stanford University Press.

17. Ferguson, Sue. 1999. Building on the Strengths of the Socialist Feminist Tradition. *New Politics,* 7, 2 (new series), whole no. 26.

18. Figart, Deborah M., Ellen Mutari, and Marilyn Power. 2002. *Living Wages, Equal Wages.* London and New York: Routledge.

19. Foner, Philip S. 1947. *History of the Labor Movement in the United States.* New York: International Publishers.

20. Frankel, Linda. 1984. Southern Textile Women: Generations of Survival and Struggle. In *My Troubles Are Going to Have Trouble with Me,* ed. Karen Brodkin Sacks and Dorothy Remy. New Brunswick, N.J.: Rutgers University Press.

21. Glenn, Evelyn Nakano. 2002. *Unequal Freedom: How Race and Gender Shaped American Citizenship and Labor.* Cambridge: Harvard University Press.

22. Goldin, Claudia. 1990. *Understanding the Gender Gap: An Economic History of American Women.* New York and Oxford: Oxford University Press.

23. Gutman, Herbert G. 1976. *Work, Culture, Society in Industrializing America.* New York: Alfred A. Knopf.

24. Hartmann, Heidi. 1976. Capitalism, Patriarchy, and Job Segregation by Sex. *Signs* 1, no. 3, part 2: 137–69.

25. Hearn, Jeff. 1996. Is Masculinity Dead? A Critique of the Concept of Masculinity/Masculinities. In *Understanding Masculinities: Social Relations and Cultural Arenas,* ed. M. Mac an Ghaill. Buckingham: Oxford University Press.

26. ———. 2004. From Hegemonic Masculinity to the Hegemony of Men. *Feminist Theory* 5, no. 1: 49–72.

27. Hearn, Jeff, and Wendy Parkin. 2001. *Gender, Sexuality and Violence in Organizations.* London: Sage.

28. Janiewski, Dolores. 1996. Southern Honour, Southern Dishonour: Managerial Ideology and the Construction of Gender, Race, and Class Relations in Southern Industry. In *Feminism & History,* ed. Joan Wallach Scott. Oxford: Oxford University Press.

29. Kanter, Rosabeth Moss. 1977. *Men and Women of the Corporation.* New York: Basic Books.

30. Keister, Lisa. 2000. *Wealth in America: Trends in Wealth Inequality.* Cambridge: Cambridge University Press.

31. Kessler-Harris, Alice. 1982. *Out to Work: A History of Wage-Earning Women in the United States.* New York: Oxford University Press.

32. Kilbourne, Barbara, Paula England, and Kurt Beron. 1994. Effect of Individual, Occupational, and Industrial Characteristics on Earnings: Intersections of Race and Gender. *Social Forces* 72: 1149–76.

33. McDowell, Linda. 1997. A Tale of Two Cities? Embedded Organizations and Embodied Workers in the City of London. In *Geographies of Economies,* ed. Roger Lee and Jane Willis, 118–29. London: Arnold.

34. Middleton, Chris. 1983. Patriarchal Exploitation and the Rise of English Capitalism. In *Gender, Class and Work,* ed. Eva Gamarnikow, David H. J. Morgan, June Purvis, and Daphne E. Taylorson. London: Heinemann.

35. Milton, David. 1982. *The Politics of U.S. Labor: From the Great Depression to the New Deal.* New York: Monthly Review Press.

36. Omi, Michael, and Howard Winant. 1994. *Racial Formation in the United States.* New York: Routledge.

37. Padavic, Irene, and Barbara Reskin. 2002. *Women and Men at Work,* second edition. Thousand Oaks, Calif.: Pine Forge Press.

38. Perrow, Charles. 2002. *Organizing America.* Princeton and Oxford: Princeton University Press.

39. Reed, Rosslyn. 1996. Entrepreneurialism and Paternalism in Australian Management: A Gender Critique of the "Self-Made" Man. In *Men as Managers, Managers as Men,* ed. David L. Collinson and Jeff Hearn. London: Sage.

40. Reskin, Barbara F., Debra B. McBrier, and Julie A. Kmec. 1999. The Determinants and Consequences of Workplace Sex and Race Composition. *Annual Review of Sociology* vol. 25: 335–61.

41. Royster, Deirdre A. 2003. *Race and the Invisible Hand: How White Networks Exclude Black Men from Blue-Collar Jobs.* Berkeley: University of California Press.

42. Seidler, Victor J. 1989. *Rediscovering Masculinity: Reason, Language,* and *Sexuality.* London and New York: Routledge.

43. Taylor, Paul F. 1992. *Bloody Harlan: The United Mine Workers in Harlan County, Kentucky, 1931–1941.* Lanham, Md.: University Press of America.

44. Wacjman, Judy. 1998. *Managing Like a Man.* Cambridge: Polity Press.

45. Williams, Eric. 1944. *Capitalism and Slavery.* Chapel Hill: University of North Carolina Press.

 # 14

Theorizing Difference from Multiracial Feminism

MAXINE BACA ZINN AND BONNIE THORNTON DILL

Women of color have long challenged the hegemony of feminisms constructed primarily around the lives of white middle-class women. Since the late 1960s, U.S. women of color have taken issue with unitary theories of gender. Our critiques grew out of the widespread concern about the exclusion of women of color from feminist scholarship and the misinterpretation of our experiences,[1] and ultimately "out of the very discourses, denying, permitting, and producing difference."[2] Speaking simultaneously from "within and against" *both* women's liberation *and* antiracist movements, we have insisted on the need to challenge systems of domination.[3] not merely as gendered subjects but as women whose lives are affected by our location in multiple hierarchies.

Recently, and largely in response to these challenges, work that links gender to other forms of domination is increasing. In this article, we examine this connection further as well as the ways in which difference and diversity infuse contemporary feminist studies. Our analysis draws on a conceptual framework that we refer to as "multiracial feminism."[4] This perspective is an attempt to go beyond a mere recognition of diversity and difference among women to examine structures of domination, specifically the importance of race in understanding the social construction of gender. Despite the varied concerns and multiple intellectual stances which characterize the feminisms of women of color, they share an emphasis on race as a primary force situating genders differently. It is the centrality of race, of institutionalized racism, and of struggles against racial oppression that link the various feminist perspectives within this framework. Together, they demonstrate that racial meanings offer new theoretical directions for feminist thought.

TENSIONS IN CONTEMPORARY DIFFERENCE FEMINISM

Objections to the false universalism embedded in the concept "women" emerged within other discourses as well as those of women of color.[5] Lesbian feminists and postmodern feminists put forth their own versions of what Susan Bordo has called "gender skepticism."[6]

Many thinkers within mainstream feminism have responded to these critiques with efforts to contextualize gender. The search for women's "universal" or "essential" characteristics is being abandoned. By examining gender in the context of other social divisions and perspectives, difference has gradually become important—even problematizing the universal categories of "women" and "men." Sandra Harding expresses the shift best in her claim that "there are no gender relations *per se,* but only

gender relations as constructed by and between classes, races, and cultures."[7]

Many feminists now contend that difference occupies center stage as *the* project of women studies today.[8] According to one scholar, "difference has replaced equality as the central concern of feminist theory."[9] Many have welcomed the change, hailing it as a major revitalizing force in U.S. feminist theory.[10] But if *some* priorities within mainstream feminist thought have been refocused by attention to difference, there remains an "uneasy alliance"[11] between women of color and other feminists.

If difference has helped revitalize academic feminisms, it has also "upset the apple cart" and introduced new conflicts into feminist studies.[12] For example, in a recent and widely discussed essay, Jane Rowland Martin argues that the current preoccupation with difference is leading feminism into dangerous traps. She fears that in giving privileged status to a predetermined set of analytic categories (race, ethnicity, and class), "we affirm the existence of nothing but difference." She asks, "How do we know that for us, difference does not turn on being fat, or religious, or in an abusive relationship?"[13]

We, too, see pitfalls in some strands of the difference project. However, our perspectives take their bearings from social relations. Race and class differences are crucial, we argue, not as individual characteristics (such as being fat) but insofar as they are primary organizing principles of a society which locates and positions groups within that society's opportunity structures.

Despite the much-heralded diversity trend within feminist studies, difference is often reduced to mere pluralism: a "live and let live" approach where principles of relativism generate a long list of diversities which begin with gender, class, and race and continue through a range of social structures as well as personal characteristics.[14] Another disturbing pattern, which bell hooks refers to as "the commodification of difference," is the representation of diversity as a form of exotica, "a spice, seasoning that livens up the dull dish that is mainstream white culture."[15] The major limitation of these approaches is the failure to attend to the power relations that accompany difference. Moreover, these approaches ignore the inequalities that cause some characteristics to be seen as "normal" while others are seen as "different" and thus, deviant.

Maria C. Lugones expresses irritation at those feminists who see only the *problem* of difference without recognizing *difference*.[16] Increasingly, we find that difference is recognized. But this in no way means that difference occupies a "privileged" theoretical status. Instead of using difference to rethink the category of women, difference is often a euphemism for women who differ from the traditional norm. Even in purporting to accept difference, feminist pluralism often creates a social reality that reverts to universalizing women:

> So much feminist scholarship assumes that when we cut through all of the diversity among women created by differences of racial classification, ethnicity, social class, and sexual orientation, a "universal truth" concerning women and gender lies buried beneath. But if we can face the scary possibility that no such certainty exists and that persisting in such a search will always distort or omit someone's experiences, with what do we replace this old way of thinking? Gender differences and gender politics begin to look very different if there is no essential woman at the core.[17]

WHAT IS MULTIRACIAL FEMINISM?

A new set of feminist theories has emerged from the challenges put forth by women of color. Multiracial feminism is an evolving body of theory and practice informed by wide-ranging intellectual traditions. This framework does not offer a singular or unified feminism but a body of knowledge situating women and men in multiple systems of domination. U.S. multiracial feminism encompasses several emergent perspectives developed primarily by women of color: African Americans, Latinas, Asian Americans, and Native Americans, women whose analyses are shaped by their unique perspectives as "outsiders within"—marginal intellectuals whose social locations provide them with a particular perspective on self and society.[18] Although U.S. women of color represent many races and ethnic backgrounds—

with different histories and cultures—our feminisms cohere in their treatment of race as basic social division, a structure of power, a focus of political struggle, and hence a fundamental force in shaping women's and men's lives.

This evolving intellectual and political perspective uses several controversial terms. While we adopt the label "multiracial," other terms have been used to describe this broad framework. For example, Chela Sandoval refers to "U.S. Third World feminisms,"[19] while other scholars refer to "indigenous feminisms." In their theory text-reader, Alison M. Jagger and Paula S. Rothenberg adopt the label "multicultural feminism."[20]

We use "multiracial" rather than "multicultural" as a way of underscoring race as a power system that interacts with other structured inequalities to shape genders. Within the U.S. context, race, and the system of meanings and ideologies which accompany it, is a fundamental organizing principle of social relationships.[21] Race affects all women and men, although in different ways. Even cultural and group differences among women are produced through interaction within a racially stratified social order. Therefore, although we do not discount the importance of culture, we caution that cultural analytic frameworks that ignore race tend to view women's differences as the product of group-specific values and practices that often result in the marginalization of cultural groups which are then perceived as exotic expressions of a normative center. Our focus on race stresses the social construction of differently situated social groups and their varying degrees of advantage and power. Additionally, this emphasis on race takes on increasing political importance in an era where discourse about race is governed by color-evasive language[22] and a preference for individual rather than group remedies for social inequalities. Our analyses insist upon the primary and pervasive nature of race in contemporary U.S. society while at the same time acknowledging how race both shapes and is shaped by a variety of other social relations.

In the social sciences, multiracial feminism grew out of socialist feminist thinking. Theories about how political economic forces shape women's lives were influential as we began to uncover the social causes of racial ethnic women's subordination. But socialist feminism's concept of capitalist patriarchy, with its focus on women's unpaid (reproductive) labor in the home, failed to address racial differences in the organization of reproductive labor. As feminists of color have argued, "reproductive labor has divided along racial as well as gender lines, and the specific characteristics have varied regionally and changed over time as capitalism has reorganized."[23] Despite the limitations of socialist feminism, this body of literature has been especially useful in pursuing questions about the interconnections among systems of dominations.[24]

Race and ethnic studies was the other major social scientific source of multiracial feminism. It provided a basis for comparative analyses of groups that are socially and legally subordinated and remain culturally distinct within U.S. society. This includes the systematic discrimination of socially constructed racial groups and their distinctive cultural arrangements. Historically, the categories of African American, Latino, Asian American, and Native American were constructed as both racially and culturally distinct. Each group has a distinctive culture, shares a common heritage, and has developed a common identity within a larger society that subordinates them.[25]

We recognize, of course, certain problems inherent in an uncritical use of the multiracial label. First, the perspective can be hampered by a biracial model in which only African Americans and whites are seen as racial categories and all other groups are viewed through the prism of cultural differences. Latinos and Asians have always occupied distinctive places within the racial hierarchy, and current shifts in the composition of the U.S. population are racializing these groups anew.[26]

A second problem lies in treating multiracial feminism as a single analytical framework, and its principal architects, women of color, as an undifferentiated category. The concepts "multiracial feminism," "racial ethnic women," and "women of color" "homogenize quite different experiences and can falsely universalize experiences across race, ethnicity, sexual orientation, and age."[27] The feminisms created by women of color exhibit a plurality of intellectual and political positions. We speak in many voices, with inconsistencies that are born of our different social locations. Multiracial feminism embodies this plurality and richness. Our intent is not to falsely universalize women of color. Nor do we wish to promote a new racial essentialism in place of the old gender essentialism. Instead, we use these concepts to examine the structures and experiences produced by intersecting forms of race and gender.

It is also essential to acknowledge that race is a shifting and contested category whose meanings construct definitions of all aspects of social life.[28] In the United States it helped define citizenship by excluding everyone who was not a white, male property owner. It defined labor as slave or free, coolie or contract, and family as available only to those men whose marriages were recognized or whose wives could immigrate with them. Additionally, racial meanings are contested both within groups and between them.[29]

Although definitions of race are at once historically and geographically specific, they are also transnational, encompassing diasporic groups and crossing traditional geographic boundaries. Thus, while U.S. multiracial feminism calls attention to the fundamental importance of race, it must also locate the meaning of race within specific national traditions.

THE DISTINGUISHING FEATURES OF MULTIRACIAL FEMINISM

By attending to these problems, multiracial feminism offers a set of analytic premises for thinking about and theorizing gender. The following themes distinguish this branch of feminist inquiry.

First, multiracial feminism asserts that gender is constructed by a range of interlocking inequalities, what Patricia Hill Collins calls a "matrix of domination."[30] The idea of a matrix is that several fundamental systems work with and through each other. People experience race, class, gender, and sexuality differently depending upon their social location in the structures of race, class, gender, and sexuality. For example, people of the same race will experience race differently depending upon their location in the class structure as working class, professional managerial class, or unemployed; in the gender structure as female or male; and in structures of sexuality as heterosexual, homosexual, or bisexual.

Multiracial feminism also examines the simultaneity of systems in shaping women's experience and identity. Race, class, gender, and sexuality are not reducible to individual attributes to be measured and assessed for their separate contribution in explaining given social outcomes, an approach that Elizabeth Spelman call "popbead metaphysics," where a woman's identity consists of the sum of parts neatly divisible from one another.[31] The matrix of domination seeks to account for the multiple ways that women experience themselves as gendered, raced, classed, and sexualized.

Second, multiracial feminism emphasizes the intersectional nature of hierarchies at all levels of social life. Class, race, gender, and sexuality are components of both social structure and social interaction. Women and men are differently embedded in locations created by these cross-cutting hierarchies. As a result, women and men throughout the social order experience different forms of privilege and subordination, depending on their race, class, gender, and sexuality. In other words, intersecting forms of domination produce *both* oppression *and* opportunity. At the same time that structures of race, class, and gender create disadvantages for women of color, they provide unacknowledged benefits for those who are at the top of these hierarchies—whites, members of the upper classes, and males. Therefore, multiracial feminism applies not only to racial ethnic women but also to women and men of all races, classes, and genders.

Third, multiracial feminism highlights the relational nature of dominance and subordination. Power is the cornerstone of women's differences.[32] This means that women's differences are *connected* in systematic ways.[33] Race is a vital element in the pattern of relations among minority and white women. As Linda Gordon argues, the very meanings of being a white woman in the United States have been affected by the existence of subordinated women of color: "They intersect in conflict and in occasional cooperation, but always in mutual influence."[34]

Fourth, multiracial feminism explores the interplay of social structure and women's agency. Within the constraints of race, class, and gender oppression, women create viable lives for themselves, their families, and their communities. Women of color have resisted and often undermined the forces of power that control them. From acts of quiet dignity and steadfast determination to involvement in revolt and rebellion, women struggle to shape their own lives. Racial oppression has been a common focus of the "dynamic of oppositional agency" of women of color. As Chandra Talpade Mohanty points out, it is the nature and organization of women's opposition which mediates and differentiates the impact of structures of domination.[35]

Fifth, multiracial feminism encompasses wide-ranging methodological approaches, and like other branches of feminist thought, relies on varied theoretical tools as well. Ruth Frankenberg and Lata Mani identify three guiding principles of inclusive feminist inquiry: "building complex analyses, avoiding erasure, specifying location."[36] In the last decade, the opening up of academic feminism has focused attention on the social location in the production of knowledge. Most basically, research by and about marginalized women has destabilized what used to be considered as universal categories of gender. Marginalized locations are well suited for grasping social relations that remained obscure from more privileged vantage points. Lived experience, in other words, creates alternative ways of understanding the social world and the experience of different groups of women within it. Racially informed standpoint epistemologies have provided new topics, fresh questions, and new understandings of women and men. Women of color have, as Norma Alarcón argues, asserted ourselves as subjects, using our voices to challenge dominant conceptions of truth.[37]

Sixth, multiracial feminism brings together understandings drawn from the lived experiences of diverse and continuously changing groups of women. Among Asian Americans, Native Americans, Latinas, and Blacks are many different national cultural and ethnic groups. Each one is engaged in the process of testing, refining, and reshaping these broader categories in its own image. Such internal differences heighten awareness of and sensitivity of both commonalities and differences, serving as a constant reminder of the importance of comparative study and maintaining a creative tension between diversity and universalization.

DIFFERENCE AND TRANSFORMATION

Efforts to make women's studies less partial and less distorted have produced important changes in academic feminism. Inclusive thinking has provided a way to build multiplicity and difference into our analyses. This has led to the discovery that race matters for everyone. White women, too, must be reconceptualized as a category that is multiply defined by race, class, and other differences. As Ruth Frankenberg demonstrates in a study of whiteness among contemporary women, all kinds of social relations, even those that appear neutral, are, in fact, racialized. Frankenberg further complicates the very notion of a unified white identity by introducing issues of Jewish identity.[38] Therefore, the lives of women of color cannot be seen as a *variation* on a more general model of white American womanhood. The model of womanhood that feminist social science once held as "universal" is also a product of race and class.

When we analyze the power relations constituting all social arrangements and shaping women's lives in distinctive ways, we can begin to grapple with core feminist issues about how genders are socially constructed and constructed differently. Women's difference is built into our study of gender. Yet this perspective is quite far removed from the atheoretical pluralism implied in much contemporary thinking about gender.

Multiracial feminism, in our view, focuses not just on differences but also on the way in which differences and domination intersect and are historically and socially constituted. It challenges feminist scholars to go beyond the mere recognition and inclusion of difference to reshape the basic concepts and theories of our disciplines. By attending to women's social location based on race, class, and gender, multiracial feminism seeks to clarify the structural sources of diversity. Ultimately, multiracial feminism forces us to see privilege and subordination as interrelated and to

pose such questions as: How do the existences and experiences of all people—men and women, different racial-ethnic groups, and different classes—shape the experiences of each other? How are those relationships defined and reinforced through social institutions that are the primary sites for negotiating power within society? How do these differences contribute to the construction of both individual and group identity? Once we acknowledge that all women are affected by the racial order of society, then it becomes clear that the insights of multiracial feminism provide an analytical framework, not solely for understanding the experiences of women of color but for understanding all women, and men, as well.

NOTES

1. Maxine Baca Zinn, Lynn Weber Cannon, Elizabeth Higginbotham, and Bonnie Thornton Dill, "The Costs of Exclusionary Practices in Women's Studies," *Signs* 11 (winter 1986): 290–303.
2. Chela Sandoval, "U.S. Third World Feminism: The Theory and Method of Oppositional Consciousness in the Postmodern World," *Genders* (spring 1991): 1–24.
3. Ruth Frankenberg and Lata Mani, "Cross Currents, Crosstalk: Race, 'Postcoloniality,' and the Politics of Location," *Cultural Studies* 7 (May 1993): 292–310.
4. We use the term "multiracial feminism" to convey the multiplicity of racial groups and feminist perspectives.
5. A growing body of work on difference in feminist thought now exists. Although we cannot cite all the current work, the following are representative: Michèle Barrett, "The Concept of Difference," *Feminist Review* 26 (July 1987): 29–42; Christina Crosby, "Dealing with Difference," in *Feminists Theorize the Political*, ed. Judith Butler and Joan W. Scott (New York: Routledge, 1992), 130–43; Elizabeth Fox-Genovese, "Difference, Diversity, and Divisions in an Agenda for the Women's Movement," in *Color, Class, and Country: Experiences of Gender*, ed. Gay Young and Bette J. Dickerson (London: Zed Books, 1994), 232–48; Nancy A. Hewitt, "Compounding Differences," *Feminist Studies* 18 (summer 1992): 313–26; Maria C. Lugones, "On the Logic of Feminist Pluralism," in *Feminist Ethics*, ed. Claudia Card (Lawrence: University of Kansas Press, 1991), 35–44; Rita S. Gallin and Anne Ferguson, "The Plurality of Feminism: Rethinking 'Difference,'" in *The Woman and International Development Annual* (Boulder. Westview Press, 1993), 3: 1–16; and Linda Gordon, "On Difference," *Genders* 10 (spring 1991): 91–111.
6. Susan Bordo, "Feminism, Postmodernism, and Gender Skepticism," in *Feminism/Postmodernism*, ed. Linda J. Nicholson (London: Routledge, 1990), 133–56.
7. Sandra G. Harding. *Whose Science? Whose Knowledge? Thinking from Women's Lives* (Ithaca: Cornell University Press, 1991), 179.

8. Crosby, 131.

9. Fox-Genovese, 232.

10. Faye Ginsberg and Anna Lowenhaupt Tsing, Introduction to *Uncertain Terms: Negotiating Gender in American Culture,* ed. Faye Ginsburg and Anna Lownhaupt Tsing (Boston: Beacon Press, 1990), 3.

11. Sandoval, 2.

12. Sandra Morgan, "Making Connections: Socialist-Feminist Challenges to Marxist Scholarship," in *Women and a New Academy: Gender and Cultural Contexts,* ed. Jean F. O'Barr (Madison: University of Wisconsin Press, 1989), 149.

13. Jane Rowland Martin, "Methodological Essentialism, False Difference, and Other Dangerous Traps," *Signs* 19 (spring 1994): 647.

14. Barrett, 32.

15. bell hooks, *Black Looks: Race and Representation* (Boston: South End Press, 1992), 21.

16. Lugones, 35–44.

17. Patricia Hill Collins, Foreword to *Women of Color in U.S. Society,* ed. Maxine Baca Zinn and Bonnie Thornton Dill (Philadelphia: Temple University Press, 1994), xv.

18. Patricia Hill Collins, "Learning from the Outsider Within: The Sociological Significance of Black Feminist Thought," *Social Problems* 33 (December 1986): 514–32.

19. Sandoval, 1.

20. Alison M. Jagger and Paula S. Rothenberg. *Feminist Frameworks: Alternative Theoretical Accounts of the Relations between Women and Men,* 3d ed. (New York: McGraw-Hill, 1993).

21. Michael Omi and Howard Winant, *Racial Formation in the United States: From the 1960s to the 1980s,* 2d ed. (New York: Routledge, 1994).

22. Ruth Frankenberg, *The Social Construction of Whiteness: White Women, Race Matters* (Minneapolis: University of Minnesota Press, 1993).

23. Evelyn Nakano Glenn, "From Servitude to Service Work: Historical Continuities in the Racial Division of Paid Reproductive Labor," *Signs* 18 (autumn 1992): 3. See also Bonnie Thornton Dill, "Our Mothers' Grief: Racial-Ethnic Women and the Maintenance of Families," *Journal of Family History* 13, no. 4 (1988): 415–31.

24. Morgan, 146.

25. Maxine Baca Zinn and Bonnie Thornton Dill, "Difference and Domination," in *Women of Color in U.S. Society* (1994): 11–12.

26. See Omi and Winant, 53–76, for a discussion of racial formation.

27. Margaret L. Andersen and Patricia Hill Collins, *Race, Class, and Gender: An Anthology* (Belmont, Calif.: Wadsworth, 1992), xvi.

28. Omi and Winant.

29. Nazli Kibria, "Migration and Vietnamese American Women: Remaking Ethnicity," in *Women of Color in U.S. Society* (1994): 247–61.

30. Patricia Hill Collins, *Black Feminist Thought: Knowledge. Consciousness, and the Politics of Empowerment* (Boston: Unwin Hyman, 1990).

31. Elizabeth Spelman, *Inessential Women: Problems of Exclusion in Feminist Thought* (Boston: Beacon Press, 1988), 136.

32. Several discussions of difference make this point. See Baca Zinn and Thornton Dill, 10; Gordon, 106; and Lynn Weber, in the "Symposium on West and Fenstermaker's 'Doing Difference,'" *Gender & Society,* 9 (August 1995): 515–19.

33. Glenn, 10.

34. Gordon, 106.

35. Chandra Talpade Mohanty, "Cartographies of Struggle: Third World Women and the Politics of Feminism," in *Third World Women and the Politics of Feminism,* ed. Chandra Talpade Mohanty, Ann Russo, and Lourdes Torres (Bloomington: Indiana University Press, 1991), 13.

36. Frankeberg and Mani, 306.

37. Norma Alarçon, "The Theoretical Subject(s) of *This Bridge Called My Back* and Anglo-American Feminism," in *Making Face, Making Soul, Haciendo Caras: Creative and Critical Perspectives by Women of Color,* ed. Gloria Anzaldúa (San Francisco: Aunt Lute, 1990), 356.

38. Frankenberg. See also Evelyn Torton Beck, "The Politics of Jewish Invisibility," *NWSA Journal* (fall 1988): 93–102.

15

"You're Not a Real Boy If You're Disabled"

Boys Negotiating Physical Disability and Masculinity in Schools

WAYNE MARTINO AND MARIA PALLOTTA-CHIAROLLI

Interviewing boys with physical disabilities highlighted my inabilities. I had to visualize the geographic terrain differently, move within the familiar world as if it was unknown—which it became as I set out to remap, relocate, rethink the meanings and logistics of time and space and place.

How to get to the interviewee, how to physically position the interviewee's mouth, arms, legs, wheelchair, laptop in order to be clearly audio-taped, printed, written. How to get the interviewee from his locality to the researcher's office. Assumptions and taken-for-granted notions of motion, travel, time and space were disrupted and demanded immediate reinscription.

In what I thought was the known and easily traversed geographical, temporal and spatial terrain of my university grounds and university office, of footpaths and other public spaces on streets and in schools, I discovered a parallel world, one that had always been there but rendered invisible through my able-bodied impairment. In this world, lift buttons were unreachable, footpaths were potholed and treacherous, sheltering from the rain was not just a matter of opening an umbrella. New paths to my office needed to be found, my own office furniture needed to be shifted.

Boys and young men needed to be assisted into my car, wheelchairs dismantled while my fingers trembled in fear of breaking such vital equipment while struggling to understand the boy's polite and patient directions. Familiar lines and bumps in the palms of my hands being remapped by wheelchair tyre grease and dirt. The knees of my jeans dirty from gravel and mud where I had knelt to figure out how to take a wheelchair apart.

What was it like to be a young man being lifted, moved, pushed by a woman? What was it like to have to ask for everyday materials to be taken out of your bag slung unreachably behind you on the chair? What was it like to request a straw for the glass of water naively placed on the wheelchair tray by the researcher, to have to request the glass be brought closer to the mouth, to have to request that a cushion under one's neck be adjusted? These questions took up residence within me.

INTRODUCTION

In this chapter, we analyse the interweaving of physical disability and masculinity. There has been an absence of educational research on the multiple intersections of disability and gender in schools. Those who have undertaken research into disability in the wider society offer critiques and interrogations that need to be taken up in educational settings (Shakespeare 1999). An exploration of diversity within the category of disability is required, as well

as the way that oppression impacts differently on students with disabilities when interconnected with other factors such as gender, ethnicity and sexuality (Meekosha and Jakubowicz 2001). It is necessary to be aware of the variety of strategies employed by different boys to negotiate their masculinities and disabilities for in some ways, men with disabilities 'are never "real men": they don't have access to physical strength or social status in the conventional way' (Shakespeare 1999: 60).

Gilbert and Gilbert summarize the breadth and depth of concerns and issues that boys with physical disabilities must negotiate, and the potential for isolation and marginalization:

> if they are unable to conform to the demands for competence in aggressive and competitive performance or play, or do not match the image of the masculine body, or if they are not accepted as potential participants in the increasingly important arena of sexual relations . . . Disabled boys are subject to the same cultural images of masculinity as others; that it involves a denial of weakness, emotions and frailty. They will often value sport as much as those who are not disabled, and seek the same success and reward. Yet, disabled boys are often stigmatized as weak, pitiful, passive and dependent. They are often perceived as either asexual innocents or animals with little control over their sexual desires. They may also be subject to further marginalization if they differ from the dominant group in terms of 'race', class or sexuality.
>
> *(1998: 145)*

The following five aspects arose in our research:

1. *Being labelled disabled:* how the use of the label 'disability' evokes differing responses and self-ascriptions in relation to the fashioning and policing of one's masculinity.
2. *The borderland existences of boys with disabilities:* how physical disability interweaves with masculinity, ethnicity and sexuality as boys negotiate their multiple positionings on the borders.
3. *The disability/heterosexuality interface:* how boys with physical disabilities use various strategies of compensation and negotiation to achieve a

measure of normalization by the performance or fashioning of a heteronormative masculinity.

4. *Being harassed and harassing:* how boys with physical disabilities are positioned and position themselves within a social hierarchy of 'normal' and 'abnormal' masculinities.

5. *School as a site of the stigmatization of disabilities:* how schools are often complicit in perpetuating harassment and ignorance, and yet recognized by many boys as potential sites for the demystification of physical disabilities.

BEING LABELLED 'DISABLED'

Our research participants, both able-bodies and with disabilities, tended to perceive schools as sites that reinforce the idealization of the hegemonic embodiment of masculinity. As boys with physical disabilities explain, their bodies' appearances and movements are major signifiers of their lower positioning within the hierarchy of masculinities. In the following, Andrew exemplifies the power of normalizing discourses and practices within which he 'passes' as able-bodied and constructs a hierarchy of disabilities within which he situates himself as closer to 'normal':

> The word 'normal' means to be physically like everybody else. I would say I'm about 95 percent normal, yes. . . like I had friends who didn't actually know I was disabled until about a year afterwards. I think they thought I'd done something to my wrist because I had it in plaster and expected that I was going through some sort of recovery. They didn't actually know, didn't actually think that I was disabled, so that was a good feeling. I know a lot of people with disabilities, but do I hang out with them, no. A lot of the people I know with disabilities are in wheelchairs, mental impediments. I don't have the patience to put up with that sort of thing, and that's really terrible of me, but that's how I feel. All my friends that I hang out with aren't disabled.
>
> *(Andrew, 16 years)*

Andrew's attempts to 'pass' as 'normal', and his inferiorization of other boys with more severe physical disabilities, reflects the emphasis by some disability theorists on normalization principles. These discourses of disability are based on instructing people with disabilities on how to conform as much as possible to a socio-culturally prescribed embodied 'norm' rather than encouraging acceptance of embodied diversity (see Morris 1993). This requires the deployment of 'passing', 'covering', 'disavowal' and 'compensatory' strategies as performances of 'normal-bodies' (see Higgins 1992; Taleporos 1999, 2001; Loeser 2002). There is no recognition of the stigma/normativity dichotomy itself as a social construct. Boys such as Andrew invoke this kind of normalization in order to minimize and invisibilize the realities of bodies with various disabilities (Meissner and Thoreson 1967; Morris 1993; Meekosha and Jakubowicz 1996; Chappell 1997).

Normalizing practices are evoked and upheld by some theorists for people with disabilities in ways similar to assimilationist practices for culturally and sexually 'inferior' groups. Meekosha and Jakubowicz explore how the heteronormative gaze which 'frames the [normal] space . . . is a male gaze, with male able-bodied points of view, drawn with middle-class and white inflections' (1996: 89). An example of this 'gaze' is provided by Nick who discusses how boys with disabilities are constructed as 'abnormal' and inferiorized by some able-bodied boys: 'They think, "He's got a disability, he's not the same as us and we don't have to listen to him, he doesn't have normal feelings, we can tease him, he's not normal, he doesn't look like he's normal"' (Nick, 13 years).

For some boys with disabilities, the boundary between able-bodied and disable-bodied was not so demarcated. Bryce, for example, situates himself as living within a borderzone where he is dependent on a technical aid which allows for a fluidity between the hierarchically constructed duality of ability/disability (see Loeser 2002). He is not disabled, he is not abled, but occupies the 'inbetween-space' (Bhabha 1990b; Trinh 1991). He is confused with and dubious of the interviewer's simplistic definition of his hearing ability and attempts to provide her with an insight into the both/and intricacy of his situation:

Maria: Now some people would say that you have a disability, would you agree or disagree?
Bryce: Disability? [*looking confused and doubtful*] How do you mean?
Maria: Well, how would you describe yourself with your hearing aid, would you call that a disability?
Bryce: No, I can still hear, but if I took my hearing aid off I would say it's pretty much a disability.

(Bryce, 13 years)

People with disabilities such as Bryce contest their identity as deficit, as medical problems, and the dichotomous logics that society neatly comprises those who are able or 'normal' and those who are not. They also challenge the way the disability becomes the prime or sole signifier or identity marker. 'The person becomes "the disabled" . . . rather than being viewed as a complex, multifaceted, fully human person (Christensen 1996: 65; see also Morris 1991; Higgins 1992).

★ ★ ★

Boys with disabilities may attempt to use normative performances of masculinity as a way of resisting the disabled label while simultaneously experiencing masculinity as an oppressive social construct (Skord and Schumacher 1982; Asch and Sacks 1983; Morris 1993; Blinde and Taub 1999; Shakespeare 1999). Gerschick and Miller identified three different interwoven patterns which arise as men with disabilities try to come to terms with societal expectations and definitions:

- *'Reformulation':* whereby men with disabilities confront able-bodied standards of masculinity 'by reformulating it, shaping it along the lines of their own abilities, perceptions and strengths' (1994a: 34–7).
- *'Reliance':* whereby men unquestionably adopt particular normalizing practices of masculinity and 'despite their inability to meet many of these ideals, (these men) rely on them heavily' (1994a: 41).
- *'Rejection':* whereby men renounce hegemonic masculinist standards and either construct

their own principles or deny the importance of hegemonic masculinity in their lives. 'They have been able to create alternative gender practices' (1994b: 29–30).

Alan displays the tension between reliance and reformulation in relation to his participation in school sport. This example also points to the role played by harassment in the 'passing' and 'covering' strategies deployed by some boys with disabilities:

I cop all of my peers' abuse because I am not good at sport. This really pisses me off because I don't want to tell them that I am slow and poorly coordinated because then they will in turn treat me different again. And now as I get older my problems get worse because my back is starting to go on me, and I will be in a wheelchair by the time I am 25. For now I have found something I can do even when I am older and can't walk. It's computers. I have a gift with them so I am f___g happy again but still you get dickheads who think it is fun to try to ruin this for me.

(Alan, 16 years)

Indeed, for most of our research participants with physical disabilities, the sporting field became a major site for normalizing one's masculinity, despite medical and other recommendations not to participate in contact sports. Other boys wanted to participate in sport but found the kinds of sports offered do not cater for physical diversity. 'I don't do PE out of fear of embarrassing myself. I just can't get into it, it's just a fear of being laughed at basically. I stuff something up and people laugh at me' (Andrew, 16 years).

Several boys with disabilities such as Marc were able to interrogate their reformulation of dominant masculinity and reflected upon the fact that if it wasn't for the disability, hegemonic masculinity would have remained 'unquestioned and unquestionable' (Schutz 1944) in their lives:

I would have been either a full sporto, one of those really egotistical pricks. I know me for who I am, and I honestly feel that I'm pretty confident about myself . . . because I sit in a wheelchair and they think, 'Oh my God, he's not normal' and then as soon as I sing and I play music they think, 'Oh, maybe he's not so different after all'. I'm just a larrikin. I've got a disability, and I'm happy with it.

(Marc, 16 years)

Due to his status as 'normal', acquired and secured by his playing in a music band, Marc appeared to be comfortable self-ascribing as disabled. Thus, we can see how the strategic deployment of reformulation negotiations, wherein compensation for physical disability in traditional sports occurs in the form of other normative successes such as playing in a band, allows Marc to make decisions about the use of a wheelchair, otherwise a very visual marker of marginality: 'I chose to go in the wheelchair and everyone accepted it, and it's like being one of the guys.'

For Sam, also in a wheelchair, being disabled meant a rejection of dominant constructs of masculinity such as independence and a broader understanding of and empathy for other social differences:

> Well, [my friend] helps me, he doesn't mind doing things with me in a wheelchair that need doing— which is a lot, because I can't do anything practically myself. I think I do things more seriously. Other boys have more time to muck around. I have more time to think and I'm tolerant of people with differences.
>
> *(Sam, 16 years)*

Indeed, Sam was very aware of how other boys with disabilities adopted reliance strategies. He said they would 'act crazy' in order to fit in with able-bodied 'cool' boys, 'to be the same as anyone else'.

Able-bodies boys often appeared to be complicit in the need for boys with disabilities to 'be normal', such as participating in sport, for they commented very favourably on those boys with disabilities who participated in sports, despite the risks they knew they were taking: 'He's always having a go at things which I think a lot people really respect in him, he has a go at sport and all those sort of things' (Simon, 16 years).

Another example of reformulating notions of hegemonic masculinity is the way in which a wheelchair becomes incorporated as part of one's male body that can be used to simulate action and speed of a vehicle such as a car or the athletic masculine

body itself. Several able-bodied boys commented with admiration on how some boys with physical disabilities utilized their wheelchairs in 'cool' or 'tough' ways: 'He's got a mechanical one [wheelchair], so he drives by himself. He goes very fast . . . he loves driving it, you can tell' (Adam, 13 years). 'Everyone loves him. They just hang around him. They just all want to push him fast' (Josh, 13 years).

Other examples of compensatory or reactive masculinist behaviour, or the reliance upon traditional strategies of asserting one's masculinity among peers, were examples of boys with disabilities becoming involved in aggressive behaviours such as fighting and classroom disruption. While some disabled students resorted to fighting, harassing other students and creating classroom disruptions in an attempt to assert a normative masculinity, they were not disciplined by teachers in the same way that able-bodied boys were for engaging in these behaviours. In this sense, teachers were perceived to be perpetuating the marginalization of these boys by treating their 'normal' disruptive behaviour as 'abnormal' behaviour for boys with disabilities. Several able-bodied and disabled boys commented on how teachers constructed the latter as victims, even when they reclaimed some masculine status through aggressive and attention-seeking behaviour:

> I think that he does things to make people deliberately pay him out. Like he just starts fights with people . . . and just makes people hate him. He tries to act tough. I think they [teachers] are [aware] but they just don't do anything about it. They said they just didn't think it was serious, and they just let it go because he was disabled.
>
> *(Andrew, 16 years)*

★   ★   ★

'I GOT SEVEN CHICKS AFTER ME'
Crossing and Negotiating the Disability/Heterosexuality Interface

Boys with disabilities also find that their disability becomes a signifier of marginal heterosexual masculinity in relation to able-bodied girls. To be male and disabled, such as in a wheelchair, is to be 'impotent, unable to be a (hetero)sexual being, and therefore not a "complete" man' (Morris 1991: 96; Robillard and Fichten 1983; see also Tepper 1997). As Andrew, 16 years, illustrates: 'People think that just because I'm disabled I shouldn't be able to relate with girls, I shouldn't be able to talk to them. It's basically solitary confinement.'

This dominant discourse then constructs a situation in which a boy with a disability may utilize heterosexual relationships and the admiration and affirmation of girls as a measure of his 'normal' masculinity. For example, Kieran, who had a very noticeable speech impediment, believed that the stigma against his self-ascribed 'disability' in the social networks at school had diminished by his being personally affirmed by his girl friend: I'm more confident now . . . I'm not worried anymore. Being in a relationship with a girl, it makes you feel like you're worth something' (Kieran, 16 years).

Regarding the construction of a heterosexual disabled masculinity, there is often tension evident in boys not necessarily wanting to relate to girls who are disabled as this reinforces their own disability. Hence, in negotiating the subordinate disability/ dominant heterosexual masculinity interface, both able-bodied girls and disabled girls may become 'props' and signifiers of a disabled boy's location within the hierarchy of masculinities. This may occur even if the boy himself is not consciously aware of the classifying of girls in this way. In the following interview excerpt, Marc moves from a position of self-confidence and successful competition with able-bodied boys as a result of able-bodied girls becoming interested in him. He shifts to interrogating how boys utilize having a girlfriend as a marker of successful heterosexual masculinity, to a realization that he is implicated in the hierarchical classification and use of girls to build his own image. He is taken aback by the question of whether he would consider going out with a girl with a disability. He shifts from a confident, breezy conversational tone in the interview to one of hesitancy and concern. The research interview became a major point of inter-

vention and interrogation into his own social practices of masculinity that had been unquestioned and unquestionable:

Marc: Oh yes, I've had that [harassment from able-bodied boys], but now who's laughing? [*laughing proudly*] They say, 'if you have sex, will you break?' Because I break bones easy, they go, 'Does your dick break in half?' And then the music and band started, and then the chicks started in Year 9. As soon as I did start going out with girls it didn't matter if they [boys] were paying me out because I was having the last laugh because I actually was with a girl. It is a goal when you're at high school to have your first girlfriend and that's really not good [*disapproving look*].

Maria: Would you ever go out with a girl with a disability?

Marc: I'm not sure. [*Long pause, frowning and looking away from the interviewer.*] I'm not sure. [*Long pause, looking troubled, still looking away from the interviewer.*] I don't know. That's a good question. [*Long pause and sounding very troubled, very uncomfortable and confused.*] I'm not sure about that one.

(Marc, 16 years)

Hearing impaired Bryce was very clear about the kinds of interactions he would have with various differently abled girls and why. His hand gestures on the table, while he discussed the boundaries and hierarchies of these interactions, visibly demarcated the symbolic relational boundaries and hierarchies in place at the school:

I've had a fair few girlfriends . . . and mostly not deaf or anything. If it was a deaf girl it would be alright. But if it's someone at integration [with more severe physical disabilities] you don't feel comfortable. When you're going out with that girl you get teased a lot. Sometimes I tease them. I really shouldn't do it, but if you talk to them, then others call you dumb as well. It's like a puzzle. [*extends his arms along the table*]. If a boy here [*indicates a zone with his left hand*] likes a girl, and you want to fit into there [*indicates a zone with his right hand above his left hand zone*], if he went out with her, everyone would tease him because they don't really like her. She's, you know, not right . . . the good girls are the normal ones.

(Bryce, 13 years)

Being a boy with a disability that can be hidden is superior to a boy with a physical disability that is very obvious. This, in turn, is superior to a boy with an intellectual disability. And all of the above masculine variations are superior to being a girl with a disability, albeit with a gradation of disabilities being classifiable within the girls' group as well. 'Boys who have disabilities seek out attractive, caring women. Boys without a disabilities seek out attractive, caring women. Girls with disabilities are not usually sought out' (Hastings 1996: 116; see also Asch and Fine 1988, 1997). Thus, it is unsurprising that girls with disabilities evidence lower self-esteem than disabled boys (Deegan 1985; Taleporos 1999, 2001).

Another consequence of heteronormative and gendernormative frameworks is that boys with disabilities are likely to be labeled as gay and experience homophobic harassment (Shakespeare 1996, 1999). This is predominantly based on their embodied appearance and movements which may be constructed as effeminate. For example, Andrew, 16 years, who has cerebral palsy, is often called 'faggot' due to his inability to control the so-called 'limp-wristed' movements of his hand. He believes 'being disabled has probably made me more aware of, probably more sensitive to people's feelings. Like if someone's homosexual, that doesn't bother me in the slightest bit. If someone's black, it doesn't bother me either'. Nevertheless, Andrew finds being called 'gay' or 'faggot' more disturbing than being called 'spastic', again demonstrating the efficacy of hierarchical masculinities where mental disability is constructed as more appropriate and acceptable than homosexual masculinities. 'It's just been a prolonged thing with people calling me names. The traditional one is spastic. I don't take quite as much offence to that as to being called gay and faggot' (Andrew, 16 years).

★ ★ ★

'TO DIFFERENT PEOPLE I TALK DIFFERENTLY'
The Borderland Existences of Boys with Disabilities

The confusion or conflict that arises in some boys with disabilities of diverse cultures and sexualities can also be traced back to normalization practices and hierarchical dualisms that reinforce constructs of monoculturalism, homogeneity and universality (Meekosha and Jakubowicz 1996, 2001; Vernon 1998; Bryan 1999). Multiple Otherness can be experienced simultaneously and singularly, depending on the context, and oppression may be modified by the presence of some privileged identities, such as being disabled, but also being a male and/or from a higher class status. 'Policies for people who have multiple disabilities, come from non-English speaking backgrounds, live in a remote rural area and are poor have not yet been created. Not to mention being a girl as well!' (Hastings 1996: 115).

In some cases, borderland boys with disabilities may find that other facets of their lives provide points of connection with their peers. For example, in relation to Abdu's dwarfism, other boys from a Turkish Muslim background supported and befriended him due to shared cultural background and understandings: 'He's good to talk to and we know what's going on with him . . . because he's Turkish, that's why it's a bit easier for me to talk to him' (Mustafa, 15 years). In other cases, having a physical disability disrupted hegemonic constructs of masculinity upheld within a particular culture. For example, Tony talks about how being disabled was seen to exclude him from the expectations placed upon able-bodied Greek boys and men:

The disability totally threw into chaos the whole Greek expectation that your parents will have of you getting married, you know, doing the whole family deal . . . because of my disability those expectations just go away or probably won't be raised.

(Tony, 24 years)

Having a disability may also mean that the boy considers himself to be part of a disability culture that is the Other to the Central able-bodied culture. This was the experience of Bryce, who located himself within 'the deaf culture' with its own language. He was also aware of how he bordered the often conflicting duality of the deaf and hearing cultures. He wanted to belong to both and move fluidly between and within each culture, utilizing the communication skills of both 'signing and talking' rather than having to choose one form of language:

> There's a school that's just for the deaf. I don't feel comfortable with that, you're always hanging around deafies in that school. There are deaf people in the deaf world and the hearing world, I'm in both. I can sign and talk. To different people I talk differently . . . some people in the deaf culture didn't want my brother to teach me English because it's more like a hearing culture and not a deaf culture. My brother knows both cultures—hearing and deaf. I learned that from TV and books and teachers. It's like an Aboriginal culture and a white people culture.
>
> *(Bryce, 13 years)*

For boys who are disabled and same-sex attracted, they are twice removed from the polarity of 'normal' masculinity and able-bodied 'abnormal' homosexual masculinity. Their physical 'abnormalities' may be seen as compounded and intertwined with sexual 'abnormality' (Rivlin 1980; Rich 1994). The denial or invisibility of homosexuality is greatly exacerbated within education for the disabled. School sex education programmes seldom address homosexuality, let alone in relation to disability, so for young people with disabilities, the articulation of their sexuality with their disability may be especially problematic (Marks 1996; Tepper 1999): Tony discusses the interweaving of his homosexuality and disability within his overall borderland experiences of being on the fringes:

> I see my sexuality as very problematic to me because it's never really been affirmed in any way by any group so that I feel good about it. I am just going back into not identifying as a gay man anymore, you know, because I was rejected by the heterosexual community, and I didn't get accepted by the gay

community and so, why did I ever bother coming here?

> *(Tony, 24 years)*

Tony highlights how his disability has resulted in his sexual expression and desire being denied by both the heterosexual and gay communities, thereby forcing him to inhabit an asexual space of limbo in which his alienation and isolation are further accentuated.

★ ★ ★

CONCLUSION

Overall, it is apparent that boys with physical disabilities are faced with unique conflicts around their masculine identities at school. This is clearly a result of a normative regime of masculinity that affirms and valorizes many of the characteristics that physical disability may take away, including independence, physical strength and (hetero)sexual prowess. The conflict forces boys to rely on, reformulate and/or reject this regime of normalizing practices. In this chapter, therefore, we have drawn attention to the interweaving of masculinity, ethnicity and sexuality for boys who live with disabilities and who are positioned and position themselves within hierarchies informed by a particular sex/gender system.

REFERENCES

1. Asch, A. and Fine, M. (1988) Introduction: beyond pedestals, in M. Fine and A. Asch (eds) *Women with Disabilities: Essays in Psychology, Culture, and Politics*. Philadelphia: Temple University Press.
2. Asch, A. and Fine, M. (1997) Nurturance, sexuality and women with disabilities, in L.J. Davis (ed.) *The Disability Studies Reader*. New York: Routledge.
3. Asch, A. and Sacks, L. (1983) Lives without, lives within: autobiographies of blind men and women, *Journal of Visual Impairment and Blindness*, 77(6): 242–7.
4. Bhabha, H. (1990b) The third space, in J. Rutherford (ed.) *Identity: Community, Culture, Difference*. London: Lawrence & Wishart.
5. Blinde, E. and Taub, D. (1999) Personal empowerment through sport and physical fitness activity: perspectives from male college students with physical and sensory disabilities, *Journal of Sport Behavior*, 22(2): 181–2.
6. Bryan, W. (1999) *Multicultural Aspects of Disabilities: A Guide to Understanding Minorities in the Rehabilitation Process*. Springfield, IL: Charles C. Thomas.

7. Chappell, A. (1997) From normalisation to where?, in L. Barton and M. Oliver (eds) *Disability Studies: Past, Present and Future*. Leeds: Disability Press.

8. Christensen, C. (1996) Disabled, handicapped or disordered: what's in a name?, in C. Christensen and F. Rizvi (eds) *Disability and Dilemmas of Education and Justice*. Buckingham: Open University Press.

9. Deegan, M. (1985) Multiple minority groups: a case study of physically disabled women, in M.J. Deegan and N.A. Brooks (eds) *Women and Disability: The Double Handicap*. New Brunswick: Transaction Books.

10. Gerschick, T.J. and Miller, A.S. (1994a) Manhood and physical disability, *Changing Men*, 27: 25–30.

11. Gerschick, T.J. and Miller, A.S. (1994b) Gender identities at the crossroads of masculinity and disability, *Masculinities*, 2(1): 34–55.

12. Gilbert, P. and Gilbert, R. (1998) *Masculinity Goes to School*. Sydney: Allen & Unwin.

13. Hastings, E. (1996) Assumption, expectation and discrimination: gender issues for girls with disabilities, in Gender Equity Taskforce, *Gender Equity: A Framework for Australian Schools*. Canberra: Ministerial Council for Employment, Education, Training and Youth Affairs.

14. Higgins, P.C. (1992) *Making Disability: Exploring the Social Transformation of Human Variation*. Springfield, IL: Charles C. Thomas.

15. Loeser, C.J. (2002) Bounded bodies, mobile selves: the significance of the muscular body in young hearing-impaired men's constructions of masculinity, in S. Pearce and V. Muller (eds) *Manning the Millennium: Studies in Masculinities*. Curtin University of Technology, WA: Black Swan Press.

16. Marks, G. (1996) Coming out as gendered adults: gender, sexuality and disability, in C. Christensen and F. Rizvi (eds) *Disability and Dilemmas of Education and Justice*. Buckingham: Open University Press.

17. Meekosha, H. and Jakubowicz, A. (1996) Disability, participation, representation and social justice, in C. Christensen and F. Rizvi (eds) *Disability and Dilemmas of Education and Justice*. Buckingham: Open University Press.

18. Meekosha, H. and Jakubowicz, A. (2001) Disability studies dis/engages with multicultural studies. Paper for the Disability with Attitude Conference, UWS, 16 February.

19. Meissner, A.L. and Thoreson, R.W. (1967) Relation of self-concept to impact and obviousness of disability among male and female adolescents, *Perceptual and Motor Skills*, 24: 1099–1105.

20. Morris, J. (1991) *Pride against Prejudice: Transforming Attitudes to Disability*. London: Women's Press.

21. Morris, J. (1993) Prejudice, in J. Swain, V. Finkelstein, S. French and M. Oliver (eds) *Disabling Barriers—Enabling Environments*. London: Sage.

22. Rich, P. (1994) Coming out blind and gay: how I survived the straight and sighted, *Changing Men*, 27: 33–6.

23. Rivlin, M. (1980) The disabled gay—an appraisal, *Sexuality and Disability*, 3(3): 221–2.

24. Robillard, K. and Fichten, C. (1983) Attributions about sexuality and romantic involvement of physically disabled college students: an empirical study, *Sexuality and Disability*, 6(3/4): 197–212.

25. Schutz, A. (1944) The stranger: an essay in social psychology, *American Journal of Sociology*, 49(6): 499–507.

26. Shakespeare, T. (1996) Power and prejudice: issues of gender, sexuality and disability, in L. Barton (ed.) *Disability and Society: Emerging Issues and Insights*. London: Longman.

27. Shakespeare, T. (1999) The sexual politics of disabled masculinity, *Sexuality and Disability*, 17(1): 53–64.

28. Skord, K. and Schumacher, B. (1982) Masculinity as a handicapping condition, *Rehabilitation Literature*, 43(9–10): 284–8.

29. Taleporos, G. (1999) The inaccessible orgasm: sexual recreation for people with disabilities, *NICAN Network News*, 8(4): 7–8.

30. Taleporos, G. (2001) Sexuality and physical disability—healing the wounds of a flesh focused society, in C. Wood (ed.) *Sexual Positions: An Australian View*. Melbourne: Hill of Content.

31. Tepper, M.S. (1997) Living with a disability: a man's perspective, in M.L. Sipski and C.J. Alexander (eds) *Sexual Function in People with Disability and Chronic Illness: A Health Professional's Guide*. Maryland: Aspen Publishers.

32. Tepper, M. (1999) Letting go of restrictive notions of manhood: male sexuality, disability and chronic illness, *Sexuality and Disability*, 17(1): 37–52.

33. Trinh, M.T. (1991) *When the Moon Waxes Red*. New York: Routledge.

34. Vernon, A. (1998) Multiple oppression and the disabled people's movement, in T. Shakespeare (ed.) *The Disability Reader: Social Science Perspectives*. London: Cassell.

 16

Choosing Up Sides

JUDY SCALES-TRENT

"Whatever he does, he had better not bring home a white girlfriend!" she exclaimed. We laughed. There were three of us, black women friends who had gotten together after a long absence, talking about our lives, our work, our men, and, of course, our children. Her son was not yet a teenager and would not be bringing anyone home for quite a while, but she was already clear about his choices.

I laughed too, but I sensed a vague discomfort at her words. It took me awhile to understand that feeling. But I finally understood that I was uneasy because she had rejected part of me, the white part, with her statement. And I was uncomfortable—fearful that my disguise might not hold, fearful that she might suddenly "see" that I was a white black woman. Michelle Cliff says it well: "She who was part-them felt on trembling ground." I also finally recognized that my laughter was dishonest: why laugh at my own rejection? But I did laugh, I laughed because, at that moment, my hunger to belong to that group of friends was stronger than my ability to be true to myself.

I thought about this for days. And what kept returning to my mind during that period were thoughts of Grandpa Tate, my father's maternal grandfather and the only white blood relative I ever heard of. I know little enough about him. I know that he was born sometime in the 1860s, and that he was a barber. I know that he married my great-grandmother Mary in 1886. I think he loved and respected her: I have a silver-plated dish inscribed "1886–1911" that he gave her on the occasion of their twenty-fifth anniversary. I know he made enough money investing in real estate to raise ten children in comfort and send them off to college. I have a picture of Grandpa Tate with his wife and children, taken around 1905. They all look healthy and well dressed and well groomed. It is clear that Grandpa Tate took good care of them. I know he was white, of Scottish origins. I also know that his wife, and therefore all of his children, were black. I think of the contribution Grandpa Tate made to my family, to me, and I am not willing to reject him. I respect and honor his memory and claim him as a cherished relative.

Racism is so deeply embedded in our consciousness that we don't often realize that society asks us, on a regular basis, to reject part of our family when we are required to take sides in this tragic war game of race and color.

"Which side are you on, black or white?
There is a war going on.
Allegiance must be clear.
Choose!"

But choosing up sides means buying into the craziness of American-style racism. For there are many black Americans with white ancestors, and there are plenty of white Americans with black family members.

This is the way the American system works: if you have one parent or ancestor with African origins, you are black. You are not a member of the white family that might also claim you. That family must renounce you, and you must renounce it. You are in the black family, as will be all of your children and your grandchildren and your great-grandchildren. It is by thus redefining "family" to exclude their black family members that white Americans keep themselves and their "family" white. The notion of "family" in white America has very controlled borders: "family" stops where "black" begins.

The result is, then, that white people are all "white," and that black people are a wide range of colors—white, rosy, olive, tan, brown, reddish, black. We are forced to choose up sides, but the American rules dictate that choice. Real facts, like who your parents and grandparents were, don't matter: only social facts count.

Several years ago, a strange and sad incident took place at the law school. It involved a moot-court program sponsored by a national association of black law students. A young woman at the school who wanted to participate decided to join the local chapter of the association. But it was not as easy to join as she had expected, for although her father was black and she had African features, her mother was Puerto Rican. There was furious debate by the students in that chapter as to whether she could—or should—participate in a program for black students. Finally, they arrived at a solution. If she would renounce her Puerto Rican mother, she could join the association.

I hope this sounds as sick to you as it does to me. Renounce her mother? Were they all mad? And yet is this not what we all require of ourselves, of our children? We do it all the time. We renounce the reality of our real families, and we embrace the unreal reality of a social construct.

Think about it for a minute: whom have you renounced today? and why?

Are we all mad?

There are two little girls whom I love. They are two years old. The world is theirs to explore, and they go at it full tilt. Anyone old enough to read these words would be hard-pressed to keep up with either of them for an afternoon. These little girls are sisters in the deepest sense of the word, for they are twins and have been together from their earliest watery memories. They speak their own language and giggle at their own secrets. But they are twins who do not look alike. One is brown, like her father; the other is fair, like her mother.

I once talked about the problems color would present them with their father, a nephew. And I wondered, would they too be forced to choose up sides? How would they choose? Whom would they renounce? How could they? And why should they be forced into such a cruel dilemma? Their father's family is from Africa and Scotland and other lands; their mother's family is from Scotland and other European lands. It is just as misleading to say that they are African American as it is to say that they are Scottish American, for their heritage is complicated and rich. And I wonder sadly if there is any chance that these little girls will ever be able to just be Americans.

Think about it, for it does not involve my family alone. It involves yours too. And we really should do better by our children.

17

*Seeing More than Black and White**

ELIZABETH "BETITA" MARTINEZ

A certain relish seems irresistible to this Latina as the mass media [have] been compelled to sit up, look south of the border, and take notice. Probably the Chiapas uprising and Mexico's recent political turmoil have won us no more than a brief day in the

---

*This article was published some years before the struggle for the rights of migrant workers, particularly Latinos, intensified.

sun. Or even less: liberal Ted Koppel still hadn't noticed the historic assassination of presidential candidate Colosio three days afterward. But it's been sweet, anyway.

When Kissinger said years ago "nothing important ever happens in the south," he articulated a contemptuous indifference toward Latin America, its people and their culture which has long dominated U.S. institutions and attitudes. Mexico may be great for a vacation and some people like burritos but the usual image of Latin America combines incompetence with absurdity in loud colors. My parents, both Spanish teachers, endured decades of being told kids were better off learning French.

U.S. political culture is not only Anglo-dominated but also embraces an exceptionally stubborn national self-centeredness, with no global vision other than relations of domination. The U.S. refuses to see itself as one nation sitting on a continent with 20 others all speaking languages other than English and having the right not to be dominated.

Such arrogant indifference extends to Latinos within the U.S. The mass media complain, "people can't relate to Hispanics"—or Asians, they say. Such arrogant indifference has played an important role in invisibilizing La Raza (except where we become a serious nuisance or a handy scapegoat). It is one reason the U.S. harbors an exclusively white-on-Black concept of racism. It is one barrier to new thinking about racism which is crucial today. There are others.

In a society as thoroughly and violently racialized as the United States, white-Black relations have defined racism for centuries. Today the composition and culture of the U.S. are changing rapidly. We need to consider seriously whether we can afford to maintain an exclusively white/Black model of racism when the population will be 32 percent Latino, Asian/Pacific American and Native American—in short, neither Black nor white—by the year 2050. We are challenged to recognize that multi-colored racism is mushrooming, and then strategize how to resist it. We are challenged to move beyond a dualism comprised of two white supremacist inventions: Blackness and Whiteness.

At stake in those challenges is building a united anti-racist force strong enough to resist contemporary racist strategies of divide-and-conquer. Strong enough, in the long run, to help defeat racism itself. Doesn't an exclusively Black/white model of racism discourage the perception of common interests among people of color and thus impede a solidarity that can challenge white supremacy? Doesn't it encourage the isolation of African Americans from potential allies? Doesn't it advise all people of color to spend too much energy understanding our lives in relation to Whiteness, and thus freeze us in a defensive, often self-destructive mode?

For a Latina to talk about recognizing the multicolored varieties of racism is not, and should not be, yet another round in the Oppression Olympics. We don't need more competition among different social groupings for that "Most Oppressed" gold. We don't need more comparisons of suffering between women and Blacks, the disabled and the gay, Latino teenagers and white seniors, or whatever. We don't need more surveys like the recent much publicized Harris Poll showing that different peoples of color are prejudiced toward each other—a poll patently designed to demonstrate that us coloreds are no better than white folk. (The survey never asked people about positive attitudes.)

Rather, we need greater knowledge, understanding, and openness to learning about each other's histories and present needs as a basis for working together. Nothing could seem more urgent in an era when increasing impoverishment encourages a self-imposed separatism among people of color as a desperate attempt at community survival. Nothing could seem more important as we search for new social change strategies in a time of ideological confusion.

My call to rethink concepts of racism in the U.S. today is being sounded elsewhere. Among academics, liberal foundation administrators, and activist-intellectuals, you can hear talk of the need for a new "racial paradigm" or model. But new thinking seems to proceed in fits and starts, as if dogged by a fear of stepping on toes, of feeling threatened, or of losing one's base. With a few notable exceptions, even our progressive scholars of color do not make the leap from perfunctorily saluting a vague multiculturalism to serious analysis. We seem to have made little progress, if any, since Bob Blauner's 1972 book *Racial Oppression in America*. Recognizing the limits of the white-Black axis, Blauner critiqued White America's ignorance of and indifference to the Chicano/a's experience with racism.

Real opposition to new paradigms also exists. There are academics scrambling for one flavor of ethnic studies funds versus another. There are politicians who cultivate distrust of others to keep their own communities loyal. When we hear, for example, of Black/Latino friction, dismay should be quickly followed by investigation. In cities like Los Angeles and New York, it may turn out that political figures scrapping for patronage and payola have played a narrow nationalist game, whipping up economic anxiety and generating resentment that sets communities against each other.

So the goal here, in speaking about moving beyond a bi-polar concept of racism, is to build stronger unity against white supremacy. The goal is to see our similarities of experience and needs. If that goal sounds naive, think about the hundreds of organizations formed by grassroots women of different colors coming together in recent years. Their growth is one of today's most energetic motions and it spans all ages. Think about the multicultural environmental justice movement. Think about the coalitions to save schools. Small rainbows of our own making are there, to brighten a long road through hellish times.

It is in such practice, through daily struggle together, that we are most likely to find the road to greater solidarity against a common enemy. But we also need a will to find it and ideas about where, including some new theory.

Until very recently, Latino invisibility—like that of Native Americans and Asian/Pacific Americans—has been close to absolute in U.S. seats of power, major institutions, and the non-Latino public mind. Having lived on both the East and West Coasts for long periods, I feel qualified to pronounce: an especially myopic view of Latinos prevails in the East. This, despite such data as a 24.4 percent Latino population of New York City alone in 1991, or the fact that in 1990 more Puerto Ricans were killed by New York police under suspicious circumstances than any other ethnic group. Latino populations are growing rapidly in many eastern cities and the rural South, yet remain invisible or stigmatized—usually both.

Eastern blinders persist. I've even heard that the need for a new racial paradigm is dismissed in New York as a California hangup. A black Puerto Rican friend in New York, when we talked about experiences of racism common to Black and brown, said, "People here don't see Border Patrol brutality against Mexicans as a form of police repression," despite the fact that the Border Patrol is the largest and most uncontrolled police force in the U.S. It would seem that an old ignorance has combined with new immigrant bashing to sustain divisions today.

While the East (and most of the Midwest) usually remains myopic, the West Coast has barely begun to move away from its own denial. Less than two years ago in San Francisco, a city almost half Latino or Asian/Pacific American, a leading daily newspaper could publish a major series on contemporary racial issues and follow the exclusively Black-white paradigm. Although millions of TV viewers saw massive Latino participation in the April 1992 Los Angeles uprising, which included 18 out of 50 deaths and the majority of arrests, the mass media and most people labeled that event "a Black riot."

* * *

. . . [W]hat has been a regional issue mostly limited to western states is becoming a national issue. If you thought Latinos were just Mexicans down at the border, wake up—they are all over North Carolina, Pennsylvania and 8th Avenue Manhattan now. A qualitative change is taking place. With the broader geographic spread of Latinos and Asian/Pacific Islanders has come a nationalization of

racist practices and attitudes that were once regional. The west goes east, we could say.

Like the monster Hydra, racism is growing some ugly new heads. We will have to look at them closely.

A bi-polar model of racism—racism as white on Black—has never really been accurate. Looking for the roots of racism in the U.S. we can begin with the genocide against American Indians which made possible the U.S. land base, crucial to white settlement and early capitalist growth. Soon came the massive enslavement of African people which facilitated that growth. As slave labor became economically critical, "blackness" became ideologically critical; it provided the very source of "whiteness" and the heart of racism. Franz Fanon would write, "colour is the most outward manifestation of race."

If Native Americans had been a crucial labor force during those same centuries, living and working in the white man's sphere, our racist ideology might have evolved differently. "The tawny," as Ben Franklin dubbed them, might have defined the opposite of what he called "the lovely white." But with Indians decimated and survivors moved to distant concentration camps, they became unlikely candidates for this function. Similarly, Mexicans were concentrated in the distant West; elsewhere Anglo fear of them or need for control was rare. They also did not provide the foundation for a definition of whiteness.

Some anti-racist left activists have put forth the idea that only African Americans experience racism as such and that the suffering of other people of color results from national minority rather than racial oppression. From this view point, the exclusively white/Black model for racism is correct. Latinos, then, experience exploitation and repression for reasons of culture and nationality—not for their "race." (It should go without saying . . . that while racism is an all-too-real social fact, race has no scientific basis.)

Does the distinction hold? This and other theoretical questions call for more analysis and more expertise than one article can offer. In the meantime, let's try out the idea that Latinos do suffer for their nationality and culture, especially language. They became part of the U.S. through the 1846–48 war on Mexico and thus a foreign population to be colonized. But as they were reduced to cheap or semi-slave labor, they quickly came to suffer for their "race"—meaning, as non-whites. In the Southwest of a super-racialized nation, the broad parallelism of race and class embraced Mexicans ferociously.

The bridge here might be a definition of racism as "the reduction of the cultural to the biological," in the words of French scholar Christian Delacampagne now working in Egypt. Or: "racism exists wherever it is claimed that a given social status is explained by a given natural characteristic." We know that line: Mexicans are just naturally lazy and have too many children, so they're poor and exploited.

The discrimination, oppression and hatred experienced by Native Americans, Mexicans, Asian/Pacific Islanders, and Arab Americans are forms of racism. Speaking only of Latinos, we have seen in California and the Southwest, especially along the border, almost 150 years of relentless repression which today includes Central Americans among its targets. That history reveals hundreds of lynchings between 1847 and 1935, the use of counter-insurgency armed forces beginning with the Texas Rangers, random torture and murder by Anglo ranchers, forced labor, rape by border lawmen, and the prevailing Anglo belief that a Mexican life doesn't equal a dog's in value.

But wait. If color is so key to racial definition, as Fanon and others say, perhaps people of Mexican background experience racism less than national minority oppression because they are not dark enough as a group. For White America, shades of skin color are crucial to defining worth. The influence of those shades has also been internalized by communities of color. Many Latinos can and often want to pass for whites; therefore White America may see them as less threatening than darker sisters and brothers.

Here we confront more of the complexity around us today, with questions like: What about the usually poor, very dark Mexican or Central American of strong Indian or African heritage? (Yes, folks, 200–300,000 Africans were brought to Mexico as slaves, which is far, far more than the Spaniards who came.) And what about the effects of accented speech or foreign name, characteristics that may instantly subvert "passing"?

What about those cases where a Mexican-American is never accepted, no matter how light-skinned, well-dressed or well-spoken? A Chicano lawyer friend coming home from a professional conference in suit, tie and briefcase found himself on a bus near San Diego that was suddenly stopped by the Border Patrol. An agent came on board and made a beeline through the all-white rows of passengers direct to my friend. "Your papers." The agent didn't believe Jose was coming from a U.S. conference and took him off the bus to await proof. Jose was lucky; too many Chicanos and Mexicans end up killed.

In a land where the national identity is white, having the "wrong" nationality becomes grounds for racist abuse. Who would draw a sharp line between today's national minority oppression in the form of immigrant-bashing and racism?

None of this aims to equate the African American and Latino experiences; that isn't necessary even if it were accurate. Many reasons exist for the persistence of the white/Black paradigm of racism; they include numbers, history, and the psychology of whiteness. In particular they include centuries of slave revolts, a Civil War, and an ongoing resistance to racism that cracked this society wide open while the world watched. Nor has the misery imposed on Black people lessened in recent years. New thinking about racism can and should keep this experience at the center.

The exclusively white/Black concept of race and racism in the U.S. rests on a western. Protestant form of dualism woven into both race and gender relations from earliest times. In the dualist universe there is only black and white. A disdain, indeed fear, of mixture haunts the Yankee soul; there is no room for any kind of multifaceted identity, any hybridism.

As a people, La Raza combines three sets of roots—indigenous, European and African—all in widely varying degrees. In short we represent a profoundly un-American concept: *mestizaje* (pronounced mess-tee-zah-hey), the mixing of peoples and emergence of new peoples. A highly racialized society like this one cannot deal with or allow room for *mestizaje*. It has never learned to do much more than hiss "miscegenation!" Or, like that Alabama high school principal who recently denied the right of a mixed-blood pupil to attend the prom to say: "your parents made a mistake." Apparently we, all the millions of La Raza, are just that—a mistake.

Mexicans in the U.S. also defy the either-or, dualistic mind in that, on the one hand, we are a colonized people displaced from the ancestral homeland with roots in the present-day U.S. that go back centuries. Those ancestors didn't cross the border; the border crossed them. At the same time many of us have come to the U.S. more recently as "immigrants" seeking work. The complexity of Raza baffles and frustrates most Anglos; they want to put one neat label on us. It baffles many Latinos too, who often end up categorizing themselves racially as "Other" for lack of anything better. For that matter, the term "Latino" which I use here is a monumental simplification; it refers to 20-plus nationalities and a wide range of classes.

But we need to grapple with the complexity, for there is more to come. If anything, this nation will see more *mestizaje* in the future, embracing innumerable ethnic combinations. What will be its effects? Only one thing seems certain: "white" shall cease to be the national identity.

A glimpse at the next century tells us how much we need to look beyond the white/Black model of race relations and racism. White/Black are real poles, central to the history of U.S. racism. We can neither ignore them nor stop there. But our effectiveness in fighting racism depends on seeing the changes taking place, trying to perceive the contours of the future. From the time of the Greeks to the present, racism around the world has had certain commonalties but no permanently fixed character. It is evolving again today, and we'd best labor to read the new faces of this Hydra-headed monster. Remember, for every head that Hydra lost it grew two more.

Sometimes the problem seems so clear. Last year I showed slides of Chicano history to an Oakland high school class with 47 African Americans and three Latino students. The images included lynchings and police beatings of Mexicans and other Latinos, and many years of resistance. At the end one Black student asked, "Seems like we have had a lot of experiences in common—so why can't Blacks and Mexicans get along better?" No answers, but there was the first step: asking the question.

II. Understanding Oppression and Privilege

Dena R. Samuels

Thou shalt not be a victim. Thou shalt not be a perpetrator.
Above all, thou shalt not be a bystander.
—HOLOCAUST MUSEUM, WASHINGTON, DC

So far, we have looked at the ways in which we identify ourselves in society and the ways others identify us. We have discussed how complicated these classifications can be and how dominant statuses often overlap in our lives, so that we are not identified by only one classification but often by many. Depending on where and in what situation we are in, we might be identified differently. So, for example, a white woman might be classified by her gender and race in parts of the South, but in Iowa, where the majority of the population is white, her race may never be identified because it would be considered the norm. This invisibility of race for most white people in most regions in the United States is considered a privilege, an unearned benefit. To be regarded as the norm and not have to be named is a luxury people of color do not get in most of the country. In this section, we will identify this particular form of privilege and other unearned advantages that are social constructions in our society. We will also explore the consequences of these unearned benefits that a portion of the population enjoys but that are denied to others based on their group memberships.

In Audre Lorde's article "Age, Race, Class, and Sex: Women Redefining Difference," she describes the "mythical norm." This is a stereotype that is perpetuated by society, against which everyone else is measured. She describes America's mythical norm as "white, thin, male, young, heterosexual, christian, financially secure." Because this myth is widely accepted, it creates a power hierarchy under which everyone falls. It is important to remember, however, that this norm is mythical because it is a social construction. In other words, the particular traits that define this myth do not inherently represent power; rather, it is only because we have been taught to believe that they do that we bestow power on those in our society who most closely possess those characteristics.

The mythical norm helps us identify which statuses within a given social location are endowed with power; thus it becomes apparent who possesses power and privilege and who does not. The hierarchies that exist in U.S. society are based on the social locations represented by the mythical norm: race, appearance, gender, age, sexual orientation, religion, and class, respectively. Using the norm as a framework, we can then make sense of the various forms of discrimination that occur based on an individual's social locations. If a person is financially unstable, for example, she or he might be the target of classism; a person of color may experience racism; a woman may experience sexism. For each social location, there is a related disadvantage that plays out in the lives of those who do not represent the mythical norm. There are also, on the other hand, connected advantages that play out in the lives of those who *do* represent the mythical norm.

In Section I, Patricia Hill Collins's "Toward a New Vision" explains how all of our social locations intersect and work together to either privilege or oppress us. As mentioned in the Introduction to this reader, she refers to this intersection of social locations as "the matrix of domination." Before we begin to make sense of the matrix of domination, however, we must review the concepts of oppression and privilege.

What is oppression? Oppression means being denied access to resources based on one's social group memberships. Allan Johnson explains: "Oppression and dominance name social realities that we can participate in without being oppressive or dominating people" (2006,10). In order to be oppressed then, one must belong to an oppressed group. In other words, oppression is based on membership in a specific social identity group such as gender, race, class, sexuality, religion, and ability.

What is privilege? Privilege means gaining access to resources that are denied to others based on one's social group memberships. In her article in this section, "White Privilege and Male Privilege," Peggy McIntosh notes, "there are two kinds of privilege: unearned entitlements are those 'things' that all people should have but often are limited to certain groups (ex: safe housing, feeling safe in public, the right to vote)." The other form she calls "conferred dominance"; and these privileges give one group power over another.

Understanding these distinctions is essential to comprehending the power and inequalities that exist in our society. To strategize about how to create change, we must analyze how these concepts play out on a societal level as well as how they directly fit into our lives. This section looks at oppression and privilege from both of these lenses so we can begin to understand the nature of inequality.

To examine oppression and privilege from a societal or macro view, we can look to one of the founders of sociology, C. Wright Mills, who explained that we must add to our analysis the social context in which we live in order to fully understand our experiences. He asserted that we must use a "sociological imagination" to link biography (the individual's specific experiences in society) with history (society's impact on the individual). Even though we may see our own personal troubles as the product of our own circumstances, we must use a sociological imagination to connect those troubles with larger societal forces. Only then can we begin to find large-scale solutions to problems that affect us all.

As such, we must consider broadly how society influences the individual in order to comprehend the full weight of inequality. If we were only to look at a single act of discrimination, for example, without understanding its connection to the institutional discrimination of a certain group of people, we would be missing an extremely important element in our analysis. Further, we would miss the implications for attempting to solve the problem if we were only analyzing the act on a micro level. We cannot gain a full understanding of society, or inequality, unless we look at both levels.

Another sociologist, Emile Durkheim, suggested that society and the individual do not exist separately, one without the other. He used an analogy of the body to explain this. According to Durkheim's theory, you can look at the systems in society or at individual acts just as you can analyze the systems in the body (circulatory, nervous) or a part of the body (a leg, an arm), but it is important to remember that these systems or acts never operate independently of society, just as these systems or parts never function independently of the body; rather, they intersect. In studying the concepts of oppression and privilege, we must examine how the macro level affects the micro level, and vice versa, and how both levels work together to privilege some and oppress others. For example, we can look at institutional oppression, the most dramatic example being slavery. We can analyze the system of slavery according to how it created inequality in our society; we can consider how slavery was adopted, how it was maintained, and how it was justified in the United States. We can study the long-term consequences to the U.S. population. We can also analyze the way in which it was abolished so that we can learn how to create institutional change.

At the same time, it is helpful to view the institution of slavery from the perspective of the captives to understand how oppression played out in individual lives. We can study the few surviving captives' autobiographies. We can learn from the stories that have been passed down through oral tradition to understand more about the lives of the individuals before they were forcibly removed from their homes. These personal accounts help us to understand the concept of oppression in a very personal way, and they teach us about personal power, strength of character, and endurance. These stories and the individuals in them serve as models and empower us to continue to fight for equality.

Using both of these lenses, we can begin to understand the systems of oppression inherent in slavery, created by individuals and sanctioned by society. Just as we can travel between the institutional lens and the individual lens of oppression, we can also examine how privilege plays out at both an institutional and an individual level. Taking again the example of slavery, we can ask how privilege has played out in this institution. Who benefited from the system of slavery? Why was it that the privilege of "pure" whiteness, an unearned benefit based on a myth of having only white ancestors, meant you did not have to spend your life as a slave (an indentured servant, perhaps, but not a slave)? How did the institution of slavery create an economic base for the United States that solidified and enhanced the capitalist system on which we rely today?

From an individual perspective, we can look at the male, white, class privilege that allowed wealthy white males to be land-owning and slave-owning. We can analyze the entitlement that came with white skin, and the invisibility of both the whiteness and the privilege that came along with it. We can ask what some wealthy white males have done with their privilege. Have they used it to their own advantage, or have they used it to become an ally for those who are oppressed? Are there role models we can look to who have used their privilege to work toward ending inequality?

Asking these kinds of questions helps us to critically analyze the institution of slavery in a way that focuses on the "oppressor" and not just on those who have been oppressed by this system. If we can understand the societal as well as the individual systems that work together to privilege some at the expense of others, we can better understand the systems of inequality that exist today. We can delve deeper into questions surrounding inequalities, such as, for example, what causes those in power to be more likely to hire others who look like them rather than creating a diverse workforce? More importantly, we can use this more complex analysis to work toward solutions.

Understanding the concepts of oppression and privilege goes beyond peering through both the institutional and individual lenses. There are many levels of oppression and privilege, and conceptualizing those levels can be helpful in conceiving of the many ways that oppression and privilege play out in each of our lives. As mentioned in the Introduction to this text, Patricia Hill Collins's matrix of domination states that based on one's social location, a person can be oppressed in some ways and privileged in others. Moreover, for every act of oppression there is an interconnected act of domination. The matrix of domination is a useful tool for understanding the ways in which different social locations interact with one another—that is, how race, gender, class, and sexuality work together to oppress or privilege. So, for example, a wealthy white lesbian might be more privileged in the social locations of class and race but might be more oppressed in the social locations of gender and sexual orientation. Collins and Lorde maintain that in order to get a full picture of the systems of privilege and oppression in our society, it is important to take all aspects of one's social locations into account. They all affect the impressions we make on others as well as how we view ourselves.

Collins asserts that the matrix helps us to understand that domination occurs on multiple levels: personal, cultural, and institutional. The Gay, Lesbian &

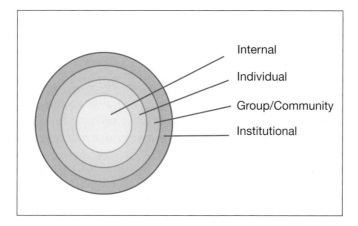

FIGURE 2.1 *Oppression Circles.*

Straight Education Network (GLSEN) (www.glsen.org) offers a model called Oppression Circles that is useful in understanding the various levels of oppression (Figure 2.1). By extending a version of this model to the concept of privilege as well, we can gain not only a visual understanding of these concepts, but also a better understanding of the intersectional aspect of oppression and privilege.

Internalized oppression, the innermost circle in the model, occurs when people who are oppressed because of their group membership in society believe the stereotypes and attitudes that are directed at their group. They feel that the stereotypes are correct and fitting. As Peggy McIntosh has stated, "internalized oppression contributes to inequality because it does the work of the oppressor for them" (April 28, 2006). Internalized oppression is an important concept not only for understanding the process of oppression, but also for thinking about creating change. For example, in Joy Harjo's poem "I Give You Back," which opens Section II, she speaks about our own culpability in believing in these stereotypes. Rather than cowering as a result of the fear that comes from our differences, her poem suggests we move forward to a place of empowerment, by acknowledging our own role in accepting stereotypes and determining instead to challenge them. Internalized oppression is a powerful means of coercion, creating fear and loathing not only of others but also of ourselves.

Internalized privilege, on the other hand, occurs when people who are privileged because of their group membership in society believe the stereotypes and attitudes about their group. This is where the elements of entitlement and invisibility come into play. Those who are privileged in a certain category are the standard against which everyone else is measured and named, and therefore they do not typically see their status as privileged but rather as the norm. For example, when we think about issues of sexual orientation, homosexuality usually comes to mind; heterosexuals are not typically cognizant of having a sexual orientation. Since heterosexuality is the norm or standard against which everyone else is measured and named, we learn to see those who are not heterosexual as having a sexual orientation, and we have many names for those who fall into those "other" categories. Heterosexuality, then, is an internalized privilege, and an invisible one at that.

The next circle in the model, *individual oppression,* is oppression that occurs between two people based on their group membership in society. Individual oppression is when a person who is oppressed in a certain social location is discriminated against by someone who has privilege in that same social location. For example, if a female is the target recipient of a sexist statement or joke made by a male, she suffers individual gender oppression. Keep in mind that oppression and privilege are based on group status. In this example, the male has individual privilege as conferred upon him by a society that benefits men. He is perpetuating oppression toward a woman, who, based on her social group membership, does not receive the same benefits that men do. Oppression is perpetuated by someone who has power against someone who lacks it. Therefore, if a woman makes a joke about a man, on the other hand, the act may be discriminatory, but it would not be considered an example of oppression because again, based on her social group membership, she does not have the power or privilege to oppress. *Individual privilege,* then, is when an individual uses her or his group membership to discriminate against another person who is oppressed in that social location. In this example of gender oppression, the male is individually perpetuating gender privilege because the statement or joke ratifies the power inequality that is already in place.

Group/community oppression occurs when a person is made to feel "less than" by the group or community she or he is in. If you are a person of color, and a group of your white friends start telling racist jokes, they are perpetuating race oppression, or racism. Moreover, as you will see in Section III, group/community oppression occurs when certain groups/communities are marginalized in society and made to feel that they do not belong, that they are not "true" Americans. In contrast, *group/community privilege* occurs when a person is made to feel that he or she is "one of us" and is welcomed solely based on the person's group membership. An example of this is when a white person walks into a store and is welcomed by the sales staff rather than being ignored or watched and tailed. Another example of group/community privilege is the fact that U.S. citizenship brings with it a sense of entitlement both within the United States and abroad, a subject that is considered in Michael Schwalbe's "The Costs of American Privilege."

Institutionalized oppression, the outermost circle, is oppression that occurs at the macro levels of society. An institution is an organization or group that provides a foundation or structure in our lives, such as family, education, religion, government, and media. Organizations that discriminate based on one's social group membership demonstrate institutionalized oppression. The vast number of states that do not currently protect against hate crimes dealing with sexual orientation is an example of institutionalized oppression. In other words, by refusing to take a stand against violence directed against gays, lesbians, bisexuals, and transgender people, these states are inadvertently perpetuating the oppression of these groups.

Institutionalized privilege, then, also occurs at the macro levels of society and springs from organizations, churches, media, and laws that have been founded on, or are based on the mythical norm, and they discriminate against anyone who is not part of that norm. For example, the assumption that everyone in the United States is Christian prompts many organizations, stores, media, and even government buildings to display "Merry Christmas" banners as part of their policy in December.

Understanding the different levels of oppression and privilege helps us to analyze how these concepts play out in our own lives. Understanding that they are based on group membership helps us to become cognizant of how stereotypes with which we are constantly bombarded teach us to make assumptions about others, regardless of their complex identities, their personalities, or how they choose to identify themselves. Once we become aware of the boxes we put others in, we can challenge those assumptions. Only when we can see how we connect to the problems of inequality can we figure out how to work toward equality.

As Allan Johnson has stated, "Privilege is the problem; oppression is the consequence" (personal communication, April 27, 2006). Systems of privilege and oppression cannot exist without the individuals that make them happen. Remember, too, though, that *equality* also cannot exist without individuals who work to make it happen. The first steps toward challenging those systems of inequality and becoming part of the solution is our willingness to understand the problem, study the consequences, connect to it so we can be aware of our own participation in the system, and choose to do something about it. Section II explains both the problem and its consequences and will assist you on your journey of understanding and action.

REFERENCES

1. GLSEN. 2004. GLSEN jump-start #6: Understanding power, privilege and oppression. New York: Gay, Lesbian & Straight Education Network. http://www.glsen.org/cgi-bin/iowa/all/library/record/1629.html. Accessed May 16, 2006.
2. Johnson, A. G. (2006). *Privilege, power and difference,* 2nd ed. New York: McGraw-Hill.
3. Johnson, A. G. 2006, April 27. Personal communication.
4. McIntosh, P. 2006, April 28. Personal communication.

I Give You Back

JOY HARJO

I release you, my beautiful and terrible
fear. I release you. You were my beloved
and hated twin, but now, I don't know you
as myself. I release you with all the
pain I would know at the death of
my daughters.

You are not my blood anymore.

I give you back to the white soldiers
who burned down my home, beheaded
    my children,
raped and sodomized my brothers and sisters.
I give you back to those who stole the
food from our plates when we were starving.

I release you, fear, because you hold
these scenes in front of me and I was born
with eyes that can never close.

I release you, fear, so you can no longer
keep me naked and frozen in the winter,
or smothered under blankets in the summer.

I release you
I release you
I release you
I release you

I am not afraid to be angry.
I am not afraid to rejoice.
I am not afraid to be black.
I am not afraid to be white.
I am not afraid to be hungry.
I am not afraid to be full.
I am not afraid to be hated.
I am not afraid to be loved.

to be loved, to be loved, fear.

Oh, you have choked me, but I gave you the leash.
You have gutted me but I gave you the knife.

You have devoured me, but I laid myself across
    the fire.
You held my mother down and raped her,
                but I gave you the heated thing.

I take myself back, fear.
You are not my shadow any longer.
I won't hold you in my hands.
You can't live in my eyes, my ears, my voice
my belly, or in my heart my heart
my heart   my heart

But come here, fear
I am alive and you are so afraid
    of dying.

 18

White Privilege and Male Privilege

A Personal Account of Coming to See Correspondences Through Work in Women's Studies

PEGGY MCINTOSH

Through work to bring materials and perspectives from Women's Studies into the rest of the curriculum, I have often noticed men's unwillingness to grant that they are over-privileged in the curriculum, even though they may grant that women are disadvantaged. Denials which amount to taboos surround the subject of advantages which men gain from women's disadvantages. These denials protect male privilege from being fully recognized, acknowledged, lessened, or ended.

Thinking through unacknowledged male privilege as a phenomenon with a life of its own, I realized that since hierarchies in our society are interlocking, there was most likely a phenomenon of white privilege which was similarly denied and protected, but alive and real in its effects. As a white person, I realized I had been taught about racism as something which puts others at a disadvantage, but had been taught not to see one of its corollary aspects, white privilege, which puts me at an advantage.

I think whites are carefully taught not to recognize white privilege, as males are taught not to recognize male privilege. So I have begun in an untutored way to ask what it is like to have white privilege. This paper is a partial record of my personal observations, and not a scholarly analysis. It is based on my daily experiences within my particular circumstances.

I have come to see white privilege as an invisible package of unearned assets which I can count on cashing in each day, but about which I was "meant" to remain oblivious. White privilege is like an invisible weightless knapsack of special provisions, assurances, tools, maps, guides, code-books, passports, visas, clothes, compass, emergency gear, and blank checks.

Since I have had trouble facing white privilege, and describing its results in my life, I saw parallels here with men's reluctance to acknowledge male privilege. Only rarely will a man go beyond acknowledging that women are [dis]advantaged to acknowledging that men have unearned advantage, or that unearned privilege has not been good for men's development as human beings, or for society's development, or that privilege systems might ever be challenged and *changed*.

I will review here several types or layers of denial which I see at work protecting, and preventing awareness about, entrenched male privilege. Then I will draw parallels, from my own experience, with the denials which veil the facts of white privilege. Finally, I will list 46 ordinary and daily ways in which I experience having white privilege, within my life situation and its particular social and political frameworks.

Writing this paper has been difficult, despite warm receptions for the talks on which it is based.[1] For describing white privilege makes one newly accountable. As we in Women's Studies work to reveal male privilege and ask men to give up some of their power, so one who writes about having white privilege must ask, "Having described it, what will I do to lessen or end it?"

The denial of men's overprivileged state takes many forms in discussions of curriculum change work. Some claim that men must be central in the curriculum because they have done most of what is important or distinctive in life or in civilization. Some recognize sexism in the curriculum but deny that it makes male students seem unduly important in life. Others agree that certain *individual* thinkers are blindly male-oriented but deny that there is any systemic tendency in disciplinary frameworks or epistemology to over-empower men as a group. Those men who do grant that male privilege takes institutionalized and embedded forms are still likely to deny that male hegemony has opened doors for them personally. Virtually all men deny that male overreward alone can explain men's centrality in all the inner sanctums of our most powerful institutions. Moreover, those few who will acknowledge that male privilege systems have over-empowered them usually end up doubting that we could dismantle these privilege systems. They may say they will work to improve women's status, in the society or in the university, but they can't or won't support the idea of lessening men's. In curricular terms, this is the point at which they say that they regret they cannot use any of the interesting new scholarship on women because the syllabus is full. When the talk turns to giving men less cultural room, even the most thoughtful and fair-minded of the men I know well tend to reflect, or fall back on, conservative assumptions about the inevitability of present gender relations and distributions of power, calling on precedent or sociobiology and psychobiology to demonstrate that male domination is natural and follows inevitably from evolutionary pressures. Others resort to arguments from "experience" or religion or social responsibility or wishing and dreaming.

After I realized, through faculty development work in Women's Studies, the extent to which men work from a base of unacknowledged privilege, I understood that much of their oppressiveness was unconscious. Then I remembered the frequent charges from women of color that white women whom they encounter are oppressive. I began to understand why we are justly seen as oppressive, even when we don't see ourselves that way. At the very least, obliviousness of one's privileged state can make a person or group irritating to be with. I began to count the ways in which I enjoy unearned skin privilege and have been conditioned into oblivion about its existence, unable to see that it put me "ahead" in any way, or put my people ahead, overrewarding us and yet also paradoxically damaging us, or that it could or should be changed.

My schooling gave me no training in seeing myself as an oppressor, as an unfairly advantaged person, or as a participant in a damaged culture. I was taught to see myself as an individual whose moral state depended on her individual moral will. At school, we were not taught about slavery in any depth; we were not taught to see slaveholders as damaged people. Slaves were seen as the only group at risk of being dehumanized. My schooling followed the pattern which Elizabeth Minnich has pointed out: whites are taught to think of their lives as morally neutral, normative, and average, and also ideal, so that when we work to benefit others, this is seen as work which will allow "them" to be more like "us." I think many of us know how obnoxious this attitude can be in men.

After frustration with men who would not recognize male privilege, I decided to try to work on myself at least by identifying some of the daily effects of white privilege in my life. It is crude work, at this stage, but I will give here a list of special circumstances and conditions I experience which I did not earn but which I have been made to feel are mine by birth, by citizenship, and by virtue of being a conscientious law-abiding "normal" person of good will. I have chosen those conditions which I think in my case *attach somewhat more to skin-color privilege* than to class, religion, ethnic status, or geographical location, though of course all these other factors are intricately intertwined. As far as I can see, my Afro-American co-workers, friends, and acquaintances with whom I come into daily or frequent contact in this particular time, place, and line of work cannot count on most of these conditions.

1. I can if I wish arrange to be in the company of people of my race most of the time.
2. I can avoid spending time with people whom I was trained to mistrust and who have learned to mistrust my kind or me.
3. If I should need to move, I can be pretty sure of renting or purchasing housing in an area which I can afford and in which I would want to live.
4. I can be pretty sure that my neighbors in such a location will be neutral or pleasant to me.
5. I can go shopping alone most of the time, pretty well assured that I will not be followed or harassed.
6. I can turn on the television or open to the front page of the paper and see people of my race widely represented.
7. When I am told about our national heritage or about "civilization," I am shown that people of my color made it what it is.
8. I can be sure that my children will be given curricular materials that testify to the existence of their race.
9. If I want to, I can be pretty sure of finding a publisher for this piece on white privilege.
10. I can be pretty sure of having my voice heard in a group in which I am the only member of my race.
11. I can be casual about whether or not to listen to another woman's voice in a group in which she is the only member of her race.
12. I can go into a music shop and count on finding the music of my race represented, into a supermarket and find the staple foods which fit with my cultural traditions, into a hairdresser's shop and find someone who can cut my hair.
13. Whether I use checks, credit cards, or cash, I can count on my skin color not to work against the appearance of financial reliability.
14. I can arrange to protect my children most of the time from people who might not like them.
15. I do not have to educate my children to be aware of systemic racism for their own daily physical protection.

16. I can be pretty sure that my children's teachers and employers will tolerate them if they fit school and workplace norms; my chief worries about them do not concern others' attitudes toward their race.

17. I can talk with my mouth full and not have people put this down to my color.

18. I can swear, or dress in second hand clothes, or not answer letters, without having people attribute these choices to the bad morals, the poverty, or the illiteracy of my race.

19. I can speak in public to a powerful male group without putting my race on trial.

20. I can do well in a challenging situation without being called a credit to my race.

21. I am never asked to speak for all the people of my racial group.

22. I can remain oblivious of the language and customs of persons of color who constitute the world's majority without feeling in my culture any penalty for such oblivion.

23. I can criticize our government and talk about how much I fear its policies and behavior without being seen as a cultural outsider.

24. I can be pretty sure that if I ask to talk to "the person in charge," I will be facing a person of my race.

25. If a traffic cop pulls me over or if the IRS audits my tax return, I can be sure I haven't been singled out because of my race.

26. I can easily buy posters, post-cards, picture books, greeting cards, dolls, toys, and children's magazines featuring people of my race.

27. I can go home from most meetings of organizations I belong to feeling somewhat tied in, rather than isolated, out-of-place, outnumbered, unheard, held at a distance, or feared.

28. I can be pretty sure that an argument with a colleague of another race is more likely to jeopardize her chances for advancement than to jeopardize mine.

29. I can be pretty sure that if I argue for the promotion of a person of another race, or a program centering on race, this is not likely to cost me heavily within my present setting, even if my colleagues disagree with me.

30. If I declare there is a racial issue at hand, or there isn't a racial issue at hand, my race will lend me more credibility for either position than a person of color will have.

31. I can choose to ignore developments in minority writing and minority activist programs, or disparage them, or learn from them, but in any case, I can find ways to be more or less protected from negative consequences of any of these choices.

32. My culture gives me little fear about ignoring the perspectives and powers of people of other races.

33. I am not made acutely aware that my shape, bearing, or body odor will be taken as a reflection on my race.

34. I can worry about racism without being seen as self-interested or self-seeking.

35. I can take a job with an affirmative action employer without having my co-workers on the job suspect that I got it because of my race.

36. If my day, week, or year is going badly, I need not ask of each negative episode or situation whether it has racial overtones.

37. I can be pretty sure of finding people who would be willing to talk to me and advise me about my next steps, professionally.

38. I can think over many options, social, political, imaginative, or professional, without asking whether a person of my race would be accepted or allowed to do what I want to do.

39. I can be late to a meeting without having the lateness reflect on my race.

40. I can choose public accommodation without fearing that people of my race cannot get in or will be mistreated in the places I have chosen.

41. I can be sure that if I need legal or medical help, my race will not work against me.

42. I can arrange my activities so that I will never have to experience feelings of rejection owing to my race.

43. If I have low credibility as a leader, I can be sure that my race is not the problem.

44. I can easily find academic courses and institutions which give attention only to people of my race.

45. I can expect figurative language and imagery in all of the arts to testify to experiences of my race.

46. I can choose blemish cover or bandages in "flesh" color and have them more or less match my skin.

I repeatedly forgot each of the realizations on this list until I wrote it down. For me, white privilege has turned out to be an elusive and fugitive subject. The pressure to avoid it is great, for in facing it I must give up the myth of meritocracy. If these things are true, this is not such a free country; one's life is not what one makes it; many doors open for certain people through no virtues of their own. These perceptions mean also that my moral condition is not what I had been led to believe. The appearance of being a good citizen rather than a troublemaker comes in large part from having all sorts of doors open automatically because of my color.

A further paralysis of nerve comes from literary silence protecting privilege. My clearest memories of finding such analysis are in Lillian Smith's unparalleled *Killers of the Dream* and Margaret Andersen's review of Karen and Mamie Fields' *Lemon Swamp*. Smith, for example, wrote about walking toward black children on the street and knowing they would step into the gutter; Andersen contrasted the pleasure which she, as a white child, took on summer driving trips to the South with Karen Fields' memories of driving in a closed car stocked with all necessities lest, in stopping, her black family should suffer "insult, or worse." Adrienne Rich also recognizes and writes about daily experiences of privilege, but in my observation, white women's writing in this area is far more often on systemic racism than on our daily lives as light-skinned women.[2]

In unpacking this invisible knapsack of white privilege, I have listed conditions of daily experience which I once took for granted, as neutral, normal, and universally available to everybody, just as I once thought of a male-focused curriculum as the neutral or accurate account which can speak for all. Nor did I think of any of these perquisites as bad for the holder. I now think that we need a more finely differentiated taxonomy of privilege, for some of these varieties are only what one would want for everyone in a just society, and others give license to be ignorant, oblivious, arrogant and destructive. Before proposing some more finely tuned categorization, I will make some observations about the general effects of these conditions on my life and expectations.

In this potpourri of examples, some privileges make me feel at home in the world. Others allow me to escape penalties or dangers which others suffer. Through some, I escape fear, anxiety, or a sense of not being welcome or not being real. Some keep me from having to hide, to be in disguise, to feel sick or crazy, to negotiate each transaction from the position of being an outsider or, within my group, a person who is suspected of having too close links with a dominant culture. Most keep me from having to be angry.

I see a pattern running through the matrix of white privilege, a pattern of assumptions which were passed on to me as a white person. There was one main piece of cultural turf; it was my own turf, and I was among those who could control the turf. I could measure up to the cultural standards and take advantage of the many options I saw around me to make what the culture would call a success of my life. *My skin color was an asset for any move I was educated to want to make,* I could think of myself as "belonging" in major ways, and of making social systems work for me. I could freely disparage, fear, neglect, or be oblivious to anything outside of the dominant cultural forms. Being of the main culture, I could also criticize it fairly freely. My life was reflected back to me frequently enough so that I felt, with regard to my race, if not to my sex, like one of the real people.

Whether through the curriculum or in the newspaper, the television, the economic system, or the general look of people in the streets, we received daily signals and indications that my people counted, and that others *either didn't exist or must be trying, not very successfully, to be like people of my race.* We were given cultural permission not to hear voices of people of other races, or a tepid cultural tolerance for hearing or acting on such voices. I was also raised not to suffer seriously from anything which darker-skinned people might say about my group, "protected," though perhaps I should more accurately say *prohibited*, through the habits of my economic class and social group, from living in racially mixed groups or being reflective about interactions between people of differing races.

In proportion as my racial group was being made confident, comfortable, and oblivious, other groups were likely being made inconfident, uncomfortable, and alienated. Whiteness protected me from many kinds of hostility, distress, and violence, which I was being subtly trained to visit in turn upon people of color.

For this reason, the word "privilege" now seems to me misleading. Its connotations are too positive to fit the conditions and behaviors which "privilege systems" produce. We usually think of privilege as being a favored state, whether earned, or conferred by birth or luck. School graduates are reminded they are privileged and urged to use their (enviable) assets well. The word "privilege" carries the connotation of being something everyone must want. Yet some of the conditions I have described here work to systematically overempower certain groups. Such privilege simply *confers dominance*, gives permission to control, because of one's race or sex. The kind of privilege which gives license to some people to be, at best, thoughtless, and at worst, murderous should not continue to be referred to as a desirable attribute. Such "privilege" may be widely desired without being in any way beneficial to the whole society.

Moreover, though "privilege" may confer power, it does not confer moral strength. Those who do not depend on conferred dominance have traits and qualities which may never develop in those who do. Just as Women's Studies courses indicate that women survive their political circumstances to lead lives which hold the human race together, so "underprivileged" people of color who are the

world's majority have survived their oppression and lived survivors' lives from which the white global minority can and must learn. In some groups, those dominated have actually become strong through *not* having all of these unearned advantages, and this gives them a great deal to teach the others. Members of so-called privileged groups can seem foolish, ridiculous, infantile or dangerous by contrast.

I want, then, to distinguish between earned strength and unearned power conferred systemically. Power from unearned privilege can look like strength when it is in fact permission to escape or to dominate. But not all of the privileges on my list are inevitably damaging. Some, like the expectation that neighbors will be decent to you, or that your race will not count against you in court, should be the norm in a just society and should be considered as the entitlement of everyone. Others, like the privilege not to listen to less powerful people, distort the humanity of the holders as well as the ignored groups. Still others, like finding one's staple foods everywhere, may be a function of being a member of a numerical majority in the population. Others have to do with not having to labor under pervasive negative stereotyping and mythology.

We might at least start by distinguishing between positive advantages which we can work to spread, to the point where they are not advantages at all but simply part of the normal civic and social fabric, and negative types of advantage which unless rejected will always reinforce our present hierarchies. For example, the positive "privilege" of belonging, the feeling that one belongs within the human circle, as Native Americans say, fosters development and should not be seen as privilege for a few. It is, let us say, an entitlement which none of us should have to earn; ideally it is an *unearned entitlement*. At present, since only a few have it, it is an *unearned advantage* for them. The negative "privilege" which gave me cultural permission not to take darker-skinned Others seriously can be seen as arbitrarily conferred dominance and should not be desirable for anyone. This paper results from a process of coming to see that some of the power which I originally saw as attendant on being a human being in the U.S. consisted in *unearned advantage* and *conferred dominance,* as well as other kinds of special circumstance not universally taken for granted.

In writing this paper I have also realized that white identity and status (as well as class identity and status) give me considerable power to choose whether to broach this subject and its trouble. I can pretty well decide whether to disappear and avoid and not listen and escape the dislike I may engender in other people through this essay, or interrupt, take over, dominate, preach, direct, criticize, or control to some extent what goes on in reaction to it. Being white, I am given considerable power to escape many kinds of danger or penalty as well as to choose which risks I want to take.

There is an analogy here, once again, with Women's Studies. Our male colleagues do not have a great deal to lose in supporting Women's Studies, but they do not have a great deal to lose if they oppose it either. They simply have the power to decide whether to commit themselves to more equitable distributions of power. They will probably feel few penalties whatever choice they make; they do not seem, in any obvious short-term sense, the ones at risk, though they and we are all at risk because of the behaviors which have been rewarded in them.

Through Women's Studies work I have met very few men who are truly distressed about systemic, unearned male advantage and conferred dominance. And so one question for me and others like me is whether we will be like them, or whether we will get truly distressed, even outraged, about unearned race advantage and conferred dominance and if so, what we will do to lessen them. In any case, we need to do more work in identifying how they actually affect our daily lives. We need more down-to-earth writing by people about these taboo subjects. We need more understanding of the ways in which white "privilege" damages white people, for these are not the same ways in which it damages the victimized. Skewed white psyches are an inseparable part of the picture, though I do not want to confuse the kinds of damages done to the holders of special assets and to those who suffer the deficits. Many, perhaps most, of our white students in the U.S. think that racism doesn't affect them because they are not people of color; they do not see "whiteness" as a racial identity. Many men likewise think that Women's Studies does not bear on their own existences because they are not female; they do not see themselves as having gendered identities. Insisting on the universal *effects* of "privilege" systems, then, becomes one of our chief tasks, and being more explicit about the *particular* effects in particular contexts is another. Men need to join us in this work.

In addition, since race and sex are not the only advantaging systems at work, we need to similarly examine the daily experience of having age advantage, or ethnic advantage, or physical ability, or advantage related to nationality, religion, or sexual orientation. Prof. Marnie Evans suggested to me that in many ways the list I made also applies directly to heterosexual privilege. This is a still more taboo subject than race privilege: the daily ways in which heterosexual privilege makes married persons comfortable or powerful, providing supports, assets, approvals, and rewards to those who live or expect to live in heterosexual pairs. Unpacking that content is still more difficult, owing to the deeper imbeddedness of heterosexual advantage and dominance, and stricter taboos surrounding these.

But to start such an analysis I would put this observation from my own experience: The fact that I live under the same roof with a man triggers all kinds of societal assumptions about my worth, politics, life, and values, and triggers a host of unearned advantages and powers. After recasting many elements from the original list I would add further observations like these:

1. My children do not have to answer questions about why I live with my partner (my husband).
2. I have no difficulty finding neighborhoods where people approve of our household.
3. My children are given texts and classes which implicitly support our kind of family unit, and do not turn them against my choice of domestic partnership.

4. I can travel alone or with my husband without expecting embarrassment or hostility in those who deal with us.
5. Most people I meet will see my marital arrangements as an asset to my life or as a favorable comment on my likability, my competence, or my mental health.
6. I can talk about the social events of a weekend without fearing most listeners' reactions.
7. I will feel welcomed and "normal" in the usual walks of public life, institutional, and social.
8. In many contexts, I am seen as "all right" in daily work on women because I do not live chiefly with women.

Difficulties and dangers surrounding the task of finding parallels are many. Since racism, sexism, and heterosexism are not the same, the advantaging associated with them should not be seen as the same. In addition, it is hard to disentangle aspects of unearned advantage which rest more on social class, economic class, race, religion, sex and ethnic identity than on other factors. Still, all of the oppressions are interlocking, as the Combahee River Collective statement of 1977 continues to remind us eloquently.[3]

One factor seems clear about all of the interlocking oppressions. They take both active forms which we can see and embedded forms which as a member of the dominant group one is taught not to see. In my class and place, I did not see myself as racist because I was taught to recognize racism only in individual acts of meanness by members of my group, never in invisible systems conferring unsought racial dominance on my group from birth. Likewise, we are taught to think that sexism or heterosexism is carried on only through individual acts of discrimination, meanness, or cruelty toward women, gays, and lesbians, rather than in invisible systems conferring unsought dominance on certain groups. Disapproving of the systems won't be enough to change them. I was taught to think that racism could end if white individuals changed their attitudes; many men think sexism can be ended by individual changes in daily behavior toward women.

But a man's sex provides advantage for him whether or not he approves of the way in which dominance has been conferred on his group. A "white" skin in the United States opens many doors for whites whether or not we approve of the way dominance has been conferred on us. Individual acts can palliate, but cannot end, these problems. To redesign social systems we need first to acknowledge their colossal unseen dimensions. The silences and denials surrounding privilege are the key political tool here. They keep the thinking about equality or equity incomplete, protecting unearned advantage and conferred dominance by making these taboo subjects. Most talk by whites about equal opportunity seems to me now to be about equal opportunity to try to get into a position of dominance while denying that *systems* of dominance exist.

It seems to me that obliviousness about white advantage, like obliviousness about male advantage, is kept strongly inculturated in the United States so as to maintain the myth of meritocracy, the myth that democratic choice is equally available to all. Keeping most people unaware that freedom of confident action is there for just a small number of people props up those in power, and serves to keep power in the hands of the same groups that have most of it already. Though systemic change takes many decades, there are pressing questions for me and I imagine for some others like me if we raise our daily consciousness on the perquisites of being light-skinned. What will we do with such knowledge? As we know from watching men, it is an open question whether we will choose to use unearned advantage to weaken hidden systems of advantage, and whether we will use any of our arbitrarily awarded power to try to reconstruct power systems on a broader base.

NOTES

1. This paper was presented at the Virginia Women's Studies Association conference in Richmond in April 1986 and the American Educational Research Association conference in Boston in October 1986 and discussed with two groups of participants in the Dodge Seminars for Secondary School Teachers in New York and Boston in the spring of 1987.

2. Andersen, Margaret, "Race and the Social Science Curriculum: A Teaching and Learning Discussion." *Radical Teacher*, November 1984, pp. 17–20. Smith, Lillian, *Killers of the Dream*, New York, 1949.

3. "A Black Feminist Statement," The Combahee River Collective, pp. 13–22 in Hull, Scott, Smith, eds., *All the Women Are White, All the Blacks Are Men. But Some of Us Are Brave: Black Women's Studies.* The Feminist Press, 1982.

19

Age, Race, Class, and Sex: Women Redefining Difference

AUDRE LORDE

Much of western european history conditions us to see human differences in simplistic opposition to each other: dominant/subordinate, good/bad, up/down, superior/inferior. In a society where the good is defined in terms of profit rather than in terms of human need, there must always be some group of people who, through systematized oppression, can be made to feel surplus, to occupy the place of the dehumanized inferior. Within this society, that group is made up of Black and Third World people, working-class people, older people, and women.

As a forty-nine-year-old Black lesbian feminist socialist mother of two, including one boy, and a member of an interracial couple, I usually find myself a part of some group defined as other, deviant, inferior, or just plain wrong. Traditionally, in american society, it is the members of oppressed, objectified groups who are expected to stretch out and bridge the gap between the actualities of our lives and the consciousness of our oppressor. For in order to survive, those of us for whom oppression is as american as apple pie have always had to be watchers, to become familiar with the language and manners of the oppressor, even sometimes adopting them for some illusion of protection. Whenever the need for some pretense of communication arises, those who profit from our oppression call upon us to share our knowledge with them. In other words, it is the responsibility of the oppressed to teach the oppressors their mistakes. I am responsible for educating teachers who dismiss my children's culture in school. Black and Third World people are expected to educate white people as to our humanity. Women are expected to educate men. Lesbians and gay men are expected to educate the heterosexual world. The oppressors maintain their position and evade responsibility for their own actions. There is a constant drain of energy which might be better used in redefining ourselves and devising realistic scenarios for altering the present and constructing the future.

Institutionalized rejection of difference is an absolute necessity in a profit economy which needs "outsiders" as surplus people. As members of such an economy, we have all been programmed to respond to the human differences between us with fear and loathing and to handle that difference in one of three ways: ignore it, and if that is not possible, copy it if we think it is dominant, or destroy it if we think it is subordinate. But we have no patterns for relating across our human differences as equals. As a result, those differences have been misnamed and misused in the service of separation and confusion.

Certainly there are very real differences between us of race, age, and sex. But it is not those differences between us that are separating us. It is rather our refusal to recognize those differences, and to examine the distortions which result from our misnaming them and their effects upon human behavior and expectation.

Racism, the belief in the inherent superiority of one race over all others and thereby the right to dominance. Sexism, the belief in the inherent superiority of one sex over the other and thereby the right to dominance. Ageism. Heterosexism, Elitism, Classism.

It is a lifetime pursuit for each one of us to extract these distortions from our living at the same time as we recognize, reclaim, and define those differences upon which they are imposed. For we have all been raised in a society where those distortions were endemic within our living. Too often, we pour the energy needed for recognizing and exploring difference into pretending those differences are insurmountable barriers, or that they do not exist at all. This results in a voluntary isolation, or false and treacherous connections. Either way, we do not develop tools for using human difference as a springboard for creative change within our lives. We speak not of human difference, but of human deviance.

Somewhere, on the edge of consciousness, there is what I call a *mythical norm,* which each one of us within our hearts knows "that is not me." In america, this norm is usually defined as white, thin, male, young, heterosexual, christian, and financially secure. It is with this mythical norm that the trappings of power reside within this society. Those of us who stand outside that power often identify one way in which we are different, and we assume that to be the primary cause of all oppression, forgetting other distortions around difference, some of which we ourselves may be practising. By and large within the women's movement today, white women focus upon their oppression as women and ignore differences of race, sexual preference, class, and age. There is a pretense to a homogeneity of experience covered by the word *sisterhood* that does not in fact exist.

Unacknowledged class differences rob women of each others' energy and creative insight. Recently a women's magazine collective made the decision for one issue to print only prose, saying poetry was a less "rigorous" or "serious" art form. Yet even the form our creativity takes is often a class issue. Of all the art forms, poetry is the most economical. It is the one which is the most secret, which requires the least physical labor, the least material, and the one which can be done between shifts, in the hospital pantry, on the subway, and on scraps of surplus paper. Over the last few years, writing a novel on tight finances, I came to appreciate the enormous, differences in the material demands between poetry and prose. As we reclaim our literature, poetry has been the major voice of poor, working class, and Colored women. A room of one's own may be a necessity for writing prose, but so are reams of paper, a typewriter, and plenty of time. The actual requirements to produce the visual arts also help determine, along class lines, whose art is whose. In this day of inflated prices for material, who are our sculptors, our painters, our photographers? When we speak of a broadly based women's culture, we need to be aware of the effect of class and economic differences on the supplies available for producing art.

As we move toward creating a society within which we can each flourish, ageism is another distortion of relationship which interferes without vision. By ignoring the past, we are encouraged to repeat its mistakes. The "generation gap" is an important social tool for any repressive society. If the younger members of a community view the older members as contemptible or suspect or excess, they will never be able to join hands and examine the living memories of the community, nor ask the all important question, "Why?" This gives rise to a historical amnesia that keeps us working to invent the wheel every time we have to go to the store for bread.

We find ourselves having to repeat and relearn the same old lessons over and over that our mothers did because we do not pass on what we have learned, or because we are unable to listen. For instance, how many times has this all been said before? For another, who would have believed that once again our daughters are allowing their bodies to be hampered and purgatoried by girdles and high heels and hobble skirts?

Ignoring the differences of race between women and the implications of those differences presents the most serious threat to the mobilization of women's joint power.

As white women ignore their built-in privilege of whiteness and define *woman* in terms of their own experience alone, then women of Color become "other," the outsider whose experience and tradition is too "alien" to comprehend. An example of this is the signal absence of the experience of women of Color as a resource for women's studies courses.

The literature of women of Color is seldom included in women's literature courses and almost never in other literature courses, nor in women's studies as a whole. All too often, the excuse given is that the literatures of women of Color can only be taught by Colored women, or that they are too difficult to understand, or that classes cannot "get into" them because they come out of experiences that are "too different." I have heard this argument presented by white women of otherwise quite clear intelligence, women who seem to have no trouble at all teaching and reviewing work that comes out of the vastly different experiences of Shakespeare, Molière, Dostoyefsky, and Aristophanes. Surely there must be some other explanation.

This is a very complex question, but I believe one of the reasons white women have such difficulty reading Black women's work is because of their reluctance to see Black women as women and different from themselves. To examine Black women's literature effectively requires that we be seen as whole people in our actual complexities—as individuals, as women, as human—rather than as one of those problematic but familiar stereotypes provided in this society in place of genuine images of Black women. And I believe this holds true for the literatures of other women of Color who are not Black.

The literatures of all women of Color recreate the textures of our lives, and many white women are heavily invested in ignoring the real differences. For as long as any difference between us means one of us must be inferior, then the recognition of any difference must be fraught with guilt. To allow women of Color to step out of stereotypes is too guilt provoking, for it threatens the complacency of those women who view oppression only in terms of sex.

Refusing to recognize difference makes it impossible to see the different problems and pitfalls facing us as women.

Thus, in a patriarchal power system where whiteskin privilege is a major prop, the entrapments used to neutralize Black women and white women are not the same. For example, it is easy for Black women to be used by the power structure against Black men, not because they are men, but because they are Black. Therefore, for Black women, it is necessary at all times to separate the needs of the oppressor from our own legitimate conflicts within our communities. This same problem does not exist for white women. Black women and men have shared racist oppression and still share it, although in different ways. Out of that shared oppression we have developed joint defenses and joint vulnerabilities to each other that are not duplicated in the white community, with the exception of the relationship between Jewish women and Jewish men.

On the other hand, white women face the pitfall of being seduced into joining the oppressor under the pretense of sharing power. This possibility does not exist in the same way for women of Color. The tokenism that is sometimes extended to us is not an invitation to join power; our racial "otherness" is a visible reality that makes that quite clear. For white women there is a wider range of pretended choices and rewards for identifying with patriarchal power and its tools.

Today, with the defeat of ERA, the tightening economy, and increased conservatism, it is easier once again for white women to believe the dangerous fantasy that if you are good enough, pretty enough, sweet enough, quiet enough, teach the children to behave, hate the right people, and marry the right men, then you will be allowed to co-exist with patriarchy in relative peace, at least until a man needs your job or the neighborhood rapist happens along. And true, unless one lives and loves in the trenches it is difficult to remember that the war against dehumanization is ceaseless.

But Black women and our children know the fabric of our lives is stitched with violence and with hatred, that there is no rest. We do not deal with it only on the picket lines, or in dark midnight alleys, or in the places where we dare to verbalize our resistance. For us, increasingly, violence weaves through the daily tissues of our living—in the supermarket, in the classroom, in the elevator, in the clinic and the schoolyard, from the plumber, the baker, the saleswoman, the bus driver, the bank teller, the waitress who does not serve us.

Some problems we share as women, some we do not. You fear your children will grow up to join the patriarchy and testify against you, we fear our children will be dragged from a car and shot down in the street, and you will turn your backs upon the reasons they are dying.

The threat of difference has been no less blinding to people of Color. Those of us who are Black must see that the reality of our lives and our struggle does not make us immune to the errors of ignoring and misnaming difference. Within Black communities where racism is a living reality, differences among us often seem dangerous and suspect. The need for unity is often misnamed as a need for homogeneity, and a Black feminist vision mistaken for betrayal of our common interests as a people. Because of the continuous battle against racial erasure that Black women and Black men share, some Black women still refuse to recognize that we are also oppressed as women, and that sexual hostility against Black women is practiced not only by the white racist society, but implemented within our Black communities as well. It is a disease striking the heart of Black nationhood, and silence will not make it disappear. Exacerbated by racism and the pressures of powerlessness, violence against Black women and children often becomes a standard within our communities, one by which manliness can be measured. But these woman-hating acts are rarely discussed as crimes against Black women.

As a group, women of Color are the lowest paid wage earners in America. We are the primary targets of abortion and sterilization abuse, here and abroad. In certain parts of Africa, small girls are still being sewed shut between their legs to keep them docile and for men's pleasure. This is known as female circumcision, and it is not a cultural affair as the late Jomo Kenyatta insisted, it is a crime against Black women.

Black women's literature is full of the pain of frequent assault, not only by a racist patriarchy, but also by Black men. Yet the necessity for and history of shared battle have made us, Black women, particularly vulnerable to the false accusation that anti-sexist is anti-Black. Meanwhile, womanhating as a recourse of the powerless is sapping strength from Black communities, and our very lives. Rape is on the increase, reported and unreported, and rape is not aggressive sexuality, it is sexualized aggression. As Kalamu ya Salaam, a Black male writer points out, "As long as male domination exists, rape will exist. Only women revolting and men made conscious of their responsibility to fight sexism can collectively stop rape."*

Differences between ourselves as Black women are also being misnamed and used to separate us from one another. As a Black lesbian feminist comfortable with the many different ingredients of my identity, and a woman committed to racial and sexual freedom from oppression, I find I am constantly being encouraged to pluck out some one aspect of myself and present this as the meaningful whole, eclipsing or denying the other parts of self. But this is a destructive and fragmenting way to live. My fullest concentration of energy is available to me only when I integrate all the parts of who I am, openly, allowing power from particular sources of my living to flow back and forth freely through all my different selves, without the restrictions of externally imposed definition. Only then can I bring myself and my energies as a whole to the service of those struggles which I embrace as part of my living.

A fear of lesbians, or of being accused of being a lesbian, has led many Black women into testifying against themselves. It has led some of us into destructive alliances, and others into despair and isolation. In the white women's communities, heterosexism is sometimes a result of identifying with the white patriarchy, a rejection of that interdependence between women-identified women which allows the self to be, rather than to be used in the service of men. Sometimes it reflects a die-hard belief in the protective coloration of heterosexual relationships, sometimes a self-hate which all women have to fight against, taught us from birth.

---

*Seabury Press, New York, 1970.

Although elements of these attitudes exist for all women, there are particular resonances of hetero-sexism and homophobia among Black women. Despite the fact that woman-bonding has a long and honorable history in the African and African-american communities, and despite the knowledge and accomplishments of many strong and creative women-identified Black women in the political, social and cultural fields, heterosexual Black women often tend to ignore or discount the existence and work of Black lesbians. Part of this attitude has come from an understandable terror of Black male attack within the close confines of Black society, where the punishment for any female self-assertion is still to be accused of being a lesbian and therefore unworthy of the attention or support of the scarce Black male. But part of this need to misname and ignore Black lesbians comes from a very real fear that openly women-identified Black women who are no longer dependent upon men for their self-definition may well reorder our whole concept of social relationships.

Black women who once insisted that lesbianism was a white woman's problem now insist that Black lesbians are a threat to Black nationhood, are consorting with the enemy, are basically un-Black. These accusations, coming from the very women to whom we look for deep and real understanding, have served to keep many Black lesbians in hiding, caught between the racism of white women and the homophobia of their sisters. Often, their work has been ignored, trivialized, or misnamed, as with the work of Angelina Grimke, Alice Dunbar-Nelson, Lorraine Hansberry. Yet women-bonded women have always been some part of the power of Black communities, from our unmarried aunts to the amazons of Dahomey.

And it is certainly not Black lesbians who are assaulting women and raping children and grandmothers on the streets of our communities.

Across this country, as in Boston during the spring of 1979 following the unsolved murders of twelve Black women, Black lesbians are spearheading movements against violence against Black women.

What are the particular details within each of our lives that can be scrutinized and altered to help bring about change? How do we redefine difference for all women? It is not our differences which separate women, but our reluctance to recognize those differences and to deal effectively with the distortions which have resulted from the ignoring and misnaming of those differences.

As a tool of social control, women have been encouraged to recognize only one area of human difference as legitimate, those differences which exist between women and men. And we have learned to deal across those differences with the urgency of all oppressed subordinates. All of us have had to learn to live or work or coexist with men, from our fathers on. We have recognized and negotiated these differences, even when this recognition only continued the old dominant/subordinate mode of human relationship, where the oppressed must recognize the masters' difference in order to survive.

But our future survival is predicated upon our ability to relate within equality. As women, we must root out internalized patterns of oppression within ourselves if we are to move beyond the most superficial aspects of social change. Now we must recognize differences among women who are our equals, neither inferior nor superior, and devise ways to use each others' difference to enrich our visions and our joint struggles.

The future of our earth may depend upon the ability of all women to identify and develop new definitions of power and new patterns of relating across difference. The old definitions have not served us, nor the earth that supports us. The old patterns, no matter how cleverly rearranged to imitate progress, still condemn us to cosmetically altered repetitions of the same old exchanges, the same old guilt, hatred, recrimination, lamentation, and suspicion.

For we have, built into all of us, old blueprints of expectation and response, old structures of oppression, and these must be altered at the same time as we alter the living conditions which are a result of those structures. For the master's tools will never dismantle the master's house.

As Paulo Freire shows so well in *The Pedagogy of the Oppressed,*★ the true focus of revolutionary change is never merely the oppressive situations which we seek to escape, but that piece of the oppressor which is planted deep within each of us, and which knows only the oppressors' tactics, the oppressors' relationships.

Change means growth, and growth can be painful. But we sharpen self-definition by exposing the self in work and struggle together with those whom we define as different from ourselves, although sharing the same goals. For Black and white, old and young, lesbian and heterosexual women alike, this can mean new paths to our survival.

We have chosen each other
and the edge of each others battles
the war is the same
if we lose
someday women's blood will congeal
upon a dead planet
if we win
there is no telling
we seek beyond history
for a new and more possible meeting.★★

20

Defining Racism:

"Can We Talk?"

BEVERLEY DANIELS TATUM

Early in my teaching career, a White student I knew asked me what I would be teaching the following semester. I mentioned that I would be teaching a course on racism. She replied, with some surprise in her voice, "Oh, is there still racism?" I assured her that indeed there was and

---

★Seabury Press, New York, 1970.
★★From "Outlines," unpublished poem.

suggested that she sign up for my course. Fifteen years later, after exhaustive media coverage of events such as the Rodney King beating, the Charles Stuart and Susan Smith cases, the O. J. Simpson trial, the appeal to racial prejudices in electoral politics, and the bitter debates about affirmative action and welfare reform, it seems hard to imagine that anyone would still be unaware of the reality of racism in our society. But in fact, in almost every audience I address, there is someone who will suggest that racism is a thing of the past. There is always someone who hasn't noticed the stereotypical images of people of color in the media, who hasn't observed the housing discrimination in their community, who hasn't read the newspaper articles about documented racial bias in lending practices among well-known banks, who isn't aware of the racial tracking pattern at the local school, who hasn't seen the reports of rising incidents of racially motivated hate crimes in America—in short, someone who hasn't been paying attention to issues of race. But if you are paying attention, the legacy of racism is not hard to see, and we are all affected by it.

The impact of racism begins early. Even in our preschool years, we are exposed to misinformation about people different from ourselves. Many of us grew up in neighborhoods where we had limited opportunities to interact with people different from our own families. When I ask my college students, "How many of you grew up in neighborhoods where most of the people were from the same racial group as your own?" almost every hand goes up. There is still a great deal of social segregation in our communities. Consequently, most of the early information we receive about "others"—people racially, religiously, or socioeconomically different from ourselves—does not come as the result of firsthand experience. The secondhand information we do receive has often been distorted, shaped by cultural stereotypes, and left incomplete.

Some examples will highlight this process. Several years ago one of my students conducted a research project investigating preschoolers' conceptions of Native Americans.[1] Using children at a local day care center as her participants, she asked these three- and four-year-olds to draw a picture of a Native American. Most children were stumped by her request. They didn't know what a Native American was. But when she rephrased the question and asked them to draw a picture of an Indian, they readily complied. Almost every picture included one central feature: feathers. In fact, many of them also included a weapon—a knife or tomahawk—and depicted the person in violent or aggressive terms. Though this group of children, almost all of whom were White, did not live near a large Native American population and probably had had little if any personal interaction with American Indians, they all had internalized an image of what Indians were like. How did they know? Cartoon images, in particular the Disney movie *Peter Pan,* were cited by the children as their number-one source of information. At the age of three, these children already had a set of stereotypes in place. Though I would not describe three-year-olds as prejudiced, the stereotypes to which they have been exposed become the foundation for the adult prejudices so many of us have.

Sometimes the assumptions we make about others come not from what we have been told or what we have seen on television or in books, but rather from what we have *not* been told. The distortion of historical information about people of color leads young people (and older people, too) to make assumptions that may go unchallenged for a long time. Consider this conversation between two White students following a discussion about the cultural transmission of racism:

"Yeah, I just found out that Cleopatra was actually a Black woman."

"What?"

The first student went on to explain her newly learned information. The second student exclaimed in disbelief, "That can't be true. Cleopatra was beautiful!"

What had this young woman learned about who in our society is considered beautiful and who is not? Had she conjured up images of Elizabeth Taylor when she thought of Cleopatra? The new information her classmate had shared and her own deeply ingrained assumptions about who is beautiful and who is not were too incongruous to allow her to assimilate the information at that moment.

Omitted information can have similar effects. For example, another young woman, preparing to be a high school English teacher, expressed her dismay that she had never learned about any Black authors in any of her English courses. How was she to teach about them to her future students when she hadn't learned about them herself? A White male student in the class responded to this discussion with frustration in his response journal, writing "It's not my fault that Blacks don't write books." Had one of his elementary, high school, or college teachers ever told him that there were no Black writers? Probably not. Yet because he had never been exposed to Black authors, he had drawn his own conclusion that there were none.

Stereotypes, omissions, and distortions all contribute to the development of prejudice. *Prejudice* is a preconceived judgment or opinion, usually based on limited information. I assume that we all have prejudices, not because we want them, but simply because we are so continually exposed to misinformation about others. Though I have often heard students or workshop participants describe someone as not having "a prejudiced bone in his body," I usually suggest that they look again. Prejudice is one of the inescapable consequences of living in a racist society. Cultural racism—the cultural images and messages that affirm the assumed superiority of Whites and the assumed inferiority of people of color—is like smog in the air. Sometimes it is so thick it is visible, other times it is less apparent, but always, day in and day out, we are breathing it in. None of us would introduce ourselves as "smog-breathers" (and most of us don't want to be described as prejudiced), but if we live in a smoggy place, how can we avoid breathing the air? If we live in an environment in which we are bombarded with stereotypical images in the media, are frequently exposed to the ethnic jokes of friends and family members, and are rarely informed of the accomplishments of oppressed groups, we will develop the negative categorizations of those groups that form the basis of prejudice.

People of color as well as Whites develop these categorizations. Even a member of the stereotyped group may internalize the stereotypical categories about his or her own group to some degree. In fact, this process happens so frequently that it has a name, *internalized oppression*. . . .

Certainly some people are more prejudiced than others, actively embracing and perpetuating negative and hateful images of those who are different from themselves. When we claim to be free of prejudice, perhaps what we are really saying is that we are not hatemongers. But none of us is completely innocent. Prejudice is an integral part of our socialization, and it is not our fault. Just as the preschoolers my student interviewed are not to blame for the negative messages they internalized, we are not at fault for the stereotypes, distortions, and omissions that shaped our thinking as we grew up.

To say that it is not our fault does not relieve us of responsibility, however. We may not have polluted the air, but we need to take responsibility, along with others, for cleaning it up. Each of us needs to look at our own behavior. Am I perpetuating and reinforcing the negative messages so pervasive in our culture, or am I seeking to challenge them? If I have not been exposed to positive images of marginalized groups, am I seeking them out, expanding my own knowledge base for myself and my children? Am I acknowledging and examining my own prejudices, my own rigid categorizations of others, thereby minimizing the adverse impact they might have on my interactions with those I have categorized? Unless we engage in these and other conscious acts of reflection and reeducation, we easily repeat the process with our children. We teach what we were taught. The unexamined prejudices of the parents are passed on to the children. It is not our fault, but it is our responsibility to interrupt this cycle.

RACISM: A SYSTEM OF ADVANTAGE BASED ON RACE

Many people use the terms *prejudice* and *racism* interchangeably. I do not, and I think it is important to make a distinction. In his book *Portraits of White Racism,* David Wellman argues convincingly that limiting our understanding of racism to prejudice does not offer a sufficient explanation for the persistence of racism. He defines racism as a "system of advantage based on race."[2] In illustrating this definition, be provides example after example of how Whites defend their racial advantage—access to better schools, housing, jobs—even when they do not embrace overtly prejudicial thinking. Racism cannot be fully explained as an expression of prejudice alone.

This definition of racism is useful because it allows us to see that racism, like other forms of oppression, is not only a personal ideology based on racial prejudice, but a *system* involving cultural messages and institutional policies and practices as well as the beliefs and actions of individuals. In the context of the United States, this system clearly operates to the advantage of Whites and to the disadvantage of people of color. Another related definition of racism, commonly used by antiracist educators and consultants, is "prejudice plus power." Racial prejudice when combined with social power—access to social, cultural, and economic resources and decision-making—leads to the institutionalization of racist policies and practices. While I think this definition also captures the idea that racism is more than individual beliefs and attitudes, I prefer Wellman's definition because the idea of systematic advantage and disadvantage is critical to an understanding of how racism operates in American society.

In addition, I find that many of my White students and workshop participants do not feel powerful. Defining racism as prejudice plus power has little personal relevance. For some, their response to this definition is the following: "I'm not really prejudiced, and I have no power, so racism has nothing to do with me." However, most White people, if they are really being honest with themselves, can see that there are advantages to being White in the United States. Despite the current rhetoric about affirmative action and "reverse racism," every social indicator, from salary to life expectancy, reveals the advantages of being White.[3]

The systematic advantages of being White are often referred to as White privilege. In a now well-known article, "White Privilege: Unpacking the Invisible Knapsack," Peggy McIntosh, a White feminist scholar, identified a long list of societal privileges that she received simply because she was White.[4] She did not ask for them, and it is important to note that she hadn't always noticed that she was receiving them. They included major and minor advantages. Of course she enjoyed greater access to jobs and housing. But she also was able to shop in department stores without being followed by suspicious salespeople and could always find appropriate hair care products and makeup in any drugstore. She could send her child to school confident that the teacher would not discriminate against him on the basis of race. She could also be late for meetings, and talk with her mouth full, fairly confident that these behaviors would not be attributed to the fact that she was White. She could express an opinion in a meeting or in print and not have it labeled the "White" viewpoint. In other words, she was more often than not viewed as an individual, rather than as a member of a racial group.

This article rings true for most White readers, many of whom may have never considered the benefits of being White. It's one thing to have enough awareness of racism to describe the ways that people of color are disadvantaged by it. But this new understanding of racism is more elusive. In very concrete terms, it means that if a person of color is the victim of housing discrimination, the apartment that would otherwise have been rented to that person of color is still available for a White person. The

White tenant is, knowingly or unknowingly, the beneficiary of racism, a system of advantage based on race. The unsuspecting tenant is not to blame for the prior discrimination, but she benefits from it anyway.

For many Whites, this new awareness of the benefits of a racist system elicits considerable pain, often accompanied by feelings of anger and guilt. These uncomfortable emotions can hinder further discussion. We all like to think that we deserve the good things we have received, and that others, too, get what they deserve. Social psychologists call this tendency a "belief in a just world."[5] Racism directly contradicts such notions of justice.

Understanding racism as a system of advantage based on race is antithetical to traditional notions of an American meritocracy. For those who have internalized this myth, this definition generates considerable discomfort. It is more comfortable simply to think of racism as a particular form of prejudice. Notions of power or privilege do not have to be addressed when our understanding of racism is constructed in that way.

The discomfort generated when a systemic definition of racism is introduced is usually quite visible in the workshops I lead. Someone in the group is usually quick to point out that this is not the definition you will find in most dictionaries. I reply, "Who wrote the dictionary?" I am not being facetious with this response. Whose interests are served by a "prejudice only" definition of racism? It is important to understand that the system of advantage is perpetuated when we do not acknowledge its existence.

RACISM: FOR WHITES ONLY?

Frequently someone will say, "You keep talking about White people. People of color can be racist, too." I once asked a White teacher what it would mean to her if a student or parent of color accused her of being racist. She said she would feel as though she had been punched in the stomach or called a "low-life scum." She is not alone in this feeling. The word *racist* holds a lot of emotional power. For many White people, to be called racist is the ultimate insult. The idea that this term might only be applied to Whites becomes highly problematic for, after all, can't people of color be "low-life scum" too?

Of course, people of any racial group can hold hateful attitudes and behave in racially discriminatory and bigoted ways. We can all cite examples of horrible hate crimes which have been perpetrated by people of color as well as Whites. Hateful behavior is hateful behavior no matter who does it. But when I am asked, "Can people of color be racist?" I reply, "The answer depends on your definition of racism." If one defines racism as racial prejudice, the answer is yes. People of color can and do have racial prejudices. However, if one defines racism as a system of advantage based on race, the answer is no. People of color are not racist because they do not systematically benefit from racism. And equally important, there is no systematic cultural and institutional support or sanction for the racial bigotry of people of color. In my view, reserving the term *racist* only for behaviors committed by Whites in the context of a White-dominated society is a way of acknowledging the ever-present power differential afforded Whites by the culture and institutions that make up the system of advantage and continue to reinforce notions of White superiority. (Using the same logic, I reserve the word *sexist* for men. Though women can and do have gender-based prejudices, only men systematically benefit from sexism.)

Despite my best efforts to explain my thinking on this point, there are some who will be troubled, perhaps even incensed, by my response. To call the racially motivated acts of a person of color acts of racial bigotry and to describe similar acts committed by Whites as racist will make no sense to some people, including some people of color. To those, I will respectfully say, "We can agree to disagree." At moments like these, it is not agreement that is essential, but clarity. Even if you don't like the definition of racism I am using, hopefully you are now clear about what it is. If I also understand how you are using the term, our conversation can continue—despite our disagreement.

Another provocative question I'm often asked is "Are you saying all Whites are racist?" When asked this question, I again remember that White teacher's response, and I am conscious that perhaps the question I am really being asked is, "Are you saying all Whites are bad people?" The answer to that question is of course not. However, all White people, intentionally or unintentionally, do benefit from racism. A more relevant question is what are White people as individuals doing to interrupt racism? For many White people, the image of a racist is a hood-wearing Klan member or a name-calling Archie Bunker figure. These images represent what might be called *active racism,* blatant, intentional acts of racial bigotry and discrimination. *Passive racism* is more subtle and can be seen in the collusion of laughing when a racist joke is told, of letting exclusionary hiring practices go unchallenged, of accepting as appropriate the omissions of people of color from the curriculum, and of avoiding difficult race-related issues. Because racism is so ingrained in the fabric of American institutions, it is easily self-perpetuating.[6] All that is required to maintain it is business as usual.

I sometimes visualize the ongoing cycle of racism as a moving walkway at the airport. Active racist behavior is equivalent to walking fast on the conveyor belt. The person engaged in active racist behavior has identified with the ideology of White supremacy and is moving with it. Passive racist behavior is equivalent to standing still on the walkway. No overt effort is being made, but the conveyor belt moves the bystanders along to the same destination as those who are actively walking. Some of the bystanders may feel the motion of the conveyor belt, see the active racists ahead of them, and choose to turn around, unwilling to go to the same destination as the White supremacists. But unless they are walking actively in the opposite direction at a speed faster than the conveyor belt— unless they are actively antiracist—they will find themselves carried along with the others.

So, not all Whites are actively racist. Many are passively racist. Some, though not enough, are actively antiracist. The relevant question is not whether all Whites are racist, but how we can move more White people from a position of active or passive racism to one of active antiracism. The task of interrupting racism is obviously not the task of Whites alone. But the fact of White privilege means that Whites have greater access to the societal institutions in need of transformation. To whom much is given, much is required.

It is important to acknowledge that while all Whites benefit from racism, they do not all benefit equally. Other factors, such as socioeconomic status, gender, age, religious affiliation, sexual orientation, mental and physical ability, also play a role in our access to social influence and power. A White woman on welfare is not privileged to the same extent as a wealthy White heterosexual man. In her case, the systematic disadvantages of sexism and classism intersect with her White privilege, but the privilege is still there. This point was brought home to me in a 1994 study conducted by a Mount Holyoke graduate student, Phyllis Wentworth.[7] Wentworth interviewed a group of female college students, who were both older than their peers and were the first members of their families to attend college, about the pathways that led them to college. All of the women interviewed were White, from working-class backgrounds, from families where women were expected to graduate from high school and get married or get a job. Several had experienced abusive relationships and other personal difficulties prior to coming to college. Yet their experiences were punctuated by "good luck" stories of apartments obtained without a deposit, good jobs offered without experience or extensive reference checks, and encouragement provided by willing mentors. While the women acknowledged their good fortune, none of them discussed their Whiteness. They had not considered the possibility that being White had worked in their favor and helped give them the benefit of the doubt at critical junctures. This study clearly showed that even under difficult circumstances, White privilege was still operating.

It is also true that not all people of color are equally targeted by racism. We all have multiple identities that shape our experience. I can describe myself as a light-skinned, well-educated, heterosexual, able-bodied, Christian African American woman raised in a middle-class suburb. As an African American woman, I am systematically disadvantaged by race and by gender, but I systematically receive benefits in the other categories, which then mediate my experience of racism and sexism. When one is targeted by multiple isms—racism, sexism, classism, heterosexism, ableism, anti-Semitism, ageism—in whatever combination, the effect is intensified. The particular combination of racism and classism in many communities of color is life-threatening. Nonetheless, when I, the middle-class Black mother of two sons, read another story about a Black man's unlucky encounter with a White police officer's deadly force, I am reminded that racism by itself can kill.

NOTES

1. C. O'Toole, "The effect of the media and multicultural education on children's perceptions of Native Americans" (senior thesis, Department of Psychology and Education, Mount Holyoke College, South Hadley, MA, May 1990).

2. For an extended discussion of this point, see David Wellman, *Portraits of White racism* (Cambridge: Cambridge University Press, 1977), ch. 1.

3. For specific statistical information, see R. Farley, "The common destiny of Blacks and Whites: Observations about the social and economic status of the races," pp. 197–233, in H. Hill and J. E. Jones, Jr. (Eds.), *Race in America: The struggle for equality* (Madison: University of Wisconsin Press, 1993).

4. P. McIntosh, "White privilege: Unpacking the invisible knapsack," *Peace and Freedom* (July/August 1989): 10–12.

5. For further discussion of the concept of "belief in a just world," see M. J. Lerner, "Social psychology of justice and interpersonal attraction," in T. Huston (Ed.), *Foundations of interpersonal attraction* (New York: Academic Press, 1974).

6. For a brief historical overview of the institutionalization of racism and sexism in our legal system, see "Part V: How it happened: Race and gender issues in U.S. law," in P. S. Rothenberg (Ed.), *Race, class, and gender in the United States: An integrated study*, 3d ed. (New York: St. Martin's Press, 1995).

7. P. A. Wentworth, "The identity development of nontraditionally aged first-generation women college students: An exploratory study" (master's thesis, Department of Psychology and Education, Mount Holyoke College, South Hadley, MA, 1994).

21

Privilege

Expanding on Marilyn Frye's "Oppression"

ALISON BAILEY

Marilyn Frye's "Oppression" (1983) is essential reading in most courses with political and feminist content. One of the merits of her essay is the way in which examples such as men opening doors for women, metaphors that equate oppression with double-binds, and birdcage-like social structures get tied to the meaning of oppression. Anyone who teaches this essay knows how difficult it is to get students initially to understand how Frye uses the term 'oppression' to refer to systems. Each time I teach this essay I try to move the conversation one step further to make connections between oppression and privilege so that, in Frye's words, these terms do not get "stretched to meaninglessness" (1983, 1). Yet when I suggest that the oppression of people of color is systematically held in place by white privilege, or that women's subordination makes male privilege possible, or that homophobia holds heterosexual privilege in place, students who otherwise embrace Frye's analysis become reluctant to extend it to cover their own unearned advantages. To my surprise, conversations about what it means to have privilege are met with responses parallel to those Frye mentions at the beginning of her essay. "Blacks and other minorities are privileged too; they get athletic scholarships and affirmative action benefits," my students say. Or, "women are privileged too; they don't have to register for the selective service and men pay for their dinner on dates." Or, " gays and lesbians are privileged; current city ordinances for domestic partnership give them special rights." If students really do understand oppression as the product of systematically related barriers and forces not of one's own making, then why do they abandon Frye's analysis when I raise

issues of privilege to explain how the oppression of one group can be used to generate privilege for another? It would appear that they have not understood the structural features of oppression well enough to grasp how their use of "privilege" to describe mere advantages, such as having someone pay for your dinner, puts the term "privilege" in danger of being stretched to meaninglessness. I've come to conclude that any understanding of oppression is incomplete without recognition of the role privilege plays in maintaining systems of domination.

This essay continues the conversation Frye began in a way that makes connections between oppression and privilege. It is my hope that by providing a parallel account of privilege in general—and white, heterosexual, male privilege in particular—I can extend Frye's analysis to clarify the political dimensions of privilege.

1. FRYE'S STRUCTURAL ANALYSIS OF OPPRESSION

In her careful analysis of oppression, Marilyn Frye argues that one of the reasons people fail to see oppression is that they focus on particular events, attitudes, and actions that strike them as harmful, but they do not place these incidents in the context of historical, social, and political *systems*. According to Frye, members of oppressed groups commonly experience "double-binds," that is, they are faced daily with situations in which their options are reduced to a very few, all of which expose them to penalty, censure, or deprivation[1] (1983, 2). These binds are created and shaped by forces and barriers which are neither accidental nor avoidable, but are systematically related to each other in ways that confine individuals to the extent that movement in any direction is penalized. To make visible the systemic character of the barriers shaping the double-bind Frye uses the metaphor of a birdcage.

> [Oppression is] the experience of being caged in. . . . Consider a birdcage. If you look very closely at just one wire, you cannot see the other wires. If your conception of what is before you is determined by

this myopic focus, you could look at that one wire, up and down the length of it, and be unable to see why a bird would not just fly around the wire . . . it is only when you step back, stop looking at the wires one by one, microscopically, and take a macroscopic view of the whole cage, that you can see why the bird does not go anywhere; and then you will see it in a moment. (1983, 5-6)

Ignoring the systemic and interlocking nature of what I call complex systems of domination (e.g., racism, ableism, sexism, anti-Semitism, or homphobia) has misleading consequences. When the effects of sexism, for example, are not understood macroscopically as the products of systemic injustices, they are understood microscopically as the exclusive problems of particular women who have made bad choices, have poor attitudes, are too sensitive, or who are overreacting to a random incident. Failure to examine sexism, homophobia, racism, and anti-Semitism as harms produced by systematically related forces and barriers blurs the distinction between harm and oppression.

For oppression to be useful as a concept, Frye argues, the differences between harm and oppression need to be sharpened. All persons who are oppressed are in some way harmed, but not all persons who are harmed are oppressed. Men who cannot cry in public or whites who are ineligible for minority loan programs may feel harmed by these restrictions, but they are not oppressed. The gender roles which make public tearfulness inappropriate for men are unfair and may indeed be harmful to men's emotional well-being, but there is no network of forces or barriers which says both crying and not crying are unacceptable and that to do either is to expose oneself to "penalty, censure or deprivation" (1983, 2). Similarly, whites who are ineligible for loan programs designated for racial or ethnic minority applicants are only oppressed if there are no other reasonable means of securing a loan open to them. If whites are eligible for a variety of existing loan options, having one avenue closed to them may feel unfair, but it does not mean they are oppressed in Frye's sense of the word. Whites who find options for financing their education severely

limited may be oppressed by their class, but not by their race. There is nothing in these cases to suggest racial barriers or forces that leave loan-seeking whites optionless.

Since oppression is a structural phenomenon that devalues the work, experiences, and voices of members of marginalized social groups, it might be said that oppression is experienced by persons *because* they are members of particular social groups. In the language of Frye's cage metaphor: "The 'inhabitant' of the 'cage' is not an individual but a group. . . . Thus, to recognize a person as oppressed, one has to see that individual *as* belonging to a group of a certain sort" (1983, 8). Before turning to my analysis of the concept of privilege, I wish to make two important comments regarding Frye's observations about group membership and its role in systems of oppression. First, because individuals are rarely members of one community, oppression is not a unified phenomenon. Group differences in race/ethnicity, sexual orientation, gender, or class cut across individual lives to the point that privilege and oppression are often experienced simultaneously. The felt experience of oppression of a working-class white woman, for example, will be different than the felt oppression experienced by a middle-class African American male. Because of the complexity of these intersections, Iris Young argues that to be oppressed persons must experience at least one or a combination of as many as five conditions: economic exploitation, social/cultural marginalization, political powerlessness, cultural imperialism, and violence (1990, 48–63). The double-bind may be *a* characteristic of an individual's experiences of oppression, but it is not *the* defining feature. Both Frye and Young, I think, would argue that the strength of the bind depends upon which of these oppressive conditions are present in a person's life, how many conditions are present, how long they are present, and whether the individual is privileged in ways that might weaken or mediate the binds.

Next, to say that women are oppressed as members of the group women, or that lesbians are oppressed as lesbians, or that African Americans, Cherokees, or Chicano/as are oppressed as members of a particular racial-ethnic group suggests that sexism, heterosexism, and racism require identifiable sexes, sexual orientations, and racial-ethnic groups. Yet to understand how oppression is experienced by these marginalized groups, it is not necessary for social groups to have fixed boundaries. In fact understanding the systemic nature of oppression requires just the opposite: it requires that one understand how the *lack* of a rigid definition of social groups is part of complex systems of domination. One of the features of privilege is the ability of dominant groups to construct, define, and control the construction of categories. In the United States, for example, the invention of the category "white" illustrates how systems of oppression are held in place by purposely unstable racial categories. The word "white" began appearing in legal documents around 1680 as a direct result of legislation enforcing the hereditary bond servitude of Negroes, antimiscegenation laws, and new anti-Negro attitudes. In time, the idea of a homogeneous "white" race was adopted as a political means of generating cohesion among European explorers, traders, migrants, and settlers of eighteenth-century North America. The borders constructed between races have never been static. Racial borders are well guarded but intentionally porous: the political nature [of] racial classification requires that these borders be redrawn as patterns of immigration challenge them and new candidates for whiteness arise. Racial designations, then, historically shift to preserve power and privilege of those who have the authority to define who counts as white.

2. THE VIEW FROM OUTSIDE OF THE BIRDCAGE: PRIVILEGE AND EARNED ADVANTAGES

When I argue that members of dominant groups—men, whites, heterosexuals, or the wealthy—have privilege by virtue of their being members of particular social groups, I do not mean "privilege," as Joel Feinberg defines it, in its philosophical broad juridical sense as synonymous with *mere* liberties or the absence of duty.[2] In this sense to say that person P

is privileged or at liberty to do action A means that P has no duty to refrain from doing A. To say that I am privileged or at liberty to take a job in Seattle means that I have no obligations to refrain from taking a job in Seattle. Although privilege, in the sense I will be using the word, does imply a greater freedom of movement and choice, there is nothing about belonging to a group such as whites or men that would imply that one does or does not have duty to refrain from choosing to move to Seattle.

Neither am I using privilege in the sense of a legal benefit that is not a right. Privilege in this sense offers valuable benefits granted to persons or organizations by institutions (e.g., the state of Illinois, the federal government, or the Catholic Church) at the discretion of those institutions. Having a driver's license, being a naturalized citizen, or holding public office are common examples of privilege in this sense. Because my driving or voting privilege may be revoked at any time, say, for speeding or treason, the privileges to drive or to vote count as *mere* privileges; the state does not have a duty to grant these to me. I have neither a prior right to get a license nor a right to retain it once I pass the examination. While legal structures have historically played a role in holding heterosexual privilege, male privilege, or white privilege in place, privilege in this sense is not captured by legal language.

My interest is in a narrower sense of privilege as unearned assets conferred systematically. My aim is to fashion a distinction between privilege and advantages that parallels Frye's distinction between oppression and harm. Just as all oppression counts as harm, but not all harms count as oppression, I want to suggest that all privilege is advantageous, but that not all advantages count as privilege. Like the difference between harms and oppression, the difference between advantages and privilege has to do with the systematically conferred nature of these unearned assets. If we want to determine whether a particular harm qualifies as oppression, Frye argues that we have to look at that harm in context (macroscopically) to see what role, if any, it plays in an maintaining a structure that is oppressive. Likewise, if we want to determine whether a particular advantage qualifies as a privilege, we need to look at that advantage macroscopically in order to observe whether it plays a role in keeping complex systems of domination in place. We need to know if the advantage enables members of privileged groups to avoid the structured system of forces and barriers which serve to immobilize members of marginalized groups.

I am interested in providing an account of privilege and advantages that further clarifies Peggy McIntosh's distinction between "earned strength" and "unearned power conferred systematically." As McIntosh argues:

> Power from unearned privilege can look like strength when it is, in fact, permission to escape or to dominate. But not all privileges . . . are inevitably damaging. Some, like the expectation that neighbors will be decent to you, or that your race will not count against you in court, should be the norm in a just society and should be considered as the entitlement of everyone. Others, like the privilege not to listen to less powerful people, distort the humanity of the holders as well as the ignored groups. Still others, like finding one's staple foods everywhere may be a function of a numerical majority. Others have to do with not having to labor under pervasive negative stereotyping and mythology. (1991, 78)

McIntosh's explanation suggests that strength is something necessarily earned and that power is something unearned. She explains that the power of unearned privilege can appear as strength, when in reality it is just permission to escape or to dominate. And later, she says that privilege may confer power, but not moral strength.

McIntosh's distinction between strength and power puzzles me. Her point can be stated more simply by distinguishing between two kinds of assets: (unearned) privilege and earned advantages. The general distinction I will make between privilege and earned advantages begins with an etymology of privilege and rests on four related claims: (1) benefits granted by privilege are always unearned and conferred *systematically* to members of dominant social groups; (2) privilege granted to members of dominant groups simply because they are members of

these groups is almost never justifiable; (3) most privilege is invisible to, or not recognized as such, by those who have it; and, (4) privilege has an unconditional "wild card" quality that extends benefits to cover a wide variety of circumstances and conditions.

To understand how the benefits granted by privilege are always unearned and conferred systematically to members of dominant social groups, privilege must first be understood as a class of advantages. The words "advantage" and "advance" have a common Latin root—*abante* meaning "in front of" or "before." To possess any kind of advantage is to have a skill, talent, asset, or condition acquired—either by accident of birth or by intentional cultivation—that allows a person or a group to rise to a higher rank, to bring themselves forward, to lift themselves up, or otherwise to make progress. Privilege, in the sense that I will be using the word, is by definition advantageous, but not all advantages count as privilege. Advantages that are not privilege I will call *earned advantages*. Earned advantages are strengths which refer to any earned condition, skill, asset, or talent that benefits its possessor and which under restricted conditions helps to advance that person. Earned advantages include things such as being awarded extra frequent flyer miles, learning a second language, working hard so that you [can] afford to live in a neighborhood with a good school system, or dutifully attending athletic practice in order to be eligible for a volleyball scholarship.

The difference between earned advantages and privilege is not hard and fast; but I want to hang onto the distinction in a way that recognizes how privilege and earned advantages do not operate independently from one another, and at the same time highlight the connections between them. So, the distinction between privilege and advantages becomes less clear when it is challenged by cases where, for example, class oppression diminishes the currency of white or male privilege. Consider the role privilege plays in one's ability to get good work, to afford to fly, to buy a house, or to rent an apartment. To earn frequent flyer miles, for instance, assumes that one can afford to fly. Regardless of race, the homeless have few, if any, chances to take advantage of opportunities to earn frequent flyer miles. Working long hours so you can afford to buy a house in a good neighborhood also assumes that you are able to get a high-paying job, that real estate agents will show you houses in the "good parts of town," and that the owners of those houses will sell to you. Regardless of economic class, practices like redlining commonly keep families of color that can afford to live in middle- or upper-class suburbs from purchasing real estate and moving into those areas. In addition, malicious stereotypes of African Americans or Puerto Ricans as lazy, dirty, or untrustworthy, or stereotypes of gays and lesbians as pedophiles, promiscuous, or diseased also discourage landowners from renting to these individuals even if they are good tenants.

The distinction between privilege and advantage is also blurred by instances where, for example, class, race, or heterosexual oppression are temporarily transcended or overlooked. I have in mind here the gay community leader or the working-class philanthropist who, by virtue of outstanding community service, earns a good reputation in the community and is granted the status and authority commonly associated with heterosexual or class privilege. Or the African American who has elevated her economic status to the point where she is granted privileges commonly associated with well-to-do whites. In these cases members of dominant groups are often willing to make exceptions for certain individuals because of their economic success, community visibility, or civic reputation. There are also instances where closeted gays or light-skinned Latinas and African Americans are granted privileges because they can pass as straight or white.

Perhaps the point here is not that earned advantages and privilege are necessarily distinct, but rather that some advantages are more easily earned if they are accompanied by gender, heterosexual, race, or class privilege. Privilege and earned advantages are connected in the sense that privilege places one in a better position to earn more advantages. The link between earned advantages and unearned privilege generates a situation in which privileged groups can earn assets (e.g., control of resources, skills, a quality education, the attention of the mayor, a good reputation, a prestigious well-paying job, political power, or a safe place to live) more easily and more frequently than those who don't have white, male, heterosexual, or economic privilege. Failure to recognize the differences between earned and unearned assets allows privileged groups to interpret *all* privilege on the same footing as earned advantages. Ann Richards' insightful remark, "George Bush was born on third base, and to this day he believes he hit a triple," is a telling illustration of the failure to make this distinction.[3]

The cases of the black entrepreneur, the working-class activist, or the gay community leader weaken the tie between privilege and birth. Privilege also helps to move a person forward, but unlike the advantages described above, privilege is *granted* and birth is the easiest way of being granted privilege. In this sense, for a person to have privilege is to be granted benefits automatically by virtue of their perceived or actual class, sex, race or sexual status that others not of that status have had to earn. Suffrage, for example, was initially granted to white property-owning males; white women and emancipated Negroes, Native Americans, and immigrants had to struggle to earn this privilege. Marriage is also a highly regulated privilege which is granted exclusively to heterosexual couples. Gay, lesbian, and bisexual couples are currently struggling to secure this privilege in ways similar to Mildred Jeter Loving and her husband, Richard, who struggled to have their interracial marriage recognized by the Commonwealth of Virginia in the early 1960s. Being granted the privilege to marry because you are heterosexual, or the privilege to vote because you own land, are male, or are white, then, is unearned in the same way that having a friend or relative who will work on your car for nothing, or having good-natured and caring neighbors is unearned; they both seem to be largely a matter of luck. In spite of their significant differences the words privilege and advantage are used interchangeably. For this reason I want to be clear about how my use of privilege—as unearned advantages or assets conferred systematically—differs from standard philosophical and conversational usage.

Like McIntosh, I recognize and am disturbed by the misleading ordinary language connotations of privilege as something positive. The privilege that gives some people the freedom to be thoughtless at best, and murderous at worst, should not be thought of as desirable (1988, 77). The etymology of the word "privilege" helps to clarify my use of privilege as unearned advantages conferred systematically. "Privilege" itself is derived from the Latin *privilegium,* a law or bill in favor of or against an individual, from *priv-us,* meaning private, individual, or peculiar, and from *lex,* or law. So, privilege literally means private or individual law.[4] As one legal definition holds: "Privileges are special rights belonging to the individual or class, and not to the mass."[5] The etymological roots of privilege as private law or special rights reveals the worrisome nature of privilege. Historically, to have a privilege meant to have a right or immunity granting a peculiar benefit, advantage, or favor, such as a right or an immunity attached to a particular position or office. The exemption of ambassadors and members of Congress from arrest while going to, returning from, or attending to their public duties is an example of this. Here, having privilege means that holders of particular offices such as queen, police officer, senator, judge, parliamentarian, or bishop are either exempt from the usual operations of public law or accountable to a less formal set of private laws (sometimes of their own making) or both. In this sense to have a privilege means that a particular individual, like the president of the United States, or a specific group, say members of the Senate, are exempt from particular burdens or liabilities of public law (e.g., having to pay their parking tickets); their activities are governed by an individual or private set of immunity-granting rules. If the contemporary connotations of privilege strike us as too positive, then surely the denotations reveal the disturbing origins of this term.

Second, since exemptions and benefits of offices are sometimes understood as arbitrary favoritism, privilege in this sense has pejorative connotations; but it could be argued that some exemptions, and thus some privilege, is justified. For example, it is reasonable to grant ambulance drivers immunity from speeding laws, since emergency care requires getting to the hospital as quickly as possible. In this sense paramedics may be said to have special rights in the sense that they are granted temporary immunity from speeding laws while they are on duty. The extension of privilege to particular practices such as ambulance driving, which enable emergency care to continue efficiently, are generally regarded as justifiable. However, by most standards of fairness it is not justifiable to grant immunities to persons simply because they are perceived to be white, heterosexual, or male. Laws granting immunities to individuals because they are perceived to be members of dominant groups, if they can be justified at all, certainly ought not to be justified on the grounds that these private laws are needed for members of dominant racial or economic groups to move through the world safely at the expense of others.

Dominant group privilege is a particular class of unearned benefits and immunities enjoyed by individuals who, by moral luck, belong to groups with race, heterosexual, gender, or class privilege. I refer to groups such as men, whites, and heterosexuals as dominant not because of their numbers, but by virtue of the fact that historically their lives and experiences define the standards for what is deemed valuable or "normal." Dominant group privileges can, as I have argued, also be extended to individuals outside of these groups. Dominant group privilege is established partly through legislation and public policy but also through informal and subtle expressions of speech, bodily reactions and gestures, malicious stereotypes, aesthetic judgments, and media images. In this way privilege is systematically created and culturally reinforced.

My third point is that one of the functions of privilege is to structure the world so that mechanisms of privilege are invisible—in the sense that they are unexamined—to those who benefit from them. What Frye's birdcage metaphor does for oppression, Peggy McIntosh's invisible knapsack and Jona Olsson's computer metaphor do for privilege.[6]

The systemic and unexamined nature of what it means to have dominant group privilege is made clearer by McIntosh's metaphor of the "invisible knapsack." White privilege, she argues,

> [is] an invisible package of unearned assets that I can count on cashing in each day, but about which I was "meant" to remain oblivious. White privilege is like an invisible weightless knapsack of special provisions, assurances, tools, maps, guides, code books, passports, visas, clothes, compass, emergency gear, and blank checks. (1988, 71)

It is worth highlighting some of the common examples of privilege in this sense. Briefly white privilege includes:

- I can if I wish arrange to be in the company of people of my race most of the time.
- I can be sure that my children will be given curricular material that testifies to the existence of their race.
- I am never asked to speak for all the people of my racial group.
- I can dress any way I want and not have my appearance explained by the perceived tastes of my race.
- Whether I use checks, credit cards, or cash I can be fairly sure that my skin color will not count against the appearance of my financial reliability.
- In most instances I can be assured of having the public trust. (1991, 78)

Heterosexual privileges include:

- Being able to publicly show affection for one's partner without fear of public harm or hostility.
- Being assured that most people will approve of one's relationship.
- Not having to self-censor gender pronouns when talking about one's partner.

The structural nature of privilege is made visible by Jona Olsson, who compares privilege to having a very user-friendly word processing program. When I open up a new document in this program, the font, margins, page length, type-point size, spacing, and footnote style are set in a commonly accepted format for me. I do not have to do anything: this preset style is the default mode. I expect this service when I open up a new document, so much so that I take the professional shape and appearance of my document for granted. The structured invisibility of the word processing program insures that the flawless professional presentation of my documents will be attributed to my own talents and individual merits, rather than to my software. Privilege offers a default mode not unlike the default position on my word processing program. White, male, and heterosexual privilege are default positions. Either I can choose to be aware of these default positions or I can ignore them and decide to experiment with new fonts, margins, or document styles. If I become unhappy or frustrated with these new modes, I can always go back to the default positions.

Like the default mode on a word processing program, the bars on the birdcage are especially difficult to see from outside of the cage. The structured invisibility of privilege insures that a person's individual accomplishments will be recognized more on the basis of individual merit than on the basis of group membership.[7] Redirecting attention away from the unearned nature of privilege and toward individual merit allows persons born on third base to believe sincerely that they hit a triple. In fact, the maintenance of heterosexual, white, or male privilege as positions of structural advantage lie largely in the silence surrounding the mechanisms of privilege. For persons situated inside the borders of privilege, the privilege associated with being white, male, wealthy, or heterosexual is difficult to name, yet for those situated outside of these borders, the benefits of privilege are seen all too clearly.[8] White, heterosexual, or male survival do not depend upon an awareness of default positions and invisible knapsacks, so whites are not encouraged to recognize or acknowledge the effects of racialization on white lives, men have difficulty seeing the effects of sexism on women's lives, and heterosexuals rarely understand the impact of homophobia on gay, bisexual, and lesbian communities. Reflecting on the racial heterogeneity within her own family, for example, Cherrie Moraga uncomfortably acknowledges that her güera (light-skinned) appearance is something she can use to her advantage in a wide variety of difficult situations.

> Then [my friend] Tavo says to me, "you see at any time [you] decide to use your light skinned privilege [you] can." I say, "uh huh. Uh huh." He says, "You can decide that you are suddenly no Chicana."
>
> That I can't say, but once my light skin and good English saved my lover from arrest. And I'd use it again. I'd use it to the hilt over and over to save our skins.
>
> "You get to choose." Now I want to shove those words right back into his face. You call this a choice! To constantly push against a wall of resistance from your own people or to fall nameless into the mainstream of this country, running with our common blood?[9]

The invisibility of the default position here means that whites are rarely aware of the times light skin and/or clear English benefits us. Since whites rarely examine their privilege, we rarely perceive the barriers and hassles faced by those who appear to others as "nonwhite."

The final claim I want to make is that privilege facilitates one's movement through the world in a way that earned advantages do not. The systemic nature of privilege gives it a wild card quality, which means that privilege has a broader currency than earned advantages. Most earned advantages will advance a person under limited conditions. For example, frequent flyer miles are only an advantage if I need to travel, living in a neighborhood with a good school system is only an asset if I have children, and being bilingual is only beneficial to me if I live in or travel to communities where speaking two languages facilitates my daily activities. Unlike earned advantages, playing the privilege card (e.g., using the passports, checks, and codebooks in my knapsack) grants extra advantages to holders in a broader variety of circumstances. This is to say that being heterosexual, male, or white will almost always count in one's favor. To have white, heterosexual, or male privilege means that the immunities and benefits you have because of your race, sexual

orientation, or sex extend beyond the boundaries of your comfort zones, neighborhood, circles of friends, or what María Lugones calls the 'worlds' in which you are at ease.[10] Although privileged persons feel ill at ease outside of their own worlds, they rarely lose privilege outside of their comfort zones. The meaning of privilege as "special rights" or "private laws" should now be clear: immunity granting passports, checks, and tickets in the knapsack are wild cards in the sense that they are accepted almost everywhere. Regardless of where I am, being a member of a dominant group will almost always count in my favor.

Andrew Hacker (1992) has designed a particularly effective exercise to illustrate the extent to which whites unconsciously understand the wild card character of white privilege. He asks his white students to imagine that they will be visited by an official they have never met. The official informs them that his organization has made a terrible mistake and that according to official records you were to have been born black. Since this mistake must be rectified immediately, at midnight you will become black and can expect to live out the rest of your life—say fifty years—as a black person in America. Since this is the agency's error, the official explains that you can demand compensation. Hacker then asks his white students: How much financial recompense would you request? The figures white students give in my classes—usually between $250,000 to $50 million—demonstrate the extent to which white privilege is valued.

3. POSITIVE AND NEGATIVE DIMENSIONS OF WHITE PRIVILEGE

The wild card quality of privilege points to the possibility that dominant group privilege is more complex than simple immunities from the systemic barriers of which Frye speaks. Members of dominant groups not only receive benefits from the default options and knapsack tools they use to maneuver themselves around barriers, they also receive *additional* benefits. Barriers are put in place with the intention of creating privilege, but it is here that we encounter the limits of

Frye's barrier metaphor. The collective package of privileges given to members of dominant groups takes two distinct forms: *negative privilege,* which can be understood simply as the absence of barriers, and, *positive privilege,* which can be understood as the presence of additional perks that cannot be described in terms of immunities alone.

The distinction between positive and negative privilege is not merely two ways of expressing the same phenomenon. I first became aware of this distinction during a conversation I had with a young white male student in my "Introduction to Women's Studies" class. Once he became aware of the unearned aspects of his male privilege, this student was eager [to] use it in politically useful ways. He suggested that one way to do this would be to accompany women on a Take Back the Night March, a historically women-only demonstration against sexual violence. Since men can go out at night with little risk of sexual assault, he reasoned, he might use this unearned privilege to, in his words, "protect the women as they marched." What this student had in mind, no doubt, was to exercise his role as protector to defend the marching women against members of his gender with predatory leanings. In other words, he wanted to use his privileged protector status in a way that supported feminist projects.

But, it might be objected, what is wrong with wanting to use male privilege to help women and girls demonstrate for their right to safe access to the streets at night? Shouldn't our male allies use privilege to open up opportunities for women and to advance feminist causes? Certainly, in some cases persons with privilege should actively seek ways of using privilege supportively, but this is not one of them. The purpose of Take Back the Night Marches is to give women and girls the opportunity to reclaim the night in ways that do not rely on male protection. On a practical level, when male protectors step in, the symbolism of the march is undermined; with male protection the marchers no longer experience the autonomy and empowerment which come with walking around at night and feeling safe.

On a theoretical level, the problem is that the gendered roles of both "protector" and "predator" are the products of the ideology of hetero-patriarchal dominance. The student fails to understand how the protector role that heterosexual male privilege grants him is the product of the systemic nature of heterosexism; that is, the benefits of the protector role depend on and cannot be secured independently of the heterosexual paradigm which casts women in male-serving subordinate roles. As Sarah Hoagland argues, "there can be no protectors unless there is a danger. A man cannot identify himself in the role of protector unless there is something which needs protection" (1988, 30). In his eagerness to help the cause he does not notice the systemic links between his heterosexual male privilege as a protector and women's oppression. He does not notice how his offer of protective services reinscribes the function of the hetero-patriarchal protector/predator gender role assigned to men.[11] In attempting to [be] supportive he falls into his scripted role as a protector.

Protector status is a wild card which can be played in a wide variety of circumstances beyond the example of the march. By virtue of a hetero-patriarchal system that casts men in the role of protector, men are granted additional credibility and power. It is expected that males will be protectors; being a protector is understood as a natural innate male trait. Men who deviate from this role are often thought of as cowardly or as sissies. The unquestioned presupposition here is that men's so-called "natural protector" status gives them additional benefits beyond protectorship. It suggests that men, by virtue of their "natural" role, are automatically the rightful heads of households, the proper leaders, the best organizers, administrators, and educators. Thus, the Take Back the Night March example reveals the tightly intertwined nature of positive and negative privilege. First, this student was aware that male privilege meant that, *as a man* he saw no barriers to his being able to move about at night (a negative privilege). Second, the student was also aware on some level that male privilege conferred upon him the status of protector (a positive privilege) that is not characterized by the absence of barriers alone.

The unearned privilege accorded to whites can also be explained in terms of both negative and positive privilege. Whiteness—the expression of white privilege—means more than just being granted immunity from demeaning stereotypes and the removal of barriers to housing or high-paying jobs. Since privilege and oppression intersect all identities, having light skin and whitely mannerisms does not automatically grant one immunity from misfortune or failure, but even for those whites who are poor or unemployed, being white does have some value. If whiteness is associated with "being an American," hardworking, or a trustworthy neighbor, then to be white in America is to have a culturally valued identity. The positive dimension of white privilege captures what, for lack of a better phrase, might be called a reputational interest in being regarded as white. In fact, this reputational interest was used as grounds for Plessy's case in *Plessy vs. Ferguson*. When Homer A. Plessy, a light-skinned man of European and African descent, boarded a railway car reserved for whites, he was arrested for violating a Louisiana Jim Crow statute mandating separate cars for white and "colored" passengers. Plessy's gripe was not that he had an additional barrier placed in his path. He charged that the refusal to seat him on the white passenger car deprived him of "the reputation [of being white] which has an actual pecuniary value."[12] Because Plessy appeared to be white, not allowing him to ride on that car reserved for whites deprived him of the white privilege to which he felt entitled. The entitlements Plessy gained from being regarded as white are not expressed negatively in terms of being denied freedom of access to the best seats on the train, but being denied the status (or positive privilege) associated with being treated as a person worthy of respect. To treat persons with respect and dignity is to listen to what they have to say, to respond to their requests, or to give their needs and concerns priority. The unquestioned presupposition that whites are in most cases hardworking, honest, good trustworthy citizens may suggest that white people will be better

candidates for jobs, scholarships, and public office.[13] By virtue of a system that understands white and male superiority to be the natural state of affairs, Plessy is granted the credibility and respect appropriate to white men.

If the structural features of oppression generate privilege, then a complete understanding of oppression requires that we also be attentive to the ways in which complex systems of domination rely on the oppression of one group to generate privilege for another. A complete understanding of the systematic features of oppression requires not only that we understand the differences between oppression and harm, but also that we understand both the differences between privilege and earned advantages and the connections between oppression and privilege. Silence about privilege is itself a function of privilege and it has a chilling effect on political discourse. Conversations that focus exclusively on oppression reinforce the structured invisibility of privilege. White women who focus solely on their oppression as women, for example, generate incomplete accounts of oppression when they fail to explore the role white privilege plays in the subordination of their sisters of color. Attention to the construction of privilege, then, is a necessary component for a full account of oppression as well as a way to make visible the role of privilege in maintaining hierarchies.

NOTES

1. María Lugones has challenged Frye's account and Marxist accounts of oppression that leave oppressed groups in the discouraging position of the double-bind. In response to these theories she suggests a more liberatory "contradictory desiderata" for oppression theory which rests on embracing a pluralist notion of the self. See "Structure and Anti-Structure: Agency under Oppression," *The Journal of Philosophy*, 88:10 (October 1990), p. 500.
2. See Joel Feinberg, *Social Philosophy*, Englewood Cliffs, N.J.: Prentice Hall, 1963, pp. 58–59, and *Black's Law Dictionary*, 6th ed., St. Paul, Minn.: West Publishing, 1990, pp. 1197–98. My remarks follow Feinberg's examples here.
3. I am grateful to Jona Olsson for demonstrating the appropriateness of Richards' remark in this context.
4. My definition here follows the *Oxford English Dictionary*. Privilege: [from old French and middle English]

privilegium, a bill in favor of or against an individual; fr. L. *priv-us,* private, peculiar + *lex, legem* law.

5. Given this definition it is ironic that current struggles for equality on the part of historically disenfranchised groups are described as "special rights" by conservatives. See, *Loans v. State, 50 Tenn.* (3 Heisk.) cited in *Words and Phrases,* permanent edition, 1658 to Date, Vol. 33A, St. Paul, Minn.: West Publishing, 1995, p. 494.

6. The word processing metaphor comes from Jona Olsson's unpublished work on white antiracism. "White Privilege" Workshop. August 10, 1994. 19th Annual Womyn's Music Festival. Hart, Michigan.

7. The term "structured invisibility" comes from Ruth Frankenburg, *White Women, Race Matters: The Social Construction of Whiteness.* Minneapolis, Minn.: University of Minneapolis Press, 1993. In another context Frye refers to this phenomenon as "structured ignorance." See Marilyn Frye, "Critique," *Philosophy and Sex,* eds. Robert Baker and Frederick Elliston, New York, N.Y.: Prometheus Books, 1984, p. 447. I'm grateful to Mark Siderits for having called my attention to Frye's phrase.

8. For instance, contrast bell hooks's account of whiteness with that of Judith Levine or Minnie Bruce Pratt. See hooks, "Representations of Whiteness in the Black Imagination," in *Black Looks: Race and Representation.* Boston: South End Press, 1992, pp. 165–79. Judith Levine, "White Like Me," *Ms. Magazine* (March/April 1994), pp. 22–24. Minnie Bruce Pratt, "Identity: Skin, Blood, Heart," *Yours in Struggle: Three Feminist Perspectives on Anti-Semitism and Racism,* ed. Elly Bulkin, Minnie Bruce Pratt, and Barbara Smith. Ithaca, N.Y.: Firebrand Books, 1984, pp. 11–63.

9. Cherrie Moraga, *Loving in the War Years, Lo Que Nunca Paso por Sus Labios,* Boston: South End Press, 1983, p. 97.

10. I'm using "world" in the sense that María Lugones uses it in her essay "Playfulness, World Traveling and Loving Perception." For those unfamiliar with Lugones's notion of world traveling, 'worlds' are not utopias; they may be an actual society as it is constructed by either dominant or nondominant groups. Worlds need not be constructions of whole societies, they may be just small parts of that society (e.g., a barrio in Chicago, Chinatown in New York, a lesbian bar, a women's studies class, an elegant country club, or a migrant farmworkers community). The notion of 'worlds' is useful in that it helps us to understand why we are constructed differently in worlds in which we are not at ease. Lugones's own example is of being constructed as "serious" in Anglo/white worlds where she is ill at ease and as "playful" in Latina worlds where she is at ease. The shift from being one person in one world, to being another person in a different world is what she calls travel. See María Lugones, "Playfulness, World-Traveling, and Loving Perception," *Hypatia,* 2:2 (Summer 1987), pp. 3–18. Lugones's observations are supported by sociologist Joe Feagin's research on the "black tax" or the added hassles African Americans face in getting through the day. See Feagin, "The Continuing Significance of Race: Antiblack Discrimination in Public Places," *American Sociological Review,* 56 (February 1991), pp. 101–22.

11. Some ways of using male and heterosexual privilege may reinscribe privilege, but it is not obvious that all will. The fact that the male student could not use the privilege his protector status afforded him in this instance does not mean that male or heterosexual privilege can never be used in traitorous ways. It does not mean that men should never use their privileges to protect women and it would be foolish for women not to ask for protection in some instances.

12. See Derek Bell, "Property Rights in Whiteness—Their Legal Legacy, Their Economic Costs," in *Critical Race Theory: The Cutting Edge,* ed. Richard Delgado, Philadelphia, Penn.: Temple University Press, 1995, pp. 75–83; Cheryl Harris, "Whiteness as Property," *Harvard Law Review,* vol. 106, no. 8 (June 1993), p. 1746; and Andrew Hacker, *Two Nations: Black and White, Separate, Hostile and Unequal,* New York, N.Y.: Scribner's, 1992, esp. pp. 31–49.

13. The political significance of whiteness as I have described it in the Plessy case is highly gendered. For example, had a Mrs. Plessy taken a seat on the train that day, the reaction would have been very different because reputation and respect have different values for women. As Frye explains: "Being rational, righteous, and [law abiding] . . . do for some of us some of the time buy a ticket to a higher level of material well-being than we might otherwise be permitted. . . . But the reason, right, and rules are not of our own making; white men may welcome our whiteliness as an endorsement of their own values and as an expression of our loyalty to them (that is, as proof of their power over us), and because it makes us good helpmates to them, but if our whiteliness commands any respect, it is only in the sense that a woman who is chaste and obedient is called . . . "respectable." See Frye "White Woman Feminist," *Willful Virgin: Essays in Feminism.* Freedom, Calif.: Crossing Press, 1992, p. 161.

REFERENCES

1. Frye Marilyn. *The Politics of Reality.* Freedom, Calif.: Crossing Press, 1983, 1–16.
2. ——. "White Woman Feminist." In *Willful Virgin: Essays in Feminism.* Freedom, Calif.: Crossing Press, 1992, 147–69.
3. Hacker, Andrew. *Two Nations: Black and White, Separate, Hostile and Unequal.* New York: Scribner's, 1992.
4. Hoagland, Sarah. *Lesbian Ethics: Toward New Value.* Palo Alto, Calif.: Institute of Lesbian Studies, 1988.
5. McIntosh, Peggy. "White Privilege and Male Privilege: A Personal Account of Coming to See Correspondences Through Work in Women's Studies." In *Race, Class and Gender: An Anthology,* eds. Margaret L. Andersen and Patricia Hill Collins. N.Y.: Wadsworth, 1991.
6. Moraga, Cherrie. *Loving in the War Years. Lo Que Nunca Paso por Sus Labios.* Boston: South End Press, 1983.
7. Young, Iris Marion. *Justice and the Politics of Difference.* Princeton, N.J.: Princeton University Press, 1990.

22

Racism Without "Racists"

EDUARDO BONILLA-SILVA

Nowadays, except for members of white supremacist organizations,[1] few whites in the United States claim to be "racist." Most whites assert they "don't see any color, just people"; that although the ugly face of discrimination is still with us, it is no longer the central factor determining minorities' life chances; and, finally, that like Dr. Martin Luther King Jr.,[2] they aspire to live in a society where "people are judged by the content of their character, not by the color of their skin." More poignantly, most whites insist that minorities (especially blacks) are the ones responsible for whatever "race problem" we have in this country. They publicly denounce blacks for "playing the race card," for demanding the maintenance of unnecessary and divisive race-based programs, such as affirmative action, and for crying "racism" whenever they are criticized by whites.[3] Most whites believe that if blacks and other minorities would just stop thinking about the past, work hard, and complain less (particularly about racial discrimination), then Americans of all hues could "all get along."[4]

But regardless of whites' "sincere fictions,"[5] racial considerations shade almost everything in America. Blacks and dark-skinned racial minorities lag well behind whites in virtually every area of social life; they are about three times more likely to be poor than whites, earn about 40 percent less than whites, and have about a tenth of the net worth that whites have.[6] They also receive an inferior education compared to whites, even when they attend integrated institutions.[7] In terms of housing, black-owned units comparable to white-owned ones are valued at 35 percent less.[8] Blacks and Latinos also have less access to the entire housing market because whites, through a variety of exclusionary practices by white realtors and homeowners, have been successful in effectively limiting their entrance

into many neighborhoods.[9] Blacks receive impolite treatment in stores, in restaurants, and in a host of other commercial transactions.[10] Researchers have also documented that blacks pay more for goods such as cars and houses than do whites.[11] Finally, blacks and dark-skinned Latinos are the targets of racial profiling by the police that, combined with the highly racialized criminal court system, guarantees their overrepresentation among those arrested, prosecuted, incarcerated, and if charged for a capital crime, executed.[12] Racial profiling in the highways has become such a prevalent phenomenon that a term has emerged to describe it: driving while black.[13] In short, blacks and most minorities are, "at the bottom of the well."[14]

How is it possible to have this tremendous degree of racial inequality in a country where most whites claim that race is no longer relevant? More important, how do whites explain the apparent contradiction between their professed color blindness and the United States' color-coded inequality? . . . I contend that whites have developed powerful explanations—which have ultimately become justifications—for contemporary racial inequality that exculpate them from any responsibility for the status of people of color. These explanations emanate from a new racial ideology that I label *color-blind racism.* This ideology, which acquired cohesiveness and dominance in the late 1960s,[15] explains contemporary racial inequality as the outcome of nonracial dynamics. Whereas Jim Crow racism explained blacks' social standing as the result of their biological and moral inferiority, color-blind racism avoids such facile arguments. Instead, whites rationalize minorities' contemporary status as the product of market dynamics, naturally occurring phenomena, and blacks' imputed cultural limitations.[16] For instance, whites can attribute Latinos' high poverty rate to a relaxed work ethic ("the Hispanics are mañana, mañana, mañana— tomorrow, tomorrow, tomorrow")[17] or residential segregation as the result of natural tendencies among groups ("Does a cat and a dog mix? I can't see it. You can't drink milk and scotch. Certain mixes don't mix.").[18]

Color-blind racism became the dominant racial ideology as the mechanisms and practices for keeping blacks and other racial minorities "at the bottom of the well" changed. I have argued elsewhere that contemporary racial inequality is reproduced through "new racism" practices that are subtle, institutional, and apparently nonracial.[19] In contrast to the Jim Crow era, where racial inequality was enforced through overt means (e.g., signs saying "No Niggers Welcomed Here" or shotgun diplomacy at the voting booth), today racial practices operate in "now you see it, now you don't" fashion. For example, residential segregation, which is almost as high today as it was in the past, is no longer accomplished through overtly discriminatory practices. Instead, covert behaviors such as not showing all the available units, steering minorities and whites into certain neighborhoods, quoting higher rents or prices to minority applicants, or not advertising units at all are the weapons of choice to maintain separate communities.[20] In the economic field, "smiling face" discrimination ("We don't have jobs now, but please check later"), advertising job openings in mostly white networks and ethnic newspapers, and steering highly educated people of color into poorly remunerated jobs or jobs with limited opportunities for mobility are the new ways of keeping minorities in a secondary position.[21] Politically, although the Civil Rights struggles have helped remove many of the obstacles for the electoral participation of people of color, "racial gerrymandering, multimember legislative districts, election runoffs, annexation of predominantly white areas, at-large district elections, and anti-singleshot devices (disallowing concentrating votes in one or two candidates in cities using at-large elections) have become standard practices to disenfranchise" people of color.[22] Whether in banks, restaurants, school admissions, or housing transactions, the maintenance of white privilege is done in a way that defies facile racial readings. Hence, the contours of color-blind racism fit America's "new racism" quite well.

Compared to Jim Crow racism, the ideology of color blindness seems like "racism lite." Instead of relying on name calling (niggers, Spics, Chinks), color-blind racism otherizes softly ("these people are human, too"); instead of proclaiming God placed minorities in the world in a servile position, it suggests they are behind because they do not work hard enough; instead of viewing interracial marriage as wrong on a straight racial basis, it regards it as "problematic" because of concerns over the children, location, or the extra burden it places on couples. Yet this new ideology has become a formidable political tool for the maintenance of the racial order. Much as Jim Crow racism served as the glue for defending a brutal and overt system of racial oppression in the pre–Civil Rights era, color-blind racism serves today as the ideological armor for a covert and institutionalized system in the post–Civil Rights era. And the beauty of this new ideology is that it aids in the maintenance of white privilege without fanfare, without naming those who it subjects and those who it rewards. It allows a President to state things such as, "I strongly support diversity of all kinds, including racial diversity in higher education," yet, at the same time, to characterize the University of Michigan's affirmation action program as "flawed" and "discriminatory" against whites.[23] Thus whites enunciate positions that safeguard their racial interests without sounding "racist." Shielded by color blindness, whites can express resentment toward minorities; criticize their morality, values and work ethic; and even claim to be the victims of "reverse racism.". . .

★ ★ ★

KEY TERMS: RACE, RACIAL STRUCTURE, AND RACIAL IDEOLOGY

One reason why, in general terms, whites and people of color cannot agree on racial matters is because they conceive terms such as "racism" very differently. Whereas for most whites racism is prejudice, for most people of color racism is systemic or institutionalized. . . . my examination of color-blind racism has etched in it the indelible ink of a "regime of truth"[24] about how the world is organized. Thus, rather than hiding my theoretical assumptions, I state them openly for the benefit of readers and potential critics.

The first key term is the notion of *race*. There is very little formal disagreement among social scientists in accepting the idea that race is a socially constructed category.[25] This means that notions of racial difference are human creations rather than eternal, essential categories. As such, racial categories have a history and are subject to change. And here ends the agreement among social scientists on this matter. There are at least three distinct variations on how social scientists approach this constructionist perspective on race. The first approach, which is gaining popularity among white social scientists, is the idea that because race is socially constructed, it is not a fundamental category of analysis and praxis. Some analysts go as far as to suggest that because race is a constructed category, then it is not real and social scientists who use the category are the ones who make it real.[26]

The second approach, typical of most sociological writing on race, gives lip service to the social constructionist view—usually a line in the beginning of the article or book. Writers in this group then proceed to discuss "racial" differences in academic achievement, crime, and SAT scores as if they were truly racial.[27] This is the central way in which contemporary scholars contribute to the propagation of racist interpretations of racial inequality. By failing to highlight the social dynamics that produce these racial differences, these scholars help reinforce the racial order.[28]

The third approach, . . . acknowledges that race, as other social categories such as class and gender, is constructed but insists that it has a *social* reality. This means that after race—or class or gender—is created, it produces real effects on the actors racialized as "black" or "white." Although race, as other social constructions, is unstable, it has a "changing same"[29] quality at its core.

In order to explain how a socially constructed category produces real race effects, I need to introduce a second key term: the notion of *racial structure*. When race emerged in human history, it formed a social structure (a racialized social system) that awarded systemic privileges to Europeans (the peoples who became "white") over non-Europeans (the peoples who became "nonwhite").[30] Racialized social systems, or white supremacy[31] for short, became global and affected all societies where Europeans extended their reach. I therefore conceive a society's racial structure as *the totality of the social relations and practices that reinforce white privilege.* Accordingly, the task of analysts interested in studying racial structures is to uncover the particular social, economic, political, social control, and ideological mechanisms responsible for the reproduction of racial privilege in a society.

But why are racial structures reproduced in the first place? Would not humans, after discovering the folly of racial thinking, work to abolish race as a category as well as a practice? Racial structures remain in place for the same reasons that other structures do. Since actors racialized as "white"—or as members of the dominant race—receive material benefits from the racial order, they struggle (or passively receive the manifold wages of whiteness) to maintain their privileges. In contrast, those defined as belonging to the subordinate race or races struggle to change the status quo (or become resigned to their position). Therein lies the secret of racial structures and racial inequality the world over.[32] They exist because they benefit members of the dominant race.

If the ultimate goal of the dominant race is to defend its collective interests (i.e., the perpetuation of systemic white privilege), it should surprise no one that this group develops rationalizations to account for the status of the various races. And here I introduce my third key term, the notion of *racial ideology*. By this I mean *the racially based frameworks used by actors to explain and justify* (dominant race) or *challenge* (subordinate race or races) *the racial status quo.* Although all the races in a racialized social system have the *capacity* of developing these frameworks, the frameworks of the dominant race tend to become the master frameworks upon which *all* racial actors ground (for or against) their ideological positions. Why? Because as Marx pointed out in *The German Ideology,* "the ruling *material* force of society, is at the same time its ruling *intellectual* force."[33] This does not mean that ideology is almighty. In fact, . . . ideological rule is always partial. Even in periods of hegemonic rule,[34] such as the current one, subordinate racial groups develop oppositional views. However, it would be foolish to believe that those who rule a society do not have the power to at least color (pun intended) the views of the ruled.

Racial ideology can be conceived for analytical purposes as comprising the following elements: common frames, style, and racial stories. . . . The frames that bond together a particular racial ideology are rooted in the group-based conditions and experiences of the races and are, at the symbolic level, the representations developed by these groups to explain how the world is or ought to be. And because the group life of the various racially defined groups is based on hierarchy and domination, the ruling ideology expresses as "common sense" the interests of the dominant race, while oppositional ideologies attempt to challenge that common sense by providing alternative frames, ideas, and stories based on the experiences of subordinated races.

Individual actors employ these elements as "building blocks . . . for manufacturing versions on actions, self, and social structures" in communicative situations.[35] The looseness of the elements allows users to maneuver within various contexts (e.g., responding to a race-related survey, discussing racial issues with family, or arguing about affirmative action in a college classroom) and produce various accounts and presentations of self (e.g., appearing ambivalent, tolerant, or strong minded). This loose character enhances the legitimating role of racial ideology because it allows for accommodation of contradictions, exceptions, and new information. As Jackman points out about ideology in general: "Indeed, the strength of an ideology lies in its loose-jointed, flexible application. *An ideology is a political instrument, not an exercise in personal logic:* consistency is rigidity, the only pragmatic effect of which is to box oneself in."[36]

Before I can proceed, two important caveats should be offered. First, although whites, because of their privileged position in the racial order, form a social group (the dominant race), they are fractured along class, gender, sexual orientation, and other forms of "social cleavage." Hence, they have multiple and often contradictory interests that are not easy to disentangle and that predict *a priori* their mobilizing capacity (Do white workers have more in common with white capitalists than with black workers?). However, because all actors awarded the dominant racial position, regardless of their multiple structural locations (men or women, gay or straight, working class or bourgeois) benefit from what Mills calls the "racial contract,"[37] *most* have historically endorsed the ideas that justify the racial status quo.

Second, although not every single member of the dominant race defends the racial status quo or spouts color-blind racism, *most* do. To explain this point by analogy, although not every capitalist defends capitalism (e.g., Frederick Engels, the coauthor of *The Communist Manifesto,* was a capitalist) and not every man defends patriarchy (e.g., *Achilles Heel* is an English magazine published by feminist men), *most* do in some fashion. In the same vein, although some whites fight white supremacy and do not endorse white common sense, *most* subscribe to substantial portions of it in a casual, uncritical fashion that helps sustain the prevailing racial order.

★ ★ ★

NOTES

1. Even members of these organizations now claim that they are not racist, simply prowhite. For David Duke's discussion on this matter, see his website, www.duke.org/.
2. Some, such as former President George H. W. Bush, use Dr. King's dictum to oppose affirmative action. Interestingly, when Bush was in Congress, he opposed most of the civil rights legislation advocated by King. Furthermore, few whites have ever read the speech in which King used this phrase. If they had, they would realize that his dream referred to the future, that he emphasized that the "Negro [was] still not free." King also emphasized that there could not be peace without justice. In his words, "There will be neither rest nor tranquility in America until the Negro is granted his citizenship rights. The whirlwinds of revolt will continue to shake the foundations of our nation until the bright day of justice emerges." See Martin Luther King Jr., *A Call to Conscience: The Landmark Speeches of Dr. Martin Luther*

King, Jr., edited by Clayborne Carson and Kris Shephard (New York: Intellectual Properties Management in association with Warner Books, 2001).

3. These views have been corroborated in survey after survey. For instance, a recent nationwide survey found that 66 percent of whites thought the disadvantaged status of blacks in America was due to blacks' welfare dependency and 63 percent thought blacks lacked the motivation to improve their socioeconomic status. Tom W. Smith, "Intergroup Relations in Contemporary America," in *Intergroup Relations in the United States: Research Perspectives,* edited by Wayne Winborne and Renae Cohen, 69–106 (New York: National Conference for Community and Justice, 2000).

4. This phrase was made popular by Rodney King immediately after his first trial. Curiously, the phrase was provided to King by his white lawyer and a movie producer. See Houston A. Baker, "Scene . . . Not Heard," in *Reading Rodney King, Reading Urban Uprising,* edited by Robert Gooding-Williams, 38–50 (New York: Routledge, 1993), 45.

5. This term was coined in Joe R. Feagin and Hernán Vera, *White Racism: The Basics* (New York: Routledge, 1995), to refer to whites' myths about race in contemporary America, particularly their self-delusions.

6. See Melvin Oliver and Thomas Shapiro, *Black Wealth/White Wealth* (New York: Routledge, 1995). See also Juliane Malveaux, "Black Dollar Power: Economics in the Black Community," vol. 10, *Essence* (October 1999), 88–92.

7. For a vivid description of the educational inequalities between blacks and whites, see Jonathan Kozol, *Savage Inequalities* (New York: Crown, 1992). For a discussion of resegregation and its consequences, see Gary Orfield, Susan Eaton, and the Harvard Project on School Desegregation, *Dismantling Desegregation: The Quiet Reversal of Brown v. Board of Education* (New York: New Press, 1996). For a discussion of racial matters in "integrated" campuses, see Joe R. Feagin, Hernán Vera, and Nikitah Imani, *The Agony of Education: Black Students at White Colleges and Universities* (New York: Routledge, 1996), and chapter 2 in Roy Brooks, *Integration or Separation? A Strategy for Racial Equality* (Cambridge, Mass: Harvard University Press, 1996).

8. William J. Collins and Robert A. Margo, "Race and the Value of Owner-Occupied Housing, 1940–1990," Working Papers Series (Annandale-on-Hudson, N.Y.: Bard College, Levy Economics Institute, August 2000).

9. Douglas Massey and Nancy E. Denton, *American Apartheid* (Cambridge, Mass.: Harvard University Press, 1993); John Yinger, *Closed Doors, Opportunities Lost: The Continuing Costs of Housing Discrimination* (New York: Russell Sage Foundation, 1995); Judith N. Desena, "Local Gatekeeping Practices and Residential Segregation," *Sociological Inquiry* 64, no. 3 (1994): 307–321.

10. Joe R. Feagin and Melvin Sikes, *Living with Racism: The Black Middle Class Experience* (Boston: Beacon, 1994); Peter Siegelman, "Racial Discrimination in 'Everyday' Commercial Transactions: What Do We Know," in *A National Report Card on Discrimination in America: The Role of Testing,* edited by Michael Fix and Margery Austin Turner, chapter 4 (Washington, D.C.: Urban Institute, March 1999).

11. Oliver and Shapiro, *Black Wealth/White Wealth;* Siegelman, "Racial Discrimination."

12. Katheryn K. Russsell, *The Color of Crime* (New York: New York University Press, 1998).

13. David A. Harris, *Driving While Black: Racial Profiling on Our Nation's Highways,* Special Report (New York: American Civil Liberties Union, June 1999).

14. Derrick Bell, *Race, Racism and American Law* (Boston: Little, Brown, 1992).

15. The work of William A. Ryan and Joel Kovel represent early efforts to understand the parameters of post–Civil Rights racial ideology. See Willam A. Ryan, *Blaming the Victim* (New York: Random House, 1976); Joel Kovel, *White Racism: A Psychohistory* (New York: Columbia University Press, 1985).

16. Melvin Thomas has found that this perspective deeply affects social science research on racial matters. Melvin Thomas, "Anything But Race: The Social Science Retreat from Racism," *African American Research Perspectives* (Winter 2000): 79–96.

17. This statement is from the top officer of a cart transport company in Chicago. William Julius Wilson, *When Work Disappears* (New York: Norton, 1996), 112.

18. These comments are from a resident of Canarsie, New York. Jonathan Rieder, *Canarsie: The Jews and Italians of Brooklyn against Liberalism* (Cambridge, Mass.: Harvard University Press, 1985), 58.

19. See my chapter with Amanda E. Lewis, "The 'New Racism': Toward an Analysis of the U.S. Racial Structure, 1960–1990s," in *Race, Nation, and Citizenship,* edited by Paul Wong, 100–150 (Boulder, Colo.: Westview, 1999). For a more recent, updated version, see chapter 3 in my *White Supremacy and Racism in the Post Civil Rights Era* (Boulder, Colo.: Rienner, 2001).

20. For general findings on housing matters, see John Yinger, *Closed Doors.* For gatekeeping practices, see Judith A. Desena, "Local Gatekeeping Practices and Residential Segregation," *Sociological Inquiry* 64, no. 3 (1994): 307–321.

21. Bonilla-Silva, *White Supremacy,* 11–117.

22. Bonilla-Silva, *White Supremacy,* 100–101.

23. CBS, "Bush Enters Affirmative Action Fray," CBS.com, January 16, 2003. For a discussion of the contradiction between President Bush opposing affirmative action and his own affirmative action-like admission to Phillips Academy and Yale, see Ellis Henican, "When it Comes to Hypocrisy, He's Brilliant!" *Newsday.com,* January 17, 2003.

24. See Michel Foucault, *The Order of Things: An Archeology of the Human Sciences* (New York: Random House, 1973).

25. A few highly visible social scientists such as Charles Murray, Arthur Jensen, Pierre van den Berghe, and Edward O. Wilson still conceive of race as a biological or primordial category. However, they are in a minority and are severely criticized by most people in academia.

26. For an example of this view, see Yehudi O. Webster, *The Racialization of America* (New York: St. Martin's, 1992).

However, this view is much more extensive and has been publicly stated by radical scholars such as Todd Gitlin. I have seen the growing influence of this stance among many "radical" scholars who now proclaim to be disillusioned with what they label as "identity politics" (in truth, they never got on board with the radical gender and racial agendas of their minority and women's colleagues) and thus argue that gender and race are divisive categories preventing the unity of the working class.

27. For a biting critique of statistical racial reasoning, see Tukufu Zuberi, "Deracializing Social Statistics: Problems in the Quantification of Race," *Annals of the American Academy of Political and Social Science* 568 (2000): 172–85.

28. It is largely irrelevant whether these authors are "racist" (that is, hold negative views about racial minorities) or not. "That knowledge [that produced by race scholars unwilling to accept the centrality of racial stratification as the basic force behind the data they uncover], sometimes wittingly, sometimes unwittingly, operates to reinforce the fear and hatred of others by providing rationales for hierarchizing differences." Thomas L. Dunn, "The New Enclosures: Racism in the Normalized Community," in *Reading Rodney King, Reading Urban Uprising,* edited by Robert Gooding-Williams, 178–95 (New York: Routledge, 1993), 180.

29. I borrow this phrase from Michael G. Hanchard, *Orpheus and Power* (Princeton, N.J.: Princeton University Press, 1994). Too many postmodern-inspired readings on race insist on the malleability and instability of all social constructions. This, they believe, is the best antidote to essentialism. In my view, however, by focusing on the instability of race as a category, they miss its continuity and social role in shaping everyday dynamics. Even worse, in some cases, the views of some of these authors come close to those of right-wing scholars who advocate the elimination [of] race as a category of analysis and discourse. From the perspective advanced in this book, the elimination of race from above without changing the material conditions that make race a *socially* real category would just add another layer of defense to white supremacy.

30. I have argued in my work that race emerged as a category of human division in the fifteenth and sixteenth centuries as Europeans expanded their nascent world system. However, other analysts believe that the category has existed since antiquity and cite evidence of "racism" from the Roman and Greek civilizations. Although I believe that they confuse xenophobia and ethnocentrism with what I call a racialized social system, our disagreement is not central to the point at hand.

31. Although many analysts resent this concept and think that [it] is inappropriate, I am persuaded by the arguments advanced by philosopher Charles W. Mills. This notion forces the reader to understand the systemic and power elements in a racialized social system, as well as the historical reality that such systems were organized and are still ordained by Western logics. For a discussion on this matter, see my book, *White Supremacy,* or consult Charles W. Mills, *Blackness Visible* (Ithaca, N.Y.: Cornell University Press, 1998).

32. I have been criticized for holding this position (see my debate with Mara Loveman in the pages of the *American Sociological Review,* December 1999), yet the view that race relations have a material foundation has a long history in American sociology. This notion formed part of the classic work of W. Lloyd Warner, in *Social Class in America* (New York: Harper & Row, 1960), and John Dollard, in *Caste and class in a Southern Town* (New York: Doubleday, 1957); later, it could be found in the work of Herbert Blumer, Hubert Blalock, Stokely Carmichael and Charles Hamilton, and Robert Blauner.

33. My emphasis. Karl Marx, *The German Ideology,* edited and with an introduction by C. J. Arthur (New York: International, 1985), 64.

34. Hegemonic rule means that dominant groups actively attempt to achieve the consent of the subordinated groups through a variety of means.

35. Margaret Wetherell and Jonathan Potter, *Mapping the Language of Racism* (New York: Columbia University Press, 1992), 91.

36. My emphasis. Jackman, *The Velvet Glove,* 69.

37. Black philosopher Charles W. Mills argues that with the advent of modern imperialism (the fifteenth and sixteenth centuries onward), whites developed a political, moral, and epistemological "racial contract" to maintain white supremacy over nonwhites. See *The Racial Contract* (Ithaca. N.Y.: Cornell University Press, 1997).

23

La Güera

CHERRÍE MORAGA

It requires something more than personal experience to gain a philosophy or point of view from any specific event. It is the quality of our response to the event and our capacity to enter into the lives of others that help us to make their lives and experiences our own.

—EMMA GOLDMAN[1]

I am the very well-educated daughter of a woman who, by the standards of this country, would be considered largely illiterate. My mother was born in Santa Paula, Southern California, at a time when much of the central valley there was still farm land. Nearly thirty-five years later, in 1948, she was the only daughter of six to marry an anglo, my father.

I remember all of my mother's stories, probably much better than she realizes. She is a fine story-teller, recalling every event of her life with the vividness of the present, noting each detail right down to the cut and color of her dress. I remember stories of her being pulled out of school at the ages of five, seven, nine, and eleven to work in the fields, along with her brothers and sisters; stories of her father drinking away whatever small profit she was able to make for the family; of her going the long way home to avoid meeting him on the street, staggering toward the same destination. I remember stories of my mother lying about her age in order to get a job as a hat-check girl at Agua Caliente Racetrack in Tijuana. At fourteen, she was the main support of the family. I can still see her walking home alone at 3 A.M., only to turn all of her salary and tips over to her mother, who was pregnant again.

The stories continue through the war years and on: walnut-cracking factories, the Voit Rubber factory, and then the computer boom. I remember my mother doing piecework for the electronics plant in our neighborhood. In the late evening, she would sit in front of the T.V. set, wrapping copper wires into the backs of circuit boards, talking about "keeping up with the younger girls." By that time, she was already in her mid-fifties.

Meanwhile, I was college-prep in school. After classes, I would go with my mother to fill out job applications for her, or write checks for her at the supermarket. We would have the scenario all worked out ahead of time. My mother would sign the check before we'd get to the store. Then, as we'd approach the checkstand, she would say—within earshot of the cashier—"oh honey, you go 'head and make out the check," as if she couldn't be bothered with such an insignificant detail. No one asked any questions.

I was educated, and wore it with a keen sense of pride and satisfaction, my head propped up with the knowledge, from my mother, that my life would be easier than hers. I was educated; but more than this, I was "la güera": fair-skinned. Born with the features of my Chicana mother, but the skin of my anglo father, I had it made.

No one ever quite told me this (that light was right), but I knew that being light was something valued in my family (who were all Chicano, with the exception of my father). In fact, everything about my upbringing (at least what occurred on a conscious level) attempted to bleach me of what color I did have. Although my mother was fluent in it, I was never taught much Spanish at home. I picked up what I did learn from school and from overheard snatches of conversation among my relatives and mother. She often called other lower-income Mexicans "braceros," or "wet-backs," referring to herself and her family as "a different class of people." And yet, the real story was that my family, too, had been poor (some still are) and farmworkers. My mother can remember this in her blood as if it were yesterday. But this is something she would like to forget (and rightfully), for to her, on a basic economic level, being Chicana meant being "less." It was through my mother's desire to protect her children from poverty and illiteracy that we became "anglocized"; the more effectively we could pass in the white world, the better guaranteed our future.

From all of this, I experience, daily, a huge disparity between what I was born into and what I was to grow up to become. Because (as Goldman suggests) these stories my mother told me crept under my "güera" skin. I had no choice but to enter into the life of my mother. *I had no choice.* I took her life into my heart, but managed to keep a lid on it as long as I feigned being the happy, upwardly mobile heterosexual.

When I finally lifted the lid to my lesbianism, a profound connection with my mother reawakened in me. It wasn't until I acknowledged and confronted my own lesbianism in the flesh, that my heartfelt identification with and empathy for my mother's oppression—due to being poor, uneducated, and Chicana—was realized. My lesbianism is the avenue through which I have learned the most about silence and oppression, and it continues to be the most tactile reminder to me that we are not free human beings.

You see, one follows the other. I had known for years that I was a lesbian, had felt it in my bones, had ached with the knowledge, gone crazed with the knowledge, wallowed in the silence of it. Silence *is* like starvation. Don't be fooled. It's nothing short of that, and felt most sharply when one has had a full belly most of her life. When we are not physically starving, we have the luxury to realize psychic and emotional starvation. It is from this starvation that other starvations can be recognized—if one is willing to take the risk of making the connection—if one is willing to be responsible to the result of the connection. For me, the connection is an inevitable one.

What I am saying is that the joys of looking like a white girl ain't so great since I realized I could be beaten on the street for being a dyke. If my sister's being beaten because she's Black, it's pretty much the same principle. We're both getting beaten any way you look at it. The connection is blatant; and in the case of my own family, the difference in the privileges attached to looking white instead of brown are merely a generation apart.

In this country, lesbianism is a poverty—as is being brown, as is being a woman, as is being just plain poor. The danger lies in ranking the oppressions. *The danger lies in failing to acknowledge the specificity of the oppression.* The danger lies in attempting to deal with oppression purely from a theoretical base. Without an emotional, heartfelt grappling with the source of our own oppression, without naming the enemy within ourselves and outside of us, no authentic, non-hierarchical connection among oppressed groups can take place.

When the going gets rough, will we abandon our so-called comrades in a flurry of racist/heterosexist/what-have-you panic? To whose camp, then, should the lesbian of color retreat? Her very presence violates the ranking and abstraction of oppression. Do we merely live hand to mouth? Do we merely struggle with the "ism" that's sitting on top of our own heads?

The answer is: yes, I think first we do; and we must do so thoroughly and deeply. But to fail to move out from there will only isolate us in our own oppression—will only insulate, rather than radicalize us.

To illustrate: a gay male friend of mine once confided to me that he continued to feel that, on some level, I didn't trust him because he was male; that he felt, really, if it ever came down to a "battle of the sexes," I might kill him. I admitted that I might very well. He wanted to understand the source of my distrust. I responded, "You're not a woman. Be a woman for a day. Imagine being a woman." He confessed that the thought terrified him because, to him, being a woman meant being raped by men. He *had* felt raped by men; he wanted to forget what that meant. What grew from that discussion was the realization that in order for him to create an authentic alliance with me, he must deal with the primary source of his own sense of oppression. He must first, emotionally come to terms with what it feels like to be a victim. If he—or anyone—were to truly do this, it would be impossible to discount the oppression of others, except by again forgetting how we have been hurt.

And yet, oppressed groups are forgetting all the time. There are instances of this in the rising Black middle class, and certainly an obvious trend of such "unconsciousness" among white gay men. Because to remember may mean giving up whatever privileges we have managed to squeeze out of this society by virtue of our gender, race, class, or sexuality.

Within the women's movement, the connections among women of different backgrounds and sexual orientations have been fragile, at best. I think this phenomenon is indicative of our failure to seriously address ourselves to some very frightening questions: How have I internalized my own oppression? How have I oppressed? Instead, we have let rhetoric do the job of poetry. Even the word "oppression" has lost its power. We need a new language, better words that can more closely describe women's fear of and resistance to one another; words that will not always come out sounding like dogma.

What prompted me in the first place to work on an anthology by radical women of color was a deep sense that I had a valuable insight to contribute, by virtue of my birthright and background. And yet, I don't really understand first-hand what it feels like being shitted on for being brown. I understand much more about the joys of it—being Chicana and having family are synonymous for me. What I know about loving, singing, crying, telling stories, speaking with my heart and hands, even having a sense of my own soul comes from the love of my mother, aunts, cousins. . . .

But at the age of twenty-seven, it is frightening to acknowledge that I have internalized a racism and classism, where the object of oppression is not only someone outside of my skin, but the someone inside my skin. In fact, to a large degree, the real battle with such oppression, for all of us, begins under the skin. I have had to confront the fact that much of what I value about being Chicana, about my family, has been subverted by anglo culture and my own cooperation with it. This realization did not occur to me overnight. For example, it wasn't until long after my graduation from the private college I'd attended in Los Angeles, that I realized the major reason for my total alienation from and fear of my classmates was rooted in class and culture. CLICK.

Three years after graduation, in an apple-orchard in Sonoma, a friend of mine (who comes from an Italian Irish working-class family) says to me, "Cherríe, no wonder you felt like such a nut in school. Most of the people there were white and rich." It was true. All along I had felt the difference, but not until I had put the words "class" and "color" to the experience, did my feelings make any sense. For years, I had berated myself for not being as "free" as my classmates. I completely bought that they simply had more guts than I did—to rebel against their parents and run around the country hitchhiking, reading books and studying "art." They had enough privilege to be atheists, for chrissake. There was no one around filling in the disparity for me between their parents, who were Hollywood filmmakers, and my parents, who wouldn't know the name of a filmmaker if their lives depended on it (and precisely because their lives didn't depend on it, they couldn't be bothered). But I knew nothing about "privilege" then. White was right. Period. I could pass. If I got educated enough, there would never be any telling.

Three years after that, another CLICK. In a letter to Barbara Smith, I wrote:

I went to a concert where Ntosake Shange was reading. There, everything exploded for me. She was speaking a language that I knew—in the deepest parts of me—existed, and that I had ignored in my own feminist studies and even in my own writing. What Ntosake caught in me is the realization that in my development as a poet, I have, in many ways, denied the voice of my brown mother—the brown in me. I have acclimated to the sound of a white language which, as my father represents it, does not speak to the emotions in my poems—emotions which stem from the love of my mother.

The reading was agitating. Made me uncomfortable. Threw me into a week-long terror of how deeply I was affected. I felt that I had to start all over again. That I turned only to the perceptions of white middle-class women to speak for me and all women. I am shocked by my own ignorance.

Sitting in that auditorium chair was the first time I had realized to the core of me that for years I had disowned the language I knew best—ignored the words and rhythms that were the closest to me. The sounds of my mother and aunts gossiping—half in English, half in Spanish—while drinking cerveza in the kitchen. And the hands—I had cut off the hands in my poems. But not in conversation; still the hands could not be kept down. Still they insisted on moving.

The reading had forced me to remember that I knew things from my roots. But to remember puts me up against what I don't know. Shange's reading agitated me because she spoke with power about a world that is both alien and common to me: "the capacity to enter into the lives of others." But you can't just take the goods and run. I knew that then, sitting in the Oakland auditorium (as I know in my poetry), that the only thing worth writing about is what seems to be unknown and, therefore, fearful.

The "unknown" is often depicted in racist literature as the "darkness" within a person. Similarly, sexist writers will refer to fear in the form of the vagina, calling it the "orifice of death." In contrast, it is a pleasure to read works such as Maxine Hong

Kingston's *Woman Warrior,* where fear and alienation are described as "the white ghosts." And yet, the bulk of literature in this country reinforces the myth that what is dark and female is evil. Consequently, each of us—whether dark, female, or both—has in some way *internalized* this oppressive imagery. What the oppressor often succeeds in doing is simply *externalizing* his fears, projecting them into the bodies of women, Asians, gays, disabled folks, whoever seems most "other."

call me
roach and presumptuous
nightmare on your white pillow
your itch to destroy
the indestructible
part of yourself

—AUDRE LORDE[2]

But it is not really difference the oppressor fears so much as similarity. He fears he will discover in himself the same aches, the same longings as those of the people he has shitted on. He fears the immobilization threatened by his own incipient guilt. He fears he will have to change his life once he has seen himself in the bodies of the people he has called different. He fears the hatred, anger, and vengeance of those he has hurt.

This is the oppressor's nightmare, but it is not exclusive to him. We women have a similar nightmare, for each of us in some way has been both oppressed and the oppressor. We are afraid to look at how we have failed each other. We are afraid to see how we have taken the values of our oppressor into our hearts and turned them against ourselves and one another. We are afraid to admit how deeply "the man's" words have been ingrained in us.

To assess the damage is a dangerous act. I think of how, even as a feminist lesbian, I have so wanted to ignore my own homophobia, my own hatred of myself for being queer. I have not wanted to admit that my deepest personal sense of myself has not quite "caught up" with my "woman-identified" politics I have been afraid to criticize lesbian writers who choose to "skip over" these issues in the name

of feminism. In 1979, we talk of "old gay" and "butch and femme" roles as if they were ancient history. We toss them aside as merely patriarchal notions. And yet, the truth of the matter is that I have sometimes taken society's fear and hatred of lesbians to bed with me. I have sometimes hated my lover for loving me. I have sometimes felt "not woman enough" for her. I have sometimes felt "not man enough." For a lesbian trying to survive in a heterosexist society, there is no easy way around these emotions. Similarly, in a white-dominated world, there is little getting around racism and our own internalization of it. It's always there, embodied in someone we least expect to rub up against.

When we do rub up against this person, *there* then is the challenge. *There* then is the opportunity to look at the nightmare within us. But we usually shrink from such a challenge.

Time and time again, I have observed that the usual response among white women's groups when the "racism issue" comes up is to deny the difference. I have heard comments like, "Well, we're open to *all* women; why don't they (women of color) come? You can only do so much. . . ." But there is seldom any analysis of how the very nature and structure of the group itself may be founded on racist or classist assumptions. More importantly, so often the women seem to feel no loss, no lack, no absence when women of color are not involved; therefore, there is little desire to change the situation. This has hurt me deeply. I have come to believe that the only reason women of a privileged class will dare to look at *how* it is that *they* oppress, is when they've come to know the meaning of their own oppression. And understand that the oppression of others hurts them personally.

The other side of the story is that women of color and working-class women often shrink from challenging white middle-class women. It is much easier to rank oppressions and set up a hierarchy, rather than take responsibility for changing our own lives. We have failed to demand that white women, particularly those who claim to be speaking for all women, be accountable for their racism.

The dialogue has simply not gone deep enough.

I have many times questioned my right to even work on an anthology which is to be written "exclusively by Third World women." I have had to look critically at my claim to color, at a time when, among white feminist ranks, it is a "politically correct" (and sometimes peripherally advantageous) assertion to make. I must acknowledge the fact that, physically, I have had a *choice* about making that claim, in contrast to women who have not had such a choice, and have been abused for their color. I must reckon with the fact that for most of my life, by virtue of the very fact that I am white-looking, I identified with and aspired toward white values, and that I rode the wave of that Southern Californian privilege as far as conscience would let me.

Well, now I feel both bleached and beached. I feel angry about this—the years when I refused to recognize privilege, both when it worked against me, and when I worked it, ignorantly, at the expense of others. These are not settled issues. That is why this work feels so risky to me. It continues to be discovery. It has brought me into contact with women who invariably know a hell of a lot more than I do about racism, as experienced in the flesh, as revealed in the flesh of their writing.

I think: what is my responsibility to my roots—both white and brown, Spanish-speaking and English? I am a woman with a foot in both worlds; and I refuse the split. I feel the necessity for dialogue. Sometimes I feel it urgently.

But one voice is not enough, nor two, although this is where dialogue begins. It is essential that radical feminists confront their fear of and resistance to each other, because without this, there *will* be no bread on the table. Simply, we will not survive. If we could make this connection in our heart of hearts, that if we are serious about a revolution—better— if we seriously believe there should be joy in our lives (real joy, not just "good times"), then we need one another. We women need each other. Because my/your solitary, self-asserting "go-for-the-throat-of-fear" power is not enough. The real power, as you and I well know, is collective. I can't afford to be afraid of you, nor you of me. If it takes head-on collisions, let's do it: this polite timidity is killing us.

As Lorde suggests in the passage I cited earlier, it is in looking to the nightmare that the dream is found. There, the survivor emerges to insist on a future, a vision, yes, born out of what is dark and female. The feminist movement must be a movement of such survivors, a movement with a future. September, 1979

NOTES

1. Alix Kates Shulman, "Was My Life Worth Living?" *Red Emma Speaks.* (New York: Random House, 1972), p. 388.
2. From "The Brown Menace or Poem to the Survival of Roaches," *The New York Head Shop and Museum* (Detroit: Broadside, 1974), p. 48.

 24

White Privilege Shapes the U.S.

Affirmative Action for Whites Is a Fact of Life

ROBERT JENSEN

Here's what white privilege sounds like:

I'm sitting in my University of Texas office, talking to a very bright and very conservative white student about affirmative action in college admissions, which he opposes and I support.

The student says he wants a level playing field with no unearned advantages for anyone. I ask him whether he thinks that being white has advantages in the United States. Have either of us, I ask, ever benefited from being white in a world run mostly by white people? Yes, he concedes, there is something real and tangible we could call white privilege.

So, if we live in a world of white privilege— unearned white privilege—how does that affect your notion of a level playing field, I asked.

He paused for a moment and said, "That really doesn't matter."

That statement, I suggested to him, reveals the ultimate white privilege: the privilege to acknowledge that you have unearned privilege but to ignore what it means.

That exchange led me to rethink the way I talk about race and racism with students. It drove home the importance of confronting the dirty secret that we white people carry around with us every day in a world of white privilege, some of what we have is unearned. I think much of both the fear and anger that come up around discussions of affirmative action has its roots in that secret. So these days, my goal is to talk openly and honestly about white supremacy and white privilege.

White privilege, like any social phenomenon, is complex. In a white supremacist culture, all white people have privilege, whether or not they are overtly racist themselves.

There are general patterns, but such privilege plays out differently depending on context and other aspects of one's identity (in my case, being male gives me other kinds of privilege). Rather than try to tell others how white privilege has played out in their lives, I talk about how it has affected me.

I am as white as white gets in this country. I am of northern European heritage and I was raised in North Dakota, one of the whitest states in the country. I grew up in a virtually all-white world surrounded by racism, both personal and institutional. Because I didn't live near a reservation, I didn't even have exposure to the state's only numerically significant nonwhite population, American Indians.

I have struggled to resist that racist training and the racism of my culture. I like to think I have changed, even though I routinely trip over the lingering effects of that internalized racism and the institutional racism around me. But no matter how much I "fix" myself, one thing never changes—I walk through the world with white privilege.

What does that mean? Perhaps most important, when I seek admission to a university, apply for a job, or hunt for an apartment, I don't look threatening. Almost all of the people evaluating me for those things look like me—they are white. They see in me a reflection of themselves—and in a racist world, that is an advantage. I smile. I am white. I am one of them. I am not dangerous. Even when I voice critical opinions, I am cut some slack. After all, I'm white.

My flaws also are more easily forgiven because I am white. Some complain that affirmative action has meant the university is saddled with mediocre minority professors. I have no doubt there are minority faculty who are mediocre, though I don't know very many. As Henry Louis Gates Jr. once pointed out, if affirmative action policies were in place for the next hundred years, it's possible that at the end of that time the university could have as many mediocre minority professors as it has mediocre white professors. That isn't meant as an insult to anyone, but it's a simple observation that white privilege has meant that scores of second-rate white professors have slid through the system because their flaws were overlooked out of solidarity based on race, as well as on gender, class and ideology.

Some people resist the assertions that the United States is still a bitterly racist society and that the racism has real effects on real people. But white folks have long cut other white folks a break. I know, because I am one of them. I am not a genius—as I like to say, I'm not the sharpest knife in the drawer. I have been teaching full time for six years and I've published a reasonable amount of scholarship. Some of it is the unexceptional stuff one churns out to get tenure, and some of it, I would argue, is worth reading. I worked hard, and I like to think that I'm a fairly decent teacher. Every once in a while, I leave my office at the end of the day feeling like I really accomplished something. When I cash my paycheck, I don't feel guilty.

But, all that said, I know I did not get where I am by merit alone, I benefited from, among other things, white privilege. That doesn't mean that I don't deserve my job, or that if I weren't white I would never have gotten the job. It means simply that all through my life, I have soaked up benefits for being white. I grew up in fertile farm country taken by force from nonwhite indigenous people. I was educated in a well-funded, virtually all-white public school system in which I learned that white people like me made this country great. There I also was taught a variety of skills, including how to take standardized tests written by and for white people.

All my life I have been hired for jobs by white people. I was accepted for graduate school by white people. And I was hired for a teaching position by the predominantly white University of Texas, headed by a white president in a college headed by a white dean and in a department with a white chairman that at the time had one nonwhite tenured professor.

There certainly is individual variation in experience. Some white people have had it easier than I, probably because they came from wealthy families that gave them even more privilege. Some white people have had it tougher than I because they came from poorer families. White women face discrimination I will never know. But, in the end, white people all have drawn on white privilege somewhere in their lives.

Like anyone, I have overcome certain hardships in my life. I have worked hard to get where I am, and I work hard to stay there. But to feel good about myself and my work, I do not have to believe that "merit," as defined by white people in a white country, alone got me here. I can acknowledge that in addition to all that hard work, I got a significant boost from white privilege, which continues to protect me every day of my life from certain hardships.

At one time in my life, I would not have been able to say that, because I needed to believe that my success in life was due solely to my individual talent and effort. I saw myself as the heroic American, the rugged individualist. I was so deeply seduced by the culture's mythology that I couldn't see the fear that was binding me to those myths. Like all white Americans, I was living with the fear that maybe I didn't really deserve my success, that may be luck and privilege had more to do with it than brains and hard work. I was afraid I wasn't heroic or rugged, that I wasn't special.

I let go of some of that fear when I realized that, indeed, I wasn't special, but that I was still me. What I do well, I still can take pride in, even when I know that the rules under which I work are stacked to my benefit. I believe that until we let go of the fiction that people have complete control over their fate—that we can will ourselves to be anything we choose—then we will live with that fear. Yes, we should all dream big and pursue our dreams and not let anyone or anything stop us. But we all are the product of both what we will ourselves to be and what the society in which we live lets us be.

White privilege is not something I get to decide whether I want to keep. Every time I walk into a store at the same time as a black man and the security guard follows him and leaves me alone to shop, I am benefiting from white privilege. There is not space here to list all the ways in which white privilege plays out in our daily lives, but it is clear that I will carry this privilege with me until the day white supremacy is erased from this society.

Frankly, I don't think I will live to see that day; I am realistic about the scope of the task. However, I continue to have hope, to believe in the creative power of human beings to engage the world honestly and act morally. A first step for white people, I think, is to not be afraid to admit that we have benefited from white privilege. It doesn't mean we are frauds who have no claim to our success. It means we face a choice about what we do with our success.

 25

The Costs of American Privilege

MICHAEL SCHWALBE

When it comes to knowledge of the U.S. government, foreign students often put American students to shame. Many of the American students in my classes don't know how Congress is organized, what cabinet members do, or how governmental powers are divided among the executive, judicial, and legislative branches. The foreign students who have shown up in my classrooms over the years tend to know about these matters and more.

The gap is even wider with regard to knowledge of U.S. behavior around the globe. When foreign students refer to exploitive U.S. trade policies, military interventions abroad, and support for repressive dictatorships—as if any educated person would of course know about such things—American students are often stunned. Foreign students are equally amazed when their remarks are greeted with blank stares.

But this level of ignorance is not so amazing, really. It's a predictable consequence of privilege. Like white privilege and male privilege in our society, American privilege brings with it the luxury of obliviousness.

Privilege comes from membership in a dominant group and is typically invisible to those who have it. Many whites do not see themselves as enjoying "white privilege," yet as Peggy McIntosh has pointed out, there are dozens of ways that whites are privileged in U.S. society.

For example, whites can live anywhere they can afford to, without being limited by racial segregation; whites can assume that race won't be used to decide whether they will fit in at work; whites who complain usually end up speaking to the white person in charge; whites can choose to ignore their racial identity and think of themselves as human beings; and, in most situations, whites can expect to be treated as individuals, not as members of a category.

Men likewise enjoy privileges as members of the dominant gender group. For example, men can walk the streets without being sexually harassed; men can make mistakes without those mistakes being attributed to their gender; men can count on their gender to enhance their credibility; men can expect to find powerful sponsors with whom they can bond as men; and, even in female-dominated occupations, men benefit from being seen as better suited to higher-paying, administrative jobs.

Whites and men tend not to see these privileges because they are taken to be normal, unremarkable entitlements. This is how things appear to members of a dominant group. What's missing is an awareness that life is different for others. Not having to think about the experiences of people in subordinate groups is another form of privilege.

In contrast, women and people of color usually see that those above them in the social hierarchy receive unearned benefits. At the least, they must, for their own protection, pay attention to what members of more powerful groups think and do. This is why women often know more about men than men know about themselves, and why blacks know more about whites than whites know about themselves.

It is no surprise, then, that foreign students, especially those from Third World countries, often know more about the U.S. than most American students do. People in those countries must, as a matter of survival, pay attention to what the U.S. does. There is no equally compelling need for Americans to study what happens in the provinces. And so again the irony: people in Third World countries often know more about the U.S. than many Americans do.

We can thus put these at the top of the list of American privileges: not having to bother, unless one chooses, to learn about other countries; and not having to bother, unless one chooses, to learn about how U.S. foreign policy affects people in other countries. A corollary privilege is to imagine that if people in other countries study us, it's merely out of admiration for our way of life.

The list of American privileges can be extended. For example, Americans can buy cheap goods made by superexploited workers in Third World countries; Americans can take a glib attitude toward war, since it's likely to be a high-tech affair affecting distant strangers; and Americans can enjoy freedom at home, because U.S. capitalists are able to wring extraordinary profits out of Third World workers and therefore don't need to repress U.S. workers as harshly.

But privileges are not without costs. Most obviously there is the cost of ignorance about others. This carries with it the cost of ignorance about ourselves.

One thing we don't learn, when we refuse to learn about or from others, is how they see us. We then lose a mirror with which to view ourselves.

Combined with power, the result can be worse than innocent ignorance. It can be smug self-delusion, belief in the myth of one's own superiority, and a presumed right to dictate morality to others.

We also bear the cost of limiting our own humanity. To be human is to be able to extend compassion to others, to empathize with them, and to reflect honestly on how they are affected by our actions. Privilege keeps us from doing these things and thereby stunts our growth as human beings.

The ignorance that stems from privilege makes Americans easy to mislead when it comes to war. Being told that they are "fighting for freedom," and knowing no better, thousands of American sons and daughters will dutifully kill and die. The ugly truth that they are fighting for the freedom of U.S. capitalists to exploit the natural resources and labor of weaker countries is rarely perceived through the vacuum of knowledge created by American privilege.

But of course it is the people in those weaker countries who bear the greatest costs of American privilege. In war, they will suffer and die in far greater numbers. In peace, or times of less-violent exploitation, their suffering will continue and once again become invisible to citizens living at the core of the empire.

There are positive aspects of American privilege, and from these we can take hope. Most of us enjoy freedom from repression in our daily lives, and we value our rights to associate and to speak out. Perhaps, then, we can appreciate the anger created when U.S. foreign policy denies other people these same rights. Perhaps, too, we can use our freedoms to more fully fight such injustices. If so, then our privileges as Americans will be put to noble and humane use.

If Americans are often afflicted with ignorance and moral blindness when it comes to the rest of the world, this is not a failing of individuals. These problems result from a system of domination that confers privilege. And so we can't make things right simply by declining privilege. In the long run, we have to dismantle the system that gives it to us.

III. How We Got Here: The Historical Context

Christina M. Jiménez

> *History, despite its wrenching pain, cannot be unlived, but if faced with courage, need not be lived again.*
> —MAYA ANGELOU

Most of us are familiar with the phrase "history is written by the winners." The standard version of U.S. history presented in grade school textbooks is written from the perspective of white privilege, class privilege, male privilege, and hetero-sexual privilege. Many texts suggest that U.S. history "begins" with the emigration of English settlers to the Americas, the establishment of the thirteen colonies, the eventual American Revolution for independence, and thus the founding of The United States of America. Does that story, however, truly incorporate the histories of the diverse peoples of the United States? Rather, if we want to write and teach our children U.S. history that includes the histories of *all* Americans, then we must rethink the privileged position of certain groups, like Anglo Americans, in the standard versions of our history.

Perhaps, for instance, we should begin the story of U.S. history in Africa where the ancestors of millions of Americans lived before their forced journey to the Americas as enslaved men, women, and children. Or perhaps we should begin the story of U.S. history hundreds of years before the arrival of Europeans with the rich history of Native American cultures throughout the present geographic territory now known as the United States of America. These other historical begin-nings of our nation and its people are not typically the points of departure for our national story. They are, however, equally if not more valid as they go back further in history and, therefore, give us a more thorough understanding of the broader historical context. Instead, white, elite, heterosexual, male Americans and their ancestors are placed at the beginning, at the center, of traditional historical accounts and thus are portrayed as the main protagonists in our national history.

As a consequence of this historical privileging, many Americans are cast in the position of other, and, at times, as the antagonist to the mythical norm of those who are seen as being true Americans. Think of the history of U.S. expansion and the sustained war against native peoples, for example, or the history of the Mexican American War when the United States took possession of over one-third of Mexico's territory and simultaneously turned thousands of Mexicans living throughout the Southwest into foreigners on their own land. In both of these cases, people of color were the rivals to be conquered by the westward expansion led by Anglo Americans. Anglo Americans are portrayed as strong, proactive heroes at the expense of Native Americans and Mexicans, who are thus cast as antagonists and as others in our national history. In this sense, the marginalization of some social groups in contemporary U.S. society is further reinforced by the way we remember and thus reconstruct our history.

Some social groups, in fact, are rendered *invisible* by our stories of the past. For example, George Chauncey in his essay "Gay New York" in Section III explains "The gay world that flourished before World War I has been almost entirely forgotten in popular memory and overlooked by professional historians; it is not supposed to have existed." Such a historical omission might lead one to think that gay men and women themselves did not exist before the 1910s. Consequently, a whole segment of the population and their particular histories are excluded from our view of the past. Similarly, our historical narratives can also render invisible the history of systematic oppression (and conversely privilege), in both subtle and overt forms. Consider the Homestead Act of 1862, which, most of us learned, "freely" distributed land in the United States in order to encourage western settlement. The Homestead Act is often cited as an example of American exceptionalism (the notion that the United States differs qualitatively from other countries due to its history and democratic traditions), particularly in terms of equality and opportunity since land was given away by the government. As Gregory Campbell suggests in his essay "Many Americas," what we often do not hear discussed about the Homestead Act, however, is that Native Americans were killed and forcibly removed from this land in order to "open" it to white "civilized" settlers. In addition, many non-white U.S. citizens, particularly recently emancipated African Americans, were denied access to this "free" land opportunity because they were deemed ineligible, since "they were not citizens under the Republic when the act was passed into law," on account of their enslavement. Viewed from the perspective of these Americans, the Homestead Act thus does not seem to confirm U.S. exceptionalism as "the land of opportunity for all," but rather suggests the privileging of certain Americans and the systematic oppression of others.

The way we remember our past through our national history often generates a basic contradiction. Many Americans, for example, note that the United States was one of the first ex-colonies of the New World to emerge as a self-governing, democratic country after declaring its independence. While theoretically a political democracy, the United States still consistently denied the rights of *personhood* to many Americans who remained enslaved for another century. Similarly, many Americans, like women and the poor, were granted only limited second-class citizenship rights based on their social identities. During the same period, while fighting for its independence, the United States actively and consistently engaged in military, territorial, and economic conquest, both within its borders and beyond. Through the nineteenth century, in fact, the concept of Manifest Destiny—the ideology that Anglo Americans had the God-given right and obligation to "tame," "civilize," and make economically productive western land—was used to justify a wide range of oppressive practices, including genocidal campaigns against Native American peoples. Indeed, our history exposes a basic "contradiction between the realities of inequality and exclusion juxtaposed against the mythical belief that American society affords equal access and opportunities regardless of class standing, racial identity, or cultural difference," states Campbell in his "Many Americas" essay. As we will discuss at length in Section IV, "Contemporary Institutionalized Oppression and Privilege," the truth of the matter is that most Americans, even today, do not have equal access to opportunities because of their social identities. These contemporary inequalities are largely the consequence of the historical dynamics of oppression and privilege, which continue to affect us all.

One of the most powerful ways in which our history shapes our present identities is through our sense of belonging and acceptance in the nation. As we witnessed in Section II, group privilege is often rooted in the feeling of belonging—in this context, belonging to the nation. Belonging confers entitlement as U.S. citizens and as Americans. White Americans, for instance, often grow up with a clear sense of their inalienable "right to" or "claim on" the nation. This entitlement further extends to the notion of belonging; they feel that they belong in the country that they call home, and, moreover, that their culture and history is deeply valued as an integral part of U.S. history. Perhaps most notable, they have the privilege of claiming what is seen as U.S. exceptionalism and progress as their own. Not all Americans, however, experience this sense of entitlement and belonging to the nation. Native Americans, disabled Americans, and gay Americans, among many other groups, are continually confronted with the oppressive history of their country toward people just like themselves, who were denied not only their civic right of "equal protection under the law," as guaranteed by the Fourteenth Amendment to the U.S. Constitution, but also their explicit rights as citizens.

Openly acknowledging and discussing the history of oppression in the United States is necessary if we are to make *visible* the often obscured histories of nonprivileged groups as well as the ways in which these dynamics have operated in our past. In order to understand where we are today as a society, we need to understand where we have come from as a nation. Therefore, in

Section III, we offer a variety of historical perspectives to expand and counter the all-too-common versions of U.S. history that exclude certain social groups and steer clear of the many ways oppression and privilege have been embedded in our practices, laws, governing institutions, social assumptions, and everyday behaviors. Fortunately, people in nonprivileged social groups have been writing their own histories for centuries. These narratives weave a thick and vibrant tapestry of U.S. history beyond the privileged center. In addition, the United States has a long and rich tradition of resistance and social activism among people across lines of race, class, gender, and sexuality. We also include in this section the history of social activism to challenge, reform, and dismantle systems of oppression. These social movements profoundly transformed our nation and thus offered a tradition upon which we can build to effect change in the future.

Learning about and integrating these histories of oppression and privilege into our understanding of the country's past can be challenging. In navigating this history together, we must be cognizant of the contrasting historical experiences of U.S. citizens from different backgrounds and how our social identities might lead us to see U.S. history from very different perspectives. Our national history intersects with our personal history in very different ways. Those from primarily privileged backgrounds often feel defensive or guilty about the past. Those from nonprivileged backgrounds feel torn about their country's treatment of their ancestors, their culture, or people just like them. A difficult situation can become more complicated when criticism of oppressive aspects of U.S. history is cast as unpatriotic or ungrateful. For various reasons, many people resist acknowledging or fully validating the historical experiences of oppressed groups of men, women, and children in the United States.

Our discomfort with these historical realities only reinforces the idea that many of us possess a skewed and oversimplified understanding of our nation's history. Resistance can stem from the pride one feels in our country and in the progress that it has made in the name of "justice for all," as our national Pledge of Allegiance states. Yet national pride and historical critique are not mutually exclusive. Other students may resist the depiction of certain groups of Americans as oppressors. But this is part of the reality of our past. Certainly, not all members of privileged groups were agents in these systems of oppression. In fact, many Americans privileged by one identity were subjects of other oppressive systems. For example, white women reaped the benefits of whiteness while at the same time experiencing oppression based on gender. On the other hand, scores of people with privilege were also political activists for social change. Many men were active in the women's suffrage movement, and many whites were abolitionists. If we are going to be able to talk about and learn from this history, we must be able to confront our discomfort, get over our resistance, and try to see our history from multiple perspectives.

How, then, do we bridge these fundamentally contrasting experiences of the history of privilege for some Americans and the history of systematic oppression for others? Fortunately, the United States also has a rich history of social change brought about by women and men who took risks and believed in a better, more equitable version of U.S. society. To explore this history of social struggle and change, we turn to the history of the civil rights movement, ethnic identity movements, the women's movement, and the gay and lesbian rights movement. These social movements are twentieth-century examples of community activism that raised people's consciousness about their social identities and societal treatment and that, consequently, produced profound political and social change. The civil rights movement of the 1950s and 1960s, for example, dismantled the legal basis for many of the institutionalized systems of oppression in the United States. Similarly, the women's movement and the gay and lesbian rights movement transformed the way people thought about their social identities and the ways in which U.S. society denied them the same rights and privileges other Americans enjoyed. In some cases, we have selected essays that highlight less familiar aspects of this history. For instance, we have included an essay on the Chicano movement as an example of ethnic identity movements rather than one on the better-known Black Power movement. Understanding this history of activism and cultural resistance is not only empowering but informative as we build contemporary movements for social and institutional change.

Section III is not a comprehensive review of the relevant history of the United States but, rather, a highly selective introduction to several key ideas, issues, events, and movements that can help us make sense of the larger topics treated in the volume. The section thus begins with four overview essays that present a "big picture" perspective of the historical dynamics of oppression and privilege. These essays map the general contours of the historical landscape around different social identities. Paul Jaeger and Cynthia Bowman's essay on the history of disability, for instance, also provides a detailed account of the justifications for discriminatory treatment based on race, gender, and ability, including those grounded in religion, morality, civility, progress, science, and public health. The essay by Karen Rosenblum and Toni-Michelle Travis demonstrates how racism, sexism, homophobia, ableism, classism, and other forms of discrimination were institutionalized, legalized, and ultimately overturned judicially through an examination of critical decisions by the U.S. Supreme Court. You are encouraged to refer back to the exact letter of the law in these case excerpts when their specific histories are cited in Section IV.

Juxtaposed with the broader histories are more topical essays in the latter half of the section. The second half of Section III opens with historical caricatures published in newspapers and magazines in the early twentieth century. These images and political commentaries illustrate the prominent role of the media in both reinforcing and challenging dominant stereotypes. Other essays are selected because their themes resonate with essays in Section IV, which examines recent examples of similar dynamics. The police practice of racial profiling discussed by John Lamberth, for instance, echoes Edward Escobar's analysis of racial profiling of Latinos in early twentieth-century Los Angeles. In this sense, many of the essays in Section III explore the historical underpinnings of current struggles around sexism, classism, racism, ableism, and homophobia.

Throughout the section a continued emphasis is placed on both the intersectionality of social identities as well as the individual and institutional perspective. Certain articles aim to make visible the commonly obscured accounts of particular social groups, such as the history of working women in the United States. Other essays provide individual representations of various groups' experiences, like Yuri Kochiyama's retelling of her internment with other Japanese Americans during World War II. Several essays present both the history of institutional oppression as well as the history of social movements to effect change. Manuel Gonzales's history of the Chicano movement, for instance, explains many of the adverse conditions faced by Mexican Americans as well as the various ways they mobilized politically, socially, and economically. As the essays convey, one significant effect of the shift in identity consciousness among ethnic Americans, women, disabled Americans, and gay and lesbian Americans in the wake of the civil rights movement was the vocal reclaiming of the nation as their own. Claiming their rights to the nation meant claiming their right of belonging, and their own sense of entitlement to the social justice and equal opportunity that America promises.

The last essay in this section treats a historical as well as contemporary issue related to racial discrimination and oppression: foreign immigration to the United States. While several of the works in this section discuss the history of immigrant politics and nativist backlash, Martin Marger's essay demonstrates how some historical dynamics have continued into the twenty-first century. Much of our contemporary debate around racial discrimination centers on the treatment and rights of foreign immigrants, including those with and without official documentation. In order to understand the ongoing debate, we must understand the historical context of U.S. immigration from the 1965 Immigration Act (The Hart-Cellar Act) to the present. The latest immigration trends—such as the rise in undocumented immigrants, security concerns, the issues around language use, and immigrant access to public services—are actually part of a much longer historical debate. As Marger explains,

> Historically, the absorption of immigrants has been a persistent theme of American political argument. In one sense, the United States has always been regarded as a "golden door," open to all seeking economic opportunity or political refuge. But, the acceptance of new groups has been countered by a

tradition of protectionism, which has manifested itself repeatedly in efforts to limit or exclude newcomers. The current public controversy is, therefore, only the latest in a long tradition.

Despite the significant progress made, over the last fifty years in particular, there still remains much to be done to dismantle and transform our social practices, institutions, and assumptions about other people's social identities and their place or lack thereof in U.S. society. If equality and democracy are indeed foundational and fundamental to our national identity, then we must be ready and willing to examine the pervasive reality of U.S. inequalities—in our laws, government policies, institutions, and everyday social practices—that are obstacles to achieving those ideals. After gaining a more balanced understanding of the histories of oppression and privilege in the United States, we are better equipped to understand the many ways in which these struggles continue all around us each day. The struggle to create and sustain social justice is the responsibility and obligation of all Americans.

I, Too

LANGSTON HUGHES

I, too, sing America

I am the darker brother.
They send me to eat in the kitchen
When company comes,
But I laugh,
And eat well,
And grow strong.

Tomorrow,
I'll be at the table
When company comes.
Nobody'll dare
Say to me,
"Eat in the kitchen,"
Then.

Besides,
They'll see how beautiful I am
And be ashamed—

I, too, am America.

A. The Big Picture: Understanding the Historical Context

Patriot

ALICE WALKER

If you
Want to show
Your love
For America
Love
Americans
Smile
When you see
One
Flowerlike
His

Turban
Rosepink.

Rejoice
At the
Eagle feather
In a grandfather's
Braid.

If a sister
Bus rider's hair
Is
Especially
Nappy
A miracle
In itself
Praise it.

How can there be
Homeless
In a land
So crammed
With houses

&
Young children
Sold
As sex snacks
Causing our thoughts
To flinch &
Snag?

Love your country
By loving
Americans.

Love Americans.

Salute the soul
& the body
Of who we
Spectacularly &
Sometimes
Pitifully are.
Love *us*. We are
The flag.

 26

Many Americas

The Intersections of Class, Race, and Ethnic Identity

GREGORY R. CAMPBELL

INTRODUCTION

America was never, ethnically or racially, a homogeneous society. From its colonial inception, American society was inescapably multi-ethnic, multi-racial, and culturally diverse. The North American continent which Europeans colonized was inhabited by at least 2.1 million and possibly, 9.8 million indigenous people.[1] They spoke more than 2,000 distinct languages and lived in a myriad of culturally distinct lifeways.[2] On the eve of Europe's conquest, the so-called "New World" was one of the most ethnically and culturally diverse places on earth.

Besides the innumerable ethnic, linguistic, and cultural identities among Native American people, many of the original European settlements were multi-ethnic and multi-racial. As early as 1619, a Dutch shipmaster brought to the Virginia colonies about 20 Africans after a foray in the West Indies. The 1625 census for Jamestown lists 23 Africans living among the European colonists, including four that had immigrated to Jamestown between 1621 and 1623.[3] Initially Africans and Europeans lived and worked side-by-side, forging the new colony.

After the formation of the 13 colonies, in sharp contrast to European nation-states, North American settlements by the mid-eighteenth century were a collage of ethnicities and "races."[4] Apart from the English, Welsh and Germans who had colonized Pennsylvania and the Carolinas, the Swedes and Finns settled Delaware, and New England was home to thousands of French Huguenots. Sephardic Jews from Holland made their home in Rhode Island, while the Dutch settled in New York.[5] Living on the frontiers and fringes of the major English settlements were Highland Scots, Irish, Scotch-Irish, who served as an ethnic buffer between the "civilized" Atlantic seaboard and "savage" wilderness filled with Native Americans.[6]

Even within the confines of the various settlements hugging the Atlantic coast, various racial and ethnic groups co-mingled. Europeans, Native Americans, as well as Africans moved freely through colonial American towns. On visiting New Amsterdam in 1643, the French Jesuit Isaac Jogues was astounded that 18 disparate languages were spoken in a town of about 8,000.[7]

Despite the multi-ethnic and multi-racial composition of the "New World" landscape, the first settlers brought with them the seeds of oppression from the world in which they left. The European colonists imported the distinctions of class and the construct of the "Other" from the Old World.[8] "The American wilderness," according to Howard Zinn, "modified and complicated these distinctions, but it did not eliminate them. And the more the population grew—the greater the wealth, the more complex the society—the sharper became the differences between the upper and lower classes."[9] As class distinctions became more focused, what explained these differences, in terms of the "Other," were color (that is, race) and culture (ethnicity).[10] It is out of this volatile mixture of class, race, and culture that a "White" consciousness and "White" racism ground itself into the fabric of American society before the American Revolution. American racism was congruent with the Old World European worldview which dictated that some men were born to rule whereas others were born to serve. This worldview about the hierarchical order of society was accepted as preordained and natural. It was a world of kings and peasants, of masters and slaves, of "civilized" and "savage" men, of upper and lower classes. Permeating all of these social dichotomies was the prevailing idea of an innate superiority and inferiority. It is these differences that defined fundamentally, from the inception of colonization, American societal hierarchical arrangements. Thus questions of class, race, and ethnicity

have been at the center of some of the most profound events in the American experience.[11]

Throughout the history of America, class, race, and ethnicity served to create the dynamic tension between who in our society is included and who is marginalized in the political economic landscape. America has never lived up to its self-professed universalistic democratic ideals of natural rights, social contracts, and human equality. It is this contradiction—the contradiction between the realities of inequality and exclusion juxtaposed against the mythical belief that American society affords equal access and opportunities regardless of class standing, racial identity, or cultural difference—that defines many Americas. . . . The transformations and interplay of class, race, and culture were applied in a multitude of ways to many different people. In each instance, American society defined who would gain a degree of inclusion and who would remain fundamentally unequal, outside America's accepted social order. It is America's tragic flaw; and our society continues to live with its explosive consequences.

THE FORMATION OF AMERICA'S RACIAL HIERARCHY

The colonial society that emerged along the Atlantic coast of North America during the early 1600's was tied—politically, economically, and ideologically—to England and her ruling elite. Initially the economic system, like that of Spain to the south and the French to the north, was a combination of state and private entrepreneurial enterprises directed toward the extraction of natural resources and the expansion of their international markets. The colonization of the Atlantic Coast with permanent European settlements was to establish and protect those political economic objectives.[12]

The colonization of North America served a dual purpose. It not only provided a valuable resource of raw materials to fuel the rapid industrial growth in Europe, the North American colonies also served as a "dumping ground" for surplus European peasants and workers being disenfranchised by the development of European capitalism.[13] Many of the colonists therefore came to North America seeking to establish small farms like the ones lost in Europe, attempting to reestablish a way of life. Thus within the colonies, two modes of production emerged—a subsistence, household mode and a mercantile capitalist mode of production, located in the merchant and plantation sectors. Both sectors, while conflicting in some arenas, required continuous access to land and labor.

Land and its natural resources were provided through the appropriation of them from Native American societies. The systematic incorporation of indigenous lands, along with the mass destruction of local indigenous populations required European colonial powers to construct an ideology of justification. Inspired by the philosophical writings of St. Augustine and others, political philosophers argued that there was an inviolable natural order in the world. The laws governing this order [are] a reflection of God's will, a pre-determined condition that existed in the mind of God before it was enacted on earth. These hierarchical laws of the natural and political order could not be challenged or overturned. It was a social contract that was not affected by historical forces and social change. The socially inferior then, had no choice in their station along the hierarchical chain of being. From the beginning of cultural contact, European scholars and theologians argued that the native people of the New World were barbaric, unreasoning, sunk in vice, incapable of learning, lacked a sophistication of language and cultural customs, and were physically different from Europeans. Hence Native Americans were lower on the scale of being, closer to a "natural" or "savage" state of humanness. Indigenous people were inferior and defective members of the human species who had to accept willingly their subjugation.[14] This ideological ranking of the social world, combined with national chauvinism, aided the course of empire-building and profit-taking across the New World.[15] All European colonial powers in their relations with indigenous people in the "New World" developed similar ideological and social constructions to delineate the boundaries between

"civilization" and "savagery," demarcating the distinctions between Europeans, Native Americans, and other ethno-racial minorities.[16]

For the English colonists, labeling Native Americans as "savages" dwelling outside the confines of "civilizations" did not require any intellectual maneuvering. Drawing on their colonial conquest of the "wild and savage" Irish and highland Scots, the English colonists entered the New World with ideological constructions of supremacy, domination, and exploitation. The colonists also knew from their interactions with the Celtic "savages" that "uncivilized" people shared a number of characteristics. They were nomadic, had no conception of private property, were dominated by an "innate sloth," and most importantly, lacked a knowledge of God.[17] The native people of North America fit this previously held definition of "savagery." In addition, the Celtic conquest taught the English two methods to control "savage people"—wars of extermination and the creation of reserves.[18] These imported ideologies and methods would become fundamental in shaping the distinctive structure of oppressive control of Native American nations.

The English colonists attempted to arrange their "New World" in the same hierarchical, intelligible order as the "Old World." The world order connected the lowest in nature with the highest in heaven, but Puritan theology viewed the message of Jesus as a radical dividing line between those residing within the grace of God and those who remained in nature unredeemed by grace.[19] The Puritans, rather than accepting human nature and the place of human kind in nature, disowned nature. Grace destroyed the nature in humans and "morality lost its centrality because morality . . . addressed itself to the conduct of natural man."[20] Puritanical ideology segregated those who were under the grace of God from those who were outside this domain.

These ideologies had dire consequences for Native Americans. Living in a perceived natural state, outside the confines of grace, meant that Indian people came to be viewed as "heathens," who were inherently evil, incapable of "civilization." The colonials regarded Native American people as members of a thinly populated, nomadic hunting race, with no fixed habitation, roaming over a virgin wilderness.[21] The myth of the nomadic savage paralleled the shift in the developing Puritan economy from one of trade with neighboring tribal-nations to an agri-based economic infrastructure.[22] Because these negative human qualities were considered inborn and were judged as "erradicable qualities of civilization," they were identified as racial markers.[23] This process of dehumanizing Native Americans allowed the New England colonists to appropriate Indian resources while destroying them through disease and warfare.[24]

Native American mortality was often interpreted as God's will. The idea of divine intent in destroying the "enemies" of civilization, as David Stannard noted, was deeply rooted in early Christian thought.[25] Native Americans, especially in light of their declining economic importance to the Puritan colonies, came to be perceived as Satanic. Wars of extermination therefore were conceived of as "Holy Wars" between God's chosen people and the minions of Satan.[26]

Throughout the Atlantic coastal region and into the western interior, indigenous populations declined because of introduced diseases, genocidal warfare, and slave raiding.[27] In the Southeast for example, the estimated Native American population in 1685 was 199,400. By 1790 the population was reduced to approximately 55,900; a decline of 71.9 percent.[28] By contrast, Europeans and Africans in the region increased their population to 1,630,100 or 31.4 percent.[29]

The precipitous decline in indigenous populations east of the Mississippi River was viewed by Euro-American society as a natural process that was divorced from the political economic realities of colonial expansion. The extinction of Native American societies, it was argued, was the fault of Indian people themselves, not European colonialism. Their inferiority and indolence inhibited Native American people from achieving the same state of economic and demographic prosperity as Europeans.[30] . . . By 1800, the European population had grown approximately to 5,308,483, while the North American

indigenous total population had declined to an estimated 600,000.[31] Depopulation, in conjunction with the rapid demographic expansion of Euro-Americans, at once offered physical confirmation that Native American people would become inevitable victims of the "laws of civilized progress." "Civilization" or extinction became the governmental-frontier battle cry as Anglo Americans pressed onward toward the Mississippi River.

Such drastic population declines across Native North America, accompanied by the loss of lands, led to a precipitous decline in cultural diversity and a cultural homogenization among surviving indigenous communities. In response, many indigenous societies underwent a variety of ethnogenetic processes to sociologically reconstitute themselves as tribal-nations or reinvent themselves ethnically as a society.[32] One of the strategies frequently employed by various Native American societies was to amalgamate themselves—sociologically and biologically—through the incorporation of other Native Americans, Africans, and Europeans.[33]

As indigenous lands fed the development of colonial farmsteads and plantations, indigenous labor was initially used to extract profits from plantation owners' lands. Demand for Indian slaves created widespread conflict and social disruption as European and Native American slave raiders attacked villages for the slave market. . . . By the early 1730's, most Siouan speaking people of the Virginia Piedmont incorporated themselves so completely among other indigenous societies ranging from Pennsylvania to the Carolinas that they "gradually gave up their language, customs, and identity."[34] Many other indigenous societies had similar fates.

Alongside indigenous slave labor, English elites filled the remaining labor void using indentured European servants. In Britain, the expansion of industrial production dislocated European farmers and peasants in the sixteenth and seventeenth centuries. To create more quickly a source of cheap, exploitable labor, England passed series of Poor Laws. The poor were viewed by the English elite as lazy, diseased, immoral, as well as ignorant. These stereotypes also were applied to the disenfranchised

Highland Scots and Irish in England's other colonies. Both the English poor and Celts were considered subhuman, each a separate "race" that could be exploited as well as enslaved both at home and in the colonies. These ideological beliefs about the disenfranchised poor, Irish, and Scots as vile subhumans were carried to the North American colonies, where poor Europeans, like Africans and Native Americans, would come to inhabit the same racial space.[35]

During the formative stages of slavery, enslaved and indentured Africans, indentured Europeans, and enslaved Native Americans worked alongside each other in the tobacco fields of Virginia and the Carolinas. They labored together, fraternized continuously, and intermarried with each other.[36] While southern "White" elites were familiar with the rigid class lines of American colonial society, they were less concerned about maintaining the racial hierarchy, especially among the lower classes.[37] Africans, Indians, and indentured "Whites" were the same—uncivilized, unclean, promiscuous, lower races.

The construction and separation of races on the basis of phenotype only emerged during the last quarter of the seventeenth century. A central criterion for the justification of oppressive chattel slavery was color. By 1661 the institution of slavery was formally recognized by Virginia. Three years later, Maryland recognized the institution. Even Quaker Pennsylvania recognized slavery by 1700.[38] Once chattel slavery was formalized as a legal economic institution, it shaped the ethnic experience of Africans until the present-day.

There were several factors that contributed to the establishment of "Black" slavery and the associated rise of "White" racism. First, agricultural production was expanding as the supply of European indentured servants was declining. European countries, because of industrialization, needed unskilled labor to exploit at home. European immigration and indentured servitude slowed to a modest pace, especially after the American Revolution. Another reason for the slowing of European immigration was Britain's passage of the *Passenger Act of 1803*. The

act raised significantly the cost of trans-Atlantic passenger tickets to discourage a "brain drain" of any skilled and talented workers who may carry with them England's industrial know-how to the United States, England's fledgling industrial competitor.[39]

Moreover, indentured servitude was a temporary status; a status that was being continually shortened in duration.[40] Freed indentured servants, whether European or African, after being released from their debt bondage, demanded lands and a decent living at a time when agricultural production in the southeastern United States demanded the concentration of land ownership into large plantations, not its fragmentation into yeoman farmsteads.[41] The establishment of small farmsteads conflicted directly with the expansion of the plantation economy.

The emergence of cotton, sugar, and later tobacco, as international commodities, demanded a stable labor force. Indentured servants were not only temporary, but rebellious, making racially mixed plantations unproblematic.[42] Bacon's Rebellion of 1676 offered the colonial elite a glimpse of how dangerous a multi-racial landless proletariat could be when united for a common purpose.[43] "Black" chattel slavery offered a greater degree of stability—economically and politically. Unlike indentured servants, African women and children worked the fields. A plantation owner could increase his profit margin by requiring more work hours while maintaining his labor force at a subsistence level.

African slavery also allowed for much greater social control, as their confinement to a single plantation, along with having no expectations of freedom or land ownership, transformed them into human-less instruments of production. That is, because African slaves ". . . can not exercise their industry for themselves, they are implicitly denied the ability to enter the transformation process: 'Day after day they drudge on without any prospect of ever reaping for themselves.' The very situation that introduces them to America precludes their participation."[44] Africans, as well as Native Americans, because of the fabrication of "Whiteness" and Anglocentricity remained outside the transformational processes of becoming fully "American."[45]

As chattel slavery evolved and became institutionalized, color as a demarcation of race and racial separation became part of the North American political economic landscape.[46] In America,

> . . . black skin became the stigma of slavery and wretchedness. The treatment of the slave degenerated to the lowest level of brutality. The image of the African became associated with savagery, paganism, immorality, ignorance, and primitiveness. In short, racism materialized.[47]

As early as 1731, Bishop Berkeley testified that American slaveowners held "an irrational contempt for blacks, as creatures of another species . . ."[48] Paralleling the rise of slavery was philosophical and scientific evidence that the "Blackness" of Africans, along with its associated inferior intellectual, moral, and social characteristics, stood separate and in direct opposition to "Whiteness" and its inherent qualities.

By 1790, fifteen years after the American Revolution, there were approximately 757,000 Africans in the United States, of which 92.1 percent were enslaved.[49] The system of forced labor created massive profits for the plantations, merchants, and other allied enterprises. . . . Slavery benefited both Anglo Americans and Europeans by producing profits for further investment, stimulating the fledgling mercantile and industrial sectors of European and American commerce. The fruits of slave labor, between 1790 to 1860, contributed directly to the growth of the United States national economy.[50] For African Americans, their oppression prior to and after emancipation, ". . . is rooted in the requirements of early capitalism."[51]

From the late 1700's until the close of the Civil War, the profits derived on the backs of African slave labor, allowed Southern "White" elites to dominate the United States political landscape. For nearly eight decades, the federal government rarely challenged the interests of the slaveholding oligarchy. The national government, throughout the entire period of slavery, played a critical role in the creation and institutionalization of racial oppression, often extending the boundaries of racism as the United States in the process [of] nation building incorporated other "races" and ethnic groups. Various presidential administrations, Congresses, and Supreme Court justices involved themselves in not only the protection of slavery as an institution, but actively engaged themselves in forcibly removing Native Americans to west of the Mississippi River and legitimizing patterns of wide disparities in the distribution of wealth among members of United States society.[52]

Further Anglo American demand for land led to a desire to extinguish remaining Native American title by the 1830's. The final solution was forced relocation of Native Americans beyond the current boundaries of civilization. It was a governmental policy rooted in the doctrine of racial decay. Native Americans, in being removed west of the Mississippi River, would find temporary respite before passing into extinction under the hegemony of civilization.[53] That sentiment was expressed by President Andrew Jackson in his 1830 *Second Annual Address.* "Humanity," President Jackson eloquently proclaimed:

> . . . has often wept over the fate of the aborigines of this country, . . . but its progress has never for a moment been arrested, and one by one have many powerful tribes disappeared from the earth. To follow . . . What good man would prefer a country covered with forests and ranges by a few thousand savages to our extensive republic . . . occupied by more than 12,000,000 happy people, and filled with all the blessings of liberty, civilization, and religion?[54]

The passage of the *Indian Removal Act* of May 28, 1830, had severe sociological and demographic consequences for relocated Native American nations.[55] Between 1828 and 1838, approximately 81,282 Native Americans were removed west of the Mississippi River. For their relocation efforts, the United States government acquired 115,355,767 acres of Indian lands and resources.[56] Under the Act, the forced removal of Native American nations from their homelands continued until 1877.[57]

Native American removal beyond the encroachments of civilization, marked a critical shift in Euro-American racial thinking about the Native Americans as well as other racial minorities. Increasingly, science was called on to explain and justify the superiority and inferiority among the different races. . . . Theological explanations for racial differences waned under the emerging cloak of scientific explanation.[58] Questions arose concerning the unity of humankind, the notion of progress, and cultural development. As its focus, American racial scholarship would collect and synthesize cultural, archaeological, linguistic, and biological data to discover empirically the mental and physical characteristics in the types of humankind. An important goal was to discern whether the varieties of humankind were separate species or not. The debate over the unity of humankind revolved around the controversy between polygeny and monogeny regarding the history of the races.[59] Both ideas were pre-evolutionary forms of scientific racism. Monogenists upheld the unity of all people from a single creation of Adam and Eve, but all races degenerated from Eve's perfection. People of European descent . . . degenerated the least, creating a racial hierarchy with Europeans superior to all other types of humankind.[60]

The polygenists, on the other hand, subscribed to the notion that human races were separate biological species. Each race had a separate origin, with innately endowed characteristics.[61] The fixedness and instinctiveness of the inferior races argued persuasively that the lower species of humankind are placed on the earth to serve higher races. For African slaves, science proved their position in American society.

One hallmark study of early nineteenth century ethnological racism was Samuel G. Morton's *Crania Americana* of 1839.[62] The work's principle aim was to delineate accurately by osteological facts whether "American aborigines of all epochs have belonged to one race or a plurality of races."[63] Drawing on the science of phrenology and craniometry, Morton, an avowed polygenist, confirmed the inferiority of American Indians. Manipulating the craniometric data, Dr. Morton concluded that Native Americans had a "deficiency of 'higher' mental powers," indicating an "inaptitude for civilization."[64] The structure of "Indian's" mind, Morton concluded, was quite different, making it impossible for Euro-Americans and Native Americans to interact socially.[65] The scientific affirmation of the polygenetic origins and inferiority of "non-White" races, by the mid-1830's was carried out as a political doctrine of racial destiny which permeated discussions about American progress.[66]

Amidst these questions, American scholarship assumed an explicit racism. Any perceived cultural differences, including the potential ability or inability to acquire the accouterments of American "civilization," were interpreted as being ineradicable, innate qualities peculiar to certain races. The varieties of humankind—Native Americans, Africans, some European ethnics, and others—were conceived of as separate species or degenerated races that possessed certain characteristics that were rooted deeply in their descent.[67] By the early nineteenth century, American scholarship provided the unifying ideological link that explained Euro-American racial and technological superiority and the oppression of indigenous people, enslaved Africans, the ethnic immigrant underclass, and other ethno-racial minorities.

Moreover, the science of race faithfully explained societal inequities and reified the destiny of the American nation-state in expanding against neighboring "inferior" people. This scientific tradition would be responsible for the exalted state of American civilization as well as determine the future social and moral progress of the nation. National progress, guided by a body of racial knowledge, would explain and determine the course, nature, and shape of America's Anglo-Saxon societal mainstream, including America's "racial" composition.[68] Mid-nineteenth century scientific inquiry supported the political ideology and governmental actions in carrying out their mission of racial destiny.

THE RACIAL PROGRESS OF A NATION

By the 1830's, the opening of "surplus" western lands for Euro-American settlement, along with the growing industrialism in the northeastern states, stimulated a wave of European immigration.[69] American states and territories actively recruited immigrants with promises of jobs or inducements of cheap land.[70] The arrival of immigrants from northern and western Europe laid the foundation for new ethno-racial conflicts to emerge. The new immigrants competed with native-born European ethnics and, to a lesser extent, free African Americans for jobs. The Northern industrial elite seized this opportunity to use various "White" ethnics as well as free "Blacks" to displace each other in the workplace. For the Northern industrialists, this "divide and conquer" strategy along ethnic and racial lines allowed them to work their laborers long hours, with minimal pay, and have total disregard for their worker's safety or well-being. Under these circumstances, the multi-ethnic and multi-racial workforce, came to view each other with disdain, often using "color" and "culture" as mechanisms for oppressing each other. Working class racism seeded itself strongly in the industrial political economy. Just as the developing industrial political economy needed a continual source of cheap, exploitable labor, it also required access to natural resources to continually feed itself.

Lands west of [the] Mississippi River offered the potential resources necessary for further industrialization. Thus [there] arose a national debate for further territorial acquisitions and a growing intolerance for western territorial holdings of competing nation-states. The arguments for national completion prompted the United States government to seek political and economic policies that would reinforce the destiny of Anglo-Saxon America. By the mid-1840's, the replacement of "inferior races" by any means necessary was considered the biosocial destiny of the "Anglo-Saxon race." Euro-Americans would outbreed, overwhelm, and replace any "inferior races" that stood in the way of creating an Anglo-Saxon nation state.[71] The ideology boldly proclaimed that it was the "White" Anglo-Saxon race's responsibility to expand against and subordinate "lesser" races. It was America's "Manifest Destiny."

A visible expression of the United States completing its racial and national destiny was the 1845 annexation of Texas from Mexico. Those Mexicans absorbed into the American domain were relegated immediately to second class citizens and treated as inferiors. American brutality was especially acute along the border, where violence erupted frequently between Euro-Americans and Mexicans. In a border territorial dispute, President James Polk declared war on Mexico, claiming that U.S. blood was shed by Mexicans on American soil. Under the banner of Manifest Destiny and armed with an ideology of racial superiority, United States military troops between April of 1846 and February 1848, marched into Mexico City. The United States federal government forced the Mexicans to sign the Treaty of Guadalupe of Hildalgo. Six years later, the United States would force Mexico into ceding southern Arizona and New Mexico as part of the Gadsden Purchase. In fulfilling its national and racial destiny, the United States incorporated Texas, Arizona, New Mexico, California, Nevada, Utah, Colorado, and portions of Oklahoma, Kansas, and Wyoming.[72]

Under the Treaty of Guadalupe of Hildalgo, the Mexicans that remained in the newly acquired U.S. territories, were guaranteed citizenship, their property, and religious freedom. Despite these assurances, Mexican Americans across the Southwest lost their lands, suffered oppressive discrimination, and were marginalized within the newly imposed American class hierarchy. The loss of Mexican American political economic power in the incorporated Southwest was the result of their *meztizo* heritage. Using their Indian ancestry against them, Anglos constructed a body of discriminatory racial laws to either steal Mexican American resources or deny them legal rights afforded them under the Treaty of Guadalupe of Hildalgo and the United States Constitution.[73]

The degree of colonization and oppression, according to Oscar Martinez:

. . . varied from place to place and among different social classes . . . The Chicano elite quickly lost economic and political power to Anglo capitalists and politicians. Texas and California, where masses of unsympathetic voters shaped the new order, are good examples of this trend. Only in New Mexico, where Hispanos remained in the majority, could local leaders retain some significant control. At the lower end of society, poor Chicanos endured lower wages than their Anglo counterparts, substandard working conditions and few opportunities for advancement. Segregation, poverty, poor education and discrimination relegated Chicanos . . . to underclass status.[74]

. . . Mexican American identity is neither static nor homogeneous. Mexican ethnic identity historically was vastly different in New Mexico, along the border of Texas, or in California. The differences in Mexican American ethnic identities across time and space are related directly to the emerging regional political economies before and after Anglo colonization. Ethnic identities have a material and social locus in that they cannot be separated from their historical and social context. Thus the construction and the perpetuation of ethnic identities is contingent on historical circumstances as people are active agents in their own history. Differential ethnic formation, whether *Indio, Mestizo,* Mexican American, or today, Chicano, is a badge of resistance to capitalism and its oppression. Within this context Vigil writes, time, place, and history do indeed matter ". . . because ethnic identity and solidarity shift across groups and historical eras, [and therefore] it is . . . inappropriate to deny the importance of social factors in molding ethnicity over time and place."[75] The formation of Chicano ethnicity is a history of conflict and survival.[76]

Across the Southwest, the rampant discrimination, exploitation, and oppression against Mexican Americans led to violence. Along the Texas-Mexico frontier in 1857, Anglo businessmen attacked Mexican teamsters who dominated the trade from San Antonio to the Texas coast. The "Cart War" of 1857 as it was called left 75 dead.[77] Despite Mexican American resistance to Anglo domi-

nation, Anglos managed to wrest control of most businesses and valuable resources owned previously by Mexican Americans. Anglo economic dominance was so complete that by the 1880's, Anglo capitalists penetrated the Mexican economies of Sonora and Chihuahua through the construction of rail routes. The railroads, taking advantage of Mexican government's establishment of a *Zona Libre* (Free Zone) along the Mexican-United States border, transported precious metals, raw materials, and human labor to the United States. Resentment among Mexicans and Mexican Americans to Anglo domination and oppression would play a pivotal role in the 1910 Mexican Revolution.[78]

The annexation of Mexican territories and the 1848–1849 California Gold Rush, opened vast new territories that offered immediate economic potential, especially in resource extractive industries. Mining, lumbering, ranching, and agriculture were labor intensive enterprises that required a cheap labor source to make a profit.

Attempting to escape the ravages of the Opium Wars, the first Chinese began to migrate to California in the late 1840's.[79] Although barred from citizenship under a 1790 federal law that afforded that privilege only to "Whites," the Chinese immigrants initially were welcomed as they offered western entrepreneurs and eastern capital investors a cheap source of labor. So welcomed were the first Chinese immigrants in 1850, the Chinese were invited to march in President Zachary Taylor's funeral procession and assisted in celebrating California's admission to statehood. With the news of *Gum San* ("Gold Mountain") reaching China, between 1850 and 1860, 41,397 Chinese arrived in the United States.[80] When many Chinese began mining for themselves in direct competition with Anglo American miners, Anglo tolerance shifted to one of resentment.[81]

Across the Atlantic Ocean, the potato blight (*Phytophthora infestans*) first appeared in Ireland in 1845, destroying 40 percent of the crop. The next year, the Irish experienced total crop failure. During the famine of 1846–1847, a million Irish died of starvation, disease, and exposure. The most affected were the poor, landless laborers, and small farmers. The British government, one of the wealthiest countries in the world, instead of offering immediate relief used the tragedy as an opportunity for massive land clearances.[82] Nearly two million Irish were forced off their lands.[83] For the British government, the famine and land clearances offered an experiment in social engineering. The political economic tragedy simultaneously eliminated fragmented landholdings and reconsolidated them in British hands while allowing the high mortality and immigration to eliminate the surplus population. As Lord Clarendon boldly proclaimed: "I would sweep the Connacht clean and turn upon it new men and English money just as one would to Australia or any freshly discovered Colony."[84] The forcible removal and massive deaths were the only solution to solving the "Irish Problem" just as forcible removals and genocide were solutions to the "Indian Problem" in America.

Once in America, Irish immigrants became targets of vicious prejudice and discrimination. Since the seventeenth century, the Irish were considered "Papists," loyal to the Catholic Church. Their Catholicism was perceived as threat to national interests, as a citizen could not have two conflicting loyalties. The "Papist" Irish were viewed as possessing an innate wickedness, immorality, and lacked intelligence. After the great migration, the Irish were believed to be a distinct "race," the "missing link" between apes, Africans, and the English.[85]

Almost every racist stereotype applied to African slaves also was levied against the Irish.[86] The dehumanizing prejudice and open hatred for the Irish in America only served to rationalize the extreme exploitation of Irish labor. The Irish, like African slaves, occupied the same rung in America's racial ladder. And the Irish, like the Chinese, increasingly were viewed by Anglo Americans as a threat to them.

By the mid-1850's nativism crystallized into a political movement that pledged to fight the influence of Roman Catholicism by voting for only Protestant, native-born Anglo American citizens and calling for a 21 year naturalization period for all immigrants. The political party called themselves the Know-Nothings. Although they vanished quickly from the political landscape, their anti-alien ideology and nativist stances would reappear later among organizations such as the Ku Klux Klan, the anti-Catholic *American Protective Association* as well as in public policy.[87] In 1854 for example California barred any Chinese person from testifying in court. In *Hall v. the people,* a "White" man was convicted on the testimony of Chinese witnesses. Judge Charles J, Murray reversed the verdict citing the *Criminal Act of 1850* which states that "No Black, Mulato person, or Indian, shall be allowed to give evidence in favor of, or against a White man."[88] The next year, California passed a law placing a $50 head tax on every Chinese immigrant and three years later passed legislation forbidding Chinese immigration into the state. Although both laws were declared unconstitutional by the United States Supreme Court in 1876, the legislation reveals the ideological legacy of nativism and xenophobic racism. Other immigrants and Americans of "color" would face similar racial hatred.

As the flow of immigrants continued unabated along with America's increasing multi-racial composition, the federal government moved to take greater control. In 1855, Congress directed the *U.S. Customs Service* to compile quarterly and annual immigration reports. Nine years later, Congress passed legislation to establish the *Bureau of Immigration.* That same year, the Republican Party advocated for a stronger national immigration policy as part of their 1864 party platform.[89] On the eve of the Civil War, the United States questioned whether immigrants were a benefit or whether they hindered national progress. It would remain an issue into the next century.

THE CIVIL WAR AND THE RISE OF SCIENTIFIC RACISM

The U. S. Civil War was, at its core, a political economic struggle between an alliance of Northern industrialists and "White" small farmers against the Southern plantation agriculturalists. The "North's" victory marked the emergence of the northern industrialism and its elite as the dominant force in the United States economy and politics.

After the Civil War, the political economic land-scape changed, laying the groundwork for a surge of nativism and xenophobia. Along with a post-war economy that required rebuilding, especially in the South, the country faced the prospect of reabsorbing Union and Confederate soldiers as well as emancipated African Americans into an eroding labor market. With the South's economic infra-structure in ruin, southern "Whites" would find it extremely difficult to reestablish a livelihood. It is out of these political economic conditions that racial questions arose surrounding immigrants, Native Americans, and African Americans.

With the 1865 passage of the 13th Amendment to the Constitution which abolished slavery and invol-untary servitude, questions arose as to whether African Americans and other racial minorities should be incorporated into the nation as voting citi-zens; one hallmark of "Whiteness." Within this legal question were two other issues for Anglo America. First, can "inferior racial stocks" be assimilated into the national fold? Last, are these "races" a benefit to national progress?

The above questions, after 1859, were answered scientifically by the application of Darwinian evo-lutionary principles to the development of social life. Societies, like species, were not wholly im-mutable; rather they changed over time. Social complexity, especially with regard to human cus-toms and institutions, was viewed as following a long history of basic, universal, evolutionary laws. The application of evolutionary theory to human cultures, as well as biology, required that there was a unity of humankind. Therefore, all the "races" must be following the same sequence of bio-social development.[90]

While evolutionism resolved the debate between polygeny and monogeny, it raised new questions and contradictions that had to be resolved, espe-cially with the intensification of racism in the decades following the Civil War.[91] If there is a unity of humankind, why did some "races" evolve more complex cultures than others? Moreover, how do these perceived differences fit into the prevailing social order of American society?

Late nineteenth century scientific racism, using evolutionary principles as [its] theoretical frame-work, used the comparative method and conjectural history to measure the course of racial and cultural progress.[92] Humans, racial evolutionists argued, emerged independently from a common proto-human ancestry, but Europeans traversed the prim-itive cultural stages long before the progenitors of the other "races," especially people of color.[93] Europeans were the result of intense, but separate, biological and cultural evolution that produced a "superior" race and cultural institutions. As evi-dence of European biological and cultural superior-ity, racial evolutionists often cited the demographic increase of "superior" European populations and the homeostasis or decline of "inferior races." No amount of education in the "art of civilized pur-suits" could compensate for thousands of years of natural selection. Non-Europeans were intellectu-ally, emotionally, and culturally unfit to survive.[94] Darwin's theory for the enlightened American read-ing public proposed a dynamic new premise on which society's social inequalities, racism, and po-litical policies could be constructed.[95] African Americans, Native Americans, Mexican Americans and "undesirable" immigrants fed the grist mill of race struggle; a struggle that could lead naturally to racial extinction.

Evolutionary theory, however, held out the re-mote possibility that some "inferior" races could be saved from extinction. Social evolution predicted that it may be possible to push some "inferior races" along the societal hierarchy toward "civiliza-tion." If inferior societies were not doomed to ex-tinction, it was the "Whiteman's burden" to alter slowly their biology and society to ". . . lift the darker fellows to liberty's plane."[96]

The solution to absorbing native-born Anglo Americans disenfranchised by the Civil War was to settle them in the West. To accomplish this task . . . required conquering and confining the remaining sovereign Native American societies. For two decades after the Civil War, the United States fed-eral government crafted policies, backed by the U. S. military, to force Native Americans from their lands. Whether by treaty or war, the remaining indigenous societies had to be separated from their lands. In many ways, it was a natural process—a "superior" race should supplant an "inferior" race.

To stimulate Anglo western settlement, Abraham Lincoln and Congress passed the *Homestead Act of 1862*. The legislation was a major wealth-building program for "Whites," providing . . . 160 to 320 acres of land for those who wished to develop the property. Most emancipated African Americans, [however,] were deemed ineligible for land under the act. The reasoning rested on the argument that they were not citizens under the Republic when the act was passed into law. Thus, African Americans, for the most part, were denied the opportunity to gain access to an important source of wealth, Indian lands.

The denial of African Americans and other racial minorities to resources across the West rested also on another legal assumption by state and territorial legislations that only "Whites" be granted full citizenship and all the rights that it entailed. To curtail state's rights to prescribe citizenship, in 1868, the United States government passed the 14th Amendment to legislate an uniform citizenship law, eliminating state's rights to establish citizenship eligibility. Despite the constitutional mandate, state and territorial legislators crafted legislation that argued the 14th Amendment only applied to "Whites" and "Blacks," not American Indians, Mexicans, Asians, and "half-breeds." It would not be until the 1897 Supreme Court decision, the *United States v. Wong Kim Ark*, that every child born in the United States regardless of race or national origin could not be denied citizenship. The exception to this ruling were Native Americans.[97]

Since most African Americans could not legally acquire western lands, they were left with two options. They could either migrate North to sell their labor or remain in the South. Both options for the freed slaves were nothing more than new forms of subordination. After Reconstruction, the Southern "White" ruling class once again reasserted itself, as agricultural entrepreneurs. After the war, there was little redistribution of lands to emancipated African Americans or poor Anglo Americans. Instead, the Southern "White" elite transformed their plantations into corporate farms by allowing African Americans and poor Anglos to work as sharecroppers or tenant farmers, exploiting their labor while holding them in a state of perpetual peonage.[98]

Those African Americans who did migrate North found themselves increasingly competing in a racially hostile environment with native-born Anglos and immigrant labor from eastern and southern Europe. The industrial elite, sufficiently barred from using "freed" Black labor to any extent because of their absorption into the Southern sharecropping system and faced with the rising demands for wage increases among native-born "White" labor, turned to eastern and southern European immigrants to fill the labor void and keep wages in check.[99]

As competitive capitalism emerged domestically, industrialists expanded their corporate activities internationally, backed by the "gun boat" diplomacy of the United States military. The penetration of American industries, supported by U. S. Navy warships, along the Pacific Rim disrupted the economies of many Asian countries. Many Asian workers and their elites had to submit to the influences of the United States. During this period, many displaced Asian workers, particularly the Chinese, were either enticed by labor recruiters or kidnapped to work in Hawaii or in the American West. By 1860, 34,933 Chinese, largely men, lived and worked in the United States. Over the next two decades, the Chinese population grew to 105,465.[100]

During the late nineteenth century, nativists and xenophobics turned their attention toward the Chinese as a danger to Anglo American "civilization." By 1882 Chinese workers were barred from entering into the United States with the passage of the *Chinese Exclusion Act*. The act banned the immigration of Chinese workers and denied citizenship to any Chinese already in the country.[101] This piece of nativist and xenophobic legislation—pushed through Congress by western Congressmen in alliance with southern legislators—was in response to the perceived threat that the Chinese posed to "White" labor and Anglo-Saxon American society. Anti-Asian hostility paralleled the downward spiral of the United States economy. The financial Panic of 1873 forced thousands of Anglo Americans living in the east to the western states. Out west, Anglos had to compete with the Chinese for jobs.[102] Across the West, Chinese workers became the targets of oppressive legislation as well as open violence. On September 9, 1885, a mob of "White" miners went into the Chinatown in Rock Springs, Wyoming to drive the 331 Chinese miners out of town. The Anglo miners killed 28 Chinese, wounded another 15, and destroyed $150,000 worth of property. The fleeing Chinese workers could only re-enter Rock Springs under military escort to gather what remained of their belongings.[103]

Coinciding with the anti-Asian movement and a growing hostility toward some European immigrants, Anglo America crafted a series of segregationist laws directed toward African Americans and other non-White racial minorities. In a landmark ruling, the Supreme Court in 1883 legally allowed the exclusion of racial minorities from hotels, restaurants, parks, public conveyances, and amusement parks. The ruling, *Robinson V. Memphis & Charleston Railroad,* also upheld the right of business owners to provide segregated services for racial minorities or refuse to serve them altogether. Thirteen years later, racial segregation was completed with the *Plessy v. Ferguson* ruling of 1896.[104]

The implementation of the Jim Crow laws served specific political economic purposes. The existence of a large class of poor "White" farmers and industrial workers which coexisted with poor "Blacks" constituted a threat to the dominant classes, particularly in the South. From the late 1870's until the 1890's, there was the real possibility through Populist Party politics that the interracial lower classes would rise and erode the privileges of the dominant elite. The implementation of the Jim Crow laws destroyed any racial and class coalitions by exacerbating racial tensions. The series of laws emphasized and bestowed "privileges" for being "White;" demarcating "color" to subvert class.

In reducing African Americans to a position of powerlessness and social inferiority, the upper, "White" classes preserved their position of economic and political power while simultaneously ending any significant political economic dissent among poor "Whites."[105]

Toward the end of the Reconstruction Era, American industry recovered sufficiently to demand the final conquest of the American West. The industrial boom coincided with the final dispossession of the western tribal-nations. By the early 1880's, the surviving Native American societies were confined to reservations. The rationale behind the reservation system was twofold: Native American resources could be further exploited with a minimum of cost and effort and, the controlled environment of the reservation would provide for a laboratory in social engineering using evolutionary theory. The reservation was conceived as a refuge for a declining race that could be forced out of their "inferior" status using forced assimilation.[106] The *Indian Office's* objective was to break-up the "habits of a savage" by introducing elements of "civilization." Ethnocide, from 1880 to 1934, became officially sanctioned as solving the "Indian Problem."

One of the most insidious expressions of late nineteenth century scientific racism carried out as reservation assimilation policy was the establishment of blood quantum. The premises that biophysical characteristics, mental attributes, and cultural capabilities were imparted through a "race's blood" or biological descent culminated into a governmental policy to manage Indian affairs.[107] The degree of "Indian blood," originally, was incorporated as part of the 1887 *General Allotment Act* to determine land inheritance among allotees.[108] Blood quantum linked forced assimilation with scientific racism through the necessity of defining legally who was Native American. The *Indian Office* used the concept to track the "civilized progress" of Indian people: cultural characteristics were linked and determined through "blood."

As Indian policy developed into the twentieth century, blood quantum expanded to determine eligibility for any federal resources and services, determine citizenship in an indigenous nation, and as per capita payments for the exploitation of resources.[109] The enumeration of Native American community members by racial criteria permitted the continued destruction of Native American communities through intermarriage with non-enrolled tribal members, whether Native American or not.[110] . . .

The implications of using blood quantum to evaluate Native American biological and cultural "purity" are evident in every aspect of Native American contemporary life. Tribal census rolls based on this eugenic concept determines citizenship in a tribal-nation. Blood quantum has resulted in the expropriation of Native American lands and resources for capitalist development at the expense of Native American rights and sovereignty.[111] The concept also has permitted "ecological racism" to occur through placing toxic waste sites, nuclear test sites, or pollutive industries on or near reservation lands affecting the health status of thousands of Native American people.[112] Furthermore, the policy has allowed the federal government to use the full-blood/mixed-blood dichotomy to erode political unity and cultural resistance.[113]

Blood quantum has divorced thousands of people from their Native American ethnic heritage through arbitrarily defining who is or is not a Native American.[114] The construction of Native American identity ultimately is tied to the continued depopulation of Native North America through the manipulation of numbers. It is a sustained effort to erode sovereignty, self-determination, and reduce the number of indigenous people in this country to the point of political, economic, and cultural insignificance.[115]

While Anglo America was creating a society based on the politics of racial exclusion, by the turn of [the] century another threat arrived on U. S. shores. The immigration of eastern and southern Europeans posed the new danger to American "civilization." Between 1899 and 1910, 2,284,601 Italians emigrated to the United States.[116] It would be an exodus that would continue into the early twentieth century.

Before the 1860's, the majority of Italian immigrants came from northern Italy. Because of their labor skills and the relatively small [number] of Italian immigrants entering the United States, the early emigrants did not face as much nativist hostility. As emigration increased beginning in the 1880's, the majority were southern Italian peasants, who like the Irish and Chinese before them, were escaping hunger and economic exploitation in their natal homelands.[117]

Italians quickly became the focus of xenophobic racism. In commenting on the undesirability of Italians, one observer remarked that "The Italian immigrant who does not become a delinquent or crazy—is a saint."[118] Another commentator wrote that the Catholic Italian "race stock is inferior and degraded; that it will not assimilate naturally or readily with the prevailing "Anglo-Saxon" race stock of this country."[119] He went on to note the "intermixture, if practicable, will be detrimental; the servility, filthy habits of life, and a hopelessly degraded standards of needs and ambitions have been ingrained in Italians . . ."[120] As a "race," they were biologically inferior—a "race" of unintelligent, immoral, disloyal, contemptible, mongrelized people. Italians and their cultural traditions were viewed as being abnormal, irrational, and sometimes, innately criminal.

Similar to the Irish, emancipated Africans, the Chinese, and Mexican Americans, the Italians found themselves relegated to the secondary labor market, segregated into ethnic ghettos, and forced to compete with other European ethnics and racial minorities for survival. Italian workers, like others who were marginalized by prejudice and discrimination, were willing to take lower wages, be used as strike breakers, and pay commissions for jobs. "That employers make capital out of racial rivalries, playing off 'Wop' against 'Hunkie,'" according to Frank Cavaioli and Salvatore J. La Gumina, ". . . is established well enough. To American laborers the procedure has naturally been obnoxious, and they have perhaps been more willing to regard the Italian as blameworthy than as victimized."[121] Thus Italians were viewed by native-born Americans as economic threats.

The mixture of economic competition, along with the cultural xenophobia of native-born Americans, erupted occasionally in violence. One of the most notorious incidences of anti-Italian violence was at New Orleans with the lynching and shooting of 11 Sicilians in 1891. Using the murder of the local police chief, local vigilante mobs arrested Sicilians for the crime. Although six were acquitted and three others had their cases declared a mistrial, the angry mob lynched the 11 in the name of "justice."[122]

From the early 1890's until the passage of the immigration restrictions in 1924, southern and eastern Europeans migrated to the United States. Industrialists used this unskilled labor to displace native-born "White" workers. As a result, many European immigrants faced prejudice, if not overt racist hostility. Between 1891 through the 1920's, Italian immigrants were lynched, shot, or viciously attacked by violent nativists.[123] Other immigrants, whether European or not, had similar fates.

To quell Anglo American nativist and xenophobic fears, Congress passed a series of bills to restrict immigration. In 1902 Congress, backed by Congressmen from far western states and labor unions, succeeded in having the 1882 *Chinese Exclusion Act* renewed indefinitely. It would not be rescinded until 1943. Eight years later, in 1910, Congress appointed a commission to solve the immigration problem. The Dillingham Commission produced a 42 volume report revealing the negative impact that immigration was having on the United States. The report began with the racist assumption, backed by scientific data, that the new immigrants from southern and eastern Europe were racially inferior to the old immigrants from northern and western Europe. The Dillingham Report led to the *Immigration Act of 1917*. The act imposed a literacy test on all immigrants over the age of 16 and no laborers were allowed from the Asiatic Barred Zone, restricting severely access to the United States.[124]

Although the federal government moved to restrict racially inferior Europeans and Asians to protect American "civilization" and labor, U. S. interests abroad stimulated other people to America. The 1898 victory of the United States in the Spanish American War resulted not only in the political economic domination of Cuba and the Philippine

Islands, but the conquest and annexation of Puerto Rico. Since at least the mid-eighteenth century, colonists of Puerto Rico carried on political economic relations with the United States. During the American Revolution, Puerto Ricans supported American revolutionary efforts by harboring American vessels and supplying them.[125] One hundred and twenty-two years later, the United States would "capture" the island, making it a colony.[126]

Before the U. S. "take-over," Puerto Rico's economy was undergoing rapid changes. The 1878–1879 economic crisis, combined with the emergence of the coffee industry, resulted in an increase in the number of landless peasants. Under the prevailing political economic conditions, some of the surplus population found employment in urban centers, but for most, chronic poverty and unemployment became a way of life. The processes of shifting wealth from the many into the hands of the few in Puerto Rico accelerated under the domination of the United States.[127]

Under the protection of the new colonial regime, the technological modernization of the island's sugar industry brought further transformations in production and land ownership creating a surplus working class. Puerto Rico's problem was not the economic transformations created by United States corporate penetration, but overpopulation. The solution for U. S. policy makers was emigration. Thus between 1900 and 1926, Puerto Rican workers emigrated to the United States and other countries as contract workers. It is an emigration flow that continues to the present-day.[128]

With the continued restriction of southern and eastern immigration, after 1910, many African Americans began to migrate north in unprecedented numbers. Attracted by job opportunities in the expanding industries, they found themselves competing with both native "White" workers, along with foreign-born European ethnics. The economic competition transformed itself into an arena whereby "Whiteness" was contrasted sharply and, sometimes violently, against "Blackness." Labor issues, as in the past, pitted various ethnic and racial groups against one another. "White" ethnics and native-born "Whites" would compete with each other using culture and color to distinguish oneself in an attempt to gain material advantage.[129] The northern industrial landscape became an arena of extensive ethno-racial hostilities and working class racism.

. . . Although there is no inherent relationship between their skin color, power, and privilege, most Euro-Americans participated in attaining and maintaining their "Whiteness." Pigmentation had to be defined against "Blackness" to be politicized. As Goldberg writes:

> "Whiteness" did not guarantee a decent job or respect, but it has provided European Americans with a legitimating claim on security, rights, and dignity historically denied African Americans and other "non-White" Americans. Tossed by the forces of capital and the cultural pretensions of already privileged "Whites," the European newcomers have staked their claim to citizenship and justice on the basis of being a "free White person." Their gains have been contested and "hard won," but they have also reinvented White racial privilege.[130]

The establishment of the racial order—the superiority of "Whiteness" to any degree over the inferiority of "Blackness"—was disseminated and sustained among the working class by a barrage of virulent racist propaganda. In books, popular magazine articles, pamphlets, plays, and motion pictures, African Americans were portrayed as a "beast," with an insatiable appetite for "White" women.

The 1915 movie, *The Birth of a Nation*, encapsulated all the racist stereotypes for Anglo Americans to absorb about African Americans. There were images of Northern carpet baggars and Negroes in the Reconstruction South forcibly preventing upstanding "White" citizens from voting. "Blacks" as state legislators in another scene pass an interracial marriage law while drinking liquor with their feet up on their desks. During the film's climax, a "White" woman is chased through the woods pursued by a sex-crazed Negro. To avoid being raped by him, she throws herself off a cliff. Her brother, the cinematic hero, leads a "White" mob to lynch

him and then organizes the Ku Klux Klan to regain control of society by "White" men. Eventually, the hero and the Klan break up rioting Negroes just in time to save a "White" girl from her forced marriage to the mulatto lieutenant-governor.[131]

These racist images, combined with the already ingrained notion that the progress of the nation depends on its "racial purity," resulted in a racial hatred for African Americans.[132] That same year, 1915, Colonel William Joseph Simmons, an Atlanta preacher, revitalized the Ku Klux Klan. His aim was to arouse "Whites" to the dangers of Negroes and "hyphenated-Americans" of every kind. The Klan must be the vanguard of Anglo-Saxon civilization, protecting it from the invasion of alien people.[133] Between 1892 and 1921, 2,364 African Americans were lynched to "keep them in their place."[134]

The construction of "Whiteness" manifested itself in the fabrication of institutionalized discriminatory barriers. "White" workers, especially in the North, fought to segregate themselves at home and in the workplace. Trade unions excluded African Americans, depriving them [of] access to skilled industrial labor, insuring that African American workers would be marginalized to the lowest paying jobs.[135] Hostilities between African American and Anglo workers were heightened during labor disputes. The industrial elite often used African American labor as strikebreakers, inciting further racial animosity. Such volatile race and labor relations led to the race riots of 1917 and 1919.[136] The political economic stage was set for industrial capitalism's rise to dominance. Class, color, and ethnicity are firmly established as arenas for exploitation, extreme inequality, and oppression.

INDUSTRIAL CAPITALISM AND RACIAL FORMATIONS, 1920's–1960's

With the advent of World War I, a labor shortage developed in the agricultural sector. That need was partially fulfilled by poor Whites, especially from the South.[137] The largest segment of the agricultural labor sector was filled by Mexican labor. The Mexican Revolution had left thousands of Mexicans across the border in a state of despair. The revolution had destroyed the economy and left many displaced from their homes. Many working-class Mexicans crossed into the United States seeking economic opportunities in the Southwest.

The flow of Mexicans into the United States was temporarily slowed with the passage of the 1917 restrictive immigration laws. The law stipulated a head tax, the ability to read English, and if under a labor contract, the laborer could only stay six months. Mexicans also feared they would be drafted into the United States military. Faced with a shortage of workers, the United States government lifted these restrictions and assured Mexican nationals they would not be drafted into military service. With the policy reversals, Mexicans again moved freely across the border into the United States to find employment.[138]

During the war years, the United States also garnered 13,000 Puerto Rican contract laborers for war related industries. The United States government in 1917 also granted Puerto Ricans citizenship under the *Jones Act*. The Act permitted a free flow of emigration to the United States, helping to alleviate the wartime labor shortages, but allowed the United States to conscript Puerto Ricans for military service. Puerto Ricans left the island in massive numbers only to find themselves concentrated in the lowest paying sectors of the U. S. economy and segregated into urban enclaves.[139]

After the success of the Russian Revolution, the United States government felt their emerging way of life, that is industrial capitalism, was threatened by the new socio-political possibilities offered by Communism. That fear became all the more apparent and real to those in power by the surge in labor organizations among the American working class. The United States government in concert with the industrial sector reacted on a number of fronts.

After World War I, nativist fears were raised over the millions of displaced southern and eastern Europeans who, possibly influenced by Bolshevism, would migrate to the United States and infect America with Communist ideologies. In 1915, President Woodrow Wilson stated that "hyphenated Americans . . . have poured the poison of disloyalty into the very arteries of our national life . . . such creatures of passion, disloyalty and anarchy must be crushed out."[140] The hysterical fear of foreign radicalism culminated in the infamous Palmer Raids. In 1919, President Wilson appointed Alexander Palmer as Attorney General of the United States. Over his three year tenure, Attorney General Palmer, using the "Red" scare as an excuse had Department of Justice agents descend in the night on immigrant neighborhoods and indiscriminately arrest people as communists or anarchists. Palmer's witch hunts equated foreign birth with subversiveness. Approximately 10,000 foreign-born workers were detained and deported without due process or evidence of their supposed anti-American politics. A young J. Edgar Hoover was in charge of the operations. His successes in ferreting out Communists led to the formation of the Federal Bureau of Investigation.

Anglo American xenophobia, combined with the perceived threat of Communism, created an ideology that foreign workers are [a] threat to American jobs and well-being as a society. This led to working class racism and violence. Because Italians were the largest southern European people immigrating to America, they bore the brunt of the "Red" scare raids and the hatred of immigrants. Such xenophobic fervor had its roots in the Know-Nothingism of the mid-1850's.[141]

★ ★ ★

By 1921, it was clear the literacy test implemented under the *1917 Immigration Act* did not inhibit the influx of southern and eastern Europeans. Given the paranoia over the spread of communism, the formation of unions, as well as the racist assumptions about inferior racial stocks polluting Anglo American society, Congress passed the *Quota Act of 1921*. The act established quotas for each admissible nationality to three percent of that nationality as recorded in the 1910 federal census. No limits were placed on immigration from western European countries.[142] The logic of the act was clear, stabilize the entry [of] inferior racial stocks, while increasing the influx of racially desirable people. In this fashion, America could engineer its racial and national destiny.

For many, the 1921 law was not rigorous enough in preserving Anglo-Saxon America. Led by Senator Albert Johnson of Washington, Congress passed the *Immigration Act of 1924*. The act reduced the admissible quotas to two percent of foreign born of that nationality recorded in the 1890 census. Since the immigration of most southern and eastern Europeans did not begin in any great numbers by 1890, the new restrictionist quotas strangled the immigration from those European countries. The act also barred all aliens ineligible for citizenship, reaffirming the exclusion of Asians. Further, the act required that all immigrants had to secure a visa from an American consul in their country of origin, meaning that America could now screen all potential applicants, considering only those "best" suited for American society.[143]

The xenophobic racism embedded in the act was invoked in a speech that Senator Johnson delivered to demonstrate the law's popular support by the American public. The American people, he proclaimed boldly:

> have seen, patent and plain, the encroachments of the foreign-born flood upon their own lives. They have come to realize that such a flood, affecting as it does every individual of whatever race or origin, cannot fail likewise to affect the institutions which have made and preserved American liberties . . . It is no wonder that Americans everywhere are insisting that their land no longer shall offer free and unrestricted asylum to the rest of the world . . .

> The United States is our land . . . We intend to maintain it so. The day of unalloyed welcome to all peoples, the day of indiscriminate acceptance of all races, has definitely ended.[144]

By 1929, the advent of the Great Depression, the 1924 national origins quota system was fully operational.

Anglo American xenophobic nativism also was extended to Mexicans. Despite their willingness to work long hours for little pay, making them ideal for the requirements of capitalism, immigration restrictionists argued there were now "too many" Mexicans in the United States. Despite the objections of nativist elements and labor unions, who argued that Mexicans hurt American workers and "damaged" American society because of their cultural "backwardness" and "inferior" intellect, the labor needs of capitalism overrode their concerns. Congress excluded immigrants from Mexico and other Latin American countries from the imposed national-origins quota system.[145]

The choking restriction of some immigrants and the selective entry of others is related to the U.S. political economy. During the 1920's, large corporations came to dominate the United States economy and politics. Eventually over-production and large scale profit taking by the corporate elite led to massive employment lay-offs, triggering the Great Depression. While the federal government labored to save the near collapse of capitalism by developing socio-economic programs, racial and ethnic hostilities increased as Americans struggled to survive. Massive unemployment created strong pressures to rid all foreign workers from the United States. In the anti-foreign fervor, Mexicans eventually became a primary target group for deportation and "repatriation." Thousands of Mexicans "voluntarily" and "involuntarily" left their homes in America for Mexico.[146] Discrimination continued against Mexican labor until the onset of World War II.

While Mexican labor was being systematically excluded, Africans Americans began to slowly dismantle legal segregation and reduce job discrimination. Beginning in the 1930's, the *National Association for the Advancement of Colored People* (NAACP) legally challenged the separate but equal doctrine of *Plessy v. Ferguson*. Paralleling these legal efforts, the *Congress of Industrial Organizations* pushed to organize African American workers. The assertion of African American rights during this period also was being felt at the voting polls. Northern "White" politicians were forced to cater to the "Black" vote in many elections in industrial states.[147]

The political economic changes brought about by World War II compelled the United States to alter its position regarding various racial and ethnic issues. A need for labor created greater, yet temporary opportunities for racial minorities and women. To meet labor demands in the agricultural sector, in 1942, Mexico and the United States created the *Los Braceros Program.*[148] Native-born Mexicans found employment in urban industries as they replaced Anglos. Puerto Rican emigration to the United States also increased dramatically since its diminution during the Great Depression. They too found temporary economic prosperity during the war.[149]

The labor needs of industry were filled by African Americans who also migrated North in great numbers to seek employment. Although they found jobs, African Americas encountered a stark racial division of labor, enforced by discrimination, exclusion, and periodic violence. "Black" workers, like other people of color attracted by the lure of jobs, were relegated to the secondary labor market, characterized by low wages, little upward mobility, and job instability. Frustration grew among many northern urban "Blacks" who experienced daily racial discrimination and exclusion.[150]

In 1941, in an effort to gain equal opportunities in the defense industry, ensure their continued employment, and "fair" treatment, A. Philip Randolph, president of the *Brotherhood of Sleeping Car Porters,* threatened to lead 100,000 African Americans on a non-violent march to Washington, D. C. The Brotherhood, according to Randolph, was ". . . the key to unlocking the door of a nationwide struggle for Negro rights."[151] The organization was a network of organizers who would carry the message of racial equality across the nation. Randolph knew that only the organization of the masses would bring about racial equality and economic betterment.

Facing international embarrassment, increasing domestic racial tension, and a hostile "Black" voting constituency in the industrial north, President Franklin D. Roosevelt made a number of governmental moves to attack the race issue. Roosevelt issued *Executive Order 8802* which enjoined employers to provide for "equitable" participation without discrimination because of race, creed, or color.[152] Although the Roosevelt Administration attempted to alleviate racial oppression, in 1943, racial disturbances broke out across the United States.[153]

Other ethnic minorities also experienced "racial" violence. Discrimination, prejudice, and unfair political practices against Mexican Americans eventually resulted in periodic urban unrest and minor periodic violence. So [as] not to offend Mexico, a war ally, the media blamed the violence not on Anglo America's racist persecution of Mexican Americans, but focused on Mexican juvenile delinquency. In particular, the media pointed to the "zoot suiters." Although "zoot suiting" crossed class, racial, and ethnic lines, "zoot suits" became synonymous with Mexican "gangsters." In June of 1943, following a murder case involving Mexican and Anglo "zoot suiters," car loads of U.S. servicemen, backed by police, drove into Mexican neighborhoods, randomly attacking any Mexican they thought was a "zoot suiter." The attacks and counterattacks by Mexican Americans lasted for a week. In the end, the brutal racist beatings were blamed ultimately on the Mexican American community. Captain E. Duran Ayers, Chief of the Foreign Relations Bureau of the Los Angeles County Sheriff's Department parroted the public attitude about the events. "The biological basis is the main basis to work from," he noted, "This total disregard for human life has always been universal throughout the Americas among the Indian population."[154] Violence, in other words, was an innate characteristic acquired biologically from their Native American ancestry. Thus, the only recourse for Anglo America is to control the violent impulses of Mexicans with violence.

With the close of World War II, the United States government and multinational corporations, supported by the military, dominated the world economy. In Puerto Rico, the federal government launched *Operation Bootstrap.* The plan was to industrialize the island through the relocation of American corporations and manufacturing firms in exchange for massive tax incentives and access to a cheap labor pool.

Politically, *Operation Bootstrap* served U.S. interests in blocking the growing Soviet Union penetration of the Caribbean and Latin America. Puerto Rico's socio-economic successes were lauded by U. S. policy makers as a model example of "democratic" development under capitalism. Puerto Rico stood as a large scale socio-economic experiment that fed America's propaganda machine about the superiority of capitalism over communism.

Although *Operation Bootstrap* between 1954 and the early 1970's did raise incomes and improve the health and education sectors, the program fostered a greater dependency on the United States. The economic plan, through technology and the shift to industry, displaced tens of thousands of farm workers and small townspeople, promoting emigration.[155] Puerto Rican emigration from the island—facilitated by public policies—served as an "'escape valve' that would ease the structural pressures of industrialization."[156]

Similar to the era surrounding the first World War, the Cold War brought about another period [of] reactionism. The fear of the global spread of communism attached itself to nativistic ideas about foreigners. Congress, expressing those fears passed the *Internal Security Act of 1950* and the *1952 McCarran-Walter Act*. The *Internal Security Act* required the exclusion or deportation of any aliens who had been or belonged to the Communist Party or any "front" organizations. National security was linked explicitly to immigration, requiring a reevaluation of immigration laws.[157]

The 1924 national origins system remained intact until the passage of the *1952 McCarran-Walter Act*. Congress, over the veto of President Harry S. Truman, passed the legislation. The act still retained the quota system, but with minor changes. Tighter quotas were placed on allowing immigration from colonies of quota receiving countries. The restriction was a response to eliminating the flow of "Black" immigrants from the British West Indies. Although the *McCarran-Walter Act* affirmed the quota system, it did abolish the category of aliens ineligible for citizenship, allowing Asians to immigrate to the United States. The quotas for China however remained at only 105 people per year and Japan was allocated a quota of 185.[158] The

slight liberalization in the policy was enacted to allow World War II veterans to return with their foreign-born wives and permit war torn refugees from western European countries to enter the country without qualifying under the nationalities quota system.

A specific feature of the act that remains intact today is the barring of anyone to the United States who is suspected of or deemed to advocate Communist ideas. In effect, the law attempted to preserve America's ethnic and racial composition as it existed in the 1920's, especially among people of color and undesirable "White" ethnics. Simultaneously, American capitalism remained relatively secure from any contesting ideologies within its borders.[159] The act, in short, sought to maintain U.S. political, economic, and cultural stability.

The political economic changes in the Cold War era brought about social and political shifts regarding "White" America's treatment of racial ethnic minorities. The wartime institutional advancements in solving America's racial questions were contested and some earlier advancements were reversed. The new governmental and societal hostility toward racial equality, [however,] remained contradictory. On one hand, segregationists attempted to erode any attempts for racial and ethnic minorities to achieve political economic parity with "White" Americans. In opposition, the Supreme Court and the Truman Administration sought to dismantle some segregated institutional arrangements in American society. This paradoxical period had differential consequences for various racial and ethnic minorities.

With the downturn of the post-War economy and the need to re-absorb returning soldiers into the domestic economy, in 1954, the United States government launched *Operation Wetback* against Mexican workers. The *Special Force Operation* was designed to rid the United States of "illegals." As with the repatriation program of the 1930's, government "raiders" rarely distinguished between "illegals" and native-born Mexican Americans. Both "illegals" and native-born Mexicans, the American public believed, took jobs away from Anglo Americans and were used as strikebreakers to suppress Anglo wages. In that year alone, over one million Mexicans were deported, creating massive social problems for the Mexican government along the border.[160] The raids and deportation continue to the present.

Under the pretext of reducing federal expenditures while giving Native Americans greater autonomy, the federal government passed the *Termination Act of 1953*. Using data gathered under a 1947 Congressional Commission, the federal government targeted various tribes for termination. The criteria for selecting those tribes to be given their "freedom," rested on their perceived control of sufficient economic resources to manage their own affairs. Implicit in that argument is the firmly established racist assumption of selecting which tribes have moved beyond the state of "dependent savagery" to a state of "civilized independence." In charge of carrying out the policy was Bureau of Indian Affairs Commissioner Dillon S. Meyer. Commissioner Meyer had supervised the internment camps for Japanese Americans during World War II. That experience made him well qualified for overseeing the destruction of Native America societies.[161]

Once Native Americans had their lives terminated, they were expected to assimilate into society. To encourage this transition, a year earlier, the *Bureau of Indian Affairs* launched its relocation program. For the next two decades, Indian people were redistributed among select urban areas. Similar to urban African Americans, Mexican Americans, Asian Americans, and some Euro-American ethnics, Indian people felt the sting of segregation, prejudice, and discrimination once in the city.[162]

The most profound changes for racial and ethnic minorities occurred as a result of the continuing struggles of African Americans. From the late 1940's into the 1950's, African American demands for racial equality broadened from issues of segregation to questioning the basic legitimacy of the American social and racial order. The momentum for this movement and ideological shift solidified with the landmark 1954 Supreme Court case, *Brown et al. v. Board of Education of Topeka et al.* In

that case, the court justices recognized the inherently unequal structure of racial segregation.[163] As Supreme Court victories mounted, the Jim Crow doctrine of separate but equal began to erode.[164] The African American Civil Rights Movement, by calling into question the meaning of race for themselves, called into direct question a fundamental element for the continued existence of and the justification for social inequity in the United States for all peoples.[165]

THE STRUGGLE FOR RACIAL AND ETHNIC LIBERATION AND THE RE-AFFIRMATION OF SOCIAL INEQUALITY, 1960's–1990's

The emerging Civil Rights Movement and its progressive allies secured in rapid succession the passage of new civil rights laws leading to President Kennedy's 1961 *Executive Order 10925*. The Executive Order, a political repudiation of segregated public life, then was followed by [the] *Civil Rights Act of 1964* and other legal acts crafted to eliminate racism.[166] Despite the impressive array of Civil Rights legislation, social and economic oppression among racial and ethnic minorities persisted and grew in epidemic proportions.

Racial and ethnic minorities, regardless of the legal protections, continued to be forced to [the] bottom of the socio-economic hierarchy. Employment opportunities remained limited, only opened by legal force. Among America's ethnic and racial minorities, there continued a concentration [of] poverty.[167]

The persistent impoverishment and economic marginalization of racial and ethnic minorities, even during the Civil Rights era, was nothing more than the continuation of processes that began from the moment of European colonization. "America," as Robert Blauner observed, "has used African, Asian, Mexican, and to a lesser degree, Indian workers for the cheapest labor, concentrating people of color in the most unskilled jobs, the least advanced sectors of the economy, and the most industrially backward regions of the nation."[168]

As racial and ethnic minorities, led by the African American Civil Rights Movement, pressed for social justice and equality, Anglo America responded with overt racial hostility. Anglo Americans, at work and at home, exacted their wages of "Whiteness" by practicing hyper-segregation. Anglo workers insisted, for the most part, that African American workers work and live separately from them. If economic exclusion and hyper-segregation did not control "Black" assertiveness, some "White" Americans resorted to outright violence.[169] The violence of "White" reactionism to upsetting the racial and class structure of America resulted in large scale urban riots across the nation.[170]

Although the riots sharpened Anglo American fears, the rise of [the] Black Power Movement instilled widespread racial paranoia. The desire of African Americans to control their own political economic destiny represented a "real" danger to America's racial and class order. And since it threatened to dismantle two central pillars of capitalism, it posed an internal hazard to capitalism itself.[171] The Black Power Movement, because it directly questioned the relationship between racial oppression and political economy in the United States, had to be discredited and eliminated from the American political economic landscape. This was especially true for the Black Panther Party, one of the most visible and confrontational arms of the Black Power Movement. To crush the Black Panther Party the Federal Bureau of Investigation launched Contelpro, a subversive operation designed to destroy any progressive social or political movement that presented a danger to the United States' internal security. By the early 1970's, central leaders of the Black Panther Party, the American Indian Movement, among others, were either dead, imprisoned, or thoroughly discredited by FBI planted provocateurs.[172] For ethnic and racial minorities living in the United States, American society remained a contradictory arena filled with "hope," the rhetoric of possible acceptance and equality against the stark realities of oppression, racial hate, and exclusion.

The legacy of the Black Power Movement, in combination with the Civil Rights Movement, spawned an awakening among other racial and ethnic minorities. The rise in ethnic consciousness and racial identity among various racial and ethnic minorities expressed itself through a variety of ethnic movements. Through mass protest, collective political mobilization, and coalition building, all protested and demanded an end to race-based social and political practices ingrained in American society.[173]

★ ★ ★

NOTES

1. Henry Dobyns, *Their Number Became Thinned: Native American Population Dynamics in Eastern North America.* (Knoxville: University of Tennessee Press, 1983), 33–45; Douglas H. Ubelaker, "Prehistoric New World Population Size: Historical Review and Current Appraisal of New World Estimates," *American Journal of Physical Anthropology.* 45(1976):661–666.
2. Ruth Underhill, *Red Man's America,* Revised Edition. (Chicago: University of Chicago Press, 1971).
3. Cited from Wesley F. Craven, *White, Red, and Black: The Seventeenth-Century Virginian.* (New York: W. W. Norton and Company, 1971), 77–78.
4. Richard Easterline, "Immigration: Economic and Social Characteristics," *Harvard Encyclopedia of American Ethnic Groups.* Stephan Thernstorm, ed. (Cambridge: Harvard University Press, 1980), 479.
5. Charlotte Erickson, "English," *Harvard Encyclopedia of American Ethnic Groups.* Stephan Thernstrom, ed. (Cambridge: Harvard University Press, 1980), 319–336; John Elson, "The Great Migration," *Time.* 142 (21, 1993): 17.
6. Because Highland Scots, the Irish, and even the Scotch-Irish were considered to be a "savage" Celtic race by the English, they were often relegated to the margins of English society. In North America this meant the frontier where the "savage" Celts could be a buffer against the "savage" Indians. For a discussion of the settlement of the Scots, Irish, and Scotch-Irish in North America see: Gordon Donaldson, "Scots," *Harvard Encyclopedia of American Ethnic Groups.* Stephan Thernstrom, ed. (Cambridge: Harvard University Press, 1980), 908–916; James Hunter, *A Dance Called America: The Scottish Highlands, the United States and Canada.* (Edinburgh: Mainstream Publishing, 1994); Maldwyn A. Jones, "Scotch-Irish," *Harvard Encyclopedia of American Ethnic Groups.* Stephan Thernstrom, ed. (Cambridge: Harvard University Press, 1980), 900–901; James Leyburn, *The Scotch-Irish: A Social History.* (Chapel Hill: University of North Carolina Press, 1962).
7. Cited from Elson, "The Great Migration," 17.
8. Thomas F. Gossett, *Race: The History of an Idea in America.* New Edition. (New York: Oxford University Press, 1997), 3–16.
9. Howard Zinn, *The Politics of History.* Second Edition. (Urbana: University of Illinois Press, 1990), 60.
10. There are a number of works that provide insights into the European concept of "Other" and how that concept shaped their perceptions during the colonization of

America. Refer to: Anthony Pagden, *The Fall of Natural Man: The American Indian and the Origins of Comparative Ethnology.* (Cambridge: Cambridge University Press, 1982); *European Encounters with the New World.* (New Haven: Yale University Press, 1993); Alden T. Vaughan, *Roots of American Racism: Essays on the Colonial Experience.* (New York: Oxford University Press, 1995).

11. See: Frank Shuffelton, ed., *A Mixed Race: Ethnicity in Early America.* (New York: Oxford University Press, 1993); Carter Wilson, *Racism: From Slavery to Advanced Capitalism.* (Thousand Oaks: Sage Publications, 1996), 55.

12. William S. Bernard, "Immigration: History of U.S. Policy," *Harvard Encyclopedia of American Ethnic Groups.* Stephan Thernstrom, ed. (Cambridge: Harvard University Press, 1980), 486–487.

13. Wilson, *Racism: From Slavery to Advanced Capitalism,* 48–50.

14. Native Americans presented European scholars with a perplexing philosophical problem. The critical issue at hand was the determination of their appropriate locale in the hierarchy of nature. Since New World indigenous populations were deemed fully human by *Papal Bull,* the continued conquest, genocide, and expropriation of indigenous resources demanded a rationalized explanation. Europeans accomplished this political task by constructing an ideology that delineated Native Americans as human beings who were residing outside the confines of "civilization." Civilization was equated with the highest form of humanity. As the "highest" social community on earth, civilization in the hierarchy of human communities stood closest to the realm of grace. Civilization and all its actions, therefore, were a divine expression. See: Don D. Fowler and Catherine S. Fowler, "The Uses of Natural Man in Natural History," *Columbian Consequences: The Spanish Borderlands in Pan-American Perspective.* Volume 3. David Hurst Thomas, ed. (Washington, D. C.: Smithsonian Institution Press, 1991), 37–41; Arthur O. Lovejoy, *The Great Chain of Being.* (Cambridge: Harvard University Press, 1936); John R. Milton, "The Origin and Development of the Concept of the 'Laws of Nature,'" *Archives of European Sociology.* 22(1981):173–195; Pagden, *The Fall of Natural Man: The American Indian and the Origins of Comparative Ethnology,* 27–56.

15. This formula for conquest became the established pattern of interaction with most indigenous nations encountered in the Americas. It is a process of dispossession and exploitation that continues to the present-day. For a general discussion of this colonial process and its ramifications for indigenous nations see: John H. Bodley, *Victims of Progress.* Third Edition. (Mountain View: Mayfield Publishing Company, 1990), 24–136; For specific regions of the Americas see: Jan Carew, "Columbus and the Origins of Racism in the Americas," Part one. *Race and Class.* XXIX(4,1988): 1–19; "Columbus and the Origins of Racism in the Americas," part two. *Race and Class.* 30(1, 1988): 33–57; Francis Jennings, *The Invasion of America: Indians, Colonialism, and the Cant of Conquest.* (New York: W. W. Norton and Company, 1975); Edward Spicer, *Cycles of Conquest: The Impact of Spain, Mexico, and the United States on the Indians of the Southwest, 1533–1960.* (Tucson: University of Arizona Press, 1962).

16. See for example: Olive P. Dickason, *The Myth of the Savage and the Beginnings of French Colonialism in the Americas.* (Edmonton: University of Alberta Press, 1984).

17. Nicholas P. Canny, "The Ideology of English Colonization: From Ireland to America," *William and Mary Quarterly.* 30(1973):585; Micheal Hechter, *Internal Colonialism: The Celtic Fringe in British National Development. 1536–1966.* (Berkeley: University of California Press), 47–123; Ronald Takaki, "The Tempest in the Wilderness: The Racialization of Savagry," *The Journal of American History,* Special Issue. *Discovering Columbus.* Fredrick E. Hoxie, ed. 79(3, 1992):893.

18. Hechter, *Internal Colonialism: The Celtic Fringe in British National Development, 1536–1966,* 47–123; William C. MacLeod, "Celt and Indian: Britain's Old World Frontier in Relation to the New," *Beyond the Frontier: Social Process and Cultural Change.* Paul Bohannon and Fred Plog, eds. (New York: Garden City, 1967), 25–41; Takaki, "The Tempest in the Wilderness: The Racialization of Savagry," 894–895.

19. Larzer Ziff, *Puritanism in America: New Culture in a New World.* (New York: The Viking Press, 1973), 8.

20. Ibid., 13.

21. Wilbur R. Jacobs, "British-Colonial Attitudes and Policies Toward the Indian in the American Colonies," *Attitudes of Colonial Powers Toward the American Indian.* Howard Peckham and Charles Gibson, eds. (Salt Lake City: University of Utah Press, 1969), 86.

22. Ziff, *Puritanism in America: New Culture in a New World,* 90.

23. Takaki, "The Tempest in the Wilderness: The Racialization of Savagry," 907.

24. Ibid., 907–912.

25. David E. Stannard, *American Holocaust: Columbus and the Conquest of the New World.* (New York: Oxford University Press, 1992), 219.

26. Ziff, *Puritanism in America: New Culture in a New World,* 168–182.

27. Stephen M. Clark, *Smallpox and the Iroquois Wars: An Ethnohistorical Study of the Influence of Disease and Demographic Change on Iroquoian Culture History, 1630–1700.* (Salinas: Coyote Press, 1981); Sherburne F. Cook, "Interracial Warfare and Population Decline Among the New England Indians," *Ethnohistory.* 20(1973):1–24; "The Significance of Disease in the Extinction of the New England Indians," *Human Biology.* 45(1973):485–508; "The Indian Population of New England in the Seventeenth Century," *University of California Publications in Anthropology.* 12(1976):1–91; John Duffy, "Smallpox and the Indians of the American Colonies," *Bulletin of the History of Medicine.* 25(1951)324–341; Wilbur R. Jacobs, *Dispossessing the American Indian.* (New York: Charles Scribner and Sons, 1972); Helen C. Rountree, *Pocahontas' People: The Powahtan Indians of Virginia Through Four Centuries.* (Norman: University of Oklahoma Press, 1990),

89–127; James H. Merrell, *The Indian's New World: Catawbas and Their Neighbors from European Contact Through the Era of Removal.* (Chapel Hill: University of North Carolina Press, 1989); Karl H. Schlesier, "Epidemics and Indians Middlemen: Rethinking the Wars of the Iroquois, 1609–1653," *Ethnohistory.* 23(1976): 129–145; Marvin T. Smith, "Aboriginal Population Movements in the Early Historic Period Interior Southeast," *Powhatan's Mantle: Indians in the Colonial Southeast.* (Lincoln: University of Nebraska, 1989), 21–34; Dean R. Snow and Kim M. Lamphear, "European Contact and Indian Depopulation in the Northeast: The Timing of the First Epidemics," *Ethnohistory.* 35 (1, 1988):150; Russell Thornton, *American Indian Holocaust and Survival: A Population History since 1492.* (Norman: University of Oklahoma Press, 1987); Bruce Trigger, *The Children of Aataentsic; A History of Huron People to 1660.* Two volumes. (Montreal: McGill University Press, 1976).

28. Peter Wood, "Re-Counting the Past," *Southern Exposure.* 16(1988):36; "The Changing Population of the Colonial South: An Overview by Race and Region, 1685–1790," *Powhatan's Mantle: Indians in the Colonial Southeast.* (Lincoln: University of Nebraska, 1989), 35–103.

29. Wood, "Re-Counting the Past," 36; See also: Craven, *White, Red, and Black: The Seventeenth Century Virginian.*

30. Brian W. Dippie, *The Vanishing American: White Attitudes and U. S. Indian Policy.* (Lawrence: University of Kansas Press, 1982), 32–44.

31. Gregory R. Campbell, "The Politics of Counting: Critical Reflections on the Depopulation Question of Native North America," *The Unheard Voices: American Indian Responses to the Columbian Quincentenary, 1492–1992.* Carole M. Gentry and Donald A. Grinde, Jr., eds. (Los Angeles: American Indian Studies Center, University of California Los Angeles, 1994), 78–79, 83–84.

32. For a description of the sociological processes indigenous people employed to survive demographically and culturally in the wake of European contact see: John H. Moore, "An Ethnogenetic Critique of Cladistic Theory," Unpublished manuscript. (Norman: University of Oklahoma, n.d.), 9–11.

33. Jack D. Forbes, "Mulattoes and People of Color in Anglo-North America: Implications for Black White Relations," *The Journal of Ethnic Studies.* 12(2, 1984): 17–61; Jack D. Forbes, *Black Africans and Native Americans: Race, Color and Caste in the Making of Red-Black Peoples.* (London: Routledge, 1988); Jack D. Forbes, "Envelopment, Proletarianization, and Inferiorization: Aspects of Colonialism's Impact upon Native Americans and Other People of Color in Eastern North America," *The Journal of Ethnic Studies.* 18(4, 1991): 95–122; Jack D. Forbes, *Africans and Native Americans: The Language of Race and the Evolution of Red-Black Peoples.* Second Edition. (Urbana: University of Illinois Press, 1993).

34. Robert S. Grumet, *Historic Contact: Indian People and Colonists on Today's Northeastern United States in the Sixteenth Through the Eighteenth Centuries.* (Norman: University of Oklahoma Press, 1995), 293–294.

35. Audrey Smedley, *Race in North America: Origin and Evolution of a Worldview.* (Boulder: Westview, 1993), 57–59; Wilson, *Racism: From Slavery to Advanced Capitalism,* 48–50.

36. Refer to Kenneth M. Stampp's work, *The Peculiar Institution: Slavery in the Anti-Bellum South.* (New York: Vintage Press, 1956), 21–22.

37. Refer to Catherine Clinton and Michele Gillespie, eds., *The Devil's Lane: Sex and Race in the Early South.* (New York: Oxford University Press, 1997).

38. Frank Cavaioli and Salvatore J. La Gumina, *The Peripheral Americans.* (Malabar: Robert F. Krieger Publishing Company, 1984), 193; Gossett, *Race: The History of an Idea in America,* 29–31.

39. Elson, "The Great Migration," 18.

40. Gossett, *Race: The History of an Idea in America,* 30.

41. Wilson, *Racism: From Slavery to Advanced Capitalism,* 52.

42. George M. Fredrickson and Dale T. Knobel, "History of Prejudice and Discrimination," *Harvard Encyclopedia of American Ethnic Groups.* Stephan Thernstrom, ed. (Cambridge: Harvard University Press, 1980), 829–847.

43. Ibid., 833.

44. Doreen Alvarez Saar, "The Heritage of American Ethnicity in Crevecoeur's: Letters from an American Farmer," *A Mixed Race: Ethnicity in Early America.* Frank Shuffelton, ed. (New York: Oxford University Press, 1993), 252.

45. Ibid., 252.

46. Wilson, *Racism: From Slavery to Advanced Capitalism,* 52.

47. Ibid., 52–53.

48. Cited from: Gossett, *Race: The History of an Idea in America,* 31.

49. U. S. Bureau of the Census, *Historical Statistics of the United States: Colonial Times to 1957.* (Washington, D.C.: U.S. Government Printing Office, 1960), 9.

50. Ronald Bailey, "The Slave(ry) Trade and the Development of Capitalism in the United States: The Textile Industry in New England," *The Atlantic Slave Trade: Effects on Economics, Societies, and Peoples in Africa, the Americas, and Europe.* Joseph E. Inikori and Stanley L. Engerman, eds. (Durham: Duke University Press, 1992), 205–245.

51. Edna Bonacich, "United States Capitalist Development: A Background to Asian Immigration," *Labor Immigration Under Capitalism.* Lucie Cheng and Edna Bonacich, eds. (Berkeley: University of California Press, 1984), 81.

52. Wilson's work, *Racism: From Slavery to Advanced Capitalism,* 62–72.

53. Dippie, *The Vanishing American: White Attitudes and U.S. Indian Policy,* 32–44.

54. Quoted from Pearce, *Savagism and Civilization: A Study of the Indian and the American Mind,* 57.

55. See for example Peter A. Brannon, "Removal of Indians from Alabama," *Alabama Historical Quarterly.* 12(1950):91–117; Angie Debo, *The Road to Disappearance: A History of the Creek Indians.* (Norman: University of Oklahoma Press, 1941); Grant Foreman, *Indian Removal: The Emigration of the Five Civilized Tribes.*

(Norman: University of Oklahoma Press, 1952); Micheal D. Green, *The Politics of Indian Removal: Creek Government and Society in Crisis.* (Lincoln: University of Nebraska Press, 1982); Francis P. Prucha, *Documents of United States Indian Policy.* Second Edition, Expanded. (Lincoln: University of Nebraska Press, 1990), 52–53; Russell Thornton, "Cherokee Population Losses During the 'Trail of Tears': A New Perspective and a New Estimate," *Ethnohistory.* 31(1984): 289–300; Russell Thornton, *American Indian Holocaust and Survival: A Population History since 1492.* (Norman: University of Oklahoma Press, 1987), 113–118.

56. Dippie, *The Vanishing American: White Attitudes and U. S. Indian Policies,* 12–32; Paul Stuart, *Nations Within a Nation: Historical Statistics of American Indians.* (Westport: Greenwood Press, 1987), 78–79; Peter Wood, "Re-Viewing the Map: 'America's Empty Wilderness,'" *Cultural Survival Quarterly.* 6(1992):59–62.

57. Gregory R. Campbell, "The Epidemiological Consequences of Forced Removal: The Northern Cheyenne in Indian Territory," *Plains Indian Historical Demography and Health: Perspectives, Interpretations, and Critiques.* Gregory R. Campbell, ed. "Memoir 23." *Plains Anthropologist.* 34(1989):90–97; Robert E. Smith, ed., *Oklahoma's Forgotten Indians.* Volume XV. (Oklahoma City: Oklahoma Historical Society, 1981).

58. The shift to "objective" scientific observations about racial differences was not a quantum leap in interpretation. The eventual development of a science of humankind, including the laws of nature governing human progress, like earlier Biblical explanations, had its origin in western European philosophical thought. Once savages were introduced into the chain of being, the next step necessarily was historical. The savage had to be affiliated to other humans and animals. To accomplish this feat, two established ideas, once separated from one another by divergent functions, were welded together, namely, the hierarchical principle of the arrangement of things and the historical or genetic principle of explanation.

Renaissance scholasticism concerning the place of the savage in the hierarchy of nature, combined with the revival of historiography during the same period, gave rise to the pre-Darwinian idea of a spatial progression of forms into an evolutionary sequence. Inherent in the intellectual tradition was the idea of cultural and biological progress and an innate superiority of "contemporary" over "earlier" social and biological forms. These were the intellectual seeds that would forge an interest in basic questions about culture and differences in cultural achievements—the intellectual seeds of scientific racism. See: Robert E. Bieder, *Science Encounters the Indian, 1820–1880: The Early Years of American Ethnology.* (Norman: University of Oklahoma Press, 1986); Jacob W. Gruber "Archaeology, History, and Culture," *American Archaeology: Past and Future;* David J. Metzer, Don D. Fowler, and Jeremy A Sabloff, eds. (Washington, D.C.: Smithsonian Institution Press, 1986), 163–186; Charles Hinsley, *Savages and Scientists: The Smithsonian Institution and the Development of American Anthropology, 1846–1910.* (Washington,

D.C.: Smithsonian Institution Press, 1981); Bruce Trigger "Prehistoric Archaeology and American Society," *American Archaeology: Past and Future.* David J. Metzer, Don D. Fowler, and Jeremy A Sabloff, eds. (Washington, D.C.: Smithsonian Institution Press, 1986), 187–215; *A History of Archaeological Thought.* (Cambridge: Cambridge University Press, 1989), 67–147; Pearce, *Savagism and Civilization: A Study of the Indian and the American Mind,* 105–134.

59. Stephen J. Gould. *The Mismeasure of Man.* (New York: W. W. Norton and Company, 1981), 31–72; Smedley, *Race in North America: Origin and Evolution of a Worldview,* 234–244.

60. Gould. *The Mismeasure of Man,* 39.

61. Ibid., 39–40.

62. Samuel G. Morton, *Crania Americana or a Comparative View of the Skulls of Various Aboriginal Nations of North and South America.* (Philadelphia: John Pennington, 1839).

63. Ales Hrdlicka, "Physical Anthropology in America," *American Anthropologist.* 16(1914):515.

64. Quoted from Stephen J. Gould, "Morton's Ranking of Races by Cranial Capacity: Unconscious Manipulation of the Data May be the Scientific Norm," *Science.* 200(1978):503–509; See also: Gould, *The Mismeasure of Man,* 56–57.

65. Gould, *The Mismeasure of Man,* 56–57.

66. Reginald Horsman's, *Race and Manifest Destiny: The Origins of American Racial Anglo-Saxonism.* (Cambridge: Harvard University Press, 1981) offers critical insight into the origins and belief in a "White," Anglo-Saxon superiority in shaping America's public policies and actions prior to 1850.

67. Fredrickson and Knobel, "History of Prejudice and Discrimination," 834; Gossett, *Race: The History of an Idea in America,* 54–83; William Stanton, *The Leopard's Spots: Scientific Attitudes Toward Race in America, 1815–1859.* (Chicago: University of Chicago Press, 1960), 24–44.

68. Leonard Dinnerstein, Roger L. Nichols, and David M. Reimers, *Natives and Strangers: Blacks, Indians, and Immigrants in America.* (New York: Oxford University Press, 1990); Ronald Takaki, *Iron Cages: Race and Culture in 19th-Century America.* (New York: Oxford University Press, 1990).

69. Easterline, "Immigration: Economic and Social Characteristics," 477, 480.

70. Bernard, "Immigration: History of U. S. Policy," 489.

71. Horsman, *Race and Manifest Destiny: The Origins of American Racial Anglo-Saxonism,* 189–303.

72. Oscar Martinez, "A History of Chicanos/Mexicanos Along the U. S.-Mexico Border," *Handbook of Hispanic Cultures in the United States: History.* Volume 3. Alfredo Jimenez, ed. (Houston: Arte Publico Press, 1994), 261–280.

73. Martha Menchaca, "Chicano Indianism: A Historical Account of Racial Repression in the United States," *American Ethnologist.* 20(3,1993):583–603; James Diego Vigil, *From Indians to Chicanos: The Dynamics of Mexican-American Culture.* Second Edition. (Prospect Heights: Waveland Press, 1998), 123–176.

74. Martinez, "A History of Chicanos/Mexicanos Along the U.S.-Mexico Border," 265.

75. Frank Bean and Marta Tienda, *The Hispanic Population of the United States.* (New York: Russell Sage Foundation, 1987), 10.

76. The formation of Chicano ethnicity is part of a larger process of creating a Latino cultural legacy in the United States. It is a process that has many historical and cultural parallels with Cuban Americans, Puerto Rican Americans, and other groups from Central and South America. See: Thomas Weaver, "Latino Legacies: Crossing National and Creating Cultural Borders," *Handbook of Hispanic Cultures in the United States: Anthropology.* Volume 2. (Houston: Arte Publico Press, 1994), 39–58.

77. Martinez, "A History of Chicanos/Mexicanos Along the U.S.-Mexico Border," 265.

78. Ibid., 266.

79. H. M. Lai, "Chinese," *Harvard Encyclopedia of American Ethnic Groups.* Stephan Thernstrom, ed. (Cambridge: Harvard University Press, 1980), 217–219; See also: Kil Zo, *Chinese Emigration to the United States, 1850–1880.* (New York: Arno, 1978).

80. Juanita Tamayo Lott, "Population Growth and Distribution," *Reference Library of Asian America.* Volume II. Susan Gall, ed. (Detroit: Gale Research, 1996), 279.

81. Connie Yung Yu, "Who Are Chinese Americans?," *Reference Library of Asian America.* Volume I. Susan Gall, ed. (Detroit: Gale Research, 1996), 41–62.

82. The British government did spend 7 million pounds on famine relief, but the relief was targeted selectively toward the upholding and consolidating the property rights of the wealthy rather than the Irish poor. Most relief came from non-British sources. The Catholic Church, Quakers, and the Choctaw tribal-nation sent relief funds. Even the Sultan of Turkey attempted to give $10,000, but his offer was rebuked because it exceeded the $1,000 donation made by Queen Victoria. The relief efforts offered by the British government throughout the famine remained not only maldistributed and inadequate, but rooted in racism. See: John Newsinger, "The Great Irish Famine: A Crime of Free Market Economics," *Monthly Review.* 47(11):14; Hazel Waters, "The Great Famine and the Rise of Anti-Irish Racism," *Race and Class.* 37(1, 1995):95–108.

83. Christine Kinealy, *The Great Calamity: The Irish Famine 1845–52.* (Dublin: Gill and Macmillian, 1994).

84. Newsinger, "The Great Irish Famine: A Crime of Free Market Economics," 15.

85. Lewis P. Curtis, *Apes and Angels: The Irish in Victorian Caricature.* (Washington, D.C.: Smithsonian Institution Press, 1971).

86. Andrew M. Greeley, *That Most Distressful Nation.* (Chicago: Quadrangle, 1972), 119–120.

87. For a thorough discussion of nativism in the United States between 1860 to 1925 refer to: John Higham, *Strangers in the Land: Patterns of American Nativism, 1860–1925.* (New Brunswick: Rutgers University Press, 1955).

88. Yu, "Who Are Chinese Americans?," 44.

89. Bernard, "Immigration: History of U. S. Policy," 489.

90. For an introduction to the development of evolutionary theory in relation to scientific views about Native American societies see: Robert F. Berkhofer, *The White Man's Indian: Images of the American Indian from Columbus to the Present.* (New York: Alfred A. Knopf, 1978), 44–61.

91. See John S. Haller, Jr., *Outcasts From Evolution: Scientific Attitudes of Racial Inferiority, 1859–1900.* (Urbana: University of Illinois Press, 1971).

92. In order to answer important sociological questions about human inequality a number of *a priori* assumptions had to be made about the development of humankind. Evolutionary theory assumed there was a uniformity of human mental characteristics and abilities over space and time. This uniformity permitted scientists to compare humans and their institutions regardless of geography or history. The comparisons could empirically measure the direction and amount of evolution that had taken place for that particular society. See: Berkhofer, *The White Man's Indian: Images of the American Indian from Columbus to the Present,* 52; Seymour Drescher, "The Ending of the Slave Trade and the Evolution of Scientific Racism," *The Atlantic Slave Trade: Effects on Economics, Societies, and Peoples of Africa, the Americas, and Europe.* Joseph E. Inikori and Stanley L. Engerman, eds. (Durham: Duke University Press, 1992), 361–396.

93. Haller, Jr., *Outcasts From Evolution: Scientific Attitudes of Racial Inferiority, 1859–1900,* 105.

94. Lubbock's argument was summarized from Bruce Trigger, *A History of Archaeological Thought.* (Cambridge: Cambridge University Press, 1989), 114–117.

95. See Richard Hofstadter, *Social Darwinism in American Thought.* (Boston: Beacon Press, 1955).

96. Haller, Jr., *Outcasts From Evolution: Scientific Attitudes of Racial Inferiority, 1859–1900,* 105.

97. Native Americans were excluded from the decision as they were not included in the *Civil Rights Act of 1866.* See: Elizabeth Hull, *Without Justice for All: The Constitutional Rights of Aliens.* (Westport: Greenwood Press, 1985); Ian F. López, "Racial Restrictions in the Law of Citizenship," *Race and Ethnic Relations 97/98.* John A. Kromkowski, ed. (Guilford: Dushkin/McGraw-Hill, 1997), 10–15; Menchaca, "Chicano Indianism: A Historical Account of Racial Repression in the United States," 592–593; Yu, "Who Are Chinese Americans?," 44–45.

98. In a probing piece of scholarship which explores the emergence of the sharecropping system as a labor arrangement which sought to rectify the conflicts between the labor and capital across the South see: Edward Royce, *The Origins of Southern Sharecropping.* (Philadelphia: Temple University Press, 1993).

99. Bonacich, "United States Capitalist Development: A Background to Asian Immigration," 112–115.

100. U. S. Bureau of the Census, *Historical Statistics of the United States: Colonial Times to 1970.* (Washington, D. C.: U. S. Government Printing Office, 1975), 14. See also: Lai, "Chinese," 219.

101. Sucheng Chan, ed., *Entry Denied: Exclusion and the Chinese Community in America, 1882–1943.* (Philadelphia: Temple University Press, 1991); Lai, "Chinese," 220; Yu, "Who Are Chinese Americans?," 48–49.

102. Rosalie Weider, "Immigration," *Reference Library of Asian America.* Volume II. Susan Gall, ed. (Detroit: Gale Research, 1996), 265.

103. Terry Hong, "Historic Landmarks of Asia America," *Reference Library of Asian America*. Volume III. Susan Gall, ed. (Detroit: Gale Research, 1996), 738.

104. Menchaca, "Chicano Indianism: A Historical Account of Racial Repression in the United States," 596–597.

105. Fredrickson and Knobel, "History of Prejudice and Discrimination," 835.

106. It is no coincidence that on March 3, 1879, the *Bureau of Ethnology* (B.A.E.) was created as an arm of the *Smithsonian Institution*. It was imperative that the government gather first-hand data of Native American lifeways to push the indigenous survivors of colonialism through the stages of cultural and biological evolution toward "civilization." The "Indian Problem" became enmeshed in federal assimilation policy. Ethnology, armed with scientific data and an evolutionary paradigm that predicted cultural progress was possible, provided the *Indian Office* with vital information to launch its social engineering assault against Native American societies. See: Charles Hinsley, *Savages and Scientists: The Smithsonian Institution and the Development of American Anthropology, 1846–1910*. (Washington, D.C.: Smithsonian Institution Press, 1981); Fredrick Hoxie, *The Final Promise: The Campaign to Assimilate the Indians, 1880–1920*. (Lincoln: University of Nebraska, 1984); Paul Stuart, *The Indian Office: Growth and Development of an American Institution, 1865–1900*. (Ann Arbor: UMI Research Press, 1979).

107. William Stannard, *The Leopard's Spots: Scientific Attitudes Toward Race in America, 1815–59*. (Chicago: University of Chicago Press, 1960).

108. David M. Holford, "The Subversion of the Indian Land Allotment System, 1887–1934," *Indian Historian*. 8(Spring, 1975):11–21.

109. M. Annette Jaimes, "Federal Indian Identification Policy," *Critical Issues in Native North America*. Document 62. Ward Churchill, ed. (Copenhagen: International Work Group for Indigenous Affairs, 1988/1989), 15–36.

110. C. Matthew Snipp, *American Indians: The First of This Land* (New York: Russell Sage Foundation, 1989), 26–35.

111. Ward Churchill, *Critical Issues in Native North America*. Document 62. (Copenhagen: International Work Group for Indigenous Affairs, 1988/1989); *Critical Issues in Native North America, Volume II*. Document 68. (Copenhagen: International Work Group for Indigenous Affairs, 1991).

112. Robert D. Bullard, ed., *Confronting Environmental Racism: Voices from the Grassroots*. (Boston: South End Press, 1993); Ward Churchill and Winona LaDuke, "Native North America: The Political Economy of Radioactive Colonialism," *The State of Native America, Genocide, Colonization, and Resistance,* M. Annette Jaimes, ed. (Boston: South End Press, 1992), 241–266; Al Gedicks, *The New Resource Wars: Native and Environmental Struggles Against Multinational Corporations*. (Boston: South End Press, 1993).

113. Campbell, "The Politics of Counting: Critical Reflections on the Depopulation Question of Native North America," 109–110. See also: Michael K. Green, ed., *Issues in Native American Cultural Identity*. (New York: Pete Lang, 1995).

114. John H. Moore, "Blood Quantum and How Not to Count Indians," Lecture held at the University of Montana, Missoula, April 9, 1992.

115. M. Annette Jaimes, "Federal Indian Identification Policy," *Critical Issues in Native North America*. Document 62. Ward Churchill, ed. (Copenhagen: International Work Group for Indigenous Affairs, 1988/1989); Robert Jarvenpa, "The Political Economy and Political Ethnicity of American Indian Adaptations and Identities," *Ethnic and Racial Studies*. 8(1985):29–48.

116. Humbert S. Nelli, "Italians," *Harvard Encyclopedia of American Ethnic Groups*. Stephan Thernstrom, ed. (Cambridge: Harvard University Press, 1980), 547.

117. Ibid., 547.

118. Cavaioli and La Gumina, *The Peripheral Americans*, 87.

119. Quoted from Eliot Lord, John J. D. Trenor, and Samuel J. Barrows, *The Italian in America*. (San Francisco: R & E Associates, 1970), 17–18.

120. Ibid., 17–18.

121. Cavaioli and La Gumina, *The Peripheral Americans*, 91.

122. Ibid., 91.

123. Richard Gambino, *Blood of My Blood: The Dilemma of Italian-Americans*. (Garden City: Doubleday and Company, 1974), 109.

124. Bernard, "Immigration: History of U. S. Policy," 495.

125. Virginia Sánchez Korrol, "In Their Own Right: A History of Puerto Ricans in the U. S. A.," *Handbook of Hispanic Cultures in the United States: History*. Volume 3. Alfredo Jímenez, ed. (Houston: Arte Publico Press, 1994), 281.

126. José Hernández, *Conquered Peoples in America*. (Dubuque: Kendall/Hunt Publishing, 1992).

127. Mansour Farhang, *U. S. Imperialism, From the Spanish American War to the Iranian Revolution*. (Boston: South End Press, 1981); Alfredo López, *Doña Licha's Island: Modern Colonialism in Puerto Rico*. (Boston: South End Press, 1988).

128. Korrol, "In Their Own Right: A History of Puerto Ricans in the U. S. A.," 284–285.

129. For a critical examination of some of the central questions surrounding the invention of "Whiteness," see: Richard D. Alba, *Ethnic Identity: The Transformation of White America*. (New Haven: Yale University Press, 1990); Theodore Allen, *The Invention of the White Race*. Volume 1. (London: Veiso, 1994); Richard Delgado and Jean Stefancic, *Critical White Studies: Looking Behind the Mirror*. (Philadelphia: Temple University Press, 1997); Noel Ignatiev, *How the Irish Became White*. (New York: Routledge, 1996); Stanley Lierson, "Unhyphenated Whites in the United States," *Ethnic and Racial Studies*. 8(1985):159–180.

130. Barry Goldberg, "Race, Class, and White Ethnicity: A Brief History," *Many Americas: Critical Perspectives on Race, Racism and Ethnicity*. Gregory Campbell, ed. (Dubuque: Kendall Hunt Publishing Co., 1998): 61-82.

131. Gossett, *Race: The History of an Idea in America*, 340.

132. Fredrickson and Knobel, "History of Prejudice and Discrimination," 835.

133. Ibid., 340.

134. U. S. Bureau of the Census, *Historical Statistics of the United States*. (Washington, D.C.: U. S. Government Printing Office, 1960), 218.

135. Stanley Lieberson, *A Piece of the Pie*. (Berkeley: University of California Press, 1980), 377–383.

136. Fredrickson and Knobel, "History of Prejudice and Discrimination," 836.

137. Jacqueline Jones, *The Dispossessed: America's Underclasses from the Civil War to the Present*. (New York: Basic Books, 1992).

138. Martinez, "A History of Chicanos/Mexicanos Along the U. S.-Mexico Border," 269.

139. Korrol, "In Their Own Right: A History of Puerto Ricans in the U. S. A.," 286.

140. Gambino, *Blood of My Blood: The Dilemma of Italian-Americans*. (Garden City: Doubleday and Company, 1974).

141. Ibid., 108.

142. Bernard, "Immigration: History of U. S. Policy," 492.

143. Ibid., 493.

144. Ibid., 493.

145. Martinez, "A History of Chicanos/Mexicanos Along the U. S.-Mexico Border," 270.

146. Ibid., 270.

147. Fredrickson and Knobel, "History of Prejudice and Discrimination," 836; Loren Miller, *The Petitioners*. (New York: Random House, 1966); Wilson, *Racism: From Slavery to Advanced Capitalism*, 147–148.

148. Martinez, "A History of Chicanos/Mexicanos Along the U. S.-Mexico Border," 273.

149. Korrol, "In Their Own Right: A History of Puerto Ricans in the U. S. A.," 290.

150. Edna Bonacich, "Class Approaches to Ethnicity and Race," *Insurgent Sociologist*. 10(Fall, 1980):9–23; Dan Lacy, *The White Use of Blacks in America*. (New York: McGraw-Hill, 1972), 143–144; Wilson, *Racism: From Slavery to Advanced Capitalism*, 118–138.

151. Elizabeth McPike and Marcia Reecer, "A. Philip Randolph, April 15, 1889–May 16, 1979," *American Educator*. Special Issue. 21(1–2, 1997):44.

152. Wilson, *Racism: From Slavery to Advanced Capitalism*, 165–166.

153. Allen D. Grimshaw, ed. *Racial Violence in the United States*. (Chicago: Aldine, 1969).

154. Vigil, *From Indians to Chicanos: The Dynamics of Mexican-American Culture*, 227–228.

155. Morrol, "In Their Own Right: A History of Puerto Ricans in the U. S. A." 291.

156. Ibid., 291.

157. Bernard, "Immigration: History of U. S. Policy," 494.

158. Ibid., 493.

159. John A. Scanlon, "Why the McCarran-Walter Act Must be Amended," *Academe*. 73(1987):5–13.

160. Carlos E. Cortes, "Mexicans," *Harvard Encyclopedia of American Ethnic Groups*. Stephan Thernstrom, ed. (Cambridge: Harvard University Press, 1980), 711–713; Wendell Gordon, "A Case for a Less Restrictive Border Policy," *Social Science Quarterly*. 56(1975):485–491; Vilma S. Martinez, "Illegal immigration and the Labor Force," *American Behavioral Scientist*. 19(1976):

335–350; Martinez, "A History of Chicanos/Mexicanos Along the U. S.-Mexico Border," 274.

161. Vine Deloria Jr., *Custer Died for Your Sins: An Indian Manifesto*. (New York: Avon, 1969), 60–71; S. Lyman Tyler, *A History of Indian Policy*. (Washington, D.C.: U. S. Government Printing Office, 1973), 161–188.

162. For select case studies see: Howard H. Bahr, Bruce A, Chawick, and Joseph H. Strauss, "Discrimination Against Urban Indians in Seattle," *Indian Historian*. 5(1972):4–11; James R. Bohland, "Indian Residential Segregation in the Urban Southwest, 1970 and 1980," *Social Science Quarterly*. 63(1982):749–761; Jack O. Waddell and Michael O. Watson, eds., *The American Indian in Urban Society*. (Boston: Little, Brown, 1971).

163. United States Supreme Court, "Brown et al. v. Board of Education of Topeka et al. from U. S. Reports, 1954," *Race and Ethnic Relations*. John A. Kromkowski, ed. (Guilford: Dushkin/McGraw-Hill, 1997), 16–18.

164. United States Commission of Civil Rights, *Freedom to the Free*. (Washington, D.C.: U. S. Government Printing Office, 1963), 109–111, 139; Wilson, *Racism: From Slavery to Advanced Capitalism*, 166.

165. Michael Omi and Howard Winant, "By the Rivers of Babylon: Race in the United States," *Socialist Review*. (13, 1983): 38.

166. Thomas F. Gossett, *Race: The History of an Idea in America*, 431–459; Anthony M. Platt, "U. S. Race Relations at the Crossroads in California," *Monthly Review*. 48(5, 1996):31.

167. U. S. Bureau of the Census, *The Social and Economic Status of the Black Population in the United States: An Historical Overview, 1790–1978*. (Washington, D.C.: U. S. Government Printing Office, 1979).

168. Robert Blauner, *Racial Oppression in America*. New York: Harper and Row, 1972), 62.

169. Neil R. McMillan, *The Citizen's Council: Organized Resistance to the Second Reconstruction, 1954–1964*. (Urbana: University of Illinois Press, 1971); James Ridgeway, *Blood in the Face: The Ku Klux Klan, Aryan Nations, Nazi Skinheads, and the Rise of a New White Culture*. (New York: Thunder's Mouth Press, 1990), 57–189; U. S. Bureau of the Census, *Historical Statistics of the United States*. (Washington, D.C.: U. S. Government Printing Office, 1960), 218.

170. Jane A. Baskin, Joyce K. Hartweg, Ralph G. Lewis, and Lester W. McCullough, Jr., *Race Related Civil Disorders: 1967–1969*. (Waltham: Lemberg Center for the Study of Violence, Brandeis University, 1971).

171. Stokely Carmichael and Charles V. Hamilton, *Black Power: The Politics of Liberation in America*. (New York: Random House, 1967); Lewis M. Killian, "Race Relations and the Nineties: Where Are the Dreams of the Sixties?," *Sources: Notable Selections in Race and Ethnicity*. Adalberto Aguirre, Jr., and David D. Baker, eds. (Guilford: The Dushkin Publishing Group. Inc., 1995), 112.

172. Ward Churchill and Jim Vander Wall, *Agents of Repression: The FBI's Secret Wars Against the Black Panther Party and the American Indian Movement*. (Boston: South End Press, 1990).

173. JoNina M. Abron, "The Legacy of the Black Panther Party," *The Black Scholar*. 17(1986):33–37; Kenyon

Chan and Shirley Hune, "Racialization and Panethnicity: From Asians in America to Asian Americans," *Toward a Common Destiny: Improving Race and Ethnic Relations in America.* (San Francisco: Jossey-Bass Publishers, 1995), 205–233; Michael Omi and Howard Winant, *Racial Formation in the United States.* (New York: Routledge and Kegan Paul, 1986); Diego Vigil, "Chicano and Latino Activism and Political Change," *Handbook of Hispanic Cultures in the United States: Anthropology.* Volume 2. Thomas Weaver, ed. (Houston: Arte Publico Press, 1994), 309–327; William Wei, *The Asian America Movement.* (Philadelphia: Temple University Press, 1993).

Mechanical Cast-Iron "Jolly Nigger" Bank. A lever in the back operates the hand.
Courtesy of Kenneth W. Goings Collection.

Postcard Depicting a Little Girl in a Watermelon Patch with a Swollen Stomach, 1952.
This card plays on two common stereotypes about African Americans: their love for watermelon and, through the suggestion of pregnancy, their wanton sexuality.
Courtesy of the Kenneth W. Goings Collection

27

Disability Discrimination and the Evolution of Civil Rights in Democratic Societies

PAUL JAEGER AND
CYNTHIA ANN BOWMAN

The worldwide population of individuals with disabilities is estimated to be as high as 550 million people (Albrecht & Verbugge, 2000; Metts, 2000). However, the practice of legally defined civil rights for individuals with disabilities is a very new concept, barely a quarter of a century old. Even in nations where legally defined civil rights have developed, disability remains at the periphery of society, as the new legal rights have yet to break established social classifications. This history demonstrates how negative social classifications of and reactions to persons with disabilities influenced the way in which they were treated by societies. This [essay] reveals the length and depth of the struggle for basic acceptance and inclusion by individuals with disabilities. For most of this history, social reactions and classifications led to negative legal classifications and social exclusion. These social conditions have progressed from complete exclusion to a recent turn toward inclusion in many societies.

To understand the magnitude of the struggle for rights for individuals with disabilities in society, familiarity with the social and political history of these individuals is vital. Discrimination against individuals with disabilities is not unique, as many other groups face institutionalized discrimination in society. However, individuals with disabilities have faced particularly harsh treatment throughout history and have gone unacknowledged for a longer period of time than most other disenfranchised groups. The history of the treatment of individuals with disabilities is exceptionally unpleasant, to put it mildly. Few rights were established for individuals with disabilities in any nation or society until well into the twentieth century. In many places, individuals with disabilities still lack basic legal rights, much less access to education, health care, information technology, or the political process. Understanding the history related to disability is essential to understanding disability in modern society.

DISABILITY IN SOCIETY BEFORE THE NINETEENTH CENTURY

For much of human history, the idea of providing legal rights to individuals with disabilities was never even considered. From ancient times to the not-so-distant past, disability was often classified as a manifestation of the anger of a deity or supernatural power (Rosen, 1968). "Conspicuously abnormal persons were surrounded by superstition, myth, and fatalism—especially fatalism" (Winzer, 1997,

p. 76). In many societies, the birth of an individual with a disability was viewed as a prophetic sign of impending doom (Warkany, 1959). Not surprisingly considering these attitudes, the inclusion of individuals with disabilities in the mainstream of society did not receive attention in most places until recent years.

Archaeologists have discovered the existence of disability dating back thousands of years in remains found in North America, South America, Europe, the Middle East, and Asia (Albrecht, 1992). Some people even had early forms of assistive technologies. Wooden prostheses were mentioned in writing in approximately 500 BCE, while a tomb from about 300 BCE was found to contain a skeleton with a bronze prosthetic leg (Braddock & Parish, 2001).

At the height of civilization in ancient Greece and Rome, what is now considered humankind's classical period, disability was kept "all but invisible, save a few blind prophets" (Edwards, 1997, p. 29). It was socially acceptable to abandon babies born with disabilities on sunny hillsides, tied or staked down, so as to perish from exposure to the sun (Garland, 1995). The law of the Greek state of Sparta, at the peak of its power, actually mandated the killing of children with disabilities, leaving the family no choice in the matter (Garland, 1995; Stiker, 1999). The fate of those who escaped death could still be most unhappy. For example, Balbous Balaesus the Stutterer, a Roman citizen, was kept in a cage along the main road to Rome so travelers could be amused by his speech problems when he tried to communicate with passersby (Garland, 1995). Blind boys in Rome were often trained as beggars, while blind girls were frequently sold into prostitution (French, 1932). Wealthy Roman households sometimes purchased individuals with disabilities to serve as amusement (Kanner, 1964). A special market even existed for the sale of these persons (Durant, 1944). Similarly, Egyptian pharaohs kept persons with disabilities both to provide entertainment and to bring good luck (Braddock & Parish, 2001).

This practice of using individuals with mental impairments as comic slaves was also common in ancient China and in pre-Columbian American civilizations (Willeford, 1969). Ancient Chinese culture, nearly 2,000 years ago, created a term to describe individuals with disabilities that translates to "disabled person, good for nothing," demonstrating an "all-too prevalent hostility and disregard for disabled people in China" (Stone, 1999, p. 137). That term is still commonly used to describe individuals with disabilities in China, and it has only started to be replaced by the slightly less derogatory term, "disabled but not useless," in recent years (Stone, 1999, p. 136). Chinese is hardly the only language that has this feature, as languages from Brazil to Zimbabwe use terms for disability that describe the person with a disability as "useless" or "afflicted as punishment" or "helpless" or "someone without freedom" (Charlton, 1998).

Worldwide, the situation really did not improve much until the recent past, as the mistreatment, abuse, neglect, and abandonment of individuals with disabilities has been commonplace throughout thousands and thousands of years of human history. Individuals with disabilities have been locked away against their will in prisons, asylums, and monasteries; they have been considered witches; and they have been thought to be suffering demonic possession. Often, forced confinement removed individuals with disabilities from any interaction with society whatsoever. Individuals with disabilities have often provoked "a kind of panic both internal and public" that has resulted in oppression, exclusion, and banishment to wretched institutions (Stiker, 1999, p. 9). That panic resulted in individuals with disabilities throughout history being killed, exiled, neglected, shunned, used for entertainment, or even treated as spiritual manifestations, both good and evil (Bragg, 1997; Hewett, 1974).

Much of the foundation for discrimination against persons with disabilities, particularly in Europe and the Americas, can actually be traced to early religious traditions and the foundations of modern religions. For many centuries, organized religions tended to express contradictory attitudes toward disabilities, with conflicting views of whether persons with disabilities should be shunned, punished, eradicated, or aided all being supported by major religious texts and leaders (Braddock & Parish, 2001; Winzer, 1997). Both the Old Testament and the New Testament of the Bible, for example, tend to equate disability with divine punishment or evidence of immoral behavior (Eisenberg, 1982; Shapiro, 1993). In the Old Testament, physical disability reflects spiritual disfavor as a result of sin, while in the New Testament persons with disabilities are viewed as possessed by evil or cursed (Shapiro, 1993). In the New Testament, the disciples even evidence the belief that disability was caused by sin, and this attitude "may be indicative of prevailing wisdom" of the time (Braddock & Parish, 2001, p. 17). These views are still reflected in many modern faiths (Shapiro, 1993). For religions that believe in reincarnation, such as Hinduism, disability poses a unique problem, as such religions typically believe that a person has a disability as punishment for something done in a previous life (Charlton, 1998). To that way of thinking, a disability always negatively reflects on the individual with a disability.

Beyond the parameters of religion, these religious views have had a tremendous social impact on the ways that persons with disabilities have been viewed and treated throughout history into the present day. "By associating sin and moral transgression with the resultant 'just retribution' of disability and illness, our society has found an apparent justification for stigmatizing the disabled" (Eisenberg, 1982, p. 5). These views have permeated many social and legal classifications of persons with disabilities.

Until the twentieth century, legal classifications of persons with disabilities were almost invariably negative. "The unwritten law of primitive society that the crippled and the disabled were to be sacrificed for the good of the group was carried over into written laws" (Funk, 1987, p. 9). Based on the Torah, Hebraic law created some classifications of individuals with disabilities (Stiker, 1999). However, "[l]egal uncleanness was attached to the disabled," denying them many social rights, leading to exclusion or denunciation in many cases (Stiker, 1999,

p. 24). Persons with hearing impairments were particularly vulnerable under biblically based laws and societies, as the Old Testament describes faith as coming through hearing, leaving individuals with hearing impairments without faith in the view of many, including the early Christian church (Daniels, 1997). Further, as Christianity, over time, became "the religion of the written revelation" with strong ties between faith and visual imagery (De Hamel, 1994, p. 11), the visually impaired were unable to participate in what was for a long time considered another key part of that faith.

Jurists interpreting Greek and Roman law were primarily concerned with disability as a cause of actions in legal cases; for example, Roman law allowed for the appointment of guardians for individuals with mental illnesses (Gaw, 1906, 1907). One curious feature of Roman law is that deaf persons who could communicate verbally had the right to be citizens, while those who could not communicate verbally did not have the right to be citizens (Gaw, 1906). The Code of Justinian, compiled beginning in 533 CE under orders of the Roman Emperor Justinian, created a unified code of civil law for the empire that had a tremendous impact on the laws of most of Europe until well into the eighteenth century. This code and companion digests of Roman case law detailed many legal rights that individuals with certain types of disability, particularly individuals with mental, visual, or hearing impairments, were not allowed to have, such as the right to inherit property (Watson, 1998). As a result, the classification of persons with disabilities as lacking social, legal, or educational rights was institutionalized for well over a millennium under legal systems derived from or influenced by the Code of Justinian, which included virtually all of Europe.

Even in the supposedly more enlightened periods of human history, individuals with disabilities still faced unfortunate popular movements that emphasized institutionalization in poorhouses or worse, segregation, eugenics, sterilization, and forced relocation to colonies. "Being different drew cruel and callous reactions from society, yet the penalties inflicted—legal sanctions, church expul-

sion, starvation, exile, or even death—were too unevenly administered to exterminate all persons with disabilities" (Winzer, 1997, p. 80). In keeping with the Roman tradition, wealthy Italian households, including those of some popes, continued for centuries to own servants with disabilities as entertainment (Hibbert, 1975). In many different societies, individuals with disabilities also were used for public spectacle or sport, often with the risk of death to the unwilling participants (French, 1932). Prior to the eighteenth century, individuals with disabilities were usually allowed to interact with society only "under supervision" (Stiker, 1999, p. 69).

If their families would not support them, individuals with disabilities often were forced to beg to survive. Begging became so important to individuals with disabilities in the Middle Ages that guilds and brotherhoods of beggars with disabilities were created (Covey, 1998). As a result, "disability became synonymous with beggary, and beggary became synonymous with failure—failure to be wholly human because human worth was increasingly being associated with work" (Branson & Miller, 2002, p. 7). Individuals with certain impairments, such as mental disorders and epilepsy, were often locked away in asylums, madhouses, and prisons, while individuals with Hansen's disease (commonly known as leprosy) were forced to live in isolated camps, with Europe having as many as 19,000 leprosy villages at one time (Braddock & Parish, 2001; Foucault, 1965). Individuals with disabilities also were commonly exiled by being sent via boat to some other community (Foucault, 1965).

The anatomical and physiological studies of human anatomy during the Renaissance, performed by Leonardo da Vinci, Vesalius, William Harvey, and others, led to better understandings of vision, hearing, and other systems of the body. Such advances, however, did not have a sizeable impact on the views of society toward persons with disabilities. During the Reformation, both John Calvin and Martin Luther advocated the classification of individuals with mental disabilities as creations of Satan (Braddock & Parish, 2001; Shorter, 2000). Luther actually favored praying for the death of individuals with cognitive disabilities or even killing them out-right, as he believed that they were masses of flesh that lacked souls (Kanner, 1964; Shorter, 2000). In Renaissance times, it was common to beat individuals with cognitive disabilities on the head as a "treatment" (Braddock & Parish, 2001). From a bleakly ironic perspective, this treatment might be considered a profoundly misguided first attempt by a society to provide rehabilitative services to individuals with disabilities.

In colonial North America, the earliest known attempt to educate an individual with a disability occurred in 1679 when a tutor named Phillip Nelson began teaching a deaf child to communicate in a systematic manner (Fay, 1899). Nelson was forced to stop his work by the community in which he and his student lived because the local church denounced his work as blasphemy for attempting to perform a miracle and threatened Nelson's life (Fay, 1899). Thus, the people of North America have the curious legacy that they almost put their first special educator to death. This irrational opposition to educating individuals with disabilities was heavily influenced by the Puritan belief that a disability was unquestionably a manifestation of divine punishment (Covey, 1998). Increase Mather, an early president of Harvard University, and his son, Cotton Mather, who is most famous for his part in the accusations and claims of witchcraft in the seventeenth century that led to the Salem witch trials, helped to popularize the perception of disability as heavenly wrath (Covey, 1998; Winship, 1994). About the same time that Phillip Nelson's life was being threatened for trying to educate a child with a hearing impairment, Jan Amos Komensky was advocating to reform education in eastern Europe so that it was provided equally to all children, regardless of class, status, or ability (Salder, 1966). Komensky's views were not widely accepted; he repeatedly faced exile and ridicule throughout his lifetime for his opinions on education (Salder, 1966).

Fortunately, the situation for individuals with disabilities began to slowly improve in the 1700s in Europe. A method for teaching communication to deaf individuals developed by a Spanish monk named Pedro Ponce de Leon around 1510 came to be widely recognized in Spain and France (Daniels, 1997). These early methods of teaching sign language inspired a number of European educators and reformers to create residential schools for children with hearing impairments, and later children with visual impairments, offering the first systematized education for individuals with disabilities (Winzer, 1997). In 1752, Benjamin Franklin and Thomas Bond founded the first general hospital in colonial America offering care and rehabilitation for individuals with disabilities (Morton, 1897). The hospital represented almost immeasurable progress for individuals with disabilities, as it was the first institution in early America to use the health care technology of the time to provide help to individuals with disabilities. Franklin and his rehabilitative hospital, sadly, did not reflect the beliefs of Franklin's famous and influential compatriots, though America would eventually become the crux of the movement toward access, inclusion, and civil rights for individuals with disabilities.

DISCRIMINATION IN THE FORMATION OF A DEMOCRACY

When the framers of the U.S. government created the Declaration of Independence, they were espousing views based on the moral imperatives of equality for all. This vision of equality, however, did not include all residents of the newly formed nation. In 1776, the colonies were in a frenzy inspired by Thomas Paine's writings, especially *Common Sense*. Paine's vision of a truly free government included universal suffrage, universal education, and universal participation. Paine's egalitarian views, however, were considered unspeakably radical by many of the people who were establishing the U.S. government on principles of equality for certain parts of society. The Declaration was nevertheless intended "as a moral statement. Human equality, they were insisting, is a moral and even a religious standard against which it is right and proper to judge a political system" (Dahl, 2001, p. 124). The practicalities of the freedoms offered by the Declaration were not all-inclusive by any means. Though it stated that all men were created equal, all men were not to have equal rights of suffrage or participation in the new government, while women were excluded completely.

The U.S. constitutional government, as a representational republic, was unprecedented in human history. Representative governments had managed to exist and grow, such as the British Parliament and the Scandinavian Tings, but they were hardly republics, with great inequalities among the population and many other highly undemocratic features (Dahl, 2001). The modern parliamentary system did not yet exist and no large republic with popular representation had ever been attempted. The only successful republican governments in history were long-gone city-states of the classical era in the Mediterranean and the Middle Ages in southern Europe (Dahl, 1998). For all the innovation of the new republic, it did not create a wholly inclusive democracy.

Before, during, and after the Constitutional Convention, the rights of various groups were hotly contested issues. In the early history of the republic, the rights of women, slaves, Native Americans, immigrants, and the poor were widely discussed. Many of the founders, in fact, were publicly in favor of emancipation of all slaves and extending the right to vote to women and the poor (Kennedy, 2003; West, 1997). However, the framers who favored a more inclusive republic were forced to accept the undemocratic features in order for the Constitution to be ratified; "as practical men they made compromises" (Dahl, 2001, p. 38). Those favoring the most inclusive republic possible had to sacrifice many ideals to have any republic at all.

One scholar lists the undemocratic elements of the Constitution as including the acceptance of slavery, the denial of suffrage to women and minorities, the system for selecting the president, the selection of senators by state legislatures, equal representation in the Senate, and the extensive power of the judiciary (Dahl, 2001). Many of the undemocratic elements of the Constitution have been altered over the course of the nation's history, through legislation, jurisprudence, or violence, or a combina-

tion of those factors. A civil war and the Thirteenth, Fourteenth, and Fifteenth Amendments to the Constitution destroyed slavery. The Fourteenth Amendment has also served to eliminate discrimination against many other groups. The protections of the Fourteenth Amendment extend to national origin (*Korematsu v. United States*, 1944), race (*Brown v. Board of Education*, 1954), alienage (*Graham v. Richardson*, 1971), gender (*Craig v. Boren*, 1976), and illegitimacy (*Trible v. Gordon*, 1977). The Seventeenth Amendment took the power to select senators away from the state legislatures and gave it to the general populace. Women gained the right to vote by the Nineteenth Amendment. The Supreme Court, however, has refused to extend the protections of the Fourteenth Amendment to include persons with disabilities (*City of Cleburne v. City of Cleburne Living Center, Inc.*, 1985).

The framers of the Declaration of Independence and the Constitution primarily held to the then-common belief that individuals with disabilities had to be protected, as they "could not fend for themselves" (Bryan, 1996, p. 4). In the colonial period, individuals with disabilities were primarily relegated to dependence on family members or the community or were placed in poorhouses (Braddock & Parish, 2001). When a person with a disability had no family that could provide support, the common practice was to contract provision of care to the lowest bidder (Funk, 1987). Individuals with disabilities often were actually turned away from communities, either through banishment or being refused the right to enter a community (Braddock & Parish, 2001; Shapiro, 1993). At the time of the American Revolution, the various colonies' laws related to disability included statutes that mandated deporting persons with physical disabilities, classifying all persons with disabilities as indigent, and requiring all persons with disabilities to wear distinguishing symbols on their garments that showed their classification (Switzer, 2003).

There were scattered concerns of what might become of war casualties, such as veterans who were amputees or otherwise permanently injured. Throughout the history of the United States, "[d]uring a war and immediately thereafter, state, federal and local governments put forth every effort to meet the needs of the veteran with a disability and his family" (Bryan, 1996, p. 6). Starting with the American Revolution, these efforts were in the form of financial compensation for physical losses (Switzer, 2003). These concerns even led to the first two federal laws related to disability, passed in 1776 and 1798, that provided compensation and medical care for soldiers who incurred disabilities while in service (Albrecht, 1992). However, after every war, the interest in veterans with disabilities has been very "short-lived" (Bryan, 1996, p. 6): The late eighteenth century, though, did include the development of a very rudimentary pension system for some people with mental disabilities in the United States (Braddock & Parish, 2001).

In the United States, social advances for individuals with disabilities first began to be made in the 1800s. Although they lacked specific legal rights, some individuals with disabilities were beginning to gain basic entrance into society. The first private education for students with visual impairments was offered in 1812, and private schooling for individuals with hearing impairments began in 1817 (Shapiro, 1993). In the 1840s, the first treatise on the education of students with disabilities was published in the United States. Eduoard Seguin's (1846) *The Moral Treatment, Hygiene, and Education of Idiots and Other Backward Children,* though featuring a title that seems brainless at this distance, actually broke ground in a very radical way by asserting that children with disabilities could be educated and were worth educating.

The creation of asylums to treat people with mental disabilities began in earnest in the mid-1840s, due in large part to the efforts of Dorothea Dix, who wrote and lectured about the pervasive mistreatment of persons with mental disabilities (Brown, 1998). Inventor Alexander Graham Bell, whose creations include the telephone, worked to popularize special education in the United States, as well as the use of the term *special education* (Winzer, 1993). Helen Keller gave disability a publicly identifiable face through her childhood accomplishments in the 1880s of learning to read, write, and speak despite being blind and deaf and not having the benefit of a trained special educator. After graduating from Radcliffe in 1904, Keller became an advocate for the rights of women, racial minorities, the poor, and, of course, persons with disabilities (Loewen, 1995). In 1905, the first special education training courses for teachers were offered in the United States (Smith, 2001).

These sporadic advances, however, were occurring in a climate where more powerful social forces still worked to oppress, marginalize, and eliminate individuals with disabilities. The tendency to separate people with disabilities from the rest of society led to the establishment of residential institutions outside of the community (Wolfsenberger, 1969), which shaped the social roles and classifications of individuals with disabilities for many years. In the nineteenth century, most children with disabilities, if provided any health care or education at all, were sent to separate residential institutions, which were nothing like the schools other students attended (Winzer, 1993). The residential schools were "warehouses where people were isolated from society" (Smith, 2001, p. 15). The individuals housed in these residential schools were "confined and isolated rather than aided toward independence" and sheltered from the world in which they were believed unable to survive (Bryan, 1996, p. 4). Overall, "[t]his socially sanctioned segregation reinforced negative societal attitudes toward human difference" (Braddock & Parish, 2001, p. 52). Into the nineteenth century, people with hearing, speech, and visual impairments were commonly assumed to have limited intellects (Pfeiffer, 1993).

Traveling "freak shows" that displayed persons with physical and mental disabilities were very popular attractions at fairs, circuses, and exhibits in the eighteenth and nineteenth centuries in Europe and North America (Bogdan, 1988; Thomson, 1997). The people used in these shows were frequently sold to the shows for life by their parents; the organizers of the shows would construct elaborate stories to exaggerate the differences of persons with disabilities (Bogdan, 1988; Thomson, 1997).

These freak shows helped to institutionalize the belief in society that disability should be equated with deviance (Thomson, 1997).

THE AGE OF EUGENICS

In the mid-nineteenth century, British scientist Francis Galton popularized a movement known as *eugenics,* which was a term of Galton's own devising. Eugenics was based on the principle that only certain people had the right to perpetuate their genetic materials through reproduction and, therefore, reproduction should be regulated based on an individual's characteristics and endowments. These beliefs were built on the revolutionary work of Charles Darwin, who was Galton's cousin. Darwin's concept of the survival of the fittest in nature led some to transfer survival of the fittest to people, though Darwin was deeply opposed to such assertions (Branson & Miller, 2002; Gould, 1996). Nevertheless, Galton was inspired to become a veritable geyser of bad ideas in relation to human fitness, including trying to quantify the attractiveness of the breeding populations of women in the British Isles by city. He ranked London highest and Aberdeen lowest, for those of you who are wondering.

One of Galton's biographers has described his ideas related to eugenics thus: "Rarely in the history of science has a generalization been made on the basis of so little concrete evidence, so badly put, and so naively conceived" (Cowan, 1985, p. 9). Galton rarely read scientific works and owned a very small library of books that mostly appeared to have never been read (Cowan, 1985). Perversely, his efforts were taken quite seriously by the scientific community and the educated public, leading Galton's concept of eugenics to burgeon into a way of thinking about disability that has threatened the existence of persons with disabilities ever since. Eugenics has been aptly described as "a rationale for atrocities" (Gray, 1999, p. 84).

In a series of curiously popular books, such as 1869's *Hereditary Genius: An Inquiry into Its Laws and Consequences,* Galton wrote of the need to eliminate what he viewed as undesirable elements through "selection of a permanent breed" of humans like purebred dogs or horses (p. 1). Along with reinforcing the rampant racism and sexism of the day, Galton advocated raising the standards of humankind by weeding out the elements that he felt were unfit, specifically persons with disabilities. Other books Galton wrote that promoted the "science" of eugenics included *Inquiry into Human Faculty* (1883) and *Natural Inheritance* (1889). The clear purpose of eugenics was to help along evolution by "reducing the number of individuals that natural selection will have to eliminate" (Levine, 2002, p. 118). Galton's followers extended his ideas to some jaw-dropping proposals. One author, for example, advocated treating unfit people the same way unfit horses are treated in the book *The Right to be Well Born or Horse Breeding in its Relation to Eugenics* (Stokes, 1917).

These biased and unscientific theories became popular in the late nineteenth and early twentieth centuries in many parts of the world under the influence of Europe. The ideas particularly took root in the United States, leading to many disturbing proposals by legislators and policymakers. Some of these upsetting ideas included placing all individuals with disabilities on islands by themselves (isolated by gender), permanently locking away all individuals with disabilities in institutions, or segregating them from the rest of society in an isolated part of a sparsely populated state (Jaeger & Bowman, 2002; Winzer, 1993). Industrialist Andrew Carnegie funded a laboratory for the study of eugenics (Ridley, 1999). In Britain, local eugenics societies were commonplace by 1900 and the name Eugene was increasingly popular (Ridley, 1999). Marie Stopes, a pioneering advocate for birth control and women's rights in Britain, also embraced eugenics, calling for the sterilization of one third of the English male population, and disowned her own son for marrying a woman who wore glasses (Cohen, 1993; Vinen, 2000). Denmark, Norway, and Sweden soon after passed compulsory sterilization laws for persons with disabilities (Vinen, 2000). As a result of the eugenics movement, public perceptions soon associated disability with a range of degenerate and antisocial behaviors (Shorter, 2000).

The theory of eugenics led to some truly horrifying laws in the United States. In 1914, the University of Washington and a self-proclaimed Foundation for Child Welfare conducted a study of the laws of the 49 states, territories, and the District of Columbia concerning individuals with disabilities (Smith, Wilkinson, & Wagoner, 1914). The results are a parade of discrimination, brutal oppression, and dehumanization, though the authors make no comments about the upsetting nature of the laws, demonstrating the social approval for them. Of the 49 jurisdictions, 38 had laws prohibiting marriage for individuals with various types of disabilities, either completely or until the woman was past the age of reproduction, a violation of which would result in imprisonment in many cases (Smith et al., 1914). Twelve of the states had detailed laws dictating the "asexualization" of individuals with many types of disabilities (pp. 16–33). Most states had laws mandating the institutionalization or banishment of individuals with any one of a number of physical, emotional, and mental disabilities to euphemistically named "villages" (Smith et al., 1914). Around the same time, the first suggestions were made for the performance of lobotomies, the surgical destruction of a portion of the brain, on individuals with mental disabilities (Noll, 1995; Shorter, 2000). The United States was not the only country to establish these types of eugenics-based involuntary sterilization and segregation laws; Australia, Canada, and most nations of Europe did as well (Baker, 2002; Bulmer, 2003; Ridley, 1999; Vinen, 2000).

For many believers in eugenics, "feeble-mindedness" had to be combated through sterilization, regardless of whether the law provided legal permission. In these cases, feeble-mindedness was used as a catchall term to encompass most disabilities. The vasectomy was actually developed by a doctor in Indiana as a more efficient means of sterilizing males with disabilities; this doctor alone would ultimately perform 600 to 700 vasectomies on males with disabilities against their will (Burgdorf, 1980). Sterilization procedures were most likely to be performed on women and on the poor (Noll, 1995). In 1916 and 1917, one institution in Virginia performed hysterectomies on 80 patients with disabilities without any legal grounds for doing so (Noll, 1995). In many states that had sterilization laws, the laws have never been formally removed from the books or struck down by courts (Pfeiffer, 1999).

The sterilization of persons with disabilities was even memorialized through early films. In the 1920s, a motion picture titled *The Black Stork* dramatized the real-life crusade of one doctor who thought that children with disabilities should be "treated" with euthanasia rather than medical attention (Pernick, 1997). From 1922 to 1937, the U.S. Public Health Service released *The Science of Life*, a set of twelve filmstrips for use in high school biology classes that equated disability to many forms of death and ugliness, including seriously ill livestock, and promoted the notion of the elimination of persons with disabilities (Pernick, 1997). Eugenics, however, did have a few prominent critics, like legal crusader Clarence Darrow and journalist Walter Lippmann, who actively campaigned against eugenics laws and policies (Richards, 1987).

For states that legally sanctioned sterilization, it was commonly viewed as very important work. A North Carolina state official asserted in a medical journal article that sterilization was "an extremely important part of any well-rounded program for combating the problems of mental deficiency and disease" (Lawrence, 1947, p. 24). Sterilization was accomplished through many different means, including removal of reproductive organs, blasting areas of the body with tremendously high levels of X-ray radiation, or directly injecting the reproductive organs with radium (Noll, 1995; Proctor, 2002). Obviously, the negative health consequences often extended far beyond infertility. Many victims of these sterilization procedures were not even told what had been done to them (Gould, 1996). The Supreme Court of the United States upheld the legality of these practices so that the United States would not be "swamped with incompetence" and to "prevent those who are manifestly unfit from continuing their kind" (*Buck v. Bell*, 1927, p. 207).

The eugenics-based assault on persons with disabilities represents perhaps the most concerted attempt in history to eradicate disability from society, most notably in Nazi Germany. The Nazis persecuted and wantonly killed members of many groups—Jews, political dissidents, intellectuals, gypsies, gays, Jehovah's Witnesses, Poles, Slavs, and many others. Persons with disabilities, in particular, were targeted by the Nazi regime for utter annihilation. In 1933, shortly after the Nazis assumed power, they passed a law designed to forcibly sterilize persons with a range of disabilities. The text of this law was, sadly, heavily influenced by the eugenics laws of California (Reilly, 1991). The German law was extremely thorough, mandating the sterilization of people with mental disabilities, mental illnesses, epilepsy, deafness, blindness, physical deformities, and alcoholism, among other conditions (Friedlander, 1995, 1999). In 1934, 181 Hereditary Health Courts were established to deliberate cases of whether specific individuals should be sterilized under the law, while in the same year the German Medical Association established a scholarly journal devoted to issues of who should be sterilized (Friedlander, 2002). In 1935, a subsequent law prevented persons with disabilities from marrying (Friedlander, 1995, 1999). These laws basically removed persons with disabilities from most social roles.

The sterilization laws created a new scientific and medical field in Germany, with manufacturers working to create new sterilization tools and 180 medical student dissertations being devoted to advances in sterilization (Proctor, 2002). These laws led to the sterilization of over 375,000 to 400,000 persons with disabilities in Germany alone (Friedlander, 2002; Reilly, 1991). The sterilization efforts of Germany in the 1930s did not go unnoticed in the United States, with officials of some states publicly lauding Germany's efforts (Noll, 1995).

The Nazi killing spree of persons with disabilities actually began in 1939, starting with children and infants with disabilities (Biesold, 1999). These activities, known as the T4 program, quickly came to include the murder of adults with disabilities in hospitals, sanitariums, institutions, schools, prisons, and concentration camps in Germany and all occupied territories (Biesold, 1999). Physicians and scientists harvested the internal organs of many of the victims for research (Friedlander, 2002; Proctor, 2002). The families of those put to death were informed by letter that their loved ones had died from a brief, highly contagious illness that necessitated that the bodies be immediately cremated and their effects destroyed (Biesold, 1999; Friedlander, 1999). The T4 program resulted in the forced abortions of uncounted fetuses and the slaughter of hundreds of thousands of children and adults with disabilities by means of starvation, lethal injections, the gas chamber, and overdoses of medication (Friedlander, 1995, 1999; Reilly, 1991).

In the mid to late 1930s, international support for sterilization began to wane. New scientific advances in biology, medicine, and other natural sciences began to undermine the principles of eugenics (Heberer, 2002). Sterilization and other eugenics-based "treatments" still had many proponents in the international scientific community, though. In 1935, a Nobel laureate argued for euthanasia for criminals and the mentally ill in a popular book, and the first lobotomy was performed (Proctor, 2002). In 1942, the *Journal of the American Psychiatric Association* published an article that argued for the killing of children with mental disabilities (Kennedy, 1942). Most of the remaining international support for eugenic theories, however, was obliterated by the revelations of Nazi war crimes (Friedlander, 2002).

California, Virginia, and North Carolina would ultimately perform the most forced sterilizations of persons with disabilities in the United States (Noll, 1995). Tens upon tens of thousands of sterilization procedures were performed between the mid-1800s and the 1970s in the United States (Pfeiffer, 1999). Involuntary eugenic sterilizations also continued to occur in Canada, Sweden, and Scandinavia into the 1970s (Gillham, 2001). To this day, China continues to perform involuntary sterilizations of persons with certain disabilities (Bulmer, 2003). Ultimately, the greatest horror of eugenics may be rooted in the fact that it used the full compulsive power of the state to completely rob persons with disabilities of the fundamental sanctity of their own bodies.

Eugenics clearly demonstrates the far-reaching consequences of negative classifications of disability.

CIVIL RIGHTS FOR INDIVIDUALS WITH DISABILITIES

The rise of industrialization did finally serve to create a sustained social awareness of disability and related issues in the early twentieth century. Industrial accidents and occupational hazards began to make physical disability a growing social concern. In the early 1900s, more than 500,000 members of the working-age population in the United States had a physical disability as a result of their work, with an average of 14,000 more workers joining those ranks each year (Zola, 1994). The trade union movement and workers' rights groups began to push for compensation for workers who suffered disabling injuries on the job; by 1920, almost every state in the United States had some form of compensation legislation (Zola, 1994). World War I created further attention to physical disability, as more than 123,000 Americans returned home with a physical disability (Gritzer & Arluke, 1985). In European nations, the numbers of persons with disabilities from the war were much greater. Germany, for example, was providing pensions for more than 750,000 veterans with war-related disabilities ten years after the end of the war (Vinen, 2000). This move to help veterans with disabilities, however, was not focused on integrating those with disabilities into society through education and health services, but rather compensating them for their lost wages and working potential (Frey, 1984). The respect for veterans with disabilities after World War I was socially limited, as well. A prominent British war hero with a combat related disability, Siegfried Sassoon, was forcibly confined to a mental institution after issuing a philosophical tract decrying the irrationality of war (Vinen, 2000).

Occasional disability rights protests did occur in the early twentieth century, such as a 1935 protest against disability discrimination by Depression-era work-relief programs (Longmore, 2003). The issue of disability was certainly becoming more pronounced in United States society by the 1950s.

Medical advances allowed many soldiers to survive World War II who would have previously died from their injuries, helped many people recover from polio, and increased survival rates for many other illnesses and injuries (Barnartt & Scotch, 2001). The end result was an increase in the number of people in the population who had some kind of disability, as people who would have previously died from many maladies now survived with a disability (Barnartt & Scotch, 2001).

Individuals with disabilities, however, continued to be socially classified as irrelevant for most of the twentieth century. For example, in the early twentieth century, some parents still were selling their children with disabilities to sideshows, freak shows, and circuses (Switzer, 2003). Randolph Bourne, a disciple of John Dewey, who had severe physical disabilities, was writing and arguing in the early part of the twentieth century that America should lead the world in working to transcend cultural identity (Menand, 2001). Though his work discussed racial and ethnic characteristics, it is worth considering the impact of his disability on his desire to overcome social classifications. Individuals with disabilities clearly were saddled with undesirable and unfortunate social classifications until the late twentieth century.

The presence of defined legal rights can be very powerful as a social classification by creating protections under the law and as a social symbol by acknowledging the importance of including a specific group of people. For persons with disabilities, the quest for legal rights was a quest to fulfill the goals of legal protection and social acknowledgment. Through the 1960s, the twentieth century had evidenced an increasing humanization in society of some persons with disabilities. However, social actions and attitudes reinforced the perception of persons with disabilities as "dependent, unhealthy deviants, who would, in the great majority, always require segregated care and protection" (Funk, 1987, p. 14).

Inspired by the civil rights movements for racial and gender equality of the 1950s and 1960s, persons with disabilities became very active in battling for legal rights in the early 1970s. The roots of the disability rights movement developed from many social and legal changes of the 1960s. In 1962, the family of President Kennedy began to publicly address issues of disability, including the fact that the president's sister had a disability (Shorter, 2000). This act began to remove some of the social stigma associated with discussing issues of disability (Shorter, 2000). Returning Vietnam veterans with disabilities provided prevalent public faces for disability, while the passage of civil rights statutes for other segments of the public spurred organization and feelings of identification between persons with disabilities (Barnartt & Scotch, 2001).

In 1971, a court held for the first time that students with disabilities had a constitutional right to receive a public education. In *Pennsylvania Association for Retarded Children (PARC) v. Commonwealth of Pennsylvania* (1971), a federal district court held that the exclusion of children with disabilities from public school was unconstitutional. Since the state had the expressed goal of providing a free public education to all the children in the state, Pennsylvania could not deny students with disabilities access to free public education. The ground breaking *PARC* ruling immediately inspired disability rights groups in 36 other states to file suits against their state governments (Spring, 1993).

In 1973, the federal government passed the first law to grant specific, affirmative legal rights to individuals with disabilities—Section 504 of the Rehabilitation Act. Section 504 was different from any previous laws that addressed disability, as it established "full social participation as a civil right" and represented a "transformation" of the legal rights of individuals with disabilities (Scotch, 2001, p. 3). The requirement that recipients of federal funds were barred from discriminating against individuals with disabilities was based on the requirements of the Civil Rights Act, which prohibited recipients of federal funds from discriminating based on race, color, or national origin. Also like the Civil Rights Act, Section 504 was intended to prevent both intentional and unintentional discrimination.

In 1973, President Nixon signed the Rehabilitation Act into law and then did absolutely nothing to implement or enforce the law. For the law to be effective, regulations and guidelines regarding requirements and enforcement had to be created by the Department of Health, Education, and Welfare (Bowe, 1979; Fleischer & Zames, 2001; Jaeger & Bowman, 2002; Scotch, 2001). After Section 504 was passed, legal scholars were still writing articles that legitimately spoke of a lack of federal government protections of persons with disabilities to receive even a minimal education (Handel, 1975; McClung, 1974; Stick, 1976). A 1976 lawsuit against the government began the chain of events that would lead to the enforcement of Section 504; in its holding, the court noted that Section 504 was not likely to implement or enforce itself (*Cherry v. Matthews,* 1976). Even a court order, however, did not get the Ford administration to start work on guidelines for Section 504; on the day the court order was issued, the executive branch immediately tried to send the matter back to Congress (Fleischer & Zames, 2001).

The problem was left for the Carter administration to address, an administration that continued to avoid the issue after taking office. These further delays spurred a series of protests by disability rights activists, including wheelchair blockades of certain government offices and of the home driveway of the Secretary of Health, Education, and Welfare, who had been threatening to issue guidelines that removed most of the power of the law (Fleischer & Zames, 2001; Shapiro, 1993). The government had also been holding closed-door meetings about the guidelines with a review committee that had no representation of disability organizations or members with disabilities (Longmore, 2003).

The protest in the San Francisco office of the Department of Health, Education, and Welfare lasted the longest, with 60 individuals with numerous types of disabilities staying 25 days and leaving only after the Section 504 regulations had been signed (Shapiro, 1993). The events that occurred during the demonstrations emphasized the bias that the protestors were fighting against. The government officials decided that the demonstrators should receive no food and should not be allowed communication outside the offices at each of the protests, while the Health, Education, and Welfare officials treated the demonstrators as misbehaving children, offering punch and cookies as a bribe to leave (Heumann, 1979; Shapiro, 1993). The demonstrators in San Francisco faced perhaps the most demeaning treatment, with a registered nurse being assigned to stay with the demonstrators to make sure they could look after themselves (Fleischer & Zames, 2001).

During their 25-day stay, the protestors in San Francisco gained national attention for the issue and received support from a wide range of people and organizations. United States Representatives Phillip Burton and George Miller ordered that food reach the demonstrators, and assistance flowed in from McDonald's, the California Department of Health Services, Safeway Markets, various unions, the Black Panthers, and San Francisco Mayor George Moscone, among others. A key event during the protests was a televised hearing held by Burton and Miller on the issue, to which the Department of Health, Education, and Welfare sent a low-ranking assistant to explain the delays (Longmore, 2003). The assistant reported that 22 major changes had to be made to the regulations before they would be promulgated, including the creation of exemptions to the requirements for accessibility features (such as ramps) for schools and hospitals, and the astounding change of not including students with disabilities in general education classrooms (Longmore, 2003). The impact of the protests, coupled with the increasingly untenable stance of the administration, finally forced the promulgation of the Section 504 guidelines. The first guidelines for Section 504, which did not dilute the impact of the law, finally were signed on April 28, 1977, and were formally issued on May 4, 1977.

The success of these protests also inspired subsequent disability rights protests. In the past 25 years, major disability rights protests have focused on issues related to education, funding for services, access to buildings, access to transportation, social attitudes and awareness, and laws and policies (Barnartt & Scotch, 2001). Over time, however, the social impact of these protests seems to be decreasing, as public, political, and media attention to disability rights protests has decreased even though the number of protests has increased (Barnartt & Scotch, 2001).

The efforts of the U.S. federal government since the belated implementation of Section 504 of the Rehabilitation Act have placed it at the forefront of articulating legal rights for persons with disabilities. In 1990, Congress passed a second extensive set of legal rights for individuals with disabilities, the Americans with Disabilities Act (ADA). Though a diverse group of organizations, politicians, and businesses lobbied against the passage of the ADA (Fleischer & Zames, 2001), the law passed easily, creating the most extensive set of legal rights for individuals with disabilities anywhere in the world. A large part of the reason for the strength of the ADA was the concerted and organized efforts by a range of disability rights and advocacy groups to ensure its success. When he signed the act, then President George H. W. Bush proclaimed, "Let the shameful wall of exclusion finally come tumbling down" (quoted in Shapiro, 1993, p. 140).

The ADA prohibits discrimination and requires equal opportunity in employment, state and local government services, public accommodations, commercial facilities, and transportation. Basically, the ADA extends the protections created by the Rehabilitation Act to most elements of society. The ADA prohibits discrimination against persons with disabilities by various private and public institutions, including state governments, and provides a mechanism for legal protection and remedies. The ADA instructs local and state governments that "no qualified individual with a disability shall . . . be excluded from participation in or be denied the benefits of the services, programs, or activities of a public entity" (42 U.S.C.A. § 12132). The Rehabilitation Act provides the same protections for federal agencies and any agency receiving federal assistance. The ADA has been determined to protect access to and use of such disparate public entities as universities (*Darian v. University of Massachusetts Boston,* 1987), courts (*People v. Caldwell,* 1995), and prisons (*Saunders v. Horn,* 1996). The ADA also prohibits discrimination by private organizations providing public accommodations, which traditionally has included hotels, restaurants, offices, housing, and shopping centers, among many others.

Since the passage of the ADA, the U.S. government has worked to continue to expand legal rights of access to new and developing technologies to individuals with disabilities. The Telecommunications Act of 1996 requires makers and providers of telecommunications equipment and services to ensure products can be used by persons with disabilities. Section 508 of the Rehabilitation Act, implemented in 2001, requires that citizens with disabilities, including federal employees, have equal access to and use of information and communication technologies used by the government. Section 508 establishes that the software applications, operating systems, Web-based information and applications, telecommunications products, video and multimedia products, self-contained or closed products, desktop computers, and portable computers of the government and organizations receiving federal funding must be accessible to individuals with disabilities. The requirements of Section 508 are extremely important to guaranteeing the delivery of technology-based information and services from the government in an equal manner for persons with disabilities.

However, despite the passage of disability rights laws and the increased role in parts of society for individuals with disabilities, there are many places where the laws clearly have not yet caused significant changes. For example, the ADA, though intended to dramatically increase the presence of individuals with disabilities in the workplace, has had limited success in this area, due to limited enforcement by the federal government and continuing lack of equal access to new information and communication technologies (Hignite, 2000; Kruse & Hale, 2003; Kruse & Schur, 2003; Lee, 2003; Wells, 2001). The Internet . . . appears to be in danger of becoming another area where the laws are not having the desired impact.

In many professions, persons with disabilities are still a rarity. Individuals with disabilities have had to fight for an equal right to attend highly specialized professional programs, like medical school and law school, and to take professional licensing exams, like the medical boards or the bar exam. Given the continued scarcity of persons with disabilities in many fields, some lack of understanding and some outright bias are hardly unexpected. However, that occasional bias can be presented in some unique ways.

While in law school, Kevin, who had an obvious disability, was asked by one of the professors to come to his office for an important discussion. Kevin did not know this professor well, so he was curious about the reasons. At the professor's office, the professor said he needed to advise Kevin not to plan on practicing law as a career. After expressing that he was only being helpful, the professor explained that he felt persons with disabilities should not be lawyers because they would only be detrimental to their clients. The professor believed that persons with disabilities would not win many court cases because juries would not be sympathetic to a client who could only afford to hire "a defective." Anyway, someone with a disability would not have the capacity to work hard enough to be a successful lawyer. After the professor had finished, Kevin left his office and found himself less angry than amazed at the lengths people will go to try to disguise their own prejudices.

THE SUPREME COURT AND DISABILITY RIGHTS

The U.S. Supreme Court, unfortunately, has been curtailing the efforts of the Congress on behalf of individuals with disabilities for more than two decades. Since 1982, the Supreme Court has been acting to limit the rights of individuals with disabilities that Congress establishes. The basic theme throughout these cases is that the Supreme Court does not believe that persons with disabilities merit the same legal rights as other minority groups. The Supreme Court first tempered the Individuals with Disabilities Education Act in 1982 by holding that the law did not mandate that a student with a disability be provided the most effective form of assistance possible to improve his or her chance of receiving an equal education. Instead, the Supreme Court decided schools are only required to provide some educational assistance to make the educational environment more conducive to learning for the student. Three years later in *City of Cleburne v. City of Cleburne Living Center, Inc.* (1985), the Supreme Court addressed the rights of persons with disabilities to seek general legal protection as a group. The court concluded that disability did not merit the same level of constitutional protection as race, gender, national origin, and other group characteristics.

The Supreme Court's next major limitation of the rights of individuals with disabilities came in 1999 with a set of cases issued on the same day. *Albertsons, Inc. v. Kirkingburg* (1999), *Murphy v. United Parcel Service* (1999), and *Sutton v. United Air Lines, Inc.* (1999) established a new limitation on who qualifies for protection under disability laws. These cases created the standard that an individual can only qualify for legal protection under disability rights law if that individual is limited in a major life activity after the maximum corrections and mitigating measures are taken. For example, a person cannot be considered to have a disability under the ADA for having profound loss of eyesight if that sight problem can be corrected into the normal range through lenses or surgery. In *Sutton,* the court wrote: "Congress did not intend to bring under the protection of the ADA all those whose uncorrected conditions amount to disabilities" (p. 475). This set of cases places a burden on persons with disabilities to prove that they still have a disability in spite of whatever corrective measures might exist. If an individual has a profound loss that cannot be corrected into the normal range with any available measures, then that individual qualifies for protection under the law. The individual, however, may have to demonstrate that he or she has a disability no matter what corrective measures are taken.

In 2001, the Supreme Court significantly limited the scope of the ADA. In *Board of Trustees of the University of Alabama v. Garrett,* the Supreme Court modified the ADA with regard to employment actions by state governments. The court held that state governments were not liable to suit for monetary damages under the ADA for employment discrimination based on disability, but still could be forced to comply with the act. Though this may not sound like a large difference, the effect is sizeable. Instead of having to pay monetary damages for violating the employment rights of persons with disabilities, state governments now must only contend with being told to stop discriminating by the courts. Perhaps most disturbing is the fact that the majority opinion in this case treats the history of discrimination against persons with disabilities as if it was relatively innocuous and inconsequential, dismissing it as anecdotal and exaggerated.

In 2002, the court went a step further in chipping away at the rights of individuals with disabilities (National Council on Disability, 2003a, p. 2). In the holding of *Toyota v. Williams* (2002), the Supreme Court constricted the definitions of disability under the ADA, limiting the coverage of the law exclusively to people who met the strictest meanings of its definition of disability. While the definitions in all other types of civil rights laws are interpreted broadly, the court held that the ADA must be "interpreted strictly to create a demanding standard for qualifying as disabled" (pp. 197–198). In 2004, one Supreme Court opinion (*Tennessee v. Lane*) at least countered the trend of limiting the scope of the ADA by holding that the ADA did definitely guarantee equal access to the courts in the United States.

These decisions by the Supreme Court have evidenced a clear intent to limit disability rights laws as much as possible, though Congress, in passing the laws, meant them to be interpreted broadly (National Council on Disability, 2002). The decisions also have resulted in considerable bias in favor of the defendant in any discrimination claims under the ADA (Burgdorf, 1997; Colker, 1999; Feldblum, 2000; Tucker, 2000). A further result of these decisions has been a wave of lower federal court decisions that make it much more difficult for people to prove that they have a disability that substantially limits a major life activity, to establish that they have taken all the possible mitigating measures, to prove they have been discriminated against, and to show that they fall within the definition of disability (National Council on Disability, 2003b). Ultimately, the Supreme Court decisions have also had a chilling effect on claims brought under disability rights laws, significantly reducing the number of claims that are even filed because many persons with disabilities now assume the courts are biased against them (National Council on Disability, 2003b).

Some state governments are actively working to counter the holdings of the Supreme Court that limit who qualifies as having a disability. Though the majority of state governments have modified their state disability rights laws to mirror the Supreme Court limitations on the rights of individuals with disabilities, California, Connecticut, Massachusetts, New Jersey, New York, Rhode Island, Washington, and West Virginia have not. California and Rhode Island have actually amended their state laws to explicitly reject federal case law that limits who is protected by disability rights laws, while the Supreme Courts of Massachusetts and West Virginia have both recently rejected the U.S. Supreme Court holdings related to disability (National Council on Disability, 2003a).

DISABILITY AS A GROWING WORLDWIDE ISSUE

The worldwide population of persons with disabilities is estimated to be as many as 550 million, but only 15 percent of persons with disabilities have had a disability since birth (Albrecht & Verbugge, 2000; Metts, 2000). As such, disability is an emerging global issue that "will be on the rise for many decades to come, fueled by population aging, environmental factors, and social violence" (Albrecht & Verbugge, 2000, p. 305). The population of persons with disabilities is expected to rise in both technologically advanced nations and less developed nations (Priestley, 2001). Though social attitudes toward persons with disabilities have improved, individuals with disabilities are still very much a minority in status and social power the

world over. "Disabled people are marginalized and excluded from mainstream society. . . . Disabled people definitely represent one of the poorest groups in Western society" (Kitchin, 1998, p. 343).

In many less developed nations, persons with disabilities literally are at the bottom of society, being described, without exaggeration, as "the poorest and most powerless people on earth" (Charlton, 1998, p. 25). In various less developed nations at this time, persons with disabilities often are deprived of education, abandoned, left in the care of inadequate state services, trained as beggars, prevented from marrying, sterilized, or even subject to infanticide or other forms of extermination (Charlton, 1998; Priestley, 2001). Persons with disabilities are so marginalized that in some societies they are treated as if they do not exist. In India, persons with disabilities are not included in the national census (Ghai, 2001). There are few greater denials of personhood than being informed that your existence is not relevant to the national census.

The nations that have created legal protections for individuals with disabilities remain in the minority (Metts, 2000). In spite of the still significant social barriers discussed in this chapter, individuals with disabilities may have more legally defined rights in the United States than anywhere else. The passage of Section 504 of the Rehabilitation Act, the Individuals with Disabilities Education Act, and the ADA place the United States in the vanguard of disability rights in the international community. Many nations, along with the United Nations, have developed laws, regulations, and policies that were inspired and influenced by the ADA. These nations have developed laws that take a range of approaches to disability rights (Blanck, Hill, Siegal, & Waterstone, 2003; Jones & Marks, 1999).

A plethora of nations, including Australia, Austria, Brazil, Denmark, Finland, Germany, Malawi, the Philippines, South Africa, Sweden, and Uganda, adopted laws or amended their constitutions in the 1990s to provide the first real legal rights for individuals with disabilities (Metts, 2000). Some emphasize defining who qualifies as having a disability, while others focus on reducing barriers to social inclusion as a result of disability (National Council on Disability, 2003a). Zimbabwe passed a law in 1992 prohibiting any social, cultural, or physical barriers to equal participation for individuals with disabilities. Australia passed a law in 1993 outlawing discrimination on the basis of specific disabilities. Venezuela adopted a law in 1994 that protects individuals with disabilities from being socially excluded as a result of a disability. In 1995, the United Kingdom passed its disability rights law, which is deeply indebted to, but not nearly as far-reaching as, the ADA. While the law does establish basic legal rights for individuals with disabilities in the United Kingdom, it has been criticized for being too limited (Doyle, 1996, 1997; Gooding, 1996). Though the legal rights established by these laws vary greatly, each represents a step forward in the effort to gain and preserve equal rights for individuals with disabilities around the world.

The United Nations (1994) has adopted the *Standard Rules on the Equalization of Opportunities for Persons with Disabilities*. These rules, which have no force of law, established basic standards that nations were encouraged to adopt to provide equal opportunities to individuals with disabilities, including rights to equal participation and rights to education and rehabilitation. The rules were partially based on an early United Nations (1982) declaration called the *World Programme of Action Concerning Disabled Persons* that argued for taking preventative actions to limit future cases of disability (such as improved health care, better diet, and limiting armed conflicts) and increasing participation in society for individuals with disabilities. The European Union (1996) has also adopted general disability guidelines that are intended to function as rules for European Union activities and basic guides for the laws of all member nations. The European Community, the predecessor of the European Union, first formally acknowledged the need for the guarantee of legal rights for persons with disabilities in 1986 (Daunt, 1991). The European Union even declared 2003 to be the Year of the Disabled in the European Union, though the accompanying activities seemed primarily designed to promote awareness of what was already happening in the nations of Europe rather than pressing for positive change in the social treatment or civil rights of individuals with disabilities.

These changes in attitudes toward persons with disabilities, however, are far from widely accepted in many parts of the world. Evidence of ingrained social classifications that are not changing can be found in the language used to describe persons with disabilities. In many regions of the world, socially accepted terms still used to identify persons with disabilities translate into useless, helpless, deserving punishment, inability to do anything for oneself, and many other terms that serve to marginalize and disempower (Charlton, 1998).

★ ★ ★

REFERENCES

1. *Albertsons, Inc. v. Kirkingburg*, 527 U.S. 555 (1999).
2. Albrecht, G. L. (1992). *The disability business: Rehabilitation in America*. Newbury Park, CA: Sage.
3. Albrecht, G. L., & Verbugge, L. M. (2000). The global emergence of disability. In G. L. Albrecht, R. Fitzpatrick, & S. C. Scrimshaw (Eds.), *The handbook of social studies in health and medicine* (pp. 293–307). London: Sage.
4. Baker, B. (2002). The hunt for disability: The new eugenics and the normalization of school children. *Teachers College Record, 10*(4), 663–703.
5. Barnartt, S., & Scotch, R. (2001). *Disability protests: Contentious politics 1970–1999*. Washington, DC: Gallaudet University Press.
6. *Bartlett v. New York State Board of Law Examiners*, 790 F. Supp. 1094 (S.D.N.Y. 1997).
7. Biesold, H. (1999). *Crying hands: Eugenics and deaf people in Nazi Germany* (W. Sayers, Trans.). Washington, DC: Gallaudet University Press. (Original work published in 1988).
8. Blanck, P. D., Hill, E., Siegal, C. D., & Waterstone, M. (2003). *Disability civil rights law and policy*. St. Paul, MN: Thomson/West.
9. *Board of Trustees of the University of Alabama v. Garrett*, 531 U.S. 356 (2001).
10. Bogdan, R. (1988). *Freak show: Presenting human oddities for amusement and profit*. Chicago: University of Chicago Press.
11. Bowe, F. (1979). Handicapping America: Barriers to disabled people. In J. P. Hourihan (Ed.), *Disability: Our challenge* (pp. 87–106). New York: Teachers College Press.
12. Braddock, D. L., & Parish, S. L. (2001). An institutional history of disability. In G. L. Albrecht, K. D. Seelman, & M. Bury (Eds.), *Handbook of disability studies* (pp. 11–68). Thousand Oaks, CA: Sage.

13. Bragg, L. (1997). From the mute god to the lesser god: Disability in medieval Celtic and Old Norse literature. *Disability and Society, 12,* 165–177.

14. Branson, J., & Miller, D. (2002). *Damned for their difference: The cultural construction of deaf people as disabled.* Washington, DC: Gallaudet University Press.

15. *Brown v. Board of Education,* 347 U.S. 483 (1954).

16. Brown, T. J. (1998). *Dorothea Dix: New England reformer.* Cambridge, MA: Harvard University Press.

17. Bryan, W. V. (1996). *In search of freedom: How persons with disabilities have been disenfranchised from the mainstream of American society.* Springfield, IL: Charles C. Thomas.

18. *Buck v. Bell,* 274 U.S. 200 (1927).

19. Bulmer, M. (2003). *Francis Galton: Pioneer in heredity and biometry.* Baltimore: Johns Hopkins University Press.

20. Burgdorf, R. L. (Ed.). (1980). *The legal rights of handicapped persons.* Baltimore: Paul H. Brookes.

21. Burgdorf, R. L. (1997). "Substantially limited" protection from disability discrimination: The special treatment model and misconstructions of the definition of disability. *Villanova Law Review, 42,* 409–585.

22. Charlton, J. I. (1998). *Nothing about us without us: Disability oppression and empowerment.* Berkeley: University of California Press.

23. *Cherry v. Matthews,* 419 F. Supp. 922 (D.D.C. 1976).

24. *City of Cleburne v. City of Cleburne Living Center, Inc.,* 473 U.S. 432 (1985).

25. Civil Rights Act, 42 U.S.C.A. sec. 1971 *et seq.* (1964).

26. Cohen, D. A. (1993). Private lives in public spaces: Marie Stopes, the mothers' clinic and the practice of contraception. *History Workshop, 35,* 95–116.

27. Colker, R. (1999). The Americans with Disabilities Act: A windfall for defendants. *Harvard Civil Rights-Civil Liberties Law Review, 34,* 99–162.

28. Covey, H. C. (1998). *Social perceptions of people with disabilities in history.* Springfield, IL: Charles C. Thomas.

29. Cowan, R. S. (1985). *Sir Francis Galton and the study of heredity in the nineteenth century.* New York: Garland.

30. *Craig v. Boren,* 429 U.S. 190 (1976).

31. Dahl, R. A. (1998). *On democracy.* New Haven, CT: Yale University Press.

32. Dahl, R. A. (2001). *How democratic is the American Constitution?* New Haven, CT: Yale University Press.

33. Daniels, M. (1997). *Benedictine roots in the development of deaf education: Listening with the heart.* Westport, CT: Bergin and Garvey.

34. *Darian v. University of Massachusetts Boston,* 980 F. Supp. 77 (D.Mass. 1987).

35. Daunt, P. (1991). *Meeting disability: A European response.* London: Cassell Education.

36. Davis, L. J. (1997). Constructing normalcy: The bell curve, the novel, and the invention of the disabled body in the nineteenth century. In L. J. Davis (Ed.), *The disability studies reader* (pp. 9–29). New York: Routledge.

37. De Hamel, C. (1994). *A history of illuminated manuscripts* (2nd ed.). New York: Phaidon Press.

38. Doyle, B. (1996). *Disability discrimination: The new law.* Bristol, UK: Jordans.

39. Doyle, B. (1997). Enabling legislation or dissembling law? The Disability Discrimination Act 1995. *Modern Law Review, 60*(1), 64–78.

40. Durant, W. (1944). *Caesar and Christ.* New York: Simon and Schuster.

41. Edwards, M. L. (1997). Deaf and dumb in ancient Greece. In L. Davis (Ed.), *The disability studies reader* (pp. 29–51). New York: Routledge.

42. Eisenberg, M. G. (1982). Disability as stigma. In M. G. Eisenberg, C. Griggins, & R. J. Duval (Eds.), *Disabled people as second-class citizens* (pp. 3–12). New York: Springer.

43. European Union. (1996). *Resolution of the council and the representatives of the governments of the member states of inequality of opportunity for people with disabilities.* Official Journal 13.01.1997. Brussels: Author.

44. European Union. (2001). *E-inclusion: The information society's potential for social inclusion in Europe.* Available: http://europa.eu.int/comm/employment_social/soc-dial/info_soc/esdis/eincl_en.pdf.

45. Fay, G. O. (1899). Hartford and the education of the deaf. *American Annals of the Deaf, 44,* 419.

46. Feldblum, C. (2000). Definition of disability under federal anti-discrimination law: What happened? why? and what can we do about it? *Berkeley Journal of Employment and Labor Law, 21,* 91–165.

47. Fleischer, D. Z., & Zames, F. (2001). *The disability rights movement: From charity to confrontation.* Philadelphia: Temple University Press.

48. Foucault, M. (1965). *Madness and civilization: A history of insanity in the age of reason* (Richard Howard, Trans.). New York: Vintage.

49. French, R. S. (1932). *From Homer to Helen Keller: A social and educational study of the blind.* New York: American Foundation for the Blind.

50. Frey, W. (1984). Functional assessment in the '80s: A conceptual enigma, a technical challenge. In A. S. Halporn & M. J. Fuhrer (Eds.), *Functional assessment in rehabilitation* (pp. 11–43). Baltimore: Paul H. Brookes.

51. Friedlander, H. (1995). *The origins of Nazi genocide: From euthanasia to the final solution.* Chapel Hill: University of North Carolina Press.

52. Friedlander, H. (1999). Introduction. In H. Biesold, *Crying hands: Eugenics and deaf people in Nazi Germany* (pp. 1–12). Washington, DC: Gallaudet University Press.

53. Friedlander, H. (2002). Holocaust studies and the deaf community. In D. F. Ryan & J. S. Schuchman (Eds.), *Deaf people in Hitler's Europe* (pp. 15–31). Washington, DC: Gallaudet University Press.

54. Funk, R. (1987). Disability rights: From caste to class in the context of civil rights. In A. Gartner & T. Joe (Eds.), *Images of the disabled, disabling images* (pp. 7–30). New York: Praeger.

55. *Galloway v. Superior Court of District of Columbia,* 816 F. Supp. 12 (D.D.C. 1993).

56. Galton, F. (1883). *Inquiry into human faculty and its developments.* London: Macmillan.

57. Galton, F. (1889). *Natural inheritance.* London: Macmillan.

58. Galton, F. (1978). *Hereditary genius: An inquiry into its laws and consequences.* New York: St. Martin's Press. (Original work published 1869)

59. Garland, R. (1995). *The eye of the beholder: Deformity and disability in the Graeco-Roman world.* Ithaca, NY: Cornell University Press.

60. Gaw, A. (1906). The development of the legal status of the deaf. *American Annals of the Deaf, 51,* 269–275, 401–423.

61. Gaw, A. (1907). The development of the legal status of the deaf. *American Annals of the Deaf, 52,* 1–12, 167–83, 229–245.

62. Ghai, A. (2001). Marginalisation and disability: Experiences from the third world. In M. Priestley (Ed.), *Disability and the life course: Global perspectives* (pp. 26–37). Cambridge: Cambridge University Press.

63. Gillham, N. W. (2001). *A life of Sir Francis Galton: From African exploration to the birth of eugenics.* Oxford: Oxford University Press.

64. Gooding, C. (1996). *Blackstone's guide to the Disability Discrimination Act of 1995.* London: Blackstone.

65. Gould, S. J. (1996). *The mismeasure of man* (rev. ed.). New York: Norton.

66. *Graham v. Richardson,* 403 U.S. 365 (1971).

67. Gray, P. (1999). Cursed by eugenics. *Time, 153*(1), 84–85.

68. Gritzer, G., & Arluke, A. (1985). *The making of rehabilitation: A political economy of medical specialization.* Berkeley, CA: University of California Press.

69. Handel, R. C. (1975). The role of the advocate in securing the handicapped child's right to an effective minimal education. *Ohio State Law Journal, 36,* 349–378.

70. Heberer, P. (2002). Targeting the "unfit" and radical public health strategies in Nazi Germany. In D. F. Ryan & J. S. Schuchman (Eds.), *Deaf people in Hitler's Europe* (pp. 49–70). Washington, DC: Gallaudet University Press.

71. Heumann, J. E. (1979). Handicap and disability. In J. P. Hourihan (Ed.), *Disability: Our challenge* (pp. 7–32). New York: Teachers College Press.

72. Hewett, F. (1974). *Education of exceptional learners.* Boston: Allyn and Bacon.

73. Hibbert, C. (1975). *The house of Medici.* New York: William Morrow.

74. Hignite, K. B. (2000). The accessible association. *Association Management, 52*(13), 36–43.

75. Individuals with Disabilities Education Act (IDEA), 20 U.S.C.A. § 1400 *et seq.* (1975).

76. Individuals with Disabilities Education Act (IDEA) regulations, 34 C.F.R. § 300 *et seq.*

77. Jaeger, P. T., & Bowman, C. A. (2002). *Disability matters: Legal and pedagogical issues of disability in education.* Westport, CT: Praeger.

78. Jones, M., & Marks, L. A. B. (Eds.). (1999). *Disability, divers-ability, and legal change.* Boston: Martinus Nijhoff.

79. Kanner, L. (1964). *A history of the care and study of the mentally retarded.* Springfield, IL: Charles C. Thomas.

80. Kennedy, F. (1942). The problem of social control of the congenitally defective: Education, sterilization, euthanasia. *Journal of the American Psychiatry Association, 99,* 13–16.

81. Kennedy, R. G. (2003). *Mr. Jefferson's lost cause: Land, farmers, slavery, and the Louisiana Purchase.* Oxford: Oxford University Press.

82. Kitchin, R. (1998). "Out of place," "knowing one's place": Space, power, and the exclusion of disabled people. *Disability and Society, 13,* 343–356.

83. *Korematsu v. United States,* 323 U.S. 214 (1944).

84. Kruse, D., & Hale, T. (2003). Disability and employment: Symposium introduction. Industrial Relations, *42,* 1–10.

85. Kruse, D., & Schur, L. (2003). Employment of people with disabilities following the ADA. *Industrial Relations, 42,* 31–66.

86. Lawrence, G. (1947). Some facts concerning sterilization based upon a study in Orange County, North Carolina. *North Carolina Medical Journal, 8,* 19–25.

87. Lee, B. A. (2003). A decade of the Americans with Disabilities Act: Judical outcomes and unresolved problems. *Industrial Relations, 42,* 11–30.

88. Levine, G. (2002). *Dying to know: Scientific epistemology and narrative in Victorian England.* Chicago: University of Chicago Press.

89. Loewen, J. W. (1995). *Lies my teacher told: Everything your American history textbook got wrong.* New York: Touchstone.

90. Longmore, P. K. (2003). *Why I burned my book and other essays on disability.* Philadelphia: Temple University Press.

91. McClung, M. (1974). Do handicapped children have a legal right to a minimally adequate education? *Journal of Law and Education, 3,* 153–173.

92. Menand, L. (2001). *The metaphysical club: A story of ideas in America.* New York: Farrar, Straus and Giroux.

93. Metts, R. L. (2000). *Disability issues, trends and recommendations for the World Bank.* Washington, DC: World Bank.

94. Morton, T. G. (1897). *The history of Pennsylvania Hospital 1751–1895.* Philadelphia: Times.

95. *Murphy v. United Parcel Service,* 527 U.S. 516 (1999).

96. National Council on Disability. (2002). *The Americans with Disabilities Act policy brief series: Righting the ADA—broad or narrow construction of the ADA.* Available: http://www.ncd.gov.

97. National Council on Disability. (2003a). *The Americans with Disabilities Act policy brief series: Righting the ADA—defining "disability" in a civil rights context: The court's focus on the extent of limitations as opposed to fair treatment and equal opportunity.* Available: http://www.ncd.gov.

98. National Council on Disability. (2003b). *The Americans with Disabilities Act policy brief series: Righting the ADA—the impact of the Supreme Court's ADA decisions on the rights of persons with disabilities.* Available: http://www.ncd.gov.

99. Noll, S. (1995). *Feeble-minded in our midst: institutions for the mentally retarded in the south, 1900–1940.* Chapel Hill: University of North Carolina Press.

100. *Pennsylvania Association for Retarded Children (PARC) v. Commonwealth of Pennsylvania*, 334 F. Supp. 1257 (E.D.Pa. 1971).
101. *People v. Caldwell*, 603 N.Y.S.2d 713 (N. Y. App. Term, 1995).
102. Pernick, M. S. (1997). Defining the defective: Eugenics, aesthetics, mass culture in early-twentieth-century America. In D. T. Mitchell & S. L. Snyder (Eds.), *The body and physical difference: Discourses of disability* (pp. 89–110). Ann Arbor: University of Michigan Press.
103. Pfeiffer, D. (1993). Overview of the disability movement: History, legislative record, and political implications. *Policy Studies Journal, 21*(4), 724–735.
104. Pfeiffer, D. (1999). Eugenics and disability discrimination. In R. P. Marinelli & A. E. Dell Orto (Eds.), *The psychological and social impact of disability* (4th ed., pp. 12–31). New York: Springer.
105. Priestley, M. (2001). Introduction: The global context of disability. In M. Priestley (Ed.), *Disability and the life course: Global perspectives* (pp. 3–14). Cambridge: Cambridge University Press.
106. Proctor, R. N. (2002). Eugenics in Hitler's Germany. In D. F. Ryan & J. S. Schuchman (Eds.), *Deaf people in Hitler's Europe* (pp. 32–48). Washington, DC: Gallaudet University Press.
107. Rehabilitation Act, 29 U.S.C.A. § 701 et seq. (1973).
108. Rehabilitation Act regulations, 34 C.F.R. § 104 et seq.
109. Reilly, P. R. (1991). *The surgical solution: A history of involuntary sterilization in the United States.* Baltimore: Johns Hopkins University Press.
110. Richards, R. J. (1987). *Darwin and the emergence of evolutionary theories of mind and behavior.* Chicago: University of Chicago Press.
111. Ridley, M. (1999). *Genome: The autobiography of a species in 23 chapters.* New York: HarperCollins.
112. Rosen, G. (1968). *Madness in society: Chapters in the historical sociology of mental illness.* Chicago: University of Chicago Press.
113. Salder, J. E. (1966). *J. A. Comenius and the concept of universal education.* New York: Barnes and Noble.
114. *Saunders v. Horn*, 959 F. Supp. 689 (E.D.Pa. 1996).
115. Scotch, R. K. (2001). *From goodwill to civil rights: Transforming federal disability policy* (2nd ed.). Philadelphia: Temple University Press.
116. Section 508 of the Rehabilitation Act, 29 U.S.C. § 794d. (1998).
117. Seguin, E. (1846). *The moral treatment, hygiene, and education of idiots and other backward children,* Paris: Bailliere.
118. Shapiro, J. P. (1993). *No pity: People with disabilities forging a new civil rights movement.* New York: Times Books.
119. Shapiro, J. P. (1994). Disability policy and the media: A stealth civil rights movement bypasses the press and defies conventional wisdom. *Policy Studies Journal, 22,* 123–133.
120. Shorter, E. (2000). *The Kennedy family and the story of mental retardation.* Philadelphia: Temple University Press.
121. Smith, D. D. (2001). Special education: Teaching in an age of opportunity. Boston: Allyn and Bacon.
122. Smith, S., Wilkinson, M. W., & Wagoner, L. C. (1914). *A summary of the laws of the several states governing marriage and divorce of the feebleminded, epileptic and the insane; asexualization; and institutional commitment and discharge of the feebleminded and the epileptic.* Seattle: University of Washington.
123. Spring, J. (1993). *Conflict of interests: The politics of American education* (2nd ed.). New York: Longman.
124. Stick, R. S. (1976). The handicapped child has a right to an appropriate education. *Nebraska Law Review, 55,* 637–682.
125. Stiker, H. J. (1999). *A history of disability* (W. Sayers, Trans.). Ann Arbor: University of Michigan Press.
126. Stokes, W. E. D. (1917). *The right to be well born or horse breeding in its relation to eugenics.* New York: C. J. O'Brien.
127. Stone, E. (1999). Modern slogan, ancient script: Impairment and disability in the Chinese language. In M. Corker & S. French (Eds.), *Disability discourse* (pp. 136–147). Philadelphia: Open University Press.
128. *Sutton v. United Air Lines, Inc.,* 527 U.S. 471 (1999).
129. Switzer, J. V. (2003). *Disabled rights: American disability policy and the fight for equality.* Washington, DC: Georgetown University Press.
130. *Tennessee v. Lane,* 2004 U.S. Lexis 3386 (2004).
131. Thomson, R. G. (1997). *Extraordinary bodies: Figuring disability in American culture and literature.* New York: Columbia University Press.
132. *Toyota v. Williams,* 534 U.S. 184 (2002).
133. *Trible v. Gordon,* 430 U.S. 762 (1977).
134. Tucker, B. P. (2000). The Supreme Court's definition of disability under the ADA: A return to the dark ages. *Alabama Law Review, 52,* 321–374.
135. United Nations. (1982). *World Programme of Action Concerning Disabled Persons.* New York: Author.
136. United Nations. (1994). *Standard Rules on the Equalization of Opportunities for Persons with Disabilities.* New York: Author.
137. United States Commission on Civil Rights. (1997). *Equal educational opportunity and nondiscrimination for students with disabilities: Federal enforcement of Section 504.* Washington, DC: Author.
138. Vinen, R. (2000). *A history in fragments: Europe in the twentieth century.* New York: De Capo.
139. Warkany, J. (1959). Congenital malformations in the past. *Journal of Chronic Disabilities. 10,* 84–96.
140. Watson, A. (Ed.), (1998). *The digest of Justinian* (2 vols.). Philadelphia: University of Pennsylvania Press.
141. Wells, S. J. (2001). Is the ADA working? *HR Magazine, 46*(4), 38–46.
142. West, T. G. (1997). *Vindicating the founders: Race, sex, class, and justice in the origins of America.* New York: Rowman and Littlefield.
143. Willeford, W. (1969). *The fool and his sceptre: A study in clowns and jesters and their audience.* London: Edward Arnold.
144. Winship, M. P. (1994). Prodigies, Puritanism, and the perils of natural philosophy: The example of Cotton Mather. *The William and Mary Quarterly, 51,* 92–105.

145. Winzer, M. A. (1993). *The history of special education: From isolation to integration.* Washington, DC: Gallaudet University Press.
146. Winzer, M. A. (1997). Disability and society before the eighteenth century: Dread and despair. In L. J. Davis (Ed.), *The disability studies reader* (pp. 75–109). New York: Routledge.
147. Wolfsenberger, W. (1969). The origin and nature of our institutional models. In R. B. Kugel & W. Wolfsenberger (Eds.), *Changing patterns in residential services for the mentally retarded* (pp. 59–171). Washington, DC: President's Commission on Mental Retardation.
148. Zola, I. K. (1994). Towards inclusion: The role of people with disabilities in policy and research issues in the United States—a historical and political analysis. In M. H. Rioux & M. Bach (Eds.), *Disability is not measles: New research paradigms in disability* (pp. 49–66). North York, Ontario: Roeher Institute.

28

A History of Women's Bodies

ROSE WEITZ

Throughout history, ideas about women's bodies have played a dramatic role in either challenging or reinforcing power relationships between men and women. We can therefore regard these ideas as political tools in an ongoing political struggle. This article presents a brief history of women's bodies, looking at how ideas about the female body have changed over time in western law and biological theory.

Beginning with the earliest written legal codes, and continuing nearly to the present day, the law typically has defined women's bodies as men's property. In ancient societies, women who were not slaves typically belonged to their fathers before marriage and to their husbands thereafter. For this reason, Babylonian law, for example, treated rape as a form of property damage, requiring a rapist to pay a fine to the husband or father of the raped woman, but nothing to the woman herself. Similarly, marriages in ancient societies typically were contracted between prospective husbands and prospective fathers-in-law, with the potential bride playing little if any role.

Women's legal status as property reflected the belief that women's bodies were inherently different from men's in ways that made women both defective and dangerous. This belief comes through clearly in the writings of Aristotle, whose ideas about women's bodies formed the basis for "scientific" discussion of this topic in the west from the fourth century B.C. through the eighteenth century (Martin 1987; Tuana 1993). Aristotle's biological theories centered around the concept of heat. According to Aristotle, only embryos that had sufficient heat could develop into fully human form. The rest became female. In other words, woman was, in Aristotle's words, a "misbegotten man" and a "monstrosity"—less than fully formed and literally half-baked. Building on this premise, Galen, a highly influential Greek doctor, later declared that women's reproductive organs were virtually identical to men's, but were located internally because female embryos lacked the heat needed for those organs to develop fully and externally. This view remained common among doctors until well into the eighteenth century.

Lack of heat, classical scholars argued, also produced a plethora of other deficiencies in women, including a smaller stature, a frailer constitution, a less developed brain, and emotional and moral weaknesses that could endanger any men who fell under women's spell. These ideas later would resonate with ideas about women embedded in Christian interpretations of Mary and Eve. Christian theologians argued that Eve caused the fall from divine grace and the expulsion from the Garden of Eden by succumbing when the snake tempted her with the forbidden fruit. This "original sin" occurred, these theologians argued, because women's nature made them inherently more susceptible to sexual desire and other passions of the flesh, blinding them to reason and morality and making them a constant danger to men's souls. Mary avoided the pitfalls of passion only by remaining virginal. Such ideas later would play a large role in fueling the witchcraft hysteria in early modern Europe and colonial America. Women formed the vast majority of the tens of thousands of people executed as witches during these centuries because both Protestants and Catholics assumed that women were less intelligent than men, more driven by sexual passions, and hence more susceptible to the Devil's blandishments (Barstow 1994).

By the eighteenth century, women's legal and social position in the western world had changed little. When the famous English legal theorist, Sir William Blackstone, published his encyclopedic codification of English law in 1769, non-slave women's legal status still remained closer to that of property than to that of non-slave men. According to Blackstone, "By marriage, the husband and wife are one person in the law, that is, the very being and legal existence of the woman is suspended during the marriage, or at least is incorporated into that of her husband under whose wing, protection and cover she performs everything" (1904, 432). In other words, upon marriage a woman experienced "civil death," losing any rights as a citizen, including the right to own or bestow property, make contracts or sue for legal redress, hold custody of minor children, or keep any wages she earned. Moreover, as her "protector," a husband had a legal right to beat his wife if he believed it necessary, as well as a right to her sexual services. These principles would form the basis of marital law in the United States from its founding.

Both in colonial America and in the United States for its first eighty-nine years, slave women *were* property. Moreover, both the law and contemporary scientific writings often described African-American women (and men) as animals, rather than humans. Consequently, neither slave women nor slave men held any rights of citizenship. By the same token, female African-American slaves were completely subject to their white masters. Rape was common, both as a form of "entertainment" for white men and as a way of breeding more slaves, since the children of slave mothers were automatically slaves, regardless of their fathers' race. Nor did African-American women's special vulnerability to rape end when slavery ended.

Both before and after the Civil War, the rape of African-American women was explained, if not justified, by an ideology that defined African-Americans, including African-American women, as animalistically hypersexual, and thus responsible for their own rapes (Gilman 1985; Giddings 1995). For example, an article published by a white southern woman on March 17, 1904 in a popular periodical, the *Independent,* declared:

Degeneracy is apt to show most in the weaker individuals of any race; so Negro women evidence more nearly the popular idea of total depravity than the men do. They are so nearly lacking in virtue that the color of a Negro woman's skin is generally taken (and quite correctly) as a guarantee of her immorality. . . . I sometimes read of a virtuous Negro woman, hear of them, but the idea is absolutely inconceivable to me.

These ideas about sexuality, combined with ideas about the inherent inferiority of African Americans, are vividly reflected in the 1861 Georgia penal code. That code left it up to the court whether to fine or imprison men who raped African-American women, recommended two to twenty years' imprisonment for white men convicted of raping white women, and mandated the death penalty for African-American men convicted of raping white women (Roberts 1990, 60). Moreover, African-American men typically were lynched before being brought to trial if suspected of raping a white woman, while white men were rarely convicted for raping white women and probably never convicted for raping African-American women.

For both free and slave women in the United States, the legal definition of women's bodies as men's property experienced its first serious challenges during the nineteenth century. In 1839, Mississippi passed the first Married Women's Property Act. Designed primarily to protect family farms and property from creditors rather than to expand the rights of women (Speth 1982), the law gave married women the right to retain property they owned before marriage and wages they earned outside the home. By the end of the nineteenth century, similar laws had been passed in all the states.

Also during the nineteenth century, both white and African-American women won the right to vote in Wyoming, Utah, Colorado, and Idaho, and a national suffrage campaign took root. Beginning with Oberlin College in 1833, a growing number of colleges began accepting women students, including free African-American women, with more than five thousand women graduating in 1900 alone (Flexner 1974, 232). At the same time, the industrial revolution prompted growing numbers of women to seek paid employment. By 1900, the U.S. census listed more than five million women as gainfully employed outside the home (Flexner 1974, 250). This did not reflect any significant changes in the lives of African-American women—who had worked as much as men when slaves and who often worked full-time post-slavery (Jones 1985)—but was a major change for white women.

Each of these changes challenged the balance of power between men and women in American society. In response to these challenges, a counterreaction quickly developed. This counterreaction combined new "scientific" ideas with older definitions of women's bodies as ill or fragile to argue that white middle-class women were unable to sustain the responsibilities of political power or the burdens of education or employment.

Ideas about middle-class women's frailty drew heavily on the writings of Charles Darwin, who had published his groundbreaking *On the Origin of Species* in 1872 (Tuana 1993). As part of his theory of evolution, Darwin argued that males compete for sexual access to females, with only the fittest succeeding and reproducing. As a result, males continually evolve toward greater "perfection." Females, on the other hand, need not compete for males, and therefore are not subject to the same process of natural selection. Consequently, in any species, males are more evolved than females. In addition, Darwin argued, females must expend so much energy on reproduction that they retain little energy for either physical or mental development. As a result, women remain subject to their emotions and passions: nurturing, altruistic, and child-like, but with little sense of either justice or morality.

Darwin's theories meshed well with Victorian ideas about middle-class white women's sexuality, which depicted women as the objects of male desire, emphasized romance and downplayed female sexual desire, and reinforced a sexual double standard. Middle-class women were expected to have passionate and even romantic attachments to other women, but these attachments were assumed to be emotional, rather than physical. Most women who had "romantic friendships" with other women were married to men and only those few who adopted male clothing or behavior were considered lesbians (Faderman 1981). Lesbianism became more broadly identified and stigmatized only in the early twentieth century, when women's entry into higher education and the workforce enabled some women to survive economically without marrying, and lesbianism therefore became a threat to male power.

With women's increasing entry into education and employment, ideas about the physical and emotional frailty of women—with their strong echoes of both Christian and Aristotelian disdain for women and their bodies—were adopted by nineteenth-century doctors as justifications for keeping women uneducated and unemployed. So, for example:

> The president of the Oregon State Medical Society, F. W. Van Dyke, in 1905, claimed that hard study killed sexual desire in women, took away their beauty, and brought on hysteria, neurasthenia [a mental disorder], dyspepsia [indigestion], astigmatism [a visual disorder], and dysmenorrhea [painful menstruation]. Educated women, he added, could not bear children with ease because study arrested the development of the pelvis at the same time it increased the size of the child's brain, and therefore its head. The result was extensive suffering in childbirth by educated women (Bullough and Voght 1984, 32).

Belief in the frailty of middle-class women's bodies similarly fostered the epidemic rise during the late nineteenth century in gynecological surgery (Barker-Benfield 1976; Longo 1984). Many doctors routinely performed surgery to remove healthy ovaries, uteruses, or clitorises, from women who experienced an extremely wide range of physical and mental symptoms—including symptoms such as rebelliousness or malaise which reflected women's constrained social circumstances more than their physical health. These operations were not only unnecessary but dangerous, with mortality rates of up to thirty-three percent (Longo 1984).

Paradoxically, at the same time that scientific "experts" emphasized the frailty of middle-class white women, they emphasized the robustness of poorer women, both white and nonwhite. As Jacqueline Jones (1985, 15) explains:

> Slaveholders had little use for sentimental platitudes about the delicacy of the female constitution. . . . There were enough women like Susan Mabry of Virginia, who could pick 400 or 500 pounds of cotton a day (150 to 200 pounds was considered respectable for an average worker) to remove from a master's mind all doubts about the ability of a strong, healthy woman field worker. As a result, he conveniently discarded his time-honored Anglo-Saxon notions about the type of work best suited for women.

Similar attitudes applied to working-class white women. Thus, Dr. Lucien Warner, a popular medical authority, could in 1874 explain how middle-class women were made frail by their affluence, while "the African negress, who toils beside her husband in the fields of the south, and Bridget [the Irish maid], who washes and scrubs and toils in our homes at the north, enjoy for the most part good health, with comparative immunity from uterine disease" (cited in Ehrenreich and English 1973, 12–13).

At any rate, despite the warnings of medical experts, women continued to enter both higher education and the paid workforce. However, although education clearly benefited women, entering the workforce endangered the lives and health of many women due to hazardous working conditions.

Although male workers could hope to improve their working conditions through union agitation, this tactic was far less useful for women, who more often worked in non-unionized jobs, were denied union membership, or were not interested in joining unions. As a result, some feminists began lobbying for protective labor laws that would set maximum working hours for women, mandate rest periods, and so on (Erickson, 1982). In 1908, the U.S. Supreme Court first upheld such a law in *Muller v. Oregon*. Unfortunately, it soon became clear that protective labor laws hurt women more than they helped, by bolstering the idea that female workers were inherently weaker than male workers.

Twelve years after the *Muller* decision, in 1920, most female U.S. citizens finally won the right to vote in national elections. (Most Asian-born and Native American women, however, were ineligible for citizenship, and most African-American women—like African-American men—were prevented from voting through legal and illegal means.) Unfortunately, suffrage largely marked the close of decades of feminist activism rather than the start of any broader reforms in women's legal, social, or economic positions.

By the 1960s, women's status had hardly changed. For example, although the fourteenth amendment (passed in 1868) guaranteed equal protection under the law for all U.S. citizens, not until 1971, in *Reed v. Reed*, did the Supreme Court rule that differential treatment based on sex was illegal. Similarly, based still on Blackstone's interpretation of women's legal position and the concept of women as men's property, until the 1970s courts routinely refused to prosecute wife batterers unless they killed their wives, and not until 1984 did any court convict a man for raping a woman to whom he was married and with whom he still legally resided.

Recognition of these and other inequities led to the emergence of a new feminist movement beginning in the second half of the 1960s (Evans 1979). In its earliest days, this movement adopted the rhetoric of liberalism and the civil rights movement, arguing that women and men were morally and intellectually equal and that women's bodies were essentially similar to men's bodies. The (unsuccessful) attempts to pass the Equal Rights Amendment, which stated that "equality of rights under the law shall not be denied or abridged by the United States or any state on account of sex," reflected this strain of thinking about gender.

★ ★ ★

Despite the differences among feminists in ideology and tactics, all share the goal of challenging accepted ideas about women's bodies and social position. Not surprisingly, as the modern feminist movement has grown, a backlash has developed that has attempted to reinforce more traditional ideas (Faludi 1991). This backlash has taken many forms, including (1) increasing pressure on women to control the shape of their bodies, (2) attempts to define premenstrual and postmenopausal women as ill, and (3) the rise of the anti-abortion and "fetal rights" movements.

Throughout history, women have experienced social pressures to maintain acceptable appearances. However, as Susan Faludi (1991), Naomi Wolf (1991), and many others have demonstrated, the backlash against modern feminism seems to have increased these pressures substantially. For example, the average weight of both Miss America winners and *Playboy* centerfolds has decreased steadily since 1978, even though the average height has increased (Wiseman et al. 1992). Current appearance norms call for women to be not only painfully thin, but muscular and buxom—qualities that can occur together only if women spend vast amounts of time on exercise, money on cosmetic surgery, and emotional energy on diet (Seid 1989).

The backlash against feminism also has affected women's lives by stimulating calls for the medical control of premenstrual women. Although first defined in the 1930s, the idea of a "premenstrual syndrome" (PMS) did not garner much attention either inside or outside medical circles until the 1970s. Since then, innumerable popular and medical articles have argued that to function at work or school, women with PMS need medical treatment to control their anger and discipline their behaviors. Similarly, many doctors now believe that menopausal women need drugs to maintain their sexual attractiveness and to control their behavior and emotions.

Finally, the backlash against feminism has restricted women's lives by encouraging the rise of the antiabortion and "fetal rights" movements. Prior to the twentieth century, abortion was generally considered both legally and socially acceptable, although

dangerous. By the mid-twentieth century, abortion had become a safe medical procedure, but was legal only when deemed medically necessary. Doctors were deeply divided, however, regarding when it was necessary, with some performing abortions only to preserve women's lives and others doing so to preserve women's social, psychological, or economic well-being (Luker 1984). To protect themselves legally, beginning in the 1960s, those doctors who favored more lenient indications for abortion, along with women who considered abortion a right, lobbied heavily for broader legal access to abortion. This lobbying culminated in 1973 when the U.S. Supreme Court ruled, in *Roe v. Wade,* that abortion was legal in most circumstances. However, subsequent legislative actions and Court decisions (including the 1976 Hyde Amendment and the Supreme Court's 1989 decision in *Webster v. Reproductive Health Services*), have reduced legal access to abortion substantially, especially for poor and young women.

Embedded in the legal battles over abortion is a set of beliefs about the nature of women and of the fetus (Luker 1984). On one side stand those who argue that unless women have an absolute right to control their own bodies, including the right to abortion, they will never attain fully equal status in society. On the other side stand those who argue that the fetus is fully human and that women's rights to control their bodies must be subjugated to the fetus's right to life.

This latter belief also underlies the broader social and legal pressure for "fetal rights." For example, pregnant women around the country—almost all of them nonwhite and poor—have been arrested for abusing alcohol or illegal drugs while pregnant, on the grounds that they had no right to expose their fetuses to harmful substances. Others—again, mostly poor and nonwhite—have been forced to have cesarean sections against their will. In these cases, the courts have ruled that fetuses' interests are more important than women's right to determine what will happen to their bodies—in this case, the right to refuse invasive, hazardous surgery—and that doctors know better than mothers what is in a fetus's best interests. Still other women have been denied jobs by employers who have argued that hazardous work conditions might endanger a pregnant worker's fetus; these employers have ignored evidence that the same conditions would also damage men's sperm and thus any resulting fetuses.

In sum, throughout, history, ideas about women's bodies have centrally affected the strictures within which women live. Only by looking at the embodied experiences of women, as well as at how those experiences are socially constructed, can we fully understand women's lives, women's position in society, and the possibilities for resistance against that position.

REFERENCES

1. Barker-Benfield, G. J. 1976. *The Horrors of the Half-Known Life: Male Attitudes Towards Women and Sexuality in Nineteenth-Century America.* New York: Harper.
2. Barstow, Anne Llewellyn. 1994. *Witchcraze: A New History of the European Witch Hunts.* San Francisco: Pandora.
3. Blackstone, Sir William. 1904. *Commentaries on the Laws of England in Four Books.* Vol. 1 edited by George Shaswood. Philadelphia: Lippincott.
4. Bullough, Vern, and Martha Voght. 1984. Women, menstruation, and nineteenth-century medicine. In *Women and Health in America: Historical Readings,* edited by Judith Walzer Leavitt. Madison: University of Wisconsin Press.
5. Daly, Mary. 1978. *Gyn/Ecology: The Metaethics of Radical Feminism.* Boston: Beacon.
6. Darwin, Charles. 1872. *On the Origin of Species.* Akron, OH: Werner.
7. Ehrenreich, Barbara, and Deirdre English. 1973. *Complaints and Disorders: The Sexual Politics of Sickness.* Old Westbury, NY: Feminist Press.
8. Erickson, Nancy S. 1982. Historical background of "protective" labor legislation: Muller v. Oregon. In *Women and the Law: A Social Historical Perspective.* Vol. 2, edited by D. Kelly Weisberg. Cambridge, MA: Schenkman.
9. Evans, Sara M. 1979. *Personal Politics: The Roots of Women's Liberation in the Civil Rights Movement and the New Left.* New York: Vintage.
10. Faderman, Lillian. 1981. *Surpassing the Love of Men: Romantic Friendship and Love Between Women from the Renaissance to the Present.* New York: William Morrow.
11. Faludi, Susan. 1991. *Backlash: The Undeclared War Against American Women.* New York: Crown.
12. Flexner, Eleanor. 1974. *Century of Struggle: The Women's Rights Movement in the United States.* New York: Atheneum.
13. Giddings, Paula. 1995. The last taboo. In *Words of Fire: An Anthology of African-American Feminist Thought,* edited by Beverly Guy-Sheftall. New York: New Press.
14. Gilman, Sander. 1985. Black bodies, white bodies: Toward an iconography of female sexuality in late nineteenth-century art, medicine, and literature. In *"Race," Writing, and Difference,* edited by Henry Louis Gates. Chicago: University of Chicago Press.
15. Griffin, Susan. 1978. *Woman and Nature: The Roaring Inside Her.* New York: Harper.
16. Jones, Jacqueline. 1985. *Labor of Love, Labor of Sorrow: Black Women, Work, and the Family from Slavery to the Present.* New York: Basic.
17. Longo, Lawrence D. 1984. The rise and fall of Battey's operation: A fashion in surgery. In *Woman and Health in America,* edited by Judith Walzer Leavitt. Madison: University of Wisconsin Press.
18. Luker, Kristin. 1984. *Abortion and the Politics of Motherhood.* Berkeley: University of California Press.
19. Martin, Emily. 1987. *The Woman in the Body: A Cultural Analysis of Reproduction.* Boston: Beacon.
20. Roberts, Dorothy E. 1990. The future of reproductive choice for poor women and women of color. *Women's Rights Law Reporter* 12(2):59–67.
21. Seid, Roberta Pollack. 1989. *Never Too Thin: Why Women Are at War with Their Bodies.* Englewood Cliffs, NJ: Prentice Hall.
22. Speth, Linda E. 1982. The Married Women's Property Acts, 1839–1865: Reform, reaction, or revolution? In *Women and the Law: A Social Historical Perspective.* Vol. 2, edited by D. Kelly Weisberg. Cambridge, MA: Schenkman.
23. Tuana, Nancy. 1993. *The Less Noble Sex: Scientific, Religious, and Philosophical Conceptions of Woman's Nature.* Bloomington: Indiana University Press.
24. Wiseman, Claire V., James J. Gray, James E. Mosimann, and Anthony H. Ehrens. 1992. Cultural expectations of thinness in women: An update. *International Journal of Eating Disorders* 11:85–89.
25. Wolf, Naomi. 1991. *The Beauty Myth: How Images of Beauty Are Used Against Women.* New York: William Morrow.

🧭 29

Thirteen Key Supreme Court Cases and the Civil War Amendments

KAREN E. ROSENBLUM AND
TONI-MICHELLE C. TRAVIS

Individuals' lives are affected not only by social practices but also by law as interpreted in the courts. Under U.S. federalism Congress makes laws, the president swears to uphold the law, and the Supreme Court interprets the law. When state laws appear to be in conflict with the United States Constitution or when the terminology of the Constitution is vague, the Supreme Court interprets such laws. We will focus here on Supreme Court rulings that have defined the roles individuals are allowed to assume in American society.

As the supreme law above laws enacted by Congress, the U.S. Constitution determines individual and group status. A brief document, the Constitution describes the division of power between the federal and state governments, as well as the rights of individuals. Only 16 amendments to the Constitution have been added since the ratification of the Bill of Rights (the first 10 amendments). Although the Constitution appears to be sweeping in scope — relying on the principle that all men are created equal — in reality the Constitution is an exclusionary document. It omitted women, Native Americans, and African Americans except for the purpose of determining a population count. In instances where the Constitution was vague on the rights of each of these groups, clarification was later sought through court cases.

Federalism provides four primary methods by which citizens may influence the political process. First, the Constitution grants citizens the right to petition the government, that is, the right to lobby. Second, as a civic duty, citizens are expected to vote and seek office. Once in office citizens can change conditions by writing new legislation, known as *statutory law*. Third, changes can be achieved through the lengthy procedure of passing constitutional amendments, which affect all citizens. Controversial amendments have often become law after social movement activists advocated passage for several years or after a major national upheaval, such as the Civil War.

Last, the Constitution provides that citizens can sue to settle disputes. Through this method, sweeping social changes can take place when Supreme Court decisions affect all the individuals in a class. Thus, the assertion of individual rights has become a key tool of those who were not privileged by the Constitution to clarify their status in American society.

An examination of landmark cases reveals the continuous difficulties some groups have had in securing their rights through legal remedy. The Court has often taken a narrow perspective on what classes of people were to receive equal protection of the law, or were covered under the privileges and immunities clause.[1] Each group had to bring suit in every area where barriers existed. For example, white women who were citizens had to sue to establish that they had the right to inherit property, to serve on juries, to enter various professions, and in general to be treated as a class apart from their husband and family. Blacks sued to attend southern state universities and law schools, to participate in the all-white Democratic Party primary election,[2] to attend public schools which had been ordered to desegregate by the Supreme Court, and to vote without having to pay a poll tax. When these landmark cases were decided, they were perceived to herald sweeping changes in policy. Yet they proved to be only a guide to determining the rights of individuals.

I. DRED SCOTT V. SANFORD *(1857)*

Prior to the Civil War the Constitution was not precise on whether one was simultaneously a citizen of a given state and of the entire United States. Slavery further complicated the matter because the status of slaves and free persons of color was not specified in the Constitution, nor were members of either group considered citizens. Each state had the option of determining the status and rights of these nonwhites.

A federal form of government permitted flexibility by allowing states to differ on matters such as rights for its citizens. Yet as a newly invented form of government, a number of issues that were clear under British law were not settled until the Thirteenth, Fourteenth, and Fifteenth Amendments were added to the United States Constitution. Federalism raised questions about rights and privileges because a citizen was simultaneously living under the laws of a state and of the United States.

Who had rights and privileges guaranteed by the Constitution? Did all citizens have all rights and privileges?

For example, what was the status of women? The Constitution provided for citizenship, but did not specify which rights and privileges were granted to female citizens. State laws considered white men and white women citizens, yet white women were often not allowed to own property, sue in court, or vote. Under federalism, each state enacted laws determining the rights and status of free blacks, slaves, white men, and white women so long as the laws did not conflict with the United States Constitution.

The *Dred Scott* case of 1846 considered the issues of slavery, property, citizenship, and the supremacy of the United States over individual states when a slave was taken to a free territory. The Court's holding primarily affected blacks, now called African Americans,[3] who sought the benefits of citizenship. Broadly, the case addressed American citizenship, a matter not clearly defined until passage of the Fourteenth Amendment in 1868.

Dred Scott was an enslaved man owned by Dr. John Emerson, a U.S. Army surgeon stationed in Missouri. When Emerson was transferred to Rock Island, Illinois, where slavery was forbidden, he took Dred Scott with him. Emerson was subsequently transferred to Fort Snelling, a territory (now Minnesota) where slavery was forbidden by the Missouri Compromise of 1820. In 1838, he returned to Missouri with Dred Scott.

In 1846 Scott brought suit in a Missouri circuit court to obtain his freedom on the grounds he had resided in free territory for periods of time. Scott won the case and his freedom. However, the judgment was reversed by the Missouri Supreme Court. Later, when John Sanford, a citizen of New York and the brother of Mrs. Emerson, arranged for the sale of Scott, the grounds were established for Scott to take his case to the federal circuit court in Missouri. The federal court ruled that Scott and his family were slaves and therefore the "lawful property" of Sanford. With the financial assistance of abolitionists, Scott appealed his case to the Supreme Court.

The Court's decision addressed these key questions:

1. Are blacks citizens?
2. Are blacks entitled to sue in court?
3. Can one have all the privileges and immunities of citizenship in a state, but not the United States?
4. Can one be a citizen of the United States and not be qualified to vote or hold office?

Excerpts from the Supreme Court Decision *in* Dred Scott v. Sanford [4]

Mr. Chief Justice Taney delivered the opinion of the Court:

. . . The question is simply this: Can a Negro, whose ancestors were imported into this country and sold as slaves, become a member of the political community formed and brought into existence by the Constitution of the United States, and as such become entitled to all the rights, and privileges and immunities, guaranteed by that instrument to the citizen? One of which rights is the privilege of suing in a court of the United States. . . .

The question before us is whether the class of persons described are constituent members of this sovereignty? We think they are not, and that they are not included, and were not intended to be included, under the word "citizens" in the Constitution, and can therefore claim none of the rights and privileges which that instrument provides for and secures to citizens of the United States.

In discussing this question, we must not confound the rights of citizenship which a State may confer within its own limits and the rights of citizenship as a member of the Union. It does not by any means follow, because he has all the rights and privileges of a citizen of a State, that he must be a citizen of the United States. He may have all of the rights and privileges of a citizen of a State, and yet not be entitled to the rights and privileges of a citizen in any other State. . . .

Undoubtedly a person may be a citizen . . . although he exercises no share of the political power, and is incapacitated from holding particular office. Those who have not the necessary qualifications cannot vote or hold the office, yet they are citizens.

The court is of the opinion, that . . . Dred Scott was not a citizen of Missouri within the meaning of the Constitution of the United States, and not entitled as such to sue in its courts: and, consequently, that the Circuit Court had no jurisdiction. . . .

II. THE CIVIL WAR AMENDMENTS

The Civil War (1861–1865) was fought over slavery, as well as the issue of supremacy of the national government over the individual states.

After the Civil War, members of Congress known as the Radical Republicans sought to protect the freedom of the former slaves by passing the Thirteenth, Fourteenth, and Fifteenth Amendments. These amendments, especially the Fourteenth, have provided the foundation for African Americans, as well as women, gays, Native Americans, immigrants, and those who are disabled to bring suit for equal treatment under the law.

Amendment XIII, 1865

(Slavery)   This amendment prohibited slavery and involuntary servitude in the United States. The entire amendment follows:

> Section 1. Neither slavery nor involuntary servitude, except as a punishment whereof the party shall have been duly convicted, shall exist within the United States, or any place subject to their jurisdiction.
> Section 2. Congress shall have power to enforce this article by appropriate legislation.

Amendment XIV, 1868

(Citizenship, Due Process, and Equal Protection of the Laws)   This amendment defined citizenship; prohibited the states from making or enforcing laws that abridged the privileges or immunities of citizenship; forbade states to deprive persons of life, liberty, or property without due process of law; and forbade states to deny equal protection of the law to any person. Over time the Fourteenth Amendment became the most important of the Reconstruction amendments. Key phrases such as "privileges and immunities," "deprive any person of life, liberty, or the pursuit of justice," and "deny to any person within its jurisdiction equal protec-

tion of the law" have caused this amendment to be the subject of more Supreme Court cases than any other provision of the Constitution. The entire amendment follows:

> Section 1. All persons born or naturalized in the United States, and subject to the jurisdiction thereof, are citizens of the United States and of the State wherein they reside. No State shall make or enforce any law which shall abridge the privileges or immunities of citizens of the United States; nor shall any State deprive any person of life, liberty, or property, without due process of law; nor deny to any person within its jurisdiction the equal protection of the laws.
> Section 2. Representatives shall be apportioned among the several States according to their respective numbers, counting the whole number of persons in each State, excluding Indians not taxed. But when the right to vote at any election for the choice of electors for President and Vice President of the United States, Representatives in Congress, the Executive and Judicial officers of a State, or the members of the Legislature thereof, is denied to any of the male inhabitants of such State, being twenty-one years of age, and citizens of the United States, or in any way abridged, except for participation in rebellion, or other crime, the basis of representation therein shall be reduced in proportion which the number of such male citizens shall bear to the whole number of male citizens twenty-one years of age in such State.
> Section 3. No person shall be a Senator or Representative in Congress, or elector or President and Vice President, or hold any office, civil or military, under the United States, or under any State, who, having previously taken an oath, as a member of Congress, or as an officer of the United States, or as a member of any State legislature, or as an executive or judicial officer of any State, to support the Constitution of the United States, shall have engaged in insurrection or rebellion against the same, or given aid or comfort to the enemies thereof. But Congress may by a vote of two-thirds of each House, remove such disability.
> Section 4. The validity of the public debt of the United States, authorized by law, including debts incurred for payments of pensions and bounties for services in suppressing insurrection or rebellion,

shall not be questioned. But neither the United States nor any State shall assume or pay any debt or obligation incurred in aid of insurrection or rebellion against the United States, or any claim for the loss or emancipation of any slave, but all such debts, obligations and claims shall be held illegal and void.

Section 5. The Congress shall have power to enforce, by appropriate legislation, the provisions of this article.

Amendment XV, 1870

(The Right to Vote) The entire amendment follows:

Section 1. The right of citizens of the United States to vote shall not be denied or abridged by the United States or by any State on account of race, color, or previous condition of servitude.

Section 2. The Congress shall have power to enforce this article by appropriate legislation.

As we have seen, the Thirteenth, Fourteenth, and Fifteenth Amendments were added to the Constitution expressly with former slaves in mind. In Section 1 of the Fourteenth Amendment, the definition of *citizenship* was clarified and granted to blacks. In the Fifteenth Amendment black males, former slaves, were granted the right to vote. For women, however, the situation was different.

During the 19th century there was no doubt that white females were U.S. citizens, but their rights as citizens were unclear. For example, although they were citizens, women were not automatically enfranchised. Depending on state laws, they were barred from owning property, holding office, or voting. The 1872 case of *Bradwell v. The State of Illinois* specifically tested whether women as United States citizens had the right to become members of the bar. More generally, it addressed whether the rights of female citizens included the right to pursue any employment.

III. MINOR V. HAPPERSETT *(1875)*

The Fifteenth Amendment was not viewed as a triumph for women because it specifically denied them the vote. Section 2 of the Fourteenth Amendment for the first time made reference to males as citizens. Since black men were included but women of all races were omitted, women were left to continue to seek changes through the courts. This was a difficult route because in subsequent cases, judges often held a narrow view that the legislators wrote the amendment only with black males in mind. Thus, a pattern was soon established in which white women followed black men and women in asserting their rights as citizens as seen in the 1875 case of *Minor v. Happersett*. In *Dred Scott* the question was whether Scott was a citizen; in *Minor* the question was whether *Minor* as a citizen had the right to vote. In both cases the Supreme Court said no.

Virginia Minor, a native-born, free, white citizen of the United States and the state of Missouri, and over the age of 21 wished to vote for president, vice president, and members of Congress in the election of November 1872. She applied to the registrar of voters but was not allowed to vote because she was not a "male citizen of the United States." As a citizen of the United States, Minor sued under the privileges and immunities clause of the Fourteenth Amendment.

The Court's decision addressed these key questions:

1. Who is covered under the term *citizen*?
2. Is suffrage one of the privileges and immunities of citizenship?
3. Did the Constitution, as originally written, make all citizens voters?
4. Did the Fifteenth Amendment make all citizens voters?
5. Can a state confine voting to only male citizens without violating the Constitution?

While women were citizens of the United States and the state where they resided, they did not automatically possess all the privileges granted to male citizens, such as suffrage. This landmark case was not overturned until the passage of the Nineteenth Amendment, which enfranchised women, in 1920.[5]

Excerpts from the Supreme Court Decision in Minor v. Happersett[6]

Mr. Chief Justice Waite delivered the opinion of the Court:

. . . It is contended [by Minor's counsel] that the provisions of the Constitution and laws of the State of Missouri which confine the right of suffrage and registration therefore to men, are in violation of the Constitution of the United States, and therefore void. The argument is, that as a woman, born or naturalized in the United States is a citizen of the United States and of the State in which she resides, she has the right of suffrage as one of the privileges and immunities of her citizenship, which the State cannot by its laws or Constitution abridge.

There is no doubt that women may be citizens. . . .

. . . From this it is apparent that from the commencement of the legislation upon this subject alien women and alien minors could be made citizens by naturalization, and we think it will not be contended that native women and native minors were already citizens by birth.

. . . More cannot be necessary to establish the fact that sex has never been made one of the elements of citizenship in the United States. In this respect men have never had an advantage over women. The same laws precisely apply to both. The Fourteenth amendment did not affect the citizenship of women any more than it did of men . . . therefore, the rights of Mrs. Minor do not depend upon the amendment. She has always been a citizen from her birth, and entitled to all privileges and immunities of citizenship. The amendment prohibited the State, of which she is a citizen, from abridging any of her privileges and immunities as a citizen of the United States.

. . . The direct question is, therefore, presented whether all citizens are necessarily voters.

The Constitution does not define the privileges and immunities of citizens. For that definition we must look elsewhere.

. . . The [Fourteenth] amendment did not add to the privileges and immunities of a citizen. It simply furnished an additional guarantee for the protection of such as he already had. No new voters were necessarily made by it.

. . . No new State has ever been admitted to the Union which has conferred the right of suffrage upon women, and this has never been considered a valid objection to her admission.

. . . Certainly, if the courts can consider any question settled, this is one. For nearly ninety years the people have acted upon the idea that the Constitution, when it conferred citizenship, did not necessarily confer the right of suffrage. . . . Our province is to decide what the law is, not to declare what it should be.

The *Dred Scott, Bradwell,* and *Minor* cases point to the similarity in the status of black men and women of all races in 19th-century America. As one judicial scholar noted, race and sex were comparable classes, distinct from all others. Historically, these "natural classes" were considered permanent and unchangeable.[7] Thus, both slavery and the subjugation of women have been described as a caste system where one's status is fixed from birth and not alterable based on wealth or talent.[8]

Indeed, the connection between the enslavement of black people and the legal and social standing of women was often traced to the Old Testament. Historically slavery was justified on the grounds that one should look to Abraham; the Bible refers to Abraham's wives, children, men servants, maid servants, camels, and cattle as his property. A man's wife and children were considered his slaves. By the logic of the 19th century, if women were slaves, why shouldn't blacks be also?

Thus, the concepts of race and sex have been historically linked. Since "the doctrines were developed by the same people for the same purpose it is not surprising to find anti-feminism to be an echo of racism, and vice versa."[9]

Additional constitutional amendments were necessary for women and African Americans to exercise the privileges of citizenship that were automatically granted to white males. Nonetheless, even after amendments were enacted, African Americans still had to fight for enforcement of the law.

IV. PLESSY V. FERGUSON (1896)

After the Civil War the northern victors imposed military rule on the South.[10] White landowners and former slaveholders often found themselves with unproductive farmland and no free laborers. Aside from the economic loss of power, white males were in a totally new political environment: Black men had been elevated to citizens; former slaves were now eligible to vote, run for office, and hold seats in the state or national legislature. To ensure the rights of former slaves, the U.S. Congress passed the Civil War Amendments and provided federal troops to oversee federal elections.

However, when federal troops were withdrawn from the southern states in 1877, enfranchised black men became vulnerable to former masters who immediately seized political control of the state legislatures. In order to solidify political power, whites rewrote state constitutions to disenfranchise black men. To ensure that all blacks were restricted to a subordinate status, southern states systematically enacted "Jim Crow" laws, rigidly segregating society into black and white communities. These laws barred blacks from using the same public facilities as whites, including schools, hospitals, restaurants, hotels, and recreation areas. With the cooperation of southern elected officials, the Ku Klux Klan, a white supremacist, terrorist organization, grew in membership. The return of political power to whites without any federal presence to protect the black community set the stage for "separate but equal" legislation to become a constitutionally valid racial doctrine.

Under slavery, interracial sexual contact was forbidden but white masters nonetheless had the power to sexually exploit the black women who worked for them. The children of these relationships, especially if they looked white, posed potential inheritance problems because whites feared that such children might seek to exercise the privileges accorded to their white fathers. In order to keep all children of such relationships subordinate in the two-tiered racial system, descent was based on the race of the mother. Consequently, regardless of color, all the children of black women were defined as black.

This resulted in a rigid biracial structure where all persons with "one drop" of black blood were labeled black. Consequently, the "black" community consisted of a wide range of skin color based on this one-drop rule. Therefore, at times individuals with known black ancestry might look phenotypically white. This situation created a group of African Americans who had one-eighth or less African ancestry.

Louisiana was one of the few states to modify the one-drop rule of racial categorization because it considered mulattoes a valid racial category. A term derived from Spanish, *mulatto* refers to the offspring of a "pure African Negro" and a "pure white." Over time, *mulatto* came to encompass children of whites and "mixed Negroes."

These were the social conditions in 1896, when Homer Adolph Plessy, a mulatto, sought to test Louisiana laws that imposed racial segregation. Plessy and other mulattoes decided to test the applicability of the law requiring racial separation on railroad cars traveling in interstate transportation.

In 1890, Louisiana had followed other southern states in enacting Jim Crow laws that were written in compliance with the Equal Protection Clause of Section 1 of the Fourteenth Amendment. These laws required separate accommodations for white and black railroad passengers. In this case, Plessy, a U.S. citizen and a resident of Louisiana who was one-eighth black, paid for a first-class ticket on the East Louisiana Railway traveling from New Orleans to Covington, Louisiana. When he entered the passenger train, Plessy took a vacant seat in a coach designated for white passengers. He claimed that he was entitled to every "recognition, right, privilege, and immunity" granted to white citizens of the United States by the Constitution. Under Louisiana law, the conductor, who knew Plessy, was required to ask him to sit in a coach specifically assigned to nonwhite persons. By law, passengers who sat in the inappropriate coach were fined or imprisoned. When Plessy refused to comply with the order, he was removed from the train and imprisoned.

Plessy v. Ferguson is the one case that solidified the power of whites over blacks in southern states. Through state laws, and with the additional federal weight in the *Plessy* decision, whites began to enforce rigid separation of the races in every aspect of life.

In *Plessy*, Justice John Marshall Harlan wrote the only dissenting opinion. Usually in Supreme Court cases, attention is focused on the majority, rather than the dissenting opinion. However, in this case Justice Harlan's dissent is noteworthy because his views on race and citizenship pointed out a line of reasoning that eventually broke down segregation and second-class citizenship for blacks.

Justice Harlan's background as a Kentucky slaveholder who later joined the Union side during the Civil War is cited as an explanation of his views. Some scholars speculate that his shift from slaveholder to a defender of the rights of blacks was caused by his observation of beatings, lynchings, and the use of intimidation tactics against blacks in Kentucky after the Civil War. In a quirk of history, when *Plessy v. Ferguson* was overturned in 1954 by a unanimous opinion in *Brown v. Board of Education*, Justice Harlan's grandson was a member of the Supreme Court.

The Court's decision addressed these key questions:

1. How is a black person defined?
2. Who determines when an individual is black or white?
3. Does providing separate but equal facilities violate the Thirteenth Amendment?
4. Does providing separate but equal facilities violate the Fourteenth Amendment?
5. Does a separate but equal doctrine imply inferiority of either race?
6. Can state laws require the separation of the two races in schools, theaters, and railway cars?
7. Does the separation of the races when applied to commerce within the state of Louisiana abridge the privileges and immunities of the "colored man,"[11] deprive him of equal protection of the law, or deprive him of his property without due process of law under the Fourteenth Amendment?

Excerpts from the Supreme Court Decision in *Plessy v. Ferguson*[12]

Mr. Justice Brown delivered the opinion of the Court:

. . . An [1890] act of the General Assembly of the State of Louisiana, provid[ed] for separate railway carriages for the white and colored races.

. . . No person or persons, shall be admitted to occupy seats in coaches, other than the ones assigned to them on account of the race they belong to.

. . . The constitutionality of this act is attacked upon the ground that it conflicts both with the Thirteenth Amendment of the Constitution, abolishing slavery, and the Fourteenth Amendment, which prohibits certain restrictive legislation.

. . . A statute which implied merely a legal distinction between the white and colored races . . . has no tendency to destroy the legal equality of the two races, or reestablish a state of servitude.

. . . The object of the amendment [the Fourteenth Amendment] was undoubtedly to enforce the absolute equality of the two races before the law, but in the nature of things it could not have been intended to abolish distinctions based upon color, or a commingling of the two races upon terms unsatisfactory to either.

Laws permitting and even requiring their separation in places where they are liable to be brought into contact do not necessarily imply the inferiority of either race to the other, and have been generally, if not universally recognized as within the competency of the state legislatures in the exercise of their police power. The most common instance of this is connected with the establishment of separate schools for white and colored children, which has been held to be a valid exercise of the legislative power even by courts of States where the political rights of the colored race have been longest and most earnestly enforced. One of the earliest of these cases is that of *Roberts v. City of Boston*, 5 Cush. 198, in which the Supreme Judicial Court of Massachusetts held that the general school committee of Boston had power to make provision for the instruction of colored children in separate schools established exclusively for them, and to prohibit their attendance upon the other schools.

. . . We are not prepared to say that the conductor, in assigning passengers to the coaches according to their race, does not act at his peril. . . . The power to assign to a particular coach obviously implies the power to determine to which race the passenger belongs, as well as the power to determine who, under the laws of the particular State, is to be deemed a white, and who is a colored person.

. . . We consider the underlying fallacy of the plaintiff's argument to consist in the assumption that the enforced separation of the two races stamps the colored race with a badge of inferiority. If this be so, it is not by reason of anything found in the act, but solely because the colored race chooses to put that construction upon it. . . . The argument also assumes that social prejudices may be overcome by legislation, and that equal rights cannot be secured to the negro except by an enforced commingling of the two races. We cannot accept this proposition. If the two races are to meet upon terms of social equality, it must be the result of natural affinities, a mutual appreciation of each other's merits and a voluntary consent of individuals.

. . . If the civil and political rights of both races be equal one cannot be inferior to the other civilly or politically. If one race be inferior to the other socially, the Constitution of the United States cannot put them upon the same plane.

It is true that the question for the proportion of colored blood necessary to constitute a colored person, as distinguished from a white person, is one upon which there is a difference of opinion in the different States, some holding that any visible admixture of black blood stamps the persons as belonging to the colored races, others that it depends upon the preponderance of blood . . . still others that the predominance of white blood must only be in the proportion of three fourths. . . . But these are questions to be determined under the laws of each State. . . .

Mr. Justice Harlan in the dissenting opinion:

. . . It was said in argument that the statute of Louisiana does not discriminate against either race, but prescribes a rule applicable alike to white and colored citizens. . . . [But] everyone knows that the statute in question had its origin in the purpose, not so much to exclude white persons from railroad cars occupied by blacks, as to exclude colored people from coaches occupied by or assigned to white persons.

. . . It is one thing for railroad carriers to furnish, or to be required by law to furnish, equal accommodations for all whom they are under a legal duty to carry. It is quite another thing for government to forbid citizens of the white and black races from traveling in the same public conveyance, and to punish officers of railroad companies for permitting persons of the two races to occupy the same passenger coach. If a State can prescribe, as a rule of civil conduct, that whites and blacks shall not travel as passengers in the same railroad coach, why may it not so regulate the use of the streets of its cities and towns as to compel white citizens to keep on one side of a street and black citizens to keep on the other? Why may it not, upon like grounds, punish whites and blacks who ride together in street cars or in open vehicles on a public road or street? Why may it not require sheriffs to assign whites to one side of a court-room and blacks to the other? And why may it not also prohibit the commingling of the two races in the galleries of legislative halls or in public assemblages convened for the consideration of the political questions of the day? Further, if this statute of Louisiana is consistent with the personal liberty of citizens, why may not the State require the separation in railroad coaches of native and naturalized citizens of the United States, or of Protestants and Roman Catholics?

. . . In my opinion, the judgment this day rendered will, in time, prove to be quite pernicious as the decision made by this tribunal in the Dred Scott case.

. . . The thin disguise of "equal" accommodations for passengers in railroad coaches will not mislead anyone, nor atone for the wrong this day done.

Thus, the *Plessy v. Ferguson* decision firmly established the separate but equal doctrine in the South until the National Association for the Advancement of Colored Persons (NAACP) began to systematically attack Jim Crow laws. It is ironic that in *Plessy* systematic social, political, and economic suppression of blacks in the South through Jim Crow laws was justified in terms of a case decided in the northern city of Boston, where the segregation of schools occurred in practice (*de facto*), but not by force of law (*de jure*). In that 1849 case (*Roberts v. City of Boston*, 5 Cush. 198), a parent had unsuccessfully sued on behalf of his daughter to attend a public school. Thus, educational access became both the first and last chapter—in the 1954 case of *Brown v. Board of Education*—-of the doctrine of separate but equal.

V. BROWN V. BOARD OF EDUCATION *(1954)*

Unlike many of the earlier cases brought by individual women, blacks, or Native Americans, *Brown v. Board of Education* was the result of a concerted campaign against racial segregation led by Howard University School of Law graduates and the NAACP. In the 1930s, the NAACP Legal Defense Fund began to systematically fight for fair employment, fair housing, and desegregation of public education. Key lawyers in the campaign against segregation were Charles Houston, Thurgood Marshall, James Nabrit, and William Hastie. Marshall later became a Supreme Court justice, Nabrit became president of Howard University, and Hastie became a federal judge.

By using the Fourteenth Amendment, *Brown* became the key case in an attempt to topple the 1896 separate but equal doctrine. Legal strategists knew that educational opportunity and better housing conditions were essential if black Americans were to achieve upward mobility. While one group of lawyers focused on restrictive covenant cases,[13] which prevented blacks from buying housing in white neighborhoods, another spearheaded the drive for blacks to enter state-run professional schools.

In 1954, suits were brought in Kansas, South Carolina, Virginia, and Delaware on behalf of black Americans seeking to attend nonsegregated public schools. However, the case is commonly referred to as *Brown v. Board of Education*. The plaintiffs in the suit contended that segregation in the public schools denied them equal protection of the laws under the Fourteenth Amendment. The contention was that since segregated public schools were not and could not be made equal, black American children were deprived of equal protection of the laws.

The Court's unanimous decision addressed these key questions:

1. Are public schools segregated by race detrimental to black children?
2. Does segregation result in an inferior education for black children?
3. Does the maintenance of segregated public schools violate the Equal Protection Clause of the Fourteenth Amendment?
4. Is the maintenance of segregated public school facilities *inherently* unequal?

5. What was the intent of the framers of the Fourteenth Amendment regarding distinctions between whites and blacks?
6. Is the holding in *Plessy v. Ferguson* applicable to public education?
7. Does segregation of children in public schools *solely on the basis of race,* even though the physical facilities and other "tangible" factors may be equal, deprive the children of the minority group of equal educational opportunities?

Excerpts from the Supreme Court Decision in **Brown v. Board of Education**[14]

Mr. Chief Justice Warren delivered the opinion of the Court:

> . . . In each of these cases [NAACP suits in Kansas, South Carolina, Virginia, and Delaware] minors of the Negro race, through their legal representatives, seek the aid of the courts in obtaining admission to the public schools of their community on a nonsegregated basis. . . . This segregation was alleged to deprive the plaintiffs of the equal protection of the laws under the Fourteenth Amendment. In each of the cases other than the Delaware case, a three-judge federal district court denied relief to the plaintiffs on the so-called "separate but equal" doctrine announced by this Court in *Plessy v. Ferguson,* 163 U.S. 537. Under that doctrine, equality of treatment is accorded when the races are provided substantially equal facilities, even though these facilities be separated. . . .
>
> The plaintiffs contend that segregated schools are not "equal" and cannot be made "equal" and that hence they are deprived of the equal protection of the laws.
>
> . . . The most avid proponents of the post–[Civil] War amendments undoubtedly intended them to remove all legal distinctions among "all persons born or naturalized in the United States."
>
> In the first cases in this Court construing the Fourteenth Amendment, decided shortly after its adoption, the Court interpreted it as prescribing all state imposed discriminations against the Negro race. The doctrine of "separate but equal" did not make its appearance in this Court until 1896 in the *Plessy v. Ferguson, supra,* involving not education but transportation.

In these days, it is doubtful that any child may reasonably be expected to succeed in life if he is denied the opportunity of an education. Such an opportunity where the state has undertaken to provide it, is a right which must be made available to all on equal terms.

We come then to the question presented: Does segregation of children in public schools solely on the basis of race, even though the physical facilities and other "tangible" factors may be equal, deprive the children of the minority group of equal educational opportunities? We believe that it does.

To separate them [the children] from others of similar age and qualifications solely because of their race generates a feeling of inferiority as to their status in the community that may affect their hearts and minds in a way unlikely ever to be undone.

We conclude that in the field of public education the doctrine of "separate but equal" has no place. Separate educational facilities are inherently unequal. Therefore, we hold that the plaintiffs and others similarly situated for whom the actions have been brought are, by reason of the segregation complained of, deprived of the equal protection of the laws guaranteed by the Fourteenth Amendment.

. . . We have now announced that such segregation is a denial of the equal protection of the laws.

VI. YICK WO V. HOPKINS *(1886)*

In the 1880s, the questions of citizenship and the rights of citizens were raised again by Native Americans and Asian immigrants. While the status of citizenship for African Americans was settled by the Thirteenth and Fourteenth Amendments, the extent of the privileges and immunities clause still needed clarification. Yick Wo, a Chinese immigrant living in San Francisco, brought suit under the Fourteenth Amendment to see if it covered all persons in the territorial United States regardless of race, color, or nationality.

The Chinese were different from European immigrants because they came to the United States under contract to work as laborers building the transcontinental railroad. When Chinese workers remained, primarily in California, after the completion of the railroad in 1869, Congress became anxious about this "foreign element" that was non-

Christian and non-European. Chinese immigrants were seen as an economic threat because they would work for less than white males. To address the issue of economic competition, the Chinese Exclusion Act was passed in 1882 to prohibit further immigration to the United States. This gave the Chinese the unique status among immigrants of being the only group barred from entry into the United States and barred from becoming naturalized U.S. citizens.

Yick Wo, a subject of the Emperor of China, went to San Francisco in 1861, where he operated a laundry at the same premise for 22 years with consent from the Board of Fire Wardens. When the consent decree expired on October 1, 1885, Yick Wo routinely reapplied to continue to operate a laundry. He was, however, denied a license. Of the over 300 laundries in the city and county of San Fracisco, about 240 were owned by Chinese immigrants. Most of these laundries were wooden, the most common construction material used at that time, although it posed a fire hazard. Yick Wo and more than 150 of his countrymen were arrested and charged with carrying on business without having special consent, while those who were not subjects of China and were operating some 80 laundries under similar conditions, were allowed to conduct business.

Yick Wo stated that he and 200 of his countrymen with similar situations petitioned the Board of Supervisors for permission to continue to conduct business in the same buildings they had occupied for more than 20 years. The petitions of all the Chinese were denied, while all petitions of those who were not Chinese were granted (with one exception).

Did this prohibition of the occupation and destruction of the business and property of the Chinese laundrymen in San Francisco constitute the proper regulation of business, or was it discrimination and a violation of important rights secured by the Fourteenth Amendment?

The Court's decision addressed these key questions:

1. Does this municipal ordinance regulating public laundries within the municipality of San Francisco violate the United States Constitution?

2. Does carrying out this municipal ordinance violate the Fourteenth Amendment?
3. Does the guarantee of protection of the Fourteenth Amendment extend to all persons within the territorial jurisdiction of the United States regardless of race, color, or nationality?
4. Are the subjects of the Emperor of China who, temporarily or permanently, reside in the United States entitled to enjoy the protection guaranteed by the Fourteenth Amendment?

Excerpts from the Supreme Court Decision in Yick Wo v. Hopkins[15]

Mr. Justice Matthews delivered the opinion of the Court:

> . . . In both of these cases [*Yick Wo v. Hopkins* and *Wo Lee v. Hopkins*] the ordinance involved was simply a prohibition to carry on the washing and ironing of clothes in public laundries and washhouses, within the city and county of San Francisco, from ten o'clock p.m. until six o'clock a.m. of the following day. This provision was held to be purely a police regulation, within the competency of any municipality.

> . . . The rights of the petitioners are not less because they are aliens and subjects of the Emperor of China.

> The Fourteenth amendment to the Constitution is not confined to the protection of citizens. It says: "Nor shall any State deprive any person of life, liberty, or property without due process of law; nor deny to any person within its jurisdiction the equal protection of the laws." These provisions are universal in their application, to all persons within the territorial jurisdiction, without regard to any differences of race, or color, or of nationality; and the equal protection from the laws is a pledge of the protection of equal laws. . . .

> Though the law itself be fair on its face and impartial in appearance, yet, it is applied and administered by public authority with an evil eye and unequal hand, so as practically to make unjust and illegal discriminations between persons in similar circumstances. . . .

> . . . No reason whatever, except the will of the supervisors, is assigned why they should not be permitted to carry on, in the accustomed manner,

their harmless and useful occupation, on which they depend for a livelihood. And while this consent of the supervisors is withheld from them and from two hundred others who have also petitioned, all of whom happened to be Chinese subjects, eighty others, not Chinese subjects, are permitted to carry on similar business under similar conditions. The fact of this discrimination is admitted. No reason for it is shown, . . . no reason for it exists except hostility to the race and nationality to which the petitioners belong, and which in the eye of the law is not justified. The discrimination is, therefore, illegal, and the public administration which enforces it is a denial of the equal protection of the laws and a violation of the Fourteenth amendment of the Constitution. The imprisonment of the petitioners is, therefore illegal, and they must be discharged.

The decision in *Yick Wo* demonstrated the Court's perspective that the Fourteenth Amendment applied to all persons, citizens and noncitizens.

VII. ELK V. WILKINS (1884)

In the late 19th century, Native Americans constituted a problematic class when the Supreme Court considered citizenship. Although Native Americans were the original inhabitants of the territory that became the United States, they were considered outside the concept of citizenship. They were viewed as a separate nation, and described as uncivilized, alien people who were not worthy of citizenship in the political community. As Native Americans were driven from their homeland and pushed farther west, the United States government developed a policy of containment by establishing reservations. Native Americans who lived with their tribes on such reservations were presumed to be members of "not strictly speaking, foreign states, but alien nations." The Constitution made no provisions for naturalizing Native Americans or defining the status of those who chose to live in the territorial United States rather than be assigned to reservations. It was presumed that Native Americans would remain on the reservations. The framers of the Constitution had not given any thought as to when or how a Native American might become a U.S. citizen. When the Naturalization Law of 1790 was written, only Europeans were anticipated as future citizens. The citizenship of Native Americans was not settled until 1924, when a statutory law, not a constitutional amendment, granted citizenship.

Elk v. Wilkins raised the question of citizenship and voting behavior as a privilege of citizenship. In 1857, the Court had easily dismissed Dred Scott's suit on the grounds that he was not a citizen. Since he did not hold citizenship, he could not sue. *Minor v. Happersett* in 1872 considered the citizenship and voting issue with a female plaintiff. In that case, citizenship was not in doubt but the court stated that citizenship did not automatically confer the right to suffrage. In *Elk,* a Native American claimed citizenship and the right to vote. Before considering the right to vote, the Court first examined whether Elk was a citizen and the process by which one becomes a citizen.

As midwestern cities emerged from westward expansion in the 1880s, a few Native Americans left their reservations to live and work in those cities. John Elk left his tribe and moved to Omaha, Nebraska, under the jurisdiction of the United States. In April 1880, he attempted to vote for members of the city council. Elk met the residency requirements in Nebraska and Douglas County for voting. Claiming that he complied with all of the statutory provisions, Elk asserted that under the Fourteenth and Fifteenth Amendments, he was a citizen of the United States who was entitled to exercise the franchise, regardless of race or color. He further claimed that Wilkins, the voter registrar, "designedly, corruptly, willfully, and maliciously" refused to register him for the sole reason that he was a Native American.

The Court's decision addressed these key questions:

1. Is a Native American still a member of an Indian tribe when he voluntarily separates himself from his tribe and seeks residence among the white citizens of the state?
2. What was the intent of the Fourteenth Amendment regarding who could become a citizen?
3. Can Native Americans become naturalized citizens?
4. Can Native Americans become citizens of the United States without the consent of the U.S. government?
5. Must Native Americans adopt the habits of a "civilized" life before they become U.S. citizens?
6. Is a Native American who is taxed a citizen?

Excerpts from the Supreme Court Decision in Elk v. Wilkins[16]

Mr. Justice Gray delivered the opinion of the Court.

. . . The plaintiff . . . relies on the first clause of the first section of the Fourteenth amendment of the Constitution of the United States, by which "all persons born or naturalized in the United States, and subject to the jurisdiction thereof, are citizens of the United States and of the State wherein they reside"; and on the Fifteenth amendment, which provides that "the right of citizens of the United States to vote shall not be denied or abridged by the United States or by any State on account of race, color, or previous condition of servitude."

. . . The question then is, whether an Indian, born a member of the Indian tribes within the United States, is, merely by reason of his birth within the United States, and of his afterwards voluntarily separating himself from his tribe and taking up his residence among white citizens, a citizen of the United States, within the meaning of the first section of the Fourteenth amendment of the Constitution.

. . . The Indian tribes, being within the territorial limits of the United States, were not, strictly speaking, foreign States; but they were alien nations, distinct political communities, with whom the United States might and habitually did deal, as they thought fit, either through treaties made by the President and Senate, or through acts of Congress in the ordinary forms of legislation. The members of those tribes owed immediate allegiance to their several tribes, and were not a part of the United States. They were in a dependent condition, a state of pupilage, resembling that of a ward to his guardian.

. . . They were never deemed citizens of the United States, except under explicit provisions of treaty or statute to that effect, either declaring a certain tribe, or such members of it as chose to remain behind on the removal of the tribe westward, to be citizens, or authorizing individuals of particular tribes to become citizens. . . .

This [opening] section of the Fourteenth amendment contemplates two sources of citizenship, and two sources only: birth and naturalization.

. . . Slavery having been abolished, and the persons formerly held as slaves made citizens. . . . But Indians not taxed are still excluded from the count [U.S. Census count for apportioning seats in the U.S. House of Representatives],[17] for the reason that they are not citizens. Their absolute exclusion from the basis of representation, in which all other persons are now included, is wholly inconsistent with their being considered citizens.

. . . Such Indians, then, not being citizens by birth, can only become so in the second way mentioned in the Fourteenth amendment, by being "naturalized in the United States," by or under some treaty or statute.

. . . The treaty of 1867 with the Kansas Indians strikingly illustrates the principle that no one can become a citizen of a nation without its consent, and directly contradicts the supposition that a member of an Indian tribe can at will be alternately a citizen of the United States and a member of the tribe.

. . . But the question whether any Indian tribes, or any members thereof, have become so far advanced in civilization, that they should be let out of the state of pupilage, and admitted to the privileges and responsibilities of citizenship, is a question to be decided by the nation whose wards they are and whose citizens they seek to become, and not by each Indian for himself.

. . . And in a later case [Judge Deady in the District Court of the United States for the District of Oregon] said: "But an Indian cannot make himself a citizen of the United States without the consent and cooperation of the government. The fact that he has abandoned his nomadic life or tribal relations, and adopted the habits and manners of civilized people, may be a good reason why he should be made a citizen of the United States, but does not of itself make him one. To be a citizen of the United States is a political privilege which no one, not born to, can assume without its consent in some form."

Mr. Justice Harlan in the dissenting opinion:

. . . We submit that the petition does sufficiently show that the plaintiff is taxed, that is, belongs to the class which, by the laws of Nebraska, are subject to taxation.

. . . The plaintiff is a citizen and *bona fide* resident of Nebraska. . . . He is subject to taxation, and is taxed, in that State. Further: The plaintiff has become so far incorporated with the mass of the people of Nebraska that . . . he constitutes a part of her militia.

By the act of April 9, 1866, entitled "An Act to protect all persons in the United States in their civil rights, and furnish means for their vindication" (14 Stat. 27), it is provided that "all persons born in the United States and not subject to any foreign power, excluding Indians not taxed, are hereby declared to be citizens of the United States.". . . Beyond question, by that act, national citizenship was conferred directly upon all persons in this country, of whatever race (excluding only "Indians not taxed"), who were born within the territorial limits of the United States, and were not subject to any foreign power. Surely every one must admit that an Indian, residing in one of the States, and subject to taxation there, became by force alone of the act of 1866, a citizen of the United States, although he may have been, when born, a member of a tribe.

. . . If he did not acquire national citizenship on abandoning his tribe [moving from the reservation] and . . . by residence in one of the States, subject to the complete jurisdiction of the United States, then the Fourteenth amendment has wholly failed to accomplish, in respect of the Indian race, what, we think, was intended by it, and there is still in this country a despised and rejected class of persons, with no nationality; who born in our territory, owing no allegiance to foreign power, and subject, as residents of the States, to all the burdens of government, are yet not members of any political community nor entitled to any of the rights, privileges, or immunities of citizens of the United States.

In all, the Court never addressed Elk's right to vote because the primary question involved Elk's citizenship. By excluding him from citizenship because he had not been naturalized and because there was no provision for naturalization, John Elk was left outside of the political community as was Dred Scott.

VIII. LAU V. NICHOLS *(1974)*

In the 19th century, Native Americans and Asian immigrants sought to exercise rights under the Fourteenth Amendment although it had been designed explicitly to protect blacks. In the 20th century, issues first raised by African Americans, such as equality in public education, again presented other minority groups with an opportunity to test their rights under the Constitution.

Brown v. Board of Education forced the Court to consider the narrow question of the distribution of resources between black and white school systems. The *Brown* decision addressed only education. It did not extend to the other areas of segregation in American society, such as the segregation of public transportation (e.g., buses) or public accommodations (e.g., restaurants and hotels). Indeed, *Brown* had not even specified how the integration of the school system was to take place. All of these questions were taken up by the Civil Rights movement that followed the *Brown* decision.

Once the separate but equal doctrine was nullified in education, immigrants raised other issues of equality. In the 1970s, suits were brought on behalf of the children of illegal immigrants, non-English-speaking children of Chinese ancestry, and children of low-income parents.

In *Lau v. Nichols*, a non-English-speaking minority group questioned equality in public education. The case was similar to *Brown* because it concerned public education, the Equal Protection Clause of the Fourteenth Amendment, and the suit was brought on behalf of minors; but the two cases also differed in many respects. The 1954 decision in *Brown* was part of a series of court cases attacking segregated facilities primarily in southern states. It addressed only the issues of black-white interaction.

In *Lau v. Nichols*, a suit was brought on behalf of children of Chinese ancestry who attended public schools in San Francisco. Although the children did not speak English, their classes in school were taught entirely in that language. (Some of the children received special instruction in the English language; others did not.) The suit did not specifically ask for bilingual education, nor did the Court require it, but *Lau* led to the development of such programs. In bilingual education, the curriculum is taught in children's native language, but they are also given separate instruction in the English language, and over time they are moved into English throughout their courses.

The *Lau* decision hinged in part on Department of Health, Education, and Welfare guidelines that prohibited discrimination in federally assisted programs. The decision was narrow because it instructed only the lower court to provide appropriate relief. The Court's ruling did not guarantee minority language rights, nor did it require bilingual education.

The Court's decision addressed these key questions:

1. Does a public school system that provides for instruction only in English violate the equal protection clause of the Fourteenth Amendment?
2. Does a public school system that provides for instruction only in English violate section 601 of the Civil Rights Act of 1964?
3. Do Chinese-speaking students who are in the minority receive fewer benefits from the school system than the English-speaking majority?
4. Must a school system that has a minority of students who do not speak English provide bilingual instruction?

Excerpts from the Supreme Court Decision in **Lau v. Nichols**[18]

Mr. Justice Douglas delivered the opinion of the Court:

> The San Francisco, California, school system was integrated in 1971 as a result of a federal court decree. The District Court found that there are 2,856 students of Chinese ancestry in the school system who do not speak English. Of those who have that language deficiency, about 1,000 are given supplemental courses in the English language. About 1,800 however, do not receive that instruction.

This class suit brought by non-English-speaking Chinese students against officials responsible for the operation of the San Francisco Unified School District seeks relief against the unequal educational opportunities, which are alleged to violate, *inter alia*, the Fourteenth Amendment. No specific remedy is urged upon us. . . .

The Court of Appeals [holding that there was no violation of the Equal Protection Clause of the Fourteenth Amendment or of section 601 of the Civil Rights Act of 1964] reasoned that "[e]very student brings to the starting line of his educational career different advantages and disadvantages caused in part by social, economic and cultural background, created and continued completely apart from any contribution by the school system.". . . Section 71 of the California Education Code states that "English shall be the basic language of instruction in all schools." That section permits a school district to determine "when and under what circumstances instruction may be given bilingually.". . .

Under these state-imposed standards there is no equality of treatment merely by providing students with the same facilities, textbooks, teachers, and curriculum; for students who do not understand English are effectively foreclosed from any meaningful education.

. . . We know that those who do not understand English are certain to find their classroom experiences wholly incomprehensible and in no way meaningful.

We do not reach the Equal Protection Clause argument which has been advanced but rely solely on section 601 of the Civil Rights Act of 1964, 42 U.S.C. section 2000d. to reverse the Court of Appeals.

That section bans discrimination based "on the ground of race, color, or national origin, in any program or activity receiving Federal financial assistance." The school district involved in this litigation receives large amounts of federal financial assistance. The Department of Health, Education, and Welfare (HEW), which has authority to promulgate regulations prohibiting discrimination in federally assisted school systems, in 1968 issued one guideline that "[s]chool systems are responsible for assuring that students of a particular race, color, or national origin are not denied the opportunity to obtain the education generally obtained by other students in the system." In 1970 HEW made the guidelines more specific, requiring school districts that were federally funded "to rectify the language deficiency in order to open" the instruction to students who had "linguistic deficiencies." . . .

It seems obvious that the Chinese-speaking minority receive fewer benefits than the English-speaking majority from respondents' school system which denies them a meaningful opportunity to participate in the educational program—all earmarks of the discrimination banned by the regulations. . . .

Lau differed from *Brown* because it was decided not on the basis of the Fourteenth Amendment but on the Civil Rights Act of 1964. In reference to *Brown*, the justices noted that equality of treatment was not achieved by providing students with the same facilities, textbooks, teachers, or curriculum. *Lau* underscores the idea that equality may not be achieved by treating different categories of people in the same way.

IX. *SAN ANTONIO SCHOOL DISTRICT V. RODRIGUEZ* (1973)

The 1973 case of *San Antonio School District v. Rodriguez* raised the question of equality in public education from another perspective. As was the case in *Brown* and *Lau*, the Fourteenth Amendment required interpretation. However, unlike the earlier cases, the issue was the financing of local public schools.

Education is not a right specified in the Constitution. Under a federal system, education is a local matter in each state. This allows for the possibility of vast differences among states and even within states on the quality of instruction, methods of financing, and treatment of nonwhite students. Whereas the *Brown* decision examined inequality between races, *San Antonio* considered inequality based on financial resources through local property taxes. *San Antonio* raised the question of the consequence of the unequal distribution of wealth among Texas school districts. As with *Brown* and *Lau*, minors were involved; however, the issue was not race or language instruction but social class. Did the Texas school system discriminate against the poor?

Traditionally, the states have financed schools based on property tax assessments. Since wealth is not evenly distributed, some communities are able to spend more on education and provide greater resources to children. This is the basis of the *San Antonio* case, where the charge was that children in less affluent communities necessarily received an inferior education because those communities had fewer resources to draw on. The Rodriguez family contended that the Texas school system of financing public schools through local property taxes denied them equal protection of the laws in violation of the Fourteenth Amendment.

Financing public schools in Texas entailed state and local contributions. About half of the revenues were derived from a state-funded program that provided a minimal educational base; each district then supplemented state aid with a property tax. The Rodriguez family brought a class action suit on behalf of school children who claimed to be members of poor families who resided in school districts with a low property tax base. The contention was that the Texas system's reliance on local property taxation favored the more affluent and violated equal protection requirements because of disparities between districts in per-pupil expenditures.

The Court's decision addressed these key questions:

1. Does Texas's system of financing public school education by use of a property tax violate the Equal Protection Clause (Section 1) of the Fourteenth Amendment?
2. Does the Equal Protection Clause apply to wealth?
3. Is education a fundamental right?
4. Does this state law impinge on a fundamental right?
5. Is a state system for financing public education by a property tax that results in interdistrict disparities in per-pupil expenditures unconstitutionally arbitrary under the Equal Protection Clause?

Excerpts from the Supreme Court Decision *in* San Antonio School District v. Rodriguez[19]

Mr. Justice Powell delivered the opinion of the Court:

. . . The District Court held that the Texas system [of financing public education] discriminates on the basis of wealth in the manner in which education is provided for its people. Finding that wealth is a "suspect" classification and that education is a "fundamental" interest, the District Court held that the Texas system could be sustained only if the State could show that it was premised upon some compelling state interest.

. . . We must decide, first, whether the Texas system of financing public education operates to the disadvantage of some suspect class or impinges upon a fundamental right explicitly or implicitly protected by the Constitution, thereby requiring strict judicial scrutiny. If so, the Texas scheme must still be examined to determine whether it rationally furthers some legitimate, articulated state purpose and therefore does not constitute an invidious discrimination in violation of the Equal Protection Clause of the Fourteenth Amendment.

. . . In concluding that strict judicial scrutiny was required, the [District] court relied on decisions dealing with the rights of indigents to equal treatment in the criminal trial and appellate processes, and on cases disapproving wealth restrictions on the right to vote. Those cases, the District Court concluded, established wealth as a suspect classification. Finding that a local property tax system discriminated on the basis of wealth, it regarded those precedents as controlling. It then reasoned, based on decisions of this Court affirming the undeniable importance of education, that there is a fundamental right to education and that, absent some compelling state justification, the Texas system could not stand.

We are unable to agree that this case, which in significant aspects is *sui generis*, may be so neatly fitted under the Equal Protection Clause. Indeed, we find neither the suspect-classification nor the fundamental-interest analysis persuasive.

The wealth discrimination discovered by the District Court in this case, and by several other courts that have recently struck down school financing in other States, is quite unlike any of the forms of wealth discrimination heretofore reviewed by this Court.

. . . First, in support of their charge that the system discriminates against the "poor," appellees have made no effort to demonstrate that it operates to the peculiar disadvantage of any class fairly definable as indigent, or as composed of persons whose incomes are beneath any designated poverty level. Indeed, there is reason to believe that the poorest families are not necessarily clustered in the poorest property districts. . . .

Second, neither appellees nor the District Court addressed the fact that . . . lack of personal resources has not occasioned an absolute deprivation of the desired benefit. The argument here is not that the children in districts having relatively low assessable property values are receiving no public education; rather, it is that they are receiving a poorer quality education than that available to children in districts having more assessable wealth. Apart from the unsettled and disputed question whether the quality of education may be determined by the amount of money expended for it, a sufficient answer to appellee's argument is that, at least where wealth is involved, the Equal Protection Clause does not require absolute equality or precisely equal advantages. . . .

For these two reasons . . . the disadvantaged class is not susceptible of identification in traditional terms. . . .

. . . [I]t is clear that appellee's suit asks this Court to extend its most exacting scrutiny to review a system that allegedly discriminates against a large, diverse, and amorphous class, unified only by the common factor of residence in districts that happen to have less taxable wealth than other districts. The system of alleged discrimination and the class it defines have none of the traditional indicia of suspectness: the class is not saddled with such disabilities, or subjected to such a history of purposeful unequal treatment, or relegated to such a position of political powerlessness as to command extraordinary protection from the majoritarian political process.

We thus conclude that the Texas system does not operate to the peculiar disadvantage of any suspect class. . . .

Education, of course, is not among the rights afforded explicit protection under our Federal Constitution. Nor do we find any basis for saying it is implicitly so protected. . . .

In sum, to the extent that the Texas system of school financing results in unequal expenditures between children who happen to reside in different districts, we cannot say that such disparities are the product of a system that is so irrational as to be invidiously discriminatory. . . .

Mr. Justice White, with whom Mr. Justice Douglas and Mr. Justice Brennan join, dissenting:

. . . In my view, the parents and children in Edgewood, and in like districts, suffer from an invidious discrimination violative of the Equal Protection Clause. . . .

There is no difficulty in identifying the class that is subject to the alleged discrimination and that is entitled to the benefits of the Equal Protection Clause. I need go no further than the parents and children in the Edgewood district, who are plaintiffs here and who assert that they are entitled to the same choice as Alamo Heights to augment local expenditures for schools but are denied that choice by state law. This group constitutes a class sufficiently definite to invoke the protection of the Constitution. . . .

In *San Antonio v. Rodriguez*, the Court did not find that the differences between school districts constituted invidious discrimination. A majority of the justices felt that Texas satisfied constitutional standards under the Equal Protection Clause. On the other hand, four justices in dissenting opinions saw a class (the poor) that was subject to discrimination and that lacked the protection of the Constitution.

X. BOWERS V. HARDWICK *(1986)*

In most of the cases we have considered, plaintiffs have sued on the basis that their rights under the Fourteenth Amendment were violated. However, cases can reach the Supreme Court by several routes, one of which is a *writ of certiorari,* which is directed at an inferior court to bring the record of a case into a superior court for re-examination and review. This was the case in *Bowers v. Hardwick,* in which the constitutionality of a Georgia sodomy statute was challenged. This became a key case in the battle for constitutional rights for gay women and men.

The case of *Bowers v. Hardwick* began on the issue of privacy because the behavior in question took place in Michael Hardwick's home. In deciding the case, however, the justices shifted from the issue of privacy to question whether gays have a fundamental right to engage in consensual sex.

Michael Hardwick's suit was based on the following facts. On August 3, 1982, a police officer went to Hardwick's home to serve Hardwick a warrant for failure to pay a fine. Hardwick's roommate answered the door, but was not sure if Hardwick was at home. The roommate allowed the officer to enter and approach Hardwick's bedroom. The officer found the bedroom door partly open and observed Hardwick engaged in oral sex with another man. The officer arrested both men, charged them with sodomy, and held them in the local jail for 10 hours.

The Georgia sodomy statute under which the men were charged made "any sexual act involving the sex organs of one person and the mouth or anus of another" a felony punishable by imprisonment for up to 20 years. When the district attorney decided not to submit the case to a grand jury, Hardwick brought suit attacking the constitutionality of the Georgia statute. Later, a divided court of appeals held that the Georgia statute violated Hardwick's fundamental rights. The attorney general of Georgia appealed that judgment to the Supreme Court.

The Court's decision on the case was split. Five justices ruled that the constitutional right of privacy did not apply to Hardwick's case; four argued that it did. While the Georgia statute did not specify that only homosexual sodomy was prohibited, the Court's majority opinion was framed in those terms. (Most legal prohibitions are directed at non-procreative acts irrespective of the sex of the participants.) The majority opinion also equated consensual sex within the home to criminal conduct within the home, an equation criticized by both gay rights activists and the dissenting justices.

> [The majority opinion] emphasized that the home does not confer immunity for criminal conduct, comparing gay sex first to drugs, firearms, and

stolen goods and then to adultery, incest, and bigamy. In so doing, the Court evoked images of dissolution, fear, seizure, and instability. . . . [and] the stereotypical fear of gay men as predators and child molesters. . . . The majority [opinion] advances, mostly by implication, its view of gay sexuality as unrelated to recognized forms of sexual activity or intimate relationships, and as exploitative, predatory, threatening to personal and social stability. [Writing for the dissent] Justice Blackmun excoriates the majority's choice of analogies and its failure to explain why it did not use nonthreatening analogies such as private, consensual heterosexual activity or even sodomy within marriage for comparison.[20]

While the majority argued that the past criminalization of sodomy argued for its continued criminalization, critics responded that "Whereas the task of the Court was to decide whether the criminalization of sodomy is consistent with the Constitution, the majority treated the fact of past criminalization as determinative. . . . It had no answer to Justice Blackmun's contention 'that by such lights, the Court should have no authority to invalidate miscegenation laws.'"[21]

The Court's decision addressed these key questions:

1. Does Georgia's sodomy law violate the fundamental rights of gays?
2. Does the Constitution confer the fundamental right to engage in homosexual sodomy?
3. Is Georgia's sodomy law selectively being enforced against gays?

Excerpts from the Supreme Court Decision *in* Bowers v. Hardwick[22]

Mr. Justice White delivered the opinion of the Court:

> This case does not require a judgment on whether laws against sodomy between consenting adults in general, or between homosexuals in particular, are wise or desirable. . . . The issue presented is whether the Federal Constitution confers a fundamental right upon homosexuals to engage in sodomy and hence invalidates the laws of the many States that still makes such contact illegal and have done so for a very long time.

We first register our disagreement with the Court of Appeals and with respondent that the Court's prior cases have construed the Constitution to confer a right of privacy that extends to homosexual sodomy. . . .

Precedent aside, however, respondent would have us announce, as the Court of Appeals did, a fundamental right to engage in homosexual sodomy. This we are quite unwilling to do. . . .

It is obvious to us that neither of these formulations [*Palko v. Connecticut*, 302 U.S. 319 (1937) and *Moore v. East Cleveland*, 431 U.S. 494 (1977)] would extend a fundamental right to homosexuals to engage in acts of consensual sodomy. Proscriptions against that conduct have ancient roots. . . . Sodomy was a criminal offense at common law and was forbidden by the laws of the original thirteen States when they ratified the Bill of Rights. In 1868, when the Fourteenth Amendment was ratified, all but 5 of the 37 States in the Union had criminal sodomy laws. In fact, until 1961, all 50 States outlawed sodomy, and today 24 States and the District of Columbia continue to provide criminal penalties for sodomy performed in private and between consenting adults. . . . Against this background, to claim that a right to engage in such conduct is "deeply rooted in this Nation's history and tradition" or "implicit in the concept of ordered liberty" is, at best, facetious. . . .

Respondent . . . asserts that the result should be different where the homosexual conduct occurs in the privacy of the home. He relies on *Stanley v. Georgia*, 394 U.S. 557, (1969) . . . where the Court held that the First Amendment prevents conviction for possessing and reading obscene material in the privacy of one's home: "If the First Amendment means anything, it means that a State has no business telling a man, sitting alone in his house, what books he may read or what films he may watch . . .".

Stanley did protect conduct that would not have been protected outside the home, and it partially prevented the enforcement of state obscenity laws; but the decision was firmly grounded in the First Amendment. The right pressed upon us here has no similar support in the text of the Constitution, and it does not qualify for recognition under the prevailing principles for construing the Fourteenth Amendment. Its limits are also difficult to discern.

Plainly enough, otherwise illegal conduct is not always immunized whenever it occurs in the home. Victimless crimes, such as the possession and use of illegal drugs, do not escape the law where they are committed at home. *Stanley* itself recognized that its holding offered no protection for the possession in the home of drugs, firearms, or stolen goods. . . . And if respondent's submission is limited to the voluntary sexual conduct between consenting adults, it would be difficult, except by fiat, to limit the claimed right to homosexual conduct while leaving exposed to prosecution adultery, incest, and other sexual crimes even though they are committed in the home. We are unwilling to start down that road. . . .

Justice Blackmun, with whom Justice Brennan, Justice Marshall, and Justice Stevens join, dissenting:

This case is no more about "a fundamental right to engage in homosexual sodomy," as the Court purports to declare, . . . than *Stanley v. Georgia*, 394 U.S. 557 (1969), . . . was about a fundamental right to watch obscene movies. . . . Rather, this case is about "the most comprehensive of rights and the right most valued by civilized men," namely, "the right to be let alone." *Olmstead v. United States*, 277 U.S. 438, (1928) (Brandeis, J., dissenting).

The statute at issue, Ga. Code Ann. section 16-6-2 (1984), denies individuals the right to decide for themselves whether to engage in particular forms of private, consensual sexual activity. The Court concludes that section 16-6-2 is valid essentially because "the laws of . . . many States . . . still make such conduct illegal and have done so for a very long time . . ." (Holmes, J., dissenting). Like Justice Holmes [dissenting in *Lochner v. New York*, 198 U.S. 45 (1905)], I believe that "[i]t is revolting to have no better reason for a rule of law than that it was laid down in the time of Henry IV. It is still more revolting if the grounds upon which it was laid down have vanished long since, and the rule simply persists from blind imitation of the past." Holmes, The Path of Law, 10 *Harvard Law Review* 457, 469 (1897). I believe we must analyze Hardwick's claim in the light of the values that underlie the constitutional right to privacy. If that right means anything, it means that, before Georgia can prosecute its citizens for making choices about the most intimate aspects of their lives, it must do more than assert that the choice they have made is an "'abominable crime not fit to be named among Christians.'"

Like the statute that is challenged in this case, the rationale of the Court's opinion applies equally to the prohibited conduct regardless of whether the parties who engage in it are married or unmarried, or are of the same or different sexes. Sodomy was condemned as an odious and sinful type of behavior during the formative period of the common law. That condemnation was equally damning for heterosexual and homosexual sodomy. Moreover, it provided no special exemption for married couples. The license to cohabit and to produce legitimate offspring simply did not include any permission to engage in sexual conduct that was considered a "crime against nature."

The Court's decision did not uphold Michael Hardwick's contention that his sexual conduct in the privacy of his own home was constitutionally protected. While the decision was seen as a blow to the assertion of gay rights, the majority's narrow one-vote margin also indicated the Court's shifting opinion on this issue.

XI. REGENTS OF THE UNIVERSITY OF CALIFORNIA V. BAKKE *(1978)*

The Supreme Court has reviewed several cases concerning equitable treatment in public education. Key cases include racially separate public schools (*Brown v. Board of Education,* 1954); the practice of English-only instruction for Chinese students in public schools (*Lau v. Nichols,* 1974); and the practice of operating public schools based solely on revenue from local property taxes (*San Antonio School District v. Rodriguez,* 1973).

African Americans not only had to fight for equity in public schools but also had to sue to gain admission to law and medical schools in state universities. See *Sipuel v. Oklahoma,* 1948; *Missouri ex rel Gaines,* 1938; and *Sweatt v. Painter,* 1950.

In 1978, race-based admissions became an issue again when a *white* person sued for admission to the medical school at the University of California at Davis. The case of *The Regents of the University of California v. Bakke,* however, must be seen in light of the policy of affirmative action, which sought to redress historic injustices against racial minorities and other specified groups by providing educational and employment opportunities to members of these groups.

In 1968, the University of California at Davis opened a medical school with a track admission policy for a 100-seat class. In 1974, applicants who identified themselves as economically and/or educationally disadvantaged or a member of a minority group (blacks, Chicanos, Asians, American Indians) were reviewed by a special committee. They could also compete for the remaining 84 seats. However, no disadvantaged white was ever admitted to the school through the special admissions program, although some applied. Bakke, a white male, applied to the medical school in 1973 and 1974 under the general admissions program. He was rejected both times because he did not meet the requisite cutoff score. In both years, special applicants with significantly lower scores than Bakke were admitted. After his second rejection Bakke sued for admission to the medical school, alleging that the special admissions program excluded him on the basis of his race in violation of the Equal Protection Clause of the Fourteenth Amendment, a provision of the California Constitution, and section 601 of Title VI of the Civil Rights Act of 1964, which provides that no person shall, on the ground of race or color, be excluded from participating in any program receiving federal financial assistance. The California Supreme Court applied a strict-scrutiny standard. It concluded that the special admissions program was not the least intrusive means of achieving the goals of the admittedly compelling state interests of integrating the medical profession and increasing the number of doctors willing to serve minority patients. The California court held that Davis's special admissions program violated the Equal Protection Clause of the U.S. Constitution. The Davis Medical School was ordered to admit Bakke.

The Court's divided opinion addressed these key questions:

1. Does the University of California, Davis Medical School's admission policy violate the Fourteenth Amendment?
2. Does giving preference to a group of nonwhite applicants constitute discrimination?
3. Does the University of California, Davis Medical School use a racial classification that is suspect?
4. Was Bakke denied admission to the University of California, Davis Medical School on the basis of race?
5. Can race be used as a criterion for admission to a university?

Excerpts from the Supreme Court Decision *in* The Regents of the University of California v. Bakke[23]

Mr. Justice Powell delivered the opinion of the Court:

The guarantees of the Fourteenth Amendment extend to all persons. Its language is explicit: "No State shall . . . deny to any person within its jurisdiction the equal protection of the laws." . . . The guarantee of equal protection cannot mean one thing when applied to one individual and something else when applied to a person of another color. . . .

. . . the [Fourteenth] Amendment itself was framed in universal terms, without reference to color, ethnic origin, or condition of prior servitude.

Petitioner [University of California, Davis] urges us to adopt for the first time a more restrictive view of the Equal Protection Clause and hold that discrimination against members of the white "majority" cannot be suspect if its purpose can be characterized as "benign."

. . . Moreover, there are serious problems of justice connected with the idea of preference itself. First, it may not always be clear that a so-called preference is in fact benign. . . . Second, preferential programs may only reinforce common stereotypes holding that certain groups are unable to achieve success without special protection based on a factor having no relationship to individual worth. Third, there is a measure of inequity in forcing innocent persons in respondent's position to bear the burdens of redressing grievances not of their making.

. . . When a classification denies an individual opportunities or benefits enjoyed by others solely because of his race or ethnic background, it must be regarded as suspect.

If petitioner's purpose is to assure within its student body some specified percentage of a particular group merely because of its race or ethnic origin, such a preferential purpose must be rejected. . . . Preferring members of any one group for no reason other than race or ethnic origin is discrimination for its own sake. This the Constitution forbids.

. . . [A] goal asserted by petitioner is the attainment of a diverse student body. This clearly is a constitutionally permissible goal for an institution of higher education. Academic freedom, though not a specifically enumerated constitutional right, long has been viewed as a special concern of the First Amendment. . . .

Ethnic diversity, however, is only one element in a range of factors a university properly may consider in attaining the goal of a heterogeneous student body.

It may be assumed that the reservation of a specified number of seats in each class for individuals from the preferred ethnic groups would contribute to the attainment of considerable ethnic diversity in the student body. But petitioner's argument that this is the only effective means of serving the interest of diversity is seriously flawed. . . . Petitioner's special admissions program, focused solely on ethnic diversity, would hinder rather than further attainment of genuine diversity.

. . . In summary, it is evident that the Davis special admissions program involves the use of an explicit racial classification never before countenanced by this Court. It tells applicants who are not Negro, Asian, or Chicano that they are totally excluded from a specific percentage of the seats in the class.

The fatal flaw in petitioner's preferential program is its disregard of individual rights as guaranteed by the Fourteenth Amendment. Such rights are not absolute.

Mr. Justice Brennan, Mr. Justice White, Mr. Justice Marshall, and Mr. Justice Blackmun, concurring in part and dissenting in part:

We conclude . . . that racial classifications are not *per se* invalid under the Fourteenth Amendment.

Unquestionably we have held that a government practice or statute which restricts "fundamental rights" or which contains "suspect classifications" is to be subjected to "strict scrutiny" and can be justified only if it furthers a compelling government purpose. . . . But no fundamental right is involved here. Nor do whites as a class have any of the "traditional indicia of suspectness; the class is not saddled with such disabilities, or subjected to such a history of purposeful unequal treatment, or relegated to such a history of purposeful unequal treatment, or relegated to such position of political powerlessness as to command extraordinary protection from the majoritarian political process.". . .

Certainly . . . Davis had a sound basis for believing that the problem of under-representation of minorities was substantial and chronic. . . . Until at least 1973, the practice of medicine in this country was, in fact, if not in law, largely the prerogative of whites. In 1950, for example, while Negroes constituted 10% of the total population, Negro physicians constituted only 2.2% of the total number of physicians. The overwhelming majority of these . . . were educated in two predominantly Negro medical schools, Howard and Meharry. By 1970, the gap between the proportion of Negroes in medicine and their proportion in the population had widened: The number of Negroes employed in medicine remained frozen at 2.2% while the Negro population had increased to 11.1%. The number of Negro admittees to predominantly white medical schools, moreover, had declined in absolute numbers during the years 1955 to 1964.

Moreover, Davis had very good reason to believe that the national pattern of under-representation of minorities in medicine would be perpetuated if it retained a single admissions standard. . . .

Davis clearly could conclude that the serious and persistent under-representation of minorities in medicine depicted by these statistics is the result of handicaps under which minority applicants labor as a consequence of . . . deliberate, purposeful discrimination against minorities in education and in society generally, as well as in the medical profession. . . .

It is not even claimed that Davis' program in any way operates to stigmatize or single out any discrete . . . or even any identifiable, nonminority group. Nor will harm comparable to that imposed upon racial minorities by exclusion or separation on grounds of race be the likely result of the program. . . .

Nor was Bakke in any sense stamped as inferior by the Medical School's rejection of him. Indeed, it is conceded by all that he satisfied those criteria regarded by the school as generally relevant to academic performance better than most of the minority members who were admitted. Moreover, there is absolutely no basis for concluding that Bakke's rejection that was a result of Davis' use of racial preference will affect him throughout his life in the same way as the segregation of the Negro schoolchildren in *Brown I* would have affected them. Unlike discrimination against racial minorities, the use of racial preferences for remedial purposes does not inflict a pervasive injury upon individual whites in the sense that wherever they go or whatever they do there is a significant likelihood that they will be treated as second-class citizens because of their color. . . .

In addition, there is simply no evidence that the Davis program discriminated intentionally or unintentionally against any minority group which it purports to benefit. The program does not establish a quota in the invidious sense of a ceiling on the number of minority applicants to be admitted. . . .

Finally, Davis' special admissions program cannot be said to violate the Constitution. . . .

. . . we would reverse the judgment of the Supreme Court of California holding the Medical School's special admissions program unconstitutional and directing respondent's admission.

Justices Stevens and Stewart, along with Chief Justice Rehnquist, concurred and dissented in part. They found that the university's special admissions program violated Title VI of the Civil Rights Act of 1964, which prohibits discrimination under any program or activity receiving federal funding assistance. This dissent found that Bakke was not admitted to the Davis Medical School because of his race.

Race-based admissions were again considered in *Hopwood v. Texas,* a 1994 case in the Western District of Texas. The suit, brought by four white Texas residents, claimed that the affirmative action admissions program of the University of Texas School of Law violated the Equal Protection Clause of the Fourteenth Amendment and Title VI of the Civil Rights

Act of 1964. The district court agreed that the plaintiffs' equal protection rights had been violated, but refused to direct the school to cease making admission decisions based on race. The case was subsequently appealed in the Court of Appeals for the Fifth Circuit, which held that the University of Texas School of Law could not use race as an admissions factor in order to achieve a diverse student body. The holding of the circuit court stands because the Supreme Court refused to hear the case.

This decision in effect overruled Justice Powell's opinion in *Bakke*, which held that universities can take account of an applicant's race in some circumstances. He asserted that the goal of achieving a diverse student body was permissible under the Constitution.

XII. TENNESSEE V. LANE *(2004)*

Historically, disabled people have been thought of as possessed or wicked. Often they were scorned and shut off from society in mental institutions. Today, however, the medical model is the dominant perspective that "those with disabilities have some kind of physical, mental, or emotional defect that not surprisingly limits their performance." Essentially, we don't expect those who are "flawed" to function as well as other people.[24]

Disabled people constantly face discrimination resulting in exclusion from housing, public buildings, and public transportation. This has prevented them from attending school, visiting museums, shopping, or living without assistance.

The 1990 Americans with Disabilities Act forbids discrimination against persons with disabilities in three key areas of public life. Title I covers employment; Title II encompasses public services, programs, and activities; and Title III covers public accommodations. In 2001 Casey Martin sued the PGA Tour,[25] under the public accommodations provisions of Title III to allow him to play golf on the tour while riding a golf cart because he suffers from Klippel-Trenaunay-Weber syndrome, a degenerative circulatory disorder that causes severe pain in his lower leg. Martin won his case when the Court held that the PGA walking rule was not compromised by allowing him to use a cart.

The provisions of Title II, which include access to the services, programs, or activities of a public entity such as a courthouse are questioned in *Tennessee v. Lane*. In this case, residents of the state who are paraplegics sued Tennessee because they were denied access to a courthouse under Title II of the Americans with Disabilities Act (ADA). Because this case involves a suit by an individual against a state, the Supreme Court has to consider the provisions of the Eleventh Amendment,[26] which provides state immunity against suits by citizens seeking equity and the enforcement clause, Section 5 of the Fourteenth Amendment.[27] After Tennessee was unsuccessful in getting the case dismissed because the plaintiffs sought damages, the case went to the Supreme Court. This issue then became an interpretation of Congress's power to enforce by appropriate legislation (Section 5) the guarantee that "no State shall make or enforce any law which shall abridge the privileges or immunities of citizens of the United States; nor shall any State deprive any person of life, liberty, or property, without due process of law; nor deny to any person within its jurisdiction the equal protection of the laws."

In 1998 George Lane and Beverly Jones, both paraplegics who use wheelchairs, filed suit against the state of Tennessee and a number of counties under Title II of the ADA, which states that no qualified individual with a disability shall, because of the disability be excluded from participation or denied the benefits of the services, programs, or activities of a public entity. Both parties claimed that they were denied access to the state court system because of their disability. Lane alleged that he was forced to appear to answer criminal charges on the second floor of a county courthouse. The courthouse had no elevator. In his first court appearance Lane crawled up two flights to reach the courtroom. When Lane had to return for a second time, he refused to crawl or to be carried to the courtroom. He was arrested and sent to jail for failure to appear for his hearing. Jones, a certified court reporter, claimed that she had not been able to obtain work because she could not gain access to several county courthouses.

The court's decision addressed these key questions:

1. Is Title II a valid exercise of Congress's Section 5 enforcement powers under the Fourteenth Amendment?
2. Does Title II enforce a variety of basic constitutional guarantees such as the right of access to the courts?
3. Does Title II validly enforce these constitutional rights?
4. Is Title II an appropriate response to this history of discrimination and pattern of unequal treatment?

Excerpts from the Supreme Court Decision in Tennessee v. George Lane et al.[28]

Mr. Justice Stevens delivered the opinion of the Court:

The ADA was passed by large majorities in both Houses of Congress after decades of deliberation and investigation into the need for comprehensive legislation to address discrimination against persons with disabilities.

. . . Title II, sections 12131–12134, prohibits any public entity from discrimination against "qualified" persons with disabilities in the provision or operation of public services, programs, or activities. The Act defines the term "public entity" to include state and local governments. . . .

Title II, like Title I, seeks to enforce this prohibition on irrational disability discrimination. But it also seeks to enforce a variety of other basic constitutional guarantees, infringements of which are subject to more searching judicial review. . . . These rights include some, like the right of access to the courts at issue in this case, that are protected by the Due Process Clause of the Fourteenth Amendment. The Due Process Clause [as] applied to the states via the Fourteenth Amendment both guarantee to a criminal defendant such as respondent Lane the "right to be present at all stages of the trial where his absence might frustrate the fairness of the proceedings.". . . The Due Process Clause also requires the States to afford certain civil litigants a "meaningful opportunity to be heard" by removing obstacles to their full participation in judicial proceedings. . . . And, finally, we have recognized that members of the public have

a right of access to criminal proceedings secured by the First Amendment.

. . . It is not difficult to perceive the harm that Title II is designed to address. Congress enacted Title II against a backdrop of pervasive unequal treatment in the administration of state services and programs, including systematic deprivations of fundamental rights.

. . . With respect to the particular services at issue in this case, Congress learned that many individuals, in many States across the country, were being excluded from courthouses and court proceedings by reason of their disabilities. A report before Congress showed that some 76% of public services and programs housed in state-owned buildings were inaccessible to and unusable by persons with disabilities. . . .

The conclusion that Congress drew from this body of evidence is set forth in the text of the ADA itself: "Discrimination against individuals with disabilities persists in such critical areas as . . . education, transportation, communication, recreation, institutionalization, health services, voting, and access to public services. . . . This finding, together with the extensive record of disability discrimination that underlies it, makes clear beyond peradventure that inadequate provision of public services and access to public facilities was an appropriate subject for prophylactic legislation.

. . . Whatever might be said about Title II's other applications, the question presented in this case is not whether Congress can validly subject the States to private suits for money damages for failing to provide reasonable access to hockey rinks, or even to voting booths, but whether Congress had the power under Section 5 to enforce the constitutional right of access to the courts. Because we find that Title II unquestionably is valid Section 5 legislation as it applies to the class of cases implicating the accessibility of judicial services, we need go no further.

. . . Title II's affirmative obligation to accommodate persons with disabilities in the administration of justice cannot be said to be "so out of proportion to a supposed remedial or preventive object that it cannot be understood as responsive to, or designed to prevent, unconstitutional behavior. . . . It is, rather, a reasonable prophylactic measure, reasonably targeted to a legitimate end.

For these reasons, we conclude that Title III, as it applies to the class of cases implicating the fundamental right of access to the courts, constitutes a valid exercise of Congress's Section 5 authority to enforce the guarantees of the Fourteenth Amendment.

XIII. THE MICHIGAN CASES

Gratz v. Bollinger et al. (2003) and *Grutter v. Bollinger et al.* (2003) considered admission standards for the University of Michigan's undergraduate program and its Law School. This marked the first time in the 25 years since the *Bakke* decision that the Supreme Court had considered the legal status of race-conscious admissions. In *Bakke,* Justice Powell held that race could be taken into consideration if it served a compelling government interest. He then held that the goal of achieving a diverse student body was a circumstance where race could be considered. However, the *Bakke* decision generated six separate opinions, but no majority opinion.[29]

The University of Michigan cases question whether Justice Powell's opinion set a precedent for considering diversity a constitutional justification for race-conscious admissions.

Gratz v. Bollinger et al. *(2003)*

Jennifer Gratz and Patrick Hamacher were both white residents of Michigan who applied for admission to the University of Michigan's College of Literature, Science, and the Arts (LSA). Both were considered qualified for admission. However, both were denied early admission, and upon further review neither was admitted to the university. The university's Undergraduate Admissions Office uses a written guideline system which includes such factors as high school grades, standardized test scores, the quality of the high school, curriculum strength, geography, alumni relationships, leadership, and race. Although the guidelines have changed since 1995, the university consistently considered African Americans, Hispanics, and Native Americans as "underrepresented minorities." The guidelines provided that all applicants from an underrepresented racial or ethnic minority group were automatically given 20 points out of the 100 needed for admission. The university never disputed the claim that practically every qualified applicant from these groups was admitted.

In 1997 Gratz and Hamacher filed a class-action suit alleging violation of their rights under the Fourteenth Amendment and the Civil Rights Act of 1964. The Equal Protection Clause of the Fourteenth Amendment provides that a state cannot act unfairly or arbitrarily toward or discriminate against a person within its jurisdiction because the individual has "the equal protection of the laws." Title VI of the Civil Rights Act prohibits discrimination on the grounds of race, color, or national origin against anyone participating in a program or activity which receives federal financial assistance.

The Court's decision addressed these key questions:

1. Under strict scrutiny does the university's use of race in its current admission policy constitute narrowly tailored measures that further compelling government interests?
2. Does the undergraduate admission policy violate the Equal Protection Clause of the Fourteenth Amendment?
3. Does the undergraduate admission policy violate Title VI of the Civil Rights Act of 1964?

Excerpts from the Supreme Court Decision in Gratz v. Bollinger et al. *(2003)*[30]

Chief Justice Rehnquist delivered the opinion of the Court:

> . . . Because the University's use of race in its current freshman admission policy is not narrowly tailored to achieve respondents' asserted interest in diversity, the policy violates the Equal Protection Clause. For the reasons set forth in *Grutter v. Bollinger* . . . the Court has today rejected petitioners' argument that diversity cannot constitute a compelling state interest. However, the Court finds that the University's current policy, which automatically distributes 20 points, or one-fifth of the points needed to guarantee admission, to every single "underrepresented minority" applicant solely because of race, is not narrowly tailored to achieve educational diversity. In *Bakke,*

Justice Powell explained his view that it would be permissible for a university to employ an admissions program in which "race or ethnic background may be deemed a 'plus' in a particular applicant's file" . . . he emphasized, however, the importance of considering each particular applicant as an individual, assessing all of the qualities that individual possesses, and in turn, evaluating that individual's ability to contribute to the unique setting of higher education. The admissions program Justice Powell described did not contemplate that any single characteristic automatically ensured a specific and identifiable contribution to a university's diversity. . . . The current LSA policy does not provide the individualized consideration Justice Powell contemplated. The only consideration that accompanies the 20-point automatic distribution to all applicants from under-represented minorities is a factual review to determine whether an individual is a member of one of these minority groups. Moreover, unlike Justice Powell's example, where the race of a "particular black applicant" could be "considered without being decisive" . . . the LSA's 20-point distribution has the effect of making "the factor of race . . . decisive" for virtually every minimally qualified underrepresented minority applicant. The fact that the LSA has created the possibility of an applicant's file being flagged for individualized consideration only emphasizes the flaws of the University's system as a whole when compared to that described by Justice Powell. The record does not reveal precisely how many applications are flagged, but it is undisputed that consideration is the exception and not the rule in the LSA's program. Also, this individualized review is only provided *after* admissions counselors automatically distribute the University's version of a "plus" that makes race a decisive factor for virtually every minimally qualified underrepresented minority applicant. . . . Nothing in Justice Powell's *Bakke* opinion signaled that a university may employ whatever means it desires to achieve diversity without regard to the limits imposed by strict scrutiny. Because the University's use of race in its current freshman admission policy violates the Equal Protection Clause, it also violates Title VI.

Grutter v. Bollinger et al. *(2003)*

Barbara Grutter, a white Michigan resident, applied to the University of Michigan Law School in 1996. She was originally placed on a waiting list but was ultimately not admitted. She alleged that her application was rejected because the Law School used race as a "predominant" factor, which gave applicants from certain minority groups "a significantly greater chance of admission than students with similar credentials from disfavored racial groups." The Law School asserted that it had a compelling interest in obtaining the educational benefits derived from a diverse student body. Law School officials contended that the admissions staff was not directed to admit a specific percentage or number of minority students, but rather to consider race among several factors. The goal was to obtain a "critical mass" of underrepresented minority students in order to realize the educational benefits of a diverse student body. The critical mass concept was never stated in terms of a fixed number, or percentage, or even a range of numbers or percentages. Admission officers acknowledged that minority group membership was a strong factor in the acceptance decisions and that applicants from minority groups were given large allowance for admission compared to applicants from nonfavored groups. However, it was asserted that race was not considered the predominant factor in the Law School's admission formula.

The Court's decision addressed these key questions:

1. Was race a predominant or a plus factor when reviewing the files of Law School applicants?
2. Did the Law School have a compelling interest in creating a diverse study body?
3. Does seeking a critical mass of minority students equal a quota?
4. Does the Law School admissions policy violate the Fourteenth Amendment and Title VI of the Civil Rights Act of 1964?

Excerpts from the Supreme Court Decision in Grutter v. Bollinger et al.[31]

Justice O'Connor delivered the opinion of the Court:

> We last addressed the use of race in public higher education over 25 years ago. In the landmark *Bakke*

case, we reviewed a racial set-aside program that reserved 16 out of 100 seats in a medical school class for members of certain minority groups. . . . The decision produced six separate opinions, none of which commanded a majority of the Court. . . . The only holding for the court in *Bakke* was that a "State has a substantial interest that legitimately may be served by a properly devised admissions program involving the competitive consideration of race and ethnic origin."

. . . Public and private universities across the nation have modeled their own admissions programs on Justice Powell's views on permissible race-conscious policies.

. . . Justice Powell approved the university's use of race to further only one interest: "the attainment of a diverse student body" . . . Justice Powell grounded his analysis in the academic freedom emphasized that nothing less than the "'nation's future depends upon leaders trained through wide exposure' to the ideas and mores of students as diverse as the nation of many peoples." . . . Both "tradition and experience lend support to the view that the contribution of diversity is substantial."

Justice Powell was, however, careful to emphasize that in his view race "is only one element in a range of factors a university properly may consider in attaining the goal of a heterogeneous student body." . . . For Justice Powell "[i]t is not an interest in simple ethnic diversity, in which a specified percentage of the student body is in effect guaranteed to be members of selected ethnic groups," that can justify the use of race. . . . Rather, "[t]he diversity that furthers a compelling state interest encompasses a far broader array of qualifications and characteristics of which racial or ethnic origin is but a single though important element."

. . . We have held that all racial classifications imposed by government "must be analyzed by a reviewing court under strict scrutiny." . . . This means that such classifications are constitutional only if they are narrowly tailored to further compelling governmental interests.

. . . The Law School asks us to recognize, in the context of higher education, a compelling state interest in student body diversity.

. . . Today, we hold that the Law School has a compelling interest in attaining a diverse student body.

. . . Our conclusion that the Law School has a compelling interest in a diverse student body is informed by our view that attaining a diverse student body is at the heart of the Law School's proper institutional mission, and that "good faith" on the part of a university is "presumed" absent "a showing to the contrary."

. . . The Law School's concept of critical mass is defined by reference to the educational benefits that diversity is designed to produce.

These benefits are substantial. As the District Court emphasized, the Law School's admissions policy promotes "cross-racial understanding," helps to break down racial stereotypes, and "enables [students] to better understand persons of different races."

. . . The Law School has determined, based on its experience and expertise, that a "critical mass" of underrepresented minorities is necessary to further its compelling interest in securing the educational benefits of a diverse student body.

. . . To be narrowly tailored, a race-conscious admissions program cannot use a quota system—it cannot "insulat[e] each category of applicants with certain desired qualifications from competition with all other applicants" (opinion of Justice Powell). Instead, a university may consider race or ethnicity only as a "'plus' in a particular applicant's file," without "insulat[ing] the individual from comparison with all other candidates for the available seats."

. . . We find that the Law School's admissions program bears the hallmarks of a narrowly tailored plan. As Justice Powell made clear in *Bakke*, truly individualized consideration demands that race be used in a flexible, nonmechanical way.

. . . We are satisfied that the Law School's admissions program . . . does not operate as a quota. Properly understood, a "quota" is a program in which a certain fixed number or proportion of opportunities are "reserved exclusively for certain minority groups."

. . . The Law School's goal of attaining a critical mass of underrepresented minority students does not transform its program into a quota. . . . "[S]ome attention to numbers," without more, does not transform a flexible admissions system into a rigid quota.

. . . The Law School affords this individualized consideration to applicants of all races. There is no

policy, either *de jure or de facto*, of automatic acceptance or rejection based on any single "soft" variable.
Unlike the program at issue in *Gratz v. Bollinger* the
Law School awards no mechanical, predetermined
diversity "bonuses" based on race or ethnicity.

. . . What is more, the Law School actually gives
substantial weight to diversity factors besides race.
The Law School frequently accepts nonminority
applicants with grades and test scores lower than
underrepresented minority applicants (and other
nonminority applicants) who are rejected.

. . . We agree that, in the context of its individualized inquiry into the possible diversity contributions
of all applicants, the Law School's race-conscious
admissions program does not unduly harm nonminority applicants.

. . . the Equal Protection Clause does not prohibit the Law School's narrowly tailored use of race
in admissions decisions to further a compelling interest in obtaining the educational benefits that flow
from a diverse student body.

NOTES

1. *Privileges and immunities* refer to the ability of one state to discriminate against the citizens of another state. A resident of one state cannot be denied legal protection, access to the courts, or property rights in another state.
2. In *Smith v. Allwright*, 321 U.S. 649 (1944), the Supreme Court held that a 1927 Texas law that authorized politi-cal parties to establish criteria for membership in the state Democratic party violated the Fifteenth Amend-ment. In effect, the criteria excluded nonwhites from the Democratic party. Since only party members could vote in the primary election, the result was a whites-only primary. The Democratic party so dominated politics in the southern states after the Civil War that winning the primary was equivalent to winning the general election.
3. Americans of African descent have been called *blacks, Negroes, colored,* or *African Americans,* depending on the historical period.
4. 19 Howard 393 (1857).
5. The Nineteenth Amendment that was ratified on August 18, 1920, stated, "The right of citizens of the United States to vote shall not be denied or abridged by the United States or by any state on account of sex. Congress shall have the power to enforce this article by appropriate legislation."
6. 21 Wallace 162 (1875).
7. Crozier, "Constitutionality of Discrimination Based on Sex," 15 *B.U.L. Review,* 723, 727–28 (1935) as quoted in William Hodes, "Women and the Constitution: Some Legal History and a New Approach to the Nineteenth Amendment." *Rutgers Law Review,* Vol. 25, 1970, p. 27.
8. Hodes, p. 45.

9. Gunnar Myrdal, *An American Dilemma: The Negro Prob-lem and Modern Democracy.* New York: Harper and Row (2d ed. 1962 [1944]), pp. 1073–74, as quoted in Hodes, p. 29. This same biblical ground has yielded the idea that a woman is an extension of her husband and his status.
10. The states under military rule were Virginia, North Carolina, South Carolina, Georgia, Florida, Tennessee, Alabama, Mississippi, Texas, Louisiana, and Arkansas.
11. The term *colored* was used in Louisiana to describe per-sons of mixed race who had some African ancestry.
12. 163 U.S. 537 (1896).
13. Restrictive covenants were written in deeds restricting the use of the land. Covenants could prohibit the sale of land to nonwhites or non-Christians.
14. 347 U.S. 483 (1954).
15. 118 U.S. 356 (1886).
16. 112 U.S. 94 (1884).
17. Native Americans and slaves posed a problem when tak-ing the census count, which was the basis for apportion-ing seats in the U.S. House of Representatives. Some states stood to lose representation if some of their slave or Native American population was not counted. Blacks were counted as three-fifths of a white man, and only those Native Americans who were taxed were counted.
18. 414 U.S. 563 (1974).
19. 411 U.S. 1 (1973).
20. Rhonda Copelon, "A Crime Not Fit to Be Named: Sex, Lies, and the Constitution," p. 182. In David Kairys (ed.), *The Politics of Law,* pp. 177–94, New York: Pantheon.
21. Copelon, p. 184.
22. 478 U.S. 186 (1986).
23. 438 U.S. 265 (1978).
24. Paul C. Higgins, *Making Disability.* Springfield, Il: Charles C. Thomas (1992), pp. 26–27.
25. *PGA Tour, Inc. v. Casey Martin,* 532 U.S. 661.
26. The Eleventh Amendment pertains to suits against the states. The interpretation is that a state cannot be sued by U.S. citizens of that state or another state nor by a foreign country.
27. Section 5 of the Fourteenth Amendment grants Congress the power to enforce the provisions of this amendment by appropriate legislation.
28. 124 S.Ct. 1978 (2004).
29. Four justices supported the University of California's ad-missions program against all objections on the ground that the government could use race "to remedy disad-vantages cast on minorities by past racial prejudice." Four other justices did not interpret *Bakke* on constitu-tional grounds, but instead struck down the program on statutory grounds. Justice Powell's position was against the set-aside admissions policy, but was also for "revers-ing the state court's injunction against any use of race whatsoever." The holding in *Bakke* was that a "State has a substantial interest that legitimately may be served by a properly devised admissions program involving the com-petitive consideration of race and ethnic origin."
30. 539 U.S. 244 (2003).
31. 539 U.S. 982 (2003).

B. Dynamics of Oppression, Dynamics of Change: The Challenges of U.S. History

※ **30**

Rape and the War Against Native Women

ANDREA SMITH

In Indian Country, there is a growing "wellness" movement, largely spearheaded by women, that stresses healing from personal and historic abuse, both on the individual and the community level. This wellness movement is based on the fact that Native peoples' history of colonization has been marked on our bodies. In order to heal from personal abuse, such as sexual abuse, we must also heal from the historic abuse of every massacre, every broken treaty, that our people have suffered. As Cecelia Fire Thunder states:

> We also have to recognize and understand that we carry the pain of our grandmothers, mothers, and the generation that came before us. We carry in our heart the pain of all our ancestors and we carry in our hearts the unresolved grief [and] the loss of our way of life. . . . There is no way we can move forward and be stronger nations without recognizing the trauma and pain that took place within our nations, our families, and within ourselves.[1]

One of the barriers, however, to healing from violence in Native communities is the reluctance to openly address violence against Native women. Native women who are survivors of violence often find themselves caught between the tendency within Native communities to remain silent about sexual and domestic violence in order to maintain a united front against racism and colonialism and the insistence on the part of the white-dominated antiviolence movement that survivors cannot heal from violence unless they leave their communities. The reason Native women are constantly marginalized in male-dominated discourses about racism and colonialism and in white-dominated discourses about sexism is the inability of both discourses to address the inextricable relationship between gender violence and colonialism. That is, the issue is

How It Would Be, If Some Ladies Had Their Own Way
Harper's Weekly, 1868.

The Declaration of Independence
Life, 1909.

not simply that violence against women happens during colonization but that the colonial process is itself structured by sexual violence. It is not possible for Native nations to decolonize themselves until they address gender violence because it is through this kind of violence that colonization has been successful. It is partly because the history of colonization of Native people is interrelated with colonizers' assaults upon Indian bodies. It is through the constant assaults upon our bodily integrity that colonizers have attempted to eradicate our sense of Indian identity.

As a multitude of scholars such as Robert Allen Warrior, Albert Cave, H. C. Porter, and others have demonstrated, Christian colonizers[2] often envisioned Native peoples as Canaanites, worthy of mass destruction as they went about the task of creating a "New Israel."[3] What makes Canaanites supposedly worthy of destruction in the biblical narrative and Indian peoples supposedly worthy of destruction in the eyes of their colonizers is that they both personify

sexual sin. In the Bible, Canaanites commit acts of sexual perversion in Sodom (Gen. 19:1–29), are the descendants of the unsavory relations between Lot and his daughters (Gen. 19:30–38), are the descendants of the sexually perverse Ham (Gen. 9:22–27), and prostitute themselves in service of their gods (Gen. 28:21–22; Deut. 28:18; 1 Kings 14:24; 2 Kings 23:7; Hos. 4:13; Amos 2:7).

Similarly, Native peoples, in the eyes of the colonizers, are marked by their sexual perversity.[4] Alexander Whitaker, a minister in Virginia, wrote in 1613, "They live naked in bodie, as if their shame of their sinne deserved no covering: Their names are as naked as their bodie: They esteem it a virtue to lie, deceive and steale as their master the divell teacheth them."[5] Furthermore, according to Bernardino de Minaya, "Their [the Indians'] marriages are not a sacrament but a sacrilege. They are idolatrous, libidinous, and commit sodomy. Their chief desire is to eat, drink, worship heathen idols, and commit bestial obscenities.[6]

Letting the Genie Out of the Bottle
The Des Moines Register & Tribune, 1943.

Cutting a Switch for a Bad Boy
McKee Barclay, *Baltimore Sun,* 1910.

Because they personify sexual sin, Indian bodies are inherently "dirty." As white Californians described in the 1860s, Native people were "the dirtiest lot of human beings on earth."[7] They wore "filthy rags, with their persons unwashed, hair uncombed and swarming with vermin."[8] The following 1885 Procter & Gamble ad for Ivory Soap also illustrates this equation between Indian bodies and dirt.

We were once factious, fierce and wild,
In peaceful arts unreconciled,
Our blankets smeared with grease and stains
From buffalo meat and settlers' veins.
Through summer's dust and heat content,
From moon to moon unwashed we went,
But IVORY SOAP came like a ray
Of light across our darkened way
And now we're civil, kind and good
And keep the laws as people should,
We wear our linen, lawn and lace
As well as folks with paler face
And now I take, where'er we go,
This cake of IVORY SOAP to show
What civilized my squaw and me
And made us clean and fair to see.[9]

Because Indian bodies are "dirty," they are considered sexually violable and "rapable." That is, in patriarchal thinking, only a body that is "pure" can be violated. The rape of bodies that are considered inherently impure or dirty simply does not count. For instance, prostitutes have almost an impossible time being believed if they are raped because the dominant society considers the prostitute's body undeserving of integrity and violable at all times. Similarly, the history of mutilation of Indian bodies, both living and dead, makes it clear to Indian people that they are not entitled to bodily integrity. Andrew Jackson, for instance, ordered the mutilation

It's for His Own Good
John T. McCutcheon, *Chicago Tribune,* 1916.

of approximately 800 Muscogee Indian corpses, cutting off their noses and slicing long strips of flesh from their bodies to make bridle reins.[10] Tecumseh's skin was flayed and made into razor straps.[11] A soldier cut off the testicles of White Antelope to make a tobacco pouch.[12] Colonel John Chivington led an attack against the Cheyenne and Arapahoe in which nearly all the victims were scalped; their fingers, arms, and ears were amputated to obtain jewelry; and their private parts were cut out to be exhibited before the public in Denver.[13]

In the history of massacres against Indian people, colonizers attempted not only to defeat Indian people but also to eradicate their very identity and humanity. They attempted to transform Indian people from human beings into tobacco pouches, bridle reins, or souvenirs—an object for the consumption of white people. This history reflects a disrespect not only for Native people's bodies but also for the integrity of all creation, the two being integrally related. That is, Native people were viewed

as rapable because they resemble animals rather than humans. Unlike Native people, who do not view the bodies of animals as rapable either, colonizers often senselessly annihilated both animals and Indian people in order to establish their common identity as expendable. During the Washita massacre, for example, Captain Frederick W. Benteen reported that Colonel Custer "exhibits his close sharpshooting and terrifies the crowd of frightened, captured squaws and papooses by dropping the straggling ponies in death near them. . . . Not even do the poor dogs of the Indians escape his eye and aim, as they drop dead or limp howling away.[14] Whereas Native people view animals as created beings deserving of bodily integrity, Bernard Sheehan notes that Europeans at that time often viewed animals as guises for Satan.[15] As one Humboldt County newspaper stated in 1853, "We can never rest in security until the redskins are treated like the other wild beasts of the forest."[16] Of course, if whites had treated Native people with the same respect that

Native people have traditionally treated animals, Native people would not have suffered genocide. Thus, ironically, while Native people often view their identities as inseparable from the rest of creation, and hence the rest of creation deserves their respect, colonizers also viewed Indian identity as inseparably linked to that of animal and plant life, and hence deserving of destruction and mutilation.

Today, this mentality continues in new forms. One example is the controversial 1992 hepatitis B trial vaccine program conducted among Alaska Native children. In this experiment, almost all Alaska Native children were given experimental vaccines without their consent. Dr. William Jordan of the U.S. Department of Health has noted that virtually all field trials for new vaccines in the United States are first tested on indigenous people in Alaska, and most of the vaccines do absolutely nothing to prevent disease.[17] As Mary Ann Mills and Bernadine Atcheson (Traditional Dena'ina) point out, this constant influx of vaccines into Native communities is a constant assault on their immune systems. They are particularly concerned about this hepatitis B vaccine because they contend it might have been tainted with HIV. They note that even Merck Sharp & Dohme seems to acknowledge that the vaccine contained the virus when it states in the *Physicians' Desk Reference* (PDR) that "clinical trials of HEPTAVAX-B provide no evidence to suggest transmission of. . . . AIDS by this vaccine, even when the vaccine has been used routinely in infants in Alaska."[18] According to Mills and Atcheson, alarming cases of AIDS soon broke out after these experiments, mostly among women and children, and now some villages are going to lose one-third of their population to AIDS.[19]

The equation between indigenous people and laboratory animals is evident in the minds of medical colonizers. The PDR manual notes that Merck Sharp & Dohme experimented both on "chimpanzees and . . . Alaska Native children."[20] Mills and Atcheson question why these drugs are being tested on Native people *or* chimpanzees when Alaska Native people did not have a high rate of hepatitis B to begin with.[21] Furthermore, they

question the precepts of Western medicine, which senselessly dissects, vivisects, and experiments on both animals and human beings when, as they argue, much healthier preventative and holistic indigenous forms of medicine are available. This Western medical model has not raised the life expectancy of indigenous people past the age of forty-seven. States Mills, "Today we rely on our elders and our traditional healers. We have asked them if they were ever as sick as their grandchildren or great-grandchildren are today. Their reply was no; they are much healthier than their children are today."[22]

Through this colonization and abuse of their bodies, Indian people learn to internalize self-hatred. Body image is integrally related to self-esteem.[23] When one's body is not respected, one begins to hate oneself. Thus, it is not a surprise that Indian people who have survived sexual abuse say they do not want to be Indian. Anne, a Native boarding school student, reflects on this process:

> You better not touch yourself. . . . If I looked at somebody . . . lust, sex, and I got scared of those sexual feelings. And I did not know how to handle them. . . . What really confused me was if intercourse was sin, why are people born? . . . It took me a really long time to get over the fact that . . . I've sinned: I had a child.[24]

As her words indicate, when the bodies of Indian people are inherently sinful and dirty, it becomes a sin just to be Indian. Each instance of abuse we suffer is just another reminder that, as Chrystos articulates, "If you don't make something pretty/they can hang on their walls or wear around their necks/you might as well be dead."[25]

While the bodies of both Indian men and women have been marked by abuse, Inés Hernández-Avila (Nez Perce) notes that the bodies of Native women have been particularly targeted for abuse because of their capacity to give birth. "It is because of a Native American woman's sex that she is hunted down and slaughtered, in fact, singled out, because she has the potential through childbirth to assure the continuance of the people."[26] David Stannard points out that control over women's reproductive abilities and destruction of women and children are essential in destroying a people. If the women of a nation are not disproportionately killed, then that nation's population will not be severely affected. He says that Native women and children were targeted for wholesale killing in order to destroy the Indian nations. This is why colonizers such as Andrew Jackson recommended that troops systematically kill Indian women and children after massacres in order to complete extermination.[27] Similarly, Methodist minister Colonel John Chivington's policy was to "kill and scalp all little and big" because "nits make lice."[28]

Because Native women had the power to maintain Indian nations in the face of genocide, they were dangerous to the colonial world order. Also, because Indian nations were for the most part not patriarchal and afforded women great esteem, Indian women represented a threat to colonial patriarchy as they belied the notion that patriarchy is somehow inevitable. Consequently, colonizers expressed constant outrage that Native women were not tied to monogamous marriages and held "the marriage ceremony in utter disregard,"[29] were free to express their sexuality, had "no respect for . . . virginity,"[30] and loved themselves. They did not see themselves as "fallen" women as they should have. Their sexual power was threatening to white men; consequently, they sought to control it.

> When I was in the boat I captured a beautiful Carib woman. . . . I conceived desire to take pleasure. . . . I took a rope and thrashed her well, for which she raised such unheard screams that you would not have believed your ears. Finally we came to an agreement in such a manner that I can tell you that she seemed to have been brought up in a school of harlots.[31]

> Two of the best looking of the squaws were lying in such a position, and from the appearance of the genital organs and of their wounds, there can be no doubt that they were first ravished and then shot dead. Nearly all of the dead were mutilated.[32]

> One woman, big with child, rushed into the church, clasping the altar and crying for mercy for herself and unborn babe. She was followed, and fell pierced with a dozen lances. . . . the child was torn alive from

the yet palpitating body of its mother, first plunged into the holy water to be baptized, and immediately its brains were dashed out against a wall.[33]

> The Christians attacked them with buffets and beatings. . . . Then they behaved with such temerity and shamelessness that the most powerful ruler of the island had to see his own wife raped by a Christian officer.[34]

> I heard one man say that he had cut a woman's private parts out, and had them for exhibition on a stick. I heard another man say that he had cut the fingers off of an Indian, to get the rings off his hand. I also heard of numerous instances in which men had cut out the private parts of females, and stretched them over their saddle-bows and some of them over their hats.[35]

American Horse said of the massacre at Wounded Knee:

> The fact of the killing of the women, and more especially the killing of the young boys and girls who are to make up the future strength of the Indian people is the saddest part of the whole affair and we feel it very sorely.[36]

Ironically, while enslaving women's bodies, colonizers argued that they were actually somehow freeing Native women from the "oppression" they supposedly faced in Native nations. Thomas Jefferson argued that Native women "are submitted to unjust drudgery. This I believe is the case with every barbarous people. . . . It is civilization alone which replaces women in the enjoyment of their equality."[37] The *Mariposa Gazette* similarly noted that when Indian women were safely under the control of white men, they "are neat, and tidy, and industrious, and soon learn to discharge domestic duties properly and creditably."[38] In 1862, a Native man in Conrow Valley was killed and scalped, his head twisted off, with his killers saying, "You will not kill any more women and children."[39] Apparently, Native women can only be free while under the dominion of white men, and both Native and white women need to be protected from Indian men rather than from white men.

While the era of Indian massacres in their more explicit form is over in North America, in Latin

America, the wholesale rape and mutilation of indigenous women's bodies continues. During the 1982 massacre of Mayan people in Rio Negro (Guatemala), 177 women and children were killed; the young women were raped in front of their mothers, and the mothers were killed in front of their children. The younger children were then tied at the ankles and dashed against the rocks until their skulls were broken. This massacre was funded by the U.S. government.[40] While many white feminists are correctly outraged by the rapes in Bosnia, organizing to hold a war crimes tribunal against the Serbs, one wonders why the mass rapes in Guatemala or elsewhere against indigenous people in Latin America [have] not sparked the same outrage. In fact, feminist legal scholar Catherine MacKinnon argues that in Bosnia "the world has *never* seen sex used this consciously, this cynically, this elaborately, this openly, this systematically . . . as a means of destroying a whole people."[41] She seems to forget that she lives on this land only because millions of Native people were raped, sexually mutilated, and murdered. Is perhaps mass rape against European women genocide while mass rape against indigenous women is business as usual? In even the white feminist imagination, are Native women's bodies more rapable than white women's bodies?

In North America, while there does not seem to be the same wholesale massacres of Indian people as in Latin America, colonizers will revert back to old habits in times of aggravated conflict. In 1976, Anna Mae Aquash (Micmac), who had been fighting U.S. policies against Native people as a member of the American Indian Movement (AIM), was found dead—apparently raped. Her killer was never brought to justice, but it is believed that she was killed either by the FBI or as a result of being badjacketed by the FBI as an informant. After her death, the FBI cut off her hands. Later, when the FBI pressured Myrtle Poor Bear into testifying against political prisoner Leonard Peltier, they threatened that she would end up just like Anna Mae if she did not comply.[42] In the 1980s when I served as a nonviolent witness for the Chippewa spearfishers, who were being harassed by white racist mobs, one white harasser carried a sign saying "Save a fish; spear a pregnant squaw."[43] Even after 500 years, in the eyes of the colonizers, Native women's bodies are still rapable. During the 1990 Mohawk crisis in Oka, a white mob surrounded the ambulance of a Native woman who was attempting to leave the Mohawk reservation because she was hemorrhaging after having given birth. She was forced to "spread her legs" to prove she had given birth. The police at the scene refused to intervene. An Indian man was arrested for "wearing a disguise" (he was wearing jeans), and he was brutally beaten, his testicles crushed. Two women from Chicago WARN (Women of All Red Nations, the organization I belong to) went to Oka to videotape the crisis. They were arrested and held in custody for eleven hours without being charged and were told they could not go to the bathroom unless the male police officers could watch. The place they were held was covered with pornographic magazines.[44]

This colonial desire to subjugate Indian women's bodies was quite apparent when, in 1982, Stuart Kasten marketed a new video game, "Custer's Revenge," in which players get points each time they, in the form of Custer, rape an Indian woman. The slogan of the game is "When you score, you score." He describes the game as "a fun sequence where the woman is enjoying a sexual act willingly." According to the promotional material,

> You are General Custer. Your dander's up, your pistol's wavin'. You've hog-tied a ravishing Indian maiden and have a chance to rewrite history and even up an old score. Now, the Indian maiden's hands may be tied, but she's not about to take it lying down, by George! Help is on the way. If you're to get revenge you'll have to rise to the challenge, dodge a tribe of flying arrows and protect your flanks against some downright mean and prickly cactus. But if you can stand pat and last past the strings and arrows—You can stand last. Remember? Revenge is sweet.[45]

Just as historically white colonizers who raped Indian women claimed that the real rapist was the Indian man, today white men who rape and murder

Indian women often make this same claim. In Minneapolis, a white man, Jesse Coulter, raped, murdered, and mutilated several Indian women. He claimed to be Indian, adopting the name Jesse Sittingcrow and emblazoning an AIM tattoo on his arm.[46] This is not to suggest that Indian men do not rape now. After years of colonialism and boarding school experience, violence has also been internalized within Indian communities. However, this view of the Indian man as the "true" rapist obscures who has the real power in this racist and patriarchal society.

Also, just as colonizers in the past targeted Native women for destruction because of their ability to give birth, colonizers today continue their attacks on the reproductive capabilities of Native women. Dr. Connie Uri, a Cherokee/Choctaw doctor, first uncovered sterilization abuses on Native women when a Native woman requested from her a "womb transplant." Dr. Uri discovered that this woman had undergone a hysterectomy for sterilization purposes but was told the procedure was reversible. The doctor began investigating sterilization abuses, which led Senator James Abourezk to request a study on IHS (Indian Health Services) sterilization policies. The General Accounting Office released a study in November 1976 indicating that Native women were being sterilized without informed consent. Dr. Uri conducted further investigations, leading her to estimate that 25 percent of all Native women of childbearing age had been sterilized without their informed consent, with sterilization rates as high as 80 percent on some reservations.[47]

While sterilization abuse has been curbed somewhat with the institution of informed consent policies, it has reappeared in the form of dangerous contraceptives such as Norplant and Depo-Provera.[48] These are both extremely risky forms of long-acting hormonal contraceptives that have been pushed on Indian women. Depo-Provera, a known carcinogen that has been condemned as an inappropriate form of birth control by several national women's health organizations,[49] was routinely administered to Indian women through IHS before it was approved by the FDA in 1992.[50] There are no studies on the long-term effects of Norplant, and the side effects (constant bleeding—sometimes for over ninety days—tumors, kidney problems, strokes, heart attacks, sterility) are so extreme that approximately 30 percent of women on Norplant want the device taken out in the first year, with the majority requesting it be removed within two years, even though it is supposed to remain implanted in a woman's arm for five years.[51] To date, more than 2,300 women suffering from 125 side effects related to Norplant have joined a class action suit against Wyeth Pharmaceuticals, the manufacturer of the product.[52] The Native American Women's Health Education Resource Center conducted a survey of IHS policies regarding Norplant and Depo-Provera and found that Native women were not given adequate counseling about the side effects and contraindications.[53]

Native women (as well as other women of color) are seen by colonizers as wombs gone amok who threaten the racist world order. In 1979, it was discovered that seven in ten U.S. hospitals that performed voluntary sterilizations for Medicaid recipients violated the 1974 DHEW guidelines by disregarding sterilization consent procedures and by sterilizing women through "elective" hysterectomies.[54] One recently declassified federal document, National Security Study Memorandum 200, revealed that even in 1976 the U.S. government regarded the growth of the nonwhite population as a threat to national security.[55] As one doctor stated in *Contemporary Ob/Gyn:*

> People pollute, and too many people crowded too close together cause many of our social and economic problems. These in turn are aggravated by involuntary and irresponsible parenthood. . . . We also have obligations to the society of which we are part. The welfare mess, as it has been called, cries out for solutions, one of which is fertility control.[56]

Consequently, Native women and women of color, because of their ability to reproduce, are "overpopulating the world" and pose "the single greatest threat to the health of the planet."[57] Consequently, Native women and women of color deserve no bodily integrity—any form of dangerous contraception is appropriate for them so long as it stops them from reproducing.[58]

Finally, completing the destruction of a people involves destroying the integrity of their culture and spirituality, which forms the matrix of Native women's resistance to sexual colonization. Native counselors generally agree that a strong cultural and spiritual identity is essential if Native people are to heal from abuse. This is because a Native woman's return to wellness entails healing from not only any personal abuse she has suffered but also from the patterned history of abuse against her family, her nation, and the environment in which she lives.[59] Because Indian spiritual traditions are holistic, they are able to restore survivors of abuse to the community, to restore their bodies to wholeness. That is why the most effective programs for healing revolve around reviving indigenous spiritual traditions.

In the colonial discourse, however, Native spiritual traditions become yet another site for the commodification of Indian women's bodies. As part of the genocidal process, Indian cultures no longer offer the means of restoring wholeness but become objects of consumerism for the dominant culture. Haunani-Kay Trask, Native Hawaiian activist, describes this process as "cultural prostitution."

> "Prostitution" in this context refers to the entire institution which defines a woman (and by extension the "female") as an object of degraded and victimized sexual value for use and exchange through the medium of money. . . . My purpose is not to exact detail or fashion a model but to convey the utter degradation of our culture and our people under corporate tourism by employing "prostitution" as an analytical category. . . .
>
> The point, of course, is that everything in Hawai'i can be yours, that is, you the tourist, the non-native, the visitor. The place, the people, the culture, even our identity as a "Native" people is for sale. Thus, Hawai'i, like a lovely woman, is there for the taking.[60]

Thus, this "New Age" appropriation of Indian spirituality represents yet another form of sexual abuse for Indian women, hindering its ability to help women heal from abuse. Columnist Andy Rooney exemplifies this dominant ideology when he argues that Native spiritual traditions involve "ritualistic dances with strong sexual overtones [that are] demeaning to Indian women and degrading to Indian children."[61] Along similar lines, Mark and Dan Jury produced a film called *Dances Sacred and Profane*, which advertised that it "climaxes with the first-ever filming of the Indian Sundance ceremony."[62] This so-called ceremony consisted of a white man, hanging from meat hooks from a tree, praying to the "Great White Spirit" and was then followed by C. C. Sadist, a group that performs sadomasochistic acts for entertainment. Similarly, "plastic medicine men" are often notorious for sexually abusing their clients in fake Indian ceremonies. Jeffrey Wall was recently sentenced for sexually abusing three girls while claiming this abuse was part of American Indian spiritual rituals that he was conducting as a supposed Indian medicine man.[63] David "Two Wolves" Smith and Alan "Spotted Wolfe" Champney were also charged for sexually abusing girls during supposed "cleansing" ceremonies.[64] That so many people do not question that sexual fondling would be part of Indian ceremonies, to the point where legitimate spiritual leaders are forced to issue statements such as "No ceremony requires anyone to be naked or fondled during the ceremony,"[65] signifies the extent to which the colonial discourse attempts to shift the meaning of Indian spirituality from something healing to something abusive.

Nevertheless, as mentioned earlier, Native women resist these attacks upon their bodies and souls and the sexually abusive representations of their cultures through the promotion of wellness. The University of Oklahoma sponsors two national wellness and women conferences each year, which more than 2,000 Indian women attend (it also sponsors smaller gatherings for Native men). These conferences help women begin their healing journeys from various forms of abuse and teach them to become enablers for community healing. The Indigenous Women's Network also sponsors gatherings that tie together the healing of individuals and communities from the trauma of this nation's history. At the 1994 conference, each of the four days had a different focus: individual healing, family healing, community healing, and political struggles in North America and the world.

I belonged to a wellness and women circle where Native women share their stories and learn from each other as they travel on the road toward wellness. At one circle, where we discussed the effect of hormonal contraceptives on our bodies, women talked about the devastating effects these hormones were having on their bodies, but the response of their medical providers was simply to give them more hormones. We began to see that we do not need to rely on the "experts" who have their own agendas; we need to trust our bodies, which colonizers have attempted to alienate from us. Our colonizers have attempted to destroy our sense of identity

Souvenirs for the Tourists

Tom Jones, *Commodity II*, 2004. Lithograph, 30 x 22 in. Printed by Jim Teskey. (Photo: Margot Geist)

by teaching us self-hatred and self-alienation. But through such wellness movements, we learn to reconnect, to heal from historical and personal abuse, and to reclaim our power to resist colonization.

NOTES

1. Cecelia Fire Thunder, "We Are Breaking a Cycle," *Indigenous Woman* II (1995): 3.
2. I shall not discuss how Jewish traditions have interpreted the Canaanite narratives, nor whether there even was a wholesale conquest of the Canaanites, which many scholars doubt. I am describing how the Christian appropriation of Canaanite narratives has impacted Native people; I make no claims either for or against Jewish colonialism.
3. Albert Cave, "Canaanites in a Promised Land," *American Indian Quarterly* (Fall 1988): 277–297; H. C. Porter, *The Inconstant Savage* (London: Gerald Duckworth, 1979), pp. 91–115; Ronald Sanders, *Lost Tribes and Promised Lands* (Boston: Little, Brown, 1978), pp. 46, 181, 292; Djelal Kadir, *Columbus and the Ends of the Earth* (Berkeley: University of California Press, 1992), p. 129.
4. Richard Hill, "Savage Splendor: Sex, Lies and Stereotypes," *Turtle Quarterly* (Spring/Summer 1991): 19.
5. Robert Berkoher, *The White Man's Indian* (New York: Vintage, 1978), p. 19.
6. David Stannard, *American Holocaust* (Oxford: Oxford University Press, 1992), p. 211.
7. Charles Loring Brace (1869), quoted in James Rawls, *Indians of California: The Changing Image* (Norman: University of Oklahoma, 1984), p. 195.
8. Hinton Rowan Helper (1855), quoted in Rawls, *Indians of California*, p. 195.
9. Andre Lopez, *Pagans in Our Midst* (Mohawk Nation: Akwesasne Notes), p. 119. It should be noted, as Paula Gunn Allen points out, that Native people in fact bathed much more frequently than did Europeans; see Paula Gunn Allen, *The Sacred Hoop* (Boston: Beacon, 1986), p. 217.
10. Stannard, *American Holocaust*, p. 121.
11. William James, *A Full and Correct Account of the Military Occurrences of the Late War between Great Britain and the United States of America* (London: printed by the author, 1818), Vol. 1, pp. 293–96, in *Who's the Savage?* ed. David Wrone and Russel Nelson (Malabar: Robert Krieger, 1982), p. 82.
12. U.S. Congress. Senate, Special Committee Appointed under Joint Resolution of March 3, 1865. *Condition of the Indian Tribes*, 39th Congress, Second Session, Senate Report 156, Washington, DC, 1867, pp. 95–96, quoted in *Who's the Savage?* p. 113.
13. John Terrell, *Land Grab* (New York: Dial Press, 1972), p. 13.
14. Terrell, *Land Grab*, p. 12.
15. Bernard Sheehan, *Savagism and Civility* (Cambridge: Cambridge University Press, 1980).
16. Rawls, *Indians of California*, p. 200.
17. Traditional Dena'ina, *Summary Packet on Hepatitis B Vaccinations* (Sterling, AK, November 9, 1992).

18. *Physicians' Desk Reference* (PDR) (Oradell, NJ: Medical Economics, 1991), pp. 1292–93.
19. Traditional Dena'ina, *Hepatitis B.*
20. PDR, pp. 1292–93.
21. Traditional Dena'ina, *Hepatitis B.*
22. Mary Ann Mills (speech delivered at a WARN Forum, Chicago, IL, September 1993).
23. For further discussion on the relationship between bodily abuse and self-esteem, see Ellen Bass and Laura Davis, *The Courage to Heal* (New York: Harper and Row, 1988), pp. 207–22, and Bonnie Burstow, *Radical Feminist Therapy* (London: Sage, 1992), pp. 187–234.
24. Celia Haig-Brown, *Resistance and Renewal* (Vancouver: Tilacum, 1988), p. 108.
25. Chrystos, "The Old Indian Granny," in *Fugitive Colors* (Cleveland: Cleveland State University Press, 1995), p. 41.
26. Inés Hernández-Avila, "In Praise of Insubordination, or What Makes a Good Woman Go Bad?" in *Transforming a Rape Culture*, ed. Emilie Buchwald, Pamela R. Fletcher, and Martha Roth (Minneapolis: Milkweed, 1993), p. 386.
27. Stannard, *American Holocaust*, p. 121.
28. Stannard, *American Holocaust*, p. 131.
29. *Cattaraugus Republican*, 11 February 1897, in Lopez, *Pagans in Our Midst*, p. 9.
30. Dominican monk Thomas Ortiz, quoted in Kirkpatrick Sale, *The Conquest of Paradise* (New York: Penguin, 1990), p. 201.
31. From Cuneo, an Italian nobleman, quoted in Sale, *Conquest of Paradise*, p. 140.
32. U.S. Commissioner of Indian Affairs, *Annual Report for 1871* (Washington, DC: Government Printing Office, 1871), pp. 487–88, cited in *Who's the Savage?* p. 123.
33. Le Roy R. Hafen, ed. *Ruxton of the Rockies* (Norman: University of Oklahoma Press, 1950), pp. 46–149, cited in *Who's the Savage*, p. 97.
34. Bartolome de Las Casas, *The Devastation of the Indies*, trans. Herma Briffault (Baltimore: Johns Hopkins University Press, 1992), p. 33.
35. Lieutenant James D. Cannon, quoted in "Report of the Secretary of War," 39th Congress, Second Session, Senate Executive Document 26, Washington, DC, 1867, printed in *The Sand Creek Massacre: A Documentary History* (New York: Sol Lewis, 1973), pp. 129–30.
36. James Mooney, "The Ghost Dance Religion and the Sioux Outbreak of 1890." In *Fourteenth Annual Report of the United States Bureau of Ethnology* (Washington DC: U.S. Government Printing Office, 1896), p. 885, quoted in Stannard, *American Holocaust*, p. 127.
37. Roy Harvey Pearce, *Savagism and Civilization* (Baltimore: Johns Hopkins University Press, 1965), p. 93.
38. Robert Heizer, ed., *The Destruction of California Indians* (Lincoln: University of Nebraska Press, 1993), p. 284.
39. Rawls, *Indians in California*, p. 182.
40. Information gathered by the Guatemalan Forensic Anthropology Team and posted by Stefan Schmitt, online at garnet.acns.fsu.edu/~sss4407/RioNeg.htm.
41. Catherine MacKinnon, "Turning Rape into Pornography: Postmodern Genocide," *Ms. Magazine* 4, no. I: 27 (emphasis mine).

42. Johanna Brand, *The Life and Death of Anna Mae Aquash* (Toronto: Lorimer), pp. 28, 140.
43. "Up Front," *Perspectives: The Civil Rights Quarterly* 14, no. 3 (Fall 1982).
44. Personal conversations with author (Summer 1990).
45. Promotional material from Public Relations: Mahoney/Wasserman & Associates, Los Angeles, CA, n.d.
46. Mark Brunswick and Paul Klauda, "Possible Suspect in Serial Killings Jailed in N. Mexico," *Minneapolis Star and Tribune*, 28 May 1987, IA.
47. See "The Threat of Life," *WARN Report*, pp. 13–16 (available through WARN, 4511 N. Hermitage, Chicago, IL 60640); Brint Dillingham, "Indian Women and IHS Sterilization Practices," *American Indian Journal* (January 1977): 27–28; Brint Dillingham, "Sterilization of Native Americans," *American Indian Journal* (July 1977): 16–19; Pat Bellanger, "Native American Women, Forced Sterilization, and the Family," in *Every Woman Has a Story*, ed. Gaya Wadnizak Ellis (Minneapolis: Midwest Villages & Voices, 1982), pp. 30–35; "Oklahoma: Sterilization of Native Women Charged to I.H.S." *Akwesasne Notes* (Mid Winter, 1989): 30.
48. For a description of the hazards of Depo-Provera, see Stephen Minkin, "Depo-Provera: A Critical Analysis," Institute for Food and Development Policy, San Francisco. He concludes that "the continued use of Depo-Provera for birth control is unjustified and unethical." For more information on the effects of Norplant, see *Womanist Health Newsletter*, Issue on Norplant, available through Women's Health Education Project, 3435 N. Sheffield, #205, Chicago, IL 60660.
49. For a statement on Depo-Provera from the National Black Women's Health Project, National Latina Health Organization, Native American Women's Health Education Resource Center, National Women's Health Network, and Women's Economic Agenda Project, contact NAWHERC, PO Box 572, Lake Andes, SD 57356-0572.
50. "Taking the Shot," series of articles from *Arizona Republic* (November 1986).
51. Debra Hanania-Freeman, "Norplant: Freedom of Choice or a Plan for Genocide?" *EIR* 14 (May 1993): 20.
52. Kathleen Plant, "Mandatory Norplant Is Not the Answer," *Chicago Sun-Times*, 2 November 1994, p. 46.
53. "A Study of the Use of Depo-Provera and Norplant by the Indian Health Services" from Native American Women's Health Education Resource Center, South Dakota, 1993.
54. "Survey Finds Seven in 10 Hospitals Violate DHEW Guidelines on Informed Consent for Sterilization," *Family Planning Perspectives* II, no. 6 (Nov/Dec 1979): 366; Claudia Dreifus, "Sterilizing the Poor," *Seizing Our Bodies*, ed. and intro. by Claudia Dreifus (New York: Vintage Books, 1977), pp. 105–20.
55. Debra Hanania-Freeman, "Norplant," p. 20.
56. *Akwesasne Notes*, p. 11.
57. Population Institute, *Annual Report*, 1991. See also Zero Population Growth, fundraising appeal, undated; "Population Stabilization: The Real Solution," pamphlet from the Los Angeles chapter of the Sierra Club—Population Committee; and Population Institute

fundraising appeal, which states that the population growth is the root cause of poverty, hunger, and environmental destruction.

58. For a more detailed discussion of the population control movement and its impact on communities of color, see Andy Smith, "Women of Color and Reproductive Choice: Combating the Population Paradigm," *Journal of Feminist Studies in Religion* (Spring 1996).

59. Justine Smith (Cherokee), personal conversation, 17 February 1994.

60. Haunani-Kay Trask, *From a Native Daughter; Colonialism & Sovereignty in Hawai'i* (Maine: Common Courage Press, 1993), pp. 185–94.

61. Andy Rooney, "Indians Have Worse Problems," *Chicago Tribune*, 4 March 1992.

62. Jim Lockhart, "AIM Protests Film's Spiritual Misrepresentation," *News from Indian Country* (Late September 1994): 10.

63. "Shaman Sentenced for Sex Abuse," *News from Indian Country* (Mid June 1996): 2A.

64. David Melmer, "Sexual Assault," *Indian Country Today* 15 (30 April-7 May 1996): 1.

65. Michael Pace, in David Melmer, "Sexual Assault," *Indian Country Today* 15 (30 April-7 May 1996): 1.

31

Race and Criminal Justice

EDWARD ESCOBAR

Between June 3 and June 10, 1943, the city of Los Angeles was wrenched by the worst rioting it had seen in the twentieth century. Incited by sensational newspaper stories and the statements of public officials, scores of white servicemen, sometimes joined by civilians and even police officers, roamed the streets of the city in search of Mexican American young men and boys wearing a distinctive style of dress called a zoot suit. When they found the zoot suiters, the servicemen attacked and beat the youths, tearing off their clothes and leaving them naked and bleeding in the gutters.[1]

The riots threw a harsh light upon the deteriorating relationship between the Los Angeles Mexican American community and the Los Angeles Police Department (LAPD) in the early 1940s. During the riots, the LAPD enforced the law selectively. Officers allowed servicemen to beat and strip the zoot suiters; only after the servicemen left the scene did police take action—arresting the Mexican American youths for disturbing the peace. Police arrested only a handful of servicemen during the riots but incarcerated over six hundred Mexican Americans.[2] With the passivity of the police, the level of violence escalated. Servicemen entered bars, theaters, dance halls, restaurants, and even private homes in search of victims. Toward the end of the rioting, the servicemen expanded their attacks to include all Mexican Americans, whether they wore zoot suits or not, and African Americans too.

At first, the Mexican American community did not respond directly to the attacks. In the initial days of the riots, neither the zoot-suit "gangs" (as the police and press had dubbed the loosely organized youth groups that had developed in Mexican American neighborhoods) nor Mexican American middle-class organizations took steps to stop the disorder. As the rioting continued and, in particular, as it became evident that the police were not protecting the community, zoot suiters began to defend themselves. According to the local press, bands of youngsters fought pitched battles with servicemen, civilians, and police in various parts of the city. The middle-class organizations also protested the increasing violence, albeit more cautiously. The rioting did not subside until the United States War Department concluded that local law-enforcement agencies could not or would not control the situation and declared parts of Los Angeles "out of bounds" to military personnel.

The Zoot Suit riots exposed a festering wound that infected the body politic of the city of Los Angeles. At its core lay a virulent anti-Mexican racism and the resultant alienation among a growing segment of Mexican American youth. The racism manifested itself as discrimination in employment, education, housing, and public accommodations. Without a doubt, however, the intertwined issues of the zoot-suit phenomenon and police misconduct received the greatest publicity and aroused the most intense passions.

The zoot-suit style and the youth subculture that accompanied it emerged from the anti-Mexican racism and its local manifestations. Much like youth subcultures in other societies, the zoot suiters were reacting to the unkept promises of mid-twentieth-century American society.[3] Educated in public schools to expect that through hard work and determination anything could be accomplished, these young people instead found their way to success barred by racial discrimination. They responded not through direct political action—a practical impossibility for them anyway—but through the symbolic rebellion of wearing an outlandish style of clothing that they knew would provoke an intense reaction from authority figures.

The reaction, however, was more dramatic than these youths anticipated and certainly greater than they wanted. Fueled by rabid and sensational newspaper coverage of juvenile crime, a public hysteria developed over an alleged zoot-suiter crime wave. One manifestation of this hysteria was the infamous Sleepy Lagoon trial that ended in January 1943. Seventeen young Mexican American men were convicted of murder without the prosecution's having presented any evidence that any of the defendants had so much as assaulted the victim. Within the context of this hysteria, police officials announced that they believed that Mexican Americans were biologically inclined toward criminality and that law-enforcement authorities needed to use harsh measures to keep the youths under control.

Because of the attitude of those in law enforcement and the resulting police practices, Mexican Americans in turn reached some harsh conclusions about the LAPD. Many believed that police regularly violated Mexican Americans' rights, that they were inclined toward chronic abuse of the community, and that the community would have to organize itself politically to combat police misconduct. They formed organizations, such as the Sleepy Lagoon Defense Committee, which sought to remedy some of the worst injustices by publicizing the anti-Mexican bias that seemed to pervade the criminal justice system. Their efforts and the often defensive response of the police and government officials contributed to the hostility and animosity that defined the relationship between much of the Mexican

American community and the LAPD in the period after World War II.

Writing from the perspective of the late twentieth century, it is hard to imagine a time when conflict was not the underlying theme in the relationship between Chicanos and the LAPD and, more broadly, in the relationship between racial minorities and police.[4] The truth is, however, that the nature and level of this conflict are phenomena of the first half of the century. While relations between the minority communities and urban police have never been "good," the fundamental assumptions upon which the current animosity is based have existed only since the end of World War II. These assumptions are the institutionalized belief within the law-enforcement community that Chicanos and other minority groups are criminally inclined and minority people's understanding that they must protect themselves from police misconduct through strident political activism. The purpose of this study is to examine how these two assumptions developed.

★ ★ ★

. . . The urban uprisings of the mid-1960s—almost all of which were sparked by violent encounters between police and minority citizens—provoked a plethora of governmental reports and scholarly studies on the relationship between the Chicano, Puerto Rican, and African American communities and American law-enforcement agencies. While these reports and studies lacked historical analysis, they became the accepted interpretation of police–minority community relations throughout the rest of the century. The studies of the 1960s and 1970s generally concluded that an adversarial relationship existed between minority groups and law enforcement and that the cause for this state of affairs lay with what the National Advisory Committee of Civil Disorders (also known as the Kerner Commission after commission chairman Otto Kerner) called "abrasive" police practices.[5]

A March 1970 report by the United States Civil Rights Commission entitled *Mexican Americans and the Administration of Justice in the Southwest* illustrated officials' and scholars' definition of abrasive police practices. The commission found "evidence of widespread . . . police misconduct against Mexican Americans." Examples included "excessive police violence," "discriminatory treatment of juveniles," "excessive use of arrests for 'investigation' and of 'stop and frisk,'" and interference with Mexican American political organizations.[6]

While the various studies generally conceded that a hostile relationship existed between police and the minority communities, they disagreed on the nature of and causes for these abrasive practices and the resulting mutual antagonism. Politically charged groups such as the Kerner Commission, which had to allow for the views of the law enforcement community, minimized the actual incidence of police misconduct and hinted that blacks were overly sensitive to standard police practices. In contrast, independent scholars acknowledged a high incidence of police misconduct as the major cause for the hostility and focused on attitudinal and structural factors as causes of abusive police practices. Most blamed racial prejudice among white officers for their egregious actions. . . .

Government commissions and independent scholars alike pointed to the increasing incidence of complaints from minority citizens and the equally decreasing responsiveness of police departments to those complaints as being among the principal factors that led to the hostility between the minority communities and the police and to the urban unrest of the 1960s. In an almost prescient analysis, the United States Civil Rights Commission issued a scathing report in March 1970 detailing antagonism between the Chicano community and the police, just five months before major rioting broke out between the two in Los Angeles. The commission found that in reaction to chronic police misconduct, "the attitude of Mexican Americans towards . . . police . . . is distrustful, fearful, and hostile. Police departments, courts, the law itself are viewed as Anglo institutions in which Mexican Americans have no stake and from which they do not expect fair treatment."[7]

The basic problem with the prevailing line of analysis that emerged from the 1960s studies, and even from some more recent reports, is not so much that it is wrong, but that it is incomplete.[8] To make the analysis more complete and robust, we must go beyond simplistic and static notions of racism, professionalism, and work culture and take into account the historical process by which these factors, and other equally important ones, have evolved. For example, societal racism has infected not just individual police officers but the police institution itself. Even more important, evolving police notions linking race and criminality have infiltrated the wider culture and have altered the way in which society defines race and racial characteristics. Society has come to equate minority communities, and especially minority youth, with violent crime. Not surprisingly, these perceptions have led to popular support for increased police budgets and autonomy, thus helping to implement the professionalism model. Finally, contrary to the victimization model employed by many liberal scholars, the minority communities, through their political activism and other forms of resistance, have themselves played a vital role in shaping their relationship with the police.

This [essay] seeks to expand on these concepts by studying the changing nature of the relationship between the Los Angeles Police Department—arguably the most important American urban police department of the second half of the twentieth century—and that city's largest racial minority group, Mexican Americans, during the years 1900–1945. . . . From the interactions between Mexican Americans and the police, the LAPD concluded that Mexican Americans, especially Mexican American youths, were a criminally inclined group that needed to be dealt with harshly. The same interactions taught many Mexican Americans that police regularly violated their rights, that they were inclined toward chronic abuse of the Mexican American community, and that the community would have to organize itself politically to combat police misconduct. Informing this narrative are the following three factors: the dynamic nature of race in American society; the role and development of the American police institution—in particular, the LAPD; and the development of the Los Angeles

Mexican American community. I will now discuss each of these factors in more detail.

Race is today generally understood, if not by the general public then at least by scholars, as a socially constructed concept. Geneticists and other biological scientists agree that the relationship between genetic structure and morphology is at best haphazard, that no one race possesses a gene or set of genes not possessed by other races, that "one's race is not determined by a single gene or gene cluster," and that there is greater genetic variation within a given race than there is between the races. Thus, there is no scientific basis for the racial categories we typically employ in everyday life.[9]

Rather, race is a socially defined and constructed concept that distinguishes among groups within a population, usually by phenotype but through other mechanisms too, for the purposes of subordination and exploitation.[10] As a socially constructed concept, race is dynamic by definition. What attributes constitute a race, which groups are defined as separate races, and how those races are treated change over time and may even vary from one race to another at any given historical moment. Thus, American society has at times viewed certain European immigrants—the Irish, Jews, and other Eastern Europeans—as separate races and other times as white. Similarly, during the nineteenth century white Americans viewed Mexicans, American Indians, and blacks as different races, but for different reasons and with the consequences of racialization differing for each group. Moreover, even when society has maintained a group in a racialized status over a long period, the basis of that racialization (the social assumptions about the group that maintain it as racially "other") changes over time.

The history of people of Mexican descent living in the United States provides an excellent example of the process of racialization. Mexicans were first racialized during the mid-nineteenth century through the rhetoric of Manifest Destiny, by which Americans sought to justify the Mexican-American War. The United States fought the war to acquire Mexico's northern territories of Texas, New Mexico, and California. American notions of fairness and international justice, however, precluded the United States from waging war against a weaker nation simply for territorial aggrandizement. The rhetoric of Manifest Destiny sought to alleviate these notions by alleging that the inherent superiority of the Anglo-Saxon race and its political, social, and economic institutions gave the United States the right, if not the responsibility, to bring under its control as much of the North American continent as possible. The racial component of this argument resulted in the dehumanization of Mexicans.[11]

Nineteenth-century American racial ideology was based on a biological essentialism that placed whites at the top of the racial hierarchy and Mexicans, along with Indians and blacks, at the bottom. Proponents of expansion justified aggression against Mexico by claiming that the Mexican people were an inherently inferior, "mongrel race" that deserved death and annihilation if they stood in the way of Anglo-Saxon expansion.

The racialization of Mexican people continued during the second half of the nineteenth century despite the fact that the United States had won the Mexican-American War. The historian Arnaldo De León has detailed the fundamental elements of American racial ideology as it applied to Mexican Americans and has concluded that whites considered Mexicans "a species of humanity different from (and inferior to) Anglos." Racial rhetoric tended to become particularly explicit whenever Mexicans and whites competed for control of vital economic resources such as land or labor. Mexicans, however, also engaged in the process of racial formation. According to the historian David Gutiérrez, nineteenth-century Mexican Americans adopted the term "la Raza" (literally, the race) to counter "the stigmatized status many Americans sought to impose on Mexicans." While Mexican Americans have consistently attempted to explain that la Raza has a connotation different from that of the English term *race*, that very effort shows the impact of its usage in American society.[12]

The biological essentialism of nineteenth-century American racial ideology carried over into the first three decades of the twentieth century. Spurred by the massive influx of Mexican immigrants into the United States, opponents of immigration used classic biological determinism to bolster their calls for restriction of Mexican immigration. Restrictionists took for granted the racial inferiority of the Mexican people and feared that continued immigration and Mexican fecundity would overrun the Southwest; many spoke of the negative "race value" of the Mexican population. In particular they feared that miscegenation between Mexicans and whites— which they labeled "mongrelization"—would lead to "the most insidious and general mixture of white, Indian, and negro blood strains ever produced in America." No wonder, then, that the Vanderbilt University economist Roy Garis argued that continued Mexican immigration to the Southwest would result in "the creation of a race problem that will dwarf the negro problem in the South" and in "the practical destruction, at least for centuries, of all that is worthwhile in our white civilization." Significantly, at least for the purposes of this study, Garis supported his argument with criminological studies that claimed that Mexicans were inherently inclined toward criminality.[13]

Proponents of continued Mexican immigration also bolstered the process of racialization, but put a positive spin on it. Employers in agriculture and other areas that profited from cheap immigrant labor generally conceded the racial inferiority of the Mexican population but attempted to use the restrictionists' argument to their own advantage. These antirestrictionists argued that the immigrants did not pose a permanent threat to white demographic dominance because Mexicans possessed a natural "homing instinct" that lured them back to Mexico. Miscegenation, they claimed, was not a problem because Mexican men did not desire white women. They did not pose other social problems because Mexicans were by nature "a very docile people." According to the Texas congressman and future vice president John Nance Garner, Mexicans "can be imposed on, the sheriff can go out and make them do anything. That is the way they are. So far as the laws of our state are concerned, they do not violate them." Finally, the antirestrictionists

argued that the restrictionists' fears flew in the face of the generally accepted racial hierarchy. "Have you ever heard," asked an Arizona agricultural spokesman, "in the history of the United States, or in the history of the human race, of the white race being overrum by a class of people of the mentality of the Mexicans?"[14]

Around the turn of the twentieth century, academicians began to question the concept of race as a biological construct and to replace it with cultural and sociological definitions. This new understanding of race was most fully articulated by Robert E. Park and his Chicago school of sociology during the 1930s and 1940s. For Park and his disciples, race was a function of ethnicity, and they equated ethnicity with the experiences of European immigrants in the United States. Like the European immigrants, racial minorities were expected to achieve social mobility and eventual assimilation into mainstream American society. To the extent that racial groups did not readily assimilate, ethnicity theorists saw their cultures as flawed. By World War II these notions of ethnicity and race had gained theoretical dominance and begun to enter popular consciousness and to influence public policy.[15]

While the abandonment of biological theories of race was a welcome circumstance, the ascendancy of ethnicity theory continued the racialization process for Mexican Americans. In equating racial groups' experiences with those of white European immigrants, ethnicity theory failed to consider the fact that the racialized status of Mexican Americans placed them in a chronically subordinated position in American society. Social scientists persisted in looking for flaws in Mexican American culture to explain the lack of social mobility or assimilation of Mexican Americans. According to such thinking, poor performance in school resulted from a present, rather than a future, orientation; low income came from a poor work ethic; and lack of political representation resulted from an inability to organize. Ethnicity theory was therefore every bit as deterministic as biological theories of race, and it served to reinforce negative attitudes among white public officials and the general public toward Mexican Americans.

Nowhere was the impact of ethnicity theory more evident or more significant than in the linkage of race and criminality. At the beginning of the century, while Mexicans were certainly seen by whites as an inferior race, they were not generally regarded by government and law-enforcement officials as inherently criminal. Even the LAPD articulated no such view. During the subsequent half century, however, the deterioration of the relationship between Mexican Americans and the LAPD, and especially the hysteria during World War II over juvenile delinquency, thrust Mexican American youth into the national consciousness as a criminal element in society. Henceforth, the youth "gang" became the metaphor through which much of white society viewed Mexican Americans. While many of the old ideas of Mexicans as lazy and stupid persisted, they eventually faded into the background, only to be replaced with the image of the vicious and treacherous gang member. This was a major reconstitution of the attributes that defined Mexican Americans as a separate race. Moreover, because the crisis achieved national and even international attention, the new definition of Mexican Americans as a criminally inclined racial group became embedded in the national consciousness. While social scientists clamored that race, as a biological construct, was no longer valid, most people, including law-enforcement officials, continued to distinguish on the basis of race. Mexican Americans had become a criminal element within the society and had to be dealt with accordingly.

At the same time, and somewhat ironically, the redefinition of Mexican Americans' racial status also had some salutary effects. The Zoot Suit riots of June 1943 and the efforts of the Mexican American groups to overcome racial injustice highlighted the dire economic conditions under which Mexican Americans lived, the hostility they faced from their white neighbors, and the discrimination—or, at best, indifference—they endured from police, school, and other governmental officials. Thus, the new definition included Mexican Americans as an oppressed and disadvantaged "minority" group whose problems had to be addressed in order to achieve civic harmony. Local business and government leaders established the Los Angeles County Human Relations Commission, whose function was to deal with the problems of racial minority groups. The designation of Mexican Americans as a racial minority elevated their political status, and they dominated the Los Angeles civil rights agenda from the 1940s until the early 1960s.

The function of police in American society has also contributed to the historically antagonistic relationship between Chicanos and the police. As agents of social control, police have historically played a conservative role. Urban elites created the first police departments during the mid-nineteenth century to control the burgeoning working class in industrializing northeastern cities. As the police institution spread and evolved throughout the rest of the nineteenth century and into the first decades of the twentieth century, it continued to concentrate its efforts on maintaining order in the working-class sections of urban America. Police patrolled city streets picking up drunks, jailing vagrants, and if not suppressing vice, at least making it invisible to ensure that the refuse of industrialized society did not disrupt the lives of the more genteel classes. On a more sinister level, police acted as the willing pawns of factory owners and chambers of commerce in suppressing labor unions, radical political organizations, and other expressions of working-class sentiment. As the legal scholar Lawrence Friedman has noted, throughout the nineteenth century and much of the twentieth century, the police functioned as "the army of the status quo."[16]

Law enforcement's essential conservatism is not an accident of history; rather, it stems from the nature of the police function. Maintaining order is a concept that can be taken either literally or metaphorically. On a literal level, police are taught to be suspicious of anything out of the ordinary. At midcentury, it became a policy for police departments to act on their suspicions. In a 1963 article in *Police* magazine on the issue of field interrogations, the author advised officers to "look for the unusual"—specifically, to be on watch for "persons who do not 'belong' where they are observed [and] automobiles which do not 'look right.'" While courts have since ruled this practice (called profiling in police parlance) unconstitutional, it still continues informally, especially in more affluent areas.[17]

On a broader level the police also enforce the existing social and economic order. Law enforcement functions as the coercive arm of the state, the role of police in any society regardless of its social or economic system. In a capitalist society with inherent class inequalities and equally apparent race distinctions that approximate class distinctions, the police play an important role in maintaining racial inequality. During the first half of the twentieth century, when racial inequality was codified through Jim Crow laws, this role for the police was explicit and overt. But even when a given action does not violate the law, police often enforce racial restrictions as part of their normal mandate to maintain order. Thus, when officers conduct a field interrogation of Chicano youth in a white neighborhood simply because they do not "belong," police not so subtly reinforce the idea that Mexicans should stay in their place. The role of the police in supporting the racial hierarchy becomes overt again when, in the name of maintaining order, they undermine the protest activities of minority groups.[18]

Modern police departments, however, are not simply the pawns of capital. As part of the state apparatus, law enforcement today often plots for itself a course that is at least seemingly independent from, and sometimes even at odds with, capitalist interests. This independent course stems from the professionalism model's major dictum of autonomy from political control. When police departments began adopting professionalism during the middle third of the century, they also began developing agendas that promoted their own bureaucratic interests while—and this is most important—still performing their essential function of supporting the capitalist economic order. Particularly in controlling minority groups, law enforcement has been extraordinarily successful in conflating both agendas. Through the concept of the "thin blue line," police function in the late twentieth century as what author Mike Davis has called the "space police,"

protecting the enclaves of the rich and powerful from the frustrated and therefore dangerous minority communities. In return, elites have generally supported law enforcement's arguments for augmented budgets and increased independence.[19]

The history of the LAPD in the first half of the twentieth century demonstrates the impact of professionalization not only on everyday police practices but also on the department's relationship with the white working class and with the minority communities. Prior to 1938, the LAPD functioned as the rather crude instrument by which local business associations maintained Los Angeles as the "citadel of the open shop." Throughout this period, but especially during the 1920s and 1930s, LAPD officers infiltrated labor unions and other "radical" organizations, sabotaged their efforts, violently broke up their meetings and picket lines, and generally harassed and intimidated organized labor and other leftist organizations in Los Angeles. Two sets of consequences resulted from these actions. First, as long as the LAPD successfully performed these functions, it could count on employer groups to support its ongoing demands for additional municipal funding. This vital support came despite the LAPD's reputation as one of the most corrupt police departments in the country. Second, while the experiences of Mexican American workers probably did not differ greatly from those of other Los Angeles unionists and radicals, police repression did help maintain Mexican workers in a subordinated status and it engendered hostility between the Mexican community and the LAPD.

Toward the end of the Depression decade, however, several phenomena converged to change the nature of the relationship between the LAPD and the community it served. First, the department adopted professionalism as its model for reform after a 1938 recall election and the subsequent dismissal of the corrupt chief of police. While the LAPD did not become fully professionalized until the 1950s, the initial efforts of the new reform administration were both controversial and costly and therefore demanded broad political support. The traditional sources of support became more problematic, however, when a general rapprochement occurred between organized labor and business groups that resulted in the LAPD losing employers' automatic backing for its budgetary requests. In order to expand its political base, the LAPD shifted its emphasis from union busting to another aspect of the professionalism model—that of conducting a "war on crime."

The LAPD's declaration of war against the city's "criminal elements" coincided with the department's linking of race and criminality. This association resulted partly from the literature in the emerging field of criminology and the way in which the department interpreted arrest statistics. In addition, the early 1940s saw the emergence of a rebellious Mexican American youth culture. This culture was most prominently characterized by young Mexican American males wearing an outlandish outfit called a zoot suit, speaking in a special argot called Caló, and assuming a definitely rebellious, if not hostile, public attitude toward authority. While a majority of Mexican American youths wore some part of the zoot suit, only a small number, the so-called pachucos, consistently engaged in pathological, antisocial behavior. Nevertheless, enough youth crime existed for the police and the press to attribute all such offenses to zoot-suit gangs. By the end of the war both police and public equated Mexican American youth with the zoot suit and the zoot suit with gangsterism.

Government officials and the public reacted with horror and consternation at this unprecedented outbreak of racial and generational defiance. They saw the zoot-suit phenomenon as a sign of the inherent social deviance in the Mexican American "race" and the pathological nature of Mexican culture. This analysis led directly to the development of a broad consensus that Mexican Americans were either biologically or sociologically inclined toward criminality. On the basis of that conclusion Los Angeles government officials, with the firm backing of the city's white majority population, gave the LAPD plentiful resources and broad latitude to institute harsh measures to deal with what the department defined as the criminal elements within the community.[20]

The LAPD, however, did not dictate its relationship with the Mexican American community. As a public entity, the department had to react to the political activism that emanated even from this largely disenfranchised minority group. While the essence of that political activism consisted of Mexican Americans' efforts to overcome their chronically subordinated status in American society, the form that the activism took changed as the Mexican American community developed.[21]

In the nineteenth century, Mexican political activity resulted from the lingering effects of the Mexican-American War (1846–1848). As noted earlier, the United States had initiated and prosecuted the war in order to acquire Mexico's northern provinces, especially California. The Treaty of Guadalupe Hidalgo ended the war, confirmed that acquisition, and guaranteed the rights of the approximately one hundred thousand Mexicans living in those territories. But the Mexicans who remained in this area, which became known as the American Southwest, never achieved equality. Indeed, as a result of the enduring effects of the racist rhetoric of Manifest Destiny that Americans had used to justify the war, Mexicans found themselves relegated to the position of a politically disenfranchised, economically subordinated, and socially ostracized racial group. They responded to their generalized subordination by developing a relatively cohesive ethnic identity and generating a series of defense mechanisms to protect themselves from the worst aspects of American racism. In addition, throughout the nineteenth century, some Mexicans, with at least the tacit support of a large part of the community, engaged in social banditry to protest their subordinated status.[22]

The arrival of as many as 1.5 million Mexican immigrants between 1890 and 1930 fundamentally altered the nature of the Mexican American community in the United States. By greatly enlarging the Mexican neighborhoods, or barrios, these newcomers reinforced the presence of Mexican culture in the Southwest. This influx did not, however, alter the low status assigned to Mexican Americans, that of an inferior racial group. This status was manifested in a number of ways, but undoubtedly the most important was in the continued economic exploitation of Mexican workers. As new workers came into the labor market they were allowed to compete only for the most menial and lowest-paying jobs. Thus, many Mexican Americans living in rural areas became migrant farmworkers and as such were the mainstay of Southwestern agribusiness. In urban areas, including Los Angeles, the overwhelming majority of Mexican Americans found jobs only in unskilled, blue-collar occupations. The resulting low income meant that Mexican American families lived in conditions that were among the most destitute of any ethnic group in the country. Mexicans also suffered from overt discrimination in many other areas, including education, housing, and public accommodations.

Throughout the twentieth century Mexican Americans have used a variety of strategies to overcome these disadvantages. In the early part of the century their efforts went largely into the economic arena, with workers in particular industries either forming overtly nationalistic Mexican labor unions or joining white-led unions. As community institutions developed, Mexican Americans turned their attention to fighting other forms of discrimination. In both cases, the resulting protest was explicit and narrowly focused, as in the work of the labor unions and the efforts of civil rights groups like the League of United Latin American Citizens (LULAC). Often, however, the protest was more symbolic and ill-defined and manifested itself through such phenomena as the zoot suit. The struggle for equality has defined much of the Chicano experience in the twentieth century.

The relationship between the Mexican American community and the LAPD developed within this context of struggle. At the turn of the century, Los Angeles Mexicans had not yet developed a clear perception of the LAPD. Early-twentieth-century Mexican immigrants concentrated their efforts on day-to-day survival, building community institutions, and demanding social and economic justice. They were not averse to protesting police misconduct when the occasion warranted it, but they did

so only in specific incidents, and, in the years before World War II, the police only periodically became a significant issue for the community. Any generalizations about the LAPD drawn by Mexicans at this time resulted from police repression of radical groups such as Ricardo Flores Magón's Partido Liberal Mexicano and from the department's constant persecution of Mexican labor unions.

Chronic conflict with the LAPD, and especially the zoot-suit crisis, transformed this relatively narrow political focus into the community-wide activism—sometimes referred to today as identity politics—that has characterized Mexican American politics since the 1940s. Crucial to the formation of this new political style was the emergence of institutions that served the Mexican American community. Spanish-language newspapers and volunteer groups such as mutual aid societies gave Mexican Americans the organizational and informational base from which to launch protests against police misconduct. Equally important was the rise of what several authors have called "the Mexican American generation."[23] As primarily the American-born and/or -raised daughters and sons of the previous "immigrant generation," members of this generation used their permanent status within the United States and their advanced education, English skills, and knowledge of American institutions to fight for the rights of Mexicans living in the United States. While this new political orientation took on many organizational forms, one organization, El Congreso de Pueblos que Hablan Español, provided an intellectual and structural bridge between the earlier labor and radical conflicts with the LAPD and the struggles of the zoot-suit era.

The crisis of the zoot-suit hysteria, aimed as it was at Mexican American youth, galvanized these forces into a community-wide effort to fight overt anti-Mexican discrimination. Spurred by official pronouncements of Mexican American criminality, by the daily barrage of newspaper stories regarding zoot-suit crime, by spectacular instances of official injustice such as the Sleepy Lagoon case, and, finally, by the riots themselves, Los Angeles Mexican Americans from a broad range of ideological affiliations engaged in an unprecedented level of political activism to defend their community. They formed organizations ranging from the Communist Party-inspired Sleepy Lagoon Defense Committee to the moderate and accommodationist, yet highly influential, Coordinating Council for Latin American Youth. Building a loose coalition, these groups succeeded to a remarkable degree in forcing white institutions to respond to Mexican American concerns. The police department, local newspapers, business and political leaders, and even the courts all took action and made decisions to accommodate the growing political power of the Mexican American minority. In short, as a result of their political activism during the zoot-suit crisis, Mexican Americans became a force with which local leaders had to reckon.

★ ★ ★

NOTES

1. The Zoot Suit riots are fully described in Jones, *Government Riots of Los Angeles;* McWilliams, *North from Mexico;* Mazón, *Zoot-Suit Riots;* Acuña, *Occupied America.*

2. *Time* magazine, June 21, 1943, quoted in Jones, *Government Riots of Los Angeles*, 29; Citizens' Committee for Latin-American Youth, Minutes, June 7, 1943; Manuel Ruiz Jr. Papers (hereafter Ruiz Papers), Box 3; *Los Angeles Times* (hereafter *Times*), June 7, 1943; *Los Angeles Daily News* (hereafter *Daily News*), June 7, 1943.

3. For a discussion of youth subcultures, see Hebdige, *Subculture.*

4. In this study, I will use the following terminology to designate people of Mexican descent living in the United States: *Mexican* will identify first-generation immigrants from Mexico; the term *Mexican American* will denote the second-generation children of the immigrants; the term *Chicano* will primarily refer to people of Mexican descent in the postwar period. In addition, the terms *white* and *Anglo* will designate Americans of European descent. In general, I will use Mexican to describe actors during the period from 1900 to 1930 and Mexican American for people from 1930 to 1945.

5. National Advisory Committee on Civil Disorders, *Report of the National Advisory Committee on Civil Disorders* (henceforth, Kerner Commission), 301.

6. United States Commission on Civil Rights, *Mexican Americans and the Administration of Justice in the Southwest,* 88.

7. U.S. Civil Rights Commission, *Mexican Americans and the Administration of Justice in the Southwest,* 88.

8. For a more recent articulation of these basic themes, see Independent Commission of the Los Angeles Police Department, *Report of the Independent Commission of the Los Angeles Police Department.*

9. Haney López, "Social Construction of Race"; also see Gould, "Geometer of Race."

10. This discussion draws heavily from Omi and Winant, *Racial Formation in the United States;* and Haney López, "Social Construction of Race." Race of course does not apply only to minority groups; people of European descent also have race and they usually fall into the category of white. For a discussion of whiteness, see Haney López, *White by Law;* Lipsitz, "Possessive Investment in Whiteness"; George J. Sánchez, "Reading Reginald Denny"; Taylor, "Hidden Face of Racism," 395–408; Williams, "Tragic Vision of Black Problems"; Lipsitz, "Toxic Racism"; and Fishkin, "Interrogating 'Whiteness,' Complicating 'Blackness.'" For the view that scholars ought not even use race as a category of analysis, see Miles and Torres, "Does 'Race Matter'?" and Fields, "Slavery, Race and Ideology in the United States of America."

11. Horsman, *Race and Manifest Destiny.*

12. DeLeón, *They Called Them Greasers*, 104; Gutiérrez, *Walls and Mirrors*, 29.

13. Reisler, *By the Sweat of Their Brow*, 151–176; Gutiérrez, *Walls and Mirrors*, 54 and 55.

14. Reisler, *By the Sweat of Their Brow*, 178–183. Reisler quotes S. Parker Fisselle saying that "like a pigeon, he [the Mexican] goes back to roost."

15. Omi and Winant, *Racial Formation*, 14–20; Haney López, "Social Construction of Race," 20–24.

16. Analyses of the origins of American urban police departments can be found in Lane, *Policing the City;* Richardson, *New York Police;* and the Center for Research on Criminal Justice, *Iron Fist and the Velvet Glove*, 19–23. The role of police protecting the interests of the capitalist class during the period in question is most thoroughly explored in Haring, *Policing a Class Society;* Friedman, *Crime and Punishment in American History,* 104.

17. Friedman, *Crime and Punishment*, 104; quoted in Skolnick, *Justice without Trial*, 45–46; *New York Times*, May 10, 1998.

18. In a democratic society the police theoretically perform their order maintenance function under the rule of law. This means that police officers are not only subject to the same laws as the rest of society, they must also perform their official duties in accordance with a whole set of rules and regulations explicitly intended to curtail their power. As the sociologist Jerome Skolnick has observed, the twin goals of "law and order" are sometimes inconsistent and often in conflict with one another. Skolnick, *Justice without Trial*, 17–22 and 230–245; also see Wilson, *Varieties of Police Behavior.*

19. For discussions on the role of the state, see Barrera, *Race and Class in the Southwest*, 157–173; Davis, *City of Quartz*, 250–253; Independent Commission, *Report.* Sometimes, however, police become too aggressive in their actions against minority groups and create disorder rather than order. In such instances elites step in and reestablish control. Such was the case in the wake of the 1991 beating of motorist Rodney King by Los Angeles police officers when the intransigence of Police Chief

Daryl Gates not only became an embarrassment but threatened to provoke a wholesale restructuring of the LAPD. The consummate corporate lawyer and power broker Warren Christopher stepped in to head a commission that called for the removal of Gates and for reforms, which came nowhere close to dealing with the mutual hostility between the minority communities and the LAPD.

20. This does not mean that Mexicans had not been racialized earlier nor that this was the first time Mexicans had been seen as a criminally inclined race. Part of the nineteenth-century stereotype that whites had of Mexicans was that they were a violent, criminal group. That view softened, however, during the early twentieth century, when American industries attracted hundreds of thousands of Mexicans to work in the factories, fields, and mines of the Southwest. In fact, while the stereotype of the violent and brutal Mexican never totally disappeared, by the 1920s it was to a great extent replaced by that of the "docile" Mexican. See Horsman, *Race and Manifest Destiny;* DeLeón, *They Called Them Greasers*, 63–74; and McWilliams, *North from Mexico*, 189–190.

21. I use the concept of politics here and throughout the study broadly to encompass all activity that seeks to change power relationships. My thinking is strongly influenced by the work of the feminist social scientists Ann Bookman and Sandra Morgen, who define "politics as activities that are carried on in the daily lives of ordinary people who are enmeshed in the social institutions and political-economic processes of their society. When there is an attempt to change the social and economic institutions that embody the basic power relations in our society—that is politics." See Morgen and Bookman, "Rethinking Women and Politics," 4.

22. For social banditry see Castillo and Camarillo, *Furia y Muerte.*

23. The generational analysis of Chicano history was first articulated in Alvarez, "Psycho-Historical and Socioeconomic Development of the Chicano in the United States." The most thorough analysis of the Mexican American generation comes in García, *Mexican Americans;* also see George J. Sánchez, *Becoming Mexican American.*

32

How Jews Became White

KAREN BRODKIN SACKS

The American nation was founded and developed by the Nordic race, but if a few more million members of the Alpine, Mediterranean and Semitic races are poured among us, the result must inevitably be a hybrid race of people as worthless and futile as the good-for-nothing mongrels of Central America and Southeastern Europe.

—KENNETH ROBERTS, QTD IN CARLSON AND COLBURN 1972:312

★ ★ ★

My parents' conclusion is that Jewish success, like their own, was the result of hard work and of placing a high value on education. They went to Brooklyn College during the Depression. My mother worked days and started school at night, and my father went during the day. Both their families encouraged them. More accurately, their families expected this effort from them. Everyone they knew was in the same boat, and their world was made up of Jews who advanced as they did. The picture of New York—where most Jews lived—seems to back them up. In 1920, Jews made up 80 percent of the students at New York's City College, 90 percent of Hunter College, and before World War I, 40 percent of private Columbia University. By 1934, Jews made up almost 24 percent of all law students nationally, and 56 percent of those in New York City. Still, more Jews became public school teachers, like my parents and their friends, than doctors or lawyers (Steinberg 1989:137, 227). Steinberg has debunked the myth that Jews advanced because of the cultural value placed on education. This is not to say that Jews did not advance. They did. "Jewish success in America was a matter of historical timing. . . . [T]here was a fortuitous match between the experience and skills of Jewish immigrants, on the one hand, and the manpower needs and opportunity structures, on the other" (1989:103). Jews were the only ones among the southern and eastern European immigrants who came from urban, commercial, craft, and manufacturing backgrounds, not least of which was garment manufacturing. They entered the United States in New York, center of the nation's booming garment industry, soon came to dominate its skilled (male) and "unskilled" (female) jobs, and found it an industry amenable to low-capital entrepreneurship. As a result, Jews were the first of the new European immigrants to create a middle class of small businesspersons early in the twentieth century. Jewish educational advances followed this business success and depended upon it, rather than creating it (see also Bodnar 1985 for a similar argument about mobility).

In the early twentieth century, Jewish college students entered a contested terrain in which the elite social mission was under challenge by a newer professional training mission. Pressure for change had begun to transform the curriculum and reorient college from a gentleman's bastion to a training ground for the middle-class professionals needed by an industrial economy. "The curriculum was overhauled to prepare students for careers in business, engineering, scientific farming, and the arts, and a variety of new professions such as accounting and pharmacy that were making their appearance in American colleges for the first time" (Steinberg 1989:229). Occupational training was precisely what drew Jews to college. In a setting where disparagement of intellectual pursuits and the gentleman's C were badges of distinction, it was not hard for Jews to excel.

How we interpret Jewish social mobility in this milieu depends on whom we compare Jews to. Compared with other immigrants, Jews were upwardly mobile. But compared with that of nonimmigrant whites, their mobility was very limited and circumscribed. Anti-immigrant racist and anti-Semitic barriers kept the Jewish middle class confined to a small number of occupations. Jews were excluded from mainstream corporate management and corporately employed professions, except in the garment and movie industries, which they built. Jews were almost totally excluded from university faculties (and the few that made it had powerful patrons). Jews were concentrated in small businesses, and in professions where they served a largely Jewish clientele (Davis 1990:146 n. 25; Silberman 1985:88–117; Sklare 1971:63–67). . . .

My parents' generation believed that Jews overcame anti-Semitic barriers because Jews are special. My belief is that the Jews who were upwardly mobile were special among Jews (and were also well placed to write the story). My generation might well counter our parents' story of pulling themselves up by their own bootstraps with, "But think what you might have been without the racism and with some affirmative action!" And that is precisely what the postwar boom, the decline of systematic, public anti-immigrant racism and anti-Semitism, and governmental affirmative action extended to white males.

EUROETHNICS INTO WHITES

By the time I was an adolescent, Jews were just as white as the next white person. Until I was eight, I was a Jew in a world of Jews. Everyone on Avenue Z in Sheepshead Bay was Jewish. I spent my days playing and going to school on three blocks of Avenue Z, and visiting my grandparents in the nearby Jewish neighborhoods of Brighton Beach and Coney Island. There were plenty of Italians in my neighborhood, but they lived around the corner. They were a kind of Jew, but on the margins of my social horizons. Portuguese were even more distant, at the end of the bus ride, at Sheepshead Bay. . . . We left that world in 1949 when we moved to Valley Stream, Long Island, which was Protestant, Republican, and even had farms until Irish, Italian, and Jewish exurbanites like us gave it a more suburban and Democratic flavor. Neither religion nor ethnicity separated us at school or in the neighborhood. Except temporarily. In elementary school years, I remember a fair number of dirt-bomb (a good suburban weapon) wars on the block. Periodically one of the Catholic boys would accuse me or my brother of killing his God, to which we would reply, "Did not" and start lobbing dirt-bombs. Sometimes he would get his friends from Catholic school, and I would get mine from public school kids on the block, some of whom were Catholic. Hostilities lasted no more than a couple of hours and punctuated an otherwise friendly relationship. They ended by junior high years, when other things became more important. Jews, Catholics, and Protestants, Italians, Irish, Poles, and "English" (I don't remember hearing WASP as a kid) were mixed up on the block and in school. We thought of ourselves as middle class and very enlightened because our ethnic backgrounds seemed so irrelevant to high school culture. We didn't see race (we thought), and racism was not part of our peer consciousness, nor were the immigrant or working-class histories of our families.

Like most chicken and egg problems, it's hard to know which came first. Did Jews and other Euroethnics become white because they became middle class? That is, did money whiten? Or did being incorporated in an expanded version of whiteness open up the economic doors to a middle-class status? Clearly, both tendencies were at work. Some of the changes set in motion during the war against fascism led to a more inclusive version of whiteness. Anti-Semitism and anti-European racism lost respectability. The 1940 census no longer distinguished native whites of native parentage from those, like my parents, of immigrant parentage, so that Euroimmigrants and their children were more securely white by submersion in an expanded notion of whiteness. (This census also changed the race of Mexicans to white [U.S. Bureau of the Census, 1940:4].) Theories of nurture and culture replaced theories of nature and biology. Instead of dirty and dangerous races who would destroy U.S. democracy, immigrants became ethnic groups whose children had successfully assimilated into the mainstream and risen to the middle class. In this new myth, Euroethnic suburbs like mine became the measure of U.S. democracy's victory over racism. Jewish mobility became a new Horatio Alger story. In time and with hard work, every ethnic group would get a piece of the pie, and the United States would be a nation with equal opportunity for all its people to become part of a prosperous middle-class majority. And it seemed that Euroethnic immigrants and their children were delighted to join middle America.[1]

This is not to say that anti-Semitism disappeared after World War II, only that it fell from fashion and was driven underground. . . .

Although changing views on who was white made it easier for Euroethnics to become middle class, it was also the case that economic prosperity played a very powerful role in the whitening process.

Economic mobility of Jews and other Euroethnics rested ultimately on U.S. postwar economic prosperity with its enormously expanded need for professional, technical, and managerial labor, and on government assistance in providing it. The United States emerged from the war with the strongest economy in the world. . . . The postwar period was a historic moment for real class mobility and for the affluence we have erroneously come to believe was the U.S. norm. It was a time when the old white and the newly white masses became middle class.

The GI Bill of Rights, as the 1944 Serviceman's Readjustment Act was known, was arguably the most massive affirmative action program in U.S. history. It was created to develop needed labor-force skills, and to provide those who had them with a life-style that reflected their value to the economy. The GI benefits ultimately extended to sixteen million GIs (veterans of the Korean War as well) included priority in jobs—that is, preferential hiring, but no one objected to it then; financial support during the job search; small loans for starting up businesses; and, most important, low-interest home loans and educational benefits, which included tuition and living expenses (Brown 1946; Hurd 1946; Mosch 1975; *Postwar Jobs for Veterans* 1945; Willenz 1983). This legislation was rightly regarded as one of the most revolutionary post-war programs. I call it affirmative action because it was aimed at and disproportionately helped male, Euro-origin GIs. . . .

EDUCATION AND OCCUPATION

It is important to remember that prior to the war, a college degree was still very much a "mark of the upper class" (Willenz 1983:165). Colleges were largely finishing schools for Protestant elites. Before the postwar boom, schools could not begin to accommodate the American masses. Even in New York City before the 1930s, neither the public schools nor City College had room for more than a tiny fraction of potential immigrant students.

Not so after the war. The almost eight million GIs who took advantage of their educational benefits under the GI bill caused "the greatest wave of college building in American history" (Nash et al. 1986:885). White male GIs were able to take advantage of their educational benefits for college and technical training, so they were particularly well positioned to seize the opportunities provided by the new demands for professional, managerial, and technical labor. "It has been well documented that the GI educational benefits transformed American higher education and raised the educational level of that generation and generations to come. With many provisions for assistance in upgrading their educational attainments veterans pulled ahead of nonveterans in earning capacity. In the long run it was the nonveterans who had fewer opportunities" (Willenz 1983:165).[2] . . .

Even more significantly, the postwar boom transformed the U.S. class structure—or at least its status structure—so that the middle class expanded to encompass most of the population. Before the war, most Jews, like most other Americans, were working class. Already upwardly mobile before the war relative to other immigrants, Jews floated high on this rising economic tide, and most of them entered the middle class. Still, even the high tide missed some Jews. As late as 1973, some 15 percent of New York's Jews were poor or near poor, and in the 1960s, almost 25 percent of employed Jewish men remained manual workers (Steinberg 1989:89–90).

Educational and occupational GI benefits really constituted affirmative action programs for white males because they were decidedly not extended to African Americans or to women of any race. White male privilege was shaped against the backdrop of wartime racism and postwar sexism. During and after the war, there was an upsurge in white racist violence against black servicemen in public schools, and in the KKK, which spread to California and New York (Dalfiume 1969:133–134). The number of lynchings rose during the war, and in 1943 there were antiblack race riots in several large northern cities. Although there was a wartime labor shortage, black people were discriminated against in access to well-paid defense industry jobs and in housing. In 1946 there were white riots against African Americans across the South, and in Chicago and Philadelphia

as well. Gains made as a result of the wartime Civil Rights movement, especially employment in defense-related industries, were lost with peacetime conversion as black workers were the first fired, often in violation of seniority (Wynn 1976:114, 116). White women were also laid off, ostensibly to make jobs for demobilized servicemen, and in the long run women lost most of the gains they had made in wartime (Kessler-Harris 1982). We now know that women did not leave the labor force in any significant numbers but instead were forced to find inferior jobs, largely nonunion, parttime, and clerical.

Theoretically available to all veterans, in practice women and black veterans did not get anywhere near their share of GI benefits. Because women's units were not treated as part of the military, women in them were not considered veterans and were ineligible for Veterans' Administration (VA) benefits (Willenz 1983:168). The barriers that almost completely shut African-American GIs out of their benefits were more complex. In Wynn's portrait (1976:115), black GIs anticipated starting new lives, just like their white counterparts. Over 43 percent hoped to return to school and most expected to relocate, to find better jobs in new lines of work. The exodus from the South toward the North and far West was particularly large. So it wasn't a question of any lack of ambition on the part of African-American GIs.

Rather, the military, the Veterans' Administration, the U.S. Employment Service, and the Federal Housing Administration (FHA) effectively denied African-American GIs access to their benefits and to the new educational, occupational, and residential opportunities. Black GIs who served in the thoroughly segregated armed forces during World War II served under white officers, usually southerners (Binkin and Eitelberg 1982: Dalfiume 1969; Foner 1974; Johnson 1967; Nalty and MacGregor 1981). African-American soldiers were disproportionately given dishonorable discharges, which denied them veterans' rights under the GI Bill. Thus between August and November 1946, 21 percent of white soldiers and 39 percent of black soldiers were dishonorably discharged. Those who did get an honorable discharge then faced the Veterans' Administration and the U.S. Employment Service. The latter, which was responsible for job placements, employed very few African Americans, especially in the South. This meant that black veterans did not receive much employment information, and that the offers they did receive were for low-paid and menial jobs. "In one survey of 50 cities, the movement of blacks into peacetime employment was found to be lagging far behind that of white veterans: in Arkansas 95 percent of the placements made by the USES for Afro-Americans were in service or unskilled jobs" (Nalty and MacGregor 1981:218, and see 60–61). African Americans were also less likely than whites, regardless of GI status, to gain new jobs commensurate with their wartime jobs, and they suffered more heavily. For example, in San Francisco by 1948, Black Americans "had dropped back halfway to their pre-war employment status" (Wynn 1976:114, 116).[3]

Black GIs faced discrimination in the educational system as well. Despite the end of restrictions on Jews and other Euroethnics, African Americans were not welcome in white colleges. Black colleges were overcrowded, and the combination of segregation and prejudice made for few alternatives. About twenty thousand black veterans attended college by 1947, most in black colleges, but almost as many, fifteen thousand, could not gain entry. Predictably, the disproportionately few African Americans who did gain access to their educational benefits were able, like their white counterparts, to become doctors and engineers, and to enter the black middle class (Walker 1970).

SUBURBANIZATION

In 1949, ensconced at Valley Stream, I watched potato farms turn into Levittown and into Idlewild (later Kennedy) Airport. This was a major spectator sport in our first years on suburban Long Island. A typical weekend would bring various aunts, uncles, and cousins out from the city. After a huge meal we would pile in the car—itself a novelty—to look at the bulldozed acres and comment on the matchbox construction. During the week, my mother and I would look at the houses going up within walking distance.

Bill Levitt built a basic 900–1,000-square-foot, somewhat expandable house for a lower-middle-class and working-class market on Long Island, and later in Pennsylvania and New Jersey (Gans 1967). Levittown started out as two thousand units of rental housing at sixty dollars a month, designed to meet the low-income housing needs of returning war vets, many of whom, like my Aunt Evie and Uncle Julie, were living in quonset huts. By May 1947, Levitt and Sons had acquired enough land in Hempstead Township on Long Island to build four thousand houses, and by the next February, he'd built six thousand units and named the development after himself. After 1948, federal financing for the construction of rental housing tightened, and Levitt switched to building houses for sale. By 1951 Levittown was a development of some fifteen thousand families. . . .

At the beginning of World War II, about 33 percent of all U.S. families owned their houses. That percentage doubled in twenty years. Most Levittowners looked just like my family. They came from New York City or Long Island; about 17 percent were military, from nearby Mitchell Field; Levittown was their first house; and almost everyone was married. The 1947 inhabitants were over 75 percent white collar, but by 1950 more blue-collar families moved in, so that by 1951, "barely half" of the new residents were white collar, and by 1960 their occupational profile was somewhat more working class than for Nassau County as a whole. By this time too, almost one-third of Levittown's people were either foreign-born or, like my parents, first-generation U.S. born (Dobriner 1963:91, 100).

The FHA was key to buyers and builders alike. Thanks to it, suburbia was open to more than GIs. People like us would never have been in the market for houses without FHA and VA low-down-payment, low-interest, long-term loans to young buyers.[4] . . .

The FHA believed in racial segregation. Throughout its history, it publicly and actively promoted restrictive covenants. Before the war, these forbade sale to Jews and Catholics as well as to African Americans. The deed to my house in Detroit had such a covenant; which theoretically prevented it from being sold to Jews or African Americans. Even after the Supreme Court ended legal enforcement of restrictive covenants in 1948, the FHA continued to encourage builders to write them against African Americans. FHA underwriting manuals openly insisted on racially homogeneous neighborhoods, and their loans were made only in white neighborhoods. I bought my Detroit house in 1972 from Jews who were leaving a largely African-American neighborhood. By that time, after the 1968 Fair Housing Act, restrictive covenants were a dead letter (although blockbusting by realtors was rapidly replacing it).

With the federal government behind them, virtually all developers refused to sell to African Americans. Palo Alto and Levittown, like most suburbs as late as 1960, were virtually all white. Out of 15,741 houses and 65,276 people, averaging 4.2 people per house, only 220 Levittowners, or 52 households, were "nonwhite." In 1958 Levitt announced publicly at a press conference to open his New Jersey development that he would not sell to black buyers. This caused a furor, since the state of New Jersey (but not the U.S. government) prohibited discrimination in federally subsidized housing. Levitt was sued and fought it, although he was ultimately persuaded by township ministers to integrate. . . .

The result of these policies was that African Americans were totally shut out of the suburban boom. An article in *Harper's* described the housing available to black GIs. "On his way to the base each morning, Sergeant Smith passes an attractive air-conditioned, FHA-financed housing project. It was built for service families. Its rents are little more than the Smiths pay for their shack. And there are half-a-dozen vacancies, but none for Negroes" (qtd. in Foner 1974:195).

Where my family felt the seductive pull of suburbia, Marshall Berman's experienced the brutal push of urban renewal. In the Bronx in the 1950s, Robert Moses's Cross-Bronx Expressway erased

"a dozen solid, settled, densely populated neighborhoods like our own; . . . something like 60,000 working- and lower-middle-class people, mostly Jews, but with many Italians, Irish and Blacks thrown in, would be thrown out of their homes. . . . For ten years, through the late 1950s and early 1960s, the center of the Bronx was pounded and blasted and smashed" (1982:292).

Urban renewal made postwar cities into bad places to live. At a physical level, urban renewal reshaped them, and federal programs brought private developers and public officials together to create downtown central business districts where there had formerly been a mix of manufacturing, commerce, and working-class neighborhoods. Manufacturing was scattered to the peripheries of the city, which were ringed and bisected by a national system of highways. Some working-class neighborhoods were bulldozed, but others remained (Greer 1965; Hartman 1975; Squires 1989). In Los Angeles, as in New York's Bronx, the postwar period saw massive freeway construction right through the heart of old working-class neighborhoods. In East Los Angeles and Santa Monica, Chicano and African-American communities were divided in half or blasted to smithereens by the highways bringing Angelenos to the new white suburbs, or to make way for civic monuments like Dodger Stadium (Pardo 1990; Social and Public Arts Resource Center 1990:80, 1883:12–13).

Urban renewal was the other side of the process by which Jewish and other working-class Euroimmigrants became middle class. It was the push to suburbia's seductive pull. The fortunate white survivors of urban renewal headed disproportionately for suburbia, where they could partake of prosperity and the good life. . . .

The record is very clear that instead of seizing the opportunity to end institutionalized racism, the federal government did its best to shut and double seal the post-war window of opportunity in African Americans' faces. It consistently refused to combat segregation in the social institutions that were key for upward mobility: education, housing, and employment. Moreover, federal programs that were themselves designed to assist demobilized GIs and young families systematically discriminated against African Americans. Such programs reinforced white/nonwhite racial distinctions even as intrawhite racialization was falling out of fashion. This other side of the coin, that white men of northwestern or southeastern European ancestry were treated equally in theory and in practice with regard to the benefits they received, was part of the larger postwar whitening of Jews and other eastern and southern Europeans.

The myth that Jews pulled themselves up by their own bootstraps ignores the fact that it took federal programs to create the conditions whereby the abilities of Jews and other European immigrants could be recognized and rewarded rather than denigrated and denied. The GI Bill and FHA and VA mortgages were forms of affirmative action that allowed male Jews and other Euro-American men to become suburban homeowners and to get the training that allowed them—but not women vets or war workers—to become professionals, technicians, salesmen, and managers in a growing economy. Jews' and other white ethnics' upward mobility was the result of programs that allowed us to float on a rising economic tide. To African Americans, the govrnment offered the cement boots of segregation, redlining, urban renewal, and discrimination.

Those racially skewed gains have been passed across the generations, so that racial inequality seems to maintain itself "naturally," even after legal segregation ended. Today, in a shrinking economy where downward mobility is the norm, the children and grandchildren of the postwar beneficiaries of the economic boom have some precious advantages. For example, having parents who own their own homes or who have decent retirement benefits can make a real difference in young people's ability to take on huge college loans or to come up with a down payment for a house. Even this simple inheritance helps perpetuate the gap between whites and nonwhites. Sure Jews needed ability, but ability was not enough to make it. The same applies even more in today's long recession.

NOTES

This is a revised and expanded version of a paper published in *Jewish Currents* in June 1992 and delivered at the 1992 meetings of the American Anthropological Association in the session *Blacks and Jews, 1992: Reaching across the Cultural Boundaries* organized by Angela Gilliam. I would like to thank Emily Abel, Katya Gibel Azoulay, Edna Bonacich, Angela Gilliam, Babelle Gunning, Valerie Matsumoto, Regina Morantz-Sanchez, Roger Sanjek, Rabbi Chaim Seidler-Feller, Janet Silverstein, and Eloise Klein Healy's writing group for uncovering wonderful sources and for critical readings along the way. . . .

1. Indeed, Jewish social scientists were prominent in creating this ideology of the United States as a meritocracy. Most prominent of course was Nathan Glazer, but among them also were Charles Silberman and Marshall Sklare.
2. The belief was widespread that "the GI Bill . . . helped millions of families move into the middle class" (Nash et al. 1986:885). A study that compares mobility among veterans and nonveterans provides a kind of confirmation. In an unnamed small city in Illinois, Havighurst and his colleagues (1951) found no significant difference between veterans and nonveterans, but this was because apparently very few veterans used any of their GI benefits.
3. African Americans and Japanese Americans were the main target of wartime racism (see Murray 1992). By contrast there went virtually no anti-German American or anti-Italian American policies in World War II (see Takaki 1969:357–406).
4. See Eichler 1982:5 for homeowning percentages; Jackson (1985:205) found an increase in families living in owner-occupied buildings, rising from 44 percent in 1934 to 63 percent in 1972; see Monkkonen 1988 on scarcity of mortgages; and Gelfand 1975, esp. chap. 6, on federal programs.

REFERENCES

1. Binkin, Martin, and Mark J. Eitelberg. 1982. *Blacks and the Military.* Washington, D.C.: Brookings.
2. Bodnar, John. 1985. *The Transplanted: A History of Immigrants in Urban America.* Bloomington: Indiana University Press.
3. Brody, David. 1980. *Workers in Industrial America: Essays of the Twentieth Century Struggle.* New York: Oxford University Press.
4. Brown, Francis J. 1946. *Educational Opportunities for Veterans.* Washington, D.C.: Public Affairs Press, American Council on Public Affairs.
5. Carlson, Lewis H., and George A. Colburn. 1972. *In Their Place: White America Defines Her Minorities, 1880–1950.* New York: Wiley.
6. Dalfiume, Richard M. 1969. *Desegregation of the U.S. Armed Forces: Fighting on Two Fronts, 1939–1953.* Columbia: University of Missouri Press.
7. Davis, Mike. 1990. *City of Quartz.* London: Verso.
8. Dobriner, William M. 1963. *Class in Suburbia.* Englewood Cliffs, N.J.: Prentice-Hall.

9. Eichler, Ned. 1982. *The Merchant Builders*. Cambridge, Mass.: MIT Press.

10. Fields, Barbara Jeanne. 1990. Slavery, Race, and Ideology in the United States of America. *New Left Review* 181:95–118.

11. Foner, Jack. 1974. *Blacks and the Military in American History: A New Perspective*. New York: Praeger.

12. Gans, Herbert. 1962. *The Urban Villagers*. New York: Free Press.

13. ——. 1967. *The Levittowners*. New York: Pantheon.

14. Gordon, Milton. 1964. *Assimilation in American Life*. New York: Oxford University Press.

15. Hartman, Chester. 1975. *Housing and Social Policy*. Englewood Cliffs, N.J.: Prentice-Hall.

16. Higham, John. 1955. *Strangers in the Land*. New Brunswick, N.J.: Rutgers University Press.

17. Hurd, Charles. 1946. *The Veterans' Program: A Complete Guide to Its Benefits, Rights, and Options*. New York: McGraw-Hill.

18. Jackson, Kenneth T. 1985. *Crabgrass Frontier: The Suburbanization of the United States*. New York: Oxford University Press.

19. Johnson, Jesse J. 1967. *Ebony Brass: An Autobiography of Negro Frustration amid Aspiration*. New York: Frederick.

20. Karabel, Jerome. 1984. Status-Group Struggle, Organizational Interests, and the Limits of Institutional Autonomy. *Theory and Society* 13:1–40.

21. Kessler-Harris, Alice. 1982. *Out to Work: A History of Wage-Earning Women in the United States*. New York: Oxford University Press.

22. Martyn, Byron Curti. 1979. Racism in the U.S.: A History of Anti-Miscegenation Legislation and Litigation. Ph.D. diss., University of Southern California.

23. Mosch, Theodore R. 1975. *The GI Bill: A Breakthrough in Educational and Social Policy in the United States*. Hicksville, N.Y.: Exposition.

24. Nalty, Bernard C., and Morris J. MacGregor, eds. 1981. *Blacks in the Military: Essential Documents*. Wilmington, Del.: Scholarly Resources.

25. Nash, Gary B., Julie Roy Jeffrey, John R. Howe, Allen F. Davis, Peter J. Frederick, and Allen M. Winkler. 1986. *The American People: Creating a Nation and a Society*. New York: Harper and Row.

26. Pardo, Mary. 1990. Mexican-American Women Grassroots Community Activists: "Mothers of East Los Angeles." *Frontiers* 11:1–7.

27. *Postwar Jobs for Veterans*. 1945. *Annals of the American Academy of Political and Social Science* 238 (March).

28. Saxton, Alexander. 1971. *The Indispensible Enemy*. Berkeley and Los Angeles: University of California Press.

29. ——. 1990. *The Rise and Fall of the White Republic*. London: Verso.

30. Silberman, Charles. 1985. *A Certain People: American Jews and Their Lives Today*. New York: Summit.

31. Sklare, Marshall. 1971. *America's Jews*. New York: Random House.

32. Sowell, Thomas. 1981. *Ethnic America: A History*. New York: Basic.

33. Steinberg, Stephen. 1989. *The Ethnic Myth: Race, Ethnicity, and Class in America*. 2d ed. Boston: Beacon.

34. Synott, Marcia Graham. 1986. Anti-Semitism and American Universities: Did Quotas Follow the Jews? In *Anti-Semitism in American History*, ed. David A. Gerber. Urbana: University of Illinois Press, 233–274.

35. Takaki, Ronald. 1989. *Strangers from a Different Shore*. Boston: Little, Brown.

36. Tobin, Gary A., ed. 1987. *Divided Neighborhoods: Changing Patterns of Racial Segregation*. Beverly Hills: Sage.

37. U.S. Bureau of the Census. 1930. *Fifteenth Census of the United States*. Vol. 2. Washington, D.C.: U.S. Government Printing Office.

38. ——. 1940. *Sixteenth Census of the United States*. Vol. 2. Washington, D.C.: U.S. Government Printing Office.

39. Walker, Olive. 1970. The Windsor Hills School Story. *Integrated Education: Race and Schools* 8(3):4–9.

40. Willenz, June A. 1983. *Women Veterans: America's Forgotten Heroines*. New York: Continuum.

41. Wynn, Neil A. 1976. *The Afro-American and the Second World War*. London: Elek.

 33

Then Came the War

YURI KOCHIYAMA

I was red, white, and blue when I was growing up. I taught Sunday school, and was very, very American. But I was also very provincial. We were just kids rooting for our high school.

My father owned a fish market, Terminal Island was nearby, and that was where many Japanese families lived. It was a fishing town. My family lived in the city proper. San Pedro was very mixed, predominantly white, but there were blacks also.

I was nineteen at the time of the evacuation. I had just finished junior college. I was looking for a job, and didn't realize how different the school world was from the work world. In the school world, I never felt racism. But when you got into the work world, it was very difficult. This was 1941, just before the war. I finally did get a job at a department store. But for us back then, it was a big thing, because I don't think they had ever hired an Asian in a department store before. I tried, because I saw a Mexican friend who got a job there. Even then they didn't hire me on a regular basis, just on Saturdays, summer vacation, Easter vacation, and Christmas vacation. Other than that, I was working like the others—at a vegetable stand, or doing part-time domestic work. Back then, I only knew of two Japanese American girl friends who got jobs as secretaries—but these were in Japanese companies. But generally you almost never saw a Japanese American working in a white place. It was hard for Asians. Even for Japanese, the best jobs they felt they could get were in Chinatowns, such as in Los Angeles. Most Japanese were either in some aspect of fishing, such as in the canneries, or went right from school to work on the farms. That was what it was like in the town of San Pedro. I loved working in the department store, because it was a small town, and you got to know and see everyone. The town itself was wonderful. People were very friendly. I didn't see my job as work—it was like a community job.

Everything changed for me on the day Pearl Harbor was bombed. On that very day—December 7—the FBI came and they took my father. He had just come home from the hospital the day before. For several days we didn't know where they had taken him. Then we found out that he was taken to the federal prison at Terminal Island. Overnight, things changed for us. They took all men who lived near the Pacific waters, and had nothing to do with fishing. A month later, they took every fisherman from Terminal Island, sixteen and over, to places—not the regular concentration comps—but to detention centers in places like South Dakota, Montana, and New Mexico. They said that all Japanese who had given money to any kind of Japanese organization would have to be taken away. At that time, many people were giving to the Japanese Red Cross. The first group was thirteen hundred Isseis—my parent's generation. They took those who were leaders of the community, or Japanese school teachers, or were teaching martial arts, or who were Buddhist priests. Those categories which would make them very "Japanesey," were picked up. This really made a tremendous impact on our lives. My twin brother was going to the University at Berkeley. He came rushing back. All of our classmates

were joining up, so he volunteered to go into the service. And it seemed strange that here they had my father in prison, and there the draft board okayed my brother. He went right into the army. My other brother, who was two years older, was trying to run my father's fish market. But business was already going down, so he had to close it. He had finished college at the University of California a couple of years before.

They took my father on December 7th. The day before, he had just come home from the hospital. He had surgery for an ulcer. We only saw him once, on December 13. On December 20th they said he could come home. By the time they brought him back, he couldn't talk. He made guttural sounds, and we didn't know if he could hear. He was home for twelve hours. He was dying. The next morning, when we got up, they told us that he was gone. He was very sick. And I think the interrogation was very rough. My mother kept begging the authorities to let him go to the hospital until he was well, then put him back in the prison. They did finally put him there, a week or so later. But they put him in a hospital where they were bringing back all these American Merchant Marines who were hit on Wake Island. So he was the only Japanese in that hospital, so they hung a sheet around him that said Prisoner of War. The feeling where he was was very bad.

You could see the hysteria of war. There was a sense that war could actually come to American shores. Everybody was yelling to get the "Japs" out of California. In Congress, people were speaking out. Organizations such as the Sons and Daughters of the Golden West were screaming "Get the 'Japs' out." So were the real estate people, who wanted to get the land from the Japanese farmers. The war had whipped up such a hysteria that if there was anyone for the Japanese, you didn't hear about it. I'm sure they were afraid to speak out, because they would be considered not only just "Jap" lovers, but unpatriotic.

Just the fact that my father was taken made us suspect to people. But on the whole, the neighbors were quite nice, especially the ones adjacent to us. There was already a 6 A.M. to 6 P.M. curfew and a five mile limit on where we could go from our homes. So they offered to do our shopping for us, if we needed.

Most Japanese Americans had to give up their jobs, whatever they did, and were told they had to leave. Executive Order No. 9066—President Roosevelt's edict[1] for evacuation—was in February 1942. We were moved to a detention center that April. By then the Japanese on Terminal Island were just helter-skelter, looking for anywhere they could go. They opened up the Japanese school and Buddhist churches, and families just crowded in. Even farmers brought along their chickens and chicken coops. They just opened up the places for people to stay until they could figure out what to do. Some people left for Colorado and Utah. Those who had relatives could do so. The idea was to evacuate all the Japanese from the coast. But all the money was frozen, so even if you knew where you wanted to go, it wasn't that simple. By then, people knew they would be going into camps, so they were selling what they could, even though they got next to nothing for it.

We were fortunate, in that our neighbors, who were white, were kind enough to look after our house, and they said they would find people to rent it, and look after it till we got back. But these neighbors were very, very unusual.

We were sent to an assembly center in Arcadia, California, in April. It was the largest assembly center on the West Coast, having nearly twenty thousand people. There were some smaller centers with about six hundred people. All along the West Coast—Washington, Oregon, California—there were many, many assembly centers, but ours was the largest. Most of the assembly centers were either fairgrounds, or race tracks. So many of us lived in stables, and they said you could take what you could carry. We were there until October.

Even though we stayed in a horse stable, everything was well organized. Every unit would hold four to six people. So in some cases, families had to split up, or join others. We slept on army cots, and for mattresses they gave us muslin bags, and told us to fill them with straw. And for chairs, everybody scrounged around for carton boxes, because they could serve as chairs. You could put two together and it could be a little table. So it was just makeshift. But I was amazed how, in a few months, some of those units really looked nice. Japanese women fixed them up. Some people had the foresight to bring material and needles and thread. But they didn't let us bring anything that could be used as weapons. They let us have spoons, but no knives. For those who had small children or babies, it was rough. They said you could take what you could carry. Well, they could only take their babies in their arms, and maybe the little children could carry something, but it was pretty limited.

I was so red, white, and blue, I couldn't believe this was happening to us. America would never do a thing like this to us. This is the greatest country in the world. So I thought this is only going to be for a short while, maybe a few weeks or something, and they will let us go back. At the beginning no one realized how long this would go on. I didn't feel the anger that much because I thought maybe this was the way we could show our love for our country. And we should not make too much fuss or noise; we should abide by what they asked of us. I'm a totally different person now than I was back then. I was naïve about so many things. The more I think about it, the more I realize how little you learn about American history. It's just what they want you to know.

At the beginning, we didn't have any idea how temporary or permanent the situation was. We thought we would be able to leave shortly. But after several months they told us this was just temporary quarters, and they were building more permanent quarters elsewhere in the United States. All this was so unbelievable. A year before we would never have thought anything like this could have happened to us—not in this country. As time went by, the sense of frustration grew. Many families were already divided. The fathers, the heads of the households, were taken to other camps. In the beginning, there was no way for the sons to get in touch with their families. Before our group left for the detention camp, we were saying goodbye almost every day to other groups who were going to places like Arizona and Utah. Here we finally had made so many new friends—people who we met, lived with, shared the time, and got to know. So it was even sad on that note and the goodbyes were difficult. Here we had gotten close to these people, and now we had to separate again. I don't think we even thought about where they were going to take us, or how long we would have to stay there. When we got on the trains to leave for the camps, we didn't know where we were going. None of the groups knew. It was later on that we learned so and so ended up in Arizona, or Colorado, or some other place. We were all at these assembly centers for about seven months. Once they started pushing people out, it was done very quickly. By October, our group headed out for Jerome, Arkansas, which is on the Texarkana corner.

We were on the train for five days. The blinds were down, so we couldn't look out, and other people couldn't look in to see who was in the train. We stopped in Nebraska, and everybody pulled the blinds to see what Nebraska looked like. The interesting thing was, there was a troop train stopped at the station too. These American soldiers looked out, and saw all these Asians, and they wondered what we were doing on the train. So the Japanese raised the windows, and so did the soldiers. It wasn't a bad feeling at all. There was none of that "you Japs" kind of thing. The women were about the same age as the soldiers—eighteen to twenty-five, and we had the same thing on our minds. In camps, there wasn't much to do, so the fun thing was to receive letters, so on our train, all the girls who were my age, were yelling to the guys, "Hey, give us your address where you're going, we'll write you." And they said, "Are you sure you're going to write?" We exchanged addresses and for a long time I wrote to some of those soldiers. On the other side of the train, I'll never forget there was this old guy, about sixty, who came to our window and said, "We have some Japanese living here. This is Omaha, Nebraska." This guy was very nice, and didn't seem to have any ill feelings for Japanese. He had calling cards, and he said "Will any of you people write to me?" We said, "Sure," so he threw in a bunch of calling cards, and I got one, and I wrote to him for years.

I wrote to him about what camp was like, because he said, "Let me know what it's like wherever you end up." And he wrote back, and told me what was happening in Omaha, Nebraska. There were many, many interesting experiences too. Our mail was generally not censored, but all the mail from the soldiers was. Letters meant everything.

When we got to Jerome, Arkansas, we were shocked because we had never seen an area like it. There was forest all around us. And they told us to wait till the rains hit. This would not only turn into mud, but Arkansas swamp lands. That's where they put us—in swamp lands, surrounded by forests. It was nothing like California.

I'm speaking as a person of twenty who had good health. Up until then, I had lived a fairly comfortable life. But there were many others who didn't see the whole experience the same way. Especially those who were older and in poor health and had experienced racism. One more thing like this could break them. I was at an age where transitions were not hard—the point where anything new could even be considered exciting. But for people in poor health, it was hell.

There were army-type barracks, with two hundred to two hundred and five people to each block and every block had its own mess hall, facility for washing clothes, showering. It was all surrounded by barbed wire, and armed soldiers. I think they said only seven people were killed in total, though thirty were shot, because they went too close to the fence. Where we were, nobody thought of escaping because you'd be more scared of the swamps—the poisonous snakes, the bayous. Climatic conditions were very harsh. Although Arkansas is in the South, the winters were very, very cold. We had a potbellied stove in every room and we burned wood. Everything was very organized. We got there in October, and were warned to prepare ourselves. So on our block, for instance, males eighteen and over could go out in the forest to chop down trees for wood for the winter. The men would bring back the trees, and the women sawed the trees. Everybody worked. The children would pile up the wood for each unit.

They told us when it rained, it would be very wet, so we would have to build our own drainage system.

One of the barracks was to hold meetings, so block heads would call meetings. There was a block council to represent the people from different areas.

When we first arrived, there were some things that weren't completely fixed. For instance, the roofers would come by, and everyone would hunger for information from the outside world. We wanted to know what was happening with the war. We weren't allowed to bring radios; that was contraband. And there were no televisions then. So we would ask the workers to bring us back some papers, and they would give us papers from Texas or Arkansas, so for the first time we would find out about news from the outside.

Just before we went into the camps, we saw that being a Japanese wasn't such a good thing, because everybody was turning against the Japanese, thinking we were saboteurs, or linking us with Pearl Harbor. But when I saw the kind of work they did at camp, I felt so proud of the Japanese, and proud to be Japanese, and wondered why I was so white, white when I was outside, because I was always with white folks. Many people had brothers or sons who were in the military and Japanese American servicemen would come into the camp to visit the families, and we felt so proud of them when they came in their uniforms. We knew that it would only be a matter of time before they would be shipped overseas. Also what made us feel proud was the forming of the 442nd unit.[2]

I was one of these real American patriots then. I've changed now. But back then, I was all American. Growing up, my mother would say we're Japanese. But I'd say, "No, I'm American." I think a lot of Japanese grew up that way. People would say to them, "You're Japanese," and they would say, "No, we're Americans." I don't even think they used the hyphenated term "Japanese-American" back then. At the time, I was ashamed of being Japanese. I think many Japanese-Americans felt the same way. Pearl Harbor was a shameful act, and being Japanese-Americans, even though we had nothing to do with it, we still somehow felt we were blamed for it. I hated Japan at that point. So I saw myself at that part of my history as an American, and not as a Japanese or Japanese-American. That sort of changed while I was in the camp.

I hated the war, because it wasn't just between the governments. It went down to the people, and it nurtured hate. What was happening during the war were many things I didn't like. I hoped that one day when the war was over there could be a way that people could come together in their relationships.

Now I can relate to Japan in a more mature way, where I see its faults and its very, very negative history. But I also see its potential. Scientifically and technologically it has really gone far. But I'm disappointed that when it comes to human rights, she hasn't grown. The Japan of today—I feel there are still things lacking. For instance, I don't think the students have the opportunity to have more leeway in developing their lives.

We always called the camps "relocation centers" while we were there. Now we feel it is apropos to call them concentration camps. It is not the same as the concentration camps of Europe; those we feel were death camps. Concentration camps were a concentration of people placed in an area, and disempowered and disenfranchised. So it is apropos to call what I was in a concentration camp. After two years in the camp, I was released.

Going home wasn't much of a problem for us because our neighbors had looked after our place. But for most of our Japanese friends, starting over again was very difficult after the war.

I returned in October of 1945. It was very hard to find work, at least for me. I wasn't expecting to find anything good, just something to tide me over until my boyfriend came back from New York. The only thing I was looking for was to work in a restaurant as a waitress. But I couldn't find anything. I would walk from one end of the town to the other, and down every main avenue. But as soon as they found out I was Japanese, they would say no. Or they would ask me if I was in the union, and of course I couldn't be in the union because I had just gotten there. Anyway, no Japanese could be in the union, so if the answer was no I'm not in the union, they would say no. So finally what I did was go into the rough area of San Pedro—there's a strip near the wharf—and I went down there. I was determined to keep the jobs as long as I could. But for a while, I could last maybe two hours, and somebody would say "Is that a 'Jap'?" And as soon as someone would ask that, the boss would say, "Sorry, you gotta go. We don't want trouble here." The strip wasn't that big, so after I'd go the whole length of it, I'd have to keep coming back to the same restaurants, and say, "Gee, will you give me another chance." I figure, all these servicemen were coming back and the restaurants didn't have enough waitresses to come in and take these jobs. And so, they'd say "Okay. But soon as somebody asks who you are, or if you're a 'Jap,' or any problem about being a 'Jap,' you go." So I said, "Okay, sure. How about keeping me until that happens?" So sometimes I'd last a night, sometimes a couple of nights that no one would say anything. Sometimes people threw cups at me or hot coffee. At first they didn't know what I was. They thought I was Chinese. Then someone would say, "I bet she's a 'Jap'." And I wasn't going to say I wasn't. So as soon as I said "Yeah," then it was like an uproar. Rather than have them say, "Get out," I just walked out. I mean, there was no point in fighting it. If you just walked out, there was less chance of getting hurt. But one place I lasted two weeks. These owners didn't want to have to let me go. But they didn't want to have problems with the people.

And so I did this until I left for New York, which was about three months later. I would work the dinner shift, from six at night to three in the morning. When you are young you tend not to take things as strongly. Everything is like an adventure. Looking back, I felt the people who were the kindest to me were those who went out and fought, those who just got back from Japan or the Far East. I think the worst ones were the ones who stayed here and worked in defense plants, who felt they had to be so patriotic. On the West Coast, there wasn't hysteria anymore, but there were hostile feelings towards the Japanese, because they were coming back. It took a while, but my mother said that things were getting back to normal, and that the Japanese were slowly being accepted again. At the time, I didn't go through the

bitterness that many others went through, because it's not just what they went through, but it is also what they experienced before that. I mean, I happened to have a much more comfortable life before, so you sort of see things in a different light. You see that there are all kinds of Americans, and that they're not all people who hate "Japs." You know too that it was hysteria that had a lot to do with it.

All Japanese, before they left camp, were told not to congregate among Japanese, and not to speak Japanese. They were told by the authorities. There was even a piece of paper that gave you instructions. But then people went on to places like Chicago where there were churches, so they did congregate in churches. But they did ask people not to. I think psychologically the Japanese, having gone through a period where they were so hated by everyone, didn't even want to admit they were Japanese, or accept the fact that they were Japanese. Of course, they would say they were Japanese-Americans. But I think the psychological damage of the wartime period, and of racism itself, has left its mark. There is a stigma to being Japanese. I think that is why such a large number of Japanese, in particular Japanese-American women, have married out of the race. On the West Coast I've heard people say that sixty to seventy percent of the Japanese women have married, I guess, mostly whites. Japanese men are doing it too, but not to that degree. I guess Japanese-Americans just didn't want to have that Japanese identity, or that Japanese part. There is definitely some self-hate, and part of that has to do with the racism that's so deeply a part of this society.

Historically, Americans have always been putting people behind walls. First there were the American Indians who were put on reservations; Africans in slavery, their lives on the plantations; Chicanos doing migratory work, and the kinds of camps they lived in; and even, too, the Chinese when they worked on the railroad camps where they were almost isolated, dispossessed people—disempowered. And I feel those are the things we should fight against so they won't happen again. It wasn't so long ago—in 1979—that the feeling against the Iranians was so strong because of the takeover of the U.S. embassy in Iran, where they wanted to deport Iranian students. And that is when a group called Concerned Japanese-Americans organized, and that was the first issue we took up, and then we connected it with what the Japanese had gone through. This whole period of what the Japanese went through is important. If we can see the connections of how often this happens in history, we can stem the tide of these things happening again by speaking out against them.

Most Japanese-Americans who worked years and years for redress never thought it would happen the way it did. The papers have been signed, we will be given reparation, and there was an apology from the government. I think the redress movement itself was very good because it was a learning experience for the Japanese people; we could get out into our communities and speak about what happened to us and link it with experiences of other people. In that sense, though, it wasn't done as much as it should have been. Some Japanese-Americans didn't even learn that part. They just started the movement as a reaction to the bad experience they had. They don't even see other ethnic groups who have gone through it. It showed us, too, how vulnerable everybody is. It showed us that even though there is a Constitution, that constitutional rights could be taken away very easily.

NOTES

1. Executive Order No. 9066 does not mention detention of Japanese specifically, but was used exclusively against the Japanese. Over 120,000 Japanese were evacuated from the West Coast.
2. American soldiers of Japanese ancestry were assembled in two units: the 442nd Regimental Combat Team and the 100th Infantry Battalion. The two groups were sent to battle in Europe. The 100th Battalion had over 900 casualties and was known as the Purple Heart Battalion. Combined, the units received 9,486 purple hearts and 18,143 individual decorations.

America

MAYA ANGELOU

The gold of her promise
has never been mined

Her borders of justice
not clearly defined

Her crops of abundance
the fruit and the grain

Have not fed the hungry
nor eased that deep pain

Her proud declarations
are leaves on the wind

Her southern exposure
black death did befriend

Discover this country
dead centuries cry

Erect noble tablets
where none can decry

"She kills her bright future
and rapes for a sou

Then entraps her children
with legends untrue"

I beg you
Discover this country.

34

The Chicano Movement

1965–1975

MANUEL GONZALES

The decade comprising the mid-sixties to the mid-seventies was a period of extraordinary ferment in the Mexican communities of the United States. Significant social changes were in the air. Immigration from Mexico, for example, increased markedly, a trend that tended to push many of the older residents of the Southwest into other parts of the country. The most momentous changes, though, were political and psychological.

Following the lead of the African-American community, which initiated a far-reaching movement for civil liberties in the fifties, many Mexicans, now calling themselves Chicanos and Chicanas, embarked on their own campaign to improve socioeconomic conditions and win full recognition of their rights as U.S. citizens.[1] While these concerns had been articulated before, notably by the Mexican-American Generation of the post–World War II period, after the mid-sixties a new aggressiveness developed in the barrios. Socioeconomic gains made in past years seemed woefully inadequate. Many Mexicans began to demand immediate reform. Some called for revolution. Convinced that changes of whatever kind could be instituted only through the acquisition of power, political action was emphasized as never before. Moreover, in contrast to their postwar predecessors, the leaders of the so-called Chicano Generation stressed pride in their ethnic roots while deemphasizing assimilation into the American mainstream. "A Chicano," Rubén Salazar, a journalist on the periphery of the movement, once said, "is a Mexican-American with a non-Anglo image of himself."[2] Tired of apologizing for their ethnic origins, Chicanos looked to Mexico, especially Indian Mexico, for inspiration. While there was much disagreement on specific methods—indeed a significant minority stood on the sidelines—most of the community was in general agreement with the goals formulated by barrio leaders: cultural regeneration and political power. Since these twin objectives are the crux of the emerging Chicano movement (also called Chicano Power or Brown Power), the struggle for Mexican-American civil rights, it seems reasonable to see this decade in terms of Chicanismo.

★　★　★

ORIGINS OF THE CHICANO MOVEMENT

. . .[T]he socioeconomic condition of the Mexican community was not notably worse in the early sixties than it had been in the past. Indeed, demographers indicate that steady progress had been made in this regard. Furthermore, despite widespread hostility, *overt* forms of racism were fading.

Discrimination was less blatant than before, thanks in part to the efforts of the Mexican-American Generation, as well as the waning of the Cold War and the demand for conformity that it fostered. Even Mexican participation in Vietnam, with its widespread disaffection, is insufficient to explain the rise of Chicanismo; Mexicans had fought and died in other U.S. wars without turning to militant antiestablishment activity. What made the difference was the changing intellectual climate in America, especially the rise of the black civil rights movement.

Brown v. the Board of Education of Topeka encouraged a new assertiveness by blacks, whose civil rights movement began in 1955, when Rosa Parks, a black woman, refused to give up her bus seat in Montgomery, Alabama. This campaign launched the career of Dr. Martin Luther King, Jr. (1929–1968), a young Baptist minister, arguably the most powerful voice for racial justice in the annals of American history. Influenced by Mohandas Gandhi and Henry Thoreau, Dr. King preached the philosophy of militant nonviolence, which had a profound and lasting impact on his contemporaries. Dr. King and the Southern Christian Leadership Conference (SCLC) spearheaded the drive for desegregation and together with the National Association for the Advancement of Colored People (NAACP) dominated the swelling movement during its first years.

By 1966, however, dissatisfied with the seemingly glacial pace of reform, more militant leaders emerged from the African-American community, particularly in northern urban ghettos, where Dr. King was less influential. They included Stokely Carmichael, head of the Student Nonviolent Coordinating Committee (SNCC); Bobby Seale, Huey P. Newton, and Eldridge Cleaver of the Black Panthers; and the most charismatic of the new leaders, Malcolm X (1925–1965), who emerged from the ranks of the Black Muslims. Labeling their movement "Black Power," they called for permanent racial separation and the use of violence.

Both moderate and radical wings of the black civil rights movement, and the riots that broke out in African-American ghettos across the country in

1964–1967, had a significant impact on American society. One of the most immediate responses was the War on Poverty, which was launched by President Lyndon B. Johnson in a quixotic attempt to create the Great Society. A myriad of federally funded programs—Job Corps, Volunteers in Service to America (VISTA), Neighborhood Youth Corps, Head Start, and Upward Bound, among them—were set up to [e]ffect the change. While not completely successful, LBJ's domestic programs did ameliorate the plight of many poor people in the country, and they also took the wind out of the sails of black militancy, which had faded by the seventies.

The black civil rights movement, though, left a powerful legacy. One of its most momentous consequences was the stimulus it provided for other people of color to stand up for their rights. These included Mexicans, who now initiated their own movement of self-awareness.

CHÁVEZ, HUERTA, AND THE UNITED FARMWORKERS

The Chicano movement consisted of hundreds of organizations focusing on a variety of issues. Broadly speaking, these groups were found in barrios, schools, and prisons. In terms of their approaches, they could be divided into those associations that sought to work through the system and those that called for a major restructuring of the system, the moderate and radical wings of the movement respectively. As the Chicano movement began, in the mid-sixties, the moderates predominated. The key organization representing their perspective was undoubtedly the United Farm Workers (UFW).

The history of labor organization among field workers goes back to the early part of the twentieth century. . . . Both the IWW, before and during the Great War, and the American Communist party, in the thirties, made abortive attempts to win concessions for farmworkers in the agricultural valleys of the West. Before the rise of the UFW, the last serious initiative in the fields was taken by the National Farm Labor Union (NFLU), formed in 1945 and led in California by Ernesto Galarza. In the late

forties, the NFLU launched a series of strikes in California, where it centered its activities. These initiatives failed not only because of the many difficulties inherent in organizing workers in the fields but also because the Bracero Program made it impossible to win concessions from growers. The termination of the Bracero Agreement in 1964, however, set the stage for the most ambitious unionization attempt to date, the UFW campaign begun in California's San Joaquin Valley during the following year. It was led by two extraordinary people: César Chávez and Dolores Huerta.

Despite his rejection of the term *Chicano*, César Chávez (1927–1993) is the single most important representative of the movimiento; indeed, he is the most well-known figure in the Mexican community, in general.[3] A legend in his own lifetime, it is difficult to separate fact from fiction in relating the outlines of his long and productive career. César Estrada Chávez was born on 31 March 1927, on a small family farm near Yuma, Arizona. During the Depression, his grandfather lost the farm, and the Chávez family was reduced to working as migratory farm laborers. For the next few years, they traveled up and down California eking out a living. Education for the Chávez children was sporadic, given their nomadic existence, and young César was forced to abandon school altogether after the eighth grade. During World War II, he joined the Navy and served in the Pacific. Upon his release in 1946, he returned to the fields, joining the ill-fated NFLU.

Eventually, Chávez settled down with his wife Helen and their growing family in San Jose, California, where he continued to do farm work. It was here that he met and was influenced by Fred Ross, who recruited him into the Community Service Organization in 1952. Hardworking and dedicated, Chávez made his way up the organizational ladder very swiftly, becoming CSO regional director in 1958. In this capacity, he tried to steer the association toward advocacy of the rights of farmworkers. He met fierce resistance among CSO members who preferred to focus attention on urban and middle-class concerns. Exasperated, Chávez quit CSO in

1961 and took his family to Delano, his wife's hometown. Using his life savings, he initiated a new union, the Farm Workers Association—known later as the National Farm Workers Association and, later still, the United Farm Workers—which was founded in Fresno on 30 September 1962.

Because the UFW always focused on the family unit, women came to play prominent roles in union activities. Among them, Helen Chávez and Jessie López de la Cruz stand out. From the very outset, though, César Chávez's most trusted lieutenant—often considered cofounder of the union—was Dolores Huerta (1930–). Although eclipsed by Chávez throughout most of her life, Huerta remains in many ways, as her biographer Richard A. García has argued, a better symbol of Chicanismo than her friend and mentor.[4]

Dolores Fernández Huerta was born in Dawson, New Mexico, in 1930. Her parents divorced when she was five; and her mother, the seminal influence on her life, took the family to California. Unlike Chávez, Dolores emerged from a middle-class background. Her mother, who started off as a waitress and cannery worker, eventually came to own a hotel in Stockton, California, where Dolores was raised in an integrated neighborhood, received her early education, and met her first husband, an Anglo. After her marriage, she earned a provisional credential by attending community college and taking night classes at College of the Pacific, and became a grammar school teacher.

In the mid-fifties, however, she determined to devote herself to fighting for the rights of the underprivileged. She joined CSO, where she received her initial training as an organizer under Fred Ross, who taught her the mobilization techniques associated with Saul Alinsky. "The emphasis of Alinsky's message," writes Richard García, "coincided with hers—a pragmatic non-ideological approach to life and change."[5]

It was in CSO in 1955 that she met Chávez, initiating a lifelong though sometimes turbulent friendship. A conservative Catholic, somewhat puritanical in his value system, Chávez would always have difficulty accepting her two divorces and the apparent neglect of her children. These personal difficulties, however, rarely impeded effective collaboration by two individuals equally dedicated to the cause of ameliorating the lives of the downtrodden. When Chávez bolted CSO in 1961, Dolores Huerta followed. Together, they forged the new union. She was in Delano when the strike began. During the next few years, it would completely consume her life.

THE DELANO STRIKE

The strike against local grape growers in the Kern County city of Delano, just north of Bakersfield, was initiated by the Agricultural Workers Organizing Committee (AWOC), a Filipino union affiliated with the AFL-CIO, on 8 September 1965. Led by Larry Itliong, Filipinos struck to gain higher pay and recognition as a union, a right given to industrial workers by the National Labor Relations Act of 1935 but denied to agricultural laborers. Since most of the field hands in the area were Mexican— by the sixties, they constituted at least two-thirds of the agricultural work force in the state—Chávez was asked to join and help conduct the strike. Fearing that his own fledgling union was unprepared, he agreed with some reluctance. However, given his union's superior numbers and his characteristic determination, Chávez soon became the acknowledged leader of the entire operation.

UFW tactics and strategy at Delano mirrored Chávez's personal philosophy. Profoundly impacted by both Gandhi and Dr. King, he had come to embrace the philosophy of militant nonviolence. Like his two renowned mentors, Chávez, a devout Catholic, was against violence on principle; but he also realized, as they did, that violence was self-defeating when directed at a power with a monopoly on armed force. On the other hand, the idea of turning the other cheek, while praiseworthy as a Christian ideal, was calculated to preserve the status quo. It was essential, he felt, that the oppressed unite and assert themselves, using a variety of strategies to gain their ends. In the case of farmworkers, those objectives were better working conditions, including higher wages, and recognition of their union. Unlike many other militants of the time, Chávez believed that the American middle class was basically responsive to the needs of poor people and would support them if given the opportunity.

During the long struggle, Chávez recruited help from various disparate sources. These included the trade union movement, especially the AFL-CIO, with which he affiliated in 1966; Christian organizations, both Protestant and Catholic; radical student associations, including the Students for a Democratic Society (SDS); and other civil rights groups. Aside from alliances, he relied, too, on demonstrations, prayer sessions, marches, and fasts. His basic tactic was the strike, the *huelga*, the time-honored weapon of organized labor. Eventually, though, he discovered that a work stoppage had limited potential in small agricultural towns like Delano, where powerful growers could generally count on the support of the local citizenry, including the Mexican petite bourgeoisie, and even many of the farmworkers themselves. Beginning in 1968, Chávez came to rely on the boycott, a consumer strike, which meant that his success would depend to a large extent on winning support in urban areas throughout the country. His boycott of non-union grapes in 1968–1975, the first nationwide boycott of any kind, was highly successful. Some 12 percent of the adult American population (17 million people) honored the appeal, effectively wiping out grower profits. Still, the strike was long and hard. It finally ended in 1970, when growers reluctantly agreed to recognize the union and sign contracts with it.

★ ★ ★

Unfortunately, successes were few and far between for Chávez during the next few years, as the public mood grew increasingly conservative, boding ill for both trade union and civil rights movements. The upsurge of undocumented workers brought unwelcome competition for agricultural jobs. Internal dissension compounded union problems. When Chávez died in 1993, the union was moribund. The UFW rebounded under his son-in-law, Arturo Rodríguez, but by 1995, when there were an estimated 1.6 million farmworkers in the country, membership was only 26,000, a stark contrast to the 70,000 members during the union's peak years in the mid-1970s. The difficulties in organizing farm labor had proved insurmountable. Growers were as strong as workers were weak; it truly was a David and Goliath battle. Mechanization, especially, had hurt unionization efforts.

Still, the failure to unionize farm labor should be seen in a wider perspective. Chávez brought about much-needed reforms in the fields, including medical, pension, and unemployment benefits. The determined UFW leader served as an important catalyst in this regard. He was also responsible for focusing national attention on the abuses of agribusiness interests, particularly monopolistic tendencies vis-à-vis land and water.

Moreover, it is a mistake to see and measure Chávez solely in terms of union activity. His movement was much more than an attempt to organize farmworkers; it was a vital wing of the civil rights movement, which partly accounts for the widespread support he found among churches. Chávez was concerned about the plight of Mexicans generally, not just those among them who happened to be campesinos. He succeeded in politicizing a large part of the ethnic community, his paramount contribution to the Chicano movement. Indeed, he even found this expanded focus to be too constricting. Like Gandhi and King, he eventually came to espouse the entire gamut of human rights, irrespective of race, perhaps his most enduring legacy.

★ ★ ★

OTHER EARLY CHICANO LEADERS

During the sixties, another extraordinary individual emerged from the ranks of the Mexican community who received national attention and, for a short while at least, had a profound impact on young Chicano activists, Reies López Tijerina (1926–).[6] Tijerina is assuredly the most fascinating and controversial of movement personalities. Born near Fall City, Texas, the son of migrant farm laborers, he was raised by his father and grandmother after his mother's premature death. At eighteen, he embraced a fundamentalist form of Protestantism and enrolled in the Assembly of God Bible Institute at Isleta (now part of El Paso), where he studied for the ministry. Expelled from the school, he became an itinerant Pentecostal evangelist. His travels took him throughout the country. . . . In 1960, Tijerina made his way to New Mexico, where he championed a new cause—the crusade to recover lost Hispano lands. Toward that end, he founded the Alianza Federal de Mercedes (Federal Alliance of Land Grants) in 1963.

This improbable crusade led by an unlikely champion gained surprising support among Hispanos, people notoriously Catholic and conservative. The reasons are largely historical. During World War II, continuing the trend initiated during the Depression, Hispanos were forced to leave their traditional villages in northern New Mexico and southern Colorado in increasing numbers. Many displaced villagers headed to California, but the majority made their way to the cities nearby, notably Albuquerque. This disintegration of village life caused profound alienation. Moreover, poverty continued to be a major problem for both rural and urban residents. The war also saw the continued immigration of Anglos into the state. Now a minority within the population—by 1960, only 28.3 percent of the state population was Spanish-speaking—Hispanos saw their political clout dissipate rapidly. The rise of Tijerina, an outsider, has to be seen in the context of these desperate and deteriorating conditions.

Disillusionment was most severe in northern New Mexico, where angry villagers blamed their problems on the loss of land. Moreover, it was here that seemingly irresponsible policies established by the National Forest Service threatened the grazing and water rights of the rural Hispano populace. It was in this northern peripheral area, centering on Río Arriba County—where half the residents were on public relief—that Tijerina built a power base. Ultimately, Alianza membership reached twenty thousand.

Tijerina believed that all the problems of "Indo-Hispanos" in the Southwest stemmed from the loss of their patrimony. He charged that this land was taken illegally. The Treaty of Guadalupe Hidalgo, he argued, guaranteed Mexicans in the United States citizenship rights, including those relating to property. Even land alienated through sale had been taken illegally. Mexicans, he concluded, needed to organize to win redress through the American court system. The repossession of lost grants was to be a prelude to an even more ambitious and utopian scheme: the creation of a free city-state, the independent Republic of Chama, that would be established in northern New Mexico. . . .

During the first years, from his headquarters in Albuquerque, Tijerina pursued a moderate path in his efforts to achieve victory. For the most part, he placed his faith on legal avenues; he hoped to regain lost lands through litigation. His research into land grants took him to the archives of Spain and Mexico, where he gathered materials to sustain his claims. He got nowhere; U.S. courts refused to hear the case.

In desperation, Tijerina sought to bring national attention to the plight of Hispanos and to force the government to hear him out through extralegal means. Increasingly, the Alianza resorted to fence-cutting and arson. In 1966, Tijerina occupied Echo Amphitheater, formerly an old land grant, now part of Kit Carson National Forest, arresting forest rangers for trespassing. On 5 June 1967, he and his supporters invaded the courthouse at Tierra Amarilla, county seat of Río Arriba, in an attempt to free jailed Alianza members and make a citizen's arrest of the local district attorney. A shoot-out ensued, with *aliancistas* making a getaway by taking two hostáges. The largest manhunt in New Mexico history resulted in the arrest of Tijerina and his closest associates. The chief prosecution witness, a deputy sheriff, was found mysteriously beaten to death in early 1968. Later that year, Tijerina was put on trial for kidnapping and assault during the 1967 shoot-out. . . . A forceful and charismatic speaker, Tijerina handled his own defense and, in a stunning turn of events, succeeded in winning acquittal.

Rey Tigre (King Tiger), as his admirers now called him, was soon in trouble with the law again, and this time his luck ran out. Tried on charges stemming from the Amphitheater episode and for destruction of federal property at a second incident at Kit Carson National Forest, he was found guilty in June 1969 and sentenced to prison. Jailed for two years, he was released on parole from federal prison in Springfield, Missouri, in July 1971, and placed on probation for five years. One of the conditions of his parole was that he sever all ties to the Alianza. He returned to public life, but the old fire was gone. Counseling moderation, he was no longer in the forefront of the Brown Power movement. . . . Tijerina remains an enigmatic figure today. His most meaningful contribution was to dramatize the plight of the impoverished Hispano communities in New Mexico.

Unlike Chávez and Tijerina, Rodolfo ("Corky") Gonzales (1929–) realized that the future of the Mexican community would be in urban areas and that the focus should be on young people.[7] Raised in the barrios of Denver, Gonzales first achieved national prominence as a prize fighter in the early fifties. When he left the ring, he turned to Democratic politics in his hometown. In 1960, he acted as Colorado coordinator of the Viva Kennedy clubs. He then served in a variety of War on Poverty programs. "In no time," according to Stan Steiner, "he was a one-man directory of poverty agencies."[8] Like many other barrio leaders, Gonzales gradually became disillusioned with conventional party politics, and in April 1966, he founded an organization that would permit him to better serve Mexicans in Denver, La Crusada Para la Justicia (the Crusade for Justice).

An organization to mobilize the ethnic community, the Crusade focused on young people and their problems. It established a whole host of services—school, nursery, gym, art gallery, and community center—as well as its own newspaper, *El Gallo.* During the course of the late sixties, as the political climate became more radical, the Crusade embraced a more militant posture. Gonzales, an ex–G. I. Forum member, began to emphasize cultural nationalism. Before too long, he came to espouse a form of separatism. Adopting a widely held view of the time among nationalists, Corky Gonzales became the foremost champion of the idea that

Aztlán, the mythical homeland of the México, was to be found in the Southwest, which he and others called "occupied America." The Crusade, going beyond Tijerina, called for the restoration of their ancestral land to Chicanos. In the meantime, Gonzales focused on direct action in the schools, launching a series of student walkouts in Denver. The Crusade also participated in Dr. King's 1968 Poor People's March on Washington, D.C., where Gonzales and Tijerina led the Chicano contingent.

By now, the idea that militant student groups throughout the country needed a unified organization had gained currency; and Gonzales, the self-appointed leader of the movement, took the initiative in sponsoring a Chicano Youth Liberation Front, a national convention of barrio youth, in Denver on 27–31 March 1969. The convention attracted more than 1,500 Chicanos. It was there that the *Spiritual Plan of Aztlán,* a call for an autonomous Chicano homeland, was unveiled, and the formation of an independent Chicano party was projected.[9] A second youth conference met in Denver in May of the following year. Gonzales was now firmly committed to the idea of a separatist political party, and immediately after the 1970 conference, he and his allies launched the Colorado Raza Unida party.

The genesis of La Raza Unida occurred four years earlier. On 28 March 1966, a number of prominent Mexican delegates walked out of a conference in Albuquerque sponsored by the Equal Employment Opportunity Commission (EEOC) in protest of that organization's failure to address the pressing problems of the barrios. "The walkout in Albuquerque," it has been observed, "marked the first time that the middle-class leadership had engaged in an act of collective protest against the government."[10] President Johnson, looking to placate the dissidents, promised a White House conference of Hispanic leaders to deal with Mexican-American issues.

★ ★ ★

THE CHICANO STUDENT MOVEMENT

To a large extent, the Raza Unida party, notably through the agency of MAYO, reflected the influence of Chicano students. By 1970, the Chicano movement, it appeared, was increasingly dominated by young people, students in high schools and universities concerned especially with the multitude of problems they experienced in these institutions. Among the issues were de facto segregation, racist instructors, the tracking system, and, in institutions of higher learning, inadequate recruitment and funding.

Student activism among Mexicans was not altogether a recent phenomenon. As with other aspects of the Chicano movement, there were notable historical roots. According to Carlos Muñoz, Jr., who has written the most complete study of the Chicano movement to date, the origins of Mexican student activism "can be traced to 1929 when Ernesto Galarza, then a twenty-four-year-old graduate student in history at Stanford University, spoke out in defense of Mexican immigrant workers."[11] More significantly, in 1942 the Mexican-American Movement, Inc. (MAM), a student association which grew out of YMCA-sponsored Mexican Youth Conferences in Southern California, was formed. Led by Paul Coronel and Félix Gutiérrez, it was dedicated to the promotion of educational opportunities for the Mexican community. The main precursor of the Chicano student movement was undoubtedly MAM.

By the mid-sixties, the ferment of the youth movement had impacted Chicanos, who eagerly embraced militant forms of protest. The intellectual sources of student militancy among Chicanos were varied. Almost any form of resistance to oppression was appealing. Students looked to their more militant elders for inspiration, preeminent among them being Chávez and Tijerina. The Black Power movement was a second major contributor. The Mexican Revolution, personified by Pancho Villa and Emiliano Zapata, was still another source of intellectual inspiration. Many students came under the sway of socialism. They looked to Marx, Mao, and especially the heroes of the Cuban Revolution, Che Guevara and Fidel Castro. The Vietnam antiwar protest had an impact, as well.

By 1970, after its formative stage, perhaps the cardinal influence on the growing youth movement was that of indigenismo. By now, students were heavily committed to the idea of cultural regeneration, which, as in the case of blacks, meant a glorification of the motherland. It was the Indian legacy, however, that they found attractive, rather than that of the Spanish, who were doubly condemned for being white and imperialist.

The Chicano *student* movement—as contrasted to other aspects of *La Causa* (the Cause)—began in the mid-sixties; that is, it emerged simultaneously with the other Chicano efforts previously described. The first of the student organizations espousing some form of Chicanismo was the Student Initiative founded at San Jose State College by Armando Valdez in 1964. Three years later, in 1967, several other militant campus organizations appeared. Texas and California took the lead. . . .

Beginning at the college level, student militancy quickly spread to younger students. On 3 March 1968, Latino dissatisfaction with the school system became evident at the high school level. On that fateful day, Chicano students in East Los Angeles, in an effort to get school administrations to address their many problems, walked out of several local high schools. They were led by Sal Castro, a Lincoln High School teacher. These "blowouts," as they were called, soon spread to other schools in what was then the largest school district in the country. Altogether, over fifteen thousand students were involved. Eventually, thirteen strike leaders, including UMAS members Moctezuma Esparza, from UCLA, and Carlos Muñoz, Jr., an ex-serviceman, now chapter president at Los Angeles State College, were indicted on conspiracy charges (dropped two years later).

The Los Angeles strike received national attention. It also stimulated student activism in other cities. During the next few months, walkouts occurred in high schools throughout the Southwest and beyond. Those in Denver and South Texas were the largest and received the most media attention. Student demands included the hiring of Mexican instructors, counselors, and administrators; bilingual and bicultural education; and closer cooperation between schools and the barrio.

★ ★ ★

In early 1969, Chicano students, dispersed in a number of student clubs, sought to achieve a measure of cohesion through the establishment of a nation-wide organization. The opportunity arose at a conference held in April at UC Santa Barbara, one of the strongholds of the mushrooming movement. The conference was called by the Chicano Coordinating Committee on Higher Education (CCHE), formed in 1968 by a group of concerned college students and professors. About one hundred delegates— students, instructors, and administrators—were present. They came from throughout the state of California and other parts of the Southwest. Among the most dynamic participants were Jesús Chavarría, a young professor at UCSB and the dominant personality at the meeting; Juan Gómez-Quiñones, who had been one of the prime movers of the meeting; and the ubiquitous Carlos Muñoz, Jr., the future chronicler of the Chicano student movement. The three-day Santa Barbara convention had two meaningful results: (1) the drafting of the *Plan de Santa Bárbara,* a program of educational reform calling for the institution of Chicano Studies programs, and (2) the establishment of El Movimiento Estudiantil de Aztlán (MECHA or MEChA, The Student Movement of Aztlán), an organization intended to supersede all other student groups by uniting them under the banner of cultural nationalism.[12] The convention, and the organization it spawned, mirrored the increasingly radical notions espoused by Corky Gonzales, whose appeal was at its height at this time. Several weeks before, a number of the delegates at Santa Barbara had attended the Denver Youth Conference, where the Spiritual Plan of Aztlán had been formulated. Gómez-Quiñones had been one of its principal authors.

★ ★ ★

THE CHICANO MOVEMENT IN THE COMMUNITY

The Chicano Power movement was not confined to students; Chicanismo was also pervasive in barrios, where it was particularly evident among the working class. The most important of the militant barrio organizations was the Brown Berets. A paramilitary group, it was founded in East Los Angeles in 1967 by David Sánchez, Carlos Móntez, and Ralph Ramírez, all of them college students at the time. The Brown Berets, however, were relatively unconcerned with the university; their focus was on the barrio, where they targeted police brutality and drug use in the community. They also took a special interest in the youth and played a conspicuous role in the 1968 school walkouts. Sánchez, Móntez, and Ramírez were among the strike leaders put on trial afterwards. In 1969, they claimed to have chapters in twenty-seven cities other than Los Angeles, including Denver and San Antonio. By this time, the Vietnam War had become a major priority.

During the previous year, antiwar sentiment in the country had been transformed into a massive movement uniting students and communities throughout the country, and Chicanos were in the forefront of the protest. Not all Mexicans opposed the war—the G.I. Forum was a firm supporter of U.S. involvement, especially under LBJ—but Chicano students found that their opposition was generally shared by their families in the barrios. This contestation was understandable: the war had escalated steadily since August 1964, when the infamous Tonkin Resolution gave LBJ carte blanche to stop Communist aggression in Southeast Asia; and, as in World War II and Korea, Mexicans played a leading role.

Inspired by patriotism, machismo, and the chance to escape dead-end jobs in rural towns and urban barrios—the primary motives cited by the soldiers themselves in Charley Trujillo's absorbing series of interviews, *Soldados: Chicanos in Viet Nam* (1990)—many Mexican youths volunteered for service. A high percentage entered high-risk branches of the service, such as the U.S. Marine Corps. The majority were drafted. Undereducated, and often ignorant of their rights, Mexicans were prime targets for draft boards. Hispanos, for example, made up 27 percent of the New Mexican population in 1970, but they supplied 69 percent of all draftees from that state. Even more than most wars, Vietnam was fought by poor people. Studies conducted by Prof. Ralph Guzmán in 1969 indicated that Mexicans and other Hispanics were overrepresented in Southeast Asia—on the battle front and on the casualty lists. Constituting about 11 percent of the population in the Southwest in 1960, Mexicans apparently represented close to 20 percent of the region's soldiers killed in battle during the following decade.

★ ★ ★

Many Mexicans distinguished themselves on the field of battle. Thirteen Hispanics were awarded the Medal of Honor, among them Marine Sgt. Alfredo González from Edinburg, Texas, who died in battle in 1968. Twenty-eight years later, he became the first Mexican American to have a destroyer named after him by the U.S. Navy. In general, the war was fought by minorities and working-class whites. It was not long before the white middle class, who had hailed the war as a moral crusade against Communism at the beginning, came to the conclusion that the escalating conflict was morally indefensible—after most deferments were abolished in early 1970 and the burden of financing the war fell increasingly on to their shoulders. The irony was that those youths being asked to lay down their lives to protect the American Way, the poor of the nation, were largely the very individuals who had gained least from it.

Spearheading Mexican opposition to the war was the Chicano Moratorium Committee, consisting of both students and members of the community in southern California. The Brown Berets was the most conspicuous of the barrio groups. David Sánchez, Brown Beret prime minister, was cochair of the Chicano Moratorium Committee, together with Rosalio Muñoz, former UCLA student body president. The Moratorium Committee was responsible for a series of protest marches in East Los Angeles in 1970–1971.

The most memorable demonstration occurred on 29 August 1970, when thirty thousand people gathered at Laguna Park to protest U.S. involvement in Vietnam and the disproportionate loss of Latino lives in the conflict. Chicano representatives came from all over the Southwest. Corky Gonzales was one of the featured speakers. Intended as a peaceful demonstration, the crowd got out of hand

when provoked by the police. In the aftermath, three Mexicans were killed. These included Rubén Salazar, who died under mysterious circumstances.[13] Salazar, a reporter for the *Los Angeles Times* and news director of KMEX-TV, was sitting at a bar with some friends when he was struck in the head by a tear-gas projectile fired by a deputy sheriff. Since he was in the process of preparing an exposé on law enforcement in Los Angeles, the circumstances of his death aroused instant suspicion. Even staunch defenders of law and order condemned the injustice: "Whatever the rights and wrongs of what Chicano activists called an Anglo police riot, there was no excuse for what, according to the coroner's inquest, was the unprovoked killing of Salazar."[14] The incident incensed the Latino community in Los Angeles—the officer who shot Salazar was never charged with a crime, though negligence was obvious to many—and angry demonstrations continued for months.

Like the Black Panthers, after whom they patterned themselves, the Brown Berets were subject to intense police repression during this time, and like the black militant group, they gradually changed their emphasis from confrontation to more productive and concrete forms of community service, including educational projects and soup kitchens. Beset by internal dissension, the Brown Berets announced their disbandment in 1972.

★ ★ ★

THE CHICANA MOVEMENT

After about 1970, a new force began to surface within the movement: feminism. While feminism has a history in the Mexican community that can be traced at least as far back as the Liga Femenil Mexicanista (Mexican Feminist League), established in 1911 by Jovita Idar (1885–1946) in Laredo, the *movimiento* at its inception in the sixties had little concern for women's liberation, a neglect it shared with other civil rights movements. Although advanced in their political ideas, many Chicanos were very traditional in their views of women and the family.[15] Consequently, in the various Chicano organizations, active participation by

Chicanas was discouraged; it seemed that they were inevitably relegated to subordinate positions, such as secretaries, cooks, and janitors. Outright sexual harassment of female members was not uncommon. Many Chicanas gradually came to realize that they were worse off than their *compañeros* (male comrades) since they were subject to triple oppression: exploitation based on race, class, *and* gender. As they sought a greater voice in the movement, they encountered considerable resistance. At the 1969 National Chicano Youth Conference in Denver, delegates, mostly male, resolved that Chicanas were opposed to their own liberation! Middle-class Chicanas also had a difficult time gaining a forum for their views. In 1970, efforts to establish a Chicana caucus at the annual convention of MAPA proved premature.

Some of the feminist criticism came from the ranks of their own sisters. As Anna Nieto-Gómez, herself an early feminist champion, has pointed out, women within the Chicano movement soon came to be divided into two general categories, which she calls the "loyalists" and the "feminists."[16] The first recognized that mujeres were oppressed within their own ethnic communities but felt that ultimately Anglo institutions were to blame. Moreover, they believed that criticism of Mexican men would serve only to sow the seeds of dissension. Feminists argued that the oppression they experienced within their own communities was as bad as that encountered from the dominant society. They felt that in returning to their cultural roots, many Chicanos had unfortunately come to glorify all aspects of the culture indiscriminately, including misogynistic elements. They insisted on speaking out against the machismo and sexual abuse rampant in the movement.

This widening schism among women activists came out in the open at the First National Chicana Conference, *Mujeres Por La Raza* (Women for La Raza), in May 1971, when six hundred delegates from the Southwest and Midwest met in Houston. The debates were extremely animated and the two sides polarized. Eventually, loyalists, almost half the delegates in attendance, walked out of the meeting in protest, ostensibly because of alleged neglect of mujeres in the barrio.

At first, feminists were put on the defensive by charges of being sellouts. Labeled traitors, they came to identify with La Malinche, who though much maligned historically for helping Cortés conquer her own people, was now adopted as a symbol of womanhood and revered as the mother of the Mexican mestizo. Moreover, their critics tried to discredit them by identifying emerging feminism with the small lesbian minority within their ranks, thus cashing in on the homophobia that pervades Mexican culture.

Undaunted, Chicana feminists began to form their own caucuses within Chicano conferences. They also initiated their own publications. While not exclusively feminist in its orientation, one of the earliest and most influential was *Regeneración*, which appeared in Los Angeles beginning in 1971. *Encuentro Femenil,* published by Nieto-Gómez and Adelaida del Castillo in 1973–1974, was the first major student publication. Chicana feminists worked with community-based women's service organizations, and before long they created their own associations distinct from those of other members of La Causa. In fact, some of them antedated the Houston Conference. Among these early women's groups were Las Chicanas at San Diego State University and Hijas de Cuauhtémoc at Long Beach State University. The Chicana movement—i.e., the movement championing the rights of Mexican women—was emerging from the shadow of the Chicano movement.

★ ★ ★

Chicanas were active in championing all the causes Chicanos espoused, but their focus was consistently on women's issues. These included welfare rights, child care, sexual discrimination in employment, abortion, and birth control. Throughout the seventies, they were also adamant in their opposition to involuntary sterilization programs that victimized poor minority women. In colleges, their main contribution was the establishment of Chicana Studies classes beginning in 1968 and Chicana Studies programs a little later. These feminist programs were rapidly adopted by institutions of higher learning throughout the Southwest. Their greatest success was in California, the stronghold of Chicana feminism. . . . But in the early seventies, the Chicana movement was only in its infancy. Ultimately, it was to survive the hard years ahead much better than the Chicano movement.

★ ★ ★

THE CHICANO LEGACY

★ ★ ★

Chicano activists were correct when they acted on the premise that American institutions respond to the needs of a minority community only when they are forced to. A good example was the War on Poverty. The programs emanating from that government-sponsored campaign were initially concessions to the black community, thanks in part to the riots of the mid-sixties, but also to the efforts of the black civil rights movement. It was largely Chicano militancy that forced LBJ to include Mexicans, who received many benefits, not the least of which was the opportunity for leadership training in government-supported programs.[17] There are literally hundreds of community service organizations today serving the Mexican community that trace their roots to the turbulent decade between 1965 and 1975.

The Brown Power movement had other benefits as well. Reform legislation was one. Bilingual and bicultural education, for example, owes its existence to Chicano pressure. In terms of higher education, the single most important contribution may well be Chicano and Chicana Studies programs, strongholds of Chicanismo, instituted in more than one hundred universities throughout the nation. A monument to the efforts of student militants, these programs continue to exist—those at UCLA, UC Berkeley, and the University of Texas at Austin seem to be the most active—serving the student community and producing innovative scholarly research on a host of topics. Virtually all Latino college professors, in or out of Ethnic Studies departments, were impacted by the movement. Through them, its values continue to be transmitted to a powerful audience, the future leaders of a multicultural society.

The movement has had a profound influence on artists. Beginning with El Teatro Campesino, established by Luis Valdez as an adjunct to the UFW in the mid-sixties, Chicanismo became a vital force in the arts. Ultimately, it spurred a cultural renaissance which continues to enrich not only the Mexican community but American society as a whole. Finally, there is the sense of pride that it fostered among Mexicans, both men and women, especially the youth. Undoubtedly, this is its single most beneficial contribution.

★ ★ ★

In sum, the movement was extremely varied. Indeed, it would be more accurate to describe several Chicano movements. Although the students were more vocal and radical, consequently grabbing the headlines, most militant organizations were not student-centered. In fact, as the historian Ignacio García argues, despite appearances, "a closer look at the Movement reveals that it remained dominated not by students or youth but by adults who had experienced Anglo-American prejudice for an extended period."[18] These activists were to be found in a variety of community groups, some operating in urban barrios, others in rural settings. Most catered to the working class.

. . . [M]iddle-class organizations were also well represented in the movement. In the decade between 1965 and 1975, older middle-class associations like LULAC, CSO, MAPA, and even the G.I. Forum embraced the concept of La Raza, albeit reluctantly at times. The spectrum within the movement extended from the moderate position endorsed by the G.I. Forum to the radical philosophy of the Brown Berets, with student groups—who were more moderate than their rhetoric would suggest—somewhere in the middle. What these various organizations had in common was that they all sought, through the tactics of confrontation, to gain political representation in order to protect their civil rights, and they all rejected breakneck assimilation into the American mainstream, opting instead for some form of cultural pluralism.

NOTES

1. For the etymology of the term *Chicano*, see Edward Simmen, "Chicano: Origin and Meaning," in *Pain and Promise: The Chicano Today*, ed. Edward Simmen (New York: Mentor, 1972), pp. 53–56.
2. Rubén Salazar, *Los Angeles Times*, 6 Feb. 1970.
3. There are a score of Chávez biographies, virtually all of them sympathetic. Though somewhat dated, the most objective biography is John Gregory Dunne, *Delano*, rev. ed. (New York: Farrar, Straus and Giroux, 1971); the most recent, Richard Griswold del Castillo and Richard A. García, *César Chávez: A Triumph of Spirit* (Norman: University of Oklahoma Press, 1995).
4. Richard A. García, "Dolores Huerta: Woman, Organizer, and Symbol," *California History* 72 (Spring 1993): 70.
5. Ibid., p. 65.
6. For a brief biographical sketch, see Matt S. Meier, "'King Tiger': Reies López Tijerina," *Journal of the West* 27 (Apr. 1988): 60–68.
7. For a useful biography, see Christine Marín, "Rodolfo 'Corky' Gonzales: The Mexican-American Movement Spokesman, 1962–1972," *Journal of the West* 14 (Oct. 1975): 107–20.
8. Stan Steiner, *La Raza: The Mexican Americans* (New York: Harper and Row, 1969), p. 382.
9. See the *Plan Espiritual in Aztlán: Essays on the Chicano Homeland*, ed. Rudolfo A. Anaya and Francisco Lomelí (Albuquerque: University of New Mexico Press, 1989), pp. 1–5.
10. Carlos Muñoz, Jr., *Youth, Identity, Power: The Chicano Movement* (London: Verso, 1989), p. 56.
11. Muñoz, *Youth, Identity, Power*, p. 21.
12. For the *Plan de Santa Bárbara*, see *Introduction to Chicano Studies*, ed. Livie Isauro Durán and H. Russell Bernard (New York: Macmillan, 1973), pp. 535–45.
13. For Salazar's work, see *Border Correspondent: Selected Writings, 1955–1970*, ed. Mario T. García (Berkeley: University of California Press, 1996).
14. L. H. Gann and Peter J. Duignan, *The Hispanics in the United States: A History* (Boulder, Colo.: Westview Press, 1986), p. 301.
15. "Mexican society," observes Carlos Fuentes, "is founded on very chauvinistic principles inherited from the Aztecs, the Spaniards, and the Arabs. We have a triple misogynistic inheritance that is very hard to overcome." Quoted by Anne-Marie O'Connor, "The Sum of Unequal Parts," *Los Angeles Times*, 24 Oct. 1997.
16. Anna Nieto-Gómez, "La Femenista," *Encuentro Femenil* 1 (1974): 34–47.
17. The political impact of Chicanismo is explored in John A. García, "The Chicano Movement: Its Legacy for Politics and Policy," in *Chicanas/Chicanos at the Crossroads*, pp. 83–107.
18. Ignacio M. García, *Chicanismo: The Forging of a Militant Ethos among Mexican Americans* (Tucson: University of Arizona Press, 1997), p. 134. See, too, Marguerite V. Marín, *Social Protest in an Urban Barrio: A Study of the Chicano Movement, 1966–1974* (Lanham, Md.: University Press of America, 1991); and Guadalupe San Miguel, "Actors Not Victims: Chicanas/os and the Struggle for Educational Equality," in *Chicanas/Chicanos at the Crossroads*, p. 159.

35

Gay New York

GEORGE CHAUNCEY

In the half-century between 1890 and the beginning of the Second World War, a highly visible, remarkably complex, and continually changing gay male world took shape in New York City. That world included several gay neighborhood enclaves, widely publicized dances and other social events, and a host of commercial establishments where gay men gathered, ranging from saloons, speakeasies, and bars to cheap cafeterias and elegant restaurants. The men who participated in that world forged a distinctive culture with its own language and customs, its own traditions and folk histories, its own heroes and heroines. They organized male beauty contests at Coney Island and drag balls in Harlem; they performed at gay clubs in the Village and at tourist traps in Times Square. Gay writers and performers produced a flurry of gay literature and theater in the 1920s and early 1930s; gay impresarios organized cultural events that sustained and enhanced gay men's communal ties and group identity. Some gay men were involved in long-term monogamous relationships they called marriages; others participated in an extensive sexual underground that by the beginning of the century included well-known cruising areas in the city's parks and streets, gay bathhouses, and saloons with back rooms where men met for sex.

The gay world that flourished before World War II has been almost entirely forgotten in popular memory and overlooked by professional historians; it is not supposed to have existed. This book seeks to restore that world to history, to chart its geography, and to recapture its culture and politics. In doing so, it challenges three widespread myths about the history of gay life before the rise of the gay movement, which I call the myths of isolation, invisibility, and internalization.

The myth of isolation holds that anti-gay hostility prevented the development of an extensive gay subculture and forced gay men to lead solitary lives in the decades before the rise of the gay liberation movement. As one exceptionally well informed writer and critic recently put it, the 1969 Stonewall rebellion not only marked the beginning of the militant gay movement but was

> the critical . . . event that unleashed a vast reconstitution of gay society: gay bars, baths, bookstores, and restaurants opened, gay softball teams, newspapers, political organizations, and choruses proliferated. Gay groups of all sorts popped up while gay neighborhoods emerged in our larger, and many of our smaller cities. This was and is a vast social revolution . . . a new community came into being in an astonishingly short period of time.

This has become the common wisdom for understandable reasons, for the policing of the gay world before Stonewall was even more extensive and draconian than is generally realized. A battery of laws criminalized not only gay men's narrowly "sexual" behavior, but also their association with one another, their cultural styles, and their efforts to organize and speak on their own behalf. Their social marginalization gave the police and popular vigilantes even broader informal authority to harass them; anyone discovered to be homosexual was threatened with loss of livelihood and loss of social respect. Hundreds of men were arrested each year in New York City alone for violating such laws.

But the laws were enforced only irregularly, and indifference or curiosity—rather than hostility or fear—characterized many New Yorkers' response to the gay world for much of the half-century before the war. Gay men had to take precautions, but, like other marginalized peoples, they were able to construct spheres of relative cultural autonomy in the interstices of a city governed by hostile powers. They forged an immense gay world of overlapping social networks in the city's streets, private apartments, bathhouses, cafeterias, and saloons, and they celebrated that world's existence at regularly held communal events such as the massive drag (or transvestite) balls that attracted thousands of participants and spectators in the 1920s. By the 1890s, gay men had made the Bowery a center of gay life, and by the 1920s they had created three distinct gay neighborhood enclaves in Greenwich Village, Harlem, and Times Square, each with a different class and ethnic character, gay cultural style, and public reputation.

Some men rejected the dominant culture of the gay world and others passed through it only fleetingly, but it played a central role in the lives of many others. Along with sexual camaraderie, it offered them practical support in negotiating the demands of urban life, for many people used their gay social circles to find jobs, apartments, romance, and their closest friendships. Their regular association and ties of mutual dependence fostered their allegiance to one another, but gay culture was even more important to them for the emotional support it provided as they developed values and identities significantly different from those prescribed by the dominant culture. Indeed, two New Yorkers who conducted research on imprisoned working-class homosexuals in the 1930s expressed concern about the effects of gay men's participation in homosexual society precisely because it made it possible for them to reject the prescriptions of the dominant culture and to forge an alternative culture of their own. "The homosexual's withdrawal, enforced or voluntary, into a world of his own tends to remove him from touch with reality," they warned in 1941, almost thirty years before the birth of the gay liberation movement at Stonewall. "It promotes the feeling of homosexual solidarity, and withdraws this group more and more from conventional folkways and confirms them in their feeling that they compose a community within the community, with a special and artificial life of their own." Once men discovered the gay world, they knew they were not alone.

The myth of invisibility holds that, even if a gay world existed, it was kept invisible and thus remained difficult for isolated gay men to find. But gay men were highly visible figures in early-twentieth-century New York, in part because gay life was more integrated into the everyday life of the city in the prewar decades than it would be after World War II—in part because so many gay men boldly announced their presence by wearing red ties, bleached hair, and the era's other insignia of homosexuality. Gay men gathered on the same street corners and in many of the same saloons and dance halls that other working-class men did, they participated in the same salons that other bohemians did, and they rented the same halls for parties, fancy balls, and theatrical events that other youths did. "Our streets and beaches are overrun by . . . fairies," declared one New Yorker in 1918, and nongay people encountered them in speakeasies, shops, and rooming houses as well. They read about them in the newspapers, watched them perform in clubs, and saw them portrayed on almost every vaudeville and burlesque stage as well as in many films. Indeed, many New Yorkers viewed the gay subculture's most dramatic manifestations as part of the spectacle that defined the distinctive character of their city. Tourists visited the Bowery, the Village, and Harlem in part to view gay men's haunts. In the early 1930s, at the height of popular fascination with gay culture, literally thousands of them attended the city's drag balls to gawk at the drag queens on display there, while newspapers filled their pages with sketches of the most sensational gowns.

The drag queens on parade at the balls and the effeminate homosexual men, usually called "fairies," who managed to be flamboyant even in a suit were the most visible representatives of gay life and played a more central role in the gay world in the prewar years than they do now. But while they made parts of the gay world highly visible to outsiders, even more of that world remained invisible to outsiders. Given the risks gay men faced, most of them hid their homosexuality from their straight workmates, relatives, and neighbors as well as the police. But being forced to hide from the dominant culture did not keep them hidden from each other. Gay men developed a highly sophisticated system of subcultural codes—codes of dress, speech, and style—that enabled them to recognize one another on the streets, at work, and at parties and bars, and to carry on intricate conversations whose coded meaning was unintelligible to potentially hostile people around them. The very need for such codes, it is usually (and rightly) argued, is evidence of the degree to which gay men had to hide. But the elaboration of such codes also indicates the extraordinary resilience of the men who lived under such constraints and their success in communicating with each other despite them. Even those parts of the gay world that were invisible to the dominant society were visible to gay men themselves.

The myth of internalization holds that gay men uncritically internalized the dominant culture's view of them as sick, perverted, and immoral, and that their self-hatred led them to accept the policing of their lives rather than resist it. As one of the most perceptive gay social critics has put it, "When we hid our homosexuality in the past, it was not only because of fear of social pressure but even more because of deeply internalized self-hatred . . . [which was] very pervasive. Homosexuals themselves long resisted the idea of being somehow distinct from other people." But many gay men celebrated their difference from the norm, and some of them organized to resist anti-gay policing. From the late nineteenth century on, a handful of gay New Yorkers wrote polemical articles and books, sent letters to hostile newspapers and published their own, and urged jurists and doctors to change their views. In the 1930s, gay bars challenged their prohibition in the courts, and gays and lesbians organized groups to advocate the homosexual cause. A larger number of men dressed and carried themselves in the streets in ways that proclaimed their homosexuality as boldly as any political button would, even though they risked violence and arrest for doing so.

Most gay men did not speak out against anti-gay policing so openly, but to take this as evidence that they had internalized anti-gay attitudes is to ignore the strength of the forces arrayed against them, to misinterpret silence as acquiescence, and to construe resistance in the narrowest of terms—as the organization of formal political groups and petitions. The history of gay resistance must be understood to extend beyond formal political organizing to include the strategies of everyday resistance that men devised in order to claim space for themselves in the midst of a hostile society. Given the effective prohibition of gay sociability and the swift and certain consequences that most men could expect if their homosexuality were revealed, both the willingness of some men to carry themselves openly *and* the ability of other gay men to create and hide an extensive gay social world need to be considered forms of resistance to overwhelming social pressure. The full panoply of tactics gay men devised for communicating, claiming space, and affirming themselves—the kind of resistant social practices that the political theorist James Scott has called the tactics of the weak—proved to be remarkably successful in the generations before a more formal gay political movement developed. Such tactics did not directly challenge anti-gay policing in the way that the movement would, but in the face of that policing they allowed many gay men not just to survive but to flourish—to build happy, self-confident, and loving lives.

One striking sign of the strength of the gay male subculture was its ability to provide its members with the resources necessary to reject the dominant culture's definition of them as sick, criminal, and unworthy. Some gay men internalized the anti-homosexual attitudes pervasive in their society. Many others bitterly resented the dominant culture's insistence that their homosexuality rendered them virtual women and despised the men among them who seemed to embrace an "effeminate" style. But the "unconventional folkways" of gay culture noted by the two 1930s researchers were more successful in helping men counteract the hostile attitudes of their society than we usually imagine. Many gay men resisted the medical judgment that they were mentally ill and needed treatment,

despite the fact that medical discourse was one of the most powerful anti-gay forces in American culture (and one to which some recent social theories have attributed almost limitless cultural power). Numerous doctors reported their astonishment at discovering in their clinical interviews with "inverts" that their subjects rejected the efforts of science, religion, popular opinion, and the law to condemn them as moral degenerates. One doctor lamented that the working-class "fags" he interviewed in New York's city jail in the early 1920s actually claimed they were *"proud* to be degenerates, [and] do not want nor care to be cured." Indeed, it became the reluctant consensus among doctors that most inverts saw nothing wrong with their homosexuality; it was this attitude, they repeatedly noted, that threatened to make the "problem" of homosexuality so intractable.

All three myths about prewar gay history are represented in the image of the closet, the spatial metaphor people typically use to characterize gay life before the advent of gay liberation as well as their own lives before they "came out." Before Stonewall (let alone before World War II), it is often said, gay people lived in a closet that kept them isolated, invisible, and vulnerable to anti-gay ideology. While it is hard to imagine the closet as anything other than a prison, we often blame people in the past for not having had the courage to break out of it (as if a powerful system were not at work to keep them in), or we condescendingly assume they had internalized the prevalent hatred of homosexuality and thought they deserved to be there. Even at our most charitable, we often imagine that people in the closet kept their gayness hidden not only from hostile straight people but from other gay people as well, and, possibly, even from themselves.

Given the ubiquity of the term today and how central the metaphor of the closet is to the ways we think about gay history before the 1960s, it is bracing—and instructive—to note that it was never used by gay people themselves before then. Nowhere does it appear before the 1960s in the records of the gay movement or in the novels, diaries, or letters of gay men and lesbians. The fact that gay people in the past did not speak of or conceive of themselves as living in a closet does not preclude us from using the term retrospectively as an analytic category, but it does suggest that we need to use it more cautiously and precisely, and to pay attention to the very different terms people used to describe themselves and their social worlds.

Many gay men, for instance, described negotiating their presence in an often hostile world as living a double life, or wearing a mask and taking it off. Each image has a valence different from "closet," for each suggests not gay men's isolation, but their ability—as well as their need—to move between different personas and different lives, one straight, the other gay, to wear their hair up, as another common phrase put it, or let their hair down. Many men kept their gay lives hidden from potentially hostile straight observers (by "putting their hair up"), in other words, but that did not mean they were hidden or isolated from each other—they often, as they said, "dropped hairpins" that only other gay men would notice. Leading a double life in which they often passed as straight (and sometimes married) allowed them to have jobs and status a queer would have been denied while still participating in what they called "homosexual society" or "the life." For some, the personal cost of "passing" was great. But for others it was minimal, and many men positively enjoyed having a "secret life" more complex and extensive than outsiders could imagine. Indeed, the gay life of many men was so full and wide-ranging that by the 1930s they used another—but more expansive—spatial metaphor to describe it: not the gay closet, but the *gay world*.

The expansiveness and communal character of the gay world before World War II can also be discerned in the way people used another familiar term, "coming out." Like much of campy gay terminology, "coming out" was an arch play on the language of women's culture—in this case the expression used to refer to the ritual of a debutante's being formally introduced to, or "coming out" into, the society of her cultural peers. (This is often remembered as exclusively a ritual of WASP high society, but it was also

common in the social worlds of African-Americans and other groups.) A gay man's coming out originally referred to his being formally presented to the largest collective manifestation of prewar gay society, the enormous drag balls that were patterned on the debutante and masquerade balls of the dominant culture and were regularly held in New York, Chicago, New Orleans, Baltimore, and other cities. An article published in the *Baltimore Afro-American* in the spring of 1931 under the headline "1931 Debutantes Bow at Local 'Pansy' Ball" drew the parallel explicitly and unselfconsciously: "The coming out of new debutantes into homosexual society," its first sentence announced, "was the outstanding feature of Baltimore's eighth annual frolic of the pansies when the Art Club was host to the neuter gender at the Elks' Hall, Friday night."

Gay people in the prewar years, then, did not speak of *coming out of* what we call the "gay closet" but rather of *coming out into* what they called "homosexual society" or the "gay world," a world neither so small, nor so isolated, nor, often, so hidden as "closet" implies. The Baltimore debutantes, after all, came out in the presence of hundreds of straight as well as gay and lesbian spectators at the public hall of the fraternal order of Elks. Their sisters in New York were likely to be presented to thousands of spectators, many of whom had traveled from other cities, in some of the best-known ballrooms of the city, including the Savoy and Rockland Palace in Harlem and the Astor Hotel and Madison Square Garden in midtown. Although only a small fraction of gay men actually "came out" at such a ball or in the presence of straight onlookers, this kind of initiation into gay society served as a model for the initiation—and integration—into the gay world for other men as well. . . .

Although the gay male world of the prewar years was remarkably visible and integrated into the straight world, it was, as the centrality of the drag balls suggests, a world very different from our own. Above all, it was not a world in which men were divided into "homosexuals" and "heterosexuals." This is, on the face of it, a startling claim, since it is almost impossible today to think about sexuality without imagining that it is organized along an axis of homosexuality and heterosexuality; a person is either one or the other, or possibly both—but even the third category of "bisexuality" depends for its meaning on its intermediate position on the axis defined by those two poles. The belief that one's sexuality is centrally defined by one's homosexuality or heterosexuality is hegemonic in contemporary culture: it is so fundamental to the way people think about the world that it is taken for granted, assumed to be natural and timeless, and needs no defense. Whether homosexuality is good or chosen or determined, natural or unnatural, healthy or sick is debated, for such opinions are in the realm of ideology and thus subject to contestation, and we are living at a time when a previously dominant ideological position, that homosexuality is immoral or pathological, faces a powerful and increasingly successful challenge from an alternative ideology, which regards homosexuality as neutral, healthy, or even good. But the underlying premise of that debate—that some people are homosexuals, and that all people are either homosexuals, heterosexuals, or bisexuals—is hardly questioned.

This [essay] argues that in important respects the hetero–homosexual binarism, the sexual regime now hegemonic in American culture, is a stunningly recent creation. Particularly in working-class culture, homosexual behavior per se became the primary basis for the labeling and self-identification of men as "queer" only around the middle of the twentieth century; before then, most men were so labeled only if they displayed a much broader inversion of their ascribed gender status by assuming the sexual and other cultural roles ascribed to women. The abnormality (or "queerness") of the "fairy," that is, was defined as much by his "woman-like" character or "effeminacy" as his solicitation of male sexual partners; the "man" who responded to his solicitations—no matter how often—was not considered abnormal, a "homosexual," so long as he abided by masculine gender conventions. Indeed, the centrality of effeminacy to the representation of the "fairy" allowed many conventionally

masculine men, especially unmarried men living in sex-segregated immigrant communities, to engage in extensive sexual activity with other men without risking stigmatization and the loss of their status as "normal men."

Only in the 1930s, 1940s, and 1950s did the now-conventional division of men into "homosexuals" and "heterosexuals," based on the sex of their sexual partners, replace the division of men into "fairies" and "normal men" on the basis of their imaginary gender status as the hegemonic way of understanding sexuality. Moreover, the transition from one sexual regime to the next was an uneven process, marked by significant class and ethnic differences. Multiple systems of sexual classification coexisted throughout the period in New York's divergent neighborhood cultures: men socialized into different class and ethnic systems of gender, family life, and sexual mores tended to understand and organize their homosexual practices in different ways. Most significantly, exclusive heterosexuality became a precondition for a man's identification as "normal" in middle-class culture at least two generations before it did so in much of Euro-American and African-American working-class culture.

One way to introduce the differences between the conceptual schemas by which male sexual relations and identities were organized in the first and second halves of the twentieth century (as well as this [essay's] use of terminology) is to review the changes in the vernacular terms used for homosexually active men, and, in particular, the way in which gay came to mean "homosexual." This does not mean reconstructing a lineage of static meanings—simply noting, for instance, that gay meant "prostitute" before it meant "homosexual." In keeping with the methodology of the study as a whole, it means instead reconstructing how men used the different terms tactically in diverse cultural settings to position themselves and negotiate their relations with other men, gay and straight alike.

Although many individuals at any given times, as one might expect, used the available terms interchangeably and imprecisely, the broad contours of lexical evolution reveal much about the changes in the organization of male sexual practices and identities. For many of the terms used in the early twentieth century were not synonymous with *homosexual* or *heterosexual,* but represent a different conceptual mapping of male sexual practices, predicated on assumptions about the character of men engaging in those practices that are no longer widely shared or credible. *Queer, fairy, trade, gay,* and other terms each had a specific connotation and signified specific subjectivities, and the ascendancy of *gay* as the preeminent term (for gay men among gay men) in the 1940s reflected a major reconceptualization of homosexual behavior and of "homosexuals" and "heterosexuals." Demonstrating that such terms signified distinct social categories not equivalent to "homosexual" and that men used many of them for themselves will also explain why I have employed them throughout this study, even though some of them now have pejorative connotations that may initially cause the reader to recoil.

Gay emerged as a coded homosexual term and as a widely known term for homosexuals in the context of the complex relationship between men known as "fairies" and those known as "queers." According to Gershon Legman, who published a lexicon of homosexual argot in 1941, *fairy* (as a noun) and *queer* (as an adjective) were the terms most commonly used by "queer" and "normal" people alike to refer to "homosexuals" before World War II. Regulatory agents—police, doctors, and private investigators alike—generally used technical terms such as *invert, pervert, degenerate,* or, less commonly, *homosexual* (or *homosexualist,* or simply *homo*), but they also knew and frequently used the vernacular *fairy* as well. In 1917, for instance, an agent of an anti-vice society reported to his supervisor on a "crowd of homosexualists, commonly known as 'fairies.'" Another agent of the society reported ten years later that he had noticed a "colored pervert" in a subway washroom, but added that in identifying the "pervert" to another man in the washroom he had used the more commonplace term: "I said, 'He is a fairy.'"

While most gay men would have understood most of the terms in use for homosexual matters, some terms were more likely to be used in certain social milieus than others. *Fag* was widely used in the 1930s, but almost exclusively by "normals" (the usual word then for those who were not queers); gay men used the word *faggot* instead, but it was used more commonly by blacks than whites. An investigator who visited a "woman's party" at a 137th Street tenement in Harlem in 1928, for instance, reported that one of the women there told him, "Everybody here is either a bull dagger [lesbian] or faggot.'" The investigator, a black man working for an anti-vice society, appears to have believed that the term was less well known than *fairy* to the "normal" white population. When he mentioned in another report that two men at a Harlem restaurant were "said to be 'noted faggots,'" he quickly explained to his white supervisor this meant they were "fairies." While gay white men also used the term *faggot* (although less often than blacks), they rarely referred to themselves as being "in the life," a phrase commonly used by black men and women.

Most of the vernacular terms used by "normal" observers for fairies, such as *she-man, nance,* and *sissy* as well as *fairy* itself, emphasized the centrality of effeminacy to their character. In the 1920s and 1930s, especially, such men were also often called *pansies,* and the names of other flowers such as daisy and buttercup were applied so commonly to gay men that they were sometimes simply called "horticultural lads." ("Ship me home," said a "nance" to a florist in a joke told in 1932. "I'm a pansy.") The flamboyant style adopted by "flaming faggots" or "fairies," as well as its consistency with outsiders' stereotypes, made them highly visible figures on the streets of New York and the predominant image of *all* queers in the straight mind.

Not all homosexual men in the prewar era thought of themselves as "flaming faggots," though. While the terms *queer, fairy,* and *faggot* were often used interchangeably by outside observers (and sometimes even by the men they observed), each term also had a more precise meaning among gay men that could be invoked to distinguish its object from other homosexually active men. By the 1910s and 1920s, the men who identified themselves as part of a distinct category of men primarily on the basis of their homosexual interest rather than their womanlike gender status usually called themselves *queer*. Essentially synonymous with "homosexual," *queer* presupposed the statistical normalcy—and normative character—of men's sexual interest in women; tellingly, queers referred to their counterparts as "normal men" (or "straight men") rather than as "heterosexuals." But *queer* did not presume that the men it denoted were effeminate, for many queers were repelled by the style of the fairy and his loss of manly status, and almost all were careful to distinguish themselves from such men. They might use *queer* to refer to any man who was not "normal," but they usually applied terms such as *fairy*, *faggot*, and *queen* only to those men who dressed or behaved in what they considered to be a flamboyantly effeminate manner. They were so careful to draw such distinctions in part because the dominant culture failed to do so.

Many fairies and queers socialized into the dominant prewar homosexual culture considered the ideal sexual partner to be "trade," a "real man," that is, ideally a sailor, a soldier, or some other embodiment of the aggressive masculine ideal, who was neither homosexually interested nor effeminately gendered himself but who would accept the sexual advances of a queer. While some gay men used the term *trade* to refer only to men who insisted on payment for a sexual encounter, others applied it more broadly to any "normal" man who accepted a queer's sexual advances. The centrality of effeminacy to the definition of the fairy in the dominant culture enabled trade to have sex with both the queers and fairies without risking being labeled queer themselves, so long as they maintained a masculine demeanor and sexual role. Just as significantly, even those queers who had little interest in trade recognized that trade constituted a widely admired ideal type in the subculture and accepted the premise that trade were the "normal men" they claimed to be.

Ultimately men who detested the word *fairy* and the social category it signified were the ones to embrace *gay* as an alternative label for themselves. But

they did not initiate its usage in gay culture. The complexity of the emergence of the term's homosexual meanings is illustrated by a story told by a gay hairdresser, Dick Addison, about an incident in 1937 when he was a fourteen-year-old "flaming faggot" in a Jewish working-class section of New York:

> A group of us hung out at a park in the Bronx where older boys would come and pick us up. One boy who'd been hanging out with us for a while came back once, crying, saying the boy he'd left with wanted him to suck his thing. "I don't want to do *that!*" he cried. "But why are you hanging out with us if you aren't gay?" we asked him. "Oh, I'm *gay*," he exclaimed, throwing his hands in the air like an hysterical queen, "but I don't want to do *that*." This boy liked the gay life—the clothes, the way people talked and walked and held themselves—but, if you can believe it, he didn't realize there was more to being gay than that!

Gay, as the story indicates, was a code word. Gay men could use it to identify themselves to other gays without revealing their identity to those not in the wise, for not everyone—certainly not the boy in this story (unless he was simply using the word's protean character to joke with the group)—knew that it implied a specifically sexual preference. But it did not simply mean "homosexual," either. For all the boys, the "gay life" referred as well to the flamboyance in dress and speech associated with the fairies. Indeed, it was the fairies (the especially flamboyant gay men), such as the ones Addison associated with, who used the word most in the 1920s and 1930s. Will Finch, a social worker who began to identify himself as "queer" while in New York in the early 1930s, recalled in 1951 that the word *gay* "originated with the flaming faggots as a 'camp' word, used to apply to absolutely everything in any way pleasant or desirable (not as 'homosexual'), . . . [and only began] to mean 'homosexual' later on."

The earliest such uses of *gay* are unknown, but the "flaming faggots" Finch remembered doubtless used the word because of the host of apposite connotations it had acquired over the years. Originally referring simply to things pleasurable, by the seventeenth century *gay* had come to refer more specifically to a life of *immoral* pleasures and dissipation (and by the nineteenth century to prostitution, when applied to women), a meaning that the "faggots" could easily have drawn on to refer to the homosexual life. *Gay* also referred to something brightly colored or someone showily dressed—and thus could easily be used to describe the flamboyant costumes adopted by many fairies, as well as things at once brilliant and specious, the epitome of camp. One can hear these meanings echo through the decades in Finch's comment in 1963 that he still "associate[d] the word with the hand waving, limp-wristed faggot, squealing 'Oh, it's *gay!*'" One hears them as well in the dialogue in several novels written in the late 1920s and early 1930s by gay men with a camp sensibility and an intimate knowledge of the homosexual scene. "I say," said Osbert to Harold in *The Young and Evil*, perhaps the campiest novel of all, "you look positively gay in the new clothes. Oh, said Harold, you're lovely *too*, dear, and gave him a big kiss on the forehead, much to Osbert's dismay." A chorus boy gushed to his friend in another, rather more overwritten 1934 novel, "I'm lush. I'm gay. I'm wicked. I'm everything that flames.'" And Cary Grant's famous line in the 1938 film *Bringing Up Baby* played on several of these meanings: he leapt into the air, flounced his arms, and shrieked "I just went gay all of a sudden," *not* because he had fallen in love with a man, but because he was asked why he had put on a woman's nightgown. The possibility of a more precisely sexual meaning would not have been lost on anyone familiar with fairy stereotypes.

The word's use by the "flaming faggots" (or "fairies"), the most prominent figures in homosexual society, led to its adoption as a code word by "queers" who rejected the effeminacy and overtness of the fairly but nonetheless identified themselves as homosexual. Because the word's use in gay environments had given it homosexual associations that were unknown to people not involved in the gay world, more circumspect gay men could use it to identify themselves secretly to each other in a straight setting. A properly intoned reference or

two to a "gay bar" or to "having a gay time" served to alert the listener familiar with homosexual culture. . . .

Younger men rejected *queer* as a pejorative name that others had given them, which highlighted their difference from other men. Even though many "queers" had also rejected the effeminacy of the fairies, younger men were well aware that in the eyes of straight men their "queerness" hinged on their supposed gender deviance. In the 1930s and 1940s, a series of press campaigns claiming that murderous "sex deviates" threatened the nation's women and children gave "queerness" an even more sinister and undesirable set of connotations. In calling themselves *gay*, a new generation of men insisted on the right to name themselves, to claim their status as men, and to reject the "effeminate" styles of the older generation. Some men, especially older ones like Finch, continued to prefer *queer* to *gay*, in part because of *gay*'s initial association with the fairies. Younger men found it easier to forget the origins of *gay* in the campy banter of the very queens whom they wished to reject.

Testimony given at hearings held by the State Liquor Authority (SLA) from the 1930s to the 1960s to review the closing of bars accused of serving homosexuals provides striking evidence of the growing use of the word *gay*. At none of the hearings held before the war did an SLA agent or bar patron use the word to refer to the patrons. At a hearing held in 1939, for instance, one of the Authority's undercover investigators testified that the bar in question was patronized by "homosexuals or fairies, fags commonly called." Another investigator also called the bar's patrons "fags," but noted that the "fags" preferred to call themselves "fairies." A few moments later he referred to a group of "normal" people having a good time at a party as "people that were gay," indicating that the term, in his mind, still had no homosexual connotations. Twenty years later, however, SLA agents casually used *gay* to mean homosexual, as did the *gay* men they were investigating. One agent testified in 1960 that he had simply asked a man at a suspected bar whether he was "straight or gay." "I am as gay as the Pope" came the knowing reply. ("Which Pope?" asked the startled investigator. "Any Pope," he was assured.)

Once the word was widely diffused within the gay world, it was introduced to people outside that world by writers who specialized in familiarizing their readers with New York's seamier side. Jack Lait and Lee Mortimer, for instance, confided to the readers of their 1948 *Confidential* guide to the city that "not all New York's queer (or, as they say it, 'gay') people live in Greenwich Village." In 1956, the scandal magazine *Tip-Off* played on the expectation that some of its readers would understand the term—and others would want to—by putting a report on homosexuals' supposed "strangle-hold on the theatre" under the headline, "Why They Call Broadway the 'Gay' White Way." By 1960, liquor authority attorneys prosecuting a gay bar were so certain a bartender in a heavily gay neighborhood such as Greenwich Village could be expected to understand the word that they used one bartender's claim that he was unsure of its meaning as a basis for questioning his candor. "You live only a few blocks from . . . the heart of Greenwich Village," an attorney demanded incredulously, "and you are not familiar with the meaning of the word gay?" The word had become familiar to hip New Yorkers and others fully a decade before the gay liberation movement introduced it to the rest of the nation, and parts of the "respectable" press began using it in the late 1960s and early 1970s.

The ascendancy of *gay* as the primary self-referential term used within the gay world reflected the subtle shifting occurring in the boundaries drawn among male sexual actors in the middle decades of the century. Earlier terms—*fairy, queer,* and *trade* most commonly—had distinguished various types of homosexually active men: effeminate homosexuals, more conventional homosexuals, and masculine heterosexuals who would accept homosexual advances, to use today's nomenclature. *Gay* tended to group all these types together, to deemphasize their differences by emphasizing the *similarity* in character they had presumably demonstrated by their choice of male sexual partners. This reconfiguration of sexual categories occurred in two stages.

First, gay men, like the prewar queers but unlike the fairies, defined themselves as gay primarily on the basis of their homosexual interest rather than effeminacy, and many of them, in a break with older homosexual cultural norms, adopted a new, self-consciously "masculine" style. Nonetheless, they did not regard all men who had sex with men as gay; men could still be trade, but they were defined as trade primarily on the basis of their purported heterosexuality rather than their masculinity (though modified as "rough" trade, the term still emphasized a man's masculine character). A new dichotomous system of classification, based on sexual object choice rather than gender status, had begun to supersede the old.

In the second stage of cultural redefinition, trade virtually disappeared as a sexual identity (if not as a sexual role) within the gay world, as men began to regard *anyone* who participated in a homosexual encounter as "gay," and, conversely, to insist that men could be defined as "straight" only on the basis of a total absence of homosexual interest and behavior. Alfred Gross, publicly a leader in psychological research and social work related to homosexuals in New York from the 1930s through the 1960s and secretly a gay man himself, derided the distinction between homosexuals and trade in a speech he gave in 1947. Fairies, he contended, "are preoccupied with getting and holding their 'man.'" But, he remonstrated, they refuse "to recognize that the male, no matter how roughly he might be attired, how coarse his manners, how brutal or sadistic he may be, if he willing to submit regularly to homosexual attentions, is every whit as homosexual as the man who plays what is considered the female role in the sex act."

A growing number of gay men subscribed to this more limited view of the behavior allowed men if they were to be labeled "straight"; by the 1970s, most regarded a self-proclaimed "piece of trade" who regularly let homosexuals have sex with him not as heterosexual but as someone unable to recognize, or accept, or admit his "true nature" as a homosexual. . . .

The ascendancy of *gay* reflected, then, a reorganization of sexual categories and the transition from an early-twentieth-century culture divided into "queers" and "men" on the basis of gender status to a late-twentieth-century culture divided into "homosexuals" and "heterosexuals" on the basis of sexual object choice. Each set of terms represented a way of defining, constituting, and containing male "sexuality," by labeling, differentiating, and explaining the character of (homo) sexually active men. Any such taxonomy is necessarily inadequate as a measure of sexual behavior, but its construction is itself a significant social practice. It provides a means of defining the deviant, whose existence serves both to delineate the boundaries of acceptable behavior for all men and to contain the threat of deviance, at once stigmatizing it and suggesting that it is confined to a "deviant" minority.

 36

A Brief History of Working Women

SHARLENE NAGY HESSE-BIBER AND
GREGG LEE CARTER

The number of women in the paid workforce has steadily increased throughout the twentieth century, from around 20 percent in 1900 to around 45 percent in 1975 and just under 60 percent in 2002 (see Figure 1).

Even so, for much of the twentieth century women were "invisible" workers, whose labor and skills were considered insignificant compared to those of men. Traditional studies perpetuated this illusion by treating the topic of labor-force participation as though it involved only men. . . .

Until the 1970s, there was little historical research on women workers, or on women in general. Studies of women's history tended to be limited to (1) institutional histories of women's organizations and movements; (2) biographies of important suffragists and "token women," such as first ladies or isolated nineteenth-century professional women; and (3) "prescriptive history," or discussions of class or societal ideals rather than actual cultural practices; for example, analyses of recommended child-rearing methods. There were few studies on women's work either inside or outside the home. Little attention was paid to the diversity of women workers, to contemporary or historical effects of race, class, or ethnicity.

Over the past three decades, however, women have become the subject of wider historical interest. The contributions over the decades of a diversity of women workers have begun to be identified. We have a better understanding of who they were, why they worked, in which occupations and industries, and what problems they encountered. A historical overview enriches our understanding of the interplay of social, economic, and political factors that have influenced and shaped women's relationship to the paid labor force. Knowing more about "where women have been" helps us understand "where women are" now and "where they are going" in the future.

★ ★ ★

THE ARRIVAL OF INDUSTRIALIZATION

The transformation from an agrarian rural economy to an urban industrial society ushered in a new era in women's work. With the advent of industrialization, many of the products women made at home—clothes, shoes, candles—gradually came to be made instead in factories. For a while, women still performed the work at home, using the new machines. Merchants would contract for work to be done, supplying women with the machines and the raw materials to be made into finished articles. The most common of these manufacturing trades for women was sewing for the newly emerging clothing industry. Since women had always sewn for their families, this work was considered an extension of women's traditional role, and therefore a respectable activity. As the demand for goods increased, however, home production declined and gave way to the factory system, which was more efficient in meeting emerging needs.

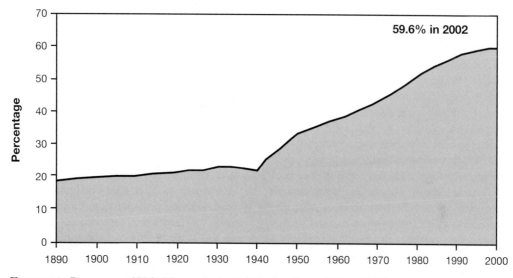

FIGURE 1 *Percentage of U.S. Women in the Paid Labor Force, 1890–2002.*
Note: pre-1945 data are for ages 14 and older; 1945–2001 are for ages 16 and older.
Sources: Bureau of Labor Statistics, 1979, 1980, 1997b; U.S. Bureau of the Census, 2002a (Table 576, p. 372).

The rise of factory production truly separated the home from the workplace. With the decline of the household unit as the center of industrial and economic activity, the importance of women's economic role also declined. Male and female spheres of activity became more separated, as did the definitions of men's and women's roles. Man's role continued to be primarily that of worker and provider; woman's role became primarily supportive. She was to maintain a smooth and orderly household, to be cheerful and warm, and thus to provide the husband with the support and services he needed to continue his work life (Kessler-Harris, 1981, p. 35). The industrial revolution created a set of social and economic conditions in which the basic lifestyle of white middle-class women more nearly approached society's expectations concerning woman's role. More and more middle-class women could now aspire to the status formerly reserved for the upper classes—that of "lady" (Chafe, 1977). The nineteenth-century concept of a lady was that of a fragile, idle, pure creature, submissive and subservient to her husband

and to domestic needs. Her worth was based on her decorative value, a quality that embraced her beauty, her virtuous character, and her temperament. She was certainly not a paid employee. This ideal was later referred to as the "cult of true womanhood" because of its rigid, almost religious standards (Gordon, Buhle, and Schrom, 1971, p. 28).

Biological and social arguments were also often used to justify women's exclusion from the labor force. Women were seen as too weak and delicate to participate in the rough work world of men. It was believed they lacked strength and stamina, that their brains were small, that the feminine perspective and sensitivity were liabilities in the marketplace. Such arguments rationalized women's accepting the roles of homemaker and mother almost exclusively, as the industrial revolution spread across the country (Kessler-Harris, 1981, p. 14).

During the early years of industrialization, however, because many men were still primarily occupied with agricultural work and were unavailable or unwilling to enter the early factories, male laborers were in short supply. American industry depended, then, on a steady supply of women workers. Yet how could society tolerate women's working in the factories, given the dominant ideology of the times, which dictated that a woman's place was at home? Single white women provided one answer. Their employment was viewed as a fulfillment of their family responsibilities, during an interlude before marriage.

The employment of young, single women in the early Lowell (Massachusetts) mills is a prime example of the reconciliation of ideology with the needs of industry. Francis Cabot Lowell devised a respectable route into employment for such women. Recruiting the daughters of farm families to work in his mill, which opened in 1821 in Lowell, he provided supervised boardinghouses, salaries sufficient to allow the young women to offer financial aid to their families or to save for their own trousseaux, and assurances to their families that the hard work and discipline of the mill would help prepare them for marriage and motherhood (Kessler-Harris, 1975). The boardinghouse was the center of social life for young factory workers, integrating them into an urban life style and factory life. The average boardinghouse erected in the mid-1830s consisted of series of apartments arranged in a long housing block. Twenty-five residents usually comprised each house, with up to six living in each room. The women had little privacy and, as historian Thomas Dublin (1979, p. 80) observes, ". . . pressure to conform to group standards must have been strong."

Work life in the mills was arduous and the hours were long. Hannah Borden, noted to be the "best weaver of her day," learned how to weave when she was eight and became one of the first weavers to work at the mills in Fall River, Massachusetts, in 1817 (Wertheimer, 1977, p. 66). Historian Barbara Mayer Wertheimer (1977, p. 65) gives us a sense of the typical daily routine for mill girls like Hannah Borden:

> The factory bell woke her at 4:00 in the morning. Taking her breakfast along, she readied her looms by 5:00, when the bell signaled the start of work. At 7:30 it announced the breakfast break, and called

workers back afterward. At noon it rang the half-hour lunch period, and at 12:30 summoned them back. It dismissed them at 7:30 each evening, unless they worked overtime. When they got back to their boardinghouses at night, they were often too tired to eat. At 10:00 the bell rang for bed and lights out. Sundays it called them to church.

Even though their work day was long, many women still found the time and strength "to organize and attend lectures, forums, and language classes, sewing groups, and literary improvement circles" (Wertheimer, 1977, p. 65). The literary journal *The Lowell Offering* was written "by and for" mill women. "The women who wrote for the *Offering* . . . found an outlet for their talents and a vindication of their role as millworkers; they portrayed themselves in a dignified light, and this gave status to their work" (Wertheimer, 1977, p. 66).

While employment in the mills gave many young women a sense of independence and filled an important economic need for their families, working life in the mills began to deteriorate in the 1830s. Absentee owners allowed the factory supervisors to have complete control over their workforce. They initiated work rules that provided little time for women to have their meals and strict punishments if they did not comply with company policy: "So little time was allowed for meals—one half-hour at noon for dinner—that the women raced from the hot humid weaving rooms several blocks to their boardinghouses, gulped down their main meal of the day, and ran back to the mill in terror of being fined if they were late" (Wertheimer, 1977, p. 66).

As the power and authority of mill management continued to become more oppressive, women's resentment toward mill owners erupted into several strikes. In February 1834 and October 1836, the women of Lowell Mill went out on strike to protest a reduction in their wages and an increase in the board rate charged for their company housing. The solidarity women gained through their years of community living, and the formation of the Factory Girls' Association in 1834, assisted them in their ability to organize. Eight hundred women took part in the in the 1834 strike, and this number nearly doubled for the 1836 strike (Dublin, 1979, pp. 86–88; Wertheimer, 1977, pp. 68, 70). The testimony of Harriet Hanson, who was only eleven years old at the time, provides a gripping account of [what] happened during the 1836 strike:

> I worked in a lower room where I had heard the proposed strike fully, if not vehemently, discussed; I had been an ardent listener to what was said against this attempt at "oppression" on the part of the corporation, and naturally I took sides with the strikers. When the day came on which the girls were to turn out, those in the upper rooms started first, and so many of them left that our mill was at once shut down. Then, when the girls in my room stood irresolute, uncertain what to do. . . . I, who began to think they would not go out after all their talk, became impatient, and started on ahead, saying with childish bravado, "I don't care what you do, I am going to turn out, whether anyone else does or not"; and I marched out, and was followed by the others. . . . I was more proud tha[n] I have ever been since at any success I may have achieved and more proud than I shall ever be again until my own beloved State gives to its women citizens the right of suffrage." (Wertheimer 1977, p. 70)

While few labor organizations arose among women textile workers in the 1830s, these early protests eventually paved the way for future strikes and the eventual movement of women into organized labor (see Dublin, 1979, pp. 88–89).

In the early industrial era, working conditions were arduous and hours were long. By the late 1830s, immigration began to supply a strongly competitive, permanent workforce willing to be employed for low wages in the factories, under increasingly mechanized and hazardous conditions. By the late 1850s, most of the better-educated, single, native-born women had left the mills, leaving newly immigrated women (both single and married) and men to fill these positions.

While women thus played a crucial role in the development of the textile industry, the first important manufacturing industry in America, women also found employment in many other occupations during the process of industrialization. As railroads and other business enterprises expanded and consolidated, women went to work in these areas as well. In fact, the U.S. Labor Commissioner reported that by 1890 only 9 out of 360 general groups to which the country's industries had been assigned did not employ women (Baker, 1964).

By 1900, more than five million women or girls, or about one in every five of those ten years old and over, had become a paid employee (Baker, 1964). The largest proportion (40 percent) remained close to home in domestic and personal service, but domestic service was on the decline for white working-class women at the turn of the century. About 25 percent (1.3 million) of employed women worked in the manufacturing industries: in cotton mills, in the manufacture of woolen and worsted goods, silk goods, hosiery, and knitwear. The third largest group of employed women (over 18 percent) were working on farms. Women in the trade and transportation industries (about 10 percent) worked as saleswomen, telegraph and telephone operators, stenographers, clerks, copyists, accountants, and bookkeepers. Women in the professions (about 9 percent, and typically young, educated, single, and of native-born parentage) were employed primarily in elementary and secondary teaching or nursing. Other professions—law, medicine, business, college teaching—tended to exclude women. The fastest growing of these occupational groups were manufacturing, trade, and transportation. In the last thirty years of the nineteenth century, the number of women working in trade and transportation rose from 19,000 to over half a million (Baker, 1964). These women also tended to be young, single, native-born Americans; immigrants and minority women were excluded from these white-collar positions (Smuts, 1971).

Only a small minority of married, working-class women, with the exception of African American women, worked away from their homes during this time. Most continued to be heavily involved in childbearing and child-rearing and in the heavy responsibility for the domestic work within the family unit. Even fewer middle-class wives worked outside of the home; those who did work tended to be divorced, widowed, or supporting disabled or unemployed husbands (Pleck, 1979, p. 367). Among many immigrant groups, cultural traditions of male authority effectively discouraged married women from working, even when the husband was unemployed and the family's economic situation was precarious. Immigrant wives with jobs not infrequently withdrew from the marketplace when family finances permitted, "to pursue the goal, often elusive, of equipping their children to join the middle class" (Brownlee and Brownlee, 1976, p. 31).

Although at least some working-class men were becoming successful in large enterprises and in the professions, working-class women were limited to low-paying jobs and unskilled jobs that carried little if any promise of advancement. The single, white woman workers were never fully integrated into the workforce, either. The young ones were assumed to be working only temporarily—until they married. Women who complained of low wages were often asked "but haven't you a male friend that helps support you?" (Baker, 1964). The older ones were considered "spinsters"—women who had been unsuccessful in getting a husband and who had substituted work for family life (Grossman, 1975).

In addition, sexual harassment was a growing occupational hazard affecting women in almost every occupation. In 1908, *Harper's Bazaar* printed a series of letters in which working women wrote of these difficulties. The following letter, from a woman seeking a job as a stenographer, describes such an experience:

> I purchased several papers, and plodded faithfully through their multitude of "ads." I took the addresses of some I intended to call upon. . . . The first "ad" I answered the second day was that of a doctor who desired a stenographer at once, good wages paid. It sounded rather well, I thought, and felt that this time I would meet a gentleman. The doctor was very kind and seemed to like my appearance and references; as to salary, he offered me $15 a week, with a speedy prospect of more. As I was leaving his office, feeling that at last I was launched safely upon the road to a good living, he said casually, "I have an auto; and as my wife doesn't care for that sort of thing, I shall expect you to accompany me frequently on pleasure trips." That settled the

> doctor; I never appeared. After that experience I was ill for two weeks. (*Harper's Bazaar,* 1908, quoted in Bularzik, 1978, p. 25)

Women's working conditions were also aggravated by women's exclusion from the organized labor movements of the day, which were steadily improving conditions for men. For the first half of the nineteenth century, unions—which were primarily for craft and skilled workers—did not accept female members (Wertheimer, 1977, p. 341). By 1920, only 7 percent of women workers belonged to trade unions, compared with 25 percent of male workers (Baxandall, Gordon, and Reverby, 1976, p. 255). In a number of industries, women formed their own unions, but these affected only a small minority of those employed. The Working Girl's Societies, the Women's Trade Union League, and other such groups tried to little avail to change the widely held beliefs that women were temporary workers whose motivation was to earn pocket money, or who, if they had other goals, were selfish creatures ignoring family responsibilities. Such attitudes persisted well into the twentieth century (Gordon et al., 1971, p. 43).

While women's labor organizations were not initially successful in directly achieving their goals, they did develop a sense of unity among working women. This was an important step in the future formation of a women's movement. The industrial revolution pushed women from the domestic sphere into the factory, where they worked alongside one another. The result was an interchange of ideas, values, and attitudes, and the subsequent ability to share common concerns and dreams—a phenomenon that would not have been possible if they remained agrarian homemakers. Economic historian Ivy Pinchbeck (1930; 1969, p. 307) observes that the movement of women into the industrial workforce benefited women by the "wider experience and more varied interests they gained by working together in a community." Pinchbeck's observation is echoed by another contemporary chronicler of the industrial revolution, Caroline Foley. Writing in 1894, Foley noted that "the factory and workshop take the girl out of 'the home,' cribbed, cabined, and confined as to space, light, air, ideas and companionship, mould her in habits of punctuality, promptness, handiness, gumption, and sustained attention and effort, spur her on to work well, bring ou[t] her capacities for comradeship and social action, and train her in self-respect, self-reliance and courage" (Foley, 1894, p. 187, as cited in Pinchbeck, 1969, p. 308).

By the turn of the century, the labor market had become clearly divided according to gender, race, and class. Fewer manufacturing jobs were being defined as suitable for white women, especially with the rising dominance of heavy industry employment for which female workers were considered too delicate. Working-class women were increasingly devalued by their continued participation in activities men had primarily taken over (such as factory work), because these activities were regarded as lacking in the Victorian virtue and purity called for by the "cult of true womanhood." As the economy expanded and prosperity came to more and more white middle-class families, middle-class women could "become ladies." A "woman's place" was still defined as at home. If these women did work outside the home, the appropriate occupation was a white-collar job (sales, clerical, and professional occupations). White women's occupations shifted from primarily domestic service—which became increasingly identified as "black women's work"—and from light manufacturing to the rapidly growing opportunities in office and sales work. These jobs were also considered more appropriate for feminine roles as defined by the cult of true womanhood. Women of color did not share in this occupational transformation. In 1910, for example, nine out of ten African American women worked as agricultural laborers or domestics, compared with three out of ten white women (Aldridge, 1975, p. 53).

The Legacy of Slavery

African American women were not part of the "cult of true womanhood." They were not sheltered or protected from the harsh realities and, "while many white daughters were raised in genteel refined circumstances, most black daughters were forced to deal with poverty, violence and a hostile outside world from childhood on" (Chafe, 1977, p. 53). After emancipation, their employment and economic opportunities were limited, in part because the skills they had learned on the plantation transferred to relatively few jobs, and those only of low pay and status.

African American women's concentration in service work—especially domestic work—was largely a result of limited opportunities available to them following the Civil War. The only factory employment open to them was in the Southern tobacco and textile industries, and until World War I most African American working women were farm laborers, domestics, or laundresses. Life as a domestic worker in 1912 sounds remarkably like life as a slave:

> I am a Negro woman, and I was born and reared in the South. I am now past forty years of age and am the mother of three children. My husband died nearly fifteen years ago. . . . For more than thirty years—or since I was ten years old—I have been a servant . . . in white families. . . . During the last ten years I have been a nurse. . . . I frequently work from fourteen to sixteen hours a day. . . . I am allowed to go home to my children, the oldest of whom is a girl of eighteen years, only once in two weeks, every other Sunday afternoon—even then I am not permitted to stay all night. I not only have to nurse a little white child, now eleven months old, but I have to act as playmate . . . to three other children in the home, the oldest of whom is only nine years of age. . . . I see my own children only when they happen to see me on the streets when I am out with the children, or when my children come to the "yard" to see me, which isn't often. . . . You might as well say that I'm on duty all the time—from sunrise to sunrise, every day of the week. I am the slave, body and soul, of this family, and what do I get for this work? . . . Ten dollars a month. (Anonymous, 1912, quoted in Lerner, 1972, pp. 227–228)

Following the abolition of slavery, African American women faced a great deal of opposition as they entered the labor force. As observed by historian Rosalyn Terborg-Penn (1985), to ensure the survival of their communities African Americans had to traverse the harsh realities of racism and sexism left by the legacy of slavery. African American women developed unique organizational forms of assistance based upon mutual aid and support that did not follow the contours of the typical labor unions that were developing among the working classes. These organizational forms were rooted in traditional African culture, "where women had a long tradition of self-organization for mutual support in relation to most life activities, including work. Labor was an essential role and responsibility in traditional Africa, and indeed, women's labor output generally far surpassed that of men" (Terborg-Penn, 1985, p. 140).

Despite the limited range of job opportunities, a relatively large proportion of African American women were employed. The legacy of slavery may partly account for the relatively high labor-force participation rate of African American women. Although women's labor-force participation rate is generally lower than men's, African American women's participation rate was historically much higher than that of white women. Thus, for example, white women's labor-force participation in 1890 was 16.3 percent, while African American women's rate was 39.7 percent (Goldin, 1977, p. 87). Even today, African American women have a higher rate of participation than their white counterparts: 62.9 percent versus 59.7 percent (Bureau of Labor Statistics, 2003b).

WORLD WAR I AND THE DEPRESSION

World War I accelerated the entry of white women into new fields of industry. The pressure of war production and the shortage of male industrial workers necessitated the hiring of women for what had been male-dominated occupations. Women replaced men at jobs in factories and business offices, and, in general, they kept the nation going, fed, and clothed. The mechanization and routinization of industry during this period enabled women to quickly master the various new skills. For the most part, this wartime pattern involved a reshuffling of the existing female workforce, rather than an increase in the numbers of women employed. Although the popular

myth is that homemakers abandoned their kitchens for machine shops or airplane hangars, only about 5 percent of women workers were new to the labor force during the war years. Figure 2 shows that there was a significant decrease in the number of white women employed in domestic occupations (cleaners, laundresses, dressmakers, seamstresses, and servants) and a sharp increase in the number of female office workers, laborers in manufacturing, saleswomen in stores, schoolteachers, telephone operators, and trained nurses.

Thus the wartime labor shortage temporarily created new job opportunities for women workers, and at higher wages than they had previously earned. This was not necessarily the case for African American women, however. Although World War I opened up some factory jobs to them, these were typically limited to the most menial, least desirable, and often the most dangerous jobs—jobs already rejected by white women. These jobs included some of the most dangerous tasks in industry, such as carrying glass to hot ovens in glass factories and dyeing furs in the furrier industry (Greenwald, 1980, p. 26).

World War I produced no substantial or lasting change in women's participation in the labor force. The employment rate of women in 1920 was actually a bit lower (20.4 percent) than in 1910 (20.9 percent). The labor unions, the government, and the society at large were not ready to accept a permanent shift in women's economic role. Instead, women filled an urgent need during the wartime years and were relegated to their former positions as soon as peace returned. As the reformer Mary Von Kleeck wrote, "When the immediate dangers . . . were passed, the prejudices came to life once more" (quoted in Chafe, 1972, p. 54).

When the men returned from the war, they were given priority in hiring and, although a number of women left the labor force voluntarily, many were forced out by layoffs. Those remaining were employed in the low-paying, low-prestige positions women had always occupied and in those occupations that had become accepted as women's domain. For example, although during the war some women

Increase (1000's)

| | 0 | 100 | 200 | 300 |

Clerks (except clerks in stores)
Semiskilled operatives (manufacturing)
Stenographers & typists
Bookkeepers, cashiers, & accountants
Saleswomen & clerks in stores
Teachers (school)
Telephone Operators
Laborers (manufacturing)
All other nonagricultural pursuits
Trained nurses
Waitresses
Housekeepers & stewardesses
Midwives and nurses (not trained)
Religious, charity, & welfare workers
Retail dealers
Barbers, hairdressers & manicurists
Forewomen/overseers (manufacturing)
Manufacturers, officials, & managers
Agents, canvassers, & collectors
Laundry operatives
Restaurant, cafe, & lunchroom helpers
Postmistresses
Actresses & showwomen

Hotel keepers & managers
Artists, sculptors, & teachers of art
Charwomen & cleaners
Compositors, linotypers, & typesetters
Tailoresses
Musicians & teachers of music
Boarding- and lodging-house helpers
Milliners & millinery dealers
Laundresses (not in laundry)
Dressmakers & seamstresses (not in factory)
Servants

| 200 | 100 |

Decrease (1000's)

FIGURE 2. *Increase and Decrease in the Number of Women Employed in the Principal Nonagricultural Occupations, 1910–1920.*

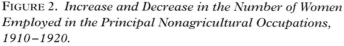

Source: U.S. Bureau of the Census, 1929).

had worked in nontraditional occupations (such as machinists) in the railroads, after the war the railroads employed women only as typists, card punchers, accountants, receptionists, file clerks, janitresses, laundresses, and railroad matrons (Greenwald, 1980). Many women resented having been encouraged to enter a nontraditional occupation only to be fired at the war's end. One who had been employed as a laborer in a machine shop during the war wrote to the director general of the railroad administration in hopes of restoring such jobs:

We are women that needed the work very much. [O]ne woman gave her only support to the army [;] one has her aged Father[;] another has a small son

[;] and I support my disabled Sister . . . We never took a soldier's place, a soldier would not do the work we did . . . such as sweeping, picking up waste and paper and hauling steel shavings . . . We are . . . respectable but poor women and were liked and respected by all who knew us . . . Women's work is so very hard to find that time of year and expenses are so high with Liberty bonds and insurance to pay and home expenses it is hard to get by. We like our job very much and I hope you will do for us whatever you can and place us back at the shop. (quoted in Greenwald, 1980, p. 135)

The common image of women workers, even in business and the professions, was still that they were "temporary" employees (Chafe, 1972, p. 65).

The Great Depression of the 1930s threw millions out of work. In 1933, a quarter of the American labor force was unemployed, compared to about 3 percent in 1929. Business failures devastated both owners and workers. Total personal income plummeted from eighty-four billion in 1929 to forty-seven billion in 1933. Due to the shortage of employment opportunities, efforts to "maintain the family's claim on women appeared almost immediately on many fronts" (Kwolek-Folland, 1998, p. 145). To secure employment opportunities for men, married women were urged to stay out of the workplace. A 1936 Gallup Poll asked if women should work if their husbands were employed; 82 percent of those polled answered "no." Business leaders were bombarded with letters from the media, politicians, and others to terminate married women workers (Kwolek-Folland, 1998, p. 145). The attitude that emerged among Americans is clear in a letter from a private citizen named Earl Leiby to President Roosevelt in 1933. It read, in part, that "homes are being wrecked daily due to the fact that married women are permitted to work in factories and offices. . . . You and we all know that the place for a wife and mother is at home. . . . These women's husbands would naturally be paid a higher salary, inasmuch as male employees demand a higher salary than females" (as quoted in Kessler-Harris, 1990, p. 57).

This national sentiment resulted in people turning to both the state and federal governments for a response. For example, in 1933 the National Economy Act only allowed one federal salary per married couple. What inevitably followed was that many women were forced to resign out of practicality, due to the fact that their husbands almost always earned higher wages (Kwolek-Folland, 1998, p. 145).

As this Depression-era situation unfolded, however, efforts to keep women—especially those who were married—out of the workforce were not very successful. In fact, during the 1930s, an increasing number of women went to work for the first time. The increase was most marked among younger, married women, who worked at least until they had

their first child, and among older, married women, who re-entered the marketplace because of dire economic need or in response to changing patterns of consumer demand (Scharf, 1980, p. 158). The disappearance of "male jobs" in manufacturing and heavy industry—combined with the rising prominence of "female jobs" in white-collar, light industry, and service arenas—allowed women to increase their numbers in the workforce during the Depression (Kwolek-Folland, 1998, p. 145). Even though these "female jobs" usually had pay scales that were significantly lower than "male jobs," the income women earned was enough to clothe and feed the children of many families that suffered from this devastating economic downturn (Kwolek-Folland, 1998, p. 145). Still, many of the jobs held by women were often parttime, seasonal, and considered marginal. In sum, women's labor-force participation increased slowly throughout this period and into the early 1940s (see Figure 1), except in the professions (including feminized professions such as elementary teaching, nursing, librarianship, and social work). The proportion of women in all professions declined from 14.2 percent to 12.3 percent during the Depression decade (Scharf, 1980, p. 86).

WORLD WAR II

The ordeal of World War II brought about tremendous change in the numbers and occupational distribution of working women. As during World War I, the shortage of male workers, who had gone off to fight, coupled with the mounting pressures of war production brought huge numbers of women into the workforce. A corresponding shift in attitudes about women's aptitudes and proper roles resulted (Trey, 1972, p. 40). Indeed, for women the "liberative potential of wartime changes is undeniable because the dislocations of a nation at war have always created important challenges to traditional assumptions and practices" (Anderson, 1981, p. 4). Women entered the munitions factories and other heavy industries to support the war effort. The War Manpower Commission instituted a massive advertising campaign to attract women to the war industries. Patriotic appeals were common:

Women, let it be understood, have a double stake in the winning of this war. Citizens of the United States of America, and partners in the United Nations, they are in and a part of the common struggle to crush Fascism—the acknowledged Number One foe of the progress of women. No women are supernumerary. All must fight with their fathers, their husbands, their brothers, their sweethearts, to make certain that never again will dictators and aggressors such as Hitler, Mussolini, and Hirohito, have the freedom to rise and persecute and enslave and murder first their own people, and then peoples of other nations. The essence of Fascism is bullying individuals and whole races of people—and women and men alike must destroy this monstrous organism of fear and cruelty once and for all. (quoted in Anthony, 1943, p. 3)

During the war years, white women had access to skilled, higher-paying industrial jobs. Many women in industrial positions had worked before, but only at lower paying unskilled service jobs. Women now became switchmen, precision-tool makers, overhead-crane operators, lumberjacks, drill-press operators, and stevedores (Baxandall et al., 1976). Women in these jobs had to "toughen up." Polly Ann Stinnett Workman describes her experience as a welder at the Stockton-Pollock Navy Yard in California:

I was the only woman welder on the graveyard shift. I was welding fifty-foot walls in the hull of the ship. The working conditions were wonderful. As far as I'm concerned, it was the best job I've ever had. It gave me a sense of accomplishment. When I went in, they were working on a cost-plus job, and the first night I was there the supervisor took me around to get me on a crew, and nobody wanted me because I was a woman. They'd say, "We have all we need." Finally, the supervisor said to the leadman, "This is your welder."

They tried every way in the world to show me up. They put me on a cost-plus job, working out in the rain, on a big tunnel they had contracted. . . The tunnel was part of a ship. This was in January, which is the worst. We had to wear those heavy leather pants and jackets, and it was so cold you just darn near froze to death. When he put me on that job, I was terrified. There was all this loud noise,

the shipwrights, the chippers, people dropping hammers and dropping metal; this was really terrifying to me but I didn't let them know it. (quoted in Wise and Wise, 1994, p. 135)

Equal work did not mean equal pay for the women in these varied wartime occupations. Although the National War Labor Board issued a directive to industries that stipulated equal pay for equal work, most employers continued to pay women at a lower rate. Furthermore, women had little opportunity to advance in their new occupations.

World War II marked an important turning point in women's participation in the paid labor force. The social prohibition concerning married women working gave way under wartime pressure, and women wartime workers demonstrated that it was possible for women to maintain their households while also assuming the role of breadwinner with outside employment. More women than ever before learned to accommodate the simultaneous demands of family and work. The experience "pointed the way to a greater degree of choice for American women" (Anderson, 1981, p. 174).

However, at the war's end, with the return of men to civilian life, there was tremendous public pressure on women to abandon their work roles; thus, for many it meant a return to the domestic sphere they had left behind before the war. Yet for some women, especially the poor and those in the working class, this return was not an option.

The post-World War II work environment for women was less than hospitable. It included a range of discriminatory employment and union practices— key among them was the preferential hiring of veterans. Women often found that the male-dominated jobs they held during the war were now out of reach; what were left were "female jobs," most of which were well below their skill levels and pay expectations (Anderson, 1981, p. 7). Thus, the late 1940s and 1950s marked the reestablishment of the sex-segregated labor market.

During this time, a new social ideology began to emerge; Betty Friedan (1963) later called it "the feminine mystique." This ideology drew in social workers, educators, journalists, and psychologists, all of whom tried to convince women that their place was again in the home. It was not unlike the "cult of true womanhood" advanced in the late 1800s to differentiate middle-class women from working-class women. As Friedan notes, in the fifteen years following World War II, the image of "women at home" rather than "at work" became a cherished and self-perpetuating core of contemporary American culture. A generation of young people were brought up to extol the values of home and family, and woman's role was defined as the domestic center around which all else revolved. Women were supposed to live like those in Norman Rockwell *Saturday Evening Post* illustrations. The idealized image was of smiling mothers baking cookies for their wholesome children, driving their station wagons loaded with freckled youngsters to an endless round of lessons and activities, returning with groceries and other consumer goods to the ranch houses they cared for with such pride. Women were supposed to revel in these roles and gladly leave the running of the world to men (Friedan, 1963, p. 14).

This image was nourished by the new psychological and child-development theories of the time. Psychoanalytic theory held that "biology is destiny" and that "a woman's personality was completely defined by her sex" (Anderson, 1981, p. 176). Meeting the needs of her family best fulfills a woman's needs, it was argued. These new "experts" maintained that women's employment during the war years had fostered certain individual neuroses and social maladjustments, which could be corrected only by women's return to a domestic (and subordinate and dependent) status. In this way, "Rosie the Riveter' was transformed with dizzying speed from a wartime heroine to a neurotic, castrating victim of penis envy" (Anderson, 1981, p. 176; also see Honey, 1984).

Along with these ideological arguments to bring women back to the home were important economic considerations. The traditional notion of women's place in the home became, after the war, integrally linked with the housewife's function as primary consumer of goods. The war had wound up the economy with massive production, inflation, growth, and low rates of unemployment. With the reduction in military spending, the country could not support full employment or continued industrial profits without an increase in a major market such as household goods. Both Federal Housing Administration-guaranteed loans and government-subsidized construction of commuter highways encouraged a general migration to the suburbs, where families would buy more household goods. Women were the key to this market, and homemaking was encouraged as a necessary stimulant to the postwar industrial economy (Baxandall et al., 1976, pp. 282–283).

Yet, unlike the post–World War I period, after World War II women did not go back to the kitchens. Instead, women's labor-force participation continued to increase throughout the post-World War II decades, so that by the late 1960s, 40 percent of American women were in the labor force, and by the beginning of the twenty-first century, 60 percent were. Who were the women most likely to be part of this "new majority" of women at work?

AFTER WORLD WAR II: THE RISE OF THE MARRIED WOMAN WORKER

Between 1890 and the beginning of World War II, single women comprised at least half the female labor force. The others were mostly married African American, immigrant, or working-class women.

The decade of the 1940s saw a change in the type of woman worker, as increasing numbers of married women left their homes to enter the world of paid work (see Figure 3). Although single women continued to have the highest labor-force participation rates among women, during the 1940s the percentage of married women in the workforce grew more rapidly than any other category. Between 1940 and 1950, single women workers were in short supply because of low birthrates in the 1930s. Furthermore, those single women available for work were marrying at younger ages and leaving the labor market to raise their families. On the other hand, ample numbers of older, married women were available, and these women (who had married younger, had had fewer children, and were living longer) were eager for paid employment.

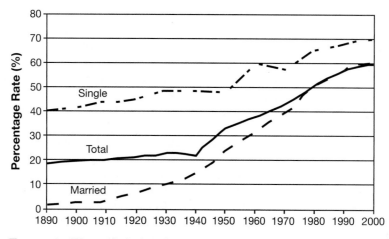

FIGURE 3. *Women's Labor-Force Participation Rates by Marital Status, 1890–2000.*

Sources: Goldin (1977); U.S. Bureau of the Census (1996a, p. 399; 2002a, Table 576, p. 372).

In 1940, about 15 percent of married women were employed; by 1950, 24 percent. This increase has continued: by 1960, 32 percent of married women; in 1970, over 41 percent; in 1980, 50 percent; and by 1995, 61 percent (U.S. Bureau of the Census, 1996a, p. 399); it continues to inch up slowly, and was 61.3 percent by the end of 2000 (U.S. Bureau of the Census, 2002a, Table 576, p. 372). Indeed, as the twenty-first century proceeds, we can see that labor-force participation rates of single and married women will become almost identical (Figure 3).

During the 1940s, 1950s, and 1960s, it was mainly older, married women entering the workforce.

In 1957, for example, the labor-force participation rate among women aged forty-five to forty-nine years exceeded the rate for twenty to twenty-four-year-old women (Oppenheimer, 1970, p. 15). During the early 1960s, young married mothers with preschool- or school-age children began to enter the workforce. This trend continued for the next four decades; by the early 2000s, more than three-quarters of married women with children between six and seventeen years of age were employed, and, most significantly, almost two-thirds of those women with children under the age of six were in the labor force (see Table 1). In short, whereas before 1970 the overwhelming

TABLE 1 Women's Labor-Force Participation Rates by Marital Status and Presence and Age of Children, 1960–2000

Year	Total			With Children Under 18			With Children 6–17			With Children Under 6		
	Single	Married	Other	Single	Married	Other	Single	Married	Other	Single	Married	Other
1960	44.1	30.5	40.0	n/a	27.6	56.0	n/a	39.0	65.9	n/a	18.6	40.5
1970	53.0	40.8	39.1	n/a	39.7	60.7	n/a	49.2	66.9	n/a	30.3	52.2
1980	61.5	50.1	44.0	52.0	54.1	69.4	67.6	61.7	74.6	44.1	45.1	60.3
1990	66.4	58.2	46.8	55.2	66.3	74.2	69.7	73.6	79.7	48.7	58.9	63.6
2000	68.6	62.0	50.2	73.9	70.6	82.7	79.7	77.2	85.0	70.5	62.8	76.6

Source: U.S. Bureau of the Census (1996a, p. 400; 2002a, Table 577, p. 373).

majority of married women stopped working after they had children, today the overwhelming majority of married women do not.

ORGANIZING WOMEN LABORERS: THE ROLE OF UNIONS

Women have participated in the labor movement both as leaders and rank-and-file members. Indeed, women factory workers in the United States were among the first labor activists.

Historian Ruth Milkman (1985, p. xi) observes that feminist scholars do not agree on how the development of the labor movement in the United States affected women. In the view of some feminists, organized labor has been an "enemy" of women workers; for example, many unions prevented women from obtaining union cards, and discriminated against those women who did. From this vantage point, unions have reinforced and promoted gender inequality in the labor force. Other feminists, however, view unions more positively — observing, for example, that women in unions have historically fared better (higher wages, more benefits, healthier working conditions) than their nonunionized counterparts.

Indeed, unionization has helped women to increase their pay and to diminish the historical income gap between men and women. In 2002, union women earned about 30.8 percent more than nonunion women ($667 versus $510 per week; see Table 2). Women, in general, and women of color, in particular, are helped even more by union membership: African American union members earned 32.1 percent more than their nonunion counterparts, and for Latino workers the union advantage is 46.5 percent (versus 33.4 percent for white women; see Table 2).

The women's labor movement began in the early 1920s as factory workers in Pawtucket, Rhode Island, participated for the first time in a strike. Historian Philip Foner (1979, p. 29) observes that "about one hundred female weavers joined with male workers to protest a wage reduction and an attempt to increase working hours." The strikes at the Lowell mills in 1834 and 1836 continued women's large-scale efforts to demand fair treatment in the workplace regarding wages. Over the next several decades, this protest would grow into a series of more permanent labor organizations for women.

The Ten-Hour Movement in the 1840s, which pressed for ten hours as the legal limit to the work day in factories, helped to forge a new labor movement emerging in the Lowell mills (Dublin, 1979, p. 108). This movement was instrumental in reforming working conditions for women laborers. By January of 1845, the Lowell Female Labor Reform Association had established—due in no small part to the efforts of a new class of female labor activists, such as Sarah Bagley and Huldah J. Stone. Within six months, almost five hundred women were members. Bagley was elected to the position of president, while Stone was voted in as secretary (Wertheimer, 1977, p. 73).

In their struggle to gain fair wages and better working conditions, women activists also came to a new understanding of their own identity concerning what it meant to be a woman worker. "In the course of the labor struggles of the 1840s, women activists came to a new sense of the 'sisterhood' of working women and developed a critique of the 'cult of true womanhood,' that ideology of women's sphere that evolved in the period and was expressed in popular women's magazines and domestic advice books" (Dublin, 1979, pp. 125–126).

Sarah Bagley was aware of the crossing of traditional gender boundaries in women's attempts at union organizing. She spoke to these concerns in a speech before the first convention of the workingmen's association in 1845: "For the last half a century, it has been deemed a violation of women's sphere to appear before the public as a speaker, but when our rights are trampled upon and we appeal in vain to legislators, what shall we do but appeal to the voice of the people?" (from *The Voice of Industry,* June 5, 1845, as quoted in Wertheimer, 1977, p. 73).

TABLE 2   Union Affiliation and Median Weekly Earnings of Full-Time Wage and Salary Workers by Sex, Race, and Latino Origins, 2002

	Percent Unionized	Median Weekly Wages Union Workers	Nonunion Workers	Ratio of Union to Nonunion Wages (%)
Men	14.7	780	652	119.6
White	12.8	804	674	119.3
African American	18.2	651	502	129.7
Latino	11.1	666	422	157.8
Women	12.8	667	510	130.8
White	10.9	695	521	133.4
African American	15.7	588	445	132.1
Latina	9.8	558	381	146.5

Source: U.S. Department of Labor (2002a, 2002b).

Women's participation in reform movements had to upend some central perspectives on women's traditional role within society, and this permeated down to the rank-and-file. As one female factory worker bemoaned society's traditional view of women's roles and the narrowness of this view:

> Woman is never thought to be out of her sphere, at home; in the nursery, in the kitchen, over a hot stove cooking from morning till evening—over a washtub, or toiling in a cotton factory fourteen hours per day. But let her once step out, plead the cause of right and humanity, plead the wrongs of her slave sister of the South or of the operative of the North, or even attempt to teach the science of Physiology, and a cry is raised against her, "of out of her sphere." (Dublin, 1979, p. 127)

By the 1850s workers were successful in seeing the ten-hour work week garner state legislative approval in some states, as Wertheimer (1977, p. 83) observes, this success was, at best, only partial:

> Workers did succeed in achieving laws in some states to limit the hours of work for children and guaranteed them several months of school a year, although these laws were seldom enforced. When

New Hampshire (in 1847), Pennsylvania, Massachusetts, and other states passed ten-hour laws, each legislature included "contracting out" clauses providing that, when necessary, employers could sign contracts with individual employees to work more than the ten hours permitted under the law. Mill owners insisted from the start on workers signing these individual contracts as a condition of employment. Workers signed . . . but not without a fight.

Labor unions sometimes supported women's organizing efforts. In 1863, for example, seamstresses working throughout the North lived in dire poverty. In New York City, seamstresses were among the most impoverished of workers. Few earned more than 17 to 24 cents per day—even though the work day was often fifteen hours long. "Moreover, they often were unable to collect from their employers even the little that was owed them" (Wertheimer, 1977, p. 152). Some New York trade unions helped to lay the foundations for women to unionize. For example, they organized a meeting of women workers in November of 1863 to strategize on how to boost their earnings and recoup unpaid wages. Wertheimer (1977, p. 152) notes that "it is likely that a successful strike of women shirtmakers that month was a direct outgrowth of this meeting."

The Era of the Craft Union

The organized labor movement in the early twentieth century all but shut out working women. The American Federation of Labor (AFL), which set the norms for union practices in this period, sought to mobilize skilled workers, the vast majority of whom were white, native-born men. Working women, on the other hand, tended to be unskilled and were quite often recent immigrants from Europe. Unions that did accept women stipulated that they should start their own locals. For many factory women, union dues were often high, which precluded may of them from joining. Women were prevented from learning certain trades through establish[ed] apprenticeship programs and this tended to confine them to low status, low-paying, unskilled jobs (Foner, 1979; Wertheimer, 1977, pp. 200–201). The attitude of the AFL and other unions at the time echoed specific views of women's traditional roles, which was captured by the rubric the "cult of true womanhood" (Triece, 2001, pp. 186–187). For the most part, women were viewed as "temporary workers," even though they dominated the textile and garment trades (Milkman, 1985, p. 307).

For African Americans, acceptance into labor unions like the AFL was virtually impossible. Institutionalized racism and sexism served to define African Americans as fit only to carry the burden of hard labor, and women as inferior workers not worthy of the monetary compensation given to men's work. Thus, this double oppression of black women workers made it almost impossible for them to attain membership into any type of labor union (Foner, 1979, p. 267).

In response to this discrimination, both white and black women laborers sometimes tried to form their own organizations. For example, in Chicago, white women formed the Women's Trade Union League. In 1897, affluent black women in New York City founded the White Rose Industrial Association to aid black women domestics whose working conditions in "the Bronx slave market" were deplorable (Terborg-Penn, 1985, p. 142).

Black women's organizations developed remedies to unfair treatment that embodied traditional African survival strategies. For example, older women in Africa were responsible for socializing, training, and providing emotional support to younger women. This tradition carried over to America and served as a means for victims of racial discrimination in the labor force to unite for purposes of teaching one another valuable skills to obtain employment as well as for mutual support against that very discrimination (Terborg-Penn, 1985, pp. 142–143).

Middle- and upper-middle class women came to the aid of immigrant and working-class women workers' plight. Such was the case with the genesis of the Working Women's Protective Union; while not a labor union, it was directed and staffed by middle- and upper-class women "concerned particularly about the powerlessness of working women, who had neither knowledge of the law nor money to hire lawyers to collect the wages due them" (Wertheimer, 1977, p. 155). The Protective Union in New York City provided women workers with free legal advice. Many prominent New York City attorneys represented these women in civil disputes against their employers. In the first decade-and-a-half of its existence, the Protective Union handled over twenty-seven thousand cases, and it managed to settle the majority of them out of court, recovering almost twenty-five thousand dollars in unpaid wages. It also lobbied successfully for the passage of a law establishing criminal penalties for business owners who failed to fully compensate their workers (Wertheimer, 1977, p. 156).

The Rise of "New Unionism"

While many of the early women's labor organizations did not survive, craft unions became the dominant model for organizing women workers. The turn of the twentieth century began to see women's unionism grow dramatically, beginning within the clothing industry. A series of tragedies and militant strikes forged a coming together of a diversity of women workers from different ethnic and racial backgrounds that led to the fortification of unions such as the International Ladies' Garment Workers

Union (ILGWU), which was founded in 1900. Another organization of garment workers, the Amalgamated Clothing Workers of America, was founded in 1914 under the leadership of Bessie Abramowitz Hillman and Dorothy Jacobs Bellanca (see Wertheimer, 1977, pp. 321–330). These two organizations, observes historian Barbara Mayer Wertheimer (1977, p. 335), were "the first unions of substance, power, and durability to include large numbers of women and to effect changes in a low-wage, traditionally female sweatshop industry, although differentials between men's and women's wages would remain for a long time."

It was through garment workers strikes, such as the 1909 uprising of the 20,000 garment workers in New York City, that served to change the ILGWU into a modern industrial union. The New York City strike demonstrated the "previously untapped potential for militancy among young female Jewish and Italian immigrant workers, and dramatically challenged the conventional stereotypes of the era, which constructed women workers as passive and uninterested in unionism" (Milkman, 1993, p. 281). The first president of the AFL, Samuel Gompers, had this to say of the great impact of this strike:

> [it] brought to the consciousness of the nation a recognition of the extent to which women are taking up with industrial life, their consequent tendency to stand together in the struggle to protect their common interests as wage earners, the readiness of people in all classes to approve of trade-union methods in behalf of working women, and the capacity of women as strikers to suffer, to do, and to dare in support of their rights. (as quoted in Milkman, 1993, p. 281)

The tragedy of the 1911 Triangle Shirtwaist Fire—which claimed the lives of 146 factory workers—was another critical turning point in organizing women garment workers. Wertheimer (1977, p. 310) describes how crowding and violation of the fire codes of the time, including the locking of factory doors and a nonexistent sprinkling system, cost women their lives:

> . . . of the 500 workers crowded into the top three floors of the Asch Building, 146, most of them women and girls, jumped to their death, were

burned, or suffocated that afternoon in a building where no fire drills had been held, where doors opened inward rather than out, where factory doors were locked each working day to keep the women in and the union organizers out, where there was no sprinkler system, and where the city's fire-fighting equipment proved totally unequal to the rescue task required.

Eye-witnesses to the fire relate the following details of the tragedy:

> . . . a "bale of dark dress goods" being thrown out of a window. Another who saw it thought the factory owner was trying to save his cloth from the fire. But then the screams began. It had not been a bundle of cloth, but a human being leaping from the windows. Then came another, and then another. (Wertheimer, 1977, p. 310)

Industrial Unionism

Women entered the mass production industries in large numbers during World War I, joining male-dominated trade and industrial unions, especially the Congress of Industrial Organizations (CIO). Union membership resulted in both positive and negative experiences for women industrial workers:

> They gained the strength of membership in permanent organizations. But there was a price. Once women had led unions of their own, ephemeral though these were. Women leaders had defied tradition to speak out on behalf of women workers. Now they would be absorbed into unions led entirely by men. This process was accelerated when the National Labor Relations Act, passed during the Great Depression of the 1930s, at last gave workers the legal right to organize and bargain collectively. Breaking from the AFL, a Committee for Industrial Organization. . . reached out to industrial workers, to blacks and other minorities, and to women. (Wertheimer, 1977, pp. 371–372)

Public Sector and Service Workers and the Influence of the Women's Movement

Women working in the public sector of society were, for the most part, not adequately represented by unions. This began to change in the 1970s, when an increasing number of unions began representing state and local government workers—many of whom were women. The most notable of these unions were the American Federation of State, County and Municipal Employees (AFSME) and the Service Employees International Union (SEIU). The unionization of government workers, in contrast to workers in the private sector, held steady during the 1980s and 1990s; and by the early 2000s, workers in the public sector had a union membership rate over four times that of the private sector: 37.5 percent versus 8.5 percent. The most unionized are locale government workers, especially teachers, police officers, and fire fighters (see U.S. Department of Labor, 2002c).

Historian Ruth Milkman (1985, p. 307) observes that during the 1950s and early 1960s, before the second wave of feminism, the American labor movement held a very traditional attitude toward women workers. They were seen as a group that needed special treatment and protection. Few women held any positions of power within the union hierarchy. However, all of this changed in the 1970s. Unionized women began meeting in caucuses and committees, taking over leadership roles, and becoming more active in general. As a consequence, union leadership improved its attitudes regarding women's issues. For example, in the early 1970s, the AFL-CIO approved the Equal Rights Amendment, and the Coalition of Labor Union Women (CLUW) held its first conference. Unions took up those issues most pressing to women, including daycare, affirmative action, and pay inequities.

WOMEN OF COLOR

Denied entrance to the factories during the rise of industrialization and, for much of the twentieth century, facing discriminatory hiring practices that closed off opportunities in the newly expanded office and sales jobs, many women of color entered domestic service. From 1910 to 1940, the proportion of white women employed in clerical and sales positions almost doubled, and there was a decline in the numbers of white women in domestic work. Private household work then became the province of African American women: The percentage of

African American household workers increased from 38.5 percent in 1910 to 59.9 percent in 1940, as shown in Table 3. For the next three decades, African American women remained the single largest group in domestic service.

African American women's economic status improved dramatically from 1940 through the 1960s, as a result of an increase in light manufacturing jobs, as well as changes in technology. African American women moved from private household work into manufacturing and clerical work, and made significant gains in the professions. Whereas in 1940, nearly six in ten of employed African American females worked in private households, by the late 1970s only two in ten did. Their job prospects continued to improve, and by the 1980s, almost half of all working African American women were employed in "white collar" jobs: clerical and sales positions as well as professional jobs in business, health care, and education. Through the 1990s and into the 2000s, the historic job-prestige gap between African American and white working women continued to close. Almost two-thirds of working African American women had jobs in the white-collar world by 2001, compared with nearly three-quarters of working white women. Moreover, as evident in Figure 4, the gap has never been narrower, and the overall trend is unmistakable; that is, we can expect this narrowing to continue.

Other Women of Color at Work

Each minority group has had a different experience in American society and has faced different opportunities and obstacles. Women in each group share with African American women the concerns of all minority women; they share with the men of their ethnic groups the problems of discrimination against that particular ethnic minority.

Native American Women   As we noted earlier, gender roles in Native American communities were disrupted during the conquest and oppression by whites. For example, Navajo society was traditionally matrilineal, with extended families the norm; Navajo women owned property and played an

TABLE 3   Percentage Distribution of Employed Women by Occupation, Race, and Ethnic Origins, 1910–2001

	Professional	Managerial & Administrative	Technical, Sales, & Clerical	Craft	Operatives & Nonfarm Laborers	Private Household Workers	Other Service Workers	Farm Laborers
1910								
White	11.6	1.5	17.5	8.2	23.7	17.2	9.2	12.1
Afr. Amer.	1.5	0.2	0.3	2.0	2.3	38.5	3.2	52.0
1940								
White	17.7	4.3	32.8	1.1	21.2	10.9	12.7	2.3
Afr. Amer.	4.3	0.7	1.3	0.2	7.0	59.9	11.1	15.9
1950								
White	13.3	4.7	39.3	1.7	22.2	4.3	11.6	2.9
Afr. Amer.	5.3	1.3	5.4	0.7	16.8	42.0	19.1	9.4
1960								
White	14.1	4.2	43.2	1.4	18.1	4.4	13.1	1.5
Afr. Amer.	7.7	1.1	9.8	0.7	15.5	38.1	23.0	4.1
Native Amer.	9.1	2.0	17.8	n/a	18.1	16.8	25.8	10.5
1970								
White	15.6	4.8	43.4	1.1	14.9	3.7	15.1	1.5
Afr. Amer.	10.0	1.4	21.4	0.7	17.6	19.4	29.0	0.5
Native Amer.	10.3	2.5	30.2	n/a	22.3	6.6	25.9	2.1
Latina	8.1	2.1	33.9	2.3	28.9	4.6	18.3	2.1
1980								
White	16.9	6.7	43.5	1.8	11.8	2.1	16.2	1.0
Afr. Amer.	12.7	3.0	31.6	1.3	16.1	8.0	26.8	0.5
Native Amer.	14.5	6.6	35.4	n/a	17.0	1.4	23.9	1.2
Latina	7.5	3.7	37.0	2.1	26.3	2.6	19.2	1.5
1990								
White	16.6	11.8	46.3	2.1	8.8	1.2	15.2	1.1
Afr. Amer.	11.2	7.5	39.1	2.3	12.2	3.1	30.2	0.3
Native Amer.	15.7	9.4	36.2	n/a	14.2	1.0	22.4	1.1
Latina	7.3	6.7	38.5	3.1	20.9	4.2	20.8	1.9
2001								
White	15.4	19.0	39.9	2.0	6.1	1.1	15.3	1.2
Afr. Amer.	11.4	14.6	38.3	1.8	9.0	1.0	23.7	0.2
Native Amer.	n/a	n/a	n/a	n/a	n/a	n/a	n/a	n/a
Latina	9.4	9.3	37.0	3.0	13.0	3.7	23.3	1.6

Note: 1910 data for ages ten and older; 1940–1960 for ages fourteen and over; 1970–2001 for ages sixteen and over. For a discussion of this and other problems associated with comparing decennial censuses, see Amott and Matthaei (1996, pp. 414–415).

Sources: Aldridge (1975, p. 53), Amott and Matthaei (1996, p. 48), Bureau of Labor Statistics (1980, p. 74, 1997c; 1997d; 2003b).

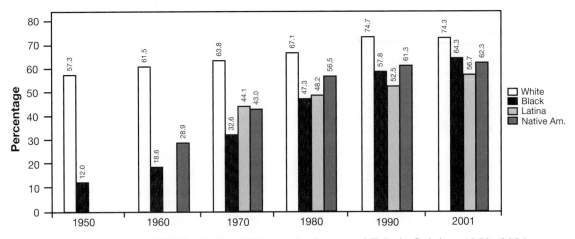

FIGURE 4. *Percentage of "White-Collar" Women by Race and Ethnic Origins, 1950–2001.*
Note: "White-Collar" = sum of (a) Professionals, (b) Executives, Administrators, and Managers, and (c) Technical, Sales, and Administrative Support Workers.

Sources: Aldridge (1975, p. 53); Amott and Matthaei (1996, p. 48); Bureau of Labor Statistics (1980, p. 74; 1997c, 1997d, 2003b); U.S. Equal Employment Opportunity Commission (2002; this source used for Native American estimate for 2001).

important role in family decisions. But, beginning in the 1930s, government policy disrupted this system by giving land only to males. As they could no longer make a sufficient living off the land, more and more Navajo men had to seek employment off the reservations. Nuclear families became the norm. Navajo women became dependent on male providers. With the men away much of the time, these women are often isolated and powerless. They often face divorce or desertion and thus economic difficulties because the community frowns on women seeking work off the reservation.

Such disruption of the traditional Native American society left Native American women in very grim economic circumstances. But, in recent decades, more and more of them have gotten jobs. Native American women's labor-force participation rate in 1970 was 35 percent (compared to 43 percent for all women). This rate rose sharply to 55 percent by the early 1990s and is now within a few percentage points of the rate for all women (56.8 percent in

2000, see U.S. Bureau of the Census, 2002b, Table P150C).

Like their African American counterparts over the past half century, Native American women have gradually moved out of low-skill farm and nonfarm work and domestic jobs into clerical, sales, professional, technical, and other "white-collar" jobs. In 1960, one in six working Native American women was employed as domestic household worker; by the early 1990s only one in a hundred was. During the same period, the proportion of Native American women involved in agricultural work also went from ten to one in a hundred. Manufacturing work was increasingly replaced by white-collar work, reflecting the overall trends in the occupational structure; more specifically, while the percentage involved in factory work (much of it in textiles and traditional crafts) fell from 18.1 to 14.2, the percentage employed in white-collar work soared from 28.9 to 61.3. Although many of these white-collar jobs are classified as "professional" (15.7 percent of all working Native American women) or "managerial" (9.4 percent), two-thirds of Native American women are still concentrated in the "secondary" sector of the labor market,* which is characterized by low wages, few or no benefits, low mobility, and high instability. They are kept there because of the "stagnation of the reservation economy," discrimination, and their relatively low level of educational attainment (Amott and Matthaei, 1996, p. 51). A significant number of Native American women do not even have a high school diploma—in 2000, more than one-quarter (28.3 percent) of all those over the age of twenty-five, compared to one-sixth (16.3 percent) of white women (see U.S. Bureau of the Census, 2002b, Tables P148A and P148C).

Latina Women The term "Latina" is used to denote populations of women with Mexican American (Chicana), Puerto Rican, Cuban, and other Central and South American origins (including, most notably, the Dominican Republic, Colombia, El Salvador, and Nicaragua). Mexican Americans (58.5 percent) and Puerto Ricans (9.6 percent) constitute the largest segments of the Latina population (see Guzmán, 2001, Table 1), and we will focus on these two groups.

Large numbers of Chicanas migrated, usually with husband and children, from Mexico to the United States during the 1916–1920 labor shortage created by World War I. They found work in the sprawling "factory farms" of the Southwest, harvesting fruits, vegetables, and cotton in the Imperial and San Joaquin valleys of California, the Salt River valley of Arizona, and the Rio Grande valley of Texas (Amott and Matthaei, 1996, p. 75). They also went to the Midwest, for instance to Michigan and Minnesota, to harvest sugar beets. Such migrant workers typically were exploited, spending

---

*The "secondary" job market comprises most of those jobs falling under the following Bureau of the Census occupational classifications: sales, clerical, operatives, nonfarm labor, household work, low-level ("other") service work, and farm labor. The "primary" job market comprises most of those jobs that are labeled as technical, executive, administrative, professional, and (skilled) craft.

long, tedious, and physically demanding hours in the fields for very low pay. Some became tenant farmers, which might seem a step up, except too often this system "created debt peonage; unable to pay the rent, tenants were unable to leave the land and remained virtually permanently indebted to their landlords" (Amott and Matthaei, 1996, p. 75).

During the 1920s, with a shortage of European immigration, new job opportunities opened up for Mexican Americans, and they began to migrate from rural farm country to the urban industrial centers, where they found work as domestics and factory workers. By 1930, a third of working Chicanas were domestics and a quarter worked in manufacturing; at the time, the share employed in agriculture, forestry, and mining had fallen to 21 percent (Amott and Mathaei, 1996, pp. 75–76). Wage scales varied according to ethnicity, however. It was not uncommon to pay Chicana workers lower wages than "Anglo" (whites of European descent) women for doing the same job, whether as domestics, laundresses, or workers in the food-processing industries of the West and Southwest (Zavella, 1987, p. 8). The Depression years of the 1930s, with the general shortage of jobs, brought a backlash against Mexican American labor, and thousands of Mexicans were deported or pressured to leave.

World War II once again opened up the American labor market for Mexican migrants, as their labor was needed to offset wartime labor shortages. However, their treatment was deplorable by modern standards. In short, Mexican workers comprised a "reserve army" of exploited labor. Through the government-sponsored Bracero or "Manual Workers" program, Mexican workers were granted temporary work visas so that they could be employed on large corporate farms and elsewhere, but too often they were treated like slaves or prisoners.

World War II and the years following saw a massive shift in the occupational and geographical distribution of Chicana workers:

Many left Texas for California, and the population became increasingly more urban. Women continued their move from the fields into garment factories throughout the Southwest. . . . [A] comparison of the 1930 and 1950 [census] data shows the magnitude of these shifts. For instance, the share of employed southwestern Chicanas working on farms dropped from 21 percent in 1930 to 6 percent in 1950, while the percentage in white-collar work doubled. (Amott and Matthaei, 1996, p. 80)

By the 1960s, the largest occupational category for Chicana workers was operatives, followed by clerical and service work. Chicanas became concentrated in particular industries: food processing, electronics (including telecommunications), and garments. Like their Native American counterparts, Chicana women have made some progress in entering professional and managerial occupations (primarily noncollege teaching, nursing, librarianship, and social work). In 1960, 8.6 percent were in these occupations; by 1980, 12.6 percent, and by the early 2000s, 18.7 percent. However, like Native American women, Chicana women are still overwhelmingly found in the secondary labor market (75.5 percent); much more so than women (59.9 percent) and men (49.2 percent) of white European heritage (see Bureau of Labor Statistics, 2003b).

The dominant reasons behind the low occupational prestige of all minority groups are the same: discrimination and low educational attainment. In the case of Chicana women, over 15 percent "are illiterate by the standard measure (completion of less than five years of schooling)," but studies of functional illiteracy during the 1970s and 1980s suggest "much higher rates—perhaps as high as 56 percent" (Amott and Matthaei, 1996, p. 86). At the other end of the educational attainment spectrum, only 10.7 percent of Latina women have completed four or more years of college—compared with 15.2 percent of African American women and 24.1 percent of white women (U.S. Bureau of the Census, 2002b, Tables P148A, P148C, and P148H). However, education is only part of the formula for success in the U.S. occupational system: Even when education is held constant and we compare only workers having a college-level education, Latina women only make 90.8 percent of what non-Latina white women do (see Bureau of Labor Statistics, 2003c; pp. 64, 84).

Beyond lack of education, Chicana women face other important obstacles in the labor market. They have high rates of unemployment and underemployment. Many of the jobs they hold are seasonal and often nonunionized. This lack of advancement translates into higher poverty rates and lower incomes compared to most other U.S. racial and ethnic groups. For Latina women (in general) with children under eighteen and no husband present, the poverty rate is 44.5 percent compared to 27.8 percent for non-Latina white women in this situation (U.S. Bureau of the Census, 2002b, Tables P150A and P150H).

Increasingly, Chicana women, like many female workers of color around the globe, are doing service or assembly work for multinational corporations, especially in the apparel, food-processing, and electronics industries. These women have often displaced men in assembly work because they can be paid less and many do not receive job benefits. The work hours are long, and women are often assigned monotonous tasks that are dangerous to their health.

In recent years, the labor-force participation of U.S. Puerto Rican women has averaged about 55 percent, somewhat less than the overall rate for women of 60 percent (U.S. Department of Labor, Women's Bureau, 2000). The employment of U.S. Puerto Rican women is complicated by frequent migration between the island and the mainland, which often leads to instability both in work and in family life. It is not unusual to find women working in the United States whose children are cared for by grandmothers or other relatives in Puerto Rico, or to find wives and children living in Puerto Rico while their husbands find work on the mainland.

Like African American women, Latina women may find that their social, cultural, and historic bonds with white women of European descent are somewhat tenuous. Latin cultures tend to be even more male dominated than in U.S. culture, with women assigned an almost exclusively familial role. In addition, the discrimination that both Latin men and women have faced tends to draw them together in the struggle against racism, making sexism almost a peripheral issue for many of these women. As Lorenzana (1979, p. 336) observes regarding Mexican American women: "When a people are undernourished, ill, socially alienated, and powerless members of a society, male chauvinism is of trivial concern." Thus, gender-based affirmative action programs are looked on skeptically because they are perceived as pitting Latin women against Latin men in the search for jobs.

★ ★ ★

REFERENCES

1. Aldridge, Delores. 1975. "Black Women in the Economic Marketplace: A Battle Unfinished." *Journal of Social and Behavioral Sciences* 21(Winter):48–62.

2. Amott, Teresa L. and Julie A. Matthaei. 1996. *Race, Gender, and Work: A Multicultural Economic History of Women in the United States*. Rev. ed. Boston: South End Press.

3. Anderson, Karen. 1981. *Wartime Women: Sex Roles, Family Relations, and the Status of Women During World War II*. Westport, CT: Greenwood Press.

4. Anthony, Susan B. 1943. *Out of the Kitchen—Into the War*. New York: Daye.

5. Baker, Elizabeth F. 1964. *Technology and Women's Work*. New York: Columbia University Press.

6. Baxandall, Rosalyn, Linda Gordon, and Susan Reverby. 1976. *America's Working Women: A Documentary History—1600 to the Present*. New York: Vintage Books.

7. Brownlee, W. Eliott, and Mary M. Brownlee. 1976. *Women in the American Economy: A Documentary History, 1675–1929*. New Haven, CT: Yale University Press.

8. Bularzik, Mary. 1978. "Sexual Harassment in the Workplace: Historical Notes." *Radical America* 12(4): 25–43.

9. Bureau of Labor Statistics. 1979. *Women in the Labor Force: Some New Data Series*. Washington, DC: Bureau of the Census.

10. ———. 1980. *Perspectives on Working Women: A Databook* (Bulletin 2080). Washington, DC: Bureau of the Census.

11. ———. 1997b. "Labor Force Statistics from the *Current Population Survey*." http://www.bls.gov/

12. ———. 1997c. "Table 1: Employed and Experienced Unemployed Persons by Detailed Occupation, Sex, Race, and Hispanic Origins." Unpublished table based on data taken from the *Current Population Survey 1996 Annual Averages*. Washington, DC: Bureau of the Census.

13. ———. 1997d. *Employment and Earnings* 44:5 (May). Washington, DC: U.S. Government Printing Office.

14. ———. 2003b. "Table 1. Employed and Experienced Unemployed Persons by Detailed Occupation, Sex, Race, and Hispanic Origin, Annual Averages 2001." Unpublished table based on 2001 data taken from the *Current Population Survey*. Washington, DC: U.S. Department of Labor.

15. ———. 2003c. "Table A-17. Usual Weekly Earnings of Employed Full-Time Wage and Salary Workers by Educational Attainment, Age, Sex, Race, and Hispanic Origin, 2001 Annual Averages." Unpublished table based on 2001 data taken from the *Current Population Survey*. Washington, DC: U.S. Department of Labor.

16. Chafe, William. 1972. *The American Woman: Her Changing Social, Economic, and Political Roles, 1920–1970*. New York: Oxford University Press.

17. ———. 1977. *Women and Equality: Changing Patterns in American Culture*. New York: Oxford University Press.

18. Dublin, Thomas. 1979. *Women at Work: The Transformation of Work and Community in Lowell, Massachusetts, 1826–1860*. New York: Columbia University Press.

19. Foner, Philip S. 1979. *Women and the American Labor Movement: From Colonial Times to the Eve of World War I*. New York: Free Press.

20. Friedan, Betty. 1963. *The Feminine Mystique*. New York: W. W. Norton.

21. Goldin, Claudia. 1977. "Female Labor Force Participation: The Origins of Black and White Differences, 1870 and 1880." *Journal of Economic History* 37(March): 87–108.

22. Gordon, Ann, Mari-Jo Buhle, and Nancy Schrom. 1971. "Women in American Society: A Historical Contribution." *Radical American* 5(4):3–66.

23. Greenwald, Maurine Weiner. 1980. *Women, War and Work: The Impact of World War I on Women Workers in the United States*. Westport, CT: Greenwood Press.

24. Grossman, Allyson Sherman. 1975. "Women in the Labor Force: The Early Years." *Monthly Labor Review* 98(11):3–9.

25. Guzmán, Betsy. 2001. The Hispanic Population: Census 2000 Brief. C2KBR/01-3 (May). Washington, DC: U.S. Bureau of the Census.

26. Honey, Maureen. 1984. *Creating Rosie the Riveter: Class, Gender, and Propaganda During World War II*. Amherst: University of Massachusetts Press.

27. Kessler-Harris, Alice. 1975. "Stratifying by Sex: Understanding the History of Working Women." Pp. 217–242 in Richard C. Edwards, Michael Reich, and David Gordon (eds.), *Labor Market Segmentation*. Lexington, MA: Heath.

28. ———. 1981. *Women Have Always Worked: A Historical Overview*. Old Westbury, New York: Feminist Press.

29. ———. 1990. *A Woman's Wage: Historical Meanings and Social Consequences*. Louisville: University of Louisville Press.

30. Kwolek-Folland, Angel. 1998. *Incorporating Women: A History of Women and Business in the United States*. New York: Twayne Publishers.

31. Lerner, Gerda. 1972. *Black Women in White America: A Documentary History*. New York: Vintage.

32. Lorenzana, Noemi. 1979. "La Chicana." Pp. 336–341 in Eloise C. Snyder (ed.), *The Study of Women: Enlarging Perspectives of Social Reality*. New York: Harper & Row.

33. Milkman, Ruth. 1980. "Organizing the Sexual Division of Labor: Historical Perspectives in 'Women's Work' and the American Labor Movement." *Socialist Review* 10(1): 95–105.

34. ——— (ed.). 1985. *Women, Work, and Protest: A Century of U.S. Women's Labor History*. Boston: Routledge and Kegan Paul.

35. ———. 1993. "Organizing Immigrant Women in New York's Chinatown: An Interview with Katie Quan," Pp. 281–298 in Dorothy Sue Cobble (ed.), *Women and Unions: Forging a Partnership.* Ithaca, NY: ILR Press.

36. Oppenheimer, Valerie Kincade. 1970. *The Female Labor Force in the United States.* Berkeley: University of California Press.

37. Pinchbeck, Ivy. 1930. *Women Workers and the Industrial Revolution (1750–1850).* London: Virago Press.

38. ———. 1969. *Women Workers and the Industrial Revolution (1750–1850).* London: Virago Press.

39. Pleck, Elizabeth H. 1979. "A Mother's Wages: Income Earning Among Married Italian and Black Women, 1896–1911." Pp. 367–392 in Nancy Cott and Elizabeth Pleck (eds.), *A Heritage of Her Own: Toward a New Social History of American Women.* New York: Simon & Schuster.

40. Scharf, Lois. 1980. *To Work and to Wed: Female Employment, Feminism, and the Great Depression.* Westport, CT: Greenwood Press.

41. Smuts, Robert. 1971. *Women and Work in America.* New York: Schocken.

42. Terborg-Penn, Rosalyn. 1985. "Survival Strategies among African-American Women: A Continuing Process." Pp. 139–155 in Ruth Milkman (ed.), *Women, Work, and Protest: A Century of U.S. Women's Labor History.* Boston: Routledge and Kegan Paul.

43. Trey, Joan Ellen. 1972. "Women in the War Economy— World War II." *Review of Radical Political Economics* 4(3):40–57.

44. Triece, Mary E. 2001. *Protest and Popular Culture: Women in the U.S. Labor Movement, 1897–1917.* Boulder, CO: Westview Press.

45. U.S. Bureau of the Census. 1929. *Women in Gainful Occupations, 1870–1920.* Census Monograph No. 9 (prepared by Joseph A. Hill). Washington, DC: U.S. Government Printing Office.

46. ———. 1996a. *Statistical Abstract of the United States: 1996.* Washington, DC: U.S. Government Printing Office.

47. ———. 2002a. *Statistical Abstract of the United States: 2001* (121st ed.). Washington, DC: U.S. Government Printing Office.

48. ———. 2002b. *United States Census 2000, Summary File 3.* http://www.census.gov/Press-Release/www/2002/sumfile3.html.

49. U.S. Department of Labor. 2002a. "Table 2. Median Weekly Earnings of Full-Time Wage and Salary Workers by Union Affiliation and Selected Characteristics." Washington, DC: U.S. Department of Labor. http://www.bls.gov/news.release/union2.t02.htm.

50. ———. 2002b. "Table 1. Union Affiliation of Employed Wage and Salary Workers by Selected Characteristics." Washington, DC: U.S. Department of Labor. http://www.bls.gov/news.release/union2.t01.htm.

51. ———. 2002c. *Union Members in 2002.* Washington, DC: U.S. Department of Labor. http://www.bls.gov/news.release/union2.nr0.htm.

52. ———2000. *Women of Hispanic Origin in the Labor Force.* No. 00–04 (April). Washington, DC: U.S. Department of Labor. http://www.dol.gov/wb/wb_pubs/hispwom2.htm.

53. U.S. Equal Employment Opportunity Commission. 2002. *Job Patterns for Minorities and Women in Private Industry, 2000.* Washington, DC: U.S. Department of Labor.

54. Wertheimer, Barbara Mayer. 1977. *We Were There: The Story of Working Women in America.* New York: Pantheon.

55. Wise, Nancy B., and Christy Wise. 1994. *A Mouthful of Rivets: Women at Work in World War II.* San Francisco: Jossey-Bass.

56. Zavella, Patricia. 1987. *Women's Work and Chicano Families: Cannery Workers of the Santa Clara Valley.* Ithaca, New York: Cornell University Press.

37

The Problem That Has No Name

BETTY FRIEDAN

The problem lay buried, unspoken, for many years in the minds of American women. It was a strange stirring, a sense of dissatisfaction, a yearning that women suffered in the middle of the twentieth century in the United States. Each suburban wife struggled with it alone. As she made the beds, shopped for groceries, matched slipcover material, ate peanut butter sandwiches with her children, chauffeured Cub Scouts and Brownies, lay beside her husband at night—she was afraid to ask even of herself the silent question—"Is this all?"

For over fifteen years there was no word of this yearning in the millions of words written about women, for women, in all the columns, books and articles by experts telling women their role was to seek fulfillment as wives and mothers. Over and over women heard in voices of tradition and of Freudian sophistication that they could desire no greater destiny than to glory in their own femininity. . . . They were taught to pity the neurotic, unfeminine, unhappy women who wanted to be poets or physicists or presidents. They learned that truly feminine women do not want careers, higher education, political rights—the independence and the opportunities that the old-fashioned feminists fought for. . . .

By the end of the nineteen-fifties, the average marriage age of women in America dropped to 20, and was still dropping, into the teens. Fourteen million girls were engaged by 17. The proportion of women attending college in comparison with men dropped from 47 per cent in 1920 to 35 per cent in 1958. A century earlier, women had fought for higher education; now girls went to college to get a husband. By the mid-fifties, 60 per cent dropped out of college to marry, or because they were afraid too much education would be a marriage bar. Colleges built dormitories for "married students," but the students were almost always the husbands. A new degree was instituted for the wives—"Ph.T." (Putting Husband Through).

Then American girls began getting married in high school. And the women's magazines, deploring the unhappy statistics about these young marriages, urged that courses on marriage, and marriage counselors, be installed in the high schools. Girls started going steady at twelve and thirteen, in junior high. Manufacturers put out brassieres with false bosoms of foam rubber for little girls of ten. And an advertisement for a child's dress, sizes 3-6x, in the *New York Times* in the fall of 1960, said: "She Too Can Join the Man-Trap Set." . . .

In a New York hospital, a woman had a nervous breakdown when she found she could not breast-feed her baby. In other hospitals, women dying of cancer refused a drug which research had proved might save their lives: its side effects were said to be unfeminine. "If I have only one life, let me live it as a blonde," a larger-than-life-sized picture of a pretty, vacuous woman proclaimed from newspaper, magazine, and drugstore ads. And across America, three out of every ten women dyed their hair blonde. They ate a chalk called Metrecal, instead of food, to shrink to the size of the thin young models. Department-store buyers reported that American women, since 1939, had become three and four sizes smaller. "Women are out to fit the clothes, instead of vice-versa," one buyer said.

Interior decorators were designing kitchens with mosaic murals and original paintings, for kitchens were once again the center of women's lives. Home sewing became a million-dollar industry. Many women no longer left their homes, except to shop, chauffeur their children, or attend a social engagement with their husbands. Girls were growing up in America without ever having jobs outside the home. In the late fifties, a sociological phenomenon was suddenly remarked: a third of American women now worked, but most were no longer young and very few were pursuing careers. They were married women who held part-time jobs, selling or secretarial, to put their husbands through school, their sons through college, or to help pay the mortgage. Or they were widows supporting families. Fewer and fewer women were entering professional work. The shortages in the nursing, social work, and teaching professions caused crises in almost every American city. Concerned over the Soviet Union's lead in the space race, scientists noted that America's greatest source of unused brainpower was women. But girls would not study physics: it was "unfeminine." . . .

The suburban housewife—she was the dream image of the young American women and the envy, it was said, of women all over the world. The American housewife—freed by science and labor-saving appliances from the drudgery, the dangers of childbirth and the illnesses of her grandmother. She was healthy, beautiful, educated, concerned only about her husband, her children, her home. She had found true feminine fulfillment. As a housewife and mother, she was respected as a full and equal partner to man in his world. She was free to choose automobiles, clothes, appliances, supermarkets; she had everything that women ever dreamed of.

In the fifteen years after World War II, this mystique of feminine fulfillment became the cherished and self-perpetuating core of contemporary American culture. . . .

For over fifteen years, the words written for women, and the words women used when they talked to each other, while their husbands sat on the other side of the room and talked shop or politics or septic tanks, were about problems with their children, or how to keep their husbands happy, or improve their children's school, or cook chicken or make slipcovers. Nobody argued whether women were inferior or superior to men; they were simply different. Words like "emancipation" and "career" sounded strange and embarrassing; no one had used them for years. When a Frenchwoman named Simone de Beauvoir wrote a book called *The Second Sex,* an American critic commented that she obviously "didn't know what life was all about," and besides, she was talking about French women. The "woman problem" in America no longer existed.

If a woman had a problem in the 1950's and 1960's, she knew that something must be wrong with her marriage, or with herself. Other women were satisfied with their lives, she thought. What kind of a woman was she if she did not feel this mysterious fulfillment waxing the kitchen floor? She was so ashamed to admit her dissatisfaction that she never knew how many other women shared it. If she tried to tell her husband, he didn't understand what she was talking about. She did not really understand it herself. For over fifteen years women in America found it harder to talk about this problem than about sex. Even the psychoanalysts had no name for it. When a woman went to a psychiatrist for help, as many women did, she would say, "I'm so ashamed," or "I must be hopelessly neurotic." "I don't know what's wrong with women today," a suburban psychiatrist said uneasily. "I only know something is wrong because most of my patients happen to be women. And their problem isn't sexual." Most women with this problem did not go to see a psychoanalyst, however. "There's nothing wrong really," they kept telling themselves. "There isn't any problem."

But on an April morning in 1959, I heard a mother of four, having coffee with four other mothers in a suburban development fifteen miles from New York, say in a tone of quiet desperation, "the problem." And the others knew, without words, that she was not talking about a problem with her husband, or her children, or her home. Suddenly they realized they all shared the same problem, the problem that has no name. They began, hesitantly, to talk about it. Later, after they had picked up their children at nursery school and taken them home to nap, two of the women cried, in sheer relief, just to know they were not alone. . . .

Just what was this problem that has no name? What were the words women used when they tried to express it? Sometimes a woman would say "I feel empty somehow . . . incomplete." Or she would say, "I feel as if I don't exist." Sometimes she blotted out the feeling with a tranquilizer. Sometimes she thought the problem was with her husband, or her children, or that what she really needed was to redecorate her house, or move to a better neighborhood, or have an affair, or another baby. Sometimes, she went to a doctor with symptoms she could hardly describe: "A tired feeling . . . I get so angry with the children it scares me . . . I feel like crying without any reason." (A Cleveland doctor called it "the housewife's syndrome.") A number of women told me about great bleeding blisters that break out on their hands and arms. "I call it the housewife's blight," said a family doctor in Pennsylvania. "I see it so often lately in these young women with four, five and six children who bury themselves in their dishpans. But it isn't caused by detergent and it isn't cured by cortisone.". . . .

A mother of four who left college at nineteen to get married told me:

I've tried everything women are supposed to do— hobbies, gardening, pickling, canning, being very social with my neighbors, joining committees, running PTA teas. I can do it all, and I like it, but it doesn't leave you anything to think about—any feeling of who you are. I never had any career ambitions. All I wanted was to get married and have four children. I love the kids and Bob and my home. There's no problem you can even put a name to. But I'm desperate. I begin to feel I have no personality. I'm a server of food and putter-on of pants and a bedmaker, somebody who can be called on when you want something. But who am I?

A twenty-three-year-old mother in blue jeans said:

I ask myself why I'm so dissatisfied. I've got my health, fine children, a lovely new home, enough money. My husband has a real future as an electronics engineer. He doesn't have any of these feelings. He says maybe I need a vacation, let's go to New York for a weekend. But that isn't it. I always had this idea we should do everything together. I can't sit down and read a book alone. If the children are napping and I have one hour to myself I just walk through the house waiting for them to wake up. I don't make a move until I know where the rest of the crowd is going. It's as if ever since you were a little girl, there's always been somebody or something that will take care of your life: your parents, or college, or falling in love, or having a child, or moving to a new house. Then you wake up one morning and there's nothing to look forward to.

A young wife in a Long Island development said:

> I seem to sleep so much. I don't know why I should be so tired. This house isn't nearly so hard to clean as the cold-water flat we had when I was working. The children are at school all day. It's not the work. I just don't feel alive.

In 1960, the problem that has no name burst like a boil through the image of the happy American housewife. In the television commercials the pretty housewives still beamed over their foaming dishpans and *Time's* cover story on "The Suburban Wife, an American Phenomenon" protested: "Having too good a time . . . to believe that they should be unhappy." But the actual unhappiness of the American housewife was suddenly being reported—from the *New York Times* and *Newsweek* to *Good Housekeeping* and CBS Television ("The Trapped Housewife"), although almost everybody who talked about it found some superficial reason to dismiss it. . . . Some said it was the old problem—education: more and more women had education, which naturally made them unhappy in their role as housewives. "The road from Freud to Frigidaire, from Sophocles to Spock, has turned out to be a bumpy one," reported the *New York Times* (June 28, 1960). . . .

Can the problem that has no name be somehow related to the domestic routine of the housewife? When a woman tries to put the problem into words, she often merely describes the daily life she leads. What is there in this recital of comfortable domestic detail that could possibly cause such a feeling of desperation? Is she trapped simply by the enormous demands of her role as modern housewife: wife, mistress, mother, nurse, consumer, cook, chauffeur; expert on interior decoration, child care, appliance repair, furniture

refinishing, nutrition, and education? . . . She has no time to read books, only magazines; even if she had time, she has lost the power to concentrate. At the end of the day, she is so terribly tired that sometimes her husband has to take over and put the children to bed.

This terrible tiredness took so many women to doctors in the 1950's that one decided to investigate it. He found, surprisingly, that his patients suffering from "housewife's fatigue" slept more than an adult needed to sleep—as much as ten hours a day—and that the actual energy they expended on housework did not tax their capacity. The real problem must be something else, he decided—perhaps boredom. Some doctors told their women patients they must get out of the house for a day, treat themselves to a movie in town. Others prescribed tranquilizers. Many suburban housewives were taking tranquilizers like cough drops. . . .

It is easy to see the concrete details that trap the suburban housewife, the continual demands on her time. But the chains that bind her in her trap are chains in her own mind and spirit. They are chains made up of mistaken ideas and misinterpreted facts, of incomplete truths and unreal choices. They are not easily seen and not easily shaken off.

How can any woman see the whole truth within the bounds of her own life? How can she believe that voice inside herself, when it denies the conventional, accepted truths by which she has been living? And yet the women I have talked to, who are finally listening to that inner voice, seem in some incredible way to be groping through to a truth that has defied the experts. . . .

I began to see in a strange new light the American return to early marriage and the large families that are causing the population explosion; the recent movement to natural childbirth and breast-feeding; suburban conformity, and the new neuroses, character pathologies and sexual problems being reported by the doctors. I began to see new dimensions to old problems that have long been taken for granted among women: menstrual difficulties, sexual frigidity, promiscuity, pregnancy fears, childbirth depression, the high incidence of emotional breakdown and suicide among women in their twenties and thirties, the menopause crises, the so-called passivity and immaturity of American men, the discrepancy between women's tested intellectual abilities in childhood and their adult achievement, the changing incidence of adult sexual orgasm in American women, and persistent problems in psychotherapy and in women's education.

If I am right, the problem that has no name stirring in the minds of so many American women today is not a matter of loss of femininity or too much education, or the demands of domesticity. It is far more important than anyone recognizes. It is the key to these other new and old problems which have been torturing women and their husbands and children, and puzzling their doctors and educators for years. It may well be the key to our future as a nation and a culture. We can no longer ignore that voice within women that says: "I want something more than my husband and my children and my home."

 38

Race and the Politics of Identity in U.S. Feminism

ESTELLE B. FREEDMAN

The investigation of the rights of slaves has led me to a better understanding of my own.

—ANGELINA GRIMKÉ,
UNITED STATES, 1838

Feminism is the political theory and practice that struggles to free all *women. . . . Anything less than this vision of total freedom is not feminism, but merely female self-aggrandizement.*

—BARBARA SMITH,
UNITED STATES, 1979

In the spring of 1920 a group of African American women met to discuss how they could integrate white organizations. In the words of Lugenia Burns

Hope, black women wanted to "stand side by side with women of the white race and work for full emancipation of all women." For such interracial cooperation to take place in the United States at this time would be highly unusual. American society divided the world into black and white, whether in neighborhoods, schools, churches, or cemeteries. So did the U.S. women's movement, despite its founding by antislavery activists. For a generation African American women had tried unsuccessfully to gain white women's support for their efforts to end racial hatred and its most virulent act, the murder of innocent blacks by lynching. Now a small opening appeared. A group of southern white women from churches, clubs, and the Young Women's Christian Association (YWCA) invited four distinguished African American women to speak to their conference in Memphis, Tennessee, in October 1920.

On the last day of the Memphis conference, North Carolina educator Charlotte Hawkins Brown reached across a wide chasm of racial distrust to deliver a talk that gave white women a firsthand account of the daily insults borne by African Americans. On the train ride to Memphis, Brown revealed, a dozen white men had forced her to leave her seat in the overnight sleeping car and ride in the segregated day coach for blacks only. Humiliated and angry, she told the audience that "the thing that grieved me most is that there were women in the car and there wasn't a dissenting voice." She asked the white women that day to put themselves in her place, to "just be colored for a few minutes." In closing her speech about the terrors of lynching and the daily insults to black womanhood, Brown reminded her white, Christian audience that "in the final analysis" they would all reach out a hand to the same God, "but I know that the dear Lord will not receive it if you are crushing me beneath your feet."[1]

In her speech that day Charlotte Hawkins Brown illustrated two critical themes in women's history: the power of personal testimony to reach across social boundaries and the role of women of color in expanding the feminist agenda. By revealing her experience of both racial insult and racial pride, Brown forced white women to think outside their own experience, to reconceptualize womanhood as a more complicated entity, and to build a politics of coalition across the racial divide. Their dialogue provided an opportunity to "pivot the center," that is, to learn from the experience of others how to question the dominant culture.[2] By doing so, women's movements can incorporate difference, not merely for the sake of inclusion or diversity but also to change their fundamental goals for social justice.

Questioning the dominant meaning of womanhood can occur in any culture where racial or class divisions complicate feminism. The particularly troubled history of race relations in the United States has compelled women's movements to grapple with the complexities of women's identities. Race became central to national politics during the same period that feminism called for women's rights. While similar issues arose in Europe, until well into the twentieth century race remained largely at the distance of empire. In the United States, in contrast, the colonized lived among the colonizers. In a nation that simultaneously championed freedom, exterminated native people, and enslaved Africans, it is not surprising that issues of race would become so central to women's movements.

Beginning in the 1830s and continuing to the present, the crucible of race has forced U.S. feminists into a dialogue about difference and dominance. In each wave of the movement, women of color have insisted upon pivoting the center so that feminism addresses the needs of all women. During the first wave, when American laws enforced white dominance over blacks, African American women led the way in formulating this critique. After the 1960s, when the U.S. population had become more diverse, women who identified as Chicana, Native American, or Asian American, as well as lesbian or disabled, insisted on the significance of their experiences to second-wave feminism. The repeated process of naming difference, organizing separately, and building political coalitions has ultimately strengthened feminism in the United States by extending its critique of inequality to all women and recognizing its historical connection to all movements for social justice.

RACE AND FEMINISM, 1830–1930

The rejection of inherited privilege that nurtured European feminisms also called into question other social hierarchies such as those of age, class, and religion, but none more vigorously than those based on the concept of race. In the era of democratic revolutions, when republican political ideas justified self-rule, racial slavery represented a stark contradiction to both the liberal principle of unfettered individualism and the socialist principle of worker control over production. Yet the expansion of capitalism that enriched democratic nations rested in part on enslavement. While the Spanish seized land and labor in Mexico and Peru, the Dutch, English, and other Europeans transported twelve million African men and women to the Americas between 1500 and 1800 to raise sugar cane, cotton, and tobacco. The profits earned by slave traders, slave owners, and merchants helped finance the industrial revolution in England and the United States.

The very notion of race served to mark the slave's subordinate status. Popular beliefs in a biological, as well as theological, basis for racial hierarchy justified both slavery and colonialism. Scientists who investigated brain size and structure relegated both women and "lower races," such as Africans, to the bottom rungs of the human hierarchy. In North America theories of white (northern and western European) racial superiority also justified the appropriation of land inhabited by Native Americans and Mexicans and fostered hostility toward immigrants from Ireland, Asia, and southern or eastern Europe.

For white feminists, race presented a particularly vexing dilemma. Just as the principle of natural rights could exclude women on biological grounds of natural sex, the concept of natural race excluded Africans, Asians, and other non-Europeans as less fully human than Europeans. White feminists could claim race privilege by insisting that they were more intelligent and deserving of rights than other demeaned groups, but doing so both negated the idea of a common womanhood and reinforced the subordination of African, Asian, Native American, and Mexican women as well as men. Would claims of universal womanhood extend to these racial others? Did the identity "woman" include all women, or only those entitled to rights based on their race or class? Just how profoundly would feminists challenge social hierarchies?

The Antislavery Movement and Women's Rights

The political birthplace of feminism in the United States was the antislavery movement. After independence, northern states gradually eliminated slave labor but the South increasingly relied upon it. Slavery politicized northern women for several reasons. Some white women opposed the system because the dispersal of slave families and the rape of female slaves offended their ideals of womanhood. Both religious principles and beliefs in female moral authority inspired them to form dozens of Female Anti-Slavery societies in the 1830s. Through pamphlets and talks they exhorted women to exercise their indirect political influence by praying to convert Americans to antislavery. Women gathered the bulk of the signatures asking legislators to abolish slavery. Taking direct action, northern women who supported the Underground Railroad hung special quilts on their clotheslines to mark safe houses for fugitives from slavery.

Yet opposition to slavery did not necessarily translate into a belief in racial equality. Some antislavery societies admitted only white women. In response, northern free black women formed their own groups and became activists on three fronts: to free the slaves, to end the race barrier within the female antislavery movement, and to gain rights as women. Their personal testimony about race initiated the dialogue on the complexities of womanhood. In 1837, for example, Sarah Forten circulated a poem at the first Anti-Slavery Convention of American Women asking white women to abandon their own race prejudice and in the name of sister-

hood welcome all women to a common Christian cause. The convention admitted black women and called for the racial integration of churches.

In the free black community, women activists faced other obstacles. When Maria Stewart spoke in public against slavery, she was effectively ostracized by other northern free blacks who objected to her unwomanly behavior. "What if I am a woman[?]" she asked in 1833. "Is not the God of ancient times the God of these modern days[?]" Citing biblical and historical women, from Deborah and Mary Magdalene to medieval nuns, Stewart justified her right to speak out politically, whatever her race or sex. Although she withdrew from public speaking under pressure, in her farewell address she chastised African American reformers: "Let us no longer talk of prejudice till prejudice becomes extinct at home. Let us no longer talk of opposition till we cease to oppose our own."[3]

White women's determination to speak out against slavery initiated a crisis over women's rights in the abolition movement. Two southern white women, Sarah and Angelina Grimké, forced the issue. Raised in a southern, slaveholding family, the sisters converted to the Quaker faith and rejected slavery as a moral sin. They attempted to subvert the institution by illegally teaching their slaves to read. The Grimké sisters' views were so unpopular that they left the South for Philadelphia, where they joined the Female Anti-Slavery Society. At first they urged women to use their influence to extend natural rights to blacks. "Try to persuade your husband, father, brothers and sons that slavery is a crime against God and man," Angelina Grimké urged in *An Appeal to the Christian Women of the Southern States* (1836). But when she spoke out in public to audiences of men and women, she shared the fate of Maria Stewart. Northern white clergy condemned her for disobediently stepping outside the female sphere. "How monstrous, how anti-Christian is the doctrine that woman is dependent on man!" she responded. "The investigation of the rights of slaves has led me to a better understanding of my own."[4]

In the process of opposing slavery the Grimké sisters recognized the broader implications of political rights. In 1838, a decade before the Seneca Falls convention, they published *Letters on the Equality of the Sexes,* which analyzed women's inferior status, refuted biblical injunctions against women's activism, and rejected female subservience to men. Abolition, Angelina Grimké recognized, had "opened the way for the discussion of other rights, and the ultimate result will most certainly be the breaking of *every* yoke, the letting the oppressed of every grade and description go free."[5] Most abolitionists did not want to dilute their movement by adding women's rights, however. Only a handful of male allies, such as William Lloyd Garrison, protested when organizers of the 1840 World Anti-Slavery Convention in London refused to seat female delegates. Two of those women, Lucretia Mott and Elizabeth Cady Stanton, pledged to respond one day. With the support of abolitionists such as former slave Frederick Douglass, they organized the first women's rights convention in 1848.

Free African American women stood at the intersection of abolitionism and women's rights. Most concentrated on antislavery. A few, such as former slave and itinerant preacher Sojourner Truth, testified from their own experience that race and gender were inseparable. At one of the women's rights conventions held throughout the northern states in the 1850s, Truth defied clergymen who claimed that women needed to be supported and protected by men. "I have as much muscle as any man, and can do as much work as any man," she told the crowd. "I have plowed and reaped and husked and chopped and mowed, and can any man do more than that?"[6] Years later the white feminist Matilda Joselyn Gage reconstructed Truth's speech with a rhetorical flourish that became legendary: "Nobody ever helps me into carriages, or over mud puddles, or gives me any best place! And ain't I a woman?"[7] Apocryphal as the precise phrases may be, Sojourner Truth's message echoed for generations, reminding feminists that middle-class white women's experiences do not encompass the full range of women's subordination. By listening to other voices the movement could refute the argument that women should be satisfied with the privileges that only a few enjoy.

After the Civil War and the emancipation of slaves, the U.S. women's movement split over a constitutional amendment to enfranchise former slaves that did not include woman suffrage. When Frederick Douglass proclaimed, "This is the Negro's hour," Sojourner Truth, then eighty years old, predicted that "if colored men get their rights, and not colored women theirs, you see the colored men will be masters over the women, and it will be just as bad as it was before." But Truth recognized that she was "about the only colored women that goes about to speak of the rights of the colored women."[8] In 1869 Douglass, along with Lucy Stone and others, supported the black suffrage amendment through the American Woman Suffrage Association (AWSA). Elizabeth Cady Stanton and her colleague Susan B. Anthony formed the National Woman Suffrage Association (NWSA) to press for black and woman suffrage. In 1870 the Fifteenth Amendment to the U.S. Constitution enfranchised black males only. The breach among black and women's rights advocates remained bitter.

Suffrage and Segregation

Over the next generation the U.S. women's movement reflected the increasingly racist national political climate. Jim Crow policies of segregation spread through the southern states, enforced by the white supremacist Ku Klux Klan (KKK), which terrorized blacks through vigilante violence and murder by lynch mobs. Northern support for reform diminished, while the economic and political plight of former slaves deteriorated. From the 1890s onward southern states found ways to disfranchise black male voters, depriving them of the power to challenge discriminatory practices.

The women's rights movement, blocked in its campaign for the vote, ignored these growing racial injustices. Some suffragists even tried to bolster their unpopular cause by exploiting racial stereotypes directed at both African Americans and the masses of Catholic and Jewish immigrants arriving from Europe. If ignorant black and immigrant men could vote, they argued, why not educated white women? They were not alone in their rhetorical tactic. In

South Africa as well, English and Afrikaner women's suffrage associations were arguing that white women needed to vote to counter the political power of black Africans. In the United States, suffrage organizations agreed to exclude black women from leadership at conventions or visibility at demonstrations, partly to accommodate their southern members. The maternalist white women's club movement segregated African American women. The YWCA had separate African American (as well as Chinese American) branches. Only rare exceptions, such as white missionary teachers in the South, worked in a common cause across race, united by a belief in "woman's work for woman."[9]

Once again, African American women struggled on several fronts: for suffrage, to improve conditions for their race, and to achieve equality with white women. Black women wanted the vote not only for themselves but also as a way to represent their race in those northern states where blacks could exercise the franchise. Mary Church Terrell rejoiced "not only in the prospective enfranchisement of my sex but in the emancipation of my race."[10] In addition, middle-class African Americans tried to uplift former slaves through education and temperance. To avoid the condescension of white women, they formed separate black chapters of the maternalist Woman's Christian Temperance Union (WCTU). They also risked their lives to oppose racial discrimination. In the 1880s, for example, Memphis newspaper editor and former slave Ida B. Wells was run out of town when she tried to expose the trumped-up charges of rape used to justify the lynching of innocent African American men by white mobs. Wells turned to northern black women for support and inspired the first African American women's clubs. By 1909 the National Association of Colored Women had established branches in twenty states. Locals concentrated on community self-help by establishing day care facilities, hospitals, and mothers groups. They also turned their attention to the most pressing problem facing African Americans, lynching.

The black women's clubs attempted to dispel several myths about race and sexuality. Racial stereotypes cast all black women as sexually immoral and available to men, a legacy of black women's vulnerability to assault during slavery. As Anna Julia Cooper pointed out in the 1890s, American prejudice "cynically assumes 'A Negro woman cannot be a lady.'"[11] White women's reluctance to work with black women rested in part on this supposed moral divide between white female purity and black female depravity. Organized black womanhood insisted that women of their race were as chaste as white women and equally offended by unwanted sexual advances. Few white women's clubs took heed of this message. Along with excluding African Americans they ignored the call to help abolish lynching. When Wells called for support in her campaign, the leader of the influential WCTU, Frances Willard, failed to speak out and even seemed to condone lynching as necessary to protect white women's virtue.

Ignoring the voices of African American women did not advance the white women's movement. In 1890, when AWSA and NWSA united as the National American Woman Suffrage Association (NAWSA), to appease southern members they permitted chapters to exclude African American women. But this strategy won little support for suffrage in the South. Only northern state legislatures, and few of them, granted the vote to women. As the suffrage movement finally gathered momentum after 1910, African American women participated but did not feel welcome. The huge suffrage parades placed them at the back, but with the help of some white allies the black women literally forced their way into the mainstream of the marches. After Congress finally passed the suffrage amendment in 1919, only one southern state joined those ratifying the measure. Although the law now extended the vote to both black and white women after ratification in 1920, Jim Crow legislation effectively disenfranchised most black women, along with black men, in southern states.

Whose Equal Rights?

In the aftermath of suffrage, white women's racial attitudes ranged from intolerance to neglect to engagement. At one extreme, the resurgent Ku Klux Klan established a Women's KKK, which in 1924 claimed a membership of a quarter million. More typical was the dismissal of race by younger radicals such as Alice Paul, the charismatic leader of the self-identified feminists, who had helped revive the U.S. suffrage movement. Borrowing the militant tactics of the British suffragettes, they had chained themselves to the White House fence and survived hunger strikes in jail. In 1923 these militant feminists, now called the National Women's Party, introduced the Equal Rights Amendment (ERA) to the U.S. Constitution to mandate that "equality of rights under the law shall not be denied or abridged by the United States or any state on account of sex." With a single focus on sex, however, they refused to discuss racial injustice, even when African American women raised the subject at their meetings.

This refusal to acknowledge racism recurred in the anti-Semitism of the women's movement. Like African Americans, Jewish women had formed their own clubs in response to exclusion from white Christian organizations. Although Jewish women supported suffrage more often than other groups, the suffrage movement had ignored their cultural life when it scheduled conventions and parades on the Jewish sabbath. Historian Elinor Lerner refers to these acts as "anti-Semitism by neglect."[12] After suffrage, Jewish women called on their Christian allies to protest anti-Semitism at home and in the growing Nazi movement in Germany in the 1920s and 1930s. The National Council of Jewish Women sought political support for amending restrictive immigration laws that prevented persecuted Jews from emigrating to the United States. They also hoped that the National Consumers League would join a boycott of German-made goods. Just as the National Woman's Party did not consider lynching a "woman's issue," most women reformers did not see anti-Semitism as part of their agenda. Former NAWSA president Carrie Chapman Catt did circulate a petition among non-Jewish feminists calling for an end to the persecution of German Jews, but neither the boycott nor the efforts to lift immigration quotas won feminist support.

Despite the legacy of racism and neglect, some postsuffrage activists began to sow the seeds of interracial cooperation. In 1924 the League of Women Voters, which had formed after suffrage to help educate women for politics, established a Committee on Negro Problems. The YWCA had begun to hold interracial conferences in 1915; in the 1920s its college branches confronted the organization's policy of segregated facilities. Charlotte Brown's 1920 Memphis speech contributed to this incipient interracial cooperation. By the 1930s the antilynching movement gained the support of several liberal white women's groups, including the Women's Trade Union League, the Women's Joint Congressional Committee (which was the major women's lobbying group in Washington), and the YWCA, which in the 1940s fully integrated and adopted the goals of racial equality and civil rights for minorities.

In the 1930s white southerner Jessie Daniel Ames responded to pleas by black churchwomen by spearheading the Association of Southern Women for the Prevention of Lynching (ASWPL). The members decided to take responsibility for preventing or exposing the murders carried out by men who claimed to be protecting the purity of white womanhood when they lynched alleged black male rapists. Echoing the earlier ideas of Ida B. Wells, Ames recognized the deep connections between race and gender subordination. Ames reported that after reviewing the history of lynching, the ASWPL resolved "no longer to remain silent in the face of this crime done in their name."[13] By rejecting the pedestal of sexual protection, the ASWPL undermined the hold of white supremacy. The group collected forty thousand signatures from southern white women pledged to stop lynching in their localities.

After 1930, both interracial and interfaith cooperation found a foothold within the U.S. women's movement. First Lady Eleanor Roosevelt's gradual rejection of the racism and anti-Semitism she had learned growing up foreshadowed a later trend. The tentative connections made across race and religious lines would nurture the rebirth of feminism in the 1960s. As in the past, African American women in particular provided a critical perspective for white women, alerting them to the integral connections between race and gender. By articulating their personal experience of race, African American women contributed the knowledge that enfranchisement alone could not ensure equality; that the female pedestal was a myth; that sexual stereotypes, whether of purity or immorality, exerted forceful social controls; that power relations always rested upon both race and gender hierarchies; that alliance across race and gender could challenge these hierarchies; and that dignified resistance in the face of seeming powerlessness could be a mighty weapon for change.

RACIAL JUSTICE, 1930–1970: SEEDBED FOR SECOND-WAVE FEMINISM

Viewed from the perspectives of race, class, and gender, the U.S. women's movement experienced significant growing pains in the decades after the suffrage victory. During the 1930s women organized as consumers, pacifists, professionals, and workers. The radical wing of the American labor movement spoke to the needs of working-class women, such as Mexican American cannery and field workers. In 1939, for example, labor organizer Luisa Moreno called on the Congress of Spanish-Speaking Peoples to form a women's committee to support the "education of the Mexican woman" and equality in wages and civil rights.[14] Women mobilized to support the war effort in the 1940s, and they did not necessarily demobilize afterward. With more women working for wages, female union membership expanded. A new generation of labor feminists revived socialist feminist goals and initiated a campaign for "equal pay for equal work." Above all, a movement for racial justice insisted that white supremacy had no place in the postwar democratic world. When the U.S. Supreme Court struck down the legality of public school segregation in 1954, it ushered in a revolution in race relations in which women played a central role.

Ella Baker, an organizer for the Southern Christian Leadership Conference (SCLC) and a founder of the Student Non-Violent Coordinating Committee (SNCC), recalled that "the movement of the 50s and 60s was carried largely by women, since it came out of church groups."[15] African American churchwomen fed, housed, clothed, and prayed for the black and white civil rights workers who mobilized throughout the South. They also helped organize and lead the movement. College professor Jo Ann Gibson Robinson and the Women's Political Council of Montgomery, Alabama, instigated and sustained the inspirational bus boycott of 1955–56 after Rosa Parks refused to move to the back of the bus. In 1964 former sharecropper Fannie Lou Hamer took the cause of black political representation to the floor of the Democratic National Convention to demand seating of popularly chosen black delegates. College students such as Anne Moody and Diane Nash bravely demonstrated at lunch counters, participated in the racially integrated Freedom Rides, and went to jail for challenging segregation.

The politics of racial justice directly inspired a revival of feminism from two political perspectives, one liberal and one radical. The Civil Rights Act of 1964 outlawed racial discrimination but also banned sex discrimination, partly at the urging of lobbyists from the aging National Woman's Party. The act established the Equal Employment Opportunity Commission (EEOC) to hear complaints about discrimination based on either race or gender. When the EEOC failed to respond to sex discrimination complaints, feminists decided they needed a political lobby akin to the National Association for the Advancement of Colored People. In 1966 three hundred charter members signed on to the National Organization for Women (NOW). They included black civil rights lawyer Pauli Murray, union leaders, professional women and men, and white feminists like Betty Friedan, whose 1963 book *The Feminine Mystique* had touched a nerve among educated suburban white women. The organization pledged "to bring women into full participation in the mainstream of American society, now, assuming all the privileges and responsibilities thereof in truly equal partnership with men."[16]

This liberal branch of the second wave of U.S. feminism emphasized antidiscrimination law, supporting court cases to achieve equal pay and promotion for women workers at all levels. The feminist magazine *Ms.* founded in 1972 by journalist Gloria Steinem, promoted these and other goals in its pages. Along with the National Women's Political Caucus, NOW encouraged the election of women to public office. It also rallied behind the ERA, which Congress passed in 1972. Although the amendment failed to be ratified by enough states to become law, the equal-rights strategy ultimately prevailed. Legislation such as the Women's Educational Equity Act and the Equal Credit Opportunity Act (1974) banned discrimination in schools and lending, and the EEOC filed suits on behalf of workers who complained of sex discrimination in hiring, training, and promotion.

Though predominantly white, the ranks of liberal feminists included politically active women of color such as Shirley Chisholm, Patsy Mink, and Aileen Hernandez, a former labor organizer who in 1971 became NOW's second president. The National Black Feminist Organization reached out to African American women to embrace liberal feminism. One of its founders, Eleanor Holmes Norton, recognized that "every problem raised by white feminists has a disproportionately heavy impact on blacks." She also knew that the white feminist movement would "only take on the color line if we who are black join it."[17]

The second, radical wing of the feminist revival grew out of both the civil rights and student movements of the 1960s. During the voter registration and community organizing drives in the southern states, young white female volunteers met strong black women activists. "For the first time," one young white woman stated, "I had role models I could really respect."[18] Working with black leaders such as Ella Baker or Septima Clark taught these white students about women's potential for activism and leadership.

Radicalized in New Left organizations such as SNCC, idealistic activists soon objected to the limitations placed on them as women. Like Maria Stewart and Sarah and Angelina Grimké more than a century earlier, they hoped to be full participants in the quest for racial justice. When men in the movement relegated them to serving coffee, cooking, and having sex, these young women applied their political analysis to gender. Ruby Doris Smith Robinson, a black activist, inspired Casey Hayden and Mary King to write a position paper on women in the movement. The contradiction of sexual subordination in a liberation movement also inspired protest from women in Students for a Democratic Society (SDS). "Having learned from the Movement to think radically about the personal worth and abilities of people whose role in society had gone unchallenged before," they wrote in 1965, "a lot of women in the movement have begun trying to apply those lessons to their relations with men."[19]

Neither white nor black men responded with much enthusiasm, and some blatantly ridiculed women for raising these issues. The rhetoric escalated. In 1967 SDS women prepared the Women's Manifesto, which compared women to Third World people—colonized by white males. They called on SDS to work for communal child care, rights to birth control and abortion, and equality within the home. "[W]e demand that our brothers recognize that they must deal with their own problems of male chauvinism in their personal, social and political relationships," they wrote.[20]

Women's Liberation

Radical women began to extend the politics of self-determination to gender. Just as a call for Black Power purged whites from some interracial organizations and separate movements formed to empower Chicanos and Native Americans, some feminists articulated separatist politics. These radical, or cultural, feminists considered gender the most important aspect of all liberation struggles. To Shulamith Firestone, for example, injustices of class and race would end only when women achieved equality. Not surprisingly, the majority of those who adopted this strategy were white and middle-class.

Breaking away from the male-dominated New Left, the women's liberation movement created a network of predominantly white, women-only organizations. In Chicago, New York, Berkeley, Boston, and smaller cities, radical feminists formed groups such as the Redstockings, the Feminists, the Furies, and Radical Women. In private consciousness-raising sessions members revealed their personal struggles as women, including stories of rape, unwanted pregnancies, lesbian desires, illegal abortions, and the dilemmas of child care and housework. In mimeographed pamphlets they insisted that "the personal is political," rejecting the ideological division of public and private spheres that dismissed women's claims of injustice as merely personal. Power, these feminists realized, operated within and through personal relations, including sexuality and the family. In addition, they questioned the liberal feminist goal of integrating women into male power structures. "We in this segment of the movement," Bonnie Kreps explained in 1968, "do not believe that the oppression of women will be ended by giving them a bigger piece of the pie as Betty Friedan would have it. We believe that the pie itself is rotten."[21]

Through direct action, radical feminists challenged cherished beliefs about women's place. They gained publicity for women's liberation when they demonstrated against the Miss America pageant, occupied the offices of the *Ladies Home Journal,* and held speak-outs about once-unmentionable topics such as abortion, rape, and prostitution. They created woman-only spaces to heal from the daily wounds of patriarchy. To replace the demeaning images of women in the media they celebrated a positive "women's culture" through alternative bookstores, publishing firms, coffeehouses, record companies, concerts, spiritual retreats, exhibit spaces, and back-to-the-land cooperatives and communes.

Explorations of sexuality contributed to a new politics of identity. Second-wave radical feminists shared with first-wave moral reformers a critique of men's sexual exploitation of women. But they differed in their exploration of an explicitly sexual bond among women as an alternative to heterosexual relations. A group called Radicalesbians drew connections between the rejection of male dominance and the assertion of sexual love for other women. Their 1970 essay "The Woman-identified Woman" began by defining a lesbian as "the rage of all women condensed to the point of explosion." Because women's "self-hate and the lack of real self are rooted in our male-given identity," they reasoned, "only women can give to each other a new sense of self."[22] By embracing lesbianism as a positive identity, they rejected the stigma of mental illness that had previously been attached to love between women.

While not all radical feminists became lesbians, the message of putting women first pervaded separatist organizing. Much of the women's culture of the 1970s was largely lesbian culture, and lesbians provided a great deal of the woman power to run feminist bookstores, concerts, and conferences. In response to attempts to exclude or closet them in mainstream feminist organizations, lesbians formed separate consciousness-raising groups and caucuses. In essays, songs, and art they expressed their alternative experience of sexuality and insisted on its legitimacy. Along with the fledgling gay liberation movement, lesbian feminists helped forge an influential concept of sexual identity.

THE LIMITS OF SISTERHOOD AND THE COMPLEXITIES OF IDENTITY, 1970–2000

Both liberal and radical feminists hoped to achieve gender solidarity through the politics of identity. Poet Robin Morgan called the anthology of feminist essays she edited in 1970 *Sisterhood Is Powerful.* As women of color pointed out from the beginning of the movement, sisterhood was also complicated. Many women of color felt excluded from a theory that elevated gender at the expense of race or class identity. By making white women's experience their standard, both liberal and radical feminists overlooked the perspectives of women of color. For example, when Betty Friedan called for liberating women from the home through employment, women of color who had always worked knew that joining the men of their race on the job meant they would still encounter discrimination. Or when the radical feminist theologian Mary Daly spoke about reclaiming women's spirituality through rituals honoring the goddess, African American poet Audre Lorde asked, "What color is your goddess?" A white female deity matched the white male deity, ignoring the heritage of African spirituality. Separatist politics troubled other women of color. For many Chicanas, the extended family represented both economic and cultural survival. "When a family is involved in a human rights movement, as is the Mexican-American family," Enriqueta Longeaux y Vásquez wrote in 1972, "there is little room for a woman's liberation movement alone."[23] Other women of color echoed the pervasive homophobia of the society when they rejected radical feminism because of its inclusion of lesbians.

Despite these tensions, women of color in the United States clearly recognized that gender as well as race affected their lives. A 1972 poll showed that two-thirds of black women, compared to only one-third of white women, were sympathetic to the women's movement. A 1976 survey of Chicana students found agreement with the goals of feminism as well as the view that the white women's movement was elitist and too focused on men as the oppressors. Many women of color longed for a more inclusive feminism. Former SNCC worker Elizabeth Martinez recalled that after the assassination of Martin Luther King Jr. in 1968 she realized "that if the struggle against sexism did not see itself as profoundly entwined with the fight against racism, I was gone." At the same time, though, she "looked hard at the sexism in the [Chicano] *movimiento*, and knew a Chicana feminism needed to be born."[24]

Women of color who shared feminist goals faced dual obstacles, from their own communities and from women's movements. Black nationalists, for example, urged women to align with racial rather than sexual politics, primarily by supporting men through women's roles as wives and mothers. Asian American feminists were criticized as traitors to their race for threatening ethnic identity, just as Chicana feminists risked being labeled *"vendidas,"* or sellouts, in the Chicano movement, especially if they accepted lesbianism. Yet when women of color did join the women's movement, they encountered overt and subtle racial bias. Given their small num-

bers, they often felt the discomfort of being treated as tokens, expected to represent their race but not to bring their own issues to the table. "Inclusion without influence," Lynet Uttal called it, or as Bernice Johnson Reagon explained, "You don't really want Black folks, you are just looking for yourself with a little color in it."[25]

The title of one collection of African American women's writing captured well the quandary of exclusion: *All the Women Are White, All the Blacks Are Men, but Some of Us Are Brave* (1982). In response to this dilemma, women of color initiated a redefinition of identity politics. They refused the pressures from both men of color who would subsume women's issues and white women who would subsume race issues. As Pauli Murray poignantly explained her "equal stake" in women's liberation and black liberation: "I have one foot in each camp and cannot split myself apart."[26] When the Chicano movement called on the women of La Raza (the race) to reject feminism, Adelaida del Castillo insisted that "true freedom for our people can come about only if prefaced by the equality of individuals within La Raza."[27]

Just as women had separated from men within the New Left, women of color established their own groups. One of these, the Combahee River Collective, issued a "black feminist statement" in 1974 that pledged to "struggle together with black men against racism, while we also struggle with black men about sexism."[28] Asian American Women United, Women of All Red Nations, and the National Black Women's Health Project served specific groups. Women from a variety of racial backgrounds formed Kitchen Table/Women of Color Press to present diverse women's stories. In 1981 they published an influential anthology, *This Bridge Called My Back: Writings by Radical Women of Color* (1981), edited by Chicana feminists Cherríe Moraga and Gloria Anzaldúa, which opened a cultural space for further explorations of multiple personal identities.

The theme of bridging different female identities recurred in other personal writing that expanded beyond the historically dominant categories of black and white. Jewish and Asian American feminists wrote passionately about the two worlds they bridged. Lesbians insisted on the inclusion of sexuality as another component of identity. Disabled women called for access to feminist events and acknowledgment of their sexual and reproductive capacities. Latinas explored how language represented both a link to family and community and a potential barrier to understanding across ethnicities. In *Borderlands/La Frontera: The New Mestiza* (1987) Gloria Anzaldúa captured well the empowering effect of articulating a mixed, or mestizo, identity: "I will have my voice: Indian, Spanish, white. I will have my serpent's tongue—my woman's voice, my sexual voice, my poet's voice. I will overcome the tradition of silence."[29]

Of all these identity groups, women of color stood at a particularly critical intersection. Frustrated by racial exclusion in the women's movement and tired of being asked to educate white women, writers such as Moraga asked, "How can we—this time—not use our bodies to be thrown over a river of tormented history to bridge the gap?"[30] Only if white women took race into account would the burden be shared. Indeed, the work of radical women of color profoundly affected white feminists. Combahee River Collective member Barbara Smith, who led antiracism workshops for white women in Boston, felt that white feminists had to "take responsibility for their racism," and she believed they were learning to do so. As she told a predominantly white audience at the National Women's Studies Association meeting in 1979, "The reason racism is a feminist issue is easily explained by the inherent definition of feminism." In Smith's view, the struggle to free *all* women had to include "women of color, working-class women, poor women, disabled women, Jewish women, lesbians, old women—as well as white, economically privileged, heterosexual women. Anything less than this vision of total freedom is not feminism, but merely female self-aggrandizement."[31]

White women contributed to the redefinition of feminism that made alliance across races, religions, and sexual identities a possibility. By recognizing cultural difference, including their own fragmented identities, many rejected the primacy of gender that characterized early radical feminism. By acknowl-

edging their own racism, they also began to question whiteness as a source of privilege. As Ruth Frankenberg put it in 1993, "Racism shapes white people's lives and identities in a way that is inseparable from other facets of daily life."[32] Recognizing white privilege did not have to be a source of immobilizing guilt; rather it could be a productive step toward applying that privilege to combating racism. Realizing that racial categories had been historically constructed—that whiteness, like any color, could change its meaning—opened an effort to "unlearn" the internalized racism that affected all women. As Gloria Yamato cautioned white women, "Work on racism for your sake, not 'their' sake."[33]

The intense conversations on identity and privilege encouraged some U.S. feminists to form coalitions across lines of race, ethnicity, gender, and sexuality. So did the political conservatism of the 1980s, which put feminists on the defensive. Whether addressing reproductive rights, the AIDS crisis, or welfare reform, feminists from diverse backgrounds built cross-cultural political support, sometimes painfully but also productively. Bernice Johnson Reagon captured the importance of this effort in a speech she gave at a women-only music festival. Separatism, she recognized, offered a safe space for groups who felt threatened by the outside world—lesbians, for example, or minorities—but it could be reactionary as well as healing. In the real world, she explained, "There is nowhere you can go and only be with people who are like you." Reagon challenged women to move from that safe space of separatism into the streets to engage in the difficult work of coalition politics.[34] Thus white women learned to protest race discrimination, heterosexual women of color to support lesbian rights, and feminist men to defend women's reproductive rights. Facing common opposition and learning to trust across difference, though never an easy task, helped sustain grassroots feminism in the face of opposition.

THE FUTURE OF IDENTITY POLITICS

For two centuries, women of color in the United States have stood in the vanguard of redefining feminism to ask not only what difference gender makes but how also women experience gender differently because of their access to or lack of social privilege. In defining a "multiracial feminism," social scientists Maxine Baca Zinn and Bonnie Thornton Dill point to the importance of going "beyond a mere recognition of diversity and difference among women to examine structures of domination." Sociologist Patricia Hill Collins refers to these structures as a "matrix of domination" in which gender is but one source of power, always connected to other forms. To recognize that matrix, to pivot the center, feminists have turned repeatedly to the lived experiences of women from diverse back-grounds.[35]

In the past two decades, some feminists have questioned whether the categories of gender and race continue to matter. For one, recognizing the multiplicity of identities within us reveals the limits of single labels. We need long strings of adjectives to locate our complex selves by race, religion, sexuality, physical ability, ethnicity, and the like. In addition, postmodern critics point out that Enlightenment ideas about fixed race and sex rest upon biological definitions that have often been used to restrict the rights of women and minorities. To Donna Haraway, who calls all identities "fabricated hybrids," our consciousness of gender, race, or class "is an achievement forced on us by the terrible historical experiences of . . . patriarchy, colonialism, and capitalism."[36] If so, refusing to be categorized by race or gender can become an act of political resistance. Claiming interracial or transgendered identities, for example, shakes up our beliefs about fixed biological categories. In her influential book *Gender Trouble* (1990), philosopher Judith Butler proposed that playing with the way we "perform" gender can also disrupt the category. In this view, exaggerated parodies of clothing and speech styles, such as the performances of drag queens or drag kings, could undermine the constraints of gender.

In contrast to those who emphasize the reactionary implications of our inherited categories, feminist critics such as Chela Sandoval and Paula Moya want to retain identity politics but refine them as well. Sandoval has insisted that identities are not necessarily imposed on us but that we may self-consciously choose among them, switching at times from an emphasis on our gender to an emphasis on our race or sexuality. Such "differential consciousness," she argues, can help forge political alliances among women. Paula Moya takes the argument further by calling for what she terms a "realist" account of identity. Since the social facts of race and gender continue to affect our personal experiences, to deny these categories overlooks "the fact that some people are more oppressed than others." Only by acknowledging this structural reality can we undermine it.[37]

The lived realities of race and sex remain as powerful in contemporary U.S. society as in the past. What has changed, however, is the political meaning of these categories. Instead of dismissing race, feminists have learned to confront its effects on all women. The acknowledgment of racial injustice has led to further explorations of personal identities that now empower many groups once relegated to the margins of women's movements. Listening to personal testimony has contributed to the feminist goal of extending the rights of women to all. The poet Audre Lorde recognized the importance of this historical process when she wrote that "those of us who have been forged in crucibles of difference—those of us who are poor, who are lesbians, who are Black, who are older," know that survival means "learning how to take our differences and make them strengths."[38] Nowhere would this lesson prove more challenging than when Western feminism reached beyond its cultural base and confronted gender inequality in the global arena.

NOTES

1. Charlotte Hawkins Brown, October 8, 1920, in *Black Women in White America: A Documentary History*, ed. Gerda Lerner (New York: Vintage Books, 1973), 467–72.
2. Elsa Barkley Brown, "African-American Women's Quilting: A Framework for Conceptualizing and Teaching African-American Women's History," *Signs* 14:4 (1989), 922. Brown credits Bettina Aptheker with this phrase (*Tapestries of Life: Women's Work, Women's Consciousness and the Meaning of Daily Life* [Amherst: University of

Massachusetts Press, 1989]); it is also adopted by Patricia Hill Collins, *Black Feminist Thought: Knowledge, Consciousness, and the Politics of Empowerment* (Boston: Unwin Hyman, 1990), 236–37.

3. "Mrs. Stewart's Farewell Address to Her Friends in the City of Boston. Delivered September 21, 1833," excerpted in Lerner *Black Women in White America:* 565–66.

4. Angelina Grimké to Catharine Beecher, Letter XII in Alice S. Rossi, *The Feminist Papers: From Adams to de Beauvoir* (New York: Columbia University Press, 1973), 320.

5. Quoted in Gerda Lerner, *The Grimké Sisters from South Carolina: Pioneers for Woman's Rights and Abolition* (New York: Schocken Books, 1971), 187.

6. Quoted in Nell Painter, *Sojourner Truth: A Life, a Symbol* (New York: W. W. Norton, 1996), 125.

7. "The Akron Convention," in *History of Woman Suffrage,* eds. Elizabeth Cady Stanton, Susan B. Anthony, and Matilda Joslyn Gage, reprinted in Rossi, *Feminist Papers,* 428.

8. Convention of the American Equal Rights Association, New York City, 1867, excerpted in Lerner, *Black Women in White America: A Documentary History,* 568.

9. Higginbotham, *Righteous Discontent: The Women's Movement in the Black Baptist Church, 1880–1920* (Cambridge: Harvard University Press, 1993), 91–105.

10. Quoted in Bettina Aptheker, *Women's Legacy: Essays on Race, Sex, and Class in American History* (Amherst: University of Massachusetts Press, 1982), 65.

11. Anna Julia Cooper, *A Voice From the South, by a Black Woman of the South* (Xenia, OH.: Aldine Printing House, 1892; repr., New York: Oxford University Press, 1988), 32.

12. Elinor Lerner, "American Feminism and the Jewish Question, 1890–1940," in *Anti-Semitism in American History,* ed. David Gerber (Urbana: University of Illinois Press, 1986), 305–28.

13. Quoted in Jacquelyn Dowd Hall, *Revolt Against Chivalry: Jessie Daniel Ames and the Women's Campaign Against Lynching* (New York: Columbia University Press, 1979), 164.

14. Moreno quoted in Vicki L. Ruiz, *From Out of the Shadows: Mexican Women in Twentieth-Century America* (New York: Oxford University Press, 1998), 101.

15. Baker quoted in Karen Anderson, *Changing Woman: A History of Racial Ethnic Women in Modern America* (New York: Oxford University Press, 1996), 211.

16. NOW mission statement in Miriam Schneir, *Feminism in Our Time* (New York: Vintage Books, 1994), 96.

17. Quoted in Susan Hartmann, *The Other Feminists: Activists in the Liberal Establishment* (New Haven: Yale University Press, 1998), 191.

18. Dorothy Dawson Burlage, quoted in Sara Evans, *Personal Politics: The Roots of Women's Liberation in the Civil Rights Movement and the New Left* (New York: Knopf, 1979), 51.

19. Casey Hayden and Mary King, "Sex and Caste," November 18, 1965, reprinted in Evans, *Personal Politics,* 236.

20. "Liberation of Women: New Left Notes, July 10, 1967," reprinted in Evans, *Personal Politics,* 241.

21. Kreps, "Radical Feminism 1," in *Radical Feminism,* eds. Anne Koedt, Ellen Levine, and Anita Rapone (New York: Quadrangle Books, 1973), 239.

22. Ibid., 245

23. Enriqueta Longeaux y Vásquez, "The Woman of La Raza," in *Chicana Feminist Thought: The Basic Historical Writings,* ed. Alma García (New York: Routledge, 1997), 31.

24. Elizabeth (Betita) Martinez, "History Makes Us, We Make History," in *The Feminist Memoir Project: Voices from Women's Liberation,* eds. Rachel Blau Duplessis and Ann Snitow (New York: Crown Publishing, 1998), 118–20.

25. Lynet Uttal, "Inclusion Without Influence: The Continuing Tokenism of Women of Color," in Gloria Anzaldúa, ed., *Making Face, Making Soul/Haciendo Caras: Creative and Critical Perspectives by Women of Color* (San Francisco: Aunt Lute Foundation, 1990), 42; Bernice Johnson Reagon, "Coalition Politics: Turning the Century," in *Homegirls: A Black Feminist Anthology,* ed. Barbara Smith (Brooklyn: Kitchen Table/Women of Color Press, 1983), 359.

26. Quoted in Hartmann, *The Other Feminists,* 205.

27. Del Castillo quoted in Ramón A. Gutiérrez, "Community, Patriarchy, and Individualism: The Politics of Chicano History and the Dream of Equality," in Vicki L. Ruiz and Ellen Carol DuBois, *Unequal Sisters: A Multicultural Reader in U.S. Women's History* (New York: Routledge, 2000), 3d ed., 591.

28. Combahee River Collective, "Black Feminist Statement," in *Capitalist Patriarchy and Socialist Feminism,* Zillah Eisenstein, ed. (New York: Monthly Review Press, 1979), 366.

29. "How to Tame a Wild Tongue," in Gloria Anzaldúa, *Borderlands/La Frontera: The New Mestiza* (San Francisco: Spinsters/Aunt Lute, 1987), 59.

30. Cherrie Moraga, "Preface," *This Bridge Called My Back: Writings by Radical Women of Color* (Watertown, Mass.: Persephone Press, 1981; repr., New York: Kitchen Table/Women of Color Press, 1983), xv.

31. Smith, "Racism and Women's Studies," in *The Truth That Never Hurts* (New Brunswick, N.J.: Rutgers University Press, 1998), 96.

32. Ruth Frankenberg, *White Women, Race Matters: The Social Construction of Whiteness* (Minneapolis: University of Minnesota Press, 1993), 6.

33. Gloria Yamato, "Something About the Subject Makes It Hard to Name," in Anzaldúa, *Haciendo Caras,* 23–24.

34. Reagon, "Coalition Politics," 359.

35. Maxine Baca Zinn and Bonnie Thornton Dill, "Theorizing Difference from Multiracial Feminism," *Feminist Studies* 22:2 (1996), 321; Collins, *Black Feminist Thought,* 326; Barkley Brown, "African American Women," 921.

36. Donna Haraway, "A Cyborg Manifesto: Science, Technology, and Socialist-Feminism in the Late Twentieth Century," in *Simians, Cyborgs, and Women* (New York: Routledge, 1991), 150, 155.

37. Chela Sandoval, "U.S. Third World Feminism: The Theory and Method of Oppositional Consciousness in

the Postmodern World," *Genders* 10 (spring 1991), 1–24; Paula M. L. Moya, "Postmodernism, 'Realism' and the Politics of Identity: Cherríe Moraga and Chicana Feminism," in *Feminist Genealogies, Colonial Legacies, Democratic Futures,* eds. M. Jacqui Alexander and Chandra Talpade Mohanty (New York: Routledge, 1997), 125–50.

38. Audre Lorde, "The Master's Tools Will Never Dismantle the Master's House," *Sister Outsider* (Freedom, Calif.: Crossing Press, 1984), 112.

BIBLIOGRAPHIC NOTES

1. Overviews of the early women's rights and feminist movements in the United States include Eleanor Flexner, *Century of Struggle: The Woman's Rights Movement in the United States* (Cambridge: Belknap Press of Harvard University Press, 1959, reprinted 1996) and Steven Buechler, *Women's Movements in the U.S.: Woman Suffrage, Equal Rights, and Beyond* (New Brunswick: Rutgers University Press, 1990). On racial conflicts in the nineteenth century, see Ellen Carol Dubois, *Feminism and Suffrage: The Emergence of An Independent Women's Movement in America, 1848–1869* (Ithaca: Cornell University Press, 1978), Louise Michelle Newman, *White Women's Rights: The Racial Origins of Feminism in the United States* (New York: Oxford University Press, 1999) and Aileen Kraditor, *The Ideas of the Woman Suffrage Movement, 1890–1920* (New York: W. W. Norton, 1965). On changing female consciousness see Nancy Cott, *The Bonds of Womanhood: "Woman's Sphere" in New England, 1780–1835,* (New Haven: Yale University Press, 1977), and *The Grounding of Modern Feminism* (New Haven: Yale University Press, 1987). In addition to Sara Evans' discussion of the origins of radical feminism in *Personal Politics: The Roots of Women's Liberation in the Civil Rights Movement and the New Left* (New York: Vintage Books, 1979), Ruth Rosen provides a thorough account of second-wave movements in *The World Split Open: How the Modern Women's Movement Changed America* (New York: Viking, 2000). Alice Echols, *Daring to Be Bad: Radical Feminism in America, 1967–1975* (Minneapolis: University of Minnesota Press, 1989) critiques cultural feminism.

2. Primary sources not otherwise cited in the text include Shulamith Firestone, *The Dialectic of Sex: The Case for Feminist Revolution* (New York: Morrow, 1970); Robin Morgan, ed., *Sisterhood Is Powerful: An Anthology of Writings from the Women's Liberation Movement* (New York: Random House, 1970); Anne Koedt, Ellen Levine, and Anita Rapone, eds., *Radical Feminism* (New York: Quadrangle, 1973). Several recent books collect sources from U.S. feminism: Karen Kahn, ed., *Frontline Feminism, 1975–1985: Essays from Sojourner's First 20 Years* (San Francisco: Aunt Lute, 1995); Barbara A. Crow, ed., *Radical Feminism: A Documentary Reader* (New York: New York University Press, 2000) and Rosalyn Baxandall and Linda Gordon, eds., *Dear Sisters: Dispatches From the Women's Liberation Movement* (New York: Basic Books, 2000).

3. On the relationship of women's movements to slavery, abolitionism, emancipation, and lynching, see Deborah Gray White, *Ar'n't I a Woman: Female Slaves in the Plantation South* (New York: W. W. Norton, 1985) and *Too Heavy a Load: Black Women in Defense of Themselves, 1894–1994* (New York: W. W. Norton, 1999); Shirley J. Lee, *Black Women Abolitionists: A Study in Activism, 1828–1860* (Knoxville: University of Tennessee Press, 1992); Lora Romero, *Home Fronts: Domesticity and its Critics in the Antebellum United States* (Durham: Duke University Press, 1997); Nell Irwin Painter, *Sojourner Truth: A Life, a Symbol* (New York: W. W. Norton, 1996); Gerda Lerner, *The Grimké Sisters from South Carolina: Pioneers for Woman's Rights and Abolition* (New York: Schocken Books, 1971); Jacquelyn Dowd Hall, *Revolt Against Chivalry: Jessie Daniel Ames and the Women's Campaign Against Lynching* (Watertown, Mass.: Columbia University Press, 1979); and essays in Kimberly Springer, ed., *Still Lifting, Still Climbing: African American Women's Contemporary Activism* (New York: New York University Press, 1999).

4. Important contemporary works by African American feminists include bell hooks, *Ain't I a Woman: Black Women and Feminism* (Boston: South End Press, 1981) and *Feminist Theory: From Margins to Center* (Boston: South End Press, 1984, reprinted 2000); Angela Y. Davis, *Women, Race and Class* (New York: Random House, 1981); Gloria T. Hull, Patricia Bell Scott, and Barbara Smith, eds., *All the Women Are White, All the Men Are Black, but Some of Us Are Brave* (Old Westbury, N.Y.: Feminist Press, 1982); Audre Lorde, *Zami: A New Spelling of My Name* (Watertown, Mass.: Persephone Press, 1982); Barbara Smith, ed., *Home Girls: A Black Feminist Anthology* (New Brunswick: Rutgers University Press, 2000), and *The Truth That Never Hurts: Writings on Race, Gender, and Freedom* (New Brunswick: Rutgers University Press, 1998); Patricia Hill Collins, *Black Feminist Thought: Knowledge, Consciousness, and the Politics of Empowerment* (Boston: Unwin Hyman, 1990, reprinted 2000).

5. Organizing among women of color is discussed in Judy Yung, *Unbound Feet: A Social History of Chinese Women in San Francisco* (Berkeley: University of California Press, 1995); Karen Anderson, *Changing Woman: A History of Racial Ethnic Women in Modern America* (New York: Oxford University Press, 1996); and Vicki L. Ruiz, *From Out of the Shadows: Mexican Women in Twentieth-Century America* (New York: Oxford University Press, 1998). On intercultural relations among women, see Peggy Pascoe, *Relations of Rescue: The Search for Female Moral Authority in the American West, 1874–1939* (New York: Oxford University Press, 1990). Paula Gunn Allen writes about Native American women's history and culture in *The Sacred Hoop: Recovering the Feminine in American Indian Traditions* (Boston: Beacon Press, 1992).

6. Contemporary Chicana feminism is the subject of Alma M. García, "The Development of Chicana Feminist Discourse, 1970–1980," in *Unequal Sisters: A Multicultural Reader in U.S. Women's History,* eds. Vicki L. Ruiz and Ellen Carol DuBois, Ist ed. (New York: Routledge,

1990), 418–31, and Alma M. García, ed., *Chicana Feminist Thought: The Basic Historical Writings* (New York: Routledge, 1997); Beatriz M. Pesquera and Denise A. Segura, "There Is No Going Back: Chicanas and Feminism," in *Chicana Critical Issues*, eds. Norma Alarcon et al. (Berkeley: Third Woman Press, 1993); Ramón Gutiérrez, "Community, Patriarchy, and Individualism: The Politics of Chicano History and the Dream of Equality," in *Unequal Sisters: A Multicultural Reader in U.S. Women's History*, eds. Vicki L. Ruiz and Ellen Carol DuBois, 3rd ed. (New York: Routledge, 2000), 587–606. Gloria Anzaldúa, *Borderlands/La Frontera: The New Mestiza* (San Francisco: Spinsters/Aunt Lute, 1987) and *Making Face, Making Soul/Haciendo Caras: Creative and Critical Perspectives by Feminists of Color* (San Francisco: Aunt Lute Books, 1990) document the politics of multiple identity since the 1970s, as does Anzaldúa and Cherríe Moraga, eds., *This Bridge Called My Back: Writings by Radical Women of Color* (Watertown, Mass.: Persephone Press, 1981). See also Cherríe Moraga, *Loving in the War Years: Lo Que Nunca Pasó Por Sus Labios* (Boston: South End Press, 1983) and M. Jacqui Alexander, ed., *Third Wave: Feminist Perspectives on Racism* (Brooklyn: Kitchen Table/Women of Color Press, 1994).

7. On women in labor, pacifist, and liberal movements, see Dorothy Sue Cobble, "Recapturing Working-Class Feminism: Union Women in the Postwar Era," in *Not June Cleaver: Women and Gender in Postwar America, 1945–1960*, ed. Joanne Meyerowitz (Philadelphia: Temple University Press, 1994), 56–83; Susan Lynn, *Progressive Women in Conservative Times: Racial Justice, Peace, and Feminism, 1945 to the 1960s* (New Brunswick: Rutgers University Press, 1992); Susan Hartmann, *The Other Feminists: Activists in the Liberal Establishment* (New Haven: Yale University Press, 1998); and Blanche Wiesen Cook, *Eleanor Roosevelt* (New York: Viking, 1992). On women's racist activities, see Kathleen M. Blee, *Women of the Klan: Racism and Gender in the 1920s* (Berkeley: University of California Press, 1991).

8. Important contemporary explorations of race, racism, and identities include Bettina Aptheker, "Race and Class: Patriarchal Politics and Women's Experience," *Women's Studies Quarterly* 10:4 (1982), 10–15; Ruth Frankenberg, *White Women, Race Matters: The Social Construction of Whiteness* (Minneapolis: University of Minnesota Press, 1993); Vron Ware, *Beyond the Pale: White Women, Racism, and History* (London: Verso, 1992); Elizabeth V. Spelman, *Inessential Woman: Problems of Exclusion in Feminist Thought* (Boston: Beacon Press, 1988); Diana Fuss, *Essentially Speaking: Feminism, Nature and Difference* (New York: Routledge, 1989); Donna Haraway, "A Cyborg Manifesto: Science, Technology, and Socialist-Feminism in the Late Twentieth Century," in *Simians, Cyborgs, and Women: The Reinvention of Nature,* (New York: Routledge, 1991); Judith Butler, *Gender Trouble: Feminism and the Subversion of Identity* (New York: Routledge, 1990); Chela Sandoval, "U.S. Third World Feminism: The Theory and Method of Oppositional Consciousness in the Postmodern

World," *Genders* 10 (1991), 1–24; Maria C. Lugones and Elizabeth V. Spelman, "Have We Got a Theory for You! Feminist Theory, Cultural Imperialism and the Demand for 'The Woman's Voice,'" *Women's Studies International Forum* 6:6 (1983), 573–81; Linda Martín Alcoff, "Cultural Feminism vs. Poststructuralism: The Identity Crisis in Feminist Theory," *Signs* 13:3 (1988), 405–36 and "Philosophy and Racial Identity," *Philosophy Today* (spring, 1997), 67–76; Paula M. L. Moya, "Chicana Feminism and Postmodernist Theory," *Signs* 26:2 (2001), 441–83, and *Reclaiming Identity: Realist Theory and the Predicament of Postmodernism*, eds. Paula M. L. Moya and Michael R. Hames-García (Berkeley: University of California Press, 2000); and essays in Teresa de Lauretis, ed., *Feminist Studies/Critical Studies* (Bloomington: Indiana University Press, 1986). On the use of experience in feminist theory, see, e.g., Patricia J. Williams, *The Alchemy of Race and Rights: Diary of a Law Professor* (Cambridge: Harvard University Press, 1991). For a critique, see Joan Scott, "The Evidence of Experience," *Critical Inquiry* 17:4 (1991), 773–97.

 39

From Outsider to Citizen

STEVEN SEIDMAN

The 1950s and 1960s were not easy times to be different. The Cold War, the red scare, and a culture of patriotism promoted a narrow ideal of the American citizen. He loved his country, worked hard, married the girl next door, and fathered happy children. (Or, loved her country, stayed at home, and was a dutiful wife and mother.) This good citizen was, of course, heterosexual, preferably white, middle class, and churchgoing, and took front and center stage with a vengeance. Think of Ward and June Cleaver. As this nation aggressively made heterosexuality into a condition of citizenship, gays became "aliens," outsiders in a nation that many had just recently risked their lives for.

Many gays in the 1950s and 1960s perhaps suffered more because they were damned to silence and invisibility than because of an open, aggressive homophobic culture (something that truly crystallized after Stonewall). We need to be mindful that gays barely registered on the screen of popular culture in the immediate postwar years.[1] Outside major urban centers it is likely that few people were either very aware of, or particularly exercised over, the issue of homosexuality. Career, marriage, family making, home, the Soviet threat—these were the preoccupations of most Americans.

Ironically, the barely noticed presence of gays allowed some of them to carve out inconspicuous social lives. These often courageous individuals cautiously sought out those few public spaces where others like themselves could be found. Despite considerable risk, gay men searched out cruising spaces (parks, tearooms, highway stops, YMCAs), while lesbians discovered each other in such spaces as bars and softball leagues.[2]

But these tentative steps into public life were marked by a sense of fear. The places where gays gathered were often under surveillance and lacked a solid institutional footing. Bars would be raided and closed down; parks and tearooms were subject to police patrols; and softball leagues were seasonal. There was risk, often great, for anyone who ventured into these public places. Gays were vulnerable to arrest, harassment, violence, and public exposure, which threatened social disgrace and worse.

In the day-to-day struggle to eke out some sense of a gay life, individuals encountered a government intent on preventing this. Gays not only lacked basic legal rights (for example, to freely associate), but they encountered governmental authorities (federal, state, and local) that were aggressively turning against them. Moral reformers, politicians, and public officials wishing to brandish their moral purity enlisted the state to persecute homosexuals. Perhaps the most infamous of the time, and now known to have been a closeted homosexual himself, was the director of the FBI, J. Edgar Hoover. In this atmosphere of heightened risk and fear, many individuals understandably chose to pass as straight. The closet was a product of both cultural defilement and the repressive, coercive power of the state.

If the social status of gays has changed between the 1950s and today, it is not only because of a change in American culture. Stepping outside the closet would not have been possible without at least some individuals and some elites (e.g., newspaper editors, writers, or politicians) redefining homosexuality as something natural and good. Yet tens of thousands of Americans can today choose to live outside the closet only because the state has retreated from its campaigns of homosexual persecution.

GAYS AS "ALIENS"

From the founding years of America through the nineteenth century, sex laws were passed with the primary aim of strengthening marriage. Nonmarital and nonprocreative sexual behaviors were proscribed. Accordingly, a wide range of sexual practices, from fornication and adultery to "lewd and lascivious" behavior, were criminalized. A culture of sexual respectability took shape that valued sex only between married adults in the privacy of their home and for the purpose of procreation.[3]

Through most of the nineteenth century, the American government was not especially involved in regulating homosexuality, at least not enough to direct the criminal justice system to aggressively suppress homosexual behavior. The very term *homosexual*, or terms like *invert* and *Urning* that circulated in Europe in the nineteenth century, were absent from the American vernacular.[4] In fact, there were no laws that focused exclusively on homosexuality.[5] Homosexual behavior was classified and punished under the category of "sodomy." Initially understood as a sinful immoral act, in the course of the nineteenth century sodomy was reinterpreted as a criminal offense that included a wide spectrum of nonprocreative, nonmarital sexual acts such as oral or anal sex or sex with an animal.[6] The fact that few individuals were convicted of homosexual sodomy until the last decades of the nineteenth century speaks to its marginal status in Victorian sexual culture.[7] At the same time, the adoption of sodomy laws by most states and the severity of the punishment for those convicted (whipping, banishment, and imprisonment) speaks to the status of homosexual behavior as outside of respectable society.

Restricting sex to a private, marital, and procreative act was the idea. Victorians believed that sex should have a high moral purpose. Sex should be a way to display moral self-control and could acquire meaning as a selfless act under the guise of the need to create a family. The realities of the time no doubt greatly disappointed the keepers of moral virtue. A world of illicit sex flourished, especially in seaports, mining towns, and large cities.[8] Regulating sexual behavior was by and large the responsibility of the family, churches, and various moral reform and purity groups. The state mostly stayed out of the business of regulating its citizens' intimate affairs. For example, although contraception and abortion [were] illegal, these practices were widespread and barely regulated by the state.

In the course of the nineteenth century, this laissez-faire state practice was criticized for being unable to address what some people viewed as threats to the Victorian ideal of sexual respectability. Pornography and prostitution were somewhat tolerated, so long as these vices were far removed from respectable society. This sexual underworld, however, began to find its way into the lives of ordinary Americans through romance novels and magazines. The very heart of Victorian culture, its ideal of marriage, seemed threatened by another, unprecedented development: the rise of divorce. By the 1920s, scholars estimate, one in six marriages was ending in divorce.[9] In short, the Victorian cultural ideal of sexual respectability was threatened by a new set of realities that were becoming undeniable: a world of sex outside marriage.

Sensing a crisis in American sexual culture, social reformers turned to the state to enforce a Victorian sexual morality. Against the grain of a long-standing American tradition that championed privacy, the state took greater responsibility for regulating individuals' sexual lives.

Between 1860 and 1890, forty states enacted anti-abortion statutes.[10] This legislation was initially spearheaded by a variety of so-called purity groups and moral crusaders. Medical doctors soon joined the battle to end abortion. A fledging American Medical Association sought to enhance its power in relation to other medical practitioners by backing the criminalization of abortion. The historians John

D'Emilio and Estelle Freedman write that "by the end of the century, the physicians campaign to criminalize abortion had succeeded. . . . Congress had outlawed the dissemination of birth control information through the mails; many states restricted the sale or advertising of contraceptive devices. . . . Comstock was waging a ceaseless battle to enforce these laws. . . . Large sectors of the medical profession were declaring against artificial methods to limit fertilization. Birth control information had virtually been driven underground."[11]

Paralleling this campaign against abortion, an alliance of suffragists, purity crusaders, and the AMA backed sweeping anti-prostitution legislation. For example, the American Social Hygiene Association proposed legislation that would give states wide latitude in regulating commercial sex. Provisions such as the "Red Light Abatement Acts" would authorize states to regulate saloons, dance halls, and bars, as well as the people that owned and managed them. Another statute permitted ordinary citizens to petition to close places suspected of harboring prostitutes. Such aggressive, far-reaching anti-prostitution laws were promoted in state after state. As the sociologist Kristin Luker notes, "By 1920, ten states had passed laws that enacted these provisions . . . and thirty-two states had laws that enacted at least some of these provisions."[12]

Social groups enlisting the state to defend the purity of women, marriage, and the family also launched an attack on public sexual images. The courts and state legislatures expanded the legal meaning of obscenity in order to suppress sexual representations in public life. "The American courts heard very few obscenity cases between 1821 and 1870. . . . Only four state legislatures enacted obscenity laws prior to the civil war." However, in 1873 the Congress passed "an act for the suppression of trade in, and circulation of obscene literature and articles of immoral use."[13] By the early twentieth century, virtually every state monitored books, art, or magazines for their sexual content; this extended beyond pulp novels and pornography to literary publications and sex-education and birth-control documents.

Finally, a powerful eugenics movement successfully enlisted the state to promote an aggressive policy of sterilization. Invoking fears of the spread of sexual immorality and mental feebleness stemming from interracial intimacy, this movement targeted people of color, the poor, rebellious youths, immigrants, and other unruly, outsider groups for sterilization. Legal scholars Linda Hirshman and Jane Larson observe, "By 1930 half of the states had enacted compulsory sterilization laws. These laws covered convicted criminals, but also persons considered 'feebleminded' or suspected of 'sexual immorality.' In the first third of the century, approximately 20,000 involuntary sterilizations were performed by order of state law."[14]

By the early twentieth century, birth control, abortion, interracial marriage, prostitution, commercial sex, forced sterilization, and public sexual representations had become the business of the state. The state now exercised unprecedented control of the sexual-intimate lives of Americans. "Sex law, once limited to prohibiting adultery, rape and whoredom or lewd behavior, by the end of the nineteenth century ran to pages of elaborate and detailed prohibitions."[15]

While the web of governmental control of heterosexual behavior expanded by leaps and bounds between the 1860s and World War I, homosexuality was only marginally targeted. For example, in his highly regarded book *Gay New York*, the historian George Chauncey argues that while laws prohibiting cross-dressing, loitering, solicitation, and public lewdness were sometimes used to control homosexuality, New York municipal authorities were erratic in their persecution of homosexuals.[16] There was an informal understanding that gays were to be tolerated so long as they moderated their public visibility. In fact, Chauncey documents a fairly robust public gay life that in many respects was integrated into the mainstream of New York. Contrary to standard accounts of the pre-Stonewall past as blanketed by silence and invisibility, Chauncey holds that, at least in New York, an open gay life flourished in bars, cafés, speakeasies, certain streets, cafeterias, and grand balls.[17]

In the years between the two world wars, the tide slowly, if unevenly, began to turn. State control of consensual heterosexual adult behavior was relaxed. For example, a flourishing birth-control movement challenged its criminalization. Restrictive birth-control legislation such as laws prohibiting the advertising of birth-control devices were repealed. One result was the takeoff of the condom industry and the easy availability of condoms. Another result was the establishment in 1942 of the Planned Parenthood Federation of America. Championing contraception as a legitimate strategy of family planning, birth-control clinics cropped up in cities and towns across the country. And while abortions were still illegal, they were widespread and rarely prosecuted. Similarly, by the 1940s sexually provocative images began to regularly appear in the public realm. Big business had discovered that sex sells, and artists and writers found in sex a powerful avenue to explore the character of personal and social life in America. This new sexual openness was met with opposition by organizations such as the National Organization of Decent Literature, but the tide had already turned.

The retreat of the state from controlling consensual adult heterosexual conduct and expression continued in the decades following World War II. State liberalization is evident in sex-law reforms and court decisions.

In 1962, the Model Penal Code became the most important guide to legal reform through the 1970s and 1980s.[18] A product of the American Law Institute, sex law was recast in a way to expand personal choice. The code aimed to decriminalize adult consensual behavior. Its guiding idea was that sex is an individual right. Sex was thought to be so integral to individual well-being that sexual choice needed to be protected from the arbitrary interference of other citizens and the government.

The code became the model for criminal legal reform; it shaped a series of key court decisions that expanded sexual rights. For example, in *Skinner v. Oklahoma* (1942) the courts struck down the practice of sterilizing individuals convicted of a wide range of nonsexual crimes. Subsequent court decisions decriminalized fornication and declared unconstitutional laws that banned or limited birth-control practices such as the use of contraceptives. In *Griswold v. Connecticut* (1965) the Supreme Court declared state laws that criminalized the use of contraceptives by married couples unconstitutional. The Court appealed to a zone of privacy in marriage that was said to be established by the Constitution. This court decision in effect recognized the legitimacy of nonprocreative sex. In *Eisenstadt v. Baird* (1972), the courts extended this protection to unmarried couples. Nowhere has the retreat of the state from intimate life been more apparent than in the sphere of the heterosexual family. One scholar has argued that "over the past twenty-five years, family law has become increasingly privatized. In virtually all doctrinal areas, private norm creation and private decision making have supplanted state-imposed rules and structures for governing family-related behavior."[19] In short, a clear trend in court rulings defined sex as an important sphere of personal expression or individual choice that, like religious or occupational choice, merits state protection.

The legal safeguarding of consensual adult heterosexual behavior in private was paralleled by the liberalization of laws regulating public sex speech. In *Roth v. U.S.* (1957), the Supreme Court ruled that "obscenity" covers only sex speech that appeals to clear prurient interests. Subsequent cases further weakened obscenity laws. In *Memoirs of a Woman of Pleasure v. Mass.* (1966), the court narrowed what was to be considered obscene to material "utterly without redeeming social importance." In *Miller v. Ca.* (1973) the Court further liberalized public sex speech by appealing to "community standards" as the criteria to determine obscenity. Commenting on the consequences of the retreat of the state from regulating public sexual materials, D'Emilio and Freedman write, "From the 1930s onward . . . the courts in the United States steadily narrowed the definition of obscenity until . . . they had virtually removed barriers . . . against the presentation of sexual matter in literature and other media."[20]

By strengthening a zone of privacy that included sex, and by expanding protections for public sex speech, the postwar state enlarged the sphere of sexual autonomy for heterosexual adults. These reforms in sex laws were a return to long-standing American traditions championing minimal state regulation of consensual adult intimate behavior.[21]

As the state was relaxing controls over heterosexual behavior, homosexuality became the focus of considerable social regulation between the 1930s and 1960s. For the first time in American history, the state mobilized its growing authority and resources to control same-sex behavior.

Gay individuals initially stepped into the public eye in the later decades of the nineteenth century. If ordinary citizens weren't directly exposed to such individuals, newspapers began to report gatherings of so-called sexual and gender deviants. Already geared up to combat vice of all kinds, the guardians of a Victorian morality expanded the scope of their crusade to include people who engaged in sodomy. The state was enlisted to suppress these acts of sexual and gender deviance. Existing laws were now being enforced, and new legislation was enacted to address this perceived social danger.[22] In particular, cross-dressing laws figured prominently because of the association of homosexuality with gender inversion. Despite agitation by moral crusaders, governmental agencies acted spottily rather than launching a full-scale methodical campaign of homosexual persecution.

This changed in the 1930s and dramatically so in the postwar period: the state stepped forward as the chief guardian of a respectable heterosexual order. Homosexuals were to be pursued, persecuted, and prosecuted. Chauncey writes,

> The very growth and visibility of the gay subculture during the Prohibition years of the 1920s and 1930s precipitated a powerful cultural reaction in the 1930s [and] . . . a new anxiety about homosexuals and hostility toward them. . . . A host of laws and regulations were enacted or newly enforced in the 1930s that suppressed the largest of the drag balls, censored lesbian and gay images in plays and films, and prohibited restaurants, bars, and clubs from employing homosexuals or even serving them.[23]

By the 1950s and 1960s, as homosexuals were being publicly demonized as an invisible, menacing threat, government agencies were issuing executive orders and enacting new laws aimed at persecuting them. Homosexuals, real or suspected, were routinely arrested and their names and places of employment often printed in newspapers; they were discharged from the military and civil service; denied immigration; harassed in bars and the streets; their businesses or businesses they frequented were closed; and their publications were censored and destroyed.

The legal scholar William Eskridge summarizes the status of the homosexual in 1960:

> The homosexual in 1961 was smothered by law. She or he risked arrest . . . for dancing with someone of the same sex, cross dressing, propositioning another adult homosexual, possessing a homophile publication, writing about homosexuality without disapproval, displaying pictures of two people of the same sex in intimate positions, operating a lesbian or gay bar, or actually having oral or anal sex with another adult homosexual. . . . Misdemeanor arrests for sex related vagrancy or disorderly conduct offences meant that the homosexual might have her or his name published in the local newspaper, would probably lose her or his job. . . . If the homosexual were not a citizen, she or he would likely be deported. If the homosexual were a professional . . . she or he would lose the certification needed to practice that profession. If the charged homosexual were a member of the armed forces, she or he might be court-martialed and would likely be dishonorably discharged and lose all veterans benefits.[24]

Eskridge concludes, "This new legal regime represented society's coercive effort to normalize human relationships around 'heterosexuality.'"[25] The effort by the state to "normalize" heterosexuality between the 1930s and 1960s helped create what we've come to call the closet.

BECOMING CITIZENS

Sex laws and policies are guided by a norm of the good sexual citizen. By criminalizing and disenfranchising certain sexual acts, identities, or intimate arrangements, the state helps to create a sexual hierarchy. Some acts or identities are tolerated but barely; others are not tolerated at all; still other sexual expressions are deemed so intolerable that those who engage in them are scandalized as "bad sexual citizens"—immoral and dangerous to society. Bad sexual citizens become the targets of social control, which may include public stereotyping, harassment, violence, criminalization, and disenfranchisement. In the early decades of the twentieth century, women who had children out of wedlock, sexually active youths, adults who sexually desired youths, and individuals who engaged in interracial sex were often labeled bad sexual citizens.

The good sexual citizen was most definitely heterosexual. However, it was only after World War II that homosexuals became perhaps the personification of the bad sexual citizen. As they took on the role of a social and moral menace, a network of controls evolved that had the effect of creating the closet. And the closet clearly marked gays as outsiders, as moral, social, and political aliens.

As the closet became the defining reality for many gay Americans, a political movement took shape that challenged this condition. This movement was and still is divided between, roughly speaking, a "liberationist" and an "assimilationist" ideology and agenda.

If assimilationists aim to broaden the notion of the good sexual citizen to include homosexuals, liberationists challenge this ideal. If the norm of the good sexual citizen defines sex exclusively as a private act, liberationists defend public forms of sexuality (for example, sex in parks, tearooms, or bath houses); if the ideal sexual citizen is gender conventional, liberationists aim to scramble gender norms such that being active or passive, aggressive or submissive, is not coded as masculine or feminine; if the good sexual citizen tightly binds sex to love or intimacy, liberationists relax the bond, allowing for legitimate sex within and outside intimacy; and if the ideal sexual citizen is married, liberationists advocate either the end of state regulation of adult intimate relationships or state recognition of a diversity of families. In short, assimilationists want homosexuals to be recognized and accepted as good sexual citizens; liberationists challenge the sexual norms associated with this ideal.

A liberationist politics emerged after the Stonewall rebellions in 1969.[26] Liberationists opposed the system of compulsory heterosexuality that produced the closet. They were also critical of the assimilationist politics of the Mattachine Society and the Daughters of Bilitis, which, they argued, left heterosexual domination in place.

Gay liberationism arose during a time of extraordinary social turmoil. The protests against the Vietnam War and the rise of militant, in-your-face movements for racial and gender justice stirred hopes of revolutionary change. Liberationists absorbed the spirit of radical feminism, lesbian feminism, and black liberation. Gays were not just the targets of prejudice and discrimination but were oppressed by a heterosexual dictatorship. Writes one liberationist, "One is oppressed as a homosexual every minute of every day, inasmuch as one is restrained from acting in ways that would seem normal to a heterosexual. Every time one refrains from an act of public affection with a lover—in the park, on the movie line—one dies a little. And gay people, of course, die a little every day. . . . Everything in society—every movie, every billboard, everything. . . reminds the gay person that what he or she is is unnatural, abnormal."[27] Liberation required dismantling the "system." The fight for gay justice was viewed as inseparable from struggles to transform gender roles, the institution of marriage and the family, and the political economy of capitalism and imperialism.[28] Challenging gay oppression meant changing America, from top to bottom.

The early 1970s were the heroic years for gay liberationism. Groups such as the Gay Liberation Front, the Fairies, the Furies, and Radicalesbians created their own political organizations, published newspapers, newsletters, and books, and forged distinctive cultures with their own ideologies. They marched, organized sit-ins, met with newspaper editors, appeared on television, published manifestos, and formed alliances with other movements. Their militancy and almost swaggering sense of

pride and confidence was for many individuals a welcome departure from the subdued, cautious politics of assimilationism that had dominated the 1950s and 1960s. For a moment it looked as if liberationism would become the chief political and cultural force in gay life.

This did not happen. By the mid-1970s, gay liberationism virtually disappeared as an organized political movement. Many liberationist groups dissolved or were greatly weakened by the incessant battles over ideology and strategy. Their Marxist or radical feminist rhetoric, which portrayed America as fundamentally corrupt and in need of a revolution, alienated many gays who gravitated toward reform-minded groups such as the Gay Activist Alliance. In the end, liberationism proved more effective in shifting gay politics away from the cautious assimilationism of the previous decades than at mobilizing mass support for its own radical vision and agenda.

Liberationists never managed more than a marginal presence in organized gay politics after the mid-1970s. Yet artists, writers, activists, and academics have sustained its critical spirit. And, in response to AIDS and an organized anti-gay politics from the late 1970s onward, a broadly liberationist political agenda surfaced in the organized politics of ACT UP, Queer Nation, Lesbian Avengers, and Sex Panic![29] Except perhaps for ACT UP, none of these groups managed more than a short-lived organizational life. Liberationism lives on primarily as a cultural sensibility.

An assimilationist agenda has been and still is the driving force of the gay movement.[30] Although there are differences among assimilationists, they share an agenda aimed at bringing the homosexual into the circle of sexual citizenship. These reformers do not wish to change America beyond altering the status of gays from outsider to citizen. An assimilationist agenda does not necessarily protest the dominant status of heterosexuality; it's about minority rights, not toppling the majority. Nor do these reformers wish to challenge the broader spectrum of sexual-intimate norms that govern behavior, such as the norm of marriage, monogamy, or gender norms of sexuality. Assimilationists press

America to live up to its promise of equal treatment of all of its citizens; they wish to be a part of what is considered a basically good nation; this requires reform, not revolution.[31]

In the initial wave of political organizing in the 1950s, the focus of an assimilationist politics was to end the harassment and persecution of homosexuals that was sanctioned and often initiated by the state. The key political organizations of the time were the male-oriented Mattachine Society and female-organized Daughters of Bilitis.[32] Without much public fanfare, these organizations cautiously but courageously, given the times, challenged state-driven discrimination. They protested the firing of homosexuals by government agencies and their persecution by the random enforcement of laws such as those prohibiting loitering, solicitation, lewdness, or cross-dressing. However, because they believed that the source of prejudice is ignorance or a misinformed view of homosexuals as different and dangerous, their chief political strategy was public education. Through sponsoring public talks, promoting research, and encouraging positive public role models to step forward, these organizations sought to persuade the public that homosexuals are no different from heterosexuals. The Mattachine Society declared that its chief task was to "dispel the idea that the sex variant is unique, 'queer' or unusual, but is instead a human being with the same capacities of feelings, thinking and accomplishment as any other human being."[33] The ultimate purpose was to end legal discrimination and public stereotyping; social integration would mean the end of the homosexual as a separate identity and subculture.

As the 1950s gave way to the 1960s a gay movement pursuing an assimilationist agenda grew more confident. Appealing to constitutional principles of privacy, due process, and basic rights of free speech and association, municipalities were taken to court to end street harassment and police entrapment, to halt bar raids and unnecessary search and seizure, and to stop government actions that shut down businesses catering to gays. For example, the California State Supreme Court and legislature took giant steps in deregulating consensual same-sex adult behavior by narrowing the meaning of public decency, lewdness, and vagrancy statutes so that they could no longer be used to persecute homosexuals. Most impressively, invoking recent judicial rulings gay organizations successfully challenged obscenity laws that were used to censor gay public speech (for example, in gay magazines, newsletters, books, art, and pornography).

By the mid-1970s, provoked and inspired by the defiant spirit of liberationism, a more assertive rights-oriented gay movement challenged laws that criminalized homosexuality. In the aftermath of the Griswold, Eisenstadt, and Stanley Supreme Court decisions, gay rights advocates argued that acknowledging the fundamental role of sexuality in personal liberty, which was at the heart of cases that extended privacy rights to adult private consensual sex, should apply to homosexuals as well. Appealing to a constitutional right to privacy and equal treatment, state laws that criminalized sodomy were challenged. By 1983, twenty-five states had decriminalized consensual sodomy, while eleven states reduced sodomy to a misdemeanor. In the 1990s, many states and cities banned anti-gay discrimination in state employment. And, while Congress has continued to block federal civil rights legislation that would include sexual orientation, the Civil Service Commission and ultimately a executive order by President Clinton, ended legal job discrimination in all federal agencies.

Strategies aimed at decriminalizing homosexuality were supplemented by deliberate efforts at gaining equal civil rights. From the mid-1970s on, the gay movement turned its attention and resources to gaining positive rights. In small towns and large cities across the country, organizations dedicated to enacting gay rights ordinances were formed. And well-financed, professional national organizations such as the Lambda Legal Defense, the National Lesbian and Gay Task Force, and the Human Rights Campaign made gaining equal civil rights the chief aim of a national gay movement. The intent of so-called gay rights laws is to get the state to recognize lesbians and gay men as citizens deserving the same positive liberties and protections as any other citizen. In the course of the 1970s, there were few victories—only forty communities passed gay rights. However, by 2000 the number had swelled to well over three hundred. Moreover, gay rights laws are no longer confined to urban centers but have been passed in small towns and suburban communities, and not just in the northeast and west, but in the south, midwest, and northwest. The wave of domestic partnership law beginning in the mid-1990s is indicative of moderate but real success at legal integration. By the late 1990s, 421 cities and states, and over 3,500 businesses or institutions of higher education offered some form of domestic partner benefit.[34]

William Eskridge summarizes the considerable gains toward legal and social integration during this period:

> The gay rights movement had won many successes by 1981—judicial nullification or legislative repeal of laws criminalizing consensual sodomy in most jurisdictions, of almost all state criminal laws targeting same-sex intimacy, and municipal cross-dressing ordinances, of the immigration and citizenship exclusions, of all censorship laws targeting same-sex eroticism, of almost all laws or regulations prohibiting bars from becoming congregating places for gay people, and of exclusions of gay people from public employment in most jurisdictions. . . . Since 1981 an increasing number of states and cities have adopted laws affirmatively protecting gay people against private discrimination and violence, recognizing gay families as domestic partnerships, and allowing second-parent adoptions by a party of a same-sex partner.[35]

This wave of legal reform made possible a "post-closeted regime where openly gay people could participate in the public culture."[36]

Legal reform has brought gays into the national community, but not as equal citizens. The battle over the meaning of legal and social equality has become the chief focus of the gay movement today.

TOLERATED BUT NOT EQUAL

The legal and social integration of gay Americans has not been an unqualified story of success, to say the least. A majority of cities and states lack laws that protect gay people from housing and job discrimination. The Federal Gay and Lesbian Civil Rights Bill, introduced in Congress in 1975, has virtually no hope of passage. The more modest Employment Non-Discrimination Act (ENDA), introduced in 1994, has few realistic prospects of passage at this time. The result: the jobs and homes of the overwhelming majority of gays and lesbians are not legally protected by any local, state, or federal laws. Moreover, anti-gay legislative proposals, at the local and state levels, may very well have exceeded positive legislative efforts in the 1990s. One analyst counts 472 cases of proposed anti-gay legislation.[37] And government policies such as "Don't ask, don't tell" and the Defense of Marriage Act and judicial decisions like *Bowers v. Hartwick* (1986) and *The Boy Scouts of America and Monmouth Council, et al. v. James Dale* (2000) underscore gays' second-class citizenship status.

Many Americans stand opposed to the social integration of gays. They would like to reinstate the conditions of the closet or at least to maintain gays' status as outsiders.

Surveys document continued widespread moral disapproval. Polls through the early 1990s indicate that an overwhelming majority of Americans believed that homosexuality is wrong or immoral.[38] Summarizing data from thirteen surveys between 1973 and 1991, two political scientists conclude, "Between 67 percent and 75 percent of respondents said that 'sexual relations between two adults of the same sex' were 'always wrong.'" However, researchers document a dramatic and unexpected shift in moral attitudes in the mid-1990s. "Surprisingly, given almost twenty years of stability, the percentage saying 'always wrong' dropped 15 percent between 1991 and 1996 [to 56 percent], suggesting the first major decline in disapproval."[39]

Moreover, as survey questions shift from abstract moral beliefs about homosexuality to the morality of discrimination, the trend toward social tolerance is even clearer. A majority of Americans—and in the late 1990s the support has climbed to around 70 to 80 percent—support a wide range of rights for gays. Assessing the available survey data, two researchers conclude, "Americans increasingly support civil liberties for gay people. Between 1973 and 1996, the percentages saying that 'a man who admits he is a homosexual' should 'be allowed to teach in a college' and 'to make a speech in your community' and who would *not* favor taking 'a book he wrote in favor of homosexuality . . . out of your public library' rose steadily by 28, 20, and 15 percent, respectively. By 1996, substantial majorities (75 percent, 81 percent, and 69 percent, respectively) supported each of these rights. Between 1977 and 1996, the percentage saying 'homosexuals should . . . have equal rights in terms of job opportunities' rose 27 percent (to 83 percent)."[40]

★ ★ ★

The push for equal citizenship has exposed the limits of state liberalization. The refusals to grant gays the right to marry and serve in the military stand as telling statements of the government's denial of gays' status as first-class citizens. This opposition may at first glance seem puzzling. After all, heterosexual dominance is hardly in jeopardy if equal rights are extended to a small minority, so what's the big deal?

I think that part of the explanation lies in the connection between the issues of gay equality and national identity. First blacks challenged a white-defined America; Latinos and other people of color followed; then women protested a masculine understanding of national identity. Establishing gay equality would challenge another core feature of American national identity. It would effectively mean, as some members of the Supreme Court understood in *Bowers v. Hartwick,* ending or weakening the historical association of nationhood with heterosexuality. It was Chief Justice White who explicitly repudiated any association of homosexuality with American nationality: "Proscriptions against that conduct [homosexual sodomy] have ancient roots. Sodomy was a criminal offense at common law and was forbidden by the laws of the original 13 states when they ratified the Bill of Rights. . . . In fact, until 1961, all 50 states in the Union outlawed

sodomy . . . Against this background, to claim that a right to engage in such conduct is 'deeply rooted in this nation's history and tradition' . . . is, at best, facetious."[41]

The sexual politics of national identity are at the heart of the conflict over gays in the military and gay marriage. If gays were to openly serve in the military and to marry, this would be a major challenge to the national ideal of the heterosexual citizen.[42]

From this perspective, the military policy of "Don't ask, don't tell" is a striking sign of gays' unequal status and their ambivalent status as not quite outsiders or citizens. The military is not an institution like, say, a bank or a hospital, but it is symbolically linked to Americans' core sense of nationhood. As many scholars remind us, citizenship is not just a legal reality but is symbolic—something we have an idea and ideals about.[43] Serving in the military or being eligible to serve are key markers of being a good American. The strong tie between the military and the nation is captured in the memorializing of soldiers and national wars in the nation's capital and in a popular culture that celebrates military triumphs and heroes. For a fully abled adult to be excluded from military service because of his or her race, national origin, or sexual identity publicly marks the individual as an outsider.

It was perhaps a mistake on Clinton's part to approach the issue of gays in the military as merely a question of rights. As Congress, the military brass, and the American public weighed in, it was apparent that the battle around gays in the military had become part of a symbolic national drama. Some supporters of ending the ban on gays in the military misread the opposition as old-style closet politics. No doubt some critics longed for a return to the days of state-supported homosexual repression. However, opponents may have also understood in a way that Clinton and some gay activists did not that incorporating gays into the military would signal the beginning of the end of the historical association of national identity and heterosexuality. The "Don't ask, don't tell" policy signaled a rejection of gay equality and of any challenge to the heterosexual meaning of American nationhood. Many Americans, not just in the military and Congress, are not ready to uncouple heterosexuality and being an American.

The institution of marriage is equally invested with national significance in American culture. Whether it's the legal restriction of marriage to heterosexuals, the state privileging of heterosexual marriage over all other intimate unions, or the idealization of marriage in popular culture and commerce (for example, the wedding industry), the ideal national citizen is married.[44] Americans may be more tolerant today toward individuals who choose to be single or cohabitate, but these choices occupy a lesser status than marriage. For this reason, the struggle to extend marital rights to gays is as much about symbolic struggles over national identity as about the politics of equality.[45]

The issue of whether the state should, as a matter of morality or law, recognize gay relationships has bounced around the courts for some time.[46] However, in the last decade or so, as lesbians and gay men have been creating stable, long-term families, and as the question of intimate rights became an urgent health-care issue because of the AIDS crisis, the gay movement has made the legal recognition of gay relationships a priority. While some individuals in the gay community oppose gay marriage because it legitimates the state's regulation of intimate life and devalues all nonmarital intimate arrangements, most gays and lesbians consider the denial of the right to marry as compromising their goal of achieving social equality. Gay marriage became a national issue after the Hawaii State Supreme Court, in *Baehr v. Lewin* (1993), ruled that not allowing gays to marry was a form of gender discrimination. However, even before the courts could resolve the issue, the Hawaii legislature acted in 1994 to restrict marriage to heterosexuality. Other states quickly followed suit, and in 1996 the U.S. Congress passed, with the overwhelming support of the Democrats and President Clinton, the Defense of Marriage Act. This reaffirmed a national ideal that defines marriage as an exclusively heterosexual institution.

To summarize, in the last decade or so the gay movement has shifted its focus from tolerance to social equality. Gays want to be equal citizens; we already have the same obligations and duties; we want the same rights, opportunities, and respect as any other American citizen. And while the state and other institutions have retreated significantly from the repressive practices that produced the closet, they have also refused to grant gays equal citizenship. Gays' continued unequal status reflects a public that is still divided over the moral status of homosexuality; it reflects, as well, a public that worries that gay equality means the end of heterosexual privilege and the ideal of a heterosexual national identity.

The declining social significance of the closet can only have the effect of intensifying demands for equality. Gays will not be satisfied with tolerance. As many of us approach being gay as an ordinary and good status, as we live outside the closet, and as our lives have individual integrity and purpose, we will demand full social inclusion and first-class citizenship. There is no turning back to the days of the closet. Efforts to reinstate the closet are a losing cause. And activists who interpret every anti-gay action as evidence of the still-dominant reality of a homophobic, repressive heterosexual dictatorship are no less stuck in the past than anti-gay crusaders. With the decline of the closet, the battleground shifts: from the politics of coming out, pride, and visibility to equality—before the law and across social institutions.

BEYOND ASSIMILATION AND LIBERATION

As a civil rights agenda has come to dominate the gay movement, some gays have raised doubts about its politics. No one questions that equal rights is a condition of personal freedom and political democracy. However, critics rightly ask, would gaining equal rights establish social equality? Would gaining rights bring about social respect, equal treatment, and full social integration? Can and should the pursuit of social equality be separated from a wider agenda of sexual and social justice?

The current debate over the politics of sexual citizenship expresses a long-standing division between the civil rights or assimilationist and the liberationist ideologies. At the heart of this political division are contrasting images of America.

Generally speaking, rights advocates view America as a fundamentally good society. America is faulted for incompletely realizing its promise of delivering individual freedom, equality, and happiness. Rights advocates expect America to live up to its ideals, to include gays in the circle of full citizenship. By contrast, liberationists tend to see America as deeply flawed; this nation is said to have betrayed its promise of freedom and equality, and not only to gays. For liberationists, a rights-oriented agenda amounts to a wish to be integrated into a flawed, repressive society. Real social progress requires something like a social revolution.

★ ★ ★

From early statements by lesbian feminists and gay liberationists to contemporary queer perspectives, liberationists hold that heterosexual dominance is maintained less by unjust laws and individual prejudice than by the very social structure and organization of American life. For example, many liberationists assert a tight fit between gender norms and heterosexual dominance.[47] America is said to be a society organized around dichotomous norms of gender. From birth, individuals are expected to exhibit a consistency in their self-presentation and behavior between their assigned sex identity as male or female and their gender identity as man or woman. Institutions from the family to schools and the mass media impose expectations that individuals should adopt masculine or feminine gender roles reflecting their status as males or females. These contrasting gender identities and roles are said to reflect the complementary physical and psychological nature of men and women. From this point of view, heterosexuality is understood as expressing the natural fit of gendered bodies, psyches, and social roles. Men and women form a natural unity, each attracted to the other and each finding fulfillment in the other.

Individuals who deviate significantly from gender norms are stigmatized as homosexual. For example, women who are masculine, aggressive, or erotically assertive may be called whores, but also dykes; men who are passive or too emotional or feminine in their self-presentation are labeled sissies, fags, or queers. These disparaging labels aim to enforce a binary gender order that also assumes the normality and rightness of heterosexuality. So long as there are binary gender norms there will be heterosexual dominance. There is little evidence that extending rights to gays weakens dichotomous gender norms. This is so because gender norms are not primarily upheld by laws but by institutions (for example, family, economic institutions, military, schools) and by culture—that is, the media, advertisements, popular music, television, film, scientific and medical knowledge, and the daily customs and practices in families and peer groups.

A rights agenda cannot stand alone. Legal equality easily coexists with social inequality. Gays' equal status will only be achieved when heterosexual dominance is ended, and that requires challenging its deep cultural and institutional supports. Urvashi Vaid has stated this position sharply and forcefully:

> Civil rights strategies do not challenge the moral and antisexual underpinnings of homophobia, because homophobia does not originate in our lack of full civil equality. Rather, homophobia arises from the nature and construction of the political, legal, economic, sexual, racial, and family systems within which we live. As long as the rights-oriented movement refuses to address these social institutions and cultural forces, we cannot eradicate homophobic prejudice.[48]

A rights-oriented political agenda should be broadened in at least three ways. First, equality is about more than political equality or equal rights; it's about social equality across the spectrum of national institutions from the government to the workplace, schools, families, and welfare and health-care institutions. And no matter how important it is to gain equal rights, opportunities, and protections, equality is also about respect and representation. Gays may have the right to vote and hold office, but we remain unequal citizens if our interests and points of view are not respected and are not represented in political agencies. For example, if we don't have spokespeople in political parties or if public officials do not promote our social interests or agendas, equal political rights will not translate into social equality. Rights without respect and representation in the institutions that make up social life is only the shell of social equality.

Second, equality is not only about becoming equal citizens and participants in social life, but also about a right to be heard and to have our interests taken seriously. Equality is not about extending equal rights to gays but only on the condition that we conform to dominant gender, sexual, familial, and social norms. Equality is about institutions encouraging dialogues in which gays participate as equals in shaping the social norms and conventions of our institutions. In other words, equality means encouraging the distinctive voices of gays to be heard and to potentially shape social life.

There is a third problem with a rights agenda: it severs any tie between the pursuit of gay equality and broader issues of sexual and social justice. Consider the politics of citizenship from a sexual justice perspective. Rights activists fight for gays to become first-class citizens. Becoming a citizen is understood as being integrated into a network of rights, duties, and state protections. But citizenship is not only about rights and duties. Citizenship also involves an ideal of the citizen or a notion of the kind of personal traits and behaviors that a nation values and would like to see in its individual members. In other words, citizenship involves a norm of "the good citizen."

In contemporary America, the good sexual citizen, roughly speaking, is an individual whose sexual behavior conforms to traditional gender norms, who links sex to intimacy, love, monogamy, and preferably marriage, and who restricts sex to private acts that exhibit romantic or caring qualities. While rights advocates protest unequal citizenship rights, they have not challenged the sexual norms associated with the good sexual citizen. Accordingly, gays might gain equal rights, but those who deviate from norms of the good citizen would still be considered outsiders. . . .

BEYOND THE POLITICS OF TOLERANCE

The closet has been at the center of gay politics in the United States since at least the 1950s. At the root of the closet has been a culture that views gays as not only different in basic ways from heterosexuals but inferior and threatening—to children, families, and to the nation's moral and military security. Accordingly, the dismantling of the closet has meant persuading Americans that gays are just ordinary people, that like heterosexuals, we can be disciplined, productive, loyal, and loving. If homosexuality is understood as a natural or ordinary human trait, the closet would be judged unfair. Gays would be welcomed into the community of Americans.

Gays are winning this cultural battle, even if some of our enemies remain resolute and the social landscape is littered with the victims of a terrorizing hatred of homosexuals. Whether we look at television, the movies, literature, art, book publishing, newspapers and magazines, science, or elite opinion (expressed in editorials and political party platforms, for example), images of gays as just people or as fully human are steadily gaining ground. Public expression of homophobia, though by no means rare, is more and more being challenged as a form of bigotry or as a marker of being unenlightened in a global, multicultural world that values a cosmopolitan respect for social diversity.

As gays are viewed as fully human and as deserving to be citizens, there is pressure for institutions to be accommodating. This has not always gone smoothly. Battles are being waged in virtually every institution. In general, institutions that cultivate a cosmopolitan outlook such as big corporations and unions, colleges and universities, and health and civil service bureaucracies are more welcoming than small businesses, secondary schools, and churches that are highly responsive to local and parochial interests and sentiments. The major exception to this rule is the military, whose resistance, I've suggested, is perhaps explained by its powerful symbolic association with American nationalism.

The public integration of gays has created new sources of tension. In particular, conflicts have surfaced around whether integration involves tolerance or equality. To date, tolerance has been the dominant type of social accommodation. Tolerance entails decriminalization and the delegitimation of blatant homophobic behavior. Gays are to be acknowledged as part of America, but not necessarily accepted or valued as equals. It is hard, however, to draw the line at tolerance. Once homophobic practices are criticized as hateful and hurtful, there is an implicit acknowledgment that gays are ordinary folk deserving of respect and equal treatment. The tension between the cultural legitimation of gays and their continuing institutional inequality is at the core of contemporary lesbian and gay politics.

It is not only that America's public culture is becoming more respectful and welcoming toward gays. More and more gay people accept themselves, define being gay as a good part of themselves, and feel a sense of entitlement—to be treated respectfully by all other Americans. This sense of personal integrity drives the political struggle for equality into every institution. Yes, equality before the law is important, but so is equality in our schools, healthcare and welfare agencies, in our churches and political parties, in our local YMCAs and American Legion clubs. The struggle for social equality across the institutional spectrum pushes a rights agenda to the left, to a more expansive understanding of equality and a broadening of its political strategies.

These escalating expectations for inclusion, respect, and equality in a context of continued resistance, indeed sometimes spirited opposition, have spurred the renewal of the spirit of liberationism. In particular, the AIDS epidemic, which simultaneously exposed a reality of intolerance as well as growing mainstream support for gay integration, was especially important in pressuring a rights agenda to edge toward the left. This radical spirit expresses something of the sense of integrity and entitlement that many of us who are living beyond the closet feel; it also exposes the real limitations of a rights agenda by grasping heterosexual dominance

as rooted in our institutions and culture, not just in laws, attitudes, and ignorance.

However, as in the past, liberationism has largely failed to find a solid organizational footing in gay political culture. No doubt there are many reasons for this. My own sense is that liberationism alienates many gays to the extent that its social vision is wedded to a romantic rejection of America. Many liberationists seem temperamentally unable to see in the present anything more than repression, exclusion, marginalization, and domination. Rights are discounted as benefiting only middle-class whites; integration and legal equality is said to reinforce a repressive social order; culturally respectful images are "exposed" as assimilationist or exclusionary. In short, a good America can only be imagined as a future possibility. This sort of romanticism, which parades as a left politics, must be abandoned. But the heart and soul of liberationism is its understanding of the social roots of heterosexual dominance and a political vision that connects rights and equality to social justice. This should also be the heart and soul of the gay movement.

NOTES

1. There was a notable exception to this cultural invisibility: pulp fiction. See Ian Young, "How Gay Paperbacks Changed America," and Michael Bronski, "Fictions about Pulp," in *Gay and Lesbian Review* 6 (November/December 2001).
2. See Jeff Escoffier, "The Political Economy of the Closet: Notes toward an Economic History of Gay and Lesbian Life before Stonewall," in *Homo Economics,* ed. Amy Gluckman and Betsy Reed (New York: Routledge, 1997); and Elizabeth Kennedy and Madeline Davis, *Boots of Leather, Slippers of Gold* (New York: Routledge, 1993).
3. John D'Emilio and Estelle Freedman, *Intimate Matters: A History of Sexuality in America* (New York: Harper and Row, 1988); Steven Seidman, *Romantic Longings: Love in America, 1830–1980* (New York: Routledge, 1991); Jonathan Ned Katz, "The Age of Sodomitical Sin, 1607–1740," in *Gay/Lesbian Almanac: A New Documentary* (New York: Harper and Row, 1983); Karen Lystra, *Searching the Heart: Women, Men, and Romantic Love in Nineteenth-Century America* (New York: Oxford University Press, 1989); and Peter Gay, *The Bourgeois Experience: Victoria to Freud, Vol. 1: Education of the Senses* (New York: Oxford University Press, 1984).
4. See Jonathan Ned Katz, *The Invention of Heterosexuality* (New York: Dutton, 1995) and *Love Stories: Sex between Men before Homosexuality* (Chicago: University of Chicago Press, 2001); and Seidman, *Romantic Longings.*

5. William Eskridge Jr., *Gaylaw: Challenging the Apartheid of the Closet* (Cambridge, Mass.: Harvard University Press, 1999), p.1.

6. See Eskridge, *Gaylaw;* Jonathan Goldberg, ed., *Reclaiming Sodom* (New York: Routledge, 1994); and Katz, "The Age of Sodomitical Sin," and *Love Stories.*

7. See Katz, *Love Stories.*

8. See D'Emilio and Freedman, *Intimate Matters,* p. 133; Steven Marcus, *The Other Victorians* (New York: Basic Books, 1964); Walter Kendrick, *The Secret Museum* (New York: Viking, 1987); and Gay, *The Bourgeois Experience.*

9. Linda Hirshman and Jane Larson, *Hard Bargains: The Politics of Sex* (New York: Oxford University Press, 1998), p. 134.

10. Ibid., p. 165.

11. D'Emilio and Freedman, *Intimate Matters,* p. 147; Mary Gordon, *Woman's Body, Woman's Rights: A Social History of Birth Control* (New York: Grossman, 1967); Rosiland Petchesky, *Abortion and Women's Choice: The State, Sexuality, and Reproductive Freedom* (Boston: Northeastern University Press, 1984), ch. 2; James Mohr, *Abortion in America: The Origins and Evolution of National Policy* (New York: Oxford University Press, 1978); and Janet Brodie, *Contraception and Abortion in Nineteenth-Century America* (Ithaca, N.Y.: Cornell University Press, 1994).

12. Kristin Luker, "Sex, Hygiene, and the State: The Double-Edged Sword of Social Reform," *Theory and Society* 27 (1998): 615. See also Ruth Rosen, *The Lost Sisterhood: Prostitution in America, 1900–1918* (Baltimore: Johns Hopkins University Press, 1982); and David Pivar, *Purity Crusade: Sexual Morality and Social Control, 1868–1900* (Westport, Conn.: Greenwood, 1973).

13. D'Emilio and Freedman, *Intimate Matters,* pp. 157–59.

14. Hirshman and Larson, *Hard Bargains,* p. 172.

15. Ibid., p. 135.

16. George Chauncey, *Gay New York: Gender, Urban Culture, and the Making of the Gay Male World, 1890–1940* (New York: Basic Books, 1994). In a similar vein, Allan Berube notes that prior to World War II gays were not officially excluded from military service. "Traditionally, the military had never officially excluded or discharged homosexuals from its ranks. From the days following the Revolutionary War, the Army and Navy had targeted the act of sodomy . . . not homosexual persons, as criminals. . . . But in World War Two a dramatic change occurred. . . . Psychiatrists . . . developed new screening procedures to discover and disqualify homosexual men." Berube, *Coming Out under Fire: The History of Gay Men and Women in World War Two* (New York: Macmillan, 1990), p. 2.

17. Ibid.

18. See Hirshman and Larson, *Hard Bargains,* pp. 185–91.

19. Jana Singer, "The Privatization of Family Law," *Wisconsin Law Review* (1992): 1444–45.

20. D'Emilio and Freedman, *Intimate Matters,* p. 287.

21. See David Richards, *Women, Gays, and the Constitution* (Chicago: University of Chicago Press, 1998), p. 246.

22. Eskridge, *Gaylaw,* ch. 1.

23. Chauncey, *Gay New York,* p. 9.

24. Eskridge, *Gaylaw,* p. 98; cf. Chauncey, *Gay New York,* ch. 12; John D'Emilio, *Sexual Politics, Sexual Communities: The Making of a Homosexual Minority in the United States, 1940–1970* (Chicago: University of Chicago Press, 1983) and "The Homosexual Menace: The Politics of Sexuality in Cold War America," in *Making Trouble: Essays on Gay History, Politics, and the University* (New York: Routledge, 1992).

25. Eskridge, *Gaylaw,* p. 18.

26. For overviews of liberationist politics, see Stephen Engel, *The Unfinished Revolution: Social Movement Theory and the Gay and Lesbian Movement* (Cambridge: Cambridge University Press, 2001); Barry Adam, *The Rise of the Gay and Lesbian Movement* (New York: Twayne Publishers, 1995); Steven Epstein, "Gay and Lesbian Movements in the United States: Dilemmas of Identity, Diversity, and Political Strategy," in *The Global Emergence of Gay and Lesbian Politics: National Imprints of a Worldwide Movement,* ed. Barry Adam, Jan Willem Duyvendak, and Andre Krouwel (Philadelphia: Temple University Press, 1999); Toby Marotta, *The Politics of Homosexuality* (New York: Houghton Mifflin, 1981); Laud Humphreys, *Out of the Closets: The Sociology of Homosexual Liberation* (Englewood Cliffs, N.J.: Prentice Hall, 1972); Martin Duberman, *Stonewall* (New York: Dutton, 1993); Alice Echols, *Daring to Be Bad: Radical Feminism in America, 1967–1975* (Minneapolis: University of Minnesota Press, 1989); Verta Taylor and Leila Rupp, "Women's Culture and Lesbian Feminist Activism: A Reconsideration of Cultural Feminism," *Signs* 19 (Fall 1993): 32–61; Terence Kissack, "Freaking Fag Revolutionaries: New York's Gay Liberation Front, 1969–1971," *Radical History Review* 62 (1995): 104–34.

27. Stuart Byron, "The Closet Syndrome," in *Out of the Closets: Voices of Gay Liberationism,* ed. Karla Jay and Allen Young (New York: New York University Press, 1992 [1972]), p. 58. Cf. Judy Grahn, "Lesbians as Bogeywomen," *Women* 1 (Summer 1970): 36–38; and Carl Wittman, "A Gay Manifesto," and Karla Jay and Allen Young, "Out of the Closets, into the Streets," in *Out of the Closets,* ed. Jay and Young.

28. See the essays by the Red Butterfly Collective, Wittman, Jay and Young, Third World Gay Revolution and Gay Liberation Front (Chicago), Woman-Identified Woman, and Martha Shelley, in Jay and Young, eds., *Out of the Closets.*

29. On the renewal of gay liberationist politics, see Urvashi Vaid, *Virtual Equality: The Mainstreaming of Gay and Lesbian Liberation* (New York: Doubleday, 1995); Michael Warner, *Fear of a Queer Planet* (Minneapolis: University of Minnesota Press, 1993); Michael Fraser, "Identity and Representation as Challenges to Social Movement Theory: A Case Study of Queer Nation," in *Mainstream(s) and Margins: Cultural Politics in the 90s,* eds. Michael Morgan and Susan Leggett (Westport, Conn.: Greenwood Press, 1966); Douglas Crimp and Adam Rolston, *AIDS Demo Graphics* (Seattle, Wash.: Bay Press, 1990).

30. For overviews of the rights-oriented gay politics of the 1980s and 1990s, see the essays collected in Craig Rimmerman, Kenneth Wald, and Clyde Wilcox, eds., *The Politics of Gay Rights* (Chicago: University of Chicago Press, 2000); Chris Bull and John Gallagher, *Perfect Enemies: The Religious Right, the Gay Movement, and the*

Politics of the 1990s (New York: Crown Publishers, 1998); David Deitcher, ed., *The Question of Equality: Lesbian and Gay Politics since Stonewall* (New York: Scribner, 1995); David Rayside, *On the Fringe: Gays and Lesbians in Politics* (Ithaca, N.Y.: Cornell University Press, 1998); James Button, Barbara Rienzo, and Kenneth Wald, *Private Lives, Public Conflicts: Battles over Gay Rights in American Communities* (Washington, D.C.: Congressional Quarterly Press, 1997).

31. For example, Bruce Bawer, *A Place at the Table: The Gay Individual in American Society* (New York: Simon and Schuster, 1993), p. 47.

32. See, for example, D'Emilio, *Sexual Politics, Sexual Communities*, Toby Marotta, *The Politics of Homosexuality* (New York: Houghton Mifflin, 1981).

33. "Editorial," *Mattachine Review* 8 (November 1962): 2.

34. For an overview of gains and losses through the mid-1990s, see National Gay and Lesbian Task Force Policy Institute, *Capital Gains and Losses: A State by State Review of Gay, Lesbian, Bisexual, and Transgender, and HIV/AIDS-related Legislation in 1997* (Washington, D.C.: NGLTRF Policy Institute, 1997); see also Jean Reith Schroedel and Pamela Fiber, "Lesbian and Gay Policy Priorities: Commonality and Difference," and James Button et al., "The Politics of Gay Rights at the Local and State Level," in *The Politics of Gay Rights*, ed. Craig Rimmerman et al. (Chicago: University of Chicago Press, 2000).

35. Eskridge, *Gaylaw*, p. 139.

36. Ibid., p. 124.

37. See Suzanna Danuta Walters, *All the Rage: The Story of Gay Visibility in America* (Chicago: University of Chicago Press, 2001), p. 9.

38. Gregory Lewis and Jonathan Edelson, "DOMA and ENDA: Congress Votes on Gay Rights," in *The Politics of Gay Rights*, ed. Rimmerman et al., p. 195.

39. Researchers have documented a dramatic and unexpected shift in moral attitudes in the mid-1990s. See Jeni Loftus, "America's Liberalization in Attitudes toward Homosexuality, 1973 to 1998," *American Sociological Review* 66 (October 2001): 762–82; Alan Yang, "The Polls—Trends, Attitudes toward Homosexuality," *Public Opinion Quarterly* 61 (1997): 477–507; Simon Dumenco, "They're Here, They're Queer, We're Used to It," *New York*, March 5, 2001, pp. 29–31.

40. Lewis and Edelson, "DOMA and ENDA"; Loftus, "America's Liberalization in Attitudes Towards Homosexuality"; Yang, "The Polls."

41. Quoted in Eskridge and Hunter, *Sexuality, Gender, and the Law*, p. 46.

42. On nationalism and sexual identity, see Jacqui Alexander, "Not Just (Any) Body Can Be a Citizen: The Politics of Law, Sexuality, and Postcoloniality in Trinidad and Tobago and the Bahamas," *Feminist Review* 48 (Fall 1994):5–23; George Mosse, *Nationalisms and Sexualites: Middle-Class Moralities and Sexual Norms in Modern Europe* (Madison: University of Wisconsin Press, 1985); Richard Herrell, "Sin, Sickness, Crime: Queer Desire and the American State," *Identities* 2 (3): 273–300; Jyoti Puri, "Nationalism Has a Lot to Do with It! Unraveling Questions of Nationalism and Transnationalism in Lesbian/Gay Studies," in *Handbook of Lesbian and Gay Studies*, ed. Diane Richardson and Steven Seidman (London: Sage, 2002); Lauren Berlant and Elizabeth Freeman, "Queer Nationality," in *Fear of a Queer Planet*, Carl Stychin, *A Nation by Rights: National Cultures, Sexual Identity Politics, and the Discourse of Rights* (Philadelphia: Temple University Press, 1998).

43. Benedict Anderson, *Imagined Communities* (New York: Verso, 1983); Liah Greenfeld, *Nationalism: Five Roads to Modernity* (Cambridge, Mass.: Harvard University Press, 1992); Lynn Spillman, *Nation and Commemoration: Creating National Identities in the United States and Australia* (Cambridge: Cambridge University Press, 1997).

44. For example, Chrys Ingraham, *White Weddings*.

45. Cf. Anna Marie Smith, "The Politicization of Marriage in Contemporary American Public Policy: The Defense of Marriage Act and the Personal Responsibility Act," *Citizenship Studies* 5 (November 2001): 303–20; Don Westervelt, "Defending Marriage and Country," *Constellations* 8 (March 2001): 106–126; Richard Mohr, *A More Perfect Union: Why Straight America Must Stand up for Gay Rights* (Boston: Beacon Press, 1994).

46. See William Eskridge Jr., *The Case for Same-Sex Marriage: From Sexual Liberty to Civilized Commitment* (New York: Free Press, 1996) and *Equality Practice: Civil Unions and the Future of Gay Rights* (New York: Routledge, 2002).

47. Regarding the intersection of gender norms and heterosexual dominance, see class gay liberationist and lesbian-feminist writing . . . .

48. Vaid, *Virtual Equality*, p. 183.

40

Race and Ethnic Relations

American and Global Perspectives

MARTIN MARGER

THE NEWEST IMMIGRATION

. . . [T]he civil rights movement of the 1960s proved to have far-reaching consequences for American society, resulting in fundamental changes in the society's ethnic order. No groups were unaffected. But something else occurred in the 1960s that, arguably, had an equally significant impact on ethnic relations in the United States. This was the revision of immigration laws, encapsulated in the Hart-Cellar Act of 1965, abolishing the restrictive quota system that had effectively limited immigration to those from Europe, especially northwestern Europe. The new legislation not only erased the country-of-origin quota system that had virtually prohibited certain groups from immigrating to the United States, but it also created a system of criteria for admission. Priority was given to those with family ties to U. S. citizens or permanent residents and to those with needed occupational skills.

Several driving forces provoked this truly radical change in immigration laws. First, the civil rights movement itself provided an initial impetus. As an adjunct to the mounting pressure for an end to discriminatory measures against African Americans, public sentiment now seemed prepared to do the same with immigrants, bringing the reality of immigration laws into line with the rhetoric of equal opportunity. Other factors contributing to the acceptability of change were the sentiments and efforts of the new presidential administration that entered Washington in 1961. John F. Kennedy, in his 1960 campaign for the presidency, had explicitly pledged to work toward the removal of discriminatory immigration regulations. As with much of the civil rights legislation of the mid-1960s, the revision of immigration laws was enacted in large measure as a tribute to Kennedy after his assassination in 1963. In 1965, when the revision was passed, few predicted the massive numbers that would enter the United States as a result, nor did they foresee the profound impact this legislation would subsequently have on the ethnic makeup of the society.

The ensuing massive and immensely diverse immigration has led to an unprecedented level of heterogeneity of the U.S. population. The two previous periods of substantial immigration, occurring in the nineteenth and early twentieth centuries, had been primarily European in origin. Though resisted by nativist forces, these immigration periods did not essentially threaten the basic cultural and racial makeup of the society. Until the last two decades, the connotation of *immigrant* in the United States was "of European descent." What has occurred in the modern period of immigration, however, is the onset of a movement which assures that the society's ethnic configuration, and thus its culture, will not be in the future what it has been for most of its history. To distinguish it from previous large-scale immigrations to the United States, the most recent wave may be referred to as the *newest immigration*.

Characteristics of the Newest Immigration

Scope   During the three decades between 1960 and 1990, 15 million people either entered the United States as legal immigrants or were granted permanent residence. Nine million came during the 1980s alone, exceeding the total of the first decade of the 1900s, when immigration to the United States was at its peak (Figure 1). Another 8 million were admitted between 1990 and 1997 (Martin and Midgley, 1999). Today legal immigration to the United States fluctuates between 700,000 and 900,000 per year, a number larger than the total immigration to all other developed countries together.

The figures for legal immigrants and refugees, of course, do not take into account those who enter illegally. No one can be certain of their numbers, but government estimates are in the range of 300,000 each year. As of 1996, an estimated 5,275,000 immigrants were residing in the United States illegally (U.S. Immigration and Naturalization Service, 2001). More than half were from Mexico alone, but undocumented immigrants come from the same broad range of countries as legal immigrants.

The foreign-born population of the United States has today reached an all-time high. Even during the peak immigration years of the early twentieth century, immigrants numbered only about half of what they do today (Martin and Midgley, 1999). However, when looked at in proportionate, not absolute, terms, immigrants today do not have as great a demographic impact as they did in the early 1900s. At that time, immigrants constituted about 15 percent of the total population, compared to 10 percent today. Even adding illegal immigrants would not increase that figure significantly. Nonetheless, it is very obvious that immigration in all forms continues to play a large role in U.S. population growth and will play an even greater role in the future (Heer, 1996; Martin and Midgley, 1999; Smith and Edmonston, 1997).

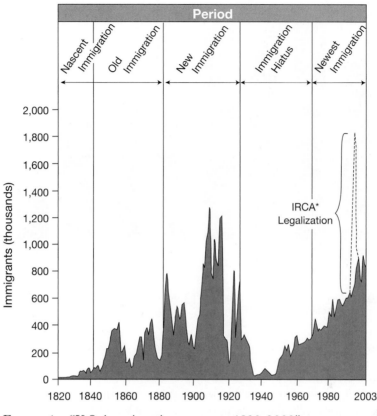

FIGURE 1   *"U.S. immigration currents 1820-2003"*

Ethnic Makeup Numbers alone do not tell the whole story of the current period of American immigration. Perhaps more important, the character of immigration has been radically changed from that of past eras. Whereas the vast majority of immigrants throughout the nineteenth and early twentieth centuries were from European societies, today most are from Latin America and Asia (Figure 2). The ramifications of that change have had a ripple effect throughout virtually all economic, political, and social institutions.

Since the 1970s, the leading countries of origin of legal immigrants to the United States have been Mexico, the Philippines, Korea, and four small Caribbean nations—the Dominican Republic, Jamaica, Haiti, and Guyana (a South American country that considers itself Caribbean in its eco-

nomic and social structure). But the sheer diversity of non-European immigrants is quite astonishing. Among the Asians, for example, are Filipinos, Koreans, Indians, Pakistanis, Chinese, Vietnamese, Cambodians, Laotians, and Hmong. From the Middle East have come Palestinians, Iraqis, Iranians, Lebanese, Syrians, Egyptians, and Israelis. Those from Africa include Somalis, Ethiopians, and Nigerians. And from Latin America, the national origins of the immigrants cover the entire Central and South American regions, in addition to the Caribbean. Figure 3 shows the leading countries of origin of immigrants in 1999.

Motivating Forces What has prompted this newest large-scale immigration to the United States? Obviously the changes in immigration law in 1965

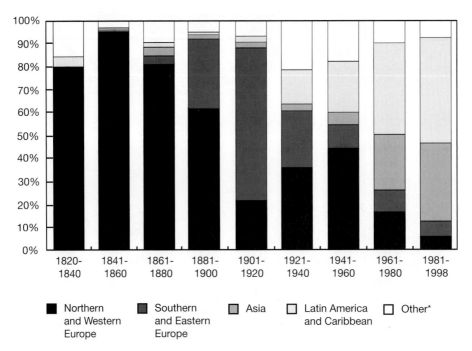

FIGURE 2 *Regions of Origin of U.S. Immigrants, 1820–1998.*

provided the favorable legal conditions and thus the necessary vehicle. But essentially the same push-pull factors that motivated past immigrations to America have been functioning for the newest wave. Although many have come as political refugees (mostly from Southeast Asia, Cuba, and Central America), most immigrants have responded to the population and economic pressures of their societies of origin. Most, in other words, seek economic betterment and improved social conditions. A national survey asked foreign-born adults living in the United States what they preferred about America in comparison with their homeland. Some answered political freedom, fair treatment under laws, safety from crime, or moral values. But the most common answer was job opportunities (Saad, 1995).

Contemporary immigration to the United States, as well as to other industrialized societies of North America, Europe, and Australia, accelerated in the 1960s in large measure because of the widening gap between rich and poor nations. The economies of the latter, many of them newly independent states,

were generally incapable of supporting rapidly growing populations, thereby creating a migration push. Most of the world's population growth has occurred since the end of World War II, and the overwhelming majority of that growth has taken place in the less developed countries. Moreover, the gains in economic development made by many of these countries during the 1960s and 1970s slowed or reversed in the 1980s due to economic recession, growing debt, and internal political conflicts. These conditions induced further pressures to migrate to the wealthier countries, like the United States, whose industrialized economies promised better employment opportunities and a superior quality of life.

Poverty and overpopulation, however, cannot alone explain the emergence and steady flow of migration streams to the United States and other industrialized countries. Additional factors help induce people to migrate. In the U.S. case, large inflows among the newest immigrants in recent years have been sustained by the changing structure of the U.S. economy, especially the expansion of low-wage jobs

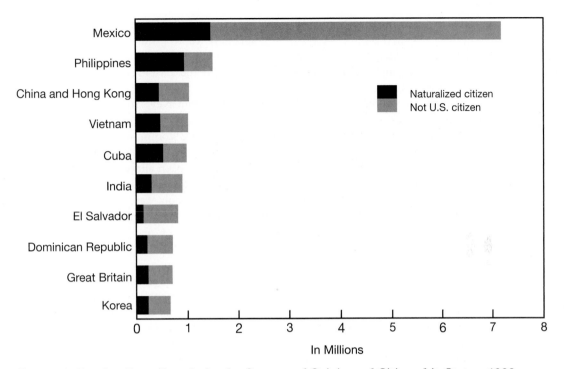

FIGURE 3 *Foreign-Born Population by Country of Origin and Citizenship Status, 1999.*

(Sassen, 1998). The newest immigration, then, must be seen as part of the internationalization of capitalist economies and the resultant globalization of the workforce (Castles and Miller, 1998; Chaney, 1979).

Ironically, much of the migration to the United States from underdeveloped societies has been induced by American political and economic influences. As American-based multinational corporations bring capital and technology to these developing economies, new wealth is created, but it remains highly maldistributed. Thus, the expectations of work and consumption opportunities are frustrated, leading to a natural gravitation to the United States, which promises to deliver these advantages. "It is only natural," notes Alejandro Portes, "that many trek North in search of the means to acquire what transnational firms and the mass media have so insistently advertised for years" (1979:434).

Geography Although the newest immigration has affected virtually all regions and states, it still is most

evident in a few states, namely California, New York, Illinois, Texas, and Florida. Similarly, though immigrant groups have dispersed widely, specific groups remain concentrated in particular regions. Asians, for example, have settled mostly in California; Mexicans, in the Southwest; Cubans and other Caribbeans in Miami; and almost all new groups have large communities in New York City. So great has the change been in California that the state has been transformed into one where non-Hispanic whites are no longer the numerical majority.

Like so many American immigrants of past generations, many today come with few expectations of remaining permanently in the United States. A great number do leave, and many (particularly from Mexico) engage in a continual back-and-forth movement. But also like their predecessors, many who at first see their immigration as temporary become firmly ensconced in their new society. The result has been, as in earlier eras of immigration, the flourishing of ethnic enclaves in cities that have attracted large numbers of new immigrants. Much as New York, Chicago, and other cities of the East and Midwest served in the nineteenth and early twentieth centuries as meccas of European immigration, cities of the Sun Belt—Los Angeles, Miami, Houston—are the focal points of the newest immigration. The immigrant population in Los Angeles, for example, is almost a third of the metropolitan area's total, equivalent numerically to the foreign-born population of New York City during the 1920s (Muller, 1993; U.S. Census Bureau, 2001m). The ethnic diversity of the metropolitan area is reflected in the fact that students in the Los Angeles School District speak more than eighty languages. In Miami the trend is much the same; over 40 percent of the metropolitan area's population is foreign-born. In 1969, 19 percent of Miami-Dade County's students were Hispanic; in 2000 they were more than half, with non-Hispanic whites only 12 percent (Nazareno, 2000).

Sun Belt cities, however, have by no means monopolized the newest immigration. New York remains a traditional port of entry for new ethnic groups. The city has absorbed especially large numbers of newcomers from the Caribbean basin, including English-speaking West Indians from Jamaica, Trinidad and Tobago, Barbados, and Guyana; French and Creole-speaking Haitians; and Spanish-speaking groups from the Dominican Republic, Cuba, Colombia, and Mexico. Hispanics from virtually every Caribbean, Central American, and South American country comprise the largest component of New York's newest immigrants, but large numbers of Asians have also settled in the city, including Chinese, Koreans, Filipinos, and South Asians from India, Pakistan, and Bangladesh. Even Europeans entered in significant numbers in the late 1970s and early 1980s, most notably thousands of Soviet Jews (Foner, 1987; Muller, 1993; Winnick, 1990). So great has been the immigrant influx that Euro-Americans now constitute less than half of the city's total population (Mumford Center, 2001c). Other eastern and Midwestern cities have also attracted large new immigrant populations.

Although most of the newest immigrants have focused on living in the largest cities, virtually no U.S. city or town has been unaffected. Many immigrants have leapfrogged over the central cities and settled in suburban communities, a pattern not common in the past. As an example, consider Bridgewater, New Jersey, an affluent township forty miles from New York City. Seemingly immune to ethnic changes occurring in the City and its surrounding communities, Bridgewater had been a solidly white, middle-class enclave. Its Asian population had been almost invisible in 1980, but twenty years later it was 10 percent Asian, and Bridgewater schools were teaching students with forty-one native languages (Chen, 1999).

Class Range   Another evident feature of the newest immigration is its class range. Unlike past great waves of immigration, in which most immigrants were either poor or of modest means, the newest influx is made up of individuals and families who span the entire class spectrum, from low-level, unskilled workers to highly educated professionals. The result of this socioeconomic variety has been equally diverse patterns of settlement and adaptation among immigrants. . . .

Gender   During previous large-scale immigration periods, male immigrants outnumbered females among most groups; the newest immigration is more gender balanced. Females actually comprise a majority among immigrants from some countries. Over half of all immigrants from the Philippines, Korea, Jamaica, and the Dominican Republic—each a source country sending large numbers to the United States—are women (Rumbaut, 1996). Immigrant women have disproportionately filled jobs in the low-wage service sector—like hotel and restaurant workers—and in certain labor intensive industries. In San Francisco, for example, the garment industry is the largest manufacturing sector, employing over 25,000 workers; 90 percent are women, most of them Asian immigrants (Louie, 2000).

Middle Eastern Americans

. . . A group that is beginning to emerge with greater clarity as part of the American ethnic mix, but one that has not been clearly classified as part of any of the society's broad ethnic categories, includes peoples from the Middle East. They serve as an excellent case to demonstrate how the United States has accommodated new and, from the standpoint of native-born Americans, culturally distant groups during the past four decades.

Small communities of people from Middle Eastern societies have actually been in the United States since the late nineteenth century, and most Middle Eastern Americans today trace their origins to immigration waves occurring prior to World War II. But, like other small groups with a relatively long U.S. history, their numbers swelled starting in the 1970s as part of the newest immigration. Although the 1990 U.S. Census described the Arab-American population as 1 million, estimates range as high as 3 million Americans with Arab origins (Telhami, 2002). Because not all Middle Eastern Americans are Arab in origin, the total Middle Eastern population is also larger than the official count.

Before World War II, most immigrants from the Middle East were poor, uneducated, and took jobs as unskilled workers. Most also were Christian, not Muslim. Many came from Lebanon and blended almost imperceptibly into the U.S. mainstream, moving rapidly into the middle class as entrepreneurs and professionals (Kayal and Kayal, 1975; Naff, 1983; Walbridge, 1999). The newest Middle Eastern immigrants, however, are far more diverse in geographical origin, ethnicity, religion, and social class. And, their absorption into American society has been far more torturous.

The most recent immigrants from the Middle East have come from over twenty countries in Southwest Asia and North Africa (Suleiman, 1999). The largest numbers have come from Iran, Egypt, Iraq, and the Palestinian territories. Some have been motivated to immigrate to the United States for reasons of economic betterment; but many have been impelled to leave their origin countries because of political unrest. The Middle East has been plagued by regional conflicts and civil wars over the past four decades, and many immigrants have sought refuge in America.

Most Americans usually perceive all Middle Easterners simply as "Arabs" and assume they are all Muslim. Neither view is correct. In fact, there are significant ethnic and religious differences among the numerous groups now comprising the Middle Eastern population in the United States. Although they are predominantly Arab, Middle Easterners comprise a diverse ethnic population. Iranians, for example, the largest component of the newest immigration from the Middle East, are not ethnically Arab, nor do they speak Arabic. As to religion, while most of the newest immigrants are Muslim, some are Christian, and a few are even Jewish (Bozorgmehr et al., 1996). Even among the Muslim immigrants, however, there are significant differences in belief and practice. For example, those from Yemen are devoutly religious, while those from Iran are predominantly secular (Walbridge, 1999). When considered in total—not simply the newest immigrants—Middle Eastern Americans are overwhelmingly Christian, not Muslim (Abraham, 1983).

Like other ethnic populations of the newest immigration, Middle Easterners are represented in a broad range of social classes. Some are poor and unskilled, but many are highly educated professionals—doctors, lawyers, engineers—and entrepreneurs who are relatively well-off. Only their geographical origin gives them commonality.

Middle Eastern communities can be found in all regions of the United States, but their major concentrations are in a few large urban areas—namely Detroit, Los Angeles, and New York. Detroit, with the largest settlement of Middle Easterners, is home to an estimated 300,000, mostly Arabs; in suburban Dearborn, Arabs now make up about a quarter of the city's population, and almost 60 percent of the students in its school are from Arab families (Hamada, 1990; Singer, 2001; Warikoo, 2001).

Because Muslims predominate among the latest cohort of Middle Easterners, they have, more than other immigrant groups, run headlong into the dominant American culture. Islam is a religion that few Americans are familiar with, and they commonly harbor misconceptions about its tenets and rituals. Many Muslim women, for example, feel an obligation to wear a head scarf in public. This practice has made them an easy target for harassment and discrimination. Young Muslim girls may face ostracism at school, and dozens of companies have refused to employ women who insist on wearing the scarf (Goodstein, 1997). Perhaps more serious is the persistence of negative stereotyping that has plagued Middle Easterners in the United States. The activities of Arab terrorists in the Middle East and elsewhere have created a sinister image of Arab and other Middle Eastern groups—an image that was greatly exacerbated by the attack on the World Trade Center in 2001. This image reaches back much further than simply the last few years, however. Political events in the Middle East during the past four decades—as well as the oil crisis of the 1970s, induced by the mainly Arab-led OPEC oil cartel—caused many Americans to view Middle Easterners in the United States with suspicion and disdain. One researcher in the 1980s documented more than 100 different pop-entertainment programs, cartoons, and documentaries relative to Arabs and concluded that negative stereotypes were virtually the only TV images of the group. The TV portrayal of Arabs, he found, perpetuated four basic myths: "they are all fabulously wealthy; they are barbaric and uncultured; they are sex maniacs with a penchant for white slavery; and they revel in acts of terrorism" (Shaheen, 1984:4). A later study (Lind and Danowski, 1998) found little change in these images, except that no longer did the media portray Arabs as fabulously wealthy. The researchers concluded that the U.S. electronic media continued to give little coverage to Arabs in general. This, of course, changed radically after the events of September 11, 2001.

The Middle Eastern population is one of the most diverse and least understood among the newest ethnic elements of U.S. society. Because the majority are Arabs, their racial/ethnic classification remains uncertain and debated both within and outside the community (Naber, 2000). Moreover, the cultural confrontation of devout Muslims with dominant American norms and values has led to a stronger sense of isolation among them than has been the case

with most immigrants to the United States. The determination of many Arab Muslim immigrants to uphold their religious convictions in the face of an overwhelming Judeo-Christian tradition and population has intensified that separateness.

Contemporary Immigration as a Global Phenomenon

As vast and diverse as immigration to the United States has been during the past three decades, it has hardly been a uniquely American phenomenon. Indeed, looking at the world's industrial societies reveals that almost all have been affected in a similar way. The numbers may be smaller than in the United States, but the relative impact has been no less deeply felt and, in some cases, has produced even greater social strain. In addition to the traditional immigrant-receiving societies like Canada, Australia, and New Zealand, many western European nations have experienced large immigration movements and, in the process, emerged as multi-ethnic societies. For countries such as Britain, France, and Germany, this has represented a profound transformation and a wrenching societal experience, the consequences of which are still unfolding. Even relatively homogeneous societies like Italy, Sweden, and Japan have begun to evince greater ethnic diversity due to immigration. And, in all of these societies, the changing ethnic composition has brought forth heated public debate, just as in the United States. Are immigrants becoming too numerous? Is the society's cultural integrity threatened? Are immigrants taking jobs from native workers? These and questions like them are heard today in many nations of the developed world.

To recognize that we are in an age of immigration should not lead us to think that immigration is a uniquely modern phenomenon. In fact, immigration has been ongoing since the very emergence of human societies. When we extend our historical perspectives far enough, we discover that the "original" inhabitants of any land were preceded by others. In a basic way, then, all societies have taken shape by migration from other societies. Nonetheless, it would hardly be exaggerating to declare that today we are in a period in which the dimensions of immigration are perhaps greater, and its consequences loom larger, than in any previous era in human history. And there appears no likelihood that the tide of international migration will recede in the foreseeable future. As long as there is a global stratification system, well-off nations with strong economies will attract people from nations with weak economies and severe population pressures. It seems apparent, then, that the issues and social consequences of large-scale immigration and increasing global diversity will follow us for many decades. . . .

ISSUES OF THE NEWEST IMMIGRATION

The prominence of ethnic issues in the United States today stems not only from the continuing socioeconomic gap between whites and nonwhites but also from the large-scale immigration of diverse peoples in the past three decades. These latest immigrants have begun to have a significant impact on the ethnic flavor of the society and have introduced new problems and questions of ethnic relations.

Economic Issues of the Newest Immigration

The economic impact of the newest immigration is widely debated. What effects are these immigrants having on the American economy? Does immigration produce net benefits for the labor force, or does it negatively affect native workers? Do immigrants become self-supporting members of the society, or do they become a drain on public services like schools and hospitals?

Immigration and the Labor Force Whereas some argue that immigrants constitute an added burden to an already swollen labor pool, others contend that the jobs they typically hold are those that native workers shun—and furthermore, that they create as many jobs as they take. Similarly, while some maintain that immigrants overburden the social welfare system, others hold that they pay in taxes

far more than they collect in benefits (Borjas, 1994; Espenshade, 1998; Simon, 1991).*

The economic impact of the newest immigration is not uniform. Instead, it appears to favor some sectors of the economy and harm others. Most of the immigrants from Mexico (the largest single group) and the Caribbean are unskilled and take their place at the lowest employment levels. They benefit employers in labor-intensive industries, such as clothing manufacturing or other work areas calling for cheap labor; but they depress the job opportunities of native low-status workers, especially African Americans (Borjas, 1998; Smith and Edmonston, 1997). . . . [N]ot all the new immigrants are impoverished and unskilled, however. A large segment of some new groups, particularly Asian Indians, Chinese, and Filipinos, are highly trained professionals and managers whose economic impact is far different from that of those entering with few occupational resources. Many immigrant doctors and nurses, for example, now staff inner city and rural hospitals, which would find it difficult to operate without them. The United States has also lagged in producing engineers and other highly trained scientific workers, and many of the newest immigrants are filling these needs (Muller, 1993; Suro, 1989; Szabo, 1989).

Those most profoundly affected by immigration are apt to express strongest support or opposition to its rate and extent. Industrialists and business owners ordinarily favor an open-door policy with few restrictions on continued immigration. Immigrants, in this view, serve as a needed workforce that helps to control wages. Those at the other end of the class spectrum, however, see immigration from an entirely different perspective. In the early 1990s, with the U.S. economy still in recession, immigration provoked negative reactions not only from whites

---

*Another argument for restricting the number of immigrants to American society is that they constitute a growing environmental problem. The United States, it is held, has limits on what it can provide while still maintaining a high standard of living. Greater numbers of newcomers strain the society's resources and create environmental problems (Beck, 1996; Bouvier, 1992).

but also from racial and ethnic minorities, who perceived the new groups as a threat to either their jobs or as an increasing pool of welfare recipients. . . .

It is especially illegal immigration that has come under public attack, since it is popularly perceived that illegals put an undue burden on public services, like schools and hospitals, at taxpayers' expense. Following the 2000 U.S. Census, estimates of the size of the illegal immigrant population rose considerably (Sachs, 2001). Because such a large proportion of illegal immigrants originate in Mexico, this is an issue with particular currency in states like Texas and California, which have large Mexican-American populations. In a 1994 referendum, California voters approved Proposition 187, which denied undocumented immigrants vital public services in education, welfare, and health care. Although the measure was subsequently declared unconstitutional, thereby preventing it from ever taking effect, the debate surrounding the referendum was extremely bitter and reflected the strong public sentiments regarding the entire illegal immigration issue.

Regarding the economic impact of the newest immigration, the debate waxes and wanes, hinging in large measure on the state of the U.S. economy. When immigrants enter during times of economic dislocation, workers are fearful of losing their jobs; immigrants, from this perspective, are seen as a potential threat, prepared to work at lower wages and under poorer conditions. Immigration is thus viewed negatively. When unemployment is low and jobs plentiful, however, arguments against immigration are muted and support wanes for reductions or restrictions on immigration levels.

These shifting trends were demonstrated in the 1990s. In the early years of the decade the U.S. economy was in recession; the rate of unemployment was relatively high and wages were stagnant or falling. Accordingly, anti-immigration attitudes seemed to be growing. By the latter part of the decade, however, a huge economic recovery was underway, with a tight labor market and rising wages. Immigrants were now seen as a valued commodity, filling labor gaps and revitalizing urban neighborhoods that the middle classes had abandoned. Many industries—hotels, restaurants, poultry-processing plants, garment factories—found themselves heavily dependent on immigrant labor, including illegal workers (Schmitt, 2001b). At the high end of the occupational hierarchy, too, a shortage of skilled workers, such as software programmers and computer engineers, gave rise to calls for the liberalization of immigration laws to permit the easier entrance of critically needed technical workers. As jobs remained plentiful, even some groups that had been staunchly critical of an open-door immigration policy were no longer pressing the issue. In 2000 the AFL-CIO, for example—long opposed to high levels of immigration, viewing immigrants as a threat to jobs and wages—called for amnesty for all illegal workers, viewing immigrants as potential union members.

In addition to the robust economy, a changed view of immigration was prompted by the increasing realization of elected officials that immigrants represented a potentially powerful political force. As a result, in the 2000 election and afterward, both Democratic and Republican parties engaged in efforts to woo immigrants. This was especially evident with the emergence of Hispanics as the largest of America's minority ethnic groups.

★ ★ ★

Social Issues of the Newest Immigration

The current immigrants are highly visible, bringing to American society cultural and physical features distant from those of the white majority. This makes them considerably different from previous immigrants who, though always viewed ethnocentrically by those already present, were nonetheless primarily European. The debate, therefore, concerns whether these new cultural and racial strains constitute a positive or negative social influence.

Some believe that currently high levels of immigration should be continued or made even higher to allow for additional immigrants. Their view is that immigrants not only create economic activity, but are a fresh cultural influence on the society. American society is in fact pluralistic, they hold, and should further develop its multicultural character, creating a more equitable society in the process (Isbister, 1996). Others, however, support highly restrictionist measures, maintaining that the new immigrants are causing a radical and unprecedented change in the social and cultural makeup of the society, which can only lead to more racial and ethnic conflict. Some see this change as undesirable in itself, suggesting that the United States remain a primarily European-origin society (Brimelow, 1995). The new groups are seen as unassimilable and thus a continual drag on the society. These issues have a familiar ring, recalling those that raged at the turn of the century with regard to southern and eastern European immigrants.

★ ★ ★

Language Questions and attitudes regarding the impact of immigrants on American culture have come together most clearly around the issue of language. In Canada, . . . the nucleus of ethnic conflict is the preservation of one group's language. A somewhat similar situation has begun to surface in certain regions of the United States, where large numbers of immigrants, particularly the Spanish speaking, use their native tongue. That these immigrants are able to maintain close links with their origin societies through easy communication and travel and through a constant influx of fellow immigrants from the homeland means that there is no pressing need to quickly relinquish the native language (Chavez, 1991; Heath, 1985; Muller, 1993). This makes their situation somewhat different from that of past immigrants. Although the latter also came speaking languages other than English, it was assumed that through the use of English in the school and other institutions, those languages would gradually be abandoned, if not by the first then by the second generation. Ethnic groups, of course, were not prohibited from maintaining their own institutions (private schools, newspapers, and so on), which often served as preservers of the native language for a time. Today, however, the assumption of language assimilation is being challenged. A greater tolerance of ethnic pluralism has led to efforts to provide public educational and other services in the language of the new groups, especially Spanish. This has created controversy among those who favor or oppose such measures (Baron, 1990; Cafferty, 1983; Chavez, 1991; Crawford, 1992).

Bilingual education has emerged as a particularly divisive political issue, especially in states with large Hispanic populations like California, Texas, New York, and Florida. In New York City, classes are now taught not only in Spanish, but in Chinese, Haitian Creole, Russian, Korean, Arabic, Vietnamese, Polish, Bengali, and French. In some of the city's neighborhoods, eight in ten school-age children live in a home where the family communicates in a non-English language (Sachs, 1999). And in Los Angles, almost half of all students have limited English proficiency (Lopez, 1996). In Miami-Dade County, almost 60 percent of public school students speak a language other than English at home; and many schools at all levels are bilingual institutions, teaching in both English and Spanish (Nazareno, 2000). The issue is not limited to these high-profile immigrant-receiving cities, however. Almost half of all U.S. school districts have at least some non-English-speaking children (Hornblower, 1995). The controversy swirls around whether such students should be instructed in their native languages or in English, and in what proportion.

Some opposing greater language diversity have sought to have English legally declared the "official" American language. By the mid-1990s, more than twenty states had passed legislation to that effect. Proponents see such legislation as a means to reverse a perceived decline in English language use and to force immigrants to more quickly adopt the dominant culture. They advocate strict limits on bilingual education, the elimination of voting ballots in languages other than English, and raised language-proficiency standards for prospective citizens. Supporters of the movement to make English the country's official language maintain that without a common language, new immigrants will resist assimilation, and the United States risks becoming linguistically divided like Canada. In response, critics of the English-only movement charge that efforts to forts to declare English the official language of the United States are a backlash against the new immigrants and essentially a mask for ethnic antagonism. Moreover, they claim that such legislation is useless because it does nothing to help promote the learning of English (Braverman, 1988; Crawford, 1992). By the late 1990s, public opinion seemed to favor the "official English" side of the controversy. A ballot initiative in California outlawing most bilingual classes was approved in 1998, and a national poll indicated that most Americans were in agreement with California voters in their opposition to bilingual education (Newport, 1998).

The issue may be moot in any case because studies indicate that, as in the past, the children of recent immigrants adopt English as their major language and gradually drift away from using their native language outside the home (Portes, 2002; Portes and Rumbaut, 1996; Saad, 1995). This shift to the English language, notes sociologist Calvin Veltman (1983), has been characteristic of every previous immigrant group and is evident among the newer groups today. "There is no language group in any region," Veltman concludes, "which possesses the retentive characteristics which would remotely sustain the theory that continued immigration is laying the groundwork for linguistic nationalism" (1983:217). Research among Latinos, for example, shows that first- and second-generation immigrants are usually bilingual, but by the third generation, English has become the primary—and for most, the only—language spoken (Fishman, 1987: Portes and Schauffler, 1996). The Latino National Political Survey revealed that among U.S.-born Latinos, 62 percent of Mexicans, 50 percent of Puerto Ricans, and 31 percent of Cubans used English predominantly or exclusively at home. More than two-thirds, regardless of national origin, were better at English or spoke no Spanish (de la Garza et al., 1992). An earlier study carried out in Miami revealed that 98 percent of Latino parents felt it was essential for their children to become competent in English (Braverman, 1988). . . . [T]he vast majority of Latinos believe that citizens and residents of the United States should learn English (de la Garza et al., 1992). What keeps Spanish

alive in the United States, therefore, is not a determination of Latinos to retain their native language but the continuation of large-scale Hispanic immigration.

Issues of Immigrant Adaptation and Integration

. . . [I]mmigration to the United States has reached epic proportions in the past two decades. Of no little significance is the fact that most of the newest immigrants are from non-European societies. How they will be absorbed into the society and the place they will eventually take in the ethnic hierarchy, as well as the ways in which they are changing the society, are issues of profound importance.

For several reasons, the typical patterns of adaptation to American society for past immigrants are not likely to be followed in quite the same way for the newest immigrants. European immigrants of the nineteenth and early twentieth centuries generally followed a path of eventual assimilation into the mainstream society, leading to upward mobility, over two or three generations. The newest immigrants may follow a more tortuous route and less certain outcome of social and economic adaptation, referred to . . . as *segmented assimilation*. Some may follow the traditional assimilation pattern, but others may retain their ethnic cultures and social structures for many generations. Still others may find themselves stuck in a low-income status, with stifling job and educational opportunities that confine them to a condition outside the mainstream society. Most of the newest immigrants are nonwhite, which automatically places a racial barrier before them that past immigrant waves, mostly European, were able to overcome relatively quickly. However, the newest immigrants face significantly different social and economic circumstances as well.

First, the labor market encountered by the newest immigrants is one in which solid industrial working-class jobs, which in the past provided immigrants with opportunities for upward mobility, have disappeared. What has taken its place is a labor market more clearly divided into two segments—high-status (highly skilled professional and technical workers) and low-status (unskilled, mostly service-sector jobs). The latter are poorly paid and essentially dead-end jobs that have been disproportionately occupied by newly entering immigrants. The fear is that a semipermanent immigrant underclass will be created, impeding integration of these groups into the mainstream society for many generations.

Second, recent immigrants enjoy communications and transportation technologies unimagined by past newcomers. To fly from New York to the Dominican Republic, for example, involves a few hours. In the mid-nineteenth century it took about 5 weeks to sail from Britain to America, though bad weather could make the trip twice as long (Van Vugt, 1999). Similarly, immigrants today can remain in constant contact with relatives and friends in the origin country by telephone and electronic mail. This ease of communication enables immigrants to retain links with the ethnic culture and to resist rapid cultural and structural assimilation. For many, the proximity of the origin country also contributes to the retention of ethnic cultures and social ties. Immigrants from Mexico, for example, make frequent trips back and forth across the border, and a similar pattern of movement is common among immigrants from the Caribbean.

The newest immigrants are likely to see a continuation of immigration from their origin societies well into the twenty-first century. This is unlike the earlier European immigrant waves, which for the most part ended in the 1920s. The older immigrant groups were therefore not constantly infused with new members. Cut off more completely as they were from their societies of origin, they were faced with a greater incentive to assimilate quickly into the mainstream society. Current immigrants and their children, by contrast, are able to continually interact with coethnics, which will likely make for longer-lasting ethnic communities and cultures (Min, 1999). On the other hand, however, the mass media have a way of homogenizing people quickly and with great force. American popular culture is a global phenomenon; most immigrants therefore have absorbed a good deal of it before they actually migrate. Gans (1999) refers to this as "anticipatory acculturation." Roberto Suro explains that it is impossible to grow up in Latin America, for example,

without being saturated with American images and information from birth. As a result, most immigrants can feel quite comfortable with U.S. culture when they arrive, at the same time feeling no need to discard their "Latino sensibilities" (Suro, 1998:71).

Finally, in recent years major institutions in the society, particularly education and the media, have moved toward an acceptance of ethnic pluralism, or multiculturalism, and away from the Anglo-conformity ideology that typified the dominant response to previous immigrant waves. The economy, too, in various ways has begun to cater to the unique needs and tastes of ethnic groups. In short, American institutions have today made it easier to retain one's ethnicity.

At the same time that social forces seem to present unique issues of social and economic adaptation, there are strong indications that the newest immigrants are, in a number of ways, following an assimilation path not radically different from past groups. . . . [L]anguage assimilation for both Latino and Asian groups is proceeding apace, as are residential integration and interethnic and interracial marriage.

Richard Alba has pointed out that assimilation has been incorrectly interpreted by some as a one-way process, in which immigrants surrender their culture and social structure to the dominant society and become carbon copies of the dominant ethnic group (1999:7). But in fact assimilation . . . is a reciprocal process between dominant ethnic groups and immigrant minorities. Thus, immigrants themselves inject change into the society's sociocultural system. As Alba has put it, "immigrant ethnicity has affected American society as much as American society has affected it" (1999:7). Moreover, a distorted conception of assimilation assumes a homogeneity of American culture that simply does not exist. Thus assimilation as it worked for past immigrants will in some regards probably work for current immigrants in a similar fashion, though not as clearly and directly. The remnants of ethnic cultures and social structures therefore will remain evident. As Alba explains, "assimilation most often occurs in the form of a series of small shifts that takes place over generations; those undergoing assimilation still carry ethnic markers in a number of ways" (1999:21). Assimilation, in other words, entails a decline of ethnic distinctions, not their absolute disappearance.

A Revitalized Nativism?

During the past decade, public views of immigration have been ambivalent. This is revealed in national surveys of the 1990s and early 2000s (*American Enterprise,* 1994; *Business Week*/Harris Poll, 1992; Gallup, 2001d, 2002; Jones, 2001; *Newsweek,* 1993, 1995b; *USA Today,* 1995).* Most Americans recognize the great historical role played by immigration in shaping their society but do not necessarily see present-day immigration in the same light. As explained earlier, tolerance for immigration seems to rise and fall with economic conditions. Even during economically good times, however, immigration is not seen positively by a substantial portion of the population. For example, in 1996, 50 percent said they would favor a law that would stop almost all legal immigration to the United States for the next five years; three years later, with the economy more robust than it had been in many years, almost 40 percent still stated their preference for a cut-off of immigration (Gallup, 2001d). Even though the newest immigrants were seen by most as very hardworking, they were also viewed by most as taking jobs away from American workers, driving down wages, and using too many government services. Although anti-immigrant sentiment is by no means as virulent as in the earlier part of the twentieth century, when it eventually led to a halt to the large-scale immigration of southern and eastern European groups, the racial and ethnic character of the newest immigrants, when combined with fluctuations in the state of the domestic economy, continually threatens to create a revitalized nativism.

The flow of international events can also affect public attitudes toward immigration. In the wake of the terrorist attacks on the United States in 2001, for example, new thinking about immigration issues surfaced quickly. A national debate ensued regarding whether adequate security measures were in place to sift out undesirable immigrants, how illegal immigration could be better controlled, and whether U.S. policy was too lenient toward immigrants generally. It is highly probable that U.S. immigration policy will be affected fundamentally by the war against terrorism, as will public attitudes toward immigration.

Whatever changes are enacted in immigration laws are unlikely to bring to an end the debate regarding the number and character of immigrants that should be permitted to enter the United States. Those seeking more stringent limits will continue to argue that immigrants have a negative economic and social influence, whereas those advocating more liberal immigration laws will maintain that immigrants ultimately have a positive impact, both economically and culturally. These are hardly new points of debate, however. Historically, the absorption of immigrants has been a persistent theme of American political argument. In one sense, the United States has always been regarded as a "golden door," open to all seeking economic opportunity or political refuge. But the acceptance of new groups has been countered with a tradition of protectionism, which has manifested itself repeatedly in efforts to limit or exclude newcomers. The current public controversy is, therefore, only the latest in a long tradition.

It is important to note that the current public debate in the United States regarding immigration and the generally negative public view of immigration are not without parallel in other societies. In an analysis of public opinion toward immigrants and immigration issues in Australia, Canada, France, Germany, Great Britain, Japan, and the United States, Simon and Lynch (1999) show that despite these countries' different current and historical immigration policies, a majority of the public in each express relatively similar views: They want fewer immigrants admitted, especially immigrants of color; they feel that priority should be given to immigrants with special skills

*This was true of ethnic minorities as well as Euro-Americans. The Latino National Political Survey showed, for example, that more than 65 percent of U.S.-born Mexicans, Puerto Ricans, and Cubans believed that there were currently too many immigrants coming to the United States (de la Garza et al., 1992).

rather than to those seeking family unification; and they believe that their country has done more than its share in accepting refugees.

REFERENCES

1. Abraham, Sameer Y. 1983. "Detroit's Arab-American Community: A Survey of Diversity and Commonality." Pp. 85–108 in Sameer Y. Abraham and Nabeel Abraham (eds.), *Arabs in the New World: Studies on Arab-American Communities*. Detroit: Wayne State University Press.

2. Alba, Richard D., 1999. "Immigration and the American Realities of Assimilation and Multiculturalism." *Sociological Forum* 14:3–25.

3. *American Enterprise*. 1994. "Immigration." (January/February): 97–100.

4. Baron, Dennis. 1990. *The English-Only Question: An Official Language for Americans?* New Haven: Yale University Press.

5. Beck, Roy. 1996. *The Case against Immigration: The Moral, Economic, Social, and Environmental Reasons for Reducing U.S. Immigration Back to Traditional Levels*. New York: Norton.

6. Borjas, George J. 1994. "Tired, Poor on Welfare." Pp. 76–80 in Nicolaus Mills (ed.) *Arguing Immigration*. New York: Touchstone.

7. ———.1998. "Do Blacks Gain or Lose from Immigration?" Pp. 51–74 in Daniel S. Hamermesh and Frank D. Bean (eds.), *Help or Hindrance? The Economic Implications of Immigration for African Americans*. New York: Russell Sage Foundation.

8. Bouvier, Leon F. 1992. *Peaceful Invasions: Immigration and Changing America*. Lanham, Md.: University Press of America.

9. Bozorgmehr, Mehdi, Claudia Der-Martirasian, and Georges Sabagh, 1996. "Middle Easterners: A New Kind of Immigrant." Pp. 345–378 in Roger Waldinger and Mehdi Bozorgmebr (eds.), *Ethnic Los Angles*. New York: Russell Sage Foundation.

10. Braverman, Marilyn. 1988. "English Yes; English Only, No." *Reconstructionist* 52(June): 29–31.

11. Brimelow, Peter. 1995. *Alien Nation*. New York: Harper Collins.

12. *Business Week*/Harris Poll. 1992. "America's Welcome Mat Is Wearing Thin." (July 13): 122.

13. Cafferty, Pastora San Juan. 1983. "The Language Question: The Dilemma of Bilingual Education for Hispanics in America." Pp. 101–127 in Lance Liebman (ed.), *Ethnic Relations in America*. Englewood Cliffs, N.J.: Prentice-Hall.

14. Castles, Stephen, and Mark J. Miller. 1998. *The Age of Migration: International Population Movements in the Modern World*. 2d ed. New York: Guilford.

15. Chaney, Elsa M. 1979. "The World Economy and Contemporary Migration." *International Migration Review* 13:204–212.

16. Chavez, Linda. 1991. *Out of the Barrio: Toward a New Politics of Hispanic Assimilation*. New York: Basic Books.

17. Chen, David W. 1999. "Asian Middle Class Alters a Rural Enclave." *New York Times* (December 27):A1.

18. Crawford, James. 1992. *Hold Your tongue: Bilingualism and the Politics of "English Only."* Reading, Mass.: Addison-Wesley.

19. de la Garza, Rodolfo O., Louis DeSipio, F. Chris Garcia, John Garcia, and Angelo Falcon. 1992. *Latino Voices: Mexican, Puerto Rican, and Cuban Perspectives on American Politics*. Boulder, Colo.: Westview Press.

20. Espenshade, Thomas J. 1998. "U.S. Immigration and the New Welfare State." Pp. 231–250 in David Jacobson (ed.), *The Immigration Reader: America in a Multidisciplinary Perspective*. Malden, Mass: Blackwell.

21. Fishman, Josua A. 1987. "What Is Happening to Spanish on the U.S. Mainland?" *Ethnic Affairs* 1(Fall): 12–23.

22. Foner, Nancy. 1987. *New Immigrants in New York*. New York: Columbia University Press.

23. Gallup Organization. 2001d. "Americans Ambivalent about Immigrants." Gallup News Service, *Poll Analyses* (May 3).

24. ———. 2002. *Poll Topics & Trends: Immigration* <http://www.gallup.com/poll/topics/immigration.asp>.

25. Gans, Herbert J. 1999. "Filling in Some Holes: Six Areas of Needed Immigration Research." *American Behavioral Scientist* 42:1302–1313.

26. Goodstein, Laurie. 1997. "Women in Islamic Headdress Find Faith and Prejudice, Too." *New York Times* (November 3):A1, A14.

27. Hamada, Tarek. 1990. "Many Arab Immigrants Invest Hope in Detroit." *Detroit News* (December 2): 1A, 10A.

28. Heath, Shirley Brice. 1985. "Language Policies: Patterns of Retention and Maintenance." Pp. 257–282 in Walker Connor (ed.), *Mexican-Americans in Comparative Perspective*. Washington, D.C.: Urban Institute Press.

29. Heer, David. 1996. *Immigration in America's Future: Social Science Findings and the Policy Debate*. Boulder, Colo.: Westview.

30. Hornblower, Margot. 1995. "Putting Tongues in Check." *Time* (October 9):40–50.

31. Isbister, John. 1996. *The Immigration Debate: Remaking America*. West Hartford, Conn.: Kumarian Press.

32. Jones, Jeffrey M. 2001. "Americans Have Mixed Opinions about Immigration." *The Gallup Poll Monthly* (July):28–32.

33. Kayal, Philip, and Joseph Kayal. 1975. *The Syrian-Lebanese in America: A Study in Religion and Assimilation*. Boston: Twayne.

34. Lind, Rebecca Ann, and James A. Danowski. 1998. "The Representation of Arabs in U.S. Electronic Media." Pp. 157–168 in Yahya R. Kamalipour and Theresa Carilli (eds.), *Cultural Diversity and the U.S. Media*. Albany: State University of New York Press.

35. Lopez, David E. 1996. "Language: Diversity and Assimilation." Pp. 139–163 in Roger Waldinger and Mehdi Bozorgmehr (eds.), *Ethnic Los Angeles*. New York: Russell Sage Foundation.

36. Louie, Miriam Ching. 2000. "Immigrant Asian Women in Bay Area Garment Sweatshops: 'After Sewing, Laundry, Cleaning and Cooking, I Have No Breath Left to Sing'." Pp. 226–242 in Timothy P. Fong and Larry H. Shinagawa (eds.), *Asian Americans: Experiences and Perspectives*. Upper Saddle River, N.J.: Prentice Hall.

37. Martin, Philip, and Elizabeth Midgley. 1999. *Immigration to the United States*. Population Bulletin (June). Washington, D.C.: Population Reference Bureau.

38. Min, Pyong Gap. 1999. "A Comparison of Post-1965 and Turn-of-the-Century Immigrants in Intergenerational Mobility and Cultural Transmission." *Journal of American Ethnic History* 18 (Spring):65–94.

39. Muller, Thomas. 1993. *Immigrants and the American City*. New York: New York University Press.

40. Mumford Center for Comparative Urban and Regional Research. 2001c. *Immigrant Enclaves in the American Metropolis, 1990–2000*. Mumford Center, State University of New York at Albany <http://www.albany.edu/mumford/census>.

41. Naber, Nadine. 2000. "Ambiguous Insiders: An Investigation of Arab American Invisibility." *Ethnic and Racial Studies* 23:37–61.

42. Naff, Alixa. 1983. "Arabs in America: A Historical Overview." Pp. 9–29 in Sameer Y. Abraham and Nabeel Abraham (eds.), *Arabs in the New World: Studies on Arab-American Communities*. Detroit: Wayne State University Press.

43. Nazareno, Analisa. 2000. "How Immigrants Reshaped Schools." *Miami Herald* (January 2) <http://www.herald.com>.

44. Newport, Frank. 1998. "Americans Support Elimination of Bilingual Education." *The Gallup Poll Monthly* (June): 17–18.

45. *Newsweek*. 1993. "Newsweek Poll." (August 9):19.

46. ———. 1995a. "Newsweek Poll." (February 13):67.

47. ———. 1995b. "Newsweek Poll." (July 10):31.

48. Portes, Alejandro. 1979. "Illegal Immigration and the International System: Lessons from Recent Legal Mexican Immigrants to the United States." *Social Problems* 26:425–438.

49. Portes, Alejandro, and Rubén Rumbaut. 1996. *Immigrant America: A Portrait*. 2d ed. Berkeley: University of California Press.

50. Portes, Alejandro, and Richard Schauffler. 1996. "Language and the Second Generation: Bilingualism Yesterday and Today." Pp. 8–29 in Alejandro Portes (ed.), *The New Second Generation*. New York: Russell Sage Foundation.

51. Rumbaut, Rubén G. 1996. "Origins and Destinies: Immigration, Race, and Ethnicity in Contemporary America." Pp. 21–42 in Silvia Pedraza and Rubén Rumbaut (eds.), *Origins and Destinies: Immigration, Race, and Ethnicity in America*. Belmont, Calif.: Wadsworth.

52. Saad, Lydia. 1995. "Immigrants See U.S. as Land of Opportunity." *Gallup Poll Monthly* (July):19–33.

53. Sachs, Susan. 1999. "From a Babel of Tongues, a Neighborhood." *New York Times* (December 26):1, 20.

54. ———. 2001. "A Hue, and a Cry, In the Heartland." *New York Times* (April 8):WK5.

55. Sassen, Saskia. 1998. *Globalization and Its Discontents*. New York: The New Press.

56. Schmitt, Eric. 2001b. "Americans (a) Love (b) Hate Immigrants." *New York Times* (January 14):1,3.

57. Shaheen, Jack G. 1984. *The TV Arab*. Bowling Green, Ohio: Bowling Green State University Popular Press.

58. Simon, Julian L. 1991. "The Case for Greatly Increased Immigration." *The Public Interest* 102(Winter):89–103.

59. Simon, Rita J., and James P. Lynch. 1999. "A Comparative Assessment of Public Opinion toward Immigrants and Immigration Policies." *International Migration Review* 33:455–467.

60. Singer, Mark. 2001. "Home Is Here: America's Largest Arab Community in the Aftermath of September 11th." *The New Yorker* (October 15):62–70.

61. Smith, James P., and Barry Edmonston (eds.). 1997. *The New Americans: Economic, Demographic, and Fiscal Effects of Immigration*. Washington, D.C.: National Academy Press.

62. Suleiman, Michael W. 1999. "Introduction: The Arab Immigrant Experience." Pp. 1–24 in Michael Suleiman (ed.), *Arabs in America: Building a New Future*, Philadelphia: Temple University Press.

63. Suro, Roberto. 1989. "Employers Are Looking Abroad for the Skilled and the Energetic." *New York Times* (July 16):IV–4.

64. ———. 1998. *Strangers Among Us: How Latino Immigration is Transforming America*. New York: Alfred A. Knopf.

65. Szabo, Joan C. 1989. "Opening Doors for Immigrants." *Nation's Business* 77(August):48–49.

66. Telhami, Shibley. 2002. "Arab and Muslim America: A Snapshot." *Brookings Review* 20(1):14–15. Washington, D.C.: The Brookings Institution.

67. *USA Today*. 1995. "The New Immigrants" (June 30–July 2):1A, 2A.

68. U.S. Census Bureau. 2001h. *Statistical Abstract of the U.S.: 2000*. Washington, D.C.: U.S. Government Printing Office.

69. ———. 2001m. *Profile of the Foreign-Born Population in the United States: 2000*. CPR P23-206. Washington, D.C.: U.S. Government Printing Office.

70. U.S. Immigration and Naturalization Service.1984. *Statistical Yearbook of the Immigration and Naturalization Service 1984*. Washington, D.C.: U.S. Government Printing Office.

71. ———. 1998. *Statistical Yearbook of the Immigration and Naturalization Service 1998*. Washington, D.C.: U.S. Government Printing Office.

72. ———. 2001. *Illegal Alien Resident Population* <http://www.ins.usdoj.gov>.

73. Van Vugt, William E. 1999. *Britain to America: Mid-Nineteenth-Century Immigrants to the United States*. Urbana: University of Illinois Press.

74. Veltman, Calvin. 1983. *Language Shift in the United States*. Berlin: Mouton.

75. Walbridge, Linda S. 1999. "Middle Easterners and North Africans." Pp. 391–410 in Elliott R. Barkan (ed.), *A Nation of Peoples: A Sourcebook on America's Multicultural Heritage*. Westport, Conn.: Greenwood Press.

76. Warikoo, Niraj. 2001. "Arab Americans Fight Redistricting." *Detroit Free Press* (July 6):A1, A14.

77. Winnick, louis. 1990. *New Pople in Old Neighborhoods: The Role of New Immigrants in Rejuvenating New York's Communities*. New York: Russell Sage Foundation.

IV. Contemporary Institutionalized Oppression and Privilege

Abby L. Ferber

> *Race relations—or, more accurately, racist relations—are not in, but rather of this society.*
>
> —JOE R. FEAGIN

- Women earn 73 cents for every dollar men earn.
- Women executives earn 68 percent of what male executives earn.
- Women with college degrees earn little more than men with only a high school degree.
- Sixty percent of women in the United States are employed in sales, service, or clerical work.
- Regardless of educational level, women and people of color who are seeking employment are more likely to be unemployed than white men and women.
- Average income for white families has increased 34 percent since 1995, but only 25 percent for families of color.
- One out of thirteen whites, one out of five Hispanics, one out of four African Americans, and one out of three Native Americans live in poverty.
- The net worth of the wealthiest one-tenth of Americans increased 76 percent between 1995 and 2004.
- A woman is battered every 15 seconds in the United States.
- Over half of all married women will experience violence in their marriage.
- One-fourth of pregnant women are physically abused.
- Approximately one-fourth of women experience rape or attempted rape.
- Among high school students, 7.3 percent of whites report being raped, compared to 10.4 percent of Hispanics and 12.3 percent of blacks.
- Over 90 percent of eating disorders are experienced by women.
- Fifty percent of fourth-grade girls and 90 percent of eleventh-grade girls are dieting.
- Every 13 seconds a child is molested in the United States.
- One-half of all homeless women and children are fleeing domestic violence.
- Twenty-eight percent of GLBT (gay, lesbian, bisexual, and transgender) youth drop out of school due to a hostile environment.
- Twenty-six percent of GLBT youth are forced to leave home.
- Sixty-nine percent of GLBT youth report experiencing harassment or violence.
- Five children per day in the United States are born with an obvious intersex condition.

- African American men live 7.1 years less than other racial groups.
- Forty percent of African American men die prematurely from cardiovascular disease, as compared to 21 percent of white men, and are five times more likely to die of HIV/AIDS.
- The two richest people in the United States own more personal assets than the sixty poorest countries combined.
- Ninety-seven percent of all students in public high schools regularly hear homophobic comments from peers; 53 percent report hearing homophobic remarks from school staff or faculty.

The numbers are staggering, yet they provide only a tiny snapshot of the full extent of inequality that exists today. This section will begin to examine the inequality that shapes and is produced by social institutions—such as the family, education, and the workplace. While previous sections have examined the dynamics of oppression and privilege, this section will take a closer look at how these patterns are institutionalized. Examining structural inequality across institutions provides a more comprehensive picture than examining any single institution in isolation. When confronted with a single statistic, we may see it as an anomaly and believe that things are generally not too bad. For instance, we may realize that women are paid less than men for the same work, but that fact may not justify in our minds seeing women as oppressed. However, the reality is much bleaker when we examine the full picture.

It is helpful to imagine oppression as a birdcage, as Marilyn Frye (1983) suggests. Each instance of discrimination may be seen as a single wire in this cage. For example, a student might research disparity between schools in primarily white and black neighborhoods and agree that it is, in fact, a problem. But this same student might not understand how that single issue can constitute a serious barrier for African Americans. She may see it as a sad fact of life but, on the other hand, feel it is not an excuse for the failure of many African Americans to succeed.

When we understand the dynamics of oppression, however, we see that this is simply one wire that is a part of the whole birdcage. School disparity in conjunction with segregated housing, unequal wages, higher unemployment rates, disproportionate arrests and prison sentences, unequal access to health care, and tremendous gaps in inherited wealth together add up to create a cage—a cage that holds back and limits the aspirations, hopes, opportunities, and success available to large numbers of African Americans and other minority groups. Sociologist Joe Feagin has spent his distinguished career documenting ongoing discrimination and inequality across institutions, leading him to conclude that "being black means living with racial oppression from cradle to grave" (2001, 173). Thus when we see the structural and systemic nature of the barriers faced by African Americans, we understand then the problem is much larger than the issues inherent in any single institution or cultural context.

It is extremely important not only to examine the construction of difference and the maintenance of inequality in specific institutions, but also to understand how they work together, reinforcing each other, and interacting in their impact on individuals' lives. We all spend our lives moving in a network of institutions, and our experiences in one sphere shape and constrain our experiences in the others. Our families shape our educational opportunities and our success in school; our experiences in both the family and school shape our career opportunities and goals. Indeed, if we do not look at the broader picture, our understanding of any single institution is compromised. For example, women of color have long argued that the reproductive rights movement, which focuses on contraception and abortion rights only, does not address the complexity of the barriers women of color face regarding their reproductive lives. Without economic equality, and access to good health care and education, the legal right to contraception and abortion is insufficient. Further, this example also demonstrates the ways in which various systems of stratification interact. For poor women and women of color, access to abortion is often not the central issue; instead, they may be primarily concerned with the right to bear and keep their children. African American, Latina, and Native American women have historically faced sterilization abuse and forced birth control in order to limit minority populations. Clearly, the categories of race, class, gender, and sexuality, as well as other identity categories, interact in shaping our experiences and opportunities in these institutions.

Due to space limitations, it is not possible to fully examine every social institution in this book, yet there is no institution that is exempt from the dynamics of oppression and privilege. Often we only hear about inequality in one or two institutions, such as education and the workplace, which may limit our understanding of how widespread and embedded these hierarchies truly are. Further, this may lead us to minimize the impact and devastation of lives wrought by this inequality. We have tried, therefore, to provide a brief snapshot of institutional inequality across numerous institutions.

To understand these institutional dynamics, we must place them within the broader context of globalization and the increasing gap between the extremely rich and everyone else. Across the globe, the structure of work has changed, as transnational corporations have relocated to other regions of the world where they can pay workers much less than U.S. workers. This trend, coupled with the policies of the International Monetary Fund, the World Bank, and the World Trade Organization, has contributed to the widening gap between the wealth of the global North and South. At the same time, the growing divide within the United States between the very wealthy and everyone else has been steadily increasing, with tremendous consequences. Further, the obligations of the upper class to the public good have been decreasing. In 1945, individuals paid 40.7 percent of federal taxes, and corporations paid 35.4 percent. In 2005, individuals were paying 47.6 percent, while corporations' shares had plunged to 10.1 percent. This increasing class inequality also impacts people differently based on their race and gender.

As Section III highlighted, social movements like the women's movement, the civil rights movement, and the gay and lesbian movements have fought for and won significant battles for social justice and equity. Many years of struggle and protest have provided us with greater workplace rights than we had a hundred years ago, and we are protected by increased legislation against discrimination (although federal law does not protect us from discrimination based on sexual orientation). An important example is the 1990 Americans with Disabilities Act, passed by Congress thanks in large part to the work of disability rights activists.

Despite tremendous gains, however, in many respects inequality has not improved, and in many domains it has, in fact, worsened. Contemporary sociologists argue that discrimination has morphed, becoming more covert and coded and thus invisible to the undiscerning eye. Many hierarchies are so embedded and institutionalized that they are part of the normal functioning of our society and often not even recognized as playing a significant role in producing inequality. Too many people believe these problems have been solved and are behind us. People with privilege generally do not realize the extent to which inequality is still pervasive. It is not uncommon to hear people argue that "if blacks and other minorities would just stop thinking about the past, work hard, and complain less (particularly about racial discrimination), then Americans of all hues could "all just get along"" (Bonilla-Silva 2003, 1). In terms of race, sociologists and other scholars have labeled this phenomenon "color-blind racism." As Eduardo Bonilla-Silva explained in Section II, color-blind racism is a recent phenomenon that denies the reality of race and racial inequality in American life. According to this perspective, legal changes have already been made, discriminatory practices are now against the law, and all people have equal opportunities to succeed. Therefore, if people are not successful, it is a result of their own poor choices (sociologists call this "blaming the victim").

This perspective justifies racial hierarchies as naturally occurring, rather than as the product of social forces. For example, from this perspective people simply *choose* to live near, work with, and marry people of the same race. Inequality is dismissed as the result of biological or cultural differences between racial groups. For example, the myth that blacks and Hispanics do not value education and hard work may be offered to explain inequality in the workplace. Asian Americans face the opposite, the stereotype of the "model minority," which assumes that they are more successful than other racial and ethnic groups due to their strong cultural values. Even this seemingly positive stereotype perpetuates the assumption that discrimination against Asian Americans does not exist, which is not the case. It also simultaneously lumps together all Asian Americans so that we tend to ignore the reality of disproportionate poverty among many Asian American minority groups. Color-blind racism minimizes and denies the seriousness of oppression. Similar essentialist ideologies are used to explain away other forms of oppression. For example, gender inequality is reinforced and justified by the pervasive opinion that women are nurturers by nature and thus less suited for careers; according to this line of reasoning, women should, therefore, be primarily responsible for child care, elder care, and domestic labor.

Social institutions play a central role not only in producing inequality but in constructing differences. We have seen in Section III how the institution of science constructed racial classifications and literally produced "raced" beings. As we examine numerous other institutions here, we will see similar processes at work, although not as overtly as those practices of the seventeenth and eighteenth centuries. It is essential to understand that inequality is not the result of differences, as we so often assume. Instead, it is the unequal practices of institutions and their efforts to maintain and reproduce that inequality that define people as different, based on race, gender, sexuality, ability, and class. Our social hierarchies do not reflect inherent, natural differences in potential. Instead, our institutions construct, reproduce, and maintain inequality and reinforce the ideology of natural differences to justify this inequality.

Institutionalized inequality begins at the very basic level of language. In "Sounds and Silences of Language: Perpetuating Institutionalized Privilege and Oppression," Dena Samuels examines the ways in which our language perpetuates inequality. It is through language that we construct and make sense of the world. These constructions are reified and communicated most significantly by the media. We live in a media-saturated environment, and the vast majority of people live in neighborhoods populated by people of the same race and class. Therefore, often it is through the media that we come to understand our own culture as well as the cultures of others. Too often the media represent narrow, stereotypical notions of race, class, gender, and sexuality, and, even more importantly, reproduce ideologies that justify inequality. In "Media Magic: Making Class Invisible," Gregory Mantsios demonstrates the power of the media to shape our understanding of reality and to minimize the problem of inequality.

Like the media, schools play a significant role in influencing our knowledge of oppression and privilege. What is being taught in our educational curriculum? Who and what are missing? Who is being privileged and who is being silenced? What messages are being sent to students about our history, about their ability to succeed (and in what areas), and most importantly, about their futures? We often assume that education is the key to increasing equality and inclusion. Unfortunately, this is not the reality. There are, and always have been, gaps in who our educational system serves. Those who are privileged receive a far different and far superior education than those who are not. Inequality shapes everything from the schools we go to and the resources available to those schools, to the images found in textbooks, to the amount and quality of attention each student receives in class. We often assume that every child starts out in school with the same chances of success as any other child, but in the excerpts included in this section from Jonathan Kozol's *The Shame of the Nation,* we see that this is not the case. Moreover, educational disparities have a significant impact on workplace opportunity.

The economy and the workplace are central sites where the dynamics of oppression and privilege operate. A wide range of mechanisms continue to discriminate, both overtly and covertly, despite legal prohibitions. The wage gap between men and women and white people and people of color endures even when they are employed in the same jobs. Furthermore, seemingly neutral organizational rules and economic processes affect social groups differently. For example, in addition to a host of other factors, the lack of flexible work schedules at most jobs makes it more difficult for women working the "second shift" at home—laundry, housework, cooking, shopping, and errands, supervising children's homework, providing child care and elder care, transporting family members to medical appointments, and so on—to advance in their careers (Hochschild 2003). Research finds that even when both parents work full time, mothers perform the majority of child care, housework, and care for extended family members.

The family is perhaps the most fundamental institution to shape human identity. The institution of marriage and the modern family order, as conceived in most Western cultures, is a relatively recent concept. The notion of a hetero-sexually identified nuclear family—consisting of a mother, father, and biological or adopted offspring—was constructed and codified in the context of industrial-ization and economic transformations in Europe and the United States. In other words, the institutionalization of the present-day norm of monogamous, hetero-sexual marriage served the pragmatic functions of preserving family ties, forging political and social relationships, and ensuring the continuity of white privilege (Coontz 2000, 2006). Many groups, particularly those subject to slavery, were legally denied the right to fully partake in this order. The ideology of the modern family has shifted dramatically in the wake of the civil rights and women's move-ments and the advent of global capitalism. Although they have always existed, alternative familial configurations—including interracial, gay, and lesbian couples and single-parent families—have as a result attracted increasing visibility and attention. In "Race, Family Values and Welfare Reform," Bonnie Thornton Dill, Maxine Baca Zinn, and Sandra L. Patton examine the dialogue around women and welfare and the racialized basis of our ideology of the family.

Violence within the family is another mechanism that maintains male privi-lege. Control over women's bodies in particular, and, more generally, violence that pertains to distinct groups and their attendant histories are an essential form of social control. Violence keeps people in their "place" and operates at the levels of both individual experience and the social collectivity. For example, this is the power of a hate crime: While there may be only one individual physically attacked, it sends a powerful message to the broader group of which that individual is a member. For many years lynching served this function. As Barbara Perry demonstrates in "Doing Gender and Doing Gender Inappropriately: Violence Against Women, Gay Men, and Lesbians," continued violence against women, gays and lesbians, and people of color functions as a powerful means of social control, which naturalizes, reifies, and maintains existing value systems and hierarchies.

For women, domestic violence and sexual assault may be the greatest threat to health and well-being. For people of color, the daily experience of racism has a tangible impact on both physical and mental health. We tend to think of health as an individual phenomenon. We assume that besides the genetics we have inherited from our families, our health is largely within our control. Yet the reality is that health and medicine, like other institutions, are shaped by the dynamics of gender, class, sexuality, and race. Health is affected by factors such as access to good nutrition, prenatal care, the quality of affordable and accessible health care, environmental quality, and education, as Melanie Johnson reveals in her essay, "SES, Race/Ethnicity, and Health." Further, the dynamics of racism, patriarchy, and other forms of inequality directly impact peoples' health. Across institutions, it is not only inequality, but difference itself, which is being produced. For example, in Leslie Feinberg's reading, "We Are All Works in Progress," we see that medical institutions play an important role in constructing gender and sexual difference. The extent to which health and medicine shape women's lives and bodies is examined further in "Medicalization of Racial Features," by Eugenia Kaw and "'A Way Outa' No Way'" by Becky Thompson.

The devastation wrought by Hurricane Katrina brought ongoing race and class inequality into stark relief for many of us. Gregory Squires argues in his reading that the impact could have been greatly minimized, that the devastation was not largely due to a natural disaster but to a social one. Our policies regarding poverty, urban infrastructure, suburbanization, and economic development created a situation far worse than the hurricane alone. Public policy and practices differentially impact social groups. Further, our public policy attempts to address specific social problems—such as poverty, child welfare, or drug use—are shaped by inequality; produce and perpetuate inequality; and contribute to the production of race, gender, sexuality, and class constructs. Consider the extent to which social problems are racialized, for example. When we think of welfare recipients, who comes to mind? What about when we think of undocumented workers? Drug dealers? Gang members? Criminals? For most people, these images are highly racialized. We imagine the African American mother on welfare, for example, despite the fact that the vast majority of those receiving welfare are white. To what extent does this racialization shape our policy and practice? In "Driving While Black," John Lamberth examines the ways in which such stereotypes shape the practices of law enforcement officers.

I began this introduction with a quote from Joe Feagin, who aptly describes inequality and the dynamics of oppression and privilege as central to the very fabric of our society. The readings in this section provide a glimpse of the structural nature of inequality. Understanding just how deeply rooted these problems are is essential to developing more successful strategies to eradicate them, to which we will finally turn our attention in Section V.

REFERENCES

1. Bonilla-Silva, E. 2003. *Racism without "racists."* Lanham, MD: Rowman & Little field.
2. Coontz, S. 2000. *The way we never were: American families and the nostalgia trap.* New York: Basic Books.
3. Coontz, S. 2006. *Marriage, a history: How love conquered marriage.* New York: Penguin.
4. Feagin, J. R. 2001. *Racist America: Roots, current realities, and future reparations.* New York: Routledge.
5. Frye, M. 1983. *The politics of reality.* Freedom, CA: Crossing Press.
6. Hochschild, A., with A. Machung. 2003. *The second shift.* New York: Penguin.

Where Is My Country?

NELLIE WONG

Where is my country?
Where does it lie?

The 4th of July approaches
And I am asked for
    firecrackers.
Is it because of my skin color?
Surely not because of my
    husband's name.

In these skyways
I dart in and out.
One store sells rich ice cream
And I pick bittersweet nuggets.

In the office someone asks me
To interpret Korean,
My own Cantonese netted
In steel, my own saliva.

Where is my country?
Where does it lie?

Tucked between boundaries
Striated between dark dance floors
And whispering lanterns
Smoking of indistinguishable features?

Salted in Mexico
Where a policeman speaks to me in Spanish?
In the voice of a Chinese grocer
Who asks if I am Filipino?

Channeled in the white businessman
Who discovers that I do not sound Chinese?
Garbled in a white woman
Who tells me I speak perfect English?
Webbed in another
Who tells me I speak with an accent?

Where is my country?
Where does it lie?

Now the dress designers flood us
With the Chinese look,
Quilting our bodies in satin
Stitching our eyes with silk.

Where is my country?
Where does it lie?

41

Doing Gender and Doing Gender Inappropriately

Violence Against Women, Gay Men, and Lesbians

BARBARA PERRY

I Identify as a woman. Whatever Insults women insults me.
I Identify as gay. Whoever Insults gays Insults me.
I Identify as feminist. Whoever slurs feminism slurs me.

—GLORIA ANZALDÚA, *LA PRIETA*

Gender, like race, is not a static category. It is not a given, natural property or master status that defines our identities once and for all. It is in fact an accomplishment: it is created through conscious, reflective pursuit and must be established and reestablished under varied situations (West and Zimmerman, 1987; West and Fenstermaker, 1993; Fenstermaker, West, and Zimmerman, 1987; Messerschmidt, 1993; Connell, 1987). That is, gender is an *activity* concerned with "managing situated conduct" according to society's normative expectations of what constitutes essential maleness and femaleness (West and Zimmerman, 1987: 127). Moreover, gender is a means by which actors express their manliness or womanliness. They do so with an eye to how their behavior is interpreted or evaluated by others. Central to this conceptualization is the notion of "accountability." At all times, and in all situations, actors are concerned with whether their behavior *will be seen to be* in accordance with approved standards for their assigned sex.

Within this essentially dichotomous understanding of sex, there is very little space for ambiguity, or for blurring the line between masculinity and femininity. On the contrary, "a person engaged in virtually any activity may be held accountable for performance of that activity as a *woman* or a *man,* and their

incumbency in one or the other sex category can be used to legitimate or discredit their other activities" (West and Zimmerman, 1987: 136). In other words, accountability involves the assessment of behavior as either conforming or deviating from culturally normative standards. Whenever we do gender—which is a recurring effort—we leave ourselves open to reward or censure.

Accomplishing gender is not solely an individual or even interpersonal process. It is also institutional, to the extent that it is reinforced by broader social relationships and structures. Consequently, "If we do gender appropriately, we simultaneously sustain, reproduce and render legitimate the institutional arrangements that are based on sex category. If we fail to do gender appropriately, we as individuals—not the institutional arrangements—may be called to account [for our character, motives, and predispositions]" (West and Zimmerman, 1987: 146).

The practice of gender occurs within the constraints of overlapping and competing structures which are simultaneously conditioned by that practice. As noted previously, the structures of labor, power, sexuality, and culture all have significant implications for the process of doing gender. They provide the context in which we "do gender." First, the sexual division of labor defines for us what is considered appropriate work for "essential" males or females, or more important, what is *not* appropriate. Issues involving both the allocation and organization of work (such as job segregation, training and pay differentials, workplace and household technologies) provide important markers and instruments for engaging in masculinity or femininity. To be an engineer or work with heavy machinery or make management decisions is to be masculine; to be a nurse or work with a typewriter or follow orders is to be feminine. To do gender appropriately, one must labor appropriately.

One must also pay homage to established relationships of power. Whether we are speaking of the restricted roles of women in decision making, or their control of institutional resources, or the nature and likelihood of access to social and political institutions, it is consistently the case that women have been disadvantaged as men seek to maintain their own privilege. Women's lived experience of unequal personal and structural power affects and limits their opportunities in all spheres of life.

Gender is accomplished in the context of patterns of sexuality and emotional attachment, or the "social patterning of desire," as well (Connell, 1987: 112). This dimension is predicated on a hierarchy of sexualities, arrayed beneath the hegemonic pattern of the heterosexual couple. The heterosexual ideal generally is characterized by an unequal relationship wherein the male is dominant. Moreover, alternative sexualities (homosexuality, interracial couplings) are subordinated if not vilified.

Underlying, often supporting, these gender structures is an array of cultural constructs that serve to define "masculine" and "feminine." Consistently, such imagery reinforces the presumed strength, aggressiveness, and mastery of the former, and the presumed weakness, passivity, and enslavement of the latter. Media images (such as Ally McBeal), legal constructs (such as female dependency), humor (such as "dumb blonde" jokes), and an array of other cultural icons reproduce feminine ideals that highlight women's sexed position in U.S. society.

Just as parallel structural and cultural scripts condition racialized violence, so too do they condition gendered violence. Moreover, while not all violence against women is necessarily bias motivated—just as not all violence against people of color is bias motivated—much of it is inspired by the anxieties and frustrated expectations of "woman's place." It is meant to teach women, both individually and collectively, a lesson about remaining accountable to their femininity.

GENDER-MOTIVATED VIOLENCE: KEEPING WOMEN IN "THEIR PLACE"

Gender-motivated violence is predicated upon widespread assumptions regarding gender and gender-appropriate deportment. In particular, these assumptions revolve around constructions of gender that represent polar extremes inhabited

by masculine and dominant men, and feminine and subordinate women. Violence is but one means by which men as a class enforce conformity of women as a class. Moreover, it is not necessary for all men to engage in violence against women, since the very threat of violent censure is constantly with women. Violence against women, then, is indeed a "classic" form of hate crime, since it too terrorizes the collective by victimizing the individual. In so doing, hate crime against women reaffirms the privilege and superiority of the male perpetrator with respect to the female victim.

Feminist scholars acknowledge the parallel between violence against women—especially sexual violence—and the lynching of black males as means to exert control and create identity (Brownmiller, 1974; Rothschild, 1993; Pendo, 1994). There is little difference in the motives. Both groups are victimized because of their identity, often for very similar illusionary "violations": "for being uppity, for getting out of line, for failing to recognize 'one's place,' for assuming sexual freedoms, or for [behavior] no more provocative than walking down the wrong road at night in the wrong part of town and presenting a convenient isolated target for group hatred and rage" (Brownmiller, 1974: 281). Just as racially motivated violence seeks to reestablish "proper" alignment between racial groups, so too is gender-motivated violence intended to restore men and women to "their place." Victims are chosen because of their gender and because of the assumptions about how they should enact their gender. The gender polarization that permeates U.S. culture is taken as a "natural," "given" fact, wherein women are expected to enact deference, men dominance. This dichotomy presupposes mutually exclusive scripts for males and females—scripts that constrain everything from modes of dress and social roles to ways of expressing emotion and experiencing sexual desire. It also defines any person or behavior that deviates from these scripts as problematic: unnatural, immoral, biologically anomalous, or psychologically pathological. Gender-motivated violence is a key means by which men and women rehearse their scripts, ensuring that women act "like women" in the bedroom, in the kitchen, in the workplace, and on the street.

GENDER, POWER, AND VIOLENCE

In each of these domains, gendered relations of power are enacted, albeit in slightly disparate forms. What unites the home, the workplace, and the street is that each historically has been a crucial site in efforts to establish an "appropriate" hierarchy in which men are dominant, women subordinate. Each has been the locus of struggles that have contributed to the empowerment of men and the relative disempowerment of women.

The United States is a male supremacist society wherein gender difference is constructed as gender inferiority and, ultimately, gender disadvantage. Consequently, women garner less power, prestige, and economic reward than men, who have consistently retained leadership and control in government, commerce, and family matters (Lorber, 1994). This is readily apparent in the legal history that has helped shape gendered relations of power. Male privilege has long been guaranteed by legal proscriptions and silences that have simultaneously excluded women from involvement in the public sphere, while failing to protect them in the context of their private lives (Taub and Schneider, 1990). On the one hand, legal exclusions on women's enfranchisement, ownership of property, and employment (in law and medicine, for example) have meant that until well into the twentieth century, women were unable to participate fully in politics or the economy. Even today, restrictions on access to abortion or to social security provisions, for example, limit the participatory power of women.

On the other hand, law has also enabled the subordination of women within the home. The same nineteenth-and twentieth-century provisions that limited (married) women's ownership of property meant that married women, in particular, ceded autonomy to their husbands upon marriage. The historical tendency to exclude from criminal proceedings husband's rapes or assaults on wives similarly ensured the dominance of men who were merely exercising their "marital rights." The continued

failure to recognize the value of women's domestic labor through some form of income support likewise helps to maintain women's economic dependence on men, both during and subsequent to marriage. This is exacerbated by inequitable divorce settlements and the intractable wage disparities between men and women.

At least with respect to family and domestic violence, men's perceived sense of "ownership" continues to provide a context for the victimization of girls and women. The structured inequality of women leaves them vulnerable to the presumption of male control by whatever means necessary. It establishes an environment in which men freely manipulate the terms of a relationship. Violence becomes one such means for him to prove that he is "the man" and therefore in control. This even extends to relationships with daughters, as in the case of incestuous assaults. Research consistently suggests that child sexual abuse within families is disturbingly common (Baskin and Sommers, 1998; Belknap, 1996). It is not unlike woman battering in the home, to the extent that it too is a display of men's control over women, and especially women's sexuality. As Elizabeth Stanko (1985) contends, incestuous assaults are an assertion of male "rights" of access to and control of the powerless female. Young girls especially are vulnerable to such victimization due to their place in the family, their lack of experience, and their femaleness, which Stanko equates with powerlessness.

The extensive research of R. Emerson Dobash and Russell Dobash has led them to identify four interrelated "sources of conflict" that, they argue, are most predictive of woman battering: "men's possessiveness and jealousy; men's expectations concerning women's domestic work; men's sense of the right to punish 'their' women for perceived wrong doing; and the importance, to men, of maintaining or exercising their position of authority" (1997: 268). Uniting these four triggers is the sense that the man has the right, perhaps the duty, to express his masculine power through violent repression. The female partner in such a relationship is seen to have challenged the masculine authority of her partner. She is seen to have transcended the boundaries of appropriate behavior and deference—perhaps she spoke too long with another man, or sought employment outside the home, contrary to the "demands" of her partner. Such behaviors throw into question the masculinity of the perpetrator. If he cannot control "his woman," perhaps he is not really a manly man after all. By striking out in violence, he reasserts his dominant and aggressive masculinity.

This male concern with taking charge and taking control of the heterosexual relationship emerges repeatedly in research on domestic violence (Websdale and Chesney-Lind, 1998; Weisburd and Levin, 1994; Wolfe and Copeland, 1994; Dobash and Dobash, 1997). This is especially true for patriarchal and usually lower-class families. In such situations, the "essential" nature of the patriarch is interpreted as the responsibility to "dominate and control their wives, and wife beating serves both to ensure continued compliance with their commands and as a resource for constructing a 'damaged' patriarchal masculinity. Thus, wife beating increases (or is intended to do so) their control over women" (Messerschmidt, 1993: 147).

That a great deal of domestic violence is in fact motivated by a presumed loss of control and ownership is apparent in the increased likelihood of victimization as women attempt to exit a relationship. When women seek to empower themselves, when they seek to achieve some personal autonomy by escaping an abusive relationship, they often become dangerously vulnerable to stalking, assault, even murder (Browne, 1995; Chaiken, 1998; Tjaden and Thoennes, 1998). In many relationships, separation is the moment when the quest for control becomes lethal. Browne's interviews with battered women who killed their partners revealed the extent to which men's attempts to retain control outlast the relationship. One participant maintained that "we were separating but I don't think that would have solved anything. Don always said that he would come back around—that I belonged to him" (Browne, 1995: 232). The spouse of another of Browne's subjects once wrote in his journal, "Every time, Karen would have ugly bruises on her

face and neck. She would cry and beg me for a divorce, and I would tell her, 'I am sorry. I won't do it again. But as for the divorce, absolutely not. If I can't have you for my wife, you will die. No one else will have you if you ever try to leave me'" (Browne, 1995: 232). Men who batter attempt to assert their proprietary masculinity through violence. It is as if they fear that all appearance of masculinity, of dominance, of control is lost in the face of women's challenges to their authority. Their violence simultaneously reestablishes the appropriate place of the male and female partners; it is both male prerogative and female punishment.

Moreover, not all men need to engage in battering for it to have a debilitating effect on women. Indeed, the power of domestic violence is that—like other forms of bias-motivated violence—it is embedded in a systemic pattern of real and potential violence against women. The violence against a particular woman in the home is a reminder that any woman in society is subject to violent control by men. In other words, "Men's power is not an individual, but a collective one. Women's lives are bounded by it. The threat of male violence outside the home . . . is an acutely intimidating reality to women who endure violence within their own homes" (Stanko, 1985: 57). Men correspondingly enact their "will to power" outside the home. Assaults, rapes, or homicides that are outside the bounds of an intimate relationship tend to be directed at individual women as proxies for the combined threats to masculine domination represented by women as a class. In their daily lives, all women, at any time, may be vulnerable to gender-motivated harassment, intimidation, and violence because they are women and because they represent the devalued, often threatening Other. Wherever a particular act lies on the continuum of violence, it is a "ritual enactment of domination, a form of terror that functions to maintain the status quo" (Caputi, 1993: 7).

As with racially motivated violence, gender-motivated violence often emerges in the context of what is perceived by men as a loss of relative position. Challenges to the collective hegemony of men often are met with aggressive attempts to reassert the "natural" dominance of men. It is, in these terms, a reactive expression of insecurity in the face of reconstituted femininities. It is no coincidence that violent crime perpetrated against women has risen so steadily in the three decades corresponding to the rise of the women's movement. Marilyn French (1992) and Susan Faludi (1991) carefully document what they refer to as the "War Against Women" and the antifeminist backlash, respectively. Both authors point to the increasing harassment and intimidation of women through violence and the threat of violence. As women have collectively striven to redefine themselves as autonomous actors, some men have been compelled to meet the challenge by resorting to the readily available resource of violence.

Marc Lepine is a case in point. On December 6, 1989, Lepine entered a classroom at Montreal's Ecole Polytechnique, systematically separated the male and female engineering students, and opened fire on the women. Before he killed himself, Lepine had murdered fourteen women and seriously injured nine others. In his verbal harangue during the shooting and in his suicide note, Lepine made it clear that his assault was intended to punish the feminists he held responsible for his personal failures— in particular, his inability to get into engineering school. Lepine's response was extreme, but nonetheless illustrative of the male response to the "erosion of white male exclusivity and privilege" (Caputi and Russell, 1992: 13).

WORKING TOWARD VIOLENCE

Lepine's case also is illustrative of one of the greatest sources of male trepidation and hostility: the reconfiguration of the gendered division of labor. This is a central component within which gendered relations of power are embedded. Misogynistic hostility often finds its roots and its focus in what are perceived to be distortions in the "natural" division of labor between men and women. Gender-motivated violence, in other words, is very likely in the context of local and global patterns that empower women with respect to the distribution and organization of work.

As noted earlier in this [essay], there is a social perception that there is "men's work" and "women's work"; each provides the structured opportunities and resources for what is deemed the appropriate performance of labor to which each gender is "naturally" suited. At the highest level of generality, this means that "woman's place" is in the home— bearing, nurturing, and raising the children, and acting as companion and sexual partner for her spouse. "Man's place" is in the corridors of the capitol, or the office, or the shop floor—making the "hard decisions, doing the "hard" work, and providing the paycheck. Beyond this illusory ideal are arranged an array of other less-valued options that reproduce the gendered relations of reproduction and production. Even in the workforce, women are expected to behave like women, occupying subordinate, nurturing, and supportive roles as secretaries, as nurses, as (elementary) schoolteachers. Correspondingly, men are expected to act like men in their capacity as leaders, managers, and manual laborers.

The gendered division of labor is manifest in a number of identifiable patterns, including wage differentials, job segregation, and uneven patterns of reproductive labor in the home. Each of these can be traced back to the deeply embedded ideologies of "gender-appropriate" labor. Not only is the work women do devalued. Traditionally, it has also been viewed as secondary. Labor inside the home is invisible and unrecognized; work outside the home is merely something she does until married, or to earn pin money. In contrast, "men's work" is deemed essential to the operation of both the national and the family economy. His is the "real" work, which earns a "real" paycheck. Consequently, women's labor tends to be both underacknowledged and underpaid (if not unpaid), while that of men tends to be highly recognized in both social and economic terms.

In concrete terms, this means that women in the United States still earn only about 75 cents to every dollar men earn. In spite of equal-pay legislation, even in similar jobs men's wages outpace those of women. This holds regardless of educational level attained. In 1991, men with less than eight years of schooling earned, on average, $19,632 annually, or $300 more than women who had completed high school ($19,336). Men without a college degree earned $33,758, or $600 more than women with a bachelor's degree or above (U.S. Department of Commerce, 1993).

Moreover, the fact that "women's work" is less prestigious contributes to low wages industrywide in those areas dominated by women. Typically, the higher the concentration of women in a particular job, the lower the median wage. In fact, some studies estimate that as much as 35 to 40 percent of the income disparity between men and women can be accounted for by occupational sex segregation (Reskin, 1993; Rosenfeld and Kalleberg, 1991). For example, in 1990, 99.1 percent of all secretaries were female and their median weekly wage was $343; 96.1 percent of all child care workers were women, and their weekly income was $203. In the same year, women represented only 13.4 percent of all police officers, who earned $645 per week, and 3.1 percent of all airline pilots or navigators, who earned $898 per week (U.S. Department of Labor, 1991).

The dual labor market that characterizes the U.S. economy maintains women in low-wage, low-prestige ghettos of service work, while simultaneously maintaining the male privilege of lucrative, skilled, and professional positions. Moreover, in keeping with the "natural" superiority of men over women, even when men are employed in traditionally female areas, the positions they occupy are more powerful. For example, while women constituted 98 percent of all clerical staff in 1992, over 40 percent of the clerical supervisors—the bosses—were men (U.S. Department of Commerce, 1993).

The gendered division of labor is reproduced in the household. In spite of the dramatic increase in women's labor force participation, they continue to bear a disproportionate share of the burden of homemaking (Ferree, 1987). The parallel construction of a gendered division of labor in the home means that "just as there is a wage gap between men and women in the workplace, there is a 'leisure gap' between them at home. Most women work one shift at the office or factory and a 'second shift' at home" (Hochschild, 1995: 444). Consequently, traditional male privilege also tends to be reproduced in the home: women's unequal structural and economic power finds its counterpart in her unequal access to personal power within the home.

It is women's "essence," after all, to nurture. This expectation lies at the heart of the sexual division of labor. What Robert Connell (1987) refers to as emphasized femininity is enacted through women's commitment to household labor: cleaning, cooking, and attending to the needs of husband and children alike. Regardless of the reality, the idealized image of femininity might resemble something from the black-and-white episodes of *Pleasantville* or *Leave It to Beaver,* or the full-color television ads of today. A nicely dressed Mommy mops the (already spotless) floor of a tidy and ordered house, then prepares a full-course meal for her provider husband and well-behaved and -coiffed children. One moment she is overseeing the children's homework, the next she is a fiery vixen satisfying her husband's sexual fantasies.

Of course, this is a simplified and monolithic vision. There is remarkable variation across class, race, and ethnicity with respect to the extent to which women are held accountable to the ideal. For example, Scott Coltrane's (1995) interviews with dual-income Chicano couples found an asymmetrical division of labor to be more prevalent among both lower-class and upper-middle-class couples than among white-collar and working-class Chicanos. A. S. Barnes's (1985) examination of African-American couples suggests also that men at the extremes of educational and occupational hierarchies rejected housework as a threat to their masculinity.

There is some consistency in gender expectations that cuts across all other lines of difference. There continue to exist "patriarchs" of all classes and races who enact their masculinity through concentrated attempts to define the terms of the labor "contract" in heterosexual relationships. As much as the "culture of fatherhood" may have changed in recent years, the "conduct of fatherhood" has not kept pace (La Rossa, 1995). In other words, in spite of the popular belief that contemporary family life is more egalitarian, the reality is that many women continue to negotiate their identities in relationships that are oppressive and decidedly unequal.

Recent years have witnessed remarkable disruptions in the traditional patterns of the public and private division of labor. Changes in the distribution and organization of work have robbed men of the predictable context and resources for the exhibition of their many characteristics: autonomy, risk taking, mastery of humans and nature. At the same time, gains of the women's movement have blurred the gendered labor lines. Together these patterns have created anxiety among those who are left without evidence of their masculinities. Kenneth Karst expresses this uneasiness in colorful terms when he asserts, "In an economy that has not produced jobs to keep up with the pool of prospective workers, a lot of men, especially young men, have become nervous about more than their flaccid incomes" (1993: 144–45). Because the labor realm has for so long been a site for the visible construction of dominant and patriarchal masculinity, recent challenges posed by resistant and empowered femininities in search of autonomy have provoked considerable backlash. All too often, women's efforts to redefine femininity in the context of their work have been countered by violence intended to remind them of the appropriate gendered balance of labor. The blurring of gender lines has proven disquieting to many who see male preserves crumbling. The working-class men interviewed by Fine, Weis, and Addleston (1997) voiced their concerns about their diminished abilities to exercise masculine prerogatives. The traditional mechanisms in and through which they could enact aggressive and patriarchal masculinity have faded in the 1980s and 1990s, "a time when the women they associated with got independent, their jobs got scarce, their unions got weak and their privileged access to public institutions was compromised by the success of equal rights and affirmative action" (Fine et al., 1997: 66). As beneficiaries of equal rights and affirmative action, women are among the blameworthy. They are seen, by virtue of their engagement in "inappropriate" labor

activities, to have impinged on men's opportunities to "do gender" without interference or competition.

One very visible reaction to these perceived threats and improprieties is evident in the ubiquitous practice of sexual harassment. Laura O'Toole and Jessica Schiffman observe that women's presence in nontraditional fields is associated with an elevated risk of harassment (1997: 134). Stanko (1985) similarly notes that the more highly educated a woman is the more likely she is to be harassed. In this context, workplace harassment becomes a frequent response to women's invasion of male bastions. It is a means to simultaneously create a particular masculinity and enforce a particular exclusive feminity. Carol Brooks Gardner's (1995) interviews with men revealed explicitly that men often perceived sexual harassment of women as a well-deserved response to their economic and professional advances. Their encroachment into male realms interferes with, indeed calls into question, men's ability to prove themselves to be men by the work they do. If women can do the job, then what does that say about the masculinity of the role players?

Sexual harassment allows for the reassertion of masculinity and femininity, and especially the "natural" differences between the two. It sexualizes the workplace, so as to reassure the men that they are at once heterosexual and empowered, and to remind the women that they are sexual objects, not laborers. The differences between masculinity—aggressive, in control, dominant—and femininity—passive, sexual, submissive—are made explicit through sexual jokes, grabbing or sexual assaults aimed toward women. The message that accompanies the acts is that women "don't belong," that they are "out of place," in short, that femininity cannot be constructed appropriately in male-dominated workplaces. This becomes very clear in the study of workplace sexual assault conducted by Beth Schneider (1993). Interestingly, she found that in approximately one-half of the incidents of workplace sexual assaults reported by respondents, the offenders coerced their victims through "challenges to femininity." In other words, they expressed the sentiments that "real women" would welcome the sexual advances. In light of their employment in male-dominated fields, women were asked to prove their femininity through sexual conduct. Perpetrators' sought to reinstate their victims' femininity by coercing them to make themselves available sexually.

That women hear the punitive message loud and clear is often evident in their reactions to the harassment. While many don't bother to report their harassment to supervisors, a disconcerting number of women leave or change jobs in the face of ongoing harassment (U.S. Merit Systems Protection Board, 1995; Gardner, 1995; Stanko, 1985). Gardner's female subjects reported that they often began to feel "untraditional" and that they did not belong in the workplace. One women who quit after a lengthy period of harassment stated that her experience "proved men are right when they say women still belong at home, because I do and now that's where I am. I should never have tried [to take a job outside the home]" (Gardner, 1995: 61).

Short of quitting their jobs, some women who stay in the workplace nonetheless reassess their self-presentation so that they might be seen as conforming to some minimum standard of "appropriate femininity" (Gardner, 1995). They act "less bitchy" or "less sexy" or even less competent or intelligent. In this way, they may become accountable to the ideal of emphasized femininity. Where this is the response, the male harasser has been effective in reaffirming the proper, or at least acceptable boundaries between men and women. As long as women remain in the workplace, they are expected to do so within redefined but nonetheless circumscribed boundaries of acceptable workplace behavior set by male workmates and superiors. In this way, the harasser resumes control of the situation. *He* takes a stand; *he* engages in behavior that renders women powerless in the workplace. By displaying his own power, and emphasizing his own aggressive heterosexuality, the harasser takes advantage of sexual harassment as "an effective (albeit primitive) resource for solidifying, strengthening, and validating a specific type of heterosexual shop-floor masculinity, while simultaneously excluding, disparaging and ridiculing women" (Messerschmidt, 1993: 132).

Moreover, women are peculiarly vulnerable to sexual harassment in the workplace. Earlier in this [essay] we saw how men are positioned structurally to exploit the labor market as a place of empowerment. In the public mind, paid employment traditionally has been the locus for the construction of masculinities rather than femininities. More important, however, where women have entered the workforce, it has been in a position of relative inferiority and subordination. Women's entry into the workforce has been on unequal terms. Consequently, men can engage in sexual harassment of women with virtual impunity. Such behavior is all too often perceived as a typical, normative interaction between unequals. Women are rarely in a position to effectively challenge their harassers who are their political, social, and usually economic "betters."

To the extent that workplace harassment is intended to make women feel like they don't belong, it parallels the intent of much violence in the home. Woman battering, too, often finds its roots and its motivation in a desire to confirm the traditional division of (domestic) labor. Disputes over whether and how women will labor outside the home, and the distribution of labor within the home, go to the heart of patriarchal violence behind closed doors. The challenge to male authority is not restricted to the workplace. As Fine et al. (1997) indicated, men also fear an erosion of their ability to perform as "real men" in their homes. They fear emasculation in the face of multiple and alternate constructions of femininity, few of which correspond to the passive and nurturing ideal.

Add to this the deskilling and loss of autonomy associated with the contemporary workplace. The resultant situation is one in which a whole class of men envision themselves with limited traditional means of testing and proving their masculinity. Violence directed toward their female partners represents a remaining weapon in the dwindling arsenal of resources available for presenting a masculine face to the world. Powerless in the workplace, he assumes power in the home. The assumption of this authority is held to extend to the violent enforcement of "his woman's" compliance to a rigid essence of femininity. It is when she resists such compliance that she is likely to become vulnerable to assault within the household. In this way, the struggle to define the terms of the domestic division of labor provides a context for both partners to do gender on relative, often antagonistic terms.

Neil Websdale and Meda Chesney-Lind's (1998) review of recent domestic violence literature reveals the consistency with which researchers are able to identify a relationship between patriarchal ideals and wife battering. For example, studies by Dobash and Dobash have revealed that battering is most likely to occur where women challenge their partners about household (economic) decisions, and where women are perceived as having failed in their "wifely duties"—refusing sex, serving cold meals, or neglecting the vacuuming. In other words, violence is a reactive performance of masculinity in the face of oppositional performances of femininity.

Interviews with batterers and their victims are illuminating in this regard. Often, both are very much aware of the existence of shared patriarchal beliefs, and the role of violence in enforcing them. A Kentucky woman interviewed by Websdale makes astute observations on the consequences of her "inappropriate" performance of an oppositional form of femininity.

Tamara: The man is the head of the household. The woman has no say. It doesn't matter about her morals and her feelings. Nothing.
Websdale: Was your husband like that?
Tamara: He tried to be. That was our biggest problem. I talked back. I had an opinion and I wasn't allowed to have an opinion. And I'd say, "I don't care if you agree or not, honey, that's how I feel." That's one reason I was hit.

Male batterers express the same ideological position, as is the case with this abusive male interviewed by Peter Adams, Alisa Towns, and Nicole Garvey:

Well, you got the male and you got the [laughing] female. And the male earns the bread and the

woman brings up the family and that. . . . And it's a fact of life that only women can be a mother. There's no, there's no other way around it. And the man's still gotta go and earn the bread and the woman's still gotta have the children. (1995: 390)

Interviews with both battered women and their partners conducted by Dobash and Dobash (1998) reflect the paramount importance men place on their needs and their partners' ability to fulfill them. Often the only provocation to violence was the woman's failure to anticipate or fulfill her partner's expectations of her domestic femininity. One woman reported that

He was late and I'd started cooking his meal but I put it aside, you know, when he didn't come in. Then when he came in I started heating it. I was standing at the sink and he just came up and gave me a punch in the stomach. . . . It was only because his dinner wasn't ready on the table for him. (1998: 147)

This theme appears again in Diana Russell's interviews with victims of marital rape. One participant revealed that

Oftentimes, he'd ask "where's my supper?" If it wasn't there, he'd hit me, even though I never knew when he'd be home because he was out with other women. (1990: 129)

A final illustration of the relationship between patriarchal beliefs and gendered violence is cited by Jane Caputi and Diana Russell:

In 1989, Curtis Adams was sentenced to 32 years in prison for torturing his wife in a ten-hour attack. After she refused anal sex, Adams handcuffed his wife, repeatedly forced a bottle and then a broomstick into her anus and hung her naked out the window—*taking breaks to make her read biblical passages adjuring women to obey their husbands.* (1992: 18, emphasis added)

In such patriarchal relationships, male batterers use violence to simultaneously prove their manliness and remonstrate "their women" for failing to prove their corresponding womanliness. An essential nature and set of roles is assumed for each, and when they are not forthcoming—when his ability to be a real man is thwarted by her refusal to be a real woman—violence often ensues. The enactment of violence is an enactment of masculine power and control, where it might otherwise be eroding.

Intuitively, this analysis implies that domestic violence perpetrated against women of color may be especially problematic. Christine Rasche (1995) maintains that many of the ethnic communities that have shaped the United States—Latinos, African Americans, Asians, and Native Americans in particular—are structured by rigid patriarchal norms that tend to render familial violence tolerable, if not invisible. However, Kimberlé Williams Crenshaw (1994) highlights the problematic nature of this assumption in light of the academic neglect of the "intersection of racism and patriarchy." What Crenshaw does make clear is that women of color are uniquely vulnerable to gendered violence because of their multiply determined structural disempowerment. They are often simultaneously oppressed by their class, gender, and racial position. That this is the case is also suggested by recent trends toward increasing domestic violence among the Navajo of the Southwest, for example (Zion and Zion, 1996). The traditionally egalitarian nature of these people has been distorted by their more recent history of racial discrimination and disempowerment. Racial and economic disadvantage, coupled with the incursion of Anglo gender ideals, has dramatically altered the place of Navajo women. Increasingly, like their white counterparts, Navajo women are expected to perform the rituals of domestic femininity as a complement to the male performance of patriarch[y].

Contrary to popular mythology, African-American gender politics are characterized by neither the extreme matriarch nor the extreme patriarch. Rather, the performance of gender historically has been fluid. According to Beverly Greene (1997), rigid expectations of femininity and masculinity have been "impractical" against the backdrop of economic marginalization of black men. While the importance of the family has been a constant, idealized notions of masculinity and femininity nonetheless have varied by class, region, and ethnicity.

This is not to say that domestic violence has not also been a constant. hooks' volumes consistently draw attention to the sexism that seems to permeate African-American culture, even where patriarchal performances of masculinity are not in question. hooks agrees that male-as-breadwinner has not always been a viable option as a resource for most young black males. Proof of masculinity instead is embedded in their aggression, their sexuality, or in their ability to discipline the family. Combine these options with the tendency to share with white males a devalued and disdainful perception of women, and the climate is ripe for domestic violence against "uppity black women" (hooks, 1981; 1992). Contemporary African Americans also can find legitimation for their violent subjugation of women in the Muslim glorification of the "feminine ideal." Women are expected to defer to men's natural superiority. Violence in this context allows men to exercise at once their aggressiveness, dominance, and holiness (hooks, 1981).

Espiritu's (1997) examination of the gender politics of Asian Americans also highlights the intersection of race, gender, and class. In contrast to what is often a very traditional division of labor and power in their homeland, Asian immigrants to the United States find that their abilities to maintain such boundaries are compromised. As Espiritu contends, Asian-American women are more likely to be employed, albeit in low-wage occupations, than either their counterparts at home or their male partners in the United States. Consequently, they assume an elevated position in the family as breadwinner and decision maker—a clear threat to the masculinity authority and place of their husbands. As in the parallel white patriarchal family, violence can come to represent a leveling influence. One immigrant male expressed his dissatisfaction with his situation in the United States:

> In Korea [my wife] used to have breakfast ready for me. . . . She didn't do it any more because she said she was too busy getting ready for work. If I complained, she talked back at me, telling me to fix my own breakfast. . . . I was very frustrated about her, started fighting and hit her. (Espiritu, 1997: 75)

Asian immigrant males' inability to sustain traditional patriarchal identities and women's challenges to an idealized and subordinate femininity have resulted in elevated rates of family violence among these families (Civil Rights Commission, 1992a). Such violence is a readily available means to resurrect "normal" relations of power, whereby women are reminded that, regardless of economic contributions, their true place is in the kitchen, their true occupation is the care of the family.

SEXUALITY AND VIOLENCE

Paralleling the presumption of a normative division of labor, there exists the presumption of normative sexualities. The latter is especially crucial in helping us to understand sexual violence as gendered violence. Sexual assault serves a particularly dramatic role in the policing of gender boundaries and the control of women's sexuality, for it is the place wherein women become objectified as predominantly sexual beings in the service of men.

To the extent that women are sexualized—in the workplace, on the street, in the home—they are held accountable to a femininity that requires sexual responsivity to men's advances. Just as the relative performance of masculinity and femininity assumes male proprietary rights, so too does it assume that sex with the woman of his choice is a man's right. Herein lies the context for gender-motivated sexual violence. As one rapist put it,

> Rape is a man's right. If a woman doesn't want to give it, the man should take it. Women have no right to say no—women are made to have sex. That's all they're good for. (Curran and Renzetti, 1994: 207)

Just as a sense of entitlement underlies domestic violence, so too does it underlie sexual violence within and outside intimate relationships. As the above quote suggests, sexual access to women as a class is perceived as the inalienable right of men as a class. Sexual assault, then, is an institutionalized, rather than aberrant, means by which men can perform their masculinity while "symbolizing and actualizing women's subordinate position"

(MacKinnon, 1991: 1302). Women's sexuality is a ready commodity, available to all. In other words, "all women are whores and, therefore, fair game; sexual violence is normal and acceptable" (Caputi and Russell, 1992: 18).

Entitlement takes on a special meaning in the context of sexual assault by intimates—both rape in marriage and acquaintance rape. In these situations, sexual assault takes on an additional validity, reinforcing the gendered power of men to control even the most intimate dimensions of women's lives. Earlier, I discussed the family as a preeminent site for the regulation of the sexual division of labor, through violence if necessary. The marital relationship is no less important for the regulation of sexuality, and women's sexuality in particular. It is the site at which men most readily and forcefully exercise their (hetero)sexual rights to a woman's body. Women are expected to "exchange" their sexual favors for a share of their husbands' paychecks, or for the dinner and a movie provided by their dates. This, according to tradition, is the appropriate way for a woman to express her gratitude, and of course, her femininity. Should she adopt an oppositional femininity—by saying "no"—she becomes vulnerable to violent reprobation. Such is the normativity of sexual entitlement, that rapists—and their victims—often don't acknowledge intimate rape as rape. Robin Warsaw (1994) reports that 84 percent of men who had committed date rape asserted that their actions definitely did not constitute rape. A victim of rape clearly articulates her victimizer's failure to recognize the severity of his assault:

> He left me a note with one of those smile faces drawn on it. The note read "Denise, I woke up and you were gone. Catch ya later! Have a nice day. Bob." Minutes later, the phone rang. The voice belonged to a cheerful Bob. I think I called him a bastard or a fucker and I told him not to ever call me again, and then hung up. He called back, sounding surprised, asking, "Hey, what's the matter?" (Warsaw, 1994: 91).

Similar assumptions of the unobstructed right of men to women's bodies [are] evident in sexual assault within cohabiting and marital relationships. Even more so than dates or boyfriends, husbands hold their wives to the presumption of unrestricted sex-on-demand. That is part of her "role" as prescribed by narrow and rigid constructions of femininity. She is the sexual companion, often sexual property, of her mate. When women rebel against such prescriptions, they become vulnerable to the violent reassertion of their partners' aggressive sexuality and manhood, in a way that also is intended to remind them how they are expected to perform. This was the interpretation of rape offered by many of Russell's (1990) subjects:

> I consented to sex with him when I didn't want to. . . . It was out of duty, I guess you'd say. He somehow conveyed to me that he expected it of me because I was his wife. (52)

> With a husband, you feel forced. I have an obligation to my husband which is very bad. It's always been a man's world. (81)

> He used to call me at work to come to him at once because he wanted sex. I used to work on Saturday and he didn't so he wanted me home. (92)

> It was a very brutal marriage. He was so patriarchal. He felt he owned me and the children—that I was his property. In the first three weeks of our marriage, he told me to regard him as God and his word as gospel. If I didn't want sex and he did, my wishes didn't matter. (123)

Women and men learn very young that male sexual access to women is "naturally" unrestricted. In some cases, this lesson is learned in the home, when young girls become the victim of child sexual abuse. This practice normalizes sexual assaults against women. It also sexualizes them very early on, so that they become defined by their "sexual capital"; girls learn that their most valuable and manipulable asset is their sexuality. As Stanko puts it, "One basic part in some children's lives, however, can be a source of confusion: as part of the pink world, incestually assaulted children learn that their female role also entails sexual availability to men" (1985: 20).

Perhaps, then, it is no accident that those victimized as children are vulnerable to revictimization as adults (Belknap, 1996).

These lessons are reinforced as girls and boys enter adolescence. Barrie Thorne's (1994) work on gender socialization in school settings suggests that adolescent girls are encouraged to cultivate a "culture of compliance and conformity" with respect to boys that may very well leave them vulnerable to sexual victimization. Conversely, boys begin to develop a sense of self that is predicated on mastery of their environment, including girls.

If women have not learned during earlier courtships that "their sexuality is not their own," the lesson often is driven home after marriage (Stanko, 1985: 73). In fact, sexual assault is the ultimate abrogation of women's choice, autonomy, and self-determination. Forced sex reproduces masculine dominance and control like few other activities. It victimizes women in ways to which they are "uniquely vulnerable" (Rothschild, 1993: 270). Men's ability to overpower women sexually—by right—establishes them as master.

O'Sullivan's comparison of gang rapists and batterers suggests that in some respects, there are remarkable similarities in the dynamics of marital rape and gang rapes. Both appear to turn on "general beliefs in male supremacy, hostility toward women, and different standards for sexual behavior in men and women" (O'Sullivan, 1998: 89). However, there is also a crucial difference: "Gang rape is 'about' the relationship among men doing it rather than their relationship to the woman they are abusing. . . . [Marital rape] is more instrumental than expressive, with the goal of regulating the relationship between the man and his wife" (O'Sullivan, 1998: 105). In other words, gang rape has a different audience in mind, with a slightly different purpose. It is a display of sexual prowess for the group. It is a communal exercise whereby men degrade women while simultaneously proving their solidarity, their sexuality, and their manhood. They share in one another's sexuality through their sharing of the victim (O'Sullivan, 1998; Martin and Hummer, 1995; Sanday, 1998). Moreover, that gang rapes are especially likely in college fraternities should not come as a surprise, since these groups tend to be consumed with constructing and displaying masculinity. Few contexts are so meticulously orchestrated around a conception of hegemonic masculinity that "stresses competition, athleticism, dominance, winning, conflict, wealth, material possessions, willingness to drink alcohol, and sexual prowess vis à vis women" (Martin and Hummer, 1995: 473). In brief, few contexts provide such a ready recipe for gang rape as a display of heterosexuality, misogyny, and loyalty.

Just as in other situations involving coerced sex, gang rapists perceive their victims as sexual commodities. Patricia Yancey Martin and Robert Hummer's (1995) investigation of fraternities suggests that sexual violence against women is seen by members as a sport or game in which women collectively are pawns, and in which the goal is to score sexually. Non-fraternity rapists share this notion of using a woman—any woman—as a vessel for a group adventure. The challenge is to perform for the group, regardless of the wishes of the interchangeable victim. As expressed by one such rapist,

> We felt powerful, we were in control. I wanted sex and there was peer pressure. She wasn't like a person, no personality, just domination on my part. Just to show I could do it—you know, macho. (Scully and Marolla, 1993: 39)

Male sexual prowess is performed at the expense of the victim's autonomy. The victims are natural and ready outlets for the satisfaction of males' "explosive" or "insatiable" sexual appetites (Sanday, 1998; Messerschmidt, 1993). While men voluntarily and enthusiastically enact what is for them normal masculinity, their female victims are involuntarily and unwillingly forced to play the feminine role into which the culture has cast them: sexual conduits whose own pleasure is unimportant.

Women who are victims of gang rape are not in a position to exercise their autonomy. The sheer fact of being outnumbered by two, three, or seven men is itself an obstacle to resistance. Peggy Sanday cites one such case, where the victim was virtually paralyzed with fear:

> The 17–year-old freshman woman went to the fraternity "little sister" rush party with two of her roommates. The roommates left early without her. She was trying to get a ride home when a fraternity brother told her he would take her home after the party ended. While she waited, two other fraternity members took her into a bedroom to "discuss little sister matters." The door was closed and one of the brothers stood blocking the exit. They told her that in order to become a little sister she would have to have sex with a fraternity member. She was frightened, fearing they would physically harm her if she refused. She could see no escape. Each of the brothers had sex with her, as did a third who had been hiding in the room. During the next two hours, a succession of men went into the room. There were never less than three men with her, sometimes more. (1998: 498)

Alternatively, the victim's ability to consent may be compromised by her state of intoxication, a factor that is unfortunately often used to "blame the victim." If she had been a "good girl," if she had acted "like a lady," she would not have put herself in the position to be so dramatically violated. Chris O'Sullivan traces this to the cultural perception that women who do not adhere to their roles as gatekeepers of sexuality are "fair game for exploitation" (1998: 85). Such popular interpretations, however, deny the complicity of the offenders in providing the liquor and in exploiting the victim when she is vulnerable.

The literature on campus gang rape, in particular, reveals the normativity of alcohol use as a precedent to gang rape (O'Sullivan, 1998; Sanday, 1998). Offenders often plan and coordinate their victims' excessive consumption of alcohol. One fraternity member boasted that

> We provide them with "hunch punch" and things get wild. We get drunk and most of the guys end up with one. . . . Hunch punch is a girl's drink made up of overproof alcohol and powdered Kool-Aid, no water or anything else, just ice. It's very strong. Two cups will do a number on a female. (Martin and Hummer, 1995: 477–478).

The "number" that such drinks do on women is to render them incapable of resistance, either because of a loss of coordination or a loss of consciousness. That women are but the vessel of men's sexuality is especially evident here, where women could not possibly be expected to attain any pleasure from the act. This bothers the participants not at all; it is in fact seen as an extension of women's normative sexual passivity. A couple of examples will suffice to illustrate the dynamics whereby fraternity men take advantage of their intoxicated victims.

> In the Florida State case, the ringleader met the victim at an off-campus drinking club and invited her back to his fraternity for a "party.". . . At the fraternity house, her host gave her a bottle of wine, which she finished. He carried her unconscious to the communal shower room and summoned three other men. His best friend left his own date waiting downstairs in the hall to join in the assault. After sexually assaulting her, the four classy men wrote fraternity slogans and "hatchet gash" on her thighs, dumped her in the entry hall of another fraternity and called 911. At the hospital, her blood alcohol level was found to be potentially lethal and semen from several different men was found in her vagina. (O'Sullivan, 1998: 101)

> It was her first fraternity party. The beer flowed freely and she had much more to drink than she had planned. It was hot and crowded and the party spread out all over the house, so that when three men asked her to go upstairs, she went with them. They took her into a bedroom, locked the door and began to undress her. Groggy with alcohol, her feeble protests were ignored as the three men raped her. When they finished, they put her in the hallway, naked, locking her clothes in the bedroom. (Sanday, 1998: 498)

Whether drunk or sober, the victim's sexuality often is invoked to justify the perpetrator's behavior. As noted previously, victims often are portrayed as "whores" or "sluts" who have violated the standards of femininity, and so deserve to be themselves violated for their impropriety. In such contexts, women are presumed to enjoy gang rape. This allows the construction of the perpetrators as men involved in the legitimate performance of heterosexuality with willing participants. Their behavior is a natural reaction to the seductress in their midst. It is not they who have schemed to assault the victim, but the victim who has somehow schemed to "fire them up." The following example illustrates the presumption of consent:

> A 19-year-old woman student was out on a date with her boyfriend and another couple. They were all drinking beer and after going back to the boyfriend's dorm room, they smoked two marijuana cigarettes. The other couple left and the woman and her boyfriend had sex. The woman fell asleep and the next thing she knew she awoke with a man she didn't know on top of her trying to force her into having sex. A witness said the man was in the hall with two other men when the woman's boyfriend came out of his room and invited them to have sex with his unconscious girlfriend. (Sanday, 1998: 498)

That victimized women are presumed to be always willing, available, and receptive to male "advances" also is apparent in the rationales of gang rapists interviewed by Diana Scully and Joseph Marolla (1993). Rapes of women hitchhikers were justified under the pretext that they must have been prostitutes and therefore "enjoyed it." Gang date rape involved the planned communal assault of one group member's date. This, too, was rendered acceptable by impugning the sexual promiscuity—read inappropriateness—of the victims: "Usually the girl had a bad reputation, or we know it was what she liked" (Scully and Marolla, 1993: 40). One participant admitted to committing twenty or thirty such assaults on "girls who were known to do this kind of thing." He also believed that "it might start out as rape, but then they [the women] would quiet down and none ever reported it to the police" (Scully and Marolla, 1993: 40). Obviously, the women "enjoyed" or even "invited" their victimization. Consequently, men imagined themselves to have established their sexual prowess by their demonstrated ability to satisfy even a protesting woman.

Such demonstrations are at the core of gang rapes. To themselves and their peers, such behavior is not deemed aberrant or deviant. Quite the contrary, it is a show of manliness and camaraderie among friends. Again, it is apparent that the intended audience is not the woman involved. She is a secondary player, interchangeable with any other available woman. What is important is that the men involved solidify their individual and collective identities as heterosexual performers. The show is for the coparticipants. The communal activity permits the concurrent display of sexuality, fearlessness, and camaraderie. O'Sullivan expresses the value of gang rape to its participants as "a performance put on for other men, proving one's masculinity through heterosexual dominance and exploitation of women. It is a way of cooperating and competing with male friends through a shared risky and risqué, socially sanctioned (in the sense that it's something to brag about among men, although not something to write home to mother about) behavior" (1998: 105). Gang rape signifies the commitment of the participants to the group and to masculine norms of behavior. It is a very public enactment of loyalty to the brotherhood of Man over Woman. And it is a confirmation of the aggressive sexuality of each of the group members. That it is seen as a crucial test of one's heterosexual mastery is evident in the finding that those who refuse to participate are branded "unmanly," possibly homosexual (Sanday, 1998; Martin and Hummer, 1995).

CULTURAL PERMISSION TO HATE

An implicit thread has run throughout this discussion of gender-motivated violence: cultural permission to hate and to victimize women is typically bestowed upon men. Abundant myths, stereotypes, images, and ideologies simultaneously support gendered and unequal relations of power, labor, and sexuality as well as the resultant gender-motivated violence. Cultural assumptions about men, women, and the relationships among and between them condone and often encourage victimization of women as women, because they commonly objectify and minimize the value of women. In other words, "men physically and emotionally abuse women because they *can,* because they live in a

world that gives them permission" (Pharr, 1988: 14). For example, actual and potential victims of sexual violence are all too often portrayed as fantasizing about and therefore enjoying their victimization. Movie images, pornographic magazines, even commercial advertising often paint a portrait in which women may initially resist, but ultimately willingly and enthusiastically participate in their own violation. Hence, "No Means Yes" and other such rape myths abound to distance the offender from culpability. "Boys will be boys," after all!

This discussion of gender-motivated violence began with the acknowledgment that our culture assumes a masculine and feminine essence—traits, characteristics, capacities that clearly distinguish Man from Woman. Part of that binary is the construction of women as either "good" or "bad," depending upon their adherence to their prescribed role (Sheffield, 1987). If femininity is enacted through nurturing, submissive, passive behavior, then the woman is good; if it is enacted through selfishness, aggression, promiscuity, or resistance, the woman is bad and so deserves whatever she gets by way of violent retribution. The Bad Woman is herself to blame for male violence directed at her: "women who are beaten by their intimate partners, raped by strangers or acquaintances, or even killed somehow deserve their victimization because of their own fallibility, misjudgement or provocation" (Miller, 1994: 232–233).

Cultural constructs surrounding women's experiences of violence overwhelmingly lay blame on the victim. If only she had not been out alone; if only she had prepared a hot, appetizing meal; if only she had not dressed so provocatively, she would not have been assaulted, battered, or raped. In other words, if she had "done femininity" appropriately rather than oppositionally, she would not have suffered. Violence is a predictable response to women who violate the gender order. In contrast, the male offender is exonerated, often rewarded. He is "doing masculinity" normally; he is performing masculinity in a socially sanctioned, legitimate manner, in accordance with his right and duty to chasten non-conforming women.

Sheffield (1989) identifies what she refers to as "gender violence myths" that perform this function of releasing males from culpability. Rape myths include:

- all women want to be raped
- no woman can be raped if she doesn't want it
- she asked for it
- she changed her mind *afterward*
- she said no but meant yes
- if she's going to be raped, she may as well lie back and enjoy it

Among the wife-battering myths:

- some women need to be beaten
- a good smack will straighten her out/shut her up
- she needs a beating to keep her in line
- she must have provoked it

Sexual harassment is often justified because:

- she was seductive/flirting
- she was in a workplace where she didn't belong
- she misunderstood "friendliness"

In the context of a culture that holds so tenaciously to these sorts of excuses, women who are assaulted become suspect. She must have done something "inappropriate" to incite the violence. Moreover, it is not just the perpetrators who cling to the popular mythologies. Friends and family of the victim are likely to question her role in the process; police officers carry the assumptions into their investigation of reports of gender-motivated violence; and judges and attorneys are infamous for their tendency to try the victim rather than the offender in cases of sexual assault and domestic violence.

Sheffield (1987) argues elsewhere that the good/bad woman dichotomy is especially problematic for women of color, who, according to strictures of the racial hierarchy, can never achieve "goodness." It is the presumption of the inherent inferiority of black women that long left them vulnerable to unpunished and unpunishable rape at the hands of white men. That black women are uniquely vulnerable to gendered violence is implicit in Opal Palmer Adisa's observation that "African American women are more likely to be raped than any other woman, are least likely to be believed, and most often watch their rapists treated with impunity or mild punishment" (1997: 196). Women of color typically are not viewed as "real" victims. More so even than white women, women of color are characterized as inviting violent assault. The latitude allowed them for enacting femininity is even more circumscribed than that allowed white women. African-American women, for example, are "safe" only when enacting the roles of "mule" or "Mammy." So narrow are these notions of black womanhood that few women could possibly live up to them. Consequently, black women are assigned the label—often by black and white cultures alike—Jezebels, matriarchs, or uppity black women. It is this intersection of race, gender, and sexuality that shapes the victimization of black women and other women of color (Crenshaw, 1994; Collins, 1993). As noted earlier, it is the Jezebel image of the black prostitute that is perhaps most damning. It constructs black women as sexually promiscuous and therefore enticing, seductive. It is "impossible" to rape a prostitute since she is always on the job.

Aída Hurtado confirms the contrasting imagery of white and black femininity. While the former share in the privilege of white men through their enactment of emphasized femininity, the latter are denied such access and are instead the objects of white masculine power and aggression:

> In many ways the dual conception of women based on race—"white goddess/black she-devil, chaste virgin/nigger whore, the blond blue-eyed doll/the exotic 'mulatto' object of sexual craving"—has freed women of color from the distraction of the rewards of seduction. Women of color "do not receive the respect and treatment—mollycoddling and condescending as it sometimes is—afforded to white women." (Hurtado, 1989: 846; quoting Joseph, 1981)

In other words, race conditions the gender imagery to which women are held accountable, especially in terms of their sexuality. While both white women and women of color are vulnerable to gendered violence, the cultural permission for such victimization varies dramatically. As argued above, white women are often victimized because they are perceived to have crossed some boundary of appropriate feminine behavior; women of color because they are perceived to be, "by nature," sexually available and provocative. In short, white men's subordination of white women and women of color "involves holding them accountable to normative conceptions of essential womanly nature in different ways" (West and Fenstermaker, 1993: 168).

ANTI-GAY VIOLENCE AND THE CONSTRUCTION OF GENDER

As the foregoing discussion suggests, the contemporary practices of gender politics result in a situation where *men in general* benefit from the subordination of women. Clearly, a dominant masculinist project is the subordination of women by men. However, no less important is the "denial of authority to some groups of men" (Connell, 1987: 109). Significantly, the intersection of the division of labor, power, sexuality, and culture, as outlined above, means that there also exists a hierarchy of masculinities in which some are subordinated to others. Relations of power operate between masculinities and femininities, but also between an array of masculinities. Not all men share in the ability to exercise control at either the macro- or micro-social level. Below a hegemonic masculinity are arrayed a series of subordinated masculinities. Working-class men are subordinate to capitalists; black men to white; homosexuals to heterosexuals. Goffman may have overstated the case only slightly when he identified ideal—or "hegemonic"—masculinity as "a young, married, white, urban, northern, heterosexual Protestant father, of college education, fully employed, of good complexion, weight and height, and a recent record in sports. . . . Any male who fails to qualify in any of these ways is likely to view himself—during moments at least—as unworthy, incomplete and inferior" (1963: 128). The crucial point here is that the nonqualifiers not only "feel" inferior, but are so judged. This is the

standard according to which the hierarchy of masculinities is created, resulting in stigmatized and marginalized "out-groups." It is among these subordinated masculinities that we find homosexuals.

Herek explicitly places homophobic violence in its sociocultural context: "Anti-gay violence is a logical, albeit extreme extension of the heterosexism that pervades American society. *Heterosexism* is defined here as an ideological system that denies, denigrates and stigmatizes any nonheterosexual form of behavior, identity, relationship or community" (1992: 89). From this point of reference, Herek goes on to trace the ideological and institutional practices that serve to denigrate and marginalize gay men and lesbians. From the exclusion of gays from civil rights and hate crime protections, to biblical condemnations of homosexuality as "unnatural," to curricular constraints on positive presentations of homosexuality, heterosexism is transmitted through cultural institutions (Herek, 1992: 90). The implication of this is that gays are subsequently rendered invisible at best, worthy of persecution at worst.

As one potential resource in the accomplishment of gender, gay-bashing plays the dual role of reaffirming the perpetrator's ability to "do gender," while simultaneously punishing the victim's propensity to "do gender inappropriately." At one and the same time, this practice serves to define, regulate, and express sexuality. It is a forceful resource by which young men, in particular, can regulate challenges to the binaries of gender and sexuality. In short, both hegemonic and subordinate forms of masculinity are shaped and maintained through active homophobia. In particular, hegemonic masculinity is accomplished through the simultaneous valuation of aggressive heterosexuality and the denunciation of homosexuality.

GAY-BASHING AS A RESOURCE FOR CONSTRUCTING MASCULINITIES

Violence against homosexuals is not a new problem (Bensinger, 1992). Historically, it has been a legally sanctioned policy, as in medieval Europe or the colonial United States where sodomy was punishable by various forms of mutilation, or even death.

Homosexuals were imprisoned and exterminated alongside German Jews in Nazi death camps (Herek and Berrill, 1992: 1). Some American "liberators," noting the pink triangles worn by gay men in the camps, returned the "deviants" to their prisons in sympathy with the Nazis' intentions (Grau, 1995; Heger, 1980; Plant, 1986). The McCarthy era in the United States was a period of extensive legal and extralegal persecution of gay men and lesbians (Duberman, 1993; Adam, 1995).

While most (but not all) American states have eliminated legislation that would criminalize the sexual practices of gays and lesbians, the gay community continues to suffer as victims of hatred, harassment, and violence. Moreover, attacks against homosexuals tend to be among the most brutal acts of hatred. They often involve severe beatings, torture, mutilation, castration, and sexual assault. They are also very likely to result in death (Comstock, 1991; Levin and McDevitt, 1993). NGLTF annual audits consistently report disproportionate evidence of "overkill" in gay-related homicides (1996; 1997; 1998). In fact, more than 60 percent of such homicides show evidence of "rage/hate-fueled extraordinary violence . . . (such as dismemberment, bodily and genital mutilation, use of multiple weapons, repeated blows from a blunt object, or numerous stab wounds)" (NGLTF, 1995: 18). Frequently, the mutilation or dismemberment follows death, as if to wipe out the victim's identity.

What accounts for the persistence of violence against gays? Perhaps a consideration of the common traits shared by its perpetrators provides some insight. Consistently, the data show that they are "predominantly ordinary young men" (Comstock, 1991: 2; Hamm, 1994). In particular, they are young white men or adolescents, often from working-class or middle-class backgrounds (Berk, Boyd, and Hamner, 1991; Berrill, 1992; Hamm, 1994a). With this in mind, Comstock is quite right to insist that sociological and sociocultural, rather than psychodynamic, processes are at work. It is vital to recognize anti-gay violence as an active exercise in the construction of gender. Such an understanding allows us to examine hate crime in its immediate subjective context by drawing attention to the interactions and implied meanings of actors and their audiences. Yet it also demands that we consider the historical and cultural contexts that inform those meanings, so that we might understand the ways in which identities are shaped both by our engagement with others and by our structural background.

Gay-bashing provides young men in particular with a very useful resource for doing gender, especially for accomplishing hegemonic masculinity. It is an interesting paradox that while masculinity is assumed to be "natural," it also appears to be so fragile "that one must always guard against losing it" (Hopkins, 1992: 123; Kaufman, 1995). Gay-bashing thus allows perpetrators to reaffirm their own masculinity, their own aggressive heterosexuality, in opposition to this nonconformist threat. As an activity, it is tailor-made for this construction of masculinity, since it allows the visible demonstration of the most salient features of manliness: aggression, domination, and heterosexuality.

Recall West and Zimmerman's (1987) contention that gender is situationally managed. Doing gender is to be understood in the context in which it occurs. The task of gender is reaccomplished in a diversity of social settings, each of which may demand different accountable activities. Thus, "even though one is recognized as a man (or boy) prior to evidenced masculinity, evidence must also be forthcoming in order to merit that continued 'unproblematic' status" (Hopkins, 1992: 124). In this context, the practice of violence against gays provides one such situational resource for men to establish their masculinity. And it does so in both negative and positive terms: by establishing what a man *is not* and what he *is*.

Gay-bashing provides proof of manhood, which is especially important for young males who are constantly challenged to prove their virility. The perpetrator proves, by his actions, that he is unafraid to fight, as any real man must be. And, he is unafraid of engaging in illegal attacks on his victims—again a sign of his manhood.

Like all social actors, gay-bashers act with an eye to their audience (Herek, 1992a; 1992b). How will they be evaluated? What is the message their actions carry? In part, violence against gays provides visible, documented proof of offenders' unquestionably straight sexuality. As Messerschmidt contends, physical violence against gay men in front of other young, white, working-class men reaffirms what they define as natural and masculine sex—heterosexuality (1993: 100). Karen Franklin takes a similar position, arguing that "in group assaults the homosexual victim can be seen as fundamentally a dramatic prop, a vehicle for a ritualized conquest through which assailants demonstrate their commitment to heterosexual masculinity and male gender norms" (1998: 12). Gay-bashing provides a resource through which young men can confirm not only what is natural, but what is culturally *demanded* of them in performance of their particular style of masculinity.

Thus, while violence against gays serves as a verification of the perpetrator's bravery and machismo, it also serves as a disclaimer of his homosexuality. The taunts the young adolescent males often favor—such as, "What are you, a fag?"—are frequent reminders of the inviolability of the artificial boundaries between the sexes. Hostility against homosexuals can be accounted for as an assertion of its opposite, that is, heterosexuality. The gay-basher could not possibly be mistaken for a homosexual, since he willingly assaults homosexuals. The active substantiation of his homophobia simultaneously removes any doubt about the offender's sexuality. Similarly, the epithets cast by the perpetrator distance him from the dreaded Other, once again offering obvious proof that he is of the "in-group" rather than the "out-group" constituted by homosexuals. The Blue Boys, an avowed homophobic group of young men interviewed by Michael Collins, offer an extreme illustration of this point:

> We chose the blue baseball bat because it's the color of the boy. The man is one gender. He is not female. There is no confusion. Blue is the color of men, and that's the color that men use to defeat the anti-male, which is the queer. (1992: 193)

As this statement implies, gay-bashing also provides the ideal context in which young men can conclusively establish what they *are*, in other words, manly, virile men. Recall the importance of accountability here: one must be seen (and interpreted) to be masculine in the prevailing sense of the term. And violence is a tried and true means to this end. However, many forms of violence carry significant risks: that of losing a fight, that of injury, that of arrest. The dynamics of gay-bashing, on the other hand, offer few such risks. Given its frequent group nature, there is little risk of loss or injury. In light of victims' fear of reporting, as well as police indifference, there is little risk of arrest (Harry, 1992). Ultimately, gay-bashing allows males to flex their muscles, to prove their masculinity with few of the hazards normally attendant with violent engagements. A youth interviewed by Eric Weissman supports this interpretation:

> We were trying to be tough to each other. It was like a game of chicken—someone dared you to do something and there was just no backing down. (1992: 172)

Similarly, a confirmed gay-basher assured Collins that his group (the Blue Boys)

> are *real* men searching for real solutions. We can't expect help from nobody but ourselves when it comes to cleaning the streets of the faggot and dyke scum. (1992: 193)

"Real men" can take care of themselves and those around them. One way of defending this circle is to eliminate the threat—in this case, homosexuals—through violence. Simultaneously, the offender can demonstrate his strength and his capacity to defend his territory, as must all hegemonic males.

The Blue Boys, and even less extreme "typical" gay-bashers are most at pains to prove the very essence of their masculinity: heterosexuality. To quote the same member:

> I tell you, (the) Blue Boys are male. We're heteros. We have girl-friends and wives. We're out there fucking chicks every night and we have nothing to do with any fag shit. (Collins, 1992: 193)

Young men's attempts to assert a particular form of sexuality in a public manner can take many forms—"cruising for chicks" or boasting of their (hetero)sexual exploits. In the case of violence against homosexuals, denial of the "unnatural" reinforces the "natural" heterosexuality of their emerging masculinity. Ironically, then, gay-bashers are not so much *violating* the norms of society (re: violence), as they are *reaffirming* a much more important set of norms revolving around sexuality. Their activities reflect the performance of the most salient features of a culturally approved hegemonic masculinity: aggression, domination, and heterosexuality.

GAY-BASHING AS A RESPONSE TO DOING GENDER INAPPROPRIATELY

Any performance of masculinity typically involves more than one audience. Perpetrators are playing to their peers, and to whatever other elements of "conventional" society happen to be watching. For them, the message is "Look at me! I'm a real man!" A very different message is transmitted to the most adversely affected audience: the victims. What they hear is "Real men are heterosexual. By definition, *you are not a real man!*" Simply put, gays are seen to be doing gender inappropriately. Thus, while violence against gays affirms the hegemonic masculinity of the actor(s), it also disparages the masculinity of homosexuals, whose behavior is no less accountable, no less open to interpretation and evaluation.

Gay men are, in fact, doing gender, just as are heterosexuals. They are constructing their own masculinity, albeit an alternate form of masculinity that is culturally subordinate to its heterosexual counterpart. On this basis, they are vulnerable to social disapprobation because they are seen to be gender traitors. Thus, while traditional hegemonic masculinity demands aggression and heterosexuality, it also requires the repression of the challenge represented by homosexuality. Violence against gays is a very powerful means by which this subordination can be maintained.

First and foremost, there is an extensive cultural mythology that facilitates anti-gay sentiment and activity. It is a mythology that constructs gay identities as dangerous and wicked. Contemporary imagery and stereotypes surrounding gay men, in particular, often resurrect the historical construction of homosexuality as sin and illness. The dominant Western perspective has been shaped by the social and moral agenda of the Euro-Christian majority. Drawing on the English common law, the colonial state determined that "what was sinful in the eyes of the church was illegal in the eyes of the state" (Biery, 1990: 10). So it was that "sodomy" and "buggery" came to be seen as immoral acts, and "crimes against nature."

While there are still proponents of the "homosexuality as sin" perspective, this religiously grounded view has been supplemented, if not supplanted, by the more "scientific" view of same-sex relations as "illness." This interpretation, "which also sees homosexuality as wrong and deviant, maintains that sexual acts are symptoms of a sickness. In contrast to the sin conception, the sickness view sees the desire to engage in homosexual activity inhering in the individual's identity" (Editors of the *Harvard Law Review,* 1990: 4).

Whether grounded in religion or science, an immutable stigma is applied to gay identity, which is perceived as a moral and physical threat to the public's well-being. By engaging in "unnatural" sexual behavior, gays are said to thwart God's law; they promote a "deviant lifestyle" to the young and pliable; they carry disease and degeneracy like rats carry the plague. Homosexuals of both sexes are perceived to be predatory and menacing. Moreover, the unspoken threat is that they are gender traitors, because they have broken ranks with dominant males, thereby threatening to destabilize carefully scripted gender relationships. Long-standing gender boundaries are uncomfortably blurred by homosexuality.

Given such pervasive negative sentiments, it is perhaps not surprising that gay men (and lesbians) still suffer considerable legal discrimination and exclusion. The anti-gay mythology is embedded in the legal order. Restrictions on their sexuality, relationships, and civil rights means that gay men and women typically do not enjoy the same freedoms as their heterosexual counterparts. *Bowers v. Hardwick,* is held to be the most significant contemporary legal statement of the status and rights of gays (Editors of the *Harvard Law Review,* 1990; Mohr, 1988; Leiser, 1997). In that case, the Supreme Court upheld the constitutionality of Georgia's sodomy statute. In his majority opinion, Chief Justice Warren Burger concluded that "to uphold that the act of homosexual sodomy is somehow protected as a fundamental right would be to cast aside millennia of moral teaching." With these words, he denied the legal right to private, consensual same-sex sodomy. Twenty states continue to criminalize same-sex sexual relations, referring to them variously as "sodomy," "unnatural intercourse," "deviate sexual conduct," "sexual misconduct," "unnatural and lascivious acts," and "crimes against nature."

While prosecutions under these sodomy statutes are rare, their presence nonetheless has a dramatic impact on gay men and lesbians. Symbolically, the legislation and its terminology marginalize and stigmatize a whole community. They send the message that same-sex activity is "unnatural," "deviant," and not to be tolerated. At the practical level, these laws are "frequently invoked to justify other types of discrimination against lesbians and gay men on the ground that they are presumed to violate these statutes" (Editors of the *Harvard Law Review,* 1990: 11). So, for example, the "criminality" of gay men or lesbians has been used to refuse parental rights, or the right to adopt, or the right to marry. The legally ambiguous status of gay men and women even can be invoked as a means of denying them freedom from discrimination in employment and job benefits (domestic partner benefits, for example). Ultimately, the persistent criminalization of homosexual behavior leaves gay men and lesbians vulnerable to public and private persecution, including violence. This designation of "deviant" has long facilitated the persistence of the criminalization and pathologizing of same-sex relations. Consequently, gay men and women have been harassed, persecuted, and disempowered for their difference: they continue to be marked as the sexual Other.

As outlined previously, "doing gender" explicitly is concerned with structuring differences between males and females, with creating "essential" natures specific to each gender. Consequently, contemporary sexuality (and marriage) is predicated upon the normalcy of opposite-sex relationships. Homosexuals apparently refuse to play this game. They do not sufficiently accomplish either maleness or femaleness; they have not even attempted to become one of the "natural" sexes. Homosexuals refuse to be forced into these binary categories of masculine or feminine. Thus, by definition, homosexuality transcends the boundaries our culture has so conscientiously erected between the genders, lapsing into the category of deviance. Additionally, gays violate the sanctity, the "naturalness" of established gender identities. That is, they are sanctioned for *presumably* failing to practice either absolute femininity or masculinity. Such violations ultimately make them vulnerable to stigmatization and finally to violent repression. William Hassel's two teenage assailants clearly were hostile to his refusal to "be a man." Throughout the attack—at knifepoint—the pair challenged his masculinity, beating him for crossing the gender line, for being a failed man. They threatened to complete his emasculation physically. According to Hassel's account,

> They made me address them as "Sir." They made me beg them to be made into a real woman. They threatened to castrate me. They threatened to emasculate me. They called me "Queer," "Faggot." One of them urinated on me. They threatened me with sodomy. (1992: 144–145)

This patterning of sexuality—cathexis—is a major axis of the sexual power relations of which gender accomplishment is so integral a part. Homosexuals' "unnatural" sexual attractions threaten the dichotomous sexual ideals. They are seen to have crossed the acceptable boundaries of sexuality. Homophobia and gay-bashing thus can be explained by "the degree to which the fact of homosexuality threatens the credibility of a naturalized ideology of gender and a dichotomized social world" (Connell, 1987: 248). Violations of the normative rules of cathexis provide an important motive for violence against gays. In West's terms, homosexuals are "called to account for" their failure to do gender as prescribed (West and Zimmerman, 1987).

It bears repeating that gender constitutes a hierarchical structure of domination not only between but within genders. This structure of power is also a constitutive part of the broader pattern of sexual power relations, in which heterosexual masculinity comes to the fore. The hierarchy of masculinities valorizes this narrow, hegemonic form of masculinity, while denying or limiting the power of "lower" forms of masculinity (and all forms of femininity). Consequently, "a series of masculinities becomes subsumed under one form of masculinity that becomes 'masculine'" (Kinsman, 1987: 104).

Because homosexuality challenges the fundamental assumptions of what it is to "be a man," it inevitably is assigned an inferior status in this gender hierarchy. The institutional norm of heterosexual masculinity is affirmed in the media, legislation and social policy, and police practices, to name but a few (Kaufman, 1987; Carrigan and Lee, 1987). The 1978 Briggs Initiative was an early attempt to expel homosexuals from the education system. Restrictions on "domestic partner" benefits disadvantage gay couples. And tax status is based on the traditional heterosexual marriage—doubly problematic since most states outlaw gay marriages.

At the level of the informal social order, gay-bashing serves a no less effective, but certainly more violent, disciplinary mechanism. Violence is used as a tool of subordination intended to maintain the powerlessness of homosexuals. Tim Carrigan et al. are worthy of a lengthy quotation on this point:

> The history of homosexuality obliges us to think of masculinity not as a single object with its own history but as being constantly constructed within the history of an evolving social structure, a structure of sexual power relations. It obliges us to see this construction as a social struggle going on in a complex ideological and political field in which there is a continuing process of mobilization, marginalization, contestation, resistance, and subordination. It forces us to recognize the importance of violence, not as an expression of subjective values or of a type of masculinity, but as constitutive

> practice that helps to make all kinds of masculinity. (1987: 89)

Violence simultaneously conditions both hegemonic and subordinate masculinities. As such, it is an integral weapon within the structure of power relations. This is especially obvious when gays collectively challenge their subordination. The last decade has seen a dramatic increase in the activity and visibility of a vibrant gay and lesbian movement. This visibility has been a two-edged sword. On the one hand, it has resulted in valuable gains in gay rights. On the other hand, it has engendered great hostility and backlash. Just as Native Americans and women, for example, are at increased risk of victimization during periods of activism, so too are gays more vulnerable when they find their voice. This is evident in the increased violence leading up to gay rights referenda in Maine, Colorado, and Oregon. Kathleen Sarris's experiences in Indiana are not atypical. She had played a leadership role in Justice, Inc.'s efforts to promote pro-gay activities. Following a widely publicized press conference, Sarris suffered weeks of telephone harassment and hate mail. The harassment culminated in a brutal beating and sexual assault by a man claiming to be

> acting for God; that what he was doing was God's revenge on me because I was a "queer," and getting rid of me would save children and put an end to the movement in Indiana. (Sarris, 1992: 202)

Such assaults are indicative of a perceived loss of white male privilege—privilege that instead has been offered up to "underserving" gays. A white male convicted of murdering a gay man in Texas justified his crime with reference to this relative imbalance. He bemoaned the fact that, while he had worked hard all his life, he nonetheless was unable to find a decent job, and yet

> here they [homosexuals] are, they're doing something that God totally condemns in the Bible. But look at everything they've got. . . . They've got these good jobs, they've got money. They've got the cars, they've got the apartments. They've got all the nice stuff in 'em. So, yeah, I resented that. (cited in Franklin, 1998: 18)

This assailant raises another crucial element underlying gay-bashing. He articulates quite openly the common perception that gay men have benefited unjustly from meaningful and profitable employment. This is in spite of the fact that gay men often are perceived to be doing gender inappropriately in terms of its final dimension, that is, in labor. As Connell (1987) explains, the sexual division of labor amounts to the historical constitution of gender-appropriate categories and processes of work. Consequently, we are left with cultural ideals with respect to who is capable of and who should perform what tasks. Moreover, actors' performance of these tasks provides an important means for demonstrating their essential masculinity or femininity. Men make decisions, women follow orders; men are professionals, women are support staff; men work with their hands, women look nice.

According to popular stereotypes, homosexuals contravene this comfortable arrangement as well. Just as they refuse to abide by the rules of gendered sexuality, so too do they buck conformity in their employment. The work of male homosexuals is not that of "manly men" but of passive, effeminate men. Again, according to popular stereotypes, gay men are hairdressers, dancers, or interior designers. Given the cultural association between homosexuality and feminine weaknesses, gay men are thought to be incapable of the "tough," "demanding" jobs like construction, or even management. We don't want "them" teaching our children, since they might seduce them. We don't want "them" raising children of their own, since they would reproduce another generation of gays.

The sexual politics of labor have little room for the sort of gender ambiguity presumed of homosexuals. The gay community, in many states, is still without statutory protection against job discrimination. Like women, who similarly are ghettoized and subordinated in the gender hierarchy, homosexual men often are left with few high-paying options and few opportunities for significant professional advancement. This economic violence complements the physical violence of gay-bashing in a number of ways. First, homosexuals who are not "out" may fear the publicity associated with reporting their victimization. That is, the risk to their job status, family affections, and so on appears greater than the benefits to be derived from reporting violence perpetrated against them. In the absence of consistent reporting, there is little to deter potential offenders. Second, there are frequently additional (social) injuries when victimization is reported, either with or without the victim's consent. Rather than winning sympathy, as do most victims of crime, homosexuals often are further victimized after the initial assault—experiencing harassment from neighbors or coworkers, even threats of job loss or demotion. Anti-gay violence in the workplace only recently has begun to receive the attention it deserves (NGLTF, 1996, 1997, 1998; Bain, 1995). A Boston victim advocate observed in an interview with an *Advocate* reporter that while such cases are not necessarily as violent or brutal as others,

> there is something especially frightening nonetheless about harassment at work, because the victims don't have the freedom to leave; it's happening in the place where they make their living. The situation can be agonizing over time, especially if the harassment is coming from a supervisor. (cited in Bain, 1995: 31)

The dynamics parallel the experiences of women harassed on the job. The implied—sometimes explicit—message is that the victims don't belong. They don't deserve the job or position they hold because they don't "fit." That is, like women in "men's" jobs, gays in the workplace represent a direct threat. Physical violence or ongoing harassment makes the victim's workplace experiences unbearable, often forcing them to seek employment elsewhere.

Ultimately, then, gay-bashing is a practice motivated by the discomfort, even hostility toward those Others who cross the gender boundaries of sexuality, power and labor, who refuse to "do gender appropriately." In almost Durkheimian fashion, violence against gays reasserts the normative order around gender by rewarding the perpetrators (explicitly or implicitly) for accomplishing masculinity in a "manly manner" while punishing the victims for refusing to do so.

MASCULINITIES, FEMININITIES, AND ANTI-LESBIAN VIOLENCE

If gay men are victimized for their failure to appropriately construct their masculinity, are lesbians subject to violence for their failure to appropriately construct their femininity? To be sure, lesbians are often victims of homophobic violence, but at a much lower rate than gay males (Berrill, 1992; Comstock, 1991; NGLTF, 1992, 1993, 1994). In part, these findings may reflect women's greater tendency not to report homophobic violence (NGLTF, 1994). Additionally, Kevin Berrill identifies several pragmatic reasons why lesbians may appear to be at lower risk of victimization: the fact that men, in general, are at a greater risk of violence; the higher visibility of gay men as opposed to gay women; the earlier recognition and "outing" of gay men; gay women's greater tendency to alter behavior, and therefore vulnerability to assault; the difficulty in distinguishing anti-woman violence from anti-lesbian violence. (1992: 28)

Theoretically, this last point is significant. Beatrice von Schulthess's (1992) study of anti-lesbian violence in San Francisco reveals close links between anti-woman and anti-lesbian violence. In fact, she argues that anti-lesbian violence is an extension of misogynistic sentiment generally. Thus the two are difficult to untangle. This confusion may, in fact, deflate the numbers of *reported* anti-lesbian hate crimes. Victims and law enforcement authorities alike often are unable (or unwilling) to identify assaults as anti-lesbian. They may, instead, be perceived as anti-woman. Women in general become conditioned to gender harassment at work, in the home, on the street (von Schulthess, 1992; NGLTF, 1995). Victoria Brownworth (1991) cites three dramatic examples where anti-lesbian sentiment was apparent in the perpetrators' actions or testimony, yet none was officially defined as homophobic violence. Similarly, she quotes a lesbian victim, who makes

clear the difficulty of distinguishing the motive in this context:

> Was my attack anti-lesbian? Or was it anti-woman?. . . I was raped because as a woman I'm considered rapeable, and as a lesbian I'm considered a threat. How can one separate these two things? (1: 52)

Lesbians and non-lesbians alike frequently report this confusion (Pharr, 1988; NGLTF, 1994). Sexual harassment—wolf whistles and "come-ons," for example—often escalates into lesbian baiting and, worse, violence. In the immediate context of the rejection of his sexual overtures, the perpetrator's masculinity is threatened—his sexual attractiveness and prowess are thrown into question. In general then, this form of social control as punishment is most likely to occur when

> our behavior is not acceptable, that is when we're being independent, going our own way, living whole lives, fighting for our rights, demanding equal pay, saying no to violence, being self-assertive, bonding with and loving the company of women, insisting upon our authority, making changes that include us in society's decision-making. (Pharr, 1988: 19)

Consequently, lesbians—and women erroneously identified as lesbians—are subject to similar social censure as gay males. Pharr reminds us that "to be a lesbian is to be *perceived* as someone who has stepped out of line, who has moved out of sexual/economic dependence on a male, who is woman identified" (1988: 181). Lesbians also may be punished for doing gender inappropriately. As a lesbian, she has forfeited all "womanly" rights to protection; she is left vulnerable to the harassment and violence that mark her as deviant and "out-of-line."

However, it remains the case that lesbians appear to be less frequent victims of anti-gay violence than men. How are we to explain the fact that while the dynamics of lesbian- and gay-bashing are similar in kind they differ in degree? Connell (1987) provides a potential line of response. He contends that the gender hierarchy demands slightly less conformity of women than of men. Whereas men are arrayed relative to a hegemonic masculinity, women are held accountable to a less rigid norm of "emphasized femininity." Thus, failures to accomplish "appropriate" masculinity are likely to elicit stronger negative social sanctions than are similar challenges to femininity: "All forms of femininity in this society are constructed in the context of the overall subordination of women to men. For this reason there is no femininity that holds among women the position held by hegemonic masculinity among men. . . . No pressure is set up to negate or subordinate other forms of femininity in the way hegemonic masculinity must negate other masculinities" (Connell, 1987: 187; see also Harry, 1992). In other words, there is slightly more latitude for gender nonconformity—especially in terms of sexuality and expression—among women than among men. Same-sex bonding, affection, and physical contact are much more readily accepted for women than men—the former may even be titillating for men to observe, as evidenced by the amount of lesbian activity pictured in magazines such as *Playboy* and *Penthouse*. Thus, women's homosexuality does not threaten the status quo in quite the same way as that of men. They can retain their femininity in spite of their sexual orientation, since they are still perceived as sexual objects. Gay men, on the other hand, do not have the same appeal. In fact, gay men threaten the very fiber of the gender hierarchy. Their violations touch the basic assumptions on which the hierarchy is predicated: that of the primacy of the heterosexual male.

Whether one speaks of anti-woman or anti-gay violence, one is speaking of action oriented around the reaffirmation of a hegemonic formation. Such violence represents efforts to keep men and women in appropriate alignment, along the axes of labor, power, sexuality, and culture. Until equality between genders is achieved, until we all can blur the boundaries between genders, we will continue to force people into rigid categories of male/female, straight/gay, normal/deviant. And we will continue to devalue and persecute the "negative" half of the equation.

BIBLIOGRAPHY

1. Adam, Barry. 1995. *The Rise of a Gay and Lesbian Movement*. New York: Twayne Publishers.

2. Adams, Peter, Alisa Towns, and Nicole Garvey. 1995. "Dominance and Entitlement: The Rhetoric Men Use to Discuss Their Violence Towards Women." *Discourse and Society*. 6(13): 387–406.

3. Adisa, Opal Palmer. 1997. "Undeclared War: African American Women Writers Explicating Rape," in *Gender Violence: Interdisciplinary Perspectives*, ed. Laura O'Toole and Jessica Schiffman. New York: New York University Press, 194–208.

4. Bain, Christian Arthur. 1995. "Anti-Gay Violence in the Workplace." *The Advocate*, June 13: 31–32.

5. Barnes, A. S. 1985. *The Black Middle Class Family*. Bristol, IN: Wyndham Hall Press.

6. Belknap, Joanne. 1996. *The Invisible Woman: Gender, Crime and Justice*. Belmont, CA: Wadsworth.

7. Bensinger, Gad. 1992. "Hate Crime: A New/Old Problem." *International Journal of Comparative and Applied Criminal Justice* 16: 115–123.

8. Berk, Richard, Elizabeth Boyd, and Karl Hamner. 1992. "Thinking More Clearly about Hate-Motivated Crimes," in *Hate Crimes: Confronting Violence against Lesbians and Gay Men*, ed. Gregory Herek and Kevin Berrill. Newbury Park, CA: Sage, 123–143.

9. Berrill, Kevin. 1992. "Anti-Gay Violence and Victimization in the United States: An Overview," in *Hate Crimes: Confronting Violence against Lesbians and Gay Men*, ed. Gregory Herek and Kevin Berrill. Newbury Park, CA: Sage, 19–45.

10. Browne, Angela. 1995. "Fear and the Perception of Alternatives: Asking 'Why Battered Women Don't Leave' Is the Wrong Question," in *The Criminal Justice System and Women*, ed. Barbara Price and Natalie Sokoloff. New York: McGraw-Hill, 228–245.

11. Brownmiller, Susan. 1974. *Against Our Will*. New York: Simon and Schuster.

12. Brownworth, Victoria, 1991. "An Unreported Crisis," *The Advocate*, November 5: 50, 52.

13. Caputi, Jane. 1993. "The Sexual Politics of Murder," in *Violence against Women*, ed. Pauline Bart and Eileen Moran. Newbury Park, CA: Sage, 5–25.

14. ———, and Diana Russell. 1992. "Femicide: Sexist Terrorism against Women," in *Femicide: The Politics of Woman Killing*, ed. Jill Radford and Diana Russell. New York: Twayne Publishers, 13–21.

15. Carrigan, Tim, Bob Connell, and John Lee. 1987. "Toward a New Sociology of Masculinity," in *The Making of Masculinities: The New Men's Studies*, ed. Harry Brod. Winchester, MA: Allen and Unwin, 63–100.

16. Chaiken, Jan. 1998. *Violence by Intimates: Analysis of Data on Crimes by Current or Former Spouses, Boyfriends and Girlfriends*. Washington, DC: Bureau of Justice Statistics, NCJ 167237.

17. Collins, Michael. 1992. "The Gay-Bashers," in *Hate Crimes: Confronting Violence against Lesbians and Gay Men*, ed. Gregory Herek and Kevin Berrill. Newbury Park, CA: Sage, 191–200.

18. Collins, Patricia Hill. 1993. "The Sexual Politics of Black Womanhood," in *Violence against Women*, ed. Pauline Bart and Eileen Moran. Newbury Park, CA: Sage, 85–104.

19. Coltrane, Scott. 1995. "Stability and Change in Chicano Men's Family Lives," in *Men's Lives*, ed. Michael Kimmel

and Michael Messner. Needham Heights, MA: Allyn and Bacon, 469–484.

20. Comstock, Gary. 1991. *Violence against Lesbians and Gay Men.* New York: Columbia University Press.

21. Connell, Robert. 1987. *Gender and Power.* Stanford, CA: Stanford University Press.

22. Crenshaw, Kimberlé Williams. 1994. "Mapping the Margins: Intersectionality, Identity and Violence Against Women of Color," in *The Public Nature of Private Violence,* ed. Martha Albertson Fineman and Roxanne Mykitiuk. New York: Routledge, 93–118.

23. Curran, Dan, and Claire Renzetti. 1994. "Introduction: Gender Inequality and Discrimination on the Basis of Sexual Orientation," in *Contemporary Societies: Problems and Prospects,* ed. Dan Curran and Claire Renzetti. Englewood Cliffs, NJ: Prentice Hall, 204–209.

24. Dobash, R. Emerson, and Russell Dobash. 1997. "Violence against Women," in *Gender Violence: Interdisciplinary Perspectives,* ed. Laura O'Toole and Jessica Schiffman. New York: New York University Press, 266–278.

25. Duberman, Martin. 1993. *Stonewall.* New York: Penguin Books.

26. Editors of the *Harvard Law Review,* 1990, *Sexual Orientation and the Law.* Cambridge: Harvard University Press.

27. Espiritu, Yen. 1997. *Asian American Women and Men.* Thousand Oaks, CA: Sage.

28. Faludi, Susan. 1991. *Backlash.* New York: Anchor Books.

29. Fenstermaker, Sarah, Candace West, and Don Zimmerman. 1991. "Gender Inequality: New Conceptual Terrain," in *Gender Family and Economy: The Triple Overlap.* ed. Rae Lesser Blumberg. Newbury Park, CA: Sage, 289–307.

30. Ferree, Myra Marx. 1987. "She Works Hard for a Living: Gender and Class on the Job," in *Analyzing Gender,* ed. Beth Hess and Myra Marx Ferree. Newbury Park, CA: Sage, 322–347.

31. Fine, Michelle. 1997. "Witnessing Whiteness," in *Off White: Readings on Race, Power and Society,* ed. Michelle Fine, Lois Weis, Linda Powell, and L. Mun Wong. New York: Routledge, 57–65.

32. ———, Lois Weis, and Judi Addelston. 1997. "(In)Secure Times: Constructing White Working Class Masculinities in the Late Twentieth Century." *Gender and Society* 11(1): 52–68.

33. Franklin, Karen, 1998. "Unassuming Motivations: Contextualizing the Narratives of Anti-Gay Assailants," in *Stigma and Sexual Orientation,* ed. Gregory Herek. Thousand Oaks, CA: Sage.

34. French, Marilyn. 1992. *The War against Women.* New York: Summit Books.

35. Gardner, Carol Brooks. 1995. *Passing By: Gender and Public Harassment.* Berkeley: University of California Press.

36. Goffman, Erving. 1963. *Stigma: Notes on the Management of Spoiled Identity.* New York: Touchstone Books.

37. Grau, Günter. 1993. *Hidden Holocaust?* London: Cassell.

38. Greene, Beverly. 1997. "Ethnic Minority Lesbians and Gay Men: Mental Health and Treatment Issues," in *Ethnic and Cultural Diversity among Lesbians and Gay Men,* ed. Beverly Greene. Thousand Oaks, CA: Sage, 216–239.

39. Hamm, Mark. 1994a. *American Skinheads: The Criminology and Control of Hate Crime.* Westport, CT: Praeger.

40. Harry, Joseph. 1992. "Conceptualizing Anti-Gay Violence," in *Hate Crimes: Confronting Violence against Lesbians and Gay Men,* ed. Gregory Herek and Kevin Berrill. Newbury Park, CA: Sage, 113–122.

41. Heger, Heinz. 1980. *The Men with the Pink Triangles.* Boston: Alyson Publications Inc.

42. Herek, Gregory. 1992. "The Social Context of Hate Crimes: Notes on Cultural Heterosexism," in *Hate Crimes: Confronting Violence against Lesbians and Gay Men,* ed. Gregory Herek and Kevin Berrill. Newbury Park, CA: Sage, 89–104.

43. ———, and Kevin Berrill. 1992. "Introduction," in *Hate Crimes: Confronting Violence against Lesbians and Gay Men,* ed. Gregory Herek and Kevin Berrill. Newbury Park, CA: Sage, 1–10.

44. Hochschild, Arlie. 1995. "The Second Shift: Employed Women Are Putting in Another Day of Work at Home," in *Men's Lives,* ed. Michael Kimmel and Michael Messner. Needham Heights, MA: Allyn and Bacon, 443–447.

45. hooks, bell. 1981. *Ain't I A Woman: Black Women and Feminism.* Boston: South End Press.
Hopkins, Patrick. 1992. "Gender Treachery: Homophobia, Masculinity, and Threatened Identities," in *Rethinking Masculinity: Philosophical Explorations in Light of Feminism,* ed. Larry May and Robert Strikwerda. Lanham, MD: Rowman and Littlefield, 111–131.

46. Hurtado, Aida. 1989. "Relating to Privilege: Seduction and Rejection in the Subordination of White Women and Women of Color." *Signs* 14: 833–855.

47. Karst, Kenneth. 1993. *Law's Promise, Law's Expression.* New Haven, CT: Yale University Press.

48. Kaufman, Michael. 1992. "The Construction of Masculinity and the Triad of Men's Violence," in *Men's Lives,* ed. Michael Kimmel and Michael Messner. New York: Macmillan, 28–49.

49. Kinsman, Gary. 1992. "Men Loving Men: The Challenge of Gay Liberation," in *Men's Lives,* ed. Michael Kimmel and Michael Messner. New York: Macmillan, 483–496.

50. La Rossa, Ralph. 1995. "Fatherhood and Social Change," in *Men's Lives* (3rd Ed.), ed. Michael Kimmel and Michael Messner. Needham Heights, MA: Allyn and Bacon, 448–460.

51. Levin, Jack, and McDevitt. 1993. *Hate Crimes: The Rising Tide of Bigotry and Bloodshed.* New York: Plenum.

52. Lorber, Judith, 1994. *Paradoxes of Gender.* New Haven, CT: Yale University Press.

53. MacKinnon, Catharine. 1991. "Reflections on Sex Equality under Law." *Yale Law Journal* 100: 1281–1319.

54. Martin, Patricia Yancey, and Robert Hummer. 1995. "Fraternities and Rape on Campus," in *Race, Class and Gender: An Anthology,* ed. Margaret Anderson and Patricia Hill Collins. Belmont, CA: Wadsworth, 470–487.

55. Messerschmidt, James. 1997. *Crime as Structured Action.* Thousand Oaks, CA: Sage.

56. ———. 1993. *Masculinities and Crime,* Lanham, MD: Rowman and Littlefield.

57. Miller, Susan. 1994. "Gender-Motivated Hate Crimes: A Question of Misogyny," in *Contemporary Societies: Problems and Prospects,* ed. Dan Curran and Claire Renzetti. Englewood Cliffs, NJ: Prentice Hall, 229–240.

58. National Gay and Lesbian Alliance. 1995. *Anti-Gay/Lesbian Violence, Victimization and Defamation in 1994.* Washington, DC: NGLTF Policy Institute.

59. National Gay and Lesbian Task Force. 1999. *Anti-Gay/Lesbian Violence, Victimization and Defamation in 1998.* Washington, DC: NGLTF Policy Institute.

60. ———. 1998. *Anti-Gay/Lesbian Violence, Victimization and Defamation in 1997.* Washington, DC: NGLTF Policy Institute.

61. ———. 1997. *Anti-Gay/Lesbian Violence, Victimization and Defamation in 1996.* Washington, DC: NGLTF Policy Institute.

62. ———. 1996. *Anti-Gay/Lesbian Violence, Victimization and Defamation in 1995.* Washington, DC: NGLTF Policy Institute.

63. ———. 1995. *Anti-Gay/Lesbian Violence, Victimization and Defamation in 1994.* Washington, DC: NGLTF Policy Institute.

64. ———. 1994. *Anti-Gay/Lesbian Violence, Victimization and Defamation in 1993.* Washington, DC: NGLTF Policy Institute.

65. ———. 1993. *Anti-Gay/Lesbian-Violence, Victimization and Defamation in 1992.* Washington, DC: NGLTF Policy Institute.

66. O'Sullivan, Chris. 1998. "Ladykillers: Similarities and Divergences of Masculinities in Gang Rape and Wife Battery," in *Masculinities and Violence,* ed. Lee Bowker. Thousand Oaks, CA: Sage, 82–110.

67. O'Toole, Laura, and Jessica Schiffman. 1997. "Introduction to Part II, Section 1," in *Gender Violence: Interdisciplinary Perspectives,* ed. Laura O'Toole and Jessica Schiffman. New York: New York University Press, 131–137.

68. Pendo, Elizabeth. 1994. "Recognizing Violence against Women: Gender and the Hate Crimes Statistics Act." *Harvard Women's Law Journal.* 17: 157–183.

69. Pharr, Suzanne. 1995. "Homophobia as a Weapon of Sexism," in *Race, Class and Gender in the United States* (3rd ed.), ed. Paula Rothenberg. New York: St. Martin's Press, 481–490.

70. ———. 1998. *Homophobia: A Weapon of Sexism.* Inverness, CA: Chardon Press.

71. Plant, Richard. 1986. *The Pink Triangle: The Nazi War against Homosexuals.* New York: Henry Holt and Company.

72. Rasche, Christine. 1995. "Minority Women and Domestic Violence: The Unique Dilemmas of Battered Women of Color," in *The Criminal Justice System and Women,* ed. Barbara Price and Natalie Sokoloff. New York: McGraw-Hill, 246–261.

73. Reskin, B. 1993. "Sex Segregation in the Workplace." *Annual Review of Sociology* 19: 241–270.

74. Rosenfeld, R. A., and A. L. Kalleberg. 1991. "Gender Inequality in the Labor Market: A Cross-National Perspective." *Acta Sociologica* 34: 207–225.

75. Rothschild, Eric. 1993. "Recognizing Another Face of Hate Crimes: Rape as a Gender-Bias Crime." *Maryland Journal of Contemporary Legal Issues* 4(2): 231–285.

76. Russell, Diana. 1990. *Rape in Marriage.* Bloomington: Indiana University Press.

77. Sanday, Peggy. 1998. "Pulling Train," in *Race, Class and Gender in the United States* (4th ed.), ed. Paula Rothenberg. New York: St. Martin's Press, 497–503.

78. Schneider, Beth. 1993. "Put Up and Shut Up: Workplace Sexual Assaults," in *Violence against Women,* ed. Pauline Bart and Eileen Moran. Newbury Park, CA: Sage, 57–72.

79. Scully, Diana, and Joseph Marolla. 1993. "Riding the Bull at Gilley's: Convicted Rapists Describe the Rewards of Rape," in *Violence against Women,* ed. Pauline Bart and Eileen Moran. Newbury Park, CA: Sage, 26–46.

80. Sheffield, Carole. 1989. "Sexual Terrorism," in *Women: A Feminist Perspective,* ed. Jo Freeman. Mountain View, CA: Mayfield, 3–19.

81. ———. 1987. "Sexual Terrorism: The Social Control of Women," in *Analyzing Gender,* ed. Beth Hess and Myra Marx Ferree. Newbury Park, CA: Sage, 171–189.

82. Stanko, Elizabeth. 1985. *Intimate Intrusions.* London, England: Routledge and Kegan Paul.

83. Taub, Nadine, and Elizabeth Schneider. 1990. "Women's Subordination and the Role of Law," in *The Politics of Law,* ed. David Kairys. New York: Pantheon, 151–176.

84. Thorne, Barrie. 1994. *Gender Play: Boys and Girls in School.* New Brunswick, NJ: Rutgers University Press.

85. U.S. Department of Commerce. 1993. *Statistical Abstract of the United States.* Washington, DC.

86. U.S. Merit Systems Protection Board. 1995. *Sexual Harassment in the Federal Workplace.* Washington, DC.

87. von Schulthess, Beatrice. 1992. "Violence in the Streets: Anti-Lesbian Assault and Harassment in San Francisco," in *Hate Crimes: Confronting Violence against Lesbians and Gay Men,* ed. Gregory Herek and Kevin Berrill. Newbury Park, CA: Sage, 65–75.

88. Warsaw, Robin. 1994. *I Never Called It Rape.* New York: HarperPerennial.

89. Websdale, Neil, and Meda Chesney-Lind. 1998. "Doing Violence to Women: Research Synthesis on the Victimization of Women," in *Masculinities and Violence,* ed. Lee Bowker. Thousand Oaks, CA: Sage, 55–81.

90. Weisburd, Steven Bennett, and Brian Levin. 1994. "On the Basis of Sex: Recognizing Gender-Biased Bias Crimes." *Stanford Law and Policy Review,* spring: 21–47.

91. Weissman, Eric. 1992. "Kids Who Attack Gays," in *Hate Crimes: Confronting Violence against Lesbians and Gay Men,* ed. Gregory Herek and Kevin Berrill. Newbury Park, CA: Sage, 170–178.

92. West, Candace, and Sarah Fenstermaker. 1993. "Power, Inequality and the Accomplishment of Gender: An Ethnomethodological View," in *Theory on Gender/Feminism on Theory,* ed. Paula England. Hawthorne, NY: Aldine de Gruyter, 151–174.

93. West, Candace, and Don Zimmerman. 1987. "Doing Gender." *Gender and Society* 1(2): 125–151.

94. Wolfe, Leslie, and Lois Copeland. 1994. "Violence against Women as Bias-Motivated Hate Crime: Defining the Issues in the USA," in *Women and Violence,* ed. Miranda Davies. London: Zed Books, 200–213.

95. Zion, James, and Elsie Zion. 1996. "Hazko's Sokee'— Stay Together Nicely: Domestic Violence under Navajo Common Law," in *Native Americans, Crime and Justice,* ed. Marianne Nielsen and Robert Silverman. Boulder, CO: Westview, 96–112.

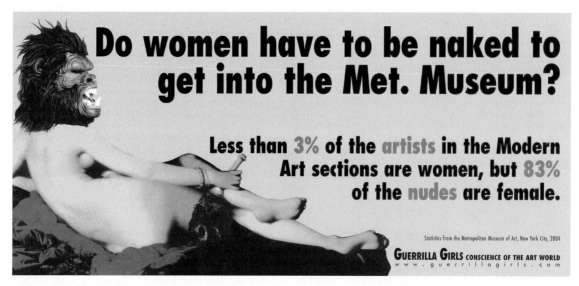

This poster by the Guerrilla Girls is one of six posters in the biennale exhibition "Always a Little Further," curated by Rosa Martinez. According to their website, "In 1989, when the GGs did the first version of this poster, less than 5% of the artists hanging in the Modern and Contemporary Sections of New York's Metropolitan Museum of Art were women, but 85% of the nudes were female. In the fall of 2004 we went back and recounted. SURPRISE. Not much had changed. In fact, there were a few less women artists than fifteen years before!"

http://www.guerrillagirls.com/posters/venicewallf.shtml. Accessed February 15, 2007.

 ## 42

We Are All Works in Progress

LESLIE FEINBERG

The sight of pink-blue gender-coded infant outfits may grate on your nerves. Or you may be a woman or a man who feels at home in those categories. Trans liberation defends you both.

Each person should have the right to *choose* between pink or blue tinted gender categories, as well as all the other hues of the palette. At this moment in time, that right is denied to us. But together, we could make it a reality. . . .

I am a human being who would rather not be addressed as Ms. or Mr., ma'am or sir. I prefer to use gender-neutral pronouns like *sie* (pronounced like "*see*") and *hir* (pronounced like "*here*") to describe myself. I am a person who faces almost insurmountable difficulty when instructed to check off an "F" or an "M" box on identification papers.

I'm not at odds with the fact that I was born female-bodied. Nor do I identify as an intermediate sex. I simply do not fit the prevalent Western concepts of what a woman or man "should" look like. And that reality has dramatically directed the course of my life.

I'll give you a graphic example. From December 1995 to December 1996, I was dying of endocarditis—a bacterial infection that lodges and proliferates in the valves of the heart. A simple blood culture would have immediately exposed the root cause of my raging fevers. Eight weeks of 'round-the-clock intravenous antibiotic drips would have eradicated every last seedling of bacterium in the canals of my heart. Yet I experienced such hatred from some health practitioners that I very nearly died.

I remember late one night in December my lover and I arrived at a hospital emergency room during a snowstorm. My fever was 104 degrees and rising. My blood pressure was pounding dangerously high. The staff immediately hooked me up to monitors and worked to bring down my fever. The doctor in charge began physically examining me. When he determined that my anatomy was female, he flashed me a mean-spirited smirk. While keeping his eyes fixed on me, he approached one of the nurses, seated at a desk, and began rubbing her neck and shoulders. He talked to her about sex for a few minutes. After his pointed demonstration of "normal sexuality," he told me to get dressed and then he stormed out of the room. Still delirious, I struggled to put on my clothes and make sense of what was happening.

The doctor returned after I was dressed. He ordered me to leave the hospital and never return. I refused. I told him I wouldn't leave until he could tell me why my fever was so high. He said, "You have a fever because you are a very troubled person."

This doctor's prejudices, directed at me during a moment of catastrophic illness, could have killed me. The death certificate would have read: Endocarditis. By all rights it should have read: Bigotry.

As my partner and I sat bundled up in a cold car outside the emergency room, still reverberating from the doctor's hatred, I thought about how many people have been turned away from medical care when they were desperately ill—some because an apartheid "whites only" sign hung over the emergency room entrance, or some because their visible Kaposi's sarcoma lesions kept personnel far from their beds. I remembered how a blemish that wouldn't heal drove my mother to visit her doctor repeatedly during the 1950s. I recalled the doctor finally wrote a prescription for Valium because he decided she was a hysterical woman. When my mother finally got to specialists, they told her the cancer had already reached her brain.

Bigotry exacts its toll in flesh and blood. And left unchecked and unchallenged, prejudices create a poisonous climate for us all. Each of us has a stake in the demand that every human being has a right to a job, to shelter, to health care, to dignity, to respect.

I am very grateful to have this chance to open up a conversation with you about why it is so vital to also defend the right of individuals to express and define their sex and gender, and to control their own bodies. For me, it's a life-and-death question. But I also believe that this discussion will have great meaning for you. All your life you've heard such dogma about what it means to be a "real" woman or a "real" man. And chances are you've choked on some of it. You've balked at the idea that being a woman means having to be thin as a rail, emotionally nurturing, and an airhead when it comes to balancing her checkbook. You know in your guts that being a man has nothing to do with rippling muscles, innate courage, or knowing how to handle a chain saw. These are really caricatures. Yet these images have been drilled into us through popular culture and education over the years. And subtler, equally insidious messages lurk in the interstices of these grosser concepts. These ideas of what a "real" woman or man should be straightjacket the freedom of individual self-expression. These gender messages play on and on in a continuous loop in our brains, like commercials that can't be muted.

But in my lifetime I've also seen social upheavals challenge this sex and gender doctrine. As a child who grew up during the McCarthyite, Father-Knows-Best 1950s, and who came of age during the second wave of women's liberation in the United States, I've seen transformations in the ways people think and talk about what it means to be a woman or a man.

Today the gains of the 1970s women's liberation movement are under siege by right-wing propagandists. But many today who are too young to remember what life was like before the women's movement need to know that this was a tremendously progressive development that won significant economic and social reforms. And this struggle by women and their allies swung human consciousness forward like a pendulum.

The movement replaced the common usage of vulgar and diminutive words to describe females with the word *woman* and infused that word with strength and pride. Women, many of them formerly isolated, were drawn together into consciousness-raising groups. Their discussions—about the root of women's oppression and how to eradicate it—resonated far beyond the rooms in which they took place. The women's liberation movement sparked a mass conversation about the systematic degradation, violence, and discrimination that women faced in this society. And this consciousness raising changed many of the ways women and men thought about themselves and their relation to each other. In retrospect, however, we must not forget that these widespread discussions were not just organized to *talk* about oppression. They were a giant dialogue about how to take action to fight institutionalized anti-woman attitudes, rape and battering, the illegality of abortion, employment and education discrimination, and other ways women were socially and economically devalued.

This was a big step forward for humanity. And even the period of political reaction that followed has not been able to overturn all the gains made by that important social movement.

Now another movement is sweeping onto the stage of history: Trans liberation. We are again raising questions about the societal treatment of people based on their sex and gender expression. This discussion will make new contributions to human consciousness. And trans communities, like the women's movement, are carrying out these mass conversations with the goal of creating a movement capable of fighting for justice—of righting the wrongs.

We are a movement of masculine females and feminine males, cross-dressers, transsexual men and women, intersexuals born on the anatomical sweep between female and male, gender-blenders, many other sex and gender-variant people, and our significant others. All told, we expand understanding of how many ways there are to be a human being.

Our lives are proof that sex and gender are much more complex than a delivery room doctor's glance at genitals can determine, more variegated than pink or blue birth caps. We are oppressed for not fitting those narrow social norms. We are fighting back.

Our struggle will also help expose some of the harmful myths about what it means to be a woman or a man that have compartmentalized and distorted your life, as well as mine. Trans liberation has meaning for you—no matter how you define or express your sex or your gender.

If you are a trans person, you face horrendous social punishments—from institutionalization to gang rape, from beatings to denial of child visitation. This oppression is faced, in varying degrees, by all who march under the banner of trans liberation. This brutalization and degradation strips us of what we could achieve with our individual lifetimes.

And if you do not identify as transgender or transsexual or intersexual, your life is diminished by our oppression as well. Your own choices as a man or a woman are sharply curtailed. Your individual journey to express yourself is shunted into one of two deeply carved ruts, and the social baggage you are handed is already packed.

So the defense of each individual's right to control their own body, and to explore the path of self-expression, enhances you own freedom to discover more about yourself and your potentialities. This movement will give you more room to breathe—to be yourself. To discover on a deeper level what it means to be your self.

Together, I believe we can forge a coalition that can fight on behalf of your oppression as well as mine. Together, we can raise each other's grievances and win the kind of significant change we all long for. But the foundation of unity is understanding. So let me begin by telling you a little bit about myself.

I am a human being who unnerves some people. As they look at me, they see a kaleidoscope of characteristics they associate with both males and females. I appear to be a tangled knot of gender contradictions. So they feverishly press the question on me: woman or man? Those are the only two words most people have as tools to shape their question.

"Which sex are you?" I understand their question. It sounds so simple. And I'd like to offer them a simple resolution. But merely answering woman or man will not bring relief to the questioner. As long as people try to bring me into focus using only those two lenses, I will always appear to be an enigma.

The truth is I'm no mystery. I'm a female who is more masculine than those prominently portrayed in mass culture. Millions of females and millions of males in this country do not fit the cramped compartments of gender that we have been taught are "natural" and "normal." For many of us, the words *woman* or *man, ma'am* or *sir, she* or *he*—in and of themselves—do not total up the sum of our identities or of our oppressions. Speaking for myself, my life only comes into focus when the word *transgender* is added to the equation.

Simply answering whether I was born female or male will not solve the conundrum. Before I can even begin to respond to the question of my own birth sex, I feel it's important to challenge the assumptions that the answer is always as simple as either-or. I believe we need to take a critical look at the assumption that is built into the seemingly innocent question: "What a beautiful baby—is it a boy or a girl?"

The human anatomical spectrum can't be understood, let alone appreciated, as long as female or male are considered to be all that exists. "Is it a boy or a girl?" Those are the only two categories allowed on birth certificates.

But this either-or leaves no room for intersexual people, born between the poles of female and male. Human anatomy continues to burst the confines of the contemporary concept that nature delivers all babies on two unrelated conveyor belts. So are the birth certificates changed to reflect human anatomy? No, the U.S. medical establishment hormonally molds and shapes and surgically hacks away at the exquisite complexities of intersexual infants until they neatly fit one category or the other.

A surgeon decides whether a clitoris is "too large" or a penis is "too small." That's a highly subjective decision for anyone to make about another person's body. Especially when the person making the arbitrary decision is scrubbed up for surgery! And what is the criterion for a penis being "too small"? Too small for successful heterosexual intercourse. Intersexual infants are already being tailored for their sexuality, as well as their sex. The infants have no say over what happens to their bodies. Clearly the struggle against gential mutilation must begin here, within the borders of the United States.

But the question asked of all new parents: "Is it a boy or a girl?" is not such a simple question when transsexuality is taken into account, either. Legions of out-and-proud transsexual men and women demonstrate that individuals have a deep, developed, and valid sense of their own sex that does not always correspond to the cursory decision made by a delivery-room obstetrician. Nor is transsexuality a recent phenomenon. People have undergone social sex reassignment and surgical and hormonal sex changes throughout the breadth of oral and recorded human history.

Having offered this view of the complexities and limitations of birth classification, I have no hesitancy in saying I was born female. But that answer doesn't clear up the confusion that drives some people to ask me "Are you a man or a woman?" The problem is that they are trying to understand my gender expression by determining my sex—and therein lies the rub! Just as most of us grew up with only the concepts of *woman* and *man,* the terms *feminine* and *masculine* are the only two tools most people have to talk about the complexities of gender expression.

That pink-blue dogma assumes that biology steers our social destiny. We have been taught that being born female or male will determine how we will dress and walk, whether we will prefer our hair shortly cropped or long and flowing, whether we will be emotionally nurturing or repressed. According to this way of thinking, masculine females are trying to look "like men," and feminine males are trying to act "like women."

But those of us who transgress those gender assumptions also shatter their inflexibility.

So why do I sometimes describe myself as a masculine female? Isn't each of those concepts very limiting? Yes. But placing the two words together is incendiary, exploding the belief that gender expression is linked to birth sex like horse and carriage. It is the social contradiction missing from Dick-and-Jane textbook education.

I actually chafe at describing myself as masculine. For one thing, masculinity is such an expansive territory, encompassing boundaries of nationality, race, and class. Most importantly, individuals blaze their own trails across this landscape.

And it's hard for me to label the intricate matrix of my gender as simply masculine. To me, branding individual self-expression as simply feminine or masculine is like asking poets: Do you write in English or Spanish? The question leaves out the possibilities that the poetry is woven in Cantonese or Ladino, Swahili or Arabic. The question deals only with the system of language that the poet has been taught. It ignores the words each writer hauls up, hand over hand, from a common well. The music words make when finding themselves next to each other for the first time. The silences echoing in the space between ideas. The powerful winds of passion and belief that move the poet to write.

That is why I do not hold the view that gender is simply a social construct—one of two languages that we learn by rote from early age. To me, gender is the poetry each of us makes out of the language we are taught. When I walk through the anthology of the world, I see individuals express their gender in exquisitely complex and ever-changing ways, despite the laws of pentameter.

So how can gender expression be mandated by edict and enforced by law? Isn't that like trying to handcuff a pool of mercury? It's true that human self-expression is diverse and is often expressed in ambiguous or contradictory ways. And what degree of gender expression is considered "acceptable" can depend on your social situation, your race and nationality, your class, and whether you live in an urban or rural environment.

But no one can deny that rigid gender education begins early on in life—from pink and blue color-coding of infant outfits to gender-labeling toys and games. And those who overstep these arbitrary borders are punished. Severely. When the steel handcuffs tighten, it is human bones that crack. No one knows how many trans lives have been lost to police brutality and street-corner bashing. The lives of trans people are so depreciated in this society that many murders go unreported. And those of us who have survived are deeply scarred by daily run-ins with hate, discrimination, and violence.

Trans people are still literally social outlaws. And that's why I am willing at times, publicly, to reduce the totality of my self-expression to descriptions like masculine female, butch, bulldagger, drag king, cross-dresser. These terms describe outlaw status. And I hold my head up proudly in that police lineup. The word *outlaw* is not hyperbolic. I have been locked up in jail by cops because I was wearing a suit and tie. Was my clothing really a crime? Is it a "man's" suit if I am wearing it? At what point—from field to rack—is fiber assigned a sex?

The reality of why I was arrested was as cold as the cell's cement floor: I am considered a masculine female. That's a *gender* violation. My feminine drag queen sisters were in nearby cells, busted for wearing "women's" clothing. The cells that we were thrown into had the same design of bars and concrete. But when we—gay drag kings and drag queens—were thrown into them, the cops referred to the cells as bull's tanks and queen's tanks. The cells were named after our crimes: gender transgression. Actual statutes against cross-dressing and cross-gendered behavior still exist in written laws today. But even where the laws are not written down, police, judges, and prison guards are empowered to carry out merciless punishment for sex and gender "difference."

I believe we need to sharpen our view of how repression by the police, courts, and prisons, as well as all forms of racism and bigotry, operates as gears in the machinery of the economic and social system that governs our lives. As all those who have the least to lose from changing this system get together and examine these social questions, we can separate the wheat of truths from the chaff of old lies. Historic tasks are revealed that beckon us to take a stand and to take action.

That moment is now. And so this conversation with you takes place with the momentum of struggle behind it.

What will it take to put a halt to "legal" and extralegal violence against trans people? How can we strike the unjust and absurd laws mandating dress and behavior for females and males from the books? How can we weed out all the forms of transphobic and gender-phobic discrimination?

Where does the struggle for sex and gender liberation fit in relation to other movements for economic and social equality? How can we reach a point where we appreciate each other's differences, not just tolerate them? How can we tear down the electrified barbed wire that has been placed between us to keep us separated, fearful and pitted against each other? How can we forge a movement that can bring about profound and lasting change—a movement capable of transforming society?

These questions can only be answered when we begin to organize together, ready to struggle on each other's behalf. Understanding each other will compel us as honest, caring people to fight each other's oppression as though it was our own.

43

Medicalization of Racial Features

Asian-American Women and Cosmetic Surgery

EUGENIA KAW

Throughout history and across cultures, humans have decorated, manipulated, and mutilated their bodies for religious reasons, for social prestige, and

for beauty (Brain 1979). In the United States, within the last decade, permanent alteration of the body for aesthetic reasons has become increasingly common. By 1988, 2 million Americans, 87% of them female, had undergone cosmetic surgery, a figure that had tripled in two years (Wolf 1991, 218). [In 2000, doctors performed about 5.7 million cosmetic procedures, 89 percent of them on women (www.surgery.org/statistics.html)—ed.] The cosmetic surgery industry, a $300 million per year industry, has been able to meet an increasingly wide variety of consumer demands. Now men, too, receive services ranging from enlargement of calves and chests to the liposuction of cheeks and necks (Rosenthal 1991). Most noticeably, the ethnic composition of consumers has changed so that in recent years there are more racial and ethnic minorities. [As of 2000, persons of color comprised about 15 percent of patients at cosmetic surgery facilities (www.surgery.org/statistics.html)—ed.] Not surprisingly, across different racial groups, women still constitute the overwhelming majority of cosmetic surgery patients, an indication that women are still expected to identify with their bodies in U.S. society today, just as they have across cultures throughout much of human history (Turner 1987, 85).[1]

The types of cosmetic surgery sought by women in the United States are racially specific. Like most white women, Asian women who undergo cosmetic surgery are motivated by the need to look their best as women. White women, however, usually opt for liposuction, breast augmentation, or wrinkle removal procedures, whereas Asian American women most often request "double-eyelid" surgery, whereby folds of skin are excised from across their upper eyelids to create a crease above each eye that makes the eyes look wider. Also frequently requested is surgical sculpting of the nose tip to create a more chiseled appearance, or the implantation of a silicone or cartilage bridge in the nose for a more prominent appearance. . . . Data from two of the doctors' offices in my study show that in 1990 eyelid surgery was the most common procedure undergone by Asian-American patients (40% of all procedures on Asian Americans at one doctor's office, 46% at another), followed by nasal implants and nasal tip refinement procedures (15% at the first doctor's office, 23% at the second).[2] [In 1999, Asian Americans comprised 4 percent of the U.S. population but 6 percent of the total number of patients who underwent facial cosmetic procedures (www.facial-plastic-surgery.org/media/stats_polls/m-stats.html)—ed.] While the features that white women primarily seek to alter through cosmetic surgery (i.e., the breasts, fatty areas of the body, and facial wrinkles) do not correspond to conventional markers of racial identity, those features that Asian-American women primarily seek to alter (i.e., "small, narrow" eyes and a "flat" nose) do correspond to such markers.[3]

My research focuses on the cultural and institutional forces that motivate Asian-American women to alter surgically the shape of their eyes and noses. I argue that Asian-American women's decision to undergo cosmetic surgery is an attempt to escape persisting racial prejudice that correlates their stereotyped genetic physical features ("small, slanty" eyes and a "flat" nose) with negative behavioral characteristics, such as passivity, dullness, and a lack of sociability. With the authority of scientific rationality and technological efficiency, medicine is effective in perpetuating these racist notions. The medical system bolsters and benefits from the larger consumer-oriented society not only by maintaining the idea that beauty should be every women's goal but also by promoting a beauty standard that requires that certain racial features of Asian-American women be modified. Through the subtle and often unconscious manipulation of racial and gender ideologies, medicine, as a producer of norms, and the larger consumer society of which it is a part encourage Asian-American women to mutilate their bodies to conform to an ethnocentric norm.

★ ★ ★

METHOD AND DESCRIPTION OF SUBJECTS

In this article I present findings of an ongoing ethnographic research project in the San Francisco Bay Area begun in April 1991. I draw on data from structured interviews with physicians and patients, medical literature and newspaper articles, and basic medical statistics. The sample of informants for this research is not random in the strictly statistical sense since informants were difficult to locate. In the United States, both clients and their medical practitioners treat the decision to undergo cosmetic surgery as highly confidential, and practitioners do not reveal the names of patients without their consent. In an effort to generate a sample of Asian-American woman informants, I posted fliers and placed advertisements in various local newspapers for a period of at least three months, but I received only one reply. I also asked doctors who had agreed to participate in my study to ask their Asian-American patients if they would agree to be interviewed. The doctors reported that most of the patients preferred not to talk about their operations or about motivations leading up to the operation. Ultimately, I was able to conduct structured, open-ended interviews with eleven Asian-American women, four of whom were referred to me by doctors in the study, six by mutual acquaintances, and one through an advertisement in a local newspaper. Nine have had cosmetic surgery of the eye or the nose; one recently considered a double-eyelid operation; one is considering a double-eyelid operation in the next few years. Nine of the women in the study live in the San Francisco Bay Area, and two in the Los Angles area. Five had their operations from doctors in my study, while four had theirs in Asia—two in Seoul, Korea, one in Beijing, China, and one in Taipei, Taiwan. Of the eleven women in the study, only two, who received their operations in China and in Taiwan, had not lived in the United States prior to their operations. The two who had surgery in Korea grew up in the United States; they said that they decided to go to Korea for their surgeries because the operations were cheaper there than in the United States and because they felt doctors in Korea are more "experienced" since these types of surgery are more common in Korea than in the United States.[4] The ages of the women in the study range from 18 to 71; one woman was only 15 at the time of her operation.

In addition to interviewing Asian-American women, I conducted structured, open-ended interviews with five plastic surgeons, all of whom practice in the Bay Area. Of the eleven doctors I randomly selected from the phone book, five agreed to be interviewed.

Since the physicians in my study may not be representative of plastic surgeons, I reviewed the plastic surgery literature. To examine more carefully the medical discourse on the nose and eyelid surgeries of Asian-American women, I examined several medical books and plastic surgery journals dating from the 1950s to 1990. I also reviewed several news releases and informational packets distributed by such national organizations as the American Society of Plastic and Reconstructive Surgeons, an organization that represents 97% of all physicians certified by the American Board of Plastic Surgery.

To examine popular notions of cosmetic surgery and, in particular, of how the phenomenon of Asian-American women receiving double-eyelid and nose-bridge operations is viewed by the public and the media, I referenced relevant newspaper and magazine articles.

For statistical information, I obtained national data on cosmetic surgery from various societies for cosmetic surgeons, including the American Society of Plastic and Reconstructive Surgeons. Data on the specific types of surgery sought by different ethnic groups in the United States, including Asian Americans, are missing from the national statistics. At least one public relations coordinator told me that such data are quite unimportant to plastic surgeons. To compensate for this, I requested doctors in my study to provide me with data from their clinics. One doctor allowed me to review his patient files for basic statistical information. Another doctor allowed his office assistant to give me such information, provided that I paid his assistant for the time she had to work outside of normal work hours reviewing his patient files. Since cosmetic surgery is generally not covered by medical insurance, doctors often do not record their patients' medical information in their computers; therefore, most doctors told me that they have very little data on their cosmetic patients readily available.

MUTILATION OR A CELEBRATION OF THE BODY?

The decoration, ornamentation, and scarification of the body can be viewed from two perspectives. On the one hand, such practices can be seen as celebrations of the social and individual bodies, as expressions of belonging in society and an affirmation of oneness with the body (Brain 1979; Scheper-Hughes and Lock 1991; Turner 1980). On the other hand, they can be viewed as acts of mutilation, that is, as expressions of alienation in society and a negation of the body induced by unequal power relationships (Bordo 1990; Daly 1978; O'Neill 1985).

Although it is at least possible to imagine race-modification surgery as a *rite de passage* or a bid for incorporation into the body and race norms of the "dominant" culture, my research findings lead me to reject this as a tenable hypothesis. Here I argue that the surgical alteration by many Asian-American women of the shape of their eyes and nose is a potent form of self, body, and society alienation. Mutilation, according to *Webster's*, is the act of maiming, crippling, cutting up, or altering radically so as to damage seriously essential parts of the body. Although the women in my study do not view their cosmetic surgeries as acts of mutilation, an examination of the cultural and institutional forces that influence them to modify their bodies so radically reveals a rejection of their "given" bodies and feelings of marginality. On the one hand, they feel they are exercising their Americanness in their use of the freedom of individual choice. Some deny that they are conforming to any standard—feminine, Western, or otherwise—and others express the idea that they are, in fact, molding their own standards of beauty. Most agreed, however, that their decision to alter their features was primarily a result of their awareness that as women they are expected to look their best and that this meant, in a certain sense, less stereotypically Asian. Even those who stated that their decision to alter their features was personal, based on individual aesthetic preference, also expressed hope that their new appearance would help them in such matters as getting a date, securing a mate, or getting a better job.

For the women in my study, the decision to undergo cosmetic surgery was never purely or mainly for aesthetic purposes, but almost always for improving their social status as women who are racial minorities. Cosmetic surgery is a means by which they hope to acquire "symbolic capital" (Bourdieu 1984 [1979]) in the form of a look that holds more prestige. For example, "Jane," who underwent double-eyelid and nose-bridge procedures at the ages of 16 and 17, said that she thought she should get her surgeries "out of the way" at an early age since as a college student she has to think about careers ahead:

> Especially if you go into business, whatever, you kind of have to have a Western facial type and you have to have like their features and stature—you know, be tall and stuff. In a way you can see it as an investment in your future.

Such a quest for empowerment does not confront the cultural and institutional structures that are the real cause of the women's feelings of distress. Instead, this form of "body praxis" (Scheper-Hughes and Lock 1991) helps to entrench these structures by further confirming the undesirability of "stereotypical" Asian features. Therefore, the alteration by many Asian-American women of their features is a "disciplinary" practice in the Foucauldian sense; it does not so much benignly transform them as it "normalizes" (i.e., qualifies, classifies, judges, and enforces complicity in) the subject (Foucault 1977). The normalization is a double encounter, conforming to patriarchal definitions of femininity and to Caucasian standards of beauty (Bordo 1990).

★ ★ ★

INTERNALIZATION OF RACIAL AND GENDER STEREOTYPES

The Asian-American women in my study are influenced by a gender ideology that states that beauty should be a primary goal of women. They are conscious that because they are women, they must conform to certain standards of beauty. "Elena," a 20-year-old Korean American, said, "People in society, if they are attractive, are rewarded for their efforts . . . especially girls. If they look pretty and neat, they are paid more attention to. You can't deny that." "Annie," another Korean American who is 18 years old, remarked that as a young woman, her motivation to have cosmetic surgery was "to look better" and "not different from why [other women] put on makeup." In fact, all expressed the idea that cosmetic surgery was a means by which they could escape the task of having to put makeup on every day. As "Jo," a 28-year-old Japanese American who is thinking of enlarging the natural fold above her eyes, said, "I am self-conscious about leaving the house without any makeup on, because I feel just really ugly without it. I feel like it's the mask that enables me to go outside." Beauty, more than character and intelligence, often signifies social and economic success for them as for other women in U.S. society (Lakoff and Scherr 1984; Wolf 1991).

The need to look their best as women motivates the Asian-American women in my study to undergo cosmetic surgery, but the standard of beauty they try to achieve through surgery is motivated by a racial ideology that infers negative behavioral or intellectual characteristics from a group's genetic physical features. All of the women said that they are "proud to be Asian American" and that they "do not want to look white." But the standard of beauty they admire and strive for is a face with larger eyes and a more prominent nose. They all stated that an eyelid without a crease and a nose that does not project indicate a certain "sleepiness," "dullness," and "passivity" in a person's character. "Nellee," a 21-year-old Chinese American, said she seriously considered surgery for double eyelids in high school so that she could "avoid the stereotype of the 'Oriental bookworm'" who is "*dull* and doesn't know how to have fun." Elena, who had double-eyelid surgery two years ago from a doctor in my study, said, "When I look at Asians who have no folds and their eyes are slanted and closed, I think of how they would look better more *awake*." "Carol," a 37-year-old Chinese American who had double-eyelid surgery seven years ago and "Ellen," a 40-year-old Chinese American who had double-eyelid surgery 20 years ago, both said that they wanted to give their eyes a "more spirited" look. "The drawback of Asian features is the puffy eyes," Ellen said. "Pam," a Chinese American aged 44, who had double-eyelid surgery from another doctor in my study two months earlier, stated, "Yes. Of course. Bigger eyes look prettier. . . . Lots of Asians' eyes are so small they become little lines when the person laughs, making the person look *sleepy*." Likewise, Annie, who had an implant placed in her nasal dorsum to build up her nose bridge at age 15, said:

> I guess I always wanted that *sharp* look—a look like you are smart. If you have a roundish kind of nose, it's like you don't know what's going on. If you have that sharp look, you know, with black eyebrows, a pointy nose, you look more *alert*. I always thought that was cool. [emphasis added]

Clearly, the Asian-American women in my study seek cosmetic surgery for double eyelids and nose bridges because they associate the features considered characteristic of their race with negative traits.

These associations that Asian-American women make between their features and personality characteristics stem directly from stereotypes created by the dominant culture in the United States and by Western culture in general, which historically has wielded the most power and hegemonic influence over the world. Asians are rarely portrayed in the U.S. popular media and then only in such roles as Charlie Chan, Suzie Wong, and "Lotus Blossom Babies" (a.k.a. China Doll, Geisha Girl, and shy Polynesian beauty). They are depicted as stereotypes with dull, passive, and nonsociable personalities (Kim 1986; Tajima 1989). Subtle depictions by the media of individuals' minutest gestures in everyday social situations can socialize viewers to confirm certain hypotheses about their own natures (Goffman 1979). At present, the stereotypes of Asians as a "model minority" serve a similar purpose. In the model minority stereotype, the concepts of

dullness, passivity, and stoicism are elaborated to refer to a person who is hard-working and technically skilled but desperately lacking in creativity and sociability (Takaki 1989, 477).

Similar stereotypes of the stoic Asian also exist in East and Southeast Asia, and since many Asian Americans are immigrants or children of recent immigrants from Asia, they are likely to be influenced by these stereotypes as well. U.S. magazines and films have been increasingly available in many parts of Asia since World War II. Also, multinational corporations in Southeast Asian countries consider their work force of Asian women to be biologically suited for the most monotonous industrial labor because the "Oriental girl" is "diligent" and has "nimble fingers" and a "slow wit" (Ong 1987, 151). Racial stereotypes of Asians as docile, passive, slow witted, and unemotional are internalized by many Asian-American women, causing them to consider the facial features associated with these negative traits as defiling.

Undergoing cosmetic surgery, then, becomes a means by which the women can attempt to permanently acquire not only a feminine look considered more attractive by society, but also a certain set of racial features considered more prestigious. For them, the daily task of beautification entails creating the illusion of features they, as members of a racial minority, do not have. Nellee, who has not yet undergone double-eyelid surgery, said that at present she has to apply makeup every day "to give my eyes an illusion of a crease. When I don't wear makeup I feel my eyes are small." Likewise, Elena said that before her double-eyelid surgery she checked almost every morning in the mirror when she woke up to see if a fold had formed above her right eye to match the more prominent fold above her left eye: "[on certain mornings] it was like any other day when you wake up and don't feel so hot, you know. My eye had no definite folds, because when Asians sleep their folds change in and out—it's not definite." The enormous constraints the women in my study feel with regard to their Asian features are apparent in the meticulous detail with which they describe their discontent, as apparent in a quote from Jo who already has natural folds but wants to enlarge them: "I want to make an even bigger eyelid [fold] so that it doesn't look slanted. I think in Asian eyes this inside corner fold [she was drawing on my notebook] goes down too much."

The women expressed hope that the results of cosmetic surgery would win them better acceptance by society. Ellen said that she does not think her double-eyelid surgery "makes me look too different," but she nonetheless expressed the feeling that now her features will "make a better impression on people because I got rid of that sleepy look." She says that she will encourage her daughter, who is only 12 years old, to have double-eyelid surgery as she did, because "I think having less-sleepy-looking eyes would help her in the future with getting jobs." The aesthetic results of surgery are not an end in themselves but rather a means for these women as racial minorities to attain better socioeconomic status. Clearly, their decisions to undergo cosmetic surgery do not stem from a celebration of their bodies.

MEDICALIZATION OF RACIAL FEATURES

Having already been influenced by the larger society's negative valuation of their natural "given" features, Asian-American women go to see plastic surgeons in half-hour consultation sessions. Once inside the clinic, they do not have to have the doctor's social and medical views "thrust" on them, since to a great extent, they, like their doctors, have already entered into a more general social consensus (Scheper-Hughes 1992, 199). Nonetheless, the Western medical system is a most effective promoter of the racial stereotypes that influence Asian-American women, since medical knowledge is legitimized by scientific rationality and technical efficiency, both of which hold prestige in the West and increasingly all over the world. Access to a scientific body of knowledge has given Western medicine considerable social power in defining reality (Turner 1987, 11). According to my Asian American informants who had undergone cosmetic surgery, their plastic surgeons used several medical terms to problematize the shape of their eyes so as to define it as a medical condition. For instance, many

patients were told that they had "excess fat" on their eyelids and that it was "normal" for them to feel dissatisfied with the way they looked. "Lots of Asians have the same puffiness over their eyelid, and they often feel better about themselves after the operation," the doctors would assure their Asian-American patients.

The doctors whom I interviewed shared a similar opinion of Asian facial features with many of the doctors of the patients in my study. Their descriptions of Asian features verged on ideological racism, as clearly seen in the following quote from "Dr. Smith."

> The social reasons [for Asian Americans to want double eyelids and nose bridges] are undoubtedly continued exposure to Western culture and the realization that the upper eyelid *without* a fold tends to give a *sleepy* appearance, and therefore a more *dull* look to the patient. Likewise, the *flat* nasal bridge and *lack of* nasal projection can signify *weakness* in one's personality and by *lack of* extension, a *lack of force* in one's character. [emphasis added]

By using words like "without," "lack of," "flat," "dull," and "sleepy" in his description of Asian features, Dr. Smith perpetuates the notion that Asian features are inadequate. Likewise, "Dr. Khoo" said that many Asians should have surgery for double eyelids since "the eye is the window to your soul and having a more open appearance make you look a bit brighter, more inviting." "Dr. Gee" agreed:

> I would say 90% of people look better with double eyelids. It makes the eye look more spiritually alive. . . . With a single eyelid frequently they would have a little fat pad underneath [which] can half bury the eye and so the eye looks small and unenergetic.

Such powerful associations of Asian features with negative personality traits by physicians during consultations can become a medical affirmation of Asian-American women's sense of disdain toward their own features.

Medical books and journals as early as the 1950s and as recent as 1990 abound with similar metaphors of abnormality in describing Asian features. The texts that were published before 1970 contain more explicit associations of Asian features with dullness and passivity. In an article published in 1954 in the *American Journal of Ophthalmology,* the author, a doctor in the Philippines armed forces, wrote the following about a man on whom he performed double-eyelid surgery:

> [He] was born with mere slits for his eyes. Everyone teased him about his eyes with the comment that as he looked constantly sleepy, so his business too was just as sleepy. For this reason, he underwent the plastic operation and, now that his eyes are wider, he has lost the sleepy look. His business, too, has picked up. [Sayoc 1954, 556]

The doctor clearly saw a causal link between the shape of his patient's eyes and his patient's intellectual and behavioral capacity to succeed in life. In 1964 a white American military surgeon who performed double-eyelid surgeries on Koreans in Korea during the American military occupation of that country wrote in the same journal: "The absence of the palpebral fold produces a passive expression which seems to epitomize the stoical and unemotional manner of the Oriental" (Millard 1964, 647). Medical texts published after 1970 are more careful about associating Asian features with negative behavioral or intellectual characteristics, but they still describe Asian features with metaphors of inadequacy or excess. For instance, in the introductory chapter to a 1990 book devoted solely to medical techniques for cosmetic surgery of the Asian face, a white American plastic surgeon begins by cautioning his audience not to stereotype the physical traits of Asians.

> Westerners tend to have a stereotyped conception of the physical traits of Asians: yellow skin pigmentation . . . a flat face with high cheek bones; a broad, flat nose; and narrow slit-like eyes showing characteristic epicanthal folds. While this stereotype may loosely apply to central Asian groups (i.e., Chinese, Koreans, and Japanese), the facial plastic surgeon should appreciate that considerable variation exists in all of these physical traits (McCurdy 1990, 1).

Yet, on the same page, he writes that the medicalization of Asian features is valid because Asians usually have eyes that are too narrow and a nose that is too flat.

> However, given an appreciation of the physical diversity of the Asian population, certain facial features do form a distinct basis for surgical intervention. . . . These facial features typically include the upper eyelid, characterized by an absent or poorly defined superior palpebral fold . . . and a flattened nose with poor lobular definition (McCurdy 1990, 1).

Thus, in published texts, doctors write about Asians' eyes and noses as abnormal even when they are careful not to associate negative personality traits with these features. In the privacy of their clinics, they freely incorporate both metaphors of abnormality and the association of Asian features with negative characteristics into medical discourse, which has an enormous impact on the Asian-American patients being served.

The doctors' scientific discourse is made more convincing by the seemingly objective manner in which they behave and present themselves in front of their patients in the clinical setting. They examine their patients as a technician diagnosing ways to improve a mechanical object. With a cotton swab, they help their patients to stretch and measure how high they might want their eyelids to be and show them in a mirror what could be done surgically to reduce the puffy look above their eyes. The doctors in my study also use slides and Polaroid pictures to come to an agreement with their patients on what the technical goals of the operation should be. The sterile appearance of their clinics, with white walls and plenty of medical instruments, as well as the symbolism of the doctor's white coat with its many positive connotations (e.g., purity, life, unaroused sexuality, superhuman power, and candor) reinforce in the patient the doctor's role as technician and thus his sense of objectivity (Blumhagen 1979). One of my informants, Elena, said that, sitting in front of her doctor in his office, she felt sure that she needed eyelid surgery: "[Dr. Smith] made quite an impression on me. I thought he was more than qualified—that he knew what he was talking about."

With its authority of scientific rationality and technical efficiency, medicine effectively "normalizes" not only the negative feelings of Asian-American women about their features but also their ultimate decision to undergo cosmetic surgery. For example, "Dr. Jones" does not want to make her patients feel "strange" or "abnormal" for wanting cosmetic surgery. All the doctors in my study agreed that their role as doctor is to provide the best technical skills possible for whatever service their patients demand, not to question the motivation of their patients. Her goal, Dr. Jones said, is "like that of a psychiatrist in that I try to make patients feel better about themselves." She feels that surgeons have an advantage over psychiatrists in treating cosmetic surgery patients because "we . . . help someone to change the way they look . . . psychiatrists are always trying to figure out why a person wants to do what they want to do." By changing the patients' bodies the way they would like them, she feels she provides them with an immediate and concrete solution to their feelings of inadequacy.

Dr. Jones and the other doctors say that they only turn patients away when patients expect results that are technically impossible, given such factors as the thickness of the patient's skin and the bone structure. "I turn very few patients away," said Dr. Khoo. And "Dr. Kwan" notes:

> I saw a young girl [a while back] whose eyes were beautiful but she wanted a crease. . . . She was gorgeous! Wonderful! But somehow she didn't see it that way. But you know, I'm not going to tell a patient every standard I have of what's beautiful. If they want certain things and it's doable, and if it is consistent with a reasonable look in the end, then I don't stop them. I don't really discuss it with them.

Like the other doctors in my study, Dr. Kwan sees himself primarily as a technician whose main role is to correct his patient's features in a way that he thinks would best contribute to the patient's satis-

faction. It does not bother him that he must expose an individual, whom he already sees as pretty and not in need of surgery, to an operation that is at least an hour long, entails the administering of local anesthesia with sedation, and involves the following risks: "bleeding," "hematoma," "hemorrhage," formation of a "gaping wound," "discoloration," "scarring," and "asymmetry in lid fold" (Sayoc 1974, 162–66). He finds no need to try to change his patients' minds. Likewise, Dr. Smith said of Asian-American women who used to come to him to receive really large double eyelids: "I respect their ethnic background. I don't want to change them drastically." Yet he would not refuse them the surgery "as long as it was something I can accomplish. Provided I make them aware of what the appearance might be with the changes."

Though most of my Asian-American woman informants who underwent cosmetic surgery recovered fully within six months to a year, with only a few minor scars from their surgery, they nonetheless affirmed that the psychologically traumatic aspect of the operation was something their doctors did not stress during consultation. Elena said of her double-eyelid surgery: "I thought it was a simple procedure. He [the doctor] should have known better. It took at least an hour and a half. . . . And no matter how minor the surgery was, I bruised! I was swollen." Likewise, Annie could remember well her fear during nose surgery. Under local anesthesia, she said that she was able to witness and hear some of the procedures.

> I closed my eyes. I didn't want to look. I didn't want to see like the knives or anything. I could hear the snapping of scissors and I was aware when they were putting that thing [implant] up my nose. I was kind of grossed out.

By focusing on technique and subordinating human emotions and motivations to technical ends, medicine is capable of normalizing Asian-American women's decision to undergo cosmetic surgery.

MUTUAL REINFORCEMENT: MEDICINE AND THE CONSUMER-ORIENTED SOCIETY

The medical system bolsters and benefits from the larger consumer-oriented society by perpetuating the idea that beauty is central to women's sense of self and also by promoting a beauty standard for Asian-American women that requires the alteration of features specific to Asian-American racial identity. All of the doctors in my study stated that a "practical" benefit for Asian-American women undergoing surgery to create or enlarge their eyelid folds is that they can put eye makeup on more appropriately. Dr. Gee said that after double-eyelid surgery it is "easier" for Asian-American women to put makeup on because "they now have two instead of just one plane on which to apply makeup." Dr. Jones agreed that after eyelid surgery Asian-American women "can do more dramatic things with eye makeup." The doctors imply that Asian-American women cannot usually put on makeup adequately, and thus, they have not been able to look as beautiful as they can be with makeup. By promoting the idea that a beautiful woman is one who can put makeup on adequately, they further the idea that a woman's identity should be closely connected with her body and, particularly, with the representational problems of the self. By reinforcing the makeup industry, they buttress the cosmetic surgery industry of which they are a part. A double-eyelid surgery costs patients $1,000 to $3,000.

The medical system also bolsters and benefits from the larger consumer society by appealing to the values of American individualism and by individualizing the social problems of racial inequality. Dr. Smith remarked that so many Asian-American women are now opting for cosmetic surgery procedures largely because of their newly gained rights as women and as racial minorities:

> Asians are more affluent than they were 15 years ago. They are more knowledgeable and Americanized, and their women are more liberated. I think in the past many Asian women were like Arab women. The men had their foot on top of them. Now Asian women do pretty much what they want to do. So if they want to do surgery, they do it.

Such comments by doctors encourage Asian-American women to believe that undergoing cosmetic surgery is merely a way of beautifying themselves and that it signifies their ability to exercise individual freedom.

★ ★ ★

CONCLUSION

Cosmetic surgery on Asian-American women for nose bridges and double eyelids is very much influenced by gender and racial ideologies. My research has shown that by the conscious or unconscious manipulation of gender and racial stereotypes, the American medical system, along with the larger consumer-oriented society of which it is a part, influences Asian-American women to alter their features through surgery. With the authority of scientific rationality and technological efficiency, medicine is effectively able to maintain a gender ideology that validates women's monetary and time investment in beauty even if this means making their bodies vulnerable to harmful and risky procedures such as plastic surgery. Medicine is also able to perpetuate a racial ideology that states that Asian features signify "dullness," "passivity," and "lack of emotions" in the Asian person. The medicalization of racial features, which reinforces and normalizes Asian-American women's feelings of inadequacy, as well as their decision to undergo surgery, helps to bolster the consumer-oriented society of which medicine is a part and from which medicine benefits.

Given the authority with which fields of "expert" knowledge such as biomedicine have come to define the commonsense reality today, racism and sexism no longer need to rely primarily on physical coercion to legal authority. Racial stereotypes influence Asian-American women to seek cosmetic surgery. Yet, through its highly specialized and validating forms of discourse and practices, medicine, along with a culture based on endless self-fashioning, is able to motivate women to view their feelings of inadequacy as individually motivated, as opposed to socially induced, phenomena, thereby effectively convincing them to participate in the production and reproduction of the larger structural inequalities that continue to oppress them.

NOTES

I would like to thank Nancy Scheper-Hughes, Aihwa Ong, and Cecilia de Mello for their help, insight, and inspiration from the inception of this research project. This research was funded by the Edward H. Heller Endowment and a President's Undergraduate Fellowship, University of California, Berkeley.

1. In a 1989 study of 80 men and women, men reported many more positive thoughts about their bodies than did women (Goleman 1991).

   According to the American Society of Plastic Surgeons, 87% of all cosmetic surgery patients in 1990 were women. In my study, in one of the two doctors' offices from which I received statistical data on Asian-American patients, 65% of Asian-American cosmetic surgery patients in 1990 were women; in the other, 62%.

2. At the first doctor's office, the doctor's assistant examined every file from 1990. In all, 121 cosmetic procedures were performed, 81 on white patients, 20 on Asian-American patients. Closely following national data, the most common procedure among white patients was liposuction (58% of all cosmetic surgeries performed on white patients).

   The second doctor allowed me to survey his patient files. I examined the 1990 files for all patients with last names beginning with the letters A through L. Of these files, all the cosmetic patients were Asian American. Thus, I do not have data on white patients from this office.

   It is important to note that at the first doctor's office, where data on white cosmetic surgery patients were available, the patients were older on average than the Asian-American cosmetic surgery patients at the same clinic. Of the Asian-American patients, 65% were in the age range of 19 to 34 years, compared with 14.8% of whites. Only 20% of Asian American cosmetic surgery patients were in the age group of 35–64 years, however, compared with 80.2% of white cosmetic surgery patients. All the other doctors in my study confirmed a similar trend in their practices. They stated that this trend results from the tendency of whites to seek cosmetic procedures to remove fat and

sagging skin that results from aging, in contrast to Asian Americans, who usually are not concerned with "correcting" signs of aging.

3. The shapes of eyes and noses of Asians are not meant in this article to be interpreted as categories that define an objective category called Asians. Categories of racial groups are arbitrarily defined by society. Likewise, the physical traits by which people are recognized as belonging to a racial group have been determined to be arbitrary (Molnar 1983).

   Also, I use the term "Asian-American" to collectively name the women in this study who have undergone or are thinking of undergoing cosmetic surgery. Although I realize their ethnic diversity, people of Asian ancestry in the United States share similar experiences in that they are subject to many of the same racial stereotypes (Takaki 1989).

4. Cosmetic surgery for double eyelids, nasal-tip refinement, and nose bridges is not limited to Asians in the United States. Asians in East and Southeast Asia have requested such surgeries since the early 1950s, when U.S. military forces began long-term occupation of such countries as Korea and the Philippines (Harahap 1982; Kristof 1991; Millard 1964; and Sayoc 1954).

   I do not mean to imply, however, that the situation within which Asian women develop a perspective on the value and meaning of their facial features is identical in Asia and the United States, where Asian women belong to a minority group. The situation in Asia would require further studies. My observations are limited to the United States.

REFERENCES

1. Blacking, John. 1977. *The Anthropology of the Body.* London: Academic Press.
2. Blumhagen, Dan. 1979. The doctor's white coat: The image of the physician in modern America. *Annals of Internal Medicine* 91:111–16.
3. Bordo, Susan. 1990. Material girl: The effacements of postmodern culture. *Michigan Quarterly Review* 29:635–76.
4. Bourdieu, Pierre. 1984. *Distinction: A Social Critique of the Judgment of Taste.* R. Nice, trans. Cambridge, MA: Harvard University Press.
5. Brain, Robert. 1979. *The Decorated Body.* New York: Harper and Row.
6. Daly, Mary. 1978. *Gyn/Ecology: The Metaethics of Radical Feminism.* Boston: Beacon Press.
7. Foucault, Michel. 1977. *Discipline and Punish: The Birth of the Prison.* A. Sheridan, trans. New York: Vintage Books.
8. Goffman, Erving. 1979. *Gender Advertisements.* Cambridge, MA: Harvard University Press.
9. Goleman, Daniel. 1991. When ugliness is only in the patient's eye, body image can reflect a mental disorder. *New York Times* 2 October:B9.
10. Gramsci, Antonio. 1971. *Selections from the Prison Notebooks of Antonio Gramsci.* New York: International.

11. Harahap, Marwali. 1982. Oriental cosmetic ble-pharoplasty. In *Cosmetic Surgery for Non-White Patients,* edited by Harold Pierce. New York: Grune and Stratton.

12. Kim, Elaine. 1986. Asian Americans and American popular culture. In *Dictionary of Asian American History,* edited by Hyung-Chan Kim. New York: Greenwood Press.

13. Kristof, Nicholas. 1991. More Chinese look "West." *San Francisco Chronicle,* 7 July: Sunday Punch 6.

14. Lakoff, Robin Tolmach, and Raquel L. Scherr. 1984. *Face Value: The Politics of Beauty.* Boston: Routledge and Kegan Paul.

15. Lock, Margaret, and Nancy Scheper-Hughes. 1990. A critical-interpretive approach in medical anthropology: Rituals and routines of discipline and dissent. In *Medical Anthropology: Contemporary Theory and Method,* edited by Thomas M. Johnson and Carolyn F. Sargent. New York: Praeger.

16. McCurdy, John A. 1990. *Cosmetic Surgery of the Asian Face.* New York: Thieme Medical Publications.

17. Millard, Ralph, Jr. 1964. The Oriental eyelid and its surgical revision. *American Journal of Ophthalmology* 57: 646–49.

18. Molnar, Stephen. 1983. *Human Variation: Races, Types, and Ethnic Groups.* Englewood Cliffs, NJ: Prentice-Hall.

19. O'Neill, John. 1985. *Five Bodies.* Ithaca, NY: Cornell University Press.

20. Ong, Aihwa. 1987. *Spirits of Resistance and Capitalist Discipline: Factory Women In Malaysia.* Albany: State University of New York Press.

21. Rosenthal, Elisabeth. 1991. Cosmetic surgeons seek new frontiers. *New York Times* 24 September:B5–B6.

22. Sayoc, B. T. 1954. Plastic construction of the superior palpebral fold. *American Journal of Ophthalmology* 38: 556–559.

23. ———. 1974. Surgery of the Oriental eyelid. *Clinics in Plastic Surgery* 1:157–71.

24. Scheper-Hughes, Nancy. 1992. *Death Without Weeping.* Berkeley: University of California Press.

25. Scheper-Hughes, Nancy, and Margaret M. Lock. 1991. The message in the bottle: Illness and the micropolitics of resistance. *Journal of Psychohistory* 18: 409–32.

26. Tajima, Renee E. 1989. Lotus blossoms don't bleed: Images of Asian women. In *Making Waves: An Anthology of Writings by and about Asian Women,* edited by Diane Yeh-Mei Wong. Boston: Beacon Press.

27. Takaki, Ronald. 1989. *Strangers from a Different Shore.* Boston: Little, Brown.

28. Turner, Bryan. 1987. *Medical Knowledge and Social Power.* London: Sage Publications.

29. Turner, Terence. 1980. The social skin. In *Not Work Alone,* edited by J. Cherfas and R. Lewin. London: Temple Smith.

30. Wolf, Naomi. 1991. *The Beauty Myth: How Images of Beauty Are Used Against Women.* New York: William Morrow.

"Lucy Hao, 24, a jewelry trader, poses with her new nose and double-eye lid next to a copy of the latest edition of Beijing weekend, where she is featured on the cover on July 28, 2003 in Beijing, China. Hao sparked a local media frenzy when she announced that within the next weeks she'll undergo cosmetic surgery 14 times in order to enhance her nose, hairline, eyes, jaws, neck, bottom, breasts and legs. Hao believes being "pretty" is essential in China's society to be successful, in her case she plans a career change to become an actress. Cosmetic clinics have popped up all over urban China as western features have become very popular with urban Chinese women who want to distinguish themselves from the masses and the majority of whom are between 20–30 years old. Hao's surgery cost $50,000."

44

SES, Race/Ethnicity, and Health

MELANIE L. JOHNSTON

INTRODUCTION

Class and race/ethnic disparities in health have been well documented. People of lower socioeconomic status (SES) tend to have poorer health, lower levels of life expectancy, earlier onset of disease, and higher mortality rates compared with their wealthier counterparts. African Americans and American Indians share similar health characteristics of low SES populations. Asian Americans and Hispanic Americans tend to be as healthy as Whites. However, the health advantage of Hispanic Americans is considered a paradox given their overall lower levels of SES. This paper discusses SES and race/ethnic differences in health, the wear and tear theory as an explanation for SES differences in health, and the Hispanic mortality paradox. Other factors related to race and SES, such as differences in health behaviors and health care access, are also discussed.

SES AND HEALTH

A large body of literature has been shown to document negative health outcomes associated with lower socioeconomic status (SES). For example, lower SES has been related to a higher prevalence and incidence of most chronic and infectious diseases (Hayward et al. 2000). A negative relationship has also been documented regarding SES and mental distress (Goldstein 1979), depression, and depressive symptoms (Adler et al. 1993). Lower SES has been associated with higher rates of nearly all major causes of morbidity and mortality (Smith 1999), and evidence suggests that this differential between SES and health is widening rather than narrowing (Crimmins and Saito 2001). *Morbidity* is the state of poor health produced by a disease, and *mortality* is the per capita death rate in a population. Overall, the

data suggest that there is a linear relationship between SES and health in that there are increasingly better health outcomes as one increases in SES levels (Crimmins and Seeman 2001).

SES is typically measured in terms of education, income, occupation, and the poverty ratio. For example, high school graduates have death rates that are two to three times higher than college graduates (Williams 2004). Furthermore, national studies indicate that low SES adults tend to get sick earlier. In other words, they tend to have levels of illness in their 30s and 40s that are not common in high SES adults until their 60s and 70s (Williams 2004).

However, SES is more than just inadequate financial resources. It is related to several other factors that potentially influence health outcomes. These include social, psychological, and behavioral factors, and life circumstances. Examples of social and psychological mechanisms include access to and use of healthcare, dangerous neighborhoods, the role of social networks/social support, and personal characteristics such as coping ability and level of control (Taylor, Repetti, and Seeman 1997). Behavioral factors include the role of personal health practices such as diet and exercise as well as preventive healthcare. Also, life circumstances are often measured by level of stress, stressful life events, and job characteristics.

Furthermore, much of the variation in SES and health is seen in the later ages (i.e., ages 45–64). In other words, the magnitude of differences in SES and health is greater during the middle to later years. This suggests that the health effects of SES are a result of cumulative processes beginning in early life (Blackwell, Hayward, and Crimmins 2001).

Cumulative Adversity and Later Life Health

Wear and tear theory can help explain the relationship between SES and health. The idea is that cumulative levels of adversity or stress may have deleterious effects on health and longevity (Finch and Seeman 1998) by "wearing out" the body's many basic and interrelated physiological systems. This results in "premature aging" among those of lower SES, with increased risk for nearly all types of negative health outcomes (Seeman and Crimmins 2001). The occurrence of an adverse or stressful event causes the body to release both adrenalin and adrenocortical hormones ("fight or flight response"), which helps the body to survive the immediate crisis (McEwen and Seeman 1999). It is the cumulative exposure to adversity that is experienced among lower SES populations that predisposes them to increased biological risk for poorer health outcomes.

An abundance of research indicates that lower SES individuals report more chronic and acute demands that arise from external and internal environments (Turner, Wheaton, and Lloyd 1995). These demands range across several life domains and are typically measured through questions on self-reported degree of environmental stress (i.e., physical environment characterized by crime, crowding, poor physical amenities, and greater exposure to physical hazards such as industrial and hazardous wastes; occupational environment characterized by inadequate and/or predictable resources, nonexistent/little job security or personal autonomy), social characteristics (sociocultural environment characterized by discrimination and impoverished social and psychological resources), and personal coping ability (individual perceptions of powerlessness, alienation, lack of self-esteem) (Seeman and Crimmins 2001).

Wear and tear theories assume that living organisms are like machines. Due to extended usage, the machine's parts wear out and the machine subsequently breaks down. Similarly, aging is seen as a gradual deterioration of the body (Perlman 1954) due to years of wear and tear. It has been suggested that the risk for poor health is due to the extent of wear and tear on the body over time from more long-term exposures to heightened physiologic activity (the body's response to stress). Biological frailty, as a result of low SES and its associated higher levels of daily stress, can act as a measure of wear and tear.

Interestingly, the wear and tear theory applies to both men and women. However, women appear to be healthier and tend to have a longer life expectancy than men, despite typically lower levels of income. Yet, it has been suggested that women may experience more "stress" over the life course as a result of reduced earning potential. Thus, other factors in addition to SES are responsible for gender differences in health.

Gender Differences in Health

An abundance of research indicates that there are differences in health and disease between men and women (Pinn 2003). Women, in general, tend to be healthier than men. In the U.S., men tend to die younger (an average of 7 years younger), have higher mortality rates from all 15 leading causes of death, are more likely to suffer from 7 out of 10 of the most common infectious diseases, and are more likely to experience severe chronic conditions and fatal diseases (Hellerstedt 2001). There are also gender differences in the ways that diseases manifest, rates at which diseases develop, the course of the disease, and responses to treatment.

Several possible reasons for these gender differences include behavioral differences, social norms, and differences in self-reported health. For example, women are more likely to exercise and use vitamin supplements. Men are more likely to engage in high-risk behaviors, such as smoking, drinking, no seat belt use, drinking and driving, and not getting health screenings. There are also cultural norms about masculinity and femininity as they relate to help-seeking behavior and self-reporting of health status. Men are more likely to lack awareness of medical conditions and are less likely to self-report poor health. Women are more likely to make health care visits than men. Although differences in the number of visits decline with increased severity of health concerns, men may still be considerably less likely to contact a physician regarding a health problem.

Despite gender differences in health behaviors, economic position, and social class, associations with health are the strongest (Hellerstedt 2001). For example, income levels are typically higher for men than for women, women are more likely to engage in unpaid work, single-adult households headed by women experience greater economic disadvantage, and women are more likely than men to experience poverty at older ages. Few studies have examined gender differences in the cumulative disadvantages of poverty. For example, one study suggested that childhood poverty had a greater effect on young men (aged 23–33 years) and women older than 33 years.

Gender differences in health reflect both behavior and socioeconomic position. However, economic factors typically play a larger role in gender differences in health. Like gender, race/ethnic differences in health are often said to be related to SES. As indicated in the next section, SES plays a large role but is not the sole contributor to race/ethnic disparities in health.

RACE/ETHNICITY, SES, AND HEALTH STATUS

The health status of U.S. ethnic groups has become an important focus of research due to the rising heterogeneity of the U.S. population and the national goal of reducing racial and ethnic disparities. The majority of studies have focused upon differences in mortality and health between non-Hispanic Whites and other major American ethnic groups, such as African Americans, American Indians, Asian Americans, and Hispanics.

African Americans

In recent years, improvements in economic status of African Americans relative to that of Whites have stagnated (Smith and Welch 1989). Low-income African American families have experienced absolute declines in family income since 1973, and this is associated with worsening health across a number of health status indicators (Williams and Collins 1995). Similarly, the gains in health status of African Americans relative to that of Whites have slowed. In fact, the gap in health status between African Americans and Whites continues to widen (Williams 2004).

On average, African Americans tend to have lower levels of income and education, which are thought to be primary determinants of their poorer health. Life expectancy for African Americans at birth is nearly 7 years shorter than that of White Americans (Rogers, Hummer, and Nam 2000). Further, at age 25, the average White male has a life expectancy of 75 years, while the average African American male can be expected to live until age 71 (Williams 2004). African Americans are more likely to die from most major diseases (Williams 2001), to report higher levels of most diseases and conditions (Hayward et al. 2000), and to experience extraordinary rates of premature aging (Hayward et al. 2000).

As mentioned earlier, the racial gap has been largely attributed to socioeconomic differences and sometimes race is used as an indicator of SES. However, differences in health status associated with race are smaller than those associated with SES (Williams 2004). Also, it has been suggested that adjustments for SES reduce but do not eliminate racial disparities in health as African Americans generally have worse health than Whites within each level of SES (Williams and Collins 1995). For example, national data on infant mortality indicate that for both White and African American women, infant mortality rates go down as years of education increase, yet a very large gap continues to exist between the two races (Williams 2004). Furthermore, it has been suggested that low SES and undereducated White women tend to have better health outcomes compared with the most advantaged college educated African American women.

Thus, both race and class interact together to contribute to health inequalities. Although race differences exist independently of class, differences are not typically due to genetics. Recent research indicates that there are more genetic variations within race/ethnic groups than there are between race/ethnic groups. Also, very few genetic differences— which directly relate to health—have been found between races (Cooper 2003; Pearce et al. 2004). Further, since the concept of race is socially constructed, race/ethnic differences in health may reflect the common environment and lifestyle experienced due to the historical and generational effects of policies based on race as well as institutional racism and discrimination (Williams 2003).

Fundamental social causes of disease, such as childhood poverty, inadequate education, marginal employment, low income, and segregated living conditions (Link and Phelan 1995), are more likely to be experienced by African Americans. At every educational level, African Americans receive less income compared with Whites. They also have lower levels of wealth at every level of income and have less purchasing power at a given level of income (Williams 2004). Also, some suggest that differences in health behaviors related to a lack of knowledge may be a partial explanation for poorer health status (Hayward et al. 2000). Part of this is related to a lack of education, but national data also indicate that African Americans receive poorer quality and less intensive medical care than Whites (Williams 2004). For example, a study found that compared with Whites, African Americans (and Hispanics) who had similar severity levels of heart disease were less likely to receive catheterization or bypass surgery (Lehrman 2004). In sum, both current economic status and factors related to economic deprivation over the life course are responsible for poorer health among African Americans.

American Indians

According to the 2000 census, American Indians consist of 1.5 percent of the U.S. population. The general consensus is that the American Indian population experiences significantly poorer health than Whites. This is consistent with data from the Indian Health Services (IHS) (Kington and Nickens 2001). It has also been suggested that the gap between the two races is narrowing. However, data on the health status and health coverage and access of American Indians (including Alaskan natives) are limited due to the population's small numbers and geographical dispersion in the United States (Zuckerman et al. 2004). Much of the data come from the Indian Health Service (IHS), which provides health care services to American Indians who live on or near reservations. Sixty percent of American Indians live on or near reservations, and little is known about the health status of those living in urban areas (Kington and Nickens 2001).

American Indians typically have higher rates of mortality (Zuckerman et al. 2004) and lower rates of life expectancy compared with Whites across the lifespan (Kington and Nickens 2001). Studies on infant mortality indicate that infant mortality rates are 70 percent higher in American Indian populations compared with Whites (DHHS 2004). American Indians are also more likely to suffer from chronic conditions. For example, they have a higher incidence of diabetes. In 2003, 14.5 percent of American Indians seen at IHS were diagnosed with diabetes (DHHS 2004). Also, it has been suggested that heart disease accounts for 20 percent of all deaths in the American Indian population (DHHS 2004).

Like the African American population, poorer health status among the American Indians is related to higher poverty rates and limited access to quality health care compared with Whites. Approximately 49 percent of American Indians have private health care coverage compared with 83 percent of Whites (Zuckerman et al. 2004). Also, 17 percent of American Indians have Medicaid coverage compared with 5 percent of Whites (Schneider and Martinez 1997) and about 48 percent of low-income American Indians are uninsured (Zuckerman et al. 2004). Further, American Indians are more likely to be dissatisfied with their health care and less likely to have a medical or dental visit in a year (Zuckerman et al. 2004).

Asian Americans

Due to high rates of immigration, the Asian American population is the fastest growing and third largest minority population (next to African Americans and Hispanics) in the United States (Markides and Black 1996). Studies comparing Asians with other race/ethnic groups indicate that Asians have a longer life expectancy. The estimated life expectancy, in 1992, of Asian Americans at birth and age 1 was 80.3 years compared with 75.1 years for Whites (Hoyert and Kung 1997).

Overall, Asian Americans tend to have lower mortality from heart disease, cancer, diabetes, liver disease/cirrhosis, pneumonia/influenza, and HIV/AIDS compared with Whites (Williams 2001). These lower mortality rates appear to be indicative of a favorable health status (Hoyert and Kung 1997). For example, Asian Americans also have lower rates of heart disease, cancer, and cardiovascular disease than Whites (Kagawa-Singer, Hikoyeda, and Tanjasiri 1997). However, these comparisons often disguise the diversity that exists within the Asian population. Chinese Americans, Filipinos, and Japanese Americans represent the three largest subgroups among Asian Americans (U.S. Bureau of the Census 1993). The remaining subgroups include the Vietnamese, Koreans, Hawaiians, Samoans, Guamanians, Cambodians, and Hmong. These diverse groups have a different culture, language, and immigration history, which results in variations in health status (Kington and Nickens 2001). For example, 1992 mortality data indicated that in comparison with the U.S. population, certain Asian subgroups such as Japanese, Asian Indians, and Koreans had lower mortality rates or longer life expectancies, while Hawaiians and Samoans had extremely high mortality rates (Hoyert and Kung 1997). Similarly, California data from 1985 to 1990 indicated lower mortality rates for Chinese, Asian Indians, and Japanese (Kington and Nickens 2001).

The general consensus is that some groups of Asian Americans are healthier on average; however, other Asian subgroups have poorer health (Kington and Nickens 2001). The favorable health status of Asian Americans in general may be related to their more advantaged socioeconomic position (Hoyert and Kung 1997). Another potential explanation is the high proportion of immigrants who may be healthier on average than their native-born counterparts (Markides and Black 1996).

Hispanics/Mexican Americans

The majority of studies on the health status of Hispanics have focused on Mexican American mortality rates with the assumption that they would be higher (similar to African Americans) than Whites since their socioeconomic profile includes high unemployment, high levels of poverty, low education, a lower likelihood of having health insurance, and poorer access to health care (Ginzberg 1991). However, the life expectancy of many Mexican Americans is similar to that of Whites (Rogers et al. 1996). Also, local, state, and national data indicate that Hispanics (including Mexican Americans) have lower all-cause mortality rates than Whites, even after controlling for demographic and socioeconomic characteristics (Liao et al. 1998). Hispanics, in general, have a lower mortality than non-Hispanics from a number of conditions including cancer (Sorlie et al. 1993), cardiovascular disease (Sorlie et al. 1993), and chronic obstructive pulmonary disease (Rosenwaike 1987). Although Hispanics have an advantage for some diseases, it has been shown that they are more likely to die from diabetes, liver disease, homicide (Sorlie et al. 1993), cervical cancer (Markides and Coreil 1986), and AIDS (Thiel de Bocanegra, Gany, and Fruchter 1993). Also, Hispanics are more likely to suffer from respiratory problems, infections, pneumonia, influenza, accidents (Markides and Black 1996), and obesity (Winkleby, Garner, and Taylor 1996). It has been suggested that differences in health behaviors do not explain the overall better health of Hispanics (Winkleby, Garner, and Taylor 1996).

The Hispanic Mortality Paradox

The favorable health profile among Hispanics, despite lower levels of SES, has been termed the Hispanic mortality paradox or epidemiological paradox (Abraido-Lanza et al. 1999). Previous research has suggested that their favorable health profile may be a reflection of data artifacts (Palloni and Arias 2004) that create an illusion of better health status. Examples include factors related to migration or being foreign born (Hummer et al. 1999), also known as the healthy migrant effect and the salmon bias hypothesis. Yet, other research has suggested that certain protective cultural factors may be responsible since one health-enhancing characteristic of the Hispanic lifestyle is the tendency to formulate closer networks compared with their White counterparts (Ramirez de Arellano 1994).

The Healthy Migrant Effect . . . The healthy migrant effect suggests that the selection of healthy migrants to the United States accounts for the Hispanic paradox (Palloni and Arias 2004). Migrants are typically physically and psychologically healthier than nonmigrants. They may also be healthier than the average individual in the receiving population. Before migration, these migrants are hypothesized to have better health behaviors, family support systems, and health status than their U.S.-born counterparts (Hummer et al. 1999). In contrast, U.S. residents tend to have higher levels of drinking and smoking as well as poorer dietary practices (Scribner 1996).

★ ★ ★

The Salmon Bias Effect The salmon bias effect has been seen among some foreign-born Hispanic subgroups (Palloni and Arias 2004), such as Mexican Americans. Like salmon that return to their place of origin before dying, some immigrants may return to their country of origin after a period of temporary unemployment or illness (Abraido-Lanza et al. 1999). . . .

Return migration leads to artificially lower mortality rates among Hispanics because there is a reduction in the number of unhealthy persons in the population, thereby leading to the illusion of reduced mortality rates. The salmon bias effect assumes that the returning migrants are typically older and frailer. In contrast, the healthy migrant effect suggests that migration to the United States is more common among the younger and healthier age groups.

Other Data Artifacts It has also been suggested that the mortality advantage of Hispanics could be due to other types of data artifacts. For example, there are three other types of data problems: ethnic identification, misreporting of ages, and mismatches of records (Palloni and Arias 2004).

Ethnic identification refers to the underreporting of Hispanic origin on U.S. death certificates. Ethnic reporting is based on self-identification and as many as 7 percent of Hispanics are not recorded as Hispanic on death certificates (Rosenberg et al. 1999). The misreporting of ages refers to the tendency of some Hispanic subgroups to overstate their ages, which could lead to a depression in mortality rates at older ages (Palloni and Arias 2004). A mismatch of records is likely to occur when there is limited data available for linking death records to a population. . . .

Others also suggest that there is significant variation in the Hispanic mortality paradox. For example, results differ by age, gender, acculturation, and cause of death (Franzini, Ribble, and Keddie 2001). It has been suggested that data artifacts (including migration) may contribute to but do not fully explain the paradox. It is concluded that the paradox is due to reasons that are multifactorial and social in origin (Franzini et al. 2001).

★ ★ ★

CONCLUSION

In conclusion, SES differences in health appear to reflect the cumulative effects of adversity or stress—which tends to exert repeated pressure on physiological regulatory mechanisms. This often leads to an increase in biological frailty or biological risk for poor health. However, SES effects on health are more than just biological and stress-related. SES also regulates access to quality healthcare and knowledge about health behaviors. Race/ethnic differences in health are often said to be related to socioeconomic levels. However, both race and SES influence health independent of each other and, at the same time, work together to influence health. Furthermore, since *race/ethnicity* is a socially constructed term, it has been suggested that race differences reflect historical policies that served to create the disparities in income, education, and access to adequate health care. The Hispanic mortality paradox appeared to be an anomaly in all of this, and some support has been found for the healthy migrant effect, yet more systematic research is needed to elicit the true explanations for the Hispanic health advantage.

REFERENCES

1. Abraido-Lanza, A. F., Dohrenwend, B. P., Ng-Mak, D. S., and Blake Turner, J. (1999). The Latino Mortality Paradox: A Test of the Salmon Bias and Healthy Migrant Hypothesis. *American Journal of Public Health,* 89 (10), 1543–1548.
2. Adler, N. E., Boyce, W. T., Chesney, M. A., Folkman, S., and Syme, S. L. (1993). Socioeconomic Inequalities in Health: No Easy Solution. *Journal of the American Medical Association,* 269, 3140–3145.
3. Blackwell, D. L., Hayward, M. D., and Crimmins, E. M. (2001). Does Childhood Health Affect Chronic Morbidity in Later Life? *Social Science and Medicine,* 52, 1269–1284.
4. Crimmins, E. M., and Saito, Y. (2001). Trends in Disability Free Life Expectancy in the United States, 1970–1990: Gender, Racial, and Educational Differences. *Social Science and Medicine,* 52, 1629–1641.
5. Crimmins, E. M., and T. E. Seeman. (2001). Integrating Biology Into Demographic Research on Health and Aging with a Focus on the MacArthur Study of Successful Aging. In C. Finch and J. Vaupel (Eds.), *Cells and Surveys: Should Biological Measures Be Included in Social Science Research?* Washington, DC: National Academy Press.
6. Cooper, R. S. (2003). Race, Genes, and Health—New Wine in Old Bottles? *International Journal of Epidemiology,* 32, 23–25.
7. Daniels, L. (2002). Diet and Coronary Heart Disease. *Nursing Standard,* 16(43), 47–52.
8. Department of Health and Human Services. (2004). Minority Health Disparities at a Glance. *HSS Fact Sheet: July 12, 2004.* Washington, D.C.: U.S. Department of Health and Human Services: The Initiative to Eliminate Racial and Ethnic Disparities in Health.
9. Erlinger, T. P., Pollac, H., and Appel, L. J. (2000). Nutrition-Related Cardiovascular Risk Factors in Older People: Results from the Third National Health and Nutrition Examination Survey. *American Geriatrics Society,* 48(11), 1486–1489.
10. Fang, J., Madhavan, S., and Alderman, M. H. (1997). Influence of Nativity on Cancer Mortality Among Black New Yorkers. *Cancer,* 80, 129–135.
11. Finch, C. E., and Seeman, T. E. (1998). Stress Theories of Aging. Pp. 81–97 in Vern L. Bengtson and K. Warner Schaie (Eds.), *Handbook of the Theories of Aging.* New York: Springer Publishing Company.
12. Franzini, L., Ribble, J. C., and Keddie, A. M. (2001). Understanding the Hispanic Paradox. *Ethnicity and Disease* 11 (3), 496–518.
13. Ginzberg, E. (1991). Access to Health Care for Hispanics. *Journal of the American Medical Association,* 265 (2), 238–241.
14. Goldstein, M. S. (1979). The Sociology of Mental Health and Illness. *Annual Review of Sociology,* 5, 381–409.
15. Hansen, K. A., and Farber, C. S. (1997). The Foreign-Born Population of the United States: 1996. *Current Population Reports: Population Characteristics,* 420–494.
16. Hayward, M. D., Crimmins, E. M., Miles, T. P., and Yang, Y. (2000). The Significance of Socioeconomic Status in Explaining the Race Gap in Chronic Health Conditions. *American Sociological Review,* 65, 910–930.
17. Health, G. W., and Smith, J. D. (1994). Physical Activity Patterns Among Adults in Georgia: Results from the 1990 Behavioral Risk Factor Surveillance System. *Southern Medical Journal,* 87 (4), 435–439.
18. Hellerstedt, W. L. (2001). Social Determinants of Gender Differences in Health in the U.S. Presentation at Healthy Generations Conference Series: Women's Reproductive Health—University of Minnesota, Center for Leadership Education in Maternal and Child Public Health, March 14, 2001.
19. House, J. S., Landis, K. R., and Umberson, D. (1988). Social relationships and health. *Science,* 241, 540–545.
20. Hoyert, D. L., and Kung, H. C. (1997). Asian or Pacific Islander Mortality, Selected States, 1992. *Monthly Vital Statistics Report,* 14, 46 (1 suppl), 1–63.
21. Hummer, R. A., Rogers, R. G., Nam, C. B., and LeClere, F. B. (1999). Race/ethnicity, nativity, and U.S. adult mortality. *Social Science Quarterly,* 80 (1), 136–153.
22. Kagawa-Singer, M., Hikoyeda, N., and Tanjasiri, S. P. (1997). Aging, Chronic Conditions, and Physical Disabilities in Asian and Pacific Islander Americans. In K. S. Markides and M. R. Miranda (Eds.), *Minorities, Aging, and Health.* Thousand Oaks, CA: Sage.
23. Kessler, R. C. (1979). Stress, social status and psychological distress. *Journal of Health and Social Behavior,* 20, 259–272.
24. Key, T. J., Allen, N. E., Spencer, E. A., and Travis, R. C. (2002). The effect of diet on risk of cancer. *Lancet,* 360 (9336), 861–868.
25. Kington, R. S., and Nickens, H. W. (2001). Racial and Ethnic Differences in Health: Recent Trends, Current Patterns, Future Directions. In N. Smelser, W. J. Wilson, and F. Mitchell (Eds.), *America Becoming: Racial Trends and Their Consequences, Volume II,* Washington, DC: National Academy Press.
26. Krause, N., and Wray, L. A. (1992). Psychosocial Correlates of Health and Illness Among Minority Elders. In E. P. Stanford and F. M. Torres-Gil (Eds.), *Diversity: New Approaches to Ethnic Minority Aging* (pp. 41–52). Amityville, NY: Baywood.
27. Kromhout, D., Menotti, A., Kesteloot, H., and Sans, S. (2002). Prevention of Coronary Heart Disease by Diet and Lifestyle: Evidence from Prospective Cross-Cultural, Cohort, and Intervention Studies. *Circulation,* 105 (7), 893–898.
28. Larsen, L. J. (2004). The Foreign-Born Population in the United States: 2003. *Current Population Reports,* P20-551, Washington, DC: U.S. Census Bureau.
29. Lehrman, S. (2004). Race and Healthcare. *http://www.alternet.org/story/16868/.*

30. Liao, Y., Cooper, R. S., Cao, G., Durazo-Arvizu, R., Kaufman, J. S., Luke, A., and McGee, D. (1998). Mortality Patterns Among Adult Hispanics: Findings From the NHIS, 1986–1990. *American Journal of Public Health*, 88, 227–32.

31. Link, B. G., and Phelan, J. (1995). Social Conditions as Fundamental Causes of Disease. *Journal of Health and Social Behavior*, 36, 89–94.

32. Markides, K. S., and Black, S. A. (1996). Race, Ethnicity, and Aging: The Impact of Inequality. In R. H. Binstock and L. K. George. (Eds.), *Handbook of Aging and the Social Sciences*, 4th ed. Washington, DC: Academic Press.

33. Markides, K. S., and Coreil, J. (1986). The Health of Hispanics in the Southwestern United States: An Epidemiologic Paradox. *Public Health Reports*, 101, 253–265.

34. McEwen, B. S., and Seeman, T. (1999). Protective and Damaging Effects of Mediators of Stress. *Annals of the New York Academy of Sciences*, 896, 30–47.

35. Meyer, J. P., and Gillatt, D. A. (2002). Can Diet Affect Prostate Cancer? *BJU Int.*, 89 (3), 250–254.

36. Milner, J. A. (2002). Strategies for Cancer Prevention: The Role of Diet. *British Journal of Nutrition*, 87 (Suppl 2), S265–272.

37. Mulatu, M. S., and Schooler, C. (2002). Causal Connections Between Socio-Economic Status and Health: Reciprocating Effects and Mediating Mechanisms. *Journal of Health and Social Behavior*, 43 (1), 22–41.

38. National Center for Health Statistics. (1993). Health Promotion and Disease Prevention: United States, 1990. *Vital Health Statistics 10*, 185. Hyattsville, MD: U.S. Dept of Health and Human Services. DHHS publication (PHS) 93–1513.

39. ——. (2000). *Health Outcomes Among Hispanic Subgroups: Data From the National Health Interview Survey, 1992–95*. Hyattsville, MD: U.S. Dept of Health and Human Services. DHHS publication (PHS) 2000–1250.

40. Odoms-Young, A. M. (2004). Obesity and Poverty. Presentation at Obesity 2004 Conference: Developing Community Strategies for a National Crisis, Case Western Reserve.

41. Palloni, A., and Arias, E. (2004). Paradox Lost: Explaining the Hispanic Adult Mortality Advantage. *Demography*, 41 (3), 385–415.

42. Perlman, R. M. (1954). The Aging Syndrome. *Journal of the American Geriatric Society*, 2, 123–129.

43. Pearce, N., Foliaki, S., Sporle, A., and Cunningham, C. (2004). Genetics, Race, Ethnicity, and Health. *British Medical Journal*, 328: 1070–1072.

44. Pinn, V. W. (2003). Sex and Gender Factors in Medical Studies: Implications for Health and Clinical Practice. *Journal of the American Medical Association*, 289, 397–400.

45. Pi-Sunyer, F. X. (1993). Health Implications of Obesity. *American Journal of Clinical Nutrition*, 53, 1595S–1603S.

46. Potter, J. D. (1997). Diet and Cancer: Possible Explanations for the Higher Risk of Cancer in the Poor. *IARC Scientific Publications*, 138, 265–283.

47. Ramirez de Arellano, A. B. (1994). The Elderly. In C. W. Molina and M. A. Molina (Eds.), *Latino Health in the U.S.: A Growing Challenge*. Washington, DC: American Public Health Association.

48. Rimm, E. B., Willett, W., Hu, F. B., Sampson, L., Colditz, G. A., Manson, J. E., Hennekens, C., and Stampfer, M. J. (1998). Folate and Vitamin B6 From Diet and Supplements in Relation to Risk of Coronary Heart Disease Among Women. *Journal of the American Medical Association*, 279 (5), 359–364.

49. Rogers, R. G., Hummer, R. A., and Nam, C. B. (2000). *Living and Dying in the USA*. San Diego, CA: Academic Press.

50. Rogers, R. G., Hummer, R. A., Nam, C. B., and Peters, K. (1996). Demographic, Socioeconomic, and Behavioral Factors Affecting Ethnic Mortality by Cause. *Social Forces*, 74, 1419–1438.

51. Rosenberg, H. M., Maurer, J. D., Sorlie, P. D., Johnson, N. J., MacDorman, M. F., Hoyert, D. L., Spitler, J. F., and Scott, C. (1999). Quality of Death Rates by Race and Hispanic Origin: A Summary of Current Research, 1999. *Vital and Health Statistics*, Series 2 (128). Hyattsville, MD: National Center for Health Statistics.

52. Rosenwaike, I. (1987). Mortality Differentials Among Persons Born in Cuba, Mexico, and Puerto Rico Residing in the United States, 1979–81. *American Journal of Public Health*, 77, 603–606.

53. Schneider, A., and Martinez, J. (1997). Native Americans and Medicaid: Coverage and Financing Issues. Kaiser Family Foundation (Pub.#2101).

54. Scribner, R. S. (1996). Paradox as Paradigm: The Health Outcomes of Mexican Americans. *American Journal of Public Health*, 86, 303–304.

55. Seeman, T. E., and Crimmins, E. M. (2001). Social Environment Effects on Health and Aging: Integrating Epidemiological and Demographic Approaches and Perspectives. *Annals of the New York Academy of Sciences*, 954, 88–117.

56. Singh, G. K., and Siahpush, M. (2001). All-Cause and Cause-Specific Mortality of Immigrants and Natives in the United States. *American Journal of Public Health*, 91 (3), 392–399.

57. ——. (2002). Ethnic-Immigrant Differentials in Health Behaviors, Morbidity, a Cause Specific Mortality in the United States: An Analysis of Two National Data Bases. *Human Biology*, 74 (1), 83–109.

58. Smith, J. P. (1999). Healthy Bodies and Thick Wallets: The Dual Relation Between Health and Economic Status. *Journal of Economic Perspectives*, 13, 145–166.

59. Smith, J. P., and Welch, F. R. (1989). Black Economic Progress After Myrdal, *Journal of Economic Literature*, 27, 519–564.

60. Sorlie, P. D., Backlund, E., Johnson, N. J., and Rogot, E. (1993). Mortality by Hispanic Status in the United States. *Journal of the American Medical Association*, 270, 2464–2468.

61. Sowers, M. F. (1997). Dietary Factors and SES. John D. and Catherine T. MacArthur Research Network on Socioeconomic Status and Health. *http://www.macses.ucsf.edu/research/allostatic/notebook/diet.html*.

62. Stephen, E. H., Foote, K., Hendershot, G. E., and Schoenborn, C. A. (1994). Health of the Foreign Born Population: United States, 1989–90. *Advance Data From Vital and Health Statistics.* No. 241 (Feb). Hyattsville, MD: National Center for Health Statistics.

63. Sterling, T. D., and Weinkam, D. (1989). Comparison of Smoking-Related Risk Factors Among Black and White Males. *American Journal of Industrial Medicine,* 15, 319–333.

64. Taylor, S., Repetti, R., and Seeman, T. (1997). Health Psychology: What Is an Unhealthy Environment and How Does It Get Under the Skin? *Annual Review of Psychology,* 48, 411–447.

65. Thiel de Bocanegra, H., Gany, F., and Fruchter, R. (1993). Available Epidemiologic Data on New York's Latino Population: A Critical Review of the Literature. *Ethnicity and Disease,* 3, 413–426.

66. Turner, R. J., Wheaton, B., and Lloyd, D. A. (1995). The Epidemiology of Social Stress. *American Sociological Review,* 60, 104–125.

67. U.S. Bureau of the Census. (1993). *We, the American Asians.* Washington, DC: U.S. Government Printing Office.

68. Wamala, S. P., Wolk, A., and Orth-Gomer, K. (1997). Determinants of Obesity in Relation to Socioeconomic Status Among Middle Aged Swedish Women. *Preventive Medicine,* 26 (5 pt 1), 734–744.

69. Williams, D. R. (1990). Socioeconomic Differentials in Health: A Review and Redirection. *Social Psychology Quarterly,* 53, 31–99.

70. ———. (2001). Racial Variations in Adult Health Status: Patterns, Paradoxes, and Prospects. In N. Smelser, W. J. Wilson, and F. Mitchell (Eds.), *America Becoming: Racial Trends and their Consequences.* Washington, DC: National Academy Press.

71. ———. (2003). Racial/Ethnic Discrimination and Health: Findings from Community Studies. *American Journal of Public Health,* 93 (2), 200–208.

72. ———. (2004). The Influence of Socioeconomic Status, Race and Geography on Health Outcomes and Health-care Access. Presented at Inequality Matters Conference. New York University: June 4, 2004.

73. Williams, D. R., and Collins, C. (1995). U.S. Socioeconomic and Racial Differences in Health: Patterns and Explanations. *Annual Review of Sociology,* 21, 349–386.

74. Winkleby, M. A., Gardner, C. D., and Taylor, C. B. (1996). The Influence of Gender and Socioeconomic Factors on Hispanic/White Differences in Body Mass Index. *Preventive Medicine,* 25, 203–211.

75. Woolhandler, S., Himmelstein, D. U., Silber, R., Bader, M., Harnly, M., and Jones, A. A. (1985). Medical Care and Mortality: Racial Differences in Preventable Deaths. *International Journal of Health Services,* 15 (1), 1–22.

76. Zuckerman, S., Haley, J., Roubideaux, Y., and Lillie-Blanton, M. (2004). Health Service Access, Use, and Insurance Coverage Among American Indians/Alaska Natives and Whites: What Role Does the Indian Health Service Play? *American Journal of Public Health,* 94 (1), 53–59.

 45

Race, Family Values, and Welfare Reform

BONNIE THORNTON DILL,
MAXINE BACA ZINN, AND
SANDRA PATTON

The national tempest in the United States over family values shows no signs of abating. Though most reasonable people acknowledge that the causes of contemporary family change are complex, public discourse is still polarized and simplistic. In the past two decades, conservatives have galvanized public opinion and public policy around an explanation of social decay rooted in the "breakdown of the family" and a decline in "family values." Progressives, on the other hand, have challenged this perspective by calling on substantial bodies of theory and research to demonstrate that changes in family life are global and primarily the result of structural, economic, and political changes that have led to major cultural shifts. And though progressives offer compelling evidence that shifting social and economic conditions are more important than declining moral standards in the creation and perpetuation of current shifts in family life, their arguments have not prevailed. Instead, in the 1990s, the conservative narrative has become broadly accepted as a way of explaining social, economic, and cultural dislocations in the U.S. landscape. Their story is one that blames single mothers and immigrants for such social ills as poverty, crime, drug abuse, and gang violence. It has become entrenched in mainstream political discourse as policy analysts and politicians have promoted these simplistic causal connections as explanations for broad socioeconomic dislocations and as justifications for dismantling the U.S. social welfare system.

At the heart of this national debate are issues of race that are only partially addressed in the progressive critique and widely exploited in the conservative narrative. In this [paper], we seek to extend the progressive challenge in three ways: first, by examining the way in which race and racial narratives are drawn on and function in contemporary public discourse regarding family values and welfare reform in the United States; second, by showing how an analysis of racialized patterns of family formation sharpens our understanding of structured inequalities; and third, by extending the discussion of race to include both black and Latino families and demonstrating a multiracial discussion of race introduces new complications into the discussion of family values and welfare reform.

We begin by outlining the conservative narrative about family values and identifying the ways that race and gender stereotypes are embedded and exploited in their discourse. We then turn to a discussion of progressive responses to the family values and welfare reform discourse, focusing on the ways in which the progressive challenge could be extended and strengthened by explicitly incorporating race into the analyses. Next, we seek to expand the progressive critique, first, by examining the way in which racial narratives function in the family values debate; second, by identifying the ways in which race structures families; and third, by examining data on family dynamics among Latinos and blacks, in order to create a more comprehensive picture of race in the family values debate. Finally, we turn to welfare reform itself and argue that the demonization of black and Latina women is part of a racialized attack on the welfare system—one that seeks to control their fertility and their work and, ultimately, to reduce the presence of poor women of color in the society.

OUR ANALYTICAL APPROACH

Our analytical strategy in this paper combines sociological and descriptive analyses with narrative analysis. This seems particularly appropriate in trying to shed light on issues that are rooted in social life but have been portrayed and given meaning through a variety of forms of language, symbols, and representations that are highly contested in contemporary U.S. society. Narrative analyses of

policy argue for the importance of recognizing that public policy dialogues are, indeed, *public* discussions situated in complex discursive, legislative, and sociopolitical histories. Legislative agendas do not exist in isolation from popular culture and public opinion, and, in our view, it is necessary to explore the relationships between shifts in public policy and widespread media narratives in order to fully understand the relations of power at work in such social shifts. As Graeme Turner explains, "What is clear is that the world comes to us in the shape of stories."[1] The political narratives embedded in public policy agendas draw on sociological data and interpretations of those data that reflect broader social stories about race, gender, family, class, and citizenship that are widely available in public discourse. The philosopher Robert Gooding-Williams argues that such representations should be read as sociopolitical allegories. His analysis suggests that we must ask, What is the social function of a particular racial representation? What does this representation of race signify beyond the particular meanings conveyed within the given text?[2] And of course, we must also seek to answer the question. Why has this narrative appeared here and now? The cultural studies scholar Hazel Carby suggests that "these narrative genealogies, in their production of this symbolic power, have significant political resonance when they are produced in response to a perceived crisis in the formation of a society."[3] Thus, Carby argues that popular narratives, in their allegorical power to signify sociopolitical "truths," function ideologically as justifications for oppression and inequality.

In this [paper], we examine the social function of racialized political narratives that blame poor single and immigrant mothers for social ills like drug addiction, poverty, crime, and gang violence. Using examples of these narratives from different points in U.S. history, we trace these themes into the present and argue that contemporary discourse on welfare reform and family values has served as justification for the passage of punitive social policies that seek to regulate the lives of low-income women of color and white women whose sexual reproductive behavior deviates from the middle-class nuclear family norm.

While we draw on critical race theory, cultural studies, family demography, and the work of political economists, our approach is most fundamentally grounded in multiracial feminism. This perspective is an attempt to go beyond a mere recognition of diversity and difference among women to examine structures of domination, specifically, the importance of race in understanding the social construction of gender. Despite the varied concerns and multiple intellectual stances that characterize the feminism of women of color, they share an emphasis on race as a primary force for situating genders differently. It is the centrality of race, of institutionalized racism, and of struggles against racial oppression that link the various feminist perspectives within this framework.[4]

THE CONSERVATIVE NARRATIVE

The conservatives, or, as they sometimes call themselves, the "pro-family" forces, believe that the traditional nuclear family is the basis of social organization and cohesion in the United States. This family form, in their view, is the one in which children are best socialized to become good citizens and in which men and women perform the roles essential to creating and maintaining social order and continuity from one generation to the next, as wives and mothers, husbands and fathers: "As the Institute for American Values [a conservative think tank] writes in its mission statement, the two-parent family, based on a lasting monogamous marriage, is the most efficacious one for child rearing."[5] Thus, in this view a lack of family values among the "underclass"—evidenced by the supposed immorality of single women bearing "illegitimate" children—causes poverty. Much of their argument turns on the notion of a "culture of poverty" that causes and perpetuates joblessness, welfare dependency, laziness, immorality, drug addiction, and crime. It is posited as the antithesis of family values—the ostensible source of middle-class stability. This narrative not only stands in direct opposition to the progressive perspective but also serves to deflect attention from economic dislocations, discrimination in the labor market, disinvestment in inner cities, and decreasing social supports for low-income families. It does this by citing a lack of hard work and family values as the cause of welfare dependency and poverty.

The critical race feminist Nathalie A. Augustin describes the contemporary narrative of the women who receive Aid for Families with Dependent Children (AFDC):

> The "welfare mother" is a deviant social creature. She is able-bodied, but unwilling to work at any of the thousands of jobs available to her; she is fundamentally lazy and civically irresponsible; she spends her days doing nothing but sponging off the government's largesse. Despite the societal pressure to be gainfully employed, she enjoys her status as a "dependent" on the state and seeks at all costs to prolong her dependency. Promiscuous and shortsighted, she is a woman who defiantly has children out of wedlock. Without morals of her own, she is unlikely to transmit good family values to her children. She lacks the educational skills to get ahead and the motivation to acquire them. Thus, she is the root of her own family's intergenerational poverty and related social ills. She is her own worse enemy. And she is Black.[6]

While the narrative about family dissolution is associated primarily with stereotypes of black women and families, racist and misogynist imagery of poor Latino families is fundamental to anti-immigrant campaigns. With rare exceptions, little connection is made between immigration and family values. Yet the link reveals a distinctive form of racism embedded in conservative pro-family rhetoric where there is said to be "too much of the former and too little of the latter."[7] When it comes to Latino immigrants, conservatives pathologize the values they champion and recast strong families as a menace to society. The immigration scholar Pierrette Hondagneu-Sotelo describes how stereotypes of Latino immigrants as breeders of large families were used in California's 1994 campaign to pass Proposition 187:

> The protagonists . . . were poor, pregnant immigrant women who were drawn to the U.S. to give birth in publicly financed county hospitals, allowing their children to be born as U.S. citizens and subsequent recipients of taxpayer-supported medical care, public assistance and education. In this scenario, immigrant families constitute a rapidly expanding underclass draining education and medical resources in the United States.[8]

Common to each of these narratives is a "bad mother," one who is seeking public funds or services to support and maintain her family and has no legitimate claim to these resources because she does not conform to traditional family values. These racialized representations of poor women guided the construction and passage of Proposition 187 in California and the Personal Responsibility and Work Opportunity Reconciliation Act of 1996 that repealed AFDC and denied benefits to legal immigrants.

The unspoken narratives embedded in this discourse draw on tenacious social myths of black family "pathology"—signified by single-parent families—infecting white women and causing a so-called epidemic of illegitimacy. It is through an assumed racialization of sexual and reproductive deviance that, in both popular and political discourse, *single mother* has come to signify *black single mother*. Sexual deviance from the patriarchal middle-class nuclear family—for white women as well as for women of color—is racialized through social narratives that link supposed black family pathology with illegitimacy, poverty, and social dysfunction.

The conservative narrative is the most recent edition of a very old story. There is a long history in the United States of social disdain for poor and single mothers, and in the nineteenth and early twentieth centuries discourse about deserving and undeserving poor women was linked to issues of race and citizenship. These earlier ideologies are reinvoked in the contemporary discourse on welfare reform and family values. In fact, part of their appeal and ready acceptance comes from the fact that they draw on ideas that are deeply rooted in American social thought.

THE PROGRESSIVE CHALLENGE

For progressives, the traditional family is not a given. Rather, family forms are socially and historically constructed, not uniform arrangements that exist for all times and places. One of the central points of contention between conservatives and progressives in these discussions concerns the causal relationships among family structure, poverty, and social problems. Three strands of thinking figure prominently in the progressive critique of family values. While they often overlap, the first emphasizes gender, the second emphasizes class, and the third emphasizes family structure.

Mainstream Feminist Perspectives

Although there is no single feminist perspective on families, it is fair to say that feminism has been at the forefront of efforts to clarify our understanding of family life. Feminists have long worked for the recognition of diverse forms of family and household arrangements, demonstrating that family forms are socially and historically constructed, not monolithic universals that exist across all times and all places. They have argued that the social and legal arrangements that govern family life are not the result of unambiguous differences between women and men. Feminists have drawn attention to the disparities between idealized and real patterns of family life, to the myths that romanticize "traditional" families in defense of male privilege, and to the fact that only a small minority of families and households has ever resembled the sentimentalized form. In challenging the dichotomy between public and private spheres, feminists have deepened our understanding of the social conditions surrounding women's family experiences.[9]

An important conclusion from the vast feminist literature on changing families is that family forms once thought to be natural and immutable are declining throughout the industrial world. Conditions of postindustrial capitalism are contributing to the demise not of the family but of an arrangement that Judith Stacey calls "the *modern* family"—an intact nuclear household composed of a male breadwinner, his full-time homemaker wife, and their dependent children.[10] This model is being replaced by rising levels of female-headed households and the growing impoverishment of women and their children. According to Stacey, marital instability and women-centered household arrangements are becoming endemic facts of life all around the world. According to Kristin Luker, "Out-of-wedlock births increased just as all industrialized societies were cutting welfare spending, so the assumption that welfare promotes such births is not borne out by the facts."[11] Stacey calls these new family forms "post-modern" because they do not fit the criteria for a "modern family."

Political Economy Perspectives

Progressive economists have contributed another strong challenge to the rhetoric of family values. Less concerned with gender relations in family life and more concerned with market forces and class formation, this work is a variant of feminist thought that directs attention to the close connections between family life and global economic developments. These thinkers call on macrostructural economic changes to explain why families are far different from what they used to be. Agreeing that families are more diverse and more easily fractured, that family members spend less time together, and that parents have less influence over their children, many political economists reason that "the current economic system is no longer congruent with traditional nuclear family values."[12] Economic realities, including men's declining wages and the pressures on women to work outside the home, mean that the family is an institution both in flux and under pressure.

As the need for certain kinds of labor diminishes, more and more working-class and middle-class families are the victims of economic dislocations. Families are profoundly affected when their resources are reduced, when they face economic and social marginalization, and when family members are unemployed or underemployed. As Lester Thurow explains, the traditional family is being destroyed by a modern economic system. Families are under attack

> not by government programs that discourage family formation (although there are some) and not by media presentations that disparage families (although there are some), but by the economic system itself. It simply won't allow families to exist in the old-fashioned way, with a father who generates most of the earnings and a mother who does most of the nurturing. The one-earner middle-class family is extinct.[13]

The argument that changes in the economy and the class structure undermine family stability is widespread within the social sciences and family studies. William Wilson's contention that supportive forces in the larger society have undergone major shifts and undermined family stability is the exemplar, but "there is no shortage of evidence of the impact of economic hardship on the family."[14] Although this position rests on growing structural inequalities rather than on the behavior of individuals or families or on their moral standards, this analysis does not discount the role of values in producing family change: "Values follow economic realities."[15] Or, as the economist David Gordon put it, "values matter, but jobs matter, at least as much if not more."[16]

Family Demography Perspectives

Conservatives believe that declining family values threaten the collective good. Yet when they say *family values,* they often mean *family structure,* or, more precisely, *nuclear family structure.* The question "What difference does family structure make?" is posed by sociologists and demographers, often quantitative social scientists. Although they do not usually engage in ideological debates about the relationship between values, single-headed households, and social problems, these scholars provide powerful evidence that social conditions are the shapers of family arrangements. This body of work empirically challenges the preoccupation with family structure as the cause of social pathologies.

By disentangling family structure from socioeconomic background, education, race, and other variables, research in this vein reveals that family structure is paramount in determining the life chances of children. Furthermore, there is a relationship between family structure and poverty.[17] Still, despite the correlation between family structure and family resources, we cannot conclude that single-parent households are the "root cause of poverty."[18]

This research finds that family structure is an increasingly important axis of racial inequality, especially between black and white children.[19] Yet it also shows that child poverty cannot be reduced to family structure for either blacks or Latinos. In the words of Sara McLanahan and Gary Sandefur, "If there were not single parents, Black children would still have much higher poverty rates."[20] To put it more precisely, for African Americans, "emulating the white family structure would close only about one-half of the income gap."[21] If Puerto Rican children lived in nuclear families, their poverty would be reduced from 41 percent to 24 percent (in other words, half is due to family structure). But poverty rates would be reduced only slightly if Mexicans and Cubans had the nuclear family structures of non-Latino white children.[22]

For feminists, progressive economists, and family demographers alike, a variety of social and economic forces has contributed to the decline of traditional family arrangements. Feminists such as Judith Stacey and Iris Marion Young have drawn from all three clusters of thought to reveal two overarching flaws in the family values position.[23] First, it reverses the relationship between family and society by treating the family as the cause of social conditions, rather than as a reflection of them. Second, it ignores the structural reasons for family breakdown.

The works of mainstream feminists, progressive political economics, and family demographers offer an extensive critique of the conservative rhetoric of family values. Each stream of work moves in different directions. Still, the critiques are similar in that they all show the link between larger economic forces and family patterns. All three argue that family life is being reconfigured more by severe structural problems than by a shift in values. Moreover, progressive scholars have taken important steps in exposing the racial scapegoating that lies at the heart of the conservative construction of family values.

RACE AND THE FAMILY VALUES DEBATE

Of particular importance to many progressive scholars are the racial images in the national discussion. Each body of literature recognizes that family breakdown is often a thinly veiled attack on the black urban underclass and that single motherhood is "often a code word for Black single mother."[24] For example, Ruth Sidel confronts the myth that most poor, single, childbearing women are black,[25] and Judith Stacey notes that racial anxiety about family structure is as old as the United States itself:

> Racial anxiety predates [Daniel Patrick] Moynihan's incendiary 1965 report. It reaches back a century to xenophobic fears about high fertility rates among Eastern and Southern European immigrants . . . [and] it reaches back much further into the history of colonial settler fears of diverse sexual and kinship practices of indigenous cultures.[26]

Progressive critics of family values are especially successful in unmasking the color-evasive language of family moralists who long for a return to a mythical time when "normal" values of "normal" Americans were sacrosanct and the law of the land.[27] Stacey interprets former Vice President Dan Quayle's criticism of Murphy Brown as an ill-fated attempt to reconstruct "Willie Horton in Whiteface":

> Without resorting to overtly racist rhetoric, the image conjured up frightening hoards of African American welfare "queens" rearing infant fodder to sex, drugs, and videotaped uprisings, such as had just erupted in Los Angeles.[28]

This pattern of discussing racial anxieties that deceptively appear to be race neutral is explained by Kristin Luker in her discussion of the ostensible *epidemic* of teenage pregnancy:

> The debate, in centering on teenagers in general, thus combined two contrasting features of American society: it permitted people to talk about African Americans and poor women (categories that often overlapped) without mentioning race or class; but it also reflected the fact that the sexual behavior and reproductive patterns of white teenagers were beginning to resemble those of African American and poor women—that is, more and more whites were postponing marriage and having babies out of wedlock.[29]

Although progressive scholarship has not been silent about race, its treatment of the concept is unsatisfactory. Three limitations prevent the progressive critique from fully exposing the racial dimensions within the pro-family position. First, while it is true that the images of low-income single mothers draw on long-held stereotypes and controlling images of black and Latina women as breeders and bad mothers and that this is a classic process of scapegoating the least powerful in times of economic crisis and social change, these patterns exist as part of broader social narratives. It is important not only to identify these narratives but to reveal the factors that make them so widely accepted and easily understood in an effort to examine the functions they serve in our society.

Second, the progressive framework does not reflect current conceptualizations of race as a macrostructural force, comparable to gender and class, that situates families differently and produces—indeed, *requires*—different arrangements. Progressives contend that the conservative view of social reality is steeped in racial prejudice that becomes a "kind of family Darwinism" that is blind to larger economic forces.[30] Such exposure of the racial bias in pro-family positions is crucial, but it does not go far enough in addressing the importance of race in shaping family life.

The third limitation rests on combined empirical and theoretical problems stemming from a black-white treatment of race. Progressive discourses on family values devote almost exclusive attention to African Americans. Except in some small clusters of scholarship by family demographers, Latinos and other people of color are ignored. Their invisibility in the national discussion is surprising since Latinos are rapidly approaching the epicenter of the current family crisis. Latinos now have the highest poverty rate in the United States. In addition, Latinos now make up the largest category of minority children in the country. These economic and demographic changes are introducing new complications into the family values debate. Yet they are invisible in most progressive literature.

Racial Narratives and Personal Responsibility

Evelyn Brooks Higginbotham uses the concept of "metalanguage" to describe the pervasiveness of racial representations in social relations in the United States. Race, she says, "speaks about and lends meaning to a host of other terms and expressions, to myriad aspects of life that would otherwise fall outside the referential domain of race. . . . It blurs and disguises, suppresses and negates, its own complex interplay with the very social relations it envelops."[31] Race is both text and subtext in the family values discussion. The images of unrestrained childbearing, freeloading, idleness, delinquency, crime, violence, abandonment, abuse, gangs, and lack of love are all associated with single mothers on welfare and inscribed on the bodies of black women nationally, Latina women—especially on the West Coast and in the Mexican border states—and Native American women in the West. In fact, a major source of the power and appeal of welfare reform is its plan to discipline and control the behavior of black and Latina women, other women of color, and, by example, white women. Placing these arguments in historical perspective illuminates how their emphasis on individual morality and personal choice masks the relationship among public discourse (that is, the social narratives and representations that shape our public debates on the issue), public policy, and the economy.

Feminists have been subject to conservative criticism, in part, for our emphasis on the social structure and the economy as *producing* diverse family forms. Those who argue for family values, on the other hand, are seen as emphasizing individual behaviors and personal responsibility. These latter arguments are constructed in such a way that social structure, as a force that *produces* certain behaviors and reinforces certain values, is essentially discredited and seen as part of a widespread failure of individuals to take responsibility for themselves. Yet what the historical analysis shows is that these ideas are themselves social products and that values are modified and even corrupted in their interaction with social structures. In our view, individual behavior must be considered in the socioeconomic context in which people's life choices are made; poverty drastically circumscribes the means through which people are able to fulfill personal values and aspirations, whatever they may be. However, drawing on the concept of a culture of poverty and a view of feminism as a form of female self-indulgence and selfishness, conservatives and centrists characterize the growth of poor single-mother families in personal, moral, and cultural terms, rather than structural and economic ones.

This association of poverty, family structure, and morality is not new. According to Michael Katz, it accompanied the transition to capitalism and democracy in early-nineteenth-century America, justifying the "mean-spirited treatment of the poor" and helping to "ensure the supply of cheap labor in a market economy increasingly based on unbound wage labor."[32] As Mimi Abramovitz has pointed out:

> The rise of the market economy brought forward a new individualistic and moralistic explanation (of poverty) which focused instead on the characteristics of the poor. . . (locating) the problem in lack of labor discipline, lack of family discipline, and the provision of relief itself.[33]

This view of poverty works in tandem with the quintessential ideology of capitalism: the myth of the American Dream, in which success is determined by personal responsibility, hard work, and good morals.

The themes that Abramovitz and Katz identify in the early-nineteenth-century arguments appear again in contemporary welfare reform discourse. The predominant explanatory system among conservatives and centrists correlates lack of a strong work ethic, laziness, present-time orientation, sexual licentiousness, and the prevalence of single-mother families with a culture of poverty that perpetuates an endless cycle of intergenerational poverty. Today, concern about lack of labor discipline has a particularly gendered construction. For example, black male unemployment is seen as the primary cause and its solution as the means of ending the rise of single-mother families among low-income black people. Latino men are seen as posing a different kind of breach in labor discipline because their unbridled desire to work in the United States is characterized as a threat to the employment opportunities of native workers. For women, work requirements have been initiated in response to the stereotype image of the black "welfare queen," who refuses to work and has babies just so that she can get more resources from the state, and the Latina woman whose stereotypic large family is seen as requiring too much undeserved support from the state. The criticism of the alleged lack of family discipline focuses primarily on women and has only recently been extended to absent fathers. For example, black single mothers are seen as unrepentantly defying traditional values regarding female sexual activity, family formation, and family structure by not marrying and by having children out of wedlock. Latinas are seen as using their childbearing as a way to illegally attain the rights and privileges of U.S. citizenship for their children, if not for themselves. These images have helped to sustain public support for provisions in the welfare reform legislation that seek to control women's fertility and reassert the values of proper family functioning and patriarchal governance over low-income women. In fact, these images have justified naming the welfare reform legislation of 1996 the Personal Responsibility Act.

Such cultural explanations for social inequality are used as a means of obscuring structural and economic causes of poverty. This, too, is a very old story. African American families and cultures have, throughout U.S. history, been alternately and sometimes simultaneously pronounced pathological, destroyed, and vanishing. The interwoven issues of black families and cultures—and questions concerning their existence, structure, and social viability—were the central concerns in the social debate between the sociologist E. Franklin Frazier and the anthropologist Melville J. Herskovitz that occurred in the 1930s and 1940s.[34] Frazier's thesis that slavery had destroyed "the black family," leaving an abnormal matriarchal family system, was the foundation of the 1965 Moynihan report.[35] Moynihan's articulation of black matriarchal families as a "tangle of pathology" was central in recent conservative and centrist arguments about the supposed epidemic of "illegitimacy" and welfare reform.

> Carla Peterson and Rhonda Williams explain: "Today, it seems that both culture and nature conspire to damn poor women in general, and poor Black women in particular. The horror of today's welfare reform lies in the truths masked by narratives of culture, nature, race, and gender.[36]

In short, in public discourse, what culture masks is power. The culture-of-poverty explanation, so widely accepted among conservatives and centrists alike, obscures the role of the state in perpetuating and enforcing inequality, even while placing the blame for the continuation of poverty on individuals and families.

The emphasis on personal values and the culture of poverty masks the interests of the state in, and its need for, a ready, willing, and available workforce and for a patriarchal family structure that controls and directs the fertility, sexuality and child rearing, and employment behavior of women. We disagree with an approach to poverty that focuses on values, obscuring the power relations involved in the state's treatment of poor families. Our concern is with the ways that social narratives about family values and single-mother families function in both popular and political discourse as explanations of and justifications

for the passage of public policies designed to police poor women's reproductive choices and to ensure the continuing availability of a low-wage workforce. In other words, we are concerned with connections among public discourse, power relations, and the political economy.

Race as Social Structure

Over the past decade, a considerable amount of attention has been devoted to race as a primary axis of inequality for situating families differently.[37] Instead of focusing on economic conditions alone, this emergent framework for studying families argues that racial inequality is also part of the larger structure in which families are embedded. Along with class and gender, race is a hierarchical structure of opportunity and oppression that has profound material consequences for family formation. The long-standing diversity of family forms by race is produced in part by an unequal distribution of social opportunities in U.S. society.

Some of the most influential work linking family formation with racial patterns of social relations is found in a conceptual framework called multiracial feminism. Grounded in multiple, interlocking hierarchies, what Patricia Hill Collins calls the matrix of domination,[38] this perspective underscores the pervasive nature of race in shaping the experiences of women and men throughout society. At the same time, this framework acknowledges how race is shaped by a variety of other social relations, especially class and gender.[39]

This perspective offers a useful set of analytic premises for thinking and theorizing about family life. It views families in relation to a racially organized social structure that provides and denies opportunities and therefore influences the way families in different social locations organize themselves to survive. One of the crucial lessons of multiracial feminism is that "race has always been a fundamental criterion in providing the kind of work people do, the wages they receive, and the kind of legal, economic, political and social support provided for their families";[40] "groups subordinated in the racial hierarchy are often deprived of access to social institutions that offer supports for family life."[41] As Collins contends, "actual families all live somewhere, and that somewhere in the United States is typically segregated."[42]

When we examine how families are positioned within intersecting inequalities, we have a better grasp of family diversity. People experience the family differently depending on their social, class, race, ethnicity, age, and sexual orientation, and from their experiences they construct different definitions of what families are and ought to be. Multiracial feminism has furthered our understanding of the racialized connections between normative family structure and social support. The family that conservative writers uphold as "legitimate" is a product of socially structured opportunities. It emerged as a result of social and economic conditions that no longer operate for most Americans and that never were operative for many poor Americans and people of color. From the original settlement of the American colonies through the mid-twentieth century, families of European descent often received economic and social supports to establish and maintain families.[43] Following World War II, as Stephanie Coontz points out, the G.I. Bill, the National Defense Education Act, the expansion of the Federal Housing Authority, and Veterans Administration loan subsidy programs, and government funding of new highways, provided the means through which middle-class whites were able to achieve the stable suburban family lives that became the ideal against which all other families were judged.[44] These kinds of support have not been widely available to people of color and, until quite recently, were actively denied them through various forms of housing and job discrimination. A careful reading of U.S. family history makes it clear that family structure is the result of far more than economic transformations.[45]

Today's economically based reorganization of U.S. society is reshaping family structure through distinctive racial patterns. Families mainly headed by women have become permanent in all racial categories, with the disproportionate effects of change most visible among racial ethnics. While the chief cause of the increase in female-headed households among whites is the greater economic independence of white women, the longer delay of first marriage and the low rate of remarriage among black women reflects, in part, the labor force problems of black men.[46] Thus, race and gender create different routes to female headship, but whites, blacks, and Latinos are all increasingly likely to end up in this family form.[47]

Latino Families and the Limits of Family Structure

Family solidarity is commonly thought to be a defining feature of the Latino population. In both the popular images and in social science literature, Latinos are regarded as "traditional" in their family convictions and behaviors.[48] Even though research shows that Latinos are not monolithically familistic, nor are their family relations uniformly traditional, "current literature is characterized by a redundancy in accounts of Latino families."[49]

The traditional Latino family archetype has always been controversial. In the earliest research on Mexican-origin families, structural functionalism and its variant, cultural determinism, attributed negative outcomes to strong family values. Mexicans were *criticized* for the strength of their family ties. Their lack of social progress was blamed on a way of life that kept them tied to family rather than open to economic advancement. During the 1960s and 1970s, many scholars vigorously refuted explanations of cultural deficiency in Mexican families, showing that family life was not deviant, deficient, or disorganized. Instead, what were once viewed as culturally deficient Mexican family lifestyles reflected adaptive responses to hardships of poverty and minority status.[50]

A new twist on the social adaptation approach has emerged in response to the family values debate. Several scholars have expressed the view that familism facilitates adaptation in difficult social settings and that strong family orientations serve Mexican immigrants in ways little understood by social scientists and policymakers. For example, David Hayes Bautista and his colleagues found that

Mexican immigrants arrive in the United States imbued with rich family values, high rates of family formation, and high labor force participation.[51] According to these researchers, "since Latinos have large families they are quite committed to fulfilling their parental roles and assuring familial obligations."[52]

Other scholars have asserted not only that strong family values facilitate immigrant adaptation, but that Latinos are better able than other groups to withstand economic hardship. Large webs of close-knit kin, a strong propensity to marry and raise large families, and, above all, "strong" family values are said to be cultural strengths that are now absent in black communities. For example, in finding that poor Mexicans in Chicago often work at two jobs, one researcher concluded that they had an intense commitment to the marital bond and to work, whereas blacks did not, presumably because of cultural differences between the two populations.[53]

Such interpretations about Latinos having strong family values and better family demographics are meant, no doubt, to challenge conservative assumptions that "Latinos as a whole have joined inner-city blacks to form one, vast, threatening underclass."[54] However, they perpetuate racial stereotypes. In their zeal to refute the negative outcomes of culture for Latinos, they use the logic of cultural determinism to "imply that Blacks and other groups do not have strong family values or a work ethic, and ironically, they ultimately reinforce the model itself."[55]

A better line of attack is to use the Latino experience to show that we cannot blame the family for social inequality. Two developments belie conservative assumptions about family. The first brings a new perspective to the discussion about the two-parent family and the impact of family structure on family well-being. The second reveals that social and economic conditions are reconfiguring living arrangements even among groups with strong commitments to marriage as the basis for family life.

Whether Latinos (or some Latino groups) have stronger family values and live in close-knit family arrangements is a question for further research. But the fact remains that the family convictions and behaviors attributed to Latinos have not prevented them from becoming the poorest racial category in the United States. As the demographers Lichter and Landale conclude, "although Latino families typically 'play by the rules,' they often remain poor."[56] These researchers found that, while substantial variation exists across Latino groups, parental work patterns are more important than family structure in accounting for poverty among Latino children. "The vast majority of Latino children live in two-parent families and almost one-half of all poor Latino children live in married-couple families, compared with 17 percent of poor African American children."[57] The conventional wisdom about the association between family structure and poverty does not hold up for Latinos. Hence, policies designed to strengthen the family will not be enough to alleviate poverty among Latinos.

Another paradox of the Latino presence in the United States underscores the importance of social and material conditions in shaping attitudes, behaviors, and family patterns. Despite high official rates of intact family characteristics upon their arrival in the United States, these characteristics are weakened in successive generations. Through the 1980s and 1990s, Latino rates of female-headed households have risen. Furthermore, research shows that life in the United States exposes immigrants (even those with strong family networks) to the current social context that gives rise to high rates of single parenthood and divorce. Although marriage is idealized in many Latin American countries, and there is a stigma attached to being divorced,[58] the U.S. social context produces family patterns that are part of a worldwide trend toward increasing maritally disrupted family structures. This generational trend is true for all immigrant groups.[59]

"ILLEGITIMATES," "ILLEGALS," AND WELFARE REFORM

Although black and Latina women are characterized differently in the family values debate, each group is demonized and their behavior depicted as threatening the basic values of American society. In the case of blacks, the central threat is single-parent families that produce "illegitimate" children, who according to the conservative and centrist narrative are likely to become unruly citizens. In the case of Latinas, the threat is undocumented immigrants who give birth in the United States and create unwanted citizens, who then become a conduit of government resources to families of "illegal" residents. Interestingly, in both cases and for quite different reasons, the family behavior of women is the focal point for criticism and complaint. For example, in his role as one of two primary Republican advisers on welfare reform in the 104th Congress, the conservative policy analyst Charles Murray testified to the House Subcommittee on Human Resources:

> "My proposition is that illegitimacy is the single most important social problem in our time—more important than crime, drugs, poverty, illiteracy, welfare or homelessness because it drives everything else. Doing something about it is not just one more item on the American policy agenda, but should be at the top."[60]

This social vision was then codified in the language of the welfare legislation passed in 1996, which itemized a long list of "negative consequences of raising children in single-parent homes," including such statements as, "Young women who have children before finishing high school are more likely to receive welfare assistance for a longer period of time"; "Children of teenage single parents have lower cognitive scores, lower educational aspirations, and a greater likelihood of becoming teenage parents themselves." On the basis of this preamble of problems, the bill states:

> Therefore, in the light of this demonstration of the crisis in our Nation, it is the sense of the Congress that prevention of out-of-wedlock pregnancy and reduction in out-of-wedlock birth are very important Government interests and the policy contained in part A of title IV of the Social Security Act (as amended by section 103(a) of this Act) is intended to address the crisis.[61]

Although Republicans were not successful in pushing through the most draconian version of the Personal Responsibility Act, the federal system of AFDC has been dismantled. Entitlements to federal benefits have been ended through the allocation of block grants to facilitate state-run assistance programs. The version of the bill that President Bill Clinton eventually signed into law places a five-year lifetime limit on benefits, requires able-bodied adults to work after two years, requires minors to be enrolled in school and living at home or with a responsible adult, requires unwed mothers to cooperate in identifying paternity, disallows support to anyone convicted of a felony drug charge, and cuts benefits to families of children with disabilities.

Although derogatory images of blacks were most prominent in public discussion of welfare reform on a national level, negative images of Latinos and other immigrants fueled debates in the states and paved the way for denying benefits to legal immigrants nationwide. The discussion surrounding California's Proposition 187 exemplify the xenophobia and anti-immigrant sentiment that resulted in the initial denial of public resources to legal immigrants as part of welfare reform.

As is evident in the language of the legislation itself, illegitimacy and single-parent families are seen as the cause of poverty and social ills; thus, it is argued, the prevention of out-of-wedlock pregnancy and the promotion of two-parent families will be in the best interest of the nation.

Although these social problems are unproblematically cited here as outgrowths of family forms that deviate from two-parent nuclear families, feminists and other progressive scholars, as pointed out earlier, typically explain such family difficulties as the consequences, not the causes, of poverty. As Judith Stacey states in her critique of the body of literature that has served as the basis for a new orthodoxy regarding the relative merits of two-parent over single-parent families:

> Most research indicates that a stable, intimate relationship with one responsible, nurturant adult is a child's surest route to becoming the same kind of adult. In short, the research scale tips handily toward those who stress the quality of family relationships over their form.[62]

The ideas of Charles Murray figure prominently in the shift in public dialogue from an acceptance of the centrist scholarship that suggests that single-parent families are harmful to children to the conservative argument that out-of-wedlock births are at the root of most contemporary social problems. In his discussion of the rising percentage of "illegitimate" births to black women (he cites 68 percent in 1991), Murray draws on one of the central theses of the 1965 Moynihan Report on black families—that single mothers are incapable of properly socializing and disciplining their sons—to explain what he sees as the social chaos of inner cities:

> But if the proportion of fatherless boys in a given community were to reach such levels, surely the culture must be *Lord of the Flies* writ large, the values of unsocialized male adolescents made norms—physical violence, immediate gratification and predatory sex. That is the culture now taking over the black inner city.[63]

Poor black women are a central concern in this narrative, not simply because as women they are seen as behaving in ways that are socially unacceptable but also because they are mothers and the primary socializers of young children. In their role as mothers, they are continually portrayed as "unfit." As the political writer Richard Cohen explained, "We fear our children, not because there are too many of them, but because too many of them lack fathers."[64]

On the surface, the concern about single-parent families among blacks appears to contrast sharply with the growth of immigrant families in the United States. After all, female-headed households are neither as prevalent statistically among these groups nor part of the dominant image of Latinos. Nevertheless, Latinos, along with blacks, became a primary target of national and local legislative efforts to reduce the provision of welfare benefits.

In his essay "Poor Suffering Bastards: An Anthropologist Looks at Illegitimacy," published in the conservative Heritage Foundation's journal *Policy Review* in 1994, the foundation fellow David W. Murray uses a striking rhetorical ploy that reveals a kind of narrative link between the issues of illegitimacy and illegality:

> Here is the pertinent meaning of the *"legitimacy"* of children: Legitimacy is nothing more nor less than the orderly transfer of social meaning across the generations. Remember that children are the ultimate *illegal aliens*. They are undocumented immigrants to our world, who must be socialized and invested with identity, a culture, and an estate. By conferring legitimacy marriage keeps this process from becoming chaos.[65]

In an important essay in which she analyzes California's Proposition 187 campaign, Pierrette Hondagneu-Sotelo argues that the anti-immigrant narrative took an important turn with this campaign. Instead of drawing on themes found in earlier anti-immigrant narratives that had generated considerable public response in the past, such as unfair job competition and "inassimilable" cultural differences, she argues that contemporary rhetoric

> targets women and children because it is they who are central to making settlement happen. Viewed in this manner, the 187 campaign is less about illegal immigration and more about rejecting Latino immigrants and their U.S.-born family members as permanent members of U.S. society.[66]

Hondagneu-Sotelo argues that this attack on the use of public resources by immigrant Mexican women and children is directed mostly toward alleviating public anxiety about the rapid increase in the Latino immigrant population in California and is less concerned with their actual use of public assistance. In fact, she cites a number of studies that document the claim that immigrants are considerably less likely than the native-born to receive public assistance.[67] The real difference between this anti-immigrant campaign and earlier ones, she contends, results from the shift on the part of immigrant Mexicans from a sojourner or temporary, work-focused pattern of engagement in the United States to a pattern of establishing permanent communities and settlements throughout California. Women, she argues, are key to this settlement pattern because they are able to find relatively stable, nonseasonal jobs; they build community through their interactions with each other and other families; and they are more likely than men to seek out and utilize the resources that make permanent settlement possible.[68]

Reforming the Children of "Unfit" Mothers

The idea that racial or cultural diversity—either native-born or immigrant—is a threat to the nation has a long venerable history in the United States. Gwendolyn Mink has eloquently and convincingly argued that motherhood became pivotal in mediating issues of diversity and citizenship in the United States as early as the late nineteenth century:

> By welding motherhood to woman's citizenship, women's politics problematized claims for gender equality. It further compromised the possibility of racial equality when it offered motherhood as the solvent for diversity in America. Arguing for policies tied to gender difference, women's politics interposed women reformers as managers of racial difference. This politics promoted an uplifted universal motherhood, one that would achieve both uplift and universality through the assimilation of Anglo-Saxon norms. Assimilated motherhood was women reformers' weapon against the blows to democracy dealt by poverty and multiculturalism.[69]

The contemporary conservative narrative picks up some of these same themes in its argument that "legitimate" nuclear families are necessary for the good of the nation. As George Will explains: "Democracy depends on virtues that depend on socialization of children in the matrix of care and resources fostered by marriage."[70] In contrast to women reformers of the late nineteenth century, at least one theme in conservative thought has abandoned the idea that low-income mothers can be uplifted and assimilated.

Once again it is the work of Charles Murray, this time in collaboration with Richard J. Herrnstein, that lays out an argument used to justify this conclusion. In their misleading and controversial book, *The Bell Curve: Intelligence and Class Structure in American Life,* they argue that IQ determines economic and social success and that the global economy is based on the manipulation of information.[71] Thus, the future economic viability of the United States is dependent on those citizens with high IQs whom they refer to as the "cognitive elite." From their perspective, "productive" citizens are defined not by hard work but, rather, by superior intelligence. Unproblematically accepting the belief that IQ tests accurately and objectively measure intelligence, they argue that African Americans are less intelligent than other racial groups, and they state that on average blacks score fifteen points lower than whites on IQ tests. Using these skewed data to account for racial stratification, they conclude that poverty among blacks is due to genetic inferiority rather than to discrimination and oppression.[72] In their circular logic, they claim that socioeconomic location is also evidence of intelligence, thereby inferring that all poor people have low intelligence. Not surprisingly, they contend that women with low IQs typically have "illegitimate" children; furthermore, given the hereditarian logic of their argument, they conclude that those children inherit their mothers' limited capacity for mental achievement and are destined to live on the margins of society, never achieving for themselves, forever draining government resources.

In their view, intelligence is so predominantly shaped by genetics (they concede a small measure of influence to environment) that social programs, such as Head Start, are doomed to failure. Yet they provide one glimmer of hope for these children: adoption. According to Herrnstein and Murray, adoption is the only social intervention radical enough to raise the IQs, and thus the chances for economic success, of poor, illegitimate children. The added bonus, they explain, is that "in terms of government budgets, adoption is cheap; the new parents bear all the costs of twenty-four-hour-a-day care for eighteen years or so."[73] They continue:

> If adoption is one of the only affordable and successful ways known to improve the life chances of disadvantaged children appreciably, why has it been so ignored in congressional debate and presidential proposals? Why do current adoption practices

make it so difficult for would-be parents and needy infants to match up? Why are cross-racial adoptions so often restricted or even banned? . . . Anyone seeking an inexpensive way to do some good for an expandable number of the most disadvantaged infants should look at adoption.[74]

Although on the face of it this argument may seem too draconian to be taken seriously, two years after those questions were written and published, the legislative infrastructure to support such policies was put in place. In the same week the Personal Responsibility Act was signed into law, legislation was also signed that provides a substantial tax deduction to couples who adopt and that bars federally funded adoption agencies from considering race in the adoptive placement of a child. It is no accident that these bills were passed at the same time. In fact, up until the final version of the welfare reform bill, the legislation to remove all restrictions to transracial adoption was part of the Personal Responsibility Act and was located in the section designed to combat the so-called epidemic of illegitimacy.

Adoption, and specifically transracial adoption, then, becomes another potential weapon in the war against illegitimate/illegal children and their mothers. The conservative narrative that constructs the mothers of these children as incapable of raising worthy citizens is already poised to be used to justify implementation of a policy that would remove the children from their birth mothers and place them in the homes of married, white, middle-class couples who are expected to do the job appropriately.[75]

In an editorial on welfare reform and adoption that was published prior to *The Bell Curve,* Murray argues that the state should actively intervene to remove children from mothers who refuse to abide by regulations that require welfare recipients to work: "What about women who can find no support but keep the baby anyway? There are laws already on the books about the right of the state to take a child from a neglectful parent."[76] There is, of course, extensive legal precedent for removing children from the homes of neglectful

parents. There is also a long history in which these provisions have been used most frequently against poor women and women of color. At issue, of course, has been the definition of the term *neglect.* In antebellum Virginia, as Victoria Bynum has argued, provisions such as these were used to remove children from the mothers of free black women and from white women who had children out of wedlock, especially those who had children by black men.[77] According to Bynum, the explicit grounds on which these children were removed were primarily that they were poor and their mothers could not provide adequately for them. Implicit, however, was the fact that their mothers lived outside the control of acceptable white male authority in an explicitly racist and patriarchal social order. Although it is clearly beyond the scope of this [paper] to trace the history of the relationship among mothers' social and economic status, child custody, and race, we point it out here to show that, while Murray's proposals may sound extreme to some, they are not without legal, historical, and social precedent.

CONCLUSION

Taken together, welfare reform legislation and the public discourse that has surrounded it can be read as a sort of *cultural eugenics* geared toward both the regulation of poor women's reproductive capacities and the social construction and socialization of economically productive citizens.[78] When compared to the eugenics movement of the early twentieth century, which sought to prevent white "race suicide" through the control of fertility among poor women and women of color, the insidious racial agenda of the recently passed legislation seems clear. The sociologist Kristin Luker discusses women's sexuality and "illegitimacy" in the context of the eugenics movement:

Whether passive victim or willing participant, the young woman who was sexually active, particularly outside marriage, and particularly when intercourse led to an out-of-wedlock birth, was perceived as deviant, unfit. And the problem did not end with her: her child represented the antithesis of reformers' hopes for societal improvement, by becoming yet another link in a chain of unfitness. Born to an immature and presumably unfit woman, the illegitimate child evoked reformers' worst fears for future generations.[79]

In the early years of this century, these social fears translated to movements for eugenic sterilization and birth control among poor women and immigrants. In the post-Holocaust and post-civil-rights-movement era, such racist and classist inclinations must adopt a more "race-neutral" veneer. While essentialist racism—the pseudoscientific explanation of the supposed inferiority of nonwhite people—was the "legitimating" knowledge that drove the eugenics of the early twentieth century, in the contemporary moment cultural determinism has joined biology as the engine of racial oppression. The earlier focus on biological heritability led to efforts at curtailing the "excess" fertility of undesirables; in a framework dominated by the culture of poverty, social engineering can be envisioned in many ways, among them reducing illegitimacy, discouraging immigration by denying social resources to both legal and undocumented immigrants, and intervening in the socialization of children through the promotion of policies such as transracial adoption.

While most of these policies have been critiqued by progressives, it is only through an analysis that extends race beyond a black-white dualism and treats it as a dynamic, macrostructural force comparable to gender and class that one can fully expose the ways in which the U.S. legacy of racial exclusion and oppression permeates contemporary discourse on family values and public policy. For example, by including Latinos in this discussion we can document that family values and family structure matter far less than conservatives claim. We also broaden our understanding of how gender, race, and family values intersect, by revealing the ways that women, as child bearers and as mothers, are particularly subject to scrutiny and stereotype, regardless of whether they are married or unmarried. In fact, in the cases of both blacks and Latinos, stereotypes of women have been used to galvanize public support for policies to control their reproductive, productive, and family behavior.

The multiracial feminist perspective that has guided this analysis has directed us to challenge the discussion of family values and the well-being of children by raising questions of which children and which family forms are privileged and, thus, whose values are enforced and fostered by social institutions. It acknowledges the differences in cultural and racial locations, the variations in access to resources, and the resulting differences in family strategies. In addition, it points us toward an examination of the cause-and-effect relationship among families, poverty, social institutions, and values, demonstrating that families are shaped through interaction with social structures. A discussion of family cannot effectively begin with values if values are seen only through the lens of individual choice and morality. We argue that the choices women make about values and morality are strongly influenced by race, class, gender, and financial resources. The stereotyping, blaming, and scapegoating of women, particularly women of color, that too frequently accompany such discussions privileges white middle-class families and sabotages attempts at addressing the needs of low-income families. This occurs in part because racial animosity and suspicion remain a fundamental (and largely unaddressed) aspect of U.S. culture. As a society, we can eradicate the scourge of racism only when we are fully cognizant of the ways it permeates and shapes our discourse and our public policies.

NOTES

This chapter was published in *Sage Race Relations Abstracts* 23, no. 3 (1998).

1. Graeme Turner, *Film as Social Practice* (New York: Routledge, 1988).
2. Robert Gooding-Williams, "Look, a Negro!" in *Reading Rodney King/Reading Urban Uprising*, ed. Robert Gooding-Williams (London: Routledge, 1993).
3. Hazel Carby, "Encoding White Resentment: Grand Canyon—A Narrative for Our Times," in *Race, Identity,*

and *Representation in Education,* ed. Cameron McCarthy and Warren Critchlow (New York: Routledge, 1993), 236.

4. Maxine Baca Zinn and Bonnie Thornton Dill, "Theorizing Difference from Multiracial Feminism," *Feminist Studies* 22 (Summer 1996): 321–31.

5. Arlene Skolnick, "Family Values: The Sequel," *American Prospect* 32 (May-June 1997): 86–94.

6. Nathalie A. Augustin, "Learnfare and Black Motherhood: The Social Construction of Deviance," in *Critical Race Feminism: A Reader,* ed. Adrein Katherine Wing (New York: New York University Press, 1997), 144.

7. Ruben Rumbaut, "Ties That Bind: Immigration and Immigrant Families in the United States," in *Immigration and the Family,* ed. Alan Booth (Lawrence Erlbaum, 1997), 1.

8. Pierrette Hondagneu-Sotelo, "Women and Children First: New Directions in Anti-Immigrant Politics," *Socialist Review* 25, no. 1 (1995): 173.

9. Bonnie Thornton Dill, Maxine Baca Zinn, and Sandra Patton, "Feminism, Race, and the Politics of Family Values," Report from the Institute for Philosophy and Public Policy (Summer 1993).

10. Judith Stacey, *In the Name of the Family: Rethinking Family Values in the Postmodern Age* (Boston: Beacon Press, 1996).

11. Kristin Luker, *Dubious Conceptions: The Politics of Teenage Pregnancy* (Cambridge, Mass.: Harvard University Press, 1996).

12. Lester D. Thurow, "Changes in Capitalism Render One-Earner Families Extinct," *USA Today,* 27 January 1997, 17A.

13. Ibid.

14. Quoted in Arlene Skolnick and Stacey Rosencrantz, "The New Crusade for the Old Family," *American Prospect* 18 (Summer 1994): 64.

15. Thurow, "Changes in Capitalism," 17A.

16. David Gordon, "Values That Work," *Nation,* 17 June 1996, 16.

17. William P. O'Hare, "A New Look at Poverty in America," *Population Bulletin* 51, no. 2 (September 1996): 347.

18. Sara McLanahan and Gary Sandefur, *Growing Up with a Single Parent* (Cambridge, Mass.: Harvard University Press, 1994), 3.

19. Daniel T. Lichter and Nancy S. Landale, "Parental Work, Family Structure, and Poverty among Latino Children," *Journal of Marriage and the Family* 57 (May 1995): 347.

20. McLanahan and Sandefur, *Growing Up with a Single Parent,* 85.

21. Andrew Hacker, "The Racial Income Gap," in *The Meaning of Difference,* ed. Karen E. Rosenblum and Toni-Michelle C. Travis (New York: McGraw-Hill, 1996), 309.

22. Lichter and Landale, "Parental Work," 347.

23. Stacey, *In the Name of the Family;* Iris Marion Young, "Making Single Motherhood Normal," *Dissent* 41 (Winter 1994): 88–93.

24. McLanahan and Sandefur, *Growing Up with a Single Parent.*

25. Ruth Sidel, *Keeping Women and Children Last* (New York: Penguin, 1996), 29.

26. Stacey, *In the Name of the Family,* 72.

27. Sidel, *Keeping Women and Children Last,* 29.

28. Stacey, *In the Name of the Family,* 72.

29. Luker, *Dubious Conceptions,* 86.

30. Valerie Polakow, *Lives on the Edge: Single Mothers and Their Children in the Other America* (Chicago: University of Chicago Press, 1993), 39.

31. Evelyn Brooks Higginbotham, "The Metalanguage of Race: Reflections on Race, History, and Feminist Theory," *Signs: Journal of Women in Culture and Society* (Winter 1992): 255.

32. Michael B. Katz, *The Undeserving Poor: From the War on Poverty to the War on Welfare* (New York: Pantheon Books, 1989), 14.

33. Mimi Abramovitz, *Regulating the Lives of Women: Social Welfare Policy from Colonial Times to the Present* (Boston: South End Press, 1989), 144.

34. Franklin E. Frazier, *The Negro Family in the United States* (Chicago: University of Chicago Press, 1939); and Melville J. Herskovitz, *The Myth of the Negro Past* (Boston: Beacon Press, 1941).

35. Daniel Patrick Moynihan, *The Negro Family: The Case for National Action* (Washington, D.C.: U.S. Department of Labor, 1965).

36. Carla Peterson and Rhonda M. Williams, "The Color of Memory: Interpreting 20th-Century U.S. Social Policy from a 19th-Century Perspective," Intersections: A Series of Working Papers of the Consortium on Race, Gender, and Ethnicity (April 1997), 10.

37. Maxine Baca Zinn, "Social Science Theorizing for Latino Families in the Age of Diversity," in *Understanding Latino Families: Scholarship, Policy and Practice,* ed. Ruth Zambrana (Thousand Oaks, Calif.: Sage, 1995), 177–87; Maxine Baca Zinn, "Family, Feminism, and Race in America," *Gender and Society* 4, no. 1 (1990): 68–82; Bonnie Thornton Dill, "Fictive Kin, Paper Sons, and Compadrazgo: Women of Color and the Struggle for Survival," in *Women of Color in U.S. Society,* ed. Maxine Baca Zinn and Bonnie Thornton Dill (Philadelphia: Temple University Press, 1994), 149–70; Patricia Hill Collins, *Black Feminist Thought: Knowledge, Consciousness, and the Politics of Empowerment* (Boston: Unwin Hyman, 1990); Patricia Hill Collins, "African American Women and Economic Justice: A Preliminary Analysis of Wealth, Family and Black Social Class, unpublished paper, 1997; Evelyn Nakano Glenn, "From Servitude to Service Work: Historical Continuities in the Racial Division of Paid Reproductive Labor," *Signs: Journal of Women in Culture and Society* 18, no. 1 (1992): 1–43.

38. Collins, *Black Feminist Thought.*

39. Baca Zinn and Dill, "Theorizing Difference from Multiracial Feminism."

40. Dill, "Fictive Kin, Paper Sons, and Compadrazgo," 166.

41. Baca Zinn, "Family, Feminism, and Race in America," 74.

42. Collins, "African American Women and Economic Justice," 18.

43. Bonnie Thornton Dill, "Our Mothers' Grief: Racial Ethnic Women and the Maintenance of Families," *Journal of Family History* 13, no. 4, (1988): 415–431.

44. Stephanie Coontz, *The Way We Never Were: American Families and the Nostalgia Trap.* (New York: Harper-Collins, 1992).

45. Bonnie Thornton Dill, Maxine Baca Zinn, and Sandra Patton, "Feminism, Race, and the Politics of Family Values."

46. William Julius Wilson and Katherine Neckernan, "Poverty and Family Structure: The Widening Gap between Evidence and Public Policy Issues," in *The Truly Disadvantaged: The Inner City, the Underclass, and Public Policy,* ed. William Julius Wilson (Chicago: University of Chicago Press, 1986), 265.

47. Baca Zinn, "Family, Feminism, and Race in America," 129.

48. On popular images, see Richard Estrada, "Myths of Hispanic Families' Wellness," *Kansas City Star,* 10 September 1989, 51; on the social science literature, see William A. Vega, "The Study of Latino Families: A Point of Departure," in *Understanding Latino Families: Scholarship, Policy and Practice,* ed. Ruth E. Zambrana (Thousand Oaks, Calif.: Sage, 1995).

49. Vega, "The Study of Latino Families," 9.

50. Baca Zinn, "Social Science Theorizing," 180.

51. David Hayes Bautista et al., *No Longer a Minority: Latinos and Social Policy in California* (University of California at Los Angeles: Chicano Studies Research Center, 1989).

52. Patricia Zavella, "Living on the Edge: Everyday Lives of Poor Chicano/Mexicano Families," in *Mapping Multiculturalism,* ed. Avery F. Gordon and Christopher Newfield (Minneapolis: University of Minnesota Press, 1996), 369.

53. Ibid., 363–64.

54. Frances Fukuyama, "Immigrants and Family Values," *Commentary* (May 1993): 29.

55. Zavella, "Living on the Edge," 370.

56. Lichter and Landale, "Parental Work," 347.

57. Ibid.

58. Scott Turner, "Single Parenthood Hurts Immigrants' Economic Gains," *Population Today* 24, no. 5 (May): 4–5.

59. Rumbaut, "Ties That Bind."

60. Charles Murray, "Testimony," House Ways and Means/House Subcommittee on Human Resources, 104th Congress, "Welfare Revisions," *Federal Document Clearinghouse Congressional Testimony,* 29 July 1994.

61. Public Law 104–193, Section 101.

62. Stacey, *In the Name of the Family,* 60.

63. Murray, "Testimony."

64. Richard Cohen, "Dealing with Illegitimacy," *Washington Post,* 23 November 1993, editorial page.

65. David W. Murray, "Poor Suffering Bastards: An Anthropologist Looks at Illegitimacy," *Policy Review* 68 (Spring 1994): 10 (emphasis added).

66. Pierrette Hondagneu-Sotelo, "Unpacking 187: Targeting Mexicans," *Immigration and Ethnic Communities: A Focus on Latinos,* ed. Refugio I. Rochin (East Lansing, Mich.: Julian Samora Research Institute, 1996), 93.

67. Ibid., 95.

68. Ibid., 98.

69. Gwendolyn Mink, *The Wages of Motherhood: Inequality in the Welfare State, 1917–1942* (Ithaca, N.Y.: Cornell University Press, 1995), 102.

70. George Will, "Underwriting Family Breakdown," *Washington Post,* 18 November 1993, editorial page.

71. Richard J. Herrnstein and Charles Murray, *The Bell Curve: Intelligence and Class Structure in American Life* (New York: Free Press, 1994).

72. For critiques of this work, see Steven Fraser, ed., *The Bell Curve Wars: Race, Intelligence, and the Future of America* (New York: Basic Books, 1995); Joseph L. Graves Jr. and Amanda Johnson, "The Pseudoscience of Psychometry and *The Bell Curve,*" *Journal of Negro Education* 64, no. 3 (Summer 1995): 277–94; Russell Jacoby and Naomi Glauberman, eds., *The Bell Curve Debate: History, Documents, Opinions* (New York: Times Books, Random House, 1995); Joe L. Kincheloe, Shirley R. Steinberg, and Aaron D. Gresson III, eds., *Measured Lies: The Bell Curve Examined* (New York: St. Martin's Press, 1996).

73. Herrnstein and Murray, *The Bell Curve,* 416.

74. Ibid.

75. Sandra Patton, *Birth Marks: An Interdisciplinary Ethnographic Study of Transracial Adoption,* Ph.D. dissertation, University of Maryland, College Park, 1997.

76. Charles Murray, "The Coming White Underclass," *Wall Street Journal,* 17 November 1993, editorial page.

77. Victoria Bynum, "On the Lowest Rung: Court Control over Poor White and Free Black Women," *Southern Exposure* (November-December, 1984): 6.

78. Patton, *Birth Marks.*

79. Luker, *Dubious Conceptions,* 36–37.

FOR FURTHER READING

1. Collins, Patricia Hill, *Black Feminist Thought: Knowledge, Consciousness, and the Politics of Empowerment* (Boston: Unwin Hyman, 1990).

2. Coontz, Stephanie, *The Way We Never Were: American Families and the Nostalgia Trap* (New York: HarperCollins, 1992).

3. Dill, Bonnie Thornton, "Fictive Kin, Paper Sons, and Compadrazgo: Women of Color and the Struggle for Survival," in *Women of Color in U.S. Society,* ed. Maxine Baca Zinn and Bonnie Thornton Dill (Philadelphia: Temple University Press, 1994), 149–70.

4. Hacker, Andrew, "The Racial Income Gap," in *The Meaning of Difference,* ed. Karen E. Rosenblum and Toni-Michelle C. Travis (New York: McGraw-Hill, 1996), 309.

5. Luker, Kristin, *Dubious Conceptions: The Politics of Teenage Pregnancy* (Cambridge, Mass.: Harvard University Press, 1996).

6. Mink, Gwendolyn, *The Wages of Motherhood: Inequality in the Welfare State, 1917–1942* (Ithaca, N.Y.: Cornell University Press, 1995).

7. Moynihan, Daniel Patrick, *The Negro Family: The Case for National Action* (Washington D.C.: U.S. Department of Labor, 1965).

8. Sidel, Ruth, *Keeping Women and Children Last* (New York: Penguin, 1996), 29.

9. Skolnick, Arlene, "Family Values: The Sequel," *American Prospect* 32 (May-June 1997): 86–94.

10. Stacey, Judith, *In the Name of the Family: Rethinking Family Values in the Postmodern Age* (Boston: Beacon Press, 1996).

46

Driving While Black

A Statistician Proves that Prejudice Still Rules the Road

JOHN LAMBERTH

In 1993, I was contacted by attorneys whose clients had been arrested on the New Jersey Turnpike for possession of drugs. They told me they had come across 25 African American defendants over a three-year period, all arrested on the same stretch of turnpike in Gloucester County, but not a single white defendant. I was asked whether, and how much, this pattern reflected unfair treatment of blacks.

They wanted to know what a professional statistician would make of these numbers. What were the probabilities that this pattern could occur naturally, that is, by chance? Since arrests for drug offenses occurred after traffic stops on the highway, was it possible that so many blacks were arrested because the police were disproportionately stopping them? I decided to try to answer their questions and embarked on one of the most intriguing statistical studies of my career: a census of traffic and traffic violators by race on Interstate 95 in New Jersey. It would require a careful design, teams of researchers with binoculars and a rolling survey.

To relieve your suspense, the answer was that the rate at which blacks were stopped was greatly disproportionate to their numbers on the road and to their propensity to violate traffic laws. Those findings were central to a March 1996 ruling by

Judge Robert E. Francis of the Superior Court of New Jersey that the state police were de facto targeting blacks, in violation of their rights under the U.S. and New Jersey constitutions. The judge suppressed the evidence gathered in the stops. New Jersey is now appealing the case.

The New Jersey litigation is part of a broad attack in a number of states, including Maryland, on what has been dubbed the offense of "DWB"—driving while black. While this problem has been familiar anecdotally to African Americans and civil rights advocates for years, there is now evidence that highway patrols are singling out blacks for stops on the illegal and incorrect theory that the practice, known as racial profiling, is the most likely to yield drug arrests. Statistical techniques are proving extremely helpful in proving targeting, just as they have been in proving systemic discrimination in employment.

This was not my first contact with the disparate treatment of blacks in the criminal justice system. My academic research over the past 25 years had led me from an interest in small group decision-making to jury selection, jury composition and the application of the death penalty. I became aware that blacks were disproportionately charged with crimes, particularly serious ones; that they were underrepresented on jury panels and thus on juries; and that they were sentenced to death at a much greater rate than their numbers could justify.

As I began the New Jersey study, I knew from experience that any research that questioned police procedures was sensitive. I knew that what I did must stand the test of a court hearing in which every move I made would be challenged by experts.

First, I had to decide what I needed to know. What was the black "population" of the road—that is, how many of the people traveling on the turnpike over a given period of time were African American? This task is a far cry from determining the population of a town, city or state. There are no Census Bureau figures. The population of a roadway changes all day, every day. By sampling the population of the roadway over a given period, I could make an accurate determination of the average number of blacks on the road.

I designed and implemented two surveys. We stationed observers by the side of the road, with the assignment of counting the number of cars and the race of the occupants in randomly selected three-hour blocks of time over a two-week period. The New Jersey Turnpike has four lanes at its southern end, two in each direction. By the side of the road, we placed an observer for each lane, equipped with binoculars to observe and note the number of cars and the race of occupants, along with a person to write down what the observers said. The team observed for an hour and a half, took a 30-minute break while moving to another observation point, and repeated the process.

In total, we conducted more than 21 sessions between 8 A.M. and 8 P.M. from June 11 to June 24, 1993, at four sites between Exits 1 and 3 of the turnpike, among the busiest highway segments in the nation. We counted roughly 43,000 cars, of which 13.5 percent had one or more black occupants. This was consistent with the population figures for the 11 states from which most of the vehicles observed were registered.

For the rolling survey, Fred Last, a public defender, drove at a constant 60 mph (5 mph above the speed limit at the time). He counted all cars that passed him as violators and all cars he passed as nonviolators. Speaking into a tape recorder, he also noted the race of the driver of each car. At the end of each day, he collated his results and faxed them to me.

Last counted 2,096 cars. More than 98 percent were speeding and thus subject to being stopped by police. African Americans made up about 15 percent of those drivers on the turnpike violating traffic laws. Utilizing data from the New Jersey State Police. I determined that about 35 percent of those who were stopped on this part of the turnpike were African Americans.

To summarize: African Americans made up 13.5 percent of the turnpike's population and 15 percent of the speeders. But they represented 35 percent of those pulled over. In stark numbers, blacks were 4.85 times as likely to be stopped as were others.

We did not obtain data on the race of drivers and passengers searched after being stopped or on the rate at which vehicles were searched. But we know from police records that 73.2 percent of those arrested along the turnpike over a 3½-year period by troopers from the area's Moorestown barracks were black—making them 16.5 times more likely to be arrested than others.

Attorneys for the 25 African Americans who had been arrested on the turnpike and charged with possessing drugs or guns filed motions to suppress evidence seized when they were stopped, arguing that police stopped them because of their race. Their motions were consolidated and heard by Judge Francis between November 1994 and May 1995. My statistical study, bolstered by an analysis of its validity by Joseph B. Kadane, professor of statistics at Carnegie Mellon University, was the primary exhibit in support of the motions.

But Francis also heard testimony from two former New Jersey troopers who said they had been coached to make race-based "profile" stops to increase their criminal arrests. And the judge reviewed police in-service training aids such as videos that disproportionately portrayed minorities as perpetrators.

The statistical disparities, Francis wrote, are "indeed stark. . . . Defendants have proven at least a de facto policy on the part of the State Police . . . of targeting blacks for investigation and arrest." The judge ordered that the state's evidence be suppressed.

My own work in this field continues. In 1992, Robert L. Wilkins was riding in a rented car with family members when Maryland State Police stopped them, ordered them out, and conducted a search for drugs, which were not found. Wilkins happened to be a Harvard Law School trained public defender in Washington. With the support of the Maryland ACLU, he sued the state police, who settled the case with, among other things, an agreement to provide highway-stop data to the organization.

I was asked by the ACLU to evaluate the Maryland data in 1996 and again in 1997. I conducted a rolling survey in Maryland similar to the one I had done before and found a similar result. While 17.5 percent of the traffic violators on I-95 north of Baltimore were African American, 28.8 percent of those stopped and 71.3 percent of those searched by the Maryland State Police were African American. U.S. District Judge Catherine Blake ultimately ruled in 1997 that the ACLU made a "reasonable showing" that Maryland troopers on I-95 were continuing to engage in a "pattern and practice" of racial discrimination. Other legal actions have been filed in Pennsylvania, Florida, Indiana and North Carolina. Police officials everywhere deny racial profiling.

Why, then, are so many more African American motorists stopped than would be expected by their frequency on the road and their violation of the law? It seems clear to me that drugs are the issue.

The notion that African Americans and other minorities are more likely than whites to be carrying drugs—a notion that is perpetuated by some police training films—seems to be especially prevalent among the police. They believe that if they are to interdict drugs, then it makes sense to stop minorities, especially young men. State police are rewarded and promoted at least partially on the basis of their "criminal programs," which means the number of arrests they make. Testimony in the New Jersey case pointed out that troopers would be considered deficient if they did not make enough arrests. Since, as Judge Francis found, training points to minorities as likely drug dealers, it makes a certain sort of distorted sense to stop minorities more than whites.

But there is no untainted evidence that minorities are more likely to possess or sell drugs. There is evidence to the contrary. Indirect evidence in statistics from the National Institute of Drug Abuse indicates that 12 percent to 14 percent of those who abuse drugs are African American, a percentage that is proportionate to their numbers in the general population.

More telling are the numbers of those people who are stopped and searched by the Maryland State Police who have drugs. This data, which has been unobtainable from other states, indicates that of those drivers and passengers searched in Maryland, about 28 percent have contraband, whether they are black or white. The same percentage of contraband is found no matter the race.

The Maryland data may shed some light on the tendency of some troopers to believe that blacks are somehow more likely to possess contraband. This data shows that for every 1,000 searches by the Maryland State Police, 200 blacks and only 80 non-blacks are arrested. This could lead one to believe that more blacks are breaking the law—until you know that the sample is deeply skewed. Of those searched, 713 were black and only 287 were non-black.

We do not have comparable figures on contraband possession or arrests from New Jersey. But if the traffic along I-95 there is at all similar to I-95 in Maryland—and there is a strong numerical basis to believe it is—it is possible to speculate that black travelers in New Jersey also were no more likely than non-blacks to be carrying contraband.

The fact that a black was 16.5 times more likely than a non-black to be arrested on the New Jersey Turnpike now takes on added meaning. Making only the assumption that was shown accurate in Maryland, it is possible to say even more conclusively that racial profiling is prevalent there and that there is no benefit to police in singling out blacks. More important, even if there were a benefit, it would violate fundamental rights. The constitution does not permit law enforcement authorities to target groups by race.

Fundamental fairness demands that steps be taken to prohibit profiling in theory and in practice. There is legislation pending at the federal level and in at least two states, Rhode Island and Pennsylvania, that would require authorities to keep statistics on this issue. This is crucial legislation and should be passed.

Only when the data are made available and strong steps are taken to monitor and curtail profiling, will we be able to assure minorities, and all of us who care about fundamental rights, that this practice will cease.

47

Dishonoring the Dead

JONATHAN KOZOL

One sunny day in April, I was sitting with my friend Pineapple at a picnic table in St. Mary's Park in the South Bronx. I had met Pineapple six years earlier, in 1994, when I had visited her kindergarten class at P.S. 65. She was a plump and bright-eyed child who had captured my attention when I leaned over her desk and noticed that she wrote her letters in reverse. I met her again a few weeks later at an after-school program based at St. Ann's Church, which was close to P.S. 65, where Pineapple and a number of her friends came for tutorial instruction and for safety from the dangers of the neighborhood during the afternoons.

The next time I visited her school, it was the spring of 1997. She was in third grade now and she was having a bad year. The school was in a state of chaos because there had been a massive turnover of teachers. Of 50 members of the faculty in the preceding year, 28 had never taught before; and half of them were fired or did not return the following September. Very little teaching took place in Pineapple's class during the time that I was there. For some reason, children in her class and other classes on her floor had to spend an awful lot of time in forming lines outside the doorways of their rooms, then waiting as long as 30 minutes for their turn to file downstairs to the cafeteria for lunch, then waiting in lines again to get their meals, then to go to recess, then to the bathroom, then return to class. Nearly two hours had elapsed between the time Pineapple's classmates formed their line to go to lunch and finally returned.

★   ★   ★

Many Americans I meet who live far from our major cities and who have no first-hand knowledge of realities in urban public schools seem to have a rather vague and general impression that the great extremes of racial isolation they recall as matters of grave national significance some 35 or 40 years ago have gradually, but steadily, diminished in more recent years. The truth, unhappily, is that the trend, for well over a decade now, has been precisely the reverse. Schools that were already deeply segregated 25 or 30 years ago, like most of the schools I visit in the Bronx, are no less segregated now, while thousands of other schools that had been integrated either voluntarily or by the force of law have since been rapidly resegregating both in northern districts and in broad expanses of the South.

"At the beginning of the twenty-first century," according to Professor Gary Orfield and his colleagues at the Civil Rights Project at Harvard University, "American public schools are now 12 years into the process of continuous resegregation. The desegregation of black students, which increased continuously from the 1950s to the late 1980s, has now receded to levels not seen in three decades. . . . During the 1990s, the proportion of black students in majority white schools has decreased . . . to a level lower than in any year since 1968. . . . Almost three fourths of black and Latino students attend schools that are predominantly minority," and more than two million, including more than a quarter of black students in the Northeast and Midwest, "attend schools which we call apartheid schools" in which 99 to 100 percent of students are nonwhite. The four most segregated states for black students, according to the Civil Rights Project, are New York, Michigan, Illinois, and California. In California and New York, only one black student in seven goes to a predominantly white school.

During the past 25 years, the Harvard study notes, "there has been no significant leadership towards the goal of creating a successfully integrated society built on integrated schools and neighborhoods." The last constructive act by Congress was the 1972 enactment of a federal program to provide financial aid to districts undertaking efforts at desegregation, which, however, was "repealed by the Reagan administration in 1981." The Supreme Court "began limiting desegregation in key ways in 1974"—and actively dismantling existing integration programs in 1991.

"Desegregation did not fail. In spite of a very brief period of serious enforcement . . . , the desegregation era was a period in which minority high school graduates increased sharply and the racial test score gaps narrowed substantially until they began to widen again in the 1990s. . . . In the two largest educational innovations of the past two decades—standards-based reform and school choice—the issue of racial segregation and its consequences has been ignored."

"To give up on integration, while aware of its benefits," write Orfield and his former Harvard colleague Susan Eaton, "requires us to consciously and deliberately accept segregation, while aware of its harms. . . . Segregation, rarely discussed, scarcely even acknowledged by elected officials and school leaders"—an "exercise in denial," they observe, "reminiscent of the South" before the integration era—"is incompatible with the healthy functioning of a multiracial generation."

Racial isolation and the concentrated poverty of children in a public school go hand in hand, moreover, as the Harvard project notes. Only 15 percent of the intensely segregated white schools in the nation have student populations in which more than half are poor enough to be receiving free meals or reduced price meals. "By contrast, a staggering 86 percent of intensely segregated black and Latino schools" have student enrollments in which more than half are poor by the same standards. A segregated inner-city school is "almost six times as likely" to be a school of concentrated poverty as is a school that has an overwhelmingly white population.

"So deep is our resistance to acknowledging what is taking place," Professor Orfield notes, that when a district that has been desegregated in preceding decades now abandons integrated education, "the actual word 'segregation' hardly ever comes up. Proposals for racially separate schools are usually promoted as new educational improvement plans or efforts to increase parental involvement. . . . In the new era of 'separate but equal,' segregation has somehow come to be viewed as a type of school reform"—"something progressive and new," he writes—rather than as what it is: an unconceded throwback to the status quo of 1954. But no matter by what new name segregated education may be known, whether it be "neighborhood schools, community schools, targeted schools, priority schools," or whatever other currently accepted term, "segregation is not new . . . and neither is the idea of making separate schools equal. It is one of the oldest and extensively tried ideas in U.S. educational history" and one, writes Orfield, that has "never had a systematic effect in a century of trials."

Perhaps most damaging to any effort to address this subject openly is the refusal of most of the major arbiters of culture in our northern cities to confront or even clearly name an obvious reality they would have castigated with a passionate determination in another section of the nation 50 years before and which, moreover, they still castigate today in retrospective writings that assign it to a comfortably distant and allegedly concluded era of the past. There is, indeed, a seemingly agreed-upon convention in much of the media today not even to use an accurate descriptor such as "racial segregation" in a narrative description of a segregated school. Linguistic sweeteners, semantic somersaults, and surrogate vocabularies are repeatedly employed. Schools in which as few as three or four percent of students may be white or Southeast Asian or of Middle Eastern origin, for instance—and where *every other child* in the building is black or Hispanic—are referred to, in a commonly misleading usage, as "diverse." Visitors to schools like these discover quickly the eviscerated meaning of the word, which is no longer a descriptor but a euphemism for a plainer word that has apparently become unspeakable.

School systems themselves repeatedly employ this euphemism in descriptions of the composition of their student populations. In a school I visited in fall 2004 in Kansas City, Missouri, for example, a document distributed to visitors reports that the school's curriculum "addresses the needs of children from diverse backgrounds." But as I went from class to class I did not encounter any children who were white or Asian—or Hispanic, for that matter—and when I later was provided with the demographics of the school, I learned that 99.6 percent of students there were African-American. In a similar document, the school board of another district, this one in New York State, referred to "the diversity" of its student population and "the rich variations of ethnic backgrounds. . . ." But when I looked at the racial numbers that the district had reported to the state, I learned that there were 2,800 black and Hispanic children in the system, one Asian child, and three whites. Words, in these cases, cease to have real meaning; or, rather, they mean the opposite of what they say.

One of the most disheartening experiences for those who grew up in the years when Martin Luther King and Thurgood Marshall were alive is to visit public schools today that bear their names, or names of other honored leaders of the integration struggles that produced the temporary progress that took place in the three decades after *Brown,* and to find how many of these schools are bastions of contemporary segregation. It is even more disheartening when schools like these are not in segregated neighborhoods but in racially mixed areas in which the integration of a public school would seem to be most natural and where, indeed, it takes a conscious effort on the part of parents or of school officials in these districts to *avoid* the integration option that is often right at their front door.

In a Seattle neighborhood, for instance, where approximately half the families were Caucasian, 95 percent of students at the Thurgood Marshall Elementary School were black, Hispanic, Native American, or of Asian origin. An African-American teacher at the school told me of seeing clusters of white parents and their children on the corner of a street close to the school each morning waiting for a bus that took the children to a school in which she believed that the enrollment was predominantly white. She did not speak of the white families waiting for the bus to take their children to another public school with bitterness, but wistfully.

"At Thurgood Marshall," according to a big wall-poster in the lobby of the school, "the dream is alive." But school assignment practices and federal court decisions that have countermanded long-established policies that previously fostered integration in Seattle's schools make the realization of the dream identified with Justice Marshall all but unattainable today.

"Thurgood Marshall must be turning over in his grave," one of the teachers at the school had told the principal, as he reported this to me. The principal, understandably, believed he had no choice but to reject the teacher's observation out of hand. "No, sister," he had told the teacher. "If Justice Marshall was still roamin' nowadays and saw what's goin' on here in this school, he would say 'Hallelujah' and 'Amen!'" Legal scholars may demur at this, but he had a school to run and he could not allow the ironies of names, or history, to undermine the passionate resolve he brought to winning victories for children in the only terms he was allowed.

In the course of two visits to the school, I had a chance to talk with a number of teachers and to spend time in their classrooms. In one class, a teacher had posted a brief summation of the *Brown* decision on the wall; but it was in an inconspicuous corner of the room and, with that one exception, I could find no references to Marshall's struggle against racial segregation in the building.

When I asked a group of fifth grade boys who Thurgood Marshall was and what he did to have deserved to have a school named after him, most of the boys had no idea at all. One said that he used to run "a summer camp." Another said he was "a manager"—I had no chance to ask him what he meant by this, or how he'd gotten this impression. Of the three who knew that he had been a lawyer, only one, and only after several questions on my part, replied that he had "tried to change what was unfair"—and, after a moment's hesitation, "wanted to let black kids go to the same schools that white kids did." He said he was "pretty sure" that this school was not segregated because, in one of the other classrooms on the same floor, there were two white children.

★ ★ ★

High school students with whom I get to talk in deeply segregated neighborhoods seem far less circumspect and far more open in their willingness to look into those problematic places. "It's like we're being hidden," said a fifteen-year-old girl named Isabel I met some years ago in Harlem, in attempting to explain to me the ways in which she and her classmates understood the racial segregation of their neighborhoods and schools. "It's as if you have been put in a garage where, if they don't have room for something but aren't sure if they should throw it out, they put it there where they don't need to think of it again."

I asked her if she truly thought America did not "have room" for her or other children of her race. "Think of it this way," said a sixteen-year-old girl sitting beside her. "If people in New York woke up one day and learned that we were gone, that we had simply died or left for somewhere else, how would they feel?"

"How do you think they'd feel?" I asked.

"I think they'd be relieved," this very solemn girl replied.

The name above the doorway of a school has little power to revise these sensitive perceptions. Still, we have these many schools bearing distinguished names that cannot fail to resonate with history. For visitors, the name of Thurgood Marshall on the doorway of a school inevitably stirs a certain expectation and reminds us of the court decision with which Marshall's name is linked forever in our memory. No matter how the meaning of *Brown v. Board of Education* may be retroactively revised, or blurred, or rendered indistinct, which seems to be almost obligatory in the speeches that are given at events commemorating the decision, the question it addressed and the resounding answer it delivered are a part of our collective memory as well.

"Does segregation of children in public schools solely on the basis of race, even though the physical facilities and other 'tangible' factors may be equal," asked the court in 1954, "deprive the children of the minority race of equal educational opportunities? We believe it does." To separate black children from white children of their age and qualifications on the basis of their race, the court went on, "generates a feeling of inferiority as to their status in the community that may affect their hearts and minds in a way unlikely ever to be undone. . . . In the field of public education, the doctrine of 'separate but equal' has no place. . . . Separate educational facilities are inherently unequal."

★ ★ ★

"There are cheap children and there are expensive children," writes Marina Warner, an essayist and novelist who has written many books for children, "just as there are cheap women and expensive women." When Pineapple entered P.S. 65 in the South Bronx, the government of New York State had already placed a price tag on her forehead. She and her kindergarten classmates were $8,000 babies. If we had wanted to see an $18,000 baby, we would have had to drive into the suburbs. But the governmentally administered diminishment of value in the children of the poor begins even before the age of five or six when they begin their years of formal education in the public schools. It starts during their infant years and toddler years when hundreds of thousands of children in low-income neighborhoods are locked out of the opportunity for preschool education for no reason but the accident of birth and budgetary choices of the government, while children of the privileged are often given veritable feasts of rich development early education.

In New York City, for example, affluent parents pay surprisingly large sums of money to enroll their youngsters in extraordinary early-education programs, typically beginning at the age of two or three, that give them social competence and rudimentary pedagogic skills unknown to children of the same age in the city's poorer neighborhoods. The most exclusive of the private preschools in New York, which are known to those who can afford them as the "Baby Ivies," cost as much as $22,000 for a full-day program. Competition for admission to these pre-K schools is so intense that "private counselors" are frequently retained, at fees as high as $300 hourly, according to The Times, to guide the parents through the application process.

★ ★ ★

. . . [I]n third grade, these children are introduced to what are known as "high-stakes tests," which in many urban systems now determine whether students can or cannot be promoted. Children who have been in programs like the "Baby Ivies" since the age of two have been given seven years of education by this point, nearly twice as many as the children who have been denied these opportunities; yet all are required to take, and will be measured and in many cases penalized severely by, the same examinations.

Which of these children will receive the highest scores—those who spent the years from two to four in lovely little Montessori schools and other pastel-painted settings in which tender and attentive grown-ups read to them from storybooks and introduced them for the first time to the world of numbers, and the shapes of letters, and the sizes and varieties of solid objects, and perhaps taught them to sort things into groups or to arrange them in a sequence, or to do those many other interesting things that early-childhood specialists refer to as prenumeracy skills, or the ones who spent those years at home in front of a TV or sitting by the window of a slum apartment gazing down into the street? There is something deeply hypocritical in a society that holds an inner-city child only eight years old "accountable" for her performance on a high-stakes standardized exam but does not hold the high officials of our government accountable for robbing her of what they gave their own kids six or seven years before.

There are obviously other forces that affect the early school performance of low-income children: levels of parent education, social instability, and frequently undiagnosed depression and anxiety that make it hard for many parents I have known to take an active role in backing up the efforts of their children's teachers in the public schools. Still, it is all too easy to assign the primary onus of responsibility to parents in these neighborhoods. (Where were these parents educated after all? Usually in the same low-ranking schools their children now attend.) In a nation in which fairness was respected, children of the poorest and least educated mothers would receive the most extensive and most costly preschool preparation, not the least and cheapest, because children in these families need it so much more than those whose educated parents can deliver the same benefits of early learning to them in their homes.

The "Baby Ivies" of Manhattan are not public institutions and receive no subsidies from public funds. In a number of cities, on the other hand, even this last line of squeamishness has now been crossed and public funds are being used to underwrite part of the costs of preschool education for the children of the middle class in public institutions which, however, do not offer the same services to children of the poor. Starting in spring 2001, Chicago's public schools began to operate a special track of preschool for the children of those families who were able to afford to pay an extra fee—nearly $6,000—to provide their children with a full-day program of about 11 hours, starting at the age of two if parents so desired. In a city where 87 percent of students in the public schools were black or Hispanic, the pay-for-preschool program served primarily white children.

Almost all these preschools were "in gentrified or gentrifying neighborhoods," The Chicago Tribune reported. "The fresh paint and new toys" in one of these programs on the North Side of Chicago were not there simply "to make preschool a happier place for the new class of toddlers" but "to keep their parents from moving to the suburbs." These and other "gold-plated academic offerings" which the city was underwriting to attract or to retain the children of the middle class had already begun to slow the "brain drain" from the public schools, The Tribune said. In the same year in which the pay-for-pre-K program was begun, 7,000 children from low-income families, many of whom were deemed to be "at risk," were waiting for preschool spaces that the city was unable to provide.

Undemocratic practices like these, no matter how strategically compelling they may seem, have introduced a radical distorting prism to an old, if seldom honored, national ideal of universal public education that affords all children equal opportunity within the borders of a democratic entity. Blurring the line between democracy and marketplace, the private subsidy of public schools in privileged communities denounces an ideal of simple justice that is often treated nowadays as an annoying residue of tiresome egalitarian ideas, an ethical detritus that sophisticated parents are encouraged to shut out of mind as they adapt themselves to a new order of Darwinian entitlements.

★ ★ ★

 48

"A Way Outa No Way"

Eating Problems Among African-American, Latina, and White Women

BECKY W. THOMPSON

Bulimia, anorexia, binging, and extensive dieting are among the many health issues women have been confronting in the last 20 years. Until recently, however, there has been almost no research about eating problems among African-American, Latina, Asian-American, or Native American women; working-class women; or lesbians.[1] In fact, according to the normative epidemiological portrait, eating problems are largely a white, middle- and upper-class heterosexual phenomenon. Further, while feminist research has documented how eating problems are fueled by sexism, there has been almost no attention to how other systems of oppression may also be implicated in the development of eating problems.

In this [essay], I reevaluate the portrayal of eating problems as issues of appearance based in the "culture of thinness." I propose that eating problems begin as ways women cope with various traumas including sexual abuse, racism, classism, sexism, heterosexism, and poverty. Showing the interface between these traumas and the onset of eating problems explains why women may use eating to numb pain and cope with violations to their bodies. This theoretical shift also permits an understanding of the economic, political, social, educational, and cultural resources that women need to change their relationship to food and their bodies.

EXISTING RESEARCH ON EATING PROBLEMS

There are three theoretical models used to explain the epidemiology, etiology, and treatment of eating problems. The biomedical model offers important scientific research about possible physiological causes of eating problems and the physiological dangers of purging and starvation (Copeland 1985; Spack 1985). However, this model adopts medical treatment strategies that may disempower and traumatize women (Garner 1985; Orbach 1985). In addition, this model ignores many social, historical, and cultural factors that influence women's eating patterns. The psychological model identifies eating problems as "multidimensional disorders" that are influenced by biological, psychological, and cultural factors (Garfinkel and Garner 1982). While useful in its exploration of effective therapeutic treatments, this model, like the biomedical one, tends to neglect women of color, lesbians, and working-class women.

The third model, offered by feminists, asserts that eating problems are gendered. This model explains why the vast majority of people with eating problems are women, how gender socialization and sexism may relate to eating problems, and how masculine models of psychological development have shaped theoretical interpretations. Feminists offer the culture of thinness model as a key reason why eating problems predominate among women. According to this model, thinness is a culturally, socially, and economically enforced requirement for female beauty. This imperative makes women vulnerable to cycles of dieting, weight loss, and subsequent weight gain, which may lead to anorexia and bulimia (Chernin 1981; Orbach 1978, 1985; Smead 1984).

Feminists have rescued eating problems from the realm of individual psychopathology by showing how the difficulties are rooted in systematic and pervasive attempts to control women's body sizes and appetites. However, researchers have yet to give significant attention to how race, class, and sexuality influence women's understanding of their bodies and appetites. The handful of epidemiological studies that include African-American women and Latinas casts doubt on the accuracy of the normative epidemiological portrait. The studies suggest that this portrait reflects which particular populations of women have been studied rather than actual prevalence (Andersen and Hay 1985; Gray, Ford, and Kelly 1987; Hsu 1987; Nevo 1985; Silber 1986).

More important, this research shows that bias in research has consequences for women of color. Tomas Silber (1986) asserts that many well-trained professionals have either misdiagnosed or delayed their diagnoses of eating problems among African-American and Latina women due to stereotypical thinking that these problems are restricted to white women. As a consequence, when African-American women or Latinas are diagnosed, their eating problems tend to be more severe due to extended processes of starvation prior to intervention. In her autobiographical account of her eating problems, Retha Powers (1989), an African-American woman, describes being told not to worry about her eating problems since "fat is more acceptable in the Black community" (p. 78). Stereotypical perceptions held by her peers and teachers of the "maternal Black woman" and the "persistent mammy-brickhouse Black woman image" (p. 134) made it difficult for Powers to find people who took her problems with food seriously.

Recent work by African-American women reveals that eating problems often relate to women's struggles against a "simultaneity of oppression" (Clarke 1982; Naylor 1985; White 1991). Byllye Avery (1990), the founder of the National Black Women's Health Project, links the origins of eating problems among African-American women to the daily stress of being undervalued and overburdened at home and at work. In Evelyn C. White's (1990) anthology, *The Black Woman's Health Book: Speaking for Ourselves,* Georgiana Arnold (1990) links her eating problems partly to racism and racial isolation during childhood.

Recent feminist research also identifies factors that are related to eating problems among lesbians (Brown 1987; Dworkin 1989; Iazzetto 1989; Schoenfielder and Wieser 1983). In her clinical work, Brown (1987) found that lesbians who have internalized a high degree of homophobia are more likely to accept negative attitudes about fat than are lesbians who have examined their internalized homophobia. Autobiographical accounts by lesbians have also indicated that secrecy about eating problems among lesbians partly reflects their fear of being associated with a stigmatized illness ("What's Important" 1988).

Attention to African-American women, Latinas, and lesbians paves the way for further research that explores the possible interface between facing multiple oppressions and the development of eating problems. In this way, this study is part of a larger feminist and sociological research agenda that seeks to understand how race, class, gender, nationality, and sexuality inform women's experiences and influence theory production.

METHODOLOGY

I conducted 18 life history interviews and administered lengthy questionnaires to explore eating problems among African-American, Latina, and white women. I employed a snowball sample, a method in which potential respondents often first learn about the study from people who have already participated. This method was well suited for the study since it enabled women to get information about me and the interview process from people they already knew. Typically, I had much contact with the respondents prior to the interview. This was particularly important given the secrecy associated with this topic (Russell 1986; Silberstein, Striegel-Moore, and Rodin 1987), the necessity of women of color and lesbians to be discriminating about how their lives are studied, and the fact that I was conducting across-race research.

To create analytical notes and conceptual categories from the data, I adopted Glaser and Strauss's (1967) technique of theoretical sampling, which directs the researcher to collect, analyze, and test hypotheses during the sampling process (rather than imposing theoretical categories onto the data). After completing each interview transcription, I gave a copy to each woman who wanted one. After reading their interviews, some of the women clarified or made additions to the interview text.

Demographics of the Women in the Study

The 18 women I interviewed included 5 African-American women, 5 Latinas, and 8 white women. Of these women, 12 are lesbian and 6 are heterosexual. Five women are Jewish, 8 are Catholic, and 5 are Protestant. Three women grew up outside of the United States. The women represented a range of class backgrounds (both in terms of origin and current class status) and ranged in age from 19 to 46 years old (with a median age of 33.5 years).

The majority of the women reported having had a combination of eating problems (at least two of the following: bulimia, compulsive eating, anorexia, and/or extensive dieting). In addition, the particular types of eating problems often changed during a woman's life span. (For example, a woman might have been bulimic during adolescence and anorexic as an adult.) Among the women, 28 percent had been bulimic, 17 percent had been bulimic and anorexic, and 5 percent had been anorexic. All of the women who had been anorexic or bulimic also had a history of compulsive eating and extensive dieting. Of the women, 50 percent were compulsive eaters and dieters (39 percent) or compulsive eaters (11 percent) but had not been bulimic or anorexic.

Two-thirds of the women have had eating problems for more than half of their lives, a finding that

contradicts the stereotype of eating problems as transitory. The weight fluctuation among the women varied from 16 to 160 pounds, with an average fluctuation of 74 pounds. This drastic weight change illustrates the degree to which the women adjusted to major changes in body size at least once during their lives as they lost, gained, and lost weight again. The average age of onset was 11 years old, meaning that most of the women developed eating problems prior to puberty. Almost all of the women (88 percent) consider themselves as still having a problem with eating, although the majority believe they are well on the way to recovery.

THE INTERFACE OF TRAUMA AND EATING PROBLEMS

One of the most striking findings in this study was the range of traumas the women associated with the origins of their eating problems, including racism, sexual abuse, poverty, sexism, emotional or physical abuse, heterosexism, class injuries, and acculturation.[2] The particular constellation of eating problems among the women did not vary with race, class, sexuality, or nationality. Women from various race and class backgrounds attributed the origins of their eating problems to sexual abuse, sexism, and emotional and/or physical abuse. Among some of the African-American and Latina women, eating problems were also associated with poverty, racism, and class injuries. Heterosexism was a key factor in the onset of bulimia, compulsive eating, and extensive dieting among some of the lesbians. These oppressions are not the same nor are the injuries caused by them. And certainly, there are a variety of potentially harmful ways that women respond to oppression (such as using drugs, becoming a workaholic, or committing suicide). However, for all these women, eating was a way of coping with trauma.

Sexual Abuse

Sexual abuse was the most common trauma that the women related to the origins of their eating problems. Until recently, there has been virtually no research exploring the possible relationship between these two phenomena. Since the mid-1980s, however, researchers have begun identifying connections between the two, a task that is part of a larger feminist critique of traditional psychoanalytic symptomatology (DeSalvo 1989; Herman 1981; Masson 1984). Results of a number of incidence studies indicate that between one-third and two-thirds of women who have eating problems have been abused (Oppenheimer et al. 1985; Root and Fallon 1988). In addition, a growing number of therapists and researchers have offered interpretations of the meaning and impact of eating problems for survivors of sexual abuse (Bass and Davis 1988; Goldfarb 1987; Iazzetto 1989; Swink and Leveille 1986). Kearney-Cooke (1988) identifies dieting and binging as common ways in which women cope with frequent psychological consequences of sexual abuse (such as body image disturbances, distrust of people and one's own experiences, and confusion about one's feelings). Root and Fallon (1989) specify ways that victimized women cope with assaults by binging and purging: bulimia serves many functions, including anesthetizing the negative feelings associated with victimization. Iazzetto's innovative study (1989), based on in-depth interviews and art therapy sessions, examines how a woman's relationship to her body changes as a consequence of sexual abuse. Iazzetto discovered that the process of leaving the body (through progressive phases of numbing, dissociating, and denying) that often occurs during sexual abuse parallels the process of leaving the body made possible through binging.

Among the women I interviewed, 61 percent were survivors of sexual abuse (11 of the 18 women), most of whom made connections between sexual abuse and the beginning of their eating problems. Binging was the most common method of coping identified by the survivors. Binging helped women "numb out" or anesthetize their feelings. Eating sedated, alleviated anxiety, and combated loneliness. Food was something that they could trust and was accessible whenever they needed it. Antonia (a pseudonym) is an Italian-American woman who was first sexually abused by a male

relative when she was four years old. Retrospectively, she knows that binging was a way she coped with the abuse. When the abuse began, and for many years subsequently, Antonia often woke up during the middle of the night with anxiety attacks or nightmares and would go straight to the kitchen cupboards to get food. Binging helped her block painful feelings because it put her back to sleep.

Like other women in the study who began binging when they were very young, Antonia was not always fully conscious as she binged. She described eating during the night as "sleep walking. It was mostly desperate—like I had to have it." Describing why she ate after waking up with nightmares, Antonia said, "What else do you do? If you don't have any coping mechanisms, you eat." She said that binging made her "disappear," which made her feel protected. Like Antonia, most of the women were sexually abused before puberty, four of them before they were five years old. Given their youth, food was the most accessible and socially acceptable drug available to them. Because all of the women endured the psychological consequences alone, it is logical that they coped with tactics they could do alone as well.

One reason Antonia binged (rather than dieted) to cope with sexual abuse is that she saw little reason to try to be the small size girls were supposed to be. Growing up as one of the only Italian Americans in what she described as a "very WASP town," Antonia felt that everything from her weight and size to having dark hair on her upper lip were physical characteristics she was supposed to hide. From a young age she knew she "never embodied the essence of the good girl. I don't like her. I have never acted like her. I can't be her. I sort of gave up." For Antonia, her body was the physical entity that signified her outsider status. When the sexual abuse occurred, Antonia felt she had lost her body. In her mind, the body she lived in after the abuse was not really hers. By the time Antonia was 11, her mother put her on diet pills. Antonia began to eat behind closed doors as she continued to cope with the psychological consequences of sexual abuse and feeling like a cultural outsider.

Extensive dieting and bulimia were also ways in which women responded to sexual abuse. Some women thought that the men had abused them because of their weight. They believed that if they were smaller, they might not have been abused. For example when Elsa, an Argentine woman, was sexually abused at the age of 11, she thought her chubby size was the reason the man was abusing her. Elsa said, "I had this notion that these old perverts liked these plump girls. You heard adults say this too. Sex and flesh being associated." Looking back on her childhood, Elsa believes she made fat the enemy partly due to the shame and guilt she felt about the incest. Her belief that fat was the source of her problems was also supported by her socialization. Raised by strict German governesses in an upper-class family, Elsa was taught that a woman's weight was a primary criterion for judging her worth. Her mother "was socially conscious of walking into places with a fat daughter and maybe people staring at her." Her father often referred to Elsa's body as "shot to hell." When asked to describe how she felt about her body when growing up, Elsa described being completely alienated from her body. She explained,

> Remember in school when they talk about the difference between body and soul? I always felt like my soul was skinny. My soul was free. My soul sort of flew. I was tied down by this big bag of rocks that was my body. I had to drag it around. It did pretty much what it wanted and I had a lot of trouble controlling it. It kept me from doing all the things that I dreamed of.

As is true for many women who have been abused, the split that Elsa described between her body and soul was an attempt to protect herself from the pain she believed her body caused her. In her mind, her fat body was what had "bashed in her dreams." Dieting became her solution, but, as is true for many women in the study, this strategy soon led to cycles of binging and weight fluctuation.

Ruthie, a Puerto Rican woman who was sexually abused from 12 until 16 years of age, described bulimia as a way she responded to sexual abuse. As a child, Ruthie liked her body. Like many Puerto Rican women of her generation, Ruthie's mother did not want skinny children, interpreting that as a sign that they were sick or being fed improperly. Despite her mother's attempts to make her gain weight, Ruthie remained thin through puberty. When a male relative began sexually abusing her, Ruthie's sense of her body changed dramatically. Although she weighed only 100 pounds, she began to feel fat and thought her size was causing the abuse. She had seen a movie on television about Romans who made themselves throw up and so she began doing it, in hopes that she could look like the "little kid" she was before the abuse began. Her symbolic attempt to protect herself by purging stands in stark contrast to the psychoanalytic explanation of eating problems as an "abnormal" repudiation of sexuality. In fact, her actions and those of many other survivors indicate a girl's logical attempt to protect herself (including her sexuality) by being a size and shape that does not seem as vulnerable to sexual assault.

These women's experiences suggest many reasons why women develop eating problems as a consequence of sexual abuse. Most of the survivors "forgot" the sexual abuse after its onset and were unable to retrieve the abuse memories until many years later. With these gaps in memory, frequently they did not know why they felt ashamed, fearful, or depressed. When sexual abuse memories resurfaced in dreams, they often woke feeling upset but could not remember what they had dreamed. These free-floating, unexplained feelings left the women feeling out of control and confused. Binging or focusing on maintaining a new diet were ways women distracted or appeased themselves, in turn, helping them regain a sense of control. As they grew older, they became more conscious of the consequences of these actions. Becoming angry at themselves for binging or promising themselves they would not purge again was a way to direct feelings of shame and self-hate that often accompanied the trauma.

Integral to this occurrence was a transference process in which the women displaced onto their bodies painful feelings and memories that actually derived from or were directed toward the persons who caused the abuse. Dieting became a method of trying to change the parts of their bodies they hated, a strategy that at least initially brought success as they lost weight. Purging was a way women tried to reject the body size they thought was responsible for the abuse. Throwing up in order to lose the weight they thought was making them vulnerable to the abuse was a way to try to find the body they had lost when the abuse began.

Poverty

Like sexual abuse, poverty is another injury that may make women vulnerable to eating problems. One woman I interviewed attributed her eating problems directly to the stress caused by poverty. Yolanda is a Black Cape Verdean mother who began eating compulsively when she was 27 years old. After leaving an abusive husband in her early 20s, Yolanda was forced to go on welfare. As a single mother with small children and few financial resources, she tried to support herself and her children on $539 a month. Yolanda began binging in the evenings after putting her children to bed. Eating was something she could do alone. It would calm her, help her deal with loneliness, and make her feel safe. Food was an accessible commodity that was cheap. She ate three boxes of macaroni and cheese when nothing else was available. As a single mother with little money, Yolanda felt as if her body was the only thing she had left. As she described it,

> I am here, [in my body] 'cause there is no where else for me to go, Where am I going to go? This is all I got . . . that probably contributes to putting on so much weight cause staying in your body, in your home, in yourself, you don't go out. You aren't around other people. . . . You hide and as long as you hide you don't have to face . . . nobody can see you eat. You are safe.

When she was eating, Yolanda felt a momentary reprieve from her worries. Binging not only became a logical solution because it was cheap and easy but also because she had grown up amid positive messages about eating. In her family, eating was a

celebrated and joyful act. However, in adulthood, eating became a double-edged sword. While comforting her, binging also led to weight gain. During the three years Yolanda was on welfare, she gained seventy pounds.

Yolanda's story captures how poverty can be a precipitating factor in eating problems and highlights the value of understanding how class inequalities may shape women's eating problems. As a single mother, her financial constraints mirrored those of most female heads of households. The dual hazards of a race- and sex-stratified labor market further limited her options (Higginbotham 1986). In an article about Black women's health, Byllye Avery (1990) quotes a Black woman's explanation about why she eats compulsively. The woman told Avery,

> I work for General Electric making batteries, and, I know it's killing me. My old man is an alcoholic. My kid's got babies. Things are not well with me. And one thing I know I can do when I come home is cook me a pot of food and sit down in front of the TV and eat it. And you can't take that away from me until you're ready to give me something in its place. (p. 7)

Like Yolanda, this woman identifies eating compulsively as a quick, accessible, and immediately satisfying way of coping with the daily stress caused by conditions she could not control. Connections between poverty and eating problems also show the limits of portraying eating problems as maladies of upper-class adolescent women.

The fact that many women use food to anesthetize themselves, rather than other drugs (even when they gained access to alcohol, marijuana, and other illegal drugs), is partly a function of gender socialization and the competing demands that women face. One of the physiological consequences of binge eating is a numbed state similar to that experienced by drinking. Troubles and tensions are covered over as a consequence of the body's defensive response to massive food intake. When food is eaten in that way, it effectively works like a drug with immediate and predictable effects. Yolanda said she binged late at night rather than getting drunk because she could still get up in the morning, get her children ready for school, and be clearheaded for the college classes she attended. By binging, she avoided the hangover or sickness that results from alcohol or illegal drugs. In this way, food was her drug of choice since it was possible for her to eat while she continued to care for her children, drive, cook, and study. Binging is also less expensive than drinking, a factor that is especially significant for poor women. Another woman I interviewed said that when her compulsive eating was at its height, she ate breakfast after rising in the morning, stopped for a snack on her way to work, ate lunch at three different cafeterias, and snacked at her desk throughout the afternoon. Yet even when her eating had become constant, she was still able to remain employed. While her patterns of eating no doubt slowed her productivity, being drunk may have slowed her to a dead stop.

Heterosexism

The life history interviews also uncovered new connections between heterosexism and eating problems. One of the most important recent feminist contributions has been identifying compulsory heterosexuality as an institution which truncates opportunities for heterosexual and lesbian women (Rich 1986). All of the women interviewed for this study, both lesbian and heterosexual, were taught that heterosexuality was compulsory, although the versions of this enforcement were shaped by race and class. Expectations about heterosexuality were partly taught through messages that girls learned about eating and their bodies. In some homes, boys were given more food than girls, especially as teenagers, based on the rationale that girls need to be thin to attract boys. As the girls approached puberty, many were told to stop being athletic, begin wearing dresses, and watch their weight. For the women who weighed more than was considered acceptable, threats about their need to diet were laced with admonitions that being fat would ensure becoming an "old maid."

While compulsory heterosexuality influenced all of the women's emerging sense of their bodies and eating patterns, the women who linked heterosexism directly to the beginning of their eating problems were those who knew they were lesbians when very young and actively resisted heterosexual norms. One working-class Jewish woman, Martha, began compulsively eating when she was 11 years old, the same year she started getting clues of her lesbian identity. In junior high school, as many of her female peers began dating boys, Martha began fantasizing about girls, which made her feel utterly alone. Confused and ashamed about her fantasies, Martha came home every day from school and binged. Binging was a way she drugged herself so that being alone was tolerable. Describing binging, she said, "It was the only thing I knew. I was looking for a comfort." Like many women, Martha binged because it softened painful feelings. Binging sedated her, lessened her anxiety, and induced sleep.

Martha's story also reveals ways that trauma can influence women's experience of their bodies. Like many other women, Martha had no sense of herself as connected to her body. When I asked Martha whether she saw herself as fat when she was growing up she said, "I didn't see myself as fat. I didn't see myself. I wasn't there. I get so sad about that because I missed so much." In the literature on eating problems, *body image* is the term that is typically used to describe a woman's experience of her body. This term connotes the act of imagining one's physical appearance. Typically, women with eating problems are assumed to have difficulties with their body image. However, the term *body image* does not adequately capture the complexity and range of bodily responses to trauma experienced by the women. Exposure to trauma did much more than distort the women's visual image of themselves. These traumas often jeopardized their capacity to consider themselves as having bodies at all.

Given the limited connotations of the term *body image*, I use the term *body consciousness* as a more useful way to understand the range of bodily responses to trauma.[3] By body consciousness I mean the ability to reside comfortably in one's body (to see oneself as embodied) and to consider one's body as connected to oneself. The disruptions to their body consciousness that the women described included leaving their bodies, making a split between their body and mind, experiencing being "in" their bodies as painful, feeling unable to control what went in and out of their bodies, hiding in one part of their bodies, or simply not seeing themselves as having bodies. Binging, dieting, or purging were common ways women responded to disruptions to their body consciousness.

Racism and Class Injuries

For some of the Latinas and African-American women, racism coupled with the stress resulting from class mobility related to the onset of their eating problems. Joselyn, an African-American woman, remembered her white grandmother telling her she would never be as pretty as her cousins because they were lighter skinned. Her grandmother often humiliated Joselyn in front of others, as she made fun of Joselyn's body while she was naked and told her she was fat. As a young child, Joselyn began to think that although she could not change her skin color, she could at least try to be thin. When Joselyn was young, her grandmother was the only family member who objected to Joselyn's weight. However, her father also began encouraging his wife and daughter to be thin as the family's class standing began to change. When the family was working class, serving big meals, having chubby children, and keeping plenty of food in the house was a sign the family was doing well. But, as the family became mobile, Joselyn's father began insisting that Joselyn be thin. She remembered, "When my father's business began to bloom and my father was interacting more with white businessmen and seeing how they did business, suddenly thin became important. If you were a truly well-to-do family, then your family was slim and elegant."

As Joselyn's grandmother used Joselyn's body as territory for enforcing her own racism and prejudice about size, Joselyn's father used her body as the territory through which he channeled the demands he faced in the white-dominated business world. However, as Joselyn was pressured to diet, her father still served her large portions and bought treats for her and the neighborhood children. These contradictory messages made her feel confused about her body. As was true for many women in this study, Joselyn was told she was fat beginning when she was very young even though she was not overweight. And, like most of the women, Joselyn was put on diet pills and diets before even reaching puberty, beginning the cycles of dieting, compulsive eating, and bulimia.

The confusion about body size expectations that Joselyn associated with changes in class paralleled one Puerto Rican woman's association between her eating problems and the stress of assimilation as her family's class standing moved from poverty to working class. When Vera was very young, she was so thin that her mother took her to a doctor, who prescribed appetite stimulants. However, by the time Vera was eight years old, her mother began trying to shame Vera into dieting. Looking back on it, Vera attributed her mother's change of heart to competition among extended family members that centered on "being white, being successful, being middle class, . . . and it was always, 'Ay Bendito. She is so fat. What happened?'"

The fact that some of the African-American and Latina women associated the ambivalent messages about food and eating to their family's class mobility and/or the demands of assimilation while none of the eight white women expressed this (including those whose class was stable and changing) suggests that the added dimension of racism was connected to the imperative to be thin. In fact, the class expectations that their parents experienced exacerbated standards about weight that they inflicted on their daughters.

EATING PROBLEMS AS SURVIVAL STRATEGIES

Feminist Theoretical Shifts

My research permits a reevaluation of many assumptions about eating problems. First, this work challenges the theoretical reliance on the culture-of-thinness model. Although all of the women I interviewed were manipulated and hurt by this imperative at some point in their lives, it is not the primary source of their problems. Even in the instances in which a culture of thinness was a precipitating factor in anorexia, bulimia, or binging, this influence occurred in concert with other oppressions.

Attributing the etiology of eating problems primarily to a woman's striving to attain a certain beauty ideal is also problematic because it labels a common way that women cope with pain as essentially appearance-based disorders. One blatant example of sexism is the notion that women's foremost worry is about their appearance. By focusing on the emphasis on slenderness, the eating problems literature falls into the same trap of assuming that the problems reflect women's "obsession" with appearance. Some women were raised in families and communities in which thinness was not considered a criterion for beauty. Yet, they still developed eating problems. Other women were taught that women should be thin, but their eating problems were not primarily in reaction to this imperative. Their eating strategies began as logical solutions to problems rather than problems themselves as they tried to cope with a variety of traumas.

Establishing links between eating problems and a range of oppressions invites a rethinking of both the groups of women who have been excluded from research and those whose lives have been the basis of theory formation. The construction of bulimia and anorexia as appearance-based disorders is rooted in a notion of femininity in which white middle- and upper-class women are portrayed as frivolous, obsessed with their bodies, and overly accepting of narrow gender roles. This portrayal fuels women's tremendous shame and guilt about eating problems—as signs of self-centered vanity. This construction of white middle- and upper-class women is intimately linked to the portrayal of working-class white women and women of color as their opposite: as somehow exempt from accepting the dominant standards of beauty or as one step away from being hungry and therefore not susceptible

to eating problems. Identifying that women may binge to cope with poverty contrasts the notion that eating problems are class bound. Attending to the intricacies of race, class, sexuality, and gender pushes us to rethink the demeaning construction of middle-class femininity and establishes bulimia and anorexia as serious responses to injustices.

Understanding the link between eating problems and trauma also suggests much about treatment and prevention. Ultimately, their prevention depends not simply on individual healing but also on changing the social conditions that underlie their etiology. As Bernice Johnson Reagon sings in Sweet Honey in the Rock's song "Oughta Be a Woman," "A way outa no way is too much to ask/too much of a task for any one woman" (Reagon 1980).[4] Making it possible for women to have healthy relationships with their bodies and eating is a comprehensive task. Beginning steps in this direction include ensuring that (1) girls can grow up without being sexually abused, (2) parents have adequate resources to raise their children, (3) children of color grow up free of racism, and (4) young lesbians have the chance to see their reflection in their teachers and community leaders. Ultimately, the prevention of eating problems depends on women's access to economic, cultural, racial, political, social, and sexual justice.

NOTES

Author's Note: The research for this study was partially supported by an American Association of University Women Fellowship in Women's Studies. An earlier version of this article was presented at the New England Women's Studies Association Meeting in 1990 in Kingston, Rhode Island. I am grateful to Margaret Andersen, Liz Bennett, Lynn Davidman, Mary Gilfus, Evelynn Hammonds, and two anonymous reviewers for their comprehensive and perceptive comments on earlier versions of this article. Reprint requests: Becky Wangsgaard Thompson, Dept. of Sociology, Simmons College, 300 The Fenway, Boston, MA 02115.

1. I use the term *eating problems* as an umbrella term for one or more of the following: anorexia, bulimia, extensive dieting, or binging. I avoid using the term *eating disorder* because it categorizes the problems as individual pathologies, which deflects attention away from the social inequalities underlying them (Brown 1985).

However, by using the term *problem* I do not wish to imply blame. In fact, throughout, I argue that the eating strategies that women develop begin as logical solutions to problems, not problems themselves.

2. By trauma I mean a violating experience that has long-term emotional, physical, and/or spiritual consequences that may have immediate or delayed effects. One reason the term *trauma* is useful conceptually is its association with the diagnostic label Post Traumatic Stress Disorder (PTSD) (American Psychological Association 1987). PTSD is one of the few clinical diagnostic categories that recognizes social problems (such as war or the Holocaust) as responsible for the symptoms identified (Trimble 1985). This concept adapts well to the feminist assertion that a woman's symptoms cannot be understood as solely individual, considered outside of her social context, or prevented without significant changes in social conditions.

3. One reason the term *consciousness* is applicable is its intellectual history as an entity that is shaped by social context and social structures (Delphy 1984; Marx 1964). This link aptly applies to how the women described their bodies because their perceptions of themselves as embodied (or not embodied) directly relate to their material conditions (living situations, financial resources, and access to social and political power).

4. Copyright © 1980. Used by permission of Songtalk Publishing.

REFERENCES

1. American Psychological Association. 1987. *Diagnostic and statistical manual of mental disorders.* 3rd ed. rev., Washington, DC: American Psychological Association.

2. Andersen, Arnold, and Andy Hay. 1985. Racial and socioeconomic influences in anorexia nervosa and bulimia. *International Journal of Eating Disorders* 4:479–87.

3. Arnold, Georgiana. 1990. Coming home: One Black woman's journey to health and fitness. In *The Black women's health book: Speaking for ourselves,* edited by Evelyn C. White. Seattle, WA: Seal Press.

4. Avery, Byllye Y. 1990. Breathing life into ourselves: The evolution of the National Black Women's Health Project. In *The Black women's health book: Speaking for ourselves,* edited by Evelyn C. White. Seattle, WA:Seal Press.

5. Bass, Ellen, and Laura Davis. 1988. *The courage to heal: A guide for women survivors of child sexual abuse.* New York: Harper & Row.

6. Brown, Laura S. 1985. Women, weight and power: Feminist theoretical and therapeutic issues. *Women and Therapy* 4:61–71.

7. ———. 1987. Lesbians, weight and eating: New analyses and perspectives. In *Lesbian psychologies,* edited by the Boston Lesbian Psychologies Collective. Champaign: University of Illinois Press.

8. Chernin, Kim. 1981. *The obsession: Reflections on the tyranny of slenderness.* New York: Harper & Row.

9. Clarke, Cheryl. 1982. *Narratives.* New Brunswick, NJ: Sister Books.

10. Copeland, Paul M. 1985. Neuroendocrine aspects of eating disorders. In *Theory and treatment of anorexia nervosa and bulimia: Biomedical sociocultural and psychological perspectives,* edited by Steven Wiley Emmett. New York: Brunner/Mazel.

11. Delphy, Christine. 1984. *Close to home: A materialist analysis of women's oppression.* Amherst: University of Massachusetts Press.

12. DeSalvo, Louise. 1989. *Virginia Woolf: The impact of childhood sexual abuse on her life and work.* Boston, MA: Beacon.

13. Dworkin, Sari H. 1989. Not in man's image: Lesbians and the cultural oppression of body image. In *Loving boldly: Issues facing lesbians,* edited by Ester D. Rothblum and Ellen Cole. New York: Harrington Park Press.

14. Garfinkel, Paul E., and David M. Garner. 1982. *Anorexia nervosa: A multidimensional perspective.* New York: Brunner/Mazel.

15. Garner, David. 1985. Iatrogenesis in anorexia nervosa and bulimia nervosa. *International Journal of Eating Disorders* 4:701–26.

16. Glaser, Barney G., and Anselm L. Strauss. 1967. *The discovery of grounded theory: Strategies for qualitative research.* New York: Aldine DeGruyter.

17. Goldfarb, Lori. 1987. Sexual abuse antecedent to anorexia nervosa, bulimia and compulsive overeating: Three case reports. *International Journal of Eating Disorders* 6:675–80.

18. Gray, James, Kathryn Ford, and Lily M. Kelly. 1987. The prevalence of bulimia in a Black college population. *International Journal of Eating Disorders* 6:733–40.

19. Herman, Judith. 1981. *Father-daughter incest.* Cambridge, MA: Harvard University Press.

20. Higginbotham, Elizabeth. 1986. We were never on a pedestal: Women of color continue to struggle with poverty, racism and sexism. In *For crying out loud,* edited by Rochelle Lefkowitz and Ann Withorn. Boston, MA: Pilgrim Press.

21. Hsu, George. 1987. Are eating disorders becoming more common in Blacks? *International Journal of Eating Disorders* 6:113–24.

22. Iazzetto, Demetria, 1989. When the body is not an easy place to be: Women's sexual abuse and eating problems. Ph.D. diss., Union for Experimenting Colleges and Universities, Cincinnati, Ohio.

23. Kearney-Cooke, Ann. 1988. Group treatment of sexual abuse among women with eating disorders. *Women and Therapy* 7:5–21.

24. Marx, Karl. 1964. *The economic and philosophic manuscripts of 1844.* New York: International.

25. Masson, Jeffrey. 1984. *The assault on the truth: Freud's suppression of the seduction theory.* New York: Farrar, Strauss & Giroux.

26. Naylor, Gloria. 1985. *Linden Hills.* New York: Ticknor & Fields.

27. Nevo, Shoshana. 1985. Bulimic symptoms: Prevalence and ethnic differences among college women. *International Journal of Eating Disorders* 4:151–68.

28. Oppenheimer, R., K. Howells, R. L. Palmer, and D.A. Chaloner. 1985. Adverse sexual experience in childhood and clinical eating disorders: A preliminary description. *Journal of Psychiatric Research* 19:357–61.

29. Orbach, Susie. 1978. *Fat is a feminist issue.* New York: Paddington.

30. ———. 1985. Accepting the symptom: A feminist psychoanalytic treatment of anorexia nervosa. In *Handbook of psychotherapy for anorexia nervosa and bulimia,* edited by David M. Garner and Paul E. Garfinkel. New York: Guilford.

31. Powers, Retha. 1989. Fat is a Black women's issue. *Essence,* Oct., 75, 78, 134, 136.

32. Reagon, Bernice Johnson. 1980. Oughta be a woman. On Sweet Honey in the Rock's album, *Good News.* Music by Bernice Johnson Reagon; lyrics by June Jordan. Washington, DC: Songtalk.

33. Rich, Adrienne. 1986. Compulsory heterosexuality and lesbian existence. In *Blood, bread and poetry.* New York: Norton.

34. Root, Maria P. P., and Patricia Fallon. 1988. The incidence of victimization experiences in a bulimic sample. *Journal of Interpersonal Violence* 3:161–73.

35. ———. 1989. Treating the victimized bulimic: The functions of binge-purge behavior. *Journal of Interpersonal Violence* 4:90–100.

36. Russell, Diana E. 1986. *The secret trauma: Incest in the lives of girls and women.* New York: Basic Books.

37. Schoenfielder, Lisa, and Barbara Wieser, eds. 1983. *Shadow on a tightrope: Writings by women about fat liberation.* Iowa City, IA: Aunt Lute Book Co.

38. Silber, Tomas. 1986. Anorexia nervosa in Blacks and Hispanics. *International Journal of Eating Disorders* 5:121–28.

39. Silberstein, Lisa, Ruth Striegel-Moore, and Judith Rodin. 1987. Feeling fat: A woman's shame. In *The role of shame in symptom formation,* edited by Helen Block Lewis. Hillsdale, NJ: Lawrence Erlbaum.

40. Smead, Valerie. 1984. Eating behaviors which may lead to and perpetuate anorexia nervosa, bulimarexia, and bulimia. *Women and Therapy* 3:37–49.

41. Spack, Norman. 1985. Medical complications of anorexia nervosa and bulimia. In *Theory and treatment of anorexia nervosa and bulimia: Biomedical sociocultural and psychological perspectives,* edited by Steven Wiley Emmett. New York: Brunner/Mazel.

42. Swink, Kathy, and Antoinette E. Leveille. 1986. From victim to survivor: A new look at the issues and recovery process for adult incest survivors. *Women and Therapy* 5:119–43.

43. Trimble, Michael. 1985. Post-traumatic stress disorder: History of a concept. In *Trauma and its wake: The study and treatment of post-traumatic stress disorder,* edited by C. R. Figley. New York: Brunner/Mazel.

44. What's important is what you look like. 1988. *Gay Community News,* July, 24–30.

45. White, Evelyn C., ed. 1990. *The Black women's health book: Speaking for ourselves.* Seattle, WA: Seal Press.

46. ———. 1991. Unhealthy appetites. *Essence,* Sept., 28, 30.

49

Sounds and Silences of Language

Perpetuating Institutionalized Privilege and Oppression

DENA R. SAMUELS

Language has tremendous power to shape attitudes and influence behavior.

—LAUREL RICHARDSON

Our language use tells us much about who we are, where we come from, and what our biases and prejudices are. Language is the way we interact with each other and the means by which we perpetuate oppression and privilege in society as well as in our own personal relationships. The words we use are either what we have been taught, or what we consciously choose to use, and often it is a combination of both.

When it comes to discussing issues of inequality in society such as sexism, racism, and heterosexism, we need language to process these volatile issues, or we may never get beyond them. Although the Civil Rights movement was relatively successful in challenging some forms of legal racism in the U.S., many people are under the false impression that our racial inequalities are a thing of the past, that we no longer need to discuss these issues because, after all, "we're all equal now." The reality is that the U.S. still has a long way to go in terms of reaching equality between all races.

In many ways, racism has become covert. Studies show that many people fear talking about race, or even mentioning someone's race, for fear of being labeled a racist (Gorski, 2004). Paul Gorski suggests that this is the reason white people created *political correctness:* "to develop a system in which everyone knew what to say in order to allow everyone to avoid . . . walking on egg shells" (p. 3).

Nevertheless, Beverly Daniel Tatum (1997), in her book *Why Are All the Black Kids Sitting Together in the Cafeteria?*, argues that race is still a taboo subject. She points out that we are socialized *not* to talk about race and learn that it is impolite to do so. In fact, adults have no idea how to respond when children bring up the subject.

> Imagine this scenario. A White mother and preschool child are shopping in the grocery store. They pass a Black woman and child, and the White child says loudly, "Mommy, look at that girl! Why is she so dirty?" (Confusing dark skin with dirt is a common misconception among White preschool children.) The White mother, embarrassed by her child's comment, responds quickly with a "Ssh!"
>
> An appropriate response might have been: "Honey, that little girl is not dirty. Her skin is as clean as yours. It's just a different color. Just like we have different hair color, people have different skin colors." If the child still seemed interested, the explanation of [different levels of] melanin could be added. Perhaps afraid of saying the wrong thing, however, many parents don't offer an explanation. . . . Children who have been silenced enough learn not to talk about race publicly. Their questions don't go away, they just go unasked. (Tatum, 36)

Parents who are proud that they have taught their children to be "color-blind" are, in fact, doing their children a disservice by teaching them to ignore differences. When other parents find out that I teach courses on Race and Gender for a living, they are quick to point out proudly, "When describing a person of color, my child *never* mentions race, but rather the clothes the person is wearing; my child does not even *see* race." The reality is, however, that everyone sees race; we are simply socialized to believe we should not mention it.

Why are parents, and even many teachers, afraid to bring up the subject of race? Unlike other physical differences like hair color, race has been given social meanings that have been used to support inequality. Being afraid to offend is one answer, but how can the subject of melanin, or simply the concept of difference, be considered offensive? There *are* differences between people. Why is that a taboo

subject? Perhaps since a productive discussion of differences leads to a discussion of inequalities, we had better just not bring it up. Further, if we are socialized to believe a discussion of differences is taboo, then we do not and will not know how to discuss our differences; we don't have the language for discussion, and further, no language is created or developed to speak about it. This is true for parents, teachers, grandparents, etc., which consequently makes it true for preschoolers. The result is that not only do we become afraid of speaking about race, but also, as a society, we literally become afraid of people of different races.

Tatum (1997) gives another example of this fear of speaking that is quite recognizable:

> My White college students sometimes refer to someone as Black in hushed tones, sometimes whispering the word as though it were a secret or a potentially scandalous identification. When I detect this behavior, I like to point it out, saying it is not an insult to identify a Black person as Black. (p. 37)

We must discuss race and racism, for ignoring these topics will not end racism; it certainly hasn't yet.

How do we learn *not* to speak about race? Consider for a moment your education. Did you learn about the contributions of peoples from any race other than white? Perhaps you were taught about Martin Luther King, Jr. and Rosa Parks during the month of February (Black History Month). You may have learned a little about Malcolm X and Gandhi. But it is likely that that was the extent of it. Robert Moore (2006) found that history books not only leave out people of color, but also use language to hide the responsibility of white men in the colonization of people of color and their cultures in the U.S. For example, D. Burgest (1973) explains the impact of using the terms "slave" and "master." If the statement "the master raped his slave" were changed to: "the white captor raped an African woman held in captivity," an altogether different implication is presented.

> Implicit in the English usage of the "master-slave" concept is ownership of the "slave" by the "master"; therefore, the "master" is merely abusing his property

(slave). In reality, the captives (slaves) were African individuals with human worth, right and dignity and the term "slave" denounces that human quality thereby making the mass rape of African women by white captors more acceptable in the minds of people and setting a mental frame of reference for legitimizing the atrocities perpetuated against African people.

Moore (2006) suggest that writers and readers of these topics try substituting "African people held in captivity" or "African people stolen from their families and societies" for the word "slaves" as it gives an entirely new and more accurate view of history.

Another example Moore examines is the words used to describe what happened to Native Americans when white men came to America.

> Eurocentrism turns . . . definitions around to serve the purpose of distorting history and justifying Euro-American conquest of the Native American homelands. Euro-Americans are not described in history books as invading Native American lands, but rather as defending *their* homes against "Indian" attacks. Since European communities were constantly encroaching on land already occupied, then a more honest interpretation would state that it was the Native Americans who were "warding off," "guarding" and "defending" their homelands. . . . Native American victories are invariably defined as "massacres," while the indiscriminate killing, extermination and plunder of Native American nations by Euro-Americans is defined as "victory." . . . Rather than portraying Native Americans as human beings in highly defined and complex societies, cultures and civilizations, history books use such adjectives as "savages," "beasts," "primitive," and "backward." (p. 479)

All of these examples demonstrate that language is a powerful tool in shaping our view of reality. Language is not only a communication tool, but clearly it constructs meaning for us depending on how it is used. Other than a few examples,[1] in most cases it is the "victor" who writes the history books, and in so doing, perpetuates historical myths about what really happened. Privilege in language use lets those who are privileged hide their atrocities, and maintain their privilege.

Another way that privilege plays out in language use is the tense used to describe horrendous acts. Julia Penelope (1990) reveals that the passive voice is often used to describe crimes against women. The research shows that overwhelmingly, rapes are reported in the media as: "women *were* raped," or "women *were* murdered," hiding the perpetrator's responsibility in the attack, and focusing instead on the victim. Jackson Katz, in the documentary, *Tough Guise* (Jhally, 1999), adds that this ignores the fact that most murders and rapes are committed by men. (In fact, 97% of sexual assault/rapes are committed by men.[2] 90% of people who commit violent physical assault are men. Males perpetrate 95% of all serious domestic violence.)[3] To ignore the role of men in these crimes is to miss an extremely important part of the equation and analysis in terms of figuring out how to curb violence against women. It also serves to protect those who are committing these crimes, perpetuating invisible male privilege.

Male privilege is also reinforced by the English language. Laurel Richardson (2002) points out that *"women* are included under the generic *man"* (p. 510). She states that most grammar books stipulate the pronoun *he* can be used as a generic form of *he* or *she*. Moreover, grammatically, *man* can refer to both men and women. So, we can interpret the following phrases as applying to both men and women: "man the oars," "one small step for man, one giant step [sic] for mankind," "man, that's tough," "man overboard," etc. (p. 510).

Many argue that it simply does not matter that we use the word *man* as generic for humans because everyone knows we mean humans, and not specifically men. However, Richardson points out:

> Research has consistently demonstrated that when the generic *man* is used, people visualize men, not women. . . . Man, then, suggests not humanity but rather male images. . . . One consequence is the exclusion of women in the visualization, imagination, and thought of males and females. (p. 510)

Richardson highlights the fact that this male-dominated language use has grave implications for the career aspirations of both males and females. For example, if young children hear the word "policeman" as opposed to "police officer," they will likely imagine a male in their minds. If young girls hear "policeman," they are much less likely to make a personal connection to this career path, rendering the belief that only boys can grow up to be policemen. This disconnect contributes to a self-fulfilling prophecy—in fact, the U.S. Department of Justice (2004) reports that the majority of police officers (88.4%) are still men. Richardson (2002) further points out that we tend to use *he* when referring to high status jobs (doctor, lawyer, judge) and *she* when referring to lower status jobs (nurse, secretary).

There are several avenues to eliminating this bias. One would be to use gender-neutral plural words such as *they.* Even the slightly unwieldy *s/he* is preferable to our current discriminatory linguistic practices. Further, we can use gender-neutral words such as *individual* or *person,* instead of *man;* and we can substitute the term *first-year student* for *freshman,* or *humanity* for *mankind.*

In a male-identified society, one might ask, what does it matter? Why make such a big deal about language when there are bigger issues to tackle? Paula Rothenberg (2000) answers this question with a thought-provoking idea. She suggests "that if the use of the pronoun is so inconsequential, we might as well use 'she' and 'her' instead of 'he' and 'him' for the next several hundred years. I have rarely met a man who shrugged his shoulders at this proposal and said 'why not!'" (p. 118).

In terms of sexual orientation, our history again shows that language has been used to privilege some and oppress others. Heterosexuality is the cultural standard and is referred to as being *straight.* In 1941, the dictionary definition for *straight* added: "conventional," especially "heterosexual," "course of conventional morality and law-abiding behavior."[4] What then does that mean for non-heterosexual people, that they are *crooked?* Although nowadays many people, heterosexual and otherwise, often use the word *straight* to refer to a heterosexual person, a linguistic hierarchy is perpetuated with this word, privileging heterosexuals while at the same time reinforcing the oppression of non-heterosexuals.

Another associated word is the term *queer,* which was historically used to mean strange or odd. Later, it was associated with gay males and used as an insult, often to debase a male and to label him weak. More recently, however, there has been an effort to "take back" the word *queer* by people in the gay and lesbian communities to highlight the diversity of sexualities in our culture. To be inclusive of many sexualities, the cumbersome term LGBTQI is often used, which encompasses: lesbian, gay, bisexual, transgender, queer, and intersex people. Each of these categories is distinct in its own right, and can, in some communities, include heterosexuals who are supportive of non-heterosexuals (adding the letter A for "allies" at the end of this already lengthy list). Many such communities have chosen simply to use the word *queer* to incorporate the diversity of sexualities, though this is not the case everywhere. The objective is to be inclusive and respectful.

It can often be empowering for certain groups to "take back" a word that was historically used to degrade them. Another example of this is the use of the word *black* to describe Americans of African descent. As Moore (2006) points out, the term *black* has been used with a negative connotation often to degrade a person or situation, yet in the 1960s it became a source of pride. The Black Power Movement challenged the prevailing myths of the time with t-shirts that proclaimed: "Black is Beautiful." This served to empower those who wore them, as well as those who saw them.

There are some words, however, that are so full of controversy that the question arises as to whether or not we should even use them. The word "nigger" is so volatile that the term "n-word" has been institutionalized for the main purpose of being able to have a discussion on the topic of race and racism. This is another example of the fact that words have meaning, and to say, "They're just words" does not reduce their impact, but rather simply demonstrates the lack of accountability on the part of the speaker.

Some people claim it depends on who uses the n-word as to whether or not it is acceptable. They often ask: why do some African-Americans think it is acceptable for them to use the n-word, but not white folks? Other say it makes a difference whether the word ends in 'er' or 'a,' though it is often difficult to hear the difference when it is spoken. *The Oprah Show* (Terry, 2005) presented a segment on the film *Crash* (Haggis, 2005) in which Oprah Winfrey hosted many of the cast members. They got into a discussion about the use of the n-word. The rapper/actor Chris "Ludacris" Bridges made the argument that he uses the n-word (with an 'a' at the end) in his lyrics to demonstrate how the word can be empowering in terms of taking it back. Actor Don Cheadle agreed, claiming that as an African-American, it is acceptable for him to use it, but that it is unacceptable for white folks to use it. He stated:

> It's transformative. We're going to take this word that you've used as a weapon against us and we're going to incorporate it so it is not a weapon within our own culture, and use it to one another, so it's not harmful to each other.

Oprah flatly disagreed, countering, "it is a racially charged, demeaning term (that is) derogatory no matter who is using it." She stated, "I don't like it because it carries too much pain with it. Every guy who was ever lynched in Mississippi, when they were hanging him, they were using that word."

Actor Terrence Howard then declared, "After thinking about it, I do believe that it should be stopped because there are too many negative associations with it, and it's perpetuating an idea." Howard's uncertainty and subsequent resolution clearly demonstrates the need for discussion on this topic so that people can make informed choices about the language they use. People need to understand the power of their words and take responsibility for how they use language.

Tim Wise (2002) sheds some light on the question of who is using what language, and the power inequalities that inform language use. In his well-known piece "Honky Wanna Cracker?" Wise reflects on the difference between a white person calling a black person the n-word, and a black person calling a white person *honky*.

> When a group of people [of color] has little or no power over you [a white person] institutionally, they don't get to define the terms of your existence, they can't limit your opportunities, and you needn't worry much about the use of a slur to describe you and yours, since, in all likelihood, the slur is as far as it's going to go. What are they going to do next: deny you a bank loan? Yeah, right.
> So whereas "nigger" was and is a term used by whites to dehumanize blacks, to imply their inferiority, to "put them in their place" if you will, the same cannot be said of honky: after all, you can't put white people in their place when they own the place to begin with. (p. 2)

In his discussion, Wise raises the important question of power: who has it and who does not. He is not suggesting that it is acceptable for anyone to call a white person *honky* or *cracker,* but rather that the significance and historical weight of these words are on a whole different level than a white person using the n-word. The words we use can either perpetuate this historical hierarchy of power or challenge it.

Our words have meaning. We do not speak in a vacuum, out of context. We have a history of inequality in our society that is perpetuated by the language we choose to use every day, in every situation we are a part of, and in every conversation or comment we make. We always have a choice in the language we choose to use.

One of my students in an Introduction to Race and Gender course wrote a reflection paper describing her experience with the derogatory use of the statement, "that's gay." She mentioned that she had used the phrase many times to mean "that's stupid" even though she said she was completely supportive of the gay community. Once she realized she was using this phrase in a derogatory manner, and how it might make others feel, she made the conscious choice not to continue to use the phrase. The result was that her very good friend finally told her he was gay. As it turned out, she was among the last of their friends that he entrusted with this information. In fact, he couldn't even say the words, he had to write them down. My student wrote:

> I couldn't help but think that most of his hesitation came from me using that phrase ("that's gay"). We really never had a discussion on homosexuality before so he never knew what my real thoughts on it were. So the only view he thought I had on it was negative because of the language I used. This really opened my eyes to the fact that the language you use does have an effect on people around you, and you might not even know it.

Again, the salient point here is that this student, like many people, regularly uses derogatory language that she never even thinks about. She did not consider herself "anti-gay"; she had just never critically analyzed her use of language because offensive language is often normalized in our culture.

Another example of this is when my son had a birthday party at our house when he turned 10. All of a sudden from the backyard I heard someone yell, "Let's play *Smear the Queer!*" This is some form of tackle game, but when I asked the kids why they used this name, they had no idea. In fact, when I asked them what *queer* meant, they had no idea. These young kids were not being deliberately offensive or homophobic; they had simply heard the game's name from others. Offensive language often permeates society surreptitiously, preparing its young members to be homophobic—preparing kids to hate.

Although some people purposefully choose to perpetuate inequality through their language use (e.g., *choosing* to use *man* as the generic form of *human*), most people simply do not recognize language as offensive or derogatory; it is simply what they have been taught and what has been accepted as the norm. And it can be quite uncomfortable to challenge these norms. It is not an easy path, but it is an important one.

We can start by thinking and talking about our language use. As Allan Johnson (2006) states:

> You can't deal with a problem if you don't name it. Once you name it, you can think, talk, and write about it, make sense of it by seeing how it's connected to other things that explain it and point toward solutions. (p. 9)

We must challenge the notion that discussion of race, gender, sexuality, and their connected privileges and oppressions have to remain taboo. We must instead find, create, and use language that will enable us to have these important discussions.

Because language that perpetuates inequality is socially constructed, it can be constructed differently. We can choose words that are not disparaging, but rather lift people up and include them, to show them that they are being accurately represented. We can take Robert Moore's (2006) suggestion and research the etymology of words to learn whether they are racist or not. We can learn how to be inclusive in our language use so women, people of color, LGBTQI folks, and others don't feel excluded. We can choose to be part of the solution to inequality.

NOTES

1. For examples of history books that tell a more accurate version of history, often from the perspectives of those who have been oppressed, see *Lies My Teacher Told Me: Everything Your American History Textbook Got Wrong* by James W. Loewen and *A People's History of the United States* by Howard Zinn.
2. U.S. Department of Justice, Bureau of Justice Statistics, Criminal Victimization in the United States, 2004 from http://www.ojp.usdoj.gov/bjs/pub/pdf/cvus0402.pdf.
3. U.S. Department of Justice, Bureau of Justice Statistics, Sourcebook of Criminal Justice Statistics Online. http://www.albany.edu/sourcebook.
4. Online Etymology Dictionary from http://www.etymonline.com/index.php?term=straight.

REFERENCES

1. Burgest, D. R. (1973). "The Racist Use of the English Language." *Black Scholar,* Sept. 1973.
2. Gorski, P. (2004). "Language of Closet Racism: An Illustration." In Vernellia R. Randall (Ed.) *Race, Racism and the Law: Speaking Truth to Power!!* from http://academic.udayton.edu/race/01race/whiteness02.htm
3. Haggis, P. (Director). (2005). *Crash* [Film]. United States: Lions Gate.
4. Jhally, S. (Director). (1999). *Tough Guise: Violence, Media & the Crisis in Masculinity* [*Featuring* Jackson Katz] [Film]. United States: Media Education Foundation.
5. Johnson, A. G. (2006). *Privilege, Power, and Difference.* 2nd ed. New York: McGraw-Hill.
6. Moore, R. B. (2006). "Racism in the English Language." In Tracy E. Ore (Ed.) *The Social Construction of*

Difference and Inequality: Race, Class, Gender, and Sexuality. 3rd Ed. Pp. 473–483. New York: McGraw-Hill.

7. Penelope, J. (1990). *Speaking Freely: Unlearning the Lies of the Fathers' Tongues.* New York: Pergamon Press.

8. Richardson, L. (2002). "Gender Stereotyping in the English Language." In Karen E. Rosenblum and Toni-Michelle C. Travis (Eds.) *The Meaning of Difference: American Constructions of Race, Sex and Gender, Social Class, and Sexual Orientation.* 3rd ed. Pp. 509–515. New York: McGraw-Hill.

9. Rothenberg, P. (2000). *Invisible Privilege: A Memoir about Race, Class, and Gender.* Lawrence: University Press of Kansas.

10. Tatum, B. D. (1997). *Why Are All the Black Kids Sitting Together in the Cafeteria?* Revised ed. New York: Basic Books.

11. Terry, J. C. (Director.) (2005, October 6). *The Oprah Show.* Chicago: Central Broadcasting System.

12. U.S. Department of Justice, Federal Bureau of Investigation Report. (2004). "Crime in the United States: Law Enforcement Personnel: Table 74" from http://www.fbi.gov/ucr/cius_04/law_enforcement_personnel/table_74.html.

13. Wise, T. (2002). "Honky Wanna Cracker?" from http://www.zmag.org/sustainers/content/2002-06/24wise.cfm.

✳ 50

Katrina's Race and Class Effects Were Planned

GREGORY D. SQUIRES

The race and class effects of Katrina were by design. The fact that poor people and racial minorities suffered by far the greatest harm from Katrina was guaranteed by decades of public policy and private practice. If the hurricane was a natural disaster, allocation of its costs were determined by political decisions grounded in longstanding social and economic inequalities.

The most obvious race and class implication, of course, is that those with the means to do so left. They had cars or money for planes and trains along with friends and contacts who could provide them shelter in other locales. Guests trapped in one luxury New Orleans hotel were saved when that chain hired a fleet of buses to get them out. Patients in one hospital were saved when a doctor who knew Al

Gore contacted the former Vice President who was able to cut through government red tape and charter two planes that flew them to safety.

More importantly, the conditions shaping the race and class effects have been building for decades. In New Orleans as in virtually all other communities, various processes of racial segregation have resulted in middle income whites being concentrated in the outlying (and in New Orleans literally higher) suburban communities while blacks have been concentrated in the central city.

Racial steering by real estate agents, exclusionary zoning in suburban municipalities, federally subsidized highways to help suburban commuters get to their jobs, tax breaks to subsidize suburban business development, and the concentration of poor people in inner city public housing projects are just some of the forces in New Orleans and elsewhere that led to the racial segregation and concentration of poverty. The sprawl machine has been operating in New Orleans to spread wealth outward and concentrate poverty in the central city.

Douglas Massey, co-author of the classic book *American Apartheid,* has long warned of the catastrophic consequences of racial segregation and concentrated poverty. He observed that "any process that concentrates poverty within racially isolated neighborhoods will simultaneously increase the odds of socioeconomic failure." The disproportionate suffering in New Orleans is illustrative of that failure.

Neglect of critical infrastructure needs also shaped the inequitable consequences of Katrina. As has now been widely reported, officals long knew the protective levees surrounding the city were inadequate leaving it vulnerable to precisely this type of disaster. But New Orleans is hardly the only city that has failed to maintain its infrastructure.

Whether it is the deteriorating subway system in New York, inadequate earthquake protection in San Francisco, the aging water mains in Chicago and Washington DC (and no doubt elsewhere), cracking roads and bridges in all regions of the country, and other declining public services, we have not maintained vital systems. Most cities are disasters waiting to happen.

In its *2005 Report Card for America's Infrastructure* the American Society of Civil Engineers concluded "Congested highways, overflowing sewers and corroding bridges are constant reminders of the looming crisis that jeopardizes our nation's prosperity and quality of life." Assessing 12 infrastructure categories the Society gave the nation a D for its maintenance efforts, noting there had been little improvement in recent years and asserting an as yet unfunded $1.6 trillion investment need over the next five years. The consequences have not been and will not be race or class neutral. As James Carr, Senior Vice President of Research for the Fannie Mae Foundation, observed[,] if the City of New Orleans had been a more diverse community it may well have had the political clout to secure the levees long ago.

Yet we persist in treating government services as costs to be reduced rather than vital services in which we should invest. The Economic Policy Institute recently reported that federal investment in key areas of the infrastructure of cities (education, transportation, and research) as a share of total economic output has declined consistently over the past 30 years by more than 35 percent. Citizens for Tax Justice reported that in recent years federal taxes rates on investment income have declined to an average of 9.6 percent while tax rates on wages and other earnings have grown to 23.4 percent. Low-income people and people of color are more dependent on public services and receive more of their income from wages than investments compared to middle- and upper-income groups, so they are disproportionately affected by these developments. They are more dependent on public transportation to get to work, local police to keep their neighborhoods safe, and emergency services of all sorts. And they have fewer private resources to serve as cushions in times of stress including periods of unemployment, unexpected illness, or natural disasters like hurricanes.

But all of us pay (though in varying degrees) when public transit systems come to a halt, earthquakes destroy bridges, and floods destroy entire neighborhoods if not cities. Even suburban employers and homeowners lose when they cannot get the workers or services they need. A combination of tax cuts for the wealthy and an expensive war in Iraq do not help this situation. But the race and class effects undermining the quality of life for all are not the outcomes of any particular Presidential administration, and it is not just the poor or racial minorities who lose. In connecting the plantation mentality that has long shaped race relations in New Orleans with the devastation that wracked the entire region, historian Christopher Morris concluded[,] "If the city never recovers, it won't be just because of the natural environment. It will be because long ago the whites of New Orleans, and whites in Washington and around the nation, made a bargain with the devil of white supremacy, and now they, we, will have now lost it all."

Some of this reflects overt racial prejudice. But it is a deeper reflection of what has become known as "color blind racism" whereby we convince ourselves that current inequalities result from the failures of those who suffer rather than the continuing effects of historical and contemporary forms of institutionalized privilege. To illustrate, then FEMA Director Michael Brown said the human suffering following Katrina could be explained by "people who did not heed evacuation warnings." The implication is that these people simply chose to remain rather than the fact that most did not have the means to escape; a car, money for and access to a train or bus ticket, or a place to go to if they could get out. United for a Fair Economy reported, for example, that 24 percent of black households and 17 percent of Latino households, compared to just 7 percent of whites, did not have a car, yet evacuation plans focused on those who had automobiles. Images of black looters, of course, reinforce traditional stereotypes and do little to encourage a broader, sociological understanding of these events. But that is the challenge we must confront, in New Orleans and elsewhere.

This hardly suggests a vast conspiracy against poor people or racial minorities. But it is evident that a series of decades-long public policies and private practices that clearly privilege middle and upper income, and predominantly white communities have made the inequitable effects of natural disasters like Katrina inevitable.

The race and class effects of Katrina should come as no surprise. We have been planning them for decades.

51

Media Magic

Making Class Invisible

GREGORY MANTSIOS

Of the various social and cultural forces in our society, the mass media is arguably the most influential in molding public consciousness. Americans spend an average twenty-eight hours per week watching television. They also spend an undetermined number of hours reading periodicals, listening to the radio, and going to the movies. Unlike other cultural and socializing institutions, ownership and control of the mass media is highly concentrated. Twenty-three corporations own more than one-half of all the daily newspapers, magazines, movie studios, and radio and television outlets in the United States.[1] The number of media companies is shrinking and their control of the industry is expanding. And a relatively small number of media outlets is producing and packaging the majority of news and entertainment programs. For the most part, our media is national in nature and single-minded (profit-oriented) in purpose. This media plays a key role in defining our cultural tastes, helping us locate ourselves in history, establishing our national identity, and ascertaining the range of national and social possibilities. In this essay, we will examine the way the mass media shapes how people think about each other and about the nature of our society.

The United States is the most highly stratified society in the industrialized world. Class distinctions operate in virtually every aspect of our lives, determining the nature of our work, the quality of our schooling, and the health and safety of our loved ones. Yet remarkably, we, as a nation, retain illusions about living in an egalitarian society. We maintain these illusions, in large part, because the media hides gross inequities from public view. In those instances when inequities are revealed, we are provided with messages that obscure the nature of class realities and blame the victims of class-dominated society for their own plight. Let's briefly examine what the news media, in particular, tells us about class.

ABOUT THE POOR

The news media provides meager coverage of poor people and poverty. The coverage it does provide is often distorted and misleading.

The Poor Do Not Exist

For the most part, the news media ignores the poor. Unnoticed are forty million poor people in the nation—a number that equals the entire population of Maine, Vermont, New Hampshire, Connecticut, Rhode Island, New Jersey, and New York combined. Perhaps even more alarming is that the rate of poverty is increasing twice as fast as the population growth in the United States. Ordinarily, even a calamity of much smaller proportion (e.g., flooding in the Midwest) would garner a great deal of coverage and hype from a media usually eager to declare a crisis, yet less than one in five hundred articles in the *New York Times* and one in one thousand articles listed in the *Readers Guide to Periodic Literature* are on poverty. With remarkably little attention to them, the poor and their problems are hidden from most Americans.

When the media does turn its attention to the poor, it offers a series of contradictory messages and portrayals.

The Poor Are Faceless

Each year the Census Bureau releases a new report on poverty in our society and its results are duly reported in the media. At best, however, this coverage emphasizes annual fluctuations (showing how the numbers differ from previous years) and ongoing debates over the validity of the numbers (some argue the number should be lower, most that the number should be higher). Coverage like this desensitizes us to the poor by reducing poverty to a number. It ignores the human tragedy of poverty— the suffering, indignities, and misery endured by millions of children and adults. Instead, the poor become statistics rather than people.

The Poor Are Undeserving

When the media does put a face on the poor, it is not likely to be a pretty one. The media will provide us with sensational stories about welfare cheats, drug addicts, and greedy panhandlers (almost always urban and Black). Compare these images and the emotions evoked by them with the media's treatment of middle-class (usually white) "tax evaders," celebrities who have a "chemical dependency," or wealthy businesspeople who use unscrupulous means to "make a profit." While the behavior of the more affluent offenders is considered an "impropriety" and a deviation from the norm, the behavior of the poor is considered repugnant, indicative of the poor in general, and worthy of our indignation and resentment.

The Poor Are an Eyesore

When the media does cover the poor, they are often presented through the eyes of the middle class. For example, sometimes the media includes a story about community resistance to a homeless shelter or storekeeper annoyance with panhandlers. Rather than focusing on the plight of the poor, these stories are about middle-class opposition to the poor. Such stories tell us that the poor are an inconvenience and an irritation.

The Poor Have Only Themselves to Blame

In another example of media coverage, we are told that the poor live in a personal and cultural cycle of poverty that hopelessly imprisons them. They routinely center on the Black urban population and focus on perceived personality or cultural traits that doom the poor. While the women in these stories typically exhibit an "attitude" that leads to trouble or a promiscuity that leads to single motherhood, the men possess a need for immediate gratification that leads to drug abuse or an unquenchable greed that leads to the pursuit of fast money. The images that are seared into our mind are sexist, racist, and classist. Census figures reveal that most of the poor are white, not Black or Hispanic, that they live in rural or suburban areas, not urban centers, and hold jobs at least part of the year.[2] Yet, in a fashion that is often framed in an understanding and sympathetic tone, we are told that the poor have inflicted poverty on themselves.

The Poor Are Down on Their Luck

During the Christmas season, the news media sometimes provides us with accounts of poor individuals or families (usually white) who are down on their luck. These stories are often linked to stories about soup kitchens or other charitable activities and sometimes call for charitable contributions. These "Yule time" stories are as much about the affluent as they are about the poor: they tell us that the affluent in our society are a kind, understanding, giving people—which we are not.* The series of unfortunate circumstances that have led to impoverishment are presumed to be a temporary condition that will improve with time and a change in luck.

---

*American households with incomes of less than $10,000 give an average of 5.5 percent of their earning to charity or to a religious organization, while those making more than $100,000 a year give only 2.9 percent. After changes in the 1986 tax code reduced the benefits of charitable giving, taxpayers earning $500,000 or more slashed their average donation by nearly one-third. Furthermore, many of these acts of benevolence do not help the needy. Rather than provide funding to social service agencies that aid the poor, the voluntary contributions of the wealthy go to places and institutions that entertain, inspire, cure, or educate wealthy Americans—art museums, opera houses, theaters, orchestras, ballet companies, private hospitals, and elite universities. (Robert Reich, "Secession of the Successful," *New York Times Magazine,* February 17, 1991, p. 43.)

Despite appearances, the messages provided by the media are not entirely disparate. With each variation, the media informs us what poverty is not (i.e., systemic and indicative of American society) by informing us what it is. The media tells us that poverty is either an aberration of the American way of life (it doesn't exist, it's just another number, it's unfortunate but temporary) or an end product of the poor themselves (they are a nuisance, do not deserve better, and have brought their predicament upon themselves).

By suggesting that the poor have brought poverty upon themselves, the media is engaging in what William Ryan has called "blaming the victim."[3] The media identifies in what ways the poor are different as a consequence of deprivation, then defines those differences as the cause of poverty itself. Whether blatantly hostile or cloaked in sympathy, the message is that there is something fundamentally wrong with the victims—their hormones, psychological makeup, family environment, community, race, or some combination of these—that accounts for their plight and their failure to lift themselves out of poverty.

But poverty in the United States is systemic. It is a direct result of economic and political policies that deprive people of jobs, adequate wages, or legitimate support. It is neither natural nor inevitable: there is enough wealth in our nation to eliminate poverty if we chose to redistribute existing wealth or income. The plight of the poor is reason enough to make the elimination of poverty the nation's first priority. But poverty also impacts dramatically on the nonpoor. It has a dampening effect on wages in general (by maintaining a reserve army of unemployed and underemployed anxious for any job at any wage) and breeds crime and violence (by maintaining conditions that invite private gain by illegal means and rebellion-like behavior, not entirely unlike the urban riots of the 1960s). Given the extent of poverty in the nation and the impact it has on us all, the media must spin considerable magic to keep the poor and the issue of poverty and its root causes out of the public consciousness.

ABOUT EVERYONE ELSE

Both the broadcast and the print news media strive to develop a strong sense of "we-ness" in their audience. They seek to speak to and for an audience that is both affluent and like-minded. The media's solidarity with affluence, that is, with the middle and upper class, varies little from one medium to another. Benjamin DeMott points out, for example, that the *New York Times* understands affluence to be intelligence, taste, public spirit, responsibility, and a readiness to rule and "conceives itself as spokesperson for a readership awash in these qualities."[4] Of course, the flip side to creating a sense of "we," or "us," is establishing a perception of the "other." The other relates back to the faceless, amoral, undeserving, and inferior "underclass." Thus, the world according to the news media is divided between the "underclass" and everyone else. Again the messages are often contradictory.

The Wealthy Are Us

Much of the information provided to us by the news media focuses attention on the concerns of a very wealthy and privileged class of people. Although the concerns of a small fraction of the populace, they are presented as though they were the concerns of everyone. For example, while relatively few people actually own stock, the news media devotes an inordinate amount of broadcast time and print space to business news and stock market quotations. Not only do business reports cater to a particular narrow clientele, so do the fashion pages (with $2,000 dresses), wedding announcements, and the obituaries. Even weather and sports news often have a class bias. An all news radio station in New York City, for example, provides regular national ski reports. International news, trade agreements, and domestic policies issues are also reported in terms of their impact on business climate and the business community. Besides being of practical value to the wealthy, such coverage has considerable ideological value. Its message: the concerns of the wealthy are the concerns of us all.

The Wealthy (as a Class) Do Not Exist

While preoccupied with the concerns of the wealthy, the media fails to notice the way in which the rich as a class of people create and shape domestic and foreign policy. Presented as an aggregate of individuals, the wealthy appear without special interests, interconnections, or unity in purpose. Out of public view are the class interests of the wealthy, the interlocking business links, the concerted actions to preserve their class privileges and business interests (by running for public office, supporting political candidates, lobbying, etc.). Corporate lobbying is ignored, taken for granted, or assumed to be in the public interest. (Compare this with the media's portrayal of the "strong arm of labor" in attempting to defeat trade legislation that is harmful to the interests of working people.) It is estimated that two-thirds of the U.S. Senate is composed of millionaires.[5] Having such a preponderance of millionaires in the Senate, however, is perceived to be neither unusual nor antidemocratic; these millionaire senators are assumed to be serving "our" collective interests in governing.

The Wealthy Are Fascinating and Benevolent

The broadcast and print media regularly provide hype for individuals who have achieved "super" success. These stories are usually about celebrities and superstars from the sports and entertainment world. Society pages and gossip columns serve to keep the social elite informed of each others' doings, allow the rest of us to gawk at their excesses, and help to keep the American dream alive. The print media is also fond of feature stories on corporate empire builders. These stories provide an occasional "insider's" view of the private and corporate life of industrialists by suggesting a rags to riches account of corporate success. These stories tell us that corporate success is a series of smart moves, shrewd acquisitions, timely mergers, and well thought out executive suite shuffles. By painting the upper class in a positive light, innocent of any wrongdoing (labor leaders and union organizations usually get the opposite treatment), the media assures us that wealth and power are benevolent. One person's capital accumulation is presumed to be good for all. The elite, then, are portrayed as investment wizards, people of special talent and skill, whom even their victims (workers and consumers) can admire.

The Wealthy Include a Few Bad Apples

On rare occasions, the media will mock selected individuals for their personality flaws. Real estate investor Donald Trump and New York Yankees owner George Steinbrenner, for example, are admonished by the media for deliberately seeking publicity (a very un-upper class thing to do); hotel owner Leona Helmsley was caricatured for her personal cruelties; and junk bond broker Michael Milkin was condemned because he had the audacity to rob the rich. Michael Parenti points out that by treating business wrongdoings as isolated deviations from the socially beneficial system of "responsible capitalism," the media overlooks the features of the system that produce such abuses and the regularity with which they occur. Rather than portraying them as predictable and frequent outcomes of corporate power and the business system, the media treats abuses as if they were isolated and atypical. Presented as an occasional aberration, these incidents serve not to challenge, but to legitimate, the system.[6]

The Middle Class Is Us

By ignoring the poor and blurring the lines between the working people and the upper class, the news media creates a universal middle class. From this perspective, the size of one's income becomes largely irrelevant: what matters is that most of "us" share an intellectual and moral superiority over the disadvantaged. As *Time* magazine once concluded, "Middle America is a state of mind."[7] "We are all middle class," we are told, "and we all share the same concerns": job security, inflation, tax burdens, world peace, the cost of food and housing, health care, clean air and water, and the safety of our streets. While the concerns of the wealthy are quite distinct from those of the middle class (e.g., the wealthy worry about investments, not jobs), the media convinces us that "we [the affluent] are all in this together."

The Middle Class Is a Victim

For the media, "we" the affluent not only stand apart from the "other"—the poor, the working class, the minorities, and their problems—"we" are also victimized by the poor (who drive up the costs of maintaining the welfare [rolls]), minorities (who commit crimes against us), and workers (who are greedy and drive companies out and prices up). Ignored are the subsidies to the rich, the crimes of corporate America, and the policies that wreak havoc on the economic well-being of middle America. Media magic convinces us to fear, more than anything else, being victimized by those less affluent than ourselves.

The Middle Class Is Not a Working Class

The news media clearly distinguishes the middle class (employees) from the working class (i.e., blue collar workers) who are portrayed, at best, as irrelevant, outmoded, and a dying breed. Furthermore, the media will tell us that the hardships faced by blue collar workers are inevitable (due to progress), a result of bad luck (chance circumstances in a particular industry), or a product of their own doing (they priced themselves out of a job). Given the media's presentation of reality, it is hard to believe that manual, supervised, unskilled, and semiskilled workers actually represent more than 50 percent of the adult working population.[8] The working class, instead, is relegated by the media to "the other."

In short, the news media either lionizes the wealthy or treats their interests and those of the middle class as one [and] the same. But the upper class and the middle class do not share the same interests or worries. Members of the upper class worry about stock dividends (not employment), they profit from inflation and global militarism, their children attend exclusive private schools, they eat and live in a royal fashion, they call on (or are called upon by) personal physicians, they have few consumer problems, they can escape whenever they want from environmental pollution, and they live on streets and travel to other areas under the protection of private police forces.*[9]

The wealthy are not only a class with distinct life-styles and interests, they are a ruling class. They receive a disproportionate share of the country's yearly income, own a disproportionate amount of the country's wealth, and contribute a disproportionate number of their members to governmental bodies and decision-making groups—all traits that William Domhoff, in his classic work *Who Rules America*, defined as characteristic of a governing class.[10]

This governing class maintains and manages our political and economic structures in such a way that these structures continue to yield an amazing proportion of our wealth to a minuscule upper class. While the media is not above referring to ruling classes in other countries (we hear, for example, references to Japan's ruling elite),[11] its treatment of the news proceeds as though there were no such ruling class in the United States.

Furthermore, the news media inverts reality so that those who are working class and middle class learn to fear, resent, and blame those below, rather than those above, them in the class structure. We learn to resent welfare, which accounts for only two cents out of every dollar in the

---

*The number of private security guards in the United States now exceeds the number of public police officers. (Robert Reich, "Secession of the Successful," *New York Times Magazine*, February 17, 1991, p. 42.)

federal budget (approximately $10 billion) and provides financial relief for the needy,* but learn little about the $11 billion the federal government spends on individuals with incomes in excess of $100,000 (not needy),[12] or the $17 billion in farm subsidies, or the $214 billion (twenty times the cost of welfare) in interest payments to financial institutions.

Middle-class whites learn to fear African Americans and Latinos, but most violent crime occurs within poor and minority communities and is neither interracial† nor interclass. As horrid as such crime is, it should not mask the destruction and violence perpetrated by corporate America. In spite of the fact that 14,000 innocent people are killed on the job each year, 100,000 die prematurely, 400,000 become seriously ill, and 6 million are injured from work-related accidents and diseases, most Americans fear government regulation more than they do unsafe working conditions.

Through the media, middle-class—and even working-class—Americans learn to blame blue collar workers and their unions for declining purchasing power and economic security. But while workers who managed to keep their jobs and their unions struggled to keep up with inflation, the top 1 percent of American families saw their average incomes soar 80 percent in the last decade.[13] Much of the wealth at the top was accumulated as stockholders and corporate executives moved their companies abroad to employ cheaper labor (56 cents per hour in El Salvador) and avoid paying taxes in the United States. Corporate America is a world made up of ruthless bosses, massive layoffs, favoritism and nepotism, health and safety violations, pension plan losses, union busting, tax evasions, unfair competition, and price gouging, as well as fast buck deals, financial speculation, and corporate wheeling and dealing that serve the interests of the corporate elite, but are generally wasteful and destructive to workers and the economy in general.

It is no wonder Americans cannot think straight about class. The mass media are neither objective, balanced, independent, nor neutral. Those who own and direct the mass media are themselves part of the upper class, and neither they nor the ruling class in general have to conspire to manipulate public opinion. Their interest is in preserving the status quo, and their view of society as fair and equitable comes naturally to them. But their ideology dominates our society and justifies what is in reality a perverse social order—one that perpetuates unprecedented elite privilege and power on the one hand and widespread deprivation on the other. A mass media that did not have its own class interests in preserving the status quo would acknowledge that inordinate wealth and power undermines democracy and that a "free market" economy can ravage a people and their communities.

---

*A total of $20 billion is spent on welfare when you include all state funding. But the average state funding also comes to only two cents per state dollar.
†In 92 percent of the murders nationwide the assailant and the victim are of the same race (46 percent are white/white, 46 percent are black/black, 5.6 percent are black on white, and 2.4 percent are white on black. (FBI and Bureau of Justice Statistics, 1985–1986, quoted in Raymond S. Franklin, *Shadows of Race and Class*, University of Minnesota Press, Minneapolis, 1991, p. 108.)

NOTES

1. Martin Lee and Norman Solomon, *Unreliable Sources*, Lyle Stuart (New York, 1990), p. 71. See also Ben Bagdikian, *The Media Monopoly*, Beacon Press (Boston, 1990).
2. Department of Commerce, Bureau of the Census, "Poverty in the United States: 1992," *Current Population Reports, Consumer Income*, Series P60–185, pp. xi, xv, 1.
3. William Ryan, *Blaming the Victim*, Vintage (New York, 1971).
4. Benjamin Demott, *The Imperial Middle*, William Morrow (New York, 1990), p. 123.
5. Fred Barnes, "The Zillionaires Club," *The New Republic*, January 29, 1990, p. 24.

6. Michael Parenti, *Inventing Reality*, St. Martin's Press (New York, 1986), p. 109.
7. *Time*, January 5, 1979, p. 10.
8. Vincent Navarro, "The Middle Class—A Useful Myth," *The Nation*, March 23, 1992, p.1.
9. Charles Anderson, *The Political Economy of Social Class*, Prentice Hall (Englewood Cliffs, N.J., 1974), p. 137.
10. William Domhoff, *Who Rules America*, Prentice Hall (Englewood Cliffs, N.J., 1967), p. 5.
11. Lee and Solomon, *Unreliable Sources*, p. 179.
12. *Newsweek*, August 10, 1992, p. 57.
13. *Business Week*, June 8, 1992, p. 86.

20 *Stereotypes and Admonitions: Housing Discrimination*

2003. Acrylic on Canvas, 20″ × 24″. Greg Kucera Gallery.

Artist Roger Shimomura is Japanese-American and draws upon both the traditions of Japanese printmaking and American pop art in his work. He interrogates stereotypes of Japanese-Americans and highlights racial inequality in the US. His series, "American Diary," depicts images of the internment of Japanese-Americans during WWII. These images are taken from his series, "Stereotypes and Admonitions," which aims to appropriate stereotypical caricatures in order to subvert them. Do you think his work is successful at doing that? Can you think of other examples of contemporary visual or performing artists or comedians whom similarly attempt to reclaim stereotypes or offensive language?

V. Be the Change

Andrea O'Reilly Herrera

Be kind, for everyone you meet is undergoing a great battle.
—PHILO OF ALEXANDRIA

To think oneself free simply because one can claim—
can utter—the negation of an assertion is not
to think deep enough.
—HENRY LOUIS GATES, *BLACK LITERATURE*
AND LITERARY THEORY

Survival is not an academic skill.
—AUDRE LORDE, *SISTER OUTSIDER*

The preliminary step toward dismantling any system of oppression and privilege is to explore and acknowledge the historical underpinnings of racism, sexism, classism, homophobia, and other forms of institutionalized inequality. As the essays in the previous sections demonstrate, contemporary systems of oppression and privilege are rooted in a complex set of historical circumstances that shape contemporary institutions and inform prevailing attitudes toward, and definitions of, race, class, gender, and sexuality. The prejudices and stereotypes we maintain can thus be understood in the context of this history; they are, moreover, the product of an elaborate and complex process of socialization that occurs at the levels of the individual and the institution.

As Allan Johnson points out, it is imperative that we acknowledge the structural and systemic character of oppression and privilege, for "social life . . . works through the relationship between individuals and social systems" (2006, 82). As a result, individuals alone cannot effect significant and long-term change; it must also occur at the level of the institution. The term *racism*, for example, refers to a system of racialized oppression as opposed to being confined to an individual's attitudes or beliefs. Distinguishing between individual and institutionalized racism, as Joe R. Feagin and Karyn D. McKinney point out, is "core" to any deep understanding of the manner in which racism operates (2003). "In most organizations and other societal settings," they observe,

> whites have the ability and opportunity to discriminate as individuals, yet much
> of their power to harm [people of color] comes from their membership in larger

517

> white-dominated social networks and organizations, what has been termed 'enforcement coalitions' . . . these white dominated networks, coalitions and other organizations typically undergird the discriminatory actions of individual[s]. Additionally, even if a white person does not discriminate individually, he or she benefits from white privilege based on group membership. (2003, 18)

Fully grasping these complex institutional practices, as examined in Section IV, provides us with the tools necessary to analyze the manner in which contemporary discriminatory practices on both the individual and institutional levels are sustained and perpetuated.

As we have argued in the introduction to this volume, the fact that oppression and privilege are interdependent phenomena is crucial to exposing the parallel fashion in which discrimination operates at the macro and micro levels. Embedded within this notion is the idea that although "everyone is undergoing a great battle," as the above quotation suggests, we are not all facing the same battles. In other words, we all experience varying degrees of oppression and privilege, as Patricia Hill Collins argues. Becoming cognizant of the circumstances that oppress and privilege us, and coming to the consequent realization that these circumstances ultimately distinguish us from one another in terms of our life potential and social status, can be jolting. Nevertheless, analyzing one's social location in relation to others' represents the epistemological foundation for determining concrete ways to initiate positive social change.

A critical first step in thinking about ways in which we can effect long-term social change is to acknowledge the manner in which we are all implicated either directly or indirectly in structures of inequality. Speaking specifically on the subject of racism, Eduardo Bonilla-Silva (2003) points out that many whites "exculpate them[selves] from any responsibility for the status of people of color" (see Bonilla-Silva's essay in Section II). Racial inequality, according to this view, is the outcome of "non-racial dynamics," or what sociologists label "color-blind racism" (2003, 2). In the introduction to this anthology we emphasize the manner in which we all participate in systems of oppression and privilege. As a result, we all share a responsibility for working toward achieving a more just and equitable society. Social justice work, when approached from this perspective, thus prompts us to evaluate our place in the world not only according to our relationship with those around us, but also according to our participation in social systems and institutions. As a result, we must weigh our actions in terms of their ultimate effect upon others.

Because we are all implicated in the matrix of oppression and privilege, we each play some role (consciously or unconsciously) as active or passive agents in either perpetuating or challenging oppressive structures of power. Whether we recognize it or not, we all have a stake in effecting social change. Assuming an active role in opposing or perpetuating discrimination thus becomes a matter of conscious choice. Choosing what Johnson refers to as *the path of least resistance*—in other words, choosing *not* to act, or to remain silent—safeguards and guarantees the perpetuation of systems of oppression and privilege (2006).

Clearly we realize that studying inequality can leave anyone feeling frustrated, angry, emotionally exhausted, and generally overwhelmed by what appear to be insurmountable odds regarding the possibility of realizing social and institutional change. Many people express their dismay at the apparent disjunction between theorizing about oppression and privilege in the classroom and the lack of viable solutions to dismantling institutionalized oppression. Although much scholarly theory and critical writing validates and sheds light upon the experiences of the oppressed, often it offers up little in the way of concrete solutions. Many people of color, for example, become weary of intellectualizing about a reality they confront on a daily basis but feel unable to alter. Theories of race, class, gender, and sexuality are sometimes so dense and opaque that they have virtually divorced themselves from the very contexts in which they were developed originally. In this sense these theories undermine their ultimate potential for transformation and for equipping individuals with concrete and pragmatic strategies for surviving and combating discrimination and institutionalized oppression. As Audre Lorde wryly observes, "survival is not an academic skill." Nevertheless, critical theory has enabled us to understand the manner in which oppression and privilege operate in a systemic manner and consequently develop concrete strategies for change. Section V, "Be the Change," thus includes a number of critical works designed to provide specific examples of, and strategies for, influencing social change and confronting oppression in all of its various manifestations.

In his examination of the ways in which systems of racial inequality are "reproduced," Bonilla-Silva (in his essay that appears in Section II) points out that oppression and privilege are maintained through "practices that are subtle, institutional, and apparently non-racial" (2003, 3). The new color-blind racism to which Bonilla-Silva refers corresponds directly to the contemporary resistance to institutional change and backlash against academic and social initiatives that advocate diversity, such as the growing movement to eliminate affirmative action programs. Understanding the ideological framework that informs present-day resistance to social justice is fundamental to determining how one can effectively enact social and institutional change. The first part of this section, "Recognizing Resistance to Change," thus includes a wide range of essays that analyze, on the one hand, the possible sources from which resistance springs, while on the other hand, examine the various forms that opposition to institutional change takes. Specifically, these works demonstrate that active and virulent backlash against changes that occurred in the wake of the civil rights, women's, and gay and lesbian movements still exists. In other words, despite the institutional change that was effected as a result of civil rights legislation and affirmative action policies, dominant society continues to harbor racist, sexist, classist, and heterosexist assumptions and practices that ultimately seek to maintain privilege and protect the status quo. More generally, these essays suggest that contemporary forms of individual and organized resistance are stumbling blocks to social justice work and ultimately prevent society from becoming more equitable.

Modeling through one's personal behavior, regardless of how insignificant it may seem, also represents a step toward working for positive social change; having the courage to speak out is the second step. In the second part of this section, "Institutionalizing Social Change," we provide students with specific examples of ways in which individuals can work together to *uproot* oppression at the level of the institution. This portion of the anthology also includes inspirational essays that detail the activities of grassroots community groups, which have organized successfully and thereby prompted institutional change at both the local and national levels.

The concluding part of Section V, "Where Do I Begin?" features a range of essays that suggest concrete and specific ways to take a stand against discrimination and *become an ally*. Because we are all implicated in this larger system of oppression, privilege, and inequality, we all possess the potential to become activists both in our daily lives and within our broader community and workplaces, regardless of our social locations. When one considers the number of individuals with whom the average person comes in contact in a single week, the possibility of making a difference becomes visible. Educating and enlightening others through our own words and deeds has exponential potential. Providing an example to children and young people is perhaps the most self-evident way to initiate change. However, some of the challenges those working for social justice face arise in their own families and immediate circles of acquaintance and influence. Often, it is painfully difficult to confront family members, friends, and colleagues who have internalized and consequently cling to deep-rooted racist, sexist, and heteronormative ideology. In this context, one must always choose one's battles carefully. However, by using a nonthreatening approach to challenging others' discriminatory views, we can introduce them to the idea that these attitudes, practices, and the value systems they generate are the products of particular historical circumstances. In other words, these discriminatory views are not tied to any essential reality or natural order. Providing specific information regarding the manner in which present-day racism, sexism, and homophobia can be located in a larger historical and social context takes the onus off the individual and reveals that racist, sexist and homophobic attitudes are symptomatic of larger social ills. More significantly, it highlights the notion that apparently incidental practices (such as telling or countenancing racist or sexist jokes) are never confined to a vacuum—they are always situated within a larger, more complex context and reproduce patterns that have over time become institutionalized, as evidenced in Section IV.

The transformative potential of scholarly research and critical theory cannot be underestimated, especially in regard to consciousness raising. Voicing one's dissent, however, as Henry Louis Gates suggests, is simply not enough, for in and of itself, it does not ensure permanent institutional change. Although the knowledge gained in race, class, gender, and sexuality studies courses is prerequisite to enacting social change, ultimately each of us must be willing to act upon this knowledge and put into practice our beliefs. We can all be a part of formulating concrete strategies for combating inequality at every level, and in everyday life.

Although significant social change must take place at the institutional level, change begins with the individual. We would, therefore, suggest that in addition to considering the concrete ways an individual or group can influence social policies that perpetuate privilege and oppression, examine your own community and identify both secular and religious organizations committed to social justice work. Your values and aspirations are shared by others in your community; and there are countless opportunities for you to ally yourself with like-minded people. Never underestimate the capacity of an individual or a united group to effect social and institutional change.

Rather than pointing out the extraordinary and offering examples of heroic figures, we stress the reality that long-term change has been initiated at the grassroots level as a result of individual and collective struggle. Social justice movements both in the United States and abroad have been possible only through the efforts of multitudes of unrecognized individuals and groups working toward a common goal over extended periods of time. The women's suffrage movement, for example, consisted of thousands of men and women who dedicated their lives to earning women the right to vote. In the same vein, personal commitments to achieving social equity and often anonymous acts of courage on the part of scores of activists of all stripes paved the way over more than a century for what culminated in the civil rights movement. These collective efforts, in turn, paved the way for the women's movement, the gay, lesbian, bisexual, and transsexual movement, and the disability rights movement. The impact that an individual can have both in the short term and over time is incalculable. As Johnson puts it, "Since people make systems happen, then people can also make systems happen differently" (2006, 82).

Each one of you can indeed make a difference, but keep in mind that change comes slowly and is not always visible. Walls are erected in the same manner that they are disassembled: stone by stone. Those of us who have committed ourselves to social justice work must by necessity be realistic about what we can and cannot alter, for not everyone has ears to hear or eyes to see. Perhaps most critical of all is that we must learn to be patient, both with ourselves and with others; for depending on our own varying degrees of oppression and privilege, and our own particular subject positions, we approach these issues and challenges from where we are located at the present moment. When one considers the time required to lay the foundations of present-day institutional racism, sexism, and homophobia, it seems logical that it may take an equal if not longer period of time to transform society. And thus, if we begin to measure our successes against history and according to a more immediate vision of social justice, the individual gesture and the collective act become the relevant things themselves. Understanding that institutionalized inequality has been constructed and shaped as a result of specific social and historical circumstances is the axis upon which the best possibility for social change rests.

"Breaking the paralysis," Johnson tells us, "begins with realizing . . . that the social world consists of a lot more than individuals. . . . Like everything else in social life, privilege and oppression exist only through social systems and people's participation in them" (2006, 78, 90). History tells us that change is possible, that each and every one of us can *choose and model alternative paths,* and thereby actively promote change in systems organized around privilege (Johnson 2006, 146–147). Therein resides the greatest hope for the future.

REFERENCES

1. Bonilla-Silva, E. 2003. *Racism without racists.* Lanham, MD: Rowman & Littlefield.
2. Feagin, J. R., & McKinney, K. D. 2003. *The many costs of racism.* Lanham, MD: Rowman & Littlefield.
3. Johnson, A. G. 2006. *Privilege, power, and difference.* New York: McGraw-Hill.

For the white person who wants to know how to be my friend

PAT PARKER

The first thing you do is to forget that i'm Black.
Second, you must never forget that i'm Black.

You should be able to dig Aretha,
but don't play her every time i come over.
And if you decide to play Beethoven—don't tell me
his life story. They made us take music
   appreciation too.

Eat soul food if you like it, but don't expect me
to locate your restaurants
or cook it for you.

And if some Black person insults you,
mugs you, rapes your sister, rapes you,
rips your house or is just being an ass—

please, do not apologize to me
for wanting to do them bodily harm.
It makes me wonder if you're foolish.

And even if you really believe Blacks are better
   lovers than
whites—don't tell me. I start thinking of charging
   stud fees.

In other words—if you really want to be my
   friend—*don't*
make a labor of it. I'm lazy. Remember.

A. RECOGNIZING RESISTANCE TO CHANGE

 ## 52

Feminists and Feminism

ALLAN G. JOHNSON

The word "feminism" is an umbrella that covers many approaches to gender and patriarchy.[1] In the most general sense, feminism is a way of thinking critically about gender and its place in social life, but from here it ranges in many directions. All forms of feminism take gender to be problematic in some way, but just what this means—how prominent the concept of patriarchy is, for example—

varies from one branch of feminism to another. As such, feminism lends itself to many different purposes. We can use it as an intellectual framework for analyzing how social life works, from love and sex to family violence to work to the meaning of art, literature, and spirituality to the conduct of science to the dynamics of ecology and global capitalism. Feminism also provides an ideological basis for change on every level of human existence, from how we behave to transforming patriarchy and its core values of dominance and control. By focusing on how we participate in the gender order, feminism challenges us to live in new ways, to question assumptions about gender and human nature, and to confront the everyday realities of women's oppression and the price men pay in return for gender privilege.

Because feminism challenges the status quo, it gets attacked from many sides. Instead of criticizing feminism as it really is, however, most critics focus on two substitutes— "issues feminism" and feminists. These are easier to deal with because they avoid confronting men and leave patriarchy largely intact. "Issues feminism" defines feminism as little more than positions on issues such as abortion or pornography.[2] The result is a fractured and divisive view of feminism as a collection of contending positions—antipornography feminism, pro-choice feminism, pro-life feminism, middle-class white feminism, black feminism, lesbian feminism, Latina feminism, and so on. This way of looking at things often does more to divide women from common struggle than to unite them. Many women, for example, refuse to call themselves feminists because they think it automatically implies a particular position on abortion or censorship or sexual orientation. Many women of color are put off by feminism because they associate it with the interests of white middle-class women to the neglect of other classes or races.

What gets lost in the heat around specific issues are basic questions about what patriarchy is, how it works, and how we participate in it. Such questions don't necessarily hinge on taking particular positions on any given issue. We don't have to be pro-choice on the abortion issue, for example, to see patriarchy as problematic and try to understand it as such; nor do we have to be white middle-class professional women bumping up against the glass ceiling. But if the focus is solely on issues such as abortion or work-place discrimination to the neglect of the system that creates and shapes them, the result is paralysis and the kind of endless, divisive debate that we've been stuck in for a long time.

When feminism isn't being fragmented into a jumble of topical issues, it is being attacked through women associated with it. Femin*ists* are regularly trashed through stereotypes portraying them as humorless, man-hating, angry, whining, antifamily, and lesbian.[3] Sam Keen, for example, applauds femin*ism* for drawing attention to patriarchy's oppressive consequences, including the obsession with control and dominance. And yet, rather than take the next step of figuring out how to take responsibility for and *do* something about patriarchy, he switches almost immediately from feminism to the behavior and motives of some feminists. He energetically attacks what he calls "ideological feminism" which is "animated by a spirit of resentment, the tactic of blame, and the desire for vindictive triumph over men that comes out of the dogmatic assumption that women are the innocent victims of a male conspiracy."[4] And having established himself as an innocent victim of such irrational, vindictive hatred of men, he never looks back or bothers to ask just what this phenomenon tells us about feminism or the women's movement as a whole. Nowhere, for example, does he ask what men might *do* with all those "enlightening perspectives and prophetic insights of the women's movement" for which he says he has such high regard.[5] That gets no more than an approving nod as he wades into what he sees as the *real* problem—women's anger at men.

Keen has a lot of company, for it's easier and safer to dwell on caricatures, extreme factions of complex movements, personal smears, and slogans than it is to understand a new way of thinking and what it might tell us about the world and ourselves in it. From Rush Limbaugh's sneering references to "femi-Nazis" to Camille Paglia's smug characterization of Gloria Steinem as Stalin,[6] stereotypes are vivid and powerful in the human imagination and potent weapons against change. Even Naomi Wolf, author of a powerful feminist analysis of the role of beauty in women's oppression,[7] goes on in a later book to confuse feminists and feminism, to the detriment of both. In *Fire With Fire,* she criticizes what she calls "victim feminism," which turns out to be a hodgepodge of a little theory, a few select issues, and, most important, a heavy dose of personal attitudes and behavior of individual feminists (who, for the most part, are left unnamed and conveniently vague as "them" or "some feminists"). She seems to see no significant difference, for example, between arguing that patriarchy is problematic and being personally humorless or rigid or grim in one's dealings with other people. Seeing both as feminism makes it impossible to distinguish feminism as a framework for thought and action—which is what threatens patriarchy most—from feminism as an attitude or style of interaction. Such fusing of feminism and feminists has taken over the public imagination, which means that to see femin*ism* clearly we have to cut through the many stereotypes about femin*ists*.

Feminists Are Antifamily   Feminists are often described as antifamily, but most feminists I've encountered in print or in person have nothing against the family per se as a group in which children are reared and people's emotional and material needs get met by loving adults. Many feminists do object, however, to the subordination of women inside the *patriarchal* family and the way this can damage the potential for nurturing, caring, and growth. They do oppose the organization of family life in ways that suffocate women's emotional and productive lives and foster a climate for the ongoing epidemic of physical abuse of women and children. They don't deny the vital importance of women's connection to children, but many do oppose how patriarchy enables and encourages men to use that connection to control women's bodies, to restrict where they go and with whom they spend their time, and to deny them the independence and autonomy that paid employment provides. If the patriarchal family is the only kind of family we can imagine, then many feminists will appear to be antifamily when in fact they are simply antipatriarchy.[8] This was especially true during the feminist heyday of the 1970s, when many women were reeling from the realization of how oppressive family life can be when it's organized on a patriarchal model. The patriarchal model was so pervasive that the only alternative often appeared to be no family life at all, which easily lent itself to the impression that feminists devalued marriage and the vital work that mothers do. This may have been true of some feminists, but the underlying theme was alarm over what had *become* of marriage and motherhood.

Feminists Are No Fun   Feminists are also accused of being angry and humorless and not knowing how to have a good time. Aside from not being true, it's a peculiar criticism to make of a group whose primary work is to deal with the reality of oppression. People of color, for example, generally lack a sense of humor around the subject of white racism and how it affects their lives, and yet whites rarely chide blacks for being angry and humorless ("Come on, lighten up; where's your sense of humor about racism?"). For women, however, getting angry is socially unacceptable, even when the anger is over violence, discrimination, misogyny, and other forms of oppression.[9] Anger is unacceptable because angry women are women in touch with their own autonomous passion and power, especially in relation to men, and this threatens the entire patriarchal order. It's unacceptable because it forces men to confront the reality of gender oppression and their involvement in it, even if only as passive beneficiaries. Women's anger challenges men to acknowledge attempts to trivialize oppression with "I was only kidding." And women's anger is unacceptable to men who look to women to take care of them, to prop up their need to feel in control, and to support them in their competition with other men—a dynamic of interdependency that doesn't exist between whites and people of color. When women are less than gracious and good-humored about their own oppression, men often feel uncomfortable, embarrassed, at a loss, and therefore vulnerable; and it places women and their concerns at center stage in a world in which men expect women to focus on them.

But what James Baldwin said about blacks, that "to be a relatively conscious African-American is to be in a rage almost all the time,"[10] is also true for women. For this reason, women and blacks often protect themselves from feeling (and appearing) perpetually angry by keeping themselves only partially aware of what's going on. But it's unreasonable to expect women to feel no anger about day-to-day oppression often lived in intimate relation to men who not only benefit from patriarchy, but typically show little interest in knowing what it's about or doing anything about it. And yet that's precisely what's expected of women who, as wives, mothers, and secretaries, are called on to please, nurture, and soothe men and never cause them discomfort, embarrassment, or alarm. As wives and employees, women are supposed to be perpetually good-natured, smiling, accepting, accessible, and yielding, lest they be thought of as cold, frigid bitches. This means that all a man has to do to challenge or discredit a woman is simply point out that she's angry or, even worse, accuse her of being angry at men. Women are a unique minority in this respect. Malcolm X, for example, was often criticized for his expressions of rage at white racism, as is Louis Farrakhan today. But while their rage may make them unpopular political figures among whites, if anything it enhances their standing as *men*.

Man-Hating Male Bashers   There is probably no more effective weapon against feminists than to accuse them of hating men and to characterize feminist criticism of patriarchy and male privilege as male bashing. The tactic works in part because to attack men is to challenge the male-identified character of society itself. In other words, since men are taken to be the standard, to criticize men in general is to take on society as a whole, which both men and women have a stake in resisting. Just the opposite is true, however, of the demeaning prejudice directed at women and other subordinate groups. Mainstream sexist and racist culture, for example, is full of negative images of women and blacks that devalue the *idea* of being female or black, but we rarely hear about "female bashing" or "black bashing" as a result. This is especially true of misogyny, which simply has no place in most people's active vocabularies in spite of, or perhaps because of, its pervasiveness as an integral part of everyday life. It is unremarkable and taken for granted. When feminists and people of color *do* call attention to sexist and racist speech, however, and demand that it stop, a hue and cry goes up about the tyranny of political correctness and infringements on free speech.

Calling feminists man-haters and male bashers protects patriarchy and male privilege by turning what otherwise would be criticism of patriarchy into questions about feminists' personalities and motives. They're accused of creating feminism and the women's movement as a way to act out personal hostility, bitterness, and discontent, all presumably fueled by being unattractive to men or wanting to be men themselves. Such feelings supposedly result from personal experience, maladjustment, and pathologies having nothing to do with patriarchy as a system or the oppression of women it produces. In short, feminism is reduced to the ravings of a bunch of bitter malcontents, and all of its critical insights into patriarchy are tossed aside.

The accusation of man-hating and male bashing also shifts attention away from women and onto men in a sympathetic way that reinforces patriarchal male centeredness while putting women on the defensive for criticizing it. In the process, it portrays men as victims of a gender prejudice that on the surface seems comparable to the sexism directed at women. Like many such false parallels, this ignores the fact that antifemale and antimale prejudice have different social bases and produce very different consequences.[11] Resentment and hatred of women are grounded in a misogynist *culture* that devalues femaleness itself as part of male privilege and female oppression. For women, however, mainstream patriarchal culture offers no comparable antimale ideology, and so their resentment is based more on experience as a subordinate group and men's part in it. It is true, of course, that men sometimes are made fun of, as in television sitcoms, and this can hurt their feelings. In almost every case, however, it is women who appear to make men laughable by turning them into fools trapped in the home as husbands, the one setting where women have some real power. It is more as *husbands* than as men that men are made to look foolish, and even in this the status of manhood is never at much risk. Even though male characters may sometimes look foolish in the narrow confines of television or the Sunday comics, they're surrounded by an overwhelmingly male-identified, male-centered world in which misandry[12] simply has no place. A few henpecked (by women) husbands may bumble their way through life for our entertainment, but it's funny precisely because it is such a departure from the exalted value placed on maleness, from which every man benefits. There wouldn't be much of an audience for a show based on a husband's ability to belittle and control his wife.

Accusations of male bashing and man-hating also work to discredit feminism because . . . people often confuse men as individuals with men as a dominant and privileged category of people. Given the reality of women's oppression, male privilege, and men's enforcement of both, it's hardly surprising that *every* woman should have moments when she resents or even hates "men."[13] Even Phyllis Schlafly, a leader in the antifeminist backlash, led the fight against the Equal Rights Amendment by arguing in part that without protective laws, mothers wouldn't be able to count on fathers to support their children, a judgment that reflects little regard for men. In spite of such mainstream criticism of men— and its thinly veiled dissatisfaction and hostility— it's politically expedient for opponents of feminism to attribute such negative judgments and feelings to feminists. It makes feminists seem marginal and extreme; it obscures the fact that many feminists have deep ties to men and thereby alienates them from other women who also depend on men; and it gives many women someone to take the heat for feelings they themselves dare not express.

There's a big difference, however, between hating a dominant group in an oppressive system like patriarchy and hating the individuals who belong to it. Angela Davis once said that as an African American she often feels hatred for *white* people, but her feelings for particular white *people* depend on the individual.[14] She hates white people's collective position of dominance in a racially oppressive society, she hates the privilege they enjoy at her expense, and she hates the racist culture that whites take for granted as unremarkable while she must struggle with the oppression it creates in everyday life. But Davis also knows that while individual whites can never be free of racism, they can participate in racist systems in many different ways, which include joining blacks in the fight against racism. The same can be said of men and women.[15]

The distinction between groups and individuals, however, is subtle and easily lost sight of when you're up to your ears in an oppressive system. Of course women are going to feel and express anger, resentment, and even hatred toward individual men who

may not have it coming in just that way or to that degree or at that moment. Of course men are sometimes going to get their feelings hurt or be called on to take responsibility for themselves in ways they may not be used to. When I heard Davis say that she sometimes hates whites, and when I've heard women talk about hating men, I've had to get clear in my own mind about how these words refer to me and how they don't, and it often takes some effort to get there. And as a white male who benefits from both gender and race privilege, I've also had to see that it's up to me—and not to women or people of color—to distinguish one from the other. Too often men react to women's anger by calling on women to take care of them, and in this way recreate the male-centered principle of the very gender order that women, feminist and otherwise, are angry about.

There do exist feminists who passionately and unapologetically hate all males simply for being male, although in all my years of work on gender I've encountered few of them. The author of the infamous 1960s *SCUM Manifesto* comes to mind as one candidate.[16] Although it's unclear whether the "Society for Cutting Up Men" ever had more than one member, I've heard men cite it as a general characterization of how feminists feel about men. Given the existence of many nonfeminists who hate men, and given how much work lies ahead of us to understand patriarchy and what we can do about it, putting the subject of women who hate men at the center of attention is nothing more than a defensive distraction.

Here Come the Lesbians   A favorite way to dismiss feminists and feminism in a single stroke is to associate both with lesbianism. It's true that many lesbians are feminists and that many feminists are lesbians; but it's also true that many lesbians aren't feminists, many feminists are heterosexual, and the women's movement is full of disagreement among feminists of varying sexual orientations.[17] More to the point, however, is that when the label "lesbian" is used to smear and dismiss feminists and feminism, it silences women who fear being labeled if they identify themselves as feminist or even talk openly about patriarchy.[18] "Lesbian-baiting" leaves no room to ask about the meaning of lesbianism and its significance under patriarchy. Adrienne Rich, for example, argues that lesbianism isn't simply about women who want to have sex with other women but is a continuum of women's sense of identification and desire to be with other women.[19] There are reasons for this to exist in any society, beginning with every girl's intimacy with her mother. In a male-identified, male-centered system, however, women must contend with paths of least resistance that encourage them to see and evaluate themselves as men would. As Ellyn Kaschak puts it, "The most notable aspect of current gender arrangements is that the masculine always defines the feminine by naming, containing, engulfing, invading, and evaluating it. The feminine is never allowed to stand alone or to subsume the masculine."[20] This means that when women look for role models, they usually find men and women who measure themselves by male-identified cultural standards—what is sometimes called the "male gaze."[21] Most Western art, for example, is created as if its intended audience were primarily male, especially when the subject is women. Similarly, when women look in a mirror, they often see themselves as they think men would see them, and judge themselves when they fail to conform to feminine ideals promoted by patriarchal culture.[22] When women leave the patriarchal frame of reference, however, by *also* turning to one another for mirroring and standards, they challenge the assumption that the world revolves around men and what men do, and that women exist primarily to please and take care of men.

Becoming more woman-identified is a critical part of feminist practice, regardless of women's sexual orientation. It is a process that *every* oppressed group goes through as part of its struggle to redefine itself. It is a way to throw off negative self-images constructed through lifetimes of gazing into cultural mirrors that devalue them in order to maintain the privilege of dominant groups. In this sense it's not surprising that many lesbians are attracted to a movement to free women from patriarchal oppression; but it also makes sense for women of *all* sexual orientations to shift toward woman-identified living even while participating in marriages and

raising families with men. As heterosexual women reclaim a positive, autonomous sense of themselves in nonpatriarchal terms, this will most likely happen as it has thus far—through other women acting as mirrors that help define what it means to be women. This means, of course, that women's movement toward being woman-identified threatens men's place at the center of women's attention and what security women have been able to attain for themselves in relation to that center. At the same time, it challenges the male-identified, male-centered core of patriarchy as a system, calling on men to develop their own sense of themselves apart from the exploitative dependency on women that patriarchy promotes. From this perspective, the persecution of lesbians and the use of "lesbian" as accusation or insult is really a defensive attack on the larger movement of women away from patriarchal existence and toward fuller and more self-defined lives. As lesbian-baiting intimidates all women into silence and blunts feminism's potential to change how they think about gender, it defends patriarchy as a whole and the male privilege that goes with it.

Feminists as Victims   A more recent attack on feminists has been the peculiar accusation that focusing on patriarchy and its oppressive consequences for women actually demeans and disempowers women by portraying them as "mere" victims. Feminists have been characterized as whining "victim feminists" and "rape-crisis feminists" who portray women as too weak to defend themselves from men who would harass, beat, sexually assault, or discriminate against them.[23] What's most bizarre about this accusation is that the women who work against male violence and exploitation are some of the strongest, toughest, most articulate and courageous people around, and to describe them as whining victims who passively sit around feeling sorry for themselves is about as far from reality as one could imagine. What makes whining so unappealing is that the whine is both a call for help and a form of focused self-pity that is so intense that nothing in the way of help has much chance of getting through. In other words, whining is a manipulative setup in which actually making things better isn't the point. But this is a far cry from feminist demands for an end to discrimination, violence, and sexual exploitation.

In spite of its loose hold on reality, the "victim feminism" criticism works because it draws attention away from men as victimizers and focuses instead on women who are victimized. In one sense, critics are correct that focusing on women as victims is counterproductive, but not because we should instead ignore victimization altogether. The real reason to avoid an exclusive focus on women as victims is to free us to concentrate on the compelling fact that men are the ones who victimize, and such behavior and the patriarchal system that encourages it are the problem. Otherwise we might find ourselves concentrating on male victimization of women as something that *happens* to women without being *done by* men. The shift in focus can be as simple as the difference between saying "Each year 100,000 women are sexually assaulted" and "Each year men sexually assault 100,000 women." Many people feel less comfortable with the second version because it draws attention to *male* violence against women and thereby to the male gender as problematic. Placing men at the center of the issue also makes it more difficult to explain away sexual violence as a matter of chance (like catching a cold or being in a traffic accident) or of women's failures to be careful enough or somehow "asking for it." Sexual violence doesn't fall on women out of thin air, and referring to women as victims doesn't tell us anything about them except that they suffered the consequences of what some men *did*. To call attention to that simple fact, as many feminists do, in no way demeans or diminishes women. It does challenge men and women to look at what's going on.

The "victim feminist" label also works because it taps a core feature of patriarchal masculinity: the importance of "taking it like a man" in order to be "one of the guys." Men's abuse of other men is a staple ingredient of patriarchal culture, from high school locker rooms to college fraternity hazing to military basic training. The man who takes abuse without complaint improves his chance of being accepted as a real man who deserves to share in male privilege. A man who objects, however, who dares identify abuse for what it is, risks being ostracized as a sissy, a mama's boy who can't take it and who belongs with "the girls" ("Aww, what's the matter? Gonna cry and run home to mama?"). In the same way, when feminists point out that sexual harassment is abusive or that coerced sex is rape, they often are chided for being the equivalent of whining sissies who don't give women enough credit for being tough and able to take it—like a man. The "like a man" part usually isn't spoken, but in a patriarchal culture it's implicit and doesn't have to be. And some of the loudest voices in the chorus are women who have achieved acceptance and success in a man's world.

As the attacks continue, many feminists are distracted and harried by having to explain and defend themselves from the latest provocation. More to the point, perhaps, is that the ongoing waves of criticism—whether warranted or not—are combined with a general absence of thoughtful public discussion of what feminism is about. Over time, this creates the illusion that patriarchy either doesn't exist or, if it does, doesn't deserve serious attention. While the reality of feminism's world-changing potential remains invisible in the public eye, gender oppression continues largely unabated. To do something about that, we need a clear sense of what feminism is about and how it can help us understand what's going on.

WHAT IS FEMINISM ABOUT?

As a matter of principle, some feminists prefer not to define feminism at all because it's so diverse that no single version of it could possibly do justice to the many forms it takes. In addition, a commitment to being inclusive and nonhierarchical makes many feminists leery of definitions, since definitions can be used to establish an exclusive "one true feminism" that separates "insiders" from "outsiders."

Nonetheless, people do use the word to describe how they think and work. Like any word, "feminism" can't be used unless it has meaning, and any meaning necessarily sets it apart from other possibilities. Without taking anything away from feminism's diversity, I think it's possible to identify some core ideas that most forms of feminism have in common. I've never encountered anything called feminism, for example, that didn't in some way begin with the assumption that gender inequality exists and that it's problematic.

How and why inequality exists, what forms it takes, and what to do about it are questions with different and sometimes conflicting answers. But the questions all reflect a common focus of attention, and this is how feminism can encompass a diversity of answers.

Having said this, it's important to emphasize the distinction between feminism as a way of thinking and two other possibilities. Feminism can refer to a set of opinions about social issues such as abortion or equal pay. It can also simply be about being "pro-woman."[24] Some people identify themselves as feminists, for example, because they favor equality for women or the right to choose abortion; but neither of these necessarily points to a particular way of analyzing gender inequality that one might call feminism. For my purposes here, feminism is a way of thinking—of observing the world, asking questions, and looking for answers—that may lead to particular opinions *but doesn't consist of the opinions themselves.* One could be pro-choice or in favor of equal pay, for example, on purely moral or liberal political grounds without any basis in a feminist analysis of gender. In this sense, feminism refers to ways of *understanding* such issues from various points of view, all of which share a common focus of concern.

Although all feminist thought begins with gender as problematic, from there it follows various paths, especially in relation to patriarchy. In general, I think it's useful to distinguish among branches of feminism according to the degree to which

- They understand various aspects of social life—such as sexual domination and violence, religion, warfare, politics, economics, and how we treat the natural environment—in relation to gender;
- They explicitly recognize patriarchy as a system, as problematic, as historically rooted, and in need of change; and
- They see men as a dominant group with a vested interest in women's subordination, the perpetuation of patriarchal values, and control over the political, economic, and other institutions through which those values operate.

Some brands of feminism, for example, have little use for the term "patriarchy" and don't see men as

particularly problematic. They may go out of their way to avoid doing or saying anything that might challenge men or make them feel uncomfortable or raise the possibility of conflict between men and women. Others define patriarchy, male privilege, gender oppression, and conflict as basic points of departure for any understanding of gender. In some cases the focus of change is quite narrow, as it was in the turn-of-the-century struggle for women's suffrage, while in others, such as ecofeminism or feminist spirituality, the focus is often global change spanning multiple dimensions of human experience.

Most feminist work draws to varying degrees on a handful of major approaches to gender that usually go by the names of liberal, radical, Marxian, and socialist feminism. These aren't the only kinds of feminist thought—psychoanalytic and postmodern feminism are two notable additions to the list—but they certainly have played a part in most attempts to understand and do something about patriarchy and its consequences. They also aren't mutually exclusive. Although liberal and radical feminism, for example, differ dramatically in some ways, they also have a lot in common and trace back to similar roots. As such, "liberal," "socialist," "Marxian," and "radical" aren't little boxes into which feminists can neatly and unambiguously fit themselves. If I tried to identify the feminist approaches that have shaped the writing of this [paper], for example, I'd find them all in one way or another even though I lean more toward some than others. It helps, then, to think of various feminist approaches as threads woven together to form a whole. While the threads are distinctive in many ways, they are strongest in relation to one another.

LIBERAL FEMINISM

The basic idea behind liberal feminism, and liberal thinking in general, is that humans are rational beings who, with enough knowledge and opportunity, will realize their potential as individuals to the benefit of themselves and society as a whole. Things go wrong primarily through ignorance, bad socialization, and limited access to opportunities. Equality of opportunity and freedom of choice are seen as the bedrock of individual well-being, which in turn makes possible an enlightened society and progressive social change. Liberalism assumes that the individual person is the highest good and the key to social life. From this perspective, societies are little more than collections of people making choices, and social change is largely a matter of changing how individuals think and behave, especially through education and other means of enlightenment.[25]

From a liberal feminist perspective, the main gender problem is that prejudice, values, and norms deny women equal access to the opportunities, resources, and rewards that society offers. Forcing women to choose between child care and employment; excluding women from positions of authority in economic, political, religious, and other organizations; segregating women in the job market, from the pink-collar ghetto to exclusion from the Catholic priesthood and combat roles in the military; devaluing, objectifying, and portraying women as inferior in a wide variety of cultural stereotypes; and socializing women and men in ways that enhance male privilege and female subordination are all identified as central to gender equality.

The liberal feminist solution is to remove the barriers to women's freedom of choice and equal participation, from restrictions on reproductive control to providing day care to breaking the glass ceiling at work. The liberal method is to persuade people to change by challenging sexist stereotypes and demanding equal access and treatment. This includes rewriting school textbooks and curricula; reforming legal codes; lobbying for child-care facilities and equal access to professions, corporate management, and elected office; breaking the glass ceiling and promoting women's advancement through networking; and providing victimized women with resources such as battered women's shelters and rape crisis services. Liberal feminism calls on men to change how they think about and behave toward women, to be less violent, harassing, and exploitative and more supportive, emotionally sensitive and expressive, and committed to their roles as fathers and partners. And it calls on women to assert and believe in themselves, to strive to

achieve and not be deterred by the barriers they must overcome. In short, liberal feminism ultimately relies on men to be decent and fair, to become enlightened and progressive as they learn the truth about gender inequality and women's true potential, to give women their due by allowing them to participate as equals in social life, and to support this by doing their fair share of domestic work. And it relies on women to believe in themselves, to strive and achieve, to push against barriers until they give way. All of this strikes a deep chord, especially in the American Dream consciousness, whose root ideology extols the virtues of individual freedom as the answer to most social problems. This is one reason why the liberal perspective has shaped so much of the women's movement and general public perceptions of what gender issues are all about.

Liberalism has improved the lives of many women, but after several decades of hard-won gains, the women's movement seems nearly swamped by a backlash and stalled by stiff resistance to further change. A recent study conducted by the U.S. Department of Labor's Women's Bureau, for example, found that a majority of working women, and especially women of color, continue to be devalued, underpaid, and not taken seriously, and still struggle with the demands of domestic responsibilities with little help from employers, government, or, most important, husbands. None of this is the fault of liberal feminism, but it does reflect its underlying limitations as a way to make sense of patriarchy and help find alternatives to it.

A basic problem with liberal feminism (and liberalism in general) is that its intense focus on the individual blinds it to the power of social systems. This is one reason why liberal feminism doesn't recognize patriarchy as something to be reckoned with. It never looks at the underlying structures that produce women's oppression and that shape the individual men and women liberal feminism aims to change. A liberal feminist approach to getting fathers more involved in child care, for example, emphasizes changing men one at a time (or perhaps in small groups). This might be done by appealing to a sense of fairness or the importance of having closer relations with children. By ignoring patriarchy, however, liberal feminism turns male privilege into an individual problem only remotely connected to larger systems that promote and protect it. In the case of child care, this misses the fact that when men don't do their "fair share" of domestic labor, they gain in terms of nondomestic rewards such as power, income, and status as "real men." In the dominant patriarchal culture, these rewards are valued far more highly than the emotional satisfactions of family life. In opinion polls, many men *say* that family life is more important than work, but when it comes to actual choices about where to invest themselves, the results reflect a different set of cultural values embedded in powerful paths of least resistance. Liberal feminism, then, often puts women in the position of negotiating from a position of weakness, depending on men to give up male privilege and endanger their standing in relation to other men because it's the right thing to do and might enrich their or their children's emotional lives.[26]

Liberal feminism's individualism also backs us into a no-win position between denying that patriarchy even exists, on the one hand, and claiming that all men are engaged in a conspiracy to oppress women on the other. If nothing significant exists beyond the rational individual, then by definition the only thing larger than ourselves that we might participate in is a conspiracy or other form of deliberate planning among individuals. Since it's easy to refute the existence of a massive conspiracy in which men gather to plot a patriarchal future, any kind of systemic understanding of gender privilege and oppression becomes virtually impossible, as does the hope of doing much about it.

Liberal feminism is also limited by its ahistorical character. It offers no way to explain the origins of the social arrangements it's trying to change, nor does it identify a social engine powerful enough to keep oppression going. Liberal feminism's main assumption is that oppression results from ignorance whose removal through enlightened education will clear the road to equality and a better life for all. But when ignorance and misunderstanding perpetuate an oppressive system grounded in privilege, they become more than a passive barrier that dissipates in the light of truth. Instead, they become part of a willful defense that puts up a fight, and a good one at that. Liberal feminism is ill-equipped to deal with this, for the closest liberalism comes to acknowledging the forces that perpetuate patriarchy is its frequent reference to "tradition" (as in "traditional roles"). There is no theory of history or systemic oppression here. Instead, we have a vague sense that things have been this way for a long time and for reasons that are apparently not worth exploring beyond "it's hard for people to change."

Liberal feminism's "tradition" catch-all obscures the underlying dynamics that make patriarchy work, and it trivializes oppression by making it seem a matter of habit. Imagine, by comparison, how unacceptable it would be to attribute racism or anti-Semitism to nothing more than tradition, as in "Racial segregation, discrimination, and violence against people of color are a matter of tradition in the U.S." or "Persecuting Jews is just the way we do things here—for as long as I can remember." "Tradition" doesn't *explain* oppression, it merely characterizes one aspect of how it's practiced and woven into the fabric of everyday life so that it's perceived as normal and taken for granted.

Liberal feminism's lack of historical perspective has serious consequences because it leads away from questions about patriarchy and systemic oppression, concepts that have little place in liberal thinking. Patriarchy is treated as a shadow concept with no serious analytical role to play in making sense of gender. Avoiding patriarchy and oppression also fits nicely with the liberal focus on individuals as the be-all and end-all of human life, with little appreciation for how feelings, motivations, thoughts, and behavior are shaped by participation in larger social contexts such as patriarchy. From a liberal perspective, for example, men who rape are merely sick individuals, and there's no reason to ask why such "sickness" is more common in some societies than others or how the violent coercion practiced by rapists might be related to the less violent "coercion" that figures so prominently in "normal" patriarchal heterosexuality, especially in some of its more romanticized versions. Unless we want to argue that men are conspiring to produce violence against women on a massive scale, we're stuck with no larger understanding of what's going on.

A deeper problem is liberal feminism's single-minded focus on the right of women to be men's equals—to do what men do in the way that men do it. In this, it doesn't ask what might be wrong with a way of organizing the world that encourages men to do what they do in the way that they do it. As a result, when women demand access to positions of power in corporations, government, the church, universities, and the professions, they also affirm the basic patriarchal character of social life. Rather than question warfare as a way to conduct international relations, for example, liberal feminism champions the right of women to serve in combat. Rather than question capitalism as a way to produce and distribute what people need in order to live, liberal feminism targets glass ceilings that keep women from moving up in corporate hierarchies. Rather than challenge the values that shape how professions are practiced—from medicine and law to science—liberalism focuses on equal access to graduate schools, legal partnerships, and the tenured ranks of university faculties.

This is essentially what Naomi Wolf promotes as "power feminism": women should beat men at their own game and run the world—hence the title of her book, *Fire With Fire*. Initially, she seems to favor the more radical goal of changing the game itself rather than merely winning at it. She disagrees with Audre Lorde's proposition that "The Master's tools will never dismantle the Master's house,"[27] arguing instead that patriarchy can be undone through the use of patriarchal forms of power and domination, whether political, economic, or interpersonal. But it soon becomes clear that Wolf isn't concerned with dismantling the Master's house, but with breaking down the door and getting into it. "Women," Wolf writes, "should be free to exploit or save, give or take, destroy or build, to exactly the same extent that men are."[28] Apparently it doesn't occur to her to ask whether *men* should be allowed to do such things to the extent that they are, or whether this is

a good standard for organizing the world. Part of Wolf's problem is that she never tells us just what the Master's house is—she doesn't define patriarchy or describe how it works. But a deeper problem is her liberal assumption that the only thing wrong with the status quo is unequal opportunity for women to participate in it as men do.

There's nothing wrong with equal opportunity, equal access, and equality under the law. These are important goals. But there are some serious unanticipated consequences to working for equal access to a system without *also* asking what kind of system this is and how it produces oppression of all sorts, especially when based on characteristics other than gender, such as race, sexual orientation, and social class. One consequence of following a liberal feminist agenda, for example, is that successful women often join men at the top of systems that oppress working-class men and women and people of color, obscuring the fact that equality for "women" comes to mean in effect equality for white women of a certain class. This does *not* mean that women shouldn't pursue power now held predominantly by men. It does mean, however, that the liberal feminist perspective that shapes and informs such striving omits huge chunks of reality. As such, it can't be our only feminist approach to understanding gender oppression or doing something about it.

Because liberal feminism has little to say about how patriarchy organizes male competitive bonding and women's oppression, it focuses on the consequences of oppression without looking at the system that produces them. Sexist behavior and sexist attitudes, for example, are discussed out of their social context, as if they were simply the result of "bad training," to be replaced with "good training" at home and in school. But socialization and education are social mechanisms that serve much larger patriarchal interests, including the perpetuation of male privilege and social institutions organized around core patriarchal values. As such, socialization isn't the problem, no more than programs that train workers in weapons factories are the key to understanding war.

Perhaps the most ironic problem with liberal feminism is that by focusing on equality only in terms of individual choice and opportunity *within* patriarchy, it actually undermines the liberal ideal of free choice. By ignoring how patriarchy shapes and limits the alternatives from which people might "freely" choose, it ignores the power to determine just what those alternatives will be. This means that the freedom to participate in the world on patriarchal terms is freedom only in a context that ignores *non*patriarchal alternatives that patriarchal culture doesn't tell us about. This also means that the limited liberal agenda for change assumes that society as it currently exists defines the limits of what is possible. But the freedom to choose among existing alternatives is only part of a larger feminist agenda:

> For although feminists do indeed want women to become part of the structure, participants in public institutions; although they want access for women to decision-making posts, and a voice in how society is managed, *they do not want women to assimilate to society as it presently exists but to change it.* Feminism is not yet one more of a series of political movements demanding for their adherents access to existing structures and their rewards. . . . [I]t is a revolutionary moral movement, intending to use political power to transform society. . . . The assimilation of women to society as it presently exists would lead simply to the inclusion of certain women . . . along with certain men in its higher echelons. It would mean continued stratification and continued contempt for "feminine" values. Assimilation would be the cooption of feminism.[29]

In the above sense, critics of liberal feminism would take feminism well beyond issues of gender equality. A broader and deeper feminism is about the very terms on which equality is figured. It is about women's right to participate as men's equals in society, but also about the power to shape the alternatives from which both women and men may choose. It's about the power to affect the forces that shape experience, thought, feeling, and behavior; it's about the power to change society itself. It's about fundamentally changing the Master's house, if not dismantling it altogether, which is a far cry

from just getting in the door. This goes well past the limits of liberal feminism to the roots, the radicals, of the patriarchal tree, which leads us into the kinds of questions that so often provoke a backlash of resistance and denial. This is a major reason why liberal feminism is so widely viewed as the only legitimate and socially acceptable form that feminism can take, because it's also the most palatable, the least threatening, and the most compatible with the status quo. This is also why one of its major alternatives, radical feminism, is so routinely maligned, misunderstood, and ignored.

RADICAL FEMINISM

As we move toward more radical areas of feminist thought, the landscape is taken up with far more than issues like sexist attitudes and unequal pay. Radical feminism of course pays attention to patriarchy's consequences and how people experience them. But unlike liberal feminism, radical feminism carries that attention to the underlying male-dominated, male-identified, male-centered, control-obsessed patriarchal system that produces gender oppression. Radical feminism aims to make sense of patriarchy in relation to history and social contexts that help explain not only where it came from, but how and why it persists and affects us so deeply.

. . . [F]or example, male violence against women is more than an individual male pathology; it is also a path of least resistance that patriarchy provides for men to follow and for women to accept. From a radical perspective, that path doesn't exist in isolation from the rest of social life but is rooted in and helps to maintain male privilege in patriarchy as a system. In similar ways, a radical perspective on family divisions of labor that still saddle women with most domestic work is quite different from a liberal view. Radical feminism sees this as more than "tradition" or an expression of female and male personality tendencies or a lack of appropriate training or encouragement for men. The family is an institution with a complex history as a vehicle for keeping women in their place, and men's resistance to domestic labor has been an important part of that dynamic.[30] Whatever reasons individual men may offer for not doing child care and housework, it is rooted in male privilege, and its cumulative effect is to reinforce that privilege.

The connection with male privilege also appears in a radical analysis of things as mundane as how difficult it is for women and men to communicate with each other. From Deborah Tannen's liberal feminist perspective, for example, power and control are secondary issues in gender communication. The real problem is that men and women speak different languages and use different "styles" that reflect men's concern with status and women's concern with intimacy and relationships. Tannen believes that the styles are "different *but equally valid*" and result from being socialized into different cultures, each with its own traditions.[31] If men interrupt and otherwise dominate conversation, for example, it's because that's "their way," just as the Spanish enjoy siesta and Japanese traditionally remove their shoes before entering a house. Since there's a lot of pressure these days to respect cultural differences, Tannen's somewhat anthropological approach to gender dynamics tends to make it off limits to criticism. Her perspective offers some comfort to those feeling stressed from gender conflict: there's no problem here that can't be cured with a good dose of education and tolerance for differences—the classic liberal remedy for just about everything. But the comfort masks the messier reality that men and women don't grow up in separate cultures in any sense of the term but share common family, school, and work environments and swim in the same cultural sea of media imagery. However soothing it might be to think of gender issues as a matter of "East meets West," it simply isn't so.

A radical critique of Tannen's feminism might begin with her liberal preoccupation with individual motives and how she confuses these with social consequences. Tannen bends over backward to discourage women's anger at men who behave in dominating, aggressive ways, arguing that men don't *mean* to be this way. What she misses is that a hallmark of privilege is not having to mean it in order to exercise or benefit from socially bestowed privilege, whether it be taking up conversational space or

being taken more seriously and given more credit for new ideas. Awareness and intention require commitment and work, in comparison to which arrogance or innocence is relatively easy. And when men's conversational style promotes privilege, whether it's intended or not is irrelevant to the social consequences that result. If anything, men's lack of intent makes change even more difficult because it reflects how far they have to go to even be aware of what they're doing and why it matters. This is why liberalism's intense focus on the individual is so limiting. We can be so preoccupied with individual guilt, blame, and purity that we don't realize that participating in the social production of bad consequences doesn't require us to know what we're doing or, in particular, to intend bad results.

A radical perspective assumes from the start that patriarchy is real, that it doesn't spring from some vague wellspring of cultural "tradition," and that it sets men and women fundamentally at odds with one another, regardless of how they might feel about it as individuals.[32] Radical feminism's historical perspective identifies patriarchy as the first oppressive system, the originator of the religion of control, power, and fear that provided a model for all other forms of oppression.[33] As such, patriarchy is also the most deeply rooted and pervasive form of oppression and the most resistant to change. It manifests itself in every aspect of social life, making women's oppression and social oppression in general part of something much larger and deeper than what they may appear to be within the rhythms of everyday life.

Since radical feminism takes patriarchy and gender oppression to be real, it looks hard at men as the prime beneficiaries and enforcers of the patriarchal order. Regardless of how individual men may behave or see themselves, they participate in a system that grants them gender privilege at the expense of women and encourages them to protect and take advantage of it. The truth of this can be seen not only in obviously sexist men but in men who consider themselves sensitive to gender issues and supportive of the women's movement, for all too often they do little about it. Sometimes known as "sensitive

New Age guys," these men rarely take the initiative to learn more about patriarchy or their participation in it; they don't speak out publicly against women's oppression; and they don't confront other men about sexist behavior. They may protest that they don't want women to be oppressed and hate the idea of benefiting from it, but they also show little interest in making themselves uncomfortable to the extent of confronting the reality of what's going on beyond the pale of their good intentions. Unless prodded into action by women, most men choose to leave things as they are, which, by default, includes their unearned gender privilege. This is especially striking when it appears in men whose politics are otherwise progressively left. In fact, radical feminism emerged from women's experience in new left civil rights and antiwar movements of the 1960s in which male colleagues often treated them as subordinate, objectified "others" whose primary purpose was to meet men's needs.[34]

The distinction between liberal and radical feminism is important not because one is right and the other is wrong, but because they focus on different kinds of questions and problems. As a result, they also lead to different kinds of answers and solutions. Liberal feminism, for example, tends to interpret sexist stereotypes as false beliefs and bad attitudes that can be corrected through exposure to the truth. The belief that women are weak and dependent, for example, can be undone by showing people how strong and independent women can be; male attitudes of contemptuous superiority can be changed by making men aware of how injurious, unfair, and groundless such views are.

Radical feminism, however, reminds us that negative stereotypes about women don't exist in a vacuum. Especially when something is so persuasive in a society, we have to ask what *social* purpose it serves beyond the motives and intentions of individuals. Whose interests does sexism support, and what kind of social order does it perpetuate? From this perspective, misogyny and other forms of sexism are more than mistaken ideas and bad attitudes. They are also part of a cultural ideology that serves male privilege and supports women's subordination.

As such, sexism is more than mere prejudice: *it is prejudice plus the power to act on it.* The belief that women are weak and dependent, for example, and the cultural identification of strength and independence with maleness combine to make women's strength and independence invisible; it masks most men's essential vulnerability and dependence on women; and it promotes the illusion that men are in control—all of which are keys to maintaining patriarchy. As a form of sexism, misogyny also helps stabilize patriarchy by encouraging men to use women as targets for the feelings of contempt, frustration, and anger that arise from their competitive relations with other men.[35] Patriarchy sets men against other men, but it also rests on male solidarity in relation to women. Using women as scapegoats for negative feelings maintains this delicate balance while minimizing the personal risk to men.

Because radical and liberal perspectives interpret sexism differently, they also suggest different solutions to it. From a radical perspective, the liberal reliance on socialization is short-sighted and futile, for anything that truly undermines the definition of women as inferior and men as superior challenges the entire patriarchal system and therefore will provoke resistance. By itself, socialization won't bring about fundamental change because families, schools, and other agents of socialization are dedicated to raising children who will be accepted and succeed in society as it is, not risk living their lives in the shunned status of troublemaker or radical. This is what makes liberal feminism so appealing and also what limits its ability to create fundamental change. After decades of liberal feminist activism, for example, a small minority of elite women have been allowed to embrace patriarchal masculine values and achieve some success in male-identified occupations; but for women as a group, sexism still abounds. The problem isn't how we train children to fit into the world; the problem is the world into which we fit them and into which they'll feel compelled to fit if they're going to "get along" and "succeed."

If sexism reflected no more than a need for the light of truth to shine on the reality of men and women as they are, then it wouldn't have much of a future, given how much knowledge is readily available. But sexism isn't simply about individual enlightenment; it isn't a personality problem or a bad habit. Sexism is rooted in a social reality that underpins male privilege and gender oppression. Sexism isn't going to disappear from patriarchal culture through appeals to people's sense of fairness and decency or their ability to distinguish stereotypes from the facts of who people are.[36]

For all its limitations—or perhaps because of them—liberal feminism is all that most people actually know of feminist thought, and it therefore defines gender issues in public discussion. Radical feminism is virtually invisible in the mainstream except for the occasional distorted sound bite references to its most provocative expressions or its ideas taken out of context. As a result, radical feminism is known primarily as an attitude (such as man-hating), or as rigid orthodoxy ("only lesbians are real feminists"), or as a form of essentialism ("women are superior and ought to rule the world"). To be sure, all of these can be found somewhere in feminist writings; but they pale beside the overwhelming bulk of the radical analysis of patriarchy, whose insights can help both men and women work for something better.

Liberal feminism has more popular appeal than radical feminism because it focuses on gender without confronting the reality of patriarchal oppression and without seriously threatening male privilege. It avoids the uncomfortable work of challenging men to take some responsibility for patriarchy rather than merely being sensitive to "women's issues" or helping women out with domestic responsibilities when it suits them. And liberal feminism allows us to stay within the relatively comfortable familiarity of an individualistic, psychological framework in which individual pathology and change are the answer to every problem.

Under the liberal umbrella, women can comfort themselves with the idea that the men in *their* lives are personally OK and uninvolved in gender oppression or male privilege. Successful women can enjoy their status without having to question the patriarchal terms on which they achieved it, except when criticizing "victim feminists" who spoil things by calling attention to patriarchy and what it does to women. Men can reassure themselves that so long as they don't behave with conscious malevolence toward women, they aren't part of the problem. Men who don't rape, harass, or discriminate against women can wash their hands of gender issues and get on with their lives, with an occasional acknowledgment of the ever-fascinating "battle of the sexes" and men's and women's "cultures" and all the ins and outs of getting along with one another and appreciating gender "differences."

Radical feminism is avoided, dismissed, and attacked precisely because it raises critical questions that most people would rather ignore in the hope that they will go away. Radical feminism forces us to confront relationships that most men and women depend on to meet their needs. It challenges us to see how patriarchy divides women and men into subordinate and dominant groups with different interests that put them at odds with one another. And it violates one of patriarchy's core principles by daring to place women rather than men at the center of the discussion, focusing women's energy on themselves and other women and encouraging even heterosexual women to identify with women rather than with a male-identified system that marginalizes and oppresses them.

It shouldn't surprise us, then, that the mass media and so many people are content to settle for negative caricatures of radical feminism, to make feminist thought invisible, discredited, and ghettoized in the underground press and the shelves of alternative bookstores. But liberalism isn't enough to work our way out of patriarchy because it can't provide a clear view of patriarchy and how it works. We wind up in Naomi Wolf's confusion between dismantling the Master's house and getting into it, a confusion based on having no clear idea of just what the Master's house *is* or what it would mean to dismantle it. To change the system, we can't just focus on individuals; we also have to find ways to focus on the *system*, and for that we have to go to its roots, which is what radical feminism is all about.

A purely liberal approach to gender—or to race or class or any other form of oppression—can take us just so far, as is painfully clear from the current antifeminist backlash, a stalled civil rights movement, and a resurgence of anti-Semitism, xenophobia, and racism both in the United States and in Europe. Liberalism is a crucial first step in the journey away from oppressive systems. But that's all that it is, because it can take us only as far as the system will allow, and in oppressive systems that isn't far enough.

PATRIARCHY AND CAPITALISM: MARXIAN AND SOCIALIST FEMINISM

From a Marxian perspective, it's economics, not love, that makes the world go around. Since nothing is possible without material necessities such as food, clothing, and shelter, Marxists argue that every aspect of social life is shaped by how those material needs are met in a society. Everything from religion to the family to literature will look different, for example, in a feudal society than it will in an industrial capitalist one or in a band of hunter-gatherers. If the family is small, mobile, and nuclear in capitalist societies, and large, fixed, and extended in agrarian ones, it's because families accommodate themselves to different economic conditions and, as a result, survive within different systems of inequality and class relations.

How production is organized in a society gives rise to various kinds of social classes. In feudal societies, for example, production centered on the land, and class inequality was defined in relation to it. The land-owning class was thereby the dominant class, while the class that worked but didn't own the land was subordinate. By comparison, in industrial capitalist societies the central importance of land has been replaced by machinery and other technology. Under capitalism, the class that owns or controls the means of producing wealth is the dominant class, and instead of agrarian peasants, we now have various kinds of workers who sell their labor in exchange for wages. In the simplest sense, Marx argued that social life is always organized around such basic aspects of economic life. The state, for example, will generally act to preserve a given economic system and the class that dominates it, such as the capitalist class's control over capital, working conditions, and profit. Schools will socialize children to accept their position in the class structure and perform appropriately, whether as obedient workers or take-charge managers. Art, literature, and popular culture all become commodities that are valued primarily by how much someone is willing to pay for them. It's hard to think of anything that can't be bought or sold in a capitalist system, and this colors almost every aspect of human existence.

Ask a strict Marxist about gender oppression, and the response will invariably center on economics. Through a Marxian lens, gender oppression is just a variation on class oppression, with men the ruling class who control the most important resources and women the subordinate class whose childrearing and other domestic labor is exploited for men's benefit. Or women's oppression is a byproduct of capitalist exploitation that feeds on women's free or cheap labor and ready availability as part-time workers who can be hired when needed and discarded when not. In short, the Marxian version of feminism argues that women's oppression has more to do with the class dynamics of capitalism than with male privilege and dominance as forces in their own right. It's true that the working class includes both women and men, and women are often exploited in different ways than men—such as by performing unpaid child care and other domestic labor that produces new workers and cares for existing ones. But Marxian feminism argues that women's oppression is nonetheless primarily a matter of economics. If women are kept out of the paid labor force, for example, it's because capitalism took production out of the home and into the factory, making it difficult for women to do both paid and domestic labor.[37] In keeping with the Marxian perspective, then, women's subordinate status is defined in terms of capitalist class relations, not gender relations per se.

Economics also lies at the heart of a Marxian feminist solution to gender oppression. This would be accomplished by closing the split between family and work and replacing capitalism with socialism or some other alternative. Such changes would integrate women into the paid labor force—making child care and other domestic work public and communal rather than private and individual[38]— and would find other ways for women to be economically independent. All of this would remove the economic basis for male privilege and men's ability to exploit women's labor, reproductive ability, and sexuality. Since Marxists see economics as the basis for all other forms of power, economic equality will bring about general social equality between women and men.

Marxian feminism is useful because it shows how economic life in general and capitalism in particular shape gender oppression. Gender oppression also exists in agrarian patriarchies, for example, but with a different basis. Rather than controlling the flow of cash income, men own the land and have authority over wives and children. Under capitalism, land ownership is no longer the major basis for wealth and power, and so the economic underpinnings of male dominance shift from the family to wage labor and controlling the occupational marketplace. As useful as Marxian feminism is, however, its single-minded focus on economics overlooks the essentially patriarchal nature of systems such as feudalism and capitalism. It tells little about how the interests and dynamics of patriarchy and capitalism overlap and support each other. Nor does it help to explain women's continued subordination in non-capitalist societies such as China and the former Soviet Union that failed to live up to socialist ideology that opposes all forms of oppression. These societies have shown that although removing capitalism can improve the status of women—as it certainly did in many ways—patriarchy can continue to exist in other forms.

Marxian feminism's limitations are understandable, given its origins. In many ways it developed as an attempt by traditional Marxists to accommodate the challenges raised by the modern women's movement. Using ideas they were most familiar with, Marxists forced gender oppression into a relatively narrow framework of capitalist class relations. This inevitably came up against the limitations of trying to reduce everything to economics. The Marxists were onto something important, however, when they identified capitalism as a powerful force to be reckoned with in opposing patriarchy. Capitalism is organized around control and domination—whether of workers or technology or markets and competitors—and economic life is one of the most important arenas in which the patriarchal dynamic of fear and control operates. Marxists also should be credited for recognizing long ago the origins of male dominance. Marx's collaborator Friedrich Engels, for example, argued that social inequality originated in the family and that historically women were the first oppressed group.[39]

Criticism of Marxian feminism produced socialist feminism, which broadens and deepens the Marxian approach by focusing on the complex connection between patriarchy and economic systems such as capitalism, especially as it operates through the family. As Heidi Hartmann argues, for example, oppression involves more than psychology and social roles, for it is always rooted in the material realities of production and reproduction.[40] In other words, historically women have been oppressed primarily through male control over women's labor and women's bodies—their sexuality and reproductive potential—especially in families. The goods women produce have been appropriated by men; women have been bought and sold in marriage arrangements between men; and control over women's sexuality and the children they bear has been a staple ingredient of patriarchal marriage. The institution of monogamous heterosexual marriage has enabled men to control women's bodies through conjugal rights of sexual access, to keep women dependent on men (through control over land or, more recently, control over the "breadwinner" role), and to ensure a clear male line of inheritance. Although women are now challenging the male monopoly of the breadwinning role, this arrangement has served men's interests for a long time, especially in the middle and upper classes. It has enabled them to benefit from women's personal services and to enhance their competition with other men over the resources and rewards that determine social class position.

One of the great values of socialist feminism is that it shows how the status of women and men has both shaped and been shaped by economic arrangements. Patriarchy and capitalism are so deeply intertwined with each other that some socialist feminists argue against even thinking of them as separate systems:

> Under capitalism as it exists today, women experience patriarchy as unequal wages for work equal to that of men; sexual harassment on the job; uncompensated domestic work. . . . Earlier generations of women also experienced patriarchy, but they lived it differently depending on the dynamics of the reigning economic system. . . . A feudal system of gender relations accompanied a feudal system of class arrangements, and the social relations of class and gender grew together and evolved over time into the forms we now know (for example, the capitalist nuclear family). To say that gender relations are independent of class relations is to ignore how history works.[41]

The basic insight of socialist feminism is that patriarchy and gender oppression are not simply about gender, but are bound up with the most fundamental aspects of social life. Justice for women involves more than changing how men and women think, feel, and behave in gendered relationships, for any deeply rooted challenge to patriarchy will profoundly affect the prevailing economic system. This also applies to other institutions such as the state, religion, education, the law, and the mass media that support and reflect both economic and patriarchal interests.

FEMINISM: BEING AND DOING

As a way of thinking, feminism is invaluable to anyone who wants to help unravel the patriarchal gender knot. It gives us a way to question everything from the nature of sex and gender to how patriarchy weaves core values of control and dominance into the fabric of everyday life. Liberal feminism provides a place to start, but sooner or later we have to move toward the roots of the problem, beyond

relatively superficial change to a more fundamental restructuring and redefinition of what life is to be about. This is precisely where we are as we approach the end of the twentieth century: standing at the edge of where liberal feminism has brought us and wondering what to do next. Some people, perhaps sensing that liberalism has taken us as far as it can, have declared a postfeminist era. But we aren't in postfeminism; we're in a backlash coming at the tail of a temporarily exhausted women's movement.

Patriarchy is like a fire burning deep underground, spreading and burning into the Earth for thousands of years. We notice what breaks through the surface and may think that's all there is. We may focus on not getting burned in the moment even though we can sense something larger and deeper down below. But if we're serious about change, we have to wake up to the fact that there's more going on than gendered brushfires springing up in episodes of miscommunication, sexual harassment, discrimination, violence, and all the other day-to-day occurrences that add up to life under patriarchy. If we're serious about this, we've got to dig, preferably with plenty of company and with a full appreciation of the fact that although we didn't start the fire, it's ours now.

Many people feel threatened by feminism, especially its nonliberal aspects, because it raises questions about gender that invite us to look more closely not only at the world, but at the complex fullness of who we are in relation to it. Feminism is a window on the world and our connection to it; and it is a mirror reflecting what our lives are about. Above all, it is a powerful framework for making sense of what we're participating in, for digging beneath the surface of status quo ideology and what we take to be reality to discover the unarticulated terms on which we actually live our lives. But at the same time that it can frighten us or make us feel uncomfortable, it can also empower us because it makes such compelling sense of what's going on and what it has to do with us. It embodies an enduring truth that patriarchy and women's oppression are real and problematic for all of us, and that not only can we understand what's happening, we must understand if we are ever to be part of the solution and not just part of the problem.

As reluctant as many women are to embrace feminism, it's even harder for men, who often see themselves as excluded members of an enemy class and therefore personally to blame for patriarchy and its consequences. Even men who don't go to this extreme are often careful not to identify too closely or too openly with feminism. This includes many men who actively support the struggle against patriarchy. The National Organization of Men Against Sexism, for example, describes itself as "pro-feminist" rather than feminist. In some ways a "feminist-once-removed" identity helps counter the dominant group tendency to coopt and take over anything of value produced by subordinate groups—from white people's appropriation of Native American spirituality to the "new men's movement" claim that it parallels the women's movement.[42] The pro-feminist label also honors the fact that whatever their politics, men cannot call themselves feminists as a kind of safe-conduct pass that obscures or denies the reality of male privilege, of their inherently problematic status *as men* under patriarchy, and of the legitimacy of women's anger. Insofar as feminism has to do with *being* rather than with *thinking* or *doing,* insofar as it reflects women's actual experience under patriarchy, then men shouldn't call themselves feminists.

But men's seemingly appropriate distance from feminism also reinforces the idea that deep down, patriarchy, like housework, is really a women's problem. This limits men to a supportive role in which they can "do the right thing" and count themselves among the "good guys." To be pro-feminist is to support women in *their* fight, but it doesn't name the fight against patriarchy as inherently *men's* responsibility and therefore their fight as well. This is especially important if we think of feminism as more than a way to think about gender oppression and how to advance women's interests in relation to men. Because patriarchy isn't simply about gender, because every major social institution is grounded in core patriarchal values, feminism is, in its broadest sense, about the way the whole world is organized.[43]

For all of feminism's potential, the simple truth is that if people want to dismiss it, they'll have an easy time of it, given how effectively feminism has been distorted and marginalized. All one need do is point to the disagreeable views of one feminist or another in order to feel the approving nod of the mainstream that "Yes, isn't that odd" or "Isn't she outrageous?" and then move along. But any complex body of thought coupled with social movements against a system as deeply entrenched as patriarchy can't help but produce enough excesses and contradictions to provide opponents with an inexhaustible supply of ammunition. Settling for that, however, accomplishes nothing more than leaving us in the mess we're in, surrounded by familiar stereotypes yet knowing on some level that something is seriously wrong with what patriarchy makes of gender and human life.

Ultimately, either we believe patriarchy exists or we don't. And if we do, we need to know more about feminism, because regardless of what branch of feminism we might lean toward, feminism is the only ongoing conversation about patriarchy that can lead to a way out. But in the patriarchal mainstream, this is just the problem, because . . . there's little there that doesn't make it harder to see patriarchy for what it is.

NOTES

1. Far more than I can cover here. For a more complete look at feminist thinking an excellent place to start is Rosemarie Tong's *Feminist Thought: A Comprehensive Introduction* (Boulder, Colo.: Westview Press, 1989); and Margaret L. Andersen, *Thinking about Women: Sociological Perspectives on Sex and Gender* (New York: Macmillan, 1993).
2. See, for example, Wendy Kaminer, "Feminism's Identity Crisis," *Atlantic,* October 1993, 51–68.
3. See Susan Faludi, *Backlash: The Undeclared War Against American Women* (New York: Crown, 1991).
4. Sam Keen, *Fire in the Belly: On Being a Man* (New York: Bantam Books, 1991), 196*ff.*
5. Keen, *Fire in the Belly,* 196.
6. Limbaugh routinely refers to feminists in this way on his radio and television talk shows. Paglia made this statement on the television show *Sixty Minutes,* 1 November 1992.
7. Naomi Wolf, *The Beauty Myth: How Images of Beauty Are Used Against Women* (New York: William Morrow, 1991).

8. For a powerful analysis of the difference between motherhood as experience and motherhood as a patriarchal institution, see Adrienne Rich, *Of Woman Born* (New York: W. W. Norton, 1976). For some insight into how patriarchy shapes fatherhood, see Robert L. Griswold, *Fatherhood in America: A History* (New York: Basic Books, 1993).

9. Women may make jokes among themselves that play off their subordinate position (as also do blacks, Jews, and other groups targeted by prejudice) that would never be tolerated coming from members of dominant groups. The difference is that when it comes from other women, it heightens awareness of their common standing as women and can help reinforce their sense of solidarity with one another; but when it comes from men it is more of an assertion of men's dominant position under patriarchy.

10. Quoted by John S. Wilson in *The Boston Globe* Magazine, 8 November 1992, p. 43.

11. I have more to say about false parallels in Chapter 6 [of *The Gender Knot*].

12. The hatred of males because they are male.

13. See, for example, Judith Levine, *My Enemy, My Love: Man-Hating and Ambivalence in Women's Lives* (New York: Doubleday, 1993).

14. At a lecture on 11 April 1991, at Trinity College, in Hartford, Connecticut, Davis made this comment in response to a young black man who supported black women's struggle for equality but felt stung by their negative comments about men in general.

15. See bell hooks, *Feminist Theory*, chap. 15.

16. Valerie Solanas, *The SCUM (Society for Cutting Up Men) Manifesto* (New York: Olympia Press, 1968).

17. See Alice Echols, *Daring to Be Bad: Radical Feminism in America 1967–1975* (Minneapolis: University of Minnesota Press, 1989), 210–241; Nancy Myron and Charlotte Bunch, eds., *Lesbianism and the Women's Movement* (Baltimore: Diana Press, 1975); and Marilyn Frye, "Willful Virgin, or, Do You Have to Be a Lesbian to Be a Feminist?" in *Willful Virgin: Essays in Feminism, 1976–1992* (Freedom, Calif.: Crossing Press, 1992).

18. See Suzanne Pharr, *Homophobia: A Weapon of Sexism* (Inverness, Calif.: Chardon Press, 1988).

19. Adrienne Rich, "Compulsory Heterosexuality and Lesbian Existence," *Signs: A Journal of Women in Culture and Society* 5, no. 4 (summer 1980).

20. Ellyn Kaschak, *Engendered Lives: A New Psychology of Women's Experience* (New York: Basic Books, 1992), 5. Kaschak provides a provocative discussion of the concept of the "indeterminate" male viewer whose gaze is everywhere in women's lives.

21. See also Marilyn Frye, "In and Out of Harm's Way: Arrogance and Love," in *The Politics of Reality: Essays in Feminist Theory* (Trumansburg, N.Y.: Crossing Press, 1983), 52–83.

22. See Wolf, *Beauty Myth.*

23. See, for example, Roiphe, *Morning After;* Christine Hoff Sommers, *Who Stole Feminism?* (New York: Simon and Schuster, 1994); and Wolf, *Fire With Fire.*

24. Naomi Wolf, for example, argues that "the right question to ask is simply how to get more power into women's hands—whoever they may be, whatever they may do with it" (*Fire With Fire,* 127).

25. For a more extensive description and analysis of liberal feminism, see Tong, *Feminist Thought,* chap. 1.

26. For some vivid portraits of what these negotiations look like and why they so often fail, see Arlie Hochschild, *The Second Shift: Working Parents and the Revolution at Home* (New York: Viking/Penguin, 1989). See also R. L. Blumberg, ed., *Gender, Family, and Economy: The Triple Overlap* (Newbury Park, Calif.: Sage, 1991); K. Gerson, *No Man's Land: Men's Changing Commitments to Family and Work* (New York: Basic Books, 1993); F. K. Goldscheider and L. J. Waite, *New Families, No Families? The Transformation of the American Home* (Berkeley: University of California Press, 1991); J. R. Wilkie, "Changes in U.S. Men's Attitudes Towards the Family Provider Role, 1972–1989," *Gender and Society* 7, no. 2 (1993): 261–279; and E. O. Wright, K. Shire, S. Hwang, M. Dolan, and J. Baxter, "The Non-Effects of Class on the Gender Division of Labor in the Home: A Comparison of Sweden and the U.S.," *Gender and Society* 6, no. 2 (1992): 25–82.

27. Audre Lorde, *Sister Outsider* (Freedom, Calif.: Crossing Press, 1984).

28. Wolf, *Fire With Fire,* 139.

29. French, *Beyond Power,* 443.

30. For more on this, see Blumberg, ed., *Gender, Family, and Economy;* C. N. Degler, *At Odds: Women and the Family in America from the Revolution to the Present* (New York: Oxford University Press, 1980); Gerson, *No Man's Land; Second Shift;* Miriam M. Johnson, *Strong Mothers, Weak Wives: The Search for Gender Equality* (Berkeley: University of California Press, 1988); Ann Oakley, *Woman's Work: The Housewife, Past and Present* (New York: Vintage, 1976); and Eli Zaretsky, *Capitalism, the Family, and Personal Life,* rev. ed. (New York: Harper and Row, 1986).

31. Deborah Tannen, *You Just Don't Understand: Women and Men in Conversation* (New York: William Morrow, 1990), 15.

32. See Tong, *Feminist Thought;* and Alison M. Jaggar and Paula S. Rothenberg, eds., *Feminist Frameworks* (New York: McGraw-Hill, 1984).

33. See Kate Millet, *Sexual Politics* (Garden City, N.Y.: Doubleday, 1970).

34. See Echols, *Daring to Be Bad.*

35. As we saw in Chapter 2 [of *The Gender Knot*].

36. I have much more to say about the problem of change in Chapters 9 and 10 [of *The Gender Knot*].

37. See Zaretsky, *Capitalism, the Family, and Personal Life.*

38. Cooking and child care, for example, might be done collectively in communal living arrangements that break down women's isolation from one another and the larger community.

39. Friedrich Engels, *The Origin of the Family, Private Property, and the State* (New York: Pathfinder Press, 1972).

40. Heidi Hartmann, "The Unhappy Marriage of Marxism and Feminism: Towards a More Progressive Union," in

Women and Revolution: A Discussion of the Unhappy Marriage of Marxism and Feminism, ed. Lydia Sargent (Boston: South End Press, 1981), 1–41: See also Tong, *Feminist Thought,* chap. 6.

41. Tong in *Feminist Thought* (185) summarizes Iris Young, "Beyond the Unhappy Marriage: A Critique of the Dual Systems Theory," in *Women and Revolution: A Discussion of the Unhappy Marriage of Marxism and Feminism,* ed. Lydia Sargent (Boston: South End Press, 1981).

42. About which I have much to say in Chapter 8 [of *The Gender Knot*].

43. See, for example, Charlotte Bunch, "Bringing the Global Home," in *Passionate Politics: Feminist Theory in Action* (New York: St. Martin's Press, 1987), 328–345. See also Irene Diamond and Gloria Feman Orenstein, eds., *Reweaving the World: The Emergence of Ecofeminism* (San Francisco: Sierra Club Books, 1990).

53

Holy War

BOB MOSER

The religious crusade against gays has been building for 30 years. Now the movement is reaching truly biblical proportions.

On June 26, 2003, the U.S. Supreme Court overturned the convictions of two Texas men arrested for having sex. Writing for the majority in *Lawrence v. Texas,* Justice Anthony Kennedy said that the two men were "entitled to respect for their private lives." The state, he declared, "cannot demean their existence or control their destiny by making their private sexual conduct a crime."

The decision was unusually popular. A national survey found that 75% of Republicans and 88% of Democrats wanted to see sodomy laws struck down. But not everyone cheered.

"Six lawyers robed in black have magically discovered a right of privacy that includes sexual perversion," said Jan LaRue, chief counsel for Concerned Women for America. "This opens the door to bigamy, adult incest, polygamy and prostitution," said Ken Connor, president of the Family Research Council.

For anti-gay crusaders, who have been fighting gay rights for three decades, *Lawrence* was the most unsettling court decision since *Roe v. Wade.* Fundamentalist groups had filed 15 briefs supporting Texas' sodomy laws, only to see their arguments—that gay sex was a threat to public health and "traditional family values," and that gay people do not deserve equal rights—shot down.

And with the Massachusetts Supreme Court widely expected to rule that fall (as it did) that gay citizens had a right to marry under that state's constitution, anti-gay leaders realized the time was ripe to ratchet up their call to arms.

★ ★ ★

The anti-gay movement was about to show why many believe it is, in the words of longtime religious right observer Frederick Clarkson, "the best-organized faction in politics." Immediately after the *Lawrence* decision, D. James Kennedy, president of Coral Ridge Ministries, issued a call to arms.

Now that America's courts were "officially off-limits to the moral framework that has allowed us to enjoy freedom and prosperity," Kennedy said the holy war on gay rights should be renewed on the battlefront of public opinion, pressing for a federal marriage amendment.

For right-wing evangelical ministries like Coral Ridge, which brings in more than $35 million annually, the stakes were never higher. Since the late 1970s, attacks on gay people and their "agenda" had helped to fuel, and pay for, the fundamentalist right's unprecedented rise to political power.

★ ★ ★

Many of its leaders have engaged in the crudest type of name-calling, describing homosexuals as "perverts" with "filthy habits" who seek to snatch the children of straight parents and "convert" them to gay sex. They have continually bandied about disparaging "facts" about gays that are simply untrue—assertions that are remarkably reminiscent of the way white intellectuals and scientists once wrote about the "bestial" black man.

But never has the anti-gay movement had the momentum it has now, and never has it been so close to achieving its larger, ultimate goal. That goal is winning, in the words of Focus on the Family founder James Dobson, a "second civil war" for control of the U.S. government.

THE POWER OF THE SWORD

★ ★ ★

. . . While fundamentalist Christians had long stayed out of electoral politics, [Rev. Jerry] Falwell and many others were "extremely unhappy with the 'rights' movements that had sprung up in the '50s and '60s," says Didi Herman, author of *The Antigay Agenda*.

"First black people, then women, now gay people? The frustration had been mounting. Their actions were catching up with their view."

Falwell was plain enough about his views; in 1964, he told a local paper that the Civil Rights Act had been misnamed: "It should be considered civil wrongs rather than civil rights." His "Old Time Gospel Hour" TV program hosted prominent segregationists like Govs. Lester Maddox of Georgia and George Wallace of Alabama.

But Falwell, like other fundamentalists, worried about "tainting" his religious message by mixing it with politics.

The Rev. Mel White . . . , an evangelical writer and filmmaker who ghostwrote Falwell's autobiography, says Falwell was led to politics in part by Dr. Francis Schaeffer, a rebellious fundamentalist who had begun spreading the word about "dominion theology" and who many see as the father of the anti-abortion movement.

Dubbed the "Guru of Fundamentalists" by *Newsweek* in 1982, Schaeffer believed that Christians are called to rule the U.S.—and the world—using biblical law. That meant winning elections.

★ ★ ★

Schaeffer was admired by a radical group of fundamentalist thinkers called Christian Reconstructionists. Led by Orthodox Presbyterian minister R.J. Rushdoony, the Reconstructionists argued that the Second Coming couldn't occur until the faithful established a "Biblical kingdom."

Democracy, which Rushdoony called "the great love of the failures and cowards of life," would be replaced by strict Old Testament law—meaning the death penalty for homosexuality, along with a host of other "abominations," including heresy, astrology, and (for women only) "unchastity before marriage."

D. James Kennedy of Coral Ridge Ministries, like James Dobson of Focus on the Family and other Christian Right luminaries, unwaveringly preaches "dominion Christianity" and hosts an annual conference devoted to "Reclaiming America for Christ."

★ ★ ★

FEAR MONGERING TO THE FORE

While conservative Christians have led historic crusades against a number of "evils" in America—witchcraft, alcohol, communism, feminism, abortion—gay sex was never more than a minor concern until 1969, when protests in New York City launched the contemporary gay-rights movement.

In *Where We Stand*, Susan Fort Wiltshire recalls some early stirrings of a new crusade: "Around 1970, ambitious small-town preachers in the Northwest Texas Annual Conference of the United Methodist Church began to exploit 'the gay issue.' They saw that virulent anti-gay rhetoric could fill football stadiums for revivals in such tiny Panhandle towns as Tulia and Clarendon and Higgins and Perryton."

The crusade went national in 1977, courtesy of Anita Bryant. The perky spokesperson for Coca-Cola, Tupperware and Florida orange juice, Bryant had converted a runner-up finish in the 1959 Miss America pageant into a lucrative career singing "wholesome family music."

Bryant later said she knew next to nothing about gay people when she attended a 1977 revival at Miami's Northside Baptist Church. The preacher railed against a new ordinance in Dade County that protected gay people from discrimination, saying he'd "burn down his church before he would let homosexuals teach in its school."

Bryant was so impressed by the dangers of this new "homosexual agenda" that she launched an initiative to overturn the anti-discrimination ordinance, winning with a 70% vote.

Bryant then founded a national group called Save Our Children and took her anti-gay message on the road, helping fundamentalists organize anti-gay ballot campaigns in the handful of American cities that had passed gay rights laws. These ballot initiatives would become the single most important organizing tool for the fundamentalist right, transforming thousands of previously apolitical churchgoers into grassroots activists.

Save Our Children's primary tactic was fear mongering. Gay people were "sick," "perverted," "twisted," and a threat to American families.

★ ★ ★

Save Our Children distributed a press kit with a paper titled, "Why Certain Sexual Deviations Are Punishable By Death." Homosexuality was of course, among those deviations. So was "racial mixing of human seed."

★ ★ ★

"Their other issues just weren't nearly as popular," says Rob Boston, assistant communications director of Americans United for Separation of Church and State and author of *Close Encounters with the Religious Right*.

. . . But gay people? Anita Bryant showed that gay-bashing could bring in some real money."

. . . Inspired by Bryant, budding "family activist" Tim LaHaye painted a full-blown portrait in his 1978 book, *The Unhappy Gays*.

LaHaye, now famous for co-authoring the blockbuster *Left Behind* series of end-of-the-world thrillers, wrote that succumbing to the demands of the gay-rights movement would be a mistake of apocalyptic proportions—literally.

"The mercy and grace of God seem to reach their breaking point when homosexuality becomes normal," LaHaye said. "Put another way, when sodomy fills the national cup of man's abominations to overflowing, God earmarks that nation for destruction."

★ ★ ★

FACTS AND FICTION

There was something missing from these dark depictions of gay people and their "agenda": evidence. It was one thing, after all, to claim that homosexuals were child "recruiters," disease-ridden, and mentally unstable. It was quite another to prove it.

Enter Paul Cameron. After losing his job teaching psychology at the University of Nebraska, Cameron set himself up as an independent sex researcher in the late 1970s, churning out scores of anti-gay pamphlets that were largely distributed in fundamentalist churches.

Cameron's "studies" falsely concluded that gay people were disproportionately responsible for child molestation, for the majority of serial killings, and for the spread of sexually transmitted diseases. Gay people, according to Cameron's research, were obsessed with consuming human excrement, allowing them to spread deadly diseases simply by shaking hands with unsuspecting strangers or using public restrooms.

★ ★ ★

Cameron's brand of "science" echoed Nazi Germany. "These themes of disease and seduction are strongly reminiscent of older, anti-Semitic discourse," writes Didi Herman in *The Antigay Agenda*. "Jews historically were associated with disease, filth, urban degeneration, and child stealing."

When the AIDS crisis broke out in the early 1980s, Cameron claimed gay people had unleashed "an octopus of infection spreading across the world," and had done it on purpose. (Jerry Falwell put it in simpler terms; he called AIDS "the gay plague.")

★ ★ ★

After being expelled from the American Psychological Association in 1983 for violating ethical standards in his anti-gay publications Cameron began referring to himself as a sociologist—until the American Sociological Association passed a 1986 resolution declaring, "Paul Cameron is not a sociologist, and [this group] condemns his constant misrepresentation of sociological research."

But despite the crackpot nature of Cameron's theories and methodology, his "research" was extolled by many in the religious right. In 1986, Summit Ministries, a right-wing Christian group in Colorado, distributed a booklet called *Special Report: AIDS*, co-written by Cameron, Summit leader David Noebel and Wayne Lutton (Lutton would later be an editor for an anti-immigrant hate group, the Social Contract Press, and act as editorial advisor to the white supremacist Council of Conservative Citizens).

Special Report argued for a drastic solution: locking up "practicing homosexuals" in the name of public health. After all, the authors wrote, "During World War II we exiled Americans of Japanese ancestry simply because we felt they were a national threat during time of war."

★ ★ ★

VICTORY AND DEFEAT

To the dismay of the anti-gay crusaders, polls showed rising public support for gay rights throughout the '80s and '90s. As a result, the crusaders began to rethink their message. "They finally started to realize the 'diseased pervert' rhetoric wasn't going to win over the majority of Americans," says *Close Encounters with the Religious Right* author Rob Boston.

In Colorado Springs, home to more than 50 Christian Right organizations by 1991, a whole new anti-gay strategy was being cooked up by Colorado For Family Values, organizers of Amendment 2, a statewide ballot initiative that would overturn gay anti-discrimination laws that had been passed by three Colorado towns and prevent any such future protections from being passed.

Realizing the old arguments weren't working, one of Amendment 2's organizers, a born-again "ex-hippie" attorney named Tony Marco, produced a fresh argument: "special rights."

"What gives gay militants their enormous power are money and the operative presumption that gays represent some kind of 'oppressed minority,'" Marco wrote. He recommended "demolishing the presumption that gays are an 'oppressed minority.'"

The best way to do that, Marco believed, was to drum up resentment against gay people— particularly among African Americans and working-class whites—by portraying them as wanting "special rights."

In a 1992 issue of Focus on the Family's *Citizen* magazine, Marco began making an economic case that gay people already had privileges that most Americans could only dream of. "Homosexuals have an average household income of $55,340," he wrote, "versus $32,144 for the general population and $12,166 for disadvantaged African-American households."

Marco's numbers were grossly misleading and, like Cameron's crackpot science, reminiscent of anti-Semitic propaganda about Jews. His source for gay income was a 1988 survey of gay magazine readers— a skewed sample, *The Antigay Agenda* author Didi Herman notes, because "readers of glossy gay men's magazines are likely to be among the most affluent members of the gay and lesbian community."

Amendment 2 got a major boost in 1991, when James Dobson began to push it on his daily radio show. Dobson had moved his multimedia empire to a campus in Colorado Springs that same year. Known to most Americans as a soft-spoken purveyor of homespun parenting advice, Dobson was now displaying a much tougher side.

★ ★ ★

When Dobson began pushing Amendment 2, its organizers had been struggling to get enough signatures to qualify for the ballot. Overnight, the campaign was flooded with volunteers and money. Amendment 2 won by a 53%–47% margin.

The anti-gay movement had won a major round—in the court of public opinion, at least. In 1996, Amendment 2 was overturned by the u.s. Supreme Court in *Evans v. Romer.* Justice Anthony Kennedy's majority decision began with a pointed reference to *Plessy v. Ferguson,* the 1896 decision that allowed "separate but equal" treatment of black people and ushered in the Jim Crow era.

The Colorado amendment, Kennedy wrote, imposed a "special disability" on gay men and lesbians, and constituted "a bare . . . desire to harm a politically unpopular group."

But by then, the anti-gay movement had been thoroughly energized. . . .

CALLING NAMES

Old-school gay-bashing did not die away with the rise of the "special rights" strategizing. If anything, the rhetoric was ratcheted up in the 1990s, when President Bill Clinton's proposal to lift the ban on gay military service inspired a verbal arms race.

★ ★ ★

Jerry Falwell worried aloud that if the ban were lifted, "our poor boys on the front lines will have to face two different enemies, one from the front and one from the rear."

★ ★ ★

In July 1998, Pat Robertson warned the citizens of Orlando, Fla., that if Disney World didn't cancel "Gay Day," their city would be subject to God's wrath, in the form of "terrorist bombs, earthquakes, tornadoes and possibly a meteor."

That same July, D. James Kennedy's Center for Reclaiming America, the Christian Coalition, Focus on the Family and other anti-gay groups launched a million-dollar ad campaign to promote "ex-gay" ministries specializing in "curing" lesbians and gay men of their sexual orientation. . . .

The ex-gay campaign was partly designed to reinforce the message that fundamentalists truly "love the sinner but hate the sin." Ex-gay people were also an essential part of the "special rights" campaign, their existence cited as proof that homosexuality was not genetic, but a matter of choice.

Most of the ex-gay ministries promoted in the campaign, including Focus on the Family's Exodus International, practiced "reparative therapy," a collection of methods that had long been thoroughly discredited in the world of psychology. . . .

★ ★ ★

"THE ULTIMATE EX-GAY"

On Oct. 6, 1998, one day before D. James Kennedy's anti-gay coalition put out a second round of ex-gay TV ads, 21-year-old college student Matthew Shepard was savagely murdered in Wyoming. Journalists jumped on the connection between the ex-gay campaign and the prejudice that fuels hate crimes.

"You call a group of people evil and sick and immoral often enough and some nutcase out there is going to act on it," wrote columnist Donald Kaul in the *Des Moines Register.*

The Advocate, a gay newsmagazine, pointedly called Shepard "the ultimate ex-gay."

★ ★ ★

In January of that year, more than 20 anti-gay groups, including Focus on the Family and the Christian Coalition, sent representatives to a church cellar in Memphis, Tenn., for the first secret meeting of the National Pro-Family Forum. The Forum, which continued to meet every three months, scored a symbolic victory that fall, when its members convinced Congress to pass the Defense of Marriage Act (DOMA), defining marriage as the union of one man and one woman.

Writing in support of DOMA, [Gary] Bauer predicted that gay marriage would have dire consequences for Americans of faith: "If they succeed, all distinctions based on sex may fall, and the worst aspects of the rejected Equal Rights Amendment will be imposed. Homosexuals will gain the 'right' to adopt children; . . . churches will be pushed outside civil law; and government power will be wielded against anyone who holds the biblical view of homosexuality."

FOREST FIRE

★ ★ ★

"What's at stake here," said Family Research Council president Tony Perkins, "is the very foundation of our society, not only of America but all Western civilization."

"I've never seen a man in my life I wanted to marry," said the Rev. Jimmy Swaggart. "And I'm gonna be blunt and plain: if one ever looks at me like that, I'm gonna kill him and tell God he died."

From the 2003 Texas sodomy decision until Election Day 2004, the gay-marriage debate seemed to bring out the warrior in everyone. The anti-gay campaign, said Human Rights Campaign Executive Director Cheryl Jacques, was marked by "the highest level of intensity and aggression ever."

In the 11 states where anti-gay marriage measures were on the ballot, television ads urged voters to "defend marriage." In Ohio, Phil Burress' anti-gay group gathered 575,000 signatures in fewer than 90 days to put their constitutional amendment on the ballot. "It's a forest fire with a 100-mile-per-hour wind behind it," Burress told *The New York Times.*

Just five months after *Lawrence v. Texas,* the Pew Research Center found that opposition to gay marriage had climbed from 53 to 59%. A new majority of Americans, 55%, now characterized gay sex as a sin. Thirty years of anti-gay crusades had begun to pay.

As Election Day drew near, James Dobson was taking no chances. His political spin-off group, Focus on the Family Action, organized large rallies in six cities. . . .

On Oct. 22 in Oklahoma City, Dobson brought the crowd to its feet with a message that Bryant might have delivered in 1977. "Homosexuals are not monogamous," he said. "They want to destroy the institution of marriage. It will destroy marriage. It will destroy the earth."

On Nov. 2, the anti-gay marriage amendments passed handily in all 11 states—including Ohio, the state that ultimately swung the election in George W. Bush's favor. Many commentators argued that the huge voter turnout in that pivotal battleground state—and therefore George W. Bush's victory—was due largely to the anti-gay amendment driving conservative voters to the polls in record numbers.

★ ★ ★

54

Color-Blinded America or How the Media and Politics Have Made Racism and Racial Inequality Yesterday's Social Problem

CHARLES A. GALLAGHER

Think for a moment about the various people who appear in television advertisements for each of these products: soda, fast food, and sneakers. Take a mental inventory of the news anchors on your favorite local television station. Now think about the major cast members in the latest big budget, over-the-top Hollywood action movie. What similarities do you see among advertisements, news anchors, and Hollywood blockbusters? In all likelihood the common denominator is a carefully staged *multiracial* cast of performers selling you Nikes or Pepsi, black, white, and perhaps Asian news anchors describing traffic gridlock in your community, or handsome actors spanning the racial continuum in a race against time to save the world from annihilation. What is relatively new is that these consciously manufactured, interracial ensembles are completely unremarkable in that they are now so commonplace.

Americans are constantly bombarded by media depictions of race relations that suggest that discriminatory racial barriers have been dismantled. Social and cultural indicators imply that America is on the verge, or has already become, a truly color-blind nation. National polling data indicate that a majority of whites now believe discrimination against racial minorities no longer exists. A recent poll by Gallup (2004) found that 61% of non-Hispanic whites believed that "blacks have equal job opportunities as whites." The number jumps to 71% when only those whites holding a high school degree or less are asked about white versus black opportunities in the labor market. The color-blind or race neutral perspective holds that in an environment where institutional racism and discrimination have been replaced by equal opportunity, one's qualifications, not one's color or ethnicity, should be the mechanism by which upward mobility is achieved. Color as a cultural style may be expressed and consumed through music, dress, or vernacular, but race as a system that confers privileges and shapes life chances is viewed as an atavistic and inaccurate accounting of U.S. race relations.

Not surprisingly, this view of society blind to color is not equally shared. Whites and blacks differ significantly—on their support for affirmative action, the perceived fairness of the criminal justice system, the ability to realize the "American Dream," and the extent to which whites have benefited from past discrimination. A majority of whites (56%) believe that the goals of the civil rights movement have been accomplished, while much of white America now sees a level playing field, a majority of black Americans see a field that is still quite uneven.

COLOR-BLINDNESS AS NORMATIVE IDEOLOGY

A 2002 Gallup poll found that 81% of whites felt that black children had "as good a chance" as the white children in their own neighborhood to get a quality education (Keifer 2003). It is simply inaccurate to suggest that the education children receive in overwhelmingly white, affluent, suburban communities is on par with the education black and brown children receive in America's inner cities. A Gallup poll conducted for AARP and released in 2004 found that a majority, 61% of non-Hispanic whites, responded that "blacks have equal job opportunities as whites" (Gallup 2004). Among those with a high school degree or less (the majority of white Americans in the United States), the numbers who believe there is now equality in the labor market went up to 71% of non-Hispanic whites (Gallup 2004). A 2003 Gallup poll asked if the goals of the civil rights movement have been achieved (Keifer 2003). Among non-Hispanic whites, 56% said all or most of the goals of the civil rights movement had been achieved. Again, it is hard to reconcile these perceptions of achieved goals when we examine quality of life indicators by race. In almost every category—unemployment, incarceration, home ownership, college attendance, wealth, and infant mortality—racial disparities among white, black, and brown populations exist. Equality of opportunity (a false assertion in itself) has somehow become synonymous with equality of results.

A huge majority (82%) of white Americans say they have a close personal friend who is not white (Gallup 2004), although half (50%) of all white Americans work in environments that are all or mostly white. Doing the math for the 82% of whites who have a black or brown close personal friend would mean that every single black and brown American would have to have about three very close

white friends. Take a moment to list your three best friends. In all likelihood they are the same race as you. A record 70% of whites in a 2003 Gallup poll said they "generally approve" of marriages between blacks and whites (Gallup 2004), although in reality these groups are the least likely among all possible racial pairings to marry. Although national polls suggest a high approval of intermarriage, ethnographic accounts of what transpires when whites cross the color line in romance provide a much more complicated and hostile account of these unions (Dalmage 2004).

The perception among a majority of white Americans that the socio-economic playing field is now level, along with whites' belief that they have purged themselves of overt racist attitudes and behaviors, have made color-blindness the dominant lens through which whites understand contemporary race relations. Color-blindness allows whites to believe that segregation and discrimination are no longer an issue because it is now illegal for individuals to be denied access to housing, public accommodations, or jobs because of their race. Indeed, lawsuits alleging institutional racism against companies like Texaco, Denny's, Coke, and Cracker Barrel validate what many whites know at a visceral level is true: firms that deviate from the color-blind norms embedded in classic liberalism will be punished. As a political ideology, the commodification and mass marketing of products that signify color but are intended for consumption across the color line further legitimate color-blindness. Almost every household in the United States has a television that, according to the U.S. Census, is on for seven hours every day (Nielsen 1997). Individuals from any racial background can wear hip-hop clothing, listen to rap music (both purchased at Wal-Mart), and root for their favorite (majority black) professional sports team. Within the context of racial symbols that are bought and sold in the market, color-blindness means that one's race has no bearing on who can purchase a Jaguar, live in an exclusive neighborhood, attend private schools, or own a Rolex. The passive interaction whites have with people of color through the media creates the

impression that little, if any, socio-economic difference exists between the races.

The achievement ideology implicit in the color-
blind perspective is also given legitimacy and
stripped of any racist implications by black neo-
conservatives like anti-affirmative action advocate
Ward Connerly, Clarence Thomas, and Asian
American Secretary of Labor Elaine Chau (Ansell
1997; Gallagher 2004). Each espouses a color-
blind, race-neutral doctrine that treats race-based
government programs as a violation of the sacrosanct belief that American society only recognizes
the rights of individuals. These individuals also
serve as important public example, of the notion
that in a post-race, color-blind society, climbing the
occupational ladder is now a matter of individual
choice. Highly visible and successful racial minorities like Colin Powell and Condeleezza Rice are further proof to white America that the state's efforts to
enforce and promote racial equality have been
accomplished.

The new color-blind ideology does not, however, ignore race; it acknowledges race while disregarding racial hierarchy by taking racially coded
styles and products and reducing these symbols to
commodities or experiences that whites and racial
minorities can purchase and share. It is through
such acts of shared consumption that race becomes
nothing more than an innocuous cultural signifier.
Large corporations have made American culture
more homogenous through the ubiquity of fast
food, television, and shopping malls, but this trend
has also created the illusion that we are all the same
through consumption. Most adults eat at national
fast food chains like McDonald's, shop at mall anchor stores like Sears and J.C. Penney's, and watch
major league sports, situation comedies, or television drama. Defining race only as cultural symbols
that are for sale allows whites to experience and
view race as nothing more than a benign cultural
marker that has been stripped of all forms of institutional, discriminatory, or coercive power. The
post-race, color-blind perspective allows whites to
imagine that depictions of racial minorities working
in high status jobs and consuming the same products,

or at least appearing in commercials for products
whites desire or consume, is the same as living in a
society where color is no longer used to allocate resources or shape group outcomes. By constructing
a picture of society where racial harmony is the
norm, the color-blind perspective functions to
make white privilege invisible while removing from
public discussion the need to maintain any social
programs that are race-based.

Comedian Chris Rock points to how erasing
the color line and color-blindness are linked when
he asked rhetorically, "What does it say about
America when the greatest golfer in the world
[Tiger Woods] is black and the greatest rapper
[Eminem] is white?" Rock's message is clear: no
role or occupation (at least in sports and music) is
now determined by skin color. By allowing anyone
to claim ownership of racial styles, color-blind
narratives negate the ways in which race continues
to circumscribe life chances. The color-blind approach requires that these preferences, while
racially bracketed, be available to all for purchase
or consumption. At its core, the color-blind philosophy holds that racial minorities can succeed if
they rid themselves of any notion that their race
entitles them to special treatment or race-based
entitlements. Racial identity can still be expressed
or acknowledged, but one's race should mean
nothing more than a tendency toward individualistic expressions like music, food, or clothes. According to the color-blind perspective, it is not
race per se that determines upward mobility but
how much an individual **chooses** to pay attention
to how race determines one's fate.

COLOR-BLIND OR BLIND TO COLOR

The beliefs voiced by whites in national survey
data and my own interviews raise an empirical
question: to what extent are we now a color-blind
nation? If educational opportunity, occupational
advancement, health, upward mobility, and equal
treatment in the public sphere can be used as indicators of how color-blind we are as a nation, then
we have failed. U.S. Census figures present a picture

of America that is far from color-blind. In 2003 over 73% of white households owned their own homes compared to 49% for blacks, 48% for Hispanics, 59% for Asians, and 56% for American Indians (U.S. Census 2003). In 2003 whites had about fourteen times more in assets than blacks and eleven times more than Latinos (Pew Hispanic Center 2002). Median family income in 2003 was $47,041 for whites, $29,939 for blacks, $34,099 for Latinos, and $54,488 for Asians. In 2004 almost 25% of whites over the age of 25 had four years of college or more compared to less than 14% for blacks and 12% for Latinos. In 2003 8.2% of whites compared to 24.3% of blacks, 22.5% of Latinos, and 12% of Asians lived at or below the poverty line (U.S. Census 2003). A national study found that even after controlling for individual credit history, blacks in 33 states were charged more for car loans than whites (Henriques 2001). Health statistics tell a similar tale. Whites have lower rates of diabetes, tuberculosis, pregnancy-related mortality, sudden infant death syndrome (SIDS), and are more likely to have prenatal care in the first trimester than blacks, Latinos, or Asians. In 2003, 13% of whites did not have public or private health care coverage compared to 21% for blacks and 34% for Latinos (National Health Interview Survey).

Blacks and Latinos are under-represented as lawyers, physicians, professors, dentists, engineers, and registered nurses. A glass ceiling study commissioned by the federal government found that when one reaches the level of vice president and above at Fortune 1000 industrial and Fortune 500 service industries, 96.6% of the executives are white males. Nationally white men comprise 90% of the newspaper editors and 77% of television news directors (Feagin 2000). In 1999, the Department of Justice found that blacks and Latinos were twice as likely as whites to be subject to force when they encounter a police officer, were more likely to be subjected to car searches during a traffic stop, and were more likely to be ticketed than whites. Although blacks and whites are just as likely to use drugs, almost two-thirds of those convicted on drug charges are black (Gullo 2001).

The 109th Congress does not represent the racial and ethnic diversity of this country. In 2000 blacks were 13% of the population, Asians and Pacific Islanders 4%, and Latinos 12%. Yet the House of Representatives was only 10% black, 6% Latino, and 1% Asian. The U.S. Senate was 1% black (that is, there is one black in the Senate), 2% Asian (two Asians), and 1% (one) American Indian. There are currently no black or Latino governors. If you are black and live in Florida, you were four times as likely as whites to have your ballot invalidated in the 2000 presidential election (Parker and Eisler 2001). We are not now, nor have we ever been, a color-blind nation. Why then do we insist we ARE a color-blind nation?

BIBLIOGRAPHY

1. Ansell, A. 1997. *New Right, New Racism: Race and Reaction in the United States.* New York: New York University Press.
2. Dalmage, H. 2004. *The Multiracial Movement: The Politics of Color.* Albany: State University of New York Press.
3. Feagin, J. 2000. *Racist America: Roots, Current Realities and Future Reparations.* New York: Routledge.
4. Gallagher, C. A. 2004. "Transforming Racial Identity Through Affirmative Action." In *Race and Ethnicity: Across Time, Space and Discipline,* edited by Rodney Coates. Brill Publishers.
5. Gallup Organization. 2004, January. "Civil Rights and Race Relations," sponsored by AARP.
6. Gullo, K. 2001, March 12. *The Atlanta Journal and Constitution,* p. A7.
7. Henriques, D. 2001, July 4. "Review of Nissan Car Loans Explains Why Blacks Pay More." *New York Times,* p. 1.
8. Keifer, M. 2003, July. *Equal Opportunity: Is it Out There.* Gallup Organization.
9. National Health Interview Survey. 2003. *Health Care Coverage by Race.* Center for Disease Control and Prevention.
10. Nielsen, A. C. 1997. *Information Please Almanac.* Boston: Houghton Mifflin.
11. Parker, L., and P. Eisler. 2001, April 6–8. *USA Today,* p. A1.
12. Pew Hispanic Center. 2002, August. *Wealth Gap Widens Between Whites and Hispanics.*
13. Roediger, D. 1993. "The White Question." *Race Traitor,* Winter.
14. U.S. Bureau of the Census. 2003. *Housing Vacancies and Home Ownership Annual Statistics.* Washington, D.C.: U.S. Government Printing Office.

55

Too Many Women in College?

PHYLLIS ROSSER

Suddenly, the media—and Laura Bush—are concerned about an education gender gap. Funny, no one was scared when men *were on top.*

Although American women still struggle for parity in many arenas, we have outpaced men in at least one: undergraduate college education. Currently, 57.4 percent of bachelor's degrees in the United States are earned by women, 42.6 percent by men. This is an almost exact reversal from 1970, when 56.9 percent of college graduates were males and 43.1 percent females.

We should be celebrated for this landmark achievement, but instead it has engendered fear. Read the headlines: "Falling Male College Matriculation an Alarming Trend," or "Admissions Officers Weigh a Heretical Idea: Affirmative Action for Men." Notice, too, that a major focus of first lady Laura Bush's new antigang task force is education for boys. As she's been quoted, "The statistics are pretty alarming. Girls are going to college much more than boys."

Few worried when college students were two-thirds men. But as early as February 1999, *U.S. News & World Report* predicted that the rising tide of women college grads could close the salary gap and move women into positions of power as heads of corporations, presidents of universities and political leaders. At the other extreme, the article suggested, college education might become devalued—considered "a foolhardy economic decision"—as has happened in other fields after women begin to predominate.

STILL RARE AT THE TOP

What *U.S. News* failed to mention was that women are still a rare presence at the top ranks of the corporate and professional world despite earning more college degrees than men for 23 years. Women undertake stronger academic programs than men in high school, and receive higher average grades than men in both high school and college, but haven't been able to translate that success into equitable money and power. Consider these disparities as well:

- Women currently earn nearly 59 percent of master's degrees, but men outstrip women in advanced degrees for business, engineering and computer-science degrees—fields which lead to much higher-paying jobs than education, health and psychology, the areas where women predominate.

- Despite women's larger numbers as undergrads and in master's programs, men outnumber women in earning doctorates (54 percent) and professional degrees (53 percent).

- This year, the number of women applying to medical school outpaced men for the second time, but they are only predicted to be 33 percent of doctors by 2010.

- Women comprise nearly half of the students entering law schools, but they're miles from parity as law partners, professors and judges.

TESTS DON'T TELL THE WHOLE TALE

Women may lose a step on the career ladder even before they enter college. That's because, despite their greater number of bachelor's and master's degrees, women remain at a disadvantage in college admissions testing—which affects their acceptance at elite schools. The main purpose of the SAT—on which women averaged 44 points lower than men last year—is to predict first-year grades. However, it consistently underpredicts the college performance of women, who earn higher college grades than men.

Women's lower scores on the SAT have been shown to arise from several factors biased toward male performance, including the fact that it's a timed test and rewards guessing—and men tend to be more confident and risk-taking than women in such test situations. Also, the SAT puts many of the questions in a male context (such as sports), which can further lower female confidence about knowing the material.

In an attempt to even the gender playing field, a writing section that includes language questions and an essay was added to the SAT this year, after the University of California insisted that the test be more attuned to the skills necessary for college success. This may raise women's SAT scores somewhat, since writing tests are an area in which they have traditionally outperformed males.

Lower SAT scores keep qualified women from both attending the most competitive schools and from receiving National Merit Scholarships and other awards based on PSAT and SAT scores. The test biases against women then continue in graduate education, with such instruments as the Graduate Record Exam (GRE), Graduate Management Admissions Test (GMAT) and Law School Admissions Test (LSAT).

Thus, women have yet to predominate at the most prestigious colleges and universities, where graduates are tracked toward top leadership positions in society. With enormous numbers of both sexes applying to these schools, the admissions offices can choose their gender ratio. In 2005, men outnumbered women at all the Ivy League schools except Brown and Columbia. Women are also significantly outnumbered at universities specializing in engineering and physical science, such as Massachusetts Institute of Technology in Cambridge and California Institute of Technology in Pasadena.

AFFIRMATIVE ACTION—FOR MEN?

The greater percentage of women earning bachelor's degrees has given rise to some reactionary theories explaining why. Conservative analyst Christina Hoff Sommers insists the gap takes root in the more "girl-friendly" elementary school environment where boys are turned off to learning. In *The War Against Boys: How Misguided Feminism Is Harming Our Young Men* (Simon & Schuster, 2000), Hoff Sommers claims that schoolboys are "routinely regarded as protosexists, potential harassers and perpetuators of gender inequity" who "live under a cloud of censure."

Even higher-education policy analyst Tom Mortensen, who has a special concern with under-represented populations in higher education, also sees the college gender gap as part of a larger societal problem for men and boys. Mortensen says K-12 teachers, 75 percent of whom are women, are not providing the role models and learning styles boys need. Of course, this was never an issue during the decades when college graduates were mainly men, and hasn't drawn much notice since the end of the Civil War—the time when women began their continuing predominance as elementary school teachers.

If these theories seem to spring from a blame-the-women viewpoint, there is a legitimate concern about the decline in male graduates at private colleges, where the gap has been greatest (although public universities have also been affected). Admissions officers worry that their colleges' value will be lowered by an imbalance of female students: The larger the female majority, some say, the less likely either males or females will want to apply.

Speaking at a College Board conference several years ago, admissions officers agreed that a 60-40 female-to-male gender ratio was their upper limit. After that, said former Macalester College president Michael McPherson, "students will take notice." Small private colleges are now using what can only be called "male affirmative action" to increase male enrollment: actively recruiting men by emphasizing their science, math and engineering courses, adding sports programs (in violation of Title IX), sending extra mailings designed to attract men and even calling men to remind them of the admissions deadline.

"Probably no one will admit it, but I know lots of places try to get some gender balance by having easier admissions standards for boys than for girls," said Columbia University Teachers College president Arthur Levine to *The New York Times* national correspondent Tamar Lewin. Robert Massa, vice president of Dickinson College in Carlisle, Penn., has said that the school now evaluates prospective male students less on grades and more on measures where they typically do better, such as SAT scores. Adds Goucher College admissions vice president Barbara Fritze, "Men are being admitted to schools they never got into before, and offered financial aid they hadn't gotten before."

Massa reported that the number of first-year males at Dickinson rose from 36 percent to 43 percent in 2001 after they took affirmative action toward men, who were admitted with lower grades but comparable SAT scores. Women, meanwhile, had to be much better than men to make the cut: Nearly 62 percent of the women accepted to the school ranked in the top 10 percent of their high school class, compared to 42 percent of the men.

This new form of affirmative action, even if begun with all good intentions, could lead to bad college-admissions policy. What if a university decides it doesn't just want more men in attendance, but more white men? The whole notion of affirmative action as a way to help disadvantaged populations succeed could be turned on its head.

THE INCOME GAP

The real reason behind the undergrad gender gap may have much less to do with one's sex and more to do with income, race and class.

Jacqueline King, director of the Center for Policy Analysis at the American Council on Education in Washington, D.C., decided that media stories about the decline of white male enrollment didn't intuitively jibe with what she saw happening, so she took a closer look at college student data, analyzing it by sex, age, race/ethnicity and socioeconomic status. She found the gender gap in college enrollment for students 18 to 24 years of age in 1995–96 occurred among low-income students of all racial/ethnic groups except Asian Americans.

In fact, since 1995, many more women than men from households making less than $30,000 attend college. The latest available data, from 2003–04, shows there is an even smaller percentage of low-income males attending college than there were in 1995, and they are from every racial/ethnic group. African American and Native American students have the largest gender gaps—males comprise just 37 percent of all low-income African American students and 36 percent of low-income Native Americans. Low-income Hispanic men reach

a slightly higher 39 percent, and low-income white males 41 percent (a drop from 46 percent in 1995). Asian Americans have the smallest gender gap, with 47 percent of that group's low-income college students being male.

Middle-income ($30,000–$70,000) male students maintained gender parity with females 10 years ago, but since then the numbers have dropped somewhat. This may mean that fewer men from the lower end of this income bracket are attending college, says Eugene Anderson, senior research associate at the American Council on Education. At the highest income level ($70,000 or more), though, men and women in all ethnic groups attend college in nearly equal numbers.

No studies have been done to determine why more low-income women than men attend college, but there are theories. Economist Lester Thurow suggests that low-income men have been lured to the comfortable salaries of mechanical maintenance jobs. Low-income women, on the other hand, don't have such opportunities, and without a college degree see themselves getting trapped in low-pay sales or service jobs, says King. Also, more men than women work in computer support or high-tech factories—jobs that don't require bachelor's degrees.

Overall, an increasing number of poor and working-class people are dropping out of college because of such reasons as escalating tuition and the attraction of high-paying factory work, according to a May piece in *The New York Times* ("The College Dropout Boom: Diploma's Absence Strands Many in the Working Class"). Harvard president Lawrence H. Summers goes so far as to call this widening of the education gap between rich and poor our "most serious domestic problem"—and recent changes in federal grant formulas may exacerbate it even further [see box].

UPRISING: MINORITIES AND OLDER WOMEN

On the bright side, ethnic minorities have made impressive gains as college students since 1976, increasing their percentage in the total student body from 10 percent to 23 percent. Minority men's share of all bachelor's degrees has gone from 5 percent to 9 percent. But, again, minority women have outstripped them, more than doubling their share of bachelor's degrees, from 5 percent to 14 percent of the total degrees awarded.

Not only is that statistic a contributing factor to the overall gender gap, but another contributing factor is that women are the majority of older (25+) students—and that demographic has been returning to college in record numbers. The "oldsters" now make up 27 percent of the undergraduate student body, and 61 percent of older students are women. King found that many of these students were African American or Latina, attending community colleges to improve future earnings in health-related fields.

"This story is not one of male failure, or even lack of opportunity," says King, "but rather one of increased academic opportunity and success among females and minorities." Indeed, there has been no decline in bachelor's degrees awarded to men; the numbers awarded to women have simply increased.

Feminists should continue to be concerned about encouraging low-income and minority students to attend college, using the current momentum to give these problems the attention they deserve. But in the meantime, we must remain vigilant about attempts to roll back our educational gains. The fact is, we're a long way from threatening corporate America, so don't put the onus on women. Maybe it's just time to let men try to catch up to us, for a change.

Will Shrinking Federal Aid Affect the Gender Gap?

KATHLEEN BISHOP

Women may outnumber men on college campuses, but they also need more financial help to get there—and for this upcoming school year, that aid might be in jeopardy.

That's because the Department of Education (DOE) is using new data to help calculate the "expected family contribution"—the amount of money a family could be reasonably expected to afford for college tuition. This helps determine how much federal grant or loan money a student can qualify for.

The DOE has used 1988 state tax information in their formula for 16 years, since the IRS hadn't released newer data. But when 2001 figures became available—showing that taxes had decreased over the 12-year span—it looked on paper as if families could afford to spend more on college. However, congressional Democrats and other education advocates argued that lumping together years of gradual tax declines would give an unfair illusion that families suddenly had extra money in the bank.

The use of the new data was blocked for a time, but last year Congress went ahead with the legally mandated formula update, prompted by concerns about the growing cost of Pell grants, the largest federal student grant program. *The New York Times* has estimated that, on average, families with the same income and assets as they had in 2000 will now have to pay an extra $1,749 for higher education this year.

Women, unfortunately will likely bear the brunt of the cut in aid. Overall, half of women in college receive federal aid, compared to 42 percent of men. According to

---

Will Shrinking Federal Aid Affect the Gender Gap? *continued*

Melanie Corrigan, assistant director of the Center for Policy Analysis at the American Council on Education, women are more often eligible for aid because they are more likely to return to school as a single parent and because, in general, they earn less than men. Additionally, more women apply for financial aid.

While everyone receiving financial aid from programs determined by the DOE formula—Pell grants, subsidized loans and some state or institutional assistance—could feel the pinch, the change might do the most damage to those families earning $35,000 to $55,000 per year. They are often on the cusp of being eligible for Pell grants and other aid for lower-income students.

Experts in the field do not predict sweeping dropouts or a widening of the college gender gap due to the new calculation, and they point out that other economic factors should rebalance the formula in the future. But for now, financially struggling women—and men—will have to work even harder to stay in school.

 ## 56

Man-Ifesting Gender

ABBY L. FERBER

For the U.S. white nationalist movement, "white men are this nation." This movement is not only concerned with issues of race and class, but just as centrally, with gender. Traditionally, scholars studying the movement have ignored issues of gender, and it was the work of Kathleen Blee who first raised the issue of gender by recovering the history of women in the Klan of the 1920s. In her most recent research, Blee focuses on women in the contemporary movement, and has found that many organizations are specifically targeting women for recruitment.

However, gender shapes the lives of everyone, not just women. If we look at a social movement and find that it consists primarily of men, that itself is an issue worth investigating. Sociologists argue

that gender is something that we all "do" or "perform" on an ongoing basis. The white nationalist movement is one arena where white men perform their masculinity. Masculinity is not something that one can prove once and for all, it is something that has to be proven again and again. For example, we know that the vast majority of hate crimes are carried out by young white men, and if we look at hate crimes directed against gay men, for example, the perpetrators often report that they felt that their own masculinity had in some way been threatened by the victim. Hate crimes aimed at gay men are one means, then, by which young white men display and "prove" their heterosexuality for others.

American society has experienced tremendous social change in recent decades, sparked by the civil rights movement, women's movement, and gay and lesbian movement. More recently, debates over affirmative action, multicultural curriculum, welfare, and other contentious topics have been perceived by many white men as attacks against them, not only against their racial privilege, but their identity as men as well. Our traditional conception of masculinity teaches men that they are to be in control, aggressive, strong, obeyed, and the breadwinner of the family. White men are taught to feel not only that this is their responsibility, but their entitlement. But what it means to be a white man is no longer secure, and white male privilege no longer proceeds unquestioned. Many feel under seige and vulnerable, facing a "crisis of masculinity." We have seen the rise of other men's movements, like the Promise Keepers, for these same reasons. As a result of these social and cultural changes, as well as economic dislocations and insecurity, many white men believe they are being denied the opportunity to achieve the American dream, which they see as their birthright.

My own research has focused largely on the discourse of this movement, and now that this discourse is reaching a far wider audience than ever before via the world wide web, it is more important that we pay close attention to it. When I began my research on this movement I was shocked by its entrenched gendered ideology. None of the studies I had read had discussed gender as a central issue for the movement. Yet I found white nationalist publications were filled with images of white girls and women with headings such as "endangered species" beneath them. Clearly white womanhood was being used as a symbol to motivate white men to action. The more I read, the more I began to see how central this gendered ideology is to the movement. It is not simply that the movement is sexist, and images of women are employed by the movement to gain converts, but I began to see that this movement is about gender, in very profound ways. Clearly what it means to be white is tied to certain notions of masculinity and femininity, and vice versa. For example, the relationship between white men and women is seen as a sign of the superiority of the white race. And the strength and independence of black women is identified as a key component of the inferiority of the black race, where gender relations are supposedly "unnatural." Furthermore, the movement's fear of white genocide leads to an obsession with controlling white women's sexuality and reproduction.

Despite the growing numbers of women in the movement, it remains centrally concerned with preserving white male privilege. It is not only about hatred of others, but about defining identity for its members and maintaining white male power. Therefore, one of the central foci of the discourse is defining both racial and gender identities as rooted in nature, either biological or God-given. By defining race and gender identities in this way, they are stabilized and naturalized. After all, if something is rooted in nature you can't change it. And this assumption undergirds the movement's critique of contemporary America—things are falling apart all around us because we are trying to change people's essential nature. Their response to all of our current social problems, whether discussing terrorism, crime, or teen pregnancy? Restore the natural social order of white men on top.

White nationalist ideology thus offers itself as the antidote to these problems, promising to empower men who feel they no longer have any power. The movement seemingly offers white men the chance to prove their masculinity. One frequent ploy is to attack white men as wimps, and then offer them the chance to prove their manliness and virility by joining the movement. White men are repeatedly attacked throughout far right publications for becoming feminized (and unsettling the natural order), and are encouraged to become real men by standing up and protecting white women, reasserting their place in the natural hierarchy, and taking over the world.

★ ★ ★

The Turner Diaries, perhaps the best known manifesto of the movement, . . . provides a plethora of examples. The novel portrays a society where white women and girls are constantly attacked by black men, yet white men never protest out of fear of being labeled "racist." As the narrator explains, "Even when gangs of Blacks took their children away or raped their women before their eyes, they offered no significant resistance" (152). The novel implores white men to take up arms to protect white womanhood and the world. Movements for race and gender equality are seen as distorting the natural race and gender order, and ultimately tied to the New World Order's elimination of national boundaries. The destruction of race, gender and national boundaries go hand in hand, and it is only through a revived white, American manhood that these can be saved.

The gender issues involved are here numerous and raise many new questions for us to think about. In terms of who joins the movement and why, women and men may be drawn to the movement for different reasons, and also may be drawn out of the movement for different reasons. Gender is central to understanding this movement's attraction and hold on members, and may be key to developing more successful strategies of resistance. We cannot fully understand this social movement without exploring its deeply gendered nature.

B. INSTITUTIONALIZING SOCIAL CHANGE

57

Uprooting Racism

PAUL KIVEL

AFFIRMATIVE ACTION

Affirmative action has been one of the primary public policy controversies of the last thirty years. Even now debates about its effectiveness continue. Following is an overview of some affirmative action issues as another example of how to think critically about public policy issues.

Affirmative action is more than a legal issue. . . . Everything you do . . . [to eliminate racism] is an affirmative action. Affirmative action to end racism should be the challenge and responsibility of every single person in our society, as well as of the institutions and organizations which have such a large

impact on our lives. Yet today we have a vocal minority who are saying we should stop affirmative action not only as a legal remedy, but also as a social commitment. They are saying we have gone too far in correcting racial injustice. Of course, they are not challenging traditional forms of preference and discrimination that favor the rich, the educated, white people and men.

Affirmative action is practiced in many areas of our society. We have hiring and recruiting preferences for veterans, women and the children of alumni of many universities, special economic incentives for purchase of U.S.-made products, import quotas against foreign goods and agricultural and textile subsidies. These practices have led to a huge overrepresentation of white people, men and people of middle, upper middle and upper class backgrounds in our universities, in well-paid jobs and in the professions. One indication that attacks on affirmative action are part of a white backlash against equality is that affirmative action in the form of preferences that primarily benefit white people is not being questioned.

Many forms of discrimination in our society are illegal. The federal government mandated affirmative action programs to redress racial inequality and injustice in a series of steps beginning with an executive order issued by President Kennedy in 1961. The Civil Rights Act of 1964 made discrimination illegal and established equal employment opportunity for all Americans regardless of race, cultural background, color or religion Subsequent executive orders, in particular Executive Order 11246 issued by President Johnson in September 1965, mandated affirmative action goals for all federally funded programs and moved monitoring and enforcement of affirmative action programs out of the White House and into the Labor Department. These policies and the government action which followed was a response to the tremendous mobilization of African Americans and white supporters during the late 1950s and early 1960s pushing for integration and racial justice.

There are many ways to attack racism. . . . I would like to address the particular legal remedy called affirmative action. It is a policy aimed primarily at correcting institutional discrimination where decisions, policies and procedures that are not necessarily explicitly discriminatory have had a negative impact on people of color. Affirmative action policies address and redress systematic economic and political discrimination against any group of people that are underrepresented or have a history of being discriminated against in particular institutions. Beneficiaries of these programs have included white men and women, people with disabilities and poor and working class people, but their primary emphasis has been on addressing racial discrimination.

There is pervasive racism in all areas of U.S. society. For example, in 1991 Diane Sawyer with ABC-TV filmed two men, one African American and one white, who were matched for age, appearance, education, and other qualities. They were followed for a day by a camera crew. The white man received service in stores while the African American was ignored, or in some cases, watched closely. The white man was offered a lower price and better financing at a car dealership, jobs where the African American was turned down, and apartments for rent after the African American man was told they were no longer available. A police car passed the white man while he was walking down the street but it slowed down and took note of the African American (Horne, pps. 40–41). Many other studies like this one demonstrate discrimination against people of color in different areas of everyday life.

Racism, rather than being self-correcting, is self-perpetuating. The disadvantages to people of color and the benefits to white people are passed on to each succeeding generation unless remedial action is taken. The disadvantages to people of color coalesce into institutional practices, . . . which, although they may be race neutral in intent, adversely affect people of color. We have to take positive steps to eliminate and compensate for these institutional effects of racism, even when there is no discernible discriminatory intent.

For example, most job opportunities are heard about through informal networks of friends, family and neighbors. Since the results of racism are

segregated communities, schools and workplaces, this pattern leaves people of color out of the loop for many jobs, advancement opportunities, scholarships and training programs. Federal law requires widespread and public advertisement of such opportunities so that not only people of color, but white women and men who are outside the circles of information, have an equal opportunity to apply for these positions.

Another area affirmative action addresses is preferential hiring programs. Many times people of color have been excluded from hiring pools, overtly discriminated against, unfairly eliminated because of inappropriate qualification standards, or have been rendered unqualified because of discrimination in education and housing. Court decisions on affirmative action have rendered illegal those qualifications that are not relevant to one's ability to do the job. They have also mandated hiring goals so that those employed begin to reflect the racial mix of the general population from which workers are drawn. There is no legal requirement to ever hire an unqualified person. There is a mandate that in choosing between qualified candidates, the hiring preference should be for a person of color when past discrimination has resulted in white people receiving preferential treatment.

Sometimes people argue that affirmative action means the best qualified person will not be hired. However, it has been demonstrated many times in hiring and academic recruitment that test and educational qualifications are not necessarily the best predictors of future success. This does not mean unqualified people should be hired. It means basically qualified people who may not have the highest test scores or grades, but who are eminently ready to do the job may be hired. Employers have traditionally hired people not only on test scores, but on personal appearance, family and personal connections, school ties and on race and gender preferences demonstrating that talent or desirability can be defined in many ways. These practices have all contributed to a segregated work force where whites hold the best jobs, and people of color work in the least desirable and most poorly paid positions.

Affirmative action policies serve as a corrective to such patterns of discrimination. They keep score on progress toward proportional representation and place the burden of proof on organizations to show why it is not possible to achieve it.

Affirmative action programs have been remarkably effective in dampening discrimination and opening up work and educational opportunities for groups of people previously excluded. When these policies receive executive branch and judicial support, vast numbers of people of color, white women and men have gained access they would not otherwise have had.

It has been argued that affirmative action benefits people of color who are already well off or have middle class advantages, not the poor and working class people of color who most need it. Affirmative action programs have benefitted substantial numbers of poor and working class people of color. Access to job training programs, vocational schools, and semi-skilled and skilled blue-collar, craft, pink-collar, police and firefighter jobs has increased substantially through affirmative action programs. Even in the professions, many people of color who have benefitted from affirmative action have been from families of low income and job status (Ezorsky, p. 64).

Middle class people of color have also benefitted from afirmative action. All people of color have experienced the effects of racial discrimination. Having more money may buffer the most extreme effects, but it doesn't protect people from everyday racial discrimination. The middle class in various communities of color is small and often fragile. Its members own less wealth and have less financial security than their white counterparts because of the past effects of racial discrimination. They also experience the full range of cultural racism and white prejudice that all people of color have to deal with.

Another argument raised against affirmative action is that individual white people, often white males, have to pay for past discrimination and may not get the jobs they deserve. It is true that specific white people may not get specific job opportunities because of affirmative action policies and may

suffer as a result. This lack of opportunity is unfortunate and we need to address the causes of the lack of enough jobs. We tend to forget that millions of specific people of color have also lost specific job opportunities as a result of racial discrimination. To be concerned only with the white applicants who don't get the job, and not with the people of color who don't, is showing racial preference.

But how true is it that white male candidates are being discriminated against or are losing out because of affirmative action programs? If we look at the composition of various professions such as law, medicine, architecture, academics and journalism, or at corporate management, or at higher-level government positions—or if we look overall at the average income levels of white men—we see that people of color are significantly underrepresented and underpaid in every category. People of color don't even make up the proportions of these jobs equal to their percentage of the population. They don't earn wages comparable to white men. White men are tremendously overrepresented in almost any category of work that is highly rewarded except for professional athletics. According to a 1995 government report, white males make up only 29 percent of the workforce, but they hold 95 percent of senior management positions (Sklar, p. 115). Until there is both equal opportunity and fair distribution of education, training and advancement to all Americans, we need affirmative action for people of color to counter the hundreds of years of affirmative action that has been directed at white males. We cannot reasonably argue that white males are discriminated against as a group if they are overrepresented in most high status categories.

We should note two other aspects of this dynamic. We have seen how all white people benefit from racism. White men receive more of the economic and other benefits of racism than white women of the same socio-economic status. White men have always been favored in families and schools and preferred for jobs, training, educational programs, athletic programs, military careers and job advancement and promotion. Men still make more than women for comparable work, are given better educational opportunities, have more leisure time and are accorded higher status than women.

The second and equally important part of this dynamic is that not all white men are equal. If you are a white male you may or may not have gained a lot from racism. If you are not well-off, well educated or well rewarded in your life, you should look at white men who are and analyze how they accumulated such rewards. Why do many corporate executives make more in a week than their workers make in a year? Why does the average CEO "earn" as much as 157 factory workers (Sklar, op. cit. p. 9)?

Business leaders are able to exploit male workers by appealing to common bonds and common fears among white men. They have played on white male fears of losing their jobs (and their manliness) to keep them working hard, claiming that only white men had the strength, skill, intelligence, independence, strength of character and virility to do the job. White workers have often bought these arguments feeling pride and increased self-esteem in their working abilities, and feeling personally threatened by the presence of people of color and white women in the workplace. Their ability to fight against low wages, unsafe working conditions, the restructuring of their jobs and plant closures has been diminished even while they thought they were protecting their jobs through race riots, anti-immigration laws, attacks on affirmative action and workplace discrimination, harassment and exclusion.

Collusion with well-off white men against affirmative action is not in the best interests of poor, working and middle class men. Yet many have bought the lie that who they are is based on the manliness of the work they do* and their ability to keep their workplaces as white male preserves.

Affirmative action programs have been effective in many areas of public life because they open up opportunities for people who would not otherwise have them, including white women and men. Attacks on affirmative action are part of a systematic attempt to roll back progress in ending discrimination and

to curtail a broad social commitment to justice and equality. Attacking affirmative action is self-destructive for all of us except the rich.

Affirmative action helps mitigate the effects of institutional racism. It also counters the effects of current discrimination, intentional or not. We know that not all white people are well intentioned. Others of us believe that everyone should have an equal chance but still hold deep seated prejudices against people of color. For a substantial number of us those prejudices lead us to practice discrimination. Without specific, numerical goals, it has been found that many people and organizations continue to practice discrimination while professing agreement with affirmative action.

There are so many subtle and not-so-subtle ways to eliminate people of color from the job application process it is not surprising that employers have found ways around affirmative action unless it is tied to visible hiring and promotion targets. In a society with such overwhelming evidence of racism, we must assume that individuals and organizations will resist efforts to end it. For instance, in 1993 the Equal Employment Opportunity Commission had a backlog of 70,000 discrimination cases (chideya, p. 110). We have to set goals and enforce and monitor standards because it is the only way we can measure compliance. These are the mechanisms we need to ensure that affirmative action is more than a facade.

Quotas have been used in the past to exclude particular groups of people from jobs or educational opportunities. They have been used to limit the number of Asian Americans or Jews in universities so white people would continue to have unequal access. Setting minimum goals for inclusion is the opposite of setting maximums. We need numerical goals to guarantee compliance with affirmative action policies. Numerical goals promote democratic access to education, jobs and job training.

Some people have claimed that affirmative action programs lower self-esteem in those who are favored by them, perhaps even in those who do not directly benefit from them. There is no systematic evidence for this effect. It seems to be something

---

*Manliness is defined differently, but no less exclusively in the computer industry than in trucking or construction.

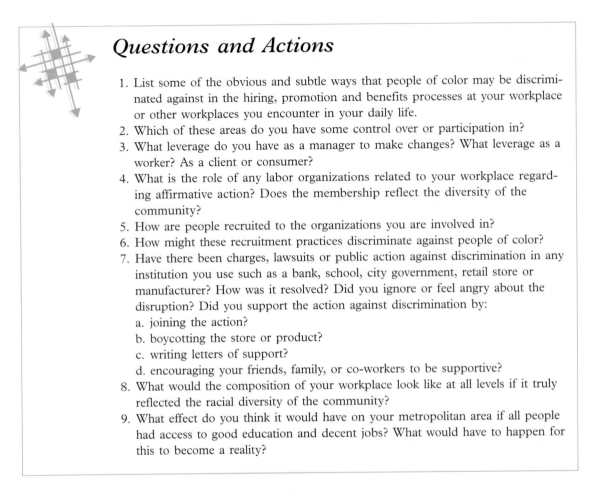

Questions and Actions

1. List some of the obvious and subtle ways that people of color may be discriminated against in the hiring, promotion and benefits processes at your workplace or other workplaces you encounter in your daily life.
2. Which of these areas do you have some control over or participation in?
3. What leverage do you have as a manager to make changes? What leverage as a worker? As a client or consumer?
4. What is the role of any labor organizations related to your workplace regarding affirmative action? Does the membership reflect the diversity of the community?
5. How are people recruited to the organizations you are involved in?
6. How might these recruitment practices discriminate against people of color?
7. Have there been charges, lawsuits or public action against discrimination in any institution you use such as a bank, school, city government, retail store or manufacturer? How was it resolved? Did you ignore or feel angry about the disruption? Did you support the action against discrimination by:
   a. joining the action?
   b. boycotting the store or product?
   c. writing letters of support?
   d. encouraging your friends, family, or co-workers to be supportive?
8. What would the composition of your workplace look like at all levels if it truly reflected the racial diversity of the community?
9. What effect do you think it would have on your metropolitan area if all people had access to good education and decent jobs? What would have to happen for this to become a reality?

that white people worry about more than people of color.

Persistent denial of equal opportunity—and therefore inadequate access to good jobs, good education and housing—leads to poor self-esteem. If we are truly worried about low self-esteem among people of color, then we need more effective affirmative action programs to counter discrimination. It is discrimination that seems to be the more important harm we should be trying to eliminate.

Affirmative action is not a cure-all. It will not eliminate racial discrimination, nor will it eliminate competition for scarce resources. Affirmative action programs can only ensure that everyone has a fair chance at what is available. They cannot direct

us to the social policies we need to pursue so we do not have to compete for scarce resources in the first place. In the larger picture we must ask ourselves why aren't there enough decent paying, challenging and safe jobs for everyone? Why aren't there enough seats in the universities for everyone who wants an education? Expanding opportunity for people of color means expanding not only their access to existing jobs, education and housing (affirmative action), but removing the obstacles that cause these resources to be limited (social justice).

Affirmative action has been a symbol of white people's acknowledgement of and serious commitment to eradicating racial discrimination. It has been interpreted as such by most people of color. It

10. Affirmative action is a tool for full inclusion and equal opportunity for all people, not only people of color. Go back through these questions and substitute women for people of color. Substitute lesbians and gay men for people of color. Substitute people with disabilities. Substitute seniors and young people.
11. What fears, doubts, questions or concerns do you have about affirmative action? Where do your fears come from? What could you do to answer your questions? Who could you talk with about your concerns?
12. Have you ever been chosen for a job, training program, college level program or housing opportunity in which you were less qualified than others? Have you ever been given preference because of family connections, economic background, age, race or gender?
13. Think again about #12 and try to understand ways that family connections, economic background, race, age or gender may have given you the benefit of the doubt compared to other applicants.
14. Do you think that veterans, sons of alumni, farmers or other people who receive preferential treatment experience self-doubt, lowered self-esteem or feelings of guilt because of it?
15. Besides numerical goals, what measures would you suggest be used to monitor racial and other forms of discrimination?
16. How are you going to respond to people who say that affirmative action unfairly discriminates against white males?
17. List three things you can do to defend or strengthen affirmative action programs in your workplace, community or state.
18. Choose one that you will start doing.

is crucial that at this stage of backlash against the gains of the last three decades, we don't abandon one tool that we know works.

When whites attack affirmative action—if they are truly committed to American ideals of justice and equality—they should be proposing other remedies for racial inequality in our society. The hypocrisy is clear when white people who say they support equal opportunity attack affirmative action, yet want to leave intact the basic economic and racial injustices it is designed to correct. Ask people who oppose affirmative action how they propose to eliminate racial discrimination. You can learn a lot about their true beliefs from their answers.

Although institutional change seems difficult to tackle, we are already involved in several institutions in our daily lives. Our workplace, the schools we or our children attend, the stores we patronize, the places we socialize, the community with which we congregate for religious worship—we have some leverage at each of these institutions. We need to analyze the institutions we are a part of, evaluate the influence we and others with us have, and devise effective strategies for challenging racism. The next sections look at some of the ways you might focus on institutions you are already involved with including your workplace, your school system, the police, the criminal justice system and your religious organization.

AT WORK

Whiteness has long been related to racism in the workplace and economy. As David Roediger explains in his book *The Wages of Whiteness,* part of the campaign to entice white male workers into industrial jobs during the 19th Century was the rationalization that at least they were not slaves. They could keep their white masculinity intact even while giving up their economic independence because they were told that being a worker in a factory was not the same as being a slave working for a master.

Male industrial workers eventually borrowed the language of slavery to describe their "waged slavery." They played on similarities between their work situation and that of slaves, at the same time trying to keep the differences clear so they could preserve industrial jobs for whites. The relationship of racism to work issues is complex. In general, early white industrial workers were manipulated by racism, and in turn, used racism to gain economic benefits. Employers manipulated racism to create a false sense of pride and opportunity among white workers, which workers then used to separate themselves from male workers of color.

Work in the United States is still highly segregated by class, race and gender. The overall economy, as well as most large organizations, is vertically segregated. Upper middle and upper class white men have access to the jobs with the most money, power and status. Women, working class whites and people of color are strung out on the economic hierarchy, but are found disproportionately at the bottom in the least secure, most unsafe, poorest paid jobs.

We saw in the section on benefits that there are many, specific economic advantages to being white. One early purpose of racism in the United States was to justify economic exploitation. Racism has always been intimately tied to the economic hierarchy. While this section focuses on the realities of fighting racism in the workplace, winning the broader struggle for economic democracy is crucial for truly ending racism.

Women comprise 50 percent of the world's population, perform two thirds of the work, earn one tenth of the world's income, and own 1 percent of the property (United Nations Report, 1980).

The United States, containing 5 percent of the world's population, consumes 30 percent of the world's total use of resources (Durning 1992).

As the above figures indicate, inequality and injustice exist at every level of our economic system. Racism contributes to an international system of economic exploitation. A key to achieving economic justice is solidarity between white workers and workers of color, between U.S. workers and workers from other countries. Racism undermines both levels of solidarity.

In addition to challenging racism where you work (see the workplace assessment below), following are some labor and race issues that deserve attention outside the workplace.

The recent collapse of the Mexican monetary system makes the interdependences of the world economy evident. What may not be so clear to us in the United States is the devastation of non-Western countries which results from the economic policies imposed by the International Monetary Fund, the World Bank and other U.S.-dominated institutions. The colonial practices of European countries, beginning in the late 15th Century and later taken up by the United States, have concentrated international power and wealth in the hands of white people and have given us the ability to dictate the economic fortunes of the rest of the world.

One way to challenge these patterns is to organize against new attempts by U.S. financial interests to further consolidate their dominance through such trade agreements as NAFTA and GATT. These agreements enhance the ability of multinational corporations to move jobs and factories from country to country, to pollute and destroy environments and, in general, to wreak havoc on the lives of hundreds of millions of people, including ourselves. These treaties encourage us to believe that our own (white) U.S. jobs will be protected at the expense of those of people of color in other countries. In reality, we get played off against foreign workers and are able to exert even less control over corporate policy.

The result of these policies is that jobs are moved overseas to countries where multinational companies and local elites buy up land that is then diverted from growing food for local consumption to growing cash crops for U.S. consumption. Foreign workers cannot grow their own food and are forced to move to the cities. If they are lucky they can find work on plantations or in multinational factories to earn enough cash to buy food that they could formerly grow. Treaties like NAFTA and GATT make it easy for companies to move to where wages are lowest and where there is the least labor and environmental regulation.

We have created an international racial hierarchy of wealth, power and control which mirrors our internal one. This international hierarchy subjects us to economic and cultural exploitation camouflaged by racist justifications that blame workers of color and foreign capitalists of color for our declining standard of living and social problems instead of blaming the decision makers in our corporate boardrooms.

We are not powerless against multinational corporations if we overcome our training in racism to work

together with people from other countries. We can challenge the dumping of toxic waste and unsafe products in other countries, the exploitation of foreign workers by U.S. companies, the sexual exploitation of women of color overseas by U.S. tourists and corporate and military personnel, the economic policies of the IMF and the World Bank, the displacement of local agricultural production to grow export crops for the United States, the manipulation of unequal trade and other agreements, the scapegoating of foreign workers for U.S. generated problems, and the scapegoating of foreign capitalists of color such as the Japanese and Arabs when (white) British and Canadian capitalists go unmentioned.★

Many of us work for these same corporations and can challenge their policies from within. We all have specific opportunities to confront racism where we work.

To identify where you have the most leverage related to your work, it is important to make an assessment of your workplace. Use the following questions. Talk with others, particularly people of color, to help you do the assessment.

★The British own as much U.S. property as the Japanese and are increasing their stake at a faster rate.

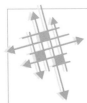

Assessment

1. What is the gender, race and class composition in your workplace? Which groups holds which positions?
2. Who, by race, gender and class, has the power to make decisions about hiring, firing, wages and working conditions in your workplace? Who gets promoted and who doesn't? Are there upper levels (glass ceilings) beyond which some groups of people (i.e., people of color, white women) cannot go?
3. Is hiring non-discriminatory? Are jobs openings posted and distributed? Do they attract a wide variety of applicants? Are certain groups excluded? Does the diversity of your workplace reflect the diversity of the wider community?
4. Do layoffs, reassignments, workplace closures or other cutbacks disproportionately affect people of color?

Assessment, continued

5. What are the salary differentials between those least well paid and those most well paid? Are salaries for comparable work equal?

6. Are there "invisible" workers, people who cook, clean or do maintenance, for example, who are not generally noticed or paid well?

7. Do the board of directors and top level management of your employer include significant numbers of people of color?

8. What is the racial composition of the people who actually own your workplace? Who makes money from the profits of your work?

9. Are there jokes, teasing, put downs or harassment of people based on race, gender, sexual orientation, age, religion or other differences?

10. Has there been or is there any racial or sexual harassment or discrimination, or charges of such, or investigations by any outside agency about such things? Do people of color describe discrimination or harassment at your workplace?

11. Does your organization provide products or services to people of color? If it does, is the clientele treated with respect and dignity? Do staff make racial comments about clients? Is there any discrimination in how people are served or treated?

12. Do the advertising and publicity images that your employer produces convey a multiracial image, or do they reinforce racial or sexual stereotypes?

13. Are there any workplace groups such as unions or affirmative action committees that monitor or respond to racial discrimination? Are they effective? Are they supported or hindered by management? Do they challenge or do they support racism?

14. Is your employer part of a larger organization with manufacturing or other facilities at other sites? Are those sites in communities of color? If they are, are workers paid the same and treated equally to workers at your site?

15. Has your employer closed down or moved facilities to areas of the United States or to other countries in order to pay workers less or to avoid unionization, workplace safety regulations or other oversight?

16. Does your company produce any kinds of toxic waste? If so, in which communities is the waste dumped?

As you can see from these questions, racism affects every level of our workplaces. Starting with an assessment you can pinpoint just how racism operates. Then you can figure out where you and other workers can start to use your own knowledge to make changes. It is difficult to do alone, although individuals can make a big difference. Even more powerful is working with others who are similarly committed to eliminating racism.

Look to the leadership of the people of color you work with, if there are any. They know where the racism lies in your organization. They may be quite clear about what kind of solidarity they need from white co-workers. Ask them how they see things, what are their priorities.

You will also need to work with other white workers, building a core group dedicated to eliminating racism. Many of your white co-workers may not have questioned the racism in your workplace. They need information and support for making changes in workplace practices and environment. You may meet with solid resistance from others who feel they have something to lose from eliminating racism. Challenging them will require more strategic thinking.

Many workers have such pressing financial and emotional needs they may not understand at first why racial equality and economic justice need to be a priority. The information provided in this [essay] can lead you to effective strategies to help them see the costs of racism in their lives.

A good way to begin, once you have the information you need, is to ask questions. "Why is this person of color paid less than that white person who was hired more recently?" "Why aren't there any people of color at management level?" "Why don't people of color stay with this organization very long?" "What effect does that kind of comment (e.g., to a racial put down) have on other people around here?"

Asking questions raises issues for people to think about. Sometimes that alone will make other people want to make some changes. Often you'll get excuses, justifications or cynicism in response. Those responses will help you and others see how white people are thinking about racism and what level of awareness they have. It will also help you map out where you'll meet resistance to further actions.

It is generally not useful to label people as racist. This strategy produces defensiveness. You will do better to document racism within the organization, build allies and propose concrete changes. If you attack people personally, they will probably counterattack. Everyone within the organization will feel unsafe. Instead, you want to focus on policies, practices and procedures.

This is not to say you won't meet resistance, innuendo, slander, isolation and threats. But where injustice and inequality are the focus, it is harder for people to present a reasonable defense of previous patterns than if they are personally attacked.

Eliminating racism is not a question of economic cost but of injustice. But in organizing against specific forms of racism, it can be a useful short-term strategy to point out the economic benefits of the changes desired or the economic costs of the old patterns. What does it cost an organization when there are high turnover rates for personnel who are people of color, when clients of color are not well served or when the leadership talent of people of color is not utilized? What does it cost when there are discrimination lawsuits, strikes, boycotts or government investigations because of racism within the organization? Organizations are differentially vulnerable to such costs. What does it cost you and those you work with when injustice is allowed to continue without protest?

An effective cost analysis may be difficult to make when corporate investment in personnel and infrastructure is scandalously low and when many company policies are based on such short-term considerations that financial payoffs must be almost immediate.

Specific struggles against racist practices can also be used to raise consciousness about management policies and economics. Each particular fight against racism is part of the long-term struggle, and even when it is unsuccessful, it can educate and organize other workers. Our long-term goal is to create a broad movement of people committed to eliminating racism in all aspects of our lives.

I am not going to romanticize the power of workers; in most circumstances multinational companies can play off workers from many sites against each other. However keeping the issue of race and gender based exploitation on the table in every workplace struggle will further the move toward economic justice. Doing so keeps people of color and white women in leadership positions, demonstrates the interconnected ways that people are exploited and produces the informed solidarity that is essential to the success of any struggle for economic justice.

REFERENCES

1. chideya, farai. *Don't Believe the Hype: Fighting Cultural Misinformation about African Americans.* New York: Plume, 1995.
2. Durning, Alan Thein. *How Much Is Enough: The Consumer Society and the Future of the Earth.* New York: W.W. Norton, 1992.
3. Ezorsky, Gertrude. *Racism and Justice: The Case for Affirmative Action.* Ithaca, NY: Cornell U P, 1991.

4. Horne, Gerald. *Reversing Discrimination: The Case for Affirmative Action.* New York: International Publishers, 1992.
5. Roediger, David R. *The Wages of Whiteness: Race and the Making of the American Working Class.* London: Verso, 1991.
6. Sklar, Holly. *Chaos or Community? Seeking Solutions, Not Scapegoats for Bad Economics.* Boston, MA: South End Press, 1995.
7. United Nations Report. 1980.

58

Las Mujeres Invisibles/The Invisible Women

SHARON ANN NAVARRO

NAFTA is a story of violence against women. It is a treaty that created violence against women and their families. There are tremendous implications, the economic implications and the whole impact it has had on women's health, their lives, their future, and their families. It is as violent as any beating, if not more destructive.

—LA MUJER OBRERA

El Paso, Texas, is a microcosm of the inherent contradictions created by the North American Free Trade Agreement (NAFTA) along the border. On the one hand, NAFTA profoundly shifted the focus of national and international commerce, moving it from an "East-West" emphasis to a "North-South" paradigm. In doing so, El Paso became the gateway to the tremendous economic opportunities available to Mexico and Latin America (Ortega 2000). At the same time, north of the U.S.-Mexican border, NAFTA acted as a catalyst, another force, or another trend, that is steadily squeezing Mexican-American women workers (in the garment industry) to the margins of the economic sector in El Paso. These Mexican-American garment workers are typically low-skilled and low-income women. As the garment industries close down their businesses and move across the border, the Mexican-American women that once worked in these businesses are being left out of the economic restructuring taking place under NAFTA. These women are being marginalized. The type of work that they have done—in some cases for more than twenty years—is now becoming obsolete and replaced by advanced technology.

★ ★ ★

For the Mexican-American garment workers in El Paso, an entire way of life and standard of living are fast disappearing. These Spanish-speaking women have worked all of their lives to provide for up to four generations of their families. Now they have lost their livelihood, their health-care insurance, their homes, and their futures. When NAFTA was first introduced in the late 1980s, various organizations with labor interests believed that NAFTA was going to be their opportunity to set labor standards for workers in the three participating countries. However, that was not at all what the crafters of NAFTA intended. Instead, labor interests were left out of NAFTA.

And so NAFTA became an incitement to discourse, an invitation to review the voices whose identities, as Spanish-speaking, female garment workers, are vehicles for political expression. This woman's nongovernmental organization mobilized to express their anxieties about the way NAFTA has affected their economic subsistence, their way of life. The struggle for this grassroots organization is not over the politics of influence, but to transform the terms and nature of the debate; it is a struggle to integrate previously excluded groups, voices, and issues into local and national politics.

Drawing on literature from political science, as well as from a wealth of new data obtained through fieldwork,[1] this study examines LMO's [La Mujer Obrera] use of central icons, traditions, history, and customs from Mexican culture to mobilize constituents in appeals to U.S. local, state, and federal government institutions. More important, this study explores how one women's organization used the

U.S.-Mexico border to highlight its struggle in the post-NAFTA era.

★ ★ ★

EL PASO: A BORDER BETWEEN TWO WORLDS

The physical designation of a boundary may serve as an observable reminder that the politics, economics, and culture of countries and subnationalities differ (Agnew, Mercer, and Sopher 1984). The uniqueness of El Paso–Ciudad Juarez stems from the fact that a city from the First World shares a border with a developing city from the Third World. Boundaries create cultures and identities that impose order on cities, communities, and individuals by shaping them in a way that embodies the values and beliefs of a society or geographic location. The physical and cultural closeness of the United States and Mexico, as well as the political, social, and economic ties that connect them, creates an intriguing bicultural arrangement that provide[s] a laboratory for studying identity formation and mobilization across borders.

In theory, a border is a line that separates one nation from another or, in the case of internal entities, one province or locality from another. The essential functions of a border are to keep people in their own space and to prevent, control, or regulate interactions among them. For the purposes of this study, the terms *border, borderland,* and *frontera* are used interchangeably. The terms are used to denote an area that is physically distant from the core of the nation; it is a zone of transition, a place where people and institutions are shaped by natural and human forces that are not felt in the core or heartland of the United States or Mexico.

For example, the U.S.-Mexico boundary is the busiest land border in the world, the longest and most dramatic meeting point between a rich and a poor country, and the site of the most intensive interaction between law enforcement and law evasion. Nowhere has the state more aggressively loosened and tightened its territorial border grip at the same time. Nowhere else do the contrasting state practices of market liberalization and criminalization

more visibly overlap. The result has been the construction of both a borderless economy (via NAFTA) and a barricaded border. More concretely, the politics of opening the border to legal economic flows is closely connected to the politics of making it appear more closed to illegal flows: illegal drugs and migrant labor.

★ ★ ★

The uniqueness of the U.S.-Mexico border, specifically the border city in question, plays a critical role in the sociopolitical construction of identities. Kimberly Grimes, in her study of migration to the United States from Putla de Guerro, Oaxaca, Mexico, suggests that identities are rooted in geography. Grimes's claim holds the key to understanding the seemingly contradictory strategy of LMO, which on the one hand embraces the Mexican culture—which is suggestive of a "borderless cultural region"—to mobilize its members, but at the same time reemphasizes the U.S.-Mexico border to highlight the struggles of displaced workers. According to Grimes, borders play an important role in distinguishing "us" from "them." Moreover, people's sense of self includes identification with particular geographical spaces. People negotiate constructed political, economic, and social (cultural) borders of self-identification. Identities are gounded in space and time, and they transform as time passes, as people move across spaces, and as national policies and global conditions transform. People react to these changes and constructions by accommodating or challenging and/or resisting them.

MEXICAN-AMERICAN WOMEN WORKERS IN EL PASO: A GENDERED LOOK AT GLOBALIZATION

For the close to 20,000 displaced workers, NAFTA and ongoing deep economic restructuring have not ushered in the new dawn of prosperity hailed by political leaders. The explosive growth of lower-paid export manufacturing jobs in the maquiladora sector in Mexico has been offset by the immense loss of jobs in the domestic manufacturing sector in the United States and Canada.

The globalization of capital necessary for economic restructuring is being deliberately hastened by most national governments, by international institutions like the International Monetary Fund and the World Bank, and by global corporations themselves. While international trade is nothing new, our system of nation-based economies is rapidly changing toward a "new world economy" (Takaki 1993). At the center of this change lies a sharp increase in capital mobility. Computer, communication, and transportation technologies continue to shorten geographical distances, making possible the coordination of production and commerce on a global scale. Lower tariffs have reduced national frontiers as barriers to commerce, thus encouraging transnational production and distribution. Corporations are becoming global not only to reduce production costs, but also to expand markets, elude taxes, acquire resources, and protect themselves against currency fluctuations and other risks, including the growth of organizations like LMO that would mobilize workers and demand that their interests and voices be heard in the new world economy (see also Brecher and Costello 1994).

Three hundred companies now own an estimated one-quarter of the productive assets of the world (Barnet and Cavanagh 1994, 15). Of the top 100 economies in the world, 47 are corporations—each with more wealth than 130 countries (Harison 1994). International trade and financial institutions like the International Monetary Fund, the World Bank, the European Union (EU), and the new World Trade Organization have cultivated powers formerly reserved for nation-states. Conversely, national governments have become less and less able to control their own economies. This new system, which is controlled by the so-called Corporate Agenda, is not based on the consent of the governed (Brecher, Childs, and Cutler 1993), and it has no institutional mechanism to hold it accountable to those whom its decisions affect.

In general, the effects of capital mobility, which is designed to increase economic efficiency, have been malignant for workers. An unregulated global economy forces workers, communities, and countries to compete with each other in an effort to attract corporate investment. Each tries to reduce labor, social, and environmental costs below the others.[2]

In the debates surrounding NAFTA, globalization and regionalization are often interpreted as homogenizing vehicles, without regard to the fact that women, and in particular women of color, are paying a disproportionate share of the costs of the processes of neoliberalism. Globalization hits especially hard racial/ethnic minorities in the United States and female factory workers in the U.S. (Larudee 1999, 123–63). It has profoundly changed the lives of women in El Paso, Texas, creating inequalities that interact with pre-existing class, ethnic, gender, and regional cleavages (Gabriel and Macdonald 1994, 535–62).

Job losses have been especially substantial in the apparel sector in El Paso and in some small communities that are heavily dependent on factories, which shut down and moved to Mexico. Since NAFTA took effect in 1994, El Paso has lost between 15,000 and 20,000 jobs.[3] Table 1 shows the number of job losses from 1994 to 2000. Table 2 shows how Texas ranks in comparison to other states with respect to displaced workers. Free trade and the reduction of tariffs made it easier for companies to close plants and move to Mexico only to continue as maquiladoras (Myerson 1998, 1C, 22C).

★ ★ ★

TABLE 1   NAFTA Job Losses in El Paso, January 1994–November 2000

Year	Number of Displaced Workers
1994	1,045
1995	2,193
1996	2,573
1997	3,435
1998	3,641
1999	2,125
2000	1,940
TOTAL	18,975

Source: Texas Workforce Commission.

TABLE 2   NAFTA-TAA Certified Workers, by State as of Mid-July 1997

Texas	★	Massachusetts	1,315
North Carolina	★	West Virginia	1,288
Pennsylvania	★	Kansas	1,184
New York	★	Kentucky	1,016
California	7,476	Alaska	780
Georgia	6,186	Louisiana	778
Indiana	5,811	Arizona	684
Tennessee	5,640	Connecticut	631
Arkansas	5,397	Montana	613
New Jersey	4,471	Maine	432
Ohio	4,413	Wyoming	392
Wisconsin	4,405	Vermont	361
Michigan	3,783	Minnesota	336
Washington	3,445	North Dakota	300
Missouri	3,329	Utah	292
Illinois	2,902	New Mexico	242
Florida	2,804	Oklahoma	230
Iowa	2,785	Nebraska	220
Oregon	2,550	New Hampshire	139
South Carolina	2,305	Maryland	86
Virginia	2,166	Idaho	83
Colorado	1,990	Nevada	76
Alabama	1,383	South Dakota	65

★The Department of Labor does not have the total number of displaced workers for the states of Texas, North Carolina, Pennsylvania, and New York, but claim they are the states with the highest numbers.
Note: Certifications are for January 1, 1994, to July 18, 1997.
Source: Department of Labor, NAFTA Trade Adjustment Assistance Office.

Approximately 80 percent of the garment workers in El Paso's garment and other manufacturing industries were Mexican-American women. Their subordinate social status limits their employment opportunities and makes them vulnerable to exploitation. As a result of NAFTA, however, thousands of Mexican-American workers, many of whom had migrated from Mexico to El Paso in search of a better life, lost their jobs. A total of 97 percent of the displaced Mexican-American workers in El Paso are Hispanic, and 80 percent are women

(Gilot 1999, 10B). One-third of these women head single households. Half are between the ages of 30 and 45, while the majority of the other half are older than 45. In addition, most of the affected workers are sustaining up to four generations of their families—themselves, their parents, their children and their grandchildren (La Mujer Obrera 1999a, 1). . . .

LMO has been working for nearly five years to make the conditions of Spanish-speaking NAFTA-displaced women workers visible locally, regionally, and nationally. The seeds of LMO were planted in 1972, when a campaign to unionize workers in the Farah plant (the biggest jean maker at the time) in El Paso intensified (see Coyle, Hershatter, and Honig 1980, 117–43). LMO was formed because women felt that the Amalgamated Clothing and Textile Workers of America, or for that matter, any union (such as the AFL-CIO), did nothing to address their needs, ignored their rights as *women* workers, and did not respect their membership as *women* members in the union (Flores 1998). This devaluation of women's work is deeply rooted in the history of U.S. labor unions. According to Glenn (1999), the old labor movement of the 1970s—including the one that organized Farah workers—"characterized itself as . . . [a]very macho kind of an organization. We (LMO) feel that the labor unions have not gotten away from that." For example, during the strike against Farah, male organizers in both the Amalgamated Clothing Workers of America and the AFL-CIO ignored women worker's concerns, such as sexual harassment, health care, child care, domestic violence, political education, and verbal abuse by their employers (Flores 1998). Moreover, employers often view the income of the female workers as "extra" or "supplemental" to their husband's income.

In 1981, following the Farah campaign, LMO was legally established as a non-profit community-based organization of women workers in El Paso. LMO has defined itself, first and foremost, as a *woman's* organization (La Mujer Obrera 1993, 3). It combines community organizing, popular education, leadership development and advocacy into a comprehensive struggle for a better quality of life for the women and their families. Like other organizations operating in a resource-poor environment, the organization relies on outside funding (La Mujer Obrera 1999, 1 and 2). The organization turns to national churches, private foundations, the federal government, and local entities for financial support (Arnold 1999a). LMO initially had a yearly budget of $150,000, and in 1998–1999 its budget was between $500,000 and $750,000 (Arnold 1999b). The organization employs a total of six women as full-time organizers. The board of directors is made up of two men and five women, all of whom have been displaced by NAFTA. The support staff consists of a paid secretary and a grant writer as well as various interns and volunteers.

The organization struggles to achieve *siete necesidades basicas* (seven basic goals): decent, stable employment, housing, education, nutrition, health care, peace, and political liberty. One of LMO's principal objectives is to educate workers so that they are able to defend their rights and to take leadership positions in their own communities. Educational programs form the basis for organizing work and raise workers' awareness of their roles as *women* and as economic producers. Like other women's movements, LMO has struggled to integrate previously excluded issues into politics by pushing women's concerns (e.g., child care and health care) (Peterson 1992, 183–206). LMO also serves at a safe place where friendships develop, experiences are shared, and where women become educated not only about their rights as workers, but, perhaps most important, their rights as women, mothers, and spouses. To this end, LMO has established a child care center where displaced workers may leave their children while they attend school, look for work, or go to their jobs.[6]

To achieve institutional changes that will lead to the creation of genuine economic alternatives for workers in the midst of globalization, La Mujer Obrera has also recently reorganized and broadened its structure (La Mujer Obrera 1998, 4). The most critical developments have been the emergence of two new quasi-independent organizations under LMO's corporate umbrella. One is the Asociacion de Trabajadores Fronterizos, which has taken on the worker and community organizing, direct action, and mass mobilization components of LMO's work (5). . . .

Through these networks, the association has the participation of more than 2,000 workers, the majority of whom are women, and a governing board of 14 displaced workers, two elected from and by each of the seven factory and school committees (26). At the same time, LMO began constructing its capacity to develop and operate community economic development programs on behalf of, and with, displaced workers. In December of 1997, LMO established El Puente Community Development Corporation as a vehicle for developing training and education, jobs, self-employment, housing, the development of microenterprises, access to credit and neighborhood revitalization strategies as a means to create jobs, income, and economic self-sufficiency for the workers and the organization. Moving into this arena has required that LMO negotiate and work with local, state, and federal agencies and officials for financial support (26–27).

By creating a space in the political and economic arena, LMO has already produced tangible results for the displaced workers. The organization succeeded in getting a $45 million grant—the largest grant ever given by the U.S. Department of Labor—to retrain displaced workers. . . .

The $45 million grant allows LMO to institute alternatives to existing federal and state retraining programs. These programs entitle displaced workers to benefits while attending English classes, courses for their general equivalency diploma (GED), and retraining within an 18-month period. Many of these programs, however, are plagued with a variety of problems, especially inadequate buildings and equipment, outdated curricula, incompetent or poorly trained teachers, and administrators who make racial/ethnic slurs and personal insults (Klapmeyer 1998).

. . . Frustrated with many of the inept retraining schools, LMO opened up its own school for displaced workers on February 1, 1999. It hired a full-time teacher to teach English, the general equivalency examination and microenterprise training. LMO has also established a business incubator that will support the self-employment initiatives of displaced workers. Further, LMO is currently in the process of developing a bilingual adult education curriculum specifically designed for displaced workers in El Paso. This curriculum will be the standard curriculum for every school in El Paso if they are to accept displaced workers in their schools. LMO has also played an instrumental role in helping El Paso win the Empowerment Zone designation that provides federal funds for economic development. As a result, the poorest area of the city—South Central—will receive much needed federal money for revitalization, which would create jobs. LMO plays a role in deciding how that money will be spent.

THE USES OF MEXICAN CULTURE FOR MOBILIZATION

For LMO, culture has become a unique dimension in women's activism. In her study of two Chicano struggles in the Southwest, Laura Pulido (1998, 31–60) points out that culture plays a key role in mobilization efforts both by "providing familiar and meaningful guideposts and by facilitating collective identity." The use of symbols, customs, traditions reminds people of who they are, of their shared traditions past and present, and of what they can achieve by uniting and acting collectively.

In the 1960s and 1970s Latinos/Chicanos became aware of how their culture not only differed from, but was also maligned by, mainstream Anglo America. Once-shameful cultural icons were reappropriated and turned into symbols of resistance. In the course of building a movement, farmworkers and activists publicly displayed statues and posters of La Virgen de Guadalupe not only as a source of solace and inspiration, but also (and far more consciously at times) as an expression of pride in the Mexican culture and a tool of mobilization. By openly engaging in ritual prayer, they asserted their identity to the larger society (see Herrera-Sobek 1990; Rodriguez 1994). LMO similarly uses La Virgen de Guadalupe as an expression of inspiration and as a vehicle of mobilization and consciousness raising. For the women of LMO, La Virgen de Guadalupe thus not only represents strength, hope, and respect, but "she is also viewed as a woman and a mother who has suffered with the death of her son and, like her, we (displaced workers) are suffering for our families and our children (Orquiz 1999).[7]

In a study of Mexican-American women in East Los Angeles, Mary Pardo examines how they transform "traditional" networks and resources based on family and culture into political assets to defend the quality of urban life. Here, the women's activism arises out of seemingly "traditional" roles, addresses wider social and political issues, and capitalizes on formal associations sanctioned by the community. Religion, commonly viewed as a conservative force, becomes intertwined with politics. Often, women speak of their communities and their activism as extensions of their family and household responsibility. Women's grassroots struggles center around quality of life and challenge conventional assumptions about the powerlessness of women as well as static definitions of culture and tradition (Pardo 1998).

LMO also identifies with the Mexican culture and its members through its landscape. Outside its building, LMO has corn (maize) stalks growing in place of an assortment of bushes or flowers. As Refugio Arrieta explains, "The maize is symbolic of our Mexican culture. It is a symbol of the resistance too. . . . It is more like the resistance that leads to maintaining the culture here and helping it live and grow here in the U.S. and not simply being forced to abandon the Mexican culture" (Arrieta 1998).

Moreover, LMO also tries to maintain and reinterpret its history and heritage with Mexico in symbolic remembrance of Emiliano Zapata and the Zapatista rebels. Hanging from some of the walls of LMO are portraits and pictures of Emilio Zapata and Zapatista *women* rebels. For LMO, Zapata and the Zapatista rebels represent the struggle of resistance against neoliberalism, specifically NAFTA.

They represent in Mexico the voice of people who have been eliminated in Mexico by NAFTA. As one member stated, "We are kindred spirits because of what the U.S. economy is doing to Mexican-American factory workers [and] what the Mexican economy is doing to the indigenous people of Mexico" (Anonymous 1998). To some extent, LMO believes, like the Zapatistas in southern Mexico, that NAFTA will eliminate them from an economy that was built on their backs.

LMO further uses the Mexican *corrido* as a mobilizing mechanism that reflects their political situation.[8] For example, during Guillermo Glenn's trial on March 17, 1999, after he was arrested for his participation in the blocking of the Zaragoza Bridge, LMO members gathered outside the courthouse in protest. With the news stations there, LMO members began to sing the "Corrido de los Desplazados" (The ballad of the displaced), which they had written themselves:

Ano de 94	In the year of '94
Comenzo la pesadilla	The nightmare started
Se robaron los trabajos,	They stole the jobs,
Nos dejaron en la orilla	They left us at the edge
Los obreros en El Paso,	The workers in El Paso,
Recuerdan bien ese dia.	Remember well that day.

The "Corrido de los Desplazados" embraces all displaced workers, raises their level of consciousness, unites them, and inspires them to mobilize. This type of cultural practice also represents the organization's strategy of activism and mobilization. It adds to more conventional forms of political participation, such as voting, in an effort to stress demands for respect, dignity, and justice of the Mexican-American workers and their traditions. Cindy Arnold (1999b), coordinator of El Puente at LMO, summed up the organization's philosophy of political participation as follows: "For us, political involvement is not based on an electoral or party process, but [is seen] in terms of on-going dialogue with political leaders at all the different levels." As a political actor, LMO emphasizes that it has no political affiliation and does not endorse any particular political party or politician.

Its legal charter as a community-based organization does not permit it to become involved in electoral politics. Now that half of its members are citizens and thus eligible to vote (a change that became evident in the last city election), it will also encourage its members to vote. . . .

★ ★ ★

In other instances, LMO activists have been accused by their spouses of neglecting their family obligations when they became involved with the organization (Olvera 1990, A12). Women in leadership roles often reveal that they have strained relationships with their husbands because they refused to adhere to the role of a traditional Mexican wife (I. Montoya 1999). Other women reported that it was okay for them to participate in LMO as long as they also did what was expected of them as mothers, housekeepers, and wives (Reyes 1999; see also Fernandez-Kelly 1990; Garcia 1981). Some women describe the difficulty of getting away from housework and their husbands. Maria Acosta describes the problem she has with her jealous husband: "Every time I get ready to come to the meetings, my husband gives me a hard time. He says that I come to [La] Mujer Obrera because I am either looking for a boyfriend or I come to meet my boyfriend."[9] According to Acosta's husband, there could be no other reason for her to come to LMO, despite the fact that it is helping her to get into a retraining program.

CONCLUSION

LMO's activism in response to global economic restructuring, as manifested in NAFTA, relies on contradictory yet successful mobilization strategy. On the one hand, LMO became visible when its members literally reemphasized the U.S.-Mexico border to highlight NAFTA's disastrous effects on Mexican-American women garment workers. On the other hand, LMO de-emphasized the U.S.-Mexico border culturally by embracing the Mexican culture. This is what makes the border city of El Paso unique. Displaced by NAFTA, the lives of the LMO women have been disrupted and forever changed by the corporate agenda driving NAFTA.

Spanish-speaking women, who once migrated to El Paso in search of a better life, have received a rude awakening after dedicating their entire lives to building the city's economy. After having been subject to exploitation and limited employment in El Paso, these women are now being marginalized and slowly eliminated from an increasingly internationalized economy.

To mobilize these women, LMO has focused on Mexican culture as a vehicle that links individual members to the organization. The use of Mexican religious symbols, traditions, histories, and customs has served to reinforce a bond between the organization and its members, as well as to contextualize the plight of the NAFTA-displaced workers. At the same time, its creation of a transnationally shared space of Mexican culture has enabled LMO to become a legitimate economic actor in the city's economic restructuring. Symbols such as the *Virgen de Guadalupe,* the cultivation of corn stalks, pictures of the Zapatistas, and the use of the Mexican *corrido* have served as icons of political resistance against a transnational agreement that has affected their lives. The success of this strategy has manifested itself in the fact that no other organization in the U.S.-Mexico border region has achieved as much as has LMO. It has helped obtain El Paso's designation as an Empowerment Zone, won a $45 million grant for displaced workers, created two umbrella organizations—the Asociacion de Trabajadores and El Puente—opened its own school for displaced workers, is currently developing the first bilingual adult curriculum for displaced workers, and has established a child-care center. All of its achievements serve as a testament to the power of a transnational culture in women's political activism. But, be that as it may, a much larger question looms: Although this essay is about one grassroots globalization movement at the U.S.-Mexico border, are there lessons to be learned from its experiences?

Certainly the first lesson points to the fact that any one specific identity—in this case the Mexican identity—may not necessarily be enough to forge a cross-border alliance. Other principal factors may come into play, such as shared gender, shared experiences, values, beliefs, ideology. For example, a much more useful and broader theme that workers could mobilize around could be the pursuit for social justice among all workers, specifically the push for "living wages." By mobilizing around the theme of social justice, LMO would broaden its support base by being inclusive of other grassroots organizations and perhaps catapult them into the international area where their voices would be much more difficult to stifle. The most recent example of this was seen in the Summit of the Americas meeting on April 20–22, 2001, in Quebec City, where numerous grassroots movements gathered to protest the expansion of economic integration (free trade) at the expense of social justice.

In addition, what becomes evident in this essay is the importance of contextualizing the workers situation under NAFTA. What this case study suggests is that mobilization depends upon the way in which an organization chooses to construct, define, identify, or contextualize itself given a certain set of circumstances. The way in which an organization chooses to identify itself and whether or not that particular identity resonates with its members has bearing on the organization's behavior and the perception external agencies, individuals, and institutions have of that organization. The perception of others outside of the organization may have significant political repercussions. For example, the identity of an organization can affect its access to resources made available only by governmental agencies.

Moreover, this essay also points to the growing participation of women in grassroots mobilization, specifically as leaders, against NAFTA, the Free Trade for the Americas Initiative scheduled for completion in 2005, as it is for the Multilateral Agreement on Investment and other similar agreements. Lisa Montoya and her colleagues correctly point out that political scientists have tended to neglect or discount Latina leadership and participation in electoral and community politics (Montoya, Hardy-Fanta, Garcia 2000, 555–61). A key issue within the debate about gender differences is whether there is an essential divide between the public and private dimensions of politics. For

Latina women, much more than men, the boundary between these supposedly distinct spheres of life is blurred, indistinct. With their emphasis on grassroots politics, survival politics, and the politics of everyday life and through their emphasis on the development of political consciousness, Latina women see connections between the problems they face personally and community issues stemming from government policies.

NOTES

1. This study is based on 56 face-to-face interviews I conducted from August of 1998 through August 1999 in El Paso, Texas, with active women who have lost their jobs because of NAFTA—that is, businesses moving from El Paso to Mexico. I have defined as "active" those women who dedicate 20 hours to LMO by either attending weekly meetings, belonging to committees within the organization, volunteering their time, or attending and helping in organizing fiestas (parties), rallies, and protests. The interviews were conducted in Spanish (and on occasion in English) at LMO, protest and rally sites, and, when it was convenient for the person interviewed, over the phone. I have also included interviews with the lead organizers of LMO, a former bilingual teacher, who was employed to teach these women English at one of the many schools that offer English classes, a public relations spokesperson from one of the last mammoth garment industries (Levi Strauss) in El Paso, politicians, and various governmental/political officials. Depending on the individual, these interviews lasted between 15 and 75 minutes. In LMO, the women speak only Spanish, range in age from 35 to 72, and more than half have no more than a fourth-grade education in Mexico. At the time of my interviews with the women of LMO, almost all of them were either in school learning English, studying for their high school equivalancy diploma, or in some retraining program.
2. According to Brecher and Costello (1994), "race to the bottom" is the reduction in labor, social, and environmental conditions that results from global competition for jobs and investment.
3. This is the only credible number that I have seen reported.
4. In speaking with John Ownby of the Dislocated Worker Service Unit at the Texas Workforce Commission, I was told that being classified as "certified NAFTA displaced worker" might not reflect the true number of displaced workers. Businesses that close up shop because of NAFTA are supposed to certify their workers with the Texas Workforce Commission, which simply means that the workers were laid off because the business closed down due solely to NAFTA. Certification by the Texas Workforce Commission ensures that the displaced worker will be eligible for retraining programs. However, the Texas Workforce Commission does not have the

manpower to see that businesses [do] in fact register their workers as certified NAFTA displaced workers. Thus, the number of certified displaced workers may not be a true account of displaced workers. Ownby believes the number to be much higher (Ownby 1999).
5. This information is based on face-to-face interviews and informal discussions with women.
6. The power of culture as a mobilizing force is not a new phenomenon. It has been instrumental in the civil rights movement, the Chicano movement, and the farmworkers movement as well as many others.
7. In both my formal and informal conversations with LMO and staff members, this was the response given by all.
8. A *corrido* is a simple narrative ballad that relates an event of interest only to a small region; it may be a love song or a comment on a political situation.
9. This name has been altered to protect the identity of the woman. The information was revealed in a private informal conversation.

BIBLIOGRAPHY

1. Agnew, John A., John Mercer, and David Sopher, eds. 1984. *The City in Cultural Context*. Boston: Allen & Unwin.
2. Anonymous. 1998. Personal interview, November 4.
3. Anonymous. 1999. Personal interview, March 17.
4. Arnold, Cindy. 1999a. Personal interview, January 9.
5. ———. 1999b. Personal interview, June 21.
6. Arrieta, Refugio, 1998. Personal interview, November 5.
7. Barnet, Richard, La Barricada, and John Cavanagh. 1994. *Global Dreams*. New York: Simon & Schuster.
8. Brecher, Jeremy, John Brown Childs, and Jill Cutler, eds. 1993. *Global Visions*. Boston: South End Press.
9. Brecher, Jeremy, and Tim Costello. 1994. *Global Village or Global Pillage: Economic Reconstruction from the Bottom Up*. Boston: South End.
10. Coyle, Laurie, Gail Hershatter, and Emily Honig, "Women at Farah: An Unfinished Story." Pp. 117–43 in *Mexican Women in the United States*, ed. Magdalena Mora and Adelaida del Castillo. (Los Angeles: Chicano Studies Research Center, University of California, 1980).
11. El Paso Greater Chamber of Commerce. 1997. "The El Paso Labor Market: A Training Gap Analysis, Final Report," December.
12. El Puente CDC/La Mujer Obrera. 1999. *Building Employment and Economic Development Bridges in South Central El Paso for Displaced Workers, Strategic Plan*. El Paso, TX: La Mujer Obrera.
13. Fernandez-Kelly, Maria Patricia, 1990. "Power Surrendered, Power Restored: The Politics of Work and Family among Hispanic Garment Workers in California and Florida." Pp. 130–49 in *Women, Politics and Change*, ed. Louise Tilly and Patricia Gurin. New York: Russell Sage.
14. Flores, Maria Antonia. 1998. Personal interview, October 13.
15. Gabriel, Christina, and Laura Macdonald. 1994. "NAFTA, Women, and Organizing in Canada and Mexico: Forging a Feminist Internationality." *Millennium: Journal of International Studies*. 23(3):535–62.

16. Garcia, Mario T. 1981. *Desert Immigrants*. New Haven, CT: Yale University Press.

17. Gilot, Louie. 1999. "Displaced Workers Want City to Help Find Jobs Quickly." *El Paso Times,* August 31.

18. Glenn, Guillermo. 1999. Personal interview, January 27.

19. Grimes, Kimberly M. 1998. *Crossing Borders: Changing Social Identities in Southern Mexico*. Tucson: University of Arizona Press.

20. Harison, Bennett. 1994. *Lean and Mean: The Changing Landscape of Corporate Power in the Age of Flexibility*. New York: Basic Books.

21. Herrera-Sobek, Maria. 1990. *The Mexican Corrido*. Bloomington: Indiana University Press.

22. Klapmeyer, Keith. 1998. Personal interview, November 19.

23. Kolence, Vic. 1999a. "Apparel Industry Was Precursor to Maquiladoras." *El Paso Times,* February 21.

24. La Mujer Obrera. 1993. *Orientation Center La Mujer Obrera*. El Paso, TX: La Mujer Obrera.

25. _____. 1998. *Progress Report*. El Paso, TX: La Mujer Obrera.

26. _____. 1999a. *Stop NAFTA? Violence against Women Workers*. El Paso, TX: La Mujer Obrera.

27. _____. 1999b. *Women Working Together: Goals and Activities*. El Paso, TX: La Mujer Obrera.

28. Larudee, Mehrene. 1999. "NAFTA's Impact on U.S. Labor Markets, 1994–1997." Pp. 123–63 in *Pulling Apart: The Deterioration of Employment and Income in North America under Free Trade*, ed. Bruce Campbell, Maria Teresa Gutierrez Haces, Andrew Jackson, and Mehrene Larudee. Ottawa, Ontario: Canadian Center for Policy Alternatives.

29. Montoya, Irma. 1999. Personal interview, February 24.

30. Montoya, Lisa, Carol Hardy-Fanta, and Sonia Garcia. 2000. "Latina Politics: Gender, Participation, and Leadership." *Political Science and Politics* 33(3).

31. Myerson, Alan. 1998. "Borderline Working Class: Texas Labor Is Feeling Trade Pact's Pinch." *New York Times,* May 8.

32. Olvera, Joe. 1990. "Hunger Strikers Face New Battle on Home Front." *El Paso Times,* September 2, p. A12.

33. Orquiz, Paz. 1999. Personal interview, January 20.

34. Ortega, Roy. 2000. "Trade Soars Both Ways after NAFTA." *El Paso Times,* July 9, pp. El–2.

35. Ownby, John. 1999. Personal interview, September 1.

36. Pardo, Mary. 1998. *Mexican American Women Activists*. Philadelphia: Temple University Press.

37. Peterson, V. Spike. 1992. "Transgressing Boundaries: Theories of Knowledge, Gender, and International Relations." *Millennium: Journal of International Studies* 21(2).

38. Pulido, Laura. 1998. *Environmental and Economic Justice*. Tucson: University of Arizona Press.

39. Reyes, Lorenza. 1999. Personal interview, January 13.

40. Rodriguez, Jeanette. 1994. *Our Lady of Guadalupe: Faith among Mexican-American Women*. Austin: University of Texas Press.

41. Takaki, Ronald. 1993. *A Different Mirror: A History of Multicultural America*. Boston: Little, Brown.

42. Templin, Neal. 2000. "Anatomy of a Jobs Program That Went Awry." *Wall Street Journal,* February 11.

59

Confronting Anti-Gay Violence

MICHAEL BRONSKI

Several weeks ago I was walking with my lover in a quiet neighborhood in Cambridge, Massachusetts, on our way to a late afternoon movie. We were holding hands in an offhanded sort of way, chatting together, when a group of young teens sitting on a front stoop across the street (the oldest was probably 14, the youngest maybe 12) yelled "faggot"; then they laughed and threw some plastic soda bottles at us before they ran off. We thought for a moment of chasing and confronting them—this didn't seem particularly dangerous and I have always felt that confronting this sort of harassment, if not immediately dangerous, is always better than ignoring it—but they were already a block away and it did not seem worth the time or energy. We went off to the movies, but the incident was deeply disquieting. Gay men and lesbians have always been aware of anti-gay violence. It becomes a way of life, just as it is for many people of color in America and for women making their way through the world everyday. In the past months we have heard—in the mainstream media—that there is a new focus on gay bashing. And the message here is that this new focus will bring about a new understanding and the end to it. Aside from the Matthew Shepard murder in Laramie, Wyoming, by Russell Henderson and Aaron McKinney, both 21, last October other murders of gay people have been deemed newsworthy:

On January 17 Kevin Tryals and Laaron Morris of Galveston, Texas, were found in a burning car on a dead-end road outside of city limits. Both bodies were severely burned. The medical examiner's office ruled that both men were dead before the car was ignited and that both men died from multiple gunshot wounds. Police have ruled out robbery and are treating the murders as anti-gay violence.

On February 20 the burned remains of Billy Jack Gaither, 39, a factory worker were discovered in Sylacauga, a small town in Alabama. He had been beaten to death (or near death) with an ax handle and thrown onto a stack of tires and set afire. His attackers, 21-year-old Charles Butler and 25-year-old Steven Mullins, claim he made a pass at them.

On March 1, the severed head of Henry Edward Northington, 39, was found on a pathway to a park known as a gay men's cruising spot outside of Alexandria, Virginia. Northington was homeless and gay. No one has been arrested.

On March 12, in Los Angeles, Juan Chavez, 34, pleaded guilty of murdering five gay men by luring them to their homes supposedly for sex and then robbing and strangling them. He also was accused of taking the victims' cars after killing them. He claimed he commited the murders to stop the spread of AIDS.

On March 15 the body of Michael Barber, 56, was discovered in his apartment in Fort Lauderdale, Florida, encased in a zippered plastic bag. He had died of multiple stab wounds. Barber, an ex-Marine, had worked as a gardener in the area. Six months ago Charles Squires, 64, of nearby Wilton Manors, Florida, was found stabbed to death and wrapped in plastic inside his home. Police are treating both as anti-gay crimes.

On March 19, Bradley Davis, 24, of San Francisco, was found bleeding and semiconscious between two parked cars at 12:15 A.M. near 18th and Castro Streets by police officers who were called to the scene. Officers arrested three suspects—Ban Doc Im, 21; Henry Sai Kwong, 19; Thang Cao Truong, 18—who were seen by witnesses attacking Davis after standing on Castro shouting anti-gay and anti–African American epithets. There is no doubt that since the Shepard murder anti-gay violence has been deemed more newsworthy, while some analysts are claiming that violence against gay, lesbian, and transgendered people is rising. The Triangle Foundation, a gay rights advocacy group in Detroit, documented two Michigan anti-gay murders in 1997 and six in 1998; by March of 1999, they were investigating five. But the reality is

that there have always been an enormous number of murders, beatings, attacks, and harassments; what has changed are both the rate of reporting and the attention of the media. Generally speaking, queer commentators and activists see this as a positive trend; it seems to me that increased visibility for homophobic violence is only a first, albeit important, but rather small step. The enormous coverage given to the Shepard murder—and we will see much more once the trial starts—is, in itself, a study of what can go wrong. It is clear that Matthew Shepard's place as a media star was predicated on several factors: his murder was brutal and shocking, and his age, race, good looks, and class status made him the perfect victim for a national media looking for a good story. But will this coverage have any lasting effect on how both the media and public policy deal with anti-gay violence? If Matthew Shepard had been an African American teenage hustler, the story would have been different: there would not have been a story. Are the media simply going to go for the most sensational stories of anti-gay violence: beheadings, public burnings, dead bodies in zippered bags? The only reason the press reported on the Castro Street beating was that it took place in the dead-center of the most famous public gay neighborhood in the world.

Anywhere else it would not be news. In the past three decades U.S. culture has made some significant changes in how some issues about violence and discrimination are perceived and acted upon. Rape (although it still occurs all the time) is now treated more seriously by the police and the courts. The same is true of domestic violence. As recent events in New York have shown, the uphill, and ferociously waged, battle to have police violence against people of color is alive, well, and even making some progress. These changes all came about because of committed, sustained grass-roots organizing, an insistence that the issues be taken seriously—as a moral imperative—and a demand that the popular media both pay attention and act more responsibly. But will this coverage of anti-gay violence engender substantive change? If it has any chance to, it must move beyond simple sentimentalization and pity for "nice" victims: the bulk of reported anti-gay assaults in Manhattan, for instance, are faced by African American and Latino transgendered sex workers. The other thing that has to change is that anti-gay violence cannot continue to be viewed outside of a broader political and social context of the personal lives of heterosexuals. This may be beginning to happen. An editorial in the *St. Louis Dispatch* on March 10 noted "the ideas allowed to fester into the kind of murderous hatred that killed Gaither and Shepard . . . sprouted long before any blows were struck, any triggers were pulled, any fires were set. Like all hatred, anti-gay hatred is learned. Don't turn a deaf ear when your kid calls another child a 'fag' on the playground. Don't laugh at homophobic jokes in the office. Support education that includes positive information on gays and lesbians. Let gay and lesbian acquaintances or friends or relatives know they have your support. To condemn the brutal slayings of these men without examining the routine homophobia in our daily lives would be hypocrisy." I have deep suspicions of the ability of the mainstream media to effect any positive social change. I think of the young men—boys, really—who shouted and threw a bottle at me in the emblematically liberal city of Cambridge. I am old enough to be their grandfather, my lover is old enough to be their father. The men—boys?—accused of killing the "innocent" Matthew Shepard were his age. How do we work on building a common consensus that hating gay people enough to attack them is wrong in a culture that supports, or doesn't care about, the most murderous aspects of U.S. foreign policy? How do we discuss "accepting"—never mind valuing—homosexuality in a country in which the complexity of race is still, for the most part, undiscussable? Gay and lesbian activists have been organizing around violence issues for decades, and to a large degree they have not been taken seriously by many other political, religious, or social institutions. It is one thing to advise that men and women not laugh at fag jokes in the office, but we have to realize that not laughing at—or rebuking the teller of—fag jokes often labels someone a fag himself. One of the main problems in

fighting anti-gay prejudice is that the specter of homosexuality is everywhere, implicating anyone who counters the sentiment. The mainstream press's coverage of anti-gay violence may be a beginning of a more complex, fruitful public discourse, but it is only one facet of how the problem is confronted. Gay activists have to begin, or continue, building coalitions with other anti-violence and social action groups. Individuals doing political work on the left also have to take more time and energy in examining the myriad ways sexuality—in all its manifestations—impacts on social, national, and international policies and politics. In the meantime I am still going to hold my lover's hand wherever and whenever I want to. But I am also going to watch my back and be more purposeful in challenging people when faced with harassment or violence. If we had chased and confronted those boys, they might have thought twice before doing this again.

 60

Privilege and Cultural Reform at the U.S. Air Force Academy

DENA SAMUELS AND
STEVEN SAMUELS

THE SOURCE OF CHANGE: REVOLUTION FROM ABOVE

After the sexual assault scandal broke in March of 2003, four of the top military officers at the Air Force Academy were ousted, to be replaced by those hand-selected and tasked to deal with the scandal. The *new* leadership entered with this mission, unequivocal in their pursuit of change. Thus, the opportunity for change existed, as did the opportunity for observation and analysis.

The problem could not be solved by simply changing a rule or adding a new regulation or forming an action team. Instead, the change must derive from the heart of the culture. Culture has been defined as "the acquired knowledge that people use to generate behavior and interpret experience" (Spradley & McCurdy, 1997:14). That is, culture is not the behavior itself, but the knowledge and mental schemas that create the behavior. One rape survivor said that the rapes "occurred because the men knew they could get away with it. They knew they could get away with it—and not only that, they would be supported by their classmates" (interview on the *Oprah Winfrey Show*, December 8, 2003). This perception illustrates the fact that this culture of gender inequality, and specifically male privilege, allowed rape, sexual assault, and sexual harassment to occur.

The first step to any change must be a general recognition of the problem. During a presentation to the Academy faculty on December 17, 2003, Brigadier General David Wagie, Dean of the Faculty, summed up the fundamental idea that had allowed the cultural change to commence: "The status quo is unacceptable." In terms of a successful transformation, culture can only change if the current culture is unacceptable to its members. The widespread buy-in of this fact is the necessary first step toward implementing large-scale social change. What is unusual about the widespread cultural change at the Air Force Academy is it originated from the empowered and in some ways was resisted by those on the bottom of the hierarchy. Finally, at the heart of this revolution, and key to its success, was the examination of the system of privilege that had been in place since the founding of the institution.

PRIVILEGE INSTILLED

One privilege Air Force Academy cadets have "enjoyed" in the past is what Robert W. Connell (1987) calls "hegemonic" masculinity. Michael Kimmel (2003) describes a hegemonic man as "a man *in* power, a man *with* power, and a man *of* power. . . being strong, successful, capable, reliable, in control. The very definitions of manhood we have developed in our culture maintain the power that some men have over other men and that men have over women" (p. 57). At the Academy, under the

old hierarchical system, cadets were taught to strive to achieve hegemonic masculinity by oppressing lower-class cadets, and eventually the female cadets who were permitted into the Academy beginning in 1976. Male cadets' position of power earned solely by surviving their four-degree year (i.e., their "frosh" year or first year of attendance) gave them hegemonic masculinity. Whether earned or unearned, the privileges many males have had access to in the past have contributed to a culture of inequality that normalized, and therefore increased, incidents of sexual assault.

It is interesting to note that privilege often is perpetuated by tradition and reification. That is, one way to justify unequal treatment is to argue, "That's the way we've always done it." This argument is especially powerful for military academies where many have argued, "Our way in the past was successful, so why change it?" Again, these rebuttals were seen in all service academies when they integrated females (e.g., Diamond & Kimmel, 2002). Most recently at The Citadel (Military College of South Carolina) in 1995, the scene of male cadets cheering as the first female cadet quit exemplifies the point. Challenging long-held traditions inevitably means that those who are privileged by a system will feel threatened by change.

CHANGE: ELIMINATION OF PRIVILEGE

Starting at the top, one of the earliest breaks with tradition, and thus perhaps the first privilege to fall by the wayside, was the appointment of Lieutenant General John Rosa, Jr.—the first superintendent not to have graduated from the Academy (or West Point). Instead of the quick fixes or short-term action teams with immediate results that the military is fond of, the Academy under Lt. Gen. Rosa has taken a longer-term approach. He created a four-year plan of phased overlapping stages, starting with several months of preparation, moving through self-assessment (although assessment continues throughout), then focusing on turning the tide, creating the new culture, and ultimately embedding the new culture.

This process of transformation demonstrated the leadership's cognizance of the socially constructed nature of culture. The Academy environment had been constructed in a way that was protective of tradition, leery of change, and perpetuated privilege. The new leadership recognized that if culture is socially constructed, it can be reconstructed. This takes time, and the understanding that it cannot be done in a single year is a key potential for its ultimate success.

Under Lt. Gen. Rosa, perhaps the most significant change was the elimination of the Fourth Class System, the ritual degradation heaped upon the four degrees by the upper classes. This harsh system of intimidation and punishment of those attempting to join the current group (who had all experienced the process during their initial year) reinforced the strict hierarchy and in many ways defined the Academy experience.

In its place, the Four Class System was instituted. While the *Fourth* Class System focused entirely on breaking down the incoming cadets, the *Four* Class System focused on the responsibilities of each of the four classes. The old system focused on harassment and humiliation as cadets had to prove their superiority. In the new system, each class is given certain responsibilities for training the classes underneath them, which has the added value of giving upper-class cadets the opportunity to learn to be effective leaders themselves. Other changes involved the removal of simplistic brutal punishments (e.g., yelling, push-ups, sprints, etc.), the addition of rewards for good behavior, and active education on how to give constructive negative feedback.

Note the privileges removed from the system. First, upper-class cadets are no longer rewarded for simply surviving. Under the old system, all senior cadets had the most privileges (e.g., parking, amount of days/times they could leave the base, etc.), followed by all juniors, then all sophomores; the four degrees had almost none. Under the new Performance Based Pass System, rewards are earned by behavior, both individual and by squadron (groups of approximately 110 cadets, each composed of all four classes). Thus, now a

four degree from an extremely high-performing squadron could earn more leave than a senior from an exceptionally poorly performing squadron.

The upper-class privilege of dominance over four degrees has also been removed. Under the old system, upper-class cadets ruled the lowest class, and their word was law. This was especially true for sophomores, who had just spent a year being dominated and now were ready and eager to dominate the new incoming class. The elimination of this position of privilege is important for this problem of sexual assault. Under the old system, obedience to upper-class cadets was required, and comments from rape survivors suggest they believed they had to follow the orders of the upper-class cadets. For example, one survivor, Beth, claimed that this cultural subservience compelled her to meet with an upper-class cadet outside of the squadron who subsequently sodomized and raped her (Zubeck, 2003:10).

EARLY EVIDENCE OF SUCCESS

There is already evidence of emerging change. One specific instance was in a session on sexual assault in Introduction to Behavioral Sciences and Leadership, a course that is required for all cadets. During the session, cadets were asked about their prototype of rape (i.e., what they imagined the "typical" rape was like). In sections made up of upper-class cadets, the response was as expected: the prototype rape is a male stranger stalking a female in a dark alley. Interestingly enough, however, the sections made up of cadets who had arrived after changes were instituted responded that there are two prototypes: one of the stranger-rape mentioned above and another of acquaintance-rape, where the assailant knows the victim and fails to respond to her pleas (note that prototypes are always comprised of male assailants and female victims). This second prototype, a much more accurate description of the majority of rape incidents, seems to have emerged from the new education the class had received from the start of their Basic Cadet Training.

Other interesting case evidence stems from research on perceptions of gender in leadership that one of the author's students was doing. When cadets were interviewed about problems that arose in leadership based on gender, one male answered, "This is 2006. That [expletive] doesn't happen anymore!" Further discussion showed this man believed there was a clear delineation between the class of 2006 (the last class that had gone through the *Fourth* Class System) and those classes since then. Of course, this statement can also be interpreted as a distancing of himself from the problem and blaming other classes for the issues. The changes may be the result of the psychological separation between the upper-class and the four degrees highlighted above. The leadership has separated them and initiated a new era of Air Force Academy cadets, cadets whose training is more focused on treating everyone with respect, as opposed to ridicule. In so doing, they are addressing the culture of masculine privilege itself and reconstructing a more egalitarian culture for the future.

IMPLICATIONS FOR THE FUTURE: USING THE CONCEPT OF PRIVILEGE FOR CHANGE

The Air Force Academy's struggle to create a culture that is more inclusive and refuses to tolerate sexual assault or harassment is a struggle between privilege and egalitarianism. In the past, the focus has been on the victims who have experienced oppression under the Academy system. Cultural transformation requires that we examine both the privileged and the oppressed to continue the change process. The leadership then must continue to focus on those who are privileged. As Allan Johnson (2001) argues:

> Women and racial minorities are often described as being treated unequally, but men and whites are not. This, however, is logically impossible. *Unequal* simply means "not equal," which describes both those who receive less than their fair share *and* those who receive more. But there can't be a short end of the stick without a long end, because it's the longness of the long end that makes the short end short. To pretend otherwise makes privilege and those who receive it invisible. So long as we participate in

a society that transforms difference into privilege, there is no neutral ground to stand on. (p. 131)

The cultural shift the Academy has begun is an attempt to create neutral ground. But this change cannot be successful until all classes of cadets learn and internalize the idea that their fellow cadets are of equal human value and must be treated accordingly. Each cadet must understand they are personally responsible for creating such a culture that perpetuates and protects that equality. By removing privilege and certain abusive traditions, they are paving the way for a more egalitarian culture at the Academy for *all* cadets, and subsequent leaders of the Air Force.

Male cadets can learn to use their privilege as males not to continue to perpetuate inequality, but to create change. For those who wish to make a difference, the framework of privilege provides a means for understanding not only those who currently experience privilege in the culture, but also those who are being oppressed by the system (in this case, the assault survivors, and perhaps, all female cadets).

As change continues to progress, the likelihood for positive momentum develops. In a culture of privilege and oppression, those who are disempowered lose their voices and thus their ability to influence change (Lorde, 1984). Under the old system, women could only voice support of the dominant culture. In a more egalitarian culture, each member is empowered to speak out against inequality and to laud positive changes.

CONCLUSION

The Air Force Academy appears to be on the path to changing their entrenched, masculinist culture. Academy leadership positions have turned over again since the 2003 changes mentioned above. For the first time in its history, two female generals were selected to run the academic side and the military training side of the Academy. Ultimately, it will be the attitudes and behavior of both male and female cadets that will tell us whether the complex attempt at reconstructing culture is on the right track. It will be future assessments that will determine whether a cultural shift has occurred, as well as research addressing the experiences of female cadets, in particular. Unfortunately, the Air Force Academy's focus on openness and release of data to the public appears to be reverting to pre-scandal levels. While 2003 and 2004 attitudinal and climate data were released quickly and disseminated efficiently, the 2005 data—collected over a year ago—have yet to be released. Without this data, it is impossible to assess the progress the Academy has made in creating cultural change. To continue its commitment to change, the Academy must be willing to continually assess its progress in an open manner. The lack of publicly available data then is an obstacle to external evaluation, and thus an impediment to fighting oppression.

If we find cultural change at the Academy is successful, this model then can be implemented at other schools. An analysis of privilege is central to understanding and eliminating inequality. It is not just a single problem that must be addressed but the entire system of male privilege that sustains it. It has been said that the military led the way in racial integration from the foxholes of WWII and Korea; it is our hope that in ten years it can be said that the Air Force Academy has led the way to create a safe and equitable environment for women as well.

NOTE

1. The authors wish to thank Abby Ferber and Michael Kimmel for their suggestions. The views expressed in this paper are those of the authors and do not necessarily represent the policy of the U.S. Air Force Academy or any other government agency.

REFERENCES

1. Connell, R. W. (1987). *Gender and power.* Stanford, CA: Stanford University Press.
2. Diamond, D., & Kimmel, M. (2002). Gender integration at the Virginia Military Institute and the United States Military Academy at West Point. In A. Datnow & L. Hubbard (Eds.), *Gender in policy and practice: Perspectives on single-sex and coeducational schooling*, pp. 172–195. New York: Routledge.
3. Johnson, A. G. (2001). *Privilege, power, and difference.* Mountain View, CA: Mayfield.
4. Kimmel, M. (2003). Masculinity as homophobia: Fear, shame, and silence in the construction of gender identity.
   In M. S. Kimmel & A. L. Ferber (Eds.), *Privilege: A reader*, pp. 51–74. Boulder, CO: Westview.
5. Lorde, A. (1984). *Sister outsider: Essays & speeches by Audre Lorde.* New York: Crossing Press.
6. *Oprah.com.* (2003, December). Gallery of comments. Retrieved December 30, 2003, from http://www.oprah.com/tows/slide/200312/20031208/tows_slide_20031208_01.jhtml;jsessionid=MMQ3SQ2ZY4KH-PLARAYHCFEQ.
7. Spradley, J., & McCurdy, D. W. (1997). Culture and ethnography. In J. Spradley & D. W. McCurdy (Eds.), *Conformity and conflict: Readings in cultural anthropology*, pp. 13–17. New York: Longman.
8. Zubeck, P. (2003, 28 December). Revived AFA working to shed scandal: Despite criticism, leaders say culture is changing. *The Gazette*, pp. A1, A10.

61

The Hidden Cost of Being African American

Assets for Equality

THOMAS M. SHAPIRO

The enormous racial wealth gap perpetuates racial inequality in the United States. Racial inequality appears intransigent because the way families use wealth transmits advantages from generation to generation. Furthermore, the twenty-first century marks the beginning of a new racial dilemma for the United States: Family wealth and inheritances cancel gains in classrooms, workplaces, and paychecks, worsening racial inequality. I see no means of seriously moving toward racial equality without positive asset policies to address the racial wealth gap.

Diagnosing causes and effects of racial inequality, while difficult and controversial enough, is easier than the seemingly overwhelming task of reversing our direction toward more inequality. Connecting the thorny dots of racial inequality means no less than confronting our historical legacy of vast material inequality, massive residential segregation, and wide gaps in educational conditions. The racial wealth gap is more than an obdurate historical legacy that lives in the present, because it also springs from contemporary public policy and institutional discrimination, not to mention individuals' behavior. I will suggest policy initiatives and principles aimed at restoring ideals of equality, the American Dream, and democracy—what I call *assets for equality.*

★   ★   ★

THE ROAD TO ASSETS

In order to address the asset deprivation of two of every five American families, I want to propose or endorse several key policy initiatives. My policy proposals do not contest the right to succeed and reap the rewards of hard work. These are start-up policies that provide families with a chance to work toward the American Dream.

Children's Savings Accounts

Children growing up in families with assets go to school secure in the knowledge that their families will support their dreams and future well-being. However, many children in America grow up without such confidence. The majority of children come from families who cannot provide a positive asset legacy. About 4 in 10 of all children grow up in asset-poor families. More distressing, over half of African American children grow up asset poor. What difference would it make if every child in America grew up knowing that (s)he had a nest egg to use to go to college, buy a home, or start a business? As a result of acquiring start-up money, they would be more confident and competent; they would feel more invested in themselves, their communities, and the future. They would have dreams and a way to risk making them come true. Benefits would accrue to individuals, families, and society as a whole.

Twelve-year-old Derek Tessler is being raised by his grandmother in the poor and black South Central section of Los Angeles. His grandmother works hard just to make ends meet and hopes the future will be better. Derek will be one of the lucky ones if he comes out of his community unscarred. Some start-up assets might keep his hopes alive and give him real choices about his life.

The Children's Savings Accounts initiative is the kind of idea that might work for Derek Tessler. There are many models for Children's Savings Accounts, such as initial government or private contribution at birth, matches of family contributions for low-income families throughout the child's formative years, and limited use of account balances at age 18 and older. Imagine, for example, that every child born in the United States had an initial deposit of $1,000 in such an account. Additional yearly deposits would be encouraged and possibly tied to achievements such as school graduations, summer employment, and community service. Acquiring financial literacy throughout the school years would be a strong program component, providing a relevant and stimulating educational context. Government funds would match contributions from low-income parents. Contributions to the account also could come from private, employer, or charitable sources. After high school, account holders could use funds for higher education or training. At age 25 or older uses of the funds might also include small-business capitalization and first-time home purchase. If accounts are still active by retirement age, people could use them to cover retirement expenses or pass them on to the next generation. With a $1,000 contribution at birth and $500 contributed annually by the family with half of that annual amount matched for poor families, a young adult by age 18 could have about $40,000 to start a productive life.

★   ★   ★

Individual Development Accounts

The vast majority of Americans have not accumulated many assets and are not about to inherit a large nest egg. This lack of assets impedes them from moving ahead, and they watch people jumping ahead who they know have not worked harder, have not tried harder, and do not deserve financial success any more than they do. Start-up assets for opportunities like education, businesses, and retirement could improve dramatically the lives of average Americans.

★   ★   ★

Individual Development Accounts (IDA) are the first and largest policy initiative in asset-development policy. . . . Individual Development Accounts reward savings by asset-poor families who aim to buy their first home, acquire postsecondary education, or start a small business. For every dollar a family saves, matching funds that typically come from a variety of private and public sources provide strong incentive. IDAs are usually managed by community-based organizations with accounts held at local financial institutions. In 1997 a multimillion-dollar IDA demonstration project, the American Dream Policy Demonstration, was launched and financed by private foundations and organizations. Since 1997 IDAs have made their way into federal policy in a wide range of federal programs. In 1998 a large federal demonstration was started through the Assets for Independence Act. Confusing many economists and others who claimed that poor people could not save because of their circumstances or values, the demonstration program provides compelling empirical evidence of poor families sacrificing to put aside money to create better lives for themselves.

★   ★   ★

Down Payment Accounts

Homeownership is a signature of the American Dream and, as I have emphasized throughout . . . , frames class status, family identity, and schooling opportunities. We also know that homeownership provides the nexus for transformative assets of family wealth. For this reason, and others, I think a hallmark policy idea is Down Payment Accounts for first-time homebuyers.

★   ★   ★

Home equity accounts for 60 percent of the total wealth of America's middle class. The gap between rising home prices and incomes that barely keep pace has widened considerably since 1995, making it more difficult for families to buy a first home; not only must they qualify for larger mortgages, but steeper purchase prices require higher down payments. As we know, substantial parental financial assistance fills this breach for many young first-time homebuyers.

The chief purpose of Down Payment Accounts is to allow families to acquire assets for down payment and closing costs. How would these accounts work? Similar to the home mortgage interest deduction, renters could deduct a portion of their rent on their tax form and have it put aside in a dedicated account to match their own savings for homeownership on a one-to-one basis. This money would be used for first-time homebuyers. . . .

Funding could also come from banks, lending institutions, and insurance companies as settlement from discriminatory lending and redlining practices. Cities could encourage new housing construction and community renovation by linking development and zoning policies with developer and construction industry participation in pooled down payment accounts. To encourage community stability, allowable uses for matching funds could include home repair and renovation for first-time homeowners. Such a program would include strong financial, homeownership, and mortgage literacy components. Inherited wealth, parental financial assistance, and savings that do not come from earnings would not qualify for matching funds. Finally, use of Down Payment Accounts would not exclude using other IDA accounts for homeownership.

WHY ASSETS?

Contrary to political rhetoric and popular belief, the American welfare policy, particularly its safety net, is the most limited among Western industrialized countries.[1] Our record of helping lift families out of poverty to better lives is shameful, as measured in absolute terms or compared to other advanced democracies. U.S. governmental policy is ineffective in reducing poverty. In the United States, current government policies reduce poverty by about 38 percent. In stark contrast, among other Western industrialized countries, government social policies reduce poverty by an average of 79 percent.[2]

A revealing contrast is that in U.S. history government policies have been very effective in giving other kinds of families start-ups to acquire property and assets. I am thinking specifically of the Homestead Act, begun in 1862, which provided up to 160 acres of land, self-reliance, and ultimately wealth to millions of American families. This remarkable government policy set in motion opportunities for upward mobility and a more secure future for oneself and one's children by giving nearly 1.5 million families title to 246 million acres of land, nearly the size of California and Texas combined. One study puts the number of homestead descendents living today at 46 million adults.[3] This means that up to a quarter of the adult population potentially traces its legacy of property ownership, upward mobility, economic stability, class status, and wealth directly to one national policy—a policy that in practice essentially excluded African Americans.

I am thinking too of the Federal Housing Administration, which changed the rules under which Americans buy homes, provided the structural stability for America's middle class, and created inheritable wealth. And the GI Bill, which allowed millions of World War II veterans to attend college and acquire human assets that became the backbone for their economic success. And Veterans Administration home loans, which made low-interest mortgages and low down payments possible and thereby made homeownership accessible to millions.

My point is not just that America has had successful asset policies helping middle-class families acquire land, homes, and wealth for well over 150 years. The poor and disadvantaged—especially African Americans—were excluded from participation in those programs that helped others acquire land, property, homes, and wealth, stuck instead with welfare policies never meant to launch mobility out of the depths of poverty.

★ ★ ★

Asset-building policies will most directly benefit the more than one in three American families (36 percent) falling beneath our conservative asset poverty line, those with less than $4,175 in financial assets. Less conservative estimates (like 125 percent of the poverty line or defining the financial safety net at six months instead of three) mean that close to one-half of American families would benefit from asset policy. An asset perspective draws the hidden fault line of inequality in a way that includes

between one-third and one-half of Americans. In contrast, the more traditional income line draws the fault line more narrowly, at one in eight. Because African American families possess fewer financial resources than whites, asset policies will have greater impact in minority communities, but they will positively include millions of white families and thus address the sedimentation of both race and class inequality.

The concept of a stakeholder society—the individual can have a stake or feel invested in all aspects of society, whether financial or not—holds much promise. . . .

Another reason for starting with asset-building policy is that it directly addresses an emerging new understanding of poverty. If welfare policy only targets those currently below the official poverty line, it focuses on about 1 in 8 Americans, but it neglects the nearly 6 in 10 Americans who will experience at least one year of poverty while they are adults. The economic fragility of those who will experience poverty would be improved vastly by building an asset safety net.

★ ★ ★

Matching Social Assistance to Asset Policy

Traditional welfare policies have failed to launch families out of poverty, just as they have failed to promote independence and self-reliance. Asset policies will not work by themselves, either. In tandem, asset and income policies promise supporting pillars for mobility. To make sure that asset-building policies do not become a shell game simply transferring costs from federal to state or from public to private—or creaming monies from social assistance—policy needs to be crafted so that asset and traditional social assistance policies synergize one another rather than cancel each other out. For example, Children's Savings Accounts should not replace a public commitment to higher education. Tuition at public institutions of higher education should not rise just because 18-year-olds have accumulated a small nest egg to make college affordable. A worst-case-scenario involves a family raiding their fledgling IDA account, losing matching payments in the process, to buy food at the end of the month because their food stamp allocation was too small. Families should not miss medical appointments, delay renewing prescriptions, stretch out the time between dental visits, or skip meals to scrape together money for monthly IDA contributions. These sacrifices to contribute to asset accounts are damaging bargains families should not be forced to consider because of public policy failures. One lesson from the national IDA demonstration project indicates that these temptations are real and should be avoided.

★ ★ ★

INHERITANCE AND WEALTH-CONCENTRATING POLICIES

★ ★ ★

Inheritance is a vexing dilemma in building a case for asset policy. There is a strongly held belief in America that when financially successful individuals die they can pass wealth to their children to secure a better future for them. It would be one thing if this money bought fancier clothes, longer and plusher vacations, bigger houses, boats, expensive meals, or even freedom from work altogether. It is something quite different, however, if this unearned wealth buys advantages in schools, communities, jobs, businesses, and social networks. Standing up for American ideals, I firmly believe, means passing an Opportunity Act that taxes the inheritance of unearned property at, say, a flat 10 percent rate, after a reasonable exemption, with revenues earmarked for asset-building policies.

Washington is running in the opposite direction, with the push to repeal the estate tax at the top of the agenda that will worsen wealth inequality. . . .

Looking at who benefits from regressive changes in the estate tax highlights the fact that it is a reverse Robin Hood tax that further redistributes wealth to the richest. By 2009, less than one-half of 1 percent of Americans will be subject to the estate tax, due to changes Congress approved in 2001.[4] There is no evidence of family farmers in Iowa having to pay the estate tax. Only 4 percent of small businesses

have a net worth of more than what the scheduled exemption will be in 2009, $3.5 million.

Instead of repealing the estate tax, I advocate reforming it to exclude family farms and small businesses and to progressively lower the exemptions while closing loopholes that allow the wealthiest families to evade this law. What is really at stake, it seems to me, is the power of very wealthy individuals to assure succeeding generations economic success and material comfort through unearned advantages, regardless of any achievements or contributions they may make. . . .

HOMEOWNERSHIP DISCRIMINATION

★ ★ ★

Mortgage discrimination against African Americans is a major reason residential segregation remains persistently high. Fair housing laws do not allow judges immediate remedies or means to punish perpetrators. The onus is on individuals and community organizations to do the expensive and time-consuming work of law enforcement because people in office have little interest in or intention of enforcing fair-lending and fair-housing laws. A large part of the solution is an enforcement agenda.

A loan-approval decision rule that is affected by an applicant's membership in a minority group is discriminatory. Discrimination also occurs when a lender's decision is affected by the location of a property in a minority neighborhood. Fair-lending enforcement must become more aggressive and effective. We do not need new laws because the present system can be improved considerably. The Fair Housing Act of 1968 and the Equal Credit Opportunity Act of 1974 prohibit discrimination in mortgage lending. Ross and Yinger in *The Color of Credit* propose steps to make fair-lending laws more effective. The responsible enforcement agencies, the Department of Justice and the Department of Housing and Urban Development, must be given adequate staffing and resources to completely review and analyze mortgage applications; weak or ineffective enforcement negates law. While the political differences between former HUD Secretary Henry Cisneros (1993–97) and Attorney General

John Ashcroft (2001–) in their passion and commitment for enforcing fair lending are important, neither Democrats nor Republicans are very keen to take on banking and construction interests for the sake of fair lending or fair housing.

Given the increasing prevalence of automated underwriting systems in scoring mortgage applications, fair-lending enforcement agencies should develop tools to test for discrimination so that factors weighted against minorities do not become codified into uniform industry standards. Especially as loan pricing according to risk becomes common practice, lenders should be discouraged from generating greater profits by designing systems that make minorities appear to be riskier borrowers and then charge higher interest to justify supposedly riskier mortgages.

Mortgage lenders and insurance redliners should be held accountable for the racially specific damages they have imposed on communities of color. Why can't we sue predatory lenders and their suppliers of capital, mortgage and insurance redliners for what they have done to cities and communities?

Without these changes, the extra capital made available to families through various asset policies and other government policies would likely fail because the two-tiered housing market would still generate more wealth for the affluent.

EDUCATIONAL EQUITY

★ ★ ★

Movement toward equality requires shrinking advantages of wealth and turning around our national drift toward plutocracy. Although we understand that awesome wealth inequality is not likely to end anytime soon, even as we work to reverse this trend, it is important to work vigorously to narrow the advantages of wealth and birth in communities and schools. Living in whatever community one wants is not in question, even using wealth to move into a higher-status community. However, public policy should work toward equity of condition in schools and communities. This means that moving to wealthier communities should not be the publicly supported ticket to higher-quality schools. Family

moves from Watts to Santa Monica, Dorchester to Harvard, or St. Louis to Sappington are not in question; the gap in school quality and resources should be in question so that these family moves do not automatically confer huge educational advantages with lifelong consequences. Clearly, this means a renewed commitment to equity-based educational reform. The way to leave no child behind in this approach is to ensure high-level equity in educational conditions, to take the school advantage out of moving to wealthier communities. Present conditions of educational inequality create reasons for families to seek richer educational environments and establish artificial markets to carry out this inequality mechanism. Public sectors like education should not legitimize, reward, and exacerbate private inequalities.

School reform is a most vexing issue because we have uncovered how educational inequality perpetuates inequality and promotes a restless nation of movers. Where a family lives largely determines school quality, and family wealth largely determines where people live. Local property taxes fund the leading portion of school finances, 45–50 percent; therefore, it is easy to understand how the wealth of a community, its resource base, governs educational resources and the opportunities that go with them. (The federal share is actually only about 5–10 percent, with the state contributing the remaining 45–50 percent.) The disadvantage of low-resource communities and the advantage of higher-resource communities can be addressed by shifting local school financing to state and federal levels.

It would be a mistake to read this as a case for vouchers. The ostensible appeal of educational vouchers is that they compensate for educational inequities by subsidizing student movement to better schools. Even if this were the real intent behind the voucher effort, the colossal mismatch between the number of students currently languishing in substandard schools and the number of open spots in high-quality schools demonstrates the folly of vouchers. In Los Angeles, one estimate is that 230,000 children occupy seats in substandard schools while there are only 100 openings in high-quality schools.[5]

From my asset perspective, . . . , the fundamental issue is condition of education and how best to foster high-quality schools. Reforms that lead to better schools also can come from within schools and outside of schools. From smaller classes to better-trained and better-paid teachers to smaller administrative units, much room exists for improving what goes on inside schools. From increased parental participation to connecting learning with working to longer and more school days, much room also exists for improving the value of education in society. Unfortunately, current choice programs like magnet schools, charter schools, and similar creative reforms, when they work, produce small islands of quality but come with a large equity price tag. Research has shown that choice programs lead to greater inequality both in who participates and in results.[6] We need to question seriously policies that result in greater inequality. However, I believe that within a context of equal conditions, all sorts of choice programs could flourish with different results. Arts-oriented schools, technology-oriented schools, math and science schools, language-immersion schools, and many other kinds could offer meaningful choices sculpted to the needs of children and parents in the context of equal educational conditions.

The goal is to achieve educational equity at a high quality level. Greatly increased educational resources more fairly distributed is the means to this goal. Since school resource levels reflect community wealth, new and significantly enhanced resources must come from federal and state governments. It is difficult to improve upon the words of educator Deborah Meier: "The primary national responsibility is to narrow the resource gap between the most and least advantaged, both between 9 A.M. and 3 P.M. and during the other five sixths of their waking lives when rich and poor students are also learning—but very different things."[7] Educational equity takes rewards out of moving for the schools, cancels advantages of

community wealth, and undermine benefits of residential segregation.

THE CHALLENGE FOR MIDDLE-CLASS AMERICA

★ ★ ★

Part of the big picture I have been describing is how communities, families, and individuals try to trap resources and hoard them for their own benefit. Because individuals believe they can personally benefit from it, and because they do not trust government to act in the civic interest, they attempt to buy their way out of social problems on a one-at-a-time basis. This encourages a privatized notion of citizenship at the expense of solutions that work for all. It creates artificial demand and artificial sources of profit, such as when people pay larger amounts for suburban homes, private schools, gated communities, car alarms, home security systems, and private police services because they feel threatened by city life. A far more cost-effective system—and a far more democratic approach—is to build an infrastructure that would help everyone. None of this can happen without an activist agenda that puts these issues on the table in a way that makes sense to people.

This agenda poses two challenges for the middle class. The first recognizes that government built the pillars of middle-class life in America by policies such as FHA and the home mortgage interest deduction that put homeownership within the reach of most families, policies from which those families personally benefit. Without family legacies of head-start assets, middle class status would not be a realizable dream for millions of Americans, especially young families. But the government-sponsored mobility ladder does not help families with few financial assets. The challenge for the middle class is to support policies that extend similar mobility opportunities to less fortunate families and do not saw off the mobility ladder behind themselves. If government policies and head-start assets are key reasons behind the success of middle-class Americans, then we need to recognize that most middle-class families, particularly white families, do not achieve that status on their own. It is time to extend those opportunities to all.

The second tough challenge for middle-class America is to participate in rebuilding a civic infrastructure for the common good. Through a steady erosion under Republican and Democratic administrations alike, our commitment to and resources targeted for building high-quality, democratic public education, supporting community development, stability, and prosperity, and enforcing civil rights, fair-housing, and fair-lending laws has deteriorated considerably. As a result, success is tougher and exacts a larger toll, quality of life declines for many, and the American Dream becomes more elusive. Largely due to deteriorating civic infrastructure, a privatized notion of citizenship—where communities, families, and individuals seek private solutions for public problems—is gaining prominence among a large portion of the middle class. Given the current choices, perhaps this is understandable, and I do not mean to assess individual responsibility or assign personal guilt. Whether it is buying out of weak schools or moving for the schools, hiring tutors and coaches, building gated communities, investing in security for cars, homes, and communities, or shunning diverse communities and schools, middle-class citizens are buying into private solutions for their own benefit that further deteriorate the civic infrastructure and make social problems worse. The answer lies in rebuilding our civic infrastructure so that what makes sense to one family does not disadvantage others. A robust, durable, opportunity-laden civic infrastructure is the best asset for equality.

It is a measure of our times and how far we have strayed from American ideals that awarding achievement and merit, not birth, sounds radical. Policies should simultaneously begin to build asset ladders out of poverty, reward achievement while narrowing inequality, and uphold rights to fair opportunity over the privilege of wealthy dead people to permanently advantage their children by giving them property. My cousin Jimmy has asked me what is wrong with improving your family. Nothing, except when improving your children's opportunities means disadvantaging others, and when inherited wealth disenfranchises the American Dream. I believe that we want to be defined as a society whose values, structures, incentives, customs, policies, and laws encourage equality of opportunity, achievement, and reward.

We can no longer ignore tremendous wealth inequities as we struggle with the thorny issue of racial inequality. Without attending to how equal opportunity or even equal achievement does not lead to equal results—especially concerning wealth—we will continue to repeat the deep and disturbing patterns of racial inequality and conflict that plague our republic. A just society would not wish racial legacies and inheritance to block opportunities and make a mockery of merit, and just individuals will rejoice to give merit and democracy a fairer chance to triumph.

NOTES

1. Rank (2004) reviews the most recent data describing the minimalist American welfare state and showing the ineffectiveness of social policy in lifting families out of poverty.
2. This is measured by looking at pretransfer poverty rates versus posttransfer poverty rates. Countries include Canada, Finland, France, Germany, the Netherlands, Norway, Sweden, and the United Kingdom. See Rank (2004) discussion of results from the Luxembourg Income Study.
3. Williams (2000).
4. See http://www.ombwatch.org site for data.
5. Huffington (2002). There may be some severe methodological problems with this estimate, but the point about the inability of any voucher plan to match needs to solutions illustrates the very limited scope of such plans. These estimates come from looking at the number of students in low-performing schools and the number of open spots in high-performing schools.
6. This research includes Lee and Burkam (2002); Lee, Croninger, and Smith (1994); Wells and Crain (1997); and Lee (1993).
7. Meier (2000).

REFERENCES

1. Huffington, Arianna. 2002. "When 'Back to School' Means 'Tough Luck Kid,'" http://www.ariannaonline.com/columns/files/090202.html. September 2.
2. Lee, Valerie. 1993. "Educational Choice: The Stratifying Effects of Selecting Schools and Courses." *Educational Policy* 7, no. 2: 125–48.
3. Lee, Valerie, and David Burkam. *Inequality at the Starting Gate.* Washington, DC: Economic Policy Institute, 2002.
4. Lee, Valerie, R. Croninger, and J. Smith. 1994. "Parental Choice of Schools and Social Stratification in Education:

The Paradox of Detroit." *Educational Evaluation and Policy Analysis* 16, no. 4: 434–57.

5. Meier, Deborah. 2000. *Will Standards Save Public Education?* Boston: Beacon Press.

6. Rank, Mark. 2004. *One Nation, Underprivileged: How American Poverty Affects Us All.* New York: Oxford U P.

7. Wells, Amy Stuart, and Robert L. Crain. 1997. "Perpetuation Theory and the Long-Term Effects of School Desegregation." *Review of Educational Research* 64, no. 4: 531–55.

8. Williams, Trina. 2000. "The Homestead Act: A Major Asset-Building Policy in American History." Paper commissioned for "Inclusion in Asset Building: Research and Policy Symposium," Center for Social Development, Washington University, St. Louis, September 21–23.

62

Why Do We Need Cross-Class Alliances?

BETSY LEONDAR-WRIGHT

The labor movement, the civil rights movement, antiwar movements, the women's movement—over and over again Americans have risen up and organized to transform their society. Each major movement has won significant reforms, satisfying the pragmatists aiming for limited concessions by power-holders. But each one has disappointed the visionaries who dreamed of deeper structural change.

Why have movements failed at their larger goals? Among other things, because all have had bases too small to shift the fundamental balance of power. Everyone who dreams of a fairer society would do well to aim to broaden our movements to include a larger percentage of the American people. But the American people have historically been too divided by race and class for a mass movement to cross many demographic lines.

Racism has been used repeatedly to divide and conquer potential allies for change. Many books document this use of racism, and many anti-racist organizations challenge it. There are also many analyses of past movements that see their limitations

as a result of tactical mistakes, geopolitical contexts, economic forces, and other causes. All these explanations contain a piece of the truth. The crucial role of class in splitting and weakening movements, however, has too often been overlooked.

The antiwar movement of the 1960s hastened the end of the war, probably preventing nuclear weapons from being used in Vietnam, and deterred later US administrations from open military invasions for more than two decades. But Students for a Democratic Society's vision of participatory democracy, in which people have a say over the decisions that affect their lives, didn't come true—nor, for that matter, did the hippies' vision of the Age of Aquarius materialize. One reason was that vast reservoirs of potential support were never tapped. Opposition to the war was in fact higher among lower-income than among higher-income Americans. Yet the movement was dominated by students and other members of the middle class, whose attitudes towards working-class people varied between romantic idealism and prejudices against "hard-hats." Counter-culture markers like long hair and flamboyantly ratty clothes were often used to define the borders of the movement, which left out many potential supporters from other subcultures. The GI movement of antiwar soldiers and the student movement formed some alliances but could have combined forces more powerfully.

The Civil Rights movement won an end to legal segregation through a mixed-class mobilization of African Americans and their allies. It was both the most class diverse movement of the twentieth century and the most successful movement. But the consolidation of its victories mostly lifted up college-educated black male leaders to national prominence, and as a result neither the "beloved community" envisioned by the movement nor the elimination of black poverty came to pass.

Earlier in the 20th century, the women's suffrage movement waged its struggle without much participation from working-class women, and the labor movement had only limited support from middle-class and owning-class allies. While the suffragettes won votes for women, the peaceful, nurturing society some of them thought would be voted in didn't materialize. While the labor movement won the 40-hour week and basic labor rights, the workers' paradise of their dreams did not come to pass. If the two movements had joined forces more, they would likely have won more reforms than they did separately.

In the 1920s, feminist groups such as the National Women's Party advocated an Equal Rights Amendment to the Constitution, without dealing with the possible loss of protective legislation for women, such as required breaks, bathrooms, weight-lifting limits, and a ten-hour day. According to Diane Balser in *Sisterhood and Solidarity,* the National Women's Trade Union League and some women's unions opposed the ERA as a way of preserving protective legislation, without dealing with women's lack of legal rights. The result was that women got neither an ERA nor protective legislation. If they had combined forces and advocated for an ERA and an extension of protective legislation to all workers, how many women's lives might have been improved?

More recent movements initiated by middle-class activists have won reforms but failed to capture the imagination of the working-class majority and thus were limited in what they could accomplish. In the 1970s, the antinuclear-power movement successfully stopped utilities from expanding the number of nuclear power plants, but the narrow base of mostly white middle-class and owning-class support was one factor in why the dream of renewable energy went unrealized.

In the 1980s, the Central America movement won a Congressional ban on aid to the Nicaraguan contra guerrillas (prompting the infamous illegal arms sales to an official "enemy" country, Iran, to fund covert aid) and helped make possible a return to limited democracy in Central American countries. But military intervention, usually on behalf of corrupt dictatorships, continued to be a common federal policy, in part because the movement did not reach out much beyond college-educated circles and thus had limited political clout. In the polarized Cold War climate, the AFL-CIO actually sided with the right-wing dictators funded by the US.

Movements initiated by working-class and low-income activists have also been limited in their accomplishments by the small amount of support they have gotten from middle-class and owning-class people. Welfare rights organizations suffered a devastating setback in the 1990s when "welfare reform" eliminated the entitlement to a safety net, and only a tiny number of middle-class allies spoke up. If middle-class feminists had responded to proposed cutbacks in welfare rights—which are the floor on which women's workplace and family status is built—in the same way they would have reacted to an equally severe cutback in reproductive rights, welfare reform would likely not have been implemented in such an extreme form.

Organized labor, which for decades had generally been closed to community coalitions, now invites more collaboration, especially the newer service worker unions such as SEIU and HERE. But old ways of doing things still create barriers. Though the student sweatshop movement, the campus living-wage movement, Jobs with Justice, and the National Interfaith Committee on Worker Justice have formed exciting alliances, only limited numbers of middle-class people have responded to their requests for support of low-wage working people. The living-wage movement, led by unions and supported by mixed-class coalitions, has had incredible success in raising wages for employees of municipal contractors in 110 places, but has not won overall increases in the minimum wage, except in New Orleans. Polls show overwhelming support for higher wages for poverty-wage jobs, but that support has not translated into sufficient voter power to force state or federal minimum wage increases.

The "Teamsters and Turtles" (unions and environmentalists) who marched together in Seattle in 1999 actually managed to nonviolently shut down the World Trade Organization meetings, and there is evidence that the WTO subsequently backed off on some decisions harmful to labor rights and the environment. But within three months after this victory, the local labor-student-NGO coalitions that had sent people to Seattle dissolved almost everywhere.

The truth that we progressives of all classes have avoided facing for the last century is that we need each other. To fundamentally transform our society to be a fairer and more sustainable one, the movement we build will have to include people of every race, every age, every geographic area—and every class.

Middle-class activists in the US have a proud history of initiating, organizing, and supporting movements for progressive social change. We also have a not-so-proud history of overlooking potential allies from other classes, failing to come through for movements led by poor and working-class people and stepping on the toes of coalition partners through classist assumptions. The purpose . . . is to help middle-class activists learn to bridge class difference and put fewer obstacles in the way of effective cross-class alliances.

63

Ideology of the Multiracial Movement

Dismantling the Color Line and Disguising White Supremacy?

EILEEN T. WALSH

The multiracial movement stands at the crossroads: will its identity politics take the path that encourages individuation to the exclusion of collective political action? Will it seek refuge in the promotion of hybrid identities that distance mixed-race persons from forging political alliances with blacks and other disenfranchised groups? Alternatively, will it coalesce around a group identity that challenges whiteness as the quintessential trope of privilege?

Despite the significant gains of the civil rights movement, racial disparities exist today in every major arena: criminal justice, education, health care, housing, and wealth accumulation.[1] The dismantling of these racial hierarchies cannot be accomplished by intellectually agreeing that social constructions of race are fiction; nor can that dismantling be accomplished by the promotion of individual rights. It is worth noting, however, that all of the rationales put forth by the following agents of change have been rooted in the rhetoric of individual rights. Jurisprudence depended on arguments regarding an individual's right to choose a partner in decriminalization of marriages across the color line.[2] Proponents of transracial adoption depended on arguments about the child's right for a loving home.[3] Multiracial people have argued for a bill of rights and recognition of microdiversity and diverse heritage.[4] These hard-won battles that focused on individual rights, however significant, cannot achieve the systemic elimination of racial hierarchies. An elimination of those inequalities requires a focus both on group rights as well as on the complex connections between racial hierarchies, gender, and social class structures. The Multiracial Movement's goal to redefine racial identity is quite likely to change not only the nature of racial classifications but also the identities and group allegiances of those who identify as multiracial. Unless the Multiracial Movement shifts its attention away from asserting the rights of individuals, however, its enduring legacy will be to sustain existing hierarchies, albeit along a color continuum instead of through a fictional racial dichotomy. If the Multiracial Movement is to succeed in eliminating race and the racial hierarchy, it must adopt and promote an antiracist, social justice agenda. Disappearing race from the vocabularies and consciousness of academics, policy makers, and the citizenry prior to dismantling the structures of inequality that persist not only puts the cart before the horse, it also serves to render white privilege invisible—a most dangerous proposition with a long legacy. Ignoring the ways in which race has been constructed as an essence, as well as marker for white group privilege, allows the mischief of race to remain hidden insidiously in our institutions while individuals, distracted from ferreting out injustice, delight in the belief that color no longer matters.

CONSTRUCTING A CATEGORY FOR HYBRID IDENTITIES CAMOUFLAGES MULTIRACIAL HERITAGE

The last decade has seen the coming of age of the first generation of children born after the U.S. Supreme Court decriminalized marriages across the color line.[5] Although such crossings have been present since colonial times, the one-drop rule of hypodescent has masked their prevalence. On both sides of the Atlantic Ocean, the one-drop rule of the United States is being questioned. Not only have children and parents of racially mixed families asserted their voices, but they also have created social pressure to rethink multiracial heritage.[6] Volumes documenting the alleged increasing number of racially mixed youngsters challenge notions about marriage and family formation across the color line.[7] Danzy Senna has declared the onset of the "Mulatto Millennium" in which "Pure breeds (at least the black ones) are out and hybridity is in. America loves us."[8]

Struggling against monoracial categories, the Multiracial Movement has staked out important territory and demanded recognition of multiracial heritages and diverse racial/ethnic identities.[9] The Multiracial Movement sought to reject the rigid racial categories that have been constructed over time to simultaneously create the fiction of both race and its corollary, racial purity, which form the basis of white supremacy. It demanded acknowledgment of hybrid identity and questioned the commonsense understandings of race in the twentieth century. Although the movement successfully has brought attention to the fiction that created existing racial categories, there is an ominous potential for the Multiracial Movement to become a pawn of the policy agendas on both sides of the political spectrum that threaten people of color.[10] The neoconservative contingent waves the "colorblind" banner over its thinly disguised policies to prop up and promote the existing racial hierarchies in which whites retain a disproportionate share of

property, power, privilege, and prestige.[11] Likewise, the neoliberal contingent eschews a frontal attack on racial injustices with the hope that economic reform will benefit all disenfranchised groups without the derisive rhetoric of race—in other words, fearful of backlash from white voters, the New Left conflates social class inequality with racial inequality.[12]

AT THE ROOTS OF RACIAL CATEGORIES: GENDER AND SOCIAL CLASS

Thinking of race as one of the distinctive threads woven into the fabric of American social structure and consciousness distorts the historical evidence about the ways that race was constructed and reconstructed as a fiber inextricably intertwined with the threads of power relations known as gender and social class. Clinging to the popular idea that race is a distinctive thread oversimplifies strategies for unraveling remaining racial hierarchies.

At various points in the United States, different criteria have been used to construct the boundaries around the racial categories of white, nonwhite, black, and other.[13] Although racial categories have changed with shifting political and economic conditions, the "history of racial categories is often a history of sexuality as well, for it is partly as a result of the taboos against boundary crossing that such categories are invented."[14] In the United States, racial classifications used to construct and maintain the racial hierarchy have been unique and contradictory. For instance, to classify the offspring of blacks and whites, the colonies broke with British tradition of patrilineal descent and created a series of inheritance laws concerning the transmission of slavery status. Laws of "partus sequitur ventrem," stated that offspring, or issue, followed the mother; this "law of the womb" determined that the child's status as free, indentured, or slave resulted from the mother's status.[15] As a consequence, a child from a union of a free white women and a black man (free or not) was granted status as a free white; conversely, the offspring of a black woman slave and a free white male was destined to the status of a black slave. The obvious inconsistency of this classification system threatened to undermine the presumed biological basis of inferiority that formed the ideological lynchpin for the enslavement of African descendants. Further complications of this classification system became apparent with the growth in numbers of offspring whose status as free or slave could not be "read" from looking at their bodies.

Extensive, recent scholarship documents the regional responses that resulted in a hodgepodge of rules for constructing racial categories and for the evolving prohibitions against crossing the color line. One consistent purpose of the laws on adultery, bastardry, and marriages across the color line, however, is the attempt to regulate white women.[16] Despite the significant regional variation and inconsistent zigzags over time in racial definitions, the intent and consequence of the diverse rules evolving between the colonial period and the Civil War consistently accomplished three outcomes. First, the rules privileged whiteness by preserving the individual rights of the children born to white women while simultaneously oppressing black women by committing all of their children to slavery—a group status. Second, the rules asserted the power of white men over all women and over black men.[17] Third, the rules privileged social class: the toleration of sexual liaisons between white women and black men in the antebellum period reflected dominant beliefs that black women seduced white men and that only *poor* white women associated with black men; this powerful ideology that conflated whiteness with feminine purity gave planter-class women a great stake in patriarchy, while at the same time it provided some of those women who had children as the result of illicit liaisons the resources and opportunity to conceal their children's paternity.[18]

During the nineteenth century many states developed racial categories based on a combination of two variables: social class standing and known ancestry that assigned persons to racial categories according to complicated assessments of the presence of a grandparent or great-grandparent of African descent.[19] Most scholars agree that with the end of slavery as a system, fluidity and inconsistency of racial categories solidified into a rigid caste system based on the fictional binary of black and white.

In sum, as the rigid binary color line evolved in this country, it reflected regional differences and frequent renegotiation of racial categories based on the interaction between gender and social class. In addition, the "law of the womb" where the status of child followed that of the mother proved problematic and gave way gradually to a set of rules based on hypodescent—ancestry with any known Negro blood precluded categorization on the "white" side of the color line.

The racial identities and consciousness prevalent in this country rely in large part on the projection of the rather recent binary racial thinking into our distant history. As a result of the shifting meanings of racial categories, it is difficult to animate and capture a sense of our long, elusive past of multiracialism in the United States. Losing sight of that historical vision, however, may create a mirage of multiracialism—an illusion of integration and equality that provides an undeserved hubris about how far we have come and blinds us to the difference between a masked multiracial heritage and an acknowledged multiracial heritage. The evidence tells us that there is a long history of individual rights that afforded some children of diverse heritages an escape from the harsh realities of membership in a group subject to discrimination and status as noncitizens or second-class citizens while other children of diverse racial heritage were consigned to group standing as blacks. The evidence suggests that the use of individual rights as a continued escape valve does not guarantee the elimination of racial hierarchies.

The construction and evolution of the color line in the United States required social processes that depended as much upon the interlinking systems of patriarchy and social class stratification that are embedded in our institutions as upon white supremacy. Gender, race, and social class have mutually constructed and supported the racial hierarchies apparent in our country today. Understanding the historical and political evolution of the color line highlights how the socially constructed categories of gender and social class were and remain as important in the creation and recreation of racial disparities as is the ideology of white supremacy that enforces and patrols the boundary between so-called whites and historically racialized peoples.

ENCOURAGING INDIVIDUATION TO THE EXCLUSION OF COLLECTIVE ACTION

Many arguments of the Multiracial Movement rest on the idea that the right to an individual identity is not possible within the racial classification system that existed in the second half of the twentieth century. The idea that the individual has a right to select a unique identity and that such a selection results from experience that is entirely individualistic parallels many of the arguments of the postmodern writers. Postmodern writers and some feminist theorists use the concept of the intersection of race, class, gender, and sexuality as a particularistic and unique location in the social structure. However, the "intersection of race, class, and gender" is a concept that is not used uniformly by all sociologists to refer to the interplay of structures affecting different groups. Used by Patricia Hill Collins and other black feminist writers, the term represents a concept that is a departure from the tradition in American sociology: it considers that race, gender, and social class (and, to a degree, age) are mutually constructing systems that shape group experience, knowledge, and praxis.

Until the last decade, within the discipline of sociology, race, class, and gender were discussed and conceptualized as variables distinct and separate from the confluence of their interactions in determining social position; much of the literature sought to weigh the relative "effects" of what were viewed as distinct, independent variables. In the positivist tradition, however, there was no recognition that race, class, and gender are experientially inseparable. Agents of knowledge cannot disaggregate their feeling experiences into distinct influences from race, gender, and social class.

Some feminist and postmodern theorists used the concept of intersections to promote an individualist approach to understanding identity and social position. Despite the practice by some authors of using the concept to locate a particular vantage point of an individual, the concept has broader theoretical use that explains both the nexus between social structure and groups and the complex interaction of structure and everyday experiences mediated through groups. The concept of intersection, as a heuristic device and a theoretical tool, can lead to understanding how members of groups come to know what they know. The concept also provides strategic insights that can empower groups to deploy situated knowledge in challenging the oppression of existing power hierarchies.

Many postmodernist writings decenter and deconstruct experience as entirely individualistic. As a result, postmodern writings emphasize difference rather than the potentials for collective action. For example, by focusing on the discourse of decentering and deconstruction, it is more likely that the situated knowledge of a homosexual black man will appear starkly in contrast to the situated knowledge of either an aging, white homosexual of the privileged class or a poor, black single mother. Difference and uniqueness are emphasized by a focus on the individual's unique positions on the axes of gender, race, and social class, which, in turn, situate the individual's knowledge, or standpoint. Such constructions of how identity affects consciousness are unlikely to promote a sense of shared oppression or a call to collective action. In fact, extreme individual analyses often critique the concept of "shared" group consciousness as a remnant of essentialist thinking—one that puts too much emphasis on the commonality of a group, as if the "essence" of being a woman or being black is somehow shared by all those with a similar status. On the other hand, black feminist writers, such as Patricia Hill Collins, warn exploited or oppressed persons to recognize their group affiliations, since, "for oppressed groups, diluting difference to the point of meaninglessness comes with real political danger."[20] Collins has noted further that "[b]ecause groups respond to the actual social conditions they confront, it stands to reason that groups constructed by different social realities will develop equally different analyses and political strategies."[21] Both truth and knowledge are largely dependent on social location of the group. Knowledge consists of the experiential information we store as well as the way we make "sense" of experience through interpersonal construction of meaning.

The postmodern conceptual tools of decentering and deconstruction can be useful to analyze power and knowledge. Yet, in terms of political action, a postmodern analysis is more likely to result in a sense of hopelessness and despair than in a realization of the possibilities for forming alliances. Rainier Spencer discusses how the "multiracial" is not based on what its members have in common backgrounds, but rather is rooted in what they are not—monoracial.[22] This raises an important issue in terms of how those who select a "multiracial" identity feel connected to various groups. Use of an individual lens on the intersections of race, gender, and social class removes the leverage that could serve to dislodge the hierarchical power structure from a potentially insightful analysis or call to action.

How then should the Multiracial Movement conceptualize the link between individual identity and strategic action with group location? Societies are constituted, reproduced, and changed by individuals behaving in structures. Emotion, intention, rationalities, and meaning are the result of how people interpret the world around them. In describing the connection between an individual's way of knowing and the dependence on a group for processing meaning and interpretations, Darnell Hunt states:

> [H]umans do not exist in a social vacuum; they are linked by various network ties to important others whose affection, approval and or respect they need and seek. Through social network discussions, individual audience members (re) negotiate their initial decodings of texts in ways they consider socially acceptable. Often this acceptability depends upon the social location of network members, upon the imprints that race, class, gender and sexuality have made on their life chances and subjectivities.[23]

Like all of us, those who identify as multiracial belong to multiple groups. If a multiracial identity

results, however, in the formation of social networks that exclude discussions with blacks and other so-called minorities in favor of networks that emphasize differences between those minorities and those of so-called diverse racial heritages, it is likely that the gaps in understandings of social situations will increase. Without ties to important others for whom race has affected life chances and shaped day-to-day experiences, multiracial identities may come at a cost of further dividing the interpretations, commitments to justice, and ability to make sense of social texts.

It is significant that this notion of knowing acknowledges the importance of affection, a moderate feeling or emotion, in making social "sense" of experiences. Taking what an individual knows and putting it into action for gaining or using power depends on emotion, an important impetus to action. The following section describes how my location on the various axes of gender, race, and social class led me from a very individualistic way of knowing to an emotional, group-based consciousness that has resulted in a commitment to social justice for all oppressed groups.

CHALLENGING WHITENESS AS PRIVILEGE THROUGH GROUP IDENTITY

As a woman, my whiteness as well as the social class trajectory I have traveled poised me to accept certain versions of how the world works and to interpret life events by accepting narratives, stories, and accounts that resonated with what I "knew" to be so. Other accounts, I discarded as flawed. Largely through a refraction of those culturally mediated accounts with my own "gut feeling," based in values and beliefs, some accounts "fit" and others did not. Openings to listen to other accounts only occurred when I was confronted with a bizarre experience or a serious injustice that did not fit either my knowledge or the accounts in circulation around me.

As one of the few students from a working-class family at an expensive, private, undergraduate university and later as one of the only women in a predominantly male workplace, I occupied outsider-within positions. From my vantage point, I was aware of the disconnections between my actual, lived experience and the cultural stories and explanations circulating around me. Throughout that time, I functioned as an individual with an awareness of my unique social location, but I did not feel any group consciousness.

Only when I came to raise a black daughter in a world befuddled by, or alternatively hostile to us, did I begin to form a sense of connectedness to an imagined community of persons categorized as black.[24] Through my intense love and caring for her, her father, and his family, and my nascent realization of the significance of race for them in this society, I began to feel like an outsider within the white world I had previously inhabited. Although it was no longer an option to remain ignorant and in denial of the true meaning and extent of white skin privilege, I might have engaged actively in attempts to extend my privilege to the two people I loved. On the other hand, I could choose a commitment to fight an all-out battle to change the oppression experienced by all people of color. The writings of black feminists resonated strongly with me: they talk of "the power of intense connectedness and of the way that caring deeply for someone can foster a revolutionary politics."[25] My love for my family motivated a sense of connection to a broader collectivity, but it was not sufficient to sustain the more difficult choices. It was anger and rage at the endless experiences of injustices I witnessed that created a reservoir of strength to take on necessary political battles. When I read Audre Lorde and bell hooks, I began to understand how my emotionally debilitating experiences with social injustice could be put to productive use:

> Every woman has a well-stocked arsenal of anger potentially useful against those oppressions, personal and institutional, which brought that anger into being. Focused with precision it can become a powerful source of energy serving progress and change. . . . But anger expressed and translated into action in the service of our vision and our future is a liberating and strengthening act of clarification, for it is in the painful process of this translation that we identify who are our allies with whom we have grave

differences and who are our genuine enemies. . . . Anger is an appropriate reaction to racist attitudes, as is fury when the actions arising from those attitudes do not change.[26]

I will never be part of the group that identifies as black. Race doesn't work that way. Nor do I feel a sense of connectedness anymore to any perceived or imagined group of whites. I have discovered too much hostility and too dense a denial there. Certainly, I have retained my white family and some of my white friends. In other cases, I have withdrawn from many who have exposed deeply held commitments to a sense of unearned superiority.

Like other white women who cross the color line, I often sense myself in disguise among other white-skinned persons to whom I have not "outed" myself.[27] Too often, in an all-white group a remark is made that reminds me that I am a complete outsider. School authorities, in particular, and others who view my family as "racially diverse," discount my interpretations of racial experiences for not being as "objective" as their white view. Although they have not been on the receiving end of racial discrimination, they are quick to position themselves as more qualified than I am to assess the motives and determine the intent of blatantly racist remarks made about people of color. Repeatedly my lived experience with racial issues has been dismissed as "a personal issue." In the world of whiteness that I once inhabited as a native, a most mystifying transformation has taken place: when my relationship to family members of color is known, my testimony as a witness to what I see and hear is discounted or dismissed.[28]

My daughter, a young woman now, self-identifies as black. I feel that I have far more at stake in the collective future of black women than I ever will with any other group. My grandchildren will be viewed as multiracial or black (depending in large part on where they live) and their future depends on our collective efforts to make this a better place. Ironically, however, it was not until I connected with a group of black women writers with whom I felt a strong affinity—connected and experienced their consciousness and commitments to social justice—that I began to understand the implications of patriarchy as another system closely linked to white supremacy. From the standpoint of black feminists, I finally got a window that allowed me to see and "get" feminism. This awareness opened my consciousness to the importance of recognizing and combating social injustice on all fronts through strategic alliances with other groups. In those ways, intersections of race, gender, and social class as a group experience, not an individual experience, bridged gaps in my knowledge and motivated political action.

Each and every person of a so-called multiracial heritage as well as their family members have choices about selecting an identity, accepting an externally derived identity, or resisting any identities imposed by others. In so doing, how one comes to feel part of the collectivity either has the potential to shift existing power relations or the potential to support existing hierarchies of domination. The path of increased sense of individual rights absent a stake in the well-being of groups who have not shared equally in the resources of our society, is a road that does not challenge white supremacy. Equally available is the path toward destabilizing the current systems of inequality by changing our group allegiances.

By its very nature the concept of intersections creates a potential instability in the power relationships: due to the multiple planes coalescing into group locations in the social structure, and the diversity of allegiances that result from those intersections, people can form alliances to support and maintain the existing power structure or to resist it and promote their own interests.

THE DANGEROUS (MIS)APPROPRIATION OF MULTIRACIAL IDEOLOGY

Every day, in every corner of America, we are redrawing the color lines and redefining what race really means. It's not just a matter of black and white anymore; the nuances of brown and yellow and red mean more—and less—than ever: the promise and perils ahead.

The captioned *Newsweek* cover story makes headlines of the "Redefining of Race in America."

The article, called "The New Face of Race," features more pictures than text.[29] Its "Gallery of Native-Born Americans" features pictures of beautiful, brown faces with straight white teeth in appealing, friendly poses. Under each picture is a list of the ethnicities of the person. One little girl is identified as "Nigerian, Irish, African-American, Native American, Russian Jewish, and Polish Jewish."[29] This litany of ethnicities defies the long-standing racial binary of black/white, renders racial categorization impossible, implies the disappearance of race as an important or salient feature of our society, and ushers in the emergence of ethnicity paradigms that gloss over the difference between the experience of racialized groups and ethnic white experience.

Such public celebrations of diversity seem aimed at calming anxiety over the shifting demographics that find whites no longer a majority in states such as California, Texas, and New York. The editors send us the message that the hybrid combines many races—happily, with no sign of conflict. The net result, of course, is an image that approximates the voluntary, symbolic ethnicity familiar to whites.

What role does ethnic identity play in the lives of white Americans? Mary Waters has concluded that it provides a sense of imagined community—because it is symbolic and somewhat arbitrary—at the same time that it provides a sense of uniqueness, for it distinguishes the individual who selects it as distinct.[30] In an attempt to understand the 1980 census data on ancestry, Waters conducted interviews in upper-middle-class, white suburbs of San Jose and Philadelphia. She interviewed Roman Catholics to determine what ancestry they would cite in response to the ethnicity census question and what it meant to them. She found a fluidity and lack of consistency within families about their ethnic identity.

> For the ways in which ethnicity is flexible and symbolic and voluntary for white middle-class Americans are the very ways in which it is not so for non-white and Hispanic Americans. The social and political consequences of being Asian or Hispanic or Black are not symbolic for the most part, or voluntary. They are real and often hurtful.[31]

Moreover, Waters found that family histories of Americans of European descent often emphasize discrimination in the past that their forbearers had overcome. In fact, most of the respondents could tell family stories about how difficult the early years were in the United States due to discrimination. "All of my respondents were sure that their ancestors had faced discrimination when they first came to the United States."[32] Likewise, Stein and Hill have argued that Americans of later generations have a "dime store ethnicity."[33] That is, the choice of a grandparent to identify with narrows down for the "identity shopper" the range of groups with whom to symbolically identify; the process is similar to the way one might shop for a product in a dime store. This ethnic "identity" is not authentic, because it is chosen, brought out to display in public by the "shopper's" volition and is not externally imposed.

The best part of the story presented by the *Newsweek* article and other media sources about both increased diversity and increased racial "mixing" is not only that race no longer matters and has no meaning, but that America has arrived at this multiracial, hybrid reality with no apparent strife. Certainly none of the white readers of *Time* or *Newsweek* has had to question white privilege; there will [be] even less possibility of a demand for "group rights," a fundamental premise of identity politics. The Multiracial Movement's focus on recognition of racially "mixed" persons in census revisions and the popular discourse play into an image that the racial hierarchy of this country has transformed into a multiracial democracy. Often, there is an implicit assumption that racism is on the wane due to this alleged increased mating across the color line. It would be well to point out that the evolution of a multiracial classification system in Brazil actually undermined civil rights by eliminating group identification with the oppressed. The mulatto class in Brazil did not feel allegiance to or identification with the *negritude* liberation movement blacks, the *preto* class. The black struggles did not have as many supporters as civil rights struggles as did those in the United States where all those of color,

defined by the rigid binary racial system, recognized their own stake.[34]

CONCLUSIONS: COMMITMENTS TO SOCIAL JUSTICE

We don't choose our color, but we can choose our commitments. We do not choose our parents, but we do choose our politics. Yes, we do not make these decisions in a vacuum; they occur within a social structure that gives value to whiteness and offers rewards for racism.[35]

To what degree are interracial couples and multiracial families sites where individuals discover the tools to dismantle the oppression of racial legacies? To what degree, if any, are interracial couples and multiracial families committed to social justice? Unless these families are sites for the systematic resistance to the structured ways that race matters in our society, we cannot assume that multiracialism is a force that works to challenge the encoded white supremacy that pervades our institutions. An aim of the Multiracial Movement must include a clear focus on the ways that whiteness, although an imaginary myth, accrues power and privilege through use of certain racial discourses. In his examination of the ways popular racial discourse is circulated by the media, John Fiske observes:

> Whiteness survives only because of its ability to define, monitor and police the boundary between itself and others and to control any movement across it. Because its space is strategic and not essential, there is movement into and out of whiteness. While arguing that whiteness is better identified by what it does than by what it is, and by defining it as a flexible positionality from which power operates, we must not forget that people with white skins have massively disproportionate access to that power base. While not essentializing whiteness into white skins or Blackness into black ones, we must recognize that whiteness uses skin color as an identity card by which to see where its interests may best be promoted and its rewards distributed.[36]

When the rhetoric about the changing face of race is put in the service of maintaining existing hierarchies by conflating the historically different experience of ethnic whites with that of nonwhites, the Multiracial Movement's accomplishments can set the stage for a replay of some of the tired old tropes used to deny that race matters.

The very processes that perpetuate racial inequalities in our society depend upon putting backstage and out of sight the ongoing legacy of white supremacy that pervades the media representations, the public school curricula, legislation, and jurisdiction that continue to disadvantage oppressed groups. And, addressing racial domination as if it has been uncoupled from the socially constructed categories of gender and social class leaves intact the forces of oppression that support the current racial hegemony.

Although the movement's contributions are laudable, an unintended consequence of the multiracial project to bend the color line in this country may be the further disenfranchisement of those people of color who do not fit the newly evolving "multiracial" racial category. The Multiracial Movement's successes can be seized and appropriated to support the backlash against civil rights. Its rhetoric about the changing face of race provides a front about the disappearance of racial prejudice and discrimination. Behind the optimistic facade of interracial harmony, the hegemonic process of white supremacy is rendered invisible. The Multiracial Movement unwittingly provides "plausible" deniability to those in power who use the image of increased diversity and the "changing face of race" to promote policies that advance the interest of the "haves" while insisting that any call for group rights for the "have nots" is a throwback to the "separate but equal" era of American life. The literature about multiracial families often confuses the possible transcendence of prejudice that allows intimacy to develop between two people and within a family, with both a loosening of the societal taboo associated with crossing the color line and with optimism about eradication of racial hierarchies. In the tradition of liberalism, it puts all of the emphasis on the individuals with no attention to the structural ways in which society continues to be organized by race. In so doing, it puts little, if any, attention on the complex workings of white supremacy, gender, and social class. A new racial order of equality is not possible without understanding those links and committing to break down the interlocking infrastructures of oppression.

NOTES

1. See Douglas Massey and Nancy Denton, *American Apartheid: Segregation and the Making of the Underclass* (Cambridge: Harvard University Press, 1994). For a thorough discussion on the state's involvement in policies that have created persisting racial gaps in wealth and income, see Melvin Oliver and Thomas Shapiro, *Black Wealth/White Wealth* (New York: Routledge, 1997).
2. See Peggy Pascoe, "Miscegenation Law, Court Cases, and Ideologies of 'Race' in Twentieth Century America," in *Interracialism: Black-White Intermarriage in American History, Literature, and Law*, ed. Werner Sollors (London: Oxford University Press, 2001). Her analysis of discourse in court decisions demonstrates that justification for antimiscegenation has a long tradition of ignoring issues about the equality of racial groups in favor of promoting the individual's right to choose a partner from another group. Her analysis includes a critique of wording in the U.S. Supreme Court's landmark decision, *Loving v. Commonwealth of Virginia*, 388 U.S. at 12.
3. Maria P. Root, *Racially Mixed People in America* (Newbury Park, CA: Sage, 1992).
4. Maria P. Root, *The Multiracial Experience: Racial Borders as the New Frontier* (Thousand Oaks, CA: Sage, 1996). Also see Naomi Zack, *Race and Mixed Race* (Philadelphia: Temple University Press, 1996) and Naomi Zack, ed., *American Mixed Race: The Culture of Microdiversity* (Lanham, MD: Rowman and Littlefield, 1995).
5. *Loving v. Commonwealth of Virginia*, 388 U.S. at 12.
6. For instance, the revision of the 2000 census to allow individuals to check more than one ethnic box is a significant change resulting from the project of the multiracial movement. This historical project is outlined by Rainier Spencer, *Spurious Issues Race and Multiracial Identity Politics in the United States* (Boulder: Westview, 1999). Also see Marion Kilson, *Biracial Young Adults of the Post-Civil Rights Era* (Westport, Connecticut: Bergin and Garvey, 2000).
7. Maria P. Root, *The Multiracial Experience*.
8. Danzy Senna, "The Mulatto Millennium," in *Half and Half: Writers on Growing Up Biracial and Bicultural*, ed. Claudine Chiawei O'Hearn (New York: Pantheon, 1998). Also refer to Barbara Tizard and Anne Phoenix, *Black, White or Mixed Race? Race and Racism in the Lives of Young People of Mixed Parentage* (London: Routledge, 1993). A compilation of essays on so-called mixed bloods can be found in William Penn, ed., *As We Are Now: Mixblood Essays on Race and Identity* (Berkeley: University of California Press, 1997).
9. As Rainier Spencer points out in *Spurious Issues*, the Multiracial Movement has demanded recognition of

those recently born to parents categorized as different races while simultaneously ignoring that for the past three centuries persons of mixed African and European heritage in the United States have been forced into a monoracial category of "black." Denying the multiracial heritage and heterogeneity of the majority of those categorized as "black," while advocating for the importance of declared multiracial identity for those born recently is one of [the] ironic ways that racial hierarchies continue to get reinscribed.

10. In this regard, I rely on discussions of racial hegemony and view the Multiracial Movement as one of several competing racial projects. "A racial project is simultaneously an interpretation, representation, or explanation of racial dynamics, and an effort to reorganize and redistribute resources along particular racial lines. Racial projects connect what race means in a particular discursive practice and the ways in which both social structure and everyday experiences are racially organized." Michael Omi and Howard Winant, *Racial Formations in the United States from the 1960's to the 1990's* (New York: Routledge, 1994), 56. The Multiracial Movement's achievement in disrupting existing racial categories is one example of how racial categories shift and slide. For a critique of the movement's failure to contest the meaning of race, see Rachael F. Moran, *Interracial Intimacy: The Regulation of Race and Romance* (Chicago: University of Chicago Press, 2001), 154–78.

11. Omi and Winant, *Racial Formations in the United States from the 1960's to the 1990's.* The authors present a discussion that exposes neoconservatism as a racial project that served to erode the progress of the civil rights movement while it simultaneously masqueraded the white supremacist agenda by creating a "commonsense" understanding of a "color-blind" rhetoric where meritocracy is allegedly the driving force. Also, see Robin D. G. Kelley, *Yo Mama's Disfunktional!: Fighting the Culture Wars in Urban America* (Boston: Beacon Press, 1997). For a review and critique of Ronald Reagan's and California governor Pete Wilson's use of the media and codes to reestablish patriarchal, white supremacy, see George Lipsitz, *The Possessive Investment in Whiteness: How White People Profit from Identity Politics* (Philadelphia: Temple University Press, 1998).

12. The seminal works that shift the rhetorical from race to class are William J. Wilson, *The Declining Significance of Race: Blacks and Changing American Institutions* (Chicago: University of Chicago Press, 1976) and William Julius Wilson, *When Work Disappears. The World of the New Urban Poor* (New York: Vintage Books, 1996). A discussion of the New Left and its conflation of class-based issues with race can be found in chapter 5 in Stephen Steinberg, *Turning Back. The Retreat from Racial Justice in American Thought and Policy* (Boston: Beacon Press, 1995) and also in Orlando Patterson, *The Ordeal of Integration: Progress and Resentment in America's Racial Crisis* (Washington, DC: Civitas, 1997). For a critique refer to Cornel West, *Race Matters* (New York: Vintage Books, 1994).

13. Ian Haney-López, *White by Law: the Legal Construction of Race* (New York: New York University Press, 1996);

David R. Roediger, *Wages of Whiteness: Race and the Making of the American Working Class* (London: Verso, 1991); Alexander Saxton, *Rise and the Fall of the White Republic: Class Politics and Mass Culture in Nineteenth Century America* (New York: Verso, 1990).

14. Martha Hodes, ed., *Sex, Love, Race: Crossing the Boundaries in North American History* (New York: New York University Press, 1999), 1.

15. Martha Hodes, *White Women, Black Men: Illicit Love in 19th Century South* (New Haven: Yale University Press, 1997); Kathleen Brown, *Good Wives, Nasty Wenches, and Anxious Patriarchs. Gender, Race, and Power in Colonial Virginia* (Chapel Hill: University of North Carolina Press, 1996); and Orlando Patterson, *Slavery and Social Death: A Comparative Study* (Cambridge: Harvard University Press, 1986).

16. Kathleen Brown, *Good Wives, Nasty Wenches, and Anxious Patriarchs.* See also Nancy F. Cott, *Public Vows: A History of Marriage and the Nation* (Cambridge: Harvard University Press, 2000) An important discussion about impact on the construction of white femininity is found in A. Leon Higgenbotham and Barbara Kopytoff, "Racial Purity and Interracial Sex in the Law of Colonial and Antebellum Virginia," in *Interracialism: Black-White Intermarriage in American History, Literature and Law,* ed. Werner Sollors (London: Oxford University Press, 2001). See also Gary B. Nash, "Hidden History of Mestizo America," in *Sex, Love, Race: Crossing the Boundaries.*

17. It should be noted that contrary to the widespread belief that black men were routinely lynched as punishment for alleged sexual relations with white women throughout colonial and antebellum periods, the preponderance of evidence is that such violent action against black men began after Emancipation with the elimination of slavery and increased white sexual anxiety directed at black men. Frederick Douglass and Ida B. Wells and W. E. B. DuBois all note the prevalence of such lynching as a post–Civil War phenomenon. A through illustration of the illicit liaisons across the color line is in Martha Hodes, *White Women, Black Men.*

18. Peter W. Bardaglio, "'Shameful Matches': The Regulation of Interracial Sex and Marriage in the South before 1900," in *Sex, Love, Race: Crossing Boundaries;* and Eva Sack, "Representing Miscegenation Law," in *Interracialism.*

19. See Joel Williamson, *New People: Miscegenation and Mulattoes in the United States* (New York: Free Press, 1980).

20. Patricia Hill Collins, *Fighting Words. Black Women and the Search for Justice* (Minneapolis: University of Minnesota Press, 1998), 149.

21. Patricia Hill Collins, *Fighting Words,* 223.

22. Rainier Spencer, *Spurious Issues.*

23. Darnell M. Hunt, *O. J. Simpson Facts & Fictions. News Rituals in the Construction of Reality* (New York: Cambridge University Press, 1999), 48.

24. In describing my daughter I deliberately choose the designator "black" rather than biracial or "mixed," for three reasons. First, it was an identity externally imposed upon her by others at school and in our social settings based on her physical appearance in a milieu that was predominantly white. Second, I prefer "black" for political reasons

over a hyphenated designator such as African-American, because it is primarily people of color whose identities are qualified as "Americans" by virtue of a hyphenated modifier (African/American, Chinese American, Japanese American, Mexican-American, etc.) Few, if any whites, identify primarily by country of origin of distant ancestors. Third, I avoid terms such as biracial, multiracial, and mixed race because they appear to reify race giving it more validity as a biological concept than is deserved. Patricia Hill Collins, *Fighting Words*, 200.

25. Patricia Hill Collins, *Fighting Words*, 200.

26. Audre Lorde, *Sister Outsider Essays and Speeches* (Freedom, CA: The Crossing Press, 1984), 127.

27. Maureen Reddy, *Crossing the Color Line: Race, Parenting, and Culture* (New Brunswick: Rutgers University Press, 1994), discusses this common experience among white women married to black men.

28. There are a number of ways this has been expressed and articulated. At one extreme are those who challenge my continued membership in the exclusive circle of whiteness: as one student in one of my courses announced upon hearing I had a black child, "You are a traitor to the race. How could you? And, how could you expect any of us to take you seriously when you don't even think right like a white person?" More common are the reactions when I express my view that one of the whites who knows my family will address one of the others and say, "You know Eileen feels strongly about this. Because of her family, she sees race when it isn't even there." By virtue of my "contamination" by relations with black family members, my interpretations are dismissed. At the other extreme are whites who call upon me to speak for blacks, which I, of course, demur. This theme is developed in my dissertation in progress, "The Edge of the Color Line: How Whites Married to Blacks Understand Race, Experience Whiteness, and Negotiate Identity through the Prism of Gender."

29. Jon Meacham, "The New Face of Race," *Newsweek*, September 18, 2000.

30. Mary C. Waters, *Ethnic Options. Choosing Identities in America* (Berkeley: University of California Press, 1990).

31. Ibid., 156.

32. Ibid., 161.

33. Howard F. Stein and Robert F. Hill, *The Ethnic Imperative: Examining the New White Ethnic Movement* (University Park: Pennsylvania State University Press, 1977).

34. See Darien J. Davis, *Avoiding the Dark: Race and the Forging of National Culture in Modern Brazil* (Brookfield: Ashgate, 1999). Also refer to Robert B. Toplin, *Freedom and Prejudice: The Legacy of Slavery in the United States and Brazil* (Westport, Connecticut: Greenwood Press, 1981). Thomas E. Skidmore *Black into White: Race and Nationality in Brazilian Thought* (New York: Oxford University Press, 1974), 70, notes:

No slave society in the Americas failed to produce a large mulatto population. It was not the fact of miscegenation, but the recognition or non-recognition of the mixed bloods as a separate group, that made the difference.

35. George Lipsitz, *The Possessive Investment in Whiteness: How White People Profit from Identity Politics* (Philadelphia: Temple University Press, 1998), vii.

36. John Fiske, *Media Matters: Race and Gender in the U.S. Politics* (Minneapolis: University of Minnesota Press, 1994).

 64

Stolen Bodies, Reclaimed Bodies

Disability and Queerness

ELI CLARE

I want to write about the body, not as a metaphor, symbol, or representation, but simply as the body. To write about my body, our bodies, in all their messy, complicated realities. I want words shaped by my slurring tongue, shaky hands, almost steady breath; words shaped by the fact that I am a walkie—someone for whom a flight of stairs without an accompanying elevator poses no problem—and by the reality that many of the people I encounter in my daily life assume I am "mentally retarded." Words shaped by how my body—and I certainly mean to include the mind as part of the body—moves through the world.

Sometimes we who are activists and thinkers forget about our bodies, ignore our bodies, or reframe our bodies to fit our theories and political strategies. For several decades now, activists in a variety of social change movements, ranging from black civil rights to women's liberation, from disability rights to queer liberation, have said repeatedly that the problems faced by any marginalized group of people lie, not in their bodies, but in the oppression they face. But in defining the external collective, material nature of social injustice as separate from the body, we have sometimes ended up sidelining the profound relationships that connect our bodies with who we are and how we experience oppression.

★ ★ ★

Disentangling the body from the problems of social injustice has served the disability rights movement well. The dominant paradigms of disability—the medical, charity, supercrip, and moral models—all turn disability into problems faced by individual people, locate those problems in our bodies, and define those bodies as wrong. The medical model insists on disability as a disease or condition that is curable and/or treatable. The charity model declares disability to be a tragedy, a misfortune, that must be tempered or erased by generous giving. The supercrip model frames disability as a challenge to overcome and disabled people as superheroes just for living our daily lives. The moral model transforms disability into a sign of moral weakness. . . .

In resistance to this, the disability rights movement has created a new model of disability, one that places emphasis on how the world treats disabled people: Disability, not defined by our bodies, but rather by the material and social conditions of ableism; not by the need to use a wheelchair, but rather by the stairs that have no accompanying ramp or elevator. Disability activists fiercely declare that it's not our bodies that need curing. Rather, it is ableism—disability oppression, as reflected in high unemployment rates, lack of access, gawking, substandard education, being forced to live in nursing homes and back rooms, being seen as childlike and asexual—that needs changing. . . .

★ ★ ★

Irrevocable difference could be a cause for celebration, but in this world it isn't. The price we pay for variation from the norm that's defined and upheld by white supremacy, patriarchy, and capitalism is incredibly high. And in my life, that price has been body centered. I came to believe that my body was utterly wrong. Sometimes I wanted to cut off my right arm so it wouldn't shake. My shame was that plain, that bleak. Of course, this is one of the profound ways in which oppression works—to mire us in body hatred. Homophobia is all about defining queer bodies as wrong, perverse, immoral. Transphobia, about defining trans bodies as unnatural, monstrous, or the product of delusion. Ableism, about defining disabled bodies as broken and tragic. Class warfare, about defining the bodies of workers as expendable. Racism, about defining the bodies of people of color as primitive, exotic, or worthless. Sexism, about defining female bodies as pliable objects. These messages sink beneath our skin.

There are so many ways oppression and social injustice can mark a body, steal a body, feed lies and poison to a body. I think of the kid tracked into "special education" because of his speech impediment, which is actually a common sign of sexual abuse. I think of the autoimmune diseases, the cancers, the various kinds of chemical sensitivities that flag what it means to live in a world full of toxins. I think of the folks who live with work-related disabilities because of exploitative, dangerous work conditions. I think of the people who live downwind of nuclear fallout, the people who die for lack of access to health care, the rape survivors who struggle with post-traumatic stress disorder. The list goes on and on.

The stolen bodies, the bodies taken for good, rise up around me. Rebecca Wight, a lesbian, shot and killed as she hiked the Appalachian Trail with her lover. James Byrd Jr., an African American, dragged to death behind a pickup driven by white men. Tyra Hunter, a transgendered person living as a woman, left to bleed to death on the streets of D.C. because the EMT crew discovered she had a penis and stopped their work. Tracy Latimer, a twelve-year-old girl with severe cerebral palsy, killed by her father, who said he did it only to end her unbearable suffering. Bodies stolen for good. Other bodies live on—numb, abandoned, full of self-hate, trauma, grief, aftershock. The pernicious stereotypes, lies, and false images can haunt a body, stealing it away as surely as bullets do.

But just as the body can be stolen, it can also be reclaimed. The bodies irrevocably taken from us, we can memorialize in quilts, granite walls, and candlelight vigils. We can remember and mourn them, use their deaths to strengthen our will. And as for the lies and false images: we need to name them, transform them, create something entirely new in their place. Something that comes close and finally true to the bone, entering our bodies as liberation, as joy, as fury, as a will to refigure the world. . . .

★ ★ ★

In the end, I am asking that we pay attention to our bodies—our stolen bodies and our reclaimed bodies. To the wisdom that tells us the causes of the injustice we face lie outside our bodies, and also to the profound relationships our bodies have to that injustice, to the ways our identities are inextricably linked to our bodies. We need to do this because there are disability activists so busy defining disability as an external social condition that they neglect the daily realities of our bodies: the reality of living with chronic pain; the reality of needing personal attendants to help us pee and shit (and of being at once grateful for those PAs and deeply regretting our lack of privacy); the reality of disliking the very adaptive equipment that makes our day-to-day lives possible. We need to do this because there are disability thinkers who can talk all day about the body as metaphor and symbol but never mention flesh, and blood, bone and tendon—never even acknowledge their own bodies. We need to do this because without our bodies, without the lived bodily experience of identity and oppression, we won't truly be able to refigure the world. . . .

65

The Motherhood Manifesto

JOAN BLADES AND
KRISTIN ROWE-FINKBEINER

In the deep quiet of a still-dark morning, Renee reaches her arm out from under her thick flowered comforter and across the bed to hit the snooze button on her alarm clock. For a few blessed (and preplanned) minutes she avoids the wakeful classic rock blaring into her bedroom from her alarm. Renee hits the snooze button exactly three times before finally casting off her covers. She does this each morning, and each morning she sleepily thinks the same thing: "It's too early. I was just at work two seconds ago, and I don't want to go back already."

Everything about Renee's morning is structured for speed and efficiency. At 5:45, with her young son, Wade, and husband, Alan, still sleeping, Renee drags herself out of bed and sleepwalks to the shower. She brushes her teeth while the shower is warming, making sweeping circles on the mirror with her hand so she can see her reflection. Renee's movements, though she's thoroughly tired, are crisp, hurried and automatic—she's repeated the routine daily for several years.

Renee knows exactly how long each of her morning tasks will take, to the minute. That, for instance, between 6 and 6:12 she needs to put on her makeup, get herself dressed, get her son's clothes out and ready for the day, and get downstairs to the kitchen to start breakfast.

All this is done with an eye on the clock and a subtle, yet constant, worry about time. Her mind loops over the potential delays that could be ahead: "Is there going to be traffic? Am I going to get stuck behind a school bus? Is my son going to act normal when I drop him off or is he going to be stuck to my leg? Am I going to get a parking space in the office garage or am I going to have to run five blocks through the city to get to work on time?" And if there isn't any garage parking, which happens often, then in order to be on time for work Renee has to run up six flights of stairs in heels because she doesn't have extra time to waste waiting for an elevator. She's done this climb more than once.

Why the stress? At her work, if Renee is late more than six times, she's in danger of losing her job. Like many American mothers, Renee needs her income to help provide for her family. In our modern economy, where more often than not two wage earners are needed to support a family, American women now make up 46 percent of the entire paid labor force. In fact, a study released last June found that in order to maintain income levels, parents have to work more hours—two-parent families are spending 16 percent more time at work, or 500 more hours a year, than in 1979.

Despite all the media chatter about the so-called Opt-Out Revolution—and all the hand-wringing about whether working moms are good for kids—women, and mothers, are in the workplace to stay. Yet public policy and workplace structures have yet to catch up.

This Mother's Day, why not step back and reflect about how we as a country can really help mothers like Renee? For example, the option of flextime would make a world of difference for Renee and her family. "Flextime would make a huge difference in my life because with my job function, there are busy days and late days. As long as I'm there forty hours a week and get my job done, then I don't know why anyone would care. I don't understand why there's such an 8AM to 5 PM 'law' in my workplace."

Seemingly mundane challenges like getting out the door in time for work and the morning commute, Renee tells us, become overwhelming when coupled with the financial anxieties that face so many families in America. Renee and Alan would like to have a second child, but they worry that they simply can't afford one right now. "By no means do we live, or want to live, extravagantly: We just want two cars, two kids and a vacation here and there," says Renee.

She and millions of other parents across the country are seriously struggling to meet the demands of work and parenthood. Vast numbers of women are chronically tired and drained. But the American credo teaches us to be fierce individualists, with the result that most parents toil in isolation and can't envision, or don't expect, help. It's time to recognize that our common problems can be addressed only by working together to bring about broad and meaningful change in our families, communities, workplaces and nation.

It's often said that motherhood is perhaps the most important, and most difficult, job on the planet. This cliché hits fairly close to the mark. While we raise our children out of an innate sense of love and nurturing, we also know that raising happy, healthy children who become productive adults is critical to our future well-being as a nation.

But right now, motherhood in America is at a critical juncture. As women's roles continue to evolve, more women than ever are in the workforce and most children are raised in homes without a stay-at-home parent. At the same time, public and private policies that affect parenting and the workplace

remain largely unchanged. We have a twenty-first-century economy stuck with an outdated, industrial-era family support structure. The result is that parents, mothers in particular, are struggling to balance the needs of their children with the demands of the workplace.

America's mothers are working, and working hard. Almost three-quarters have jobs outside their homes. Then, too, America's mothers are working hard but for less money than men (and less money than women who are not mothers). In fact, the wage gap between mothers and nonmothers is greater than that between nonmothers and men— and it's actually getting bigger. One study found that nonmothers with an average age of 30 made 90 cents to a man's dollar, while moms made only 73 cents to the dollar, and single moms made 56 to 66 cents to a man's dollar.

"It is well-established that women with children earn less than other women in the United States," writes Jane Waldfogel of Columbia University in *The Journal of Economic Perspectives*. "Even after controlling for differences in characteristics such as education and work experience, researchers typically find a family penalty of 10–15 percent for women with children as compared to women without children."

What's more, it's still common for women and men to hold the same job and receive different pay. In fact, women lost a cent between 2002 and 2003, according to the US Census, and now make 76 cents to a man's dollar. Most of these wage hits are coming from mothers, because the lower wages they receive drag down the overall average pay for all women.

The United States has a serious mommy wage gap. Why? Because, as Waldfogel writes, "The United States does at least as well as other countries in terms of equal pay and equal opportunity legislation, but . . . the United States lags in the area of family policies such as maternity leave and childcare." Studies show that this mommy wage gap is directly correlated with our lack of family-friendly national policies like paid family leave and subsidized childcare. In countries with these family policies in place, moms don't take such big wage hits.

Consider one family-friendly policy: paid family leave. The United States is the only industrialized country that doesn't have paid leave other than Australia (which does give a full year of guaranteed unpaid leave to all women, compared with the scant twelve weeks of unpaid leave given to those who work for companies in the United States with more than fifty employees). A full 163 countries give women paid leave with the birth of a child. Fathers as well often get paid leave in other countries—forty-five give fathers the right to paid parental leave.

By way of example, our close neighbor to the north, Canada, gives the mother fifteen weeks of partial paid parental leave for physical recovery, and then gives another thirty-five weeks of partial paid leave that has to be taken before the child turns 1. These thirty-five weeks of parental leave can be taken by the mother or the father, or can be shared between the two.

Sweden, with about a year of paid family leave and some time specifically reserved for fathers, is often held up as a model. Not surprisingly, with this support, Ann Crittenden writes in *The Price of Motherhood*, "Swedish women on average have higher incomes, vis-à-vis men, than women anywhere else in the world."

America, on the other hand, generally leaves it up to parents to patch together some type of leave on their own. Some states are starting to give more support to new parents, but only one of our fifty states, California, offers paid family leave. The federal government simply doesn't offer a paid family leave program at all. A weighty consequence emerges from this lack of family support. Research reveals that a full 25 percent of "poverty spells," or times when a family's income slips below what is needed for basic living expenses, begin with the birth of a baby.

Speak to mothers across the nation and you will hear that the vast majority of them find they hit an economic "maternal wall" after having children. By most accounts, this wall is why a large number of professional women leave the workforce, and it's a core reason so many mothers and their children live in poverty. Amy Caiazza, from the Institute for Women's Policy Research, notes, "If there wasn't a wage gap, the poverty rates for single moms would be cut in half, and the poverty rates for dual earner families would be cut by about 25 percent."

But mothers across America are not just crying out for better (or at least fair and equal) pay; they are also yearning to live a life in which they aren't cracking under pressure, a life in which they know that their children will be well cared for, a life in which it's possible to be at home with their son or daughter even just one afternoon a week without worrying about sacrificing a disproportionate amount of their income and benefits—or losing their job altogether. Some would argue that mothers just need to find the proper balance between parenting and career. We believe there's more to it than that.

While Renee's story captures the essence of what millions of working American women face each morning, Kiki's daunting experience simply trying to find a job shows just how deeply rooted, and widely accepted, discrimination against mothers has become.

A single mother of two, Kiki moved to a one-stoplight Pennsylvania town in 1994. She was truly on her own. Her husband had left several years earlier, when her children were 2 and 4. Kiki hadn't known how she'd make it as a single parent until her mother, a petite powerhouse and survivor of a World War II Russian gulag, stepped in to help. But when Kiki's mother died, there was nothing to keep Kiki in the Long Island town where she'd been living. The rapid property-tax increases in Kiki's carefully landscaped neighborhood of gorgeous Colonial houses were quickly exceeding her economic reach as a single working mother. So Kiki left in search of a smaller town with a lower cost of living.

With this move, Kiki and the kids were alone in a new town that had just two supermarkets. Several diners served a variety of aromatically enticing pork, sauerkraut and dumpling dishes. It was just the change she wanted. Kiki was able to buy a

Dutch Colonial house at the top of a small mountain in the Poconos with nearly two acres of land for a fraction of the price of her old house. It seemed ideal, until she started looking for a job to support her family.

On a hot, humid August day, at an interview for a legal secretary position in a one-story brick building, Kiki sat down in a hard wooden chair to face a middle-aged attorney ensconced behind a mahogany desk. His framed diplomas lined the walls, and legal books filled the shelves behind him. Kiki remembers the attorney clearly, even his height of 5'10" and the color of his light brown hair. The interaction was significant enough to remain seared in her mind a decade later. "The first question the attorney asked me when I came in for the interview was, Are you married? The second was, Do you have children?"

It was the eleventh job interview in which she'd been asked the very same questions. After answering eleven times that she wasn't married, and that she was the mother of two, Kiki began to understand why her job search was taking so long.

She decided to address the issue head-on this time. "I asked him how those questions were relevant to the job, and he said my hourly wage would be determined by my marital and motherhood status." What's that? "He said, If you don't have a husband and have children, then I pay less per hour because I have to pay benefits for the entire family." The attorney noted that a married woman's husband usually had health insurance to cover the kids, and since Kiki didn't have a husband, he "didn't want to get stuck with the bill for my children's health coverage."

The attorney insisted that this blatant discrimination was perfectly legal—and he was right. Pennsylvania, like scores of states, does not have employment laws that protect mothers.

Recent Cornell University research by Shelley Correll confirms what many American women are finding: Mothers are 44 percent less likely to be hired than nonmothers who have the same résumé, experience and qualifications; and mothers are offered significantly lower starting pay. Study participants offered nonmothers an average of $11,000 more than equally qualified mothers for the same high-salaried job. Correll's groundbreaking research adds to the long line of studies that explore the roots of this maternal wage gap. "We expected to find that moms were going to be discriminated against, but I was surprised by the magnitude of the gap," explains Correll. "I expected small numbers, but we found huge numbers. Another thing was that fathers were actually advantaged, and we didn't expect fathers to be offered more money or to be rated higher." But that's what happened.

The "maternal wall" is a reality we must address if we value both fair treatment in the workplace and the contributions working mothers make to our economy.

Stories like those of Renee and Kiki confirm that something just isn't right about what we're doing—or not doing—to address the needs of mothers across our nation. Some companies and states are experimenting with family-friendly programs, but such programs are not the norm. We need to open a whole new conversation about motherhood by illuminating the universal needs of America's mothers and spelling out concrete solutions that will provide families—whether working- or middle-class—with real relief.

National policies and programs with proven success in other countries—like paid family leave, flexible work options, subsidized childcare and preschool, as well as healthcare coverage for all kids—are largely lacking in America. The problems mothers face are deeply interconnected and often overlap: Without paid family leave parents often have to put their infants in extremely expensive or substandard childcare facilities; families with a sick child, inadequate healthcare coverage and no flexible work options often end up in bankruptcy.

Fixing even one of these problems often has numerous positive repercussions. Companies that embrace family-friendly workplace policies are thriving, with lower employee turnover, enhanced productivity and job commitment from employees, and consequently with lower recruiting and retraining costs.

Flexible work options also allow parents to create work schedules that are well suited to raising happy, healthy children.

The good news is that more enlightened policies would provide practical benefits to the whole society. But we need a genuine motherhood revolution to achieve this sort of change. We believe the following Motherhood Manifesto points are a good place to start:

• **M** = Maternity/Paternity Leave: Paid family leave for all parents after a new child comes into the family.

• **O** = Open, Flexible Work: Give parents the ability to structure their work hours and careers in a way that allows them to meet both business and family needs. This includes flexible work hours and locations, part-time work options and the ability to move in and out of the labor force without penalties to raise young children.

• **T** = TV We Choose & Other After-School Programs: Offer safe, educational opportunities for children after school doors close, including a clear and independent universal television rating system for parents along with technology that allows them to choose what is showing in their own homes; quality educational programming for kids; expanded after-school programs.

• **H** = Healthcare for All Kids: Provide quality, universal healthcare to all children.

• **E** = Excellent Childcare: Quality, affordable childcare should be available to all parents. Childcare providers should be paid at least a living wage and healthcare benefits.

• **R** = Realistic and Fair Wages: Two full-time working parents should be able to earn enough to care for their family. And working mothers must receive equal pay for equal work.

By tackling these interconnected issues together, we can create a powerful system of support for families, improving the quality of our lives and making sure our children inherit a world in which they will thrive as adults and parents. The Motherhood Manifesto is a call to action, summoning all Americans— mothers, and all who have mothers—to start a revolution to make motherhood compatible with life, liberty and the pursuit of happiness.

 66

An Indian Father's Plea

ROBERT LAKE
(MEDICINE GRIZZLYBEAR)

Dear Teacher,

I would like to introduce you to my son, Wind-Wolf. He is probably what you would consider a typical Indian kid. He was born and raised on the reservation. He has black hair, dark brown eyes, and an olive complexion. And, like so many Indian children his age, he is shy and quiet in the classroom. He is five years old, in kindergarten, and I can't understand why you have already labeled him a "slow learner."

He has already been through quite an education compared with his peers in Western society. He was bonded to his mother and to the Mother Earth in a traditional native childbirth ceremony. And he has been continuously cared for by his mother, father, sisters, cousins, aunts, uncles, grandparents, and extended tribal family since this ceremony.

The traditional Indian baby basket became his "turtle's shell" and served as the first seat for his classroom. It is the same kind of basket our people have used for thousands of years. It is specially designed to provide the child with the kind of knowledge and experience he will need to survive in his culture and environment.

Wind-Wolf was strapped in snugly with a deliberate restriction on his arms and legs. Although Western society may argue this hinders motor-skill development and abstract reasoning, we believe it forces the child to first develop his intuitive faculties, rational intellect, symbolic thinking, and five senses. Wind-Wolf was with his mother constantly, closely bonded physically, as she carried him on her back or held him while breast-feeding. She carried him everywhere she went, and every night he slept with both parents. Because of this, Wind-Wolf's educational setting was not only a "secure" environment, but it was also very colorful, complicated, sensitive, and diverse.

As he grew older, Wind-Wolf began to crawl out of the baby basket, develop his motor skills, and explore the world around him. When frightened or sleepy, he could always return to the basket, as a turtle withdraws into its shell. Such an inward journey allows one to reflect in privacy on what he has learned and to carry the new knowledge deeply into the unconscious and the soul. Shapes, sizes, colors, texture, sound, smell, feeling, taste, and the learning process are therefore functionally integrated— the physical and spiritual, matter and energy, and conscious and unconscious, individual and social.

It takes a long time to absorb and reflect on these kinds of experiences, so maybe that is why you think my Indian child is a slow learner. His aunts and grandmothers taught him to count and know his numbers while they sorted materials for making abstract designs in native baskets. And he was taught to learn mathematics by counting the sticks we use in our traditional native hand game. So he may be slow in grasping the methods and tools you use in your classroom, ones quite familiar to his white peers, but I hope you will be patient with him. It takes time to adjust to a new cultural system and learn new things.

He is not culturally "disadvantaged," but he is culturally "different." If you ask him how many months there are in a year, he will probably tell you 13—not because he doesn't know how to count properly, but because he has been taught there are 13 full moons in a year and really 13 planets in our solar system and 13 tail feathers on a perfectly balanced eagle, the most powerful kind of bird to use in ceremony and healing.

But he also knows that some eagles may have only 12 tail feathers, or seven, that they do not all have the same number. He knows that the flicker has exactly 10 tail feathers; that they are red and black, representing the directions of east and west, life and death; and that this bird is considered a

"fire" bird, a power used in native doctoring and healing. He can probably count more than 40 kinds of birds, and tell you and his peers what kind of bird each is, where it lives, the seasons in which it appears, and how it is used in a sacred ceremony.

He may have trouble writing his name on a piece of paper, but he knows how to say it and many other things in several different Indian languages. He is not fluent yet because he is only five and required by law to attend your educational system and learn your language, your values, your ways of thinking, and your methods of teaching and learning.

So you see, all of these influences together make him somewhat shy and quiet—and perhaps "slow" according to your standards. But if Wind-Wolf was not prepared for your world, neither were you appreciative of his. On the first day of class, you wanted to call him Wind, insisting that Wolf somehow must be his middle name. The students in class laughed at him.

As you try to teach him your new methods, helping him learn new tools for self-discovery and adapt to his new learning environment, he may be looking out the window as if day-dreaming. Why? Because he has been taught to watch and study the changes in nature. It is hard for him to make the appropriate psychic switch from the right to the left hemisphere of the brain when he sees the leaves turning bright colors, the geese heading south, and the squirrels scurrying around for nuts to get ready for a harsh winter. In his heart, in his young mind, and almost by instinct, he knows that this is the time of year he is supposed to be with his people gathering and preparing fish, deer meat, and native plants and herbs, and learning his assigned tasks in this role. He is caught between two worlds, torn by two distinct cultural systems.

Yesterday, for the third time in two weeks, he came home crying and said he wanted his hair cut. He said he doesn't have any friends at school because they make fun of his long hair. I tried to explain that in our culture, long hair is a sign of masculinity and balance and is a source of power. But he remained adamant.

To make matters worse, he recently encountered his first harsh case of racism. Wind-Wolf had managed to adopt at least one good school friend and asked his new pal if he wanted to come home to play with him until supper. That was OK with Wind-Wolf's mother, who was walking with them. But the other boy's mother lashed out, "It is OK if you have to play with him at school, but we don't allow those kind of people in our house!" When my wife asked why not, she answered, "Because you are Indians, and we are white, and I don't want my kids growing up with your kind of people."

So now my young Indian child does not want to go to school anymore (even though we cut his hair). He feels he does not belong. He is the only Indian child in your class, and he is well aware of it. Instead of being proud of his race, heritage, and culture, he feels ashamed.

When he watches television, he asks why the white people hate us and always kill us in movies and take everything from us. He asks why the other kids in school are not taught about the power, beauty, and essence of nature or provided with an opportunity to experience the world around them firsthand. He says he hates living in the city and that he misses his Indian cousins and friends. He asks why one young white girl at school who is his friend always tells him, "I like you, Wind-Wolf, because you are a good Indian."

Now he refuses to sing his native songs, play with his Indian artifacts, learn his language, or participate in his sacred ceremonies. When I ask him to help me with a sacred ritual, he says no because "that's weird" and he doesn't want his friends at school to think he doesn't believe in God.

So, dear teacher, I want to introduce you to my son, Wind-Wolf, who is not really a "typical" little Indian kid after all. He stems from a long line of hereditary chiefs, medicine men and women, and ceremonial leaders whose accomplishments and unique forms of knowledge are still being studied and recorded in contemporary books. He has seven different tribal systems flowing through his blood; he is even part white.

I want my child to succeed in school and in life. I don't want him to be a dropout or juvenile delinquent or to end up on drugs and alcohol because he is made to feel inferior or because of discrimination. I want him to be proud of his rich heritage and culture, and I would like him to develop the necessary capabilities to adapt to, and succeed in, both cultures. But I need your help.

What you say and do in the classroom, what you teach and how you teach it, and what you don't say and don't teach will have significant effect on the potential success or failure of my child. Please remember that this is the primary year of his education and development.

All I ask is that you work with me, not against me, to help educate my child in the best way. If you don't have the knowledge, preparation, experience, or training to effectively deal with culturally different children, I am willing to help you with the few resources I have available or direct you to such resources.

Millions of dollars have been appropriated by Congress and are being spent each year for "Indian Education." All you have to do is take advantage of it and encourage your school to make an effort to use it in the name of "equal education." My Indian child has a constitutional right to learn, retain, and maintain his heritage and culture. By the same token, I strongly believe that non-Indian children also have a constitutional right to learn about our Native American heritage and culture, because Indians play a significant part in the history of Western society. Until this reality is equally understood and applied in education as a whole, there will be a lot more school children in grades K–2 identified as "slow learners."

My son, Wind-Wolf, is not an empty glass coming into your class to be filled. He is a full basket coming into a different environment and society with something special to share. Please let him share his knowledge, heritage, and culture with you and his peers.

C. WHERE DO I BEGIN?

※ 67

Interrupting the Cycle of Oppression

The Role of Allies as Agents of Change

ANDREA AYVAZIAN

Many of us feel overwhelmed when we consider the many forms of systemic oppression that are so pervasive in American society today. We become immobilized, uncertain about what actions we can take to interrupt the cycles of oppression and violence that intrude on our everyday lives. One way to overcome this sense of immobilization is to assume the role of an ally. Learning about this role—one that each and every one of us is capable of assuming—can offer us new ways of behaving and a new source of hope.

Through the years, experience has taught us that isolated and episodic actions—even dramatic, media-grabbing events—rarely produce more than a temporary blip on the screen. What does seem to create real and lasting change is highly-motivated individuals—usually only a handful at first—who are so clear and consistent on an issue that they serve as a heartbeat in a community, steadily sending out waves that touch and change those in their path. These change agents or allies have such a powerful impact because their actions embody the values they profess: their behavior and beliefs are congruent.

WHAT IS AN ALLY?

An ally is a member of a dominant group in our society who works to dismantle any form of oppression from which she or he receives the benefit.

Allied behavior means taking personal responsibility for the changes we know are needed in our society, and so often ignore or leave to others to deal with. Allied behavior is intentional, overt, consistent activity that challenges prevailing patterns of oppression, makes privileges that are so often invisible visible, and facilitates the empowerment of persons targeted by oppression.

I use the term "oppression" to describe the combination of prejudice plus access to social, political, and economic power on the part of a dominant group. Racism, a core component of oppression, has been defined by David Wellman as a system of advantage based on race. Wellman's definition can be altered slightly to describe every other form of oppression. Hence we can say that sexism is a system of advantage based on gender, that heterosexism is a system of advantage based on sexual orientation, and so on. In each form of oppression there is a dominant group—the one that receives the unearned advantage, benefit, or privilege—and a targeted group—the one that is denied that advantage, benefit, or privilege. We know the litany of dominants: white people, males, Christians, heterosexuals, able-bodied people, those in their middle years, and those who are middle or upper class.

We also know that everyone has multiple social identities. We are all dominant and targeted simultaneously. I, for instance, am simultaneously dominant as a white person and targeted as a woman. A white able-bodied man may be dominant in those categories, but targeted as a Jew or Muslim or as a gay person. Some people are, at some point in their lives, entirely dominant; but if they are, they won't be forever. Even a white, able-bodied, heterosexual, Christian male will literally grow out of his total dominance if he reaches old age.

When we consider the different manifestations of systematic oppression and find ourselves in any of the categories where we are dominant—and therefore receive the unearned advantages that accrue to that position of advantage—we have the potential to be remarkably powerful agents of change as allies. Allies are whites who identify as anti-racists, men who work to dismantle sexism, able-bodied people who are active in the disability rights movement, Christians who combat anti-Semitism and other forms of religious prejudice. Allied behavior usually involves talking to other dominants about their behavior: whites confronting other whites on issues of racism, men organizing with other men to combat sexism, and so on. Allied behavior is clear action aimed at dismantling the oppression of others in areas where you yourself benefit—it is proactive, intentional, and often involves taking a risk.

To tether these principles to everyday reality, just think of the group Parents, Families and Friends of Lesbians and Gays (PFLAG) as the perfect example of allied behavior. PFLAG is an organization of (mainly) heterosexuals who organize support groups and engage in advocacy and education among other heterosexuals around issues of gay and lesbian liberation. PFLAG speakers can be heard in houses of worship, schools, and civic organizations discussing their own commitment to securing gay and lesbian civil rights. Because they are heterosexuals speaking (usually) to other heterosexuals, they often have a significant impact.

The anti-racism trainer Kenneth Jones, an African-American, refers to allied behavior as "being at my back." He has said to me, "Andrea, I know you are at my back on the issue of race equity—you're talking to white people who cannot hear me on this topic, you're out there raising these issues repeatedly, you're organizing with other whites to stand up to racism. And I'm at your back. I'm raising issues of gender equity with men, I am talking to men who cannot hear you, I've made a commitment to combat sexism."

Available to each one of us in the categories where we are dominant is the proud and honorable role of ally: the opportunity to raise hell with others like us and to interrupt the cycle of oppression. Because of our very privilege, we have the potential to stir up good trouble, to challenge the status quo, and to inspire real and lasting change. William Stickland, an aide to Jesse Jackson, once said: "When a critical mass of white people join together,

rise up, and shout a thunderous 'No' to racism, we will actually alter the course of history."

REDUCING VIOLENCE

When I ponder the tremendous change a national network of allies can make in this country, I think not only of issues of equity and empowerment, but also of how our work could lead to diminishing levels of violence in our society. Let us consider for a moment the critical connection between oppression and violence on one hand, and the potential role of allied behavior in combating violence on the other.

A major source of violence in our society is the persistent inequity between dominant and targeted groups. Recall that oppression is kept in place by two factors:

1. Ideology, or the propagation of doctrines that purport to legitimize inequality; and
2. Violence (or the threat of violence) by the dominant group against the targeted group.

The violence associated with each form of systemic oppression noticeably decreases when allies (or dominants) rise up and shout a thunderous "No" to the perpetuation of these inequities. Because members of the dominant group are conferred with considerable social power and privilege, they carry significant authority when confronting perpetrators of violence in their own group—when whites deter other whites from using violence against people of color, when heterosexuals act to prevent gay bashing, and so on.

Research studies have confirmed what observers and allies have been saying for years: that when a woman is the victim of ongoing, violent domestic abuse, it makes no difference to her chances of survival if she has counseling, takes out a re-straining order, or learns to fight back. According to the studies, the only factor that statistically increases a woman's chances of survival is if the victimizer himself is exposed to direct and ongoing anti-battering intervention.

These studies have inspired the creation of model mentoring programs in places like Quincy, Massachusetts, Duluth, Minnesota, and New York

City—programs in which men prone to violence against women work with other men through a series of organized interventions. The success of these programs has demonstrated that it is actually possible to interrupt and stop the cycle of violence among batterers. In 1992, for instance, the model program in Quincy helped cut the incidence of domestic homicide to zero. The Batterers Anonymous groups, in which men who are former perpetrators work with men who are current batterers, have also had remarkable success in breaking the habit of violence. These groups are allied behavior made manifest; their success in reducing the incidence of violence against women is now statistically proven.

In our society, oppression and violence are woven together: one leads to the other, one justifies the other. Furthermore, members of the dominant group who are not perpetrators of violence often collude, through their silence and inactivity, with those who are. Allied behavior is an effective way of interrupting the cycle of violence by breaking the silence that reinforces the cycle, and by promoting a new set of behavior through modeling and mentoring.

PROVIDING POSITIVE ROLE MODELS

Not only does allied behavior contribute to an increase in equity and a decrease in violence, but allies provide positive role models that are sorely needed by today's young people. The role of ally offers young people who are white, male, and in other dominant categories a positive, proactive, and proud identity. Rather than feeling guilty, shameful, and immobilized as the "oppressor," whites and other dominants can assume the important and useful role of social change agent. There have been proud allies and change agents throughout the history of this nation, and there are many alive today who can inspire us with their important work.

I often speak in high school classes and assemblies, and in recent years I have taken to doing a little informal survey from the podium. I ask the students if they can name a famous living white racist. Can they? Yes. They often name David Duke—he ran for President in their lifetime—or they sometimes name Senator Jesse Helms; and when I was in the midwest, they named Marge Schott, the owner of the Cincinnati Reds. It does not take long before a hand shoots up, or someone just calls out one of those names.

Following that little exercise, I ask the students, "Can you name a famous living white anti-racist (or civil rights worker, or someone who fights racism)?" Can they? Not very often. Sometimes there is a whisper or two, but generally the room is very quiet. So, recently, I have been saying: forget the famous part. Just name for me any white person you know in your community, or someone you have heard of, who has taken a stand against racism. Can they? Sometimes. Occasionally someone says "my mom," or "my dad." I have also heard "my rabbi, my teacher, my minister." But not often enough.

I believe that it is difficult for young people to grow up and become something they have never heard of. It is hard for a girl to grow up and become a commercial airline pilot if it has never occurred to her that women can and do fly jet planes. Similarly, it is hard for young people to grow up and fight racism if they have never met anyone who does.

And there *are* many remarkable role models whom we can claim with pride, and model ourselves after. People like Laura Haviland, who was a conductor on the Underground Railroad and performed unbelievably brave acts while the slave-catchers were right on her trail; Virginia Foster Durr, a southern belle raised with great wealth and privilege who, as an adult, tirelessly drove black workers to and from their jobs during the Montgomery bus boycott; the Rev. James Reeb, who went south during the Mississippi Freedom Summer of 1964 to organize and march; Hodding Carter, Jr., editor and publisher of a newspaper in the Mississippi Delta who used his paper to battle for racial equity and who took considerable heat for his actions. And more: the Grimke sisters, Lucretia Mott, William Lloyd Garrison, John Brown, Viola Liuzzo.

There are also many contemporary anti-racists like Morris Dees, who gave up a lucrative law practice to start the Southern Poverty Law Center and Klan

Watch in Alabama and bring white supremacists to trial; Anne Braden, active for decades in the civil rights struggle in Kentucky; Rev. Joseph Barndt, working within the religious community to make individual churches and entire denominations proclaim themselves as anti-racist institutions. And Peggy McIntosh, Judith Katz, and Myles Horton. And so many others. Why don't our young people know these names? If young people knew more about these dedicated allies, perhaps they would be inspired to engage in more anti-racist activities themselves.

CHOOSING OUR OWN ROLES

We also need to consider our role as allies. In our own communities, would young people, if asked the same questions, call out our names as anti-racists? In areas where we are dominant, is our struggle for equity and justice evident? When we think about our potential role as allies, we need to recall a Quaker expression: "Let your life be your teaching." The Quakers understand that our words carry only so much weight, that it is our actions, our daily behaviors, that tell the true story.

In my own life I struggle with what actions to take, how to make my beliefs and my behaviors congruent. One small step that has had interesting repercussions over the last decade is the fact that my partner (who is male) and I have chosen not to be legally married until gay and lesbian couples can be married and receive the same benefits and legal protection that married heterosexual couples enjoy. A small step but it has allowed us to talk with folks at the YMCA about their definition of "family" when deciding who qualifies for their "family plan"; to challenge people at Amtrak about why some "family units" receive discounts when traveling together and others do not; and to raise questions in the religious community about who can receive formal sanction for their loving unions and who cannot. These are not earth-shattering steps in the larger picture, but we believe that small steps taken by thousands of people will eventually change the character of our communities.

When we stop colluding and speak out about the unearned privileges we enjoy as members of a dominant group—privileges we have been taught for so long to deny or ignore—we have the potential to undergo and inspire stunning transformation. Consider the words of Gandhi: "As human beings, our greatness lies not so much in being able to remake the world, as in being able to remake ourselves."

In my own community, I have been impressed by the efforts of three middle-aged males who have remade themselves into staunch allies for women. Steven Botkin established the Men's Resource Center in Amherst, Massachusetts twelve years ago and put a commitment to eliminating sexism in its very first mission statement. Another Amherst resident, Michael Burkart, travels nationwide and works with top executives in Fortune 500 companies on the issue of gender equity in their corporations. And Geoff Lobenstine, a social worker who identifies as an anti-sexist male, brings these issues to his work in Holyoke, Massachusetts.

Charlie Parker once said this about music: "Music is your own experience, your thoughts, your wisdom. If you don't live it, it won't come out of your horn." I think the same is true about us in our role as allies—it is our own experience, our thoughts, our wisdon. If we don't live it, it won't come out of our horn.

PREPARING FOR THE LONG HAUL

Now I would be the first to admit that personally and professionally the role of ally is often exhausting. I know that it involves challenges—being an ally is difficult work, and it can often be lonely. We must remember to take care of ourselves along this journey, to sustain our energy and our zest for those ongoing challenges.

We must also remember that it is hard to go it alone: allies need allies. As with any other struggle in our lives, we need supportive people around us to help us to persevere. Other allies will help us take the small, daily steps that will, in time, alter the character of our communities. We know that allied behavior usually consists of small steps and unglamorous work. As Mother Teresa once said: "I don't do any great things. I do small things with great love."

Finally two additional points about us in our role as allies: First, we don't always see the results of our efforts. Sometimes we do, but often we touch and even change lives without ever knowing it. Consequently, we cannot measure our success in quantitative terms. Like waves upon the shore, we are altering the landscape—but exactly how, may be hard to discern.

Doubts inevitably creep up about our effectiveness, about our approach, about the positions we assume or the actions we take. But we move forward, along with the doubts, the uncertainty, and often the lack of visible results. In our office, we have a famous William James quote on the wall to sustain us: "I will act as though what I do makes a difference." And, speaking personally, although my faith gets rattled, I try to act as though what I do does make a difference.

Second, there is no such thing as a perfect ally. Perfection is not our goal. When I asked my colleague Kenneth Jones what stood out for him as the most important characteristic of a strong ally, he said simply: "being consistently conscious." He didn't say "never stumbling," or "never making mistakes." He said: "being consistently conscious." And so we do our best: taking risks, being smart, making errors, feeling foolish, doing what we believe is right, based on our best judgment at the time. We are imperfect, but we are steady. We are courageous but not faultless. As Lani Guinier said: "It is better to be vaguely right than precisely wrong." If we obsess about looking good instead of doing good, we will get caught in a spiral of ineffective action. Let's not get side-tracked or defeated because we are trying to be perfect.

And so we move ahead, pushing ourselves forward on our growing edge. We know that although none of us are beginners in dealing with issues of oppression and empowerment, none of us are experts either. These issues are too complex, too painful, and too pervasive for us to achieve a state of clarity and closure once and for all. The best we can hope for is to strive each day to be our strongest and clearest selves, transforming the world one individual at a time, one family at a time, one community at a time. May we summon the wisdom to be devoted allies today. May we walk the walk, living as though equity, justice and freedom for all have already arrived.

Like most activists, I carry a dream inside me. As I travel nationwide for my work, I can actually see signs of it becoming true. The dream is that we will create in this country a nonviolent army of allies that will challenge and break the cycle of oppression and usher in a new era of liberation, empowerment, and equity for persons historically targeted by systemic oppression. Within each individual is the potential to effect enormous change. May we move foward, claiming with pride our identities as allies, interrupting the cycle of oppression, and modeling a new way of behaving and believing.

 68

The Transformation of Silence into Language and Action

AUDRE LORDE

I have come to believe over and over again that what is most important to me must be spoken, made verbal and shared, even at the risk of having it bruised or misunderstood. That the speaking profits me, beyond any other effect. I am standing here as a Black lesbian poet, and the meaning of all that waits upon the fact that I am still alive, and might not have been. Less than two months ago I was told by two doctors, one female and one male, that I would have to have breast surgery, and that there was a 60 to 80 percent chance that the tumor was malignant. Between that telling and the actual surgery, there was a three-week period of the agony of an involuntary reorganization of my entire life. The surgery was completed, and the growth was benign.

But within those three weeks, I was forced to look upon myself and my living with a harsh and urgent clarity that has left me still shaken but much stronger. This is a situation faced by many women, by some of you here today. Some of what I experienced during that time has helped elucidate for me much of what I feel concerning the transformation of silence into language and action.

In becoming forcibly and essentially aware of my mortality, and of what I wished and wanted for my life, however short it might be, priorities and omissions became strongly etched in a merciless light, and what I most regretted were my silences. Of what had I *ever* been afraid? To question or to speak as I believed could have meant pain, or death. But we all hurt in so many different ways, all the time, and pain will either change or end. Death, on the other hand, is the final silence. And that might be coming quickly, now, without regard for whether I had ever spoken what needed to be said, or had only betrayed myself into small silences, while I planned someday to speak, or waited for someone else's words. And I began to recognize a source of power within myself that comes from the knowledge that while it is most desirable not to be afraid, learning to put fear into a perspective gave me strength.

I was going to die, if not sooner then later, whether or not I had ever spoken myself. My silences had not protected me. Your silence will not protect you. But for every real word spoken, for every attempt I had ever made to speak those truths for which I am still seeking, I had made contact with other women while we examined the words to fit a world in which we all believed, bridging our differences. And it was the concern and caring of all those women which gave me strength and enabled me to scrutinize the essentials of my living.

The women who sustained me through that period were Black and white, old and young, lesbian, bisexual, and heterosexual, and we all shared a war against the tyrannies of silence. They all gave me a strength and concern without which I could not have survived intact. Within those weeks of acute fear came the knowledge—within the war we are all waging with the forces of death, subtle and otherwise, conscious or not—I am not only a casualty, I am also a warrior.

What are the words you do not yet have? What do you need to say? What are the tyrannies you swallow day by day and attempt to make your own, until you will sicken and die of them, still in silence? Perhaps for some of you here today, I am the face of one of your fears. Because I am woman, because I am Black, because I am lesbian, because I am myself—a Black woman warrior poet doing my work—come to ask you, are you doing yours?

And of course I am afraid, because the transformation of silence into language and action is an act of self-revelation, and that always seems fraught with danger. But my daughter, when I told her of our topic and my difficulty with it, said, "Tell them about how you're never really a whole person if you remain silent, because there's always that one little piece inside you that wants to be spoken out, and if you keep ignoring it, it gets madder and madder and hotter and hotter, and if you don't speak it out one day it will just up and punch you in the mouth from the inside."

In the cause of silence, each of us draws the face of her own fear—fear of contempt, of censure, or some judgment, or recognition, of challenge, of annihilation. But most of all, I think, we fear the visibility without which we cannot truly live. Within this country where racial difference creates a constant, if unspoken, distortion of vision, Black women have on one hand always been highly visible, and so, on the other hand, have been rendered invisible through the depersonalization of racism. Even within the women's movement, we have had to fight, and still do, for that very visibility which also renders us most vulnerable, our Blackness. For to survive in the mouth of this dragon we call america, we have had to learn this first and most vital lesson—that we were never meant to survive. Not as human beings. And neither were most of you here today, Black or not. And that visibility which makes us most vulnerable is that which also is the source of our greatest strength. Because the machine will try to grind you into dust anyway, whether or not we speak. We can sit in our corners mute forever while our sisters and our selves are wasted, while our children are distorted and destroyed, while our earth is poisoned; we can sit in our safe corners mute as bottles, and we will still be no less afraid.

In my house this year we are celebrating the feast of Kwanza, the African-american festival of harvest which begins the day after Christmas and lasts for seven days. There are seven principles of Kwanza, one for each day. The first principle is Umoja, which means unity, the decision to strive for and maintain unity in self and community. The principle for yesterday, the second day, was Kujichagulia—self-determination—the decision to define ourselves, name ourselves, and speak for ourselves, instead of being defined and spoken for by others. Today is the third day of Kwanza, and the principle for to-day is Ujima—collective work and responsibility—the decision to build and maintain ourselves and our communities together and to recognize and solve our problems together.

Each of us is here now because in one way or another we share a commitment to language and to the power of language, and to the reclaiming of that language which has been made to work against us. In the transformation of silence into language and action, it is vitally necessary for each one of us to establish or examine her function in that transformation and to recognize her role as vital within that transformation.

For those of us who write, it is necessary to scrutinize not only the truth of what we speak, but the truth of that language by which we speak it. For others, it is to share and spread also those words that are meaningful to us. But primarily for us all, it is necessary to teach by living and speaking those truths which we believe and know beyond understanding. Because in this way alone we can survive, by taking part in a process of life that is creative and continuing, that is growth.

And it is never without fear—of visibility, of the harsh light of scrutiny and perhaps judgment, of pain, of death. But we have lived through all of those already, in silence, except death. And I remind myself all the time now that if I were to have been born mute, or had maintained an oath of silence my whole life long for safety, I would still have suffered, and I would still die. It is very good for establishing perspective.

And where the words of women are crying to be heard, we must each of us recognize our responsibility to seek those words out, to read them and share them and examine them in their pertinence to our lives. That we not hide behind the mockeries of separations that have been imposed upon us and which so often we accept as our own. For instance, "I can't possibly teach Black women's writing—their experience is so different from mine." Yet how many years have you spent teaching Plato and Shakespeare and Proust? Or another, "She's a white woman and what could she possibly have to say to me?" Or, "She's a lesbian, what would my husband say, or my chairman?" Or again, "This woman writes of her sons and I have no children." And all the other endless ways in which we rob ourselves of ourselves and each other.

We can learn to work and speak when we are afraid in the same way we have learned to work and speak when we are tired. For we have been socialized to respect fear more than our own needs for language and definition, and while we wait in silence for that final luxury of fearlessness, the weight of that silence will choke us.

The fact that we are here and that I speak these words is an attempt to break silence and bridge some of those differences between us, for it is not difference which immobilizes us, but silence. And there are so many silences to be broken.

69

Healing into Action

CHERIE BROWN AND GEORGE MAZZA

EVERYONE COUNTS

While workplaces and educational institutions need to be particularly sensitive to creating environments that welcome women and people of color, it is also important to remember that every person is important, even those who belong to majority groups. For

Activity

Consider the various ways you identify yourself (e.g. First Nation/Native-American, African heritage, European, male, Lutheran, bisexual, owning class, overweight, divorced, Canadian, etc.). Is there a part of your identity of which you are not proud, or that you tend to hide from people? One of the most profound blows to oppression is claiming legitimate delight in who we are. Try the phrase, "It's great to be _____ !" Notice where you struggle in claiming pride in who you are.

example, if White men feel that their concerns are insignificant, they may react with a backlash.

At a Southwestern US university, ugly, racist flyers that targeted Latino students were circulated on campus. To respond to the incidents, the university held a day-long assembly for all students in a huge auditorium.

At one point, a White male student mentioned that he was ashamed of being White and male. The group facilitators encouraged him to heal the shame by leaping into the air and shouting, "It's great to be a White man!" While he was leaping, they asked the rest of the students to applaud.

The next day, the dean of the campus said she was pretty sure she knew who had passed around the racist flyers. The student had come into her office and said, "If White men can also get applauded in diversity work, then I want to learn how to be part of leading prejudice reduction workshops here on campus."

When we take the time to listen to all voices, we can build even stronger intergroup coalitions.

ENCOURAGE ALL VOICES TO SPEAK

Building an environment that welcomes diversity requires gaining the active participation of all the people in the community. We can easily overlook the fact that most meetings favor people who are articulate and willing to speak in public. Because they have been told that their opinions are unimportant,

Activity

Here are ways to encourage greater participation at group meetings and ensure that key voices are heard:

- When a topic is up for discussion, ask the entire group to form pairs. Within the pairs, each person takes a set amount of time to think out loud. Without comment, one person simply listens attentively to the other person. Once the group reconvenes, everyone already has a point of view to contribute.
- Set ground rules. For example, you might establish the rule that no one speaks a second time before everyone has a chance to speak once.
- Ask group members to set personal goals. For those who tend to dominate discussions, ask them to listen and encourage the participation of others. For those who tend to become invisible in groups, ask them to try responding to every question.

Activity

At work or in your neighborhood, practice asking people who belong to groups other than your own how they may continue to experience discrimination. We may be embarrassed, thinking that by just asking such questions we're demonstrating how uninformed we are. The opposite is actually true. There is no way we can know about the experience of others without asking.

Imagine what workplaces could be like if we were open to asking about and listening to how our colleagues experience mistreatment as members of particular groups.

---

members of minority groups often find it hard to speak up in mixed groups.

A number of women who attended the United Nations Women's Conference in China in 1995 noticed that women from developing countries would not readily speak in the sessions, while women from western countries always had plenty to say. Even when the session moderator would specifically encourage women from non-western countries to contribute, US women would quickly jump in and dominate the discussion.

Eventually, attentive moderators had to set ground rules that encouraged the participation of the whole group.

INDIVIDUALS HAVE DIFFERENT NEEDS

A common response to diversity programs is, "Why are we always focusing on group differences? Wouldn't it be better if we simply treated everyone as a unique human being?" Although that is a worthy goal, it is also important to remember that many people have been mistreated as members of a group. When we ignore the ways in which groups have been historically oppressed, we may fail to see the important needs of individuals in that group.

Two colleagues, Barbara, an African-American woman, and Connie, a White woman, were on a business trip together. After a day of meetings, they decided to have dinner together at the small country

inn where they were staying. Barbara had invited a male colleague, who was also African-American, to join them.

While they were waiting, Barbara kept nervously rushing out to the lobby to see if her friend had arrived. After the third time, Connie said, "Hey, relax! This is a small inn. He'll find us. What's going on?"

Barbara responded, "I can't just relax. Black men always get stopped in hotel lobbies, because the hotel staff often automatically assume that a Black man couldn't possibly have any business in a place like this. I want to make sure he gets treated right."

By thinking that her Black colleague had the same experiences she had, Connie was unable to see how Barbara was still having to handle racism.

PAST TRAUMAS OFTEN COLOR THE PRESENT

The fierce battles we carry on in the present often have nothing to do with the present, but can be traced to similar situations in the past. Unless we actively seek to heal the past and separate it from the present, we are bound to repeat inappropriate behavior. Whenever a person or situation is making us excessively angry or frightened, chances are good that those reactions have only a little to do with the actual situation in the present and a whole lot to do with unhealed wrongs in the past.

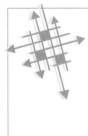

Activity

Think of a person or situation in the present that is giving you a hard time. Ask yourself the following questions:

1. Of whom does this person remind me?
2. How is this person similar to that person (or situation) from the past? How is this person (or situation) different?
3. What do I still need to say to that person in the past that will enable me to separate that relationship from this one?
4. If I were to see the present situation as a completely new opportunity, unencumbered by past experiences, how would I take charge of it?

A supervisor was about to fire a member of her staff who had come late to work several mornings in a row. When the supervisor described the situation, she said, "I feel violated by the staff person's behavior. After all I've done for her, she's completely abandoning me."

As it turned out, this supervisor had been abandoned by a parent early in life and tended to see the world through a lens of pending abandonment.

In response to her supervisor's concerns, the staff person said, "It's none of her business why I was late. I don't need to tell her everything about my personal life." The staff person was raised by a domineering mother who demanded to know her daughter's whereabouts at all times. Carrying this injury with her, the staff person did not want to tell her supervisor that personal crises at home caused her to be late.

Both the supervisor and the staff person were playing out past unhealed patterns, which, if left unchallenged, would undermine their current work together.

WE CHOOSE OUR ATTITUDES

We may not have control over what people say, but we do have control over our attitudes. Instead of getting upset when we listen to painful or abusive talk, we can decide, "This is a wonderful opportunity to make contact with someone, to have a useful and open dialogue that might change someone's perspective."

A Korean-American mediator was asked to work with a Washington, DC, neighborhood in which a conflict arose between African-American residents and Korean-American merchants. The Black community decided to boycott Korean shops in the

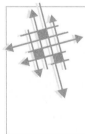

Activity

Welcome whatever negative comments come your way. Cultivate the attitude that you are lucky when someone hands you an offensive comment, because you can't wait to try handling it in a way that may lead to genuine change. Stepping beyond powerlessness, it is possible to choose an attitude that puts you in charge of any situation.

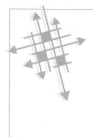

Activity

In a tense situation, remember how good the other person is and how hard he or she may be struggling to do the right thing. For example, you might say, "I know how committed you are to having this project go well, and I appreciate how much effort you are putting into working things out with me."

aftermath of the killing of a Black teenager. The young man had been robbing a small Korean shop when the owner shot him.

The mediator met with an African-American woman, who was a leader in the neighborhood. The woman screamed, "You come into our neighborhoods, and you have no concern for our community! You just take our money and run."

Instead of attacking back or challenging the woman, the mediator responded, "This is exactly the kind of honest dialogue I've been looking to hear. I'm so glad you're telling me all this. I want to know more."

Later, the Korean-American mediator commented, "I don't think this was what she expected to hear from someone with an Asian face like mine, because the woman looked at me in complete shock. Then, the woman's attitude shifted, and she said, 'I do know how your people must feel. Some of these young kids come into the neighborhood and have no respect for anyone, even for their own people. We both, Koreans and Blacks in the neighborhood, need to figure out what to do together.'"

REACH FOR HIGHER GROUND

We begin with the assumption that humans are always doing the best they can. No one wants to be ineffective. Therefore, there is no room for blame, but plenty of room for reminding people how good they are and how well they are already doing.

While Alvin and Cherie were waiting in the airport for their next flight, they saw a mother traveling with two young children, a boy and a girl. The mother lost her temper and smacked the girl hard

across the face. The daughter shrieked, tears flowed down her cheeks. The other passengers in the area muffled gasps and cast their eyes to the floor.

Deciding they had to do something, Al and Cherie said to the mother, "Having a hard day?"

The mother answered, "I'm having a horrible day. My husband couldn't be with us, and the kids are fighting and driving me crazy."

While Al continued to listen to the mother, Cherie struck up a conversation with the little girl. Al and Cherie listened to them without offering advice and in the process, both mother and daughter relaxed considerably. It only took five minutes.

It never weakens us to be generous, to assume the best of each other. Prejudice reduction work requires tremendous patience and generosity. We never know the difficulties that another person is bearing.

70

Vanilla Voices

Researching White Men's Diversity Learning Journeys

MICHAEL WELP

How do White men learn about diversity? What triggers awareness, learning, and advocacy toward inclusion and equity? These are questions I explored in my research and apply in my diversity work. I have several reasons for being interested in this topic. First, as a White man, I strive to continue my own learning and development. Second, I feel I can best contribute to diversity by helping those like myself start or continue their journey in learning to become full partners in diversity for their organizations. Through this process, I have changed both how I approach research and the way I facilitate learning in groups. In this article, I will explore my journey and insights I've gained along the way.

First, I must sketch out my background. Growing up in Iowa did not expose me to many elements of racial and ethnic diversity. Later, living in Washington, D.C., I began to understand racism, sexism, and heterosexism because I was involved in a graduate program that included intensive group learning on diversity issues.[1] I began to see the subtle threads of racism, sexism, and homophobia woven into my upbringing. I was hungry to learn more and spent a year working in South Africa facilitating interracial team building for mining groups and other South African corporations. I realized I could contribute most by returning to the United States and working on these issues with people like myself.

Back in the United States, it was in the context of a doctorate program that I began researching the learning journeys of White men who are strong advocates for diversity (Welp, 1997).

THE SEARCH FOR VALIDITY: CROSSING DIFFERENCES

My first challenge was to figure out how to identify men who fit the strong advocate description. Who am I, a White man, to say someone is living his or her life in a way that demonstrates advocacy toward diversity? Research done by a colleague, Mark Scanlon-Greene (1996), indicated that White men as a group have negative credibility when it comes to diversity and must compensate by establishing credibility as an individual. Could I be seen as credible as a White man researching White men and diversity? The media image often portrayed is of the angry White male, and rumors in many organizations quietly talk about the cluelessness of White men when it comes to diversity. How could I establish credibility, and how would I gain perspective that I may be missing as a White

man? Here I realized the importance of validating across difference and created two structures for accomplishing this aim.

First, my dissertation committee served as a source of multiple group perspectives. My committee consisted of an African American woman and man, a White woman, and three White men. This diversity allowed for perspectives across difference to be incorporated into the design and execution of my research at each stage.

Second, my committee chair and I created a nomination process to identify candidates for my study that we hoped would validate across differences. We created a nomination committee consisting of 6 people from each of the following categories: men of color, women of color, White women, and White men. All 24 nominators were senior practitioners in my field of organization development. Each of them nominated 10 White men whom they saw as strong advocates for diversity. I was curious who would be nominated by at least 1 White woman, 1 woman of color, 1 man of color, and another White man. I found 8 candidates who were identified at least once by someone from each of these four nominator categories. This approach to developing a specialized pool of research participants is in accord with the naturalistic inquiry principle of purposive sampling (Lincoln & Guba, 1985). By using this nomination approach, I was in essence triangulating the nomination process with those who view issues of inclusion and equity from different perspectives. There was a consensus across key elements of difference that created validation of my study sample. As a White man studying White men, my research was strengthened by including perspectives across difference.

All 8 candidates agreed to be in my study. Most of the White men in my study work as consultants, with their work representing a key avenue through which they demonstrate their advocacy. In defining advocacy, I have drawn from Rob Williams's (1989) dissertation on the process of becoming a social advocate. He noted that the Latin root for *advocate* comes from the Latin verb *advocatus*, which means "to give voice to." Williams defined social advocate as one who:

1. represents a minority expression concerning social or economic change;
2. . . . [demonstrates] commitment of significant personal resources;
3. . . . uses direct action, including civil disobedience and resistance, to effect social changes;
4. . . . [is part] of a small group who first brings to public attention a social issue; and
5. . . . [is] generally recognized by those he or she speaks for, by the media and by other institutions as a spokesperson. . . .

I then adapted his criteria for my own definition of advocacy to include:

• willing to take a stand to support inclusion and equity in the face of resistance;
• being one of a small group who brings attention to these issues;
• recognized by women, people of color, and gay, lesbian, bisexual, disabled, and other marginalized groups as an advocate as well as by other White men;
• demonstrated commitment of significant time and resources.

All participants were between 50 and 60 years of age, except one who was 45. All currently serve as external consultants, blending the areas of organization change and development with diversity issues. For most, consulting is their primary career, except for 1 who is a full-time professor of sociology. Four participants were raised Catholic, 2 Lutheran, 1 Jewish, 1 Methodist, and 1 described his background as Christian. All participants declared themselves straight, making this a study of 8 heterosexual White men. Participants all were either married or had been married. All had either raised or are currently raising children. I noted no physical disability and heard of no learning disabilities. All declared themselves as middle class or upper-middle class in their current lives. With these similarities and differences, a common pattern of their journey toward advocating diversity emerged.

KEY RESEARCH FINDINGS

Crossing differences turned out to be a key element in catalyzing learning. A key finding in my research was that nearly all of the diversity learning for the White men in my study came through relationships across difference. As described by one participant:

There is something about becoming friends with somebody who's very different with you, and yet, in a personal way, in ways where you're vulnerable, in which people really are able to see all of—where I'm hanging out there who I am. . . . My experience [was] that [in] those kinds of experiences when I developed intimate personal relationships with somebody, it felt like it ratcheted my understanding, my ability to understand myself, and my willingness to take risks in relationships and in speaking out for what I felt was important.

As noted in the following example, these relationships with White women and people of color provided the critical synergy of both support and challenge for diversity learning to occur:

I think it's fair to say, yeah, I got challenged. In some ways the challenges always came out of a relatively supportive place. I got plenty of feedback about things that were inappropriate. . . . I would say the most effective challenges came from the people that were most supportive and probably vice versa—the most supportive people were also challenging.

Within the context of these relationships, the White men often were able to reinterpret their earlier life experiences of engaging with differences from a broader context, sometimes seeing systemic oppression for the first time. As demonstrated by one participant, a critical step in the learning process was shifting from a sole focus on seeing people as individuals to also seeing a systemic perspective:

Understanding oppression . . . was a big one. I [had] never thought of that. You know, 10 years ago, I couldn't have talked about oppression, that we're in a system that seems to feed on itself and build on itself regardless of what we do. That was a big jump for me, [as was] the notion of the difference between individual, group, and system. I mean, I couldn't understand as an individual how [anyone could] think I was racist. . . . And yet, my colleagues would see me as a White man. I couldn't understand that. So, at a group level I worked to understand it. On a systemic level I understand it very well now. Until I made that shift I couldn't be successful.

Finally, another major finding was the lack of other White male role models for these men. This was evident in each of their journeys, with the exception of the youngest man. In fact, most of the White men found it difficult connecting with other White men. There seemed to be an early separation in many of their journeys from the White male culture. Many are still searching for a way to reconnect in a more satisfying way with White men as a group:

I spent a lot of years really being angry at White men and sort of up on my own soapbox about how good I was and how stupid they were. And I still find myself being really angry sometimes with White men. But I think as time has gone on what I realize is that we are so deeply, as my son would say, psychologicalized, around our dominance, and our importance, and the arrogance which isn't seen as arrogance, that it's very hard work to undo your own work, and then to begin to change the system. . . . So, I think part of what I decided, some time ago, was if you hang in there and at least treat people with respect, even though I get angry and sometimes say to them, you know, you are the problem . . . I say that in a way that it doesn't just piss them off and alienate them about doing anything.

Learning how to connect to other White men as a group is an ongoing challenge for all White male advocates in this study. One participant described one aspect of this transition as movement away from a "reacting-against mentality" and toward an "acting-for mentality." This involved a shift of motivation away from a base of anger and toward more love, compassion, and faith:

I came out of that much more balanced psychologically, much gentler, much [more] able to embrace White men in their struggle, much less likely to trash White men. . . . [I was more able] to embrace and enter, because I could enter myself in a new way, so I could enter other people in a new way.

He later summed up his learning by saying, "The only way to connect to other White males is

through love." How this happens and how it incorporates the critical aspects of support and challenge are still being discovered. This is at the heart of my diversity work today with White men.

As mentioned earlier, White men do not look to other White men for learning about diversity, and relationships across difference had been the sole source of knowledge and wisdom. In sharing this finding at a national conference, a woman of color was agitated: "If we are the ones who will educate all the White men, that's overwhelming." It is a burden for White women and people of color to always be the ones to educate White men about differences.

To address this burden, after my dissertation research I partnered with another White man and began exploring ways White men could support and challenge each other to further our own diversity learning journeys. For the last 4 years, my colleague, Bill Proudman, and I have been offering 3-day intensive workshops for White men called the White Men's Caucus on Eliminating Racism, Sexism, and Homophobia in Organizations[2] (see Atkinson, 2001). In these workshops, we create a new possibility—a new opening. White men learn how to challenge and support each other to further each other's diversity learning journeys. The result is that relationships across difference can be just that—relationships—and not a one-way burden for others educating White men about differences.

VALIDATING OUR OWN VOICES: WORKING WITHIN DIFFERENCE

Part of the first step for White men in learning from each other (learning within differences vs. across differences) is in validating our own voices. The men in my study were given the power to alter the narrative I wrote about them after an extended interview. The interview stimulated extensive reflection for many of them, beginning to counter the notion that as White men, we do not see ourselves as a source of wisdom on this topic. Because advocating diversity is an important part of their identity, they all chose to use their real names in my research so that the dissertation itself became another avenue for their voice and advocacy. Their voices ran counter to the dominant social narrative that White men are clueless around diversity and consequently, validated an alternative narrative of White men advocating diversity.

After doing the interviews, I also found I needed to reflect on my own diversity learning journey. My own selfish interest was that I wanted to learn how these men grew in their diversity learning so that I could discover more of my own pathway. Indeed, each man's story was both a window into their journey and a mirror to reflect on my journey. I was hungry to hear how they had resolved some dilemmas I was facing. For instance, how do you balance the need to continually challenge yourself to step up to the work of challenging oppression yet also accept yourself for the White man you are? How do you love the White male part of you that you have learned is privileged and triggers rage in others? How do you approach other White men? Do you educate other White men on diversity from a place of anger or love? Rather than pretend I was an "objective" researcher, I recognized my own questions, confusion, and insights as part of the research process. In fact, halfway through my data analysis phase, I had to stop and create my own diversity learning life map to keep my own issues and perspectives sorted during the data analysis. Researching within difference triggered self-reflection that enhanced the data collection process. My dissertation became a process of my claiming my own voice and "coming out" as a strong White male advocate for diversity.

Since then, the opportunity to work with White men on diversity issues from a variety of organizations has produced fruitful learning. What follows are some pertinent insights that help White men understand themselves.

VANILLA IS A CULTURE

Most White men in America don't believe they have a culture. Culture is something others have. Upon reflection, some White men would name it a "watered down European culture." Some say they feel "vanilla." Most White men never have to leave their culture and assume their reality is universal reality.

Similarly, a fish that never leaves water doesn't totally grasp what water is and that life can be different elsewhere. The paradox is that you don't really understand your culture unless you leave it. My experience is that what we refer to as "dominant American culture" is often White male culture. Gert Hofstede's (1980) classic study of American culture turned out to be essentially all White men who worked at IBM. Most institutions were formed by White men and exemplify White male culture. I once described White male cultural attributes to a major multinational corporation, and their first reaction was that it was a perfect description of their performance appraisal system. Women, people of color, and other groups can often describe White male culture because they have to assimilate into it. White men look around and see diversity but don't realize the quiet pressure others feel to conform to a culture most White men assume is universal reality. The hidden cost to White men is that they live in a White male "cultural box" that limits their identity, freedom, and quality of relationships. Embracing diversity ultimately offers White men awareness and choice about who they want to be.

So, what is this White male cultural box? Describing White male culture is tricky. Culture defines shared group assumptions and characteristics and does not fully describe everyone in that group. It is a both/and: White men are both unique individuals and members of a group, that share a culture. My descriptions pertain most to heterosexual White men. My colleague and I have described heterosexual White male culture in more detail elsewhere. Here is a brief summary of some of the elements of heterosexual White male culture (Proudman, 2001; Welp, 2001):

- rugged individualism with a survivor mentality;
- focus on doing, action, and task completion;
- focus on rationality;
- time is linear, focus on the future;
- low tolerance for uncertainty;
- focus on status and rank over connection.

There are several direct implications of heterosexual White male culture on the diversity learning process for White men. Perhaps the most challenging is the aspect of rugged individualism. Most White men see themselves as individuals and do not see themselves as part of a "White male" group. They may see women and people of color as a group, but see other White men as a collection of individuals. This makes it extremely difficult to understand that they may belong to a group that has systemic advantage. This can be especially true if at the individual level they do not feel any sense of advantage or privilege in their day-to-day lives.

The label *White male* in our culture also brings up connotations of extremist groups, thus creating more resistance to exploring the White male part of themselves. In addition, who gets included in the group called *White men* has some ambiguity to it. Some White men differentiate themselves from being a White man based on religion, class, ancestry, sexual orientation, or physical ability.

Other aspects of White male culture influence learning as well. The cultural attribute Hofstede (1980) called "low tolerance for uncertainty" predisposes White men to want to simplify the complex issue of diversity. Often this means thinking in either/or terms, such as I am either an individual or a member of the White male group but not both. Part of the challenge of learning about diversity is accepting the complexity of the issues diversity touches. The White male cultural predisposition toward action and doing means we often feel a need to solve the problems of diversity as we become aware of them. The individualistic Marlboro man/lone ranger needs to ride off and fix it rather than hanging in there to develop a comprehensive understanding of it or to look deeper inside himself. Furthermore, the high value placed on rationality over emotions leads White men to try to understand diversity from the head although much of the learning comes from stories of other groups' experiences that can best be comprehended from the heart.

Having groups of White men meeting together in a caucus for 3 days has offered a special opportunity where White men begin to become aware of White male culture and its effect on them in the here and now. The culture plays itself out, and we can call attention to it. Tannen (1995) described the tendency for men to focus on status and rank over connection, and it is often visible here. One morning in a caucus I wrote on a flipchart the following reflection question: How much of your energy is going toward comparing status and rank with other White men in the room, and how much of your energy is going into connecting and affirming each White male present? Just having the men conscious of this question changed the dynamic in the room toward deeper sharing and openness. As facilitators, Bill and I have shifted from a neutral facilitator to doing our own work and modeling engagement in the learning processes we are attempting to create for others. Not doing my own work would give the other men in the room permission to do the same. White men working within difference can engage in learning processes that transform White male cultural norms.

HOLDING WHITE MEN UP TO THE LIGHT OF DIVERSITY

The focal point of diversity is rarely on White men. With race, the focus is on people of color; with gender, the focus is on women; and with sexual orientation, the focus is on gays, lesbians, and bisexuals. What never gets examined is heterosexual White men. White men internalize this pattern to think diversity is not about them. Diversity is seen as everyone else's problem. Being together with other White men and exploring diversity allows White men to discover their own self-interest and realize there are costs for them of the current system. The ultimate privilege for White men is that they never have to leave their culture and thus rarely have to think about diversity. The ultimate cost for this privilege is low self-awareness of White male culture. This translates into lack of choicefulness of who one is and who one wants to be. The gifts of diversity for White men include the freedom to be truly themselves as individuals and deepening relationships through transcending the limitations of the status and rank aspect of White male culture. This deeper journey of diversity learning comes from learning within difference and allows one to be much more effective across difference.

NOTES

1. My graduate degree program was the American University/NTL Institute's Master's Program in Organization Development. See www.auntl.org.
2. See www.WMFDP.com.

REFERENCES

1. Atkinson, W. (2001). Bringing diversity to White men. *HR Magazine*, 46 (9).
2. Hofstede, G. (1980). *Culture's consequences: International differences in work related values.* Beverly Hills, CA: Sage.
3. Lincoln, Y. S., & Guba, E. G. (1985). *Naturalistic inquiry.* Beverly Hills, CA: Sage.
4. Proudman, B. (2001). *Understanding American White male culture.* Unpublished manuscript.
5. Scanlon-Greene, M. E. (1996). *White males and diversity work: A grounded theory study.* Unpublished doctoral dissertation, The Fielding Graduate Institute.
6. Tannen, D. (1995). *Talking from 9 to 5: Women and men in the workplace; Language, sex and power.* New York: Avon.
7. Welp, M. G. (1997). *Pathways to diversity for White males: A study of White males' learning experiences on the path toward advocating for inclusion and equity.* Unpublished doctoral dissertation, The Fielding Institute.
8. Welp, M. G. (2001). The treasures and challenges of diversity for White males. In A. Arrien (Ed.). *Working together: Diversity as opportunity.* San Francisco: Berrett-Koehler.
9. Williams, R. L. (1989). *Finding voice: The transition from individualism to social advocacy.* Unpublished doctoral dissertation, The Fielding Graduate Institute.

✻ 71

Real Men Join the Movement

MICHAEL KIMMEL

Cory Shere didn't go to Duke University to become a profeminist man. He was going to be a doctor, covering his bets with a double major in engineering and premed. But his experiences with both organic chemistry and feminist women conspired to lead this affable and earnest 20-year-old Detroit native in a different direction. Now in his junior year, he still has a double major—women's studies and psychology. And he works with a group of men to raise awareness about sexual assault and date rape.

Eric Freedman wasn't profeminist either, when he arrived at Swarthmore College three years ago. A 20-year-old junior literature major from Syracuse, New York, he became involved in a campus antiracism project and began to see the connections among different struggles for equality. At an antiracism workshop he helped organize, he suddenly found himself speaking about male privilege as well as white privilege. This fall, he's starting a men's group to focus on race and gender issues.

Who are these guys? And what are they doing in the women's movement?

They are among a growing number of profeminist men around the country. These aren't the angry divorcés who whine about how men are the new victims of reverse discrimination, nor are they the weekend warriors trooping off to a mythopoetic retreat. They're neither Promise Keepers nor Million Man Marchers vowing to be responsible domestic patriarchs on a nineteenth-century model.

You might think of profeminist men as the "other" men's movement, but I prefer to consider it the "real" men's movement, because by actively supporting women's equality on the job or on the streets and by quietly changing their lives to create that equality at home, profeminist men are also transforming the definition of masculinity. Perhaps this is the movement about which Gloria Steinem rhapsodized when she wrote how women "want a men's movement. We are literally dying for it."

Profeminist men staff the centers where convicted batterers get counseling, organize therapy for rapists and sex offenders in prison, do the workshops on preventing sexual harassment in the workplace or on confronting the impact of pornography in men's lives. On campus, they're organizing men's events during Take Back the Night marches; presenting programs on sexual assault to fraternities, dorms, and athletic teams; taking courses on masculinity; and founding campus groups with acronyms like MAC (Men Acting for Change), MOST (Men Opposed to Sexist Tradition), MASH (Men Against Sexual Harassment), MASA (Men Against Sexual Assault), and, my current favorite, MARS (Men Against Rape and

Sexism). Maybe John Gray was right after all— real men *are* from Mars!

FEMINISM AND MEN'S LIVES

I first met Cory, Eric, and about a dozen other young profeminist men in April at the Young Feminist Summit, organized by NOW, in Washington, D.C. They were pretty easy to spot among the nearly one thousand young women from colleges all over the country. As we talked during an impromptu workshop, I heard them describe both the exhilaration and isolation of becoming part of the struggle for women's equality, the frustrations of dealing with other men, the active suspicions and passive indifference of other students.

It felt painfully familiar. I've spent nearly two decades in feminist politics, first as an activist in antirape and antibattery groups, and later helping to organize the National Organization for Men Against Sexism (NOMAS), a network of profeminist men and women around the country. More recently, I've tried to apply the insights of academic feminist theory to men's lives, developing courses on men, debating with Robert Bly and his followers, and writing a history of the idea of manhood in the United States.

Of course, men like Cory and Eric are a distinct minority on campus. They compete with the angry voice of backlash, those shrill interruptions that scream "Don't blame me, I never raped anyone! Leave me alone!" They compete with that now familiar men-as-victims whine. Men, we hear, are terrified of going to work or on a date, lest they be falsely accused of sexual harassment or date rape; they're unable to support their scheming careerist wives, yet are vilified as bad fathers if they don't provide enough child support to keep their ex-wives in Gucci and Donna Karan after the divorce.

In the public imagination, profeminist men also compete with the mythopoetic vision of the men's movement as a kind of summer-camp retreat, and the earnest evangelical Promise Keepers with their men-only sports-themed rallies, and the Million Man March's solemn yet celebratory atonement. All offer men solace and soul-work, and promise to heal men's pain and enable them to become more nurturing and loving. All noble goals, to be sure. But to profeminist men, you don't build responsibility and democracy by exclusion—of women, or of gays and lesbians.

And profeminist men compete with the most deafening sound coming from the mouths of American men when the subject is feminism: silence. Most men, on campus and off, exude an aura of studied indifference to feminism. Like the irreverent second child at the Passover seder, they ask, "What has this to do with me?"

A lot. Sure, feminism is the struggle of more than one-half of the population for equal rights. But it's also about rethinking identities, our relationships, the meanings of our lives. For men, feminism is not only about what we *can't* do—like commit violence, harassment, or rape—or *shouldn't* do, like leave all the child care and housework to our wives. It's also about what we *can* do, what we *should* do, and even what we *want* to do—like be a better father, friend, or partner. "Most men know that it is to all of our advantage—women and men alike—for women to be equal," noted NOW President Patricia Ireland, in her Summit keynote address. Far from being only about the loss of power, feminism will also enable men to live the lives we say we want to live.

This isn't the gender cavalry, arriving in the nick of time to save the damsels from distress. "Thanks for bringing this sexism stuff to our attention, ladies," one might imagine them saying. "We'll take it from here." And it's true that some men declare themselves feminists just a bit too effortlessly, especially if they think it's going to help them get a date. (A friend calls it "premature self-congratulation," and it's just as likely to leave women feeling shortchanged.)

In part, this explains why I call them "profeminist men" and not "feminist men" or "male feminists." As an idea, it seems to me, feminism involves an empirical observation—that women are not equal—and the moral position that declares they should be. Of course, men may share this empirical observation and take this moral stance. And to that extent men support feminism as an ideal. But feminism as an identity also involves the felt experience of that inequality.

And this men do not have, because men are privileged by sexism. To be sure, men may be oppressed—by race, class, ethnicity, sexuality, age, physical ability—but men are not oppressed *as men*. Since only women have that felt experience of oppression about gender, it seems sensible to make a distinction in how we identify ourselves. Men can support feminism and can call ourselves "antisexist" or "profeminist." I've chosen profeminist because, like feminism, it stresses the positive and forward-looking.

In a sense, I think of profeminist men as the Gentlemen's Auxiliary of Feminism. This honorable position acknowledges that we play a part in this social transformation, but not the most significant part. It's the task of the Gentlemen's Auxiliary to make feminism comprehensible to men, not as a loss of power—which has thus far failed to "trickle down" to most individual men anyway—but as a challenge to the false sense of entitlement we have to that power in the first place. Profeminism is about supporting both women's equality and other men's efforts to live more ethically consistent and more emotionally resonant lives.

★ ★ ★

The routes taken by today's profeminist men are as varied as the men themselves. But most do seem to have some personal experience that made gender inequality more concrete. For some, it involved their mother. (Remember President Clinton describing how he developed his commitment to women's equality when he tried to stop his stepfather from hitting his mother? Of course, one wishes that commitment had facilitated more supportive policy initiatives.) Max Sadler, a 17-year-old senior at Trinity High School in New York City, watched his professional mother hit her head on the glass ceiling at her high-powered corporate job—a job she eventually quit to join a company with more women in high-level positions. Max shared her frustration and also felt ashamed at the casual attitudes of her male colleagues.

Shehzad Nadeem, a 19-year-old student at James Madison University in Virginia, remembered the way his older sister described her experiences. "I could barely believe the stories she told me, yet something deep inside told me that they were not only true, but common. I realized that we men are actively or passively complicit in women's oppression, and that we have to take an active role in challenging other men." Shehzad joined MOST (Men Opposed to Sexist Tradition), which has presented workshops on violence and sexual assault at Madison dorms.

★ ★ ★

Or perhaps it was having a feminist girlfriend, or even just having women friends, that brought these issues to the fore for men. "I grew up with female friends who were as ambitious, smart, achieving, and confident as I thought I was—on a good day," recalls Jason Schultz, a founder of MAC at Duke, who now organizes men's programs to combat campus sexual assault. "When I got to college, these same women began calling themselves feminists. When I heard men call women 'dumb chicks' I knew something was wrong."

★ ★ ★

THE PROFEMINIST "CLICK!"

But there has to be more than the presence of feminist role models, challenges from girlfriends, brilliant assignments, or challenging support from professors. After all, we all have women in our lives, and virtually all of those women have had some traumatic encounter with sexism. There has to be something else.

Feminists call it the "click!"—that moment when they realize that their pain, fears, confusion, and anger are not theirs alone, but are shared with other women. Do profeminist men have "clicks!"? Yes, but they don't typically come from righteous indignation or fear, but rather from guilt and shame, a gnawing sense of implication in something larger and more pervasive than individual intention. It's that awful moment when you hear women complain about "men" in general and realize, even just a little bit, that you are what they're talking about. (Much of men's reactive defensiveness seems to be a hedge against these feelings of shame.)

Suddenly, it's not those "bad" men "out there" who are the problem—it's all men. Call it the Pogo revelation: "We have met the enemy, and he is us."

That's certainly the way it felt for Jeff Wolf (not his real name). A sexually naive college sophomore, he found himself growing closer and closer to a woman friend, Annie, during a study date. They talked long into the night and eventually kissed. One thing began to lead to another, and both seemed eager and pleased to be with the other. Just before penetration, though, Jeff felt Annie go limp. "Her eyes glazed over, and she went kind of numb," he recalled, still wincing at the memory.

This is the moment that many a college guy dreams of—her apparent surrender to his desire, even if it was induced by roofies or alcohol. It's a moment when men often space out, preferring to navigate the actual encounter on automatic pilot, fearing that emotional connection will lead to an early climax.

As Annie slipped into this mental coma, though, Jeff stayed alert, as engaged emotionally as he was physically. "What had been so arousing was the way we had been connecting intellectually and emotionally," he said. After some patient prodding, she finally confessed that she'd been raped as a high school sophomore, and ever since, had used this self-protective strategy to get through a sexual encounter without reliving her adolescent trauma. Jeff, it seemed, was the first guy who noticed.

★ ★ ★

Others say their "click!" experience happened later in life. In the 1970s, psychologist David Greene was deeply involved in political activism, when he and his wife had a baby. "Not that much changed for me; I still went around doing my thing, but now there was a baby in it." On the other hand, his wife's life was totally transformed by the realities of round-the-clock child care. She'd become a mother. "After several weeks of this, she sat me down and confronted me," he recalls. "The bankruptcy of my politics quickly became clear to me. I was an oppressor, an abuser of privilege—I'd become the enemy I thought I was fighting against." The couple meticulously divided housework and child care, and David learned that revolutions are fought out in people's kitchens as well as in the jungles of Southeast Asia. Terry Kupers, a 54-year-old psychiatrist, and author of *Revisioning Men's Lives,*

remembers his first wife initiating some serious talks about the "unstated assumptions we were making about housework, cooking, and whose time was more valuable." Not only did Kupers realize that his wife was right, "but I also realized I liked things better the new way."

★ ★ ★

PROFEMINISM TODAY—AND TOMORROW

And just as sisterhood is global, so too are profeminist men active around the world. Men from nearly 50 countries—from Mexico to Japan—regularly contribute to a newsletter of international profeminist scholars and activists, according to its editor, Oystein Holter, a Norwegian researcher. Scandinavian men are working to implement a gender equity mandated by law. Liisa Husu, a senior advisor to Finland's gender equity commission, has developed a parliamentary subcommittee of concerned men. (When I met with them last fall, we spent our day discussing our mutual activities, after which they whisked me off to an all-male sauna resort on the shore of an icy Baltic Sea for a bit of male-bonding as a follow-up to all that equity work.) Scandinavian men routinely take parental leave; in fact, in Sweden and Norway they've introduced "Daddy days," an additional month of paid paternity leave for the men to have some time with their newborns after the mothers have returned to work. About half of Swedish men take paternal leave, according to fatherhood expert Lars Jalmert at the University of Stockholm.

The world's most successful profeminist organization must be Canada's White Ribbon Campaign. Begun in 1991 to coincide with the second anniversary of the Montreal Massacre—when a young man killed 14 women engineering students at the University of Montreal on December 6, 1989—its goal was to publicly and visibly declare opposition to men's violence against women by encouraging men to wear a white ribbon as a public pledge. "Within days, hundreds of thousands of men and boys across Canada wore a ribbon," noted Michael Kaufman, one of the campaign's founders. "It exceeded our wildest expectations—even the prime minister wore a ribbon." This year, WRC events are also planned for Norway, Australia, and several U.S. colleges; in Canada, events include an Alberta hockey team planning a skating competition to raise money for a local women's shelter. WRC organizers have also developed curricula for secondary schools to raise the issue for boys.

But just as surely, some of the most important and effective profeminist men's activities are taking place in American homes every day, as men increasingly share housework and child care, reorganize their schedules to be more responsive to the needs of their families, and even downsize their ambitions to develop a family strategy that does not revolve exclusively around *his* career path. "Housework remains the last frontier" for men to tame, argues sociologist Kathleen Gerson in her book *No Man's Land.* . . .

But the payoff is significant. If power were a scarce commodity or a zero-sum game, we might think that women's increased power would mean a decrease in men's. And since most men don't feel very powerful anyway, the possibilities of further loss are rather unappealing. But for most men, all the power in the world does not seem to have trickled down to enable individual men to live the lives we say we want to live—lives of intimacy, integrity, and individual expression. By demanding the redistribution of power along more equitable lines, feminism also seeks a dramatic shift in our social priorities, our choices about how we live, and what we consider important. Feminism is also a blueprint for men about how to become the men we want to be, and profeminist men believe that men will live happier, healthier, and more emotionally enriched lives by supporting women's equality.

Part of profeminist men's politics is to visibly and vocally support women's equality, and part of it is to quietly and laboriously struggle to implement that public stance into our own lives. And part of it must be to learn to confront and challenge other men, with care and commitment. "This cause is not altogether and exclusively woman's cause," wrote Frederick Douglass in 1848. "It is the cause of human brotherhood as well as human sisterhood, and both must rise and fall together."

72

Learn the Facts About Lesbian and Gay Families

CLINTON ANDERSON

Many lesbians and gay men are parents. In the 2000 U.S. Census, 33 percent of female same-sex couple households and 22 percent of male same-sex couple households reported at least one child under the age of 18 living in the home. Despite the significant presence of at least 163,879 households headed by lesbian or gay parents in this country, many American policymakers continue to voice concerns about the soundness of lesbian and gay parents.[1]

There is no scientific basis for concluding that lesbian mothers or gay fathers are unfit parents on the basis of their sexual orientation.[2] While exposure to prejudice and discrimination based on sexual orientation may cause acute distress for lesbian and gay people,[3] there is no reliable evidence that homosexual orientation per se impairs psychological functioning.[4] Research also shows that lesbian and heterosexual women do not take markedly different approaches to child rearing.[5] Members of gay and lesbian couples with children divide the work involved in child care evenly and are generally satisfied with their relationships with their partners, research has shown.[6] In fact, the results of some studies suggest that lesbian mothers' parenting skills may be superior to those of matched heterosexual parents.[7] Overall, the research on lesbian and gay parents suggests that they are as likely as heterosexual parents to provide supportive and healthy environments for their children.[8]

Research also leads us to conclude that sexual identities (including gender identity, gender-role behavior, and sexual orientation) develop in much the same ways among children of lesbian mothers as they do among children of heterosexual parents.[9] Studies of other aspects of personal development (including personality, self-concept, and conduct) similarly reveal few differences between children of lesbian mothers and children of heterosexual parents.[10] (Although the research on gay fathers is less extensive than that on lesbian mothers,[11] the APA equally supports the rights of gay fathers and their children.) Evidence also suggests that children of lesbian and gay parents have normal social relationships with peers and adults.[12]

Generally, children of gay parents appear to be engaged in social life, comfortable interacting with peers, parents, family members, and friends. Fears about children of lesbian or gay parents being sexually abused by adults, ostracized by peers, or isolated in single-sex lesbian or gay communities have received no scientific support. Overall, results of research suggest that the development, adjustment, and well-being of children with lesbian and gay parents do not differ markedly from that of children with heterosexual parents.

The APA supports policy and legislation that promote safe, secure, and nurturing environments for all children.[13] We also have a long-established policy to deplore all public and private discrimination against gay men and lesbians and to urge the repeal of all discriminatory legislation against lesbians and gay men.[14] Discrimination against lesbian and gay parents deprives their children of benefits, rights, and privileges enjoyed by children of heterosexual married couples. Some jurisdictions prohibit gay and lesbian individuals and same-sex couples from adopting children, notwithstanding the great need for adoptive parents.[15] It's time to set the record straight, take a public stance for equality, and stop making public policies and laws based on misconceptions and prejudice.

NOTES

1. C.J. Patterson, M. Fulcher, and J. Wainright. "Children of Lesbian and Gay Parents: Research, Law, and Policy." In B.L. Bottoms, M.B. Kovera, and B.D. McAuliff (Eds.), *Children, Social Science and the Law.* New York: Cambridge University Press. 2002. pp. 176–199.

2. J.C. Armesto. "Developmental and Contextual Factors That Influence Gay Fathers' Parental Competence: A Review of the Literature." *Psychology of Men and Masculinity.* 3 (2002): pp. 67–78.
   C.J. Patterson. "Family Relationships of Lesbians and Gay Men." *Journal of Marriage and Family.* 62 (2000): pp. 1052–1069.
   F. Tasker and S. Golombok. *Growing Up in a Lesbian Family.* New York: Guilford Press. 1997.

3. J.J. Conger. Proceedings of the American Psychological Association, Incorporated, for the Year 1974: Minutes of the Annual Meeting of the Council of Representatives. *American Psychologist.* 30 (1975): pp. 620-651.
   V.M. Mays and S.D. Cochran. "Mental Health Correlates of Perceived Discrimination among Lesbian, Gay, and Bisexual Adults in the United States. *American Journal of Public Health.* 91 (2001): pp. 1869-1876.
   I.H. Meyer. "Prejudice, Social Stress, and Mental Health in Lesbian, Gay, and Bisexual Populations: Conceptual Issues and Research Evidence." *Psychological Bulletin.* 129 (2003): pp. 674–697.

4. C.J. Patterson. "Family Relationships of Lesbians and Gay Men." *Journal of Marriage and Family.* 62 (2000): pp. 1052–1069.
   C.J. Patterson. "Lesbian and Gay Parents and Their Children: Summary of Research Findings." *Lesbian and Gay Parenting: A Resource for Psychologists.* Washington, DC: American Psychological Association. 2004.
   E.C. Perrin and the Committee on Psychosocial Aspects of Child and Family Health. "Technical Report: Coparent or Second-Parent Adoption by Same-Sex Parents." *Pediatrics.* 109 (2002): pp. 341–344.

5. C.J. Patterson. "Family Relationships of Lesbians and Gay Men." *Journal of Marriage and Family.* 62 (2000): pp. 1052–1069.
   F. Tasker. "Children in Lesbian-Led Families: A Review." *Clinical Child Psychology and Psychiatry.* 4 (1999): pp. 153–166.

6. C.J. Patterson. "Family Relationships of Lesbians and Gay Men." *Journal of Marriage and Family.* 62 (2000): pp. 1052–1069.
   C.J. Patterson. "Lesbian and Gay Parents and Their Children: Summary of Research Findings." *Lesbian and Gay Parenting: A Resource for Psychologists.* Washington, DC: American Psychological Association. 2004.

7. D. Flaks, I. Ficher, F. Masterpasqua, and G. Joseph. "Lesbians Choosing Motherhood: A Comparative Study of Lesbian and Heterosexual Parents and Their Children." *Developmental Psychology.* 31 (1995): pp. 104–114.

8. C.J. Patterson. "Lesbian and Gay Parents and Their Children: Summary of Research Findings." *Lesbian and Gay Parenting: A Resource for Psychologists.* Washington, DC: American Psychological Association. 2004.

9. C.J. Patterson. "Lesbian and Gay Parents and Their Children: Summary of Research Findings." *Lesbian and Gay Parenting: A Resource for Psychologists.* Washington, DC: American Psychological Association. 2004.

10. E.C. Perrin and the Committee on Psychosocial Aspects of Child and Family Health. "Technical Report: Coparent or Second-Parent Adoption by Same-Sex Parents." *Pediatrics.* 109 (2002): pp. 341–344.
J. Stacey and T.J. Biblarz. "(How) Does Sexual Orientation of Parents Matter?" *American Sociological Review.* 65 (2001): pp. 159–183.
F. Tasker. "Children in Lesbian-Led Families: A Review." *Clinical Child Psychology and Psychiatry.* 4 (1999): pp. 153–166.

11. C.J. Patterson. "Gay Fathers." In M.E. Lamb (Ed.), *The Role of the Father in Child Development.* New York: John Wiley. 2004.
"Ethical Principles of Psychologists and Code of Conduct." *American Psychologist.* 57 (2002): pp. 1060–1073.

12. C.J. Patterson. "Family Relationships of Lesbians and Gay Men." *Journal of Marriage and Family.* 62 (2000): pp. 1052–1069.
C.J. Patterson. "Lesbian and Gay Parents and Their Children: Summary of Research Findings." *Lesbian and Gay Parenting: A Resource for Psychologists.* Washington, DC: American Psychological Association. 2004.
E.C. Perrin and the Committee on Psychosocial Aspects of Child and Family Health. "Technical Report: Coparent or Second-Parent Adoption by Same-Sex Parents." *Pediatrics.* 109 (2002): pp. 341–344.
J. Stacey and T.J. Biblarz. "(How) Does Sexual Orientation of Parents Matter?" *American Sociological Review.* 65 (2001): pp. 159–183.
F. Tasker. "Children in Lesbian-Led Families: A Review." *Clinical Child Psychology and Psychiatry.* 4 (1999): pp. 153–166.
F. Tasker and S. Golombok. *Growing Up in a Lesbian Family.* New York: Guilford Press. 1997.

13. P.H. DeLeon. Proceedings of the American Psychological Association, Incorporated, for the Year 1992: Minutes of the Annual Meeting of the Council of Representatives, August 13 and 16, 1992, and February 26 to 28, 1993, Washington, D.C. *American Psychologist.* 48 (1993): p. 782.
P.H. DeLeon, Proceedings of the American Psychological Association, Incorporated, for the Year 1994: Minutes of the Annual Meeting of the Council of Representatives, August 11 and 14, 1994, Los Angeles, and February 17 to 19, 1995, Washington, D.C. *American Psychologist.* 49 (1995): pp. 627–628.
R.E. Fox. Proceedings of the American Psychological Association, Incorporated, for the Year 1990: Minutes of the Annual Meeting of the Council of Representatives, August 9 and 12, 1990, Boston, and February 8 to 9, 1991, Washington, D.C. *American Psychologist.* 45 (1991): p. 845.
R.F. Levant. Proceedings of the American Psychological Association, Incorporated, for the Legislative Year 1999: Minutes of the Annual Meeting of the Council of Representatives, February 19 to 21, 1999, Washington, D.C., and August 19 and 22, 1999, Boston; and Minutes of the February, June, August, and December 1999 Meetings of the Board of Directors. *American Psychologist.* 55 (2000): pp. 832–890.

14. J.J. Conger. Proceedings of the American Psychological Association, Incorporated, for the Year 1974: Minutes of the Annual Meeting of the Council of Representatives. *American Psychologist.* 30 (1975): pp. 620–651.
"Ethical Principles of Psychologists and Code of Conduct." *American Psychologist.* 57 (2002): pp. 1060–1073.

15. *Lofton v. Secretary of Department of Children and Family Services,* 358 F.3d 804 (11th Cir. 2004).

73

Steps to Becoming a More Informed Ally to Working-Class and Low-Income People

BETSY LEONDAR-WRIGHT

1. Read Howard Zinn's *The People's History of the United States* and other books about low-income revolts, labor struggles, and working-class life stories.

2. Join Jobs with Justice (www.jwj.org) and read their alerts about local labor struggles that need support. Act on them when you can.

3. Subscribe to the newsletter of a local low-income-led group. (If you can't find one locally, subscribe to *Survival News* [102 Anawan Ave, West Roxbury, MA 02132].) (www.survivorsinc.org).

4. Attend conferences where working-class and low-income people speak, for example Labor Notes (www.labornotes.org).

5. Don't cross picket lines. Stop and ask why they're picketing.

6. Donate money to organizations working for a stronger social safety net and decent wages, for example the Kensington Welfare Rights Union (www.kwru.org) and the Coalition of Immokalee Workers (www.ciw-online.org).

7. Be a loyal and supportive friend to low-income and working-class people in your personal life. Ask them how they see various political and

interpersonal situations. (Remember, people who work for you in any capacity may never tell you their honest opinions.)

8. In organizations you're associated with, ask the lowest people on the totem pole, and anyone from a working-class background, how they see the organization. Keep asking and listening, as the first answer you hear may not be their whole story.

74

Uprooting Racism

Home and Family

PAUL KIVEL

Very often we think of racism as an issue out there, in the community. We don't think of social action as including how we live with other family members. The walls separating us from the community are permeable, and racism doesn't stop at the door. This section will give you ideas for eliminating racism in the ways you live with others and raise your children.

Although your family members may all be white and your neighbors appear so, there may well be people of other cultures, people in interracial families, people of mixed heritage or people who are passing as white among your friends. People of color may also be providing services for you, your children, your apartment, house or yard. Our environment is seldom as white as we assume it to be because we generally don't notice people of color when their presence doesn't challenge our sense of their proper role.

Our homes are less separable from the greater community than they have ever been. They are connected to the outside world through TV, including cable channels, computer games, the internet, toys, music from CD's, cassettes and radio, books, magazines, the daily newspaper and direct market catalogs. Each of these provide vehicles for racism to enter your home and opportunities to respond to it.

Is racism talked about where you live? When you and other family members watch a movie, discuss the news or talk about daily events is racism noticed and talked about?

Talking about racism is not easy for most of us to do. Few of us grew up in homes where racism or other difficult and emotional issues were talked about at all. We come from backgrounds of silence, ignorance or a false belief that to talk about racism is to further it. When talk about race did occur, some of us experienced conflict with family members because we disagreed over racial issues. We can acknowledge and overcome these past experiences and create an atmosphere in our own homes where issues of race, gender or class can be openly and respectfully talked about.

We have an impact on family, friends and neighbors by the physical environment we create in our home. Do the calendars, pictures and posters on your walls reflect the diverse society we live in? Are there books by women and men, lesbian, straight and gay people from many different cultures? Are there magazines from communities of color? We don't get extra points if there are. Nor are we trying to create an ethnic museum. But paying attention to our environment broadens our perspective and counters the stream of negative racial stereotypes which otherwise enter our home through the media.

It is even more important to discuss racism and to pay attention to our home if we have children. As responsible parents we need to think about the toys, games, computer games, dolls, books and pictures that our young ones are exposed to. It is not just children of color who need Latino/a, Asian American, Native-American, and African American dolls. It is not just children of color who are hurt by computer games that portray people of color as evil, dangerous and expendable.

I am not recommending that you purge your house of favorite games and toys or become fanatical about the racism you find in your child's life. Children don't need to be protected from racism. They see it all the time. They need to be given critical thinking tools for recognizing, analyzing and responding to the different forms that racism

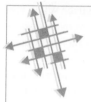

Questions and Actions

1. Were people of color and racism talked about in your childhood home? Think about particular incidents when it was. Was there tension around it? What was the general tone? Who initiated discussions and who resisted them?

2. Were Jews, the Holocaust, or anti-Semitism talked about? Think about particular incidents. What was the general tone? Who initiated discussions, and how was tension handled if there was any?

3. Was there silence in your home on issues of racism or anti-Semitism? What did you learn from the silence?

4. Was there conflict within your family because of racism or anti-Semitism (over integration, interracial or interfaith dating, music, busing)? Think of particular incidents. How was the conflict dealt with?

5. Were there people of color who cared for you, your parents, building, house or yard? If so, how were they treated? How did their presence and your family's attitudes toward them influence you?

6. As a child, what stories, TV shows or books influenced you the most in your attitudes about people of color? About Jews? What do you carry with you from that exposure?

7. Talk with your partner, housemates and friends about these issues. Notice the whiteness of your surroundings out loud to family and friends. This needn't be done aggressively or with great anger. You don't need to attack other people. Ask questions, notice things out loud, express your concerns and give other people room to think about and respond to what you say.

8. If you did a room-by-room assessment of your home today would you find a diversity of images and items?

9. If the answer to #8 is no, what do you and other family members lose because of that lack? How does it contribute to racial prejudice and discrimination?

10. Bring up feelings or thoughts about reading this book at dinner or other family time. What is difficult or awkward about doing this? What is the response?

11. Do an assessment of your home including the following items:
    a. books
    b. posters

takes. Discussing the racism (or sexism) in a children's book or movie, helping them think about the injustices of racism, and providing alternative, anti-racist materials—all these contribute to your children's awareness and their ability to respond to injustice.

You might want to initiate family discussions about racism by talking about this book and how you don't want your home to support racism. You can describe what racism is and how it affects white people and people of color in terms appropriate for the ages of your children. You can solicit their help

    c. cookbooks

    d. calendars

    e. paintings

    d. magazines

    f. newspapers

    g. videos

    h. games

    i. computer games

    j. toys

    k. art materials

    l. religious articles

    m. sports paraphernalia

    n. music

12. What would you like to remove?

13. What would you like to add to what you have? (Try to go beyond the tokenism of putting up pictures of Martin Luther King, Jr. or Michael Jordan or adding a book or two to your children's collection). Explore the roles and contributions of people of color in areas where you and other family members share an interest, such as sports, science, music, reading or movies.

14. Are women well represented in the items in your home? Are poor and working class people? Are people with disabilities? Are Moslems, Jews and Buddhists? Are lesbians and gay men? Are children? Are the creations of children themselves included?

15. Do you employ people of color? How well are they paid? How well are they treated? How do your children respond and relate to them? How will you talk with your children about these relationships? How will you balance these relationships with friends and neighbors from different cultures who are not employees? Are your children exposed to professionals such as teachers, doctors and dentists who are people of color? How could you increase such exposure?

in doing an assessment of your home and thinking about how different games, books, videos or posters might be racist.

Let your children help decide what to do to make your home different. It is one thing to create an anti-racist, multicultural environment by yourself. It is an entirely different level of education, empowerment and activism to include your children as valued participants in the process. The goal is not to create an ethnic museum but to acknowledge and celebrate the diversity of people and cultures represented in our society.

Obviously, this kind of assessment and interactive process should address issues of gender, class, disability, sexual orientation and religious and cultural difference as well as race. We don't want to foster stereotypes that people of color are not also women, poor or working class, people with disabilities, lesbian, gay or bisexual and/or Moslem, Buddhist or Jewish. These issues are inseparable. When dealt with in a context of social justice, young people are quick to develop principles of fair treatment and equality, eager to become co-participants in creating a healthier environment and challenging injustice. They may well end up inspiring and leading us with their readiness to challenge authority, take risks and stand up for fairness.

These are small, personal steps, but they have two important consequences. The more contact we have with people of color and with images and information about them, the more we are motivated and equipped to challenge racism. We are able to see more clearly the tremendous gap between average white perceptions about people of color and the lives and communities of people of color themselves. This awareness can guide our action and enrich our lives.

Second, we prepare our children to notice how racism operates and to become champions for racial justice. . . .

 75

Is Your World Too White?

A Primer for Whites Trying to Deal with a Racist Society

KAREN ASHMORE

Over fifteen years ago I started a chapter of the National Organization for Women. Since NOW and the women's movement in general are often associated with white middle class women, we named the group Rainbow NOW to emphasize the fact that it was for women of all colors. African American, Caucasian, Chicano and Native American women participated in the group. After several racially divided votes, we held anti-racism workshops every Saturday to try to grapple with the root causes of racism within the organization.

After twelve long months of dealing with the issue, the group members finally began to understand each other and work as a cohesive unit. It was a long, hard painful process, and some white women weren't too happy about sharing the power or working on their racism. Some white women left the group, but the ones who were committed on working on the issues of racism stuck with it, and the group turned out much stronger and much better.

The following points were a result of our Saturday discussions. How white is your world? What can you do to make it more colorful?

1. **Be honest about racism.** Racism is race prejudice plus the power of the institutional system to uphold that prejudice. In this country the institutional system supports the dominance of white people. If you doubt this, answer the following questions: How many black presidents have we had? Latino senators? American Indian CEOs of Fortune 500 companies?

Racism is a systematic form of oppression by the dominant culture in power in which people are oppressed economically, socially and politically solely based on skin color. Since people of color do not have the institutions to empower their prejudices, they cannot be racist. In other words, people of color can be prejudiced, but they cannot be racist without the institutional support.

There are varying degrees of racism just as there are degrees of sexism ranging from rape to tasteless jokes. Racism can range from overt violence such as lynching to more indirect examples such as insensitive remarks. Most people exhibit more subtle forms of racism, but it is important to acknowledge conscious or unconscious participation in a racist society.

*TYPES OF PREJUDICE: BASED ON SKIN
COLOR, GENDER, SEXUAL ORIENTATION
INSTITUTIONAL POWER + PREJUDICE =
RACISM, SEXISM, HETEROSEXISM
RACE PREJUDICE + INSTITUTIONAL
POWER = RACISM*

2. **Acknowledge white privilege.** More frequently than not, white people take advantage of privileges generated by a racist society. White people are often unwilling to grant that they are over-privileged, even though most are willing to concede the flip side of the coin, that people of color are disadvantaged. Most white people are in denial about the advantages that white people gain from the disadvantages of people of color. In an article on white privilege, Peggy McIntosh describes white privilege as an "invisible package of unearned assets which I can count on cashing in each day. White privilege is like an invisible knapsack of special provisions, maps, passports, code books, visas, tools and blank checks."

White people are given no training in seeing themselves as the oppressor, as an unfairly advantaged person. Whites are taught that racism is violence or meanness such as the Ku Klux Klan but are not taught that racism can be manifested in systems that allow dominance by whites. Author Beverly Daniel Tatum defines racism as "a system of advantage based on race." It is up to aware white people to open their eyes and show them the consequences of being a participant in a dysfunctional racist culture.

The following are examples of white privilege I can rely on but my African American friends cannot count on most of the time:

• I can be sure of being able to rent or get a mortgage for a house in an area which I can afford and in which I would want to live.
• I can be sure that I will be welcome in that new neighborhood.
• I can go shopping and not be followed or harassed.

• I can go shopping and get waited on promptly.
• I can go to a bar and get service.
• I can turn on the TV or read the newspaper and see people who look like me depicted as leaders and influencers.
• When I am told about our national heritage, I can be sure that I will be told that people of my race made it what it is.
• If a traffic cop pulls me over, I can be sure I haven't been singled out because of my race.
• If I ask to speak to the person in charge, I can be pretty sure I will be talking to a person of my race.
• If I have to go to court, I can be sure my race won't be held against me.

These are just a few examples of privilege that white people take advantage of every day. Most people have seen the comparison done by a national TV newsmagazine, sending a white male and black male with equal credentials to buy a car, look for a job, and hunt for an apartment. Time after time the black man came back empty-handed or cheated while the white male got the job, the apartment, and the best car deal.

Perhaps former Texas Governor Ann Richards described best the privilege of being male, white, and wealthy when she quipped, "George Bush thinks he hit a triple when actually he was born on third base."

3. **Start to heal.** Racism is a disease like alcoholism. You never recover from alcoholism and heal until you first admit you have a problem. The same thing goes for racism. You are never going to heal until you first admit there is a problem. This step is mandatory in order to continue to learn and grow. Acknowledge your privilege and participation in a racist society, begin healing, and continue down the path of growth and awareness.

4. **Be comfortable with accusations against white people in general without taking it personally.** Whites have persecuted and oppressed people of color for hundreds of years.

People of color can verbalize this oppression without you taking it personally. Release your guilt for past transgressions of other whites. Be comfortable with yourself because you know you are working for change.

5. **Learn about another culture.** People of color are often bicultural and bilingual. They know their own culture and own tongue yet also have to know the white culture and English tongue in order to survive economically. For example, many African Americans know Black English (Ebonics) and the "King's English" and many Latinas know Spanish and English.

The least you can do as a white person is get to know another culture. Go to an African American gospel extravaganza, a Native American pow wow, or a Mexican fiesta. If you are the only white person there, you will not be attacked. In fact most people of color will welcome you for taking the time to acquaint yourself with their culture.

The following are some suggested activities: Participate in Latino festivals. Cinco de Mayo (May 5) and Dies y seis de Septiembre (September 16) are important Mexican liberation festivals. Juneteenth (June 19) is the day African Americans in Texas found out they were freed from slavery, one year and six months after the fact. This date is marked by numerous celebrations in the African American community all over the country.

Kwanzaa is an African American cultural celebration from Dec. 26 to Jan. 1. Each day represents a different principle (unity, self-determination, collective work and responsibility, cooperative economics, purpose, creativity, and faith).

In the arts area, research cultural performance groups in your area. Chicano theater groups, African dance troupes, and Japanese taiko drumming groups are common in many parts of the country. If you live near a reservation, find out when pow wows and ceremonies are held. Many sacred ceremonies are not open to non-tribal members, but most reservations will open activities to the public at least once a year.

6. **Keep up with media aimed at people of color.** Research local newspapers aimed at people of color. Many communities have newspapers targeting African American, Latino, Asian, and Native American communities. Most major metropolitan areas now have Spanish language radio and TV stations. Most public radio stations and alternative radio stations have special programs hosted by diverse hosts and dealing with a variety of cultural issues. Call your local radio and TV stations and find out when these programs are aired. With the internet, it is simple to do a quick search of websites devoted to different cultures.

7. **Question yourself.** Why are you threatened by change? What threatens you about a Latino or a Haitian American representing you in the legislature or City Council? Whites have represented people of color for hundreds of years. People of color are often bicultural and thus more able to represent diverse populations.

8. **Try to learn from your mistakes.** When a person of color challenges you or corrects you about a racist or insensitive statement, that does not mean she does not like you. She cares enough about you to inform you of your misconceptions so that you can grow and be a more whole person. If she felt you were a hopeless case, she wouldn't have even bothered.

9. **Acknowledge the skills and experience of people of color.** Many times a person of color comes to an organization with more leadership skills than Anglos. People of color have been organizing and fighting for civil rights actively as a group for many, many years. African Americans and other oppressed groups have to be emotionally and spiritually strong to endure the inequities, discrimination, lynchings, and hatred for generations and still persevere as a race. Acknowledge these leadership skills and strengths as well as your own limitations. Try to learn from your sisters and brothers.

10. **Never be afraid to ask questions.** People of color are often well-versed in BS detection.

They can tell if you are sincere and will answer your questions or help you understand any misassumptions.

11. **Learn the history and struggles of another culture.** If you have never seen the award-winning civil rights documentary "Eyes on the Prize," rent/borrow the DVD. PBS often airs it during February, Black History Month. It is also available in book form. Much civil rights history for Latino(a)s took place in the Southwest. Learn about the Crystal City boycotts in South Texas. There is a documentary called "Chicano! History of the Mexican-American Civil Rights Movement" that airs periodically on PBS. Take the time to explore the history of another culture.

12. **Join another organization oriented towards another culture.** National organizations like League of United Latin American Citizens (LULAC), SCLC (Southern Christian Leadership Conference founded by Dr. Martin Luther King), NAACP (National Association for the Advancement of Colored People), AIM (American Indian Movement), JACL (Japanese/Asian Citizens League) welcome sincere white supporters. Sometimes you may have to join an organization as an associate member or supporter, but you can still participate in activities.

13. **Try to put yourself in the other person's shoes.** If you have trouble relating, try looking at an analogous situation. For example, at a recent meeting of a community organization, some white people could not understand why people of color did not come back after an initial visit. I presented an analogous scenario: Imagine an organization founded for women but you attended a meeting dominated by men who did not understand the issues of women. Would you come back? Probably not. Likewise, if an organization wants to recruit people of color but the meeting is dominated by whites, people of color are not likely to return because they will probably not feel like they have a place there.

14. **Learn to share the power.** Don't be afraid to be led by people of color. We, as whites, must become more comfortable with accepting leadership by people of color. This is especially important for the coming decade as people of color become the majority and assume more leadership roles throughout the country.

15. **Realize the enemy is not people of color.** The force to be dealt with is oppression—racism, sexism, classism, homophobia, ableism, etc. Understand the connections between the "isms." Racism, sexism, and other isms are about power and control and fear of those who are different.

16. **Read feminist literature by women of color.** Women of color face two biases: sexism and racism. Open your eyes by reading from their perspective. A good reading list includes:

- *This Bridge Called My Back* by Cherrie Moraga and Gloria Anzaldúa (multi-cultural)
- *Women, Race and Class* by Angela Davis (African American)
- *Women, Culture and Politics* by Angela Davis (African American)
- *Ain't I a Woman* by bell hooks (African American)
- *A Gathering of Spirit* by Beth Brant (American Indian)
- *Sister Outsider* by Audre Lord (African American)
- *Yours in the Struggle* by Elly Buskin, Minnie Pratt, and Barbara Smith (anti-Semitism and racism)
- *When and Where I Enter* by Paula Giddings (racism in the women's movement)
- *Three Asian American Writers Speak Out on Feminism* by Nellie Wong, Merle Woo, and Mitsuye Yamada (Asian American)
- *Mexican Women in the United States: Struggles Past and Present* by Magdalena Mora and Adelaid Castillo (Mexican American)
- *Breath, Eyes, Memory* by Edwidge Danticat (Haitian American)

17. **Expand your spiritual horizons.** If you are a spiritual person, acknowledge the female

aspect of the Creator. If you study theological history, you will learn that female aspects of the deity were included in the original scriptures of the Bible but were edited out with the King James version for political reasons. Hasn't it ever occurred to you to question why one half of the population is not revered in the Bible? Why would a document only acknowledge a trinity of the Father, Son, and Holy Ghost when women are the givers of life, the nurturers, the ones who understand the essence of life?

According to contemporary archeological findings, all civilization began in Africa, thus we are all African descendants. White people are thought to be mutations who survived over the years after migrating to the colder climates in the Caucasus Mountains. Early civilizations regarded a Black Woman as the Creator. I strongly recommend reading *When God Was a Woman* by Merlin Stone and *The Great Cosmic Mother* by Barbara Mor and Monica Sjoo.

18. **Visit the church of another culture.** A good way to learn about another culture is by sharing in their worship service. Churches, mosques, temples, synagogues abound for Islamic, Protestant, Gaian, Jewish, Kemetic, Catholic, Vodoun, Sikh, Buddhist, Quaker, Mormon, and other worshipers.

19. **Look at the people you have a choice in selecting—friends.** How many of your close friends are of another race? If none of your close friends are of a different culture, analyze the reasons why. Do you fear diversity? Why do you not seek out friends of color? Do you limit yourself to Anglo-oriented activities, neighborhoods, employers?

20. **What kind of music do you enjoy?** If you are a mainstream rock fan, have you ever explored reggae, salsa, konpa, or music of other cultures? Have you ever frequented a reggae club? Ever been to a pow wow or a taiko drumming performance?

21. **Explore neighborhoods and communities of color.** Have you ever acquainted yourself with cultural institutions in your city? Do you know where the Haitian, Cuban, or Ethiopian neighborhood is? Have you ever shopped in those neighborhoods? Do you know where the closest Indian reservation is?

22. **Support minority-owned businesses.** Do you shop mostly at white-owned businesses? Try some affirmative action with your pocketbook. Is all the art on your living room walls Anglo art? Try some diversity in your home decorating and check out local shops that specialize in ethnic art. Join the Black, Haitian, Hispanic, American Indian, or Asian Chambers of Commerce and get a copy of their business directories. Support minority vendors whether it is for furnishing your home or for business purchasing decisions.

23. **Support non-profit organizations that empower minority populations.** Volunteer time, donate money, or attend special events sponsored by such groups as the Lambi Fund of Haiti, Native American Rights Fund, and other groups organized to empower people of color. Check out local non-profit organizations that are specific to your community. Remember your goal is empowerment, not patronization. Don't volunteer with a condescending attitude that you're going to "save these poor people."

24. **Think globally, act globally.** Remember that the majority of the world lives on less than a dollar a day. The environmental and economic conditions in other countries are beyond your comprehension. Make an effort to plant a tree in Haiti, sponsor an AIDS orphan in Kenya, or help people in developing countries become self-supporting. Plant hope, trees, dignity, and self-determination. These are ways you can truly make a difference.

25. **Make a commitment to broaden your perspectives beyond your narrow eurocentric world.** You will be amazed at how enriched your life becomes.

76

Action Continuum

PAT GRIFFIN AND BOBBIE HARRO

Actively Participating	Denying, Ignoring	Recognizing, No action	Recognizing, Action	Educating Self	Educating Others	Supporting, Encouraging	Initiating, Preventing

Supporting Oppression ⟵⟶ **Confronting Oppression**

Actively Participating: Telling oppressive jokes, putting down people from target groups, intentionally avoiding target group members, discriminating against target group members, verbally or physically harassing target group members.

Denying: Enabling oppression by denying that target group members are oppressed. Does not actively oppress, but by denying that oppression exists, colludes with oppression.

Recognizing, No Action: Is aware of oppressive actions by self or others and their harmful effects, but takes no action to stop this behavior. This inaction is the result of fear, lack of information, confusion about what to do. Experiences discomfort at the contradiction between awareness and action.

Recognizing, Action: Is aware of oppression, recognizes oppressive actions of self and others and takes action to stop it.

Educating Self: Taking actions to learn more about oppression and the experiences and heritage of target group members by reading, attending workshops, seminars, cultural events, participating in discussions, joining organizations or groups that oppose oppression, attending social action and change events.

Educating Others: Moving beyond only educating self to question and dialogue with others too. Rather than only stopping oppressive comments or behaviors, also engaging people in discussion to share why you object to a comment or action.

Supporting, Encouraging: Supporting others who speak out against oppression or who are working to be more inclusive of target group members by backing up others who speak out, forming an allies group, joining a coalition group.

Initiating, Preventing: Working to change individual and institutional actions and policies that discriminate against target group members, planning educational programs or other events, working for passage of legislation that protects target group members from discrimination, being explicit about making sure target group members are full participants in organizations or groups.

77

I Came to Help: Resistance Writ Small

JULIA ALVAREZ

★ ★ ★

. . . Camila, . . . lived a placid, seemingly conservative life, teaching Spanish at Vassar for 20 years. But finally, in 1960 when she was 64, she gave up her tenure and her pension to go to Cuba and be part of the literacy brigade there. When asked years later by her students and colleagues why she gave up her security and status at Vassar to come to Cuba at a time when so many were leaving the island, she said simply, without any fanfare, "Vine a ayudar." I came to help.

This comment by Camila gives me courage by reminding me that the way we really change things is often through very simple actions, small and quiet enough not to draw too much attention: a group of women wearing kerchiefs and black dresses and practical tie shoes circle a plaza in Argentina. A young woman in a threatened forest hugs a tree. Another and another join her. A handful of women in a Greek village refuse to sleep with their husbands until they end a war. A housewife in Southern France opens the back door and ushers her Jewish neighbors to the cellar of her house.

Vine a ayudar. I came to help.

I love the simplicity and sweetness of the statement, the respect for human life at its most humble level, the hand outstretched. Toni Morrison put it this way: The function of freedom is to free someone else. This is the smallest atom of liberation that dictatorships and even revolutionaries often miss—dictatorships because they are looking out for the big counteroffensives, enemies, and revolutionaries because they often mistakenly copy the power structures of those they are struggling to resist.

I want to posit the small, sometimes invisible but utterly powerful way that we can be a force for change.

I trust that connective, consensus-building, hands-on process which I think of as a traditionally female process with its roots in the kitchen, women working together. Here, let me help you with that.

Credits

Photo Credits

Page 50: Ernst Keil, 1893. Courtesy of The Jewish Museum, New York; *56:* The Colored American Magazine, 1903; *217, 218:* Courtesy of the Kenneth W. Goings Collection; *278:* (both) Harper's Weekly, 1868; *279:* Life, 1909; *280:* (left) The Des Moines Register & Tribune, 1943, (right) Courtesy of the Baltimore Sun; *281:* Courtesy of the Chicago Tribune; *287:* Courtesy of Sherry Leedy Contemporary Art and the Artist; *437:* © by Guerrilla Girls, Inc. Courtesy of www.guerrillagirls.com; *454:* © Iko Lee/Getty Images; *512, 513:* Courtesy of Roger Shimomura

Text Credits

Page iv: "Afterword" by Leslie Feinberg from STONE BUTCH BLUES. Reprinted by permission of Sll/sterling Lord Literistic, Inc. Copyright by Leslie Feinberg.

Section I

Page 15: "I am not your Princess" by Chrystos. Used by permission of the author, Chrystos © 1988.

Page 16: Excerpts from Becoming a Visible Man. Jamison Green. Vanderbilt University Press, 2004. pp. 1–8. Copyright © 2004. Reprinted with permission of Vanderbilt University Press.

Page 21: "Gender Relations" R.W. Connell. Gender. Cambridge: Polity Press, 2002. (excerpted). Reprinted by permission.

Page 36: "The Invention of Heterosexuality" Jonathan Ned Katz from *Socialist Review* 20 (January–March 1990): 7–34. Reprinted by permission.

Page 44: Excerpts from "Masculinity as Homophobia" Michael Kimmel. Reprinted from Theorizing Masculinities Harry Brod (ed.). SAGE publications: California, 1994. Reprinted by permission of Sage Publications, Inc.

Page 51: "Racial Formations" from Michael Omi and Howard Winant. Racial Formations in the United States: From the 1960s to the 1980s. London: Routledge, 1986. Reprinted by permission of Routledge via Copyright Clearance Center.

Page 59: "Failing to See" from RACIAL HEALING by Harlon L. Dalton, copyright © 1995 by Harlon L. Dalton. Used by permission of Doubleday, a division of Random House, Inc.

Page 59: "Los Intersticios: Recasting Moving Selves." Evelyn Alsultany in This Bridge We Call Home. Gloria E. Anzaldua and AnaLouise Keating, (eds.) Routledge, 2002. Reproduced by permission of Routledge, a division of Taylor & Francis Group.

Page 60: "Social Class Matters." Brenda J. Allen. Difference Matters: Communicating Social Identity, Waveland Press, Inc, 2004, pp. 95–116. Reprinted by permission of Waveland Press, Inc. (Long Grove, IL: Waveland Press, Inc., 2004). All rights reserved.

Page 75: "Bringing Classism into the Race & Gender Picture" Chuck Barone. *Race, Gender & Class,* 6 (3), pp. 6–32, 1999. Reprinted by permission of Race, Gender & Class.

Page 91: "The Social Construction of Disability," Susan Wendell. The Rejected Body. Routledge, 1996. Reprinted by permission of Taylor & Francis Group LLC.

Page 95: "One" by Sharon Hwang Colligan in BI ANY OTHER NAME: Bisexual People Speak Out, ed. Loraine Hutchins and Lani Kaahumanu, Boston: Alyson Publications, Inc. 1991, pp. 240–243. Reprinted by permission.

Page 96: "Toward a New Vision" Patricia Hill Collins. *Race, Sex, & Class,* 1, no. 1, Fall 1993. Reprinted by permission of Patricia Hill Collins.

Page 106: "What White Supremacists Taught a Jewish Scholar About Identity" by Abby Ferber in *Chronicle of Higher Education.* May 7, 1999. Reprinted by permission of Abby Ferber.

Page 108: "Is Capitalism Gendered and Racialized?" Joan Acker in Class Questions: Feminist Answers. Rowman & Littlefield Publishers, 2006. Reprinted by permission.

Page 116: "Theorizing Difference from Multiracial Feminism" by Maxine Baca Zinn and Bonnie Thornton Dill. Originally published in *Feminist Studies* 22, No. 2 (Summer 1996): 321–331.

Reprinted by permission of the publisher, Feminist Studies, Inc.

Page 122: "You're Not a Real Boy if You're Disabled." Wayne Martino and Maria Pallotta-Chiarolli in So What's a Boy? Addressing Issues of Masculinity and Schooling. Philadelphia: Open University Press, 2003. Reprinted by permission of Open University Press.

Page 130: "Choosing Up Sides" Judy Scales-Trent. Notes of a White Black Woman: Race, Color, and Community. University Park: The Pennsylvania State University Press, 1995. pp. 61–65. Reprinted by permission of Penn State University Press.

Page 131: "Seeing More Than Black and White." Elizabeth "Betita" Martinez. Reprinted by permission of the author.

SECTION II

Page 144: "I Give You Back" from the book SHE HAD SOME HORSES by Joy Harjo. Copyright © 1983, 1997 Thunder's Mouth Press. Appears by permission of the publisher, Thunder's Mouth Press, A Division of Avalon Publishing Group, Inc.

Page 144: "White Privilege and Male Privilege: A Personal Account of Coming to See Correspondences Throughout Work in Women's Studies" Peggy McIntosh. Copyright 1988 by Peggy McIntosh, Working Paper 189, Wellesley College. Center for Research on Women, Wellesley College, Wellesley, MA 02481. May not be reprinted without permission of the author.

Page 157: "Defining Racism: Can We Talk?" Beverly Daniel Tatum. Why Are All the Black Kids Sitting Together in the Cafeteria? (Rev. Ed.) Basic Books, 1999, pp. 3–13. Reprinted by ermission of Basic Books, a member of Perseus Books Group.

Page 163: "Privilege: Expanding on Marilyn Frye's 'Oppression'" Alison Bailey from JOURNAL OF SOCIAL PHILOSOPHY, Winter 1998, pp 104–119. Reprinted by permission of Blackwell Publishing Ltd.

Page 174: Racists. Eduardo Bonilla-Silva. Lanham, MD: Rowman & Littlefield, 2003, pp. 1–4, 8–11. Reprinted by permission of Rowman & Littlefield.

Page 179: "La Guera" Cherrie Moraga in This Bridge Called My Back. (3rd Ed.) Cherrie Moraga and Gloria Anzaldua, (eds.) 3rd Woman Press, 2002.

Page 183: Reprinted with permission from SISTER OUTSIDER by Audre Lorde. Copyright 1984 by Audre Lorde, The Crossing Press, a division of Ten Speed Press, Berkeley, CA, www.tenspeed.com.

Page 184: "White Privilege Shapes the U.S." Robert Jensen. *Baltimore Sun.* July 19, 1998. Reprinted by permission of The Baltimore Sun via Copyright Clearance Center.

Page 186: "The Costs of American Privilege" Michael Schwalbe. *CounterPunch.* October 4, 2002. <http://www.counterpunch.org/schwalbe1004.html. Reprinted by permission of CounterPunch.

SECTION III

Page 195: "I, Too", from THE COLLECTED POEMS OF LANGSTON HUGHES by Langston Hughes, edited by Arnold Rampersad with David Roessel, Associate Editor, copyright © 1994 by The Estate of Langston Hughes. Used by permission of Alfred A. Knopf, a division of Random House, Inc. and Harold Ober Associates. "Patriot" from ABSOLUTE TRUST IN THE GOODNESS OF THE EARTH: New Poems by Alice Walker, copyright © 2002 by Alice Walker. Used by permission of Random House, Inc. and David Higham Associates.

Page 196: "Many Americas: The Intersection of Class, Race, and Ethnic Identity," Gregory Campbell Many Americas: Critical Perspectives on Race, Racism and Ethnicity. Kendall Hunt Publishing Co., 1998, pp. 3–21. Reprinted by permission.

Page 224: "Disability Discrimination and the Evolution of Civil Rights in Democratic Societies." In Understanding Disability: Inclusion, Access, Diversity, and Civil Rights. Paul Jaegar and Cynthia Ann Bowman. Westport: Praeger, 2005, pp. 25–47. Reprinted by permission of Greenwood Publishing Group.

Page 244: A History of Women's Bodies" Rose Weitz in The Politics of Women's Bodies. Rose Weitz, (ed.) New York: Oxford University Press, 2003, pp. 3–11. Reprinted by permission of Oxford University Press.

Page 249: "Thirteen Key Supreme Court Cases and the Civil War Amendments," Karen E. Rosenblum and Toni-Michelle C. Travis, The Meaning of Difference. McGraw-Hill, 2006.

Page 278: "Rape and the War Against Native Women" by Andrea Smith, in Reading Native American Women: Critical/Creative Representations. Ines Hernandez-Avila, (ed.), 2005, Alta Mira

Press, Lanham. Reprinted by permission of Rowman & Littlefield.

Page 289: "Race and Criminal Justice" Edward Escobar. Race, Police, and the Making of a Political Identity. Copyright © 1999 The Regents of the University of California. Reprinted by permission of The University of California Press.

Page 299: "How Jews Became White" by Karen Brodkin Sacks. How Jews Became White Folks and What that Says About Race in America. New Brunswick, NJ: Rutgers University Press. pp. 25–52, excerpted. Copyright © 1998 by Karen Brodkin. Reprinted by permission of Rutgers University Press.

Page 306: "Then Came the War" Yuri Kochiyama in Asian Americans. J.F.J. Lee (ed.) New York: The New Press, 1992. Reprinted by permission of Yuri Kochiyama.

Page 312: "America", copyright © 1975 by Maya Angelou, from OH PRAY MY WINGS ARE GONNA FIT ME WELL by Maya Angelou. Used by permission of Random House, Inc. and Little, Brown Book Group Limited.

Page 312: Excerpts from "The Chicano Movement: 1965–1975." Manuel Gonzales. Mexicanos: A History of Mexicans in the United States. Indiana University Press, 1999, pp. 191–222. Reprinted by permission of Indiana University Press.

Page 324: From GAY NEW YORK by George Chauncey, pp. 1–8, 12–23. Reprinted by permission of Basic Books, a member of Perseus Books Group.

Page 334: "A Brief History of Working Women." Sharlene Nagy Hesse-Biber and Gregg Lee Carter. Working Women in America: Split Dreams. Oxford University Press, 2005, pp. 30–59. Reprinted by permission of Oxford University Press.

Page 356: "The Problem That Has No Name", from THE FEMININE MYSTIQUE by Betty Friedan. Copyright © 1983, 1974, 1973, 1963 by Betty Friedan. Used by permission of W. W. Norton & Company, Inc. and The Orion Publishing Group Ltd.

Page 360: From NO TURNING BACK by Estelle B. Freedman, copyright © 2002 by Estelle B. Freedman. Used by permission of Ballantine Books, a division of Random House, Inc.

Page 374: Steven Seidman, Beyond the Closet: The Transformation of Gay and Lesbian Life (New York: Routledge, 2002), pp. 163–196. Reprinted by permission.

Page 389: From RACE AND ETHNIC RELATIONS, America and Global Perspectives, 5th Edition by Marger, 2003. Reprinted with permission of Wadsworht, a division of Thomson Learning: www.thonmsonrights.com. Fax 800 730-2215.

Section IV

Page 412: "Where is my country?" Nellie Wong. Reprinted by permission of the author.

Page 413: "Doing Gender and Doing Gender Inappropriately: Violence Against Women, Gay Men and Lesbians." Barbara Perry. In the Name of Hate, Understanding Hate Crimes. Routledge, 2001, pp. 81–118 (excerpts). Reproduced by permission of Routledge, a division of Taylor & Francis Group.

Page 440: "We Are All Works in Progress" from TRANS LIBERATION by Leslie Feinberg. Copyright © 1998 by Leslie Feinberg. Reprinted by permission of Beacon Press, Boston.

Page 445: "Medicalization of Racial Features: Asian-American Women and Cosmetic Surgery" Eugenia Kaw from MEDICAL ANTHROPOLOGY QUARTERLY, New Series, Vol. 7, No. 1 (March 1993), pp. 74–89 as appeared with notes in The Politics of Women's Bodies. Rose Weitz, (ed.), New York: Oxford University Press, 2003. Reprinted by permission of American Anthropological Association and Oxford University Press.

Page 455: "SES, Race/Ethnicity and Health" by Melanie L. Johnston in INTERSECTIONS OF GENDER, RACE AND CLASS (2007) edited by Segal, Marcia T. and Martinez, Theresa. Reprinted by permission of Oxford University Press.

Page 464: "Race, Family Values, and Welfare Reform" by Bonnie Thornton Dill, Maxine Baca Zinn and Sandra Patton in SAGE RACE RELATIONS ABSTRACTS, 1998, Volume 23, issue 3, pp. 4–31. Reprinted by permission of Sage Publications Ltd (UK).

Page 481: "Driving While Black: A statistician proves that prejudice still rules the road" John Lamberth. *The Washington Post.* August 16, 1998. Reprinted by permission of the author.

Page 484: From THE SHAME OF THE NATION by Jonathan Kozol, copyright © 2005 by Jonathan Kozol. Used by permission of Crown Publishers, a division of Random House, Inc. and the author.

Page 489: "'A Way Outa' No Way,' Eating Problems among African-American, Latina, and White Women," Becky W. Thompson, *Gender & Society*, Vol. 6, No. 4, 546–561 (1992). Reprinted by permission of Sage Publications, Inc.

Page 499: "Sounds and Silences of Language: Perpetuating Institutionalized Privilege and Oppression." Dena Samuels. Written especially for this volume.

Page 505: "Katrina's Race and Class Effects Were Planned." Gregory D. Squires. *Progressive Planning*. No. 167, Spring 2006: 10–11. Reprinted by permission.

Page 507: "Media Magic: Making Class Invisible" by Gregory Mantsios from RACE, CLASS & GENDER IN THE UNITED STATES, Paula Rothenberg, editor (Worth, New York). Reprinted by permission of Gregory Mantsios.

SECTION V

Page 520: Poem: "For the White Person Who Wants to Know How to Be My Friend." Pat Parker. Movement in Black. New York: Firebrand Books, 1999. Reprinted by permission of Firebrand Books.

Page 521: "Feminists and Feminisms" Allan Johnson in The Gender Knot: Unraveling Our Patriarchal Legacy. pps. 102–113 and 129–130. Philadelphia: Temple University Press, June 2005. Reprinted by permission of Temple University Press.

Page 522: © Tom Tomorrow. Used by permission.

Page 541: "Holy War." Bob Moser. *Southern Poverty Law Center Intelligence Report*, Spring 2005. http://splcenter.org/intel/intelreport/article.jsp?aid =522&printable=1. Reprinted by permission from Southern Poverty Law Center's Intelligence Report.

Page 546: "Color-blinded America or How the Media and Politics Have Made Racism and Racial Inequality Yesterday's Social Problem." Charles Gallagher. Written for this volume. Page 550: "Too Many Women in College?" Phyllis Rosser. *Ms. Magazine*, Fall 2005. Copyright © 2005. Reprinted by permission of MS Magazine.

Page 554: "Man-ifesting Gender" by Abby Ferber from *Dignity Report*, Spring 2002. Reprinted by permission of Abby Ferber. Page 556: "Affirmative Action" and "At Work" by Paul Kivel in UPROOTING RACISM. Copyright 1995. Reprinted by permission of New Society Publishers.

Page 566: "Las Mujeres Invisibles/The Invisible Women" Sharon Ann Navarro in Women's Activism and Globalization: Linking Local Struggle and Transnational Politics. Nancy A. Naples and Manisha Desai (eds.). Copyright © 2002 by Routledge. Reproduced by permission of Routledge, a division of Taylor & Francis Group.

Page 575: "Confronting Anti-Gay Violence" Michael Bronski originally appeared in *Z Magazine*, April 9, 1999. Reprinted by permission of the author.

Page 577: "Privilege and Cultural Reform at the US Air Force Academy" Dena Samuels and Steven Samuels. (written especially for this volume).

Page 581: "Assets for Equality" Thomas Shapiro. The Hidden Costs of Being African American: How Wealth Perpetuates Inequality. New York: Oxford University Press, 2004. Reprinted by permission of Oxford University Press.

Page 589: "Why Do We Need Cross-Class Alliances?" by Betsy Leonar-Wright from CLASS MATTERS: Cross-Class Alliance Building for Middle Class Activists. Copyright 2005. Reprinted by permission of New Society Publishers.

Page 591: "Ideology of the Multiracial Movement: Dismantling the Color Line and Disguising White Supremacy?" Eileen T. Walsh in The Politics of Multiracialism: Challenging Racial Thinking. Heather M. Dalmage (ed.). SUNY Press, 2004, excerpts from pp. 219–235.

Page 601: "Stolen Bodies." Eli Claire from "Stolen Bodies, Reclaimed Bodies: Disability and Queerness. Boxed Insert in Feminist Frontiers" from *Public Culture* 13 (3): 359–365. Duke University Press, 2001. Copyright, 2001, Duke University Press. All rights reserved. Used by permission of the publisher.

Page 603: "The Motherhood Manifesto," Joan Blades and Kristen Rowe-Finkbeiner. *The Nation*. May 22, 2006, excerpts from pp. 11–16. Reprinted with permission of The Nation. For subscription information, call 1-800-333-8536. Portions of each week's Nation magazine can be accessed at http://www.thenation.com.

Page 607: "An Indian Father's Plea" by Robert Lake (Medicine Grizzlybear) as appeared in TEACHER Magazine, November 1990. Reprinted by permission of Robert Lake-Thom.

Page 610: "Interrupting the Cycle of Oppression: The Role of Allies as Agents of Change." Andrea